UPGRADING AND REPAIRING NETWORKS

Fourth Edition

Terry William Ogletree

800 East 96th Street
Indianapolis, Indiana 46240

Contents at a Glance

Upgrading and Repairing Networks, Fourth Edition

Copyright © 2004 by Que® Publishing

International Standard Book Number: 0-7897-2817-6

Library of Congress Catalog Card Number: 2002110537

Printed in the United States of America

First Printing: August 2003

06   05   04   03   4   3   2   1

Trademarks

Warning and Disclaimer

Bulk Sales

Que Publishing offers excellent discounts on this book when ordered in quantity for bulk purchases or special sales. For more information, please contact:

> **U.S. Corporate and Government Sales**
> **1-800-382-3419**
> **corpsales@pearsontechgroup.com**

For sales outside of the U.S., please contact:

> **International Sales**
> **+1-317-581-3793**
> **international@pearsontechgroup.com**

Publisher
Paul Boger

Associate Publisher
Greg Wiegand

Executive Editor
Rick Kughen

Development Editors
Todd Brakke
Mark Reddin
Rick Kughen

Managing Editor
Charlotte Clapp

Project Editor
Tricia Liebig

Copy Editor
Cheri Clark

Indexer
Larry Sweazy

Proofreader
Jessica McCarty

Technical Editor
Jeff Ferris

Team Coordinator
Sharry Lee Gregory

Multimedia Developer
Dan Scherf

Interior Designer
Anne Jones

Cover Designer
Anne Jones

Page Layout
Kelly Maish

Graphics
Tammy Graham

Contents

VIII System and Network Security   845

46 Basic Security Measures Every Network Administrator Needs to Know   847

47 Auditing and Other Monitoring Measures   865

48 Security Issues for Wide Area Networks   889

To my parents, Charles and Billie Jean Ogletree

And

Zira (1994–2002)

About the Authors

Terry William Ogletree is a consultant currently working in New Jersey. He has worked with networked computer systems since 1980, starting out on Digital Equipment PDP computers and OpenVMS-based VAX systems. He has worked with Unix and TCP/IP since 1985 and has been involved with Windows NT and Windows 2000 since they first appeared, as well as the newest additions to the family, Windows XP and the Windows Server 2003 family of servers. Besides being the lead author of the third edition of this book, he is the author of *Windows XP Unleashed*, *Practical Firewalls*, and *The Complete Idiot's Guide to Creating Your Own CDs* (with co-author Todd Brakke), and he has contributed chapters to many other books published by Que, including *Microsoft Windows 2000 Security Handbook* and *Special Edition Using Unix, Third Edition*. He is also the author of *Fundamentals of Storage Area Networking*. When not writing for Que, he has on occasion contributed articles to *PC Magazine*.

You can email him at t@w2003tech.com or visit his home page at www.w2003tech.com. When between jobs and not writing for Que, he can often be found on street corners holding a sign that reads "Will work for hundreds of thousands of dollars."

Thomas Crayner (Chapter 2) currently is the Director of Applications and Infrastructure Services at a leading pharmaceutical company, where his department keeps 300 servers running in support of R&D operations. Starting with Unix and TCP/IP in the mid-1980s as an applications developer, he slowly worked his way into infrastructure development. During the course of his career, Tom has designed and implemented systems and networks of all shapes and sizes. On the weekends, he can still be found enjoying his original hobby: system and application development.

Dwight Tolay, Jr. (Chapter 6) started out as a computer test technician in the 1970s. Branching out into the electrical construction industry, he became familiar with data and fiber-optic cabling, has worked with coax Ethernet and IBM Token-Ring, and has followed the evolution up to today's Category 6 and Gigabyte cabling methods. Currently, he is a general supervisor for Ortlip Electric Co. He is a graduate EE, an ISA certified Level III control systems technician, a licensed electrical contractor, and a certified high-voltage test technician. In addition to being a certified fiber-optic and teledata instructor at a local trade school for the past 13 years, he has contributed as technical editor on various books and currently is involved in a book on Home Data and Electrical Systems Integration.

Scott and Kalinda Reeves (Chapters 32 and 33) are a married couple who live in Heron, Montana, where they have written several networking exam books.

Scott has accrued his certifications as a Master Certified Novell Engineer (MCNE), Microsoft Certified Professional (MCP) in Windows NT, Compaq Accredited Systems Engineer (ASE), Comptia Network+ professional, and Comptia A+ certified technician. He has more than 15 years in the computer industry, and he has worked in the networking field for more than 11 years.

Kalinda has more than 16 years' experience writing research, business, technical, and engineering documentation for government, military, and civilian customers. The topics include system- and circuit-level hardware; uniquely developed, hardware-specific programs; and programs that are implemented across government and military communications systems. Kalinda currently works as a freelance writer.

Acknowledgments

Most of the credit for getting this book done must be given not to the author, but to Rick Kughen, Que's executive editor, and to Todd Brakke and Mark Reddin, the development editors of this book. There is no way I could ever have gotten this book finished without their consistent, persistent, wonderful help. Todd Brakke has worked with me on four other books, and I think both he and Mark Reddin deserve a lot of credit for the material you'll find inside. Along with Rick Kughen, they have contributed both questions and ideas about the new material that we've included, as well as contributing to the organization of each chapter. Tricia Liebig expended a lot of effort coordinating various people involved in this project—a job I would not envy! As I am not the best writer in the world, I must also give credit to Cheri Clark, the copy editor, for correcting my grammatical errors and for making helpful suggestions about better ways to write this book's text. Writing for Que is a team effort!

I also would like to acknowledge Sharon Terdeman, the Solutions Editor of *PC Magazine.* Several of the articles she assisted me with spurred further research that resulted in more coverage of those topics in this book. Additionally, Sharon is a good teacher when it comes to learning how to write concise, informative text. She can take ten sentences and condense them into one, and still make the same point. Helps a lot in a long book such as this one!

Most of my contracting jobs during the past five years have been the result of the efforts of John Rogue and Angelo Simeo of The Computer Merchant firm in Norwell, Massachusetts. The jobs they have been able to find for me not only pay the bills, but also have enabled me to greatly further my knowledge of computers and networking. I can recommend this firm to anyone who is looking for highly skilled employees or consultants in the computer and networking fields (www.tcml.com).

A special thanks to Carl and Nanette Chiappetta for helping me stay focused on work and enjoy life to its fullest. Thanks again to Jo and Jeff Johnson for being such good friends, and the same for Jordan Scoggins, Andy Jones, James Garrett, Sari Gurney, Rick Clayton, and Rodney Foster. Thanks also to Vicki Harding, my agent, for helping me get many writing assignments (www.future-prod.com).

It goes without saying that without the help of Michael D. Parrott and Associates (and Michael's lovely and incredibly brilliant wife, Brenda), I never would have been able to find time to write. MDP&A is the ultimate super-accounting firm that goes more than the extra mile to take care of matters I just don't have time for (www.mdp-a.com).

As always, I would like to acknowledge my family. My brother, Gordon Ogletree, is a Solaris Wizard and my sister, Susan Harris, is a fantastic manager and organizer. And, of course, I wouldn't be here if it were not for my parents. This book should be arriving at your local bookstore at about the same time they celebrate their 53rd wedding anniversary. I hope we have 50 more reasons to celebrate.

We Want to Hear from You!

As the reader of this book, *you* are our most important critic and commentator. We value your opinion and want to know what we're doing right, what we could do better, what areas you'd like to see us publish in, and any other words of wisdom you're willing to pass our way.

As an associate publisher for Que, I welcome your comments. You can fax, email, or write me directly to let me know what you did or didn't like about this book—as well as what we can do to make our books stronger.

Please note that I cannot help you with technical problems related to the topic of this book, and that due to the high volume of mail I receive, I might not be able to reply to every message.

When you write, please be sure to include this book's title and author, as well as your name and phone or fax number. I will carefully review your comments and share them with the author and editors who worked on the book.

Email: feedback@quepublishing.com

Mail: Greg Wiegand
          Que
          800 East 96th Street
          Indianapolis, IN 46240 USA

For more information about this book or another Que title, visit our Web site at www.quepublishing.com. Type the ISBN (excluding hyphens) or the title of a book in the Search field to find the page you're looking for.

Introduction

Since the last edition of this book, there have been many changes in the information and other technology sectors. After the downturn in the dot com industry, it looked as if a career in networking might not be such a good choice after all. In the months leading up to the publication of this book, however, things have started to change. The major baby bells and other large-scale network providers have begun to expand their fiber networks and offer digital services to customers who were not within their reach before. This is being fueled on the assumption that in the near future voice services will be less of a revenue source than newer technologies such as end-to-end IP. XDSL and cable modems have enabled both home users and business customers to connect even faster to the Internet. These large corporations are laying the groundwork for what appears to be a very bright future. If you think that networking and the Internet are futuristic now, just wait to see what will happen tomorrow.

When put into perspective, the IT field grew dramatically leading up to the "year 2000" concerns. And the continued growth of the Internet has been phenomenal—seemingly indifferent to the economy at this time.

The growth in other IT fields, however, is historically unusual, and thus could not be sustained, from a business standpoint. When investors are willing to throw money at just about any new startup company because it seems like a safe ride, you can expect that there will be a backlash, as has been the case. The downturn in the economy a few years ago forced many large companies to put off purchases of network hardware, and also to lay off many employees. In general, the economy has always been a cyclic one, with a recession followed by a boom market. There is no reason to expect this to change. But the good news is that the worst is probably behind us, and the future is looking bright, especially because vendors have continued to develop new hardware and software, just at a slower place. For example, look at how quickly wireless networking has grown, despite the economy.

The next few years will most likely show a slower growth rate for IT jobs, but it will be a *sustainable* growth; the future for networking jobs has never been brighter for the long term. Because of my belief in this trend, it was much easier to write this fourth edition of *Scott Mueller's Upgrading and Repairing Networks*. I was enthusiastic because over time I have been able to add new topics, expand on others, and move some older material (which may still be relevant to your job) to the upgradingandrepairingpcs.com Web site that accompanies this book. I believe that with each new edition of this book, it just gets better and better. And with great development and technical editors at Que helping to make this a better book, I think you will find it the most comprehensive book on networking on the market today.

Who Should Use This Book?

Although this book is organized so that you can read it cover to cover, with each chapter or section building on the preceding one, it can also be used as an encyclopedia. If you are new to the networking field, you can use this book as a textbook. If you are a seasoned network administrator, and your network is changing fast or you are considering using new technologies, then this book can be a valuable reference enabling you to get up to speed on most any topic quickly. If you purchased any of the previous editions, please peruse this edition to see what has changed. Many sections, such as the one on TCP/IP and wireless networking, have been revamped to make the material a lot easier to understand.

What Will You Find Inside?

You will find a few chapters in this book that I did not write. This is because I was able to find someone who could write a better chapter due to his or her deep knowledge of the subject matter.

Part I, "Up Front: Network Planning and Design Concepts," starts off with a short chapter about the history of computer networks so that you can see how far computer interconnection technologies have developed in just a few short years. Following that is a great chapter written by Tom Crayner about network topologies—might as well start with the basics. Today you need careful planning to create a large, complex network, and Tom will show you the options to consider before you even begin to think about network protocols or other topics covered in this book. This part also contains information that will help you put together a network design or upgrade strategy, as well as some ideas about preventive maintenance that can be used to keep problems from happening in the first place.

Part II, "Physical Networking Components," covers the physical components that make up your network, from the network cables and network adapter cards to the devices that are used to connect these components. Chapter 6, "Wiring the Network—Cables, Connectors, Concentrators, and Other Network Components," was written by Dwight Torlay, an engineer who not only works in this capacity every day, but also teaches classes on these topics. In this edition the chapter has been updated, and you can learn a lot about components that are usually installed by contractors. If you want to know what they are doing, and why, then read this chapter so that you can ask the right questions and make the correct decisions when it comes to the physical cable plant and other devices that will connect your network.

Of course, you'll also find a chapter here on network adapter cards, which connect your computers to the network. If you want to expand your knowledge further on this topic, you should consider using *Scott Mueller's Upgrading and Repairing PCs*. That book will give you information about network adapter cards. The basics are covered here, such as different bus types and troubleshooting. However, Scott's book can give you greater insight about choosing the correct card, and the differences between cards on the market. It can also show you exactly how to install the hardware.

The upgradingandrepairingpcs.com Web site that comes with this book now contains chapters on older technology, such as repeaters, bridges, and hubs. Just because these chapters are now on the Web site doesn't mean you should ignore them. Many certification exams still require that you know the basics of computer networking, and these devices were revolutionary for their time. Chapter 8 gives you a quick lesson on network switches, which have now replaced hubs in most all networks. For the price of a hub a few years ago, you can now use a switch, and achieve a greater bandwidth on your network. Chapter 9 discusses virtual LANs (VLANs), which make managing a large network easier, and Chapter 10 discusses routers—those devices that can be used to connect different segments of your LAN or intranet, as well as connect your network to the Internet.

A new topic for this book can also be found in Chapter 11. And it should not be underestimated by the simple title: "Network Attached Storage and Storage Area Networks." With the need for terabytes of storage, technologies such as SCSI interfaces can no longer suffice for a large network because of distance limitations and expandability. In this chapter you can learn the difference between connecting additional storage to your LAN and adding a separate network that contains the storage that your servers need to have fast access to. This chapter alone could be the topic of an entire book.

Part III, "Low-Level Network Protocols," is where you'll find information about many types of technologies you can use to transmit data across your network. This section starts with a quick review of the IEEE 802.11 standards, followed by a chapter on the oldest LAN technology still in widespread use today: ARCnet. If you think that older solutions are always supplanted by newer ones that perform the same functions more efficiently, then read that chapter. And the next time someone asks you whether you want fries with that burger, you just might find that ARCnet is still there, as a viable solution to small networks that cannot afford a full-time network administrator. Because of ARCnet's simplicity, it is still employed in various situations, such as in point-of-sale registers and on some factory floors.

Today the major LAN wire protocol is Ethernet. It's been here for years, and will continue to be around as it evolves to meet newer demands for bandwidth and adapts to newer devices and technologies.

Token-Ring is still being used by a small percentage of networks, supported mainly by IBM and a few other vendors. However, because of its miniscule market share, and because there is very little development in process to update the technology as compared to Ethernet, this updated chapter is now found on the upgradingandrepairingpcs.com Web site.

Part IV, "Dedicated Connections and WAN Protocols," is written for both network administrators who need to connect LANs across large distances and those who need a local dedicated connection to another LAN or the Internet. Here you can find the choices available to you from the high-end T-class connections that give you huge bandwidth data paths. You will also find information about other dedicated connections, such as cable and DSL access. Keep in mind that cable and DSL access are not just for home users. Many of the large providers of these services are now targeting small businesses. If this is your environment, you might find this a less expensive method for giving your company an Internet presence.

Part V, "Wireless Networking Protocols," covers just what it says. In the previous edition of this book, wireless networking was just making its way into the marketplace. Even Bluetooth—used for very close connections, such as to replace cables used between keyboards, mice, and other devices to your computer—has probably finally arrived. In the past few years there has been much marketing hype about this technology, and it finally seems to have made it. You can also learn here about the major wireless technologies—many available at the consumer level as well as for the corporate network—including both IEEE 802.11b and IEEE 802.11a. The newest protocol in this section is IEEE 802.11g, which combines the best of both of the other two protocols. The 802.11g network devices are backward compatible with IEEE 802.11a and b, and can offer bandwidths up to 54Mbps. For wireless networks, you won't notice much of a difference from this sort of connection to your company's network than if you had a 100Mbps 100BASE-T connection. To top off this section, there is a chapter on other wireless developments, including everything from wireless security to new uses for wireless technology.

Part VI, "LAN and WAN Network, Service, and Application Protocols," contains such subjects as the all-important TCP/IP suite of protocols, applications, and troubleshooting utilities. Because TCP/IP is the main protocol used in LANs today, this is a must-read section for new readers as well as a refresher course for those who already are familiar with the topic. In addition to the basics of TCP/IP, this section covers everything from email protocols to directory services, routing protocols, and SSL, among many others.

Part VII, "Network User and Resource Management," will help you learn about managing users and controlling access to network resources. Coverage here includes Windows, NetWare, and Unix/Linux. One of the newest additions to this section is Windows 2003 and how you can use it and the updated Active Directory to manage and secure the network. A chapter devoted to network printing protocols has been updated to include the latest coverage of the Internet Printing Protocol (IPP), which is now supported by all the major operating systems. This is a topic that will revolutionize printing in the next few years, and it's a good idea to start brushing up on your skills today.

Part VIII, "System and Network Security," contains chapters to help you learn the basics about protecting your system. Topics include everything from creating policies and procedures for the workplace, to computer viruses and auditing the actions users perform on the network. Encryption technology is also covered in its own chapter, as are Virtual Private Networks (VPNs) and firewalls. If you connect to the Internet, or if you operate a large enterprise network, then this section has a lot of good security issues you should be cognizant of.

Part IX, "Troubleshooting Networks," complements most of the previous chapters. Tools you can use for troubleshooting and strategies for going about this process are found here. For small office/home office (SOHO) network users, there is an entire chapter devoted to your network. Because many SOHO networks are operated by small business owners, this chapter can help you understand more complex topics without having to read this entire book. Off-the-shelf cable/DSL routers and inexpensive firewall solutions might make you feel comfortable about your network, but everyday there are new threats that can make your small network a target.

Part X, "Upgrading Network Hardware," is a valuable reference for those who want to make use of the latest hardware devices, while trying to protect your investment in existing equipment where possible. A special chapter gives a good overview of adding wireless networking to your wired network.

Part XI, "Migration and Integration," covers the other side of the coin, upgrading from one operating system to another, as well as using multiple operating systems on the same network. This section discusses the many things that are common to most operating systems, as well as tools that can be used to help you integrate a diverse collection of systems into a single heterogeneous network. Topping off this section is another chapter of interest to SOHO users that discusses how you might go about setting up a LAN for your business. Again, you don't need to be versed in all the topics covered in this book in order to operate a small LAN. This chapter does refer to topics in other parts of the book, but it is a good starting place for those who either have a small LAN that needs to be upgraded, or are just starting out.

Finally, the appendixes contain information that can be used as a quick reference. You can get an overview of the OSI network reference model, as well as a concise explanation of how directory services work, specifically the Lightweight Directory Access Protocol (LDAP). An important resource here is a comprehensive glossary of networking terms. If you are reading a chapter in this book and find yourself stymied about a term or an acronym, then just look to this appendix for help.

As discussed earlier in this introduction, the upgradingandrepairingpcs.com Web site contains several chapters that had to be moved out of the main text. This is due to several factors. First, some of these topics apply to older networks and, second, this book would cost you a lot more if the page count were to increase by a few hundred pages! The chapters on the Web site, however, should not be dismissed as irrelevant. You may have a network that still uses the technologies found in these chapters. And, when studying for a certification exam, you should understand older technologies because they will probably turn up as questions when you sit down to take the test.

What's New in This Edition

Upgrading and Repairing Networks, Fourth Edition, contains a lot of updated content and has been reorganized to make it easier to find the information you need. Entirely new topics have been added based on feedback to the third edition and on many new technologies that have become important since the previous publication, especially Windows 2003 Server and Windows XP, wireless networking, and directory services.

Several contributing authors were brought on board to assist in making this book better than its predecessor, each a veteran in the computer book publishing field, as well as experts in their areas of networking. I'm sure you'll like what you find inside, and I'm sure you'll find that what you are looking for is easier to find in this edition. Also, don't forget to check out the Web site. In addition to the chapters mentioned previously, you will find a large collection of useful programs—from freeware to shareware and some demo programs—that can help you administer your network.

What's Missing from This Edition?

If there are topics that you think need to be included in a book like this, but that you do not find, let me know. Each time this book is written, feedback from readers is always used to add new chapters, as well as update older ones. You can send email to the publisher, or to me. If you have questions on some of the topics found in this book, I'll try to answer them for you the best I can. Feedback will just make this book a more valuable resource in the future. You can reach me at www.twoinc.com, or email me at two@twoinc.com. Happy reading!

Up Front: Network Planning and Design Concepts

SOME OF THE MAIN TOPICS FOR THIS PART ARE

A Short History of Computer Networking

Overview of Network Topologies

Network Design Strategies

Upgrading Strategies and Project Management

Protecting the Network: Preventative Maintenance Techniques

PART I

A Short History of Computer Networking

Today, computer networks are taken for granted much as the telephone network is. And the telephone network was, until the explosive growth of the Internet, the largest network in the world. It just wasn't a computer network. You could use modems to connect computers to each other on a one-by-one basis, but this wasn't networking in the sense we think of it today. And those early modems—300 baud or less—didn't make the transfer of data an inexpensive matter, especially when long-distance calls were required. In a funny twist of fate, voice communications are now creeping into the networking world (such as voice over IP, or VOIP), making the telephone network itself less important. To that end, many telephone companies are expanding rapidly into the data networking field so that they can offer data, voice, video, and other services.

Computer networking has been evolving since the late 1960s. Early work on the ARPANET began in the 1960s, and in 1969 a four-node network using primitive packet switching was created. The growth of this predecessor of today's Internet wasn't quite the phenomenon you see today.

As discussed in Chapter 14, "Ethernet: The Universal Standard," the ALOHAnet was created to establish connections between several computers in Hawaii. Robert Metcalf was later to use the basic principles from ALOHAnet to create what eventually became the Ethernet local area networking wire protocol still used today. Ethernet was simply a means to get a signal from one place to another—it was another thing to decide what kind of signaling to use. On the ARPANET, TCP was being created, and refined. If you examine the OSI Seven-Layer Networking Reference Model (see Appendix A, "Overview of the OSI Seven-Layer Networking Reference Model"), you can see that Ethernet works at a low level in the model, and is used to transmit packets of information from higher-level protocols. TCP was the first major higher-level protocol created. One of the first refinements of TCP was to break it into several parts (or layers), which is why the protocol "suite" is known today as TCP/IP.

TCP (the Transmission Control Protocol) and IP (the Internet Protocol) are the basis of the Internet. Another break-out from TCP was the User Datagram Protocol (UDP). Both TCP and UDP provide different types of service, yet both use IP as the workhorse protocol that is used to route packets (or datagrams) on the Internet, as well as any intranet. And what does IP use to send data across the wire (or the air, in case of a wireless network)? Ethernet in most cases. For the long-haul, there are other protocols that can be used, and you will read about them in Part V of this book, "Wireless Networking Protocols."

It is important to keep in mind that Ethernet and other wire-level protocols simply provide the means to frame data—create discrete units of data for transmission—and then use a specified method to send data across the network media. For example, simply varying the voltage on a wire can be used to send data from one point to another. An early transmission method, called non-return to zero (NRZ) encoding, used just this method. A high value was used to specify the bit value of one, and a low value was used for zero. A drawback to this encoding scheme is that a long stream of either ones or zeros can be difficult to decipher at the receiving end. The term "clock" is used to mean that each end of the transmission understands where a bit starts and where it ends during the transmission. Because it would be very expensive to have a physical clock at each end that could precisely time each bit transmission, this encoding method does not scale well.

Early Ethernet networks used a technique called Manchester encoding. This method does provide a clocking mechanism that is built into the coding scheme itself. Instead of using a high- or low-voltage state to indicate a specific bit, Manchester encoding uses the change from one state to another, during a specific interval.

While TCP/IP continued its development on the ARPANET, computer vendors began to recognize the importance of networking, and many proprietary protocols were developed. Digital Equipment Corporation (DEC) created DECnet (and numerous other protocols), which was used to connect its PDP computers and, later, VAX and AlphaServer computers. Today DECnet is still used, although

TCP/IP has pretty much replaced it for most installations. For a short time in the 1980s, however, DEC operated the largest computer network in the world, short of the Internet. What protocol was used? DECnet, of course. During that same period, the OSI model was created, and Digital incorporated the concepts of that model, as well as the protocols that were developed by ISO based on the OSI model, into DECnet. Because the VMS (Virtual Memory System) operating system used on DEC's VAX computers was adopting these open standards, the name of the operating system was changed to OpenVMS. However, few other vendors chose to incorporate the high-overhead concepts of these open protocols, and this first attempt to standardize networking protocols between different computers failed to come about.

Other computer manufacturers also produced their own proprietary network protocols. For example, IBM's work in this direction resulted in SNA, which combined networking protocols from the high end (application) down to the low end (wire protocols). As networking began to become an important part of the computing world, other vendors, such as Xerox (XNS), also came up with their own protocols.

The result was that if you wanted to create a network of computers for your business, you had to stick with a single vendor. Proprietary protocols, then, were not a good solution to the problem of exchanging data between computers.

During the early days of PCs, the same sort of situation occurred. Although PCs were basically the same when it came to the operating system (DOS at the start), you could buy a network setup from many different vendors. One that comes to mind is NetWare (which is still around today, although in recent years TCP/IP has replaced the proprietary IPX/SPX NetWare protocols). LAN Manager was Microsoft's entry into the field, with a legacy of NetBEUI and NetBIOS still lurking around on many Windows computers prior to Windows 2000. When DEC started to build its own PCs, it licensed LAN Manager technology and created Pathworks. You might still find Pathworks in some networks, although, like LAN Manager, it is considered history today.

Other networking packages included Banyan Vines and LANtastic, both of which are still around today. However, these products are today vastly different than when they first appeared.

In Chapter 13, "The Oldest LAN Protocol Is Still Kicking: ARCnet," you can read about an old protocol that is still used pretty much the same as it was when first created. It allows a limited number of computers to be connected, uses a simple token passing scheme, and requires minimal setup. ARCnet is typically found in point-of-sale computers and factory automation today.

The Internet changed the entire landscape. As TCP/IP continued to mature into the stable protocol suite that it is today, the PC landscape, as well as mainframe and minicomputers, began to adopt TCP/IP. Although the ISO first attempted to define open protocols so that computers from different vendors could interact to exchange data, it turns out that TCP/IP is the winner in the end. And when IPv6 (IP version 6) finally reaches from the inner core of the Internet to the edge, you will find that TCP/IP continues to add new features, enhance security, and provide more robust features.

Other protocols, such as ATM and Frame Relay, are used for long-distance transfer of data, and can encapsulate other protocols such as TCP/IP. Fibre Channel is a wire protocol that is the most widely used protocol in Storage Area Networks today (see Chapter 11, "Network Attached Storage and Storage Area Networks").

The old standard Ethernet has itself continued to be enhanced to keep up with the need for speed. Early versions operated at 2–5Mbps, and most desktops today use 100BASE-T, or 100Mbps Ethernet. Gigabit and 10Gigabit Ethernet are now on the market, although these newer versions do not use the same signaling techniques as earlier versions. The capability to provide backward compatibility with earlier versions, however, is another important factor for the continued use of Ethernet.

Today you will find that most desktop computers in a company's LAN use TCP/IP. Although other protocols may encapsulate TCP/IP for transmission over a long distance, the TCP/IP protocol is still the de facto standard for computer-to-computer communications. TCP/IP is also supported by networked printers and wireless communications.

Because of this standardization, prices for equipment that support Ethernet and TCP/IP are dramatically less than a decade ago. Network adapters themselves may become history because many computer motherboard manufacturers are starting to incorporate that functionality directly onto the motherboard.

So what does this all mean? It means that whether you operate a business or a home network, or if you just connect to the Internet from home, it has been a long process to get to where we are today. In this book you will find topics that cover many of the important protocols in use today, as well as topics on newer developments.

Overview of Network Topologies

SOME OF THE MAIN TOPICS IN THIS CHAPTER ARE

CHAPTER 2

Before you can begin to upgrade and repair your network, you need to understand how it's laid out, how it functions, and how the various parts are related to one another. Knowing how your network components are related makes the extension, expansion, and troubleshooting of your environment more focused and productive. Because network uptime is related directly to productivity, a solid grasp of network concepts is a necessity when you're facing a troubled LAN.

In this chapter, you will review the topologies in use today and learn the strengths and weaknesses of each.

LAN Topologies

Several unique network technologies have been developed over the past three decades. Different types of networks have different design criteria and, thus, various topologies have come into use. One important distinction needs to be made before we enter into a serious discussion on topology: physical topology versus logical topology. The *physical topology* describes the layout of a network media (such as copper and fiber-optic cables and, more recently, wireless equipment) and the devices that connect to it. The *logical topology* is concerned not with the actual physical connections but with the logical path through the network that data can take from one place to another. The differences will be more evident as the different topologies are discussed.

The basic topologies you will find in most LANs today include the following:

- Bus
- Star
- Ring
- Mesh
- Hybrids

Bus Topology

The simple bus topology structure was the first type used in Ethernet networks. The typical bus physical topology consists of a coaxial cabling common to all computer systems connected to the LAN. This coax is tapped in multiple places along its length, with each tap being used as a point of connection for a computing system. Taps can be physical cores cut into the coax (sometimes called a "vampire tap") or BNC-style "T-connectors" that join several individual pieces of coax together to form the common bus (see Figure 2.1 and Figure 2.2 for a comparison of the two methods).

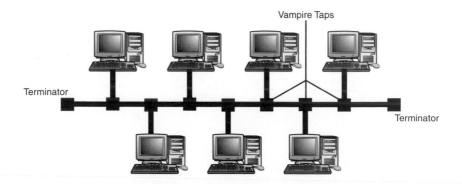

Figure 2.1   Computers can connect to coaxial cables on a bus by tapping directly through the core of the cable. The vampire taps pierce the thicknet cable but not the BNC.

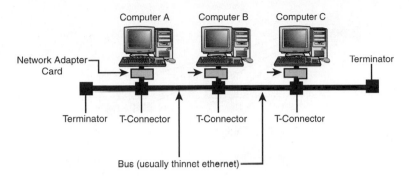

Figure 2.2 BNC-style T-connectors make attaching computers to a bus a simpler operation.

▶▶ You can learn more about how 10BASE-2 and 10BASE-5 Ethernet networks are created using coaxial cables and the bus topology in Chapter 14, "Ethernet: The Universal Standard."

A bus is also a logical topology. From a device's viewpoint, all other systems communicate through the same, shared path. Because it is a shared media technology, mechanisms must be put into place to arbitrate network traffic over the cable. Typically, collision detection (CD) or collision avoidance (CA) algorithms are used in bus topologies to arbitrate network access along with concepts such as "broadcasts" to reach every device on the cable. This subject is covered in detail in Chapter 14.

The bus topology is very simple and inexpensive to implement due to its low cost requirements for cable installation (there's only one main trunk). But some serious deficiencies make bus topology LANs unattractive to deploy:

■ Bus topologies require proper terminations on both ends of the bus to effectively dampen the network signal and to avoid a "reflection" or reoccurrence of a previous transmission. Without the proper terminations in place, expect a very slow or inoperable network.

■ The cable itself is a single point of failure. One break, cut, or poor connection negatively impacts the entire LAN.

■ Because all workstations or devices share a common cable, troubleshooting can be difficult when problems occur. You must temporarily break the terminations in the network to isolate a device. After you think you've resolved the network problem, you must disrupt LAN service again to reattach the device to the network. This makes for a cumbersome and disruptive process.

Due to these limitations, the bus topology is typically found only in the smallest or most austere of installations. Some proprietary manufacturing process control systems use a bus topology, but these aren't covered in this book.

For the most part, the bus topology is a historical relic. However, it is something you should be cognizant of in order to understand why other topologies are the norm today. Early networks were composed of only a few computers and there was no need to provide for today's high-bandwidth networks that use switches and other devices to connect a diverse collection of computers and other networked devices.

Star Topology

The concept behind the star topology is simple. Every node on the LAN has a dedicated cable that is pulled back to a centralized point, typically a wiring closet. All cables are terminated in a network component within the closet, such as a hub or, more typically today, a switch, which handles the repeating or switching of traffic out to the other nodes on the network (see Figure 2.3).

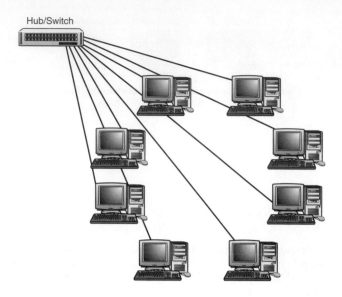

Figure 2.3   The star topology enables you to centralize wiring for a network.

The shortcomings of a star topology network are obvious: The network component (hub or switch) is a single point of failure, and a great deal of wiring is involved to implement the star.

However, there are tremendous benefits to a star topology:

- Management of the network is centralized around the hub and switch components. Most of these components have features that allow an administrator to spot congestion and network errors at the port level, which makes troubleshooting problems quick and simple.

- "Smart hubs" can automatically disable ports that exceed use or error thresholds, providing additional stability to the LAN. They are also a central point for watching bandwidth usage and overall network health.

- Wiring installation is less obtrusive and therefore does not disrupt LAN service with the addition or deletion of nodes.

- A cable cut or bad connector does not take down the entire LAN segment. No terminators are required as in the bus topology model.

You should note that nearly every popular network technology today uses a star topology for its physical implementation. This is due to several factors, including the ease of wiring, the fact that a single misbehaving computer can be removed from the topology, and the fact that it's a simple matter to set up a hub or switch.

Note

When troubleshooting a star topology network, be sure to check error counters and status indicators on your network components. These can provide valuable information in helping you find what is at fault.

Ring Topology

Ring topologies are more complex than the bus and star topologies discussed in previous sections, but they offer some attractive features. Nodes logically communicate in a ring formation, with each node communicating only directly with its upstream and downstream neighbors (see Figure 2.4).

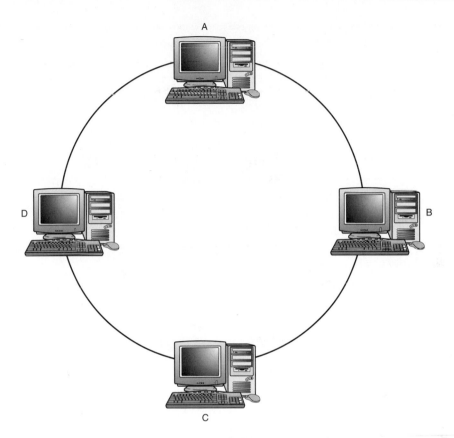

Figure 2.4   The ring topology links each node on the network to two other nodes on the network.

You can probably picture what a mess the wiring would be in an office with hundreds of computer systems, if a network like this were implemented as a physical ring. So ring topologies are typically implemented in a physical star topology (see Figure 2.5).

In a ring topology, access to the network is controlled through a token that is passed from node to node as the arbitration mechanism. Each node takes its turn at claiming the token as the token passes from neighbor to neighbor, and when a node possesses the token, it takes its turn to transmit onto the ring. A data packet is transferred from one node to the next until it reaches its destination node. After the destination node has received the packet, it modifies the packet to acknowledge receipt and passes it on. Eventually, the packet makes it completely around the ring, and the transmitting node receives it and notes that the receipt has been acknowledged. When the transmitting node is finished, it releases the token to its neighbor, and the process repeats.

Note

Token-Ring networks are the primary LAN technology that uses a ring topology. Although Token-Ring technology today represents only a small percentage of network installations, another network, the Storage Area Network (SAN) still uses the concept of a ring topology, with a different method for gaining access to the network media than the method used by Token-Ring networks.

In Chapter 11, "Network Attached Storage and Storage Area Networks," you will find that *Arbitrated Loops* continue to use the ring topology to provide access to storage devices, such as disk and tape drives, to high-end servers. The

Arbitrated Loop maintains a ring topology but uses an arbitration priority method based on device addresses to gain access to the loop instead of the token-passing mechanism used by Token-Ring networks.

Newer SANs are built using a switched network technology often referred to as a SAN fabric. As you will read in Chapter 11, it is possible to attach an Arbitrated Loop to a SAN fabric to preserve your current investment.

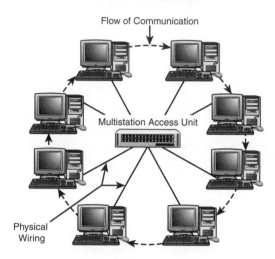

Figure 2.5 The ring topology is usually implemented as a physical star to simplify wiring management.

The benefits of this kind of topology can be readily observed:

- Token-controlled access provides greater overall bandwidth use, because there are no collision avoidance and collision detection algorithms to throttle transmissions on the media.

- Data packet transmission happens within a determinable time interval. Because each node gets a chance to claim the token and ring for itself, it's easy to determine the amount of time before the next transmission can occur (it's based on the number of nodes on the ring). This quality of ring topologies has made it a staple in manufacturing environments in which timing is essential.

- Because each node knows its upstream and downstream neighbors, this information can be used to determine where problems have occurred on the ring.

Another ring topology called Fiber Distributed Data Interface (FDDI) uses dual fault-tolerant rings. This technology requires that the two rings have tokens passing in opposite directions of one another. A breakdown in one ring causes the nodes to shift over to the secondary ring to continue communications.

▶▶ FDDI is another networking technology that uses the ring topology and token-passing for media access. Please visit the **upgradingandrepairingpcs.com** Web site for the chapter "Fiber Distributed Data Interface (FDDI)," which covers this topic in detail.

The down side of a ring topology is simple: The firmware required to manage the ring is somewhat complicated and must be on every network card that participates in the ring. Because Ethernet dominates the marketplace today, you can purchase an inexpensive 100Mbps Ethernet network adapter for $20 to $30. Token-Ring network adapters are a bit more difficult to find, and they tend to be more expensive devices than their Ethernet counterparts. As a result, technologies such as Ethernet have transitioned rapidly to higher networking speeds while ring topologies have never quite jumped the speed gap. The ring topologies that exist today have changed little in the past 10 to 15 years.

Mesh Topology

A *mesh* topology is an interlacing of multiple connections among several nodes. Typically, a mesh is done for one purpose: redundancy. Any serious campus network must incorporate a mesh to achieve the level of redundancy and fault tolerance that businesses demand from their data networks. There are two types of mesh: full and partial.

Except in the smallest network, a full mesh is not very practical, but it is mentioned here for completeness. Full mesh means that every node contained in a network has a connection to every other node contained in the network. It should be fairly obvious at this point why full meshes are not very practical (see Figure 2.6). The cost for such infrastructure would be exorbitant, and 90% of it would never be put to use.

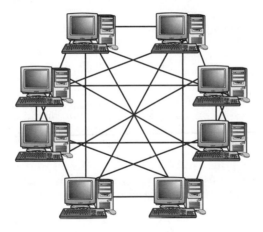

Figure 2.6   A full mesh topology is not a very practical way to wire a network.

Partial meshes are designed to provide redundancy where it is needed. By using a little forethought in design, a network architect could place some additional connectivity where it can provide needed bandwidth and fault tolerance to the network. Suppose for a moment that an important resource were attached to node A, as shown in Figure 2.7.

You can spot several paths that could fail, yet all the nodes of your network would still be able to reach node A as a destination. The true merits of partial mesh are realized when you look at WAN and campus topologies.

Hybrid Topologies

Hubs or switches can be attached to one another to create larger LANs capable of supporting more devices. After this happens, you start getting some interesting hybrid topologies. Three popular hybrids are tree, hierarchical star, and star-wireless.

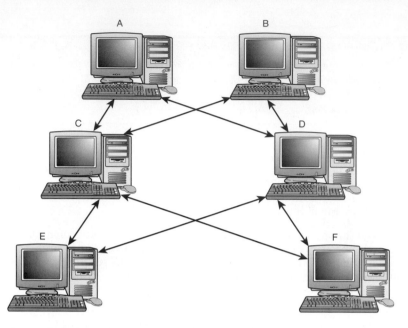

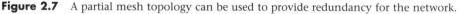

Figure 2.7   A partial mesh topology can be used to provide redundancy for the network.

Tree

Figure 2.8 shows a combination topology that groups workstations in a star and joins the stars along a linear bus. The majority of the problems of the bus are eliminated because a single workstation cannot bring the entire LAN to a halt. You still can add or change workstations by plugging them into a different port on the same hub, or on another hub. If one hub malfunctions, it disables only the workstations that are attached to it from communicating on the network. The remaining workstations on the other hubs can continue to function normally.

This is an inexpensive method that can be used to join different work departments in a building. Each local workgroup can have an administrative person who is responsible for managing the connections on the local hub. The network administrator can regulate when and where new hubs are attached to the network. This also can be used to help extend the distance of a LAN. For example, you can use 10BASE-2 cabling to connect two 10BASE-T networks that are in separate buildings. However, today that connection would most likely be accomplished using more modern techniques, such as with fiber-optic cabling.

The major problem with this type of hybrid topology, however, is that if there is a problem with the backbone bus cable, the network becomes segmented into individual hubs. Workstations on each hub can communicate with each other, but data transfers through the network to workstations on other hubs will be disrupted until the cable problem is diagnosed and corrected.

Hierarchical Star

Another method that can be used to connect hubs is a hierarchical star. This method, shown in Figure 2.9, uses a central hub to link several hubs that have workstations attached.

This method can be used to build very large LANs; however, there are restrictions on the size of the LAN. Timing issues as well as address space are driving factors in how many hubs or switches you are able to attach in the hierarchical star topology without the introduction of routing technology. The various restrictions of different network technologies are discussed in later chapters.

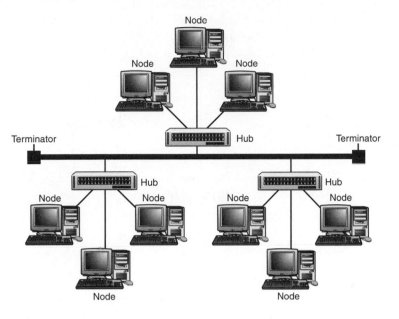

Figure 2.8 A combination of the bus and star topologies groups workstations in a star and joins them along a linear bus.

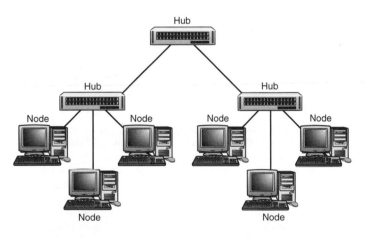

Figure 2.9 The hierarchical star topology is made up of cascading hubs.

Star-Wireless

The most recent hybrid topology has arrived with the advent of wireless technology. Wireless LAN technology in its current implementation requires a user to be in the vicinity of an *access point* attached to the wired data network. A configuration such as this gives you an amorphous hybrid topology of star combined with wireless (see Figure 2.10).

The star topology is necessary to combine the many access points spread across a building to ensure wireless coverage. All the access points collapse back into the main star hub, where server resources would reside on the network. As wireless technologies continue to evolve, so will the topologies that support them.

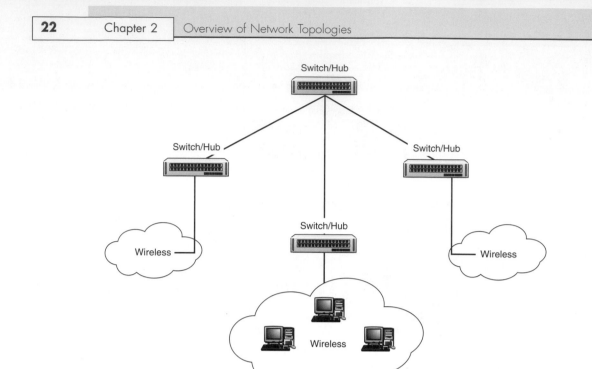

Figure 2.10   Wireless technology adds a new dimension to network topologies.

▶▶   For more information about using wireless technology in your network, see Part V, "Wireless Networking Protocols," which covers the current and emerging wireless technologies.

Shared and Nonshared Network Media Topologies

As mentioned earlier, you must abide by some constraints when constructing very large LAN environments. One item that often is overlooked is the size of the broadcast domain for a LAN segment.

Hubs take inbound traffic and broadcast it outbound on all their other ports. This means that each time a node makes a network request, the request is flooded to all other nodes. The more nodes you have on your LAN, the more traffic you have being flooded throughout the LAN segment. If you are running an Ethernet network, all this chatter can keep your LAN segment so busy that other nodes might have trouble finding an opportunity to transmit. The term *broadcast domain* is used to describe the total collection of devices that use the same network media, and thus have to contend for access to the media. This is the main reason switches have become the device of choice to replace hubs. Using a switch, the broadcast domain consists of just the switch and the device attached to the switch (if using a half-duplex connection). For a full-duplex connection—in which both the switch and the attached device can transmit data at the same time, using separate wires—the broadcast domain is eliminated, because there is no shared media.

▶▶   Switches have generally replaced hubs as the wiring concentrator of choice in most LANs. You can learn more about switches and how they work by reading Chapter 8, "Network Switches."

A solution for this problem is the introduction of a switch into the network environment. By deploying a switch in place of a hub, you dramatically reduce the number of flooded packets. Switches don't just blindly repeat network traffic, they make intelligent port-forwarding decisions based on the addresses they recognize within the packets. The net effect of introducing switches into your environment in place of hubs is that your nodes see very little flooded traffic (unless it is addressed to them) and the contention problem is greatly reduced (see Figure 2.11).

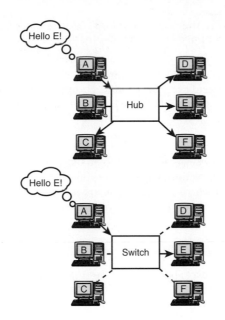

Figure 2.11 Switches can centralize wiring and also provide a greater available bandwidth to the network.

Don't forget that you still have the network broadcasts to contend with. Broadcasts get flooded to all ports within a network segment, regardless of whether you use hubs or switches. So always consider the amount of broadcast traffic added to your environment when expanding your LAN.

Full-Duplex Versus Half-Duplex

The discussion of shared and nonshared media would not be complete without the mention of full-duplex technologies. Everything that has been covered so far has assumed a half-duplex environment, which means that a node can either receive or transmit but cannot do both at the same time. In a full-duplex environment, a node can transmit and receive at the same time using separate receive and transmit pairs. If you realize that having separate pairs for transmit and receive means that there is no chance for packet collisions, you are absolutely correct! If you can afford full-duplex hubs, switches, and NICs for your environment, you should strongly consider them because they remove a major impediment in LAN design and performance.

You might ask yourself why a network topology would ever use half-duplex to begin with. The answer is simple: It's historical. Recall that at the time Ethernet was invented it was a bus topology with a coax cable; there was no opportunity for a dedicated transmit and receive pair.

Bridged Versus Routed Topologies

This section reviews bridged and routed topologies to give you a sense of how each technology can be used. Refer to the chapter "Bridges, Repeaters, and Hubs" on the upgradingandrepairingpcs.com Web site, for an in-depth overview of bridges. Details about routers can be found in Chapter 10, "Routers."

Bridging

Bridges are intelligent network devices that monitor the MAC level (layer 2) addresses within a packet. A bridge creates a table in its memory and stores the MAC address and port address of each network resource that it sees as a source of network traffic, in effect "learning" which ports are connected to a particular node.

When a bridge fails to recognize the destination MAC address of a packet it has received, it floods the packet to all its ports. When a bridge knows the destination port, it just forwards the packet to that one port.

Using this methodology, the bridge quickly accumulates an understanding of where all devices reside from its viewpoint and intelligently forwards traffic. Sounds a lot like the switch that was used earlier to replace the hub technology, doesn't it? Indeed, switches are basically just high-speed bridges with a high port density.

Routing

Routers are intelligent network devices that work at the Network level (layer 3). It is at this level that protocols such as TCP/IP, IPX/SPX, and AppleTalk are defined. Routers understand the routing topology; that is, they have an idea where all LAN segments reside. They perform routing tasks by using special "routing protocols" to communicate with other routers within a network.

▶▶ The topic of routing is covered in two other chapters. Chapter 10, "Routers," discusses how the actual router devices work, and Chapter 37, "Routing Protocols," describes how routers exchange information and maintain the routing tables that make connecting different networks possible.

Routers intelligently forward packets based on the destination segment information contained in the network protocol within a packet. A nice feature of routing is that routers do not propagate broadcasts. Broadcasts stay within a network segment, and routers are the devices that segment the network.

VLANs

When manufacturers first came out with hubs, these devices could support only one network segment. But what if you needed to support multiple network segments out of the same wiring closet? The answer was simple: You needed more hubs! Virtual local area networks (VLANs) solved this problem by providing trunking protocols that allowed the traffic of multiple LAN segments to be multiplexed across the same riser cable. After the traffic was received, the switch or hub device demultiplexed the traffic and forwarded it to the appropriate ports. In this manner, many subnets could be supported out of a single network component, and collision-domain size could be controlled by carving a large LAN into several small VLANs. A side benefit of VLANs is the security gained by being able to partition workgroups with sensitive security needs off onto their own VLAN for an extra measure of protection.

▶▶ Virtual LANs (VLANs) have become popular in large environments. They simplify subnet and client management and help to centralize wiring. Chapter 9, "Virtual LANs," gives you more information about this technology.

Layer-3 Switching

Layer-3 switching is a hybrid technology that combines the speed of a switch with the LAN segment analysis of a router to make packet forwarding decisions. Layer-3 switching is the best of both worlds because you get the broadcast isolation and segmenting capabilities of a router, yet you have the lightning-fast forwarding decisions of a wire-speed switching device. A layer-3 switch can typically forward a packet 10–20 times faster than a router!

Building and Campus Topologies

Constructing a LAN within the confines of a building or campus immediately focuses you on the physical topology of your LAN environment. Let's take a look at how you can apply the topologies we've discussed to a physical implementation.

Connecting Network Segments Within a Building: The Backbone

You can think of a backbone as the spine of your network. The backbone integrates all the other LAN segments in one cohesive structure and facilitates the communication among these different segments. Take a look at Figure 2.12. You can see how a star topology–based backbone has been used to tie together three separate segments in this fictitious three-story building.

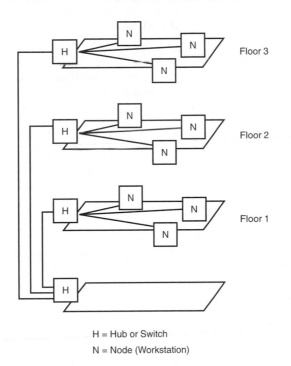

H = Hub or Switch
N = Node (Workstation)

Figure 2.12 A network backbone connects other LAN segments to create a larger network.

Backbones can be implemented with copper wiring, but fiber-optic cables are far more popular for a few reasons:

- The distance up through the risers of a building can be too long for copper wiring. Fiber-optic cables can usually handle a signal for far greater distances and therefore are a more popular medium for backbones. It is rare today to find a large network that uses coaxial cabling for a network backbone segment. There is still a large installed base of backbone segments using twisted-pair copper cables (usually running at 100Mbps), but new installations typically use fiber-optic cabling.

- Usually, electrical trunks servicing power for the building are inside the risers. Noisy electrical subsystems can wreak havoc with high-speed data communications, and copper wiring is sensitive to this electrical interference. Fiber optic, on the other hand, uses LEDs or lasers for its signaling and is not prone to electrical interference.

■ Because fiber optic does not succumb to electrical interference, it can support far higher network speeds, making it the perfect medium for a backbone. With backbones, you might want to jump to higher-speed LAN technologies as they become available. Higher-speed LAN technologies are not always readily supported on old copper wiring standards and can force you to perform costly wiring upgrades.

Note

After you've decided on a topology for your network, you'll need to determine which types of cables, connectors, and other devices to use. Chapter 6, "Wiring the Network—Cables, Connectors, Concentrators, and Other Network Components," is a useful reference.

Backbones can also span buildings. Once again, an important point to keep in mind is the distances with which you are working. If you design beyond the specifications of the network technology you are using, be prepared for a poor performing or inoperable LAN environment.

Design Considerations in a Campus LAN Environment

Integrating the LANs of several buildings creates a campus network. As a LAN grows to this scale, you face a few more design challenges: scalability, redundancy, and fault tolerance. Now give some thought to just some of the design considerations you have to keep in mind when designing a campus LAN environment (see Figure 2.13).

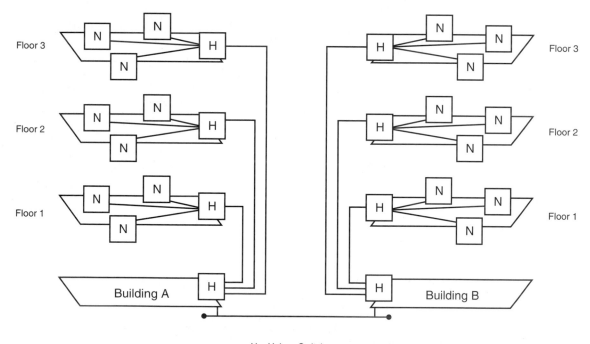

H = Hub or Switch
N = Node (Workstation)

Figure 2.13   The topology for a campus network is more complex than a simple bus or star.

You will notice two buildings that are three stories tall as you look at Figure 2.13. Suppose that each "node" represents 100 computer workstations. If this were the case, you would have 300 computer workstations per floor, 900 per building, and 1,800 for the entire campus.

Scalability

Scalability is the capability of the design to meet all the network traffic requirements and to continue to accommodate them as the company grows. The scalability question enters into several areas in your network design. Let's consider just a few of them:

- Where will you place critical server resources that your computer workstations will be using?
- Will the network technology used in your risers be capable of supporting the 300 workstations you have placed on each floor?
- Will the backbone that ties your campus together be capable of supporting cross-building traffic among the 1,800 workstations?
- Will the hubs or switches have enough bandwidth capacity to process the traffic among the three floors and two buildings?
- Will the network protocols allow you to properly address every workstation in this environment?
- Will the LAN environment be capable of accommodating the volume of broadcasts?
- Will the overall distance between the two farthest nodes on the network be outside the bounds of the *network technology you have chosen*?
- Are there workgroups that have particularly high network demands? How will you accommodate them?

Redundancy

Redundancy is the capability of the network to fail-over to secondary paths when your primary paths are cut or experience some other type of hardware failure. How much redundancy to deploy is often a cost issue. The more redundancy in a network, the greater the cost in implementation. On the other hand, if nodes or some part of your network infrastructure should fail, added redundancy can insolate your network from extended periods of downtime, which can be even more costly. Referring to Figure 2.13, consider the design from a redundancy standpoint, giving some thought to the following questions:

- How many single points of failure do you have in the network design?
- Can the environment afford to accommodate downtime during normal hours of operation? Should you consider redundancy between buildings, within buildings, or both?
- Where can you place critical resources so that clients could still work even if you were to lose an entire floor of the building?
- Where will you place resources on the LAN that are critical to the entire campus?
- What if a backhoe were to cut through your cross-building backbone?

Fault Tolerance

Fault tolerance is the aspect of your network that defines how resilient it is to the various problems that will inevitably crop up. Keeping the fault tolerance of the design in mind, consider just a few questions on this topic:

- Could a problem with a single workstation negatively impact the entire campus LAN?
- How would the LAN environment react to a broadcast storm?
- Do you have any isolation features to keep problems from propagating throughout the campus environment?

Whew! And you thought designing a campus LAN would be easy! But don't worry, everything you need to know is discussed in detail in the following chapters.

A Multi-Tiered Network Topology

By combining what you have learned so far about network topologies, you can develop a design that can meet most of the objectives mentioned in the preceding section concerning the campus network design. Several powerful features of the new campus design appear in Figure 2.14.

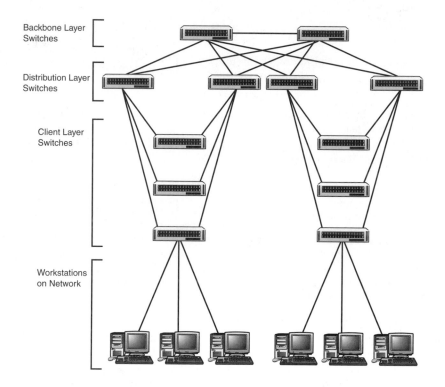

Figure 2.14   The partial mesh topology can be used to provide scalability, fault tolerance, and redundancy.

Note that the design is a partial mesh star topology. In the next few sections we'll look at how this topology can be used to provide for scalability, redundancy, and fault tolerance for your network.

Scalability

With the advent of a distribution layer, you have the ability to offload some of the network capacity requirements at a lower level of the network. For example, if you placed your file servers at the distribution layer, the backbone layer would be freed of significant burden and could focus its resources on cross-building and data-center level traffic requirements. The distribution layer would turn around about 80% of all the network traffic and respond directly to the client layer, speeding network access. By offloading file and print servers at a lower level in the network, you would have a great deal of scalability.

Note the mesh between the distribution layer and the backbone layer. You could use a high-speed network technology such as gigabit Ethernet to deliver the aggregate bandwidth you needed at the top layers of the network to process whatever requests were coming out of the client layers. Having separated this mesh from the client layer switches means you could slip higher-speed technologies into the mesh as they came along without costly downtime to your clients and expensive rewiring of your buildings.

Finally, by using VLANs from the distribution layer down into the client layer, you can ensure smaller broadcast domains to further drive down network use.

Redundancy

Significant gains in redundancy have been added by inserting a distribution layer of switching technology between client layer switches and backbone layer switches. This design would not have been possible with hub technology because the redundant connectivity would cause loops in the network, something a switch controls with a process called the *Spanning Tree Protocol*.

A failure at the distribution layer causes the client layer switches to fail-over to a secondary distribution switch. Likewise, if a failure occurs at the backbone layer, the traffic reroutes to the secondary backbone switch. Another nice feature is that because the distribution and backbone have a primary and secondary switch device, you can dual-home your most critical servers at these layers and still have network connectivity if you have a NIC card failure on your server.

Fault Tolerance

By using VLAN technologies, you can control the spread of broadcast, which provides an extra layer of control and fault tolerance to your network. Also, by incorporating some layer-3 switching technology, you can provide further isolation for robustness. Recall that routing does not forward segment broadcasts, so by using layer-3 switching, you also provide a means of isolating problems to a particular segment.

As you can see, a combination of old and new topologies and technologies provides a solid foundation that can be scaled to great size without sacrificing stability and performance.

Network Design Strategies

Many types of networks were discussed in Chapter 1, "A Short History of Computer Networking," from ARCnet to TCP/IP. And in Chapter 2, "Overview of Network Topologies," you learned about the various topologies you can employ when designing and creating a local area network (LAN), and we also looked at some scenarios in which several networks were connected to form a wide area network (WAN). In this chapter, we will look at another aspect of creating a network: the network's logical and physical design. The physical aspects of your LAN will depend on the underlying physical transport technology—Ethernet or Token-Ring, for example, or possibly ATM, which is now supported in products such as Windows 2000/XP and Server 2003 as a LAN protocol. Depending on which technology you use, there will be one or more LAN topologies from which to choose.

Note

Although there are other LAN technologies, such as ARCnet and Novell's IPX/SPX, these are basically legacy products that are no longer being deployed in newer networks. For example, ARCnet is now used mostly in vertical-market applications (such as on the factory floor, or for point-of-sale cash registers). If you don't need the features that TCP/IP provides, and don't need an Internet connection, then these older protocols may be a good solution for your network. Novell's NetWare products, while allowing for backward compatibility with the IPX/SPX protocol, have finally caught up with the times, and new installations will more than likely use the IP protocol. Other protocols, such as Microsoft's LAN Manager, are used only in older networks. If you are still using older proprietary protocols, you should consider upgrading to TCP/IP, which is now the de facto standard, from the worldwide Internet down to the LAN.

Before you can begin to design a physical network, however, you first must determine your needs. What services must you provide to your user community? What are the resources you'll need? If you have to compromise, what will it take to satisfy the most users or to provide the more important services? You then will have to take into account network protocols, applications, network speed, and, most important, network security issues; each of these figures into a network's logical design. Another important factor your management will probably force you to consider is cost—you can't forget the budget. These factors make up the logical design for your network. You first should decide what you need and what it will take to provide for those needs.

If you are creating a new network and purchasing new applications, you will probably spend most of your time considering the licensing and other financial costs (training users, network personnel, and so on). If you are upgrading older applications, several other factors come into consideration. Many applications that were coded using COBOL, BASIC, FORTRAN, and other languages that helped jump-start the computer age may have built-in network functionality based on older proprietary network protocols. If this is the case with your network, you have to consider several things. What will it cost to update thousands of lines of code (or more) to more modern versions of the same programming language? What will it cost to upgrade these programs to newer object-oriented languages? To save money, can you upgrade part of your network and use gateway hardware/software to connect to older network components?

Because of the costs associated with coding applications that were created many years ago, and the expenses that will be required to update them to modern programming languages, you may be forced to maintain legacy applications for a few years while replacement applications are designed and created. You may find a packaged application that can be used to replace older programs. This problem will apply mostly to proprietary computer architectures, instead of Windows or Unix platforms. If you can simply make minor changes and compile the source code so that it will run on a newer operating system, your costs will be much less than if you have to re-create the applications your users need from scratch. Another cost associated with upgrading to new programs is training users and help-desk personnel.

Planning a Logical Network Design

When you plan a logical network design, you can start from one of two places. You can design and install a new network from scratch, or you can upgrade an existing network. Either way, you should gather information about several important factors before you begin the logical design. For example, depending on the services that will be provided to clients, you might need to analyze the possible traffic patterns that might result from your plan. Locate potential bottlenecks and, where possible, alleviate them by providing multiple paths to resources or by putting up servers that provide replicas of important data so that load balancing can be provided. The following are other factors to consider:

- Who are the clients? What are their actual needs? How have you determined these needs—from user complaints or from help-desk statistics? Is this data reliable?

- What kinds of services will you provide on the network? Are they limited in scope? Will any involve configuring a firewall between LANs? And if so, that still doesn't account for configuring a firewall to enable access to the Internet.

- Will you need to allow an Internet connection for just your internal network's users, or will use you need to allow outside vendors access to your network? One example that comes to mind is the Internet Printing Protocol (see Chapter 25, "Overview of the TCP/IP Protocol Suite"). What will it cost to evaluate what kind of services user groups need to access from the Internet? Will you need to allow all users to use email—both within the internal network and through the firewall on the Internet? The same goes for what sites users will be allowed to access using a network browser and other network applications. Will you have users who work from home and require dial-in or VPN access through the Internet?

Note

A hot topic in many companies revolves around just how important it is to let all users have unlimited access to the Internet. If users need to exchange email with vendors, outside consultants, or customers, for example, then you should be sure to send this traffic through a content filter or firewall, and use virus-protection software to detect and prevent malicious code or virus-infected attachments.

Applications such as FTP allow users to send or receive files from remote systems. Can you trust each employee to use this application without abusing it? From a security point of view, it is usually considered very improper to allow any new application to be loaded on any computer—desktop or server—without first submitting the application to testing to ensure that is necessary and is not a security risk. Don't leave any backdoors into or out of your network. More information about securing your network can be found in Chapter 48, "Security Issues for Wide Area Networks," and Chapter 49, "Firewalls."

- Can your users tolerate a little downtime now and then due to network problems, or is it necessary to provide a high-availability network? Will you need clustered servers to provide for a high degree of uptime, or do your users' applications not suffer from a temporary loss of the use of a server? To provide for maximum uptime, can you afford to build redundancy into your network? For example, Chapter 2 discusses redundant topologies that can be used to prevent a single point of failure from making the network (and its resources) unavailable. Chapter 11, "Network Attached Storage and Storage Area Networks," describes methods you can use to mirror data at geographically distant locations.

- In an existing network, will you keep the current protocol or upgrade to a different protocol standard? If you create a network from scratch, what factors should affect your network protocol decision? Ethernet is the most popular LAN technology in the world today. TCP/IP is the most popular protocol suite that runs on Ethernet. Yet there are cases in which other technologies have their niches. Consider the implications (such as support costs) to maintain older, proprietary protocols.

Who Are Your Clients?

This seems like a very simple question. However, I'm not saying, "What are your clients' names and how well do you know their children?" I am referring instead to your knowledge of the job descriptions for the users on the network. You need to assess work patterns for various departments so that you can appropriately place servers, high-bandwidth links, and other such things in the appropriate physical location of the network. If most of the network traffic you expect to see will come from the engineering department, you'll need to provide that department with a large data pipe. In Chapter 4, "Upgrading Strategies and Project Management," you'll find more information about surveying the user community to come up with a plan that places resources where they are needed.

What Kinds of Services or Applications Will the Network Offer?

Of course, everyone knows that the most important function of a network today is to support multi-user gaming. Seriously, though, you need to make a list of the kinds of applications currently in use, as well as a list of those requested by users. Each application should have a written risk assessment document that points out potential security problems, if any. Typical network applications today include FTP, telnet, and, of course, browsing the Web. There are "secure" versions of these applications and there are versions that leave a door wide open into your network. Whatever list of applications you chose to support over the network, keep in mind two things:

- Is the application safe? Most applications today come in secure versions or can be used with a proxy server to help minimize the possibility of abuse. Yet, as we all have seen, even the largest corporations are targets at times, and those companies have the staff that should be able to prevent these things from happening. Because proxy servers are an important component of firewalls, this subject is covered in greater detail in Chapter 49. If you want a secure network, this is highly recommended reading!

- Does one application overlap another? Every user has his or her favorite application. Some people like one word processor, whereas others prefer a different one. But when dealing with applications or application suites (such as Microsoft Office), you'll find it better to make a decision and stick with a single product if it can satisfy the needs of your users. They might not like it, and training might be necessary, but supporting multiple applications that do the same thing wastes money and leads to confusion.

A commonly overlooked method for getting data files out of a network and onto the Internet is to simply send the files as an attachment to an email. So if you think you've blocked file transfers by disabling FTP access through the firewall, this example should show that you really do need to do a thorough evaluation of any new application or service you will allow on the network. New applications should be justified with facts that show why they are needed. If an existing application can be used to accomplish the same goal, why do you need another application? Should you retire the older application and use a newer one? Pay attention to the details. And don't forget to test new applications to ensure that they perform as expected. The same goes for older applications—will they work on the new or upgraded network?

Lastly, do you monitor network usage? Do you want to permit users to spend their days browsing the Net, or checking personal email while at work? Many companies have policies that apply to using the telephone for personal business. Do you overlook this situation when giving users email capability? Are you preventing access to sites that are obviously not business-related?

What Degree of Reliability Do I Require for Each Network Link?

Just how much downtime is acceptable? For most users, the answer would be zero. Important components of your network, such as file servers, should have fault tolerance built in from the bottom up. In large servers, you'll find dual-redundant power supplies (each connected to a separate UPS), and disk arrays set up using RAID techniques to provide for data integrity in the event that a disk goes south. If a link between two offices needs to be up 100% of the time, you should plan for multiple links between the two sites to provide a backup capability. In this case, you also can justify the cost of the extra link by using load balancing so that network response time is improved. And, if you are using multiple links to remote sites, it's always a good idea to have more than a single path to the site. At one site this author worked at, there were redundant power lines bringing electricity into the site—side-by-side. If a tree falls, will it bring down one or both of those power lines?

Note

In addition to dedicated links between sites, the use of Virtual Private Networking (VPNs) is becoming a popular method for connecting to remote sites. The advantages of using a VPN are that you can send data across the Internet, which is less expensive than using a dedicated link, and mobile users can also use a VPN connection to connect to your network as they move from place to place. The only problem with this approach is that a remote site, as well as your main site, should use two ISPs to ensure that if one goes down, you still have a connection to the Internet. For a mobile user, this can be problematic if using an Internet service provided by the hotel. You can solve this problem by giving your users access to two different nationwide ISPs.

Another technology that can be used to provide an extra layer of redundancy, as well as high-speed access to storage devices, is the Storage Area Network (SAN). A SAN is a network that is separate from the LAN and contains only storage devices and servers that need to access those devices. Because the network bandwidth is not shared with LAN users, multiple servers can access the same storage. If one server fails, other servers can be configured to provide redundant access to the data. Also, the same RAID and other redundancy techniques used for storage devices that are directly attached to a server (such as the SCSI hardware and protocols) can be used on a SAN.

▶▶ The terms *RAID* and *UPS* are important in today's networks, as is the concept of load balancing and dual-redundant power supplies in large networks. You can find out more about RAID (Redundant Array Of Independent Disks) and UPSs (uninterruptible power supplies) by reading Chapter 5, "Protecting the Network: Preventative Maintenance Techniques." For more information about SANs, see Chapter 11.

The old saying "If it ain't broke, don't fix it" doesn't apply to networks. You should always be proactively looking for potential single points of failure and doing something to fix them. By building redundancy into the network design at the start, you'll save yourself a lot of grief in the future.

Chapter 5 can give you more suggestions about using clustering, backups, uninterruptible power supplies, and other techniques that can keep the network up and running.

Choosing a LAN Protocol

Today the de facto protocol of choice has to be TCP/IP. However, other protocols have their place in some vertical markets. In this book, we talk about NetWare and ARCnet. ARCnet fills a special niche, especially in the factory automation environment. NetWare has been around so long that you might find you have no choice when designing an upgrade but to keep using IPX/SPX, depending on the applications your network uses. However, even NetWare has moved toward using TCP/IP as the underlying protocol. This is basically the case for version 5.x and 6.x of NetWare. Older NetWare networks should upgrade, if possible, to one of these newer versions. If you will be connecting the network to the Internet, TCP/IP will be a necessity. Even if you don't expect to have an Internet connection, you'll find that choosing TCP/IP is a more practical choice today because most applications work with it and there is a large market of trained professionals who can be hired to manage a network built on TCP/IP. NetWare 6.x provides backward compatibility with IPX/SPX for the most part, but newer features such as the iPrint—which uses the Internet Printing Protocol—require TCP/IP.

Note

Although Novell has not made statements to this point, it appears to this author that the company is beginning to de-emphasize its networking capabilities and is instead making a change toward selling Web services (iPrint and iFile, among others). NetWare 6 contains many features that can be used to create an Internet portal and enable remote access by users and customers. If you are a current NetWare user, you should read Chapter 32, "Overview of Novell NetWare IPX/SPX," and Chapter 34, "Expanding and Enhancing NDS: NetWare's eDirectory."

In addition to transport protocols such as TCP/IP and IPX/SPX, you must consider application protocols that can be used on the network. For example, to simplify administering configuration information for a large number of computers, you might want to use the Dynamic Host Configuration Protocol (DHCP), which is discussed in Chapter 29, "BOOTP and Dynamic Host Configuration Protocol (DHCP)." If you want to provide a central name resolution service, you might choose the Domain Name Service (DNS), which is covered in Chapter 30, "Network Name Resolution." If you are going to operate a Windows network that has pre–Windows 2000/XP clients, you might need to use the Windows Internet Naming Service (WINS) for backward compatibility.

So when thinking about a network protocol, remember that it's not just one protocol you need to worry about. After you've decided which protocols are necessary, research the security implications of each.

It's Almost Universal: TCP/IP

For all practical purposes, the standard LAN protocol today is TCP/IP. This is partly due to the rapid growth of the Internet, and the necessity of most businesses of having a Web presence, as well as the large number of vendors that have adopted this protocol suite. If your LAN is still using an older proprietary network protocol, you should seriously consider what it would take to upgrade to TCP/IP. Currently, TCP/IP version 4 is the most widely used protocol. In the future you can expect that the next version (IPv6) will start to find its way from the core of the Internet out to the edge, where your network resides. While technologies such as Network Address Translation (NAT) are widely employed to remedy the problem associated with the limited address space provided by IPv4, IPv6 will enable a much larger address space. Combine that with Network Address Translation, and the long-term bets are going to be on IPv6, or possibly some of the features that are part of IPv6. In addition to giving you a larger address space, IPv6 includes other important features. Those that will affect your network the most are security mechanisms, which will only become more important as Internet commerce continues to grow.

▶▶ For a detailed introduction to TCP/IP, see Chapter 25, "Overview of the TCP/IP Protocol Suite"; Chapter 26, "Basic TCP/IP Services and Applications"; and Chapter 28, "Troubleshooting Tools for TCP/IP Networks."

There is one very important reason you should consider TCP/IP as a LAN protocol: There are more trained professionals knowledgeable in TCP/IP than any other LAN protocol at this time. It is interesting to note that in Windows NT 3.51, the default network protocol was Microsoft's implementation of IPX/SPX (NWLink). In Windows NT 4.0 (and successive operating systems, from Windows 2000, XP, and Server 2003), the default network protocol is TCP/IP.

If your network is composed of several operating systems, from Windows to NetWare to Unix and Linux, then the bottom line is that TCP/IP is the lowest common denominator that will allow the easiest connectivity and interaction between all of these. Even Microsoft's now-legacy NetBIOS/NetBEUI protocols have been adapted to run over TCP/IP.

Novell's NetWare Version 6

NetWare was perhaps the first attempt at seriously providing a LAN protocol that was easy to use. The basic file and print services offered by early versions of NetWare were much better than other solutions available at that time. After it became established in the business community, NetWare became the network solution of choice in many business environments that used the PC. Microsoft countered this success with its LANManager products, which were also marketed by other vendors in their own way, such as the Pathworks solution from Digital Equipment Corporation.

Today NetWare is a totally revamped solution to LAN connectivity. It provides many new features that are addressed to specifically make use of the Internet, and allow mobile users to connect to their home networks, as well as to enable NetWare users to make connections to outside networks. For example, the iPrint feature enables NetWare users to print to a printer on a remote network. For example, instead of sending a catalog that may be out of date in a month or so, you can use iPrint to periodically send specific information relevant to each customer, by printing it directly to the customer's printer.

And NetWare's iFolder allows mobile users to synchronize data stored on remote computers (such as a laptop computer) with the data stored on the company's network. Microsoft and other vendors offer similar features. However, the point to remember is that if you already are a NetWare user, you don't have to throw out your existing investment and move to a Microsoft network, or even a Unix/Linux environment. NetWare has changed as the market has changed, and you might find it less expensive to upgrade to NetWare 6 than to migrate to another platform. The bottom line involves not just the cost of migrating to another operating system, but the costs involved with retraining your network administrative personnel in new technology.

Because NetWare 6 is so tightly integrated with the IP protocol, and also offers backward compatibility with IPX/SPX, admins for existing NetWare networks should consider upgrading to NetWare 6 as well as considering other options.

Other LAN/WAN Protocols

The distinction between LAN and WAN (wide area networking) protocols is beginning to blur. Ethernet was once considered to be a LAN protocol. As time has passed, other technologies, such as Token-Ring, have become minor players in the LAN world. Yet the opposite is true of Ethernet. It has grown from a modest specification endorsed by Intel, DEC, and other vendors, such that it now can be considered a WAN protocol. The capabilities introduced by current LAN technologies are beginning to erode the differences between a LAN and a MAN (metropolitan area network). Since the third edition of this book was published, Gigabit Ethernet devices have become very inexpensive (when you consider the bandwidth offered by this technology). 10Gigabit Ethernet is now coming to market with a strong driving force that will probably make it the most widely used MAN protocol in the next year or two. Today you may be using 100BASE-T for connecting client computers to the network, and Gigabit Ethernet to connect network segments via the network backbone.

What does this mean to a network administrator today? With 10Gigabit Ethernet, you can use TCP/IP not only to create a local area network backbone, but to extend that reach to a metropolitan area network. And because TCP/IP is so intertwined with Ethernet, you can achieve an end-to-end MAN link that uses TCP/IP over faster Ethernet connections. Instead of employing more expensive solutions, such as SONET, you can now connect branch offices in the same geographical area using just TCP/IP.

You may not have to worry about installing expensive equipment used by SONET and other typical MAN protocols. Still, for the long haul—for example, between different cities—other protocols such as ATM and Frame Relay will come into play.

▶▶   For more information about SONET, ATM, and Frame Relay, see Chapter 16, "Dedicated Connections."

Planning and Design Components

When it is time to create a plan, what should the product of this effort be? Depending on the scope of the project, the end result might be a simple short document with a step-by-step checklist for adding a few network devices to the network to segment traffic. As the scope grows larger, so do the *receivables* that should be prepared for upper management as part of the plan. Some of the things you might want to consider including are listed here:

- **Documentation**—What kind of documents will be required to implement the plan? This can be in the form of checklists for both simple and complex upgrades, sign-off sheets, informational documents provided to end users, and so on. Don't forget training documentation that will be needed in a major upgrade. Training documentation should be prepared for both administrators and the highly skilled end users (power users) of new technology. Of course, you should have a document that shows the physical and logical layout of the network that is being implemented or upgraded. This sort of document can be very useful when something goes wrong and you are trying to troubleshoot a problem. You might find, for example, that the physical network you've designed cannot handle the load that users and applications will place on the network at certain points.

- **Overall project plan**—Any large project must be implemented in an orderly manner to be sure that the goals set for the plan are met, or possibly adjusted if necessary. A mechanism for feedback should always be included because the best of planning can always overlook some important features or applications that the current network offers. Creating a project plan with a liberal timeline can be very helpful for keeping the project on track by setting milestones to be met. By making the schedule a liberal one, you automatically build in extra time to be used when things don't go quite as you expected they would. If everything works perfectly, you get gold stars from management for bringing a project in early! Experience has shown that any large network upgrade plan will not perfectly match the first plan you develop.

- **Policies and procedures**—As with any technology, you should plan to develop documents that detail policies and procedures to follow when the new network begins operating. Policies dictate how the network is to be used. For example, you might not allow employees to use email for personal use or the Web browser to view pages not related to your business. Procedures are detailed instructions on how to perform certain actions. With new technology, both policy and procedure should be considered important factors.

Document Everything

Documentation is everything. People have very short memories of things that appear to have only a limited lifetime, such as work projects. It is important that a good project contain several important documents, listed here, but not limited to these:

- **An executive overview**—You must have some overall plan to present to upper management that explains, without too many technical details, the reasons the upgrade (or new network) is needed, and what benefits the business will obtain from the upgrade. In this sort of document, less is more. *Bulleted* items make a better point than long, prose-filled paragraphs. Point out the need for the network or the upgrade, and be sure to list the benefits for each point you make. If a benefit can be measured in dollars, be sure to include that information. You can include here the feedback you've obtained from the user community to show management why a change is necessary.

- **A technical project plan**—This is a difficult document to create. After you've identified the parts of the network to upgrade, you need to create lists of steps detailing the replacement of old equipment with the new, with little disruption to the user community. If you are building a network from scratch, or planning a major upgrade in which most of the existing equipment will be replaced, this kind of document works best when done in sections. A three-ring binder can be used, and individual sections can be assigned to technologically proficient team members for the initial writing of, and any possible updates to, sections of this document. In a larger network, it is more likely that you will have separate teams of network personnel implementing the project plan. If this is your case, create an overall plan, similar to the executive overview, and then create individual plans for each team to use for implementing their goals.

Note

Goals! If you include goals in your project plan (and you should), you can identify certain accomplishments that will be attained during the implementation of the project. These goals can be used to measure the performance of the plan, and can be used to adjust the schedule you have set for the project plan. Feedback from each project team can be used to modify the goals that you have set. It is rare that a project plan succeeds without some modifications. Plan for this, by reviewing each step in the process and creating alternative documents that can address each problem as it arises.

- **Detailed checklists**—For each task that must be performed, a detailed checklist can help ensure that an important step is not left out. This is a simple process, but it's a lot easier to get it right the first time if you use a checklist. However, creating a perfect checklist means that you've anticipated each and every possible situation that can occur. In large networks this is not always an easy task, because many applications tend to be user-centric. Be prepared to modify these checklists. As with disaster recovery plans, you should be sure to pass these checklists by lower-level administrative personnel, and provide some mechanism for testing them. Use the feedback you get to adjust your checklists as necessary.
- **Risk matrix**—Identify potential risks early in the project, as well as mitigation steps that may help avoid these risks, and a description of the impact to the project that will result if the issue does occur. Impact can include items such as timeline slip, features or benefits that will need to be dropped, additional equipment or budget needed to overcome an obstacle, or even complete project failure.

Test, Test, and Then Test Some More

After you have developed a plan and the requisite documentation, don't assume that all of your assumptions and calculations are accurate. The only way to determine that the products or applications you will use in the upgraded network will function as expected is to perform extensive testing. Microsoft resource kits always point out that for larger networks you should create a testing laboratory and try to test different combinations of applications and operating-system configurations and determine whether the results match the expectations of your plan.

For example, directory services are an important issue for large networks. Creating the directory structure may seem at first to be a simple task. You might simply create objects that match up to your company's organizational chart. Yet, what kind of interaction needs to occur between different departments? How can you structure the directory to make the job of granting access to other directory objects an easy task? Just as structured programming techniques make it easier to manage changes in applications as they are modified over time, creating a directory structure for a network should be done in a similar manner. Another reason why a well-designed directory structure is important is that it is through the directory that you can delegate management responsibilities to different administrators, without having to grant an administrator carte blanche access to directory objects that do not fall within their responsibility.

It is a good idea to solicit representatives of your user community for testing scenarios. Remember that the users are the most important part of your network. You can spend all the money in the world to buy the latest technology, but it will give you little value in return unless the user can continue to work efficiently.

Creating Policies and Procedures for Network Usage

Policies, mentioned earlier, are statements about how something should or should not be used. Policy documents are important for several reasons. First, you can't very well discipline an employee for abusing a network resource if you haven't created a usage policy that prohibits the particular abuse. If you don't want your network users to spend their lunch hours shopping for bargains on eBay.com, you should spell this out in an acceptable usage policy.

Policies are important in the design phase of the network because they detail how some resources are to be used. Using the example from the preceding paragraph, if you select an Internet connection after calculating what you expect your bandwidth requirements to be, you might find your network underperforming as users begin to use the connection for nonbusiness needs. Another situation in which policies come into play—to the point of being a necessity—is when you use a firewall. In Chapter 49, you'll learn more about how important it is to first create a security policy and *then* implement that security policy using firewall technology. If you don't know what kind of network traffic you want to allow through the firewall, setting one up is going to be difficult. For example, most secure sites prohibit users from the Internet to use the standard telnet application to gain access to computers inside the local network from computers located elsewhere on the Internet. Yet you might have users who work from home.

▶▶   In addition to Chapter 49, use all the other chapters in Part VIII, "System and Network Security," of this book to learn more about network security. You'll find chapters on basic security measures, both in the local LAN and in a wide area network (WAN), as well as chapters on encryption and virtual private networks (VPNs).

You can still keep your no-incoming-telnet policy and provide your users with a remote access server that can authenticate dial-in users or by using VPN technology. By finding out what users need in advance, you can include the necessary technology up front in the network design and might not have to make exceptions to policies later.

Procedures help prevent mistakes from happening in the first place. They are proactive measures that assist technical and nontechnical people when it comes to performing functions on the network. For example, in your network design you might have a team trained to set up several hundred desktop computers and attach them to the network. Although plugging the network card into the wall socket is simple, configuring the desktop machine can be a little more difficult. You'll need to either configure the desktop machine with valid addressing configuration information or set it up to use Dynamic Host Configuration Protocol (DHCP). Even though you might be doing this on a lot of computers, it's very easy to make a mistake when performing repetitive tasks. By using a checklist for each computer, you can improve your odds of getting it right the first time. Don't wait until you've created the network and then start looking for fires to put out. Instead, create procedure documents for commonly performed tasks. This includes tasks involved in the initial setup of the network, as well as procedures for performing daily tasks after the network is up and running—backups, connecting network drives, and so on.

Providing Training for Technical Personnel

Technical users who will be responsible for helping manage the network should be trained in the procedures for which they will be responsible. Again, this means you should provide training for those who will help you set up the network as well as those who will manage it after it is functioning. Training classes can be conducted by in-house personnel already familiar with the technology, or by one of the many hundreds of consulting services that make their living doing just this sort of thing.

When it comes to training, consider cross-training support personnel so that if one person is out for the day (or longer), you still have a technician who can assist with the problem. The alternative is to have more than one person trained for specific areas of responsibility, and thus pay more in overhead costs.

Remember that the technical staff who support the network are the persons your users must depend on when a problem occurs. Perhaps the most expensive thing that can happen in most networks is *downtime*. RAID technology and backups can be used to protect data, but if you have hundreds (or even thousands) of idle workers getting paid to sit around while someone is reading a technical manual trying to determine the cause of a network problem, you might want to get your resume in order. Up-front training is not inexpensive, but downtime can be far more expensive than training the technical staff in the first place.

You Can't Forget the Budget (or Can You?)

When planning a network or an upgrade to a network, it is always tempting to use the latest, greatest gizmos. Sometimes, however, you can accomplish the same thing using a much less expensive gizmo. For example, if you have a small home office, you don't need a $2,000–$3,000 router and a T1 line to connect to the Internet. A simple cable or DSL modem and the appropriate broadband service should suffice in most instances. Inexpensive cable/DSL routers can be used to allow several computers on a small network to use this single connection (although some providers discourage, or even disallow this—check the details on your contract!). There is some debate as to whether the NAT and other firewall technology built into cable/DSL routers can serve as an adequate firewall. There are other protective steps that SOHO networks can employ, such as combining a router with NAT technology with a more complex software-based firewall and frequently updated virus-protection programs.

Plan the budget liberally, but don't include items that really aren't necessary. When you present a list of items to upper management that shows them what the new network will do for the company, the benefits should always outweigh the costs you've come up with. Although this might not be such an issue in a growing company, it's better to manage your network project responsibly so that you will maintain a good rapport with management. When you find that something you have planned and implemented isn't working as you expected, and you need to make changes, management will probably be more responsive if you've been frugal with the initial expenses incurred in building the network.

The Physical Network

After you've decided on the network protocols and the services you need to offer on the network, identified potential bottlenecks, and evaluated the security problems associated with your network needs, you can then design the physical aspects of the network.

The preceding chapter discussed different physical network topologies. There are tools you can use, such as Visio, to draw a physical network diagram. Tools such as these are expensive but make a much better presentation to management than hand-drawn network layouts. Whichever tool you decide to use to create the actual network drawings, just be sure that the drawings are clear and concise. Looking back at your network application requirements, bandwidth requirements, and the like, you can then start designing the physical network, deciding where to place important servers and redundant devices.

Planning Resources

Finally, keep in mind that technology changes rapidly in the computer and networking fields. Although hubs might have been sufficient a few years ago, today these are now legacy devices that have been replaced by switches that operate much faster and cost about the same as a hub used to cost. Although Bill Gates might have thought (way back when) that no one would ever need more than 640KB of memory, that prediction proved false almost as soon as it left his mouth. As we all know, change is the only constant thing in this universe. With technology, this is especially the case today.

If you are about to set yourself on a course of designing a network, become familiar with all the latest technologies, and don't depend solely on past experience. The best way to keep up with new technologies is to read about them. You can use books, such as this one, and resources on the World Wide Web, and you can also talk to knowledgeable consultants who are experts in their field.

Finally, Appendix C, "Internet Resources for Network Administrators," can point you to some interesting books and Web sites that contain helpful information. You'll find links in the appendix to sites that specialize in security, network protocols, and so on. You'll also find sites that maintain copies of Internet Request for Comments (RFC) documents, which spell out standards that are used on the Internet.

Upgrading Strategies and Project Management

SOME OF THE MAIN TOPICS IN THIS CHAPTER ARE

CHAPTER 4

This chapter discusses some things you should consider when deciding whether an upgrade is needed for the network, and some of the steps necessary to accomplish the task. It is not a simple task to undertake a major network upgrade. It is not a simple task to undertake an upgrade of even a single departmental network, depending on the applications, servers, network bandwidth required, and other factors. Any sort of upgrade contemplated in this book should be done so in an orderly fashion, and the appropriate documentation (before and after) needs to be created. Documentation does not mean that you have an absolute set of directions that *must* be followed. Instead, it is a set of documents you can create before the upgrade, and then modify as circumstances reveal new problems or opportunities that may arise during the upgrading process.

Where Do You Start?

You have to start somewhere, and sometimes it's best to keep the process fairly simple. Consider the following steps:

1. Determine the need for an upgrade.
2. Set goals.
3. Create a plan to guide the process.
4. Carefully investigate the plan to help ensure success.

This may seem too simplistic at first glance, but stop and think: Why are you performing an upgrade? Is it because you just read about the newest technology and your budget lets you buy it? Or does the new technology solve a network problem related to your business? After you have determined a real need to make an upgrade to all or (more likely) part of your network, you need to justify these changes to management (to get the funding) and make sure that you set goals that satisfy the needs of your network clients. It doesn't mean anything if you spend a half-million dollars (or more) installing the latest Storage Area Network (SAN) if your clients don't notice some improvement in performance or uptime.

However, if your hardware is old, you are likely to find that the vendor will continue to raise support costs to maintain this equipment. In that case, an upgrade can be justified by the cost of maintaining the older hardware, as well as the possibility that replacement parts may not be available in a few years. Because a major upgrade can sometimes take a year or more, you might consider an upgrade before you are forced to do so by your hardware vendor. Another thing to consider is whether there is an actual need to upgrade. For example, implementing a SAN might solve many problems, such as centralizing storage management on the network as well as providing additional capacity. SANs also can be created in such a way that you can incrementally add storage on an as-needed basis.

Note

Storage Area Networks are not only a hot topic today, but they are becoming an absolute necessity for large networks, or for those that are dedicated to Internet services. For more information about SANs, see Chapter 11, "Network Attached Storage and Storage Area Networks."

The next part of this chapter will enable you to create goals for a network upgrade, as summarized in the following list:

- **Evaluation**—Understanding the current environment. You can obtain this from your current resources and feedback from users.
- **Determining needs**—Why are you upgrading? As stated previously, do you really need the upgrade? If it doesn't solve a problem for your network, you may find yourself simply spending money because it is available. Yet if you have the foresight to see that the upgrade will fulfill a future requirement (such as pulling fiber-optic cables to replace copper cables), then you might justify the cost based on future, more expensive labor costs.

- **Setting goals**—What will the upgrade accomplish? Will you improve the user's perspective of the network? Will you provide additional services (think of certificate services and security) that will benefit the corporation as a whole?

- **Budgeting**—Determining what financial resources are available and setting a budget. Despite the fact that most administrators fail to understand budgeting, this is a basic premise of running a company. If you can't afford it, you can't afford it! Sometimes you just have to make do with older technology and plan the upgrade for the future. Many networks still use Windows 98 or Windows NT, and have Windows 2000 or the latest Windows Server 2003 in their distant future.

- **Planning**—Creating a detailed plan for the upgrade. This is where you will make or break your argument with upper management. If you cannot show them why an upgrade will benefit the company—based on costs of maintaining the network to user productivity—then they have no reason to approve your project.

- **Testing**—Evaluating components of the upgrade in a laboratory or pilot project environment. This is emphasized in many other books for good reason. It's crucial to put the plan to the test and prove that a plan is feasible and appropriate. For example, Microsoft's Resource Kits usually contain information on deployment and planning, which can be very helpful to you if you are rolling out an upgrade in an enterprise network.

- **Training**—Will users need to be trained on any new applications or features? Training is one of the more expensive items for any new network upgrade.

- **Backing out and recovering**—Coping with the unexpected. No matter how well you plan, something can always go awry. And when it does, your job may be on the line if you can't restore the network to its previous state. Upper management doesn't care as much about perceived new benefits from newer network technology as they do about keeping the business humming along.

- **Deployment**—Implementing the upgrade plan. This involves a team of technicians, each of whom is an expert in the technology that is their responsibility in the upgrade plan. Just because you are the network administrator (or manager of such) doesn't mean that you should rely on your own knowledge to micro-manage every aspect of the project. You should instead concentrate on managing the individuals whose job it is to get things done.

- **Post-implementation review**—Did the plan work as expected? Are the results what were expected, possibly more? There is nothing more satisfying than presenting to upper management a document (whether they read it or not) detailing how your upgrade plan worked, and the benefits that have now been accomplished. This helps you keep your job!

Determining When an Upgrade Is Necessary—The Evaluation Process

A data network in a business is much like a nervous system in a living organism. Usually, when the business grows, the network also must grow to keep up with new users and newer functions. When a business suffers and shrinks, the costs associated with a larger network must be re-evaluated to determine whether they are still feasible under a smaller business organization. A network rarely goes unchanged year after year.

Before you begin to write an upgrade plan for part or all of a network, you first must determine that there is a need for an upgrade. There are several reasons to upgrade a network:

- **User complaints**—When top-performing users complain, their managers usually do their best to make them happy. Keep in mind also that there are always going to be people who complain about the network. Investigate user complaints to determine whether they are valid.

- **New technology has been adopted**—Sometimes the upgrade can be application driven. A new kind of hardware or software needed by a business unit demands a network with higher performance capabilities or different features.

- **Business mergers and expansions**—After figuring out a way to join two networks when companies merge, a long-range plan must be developed to make the network work best for the new business entity. This can include performance enhancements, adoption of standards, and elimination of duplicated components. This also can result in a major headache if you have to find a way to combine user authorization data from different operating systems.

- **Business is good; let's spend money**—This is not an uncommon motive for making a new system or network purchase. Sometimes when economic times are good for a business it's also a good time to make long-range plans and upgrade part of the infrastructure. Yet, as stated previously, don't spend the money on just the latest, greatest technology. Consider this a windfall and evaluate the network components that can benefit from this additional cash. Do you have a need to provide mobile users with wireless capabilities? Do you need to upgrade your firewall capabilities to ensure the security of your network? Don't waste money when it is available. Think of the long term.

The first of these reasons, user complaints, probably will never go away. No matter how fast the network or how powerful the machine, there will always be someone who wants more. Usually a network administrator has a good overview of the people or departments that are major consumers of network resources and can filter out unrealistic complaints. So when deciding when and whether you need to perform some kind of overhauling of the network, you should carefully research your current network's capacity and compare it to the business needs currently loading the network.

Sometimes a simple overview of the network can reveal that all you must do to satisfy one or two small bottlenecks is reconfigure part of the network. Usually a reconfiguration is cheaper and easier to implement than a major upgrade. It's much easier to upgrade a single, growing department to a faster switch than it is to overhaul the entire network.

When reconfiguring the network will not solve capacity problems, it might be time to look at other media to handle the network traffic. Chapter 6, "Wiring the Network—Cables, Connectors, Concentrators, and Other Network Components," gives a good overview of the specifications and capabilities of this most basic part of the network. Whether you are planning an upgrade or simply extending your network into a larger geographic space, it's not necessarily a good idea to shop around and settle for the cheapest solution. Installing cabling in ceilings, walls, and floors is a labor-intensive, expensive item in an upgrade budget. Yet if you spend the money up front to install good-quality cables, connectors, and the like, you will probably quickly recoup the cost in a few years when upgrading to even faster networking technologies. The best example of this is Category 5 cabling. If you have a 10Mbps network and use Category 5 cabling, upgrading to Fast Ethernet or even Gigabit Ethernet won't require that you rewire the entire network.

Tip

When you get around to pulling new cables, don't think just one generation ahead. Pulling cables, connecting them to the user's faceplate at the terminal point, and connecting them to patch panels or other devices in the wiring closets can often be the most expensive component of your network. It's easy to replace a workstation. It's somewhat more expensive to replace a server. Pulling cables is very expensive, and it can involve replacing not just the cables, but also the connectors (at both ends of the connection). It can also involve replacing network adapter cards at both ends. If you are replacing cables today, consider fiber-optic cabling for backbone connections, as well as connections between wiring closets. In a few years the same may even apply to connections from the wiring closet to the desktop. It's all based on applications, and the bandwidth they require is constantly growing.

There are other chapters you might want to consult when planning an upgrade. Chapter 7, "Network Interface Cards," covers the basics of this topic. You also can find information there about some of the newest functionality being incorporated into NICs, such as Wake on LAN and server NIC load balancing. After you have the wiring and NIC issues settled, Chapter 8, "Network Switches," will guide you in the process of replacing overloaded department hubs with switches to improve performance and connect dissimilar LAN segments. Consider that Ethernet hubs are now legacy equipment.

Adopting new technology usually entails additional tasks such as training users and administrative personnel in the use or management of new products. For example, a major paradigm shift, such as migrating an all-Novell network to Windows 2000/.NET, would have to include months of training for network administrative personnel. For all practical purposes, TCP/IP is now the de facto networking standard for LANs. If you are still running an AppleTalk or IPX/SPX network, you might want to think about future support for these products. Novell already offers TCP/IP support, and there are products that allow interaction between Novell Directory Services (NDS) and Windows Active Directory. Although NDS still might be a useful tool, IPX/SPX LANs are good candidates for upgrading to TCP/IP, especially if your business connects to the Internet.

Tip

Although Novell's NetWare 6.x has brought a lot of raves from its implementers, it is my considered opinion that the traditional capabilities of NetWare are a thing of the past. There are many directory services (most notably Microsoft's Active Directory) that make this major capability now a minor concern. Novell is now concentrating on its other products, such as ZENworks, DirXML, and standalone components broken out of NetWare 6.x, such as iPrint and iFolder.

Another technology that might be ready for a change is the Token-Ring LAN. Although Token-Ring technology is a great LAN solution, it's not likely to keep up with the speeds being achieved by newer versions of Ethernet. And when it comes to the budget, the number of manufacturers of Ethernet equipment dwarfs those who make Token-Ring hardware. Because of the economics of scale, and competition, Ethernet is a far cheaper solution in most cases.

▶▶ For more information about the state of Token-Ring networks, see the chapter, "Token-Ring Networks," located on the `upgradingandrepairingpcs.com` Web site.

For newcomers, Chapter 14, "Ethernet: The Universal Standard," and Chapter 25, "Overview of the TCP/IP Protocol Suite," will get you started on the planning process. Other chapters can fill in the details of some aspects typical of TCP/IP-based networks. For example, Chapter 26, "Basic TCP/IP Services and Applications," will help you determine which of the basic TCP/IP-based applications will be useful in your network. Chapter 29, "BOOTP and Dynamic Host Configuration Protocol (DHCP)," and Chapter 30, "Network Name Resolution," cover the basics of automating network addressing and name resolution.

Finally, one "upgrade" that every network administrator should plan for, if it has not happened yet, is to provide a firewall between the company network and any outside network connection. Chapter 49, "Firewalls," covers this area. The chapters immediately preceding cover other aspects of network and systems security.

Today a firewall is not a luxury. It is a necessity. It doesn't matter if you are connecting different LAN segments within a company intranet, or if you are making a connection to the Internet. A good firewall is now something you cannot ignore. Even SOHO users should use some type of firewall to protect themselves from the malicious problems that can result from a wide area connection. For a corporate connection to the Internet, a good firewall, no matter what the cost, is an absolute necessity. And in some professions, such as the pharmaceutical industry, or for those corporations that do business with the government, it is required.

Determining User Requirements and Expectations

One of the simplest methods of finding out what is needed on the network is to ask the users. Although this technique might not give you the most accurate results, it will at least give you an idea of what the user community expects from the network. Conducting a simple written survey can bring light to factors that administrative and support personnel might not be aware of.

Similar to surveying end users is soliciting suggestions from support staff who encounter user problems daily. Logs of support calls can be a valuable source of information. If users are making the same mistakes over and over again, then training, not upgrading, usually can solve the problem. When examining help-desk logs, don't limit your scope to the problems. Carefully examine what was done to solve the problems. Maybe your help-desk personnel aren't giving out the best advice.

However, the most basic way to determine overall capacity needs is to establish baseline data for your network components and then make comparisons on a regular basis with the production network. By keeping data that reflects the baseline mode of operation, you will have empirical data that can be used to make projections about future use. By regularly benchmarking your systems and keeping track of the data, you also can become aware of capacity problems that begin to creep up before your projections or expectations. Most operating systems provide for monitoring of a sort. Windows 2000 Performance Monitor, or Windows 2003/XP's System Monitor, for example, can give you very detailed statistics on a server's performance, including network performance. Chapter 5, "Protecting the Network: Preventative Maintenance Techniques," gives an overview of this tool. In larger networks, using a management console that understands SNMP and RMON can help you baseline and monitor many different components in the network. Analysis software can help prepare reports that can be used to justify network changes. Both SNMP and RMON are examined in Chapter 53, "Network Testing and Analysis Tools."

Other factors that can be reviewed to determine whether changes are merited include the following:

- **Maintenance costs**—The network might be functioning nicely with equipment that is several years old. However, the maintenance costs associated with older equipment might be justification for upgrading to newer, more reliable equipment.

- **Existing contracts**—Leased equipment can usually be purchased or returned to the lessor at the end of the lease period. Contracts that are about to expire should be examined and taken into consideration when deciding whether to keep the existing equipment or upgrade. Keep in mind the costs associated with migrating to newer hardware. For example, software licensing might be more expensive on higher-capacity servers, whether or not you need or use that capacity. Yet it is often the case that newer components will provide a better return-on-investment (ROI) than older technology. You should examine the costs for both of these options. The older the equipment is, the more likely the vendor will charge more for a maintenance agreement. The newer equipment may cost more, but you might find the maintenance costs much lower for the next year or two. Keep in mind that newer technologies are now based on a few years, not decades.

- **Network traffic**—Regular monitoring of network traffic to locate bottlenecks or congested areas can be helpful. It may be that user work habits or procedures can be changed so that problems that occur only at peak hours or on specific days do not lead you into spending too much on a small problem that can be better solved by other methods.

Maintaining Support for Legacy Applications

There comes a time in every application's life when it really should just die and go away. However, when you consider the costs associated with replacing a legacy software application with one that is state-of-the-art, sometimes what you find might lead you to listen to users who like their software and want to keep the application around a little longer.

The following are some hidden costs you might overlook at first glance:

- Ongoing maintenance or support costs
- Employee support costs
- Infrastructure overhead costs

Maintenance and support costs can be hidden in part of the budget for the department that an application or a hardware platform supports. When multiple suppliers are involved, you will usually find multiple contracts, some of which even overlap each other. Another problem with ongoing support costs is that manufacturers raise these costs when products become outdated to help encourage users to adopt newer ones.

The number of employees you dedicate to a particular part of the network is an important cost. If you have a large staff whose responsibility is mostly maintaining an old application, consider the costs associated with them, from salary to overhead, and decide whether it might be better spent training them on newer technology and replacing the legacy system.

Legacy applications are usually either loved or hated by their users. Some people think with the mindset "but we've always done it that way" and do not want to change for fear of the unknown and love of the familiar. Other users who are used to better technology might hate a legacy application. The point to remember here is that it does not always matter what the user thinks about the application. What is most important to the business's bottom line is how the costs associated with the change compare with the benefits the company receives.

What Resources Are Needed for the Upgrade?

If you already have a good inventory of the network, you are ahead of the game. Keeping an up-to-date listing of network components—including hardware and software, along with other pertinent information such as network addresses, serial numbers, manufacturers' help-line numbers, and so on—is a task that, when done on a regular basis, will yield great results down the line.

Without a good network map document, you won't necessarily be sure that you're not violating some of the topology rules for your network. Before beginning to plan an expansion or the addition of new equipment, review documentation for that which you already possess. You might have some devices that do not need to be replaced. For example, if you already have network adapter cards that are 10Mbps/100Mbps, you will not need to add the cost of new cards to an upgrade plan when going from a 10BASE-T network to a 100BASE-T network.

Note

Although 10BASE-T is discussed in this section, you should consider that now is the time to upgrade to 100BASE-T. The network cards are very inexpensive (less than $20 for a 10/100Mbps card), and switches are respectively priced at a much lower rate. You will gain a large increase in performance by upgrading, at a minimal cost.

Items that you should be sure to inventory include the following:

- Workstations and servers.
- Network adapters.
- Hubs, routers, and switches. Consider replacing hubs with switches, because there is little if any price difference, and switches operate at a much faster bandwidth.

- Test equipment. Depending on your equipment (from hand-held cable testers to high-end network analyzers), this can be an expensive item.

- Workgroup and end-user software applications. Most of the newer applications require a much higher bandwidth.

- Mechanisms used to exchange data with contacts outside the company. You may still be using an older 10BASE-T network, but a good vendor is going to be operating at a much higher bandwidth.

- Management and control applications, such as SNMP, DHCP, DNS, and NIS.

Looking at your inventory, determine how the existing pieces can be used in an upgraded network. For example, it won't do a lot of good to install a faster switch and hook a server to a faster port if the server is not capable of supporting the bandwidth. In such a case, upgrades to the server (or a replacement) would have to be considered as part of the plan. Although installing switches can dramatically improve performance in a departmental LAN, an older hub might be sufficient for a few more years in an office where network utilization is not high. Test equipment and management applications are not generally inexpensive items. Be sure to include the costs of upgrading these management tools when calculating the cost of the upgrade.

When determining your resources, don't forget people. A major project of any kind should always have an identified set of team players that will be responsible for the project. A clearly defined project team will identify the person responsible for each aspect, such as purchasing, infrastructure, systems, and documentation. This will greatly improve communication during the length of the project, because a point of contact is identified for specific areas.

A project leader should be designated to be the focal point both for the project team and for others in the company who need to get information about the project or its progress. Each project team member should have a clearly defined role and area of responsibility. The area of responsibility is a very important one. As in any social interaction, overlapping duties can generate personal resentment between people working on the same project. When a clear, defined set of job responsibilities and duties is spelled out in writing, you have a better chance of achieving harmony among the team members.

A project team will work best when it is dedicated to the project. Giving users multiple roles to fill in their jobs can lead to confusion, unexpected priorities, and degradation in the progress of the overall project. Although the current support staff might be knowledgeable in the network and its quirks, bringing in additional help, by using experienced contact workers, for example, might keep the project focused on its goals and the time frame associated with them.

Planning an Upgrade

Planning is the process of deciding what actions are needed to accomplish a goal. This necessarily implies that the plan will describe the specific goals to be achieved and the benefits that will come from them. However, the steps that are required in a plan are dictated not only by the goals that are to be accomplished, but also by the following considerations:

- How a network upgrade affects users (downtime)

- What established corporate standards must be followed (or possibly re-examined)

- What criteria can be used to measure the progress or success of the plan

Planning for an upgrade should include input from both technical staff members and the user community. After user requests (and complaints!) have been reviewed and a decision has been made as to what issues will be addressed, measurable goals can be established and written documentation can be produced that details the plan, its goals, and how the goals are to be achieved.

Documenting the Plan

Planning is essential in a complex environment to ensure that a project will be successful. Planning can encompass more than one document. For example, there can be a detailed plan that contains checklists for tasks that need to be accomplished, along with time-frame assumptions and resource requirements. For top-level department heads, an executive overview can serve to garner support for the project without forcing management to get bogged down in details they do not understand.

Whatever planning you undertake must be put into the form of a written document. Representatives of the areas that will be affected should carefully review any plans in order to solicit their feedback and ensure their cooperation. However, as with most things in life, even a good plan is likely to undergo changes during its execution. It is important to create a process that can be used to evaluate changes and incorporate them into the plan in an orderly manner. Put the process in writing along with the other details of the plan. If you have the plan in writing, it becomes much more difficult for a disagreeable person to protest when deadlines must be met and resources are limited. An orderly change process can always include a method for recording potential change ideas so that a decision can be postponed to a later date.

Reminding those who are working on the plan about recent accomplishments and upcoming deadlines can help facilitate cooperation. For example, a short meeting on Monday morning that quickly reviews the previous week's work and includes a discussion about goals for the upcoming week might be helpful.

Evaluating the Plan As It Applies to Corporate Policies and Procedures

Before beginning to write any kind of plan that will be used for a major upgrade project, be sure to review the current corporate standards. A company should have one standard word processor that is used throughout the company, or at least throughout any major division of the business.

Most applications today that perform ordinary tasks, such as spreadsheets, word processing, or database functions, also come with tools that enable you to interchange data with other vendors' products. Although this might seem to alleviate the problem of using multiple products for the same purpose, there is another factor to consider: end-user support. Even if data can be easily exchanged, the extra expense of having to support more than one application for a single function is an ongoing cost that doesn't go away.

When developing the plan, first examine the current standards. Then, taking into consideration the future expansion of the network, the capabilities of products currently in use, and the direction certain technologies seem to be taking, develop a revised list of standards and sell it to the organization.

Of course, there will always be exceptions. For example, the corporate standard might require that the Oracle database application be used throughout the company. However, a specific vertical market application used in a research lab might work only with another database product. When there aren't various vendors from which to choose, you might be forced to accept a deviation from the standard here and there.

Setting Goals

Any good plan will have a clearly defined set of goals to provide some kind of benefit to the business. Although an overall view of the project's goals can be used to help sell the idea to upper-level management, the goals that should be included in a detailed project plan must be more specific. The following are two important reasons why you should have a defined set of goals:

■ If defined with enough detail, goals can give you something to gauge the progress of the upgrade project.

■ Goals can keep you on track, preventing you from getting sidetracked by other ideas that will inevitably come up during the project.

After you come up with a written list of the goals that will serve to guide the project, prioritize the list. When initially developing a list of project objectives, your staff might be over-enthusiastic, and you can find yourself with a large shopping list that attempts to solve every problem and please every department. Set realistic priorities based on the benefit each goal is expected to provide, and then remove items from the list that provide little benefit or do not address an immediate need.

Scheduling Downtime

Users should not be expected to understand what goes on behind the scenes in the complicated area of networked computer systems. They might only know that they can or cannot get their job functions performed in a timely manner because "the network is down." By planning ahead and letting everyone know when resources will be unavailable, you will find that users are more likely to cooperate.

Milestones and Criteria

Based on the goals that the project is expected to achieve, build into your plan the procedures that will be used to measure success. Select items from your list of objectives that represent major changes to the network and define the metrics that will be used to determine whether the goal has been met.

For example, a goal can consist of achieving a reduction in network utilization for overloaded segments. Monitoring utilization with a LAN analyzer can be done before and after the upgrade to obtain factual information that can be used to establish the success of this upgrade. Other metrics might include items such as network response times, user satisfaction, or new functionality. The last item is a little more abstract than the others are. How do you measure the impact of new functionality offered by a new application or network configuration? Look at the business function that it provides and find aspects you can measure. For example, if the turnaround time for a monthly billing cycle is usually 48 hours, and new faster servers or software cuts that time to only 12 hours, then this achievement should be measured and reported to management to justify the upgrade costs.

If you find that you are having trouble deciding what benefits you will gain from the upgrade and cannot devise a list of metrics, it is possible that you haven't fully thought through what you are trying to accomplish. In that case, take time to re-examine your thought process that led you to decide on an upgrade. After you identify specific goals, rewrite your plan.

Back-Out Procedures

Nobody is perfect, and no plan can ever be precise enough that you can bet your life that everything will go as expected. Whenever possible, for any major modification you intend to make to the network, you should also have a plan that can be used to restore the network to its previous state. Having good up-to-date documentation about the network can be useful for troubleshooting. When you have scheduled downtime with users and are under a deadline to finish a task or a project, it is more useful to have a definite set of procedures to follow if problems arise that prevent the execution of a task or tasks in the project plan.

A back-out plan does not have to include abandoning the entire plan. Most network upgrades do not occur all at once, but are instead done in stages. At each major step in the plan, have a procedure that can be used to undo the change.

Testing the Plan

The complexity of networking technology today makes it important that you test new equipment and software before committing it to production use. You might find that devices do not function as you expected when deployed using your planned configuration. Management software might be cumbersome and difficult for technicians to understand. In the end, if the technicians and end users are not satisfied and cannot perform their jobs efficiently using the tools you provide, it is likely they will complain to your management. Some of them may even try to find their own solutions, which can significantly increase the hidden costs of your upgrade.

During the testing phase is when you'll probably find the most changes to the plan. When tests show that performance doesn't meet your expectations, the plan will be changed and performance measured again. During testing, the laboratory environment should closely mimic the proposed production network.

Evaluating Competing Products

Careful selection of new equipment or software up front can save time and money after the upgrade is finished. Evaluate competing products carefully so that you can select those that best meet the goals of your upgrade plan. When looking at different vendors' products, try before you buy. For a large hardware purchase, many vendors will loan equipment for a trial period so that you can make a better determination as to its suitability to satisfy your needs. Almost all major software applications can now be obtained from a vendor in a "demo" or "evaluation" copy so that you can test the features.

Another very important factor to consider is the vendor itself. You might find a great product that looks as though it will work miracles for your network. However, if the vendor is not reliable, what will you do when you encounter problems later? Things to think about when choosing vendors include the following:

- **Responsiveness**—Do you get through to the help you need when you call the vendor, or do you have to play telephone-tag to get answers?

- **Availability**—Does the vendor have a good stock of products, or will you be subjected to back orders that can take days or weeks? When you have to replace a part due to malfunction, can your network wait until the part arrives?

- **Service**—Does the vendor provide service for the product? Is on-site service available or do you have to return the item to the vendor for repair?

- **Training**—Does the vendor provide training for the product? Is the training of good quality?

- **Price**—Price usually comes into play when a product is a commodity item. For specialized products or applications, price might not be as important as the other items listed here.

The Pilot Project

Every good plan should include a pilot project. This involves taking a small part of the network, such as a network-friendly department, and implementing part or all of the project modifications in that localized area. Not only will it help you determine whether you have made the right choices for new hardware or software, but it also will help you further refine the installation procedures that will be used to execute the rest of the plan.

If it is not possible to do this in a "live" environment, create a test lab where you can simulate the production environment or network. Use script files to automate processing and perform stress testing on the new components or applications to see whether they really perform as you expect.

The results of a pilot project or a test lab setup can be used to refine and modify the plan and make it more likely to succeed.

Deployment

After you have evaluated and re-evaluated, tested, and retested, and are sure that your plan is a sound one, implement the plan to upgrade the network. Depending on the scope of the upgrade, the deployment stage can be done all at once, or it can be done in a migration process over time. Adding segments to a network for new offices or replacing older cables can be a simple matter accomplished over a weekend. Migrating a large network to a faster topology might require that you deploy only small segments at a time to ensure that disruptions for users are minimized. An application upgrade can take longer to implement because of such factors as data conversion and user training.

Team Personnel

The personnel who are employed to perform upgrade functions should be well trained far in advance of the actual deployment stage. Each person should be knowledgeable in the area of expertise for the functions he or she will perform. To aid the upgrade team, it is a good idea to have specific written task lists that describe what is to be done. For example, a recent network upgrade in which I participated required that network adapter cards be replaced in a large number of workstations. The process involved the physical action to remove the old card and replace it with a new one.

After the card replacement, however, there were additional chores to do. For example, each card had to be configured with the correct drivers so that the operating system would be capable of using of it. Each workstation had to be tested for connectivity to ensure that the card was correctly configured to work with the network. The task list for this was written in detail describing each step the team member needed to perform, and included a check-off box for each step. Why a check-off box? If you have to take the time to check off each step, you are less likely to forget one. When a person is performing the same actions over and over, moving from workstation to workstation, the odds are likely that mistakes will be made.

It is also a good idea to designate one or more persons to be a resource focal point that team members can use when problems arise. If one person is aware of the problems that are occurring, it is easy to implement a fix throughout the project so that the same problem doesn't have to be solved over and over.

Keeping Users Informed

Network users should be kept current about the progress of the upgrade. At the beginning of the deployment stage, present the users with an overview of what will be happening, when it will happen, and how it will affect their work. As specific tasks are ready to be done, let the users who will be immediately affected know shortly before you begin. For example, if you plan to replace workstations throughout the enterprise, create a list of replacement candidates each week and notify the affected users via a memo or an email so that they will be reminded. For an extended project, it is easy for users to forget what you told them weeks or months earlier.

Along this same line, it is a good idea to get some kind of response from a user when you have made changes to his workstation. For example, having a user test the system for a day or so and then "sign off" on the work lets him know that (for him at least) the process is complete; this is known as user-acceptance testing.

Tracking Progress

Use the metrics that you designed to measure the progress you make as you implement the plan. It is important to keep track of the progress so that you can coordinate your people, your resources, and the delivery of additional equipment or outside services. If you are falling behind in one area, you may have to reschedule tasks in other related areas. Keeping a close watch on progress is necessary so that you can quickly detect when something is not going as expected and begin to come up with an alternative method for getting things done.

The mechanisms you can use to track implementation of the plan might include a spreadsheet, a diary-like text file, checklists, and so on. To present information to upper-level management, you might find that weekly or monthly summary reports help in keeping their support. If you find yourself in a position where you need to report on progress to high-level managers, graphical displays, such as graphs or charts, can help get your point across. If you are creating a presentation, it can be helpful to restrict your use of clip art to illustrations that convey additional information. No one will be impressed by your ability to use every stick-figure included in PowerPoint's clip art arsenal.

User Training

The topic of training can cover a large territory. Users should be trained to acquire the necessary skills needed for new applications or new ways of doing ordinary tasks when the network changes. In-house personnel who have the skills and the time to devote to the process can do training. For large projects it might be more economical to employ outside resources for training users. Additionally, there are various training resources you can make available to your users for most popular applications. These include training videos, computer-based training (CBT) applications, programs presented by user groups, and so on.

Make users aware of the resources at their disposal from the beginning, and begin training before major changes are made so that the users will be better able to cope with the new environment. Users who are trained in advance for a new application or procedure are less likely to cause a strain on the upgrade team's resources while the upgrade is proceeding.

Closing the Book—Documenting What Has Changed and Why

When a major project comes to a close, it is a good idea to compile a short report that details the project, from the evaluation and planning stages all the way through to the deployment and user-acceptance stage. This historical document can serve in the future when it comes time to take on another project of a similar scope. It also can be presented to management to make them aware of the scope of what has been accomplished. This visibility can be very beneficial to a network administrator's career!

Other Considerations for Upgrading

Undertaking a major upgrade to a network is not a task to be taken lightly. As with any large undertaking, it is best to try to accomplish your main goals with the least amount of excess baggage. With a large number of users, it is easy to become overwhelmed with the volume of suggestions or requests when the user community finds out that major changes are being planned. However, *for each additional task you add to your plan, you also add to the probability that something will go wrong.* So, after deciding on the basic goals, try to stick to only the tasks that will be needed to accomplish those goals and do not get sidetracked by unimportant issues that can be best settled later.

However, you should consider this time to be an opportunity that can be used to incorporate new technologies or functionality into the network that otherwise would require additional downtime for the network. For example, if you are about to begin upgrading user workstations throughout a department or an enterprise and you have been considering adopting DHCP, what better time to do so than now? If you are already going to put the user out of work for a short period, and the workstation is off the network, this kind of situation is ideal for bringing in a new administrative tool such as DHCP.

Housekeeping is another function that can fit nicely into an upgrade plan: Out with the old and in with the new, so to speak. Old programs that never quite went away can be removed during an upgrade process. An upgrade can be a good time to set a deadline for users who have not yet abandoned older applications that can be better performed by newer applications.

Protecting the Network: Preventative Maintenance Techniques

SOME OF THE MAIN TOPICS IN THIS CHAPTER ARE

CHAPTER 5

This chapter looks at some important preventive maintenance ideas to consider employing in your network. The size and composition of your network will determine which of the ideas in this chapter you should use. Not all are appropriate for every network. Some are prohibitively expensive for smaller networks. Yet it is important to be aware of the possibilities so that as your network grows and you plan for upgrades, you also can make plans for additional procedures and devices that can protect the growing network from downtime and preserve your valuable data.

Power Conditioning and Uninterruptible Power Supplies (UPSs)

Without electricity, you have no network at all, and computers require a well-conditioned electrical source to function properly. The power supply in a computer can't handle an incoming spike of electricity caused by a lightning strike, for example. Similarly, a brownout, in which the voltage level drops for a short period, can cause a computer to crash.

Large-scale computer systems used in corporate environments, such as minicomputers or mainframes, also need a good source of power. To ensure this, most large computer rooms use a heavy-duty UPS to interface between the outside source of electricity and the computers and other devices in a computer room.

In most large computer rooms, for example, you'll find that computers—whether they're PC servers or larger systems—are rack-mounted in cabinets, along with tape drives, disk drives, and other peripheral equipment. The cabinet usually contains one or more power distribution units that are used to supply power to components mounted in the cabinet (see Figure 5.1).

As you can see from this figure, several computer systems and the tape drives they use are housed in a single cabinet. Two power distribution units located at the bottom of the cabinet supply power to all devices in the cabinet. These two power distribution units are configured in a dual-redundant manner so that if one fails the other continues to supply power to the cabinet. Each of these power distribution units is connected to a separate UPS in the computer room. This is important for several reasons. First, not all power failures are due to outside problems, such as a downed power line. Sometimes, UPSs themselves fail. An electrician might disconnect the wrong cable during routine maintenance or installation tasks. A mouse could chew into the wires, causing a short. Sometimes, things just happen. You need to prepare for the unexpected.

To carry the concept further, each UPS in the computer room that the system uses is connected to a separate outside source of power. Thus, if a tree falls and knocks down a power line, an alternative power line is still feeding electricity into the computer room to redundant UPS systems. Because of this second source of power, computers and other devices on the network stay up and running.

Power Is Money

There is an old saying that "money is power." The opposite also is true.

The setup described in the preceding section might seem extreme to a network administrator running a small network of PCs in which some downtime can be tolerated. However, in a high-availability computer environment—such as in a large corporation—the cost of downtime can be prohibitively expensive for several reasons:

■ Hundreds or maybe thousands of employees remain idle while the computers they use are down. Employees are still being paid even though they can't work. Add up the dollars and you'll see that each minute of downtime is expensive.

■ Customers might be unable to place orders or check on the status of existing orders. Fickle customers might just call someone else. No one likes to hear, "Our computer is down right now; please call back later." After your customer talks to another supplier, you might never hear from that customer again. So you lose the current order, and possibly future business.

■ An unexpected system crash due to a power failure can cause corruption to data. After the power is restored, it can sometimes take hours (or even days) to determine which files are corrupted and then restore them to a known state from backup tapes. Many large networks, such as those operated by Internet Service Providers, now measure data in terabytes. Restoring an entire database can be very expensive and time-consuming. This additional downtime can potentially be more costly than the original power outage that caused it.

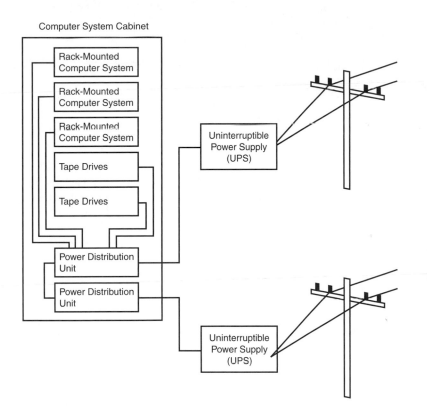

Figure 5.1 Several points in the power supply can be constructed to prevent a single point of failure for powering the network.

If you operate in a large-scale environment like this, you are probably already aware of how important it is to keep computer systems up and running. If you don't provide a steady, secure source of power up front, all your other preventive maintenance measures might prove of little value the next time the power goes out.

A UPS is not an eternal source of power. It is a conduit through which your external power source is routed before it gets to your computer systems. UPSs operate by storing electricity in one or more batteries so that when the outside source of electricity is unexpectedly lost, the batteries can be switched into use in a few milliseconds. However, batteries can be used only for a limited amount of time. If you are using only a single UPS connected to a single power source, the UPS buys you the time needed to notify users to log off the systems affected and gracefully shut down the computers so that no data is compromised. Although you'll still have idle employees, you won't have to recover data after power has been restored.

For a large network consider planning for power outages one step further: Diesel generators. Although these would be too expensive to keep a large number of desktop users working, they can be used to keep servers up so that you can relocate users to a disaster recovery site that has been set up in advance to give users a temporary workplace. For example, in most situations not all network applications are critical and require 24/7 uptime. Thus, you should provide backup power systems for servers that are critical. If your operation is a retail one, for example, you would want to keep servers running that interface with your customers—such as your Web site. Other applications, such as word processing for the legal department, and other job functions that can wait can be recovered later.

Advanced Configuration and Power Interface (ACPI) and Standalone UPS Systems

For PCs and small servers, you can buy inexpensive UPS systems for a few hundred dollars that can be used in an environment in which downtime can be tolerated but data corruption cannot. A typical UPS, such as one from American Power Conversion Corp. (APC), can be installed in just a few minutes. Depending on the model, it can provide both a battery backup and some power conditioning.

Be aware that power strips, even those that claim to be able to prevent power spikes from getting through, don't always work as claimed by the manufacturer. The inexpensive models you buy at local discount stores are notorious for not providing the protection they claim to provide. If you depend on the simple mechanics of a fuse or breaker in a cheap power strip to protect your computer, also plan on buying a new computer the next time lightning strikes. For true protection, you really need to spend the extra hundred dollars to get a small UPS for your server or other network devices if you don't use a large-scale UPS.

Tip

Keep in mind that all hardware connected to your computer must be protected against surges and such. If your computer is connected to a surge-protecting UPS, but your monitor and cable modem are plugged directly into the wall, and then into your computer, a surge could still travel from the wall to the monitor to the computer. Or if lightning hits your cable box, the power surge could probably get through the cable from the wall to the monitor to the computer. In other words, if any hardware component is connected in any way to your computer, use UPS connections for each and every device.

To allow you to gracefully shut down the operating system when the power goes out and the batteries take over, an industry initiative (involving major players such as Intel, Microsoft, and others) developed the Advanced Configuration and Power Interface (ACPI). ACPI covers a lot of territory, including power management for laptops and other computers. However, ACPI also allows a standard way for a standalone UPS to communicate with a computer and instruct it to shut down when the UPS battery supply takes over from the outside source of electricity.

Note

You can visit the ACPI Web site using the URL `http://acpi.info` to get more information about specifications and other information about how ACPI interacts with the BIOS code for computers. You will also find here a selection of tools, including tools (such as compilers) that use the ACPI Source Language, which is used to create the firmware code used on your computer's motherboard. This is not light reading but is suggested for those who like to dig into the details to "find out how things work." There is also a disassembler you can use to turn the firmware's machine language code back to ASL to make existing code easier to read. ACPI is also being adopted into Linux-based computers. There are several URLs that can provide you with more information, including `http://mobilix.org/apm_linux.html` and `http://sourceforge.net/projects/acpi`.

ACPI is not limited to just external UPS devices. The specification also includes other power-management capabilities that are standard for the major operating systems today. For example, if you open the Power Options icon in the Windows 2000/XP/2003 Control Panel, the settings that can be enabled or disabled there interact with ACPI. Another interesting feature that is just now being adopted is the capability to start your computer by simply pressing a key.

This communication is accomplished by connecting the power cable from the computer to the power UPS, and also attaching a small cable (usually a serial cable) to the UPS and the computer system, and then enabling the UPS service in the operating system. Windows 2000 and Windows 2003 servers have a UPS service you can run in conjunction with an attached UPS that supports ACPI. You'll even find this service in Windows 2000 Professional as well as Windows XP, and some Linux/Unix systems. The UPS communicates with the service and instructs the system to perform an orderly shutdown when the loss of power is detected and the batteries take over. Things to look for in a small UPS include the following:

- **Audible alarms**—I remember waking up to an alarm from my UPS several years ago to find out I was sleeping through a hurricane. Glad I had that UPS hooked up. Saved the computer; saved me.

- **Multiple outlets**—Most small UPSs allow you to connect two to four devices to the unit so that you don't have to buy one for your computer, one for your printer, one for your router, and so on. This feature can be useful in a Small Office/Home Office (SOHO) environment where the devices that need protection are in close proximity. In addition, look for a UPS that offers connections for other important devices, such as your broadband connection or other network interface, and a phone line, among other items that are connected to your computer.

- **Battery indicators**—Be sure the UPS provides some mechanism (usually an indicator light) for notifying you when the battery is fully charged or is charging. Batteries (and UPSs) don't last forever. Additionally, an indicator light should let you know whether the unit is powering your system by battery power or the outside source.

- **Overload indicator**—Even though multiple outlets are available on a UPS, it might not be capable of supplying sufficient power to the devices you plug into it. A good UPS will indicate (again, usually with a light) that you are straining the UPS to its limit. In such a case, you'll need more than one UPS. The documentation that accompanies the UPS should indicate the amount of current it can supply. Documentation for computers and peripheral devices likewise should contain information about the power they consume. Do the calculations to ensure that the UPS is sufficient for your needs.

- **Circuit breaker**—If you choose to ignore an overload indicator, the UPS should be equipped with a circuit breaker, usually a small button that can be reset, to disconnect itself from the outside power source if you continue to attempt to pull more power through the unit than it can tolerate. When the UPS finds itself at risk, it can trip the breaker, use the battery for a power source, and then instruct your computer to shut down.

Although a large number of vendors manufacture and sell small UPS systems of this type, the Web site for American Power Conversion Corp. (www.apcc.com) has information (including documentation) for products that scale from the desktop to full-fledged computer-room UPS systems.

As with power strips, when making a purchasing decision about a UPS system, you generally get what you pay for. Balance the cost of the unit with what it would cost you to replace the devices you are going to use it to protect, as well as the cost of downtime, data corruption, and so on.

Network Devices

UPS systems aren't just for computers. After all, this book is about networking. Don't forget the routers, switches, and other devices in your network. Although it might be acceptable to let a printer be offline for a while during a power problem, it won't matter whether your computers are up and running if users can't access them through the network. In a large computer room, routers and other such devices should be connected to plugs that terminate in the UPS. In a small office or home-office environment, don't forget to connect your broadband switch/router to the UPS just as you do your computer.

Network Monitoring

The Simple Network Management Protocol (SNMP) and Remote Monitoring (RMON) protocol are powerful tools that can be used to manage a medium to large network. In a small LAN, such as in a home office, these capabilities are not needed. If a device such as a cable/DSL modem or router is not working, you will probably be able to determine that quickly. This applies also to your printer (it has run out of toner or ink), and your computer(s) (it hangs or crashes). However, when a network is spread out over a large geographical area, or when a large number of network devices and computers are on the network, these two protocols can be used with management consoles to help you diagnose problems remotely and gather statistical information about your network. SNMP and RMON also can help you spot trouble before it becomes a real problem.

SNMP basically collects data about computers and other devices on the network, and is used with a management console application to provide a central reporting station. RMON is similar to SNMP but supports additional features, especially on the remote devices. By choosing a good management station application, you can set up thresholds for certain events (such as network traffic, errors, and other statistical information) so that automatic alerts are issued to warn you when something is amiss.

▶▶   SNMP and RMON are covered in greater detail in Chapter 53, "Network Testing and Analysis Tools." If you manage a large network, the central network management application that you use (such as HP OpenView or IBM's Tivoli suite of products) uses these protocols to obtain information from networked devices or, in the case of RMON, to set variables in the Management Information Base (MIB) of these devices.

Server and Workstation Backups

Did you ever lose your address book? Did you have another copy? I guess I'm showing my age again, because most people who have computers don't use an address book, but instead store that information on their laptop or possibly a personal digital assistant (PDA). So let me rephrase the question: Did you ever lose the data on your PC? Did you have a backup? Trivial as it might seem, this is about the most important point to be made in this chapter.

Nothing will save your neck more often than a good backup of all computer systems in your network. It doesn't matter whether you've spent hundreds of thousands of dollars (or even millions) getting state-of-the art RAID (Redundant Array of Independent Disk) disk arrays that have multiple copies of data stored on separate disks. Many financial institutions even have online mirroring of data between distant geographical sites to prevent a natural disaster from causing loss of data. However, no matter how well you prepare your online storage to be fully redundant, there are other reasons you should establish a good schedule of regular backups of all important data on the computer systems in your network.

It's a RAID!

Actually, when the concepts were first developed, RAID stood for Redundant Array of *Inexpensive* Disks. Obviously, the name has been changed because most disks used in large-scale RAID systems are anything but inexpensive! If you want to know more about RAID techniques, from simple disk mirroring to disk striping, and combinations of the two, visit the Web site at `www.raid-advisory.com/`. This is the home Web page for the RAID Advisory Board, a group whose members include manufacturers, testing organizations, universities, and others. You'll find excellent documentation here for the various flavors of RAID technology that have been developed.

Also, when purchasing RAID solutions from a vendor, keep in mind that the buzzword "RAID" doesn't have to imply that the solution offered will protect your data. RAID is an overall encompassing term for several disk technologies. Some of these technologies are concerned with preserving multiple copies of data, such as disk mirroring, whereas others are concerned with fast read or write access, such as disk striping. Combinations of the two are usually employed in an environment that requires fast access to online storage with provisions for data protection.

Lastly, although RAID technology is usually covered in a hardware book, such as Scott Mueller's *Upgrading and Repairing PCs*, it is also mentioned in this book because of the importance it plays in today's larger networks. You will find a more detailed discussion of RAID in Chapter 11, "Network Attached Storage and Storage Area Networks."

For example, even if you use disk mirroring and other RAID techniques, what are you going to do if a meteor falls out of the sky and lands on your computer room? Boom! There go all your computers, your data, and, of course, a few operators. You can replace the computers and the operators (with a little training, of course), but can you replace the data?

▶▶ There is one other technology that can help you out when entire storage systems fail at your local site. Storage Area Networks (SANs) can be used to replicate data between sites that are located several miles away. You can also connect SANs over much longer geographical distances (from coast to coast) by channeling the SAN traffic through standard long-haul protocols such as ATM or Frame Relay. For more information about SANs, see Chapter 11.

For a more practical reason to perform frequent, regular backups, just think of your users. When was the last time a user deleted a file (or worse yet, a directory of files) and asked you to restore it? Backups can protect you from more than just computer failures and natural or unnatural disasters—do you really trust all of your employees? Bad mistake. As the old saying goes, trust everyone but cut the cards first. In a large organization it's difficult to keep all employees happy. Some studies have shown that most of the damage inflicted on individual computers or networks is an "inside job." You need to protect your network from both internal and external problem sources.

Nothing can substitute for a good backup, short of a new job (job security tends to drop some if you lose months of corporate data or even a single day's worth, depending on your industry).

Backup Media—Tape, Optical Storage, and CD-R

The standard mechanism used by most sites to create backups of computer data is magnetic tape. You'll find all sorts of tape backup devices, ranging from QIC (quarter-inch tape) cartridges to the more modern high-capacity Digital Linear Tape (DLT) cartridges. You might even still see the old-fashioned, reel-to-reel nine-track tape lying around a computer. However, you should choose the backup media based on several things:

- Is the backup needed for the short or long term?
- If a restore is necessary, can the backup media perform up to your expectations?
- How expensive is the backup media?
- Do you need to exchange data with other sites, such as companies that provide a disaster recovery hot site?

If you have data that is transient and you only need to recover your systems to a known state that doesn't go far back in time, you can use many kinds of backup media. Most likely, your choice will depend on the speed at which you want to create backups and the speed at which the data can be restored. In this case, tape is probably your best choice. High-speed magnetic tape solutions are available that can back up and restore many gigabytes per hour. Magnetic tape also is good for short-term to long-term storage, provided it is cared for properly as specified by its manufacturer. However, for long-term storage, be sure to pick media that can be used in standard devices. For example, nine-track tapes were used for a long time as the standard in the industry for computer backups. However, if you are required to keep backups for several years due to regulatory requirements, for example, be sure to also keep around tape drives that can be used to read back the data stored on those tapes.

Note

At one of my jobs, I recently watched the company spend a large sum of money to transfer a large stock of old nine-track tapes to more modern DLT media. Occasionally, a tape was found that was unreadable; however, most of the data was recovered and is now sitting in storage awaiting the next expensive conversion. Government regulations!

For long-term storage, you really don't have much choice because technology is changing so fast. However, be sure to look for a backup technology that is from a reliable manufacturer, whom you expect to be in business for a few years to come.

In an emergency, the amount of time required to restore data from a backup can be more important than the amount of time it takes to create the backup in the first place.

For example, it might be possible to break a mirror set cleanly, use one of the mirrored disks to create a backup, and then re-create the mirror set using the software provided by your RAID subsystem. This allows your users to continue using the system with minimal interference from the backup process. If you use a disk-mirroring setup that uses three or more mirrored disks for each mirror set, you can still provide for fault-tolerance while the backup is being produced because multiple disks in the system contain copies of the current data.

Restoring data to a RAID subsystem might take longer than the backup, or it might proceed along at the same rapid pace, depending on the disk controllers, device firmware, and other factors. When choosing a backup solution, don't forget that you need to consider the opposite of the backup: the restore. You might purchase a high-tech, whiz-bang disk subsystem that supports many different levels of RAID techniques, including online backup. However, if restoring data to multiple disks takes significantly longer than restoring to a single disk, you might want to consider an alternative solution.

In case the absolute worst thing that can happen happens—your site is down, not just the computers, due to some disaster such as a fire—you must be sure that the backup media you have is compatible with the equipment you will use in a disaster-recovery scenario. This is easy to overlook when shopping around for an off-site, hot-site provider. In this kind of situation, don't take the vendor's word for it. Test it. Take your backup tapes to the hot site and perform a restore. Time the restore. Be sure the media you are using is compatible with the hot site, and be sure the tape drives (or other media drives) are fast enough to get you back up and running in a short time.

Magnetic tape is not the only backup method available today. You'll find a wide assortment of media, from magnetic-optical discs to recordable CDs and DVDs. The problem with recordable (and rewritable) CDs and DVDs is that they are still extremely slow (even if you have one of the faster drives) when compared to the speed at which magnetic tape can be used, for both the backup and the restore process. That said, recordable CD and DVD technology offers a rather inexpensive method for backing up a small computer system used in a SOHO environment. Because hard disk drives are measured in units of gigabytes, and CD-R discs in megabytes, you should consider recordable CD technology only for situations such as a small office or home office in which you just need to put a small amount of data in offline storage for backup purposes. Recordable DVDs, however, offer 4.7 gigabytes of recording capacity per disc, which makes them very suitable for larger backup jobs (though not for full hard-disk backups, for which tape drives remain the most ideal solution).

Note

Although recordable and rewritable DVD media and drives are more expensive than CD-R/RW media and CD-RW drives, the price should be compared with the amount of data that can be archived using this emerging technology. There are currently several, incompatible standards on the market. For a basic introduction to the world of recordable and rewritable CDs and DVDs, you might want to check out *The Complete Idiot's Guide to Creating Your Own CDs and DVDs* (Alpha Books, ISBN#0-0286-4484-0).

When using rewritable (RW) discs for backup purposes, you're utilizing a medium that can be added to, erased, and reused. You can do this with many of the popular CD-burner software packages on the market today (Nero Burning ROM, Easy CD and DVD Creator, and so on). Microsoft Windows XP also includes CD-burning technology built into the operating system. Note, however, that the software incorporated into Windows XP is not as easy to use as some third-party applications. For a SOHO user, Windows XP's capabilities may be all you need to use. For a more advanced user, you will probably be better off using another product.

Backup Rotation Schedules

When you create backups, first determine what data needs to be backed up and how long it must be accessible for restore purposes. If you have a volatile environment in which data older than a few weeks or months is no longer of use, you won't need to keep tapes or other media in long-term storage. However, for most companies, it's important to be able to produce data from months if not years ago to meet financial or regulatory requirements. In this case, you should create a backup rotation schedule appropriate for your needs.

For example, you might perform a full backup of all the data on your systems each night. Or you might want to produce a full backup once a week, and then produce incremental backups during the week—that is, back up only the files that have changed since the full backup. Using the combination of the full backup and the incremental backup media, you can restore the system to the state it was in at any of the backup points.

In this kind of situation, when the next full backup is performed, the incremental backups might no longer be needed. If that is the case, you can reuse the tapes. The rate at which tapes or other media can be reused is called the *rotation schedule*. A good generic policy (depending on your environment, of course) is to create a weekly backup of all data and perform incremental backups during the week. This allows you to schedule the full backup for a time (such as the weekend) when it won't impact your users. The weekly incremental backup media can be reused during the next week if the next full backup is successful.

The full backups done on a weekly basis can be stored for a month and then reused. Additionally, you might want to keep one of the end-of-month full backups for long-term storage, depending on the nature of your applications.

The full/incremental backup method has been developed to help reduce the *backup window*. This term is used to refer to the time that is available to the backup program when users do not need to have access to the system. However, as storage requirements continue to increase, and because data access in many industries is now a round-the-clock requirement, there is another technology that can be useful in these situations. As mentioned earlier in this chapter, Storage Area Networks can be used to offload storage devices from servers. SANs solve many problems associated with the standard SCSI devices. First, SCSI is limited in the number of devices that can be attached to a SCSI bus, as well as the short distances that SCSI hardware can be used over. SANs allow you to connect storage devices, both disk and tape, over much longer distances without any reduction in the access time. SANs also can be used to offload the backup process from a server's CPU. The SAN can instead be used to back up disk drives to tape drives, with no intervention by the server(s) that use the SAN.

Whatever rotation schedule you decide to use for your backup media, be sure that it meets the needs of your users and the applications they use. In addition, you should implement some type of mechanism—such as a database storing information about each tape—so that you can discard the tape after it has been reused a certain number of times. Magnetic tape does degrade with each usage, and can even deteriorate when stored in a place where such things as temperature and humidity exceed the limits recommended by the manufacturer.

Using barcodes, or simply labeling tapes using a serial numbering method, can enable you to identify each tape in the database, and you can update the database each time a tape is used. When a tape has passed its recommended useful lifetime, zap it with some utility to make the data unreadable, and toss the tape into the trash. It is a good idea to have a company policy on the disposal of all materials (including printouts as well as tapes, among other things) for security purposes. Who is looking in your trash dumpster? Better to be safe than to give someone else valuable information about your company's data.

Off-Site Storage

The backup media is helpful only if it's safely stored as well. If you need to restore only a single file because a user has made a mistake and deleted it, having a tape stored in the computer room makes this a quick and easy job. Pop the tape in the tape drive, restore the file, and then call the user. However, storing backup tapes in the same place that you house your computers is not always such a good idea. For example, this might not help you in the event of some kind of disaster, such as a fire. Not only are your computers lost, but your backups are gone as well.

For important data, the backup media should be sent to an off-site storage location as soon as practical after the backup has finished. In this scenario, if a disaster strikes your site, your tapes are safely stored away at another site and you can use them to recover when you move to a hot site or when you replace the destroyed equipment.

That said, what constitutes off-site storage? You can use several different places for off-site storage, depending on your needs. Consider first how safe the storage site is. Second, consider the amount of time it takes to retrieve the backup media. Third, consider the expense involved. Some sites to consider:

- Use a company whose business is to pick up, store, and deliver backup media. There are many companies in this business. You'll want to visit their storage site to be sure that the storage conditions are conducive to long-term storage of sensitive backup media. Test the promised restore-time window by requesting the retrieval of tapes now and then. Be sure that the site offers 24-hour access to your data.

- If you employ the service of a hot site that can be used to re-create your computer system or network during a disaster, the hot-site vendor often can provide services for off-site storage of backup media. In this case, you can save time during an emergency because you won't have to retrieve the tapes from a third party when you activate the hot site.

- If you are a large company, it might be practical to store your backup media at another company site. The odds of a disaster striking multiple sites at the same time should be taken into consideration, as well as the storage conditions at the other site. For example, if the sites are within close proximity, this might not be a good idea. A natural disaster such as a hurricane or flood might cause a disaster at both places. Consider also the expense in having to regularly send tapes to your other company site. It might be less expensive to pay a professional service to store your tapes than to have employees transferring tapes from one site to another.

■ Take the tapes home and stick them under your bed. This is no joke. I once worked at a small company in which the system manager would take the monthly backup home and store it under her bed until the next month. Along the same lines, if you operate a small office at home, you might consider taking your weekly or monthly backup tape to a safety deposit box at your local bank for off-site storage. The point is to make sure that the data is stored away from the computer system so that you can reduce the odds of a disaster destroying both your systems and your backups.

Routine Maintenance

Although the focus of this chapter is preventive maintenance, routine maintenance for computers and network devices needs to be performed on a regular basis. Routine maintenance helps prevent hardware failures due to fatigued or old equipment that breaks down. For example, although all computers, from the small desktop to the large rack-mounted systems, use fans to ensure the smooth flow of air through the system to keep components from overheating, you should periodically make sure that dust and other contaminants are not being sucked into the system, where electrical charges can cause them to adhere to system components.

Opening the system box and using canned compressed air to get rid of this kind of contamination can be a good preventive technique to use once or twice a year. If you have a home office, this is easily overlooked. If you have a smoker at home, for example, you'll find that cigarette smoke can produce a fine layer of dust on computer components over time. This can also happen, as I know from experience, with cat hair. Don't leave the box closed forever. Open it up and look inside now and then to clean things up. Even the larger servers that are stored away in a locked computer room can use cleaning now and then. No matter how "clean" you think your computer room is, just take a look at the dust that accumulates over time. You might be surprised. This is one of the problems associated with the "lights out" computer-room scenario. If you don't look into the computer room now and then, you may have a problem slowly accumulating. It's always best to find a problem before it seriously impacts your hardware.

Tape drives need to be cleaned periodically because the magnetic tape comes in contact with the tape heads inside the unit. A cleaning tape should be run on a schedule recommended by the manufacturer. DLT tape drives usually have an indicator light that comes on when a sufficient amount of contamination has accumulated on the tape head such that parity errors are occurring. If the cleaning tape light comes on more frequently than the cleaning schedule recommended by the manufacturer, you might want to consider looking at which backup tapes were used just before this happened. You might have an old tape that needs to be discarded, or even a tape drive that needs to be recalibrated or replaced.

Building Redundancy into the Network

It doesn't matter what kind of support maintenance contract you have with your vendor if it takes the vendor hours or days to get the parts necessary to replace a failed system. For this reason, it's a good idea to build redundant paths in your network from the design phase so that, for example, if a router goes down, another path through the network will allow users to keep accessing the data they need. Providing for fault-tolerant servers using clustering technology also can be used to ensure maximum uptime for critical systems.

◀◀   In Chapter 2, "Overview of Network Topologies," you will find a good discussion of using partial-mesh topologies to build redundancy into your network. If you skipped the earlier chapters, you might want to go back and take another look.

If the time needed to get replacements is excessive (when compared to the cost of paying idle users, the overhead involved in office space, and so on), it might be wise to keep a duplicate device on-site so that you can swap it into service to replace a failed device in an emergency. In the case of a router or switch, it's easy to replace the failed device, follow a carefully written plan to reconfigure it, and put the network path back in service.

Recovery Planning

Nothing (other than a backup) is more helpful during an emergency than a well-thought-out recovery plan. Actually, this is an overall term because you should plan for network or server outages—from the loss of a single disk drive to the loss of a single computer system, and even to the loss of your entire network. Chapter 3, "Network Design Strategies," stresses that you should always document the network and its components. Recovery procedures should be part of this documentation.

The problem with disasters is that you can't schedule them. They don't always occur during normal business hours when you are wide awake and functioning well. In the middle of the night after a long day at work, you might get called in to restore a system without having the advantage of a good night's sleep. A good disaster-recovery plan can be helpful if only to keep you from making a mistake during the recovery process.

A good disaster recovery plan includes several items:

- Contact information for key personnel who need to be involved in the recovery effort, as well as personnel who need to be informed of the event, such as application client representatives. Don't forget to keep this information up-to-date.

- Contact information for vendors of both the hardware and the software components of the system or network. This should include both technical support telephone numbers and contact information for local field personnel who might need to come in and assist you with setting up or repairing the damage.

- Step-by-step procedures for remedying the situation. This can involve such things as how to completely rebuild a particular computer system from scratch by reinstalling the operating system and applying the backup tapes. Configuration information for routers and other devices should be documented in the recovery plan.

- After the disaster has been remedied according to your plan, there needs to be a set of tests you can perform on the operating system, the hardware, and the applications to ensure that the recovery effort has been successful.

Justifying Preventative Maintenance

Some of the approaches that have been discussed in this chapter are expensive. Because of this, you might experience problems obtaining funding from upper management for these items. You can do several things to help yourself out in these situations.

Be sure to document all the downtime you experience for each system in the network, and try to associate a cost with it. Although you might not be able to get data that allows you to show the impact on your customers, you usually can determine the number of users who are impacted. Assuming that these users can perform only a certain percentage of their daily work without access to the computer or network, try to assign the number of hours lost due to the downtime and multiply it by an average hourly rate for the employees affected by the downtime. Most likely, you won't have access to accurate pay rates for other employees. However, a way to get around this is to multiply the hours times the minimum hourly wage and show this to upper management if it results in a significant amount. Point out that you've based your costing on the minimum wage. Because those in upper management are more likely to know the average salaries of experienced computer users, this figure still gives them a good idea of what downtime costs. In other words, if you come up with a large figure during your calculations based on the minimum wage, they'll quickly determine that the actual figure is magnitudes larger than that, and you just might get support for your preventative maintenance efforts.

Physical Networking Components

SOME OF THE MAIN TOPICS FOR THIS PART ARE

Wiring the Network—Cables, Connectors, Concentrators, and Other Network Components

Network Interface Cards

Network Switches

Virtual LANs

Routers

Network Attached Storage and Storage Area Networks

PART II

Wiring the Network— Cables, Connectors, Concentrators, and Other Network Components

CHAPTER 6

Bridging the gap between the stated standards and the actual implementation of bringing a network to a user's desktop workstation is not the simple task you might expect. Connecting tens, hundreds, or even thousands of computers can become an exercise in futility if proper planning is not done. Planning and installing your cable plant carefully is vital for ease of future upgrading and expanding your network.

◄◄   For more information about the planning necessary for a successful network implementation, see Chapter 2, "Overview of Network Topologies," and Chapter 3, "Network Design Strategies."

This chapter covers quite a few technical details that relate to the network cables and other components used in your network. Although the definitions and other material you'll find in this chapter might seem overwhelming at first, this chapter is a good reference when you encounter some of these terms later in the book.

Structured Wiring

In the 1980s, the Telecommunications Industry Association (TIA) and the Electronics Industries Association (EIA) formed a task force to establish a set of standards for installing network wiring in buildings. The first draft was completed in 1991 and became known as EIA/TIA-568 (referred to in this chapter as 568). A more recent standard is named ANSI/TIA/EIA-569-A (referred to in this chapter as 569-A). These standards documents encompass structured wiring, cables, network topology, connectors and hardware, electrical performance specifications, physical termination, and support mechanisms.

Note

ANSI is an acronym for American National Standards Institute. ANSI was founded in 1918 and is the major standards organization for the United States. ANSI is also a member of other standards organizations, such as ISO. Programmers might recognize one of the standards that ANSI adopted many years ago: American Standard Code for Information Interchange (ASCII). Unicode and other standards have been developed to add support for other language character sets. You can find ANSI online at **www.ansi.org**.

The 568 and 569-A standards describe the physical layout and specifications for the physical plant as it relates to the various topological standards. The physical plant, in this context, comprises everything having to do with what leads up to your desktop, from routers, cables, patch panels, and so on.

These are the basic topics covered in the standards:

- **The work area**—The termination point of the network at a user's work space.

- **The backbone cabling system structure**—Connections between multiple telecommunication rooms, equipment rooms, and entrance facilities.

- **The horizontal cabling system structure**—Connection from the telecommunications outlet in the work area, terminating in the telecommunications room.

- **The telecommunications closet**—The central wiring point for a floor. The telecommunications closet can contain both network devices and concentrators (such as switches), as well as telephone equipment.

- **Other specifications**—Such issues as intrabuilding connections and such factors as electromechanical interference.

In the following sections you will learn about these topics, as well as others. For a more complete explanation of the standards, it is suggested that you obtain the standards and read them. It is beyond the scope of this book to describe the standards in detail. Instead, those that apply to networks are discussed. In addition, several terms are defined for those who are not well versed in the terminology used by these standards. Many of these terms are also used throughout other chapters in this book. Between this chapter and the glossary, you should be able to locate the definition of almost any word used by network administrators, and those who put together LANs, MANs, and WANs.

The Work Area

The work area includes the telecommunications outlet (that is, the faceplate into which you plug your computer's network cable at your desk), which serves as the work area interface to the entire network cabling system. Work area equipment includes cables used to connect to the telecommunications outlet. The following are the work area cabling specifications:

- Equipment cords are assumed to have the same performance as patch cords (in the telecommunications closet) in the same typing category, for example, Category 5 and 6 network cables.

- When used, adapters are assumed to be compatible with the transmission capabilities of the equipment to which they connect.

- Horizontal cable links are specified with the assumption that a maximum cable length of 5 meters (16 feet) is used for equipment cords in the work area. This can depend on the actual length of cabling used to connect the work area back to the telecommunicatons closet. The important factor to remember is that there is a maximum distance that all cables can add up to, depending on your topology. Thus, if the cable from the telecommunications closet is less than the specified length allowed by the standards, you can use a longer cable from the termination point at the work area.

The Backbone Cabling System Structure

The backbone cabling system of the standard provides interconnections between telecommunication rooms, equipment rooms, and entrance facilities (see Figure 6.1).

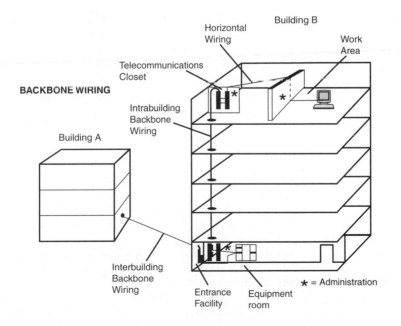

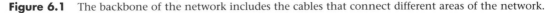

Figure 6.1   The backbone of the network includes the cables that connect different areas of the network.

This cabling system includes backbone cables, intermediate and main cross connects, mechanical terminations, and patch cords or jumpers used for backbone-to-backbone cross connections. The backbone also extends between buildings in a campus environment.

There are some points specified for the backbone of the cabling system:

- Equipment connections to the backbone cabling should be made with cable lengths of 30 meters or less.
- The backbone of cabling should be configured as a star topology.
- The backbone is limited to no more than two hierarchical levels of cross connects—main and intermediate. No more than one cross connect can exist between a main and a horizontal cross connect, and no more than three cross connects can exist between any two horizontal cross connects.
- A total coax backbone distance of 90 meters is specified for high-bandwidth capability over copper. This distance is for uninterrupted backbone runs.
- The distance between terminations in the entrance facility and main cross connect should be documented and made available to a service provider.
- Recognized media can be used individually or in a combination, as required by the installation.
- Multipair cable is allowed, as long as it satisfies the requirement of a minimum of cross-talk.
- The proximity of cabling to sources of electromagnetic interference should be taken into account.
- Cross connects for different cable types must be located in the same facility.

Note that in these specifications, bridge taps and splitters are not allowed.

Caution

A *bridge tap* is an extraneous piece of cabling that is left over from a previous connection to a communications line. If not removed, a bridge tap acts similarly to an antenna, and causes impedance mismatches and other problems with the signal that travels down the copper wire. Bridge taps are one of the reasons why it can be difficult to obtain DSL service from your local phone company. As phones are added to your local loop and then disconnected, many dangling wires can be left behind because it's simply too costly to remove them. In a properly cabled network, bridge taps should not exist.

Tip

Splitters are devices that are used to separate higher frequencies from lower frequencies on a copper wire. Again, splitters serve no purpose on a properly cabled LAN. However, on the public switched telephone network (PSTN), splitters can be installed to make it possible to obtain voice-grade telephone service and DSL service using the same copper wire pair, with a minimum of interference between the frequencies used on the wire for voice and DSL services.

For more about DSL, see Chapter 16, "Dedicated Connections."

The Horizontal Cabling System Structure

The horizontal cabling system (shown in Figure 6.2) extends from the telecommunications outlet in the work area and terminates in a horizontal cross connect in the telecommunications room. It includes the telecommunications outlet.

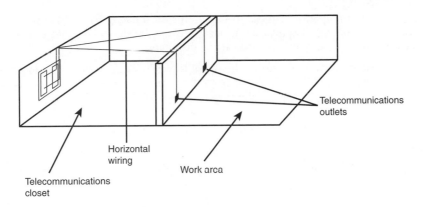

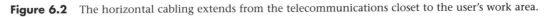

Figure 6.2 The horizontal cabling extends from the telecommunications closet to the user's work area.

The distance covered by the horizontal cabling is limited by the network topology chosen for your network. For example, in most Ethernet networks, this distance is 90 meters. Token-Ring has various specifications, depending on the cables used. For more information about Token-Ring, see the chapter "Token-Ring Networks," located on the upgradingandrepairingpcs.com Web site.

The Telecommunications Closet

Telecommunications rooms generally are considered to be floor-serving facilities for horizontal cable distribution. They also are used for intermediate and main cross connects. The telecommunications room is where you place patch panels, as well as hubs or switches that are used to connect individual workstations or servers to the network backbone.

Important Definitions

In discussing network cables and troubleshooting wiring problems, there are several important terms and concepts to understand. This section contains definitions of some of the terms used earlier in the chapter. This section should be considered as an expanded glossary of terms associated with the Physical layer of the OSI model (discussed in Appendix A, "Overview of the OSI Seven-Layer Networking Reference Model"). In other chapters you will find references to these terms. Although it is not required reading for the casual reader, the following can serve as an invaluable reference when making purchasing decisions, as well as in the design phase of a new network or when upgrading an existing one.

Attenuation to Cross-Talk Ratio (ACR)

ACR is a critical factor in determining the capability of an unshielded twisted-pair cable or shielded twisted-pair cable. Attenuation to cross-talk ratio (ACR) is the value of the attenuation less the cross-talk value, both expressed in decibels (db) at a particular frequency. This is a quality factor for cabling. Before you can understand this ratio, you need to understand what the term *attenuation* means.

Attenuation

Attenuation is the decrease in magnitude of the signal as it travels through any transmitting medium, such as wire or glass. Attenuation is measured as a logarithm of the ratio between the input and the output power or between the input and the output voltage of the system. It's expressed in db. All good things must come to an end, and this is the case with electricity as well as light. As the signal travels down the copper wire (or the fiber-optic cable), some of the signal is lost. This is why it is necessary in a network topology to impose specific limits on the lengths of cable you can use. After you get past certain limits imposed by a particular topology, the signal becomes so degraded that the data transmitted cannot be reliably recovered at the destination.

Figure 6.3 shows that attenuation occurs as the signal travels down the wire. The amplitude of the electrical signal decreases the farther it travels from the transmitting side of the communications channel.

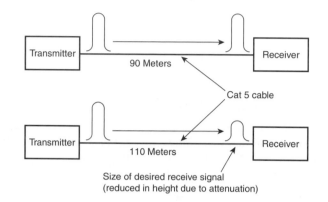

Figure 6.3   An electrical signal degrades as it travels through a copper cable (attenuation).

Bandwidth

Bandwidth is the range of frequencies required for proper transmission of a signal. This is expressed in hertz (Hz) as a difference of frequencies. For example, the bandwidth used on a copper wire for voice communications (via the PSTN) is 4MHz. Because copper cables are capable of carrying frequencies well above this 4MHz limit, DSL transfers are possible via use of frequencies above the 4MHz used by voice communications.

Characteristic Impedance

Characteristic impedance is the value of impedance (a combination of resistance and reactance) of a transmission line measured over a specific frequency range. Impedance is expressed in units of Z, because it is a calculation based on both resistance and reactance of the network media. Whereas resistance is the capability of a medium to resist the transmission of electrons, reactance is another thing altogether. Reactance, for alternating current (AC), is the medium's tendency to store and then release the current as it flows through the medium.

Cross-Talk

Cables are made up of two or more copper wires that are bundled together with an outer cover so that it's easier to route them through the conduits that form the path your physical network takes. The coupling of signals from one pair of wires in a cable to another pair of wires in the same cable actually can cause the signals to interfere with each other. The electrical signal in a copper wire not only travels down that particular wire, but also *radiates out* perpendicularly and can interfere with other copper wires in the same cable or bundle. This is called cross-talk. This coupling also can occur between wires of different cables that are close to one another. In Figure 6.4, you can see that some of the signal has radiated from one wire and produced noise on another.

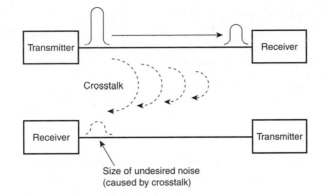

Figure 6.4 A portion of an electrical signal radiates from an adjacent wire, producing interference (cross-talk).

Dialectic

To keep the individual copper wires separated from each other within a cable, an insulating material called *dialectic material* is used to help prevent interference between two conductors. It can be a simple plastic nonconducting material, or a more complex formulation used in some high-capacity wire bundles.

Electromagnetic Field

As electrons move through a medium, two fields are associated with this movement: electric fields and magnetic fields. These fields exist at varying distances from the conductors (the wires) as they are brought closer together.

Electromagnetic Interference

Electromagnetic interference (EMI) refers to the interference that electromagnetic signals produce by frequent changes of electrons moving through certain media. Network wiring and equipment can be very susceptible to EMI, and they also emit EMI.

Far-End Cross-Talk (FEXT)

Far-end cross-talk occurs between two twisted pairs of the cable at the far end (destination) of the cable from the measuring source. The transmitting end of a cable pair produces the stronger electrical signal (because the signal attenuates, or becomes weaker, as it passes through the copper wire or fiber-optic cable), so FEXT can be a more difficult problem to tackle. However, you should be cognizant that connectors are properly created at the far end of a connection to prevent interference between copper wires at that point. The signal might be weaker at the end point of a connection, yet it still exists. This is why the specifications allow only a *very small amount of exposed copper wire* when connecting a cable to an actual connector (such as an RJ-45 jack).

Frequency

Frequency is a measurement of the number of times a periodic action occurs in a measure of time. In terms of alternating current, this is the number of cycles per second and is usually expressed in hertz.

Full-Duplex and Half-Duplex Communications

Full-duplex communications means that communications between two network nodes can occur in both directions simultaneously. Obviously, this is a communications method in which both transmitted and received signals are not simultaneously present. They alternate in time on the transmission medium. Another method for creating a full-duplex connection is to use separate wires for transmission and reception. Using this method, both ends of a communications link can send or receive data simultaneously. Using half-duplex communications, only one side of the communications line can transmit at any point in time.

Impedance

Impedance is the total resistance and reactance offered by a circuit component. The units are expressed in ohms. The common symbol for impedance is the Greek letter zeta, or Z. This is a complex numerical value, mathematically expressed as either a complex number or the polar coordinate number.

Impedance Match

Impedance match is a condition in which the impedance of a device or wiring system is matched to another wiring system or device.

Leakage

Leakage is the undesirable passage of current through an insulator or over the surface of a conductor. This can occur in older cable bundles in which the insulating material has become degraded over time and signals from one wire in the bundle interfere with signals in other wires in the same bundle. This could happen, for instance, if a small animal were to attempt to chew through a cable. Feel sorry for the rat, but feel sorrier for yourself when you have to replace the cable!

Near-End Cross-Talk (NEXT)

Near-end cross-talk is cross-talk that occurs between two twisted pairs measured at the same location, and it usually occurs between wires in a twisted-pair cable. One of the conditions that can introduce this interference is a crushed cable, so care must be used when pulling network cabling and attaching connectors.

Nominal Velocity of Propagation

Nominal velocity of propagation is the speed at which a signal travels through a medium expressed as a decimal fraction of the speed of light in a vacuum.

Power SUM

Power SUM is a measured parameter that includes the sum of the contributions of power from all pairs of a cable system, excluding the pair under test. This is done with all the other pairs of the cable having signals present.

Radio Frequency

Radio frequencies are frequencies in the electromagnetic spectrum that are used for radio communications. These generally occur above 300KHz.

Radio Frequency Interference (RFI)

Radio frequency interference is electromagnetic interference at radio frequencies.

Shield

A *shield* is a metallic foil or wire screen-mesh that encircles a cable or wires in a cable to prevent electromagnetic or radio frequency fields from entering or leaving a cable. This prevents interference with other cables in the same cable bundle or cables that are in close proximity to the shielded cable. You've probably heard the term *STP* used in connection with network cables. This is an abbreviation for shielded twisted-pair cabling, typically found in Token-Ring networks. Although shielding cables were considered to be important in earlier network implementations, unshielded twisted-pair cables (in which the twisting of wires helps to reduce interference) are the norm today for cables connecting the work area to the telecommunications closet.

Time Domain Reflectometry (TDR)

Time domain reflectometry is a method of measuring cable length or faults by timing the period between a test pulse and its reflection from an impedance discontinuity on the cable. A TDR measuring instrument can enable you to determine the approximate location of a problem on a cable. It can also be used to determine any defects in a spool of cable before you deploy it in your network. You can learn more about TDR in Chapter 53, "Network Testing and Analysis Tools."

Physical Cable Types

Much attention is given to the specifications used for Ethernet and Token-Ring networks. Most of these specifications deal with the physical makeup of the cabling involved in connecting the individual components of the network. Understanding the cable types, the number of wires in a cable (both shielded and unshielded varieties), and several other electrical factors is critical to successfully upgrading or maintaining your network system. The type of cable you use depends on the type of LAN you are creating. The connectors, terminations, and distances that can be covered by particular cable types will be a factor in determining any cable length restrictions and overall quality of LAN you can create. For example, an Ethernet network card and a Token-Ring network adapter card use different connectors and cables.

Twisted-Pair Cabling

The most basic wire type used for LAN wiring is twisted-pair wiring. This wire type also is referred to as unshielded twisted pair, or UTP. This wire is a derivative of the more common cable that was used in telephone installations in most commercial facilities for years. This type is versatile, is easy to install, and has favorable performance characteristics. It comes in various colors, wire gauges, insulation materials, twisting methods, and outer jacket materials.

The basic cable assembly for UTP cable can contain a large number of conductors (or copper wires). Most conductors are grouped into pairs that are twisted around each other. Telephone cables are available in 2, 4, 6, 25, 100, and even larger groupings of conductors. Most of the cable that is used for LAN wiring comes as cable consisting of four pairs of wires.

The four-pair cable has become a standard and is referenced in the EIA/TIA-568B cabling standards. This is the cable around which most of the cable standards and performance tests are based. Several of the LAN topology configurations use only two of the four-wire pairs; however, some use all four pairs. Another common cable type that is found in twisted-pair installations is a 25-pair jumper cable. This cable type is primarily used between patch panels and connector type punchdown blocks.

Note

A punch block is a big rack with wires coming out of it that connects to various other devices, such as switches. You then take cables, such as those that extend to the desktop, and plug them into one of the sockets on the punchdown block. This is similar in concept to what you might find in a telephone communications room, though some of those "wrap" the wire instead of "punching" it into a slot.

The main difference between typical telephone wiring and LAN wiring is the grading of the assembly of the twisted pairs within the cable. The primary factor that differentiates one cable type from another is the number of *twists per foot* that each individual pair of conductors has *within the cable*. The twisting of the individual pairs to the cable is significant. The twisting of the two wires has a twofold effect electrically on the cable assembly. First, it causes the interline capacitance to be reduced. This is a good thing because the reduction of capacitance reduces any signal shorting between the conductors at high frequencies. Second, twisting the wire couples the electromagnetic fields equally, thus helping to cancel out any interfering signals. This operation is referred to as a balanced transmission. One effect of achieving a balanced transmission is that the high frequencies of a LAN signal do not interfere with the other use of the wires in a cable assembly. Some radiation of the signal does occur, but because the transmitted signal is kept to a low amplitude, random emissions remain within acceptable limits.

Typically, wire sizes for UTP cable range between 18 AWG and 32 AWG. AWG, which stands for American wire gauge, is the standard for sizing wires in the U.S. Wire size is based primarily on the current-carrying capacity of the wire as set by the National Electrical Code. As the wire gauge increases, the physical diameter of the wire decreases. So a number 10 AWG wire is physically smaller than a number 8 AWG wire. Number 10 AWG wire is approximately 0.1 inch in diameter and usually can carry approximately 30 amps of current.

So for telephone wiring or LAN wiring, the number 18 AWG wire is much larger than the 32 AWG wire. Common sizes for LAN wiring are typically 22 to 24 AWG. This wire is typically solid, not stranded, for ease in termination on insulation displacement connectors.

Categories of Twisted-Pair Cables

As mentioned previously, the twisting of the wire pairs of conductors that make up cables is important—so important that the cable used for LAN wiring is graded into categories. Category 1 was used for POTS (or plain old telephone service). Category 2 was used in early networking wiring schemes, such as ARCnet (see Chapter 13, "The Oldest LAN Protocol Is Still Kicking: ARCnet"), and for connecting terminals to multiuser computer networks. Category 3 uses four twists per foot and is still graded for operating as a LAN wiring system. Category 3 is rated for speeds up to 16MHz and is still used as a cable in some Token-Ring networks. Category 4 is rated up to 20MHz. Category 5 is rated for up to 100MHz operation. Category 5, which was until recently the de facto standard for LAN wiring, has now been replaced by a new category.

A new transmission characteristics standard is designated as Category 5E. This is referenced to 568B.1 and B.2 and additional Class D requirements of the ISO/IEC 11801. These requirements are a specified tunable frequency limit of 100MHz and are a superset of Category 5 and Class D.

During the first quarter of 2001, Category 6 cabling was certified for use as a standard. Transmission characteristics are specified up to 250MHz. Also called Class E according to ISO/IEC, this cable probably will represent the last generation of unshielded twisted-pair cabling that is used in LAN wiring. This cable is different from the standard UTP cable because it contains filler material to separate the twisted pairs from each other, and thereby reduces cross-talk between wire pairs. One of the biggest problems with using higher frequencies through the pairs of the cables is that adjacent conductor capacitance is reduced and cross-talk increases. Separating these conductors reduces this capacitance and cross-talk. This also is a consideration when installing cables because if cables are bundled too tightly there can be a resulting chance of interference of data signals between individual cables. Hence, modern standard practice dictates that when cables are installed, they are to be installed with either loose cable ties or Velcro straps.

A new category, Category 7 UTP cabling, offers a different approach to twisted-pair cabling architecture. The cable is assembled with an overall shield and individually shielded pairs. The most significant improvement with this type of cable will be in the higher performance bandwidth achieved.

Cable rating will be up to 600MHz. There likely will be a new interface design—jack and plug. There also will be a requirement that this new category be backward-compatible with lower-performance categories and classes. It is interesting to note that TIA is not actively developing a standard for Category 7. This organization probably will try to assimilate a standard with class F standards put forth by the ISO.

Performance Comparison

The choice of cabling insulation material is important. Requirements set forth in the National Electrical Code (NEC) specifically and stringently place requirements on the type of cable insulation allowed in certain portions of buildings. There's an increasing use of large amounts of cable for LAN wiring, and these cables are usually installed above drop ceilings and below computer-room raised floors (also known as the plenum space). Unfortunately, these areas are most often used to handle cooling and environmental air. Conventional wire installations installed in these locations were found to be flammable at the very least, and at their worst, would produce toxic gases from the materials that surround cable bundles that would be carried with the cooling or environmental air, thus placing people in the other parts of the building at risk. Additionally, fire can actually be spread through the plenum areas.

Manufacturers soon developed cable installations that were less flammable and could be used in plenum-rated areas. The National Electrical Code differentiates cable types by voltage, power classifications, and insulation types. It should be noted that there is a definite difference between plenum- and riser-rated cable. It would seem that riser-rated cable would be classified higher than plenum-rated cable, because riser-rated cable is intended for use in vertical shafts that run between floors. The shafts are not normally used to handle environmental or cooling air except in ductwork. Thus, the cable installed in risers does not have to have insulation rated as stringently as that for cabling installed in plenum-rated areas.

The special requirements for cabling insulation and power ratings are covered in detail in the NFPA National Electrical Code Sections 770 and 800, for those who want to pursue these details.

Color Coding and Marking

Each pair of wires in a twisted-pair cable assembly is color coded so that each wire can be identified at each end of the cable assembly and terminated properly. This color code is shown in Figure 6.5.

• Color-coding
white/blue - blue
white/orange - orange
white/green - green
white/brown - brown

Figure 6.5   Wire pairs in a cable are color coded.

As you can see, each pair of the cable is color coded in a complementary fashion. Pair-one wires are color coded white-blue and blue-white. The blue-white wire has as its base color blue insulation with a white stripe molded at intervals along its length. The stripe is sometimes called a tracer. The white-blue wire is color coded in reverse, with a white wire that has a blue tracer. The color code is unique for each pair and is repetitive.

The color coding is important in LAN wiring because the system signals are polarity sensitive. If pairs on the cable are reversed, the signals are reversed, causing a failure in the receiving equipment. The terms *tip* and *ring*, used to designate the polarity of each pair of wires, stem from the days of the old telephone patch panels. The equipment used consisted of quarter-inch phone plugs, which fit into corresponding jacks on a patch board or switchboard. The switchboard plug consisted of two parts. The tip of the plug was wired through the sleeve or ring of the plug. The plug used on audio equipment and musical instruments is the same plug. The primary color was wired to the ring and the secondary color was wired to the tip.

As mentioned before, there is also a use for 25-pair jumper cable. This color code, broken down by pair, is shown in Table 6.1.

Table 6.1 Color Coding for a 25-Pair Jumper Cable As Specified by the ICEA

Tip Color	Pair	Ring
white/blue	pair 1	blue/white
white/orange	pair 2	orange/white
white/green	pair 3	green/white
white/brown	pair 4	brown/white
white/slate	pair 5	slate/white
red/blue	pair 6	blue/red
red/orange	pair 7	orange/red
red/green	pair 8	green/red
red/brown	pair 9	brown/red
red/slate	pair 10	slate/red
black/blue	pair 11	blue/black
black/orange	pair 12	orange/black
black/green	pair 13	green/black
black/brown	pair 14	brown/black
black/slate	pair 15	slate/black
yellow/blue	pair 16	blue/yellow
yellow/orange	pair 17	orange/yellow
yellow/green	pair 18	green/yellow
yellow/brown	pair 19	brown/yellow
yellow/slate	pair 20	slate/yellow
violet/blue	pair 21	blue/violet
violet/orange	pair 22	orange/violet
violet/green	pair 23	green/violet
violet/brown	pair 24	brown/violet
violet/slate	pair 25	slate/violet

This cable must be rated for the category for which it's to be used. Physically, it mostly is used between patch panels and punchdown blocks, or between patch panels to patch panel installations. Cable sizes above 25 pairs are usually in groups of 25-pair cables. Each of these groups of cables is marked within the larger bundle with a wrapped colored leader that, by design, is color coded with the same color code that is used on the twisted-pair cabling scheme. Thus, on a 50-pair cable, which would have two 25-pair cables, the 25-pair bundle has an outer spiral wrap of a blue plastic streamer, and the second group of 25 has a group wrapped with an orange streamer. This color code can be repeated ad infinitum for a very large group of 25-pair cables.

Coaxial Cables

Coaxial cables are the original LAN cable. This cable was first used in Ethernet networks, IBM PC net broadband networks, and ARCnet networks, besides being used for video and cable television applications. It still is in use in many older locations, even though newer installations have converted to twisted pair. Coaxial cable has been around long enough that it has a mature construction technology and is relatively inexpensive. The primary advantages of coaxial cable are its self-shielding properties, its low attenuation at high frequencies, and its moderate installation expense. For example, if you have a cable modem in your house, a coaxial cable is used for both the video signals and the cable modem frequencies.

Coaxial cables consist of the conductor centrally positioned in a cable surrounded by an insulating medium, which then is enclosed by a shield (see Figure 6.6). The shield can consist of a foil wrapping within an integral drain wire or a wire braid. The coax that is used for thick Ethernet might have a double-shield layer.

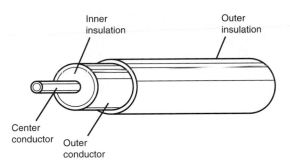

Figure 6.6 Coaxial cable consists of a shielded copper wire.

Placing the center conductor in an insulating medium surrounded by a shielding material theoretically traps all the electromagnetic fields inside the cable assembly. Because this shield has to be grounded, the mode of propagation of the signals in the cable is analogous to that of a mechanical pipeline. The grounded shield helps prevent interfering signals outside the cable from impinging on the center conductor. Conversely, the grounded shield also prevents signals from leaking out of the cable structure. Grounding is very important in this cabling system. A cable installation without proper grounding is susceptible to outside EMI and RFI interference.

Types of Coaxial Cabling

Two types of coax cabling are used in wiring local area networks. One type is called thicknet and the other is referred to as thinnet. Thicknet was used in the original Ethernet coax trunk distribution cable now known as 10BASE-5. The cable has a large center diameter conductor of number 12 AWG and has an overall diameter of approximately 0.4 inch. This cable typically was run close to a workstation either in the ceiling or in the walls. A connection is made to the cable by literally tapping to the wire by punching a hole through it (commonly known as a vampire tap), and then the connection is directly made by running a cable from the tap to the networked device, such as a terminal or a PC. The term *thicknet* was introduced because this coaxial cable is almost a half-inch in diameter, and when newer, smaller diameter coaxial cable was introduced it looked very large.

A newer standard cable, which is approximately a quarter-inch diameter and is much more flexible, was named thinnet (10BASE-2). This type of cable uses BNC connectors with T-adapters. It is less expensive, but the distances for a thinnet Ethernet segment are limited compared to those for thicknet.

ARCnet is another LAN topology that uses coaxial cable. In this topology, the workstations are connected directly to the coax in a star arrangement. Each leg terminates in an active or a passive hub.

▶▶ ARCnet is one of the oldest networking technologies still in use today, although you're more likely to find it used in point-of-sale mechanisms, linking electronic cash registers, for example. You can learn more about how ARCnet works by reading Chapter 13, "The Oldest LAN Protocol Is Still Kicking: ARCnet."

Typically, the sizes for coaxial cables are designated by an RGB number or a manufacturer's numbering system. A summary of cable types follows:

- **Cable RG 59/U-1 (105 482 624)** is a 75-ohm coaxial cable with a 22 AWG (7×30) center conductor, a foamed polyethylene dielectric, a bare copper braid (mm. 95% coverage) outer conductor, and a PVC jacket. (Similar to RG 59/U type.) UL style 1354.

- **Cable RG 59/U-1A (105 521 561)** is a 75-ohm coaxial cable with a 22 AWU (7×30) center conductor, a foamed polyethylene dielectric, a bare copper braid (mm. 95% coverage) outer conductor, and a PVC jacket. (Similar to RU 59/U type.) UL style 1354, UL Listed Type CL2.

- **Cable RG 59/U-2 (105 482 632)** is a 75-ohm coaxial cable with a 22 AWG copper covered steel center conductor, a polyethylene dielectric, a bare copper braid (mm. 80% coverage) outer conductor, and a PVC jacket. (Similar to RU 59/U type commercial.) UL style 1354.

- **Cable RG 59/U-2A (105 521 579)** is a 75-ohm coaxial cable with a 22 AWG copper covered steel center conductor, a polyethylene dielectric, a bare copper braid (mm. 80% coverage) outer conductor, and a PVC jacket. (Similar to RU 59/U type commercial.) UL style 1354. UL Listed Type CL2 per 1987 NEC.

- **Cable RG 59/U-5 (105 482 665)** is a 75-ohm plenum coaxial cable with a 22 AWG copper covered steel center conductor, an FEP dielectric, a bare copper braid (mm. 95% coverage) outer conductor, and an FEP jacket. (Similar to RU-59/U type.) UL Listed Type CL2P per 1987 NEC.

- **Cable RG 62 A/U-1 (105 482 723)** is a 93-ohm coaxial cable with a 22 AWG copper covered steel center conductor, an air dielectric polyethylene dielectric, a bare copper braid (mm. 95% coverage) outer conductor, and a PVC jacket. (Similar to RU 62 A/U type.)

- **Cable RG 62 A/U-1A (105 521 660)** is a 93-ohm coaxial cable with a 22 AWU copper covered steel center conductor, an air dielectric polyethylene dielectric, a bare copper braid (mm. 95% coverage) outer conductor, and a PVC jacket. (Similar to RU 62 A/U type.) UL Listed Type CL2 per 1987 NEC.

- **Cable Ethernet (105 482 798)** is a 50-ohm coaxial cable with a 0.0855 AWU solid tinned copper center conductor, a foamed polyethylene dielectric, a foil shield bonded to dielectric, and a PVC jacket. (Similar to Ethernet Type.) UL style 1478 DEC approved.

- **Cable Ethernet-1A (105 538 037)** is a 50-ohm coaxial cable with a 0.0855 AWU solid tinned copper center conductor, a foamed polyethylene dielectric, a foil shield bonded to dielectric, a tinned copper braid (mm. 93% coverage), a foil shield, a tinned copper braid (mm. 90% coverage), and a yellow PVC jacket. (Similar to Ethernet Type.) UL style 1478. UL Listed Type CL2 per 1987 NEC.

- **Cable Ethernet-2 (105 482 806)** is a 50-ohm plenum coaxial cable with a 0.0855 AWU solid tinned copper center conductor, a foamed FEP dielectric, a foil shield, a tinned copper braid (mm. 93% coverage), a foil shield, a tinned copper braid (mm 90% coverage), and an FEP jacket. (Similar to Ethernet.) UL Listed Type CL2P per 1987 NEC. DEC approved. Xerox specifications/IEEE 803.

Characteristic Impedance

As you can see from the preceding list, the characteristic impedance is the first electrical consideration mentioned. This is because this cable was first used for the needs of RF signal propagation, and the coax impedance was specified so that proper load matching could be made at the head end of the RF equipment. Standard impedances for coaxial cable are 50 ohms, 75 ohms, and 92 ohms. The diameter of the center conductor, the dialectic material, and the mechanical properties of the shield contribute and also help define the coaxial cable's characteristic impedance. This impedance value is the value of the impedance at the maximum frequency for which the cable is designed.

For example, if you were using coaxial cable for video service, you would expect to see 75-ohm impedance exhibited at the maximum operating frequency of 900MHz. For cable, there's always a trade-off between frequency headroom and attenuation per cable length. Typically for most coax cable, the attenuation is less than 1.5 decibels per hundred feet at 10MHz. At 100MHz, the attenuation is up around 5 decibels per hundred feet; consequently, as you increase your cable run, your attenuation goes up. When installing coax, there's always a trade-off in signal strength versus cable length versus frequency bandwidth.

A 10Mbps Ethernet segment can be up to 500 meters or approximately 1,640 feet in length using thicknet cable. For thinnet cable, the length can be up to 185 meters or 607 feet. Attenuation and frequency-based signal distortion limit segment lengths in Ethernet systems, whereas network lengths are limited by timing constraints that will be seen as bit-rate errors. Of course, at 100MB per second the maximum length is again reduced.

▶▶ The network topology and distances that can be covered in a typical Ethernet network are discussed more fully in Chapter 14, "Ethernet: The Universal Standard."

The two most common types of connectors are the BNC and the TNC. These are both named after their designers. The BNC connector has been around since World War II. It is a bayonet type and can be installed as a crimp type, a three-piece type, or a screw-on connector.

BNC connectors are similar to those used by cable companies to connect coax cabling to your set-top box. There is a single wire in the middle of the connector that carries the signal. To attach this connector to a cable, a crimping tool is used. A small portion of the cable is peeled back and inserted into the rear of the connector. The crimping tool then applies pressure to hold the cable to the connector. A three-piece type looks like a T-shaped connector, so you can connect cables to each side of the connector and use the third to screw into the receptacle on your computer. This last type was crucial in allowing a connection to a computer using coax cabling, yet letting the signal flow through the connector if the third part of the connector was removed from the computer.

The TNC connector usually is configured as a screw-on type and has been specifically developed for ease of installation with video-type cable. It is not used much in computer networking.

These are the advantages of coaxial cables:

- Low susceptibility to EMI and RFI pickup
- High-frequency bandwidth
- Longer segment lengths than with twisted-pair cables
- Can be matched with fiber-optic and twisted-pair cables
- Lower signal distortion
- Less cross-talk between cables
- Better information security than with twisted-pair cable

These are the disadvantages of coaxial cable:

- More difficult to install than twisted-pair cable
- Heavier than twisted-pair or fiber-optic cables
- Usually must be daisy-chained or home-run to workstations
- Does not have the adaptability of twisted-pair cable
- Is more expensive and takes more time to install

Note

Coaxial cables are rarely used in LANs today. However, the development of cable modems has given a new life to these cables, when applied to networking. Just as your cable television uses coaxial cables, cable modems also use frequencies on these cables to transmit and receive data to and from the Internet.

Fiber-Optic Cables

Fiber-optic technology is significantly different from copper and uses light transmitted through hair-thin fibers. Fiber-optic cable offers higher bandwidth and lower signal losses. It also allows higher data rates over longer distances.

These are the advantages of using fiber-optic cables:

- **Information carrying capacity**—Fiber-optic bandwidth capacities are well in excess of what's required by today's network applications. The 62.5/125 Micrometer fiber recommended for building use has as its minimum bandwidth a capacity of over 160MHz per kilometer. The bandwidth at over 100 meters is well over 1.5Gbps. If the wavelength is different, the actual bandwidth can rise to 5Gbps. With the advent of Gigabit Ethernet, and 10Gigabit Ethernet, signaling techniques have greatly increased the bandwidth available on fiber-optic cables.
- **Low signal loss**—Optical fibers offer low signal loss. This low signal loss permits longer transmission distances. In comparison with copper, the longest recommended copper horizontal link is 100 meters; when using fiber it is 2,000 meters or more. Again, this distance can increase as newer signaling techniques are used. In addition, long-distance runs of fiber-optic cables, joined with repeaters and other similar devices, can increase the distance achieved by fiber-optic cables dramatically.

The biggest drawback in using copper cable is that signal loss *increases* with signal frequency. Attenuation, or signal loss, is higher at 100MHz than at 10MHz. Consequently, high data rates increase power loss and decrease practical transmission distances. Loss does not significantly change with signal frequency in fiber-optic systems. Attenuation does change with frequency of the light transmitted through the fiber, but the data rate does not. So if you have both a 10MHz and a 100MHz signal traveling through the fiber, they are attenuated alike.

Electromagnetic Immunity

The basic transmission medium in a fiber-optic cable consists of either plastic or glass material. Both of these are considered to be insulators or dielectrics, so these materials are immune to electromagnetic interference. The transmitted signals consist mainly of modulated light signals that are tunneled through the fiber medium and do not escape. No signals emanate outside the cable, so it does not cause cross-talk, which is the main limitation in twisted-pair cable. It can be run in electrically noisy environments such as high-density computer-room installations, factory floors, and other electrically dense environments without concern because the cables are immune to outside noise sources. Yet, as you will learn in other chapters, fiber-optic cables do suffer some signal interference within the cable itself. For example, single-mode fiber, in which only one signal is transmitted, can cover a longer distance than multi-mode fiber, which injects multiple modes of light into a larger fiber-optic cable. In such a case, multi-mode fiber can suffer from degradation of the signal as different wavelengths of light interfere with other wavelengths.

Size and Weight

Fiber-optic cable weighs considerably less than copper cable. It is typically 22% to 50% lighter than comparable four-pair Category 5 cable. Less weight makes fiber-optic cable easier to install depending on its durability, which has improved over time. Typical weights for 1,000 feet are as listed here:

- Two-fiber cable: 11 lbs.
- 12-fiber cable: 33 lbs.
- 4-pair Category 5 UTP: 25 lbs.
- 25-pair backbone UTP: 93 lbs.
- 10BASE-2 coax: 24 lbs.

Fiber-optic cable is smaller than copper cable. Typically, it's about 15% less in volume than Category 5 twisted-pair cable.

Safety

As stated before, the glass and plastic that compose the transmission medium of fiber-optic cable are dielectrics, or insulators, and thus do not conduct electricity. Fiber-optic cable therefore does not present a spark hazard and can be used in explosive environments. It also does not attract lightning. Fiber-optic cable has jacket ratings that are comparable to the copper cable jackets and has the same flammability ratings that meet code requirements in buildings.

Security

It wasn't until just recently that the capability to physically tap fiber-optic cables was developed. This requires extremely expensive equipment and a skilled operator. Typically, because fiber-optic cables do not emanate electromagnetic radiation, they are fairly secure against tapping. When compared to other methods of transmission, fiber-optic cable is the most secure medium for carrying sensitive data.

Fiber Construction and Operation

Fiber optics is a technology in which signals are converted from electrical into light signals. The signals then are sent or transmitted through a thin glass or plastic fiber and converted back to electrical signals. The fiber-optic cable consists of three concentric layers differing in optical parities. As shown in Figure 6.7, a fiber-optic cable consists of the following:

- **The core**—The inner, light-carrying portion of the cable.
- **The cladding**—The middle layer, which confines the light in the core.
- **Buffer**—The outer layer, which serves as a shock absorber to protect the core and the cladding from damage.
- **Outer jacket**—The covering, which protects the cable.

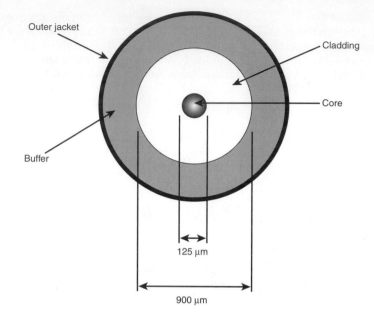

Figure 6.7 Components of a fiber-optic cable.

How Light Travels Through a Fiber-Optic Cable

Light transmission is not random. It is channeled into *modes*, which are possible paths for light rays to travel. There can be as few as one mode (single-mode fiber) or as many as several thousand modes in the design of the fiber (multi-mode fiber).

Although the number of modes is significant, it actually relates to determining the fiber's bandwidth. More modes means *lower* bandwidth. The cause of this is dispersion. As a pulse of light travels through the fiber, it spreads out over distance. Although there are several reasons for such dispersion, the two principal concerns are modal dispersion and material dispersion. Different path lengths followed by light rays as they bounce down the fiber cause modal dispersion. Material dispersion is caused by different light wavelengths traveling at different speeds. To limit material dispersion, you limit the wavelengths of light transmitted. In other words, don't use multi-mode fiber if you need to transmit a lot of data from one place to another. Use single-mode fiber for long distances. Use several cables of multi-mode fiber when you need to increase the bandwidth, without compromising on the actual bandwidth that can be achieved. Multi-mode fiber does allow for more than one data channel to travel through the same fiber-optic cable, but it should be limited as distance increases.

Fiber-optic cable can be modified in several ways to achieve different signal transmission characteristics. Modifications can be made to affect bandwidth and attenuation, and to facilitate coupling the light into and out of the fiber.

The stepped index multi-mode fiber has a large core with uniform optical properties. This fiber supports thousands of modes of operation and offers the highest dispersion and, hence, the lowest bandwidth (see Figure 6.8).

The graded index multi-mode fiber has different optical properties in the core. This type reduces dispersion and increases bandwidth. The graded index makes light following longer paths travel slightly faster than light following shorter paths. The net result is that the light does not spread out as much. Nearly all multi-mode fiber that is used in networking and data communications has a graded index score.

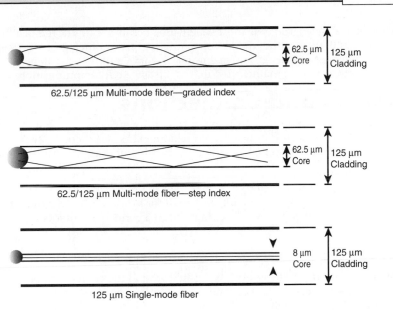

62.5 μm Core — 125 μm Cladding
62.5/125 μm Multi-mode fiber—graded index

62.5 μm Core — 125 μm Cladding
62.5/125 μm Multi-mode fiber—step index

8 μm Core — 125 μm Cladding
125 μm Single-mode fiber

Figure 6.8 Light can reflect off the internal cladding as it travels through the fiber-optic cable.

The single-mode fiber has the highest bandwidth and the lowest loss of performance. The core of single-mode fiber is smaller than that of multi-mode fiber. The bandwidth that this fiber exhibits is much greater than the capacities of today's electronics. This fiber can support speeds in excess of many gigabytes per second.

The most common fiber for networking is the 62/125-micron fiber (multi-mode). The two numbers designate the core diameter and the cladding diameter, respectively. In this case the core diameter is 62.5 microns and the cladding diameter is 125 microns. Other common sizes are 50/125-micron and 100/140-micron cable.

To summarize:

- Graded index multi-mode fiber is the preferred fiber for horizontal cable and most backbone applications.
- Single-mode fiber, by virtue of its immense bandwidth and long transmission capabilities, is the best choice for covering longer distances.

Attenuation in Fiber-Optic Cables

Similar to the degradation of an electrical signal in copper wires, attenuation in fiber-optic cables is a loss of power. During transmission, light pulses lose some of their energy, which shows up as a loss in signal strength. Attenuation is specified for fiber in decibels per kilometer. Attenuation ranges from under one decibel per kilometer for single-mode fibers and up to 2,000 decibels per kilometer for large-core plastic fibers.

Attenuation varies with the wavelength of light. There are three prime low-loss windows of wavelengths that are used today:

- 850 nanometers
- 1,300 nanometers
- 1,550 nanometers

The 850-nanometer wavelength is the most widely used because it was developed first, and optical devices such as LEDs (light-emitting diodes) operating at 850 nanometers are inexpensive and plentiful. The 1,300-nanometer wavelength offers low loss with a slight increase in cost for LEDs. The 1,550-nanometer wavelength is mainly used in long-distance telecommunications applications.

Terminations and Connections

For copper cabling, the main criterion is to provide an intimate, gas-tight joint between the connector contacts and the cable conductor. In reality, this seldom exists and there are two approaches to terminations in premise cabling: crimping the center conductor and using an insulation displacement contact.

When doing either type of connection, it is important to use the correct size and type of wire and also the correct tool. For example, if a contact is rated for a 24-gauge solid conductor, using a stranded or smaller wire, such as a 28-gauge wire, would result in a connection that could become loose or could fail.

Crimping

When a conductor is crimped, the contact is crushed around the center conductor. This cold-welds the contact to the center conductor. Many crimping tools are available today for almost any type of connection and cable type. You must use the proper tool for a successful crimp. Crimping tools are designed to provide the correct pressure by closing the dies a fixed amount. Using the wrong tool or die can result in either an under-crimp or an over-crimp. Under-crimping results in either a high resistance or a loose connection. Over-crimping can crush the wire or the connector so badly that it will be damaged and fail.

Insulation Displacement Contact

Insulation displacement contact uses a slotted beam. The wire is driven between the slotted beams. The beams are under spring tension and pierce the wire insulation and provide contact to the conductor inside. The contact can be either a flat form bar or a slotted barrel. These terminations are the most common in premise cabling applications.

Modular Jacks and Plugs

Modular jacks and plugs have been around a long time and are familiar to everyone as the connectors that plug into telephone handsets, bases, and wall outlets. The connectors and jacks that are used in premise wiring are different. Residential wiring and equipment use four-position plugs and jacks. The ones used for premise wiring are eight-position and terminate all four pairs of the cable. In typical nomenclature, the plug is the male end and the jack is the female end.

Modular jacks and plugs often are referred to as RJ connectors. The RJ comes from the term *registered jack*, and is specified in the USOC specification. USOC stands for Universal Service Order Code. This is a Bell Telephone specification that was developed for specific wiring connections, patterns, and applications within the telephone system.

An RJ-11 is a six-position connector and an RJ-45 is commonly referred to as an eight-position connector. Each of these basic jack styles can be wired for different RJ configurations. For example, the six-position jack can be wired as an RJ-11 C, which is a one-pair jack. It can also be wired as RJ-14 C, which is a two-pair, or an RJ-25 C, which is a three-point configuration. An eight-position jack can be wired for configurations such as RJ-61 C, four-pair, and RJ-48 C. The key eight-position jack can be wired for RG-45 RAS, RJ-46 S, and RJ-47 S. The fourth modular jack style is a modified version of the six-position jack, commonly called an MMJ. It was designed by Digital Equipment Corporation, along with the modified modular plug, to eliminate the possibility of connecting DEC data equipment to voice lines and vice versa. See Figure 6.9 for an example of these types of jacks.

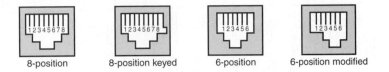

8-position **8-position keyed** **6-position** **6-position modified**

Figure 6.9   Several types of modular jacks can be used for network cabling.

Modular Plug Pair Configurations

It is important that the pairing of wires in the modular plug match the pairs in the modular jack as well as the horizontal and backbone wiring. If they do not, the data being transmitted might be paired with incompatible signals. Modular cords wired to the T 568A color scheme on both ends are compatible with the 568B systems and vice versa. See Figure 6.10 for a breakdown of jack types and how they are wired.

MODULAR JACK PLUG PAIR CONFIGURATIONS

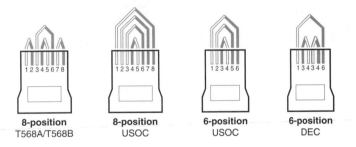

8-position **8-position** **6-position** **6-position**
T568A/T568B USOC USOC DEC

Figure 6.10   A color scheme is used to match up wires at each end of a cable when joining the cable to a modular jack.

Common Outlet Configurations

Several outlet configurations were shown in Figure 6.9; however, it should be noted that the T 568A and T 568B have been adopted by the 568B.1 and 11801 standards. They are nearly identical except that pairs two and one are reversed. T 568A is the preferred scheme because it is compatible with one- or two-pair USOC schemes. Either configuration can be used for an ISDN service or high-speed data applications. Transmission categories 3, 5, 5E, and 6 are applicable only to this type of pair of grouping.

As shown in Figure 6.11, USOC wiring is available for one-, two-, three-, or four-pair systems. Pair one occupies the center conductors, pair two occupies the next two contacts out, and so forth. One advantage to this scheme is that a six-position plug configured with one, two, or three pairs can be inserted into an eight-position jack and still maintain pair continuity. The disadvantage is the poor transmission performance associated with this type of pair sequence. None of these pair schemes is cabling-standard compliant.

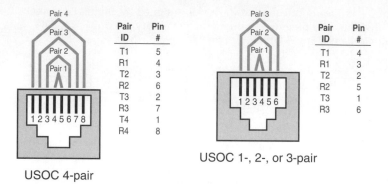

Figure 6.11 USOC wiring is available for one, two-, three-, or four-pair systems.

Various other standard schemes appear in Figure 6.12.

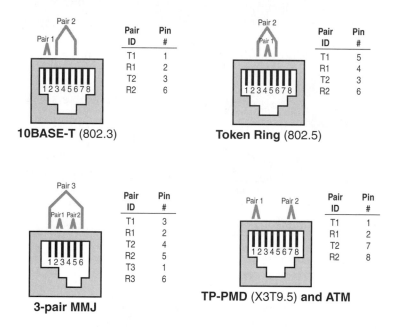

Figure 6.12 Different network cables require different wire connections to standard jacks.

There are a few guidelines you should follow when using the modular jacks and plugs:

- For each category application, you must use plugs and jacks for that category.
- You must be sure that you're using the correct plug or jack for your conductor type.
- You must follow termination procedures carefully. With the higher category cables in particular, proper installation procedures are essential to meet performance specifications.
- ANSI TIA/EIA-568B standards specify that all pairs be terminated at the outlet.
- The length of exposed wire (untwisted) shall not exceed 13mm for Category 5 or higher cables.
- The length of exposed wire (untwisted) for Category 3 shall be within 75mm from the point of termination.

Patch Panels

Patch panels provide a means of rearranging circuits so that adding, subtracting, and changing workstations is made easier. Patch panels are where the circuits are connected and reconnected. Several patch panels use a feed-through connector set into which a cable can be plugged on both sides. Some configurations can have the horizontal cables going to the work areas plugged into one side of the panel.

Typically, feed-through patch panels are not suited for high-speed operation. Category 5 and higher panels feature IDC contacts on the back and modular jacks on the front. Modular jacks are usually 110-style or barrel style. This configuration offers a better electrical performance to reduce NEXT. Fiber-optic patch panels often offer a transition between different connectors. Transition among S C, FDDI, and S T are common.

There are also other ways of connecting and terminating cabling. Two of these use IDC connections. The first is the Type 66 cross connect block. This type of block has 50 rows of IDC contacts to accommodate the 50 conductors of 25-pair cable. Each row contains four contacts. Type 66 blocks represent an older style designed originally for voice circuits. Some of the newer designs meet Category 5 requirements. You should check to be sure that the block is rated for the category you're installing, because older block designs have high cross-talk, which makes them unsuitable for high-data-rate designs.

A 110 cross connect consists of three parts: mounting legs, wiring block, and connecting block. The legs provide cable routing management and also hold the wire block. The wire block is composed of small plastic blocks that position the cable with index strips. Conductors are placed in the slot of the index strip. The strip usually has 50 slots to accommodate a 25-pair cable. It is marked every five pairs to help visually simplify the installation and reduce errors. This is also color-coded using the standard blue/orange/green/brown/slate color code. Wires used are punched into place with the 110-installation tool. This, however, does not terminate the conductors; it simply positions them. The device that does the termination is the connecting block. The IDC connecting block has contacts at both ends. One set of contacts terminates the contacts of the wiring block, and the other set on the outside is used for performing the cross connect.

This wiring system can accommodate as many as 300 pairs. Each horizontal strip can handle 25 pairs. A 100-pair cross connect requires four index strips. A 200-pair cable requires eight index strips, and so forth.

The system can be used as a prewired assembly for specific applications. One variation uses a 25-pair connector. In this situation, the block is prewired to the connector to allow a 25-pair cable from a hub or PBX to simply plug into the cross-connect.

There are pros and cons to using cross-connect blocks. They offer higher densities and require less space than patch panels, and also are less expensive. On the other hand, they are the least friendly for making moves, additions, and changes to the configuration. Skill is involved in removing and rearranging cables. When using patch panels, almost anyone can rearrange the system. In both situations security, ease of attachment, expense, and physical space are all considerations.

Terminating Fiber

What used to be a challenging task in the past, and is still an important task today, is terminating fiber-optic cable. There is a big difference between terminating electrical wiring and terminating a glass fiber that is only 62.5 microns in diameter. For one, electrical connections require a low resistance connection; the fiber requires a tight tolerance alignment. Misalignment in fiber connections will cause energy to be lost as light crosses a junction of the connector.

There are three functions of the termination process:

■ To prepare a smooth, flat, or rounded surface capable of accepting as much transmitted light as possible.

■ To provide a precise alignment of the clad fiber within the connector or splice to allow maximum coupling effectiveness.

■ To provide a secure physical attachment of the connector or spliced unit to the buffer cable.

Several varieties of common connectors are used in fiber optics. The following list does not include all connectors but does include those most commonly used for communication applications:

■ ST

■ SC

■ Biconic

■ SMA

■ Mini BNC

■ Data Link

■ Dual Fixed-Shroud (FDDI)

You can see examples of some of these in Figure 6.13.

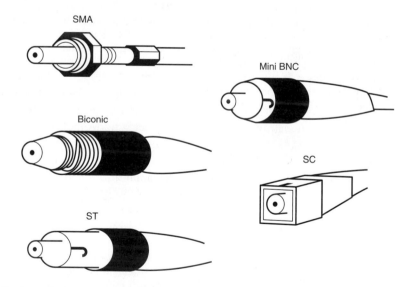

Figure 6.13   Several kinds of connectors are used with fiber-optic cables.

Various techniques are used for installing fiber-optic connectors, but five tasks are common to any termination process:

1. The outer jacket, strength members, buffer tube, and coating must be removed.

2. The fiber must be threaded through the connector housing.

3. Fiber must be secured inside the connector.

4. The connector must be securely attached to the outside of the fiber.

5. The end of the clad fiber extending through the tip of the connector must be cut in preparation to accept the light signal.

The correct installation of fiber-optic connectors requires training, specific equipment, and consumable materials. Thankfully, manufacturers are constantly reducing the amount of time and training required to install the fiber-optic equipment they produce.

Epoxy terminations have long been used to ensure that the fiber is properly held in the connection ferrule. It does have its drawbacks, however. It is an extra step in the process, it's potentially messy, and it requires curing the epoxy. Curing time can be shortened by utilizing an oven. This requires having another piece of equipment. There is also a possibility of spilling the epoxy on carpets and furniture in the finished building.

The epoxyless connectors require only a crimping tool and eliminate the need for epoxy. The simplest connectors use an internal insert that is forced snugly around the fiber during crimping. Inserts clamp and position the fiber while the crimp secures the cable strength members.

Another variation uses a short piece of fiber, which is factory-assembled and polished and inserted into the end of the connector ferrule. The inserted cable fiber butts up against this internal fiber, which is enclosed by an index-graded gel, and then the cable is crimped in place.

There also is a connector that uses a hot melt adhesive that is preloaded into the connector. This eliminates external mixing and loose components. Next, the connector is placed into an oven for a minute or so to soften the adhesive. The prepared fiber then is inserted in the assembly and is left to dry. Finally, the prepared connector is lightly polished.

The main benefit of epoxyless connectors is that they take less time and hence increase productivity. Remember that installing cables is perhaps the most expensive part of your network. Although servers and desktops computers are not cheap, the cost of labor and cabling to connect those computers to an enterprise network can be quite expensive.

Fiber-Optic Splicing

The preceding section discussed connecting fiber-optic cables to terminators. This section focuses on connecting segments of the fiber-optic cable itself. The splicing techniques are used only for extending the distance of the cable segment by adding another segment to it, or for repairing a cut or a damaged fiber cable. Now, splicing techniques and products have become user-friendly and often are considered a fast, low-loss alternative to traditional connector terminations.

There are two main types of fiber-optic splicing: fusion and mechanical.

Fusion Splicing

Fusion splicing is a process in which two sections of fiber are heated and, in effect, welded together. Fuse splices typically are good connections with attenuation losses as low as 0.1 db. Mechanical strength exhibited by this splice is often as strong as the original fiber.

The steps of a fusion splice include the following:

1. The ends of both fiber sections are prepared.

2. Both fibers are inserted into the splicing unit and precisely aligned.

3. Heat is applied at the interface of both fiber surfaces, and they are fused.

4. This place is tested for light loss.

Mechanical Splicing

Mechanical splicing is the process in which two sections of fiber are aligned and either glued or crimped in place within a permanent hood or shell. Mechanical splices are less labor-intensive than fuse splices. In some cases the splices can be installed in less than one minute per unit. Until recently, mechanical splices were relatively high-loss connections and were used for very limited applications. In the past several years, manufacturing processes have developed very low-loss mechanical splice units.

The low-loss connection attributes of today's mechanical splice units created a new technique for terminating fiber. After cleaning and polishing each installed fiber, installers have the option of purchasing fiber jumpers or tails with connectors on one end and quickly splicing these tails to the installed fiber.

Fiber-Optic Patch Panels

Fiber-optic panels are termination units, which are designed to provide a secure, organized chamber for housing connectors and splice units. The typical termination unit consists of the following components:

- **Enclosed chamber**—This can be a mountable wall or equipment rack.
- **Coupler panels**—These hold the connector couplers.
- **The connector couplers.**
- **Splice tray**—Organizes and secures splice modules.

Tip

It usually is a good practice to design termination units and jumper cables into fiber-optic installation because such units provide for growth and flexibility. The termination unit can use a patch panel in respect to making changes or additions to a system. It also can be a test point for troubleshooting the system.

General Considerations for Fiber-Optic Cabling

For the insulation of optical fiber connecting hardware, the following recommendation should apply. Connectors should be protected from physical damage and moisture. Optical fiber cable connecting hardware should incorporate high-density termination to conserve space, provide for ease of optical fiber cable, and patch cord management on installation. Optical fiber cable connecting hardware should be designed to provide flexibility for mounting on walls, racks, or other types and distribution frames, and standard and mounting hardware.

You should insist that a minimum of 1 meter of two-fiber cable be accessible for termination purposes. Testing is recommended to ensure correct polarity and acceptable link performance. Clause 2 of 568B.1 provides recommended optical fiber link performance testing criteria.

Connections

Telecommunication outlet and connector boxes should be securely mounted at planned locations. The telecommunications outlet box or connector box should provide cable management means to assure a minimum bend radius of 25mm and should have slack storage capability.

The fiber types should be identified:

- Multi-mode connectors or visible portions of it and adapters are to be identified with the color beige.

- Single-mode connectors or visible portions of it and adapters are to be identified with the color blue.

- The two positions in a duplex connector are referred to as position A and position B.

Small Form Factor Connectors (SFF)

Figure 6.14 shows a popular connector on the market today.

Figure 6.14   Small form factor (SFF) fiber-optic connectors are available today.

Some advantages of SFF connectors include compact size, modular compatibility with the eight-position modular copper interface, and adaptability to high-density eight-network electronics. Qualified SFF duplex and multi-fiber mode connector designs can be used in the main cross connect, intermediate cross connect, horizontal cross connect, and consolidation points and work areas. A TIA fiber-optic connected inter-mateability standard shall describe each SFF design. This design should satisfy the requirements specified in Annex A of the 568 B-B.3 standard.

Centralized optical fiber cabling provides users with flexibility in designing optical fiber cabling systems for centralized electronics typically in single tenant buildings.

Telecommunications Rooms

There have been some major changes from the EIA/TIA 568A to the EIA/TIA 568B and 569 standards transition. One of the major changes is that the telecommunications closet has evolved into the telecommunications room. These rooms are generally considered to be floor-serving facilities for horizontal cable distribution, and they also can be used for intermediate and main cross connects.

The telecommunications room is now defined for design and equipment according to ANSI/TIA/EIA 569A. Some of the specifications include specifications for wire management, relieving stress from tight bends, cable ties, staples, and so on. Horizontal cable terminations cannot be used to administer cabling system changes. Jumpers, patch cords, or equipment cords are required for reconfiguring cabling connections. There's also a further restriction that application-specific electrical components cannot be installed as part of the horizontal cabling.

Open Office Cabling

Additional specifications for horizontal cabling in areas with movable furniture and partitions have been included in TIA/EIA 568B.1. Horizontal cabling methodologies are specified for open office environments by a means of multiuser telecommunications outlet assemblies (MUTO). It is preferable to use MUTOs only when the entire length of the work area cord is accessible to facilitate tracing and to prevent erroneous disconnection. Up to 22 meters or 71 feet of work area cable are allowed.

Consolidation Points

Consolidation points or transition point connectors are interfaces between the patch panels and MUTOs.

General Horizontal Cabling Subsystem Specifications

Note that the ISO/IEC 11801 allows 120 and unshielded twisted-pair horizontal cabling. Grounding must conform to applicable building codes as well as ANSI/EIA/TIA 607. You must have a minimum of two telecommunications outlets in the work area. The first outlet must have a 100-ohm twisted-pair category 5E, and the next outlet must also have one outlet with twisted-pair Category 5E. Two-fiber multi-mode optical fiber must also be installed.

Additional outlets can be provided. These outlets are in addition to and cannot be replaced by the minimum requirements of the standard. Bridged taps and splices are not allowed for copper-based horizontal cabling. Additional specific components cannot be installed as part of the horizontal cabling. When needed, they must be placed external to the telecommunications outlet or horizontal cross connects.

Finally, the proximity of horizontal cabling to sources of electromagnetic interference should be taken into account.

Documenting and the Administration of the Installation

When in place, the wiring plant is not a static, immobile structure. It is a dynamic and evolving part of your network. If the plant is not maintained with an up-to-date documented record, then any additions, changes, moves, and upgrading are out of the question.

The TIA/EIA-606 standard provides a guide to documenting a cabling system to make its administration efficient and effective. This provides the administrator with several benefits:

- Allows better asset management
- Increases network reliability and up time
- Speeds and simplifies troubleshooting
- Facilitates movement, additions, and changes
- Allows for disaster recovery plans
- Allows for capacity planning, upgrading, and acceptance of new emerging applications
- Allows the generation of management reports

Documentation should include equipment and component labels, electronic or real records, drawings, work orders, and reports. Realistically, every piece of the physical plant should be labeled. This includes cables, termination hardware, cross connects, patch panels, closets, and anything else that will assist you in developing a meaningful overall view of your system.

Good labeling requires a unique coding scheme that makes sense to you. The label can include a location scheme, a component scheme, or a combination of both. You must realize that a label cannot have all the required information for a specific component, so it should contain enough information to uniquely define the component and point to a specific record. These pointers, sometimes referred to as linkages, will point to other records.

Records

The TIA/EIA 606 standard divides a record into four types of information:

- **Required information**—The essential information about the component.
- **Required linkages**—Links to other records.

- **Optional information**—Additional information that makes the record understandable and comprehensive.

- **Optional linkages**—Links to additional records that might be helpful to include. For example, if you are connecting a new PC in a new work area, you might want to include a linkage from the PC record to the record for the new workstation.

Drawings

Drawings are an essential part of your physical plant. They are necessary to locate components within a building. Drawings, especially "as built" drawings, will show the locations of conduits, pull boxes, and other components hidden from view behind walls and ceilings and under floors. These enable you, your installers, and network administrators to define and control space requirements, estimate cable densities, and keep track of equipment. In other words, you need to document your network. In Chapter 3, "Network Design Strategies," you can learn about several applications and techniques that can be used to assist you in keeping track of your cable installations, as well as other components in your network.

Work Orders

Work orders should record all equipment and cabling moves, adds, and changes. This should form a history of the cabling system's life or evolution. The records of the pertinent equipment involved should be updated every time the work order is performed.

Reports

A *report* is a group of records organized in a specific manner. This can be in the form of a database that can be selected to show a selected part of a record. For example, a report might show the number of hard drives on a specific server, or it can show the cables running to the device. You can include the hard drive identifiers or, in the case of the cables, the cable numbers.

Several types of cable management software are available that can be used to maintain records and generate reports. There are also specific programs aimed at managing a cabling system. These programs are compatible with structured cabling systems and conform to the TIA/EIA standards.

Network Interface Cards

7

SOME OF THE MAIN TOPICS IN THIS CHAPTER ARE

CHAPTER 7

The *network interface card* (*NIC*) is the piece of hardware that links a computer or workstation to the network media. The standard Ethernet NIC resides at the Physical level of the OSI Seven-Layer Reference Model and is the device responsible for translating data into zeros and ones for transmission on the network media for the network using electricity or light. To send data to and from other computers, the NIC's driver software interfaces with the NIC's hardware elements and with the protocol stack that runs on the computer.

Although this chapter concentrates mainly on network adapters that are used on Ethernet networks, be aware that there are other cards that function differently. For example, cards made for ARCnet do more than provide the functions of the Physical layer of the OSI model. They also provide the data link functionality. Token-Ring cards also work differently than standard Ethernet cards. Host Bus Adapters (HBAs) used by Storage Area Networks also incorporate more functionality on the card, thus relieving the server of having to expend CPU cycles managing some of the protocol details. However, the general troubleshooting methods discussed in this chapter can usually be applied to all these card types.

Most cards manufactured today support Plug and Play (PnP), but not all operating systems do—if only life were so simple. So, although you might find that installing a new workstation or upgrading an old one with a new network adapter card is an easy task, this might not always be the case if you are working on older equipment. In this chapter, we'll look at the differences between card types and the items that are typically configurable for NICs. After that, we'll list some of the methods you can use to troubleshoot network problems when you suspect that the NIC might be the problem.

Choosing a Hardware Bus Type

When you install a card in a workstation or server, whether it is a network adapter card or a SCSI disk adapter card, you insert the card into a slot that connects the card to a *bus*. A bus is nothing more than a communications channel that devices can use to exchange information with the computer's CPU and memory. Different kinds of cards can be inserted into slots to connect them to the bus in the computer. Before you make a decision on what kind of network card to purchase, you need to know what kinds of bus slots are available on the computer. In addition, you may have more than one type of bus in your computer. For example, all major computer manufacturers today use the Peripheral Component Interconnect (PCI) bus (or a newer PCI standard, such as Mini-PCI in notebooks and small form-factor desktops). However, the universal serial bus (USB) is now pretty much a standard on desktop computers, and there are network adapters you can use with USB. The FireWire (IEEE 1394) bus is another competitor that offers a higher bandwidth than USB. PCI cards for both FireWire and USB can be purchased inexpensively if your computer does not come with them. As you read this chapter, keep in mind (1) the number of available slots you can use in an ISA/EISA bus or PCI bus, and (2) the number of devices you will use the USB or FireWire bus for. If your workstations are all newer models, you are most likely to find that only PCI slots are available. The need for older EISA slots has fallen dramatically since the PCI bus has become the norm for computers today.

Note

In addition to a computer's bus, you will find on the market today network adapters that do not need a bus at all. For example, there are USB-compatible network adapters. Just plug them in and configure the IP information, and you're on the network. Windows systems that support USB serial ports will automatically recognize and configure these types of devices.

Another network adapter that has just recently become an inexpensive solution for networking computers is the wireless network adapter, of which there are several types. The portability that wireless networking enables is one of its best features. There are some considerations, such as security, that are being addressed with newer standards. Because wireless networks are just now coming into the mainstream marketplace, wireless adapters are discussed in several chapters in Part V, "Wireless Networking Protocols."

In this discussion we'll start with the older technologies (some of which are still widely used) and then go on to discuss newer network adapter cards.

Note

Another matter to think about when installing a network adapter card is the underlying network. Most large networks use Ethernet for the wire protocol, and thus Ethernet cards are discussed in this chapter more than others. Yet, to accommodate home users, as well as small office/home office (SOHO) users, there are several other network technologies, such as wireless adapters and HomePNA (creating a network using your home's phone lines). Yet another thing to consider is that there are also two major serial port technologies that allow you to connect to peripheral devices, such as USB and FireWire. Both of these support network adapter cards as well as disk drives and other devices. This section covers the basic bus types used in computers that are in wide usage today, such as the desktop and laptop computers. Later in this chapter you will learn more about the different network cards, and how they fit into the picture.

ISA

The ISA (Industry Standard Architecture) bus was created in the 1980s and was the bus used by the first IBM personal computer architecture. Manufacturers adopted the term ISA as the IBM computer became a standard and vendors began to create many kinds of cards to expand the capabilities of the PC.

The first version of this bus provided for an 8-bit data channel. The IBM AT computer architecture used an enhanced version of the original ISA bus, allowing for data transfers at a rate of 8MHz, using a 16-bit data channel. This architecture was later expanded on, and the Extended ISA (EISA) bus was created. Although the EISA bus still operates at only 8MHz, it allows for a 32-bit path, allowing more data to be channeled through the bus. When you open a computer and look at the available slots, the EISA slots are usually the longer ones. The shorter ones are usually PCI (Peripheral Component Interconnect) slots. Figure 7.1 shows a picture of both EISA and PCI network adapter cards. The shorter footprint of the PCI card makes it easier to create PCs that have a much smaller design than in the past.

Note

As mentioned earlier in this chapter, most newer PCs—particularly those built since 2000—are unlikely to include ISA slots on the motherboard.

Note

Another slot you might find in your computer is the Accelerated Graphics Port (AGP). You can usually distinguish this slot from other types of slots by its pin-out—only an AGP card fits into the slot—and its color, which is usually a beige or light reddish-brown. AGP slots generally are offset slightly from the PCI and ISA slots (if your motherboard includes them).

PCI

The PCI bus specifications have many advantages over previous standards, including dramatically faster data transfer rates and 32-or 64-bit-wide data paths. Devices on the PCI bus can also use a feature called *bus mastering*, whereby a card can take control of the bus and directly transfer large amounts of data to system memory without using the CPU. Some PCs today contain a mix of both PCI and EISA slots. However, most PC vendors are ending support for older ISA and EISA products, a trend that will increase over the next few years. It is more often the case now that you will find only PCI slots in newer computers. The ISA/EISA buses have become legacy hardware.

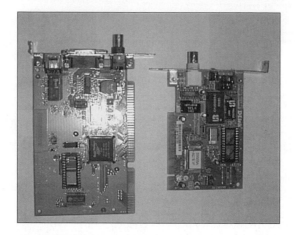

Figure 7.1   The network interface card on the left has an EISA interface, whereas the one on the right is designed for use in a PCI slot.

Besides its performance advantage over the EISA bus, the PCI bus also allows for auto-configuration. A PCI card contains internal registers that hold information used for configuration when the system is booted. The kind of information that is stored in these registers includes a 3-byte class code, which indicates the card's base class. For network cards, the value found in this register is 02h. Other possible classes include mass storage controllers (value = 01h), display controllers (value = 03h), the memory controller (value = 05h), and so on. There's even a class represented by the value 00h, which is used for cards that were created before the definitions of class codes were finished, and a class using the value FFh, which indicates that the device doesn't belong to any of the defined classes.

Other information contained in the PCI card's registers tells the system-specific configuration information about the PCI card, such as IRQ (Interrupt Request, or in older documentation, Interrupt Request Line) and memory information.

Note

An IRQ is a hardware component of the computer that devices can use to send an *interrupt* signal to the CPU in an attempt to get the attention of the processor. For example, when a network adapter needs to transfer data from its buffer into the computer's memory, it will use the IRQ assigned to it to notify the CPU that a request is pending. Using the IRQ line does not guarantee that the device will get an immediate response from the CPU, however. The CPU might be executing instructions that cannot be interrupted. This kind of interrupt, also referred to as a *maskable interrupt*, is the most used type of interrupt. Another type of interrupt is called a *non-maskable interrupt*, which is used to signal the CPU that a more serious condition exists and needs to be addressed. For example, a memory error or a critical hardware error is likely to generate a non-maskable interrupt. Although the CPU can ignore a non-maskable interrupt by setting a flag, this is rarely the case.

Usually the PCI card is configured to use an available IRQ when the system detects it. If an unused IRQ isn't found, the card can, under some circumstances, share an IRQ with another card. In that case, the system interrogates each card that shares the IRQ when the CPU receives the interrupt request. The card making the request can then communicate with the CPU to satisfy the request. Sharing IRQs should usually be done among similar devices.

Note

In addition to the bus types discussed in this chapter, you might occasionally hear about the MCA bus. MCA stands for Micro Channel Architecture. This bus was a proprietary standard that IBM created in 1987. Although MCA was, in most respects, superior to the other bus specifications *at that time*, it is not compatible with other buses. Because incorporating MCA technology required licensing it from IBM, card manufacturers never widely adopted MCA. Instead, the EISA specification was developed partly in response to the proprietary nature of MCA. And now the EISA bus has become obsolete.

PCMCIA

Although PCI slots are used in most desktop and server computers for holding adapter cards, smaller computers, such as laptops, are another matter altogether. Because of their size, it's not possible to include a similar setup of expansion slots that conform to conventional PCI specifications. PCI cards just won't fit into the smaller form factor provided by laptop computers.

PCMCIA cards are credit-card–size cards that can be used in laptops and other small computers. The acronym does *not* stand for "People Can't Memorize Computer Industry Acronyms," which is a popular phrase used to remember the acronym. Instead, PCMCIA is the Personal Computer Memory Card International Association, which is a nonprofit organization responsible for promoting standards for making cards for smaller computers, such as laptops. Although the first cards that were produced according to specifications by this organization were memory cards, you can now find all sorts of add-in cards for laptop computers, including network adapter cards. The term *PCMCIA* has been used in the past to describe these cards, but current products now use the name *PC Card*. Several varieties of cards currently are on the market, but most use a standard 68-pin connector. If you have to connect a laptop to the local LAN, you'll need to evaluate this card to find one that works with your operating system. In Figure 7.2, you can see an example of an Intel PC Card network adapter.

The PCI bus also has several variants, such as the Mini PCI, CompactPCI, Low-Profile PCI, Concurrent PCI, and PCI-X specifications, each of which is used to create a PCI-compliant bus in different computer configurations. For example, the Mini PCI bus is generally used in laptop or smaller computing devices. This PCI bus is implemented as a card that you can install in one of these smaller computer devices to enable connections to other peripheral devices, such as modems and (the topic of this chapter) network adapter cards.

Note

You can use the URL **www.pcmcia.org** to find more information about PCMCIA cards. This trade organization has been around for many years and has been responsible for many developments in this small form factor card for use in laptop computers and, more recently, consumer devices such as digital cameras and set-top boxes for cable television. In addition, this organization also defined the standards for the PC-Card specifications, which have supplanted the older PCMCIA cards for the most part.

In addition, the PCMCIA organization has another Web site that provides a large directory of PC Card devices, as well as resources for developing PC Cards. Use the URL **www.pc-card.com** to access this site.

Figure 7.2 PC Cards are much smaller than standard network adapter cards.

CardBus

In 1996, the PCMCIA organization developed the CardBus for use in small computing devices, such as laptop computers. This standard provides a 32-bit data path, which can enable PC Card devices to operate four to six times faster than earlier 16-bit cards. In addition, CardBus devices consume less power than older cards. In most cases a computer that uses CardBus is backward-compatible with older PC Card devices.

So, which kind of card should you choose for your networking needs? That can depend on many factors. For example, you might be limited on the kind of card by how many slots are available in the computers, and of what type. If you have a workstation that already has filled all its PCI slots, you might be forced to use an EISA card if you can't sacrifice one of the existing PCI cards to free a slot. However, if your hardware supports them, the obvious choice is to purchase newer PCI-based cards.

Note

If you want to get a greater understanding of how the types of buses discussed in this chapter work, I recommend that you check out *Upgrading and Repairing PCs*, by Scott Mueller, which also is published by Que. Visit www.upgradingandrepairingpcs.com to learn more about this industry classic.

InfiniBand Still Has Many Opportunities

Recently many of the larger hardware vendors, such as Intel, have stopped developing low-level chips for InfiniBand. This doesn't mean that InifiniBand is not going to be a major standard in the future. Indeed, InfiniBand is the next logical solution for a very complicated problem: the increasing need to relieve a CPU from I/O devices. Today the economics for large corporations make it a more practical venture to let smaller chip vendors develop silicon for this type of architecture, which can later be incorporated into InfiniBand products by the higher-level manufacturers who can license the technologies from smaller companies.

Note

Another new technology that will be in the marketplace soon just might take over the role of network adapter cards on large servers. The technology? InfiniBand. InfiniBand was developed to solve many problems associated with I/O between the computer's CPU/memory and external devices. By using fiber optics and a switched network, InfiniBand greatly extends the connectivity between the CPU, memory, and other components of a high-end system. You can learn more about InfiniBand at the Web site for the InfiniBand Trade Association: **www.infinibandta.org**. InfiniBand essentially removes the SCSI interface from a server and substitutes a switched network of devices, much like those used in a Storage Area Network (see Chapter 11, "Network Attached Storage and Storage Area Networks").

Different Cards, Different Speeds

Another factor to consider when making a network card purchase is the speed of your network. Standard 10BASE-T networks operate at 10Mbps. If you are upgrading, it is more likely that you'll be using or upgrading to at least a 100Mbps network. If so, you'll probably be upgrading the backbone cabling that connects your switches/routers also to a higher bandwidth, such as Gigabit Ethernet.

If you are creating a new network, simply choose 100Mbps cards. If you are upgrading an existing network, and if the cabling infrastructure supports 100Mbps, you can slowly migrate users to 100Mbps by purchasing cards that operate at both speeds. Most 10/100Mbps cards also support *autosensing*, which means that they can detect the speed of the network connection and adjust accordingly. When you swap out hubs or switches to upgrade to a faster network, you won't have to worry about reconfiguring or buying new adapter cards for end-user workstations. Therefore, if you are currently operating in a 10Mbps environment but know that you will have to upgrade to 100Mbps in the next year or two, spend the extra few dollars to buy cards that operate at both speeds. And those old machines still using 10Mbps should be destined for the recycling bin shortly anyway.

▶▶   Besides making purchasing choices for network adapter cards, plan ahead for other equipment you might need to buy, such as a new hub (or more likely a switch) to accommodate the speed of the network adapters that are used on your network. *If necessary*, get one that supports both speeds and autosensing (to detect the speed of the card/switch), and preferably one that works in dual 10/100 mode. For more information about hubs and switches, and these features, see the chapter "Bridges, Repeaters, and Hubs," on the **upgradingandrepairingpcs.com** Web site. Also check out Chapter 8, "Network Switches."

Network Cable Connectors and Terminators

In Chapter 6, "Wiring the Network—Cables, Connectors, Concentrators, and Other Network Components," the various kinds of network cables and connectors that can be used to create a LAN were examined. Although most older 10BASE-2 networks have already been upgraded to 10BASE-T (or faster) networks, there are still a few around that use thinnet coaxial cable with BNC connectors and terminators. If you are operating a LAN of this kind, be sure that any new network card purchases are "combo cards," as shown in Figure 7.3. These cards let you either connect a BNC T-connector to the card or use an RJ-45 jack for the newer 10BASE-T networks. In all probability, you will have a difficult time finding network cards that support only BNC connectors anymore. Purchasing combo cards means that you can still use the adapter when you upgrade to 10BASE-T. However, I suspect that this will be a rare situation. If you are still operating with coaxial cables in your Ethernet network, you need to immediately turn to the upgrading section of this book and start your planning there.

Figure 7.3   A combo card contains both a BNC and an RJ-45 receptacle and can be used on both types of networks.

The Wired for Management (WfM) Initiative and Wake on LAN (WOL) Technology

So far, this chapter has discussed some of the more typical factors to consider when choosing a network card for an upgrade or for retaining existing network cards for use in new computer acquisitions. However, depending on the size of your network, there is another factor to consider: the total cost of managing the computers on your network. The Wired for Management (WfM) initiative is a framework that most of the industry's major players, from IBM to Compaq and Dell, are adopting. You'll find most of the information about WfM at Intel's developer's Web site (www.intel.com/labs/manage/wfm/index.htm), including one particular key component: Wake on LAN (WOL) technology for network adapter cards.

To understand how WOL fits into this scheme, it's best to start with a simple understanding of the key components of WfM:

- Universal Network Boot
- Asset Management
- Power Management
- Remote Wake-Up (Wake on LAN and Wake on Ring)

Universal Network Boot

The Universal Network Boot component is based on technology that allows a computer to boot over a network and download an operating system, or other software, from a management server. The Preboot Execution Environment (PXE) technology is the key part of this component. PXE allows a computer to be remotely booted after the remote wakeup function is invoked. By using industry standard techniques, such as DHCP, TFTP, and TCP/IP, adopting PXE technology does not require extensive changes to incorporate it into new PCs. It also allows for older systems, which do not understand the extended uses of these standard protocols, to continue to function because they can simply ignore the extensions.

▶▶   For more information about the specifics of how PXE uses DHCP, TFTP, and TCP/IP and other protocols, see Chapter 29, "BOOTP and Dynamic Host Configuration Protocol (DHCP)."

Asset Management

The Asset Management component includes a database that keeps an inventory of software and hardware for systems on the network, and allows polling computers to get this information.

This means that a computer which hosts a database of the software and hardware components for other computers in the network can periodically query other computers on the network to ensure that those computers do indeed have the hardware/software components installed that the Asset Management software has stored in its database. This technology can detect such things as hardware additions (or software downloads performed by users).

From a security standpoint this is *very* important. For example, one of the major security problems in a large network is a user installing a modem (and thus bypassing all your network security mechanisms, such as a firewall). For software downloads, this component can also be an important security measure to ensure that "shareware" and other products are not downloaded to desktop computers. Any software that will be placed on desktop computers should undergo testing by your network administrative personnel before it is deployed on computers in the network.

Power Management

The Power Management component is included to provide support for the Advanced Configuration and Power Management Interface (ACPI) and for Advanced Power Management (APM), which helps reduce costs by reducing power consumption that PCs and assorted peripherals use. ACPI is a newer technology that is expected to replace APM. By placing a computer and its peripherals into a lower power state after a predefined time has passed with no user interaction, the computer's electricity use is greatly reduced. This results in money saved and, in some cases, less stress on the computer's components.

Remote Wake-Up

The Remote Wake-Up component is the component that is most relevant to this chapter. The WfM initiative supports two kinds of remote wake-ups for computers: by the LAN to which the system is connected, or through a telephone line connected to a modem (Wake on Ring). This second component is considered optional, but the capability to power up a computer by sending a specialized datagram to the computer is a key component that makes other components possible.

For example, taking inventory of existing software, or installing new software on a user's computer, usually must be done during normal working hours. This can result in lost productivity because the user is not able to use his workstation. Performing this same function during off-hours, such as in the middle of the night, removes this expensive obstacle. One alternative is to tell users to leave their computers up and running so that you can use an automated software package to perform the inventory or software installation functions. Yet there will always be someone who forgets. And there's the fact that while that computer is up and running, waiting to be inventoried or upgraded, electricity is being consumed. When you're talking about hundreds of computers, that also can be an important cost factor.

To wake up a computer from a low-power state or to boot the system if it has been powered off, the network adapter must be capable of sensing a "magic packet" that is directed to it, or to use the newer "packet filtering" method.

The WOL Network Adapter Card

The network adapter that is used in a WOL situation can be a PCI card that you install in a computer just like any other network card. There is also a new LAN on Motherboard (LOM) that places the network card function directly on the motherboard, eliminating the need for a separate card that uses up an expansion slot. The most common method at this time is to use a network card that you have to install, however.

Because the adapter card must be capable of listening to the network, awaiting a signal telling it that it's time to wake up the computer, the card must have a power source. In Figure 7.4 you can see an example of this kind of card. The small cable is used to connect the adapter card to the motherboard to supply a power source so that the card is always listening for wake-up packets.

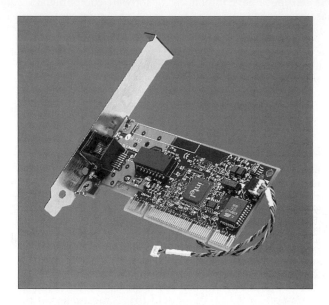

Figure 7.4 A small cable is used on some WOL cards to connect the card to the motherboard so that power can be supplied to the card.

You don't have to do anything for motherboard solutions. The network adapter circuitry on the motherboard is already connected to the computer's power source. However, most PCI cards available today require that you make a connection between the PCI card and the motherboard, using a small power cable supplied with the card just for this purpose. Read the documentation if you decide to use WOL cards on your network. Note that not only must the LAN card be WOL compliant, but the motherboard also must support this connection. Check the documentation!

The Alarm Clock: Magic Packets and Packet Filtering

There are two recommendations for signaling the LAN card that it's time to wake up the computer:

- **Magic Packets**—The first method uses a "magic packet," which is a special packet designed just for this purpose. When a specialized circuit in the network adapter card sees this packet on the network, it initiates the system wake-up.

- **Packet Filtering**—In the second method, which is the preferred method in version 2.0 of the WfM specifications, the card recognizes ordinary network packets addressed to it, instead of a specialized magic packet. This second method is referred to in the specifications as *packet filtering* and is not to be confused with the same term when applied to firewall technology.

Whichever method is used, either the computer can be booted when the LAN card receives a wake-up call, or it can simply resume normal operations if the computer has been put into a suspended low-power state without performing a complete shutdown. The preferred method is that the computer be placed in a suspended low-power state, but this is not an absolute requirement.

The "magic packet" method uses a special datagram that contains a source and destination address. The destination address can be a particular workstation's address, or it can be a broadcast address used to wake up multiple systems. The data portion of the packet contains synchronization bytes and the workstation's address repeated 16 times. Optional fields are also present in this datagram, but the point is that, by using this special kind of packet, the WOL network adapter to which it is addressed can begin the wake-up sequence of events. This allows it to either boot the computer or revive it from its low-power suspended state.

Should You Use WOL-Compliant Network Cards?

Whether this new technology is suitable for your LAN depends on how you manage your network. If you have frequent software updates or must be able to remotely manage workstations without having a technician sitting at the keyboard entering commands, you should consider using WOL and other WfM technologies. To do so you'll also have to use management software capable of formulating and sending out WOL packets, if the network adapter requires it. Using the newer specifications, you might want to purchase cards that can wake the dead, so to speak, by detecting any network traffic directed to them.

If you don't foresee a need for these capabilities in the near future, save the cash and just purchase ordinary, cheaper network adapter cards. If you manage a small network and need to make only infrequent changes, or if all of your computer systems are located in close proximity to each other, you might find it cheaper to do things the old-fashioned way, by visiting each computer when an upgrade is needed or a problem arises.

As vendors more widely adopt WOL and WfM, the prices for all components, network cards, and management software will most likely drop, making an upgrade in a few years a more cost-effective solution. Because most desktop computers are practically out of date within three to five years, don't feel you need to adopt new technology just because it's available. Evaluate your needs, balance them with the expenses involved, and make a decision based on those factors.

By the time you read this, WfM and WOL may already be a standard item on even the most inexpensive 10/100Mbps network cards.

Multi-Homed Systems

Some computers need more than one network card. For example, if you have two subnets in your LAN that both need to connect to the same server, the server computer needs more than one network adapter. Although you can use a router to connect different subnets, it is probably cheaper to simply multi-home a server for a small network than to bother with the administrative overhead of configuring and maintaining a router.

In this case, the server can function both as a file or print server to both subnets and as a router. It is also possible, depending on the type of computer, to attach more than one network card to the same subnet. In any case, each network card must be set up with its own network address and host name. For example, a high-performance server might be used on an intranet to provide a WWW service and an FTP service to clients. If the server is capable of processing the requests at the required rate but the network adapter card is a limiting factor, you can install multiple cards and assign an address and host name for each service.

One popular reason for multi-homing a server today is to provide a hardware platform that can function as a *proxy server* for a network firewall. In this configuration, the proxy server application intercepts all traffic that passes between the two subnets to which it is connected, and acts as a go-between to enhance security on the network. The proxy server accepts service requests from one adapter and interacts with the service provider through the other adapter. The proxy server examines responses from the service and, if allowed, returns them to the requesting computer using the first network adapter.

▶▶ For more information about proxy servers, see Chapter 49, "Firewalls."

Load Balancing and Dual-Redundant Network Controllers

For important servers, a single network card that is used to interface with the network is a single point of failure. If the card goes bad, the costs involved can be quite high if a large number of users access the server. For many years computer manufacturers have come up with solutions to minimize downtime for important systems. The two most basic techniques that come to mind are *clustering* and *redundancy*. Clustering technology allows two or more computers to operate in a manner such that one or more computers in the cluster can service user requests at the same time, as in HP's OpenVMS clusters. Another clustering technique, which is used in Windows 2000/2003 clusters, uses a fail-over technique. One or more computers in the cluster are on standby and ready to take over if another member of the cluster fails.

This second technique is also an example of redundancy. For many years it has been possible to buy disk controllers that operate in a redundant fashion. Redundant node clusters, disk controllers, multiple CPUs, and other mechanisms have made the task of providing maximum uptime for computers an easy task. However, the network card remains a single point of failure.

That problem has been remedied. You can now purchase network adapter cards that work in a dual-redundant manner. That is, one card services network requests while the other waits in standby mode, checking periodically to be sure the other adapter is functioning properly. There are even versions of dual-redundant network adapters that both operate at the same time, providing a load-balancing capability as well as a fail-over mechanism.

For example, one manufacturer produces NICs that use a technique in which each NIC has its own MAC address, yet all cards that the administrator places in a "group" share the same IP address. Each group can contain from two to eight network cards, which should provide enough redundancy for almost any server. The added benefit of load-balancing to maximize network traffic throughput makes this an ideal solution for a high-end enterprise server that is used by a large client base.

Different methods can be used when load-balancing is implemented with network adapter cards. For example, one scheme is to use a round-robin technique for each packet sent out on the network. Another is to use the client's MAC address and assign traffic for those packets to a specific controller. This technique might not be a good solution if most of the traffic is coming from a router because all the packets from the router share the router's MAC address.

Although dual network adapters are not a factor in the desktop environment, they can provide security at that vital link in the network between an important enterprise server and the network. The cost of redundant network adapters, when compared to the expensive server hardware, makes this a cheap solution to a big problem. Because this technology has been around for only a few years, I suggest you check out several vendors, inquiring about the methods used for load-balancing and redundancy. Take into consideration also the management software, if any, that you will need to use to configure or troubleshoot the adapters.

Software Drivers

When networks were composed of mainly proprietary solutions for a particular vendor's systems, the vendor could write a simple software driver that could handle all the functions for the protocols that the vendor chose to implement. In networks today, it is usually necessary to use more than one type of protocol on a network, so now software drivers must be capable of handling more than one protocol.

In the case of servers or routers, another factor to be considered is a system that has multiple network cards installed. The driver software must be capable of distinguishing the different NICs, as well as the protocols supported on each.

The two main types of NIC software drivers that you can find today are ODI and NDIS. Predating both of these, however, is a driver called a Packet Driver, which FTP Software developed in 1986. Because different operating systems or networking software might work only with a specific kind of driver, you must be aware of the kinds of drivers that a network card can be used with if you are planning to upgrade NICs or, perhaps, undergo a more complex change, such as migrating to a new operating system. For example, if you are thinking of migrating to a Novell network, you should concentrate on devices that support ODI drivers. In a Microsoft networking environment, you would need to look for devices that support NDIS.

Packet Drivers

In the early days of PC networking, one of the main problems with network cards and protocol stacks was that they were too closely interrelated; that is, purchasing a network protocol software package meant you had to be sure that it supported the network card you were using. The operating system did not provide the code to interface with the card, but rather the specific protocol package. This, of course, meant that developers of protocol stacks had to spend lots of time developing code to support the many types of network cards that were on the market.

FTP Software developed the Packet Driver to create an interface that protocols could use to access functions the network card provides. Protocol stacks that use the Packet Driver can exist on the computer and use the network card at the same time. Previously, network drivers were tightly bound to the network card at boot time, and you had to make changes to configuration files and reboot the computer each time you wanted to use a different network protocol.

The Open Data-Link Interface (ODI)

Novell and Apple Computer developed ODI in 1989 with a goal of providing a seamless interface at the Network, Transport, and Data Link levels, as shown in the OSI reference model. The ODI specification can be divided into three components:

- **Multi-Link Interface Driver (MLID)**—This component controls communication between the network card and the link support layer. It consists of a section of code written by Novell called the Media Support Module (MSM) and the Hardware-Specific Module (HSM), written by the card vendor. The MSM provides the functions that implement standard network functions for the media types that are supported by ODI. The vendor writes the HSM code to handle the details of its particular card; the HSM code communicates with the MSM.

- **Link Support Layer (LSL)**—This layer enables multiple protocols to exist on a single network card. The LSL is a gateway that determines to which protocol stack a network packet belongs and sends it on its way.

- **Protocol Stack**—This component gets packets from the LSL and then sends the packet to another higher-level protocol or application.

Because ODI is modular, it makes writing protocol stacks or software drivers easier for third-party vendors. The code developer who works on the software to implement a protocol needs only to write to the specifications of the ODI interface, without regard to the underlying network card or the network media. The network card vendor has to worry only about writing code that can communicate with the MSM to implement the functions that are implemented by the card's hardware.

The Network Driver Interface Specification (NDIS)

Microsoft and 3Com Corporation initially developed NDIS, with Microsoft continuing that development with more recent versions. NDIS serves the same purpose, more or less, that ODI does in that it allows for the development of software for multiple protocol stacks to exist on multiple network adapters in a single computer. The actual implementation details, however, are quite different.

In Windows NT/2000/2003/XP, transport protocols span a portion of the Transport layer, the Network layer, and a portion of the Data Link layer. Transport protocols, such as NetBEUI Frame (NBF) and TCP, are implemented by calling services in the NDIS interface. NDIS doesn't completely hide the underlying network media from the protocol stack the way that ODI does. This limits most drivers to using Ethernet 802.3 or Token-Ring 802.5. Most drivers for ARCnet, for example, are written to take this into account and make the media look like Ethernet or Token-Ring to the software layers above.

Both ODI and NDIS provide support for each other. ODI provides a program called ODINSUP to support NDIS drivers. Windows computers come with NWLink, which is Microsoft's implementation of the IPX/SPX protocols. Microsoft also offers an inexpensive product (Services for NetWare). In addition, Windows NT/2000/2003/XP also come with Client Services for NetWare, which allows Windows NT clients to access resources on NetWare servers. Gateway Services for NetWare perform similar functions using a single Windows server computer as a gateway to NetWare services. A separate product called File and Print Services for NetWare is available from Microsoft, and can be used on a NetWare client to give it access to resources in a Windows server network.

In Part VI of this book, "LAN and WAN Network, Service, and Application Protocols," you will find more details about the various networking protocols that are available.

IRQs and I/O Ports

Although many new network adapter cards support plug-and-play capabilities, which means the operating system can automatically detect and configure them, this capability is not implemented in all operating systems, such as many Unix variants. Because of this, you might find yourself having to configure a card manually when upgrading a system with a new card, or when adding other devices that might conflict with the NIC. The two main items you will commonly have to modify are the values for the IRQ and the base I/O port.

IRQs

When a device on the computer's bus needs to get the attention of the CPU, it uses a hardware mechanism called the *Interrupt Request Line* (*IRQ*). Hardware interrupts are executed by signaling the CPU through a set of wires that are connected to the pins that attach the CPU to the motherboard. It is a direct connection. Because various devices might need to get the CPU's attention at any particular time, one IRQ is not sufficient. Instead, in most cases each device has its own interrupt line. When a device signals the CPU using an interrupt, it is telling the CPU that it has a processing request that needs to be satisfied as quickly as possible.

When the CPU receives an interrupt, it grants the device its attention for a short period—as long as it is not currently servicing another interrupt of a higher priority. It is also possible that the CPU is performing some task that is too critical to allow for an interrupt. When that is the case, the CPU does not allow a hardware interrupt to distract it. For that reason, this type of interrupt is called a *maskable interrupt*. This means that the CPU can be put into a mode in which it masks out these interrupts while it is busy on an ultra-important task, and then re-enables the interrupts when it is again capable of processing them.

The number of IRQs that are available on the system depends on the system bus type. Early PCs that were based on the ISA bus type had only eight hardware interrupts, numbered from 0 to 7, as shown in Table 7.1.

Table 7.1 ISA Bus Hardware Interrupts

IRQ	Function
0	System Timer
1	Keyboard Controller
2	Available
3	Serial Port 2 and 4 (COM2:, COM4:)
4	Serial Port 1 and 3 (COM1:, COM3:)
5	Hard Disk Drive Controller
6	Floppy Disk Drive Controller
7	Parallel Port 1 (LPT1:)

This small set of IRQs was sufficient for a small system with few devices. As you can see, only one IRQ—2—is available for an additional device in this layout. When the EISA bus was developed, the number of interrupts doubled to 16 (numbered 0 through 15). However, to do this, two interrupt controllers were needed on the system; one of them funnels its interrupts through IRQ2. This means that there are actually only 15 interrupts available for use by other devices on the system. Table 7.2 shows the devices that usually use these IRQs.

Table 7.2 EISA Bus Hardware Interrupts

IRQ	Function
0	System timer
1	Keyboard controller
2	Second interrupt controller
8	Real-time clock
9	Network card
10	Available
11	SCSI card
12	Motherboard mouse port
13	Math coprocessor
14	Primary IDE (hard disk drive) controller
15	Secondary IDE (hard disk drive) controller
3	Serial port 2 and 4 (COM2:, COM4:)
4	Serial port 1 and 3 (COM1:, COM3:)
5	Sound card or parallel port 2 (LPT2:)
6	Floppy disk drive controller
7	Parallel port 1 (LPT1:)

Notice that the IRQ numbers in Table 7.2 are not in numerical order. Instead, they are listed in order of *priority*, with those at the top of the table having a higher priority than those at the bottom. Because the additional eight IRQs were added by a mechanism that uses the original IRQ2, those IRQs all have a higher priority than IRQs 3–7. On some systems, IRQ9 is used to perform the same functions that were done by IRQ2 in the earlier design. For this reason, you might see this IRQ on a card labeled as 2, 9, or possibly IRQ 2/9.

If your computer is a plug-and-play system, you might find that you do not need to make any changes to the card or the system software to select the IRQ. If you do, however, be sure to consult the documentation that comes with the card to determine which interrupts it can use and how they are set. IRQs in non–plug-and-play cards are usually set by jumpers on the card, but sometimes through a software configuration utility. A jumper consists of a set of pins that can be connected to form a complete circuit by placing a connector between them.

Base I/O Ports

Again, if you find yourself in a situation in which your computer's operating system does not provide plug-and-play capabilities, you might have to manually configure the value of the memory address that the network card uses to transfer data to and from the system. After the network card signals to the CPU that processing needs to be done, it uses a memory address called the *base I/O port address* for this purpose. Because many devices in the system might use memory port addresses, it is important to configure each device to use a different address so that any data transfers that are performed do not conflict with each other.

On most systems, 64KB of memory is set up to be used for I/O ports, so they do not represent a limited resource like the IRQ does. Consult your operating-system documentation to determine how to display the current memory assignments for this area of memory.

For example, in Microsoft Windows 2000/2003, a utility called Microsoft Diagnostics can be used to display various hardware and software configurations. In Figure 7.5 you can see the utility, displaying the I/O ports on a Windows 2003 Server computer. Note the other selections on the left side of the MMC window. You can check IRQs, memory usage, and other things when trying to diagnose problems with network cards and other devices.

To run the diagnostic utility on a Windows 2000/2003 Server system, select Start, Programs (All Programs for Windows 2003 systems), Accessories, System Tools, System Information. When the utility appears, select the Hardware Resources tab. Click the I/O Port selection on the left side of the MMC and your screen should look similar to that shown in Figure 7.5.

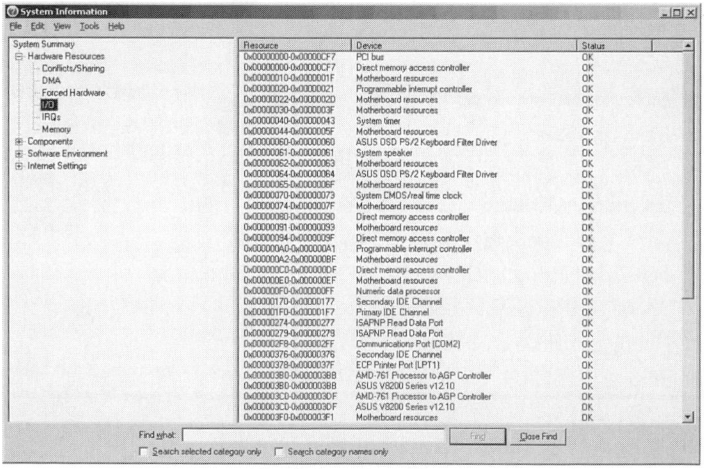

Figure 7.5 The Windows 2003 Diagnostics utility can show you how I/O ports are assigned.

Notice that the first item listed is Conflicts/Sharing. Using this item, you can determine whether more than one device on this system is sharing an interrupt.

In addition to the base I/O port, some devices use a section of memory to buffer data temporarily. For this, they require a *base memory address*, which points to the start of the buffer. Your network card might or might not use the computer's RAM, so check the documentation carefully if a conflict arises.

Troubleshooting Network Cards

When you install or replace a network adapter card and find that it does not function, there are several things you can examine to attempt to diagnose the problem. The cause might be a hardware problem with the card itself or with the computer. Or it might be the cable that links the card to the hub or switch, or the hub or the switch itself. It might be a simple problem of changing the configuration for the device. If you're having a bad day, it might even be a combination of these things!

If you are using Windows, check the system error log using the Event Viewer to see whether any errors are being logged when the computer boots and is in the process of checking devices. Using the Event Viewer, you might find that you have a software configuration problem.

When adding a new network card to a workstation, you want to first review the documentation that comes with the card to determine what values you can use for the IRQ, base I/O port address, and so on. You might also need to look at documentation for other devices on the system because resolving a conflict might require you to change some other device instead of the network card.

The good news is that if all the cards in your system are plug-and-play compatible, you can be sure that an IRQ or memory address conflict is not causing the problem. In that case, begin troubleshooting efforts by checking the cable, hub, switch, and other hardware components that connect the computer to the network.

Checking the NIC Configuration on Linux

On Red Hat Linux 8.0 systems, if a network card is detected during setup, you are prompted to enter static IP addressing information, or to use DHCP. If you choose DHCP, and there is a DHCP server on your network, then you will probably do okay. However, if you can't communicate on the network, there are some things you should check on Linux to ensure you have set up the system correctly for network activity.

Note

The following examples are based on using the Gnome desktop for Linux. Your choices may differ if using another desktop, such as KDE.

Finding Information About Your Network Card

To find out information such as the driver used by your network card, as well as to diagnose problems with the device, click on Start (the Red Hat for Red Hat Linux), System Tools, and then Network Device Control. In Figure 7.6 you can see that the current Ethernet device (eth0) has a status of inactive. Something is incorrect.

Clicking on the Configure button brings up another window (shown in Figure 7.7) that you can use to further make changes to the settings for this particular network adapter card.

The Hardware, Hosts, and DNS tabs may be helpful, along with the Devices tab that starts this set of properties sheets. On the Hardware tab, for example, you can add or delete a particular device.

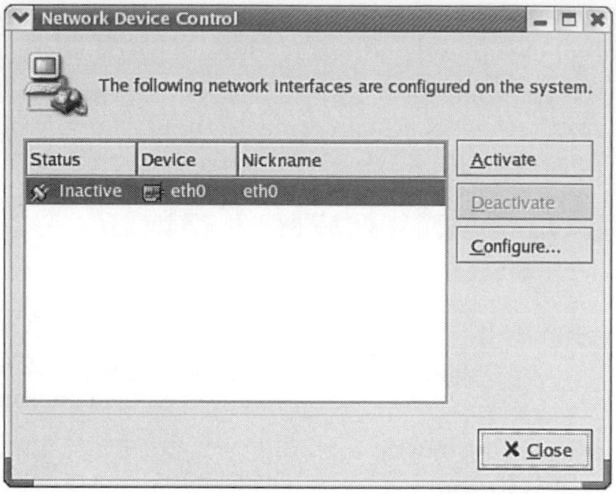

Figure 7.6   Linux will show you the network adapters connected to your system, and their current status.

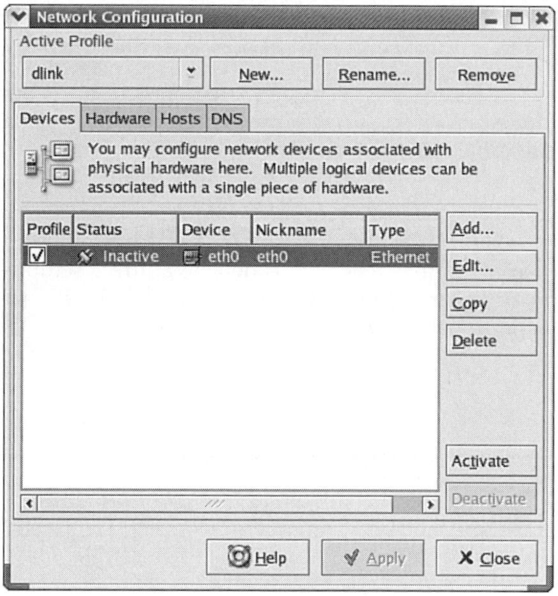

Figure 7.7   You can make changes to the settings of the network card here.

If you choose to add a device that is not recognized already by the operating system, the window shown in Figure 7.8 will appear.

After you've filled in the necessary information, you can click OK and then exit the Network Configuration utility. You can then use the standard TCP/IP tools (such as `ping` and `traceroute` to check network connectivity).

In addition, you can always check the network configuration files (using such utilities as a text editor) if you are a more advanced user and want to be sure the system information is correct. If you are not an advanced user, at least make a backup of any file you edit, or use the GUI interfaces provided for these functions.

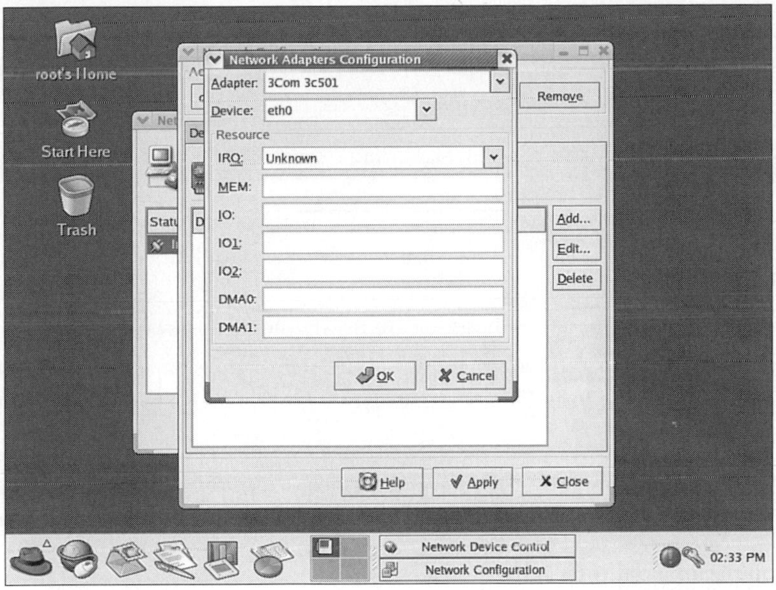

Figure 7.8 You must have the necessary technical information to install a network adapter card that is not recognized by the Linux operating system.

The files you might want to investigate include the following:

■ /proc/net/sockstat—To show raw statistics about TCP and UDP.

■ /proc/net/dev—To view statistics about a network interface.

■ /if_inet6—To view statistics about an IPv6 network interface.

Although these files can be used to watch what is happening on your network, there are others you should review to ensure that your network configuration is correct. Because new network vulnerabilities occur every few weeks, it is a good idea to keep these files as "high-advisability" items.

Checking the LEDs—Activity and Link Lights

All network interface cards have some combination of status LEDs (light emitting diodes) located on them. To determine the actual meaning of any LEDs, be sure to review the documentation for your specific brand and model of card. For example, some cards have an LED that is used to indicate the link status. In most cases, if the light is on, the link is okay—the NIC and the hub/switch can communicate with each other. If the light is flashing, there is a problem, which may lie in a bad cable, connectors, or even simple things such as having the transmit/receive wires reversed. NICs often use another LED to indicate network activity (when blinking rapidly, the network card is sending or receiving data). Because the standards used can vary on different network cards, refer to the manufacturer's documentation to discover the meaning behind LEDs on your network adapter.

Network cards usually have at least one LED, which you can see on the outside of the computer—one for link status and one for network activity. Generally, if the card has only one LED (link) it should be lit if the card is capable of communicating with the hub or switch. Most switches also have an LED status light for each port, so it is a good idea to check that also. The problem might be in the hub, switch, or network card. It might even be the cable that connects them.

Tip

Today many network cards as well as switches can tell you more than just that network connectivity has been established (one LED), and that network communications are taking place (the second LED). Newer ports on both ends can let you know if the card/port is functioning in 10 or 100Mbps, half- or full-duplex mode. This can be very useful when troubleshooting slower network nodes. You should, of course, check the operating-system settings for a network device to be sure it is set for the correct mode.

If it appears that there is a problem with the link, localize the problem and determine where the fault is by trying the following:

- Check all connectors to be sure that they are firmly plugged into their sockets.

- Be sure that the card and the hub/switch port are set for the same type of link; that is, the switch might be set to full duplex while the card is not, or one end might be set to 10Mbps while the other is set to 100Mbps.

- If your card supports auto-negotiation, try to enable or disable this feature on the switch or hub. If the card's documentation indicates that it does support auto-negotiation, it might not be functioning properly. You might have to manually set the hub or switch port to the proper setting.

- Try another port on the hub or switch.

- Try a different cable, preferably one that you know is in good working condition. If you are connecting directly to the hub or switch over a short distance, this should be relatively easy. If you are connecting from a switch to a patch panel to a run through the walls to a jack at a desk and then to the computer, you might have to try replacing a number of cables.

- Try to reseat the card in the slot.

- Try to move the network adapter to a different slot in the computer.

- Check the BIOS settings for the computer. Check the manual for your computer to determine whether you need to reserve certain IRQs for older adapters to keep PCI cards from trying to use the same values. In some computers it is possible to enable or disable a PCI slot by using the BIOS setup program. Be sure the slot is enabled if your BIOS supports this feature.

- Substitute a card that you know is good to see if the problem still presents itself.

If none of the preceding seems to work, try the card in another computer where no problem exists. If it works there, then the problem obviously does not lie in the NIC, and you might have a software or hardware configuration problem on the computer in question.

Running the Adapter's Diagnostic Program

Almost all cards, even those labeled as plug-and-play, come with a floppy disk that contains software drivers and a diagnostic program. Usually you will find that it is necessary to boot the computer into DOS to run the diagnostic program, and indeed some cards come with a floppy disk that is also DOS bootable. When using a diagnostic program like this, you should be careful that no other drivers or memory managers are loaded when you perform the test to help eliminate conflicts that can result in inaccurate results. Note that "DOS" does not mean a command-prompt window in Windows XP or Windows 2000/2003. It means booting the computer into the actual DOS operating system.

The kinds of tests that can be run vary, but you will probably get a menu that allows you to run one or all of the tests that the program is capable of executing. This can include simple hardware-specific checks and loopback tests. Some cards provide for an echo test, in which two cards from the same manufacturer can send and receive packets from each other for a diagnostic test. If the card cannot pass all the diagnostic tests that the vendor supplies, and if you are sure there are no other problems (such as a bad slot in the computer's system bus), then you probably have a bad card and need to replace it.

This method is also used for installing new network cards. Although most can be installed using the Add/Remove Hardware Wizard in the Control Panel, others need to be installed by setup programs on the floppy disk or CD that comes with the adapter.

Configuration Conflicts

If the card passes the vendor's diagnostic tests and you can find nothing wrong with the physical components of the card, the computer system, or the hub/switch, then it is time to check the configuration of the card. Earlier in this chapter (in the section "Base I/O Ports"), you saw how the Microsoft Diagnostics utility under Windows NT (or the MMC System Information utility in Windows 2000) can be used to determine which memory address a device has been configured to use. You can also use these utilities to determine the IRQ and other configuration information for the devices installed in the computer. In Figure 7.9 you can see the Windows 2000 System Information window with the Conflicts/Sharing item selected.

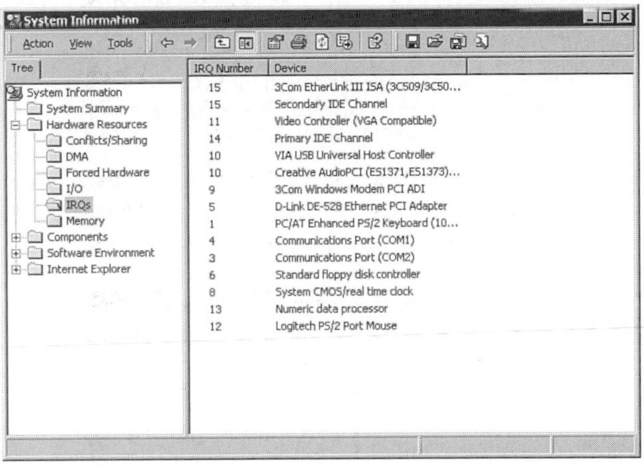

Figure 7.9 You can use the System Information MMC utility to check for device conflicts.

If you are working with a Windows 98 or Windows NT 4.0 computer, you can use the Resources tab in the Microsoft Diagnostics utility to compare device settings. Check the Conflicting Device List field. If you find that other devices appear here, you can take appropriate action and reassign the IRQs or memory addresses as needed until all devices are functioning correctly. Reassigning these values will likely involve using software that comes with the particular adapter card.

Note

Remember that the PCI bus allows for the capability to share IRQs. Thus, if you notice that more than one device is using the same IRQ number, it might not really be the source of your problem. In general, only similar devices should be sharing the same IRQ. When the IRQ line signals the CPU for a shared IRQ, the system interrogates each device that shares the IRQ to determine which device is actually requesting attention from the CPU.

If you are using an older ISA card, you will probably have to use a jumper or a small switch on the card to change configuration information. If you're using an EISA card, the ECU program can usually be used to help adjust configuration information.

For Unix users the situation is more complicated. In many older systems adding new hardware requires that you recompile the kernel and reboot. Many newer systems support plug-and-play and can recognize well-known hardware components and configure them automatically, but this is not always the case. Depending on the version of Unix, you might be able to examine configuration files to determine the interrupts and memory addresses a particular device uses. Check your system's documentation for further information.

Because there are many releases of both Unix and Linux, your best bet when troubleshooting NIC problems is to start with the card manufacturer's resources. Some cards can be configured by running a program that comes with the adapter, whereas others must be installed and configured using utilities the operating-system vendor supplies.

Checking the Computer's Network Configuration

If none of the previous troubleshooting steps has uncovered the source of your problem, the problem just might lie farther up the protocol stack and might not be a problem with the hardware components. For example, if you are using a DHCP server to allocate IP addresses on the network, the computer might not have been able to successfully obtain configuration information from a DHCP server. Or, if you have configured the IP information manually and have a statically assigned address for the computer, check to be sure you didn't mistakenly use the same address for more than one computer. Be sure that the address you assigned to the computer (and the subnet mask) is the correct one for the subnet to which the computer is attached.

After you've eliminated the hardware components as the problem source, there are other tools you can use to diagnose protocol and routing issues. Chapter 28, "Troubleshooting Tools for TCP/IP Networks," covers the standard utilities that come with most TCP/IP implementations. These programs allow you to look at the actual frames flowing through the network, giving you a detailed look at what is actually going on. Even though everything else might check out okay, such as the link LEDs, your network adapter card might be sending out corrupted frames. In that case, toss it and buy a new card.

Preventative Steps to Take

Keeping track of system information for the computers in your network can make troubleshooting tasks a lot easier. For example, a spreadsheet that lists all the nodes on your network, along with configuration information, is very useful when you need to upgrade or replace a particular component. If you have this information already available before a problem arises, you will be able to devote more of your time to solving the problem. After you've ensured that the network card is functioning, troubleshooting is a lot simpler if you have a map to follow to determine where the network cable connects to another network device.

Network Switches

8

SOME OF THE MAIN TOPICS IN THIS CHAPTER ARE

Hubs are legacy network devices that enabled creating larger LANs—extending the distance of the network—by connecting and centralizing the wiring of multiple physical LAN segments. Bridges were developed to connect separate LAN segments and reduce the collision domain. This chapter explains network switches, which have replaced hubs in all but the oldest networks. In a small home office, a hub might be sufficient to provide LAN connectivity for a few computers. However, in a large, modern network, a more powerful device is needed. It isn't enough to extend the distance of a LAN, which a simple repeater or bridge can do. It isn't enough to centralize wiring, which a hub can do.

Note

The term *collision domain* generally refers to the first Ethernet devices, those based on coaxial cable networks, and even those based on hubs. Because early Ethernet networks used a shared network media, each node on the network had to contend for access to the network. The mechanism used to get access to the shared media is called Collision Sense Multiple Access/Collision Detect (CSMA/CD). A computer attempting to transmit data on the shared media first listens to ensure that no one else is already transmitting (collision sense). If the line is free, the computer can begin to transmit data. Yet, because the length of the cables and/or hubs that make up the shared media can be lengthy, it's possible that another node may sense the media to be available at the same time, and start transmitting (multiple access). When this happens, a collision occurs. The collision can be detected because it generates a higher voltage on the wire. The collision domain consists of all those computers (or other devices) that must compete in the same shared media, be it a single cable or many cables interconnected by hubs. Switches have solved this problem in modern Ethernet equipment.

Today's large networks need to provide far more to client and server computers alike, and the device that has become predominant in the LAN for this purpose is the switch. In this chapter, you'll learn that a switch is nothing more than a combination of earlier technologies, with improvements. Without switches, Ethernet networks would have been maxed out a few years ago with 100BASE-T (Fast Ethernet) hub solutions.

Note

Routers can be used to extend a network. However, the difference between a network router and a LAN switch is significant. *Routers* are used to direct network frames to the correct network or subnet on which the destination host resides, or to another router that may know of the destination network that lies in the path to the destination network.

Although routers can be used within large networked environments to segregate physical network segments, they are generally considered to be WAN devices—used to connect a LAN to the Internet or a larger private intranet. *Switches*, in the form most used today, are used to get past the limitations imposed by traditional LAN technologies, including the bus topology, the hub, and the bridge. However, at the end of this chapter, you'll see how switching technology has also moved up the ladder into the WAN market.

A major difference between routers and LAN switches is that a router makes decisions based on the network portion of the IP address, whereas switches work at a lower level and make decisions based on the Media Access Control (MAC) address burned into the network card by the manufacturer. Because the MAC address space is random, and the IP address space is hierarchical, LAN switches would need a routing table so large that it would not be possible to store every MAC address for every computer in the world today. Yet routers can use the network portion of an IP address to send a packet on its way because of the very nature of the hierarchical address space (network address/client address) provided by IP. LAN switches can work quickly because they only need to look at the MAC address, which is always located in the same part of the Ethernet frame that carries the IP packet as its payload.

How Switches Work

In a traditional Ethernet LAN, you are limited to the number of workstations you can attach to any particular LAN segment or hub. You are limited by the total available bandwidth, which usually is 10Mbps or 100Mbps using older hub technology. The group of network devices—including workstations, servers, and hubs—that are all capable of broadcasting a packet to any other device on the network makes up a broadcast domain. Even if you follow the topological rules for creating a traditional Ethernet LAN, it won't matter how many computers you are able to connect to the LAN if network traffic becomes a problem. This can happen when you have several high-end servers or workstations that make heavy demands on the network.

Hubs do not diminish the broadcast domain, because all devices connected to the hub must still use the Ethernet CSMA/CD method to gain access to the network media. On the other hand, a bridge is used to connect two network segments and reduce the broadcast domain by passing network traffic from one segment to another based on a table that the bridge uses to determine which computers are located on which physical segments. What is all this leading up to? A switch is basically a combination of a hub and a bridge. Consider a switch to be a device that uses circuitry to create multiple bridges between the ports it provides.

If you are not familiar with hubs or bridges, these older network components are covered in detail in the chapter "Bridges, Repeaters, and Hubs," which can be found on the upgradingandrepairingpcs. com Web site.

The solution to this problem is to limit the broadcast domain. In the preceding chapter, bridges were discussed for this purpose. However, legacy bridges just aren't sufficient for the high-speed networks that are required by today's applications, such as streaming audio and video, alongside more traditional network traffic, such as file and print services.

A switch is a cross between a bridge and a hub. You can think of a switch as several bridges, centralized in a single device like a hub, with added monitoring and management capabilities. Switches centralize wiring and cut down on unnecessary broadcasts on the LAN by *switching* network packets from an incoming port to the outgoing port that will get the packet to its destination. A switch thus limits the broadcast domain to just two devices: the switch port and the network adapter card on a computer. This eliminates the need for other workstations attached to the switch to examine each packet broadcast on the network. The other workstations never see the packet to begin with. The outgoing port may be connected to the destination of the frame, or it may be connected to another switch, or perhaps a router, that will forward it until it reaches the destination computer.

Switches and bridges aren't that different. They perform just about the same function. However, early bridges usually had only two ports to connect two LAN segments and, thus, divide the broadcast domain in half. As technology developed rapidly in the 1990s, it became possible to create multiport bridges you could use to attach multiple LAN segments. Switches today can be used to connect multiple LAN segments or to connect individual workstations or servers to the network.

So although the term *switch* may sound new, it's just an evolutionary update of an older technique—bridging, combined with the central wiring concentrator function provided by a hub. You can use switches to perform the same functions that were performed earlier using bridges, but switches allow you to connect a lot more computers to your LAN. Switches have been around for many years in the high-end marketplace for large LANs. Recently they have replaced smaller SOHO hubs at the low end. Today you can purchase a small switch for the same price a hub would have cost just a year or two ago. For larger networks, rack-mounted larger switches have also come down in price. This is due to the fact that there are a lot of manufacturers (for both markets) and switches are now commonplace in high-end networks.

Note

One important distinction between earlier bridges and modern switches needs to be made. Bridges were initially designed to connect two or more LAN segments together. Each LAN segment could have a single computer or multiple computers connected to it. Bridges generally were used to segment the broadcast domain by connecting LAN segments that had multiple computers attached. Switches, however, are used to connect a single computer to a switch port, which can switch the data out another switch port to another target computer, or another switch that can deliver the packet to the target device.

Segmenting the Collision Domain

In Chapter 14, "Ethernet: The Universal Standard," you'll learn more about the limitations imposed for configuring a network based on the technology used. Each type of Ethernet, from 10BASE-2 to Gigabit and 10Gigabit Ethernet, has its own rules about the number of computers that can be connected, the length of cables, and so on. After you reach the maximum allowed length or number of computers imposed by the particular topological rules, you have to create a new LAN and, usually, connect them with a router. Gigabit and 10Gigabit Ethernet are currently used as part of a network backbone because of their large bandwidth. Yet, as desktop computers continue along their evolutionary line and get faster, and as the same thing happens with application software and data, you will probably find Gigabit Ethernet to the desktop workstation to be common in a few years. The equipment for this is already on the market. Applications that use large amounts of data, such as video editing, can benefit from this large bandwidth to the desktop. A word processor, however, would use only a very small fraction of Gigabit Ethernet!

In Figure 8.1 you can see that a switch is used to connect individual workstations, servers, and other network devices.

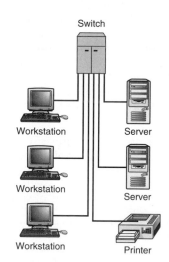

Figure 8.1   You can connect individual computers to a switch port.

The benefits of using a switch should quickly become apparent. The broadcast domain, when using the standard half-duplex Ethernet CSMA/CD technology, is limited to just two devices: the switch port and the computer attached to it. In this standard half-duplex mode, however, collisions still can occur if the switch and the computer attached to it sense that the network media is silent and both attempt to transmit at the same time. This is exactly what happens in a traditional Ethernet LAN when the CSMA/CD mechanism described in Chapter 14 is used. However, with only two devices competing for network access, bandwidth is greatly improved.

If you were to substitute a hub for the switch in Figure 8.1, the network traffic from all the workstations attached to the hub would have to compete for access to the network media. This means that if you were to use a hub, the actual bandwidth available to each workstation would be less than when a switch is used. As more and more workstations on a hub begin to generate large amounts of network traffic, the effective use of the network media begins to lessen as more and more collisions occur. Using a switch solves this problem.

Full-Duplex Ethernet Switches

The switch makes another new concept in Ethernet technology possible: full-duplex communication. As discussed in the preceding section, in a standard Ethernet implementation, each device must contend with all others that want to use the transmission medium. The CSMA/CD mechanism is used so that only one device successfully ends up talking on the wire at any particular time. The more stations that are added to the collision domain, the lower the total throughput because collisions increase and retransmissions become more frequent.

When a single workstation is connected to a switch, you want to further increase bandwidth by eliminating the collision domain altogether. This is exactly what happens when you use a switch that supports full-duplex communication. In this type of switch, separate wires in the network cable are used for transmitting and receiving. Thus, the switch port can be transmitting frames to the workstation on one set of wires, while the workstation is transmitting frames to the switch port on another wire pair in the cable.

Because there are no competing devices, the switch and the workstation can send and receive from each other at the same time, the result of which is a full-duplex operation. No collisions occur *because there is no contention for the wire*. Not only can you achieve the actual 10Mbps or 100Mbps throughput capabilities of the wire for each port attached to a full-duplex switch, but you can double those speeds—100Mbps in each direction because each side of the connection can use the full 100Mbps bandwidth. And as Gigabit Ethernet is deployed to the edge of the network, you can expect to see even greater throughput. This will become very important in the next year or two as higher-end PCs and workstations become widely used for large graphics and video applications.

Most network adapter cards, even the very inexpensive ones you can find at a local computer store, now support both 10Mbps and 100Mbps full-duplex communications. You can find a generic store brand usually for under $15. At this price, it only makes sense to throw out those older cards (which probably cost you a lot more!) and upgrade to a newer card. However, most switches, both inexpensive SOHO devices and those intended for use in an enterprise network, still support both 10 and 100Mbps. The main reason why you will see some network adapters priced at higher levels ($50–$100) is that they offer advanced features, which may be useful to your environment. And, as you learned in Chapter 7, "Network Interface Cards," there are other new features that are generally useful only in enterprise networks, such as Wake on LAN and Preboot Execution Environment (PXE) Boot. See Chapter 7 for a description of these and other types of services offered by high-end network adapter cards.

Note

Full-duplex communications are the key to faster Ethernet technologies. After you pass the 100BASE-T speed of 100Mbps, the packet size and round-trip timing required for Ethernet networks just doesn't scale very well. Newer technologies, such as Gigabit Ethernet and 10 Gigabit Ethernet, depend on this full-duplex capability and the removal of the CSMA/CD media access control mechanism.

You can increase the availability of the server to its clients, and incur only the expense of a new network card for the server, by replacing the network card on the server with a full-duplex card and plugging it into a port on the switch that supports full-duplex operations. You can increase the response time of the PC or workstation by doing the same.

To make upgrading to a 100Mbps switch easier, most vendors provide the capability of dual-speed ports. This is similar to the dual-speed 10/100Mpbs network cards. Thus you can continue to use older network cards with a new switch until your budget allows for upgrading the cards installed in individual workstations. Just about every switch on the market today can autosense the network speed of the workstation attached to the port. However, some older models require that you manually set the speed, using management software. The best switches support both autosensing and a good management program that can be used to configure ports.

Note

The best laid plans...can often go awry. Even though there are standards organizations and trade associations that set standards for all sorts of network devices, such as network adapter cards, this doesn't mean that a card (or switch) will always work as expected. This author recently had a problem with several high-end servers (AlphaServers running OpenVMS) that were capable of handling several thousand user connections at any point in time. The servers used autosensing 10/100Mbps full-duplex cards, yet for some reason the throughput was operating in a 10Mbps half-duplex mode. After user complaints, the problem was resolved by manually configuring the switch port to use 100Mbps, full-duplex communications for the particular port. In other words, if you don't find your expectations met when you install new equipment, check the alternatives.

Using Switches to Create a Collapsed Backbone

Because switches can effectively eliminate the broadcast domain, you also can use them to eliminate the traditional backbone used to connect multiple hubs or other devices. For example, it's easy to set up a hub or switch in a wiring closet on each floor of a building, and then run a single cable through the floors to connect each hub (as shown in Figure 8.2). This cable is the *backbone* for the network. However, this does nothing to eliminate the collision domain for all the traffic it receives from the switches or hubs.

In Figure 8.2, each workstation that is attached to the switch on its floor easily can exchange data with other workstations that are attached to the same switch. However, if a workstation needs to communicate with a server or another resource that is not directly connected to that switch, the network traffic flows over the backbone that connects the other departmental switches. Again, this isn't a problem if you have a network in which you can locate important servers closer to the actual clients that use them and prevent traffic from entering the backbone at all.

In today's environment, however, it's common to find many business functions centralized in data centers, in large servers, or possibly in clustered servers that manage huge databases. In this type of scenario, it isn't always easy to move a server closer to the client. And, with the advent of email and other Web-based applications, it's more likely that the old 80/20 rule—80% of network traffic stays within the local LAN, whereas only 20% is destined for other locations—has been turned around. Now most clients need to exchange only a small amount of data with local computers, sending the 80% figure to the larger network. As newer technologies, such as Windows 2003 Servers, begin to distribute components of applications among multiple computers, this problem becomes a more important consideration when planning a network. With the centralization of larger servers, most likely you'll see this paradigm in all but the smallest networks in the future.

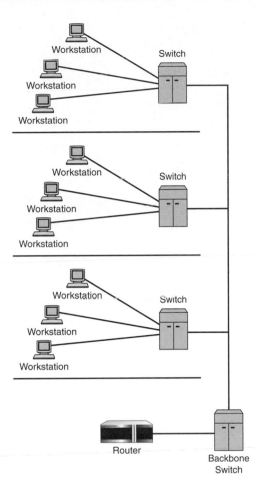

Figure 8.2   A single backbone becomes a bottleneck in a large network.

In Figure 8.3, switches are cascaded so that the switch can become a network backbone-in-a-box. *Each switch* in the building is connected to a central switch that serves as the backbone, again limiting or eliminating the collision domain, depending on whether full- or half-duplex switch ports are used.

Of course, in this example, the switches appear on each floor, but you could just as easily attach hubs at the department level or use a mixture of both hubs and switches. No need to throw out a hub if it provides the bandwidth you need for a specific situation. In Figure 8.3, it's important to note that, instead of sharing a single backbone network cable, each departmental switch has its own cable to the switch, so the full bandwidth of the network media is available to each switch. The backbone no longer becomes a bottleneck. This does, however, mean that switched connections between devices on one switch with devices on another switch may suffer some minor degradation in bandwidth, but in most cases this problem can be resolved by isolating the computers or servers that need a high-speed link and simply relocating their network connections to different switches to ensure a larger data pipe.

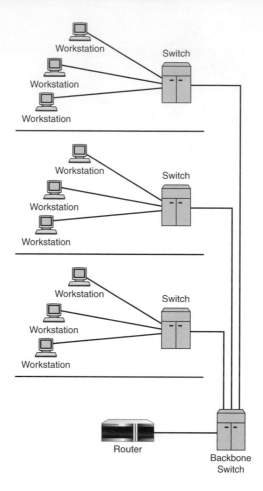

Figure 8.3   A hub can serve as a collapsed backbone to concentrate departmental switches.

Switch Hardware Types

So far, switches seem to be a network administrator's dream come true. And in most cases this is the truth. But when you decide to incorporate switches, there is something else to consider: Not all switches use the same technology. The importance of this distinction depends on which of these functions of a switch is the most important to you:

- Increasing the bandwidth for computers attached to a switch.

- Decreasing the possibility that frame errors will be propagated end-to-end in a network link.

Many architectures are used for switching, as described in the following sections. Because switching is a hot technology, many approaches are being tried. Some involve software that makes decisions much like a router and sends frames on their merry way. Others are hardware-based and can perform much better because no single component, such as a CPU, can be bogged down when too much traffic passes through the switch. Two basic modes of operation can be used by a switch when it forwards a packet out of a selected port: cut-through mode and store-and-forward mode.

Cut-Through Switches

A cut-through switch begins transmitting the incoming frame on the outgoing port after it receives the header information, or about 20 or 30 bytes. All the switch needs to determine on which port to output the frame is the *destination address* (hardware address), which is determined by the MAC address found in the frame header. The switch continues to receive information and transmit it until the frame has been "switched" from one port to another. The advantage to this mode of operation is *speed*. As long as nothing else goes wrong, the packet continues on to its destination at a fast pace with little time involved in the switch. The switch is said to be switching at *wire speed*. That is, the delay introduced by the switching function is so insignificant that to the end workstations, the full bandwidth is available for use.

This method has several disadvantages, however. The switch begins to send the packet out before it knows whether the frame is damaged in any way. If the frame has corrupted data, the switch won't be able to detect it unless it first receives the entire frame and then computes the CRC (cyclic redundancy check) value stored in the frame check sequence field. If a frame is badly malformed, as when an NIC sends out a frame that is too long, a cut-through switch might think it is a broadcast packet and send it out of all ports, causing unnecessary traffic congestion.

Store-and-Forward Switches

In the store-and-forward switch, the switch buffers the frame in its own memory before beginning to send it out of the appropriate port. This technique boasts two main advantages:

- The switch can connect two different topologies, such as 10Mbps and 100Mbps networks, without having to worry about the different speeds.

- The switch can operate like a bridge and check the integrity of the frame, allowing it to discard damaged frames and not propagate them onto other network segments. This means that a malformed frame received from a local port can be discarded immediately, instead of being sent through the entire switched network until the end-node discovers that an error has occurred.

Although the store-and-forward technology increases the latency factor, this delay usually is not a big concern when you consider the increased throughput you can achieve with a switch.

Layer 3 Switches

Just as switches are on an evolutionary upgrade path from hubs and bridges, a new breed of networking device is becoming increasingly popular in large networks. Layer 3 of the OSI model is the Network layer, on which higher-level protocol addresses are introduced into the network. Generally, switches are deployed in a LAN, whereas routers, which use layer 3 addresses (such as an IP address), are used to connect LANs that are separated by some distance, such as in a campus LAN, or to connect WANs. The main difference here is that the switch must examine only a small amount of the frame header to determine the hardware address of a frame and then send the frame out of the correct port. Routers, however, need to dig further into the packet to find the higher-level protocol address, such as an IP address. Routers also must modify the frame header, substituting the router's MAC address as the source address of the frame, examining and modifying the TTL field in the packet and performing checksum calculations to ensure the integrity of the packet. Because of the extra processing involved, routers generally operate at a lower speed than do switches.

Standard routers operating at slower speeds than switches tend to become bottlenecks in a network. To solve this problem, layer 3 switching devices usually take a different approach to the functions a router performs. Routers are like computers (indeed, sometimes a computer with multiple network adapters is used for routing in a small network), and a processor must examine each packet and perform all the functions just mentioned. Layer 3 switches usually implement these functions in application-specific integrated circuits (ASICs). By implementing these functions in hardware, some layer 3 switches can operate at just about wire speed, which ordinary routers cannot do.

Some layer 3 switches use proprietary technologies, because standards are not complete for this type of device at this time. Whatever method they use, the idea is to identify streams of traffic that are all traveling to the same destination, and output them on the appropriate port as fast as possible.

Most products that advertise themselves as layer 3 switches also function as routers. Layer 3 switching is employed for traffic streams that are easily identifiable. For small traffic loads, the device operates much like a router. In the next few years, you can expect to see layer 3 switching come down in price, making it feasible in smaller networks. For now, however, the cost might not justify the increase in speed you will achieve. For example, if a router is a bottleneck in your network that sits between client computers and servers, consider moving servers closer to the clients so that the network traffic flow doesn't have to pass through the router.

Another interesting development in routing technologies, called Multi-Label Protocol Switching, is discussed in Chapter 37, "Routing Protocols." This method of wire-speed switching, generally found in high-end Internet core routers, is defined by RFC documents, which are either proposed standards or informational documents. Here are some of them:

- RFC 3034, "Use of Label Switching on Frame Relay Networks Specification"
- RFC 3270, "Multi-Protocol Label Switching (MPLS) Support of Differentiated Services"
- RFC 3468, "The Multi-Protocol Label Switching (MPLS) Working Group Decision on MPLS Signaling Protocols"
- RFC 3471, "Generalized Multi-Protocol Label Switching (GMPLS) Signaling Functional Description"

Putting a Switch in Your Home Office

Switches, similar to hubs, come in all sizes and shapes. As stated at the beginning of this chapter, the switch has replaced the hub for all practical purposes. There is no longer a major cost difference between switches and hubs. In fact, it can be rather difficult to find new hubs. Even hubs for small home networks have been replaced by switches. The small four-port switch is an ideal solution for connecting a few devices in a SOHO network.

Installing a switch of this sort requires very little effort. You basically plug the network cables from your computers into the ports on the back of the switch and then power up the switch. If you expect your network to grow during the next year or two, you should know that most switches have an "uplink port" also. If this is the case, the documentation for your switch will point out which port is used for this function. The uplink port is used to attach your switch to another switch should your network grow and you need additional ports to connect the new computers. If your switch doesn't have an uplink port, you can use a cross-over cable to connect two standard switch ports to achieve the same result. A cross-over cable basically just swaps the transmit and receive wires so that the ports can communicate. Additionally, some uplink ports can be converted to a regular port so that you can attach a computer instead. There is usually a button or switch that can perform this function. Check the documentation!

Stackable and Chassis Switches

For larger networks, you'll find that switches come in stackable and chassis models. Stackable switches have an interconnect port you can use to link them together, so you can add capacity as your network grows. Chassis switches fit a lot of switching capacity into a very small space, providing a large number of ports. Chassis switches can be placed into computer racks and take up much less room than other types of switches. The term "blade" has come into vogue recently to describe servers, switches, and other devices that can be located in a densely populated computer rack. These kinds of switches also provide other functions, such as better management capabilities, support for the Simple Network Management Protocol (SNMP) and Remote Monitoring (RMON), and the capability to create virtual LANs, which is the subject of the next chapter.

Switch Troubleshooting and Management

You troubleshoot a switch just like you troubleshoot a hub. If the switch has a link light (or LED), be sure it's on, indicating that the port is operating as it should and receiving a signal from the network adapter attached to the client computer (or another switch, as the case might be). Management software for the switch can be based on the SNMP or RMON specifications, or it might be proprietary in nature. In either case, all but the low-end home-office switches provide the capability to examine, test, and set parameters for each port on the switch.

▶▶   Information about troubleshooting hubs can be found on the **upgradingandrepairingpcs.com** Web site, in the chapter "Bridges, Repeaters, and Hubs."

For example, if you have a client computer connected to the switch, and the client's network adapter is autosensing, meaning that it can determine the network speed, it might not be compatible with the autosensing functionality of the switch. In that case, you might have to manually configure the switch port to match the higher speed that the network adapter can support.

For more information about troubleshooting switches using SNMP and RMON, see Chapter 53, "Network Testing and Analysis Tools."

Virtual LANs

SOME OF THE MAIN TOPICS IN THIS CHAPTER ARE

CHAPTER 9

Chapter 8, "Network Switches," discussed switches that can be used to reduce the broadcast domain limit imposed by earlier networking technologies, such as hubs and bridges. LAN switches can be used to solve more problems than just reducing network traffic, however. This chapter discusses a new application for switches: virtual LANs, or VLANs. Besides reducing the broadcast domain, switches configured for use in a VLAN can be used to solve many other problems:

- The changing physical topology of the LAN
- Security on the LAN
- Performance issues
- Centralized management of multiple LANs
- Limiting multicast traffic

Although a router can also be used to reduce a broadcast domain and create separate subnets in a network, switching technology works at a much faster pace. Thus, using VLANs in your network probably can enable you to get rid of a few slow routers that currently are being used to segment a LAN.

Virtual LANs and Network Topologies

When discussing local area networks, most network administrators think of the physical topology of the LAN—that is, the switches, servers, and workstations, and how they connect to form the LAN. The physical topology, as you learned in Chapter 2, "Overview of Network Topologies," doesn't have to match the logical *topology* of the LAN. As an early example, the Token-Bus network topology (IEEE 802.4 standard) uses a single coaxial cable to connect computers into a LAN. However, the order in which individual computers gain access to this shared cable is not the order in which they exist on the cable. In Figure 9.1, you can see that six computers are connected to a single cable. In this example, you can assume that the computers are numbered in a manner that represents their actual network address (Token-Bus addresses actually can range in size from 2 to 5 bytes). For this figure, the numbers 1–6 are used instead of the network address. In a token-passing network, a token frame is passed from one computer to another, and it is this token frame that gives a computer the right to transmit data on the network.

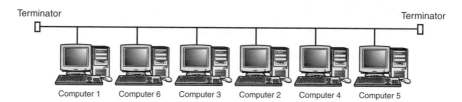

Figure 9.1   An early Token-Bus network uses a token frame to determine which computer can transmit data on the cable.

Although in this figure it might seem logical that the token frame would be passed from Computer 1 to Computer 6, and then to Computer 3, that is not how Token-Bus networks function. The physical topology is a linear bus, in which a message broadcast on the cable by Computer 1 travels down the wire until it reaches the terminator that is placed after Computer 5 at the end of the segment.

The logical topology of a Token-Bus network, however, is that of a ring. Although all computers on the same cable segment can "hear" the broadcast that every other computer makes, communications take place in an orderly manner. The token frame is "passed" in numerical address order from Computer 1 to Computer 2, then to Computer 3, and so on. This example is intended to show you the difference between a logical and a physical topology. The physical layout of the network is a linear bus. The logical topology of this network is a ring.

So what does this have to do with virtual LANs? A lot. Early LAN technologies, such as Ethernet, were limited in their size and distance by the physical topology of the LAN. You can read about this in Chapter 14, "Ethernet: The Universal Standard." Even Token-Ring networks are limited in size based on the physical topology of the network. Switches, as you learned in the preceding chapter, enable you to greatly expand the number of computers you can place on a LAN, and you can use high-speed communication links between switches to greatly expand the distance of a LAN.

However, using switches to create a huge LAN solves only the problem of the broadcast domain and the number of devices that can be attached to the network. In a modern networking environment, there are other factors to consider, such as security, configuration, and management. Perhaps you don't want all your computers connected to the same LAN, though they may be in close proximity to the same LAN switch. The more computers you have on a single LAN, the greater the odds are that a security breach will occur—giving an intruder access to other computers on the LAN.

Virtual LANs, which can be created using switches, enable you to *separate* the *physical topology* from the *logical topology*. That is, although you might have all your computers interconnected using a switch or several switches, appropriately configured switches make it possible to configure individual virtual LANs that are independent of the physical topology. Legacy hubs allow all computers on the LAN to see every network frame that is transmitted by every other computer in the same broadcast domain. Switches make connections only between the transmitting computer and the switch port that will get the network frame to its eventual destination. By limiting the network frame to just the sending and receiving stations, and the switches that stand between them, you take a big step toward preventing eavesdropping on the LAN.

Note

If you have not yet read the preceding chapter, "Network Switches," you should do so before attempting to understand the concepts covered in this chapter. For those readers who have been working in the networking industry for a long time, be aware that switches have replaced hubs in every LAN except for the oldest because switches provide a dramatic increase in performance versus cost. If you don't understand how a switch works, you will probably not get a lot of useful information out of this chapter.

Switching Based on Network Frames

It should be obvious that, using various techniques, it is possible to physically connect a large number of computers using switches, and then use software to program the switches to limit which computers can transmit frames to other computers. In other words, you can define LANs using software inside the switch, instead of creating LANs based on the actual physical cabling (see Figure 9.2). This single switch connects several computers, printers, and a server. However, the switch separates these devices into three separate virtual LANs.

Of course, this is a very simplistic example. If you have such a small number of computers, one of the only reasons you would want to create virtual LANs would be for security purposes. This example is meant to show that you can connect multiple network devices (computers, printers, print servers, file servers, routers, and so on) to the same switch, or a set of switches, and then use software that comes with the switch(es) to assign each computer to a separate *virtual LAN*. Computers on the same virtual LAN can communicate with each other just as if they were joined by a single switch. However, just because all these networked devices are connected to the same switch doesn't mean that they can send or receive data with devices that are configured on a different virtual LAN. In essence, it appears that you are partitioning the ports on the switch as though they were separate switches. That doesn't have to be the case, but it was the first step in creating VLAN switches.

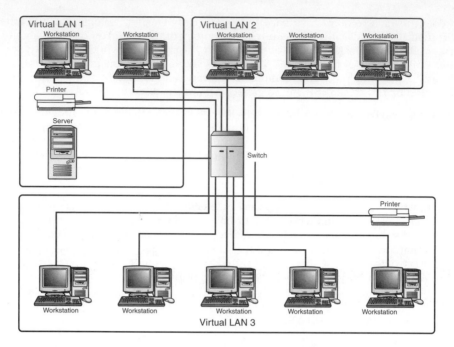

Figure 9.2   Virtual LANs can be created so that separate LANs exist on the same switch.

Note

In this chapter it is easy to state that you can create several VLANs using a single switch. From a practical standpoint, however, a single switch is not a limiting factor. Indeed, it is usually the case that multiple switches are installed in a computer rack, and the management software that controls the switches enables you to assign ports from different switches to a VLAN. It is also possible for a switch port to be a member of more than one VLAN.

Port-Based VLANs

The earliest switches that were used to create VLANs made assignments based on the switch's ports. That is, the administrator could simply designate what VLAN each port would be a member of. This is a fast way to switch frames in a VLAN because no processing needs to be done on the frame itself. Instead, the switch merely outputs the frame on all ports that are in the same VLAN as the incoming port. To place a particular workstation or another network device into a VLAN, you simply have to connect it to a port that is a member of that particular VLAN.

For the most part, the ports are configurable through software, so you can assign an identifier to each port to tell it which VLAN it is a member of. Using software management tools to configure a VLAN in this way means that when a user is moved to another VLAN but his physical location doesn't change, you don't have to make any cabling changes or plug the user into a different port. You just use the management software that comes with the switch to reassign the port to the new VLAN.

Port-based VLANs are the easiest type of VLAN to implement because the switch must do less work. The switch doesn't have to look up an IP address, a hardware address, or anything else to make a forwarding decision. It just looks up the port on which the frame arrives and outputs it on all other ports configured for that particular VLAN. This can be a security issue, though, if you do not physically secure connections to the switch. If the switch is not locked away securely, it's quite possible for someone to plug in a computer to a port and become a member of that VLAN. Of course, you'd probably configure the ports so that any unused ports are not part of *any* VLAN. However, what's to prevent some informed intruder, such as an unhappy employee, from unplugging one cable and plugging in another? Keep important network devices such as switches and routers locked away!

Implicit and Explicit Tagging

In more modern VLAN switches, the individual network devices or ports are not used to define the VLAN; the network frames—each handled on a case-by-case basis that the switch receives—are used. A modern VLAN, then, is based on frames, not on the computers that generate them or those to which they are addressed, or the ports to which either is attached.

In VLAN terminology, the term *tagging* is used to indicate what data is used to associate a frame with a particular VLAN. There are two kinds of tagging: implicit and explicit.

Implicit Tagging

Implicit tagging means that the decision is based on data that is already present in the existing frame format, such as an Ethernet frame. The data is already there, and nothing has been added; so the switch simply must examine data in the frame header and implicitly decide to which VLAN it belongs. When this type of tagging is used, no additional data needs to be added to the frame by the sending computer, so the devices on the network are considered to be VLAN-unaware. That is, they operate just as they normally would and have no idea that they are on one or another VLAN. You might as well just call this "nontagging," but the writers of the specifications have chosen to call this implicit tagging.

When implicit tagging is used, the frame data that typically is used to create VLAN association rules is generally one of the following:

- **Protocol**—The network protocol, such as IP or AppleTalk.
- **Data Link Source Address**—The hardware address of the source of the frame. Remember that hardware addresses, also known as MAC addresses, are unique addresses burned into the card at the factory when the card is manufactured. They provide a flat address space, but they should be unique from any other such address through the world.
- **Upper-level protocol identifiers**—In addition to a protocol type, such as IP, a subnet address identifier may be used to identify which VLAN a frame is associated with.

Another method that can be used for implicit tagging involves upper-level applications. However, because this can create literally hundreds of rules, it often is not used except in large WANs. This technology is called "explicit tagging."

Explicit Tagging

Explicit tagging refers to actually attaching an extra few bits of data to a network frame to specify its VLAN association. For this method to work, however, the sending station must be aware that VLANs exist. The switch itself also must understand explicit tagging and know where in the frame to look for the tagging data. For example, in a VLAN-aware network adapter, it is common to place a few bytes after the source address in the Ethernet frame. These additional bytes provide the explicit VLAN tag that the switch can examine to determine which VLAN the frame belongs to. Instead of having to apply a set of rules, the VLAN-aware switch can simply examine this value and quickly switch the frame to the correct output port. Because the tag is placed inside the Ethernet frame after the source and destination address, however, a switch that is not VLAN-aware (that is, does not use explicit tagging) cannot make decisions based on protocol type or other fields. This is because additional fields will be offset a number of bytes, depending on the length of the explicit tag. This can lead to non-aware switches or computers misinterpreting the tagging data and producing unpredictable behavior.

The solution to this problem is to use "edge switches" that receive explicitly tagged frames from VLAN-aware devices and remove the tags when they forward the frame to a port connected to another switch or device that is not equipped to handle explicitly tagged frames.

Explicit tagging does have some advantages over implicit tagging, however. Because the switch only has to look at the tag, and it's always in the same place (for a given protocol), it's easy to implement in hardware a quick switching fabric that can handle a large number of frames in a short period. Implicit tagging must check the rule set to determine what VLAN a frame belongs to, and this can involve more processing time. Although the amount of time might be just a few milliseconds, which seems like a short time to you or me, that's a lot of time when you're switching hundreds of thousands of packets in a short period. As you'll find out in the next chapter, a similar situation occurs with routers. A switch forwards a network frame quicker than many routers because the router must spend time digging into the frame to find the protocol address, and then perform a lookup in a routing table to determine how to deal with the frame and recalculate the frame check sequence (FCS).

On the downside, when a switch that uses explicit tagging has to forward a frame to a switch or device that does not, it must remove the tag. When this happens, it's necessary to recalculate the FCS value because some of the frame bits have been removed. Another drawback is that attaching an explicit tag to a large frame can cause the frame to exceed the maximum size allowed by the transport protocol, and the frame will be dropped.

MAC Address VLANs

If you have a lot of mobile users, creating a VLAN that bases its membership on a list of MAC addresses can be a good idea. Because these addresses are unique, when you plug into any switch port, a quick lookup is all that's necessary for the switch to determine which VLAN your computer's MAC address belongs to. And because MAC addresses are typically the way traditional switches work, there's not much more circuitry or software that has to be tweaked to create this kind of VLAN-capable switch. The downside is that the administrator must manually assign each hardware address to the correct VLAN in the first place. However, that's not a difficult chore when you are simply adding a few new computers to a VLAN. When implementing a set of VLANs that involve hundreds or thousands of computers, you can get tired fingers!

If you decide to use this type of switch, there is one thing you should check before purchasing the switch. What happens when a computer is connected to a port and the computer's address is not a member of any of your configured VLANs? Some switch manufacturers will implement a mechanism that looks into the frame further and then forwards the frame based on a higher-level protocol address. This allows anyone to connect to your switch, provided that you've not taken the necessary physical security precautions and locked your switching equipment away in a secure computer room. Check to be sure that frames which have no VLAN mapping for a MAC address are dropped before using this type of switch.

Protocol Rule-Based VLANs

In a virtual LAN, a switch's decision as to whether to output a frame on a particular port can be based on a set of *association rules* that are based on the network protocols used on the network. Each frame received on a switch port is examined and, based on a set of rules, is output on one or more other ports. The set of rules can be based on many things, such as the IP subnet addresses. However, it's quite possible to create VLANs that subdivide even a subnet.

▶▶ For more information about IP subnets and how they can be used to segment the IP address space into smaller units, see Chapter 25, "Overview of the TCP/IP Protocol Suite."

Other protocol-based VLANs can be created so that AppleTalk- or NetWare-based (IPX/SPX) networks all can exist on the same set of switches—each on its own virtual LAN. In this kind of protocol-based VLAN switch, you usually can further subdivide each major protocol into smaller VLANs based on identifiers used in the protocol headers.

One factor to consider about protocol-based VLANs is that if the computer is running multiple protocol stacks (such as TCP/IP and IPX/SPX), the switch can be configured to allow the device to participate in separate VLANs based on these protocols. Because this kind of switch enables you to join diverse kinds of networks, it still is quite popular, and you'll find that it is possible to buy this type of switch inexpensively. Decision trees that are used to map different protocols into separate VLANs have been implemented in hardware, which is faster than having to use software and a processor to examine frames, extract the protocol information, and then make the forwarding decisions.

For the standard IP-based network, using a switch that bases VLANs on IP subnets has another advantage. If you don't choose to divide the subnet itself into further VLANs, the switch can, after you've associated an IP address with the LAN adapter card, extract the MAC address from the frame, and from then on use the hardware MAC address to make decisions. Thus, when you move a computer from one location to another on the switch (or a series of interconnected cooperating switches), you won't have to change the IP address of the computer. The new port simply looks at the IP subnet address and creates an entry in its table for the MAC address, and it's basically plug-and-play (or I guess that should be "plug-and-work"!).

Using Explicit Tagging on the Network Backbone

It should be obvious by now that most of the network adapter cards that exist in the world today were not created with explicit tagging in mind. Switches that use explicit tagging are used for the most part in large WANs, such as the Internet. However, LAN switches have evolved to the point that for most small LANs, a VLAN-unaware switch will serve just fine in a small network of a few hundred computers.

However, when you connect a large number of these VLAN-unaware LANs to the network backbone in a larger network, as in a college campus or a large business, the core switches that connect these LANs must handle a much larger amount of network traffic. Thus, it's typical to use explicit tagging for large, high-capacity network switches than it is in smaller LAN environments (see Figure 9.3).

Here, the core switches that use explicit tagging are able to forward packets they receive within their switched network that understands the tags applied by the edge switches. The edge switches, however, add tags to frames they receive from the VLAN-unaware workstations, based on implicit tagging rules the administrator has set up. They remove the tags when they output frames to the individual workstations that are VLAN-unaware. Of course, these edge switches could just as easily have other switches attached to them, cascaded until you reach the end workstation or other network device. In this illustration, separate workstations are used to simplify the example. The edge switches could be connected to other switches that further subdivide the network and could use implicit tagging to forward the frames they receive from the edge switches.

▶▶ A technique known as Multi-Protocol Label Switching (MPLS) uses a similar tagging technique and is commonly used in the core routers (or I guess you can now call them switches) that form the heart of the Internet. You can read more about MPLS in Chapter 37, "Routing Protocols."

Within the core of switches that do understand tagging, switching is done at a fast pace. Although some people still debate the use of MPLS, it is now used as a major protocol in the Internet core switches, due to the lack of any other *standard* protocol that might be used to replace it.

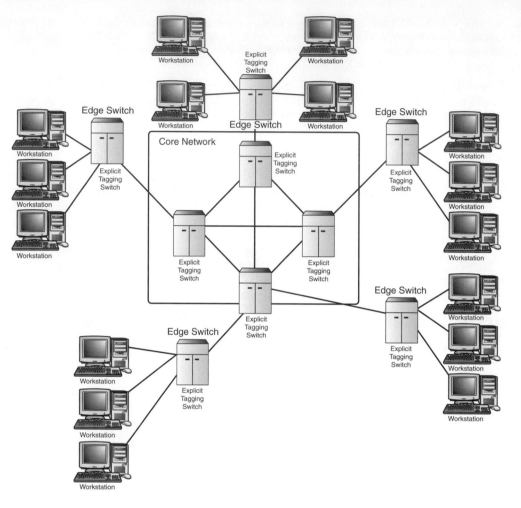

Figure 9.3 Explicit tagging can be employed in the network backbone to connect LANs that are not capable of using explicit tagging.

Switch Standards—The IEEE Standards

There currently are two standards on which many VLANs are based. The first is called IEEE 802.1D, and the second is called IEEE 802.1Q. For the most part, the newer standard builds on and extends the IEEE 802.1D standard. The basic difference is that the IEEE802.1D standard defines switches that are VLAN-unaware, whereas the newer IEEE 802.1Q standard provides for VLAN-aware switches.

The actual details of these standards are beyond the scope of this book, much less this chapter. However, there are a few details that should be covered so that you'll be more VLAN-aware when you make purchasing decisions:

■ IEEE 802.1Q includes backward compatibility with switches that were based on the IEEE802.1D standard.

- The default behavior of a switch that is IEEE 802.1Q compliant—*in the absence of any association rules*—is to function as though VLANs were based on ports. This does not mean that IEEE 802.1Q provides for simply port-based VLANs. It just means that it is the default if the vendor doesn't implement any other techniques for using a set of rules to create VLANs.

- The IEEE 802.1Q standard talks about how association rules should be processed, but it does not require that any particular kind of rule be implemented on a switch. It's more a guideline to be used if a vendor decides to use one or more rule-based mechanisms for creating VLANs.

- The IEEE 802.1Q standard applies only to switches, not to the creation of network adapter cards that are VLAN-aware. That means if you do purchase adapter cards that support explicit tagging, you should be sure that it's the same method used by your switch.

The IEEE 802.1Q standard adds a filtering database that can be used to map devices to certain ports, and it describes algorithms that can be used with this filtering database to determine which VLAN a frame is a member of. The earlier standard provided for a filtering database, but the newer standard expands on its functionality. Perhaps more important to an administrator in a large network, the standard defines a MIB (management information database) that can be used to manage switches.

▶▶ For more information about SNMP, RMON, and the MIBs they use, see Chapter 53, "Network Testing and Analysis Tools."

For explicit tagging, the IEEE 802.1Q standard defines standard tag formats so that you don't have to worry about different tagging schemes used by proprietary solutions implemented in earlier switches by different vendors.

This standard also defines a priority mechanism, which is not really necessary for VLAN operation but was added because some protocols, such as Ethernet, don't have a mechanism for this. Although this is not specifically related to the concept of a VLAN, it was decided during the standards process to include a priority mechanism simply to avoid having to go back later and create another standard for prioritizing Ethernet frames. Strange, but true.

Another important concept is that the newer standard sets forth the methods used when a switch is used to connect dissimilar network types—such as Ethernet and Token-Ring (and FDDI, though that technology is slowly becoming a dinosaur in today's market). This detail might not seem important, but there are many differences in the frame types used by these different network protocols (such as the big- or little-endian method of encoding bits—in other words, which bit that is transmitted for a byte is the most significant, and which is the least significant?). The newer standard defines the mechanisms for encapsulating dissimilar frames types within the frame type used on the network. For example, it tells which method to use for sending Token-Ring frames through an Ethernet network, and vice versa. Although it seems that Token-Ring has seen its better days, there are legacy systems out there that still use it. Using a switch that is IEEE 802.1Q compliant enables you to connect Token-Ring networks across a link that supports a faster technology, such as Gigabit Ethernet.

The final topic I'll touch on is the fact that IEEE 802.1Q also sets forth a protocol (called GVRP) that can be used by switches to exchange information about VLAN membership. This is perhaps one of its more important concepts. This means that you won't have to configure each switch in the network when VLAN membership is changed.

The IEEE standards cover a lot more territory than I can go into in this chapter. There are entire books on this subject, and if you are seriously considering implementing VLANs in a large network, you should pursue further reading, specifically purchasing the standards from the IEEE and using them to evaluate products to determine whether they meet the standards. However, for most networks today, as long as you use switches from the same manufacturer or from those who state that their products will interoperate with other vendors, you should not encounter many difficulties in setting up VLANs on your network.

What Kind of Switch Should You Buy?

Now that we've covered the basic idea of creating VLANs, let's look at some of the ways this is done. There are standards, and then there are proprietary solutions. When upgrading a network, you should consider several questions when it comes to implementing VLANs in your network:

■ Does the switch support VLANs? Small switches you buy at the local computer store for home or small office don't. Medium to high-end switches used in a large network usually do.

■ What is the port density of the switch? In a small computer room you might not have space for a large number of interconnected switches. Instead, switches with a larger number of ports can be a better choice.

■ If you are using a chassis switch, how many cards can you plug into the chassis? Can you start out with just a few cards for your current needs, and then add port cards as your network expands?

■ Do ports on the switch have LED indicator lights you can use to check for link connectivity and use, or do you have to rely on software to track down bad or misconfigured ports?

■ Does the switch limit broadcast traffic to specific VLANs, or does it broadcast this traffic to all the virtual LANs on the switch? This might be desirable, or it might not, depending on your circumstances.

■ Does the switch support multiple network speeds (that is, 10/100Mbps or even Gigabit Ethernet speeds for high-end servers)? Does the switch support high-speed connections to other switches and routers?

■ Although TCP/IP has for all practical purposes overtaken other LAN protocols, such as AppleTalk and IPX/SPX, as the network protocol of choice, does the switch support multiple protocols? If you have a multiprotocol environment, will the switch support creation of VLANs to separate these distinct protocols into separate virtual LANs?

■ Is your equipment purchase going to be used for a short period (say, a year or two) or is it going to be used longer? If you're in this for the long haul and won't be able to replace expensive VLAN switches for a while, choose a vendor that's known for providing an easy upgrade path (such as a firmware or software upgrade for the switch), or choose one that adheres to a known standard so that you can simply add switches as your capacity needs grow.

■ What management software is available for the switch? If you want to move a user from one VLAN to another, do you have to physically unplug the user from one switch port and reconnect him to another port? Or, as is more often the case, can you simply use the switch management software to reconfigure that user's port to become a member of another VLAN?

Although not as important as the considerations in the preceding list, some VLAN-aware switches enable you to associate a port with more than one VLAN. For example, in Figure 9.2 we created three distinct VLANs. However, VLAN 1 has a server and a printer as well as workstations configured within its boundaries. In some situations, it might be desirable for a server to be able to participate in more than one VLAN. In that case, you want to be able to specify that the switch port to which the server is connected be part of more than one VLAN. This would not give other computers in the separate VLANs access to other VLANs, but instead it would work in reverse, allowing members of different VLANs to establish sessions with a server, or perhaps a printer or another networked device, that is a member of more than one VLAN.

Routers

10

SOME OF THE MAIN TOPICS IN THIS CHAPTER ARE

CHAPTER 10

Routers are perhaps one of the most misunderstood devices found in a network. After you create a LAN using simple devices such as switches—which require little or no configuration—managing a router can be very intimidating. Some of the reasons for this include the following:

- Most people do not understand the difference between a connectivity device, such as a switch, and a router. They both can be used to connect computers to a LAN, right?

- Unless you use sophisticated network console management software, the management and configuration interface for most routers often seems to be very cryptic.

- Like computers, routers have an "operating system" that controls how they function. There is no universal operating system that can be learned for use with routers from different vendors.

- Routers come in all sizes and shapes. You can find a small, inexpensive router to connect a small office LAN to a broadband connection (such as DSL or a cable modem). Still larger standalone and rack-mounted units can be used for Enterprise networks. At the high end of this market are powerful machines used as Internet core routers.

In this chapter you will learn about the functions performed by routers—from those at the low end of the scale to the top of the line. In addition, this chapter introduces some of the topics that enable routers to be used in a firewall.

▶▶   Firewalls are discussed in more detail in Chapter 49, "Firewalls."

What Routers Do

Bridges and repeaters can be used to add to the number of computers and extend the distance covered by an older Ethernet or Token-Ring LAN. Bridges, intelligent hubs, and most switches operate at level 2 in the OSI network model, making decisions by hardwired MAC addresses of the installed network card for each system on the LAN. Remember that the hardware addressing scheme produces a flat address space. If you want to create a switch that communicates easily with all the computers hooked up to the Internet, it would need to store millions upon millions of these unorganized addresses in memory—an impossible task indeed.

Note

Although it is convenient to think of switches, routers, and hubs as separate devices, in reality you often find network devices that perform multiple functions. For example, although routers generally are used to connect different LAN segments or networks, you also will find routers that contain built-in hubs, as well as support for bridging and other tasks. In this chapter, the focus is on routing. Don't be surprised if the equipment you purchase offers other capabilities.

Also, older Ethernet bridges, hubs, and repeaters are now considered to be legacy equipment. You can read about these devices in the chapter "Bridges, Repeaters, and Hubs," located on the **upgradingandrepairingpcs.com** Web site.

Routers operate one step farther up the OSI model at the third layer, the Network layer. The Network layer offers a logical address space, which makes it easier to organize networks and route traffic between networks. This overcomes the flat address space provided by lower-level devices that use Media Access Control (MAC) addresses. Each router contains two or more network interfaces. One or more of these interfaces can be used to connect the router to a wide area network, whereas other interfaces can be used to connect to local network segments. Routers receive input from one network interface, and then make routing decisions based on which interface can best get the packet to its eventual destination. The port on which the packet is retransmitted can lead to another router or another LAN segment directly connected to the router.

   Switches are covered in Chapter 8, "Network Switches," and in Chapter 9, "Virtual LANs."

▶▶ If you're interested, the OSI network reference model is covered in Appendix A, "Overview of the OSI Seven-Layer Networking Reference Model."

Hierarchical Network Organization

The important difference between MAC addresses and logical network addresses (such as TCP/IP and IPX/SPX) is that the logical network addresses allow for the organization of a collection of networks into a hierarchy. This logical distribution of network addresses can be modeled after the logical organization of your business, as in a collection of departmental LANs based on an organizational chart. Or it can represent a geographical model of a business, with individual LANs located in branch offices. Or, as is usually the case, it can be a combination of both of these.

The router is the device that can connect all these different LAN segments so that larger networks can be created that go beyond the limits imposed by LAN topology standards, such as Ethernet and Token-Ring. The Internet is the prime example of a large collection of separate networks, all managed in a decentralized manner, but organized in a logical hierarchical address space. Routers connect these many thousands of networks and make decisions on how best to deliver network information from one client to another on a different network, all based on constantly changing, constantly updating routing information. They do this by storing information about how to deliver packets to different networks on the Internet.

A routing table keeps track of these routes, which can include multiple routing hops on the way to the eventual destination. A router does not always know the entire route that a packet will take to get to its destination. If the destination is on another LAN segment attached to the router, the router might not know the immediate network destination. If this is the case, the router uses a catch-all "default gateway" to send the packet to. On the Internet, a packet usually passes through many routers to reach its destination. In this case, a router simply keeps in its routing table the "next hop" that the packet needs to be sent to in order to reach its destination. Each router on the way to the destination knows the next hop in the path, or uses its default gateway entry in the routing table.

Routers are not limited to using the TCP/IP protocols, though perhaps most of the routers in the world today—on the Internet—are used for IP routing. Most routers can be configured to route many other protocols, such as IPX/SPX and AppleTalk, in addition to TCP/IP, and do it all at once.

Note

Although most of us tend to think of routers as just another kind of network device, computers—from PCs all the way up to mainframes—also can perform routing functions. All that is needed is for the computer to be equipped with more than one network adapter, connections to more than one network, and routing functionality in the protocol stack. For example, you can set up Windows 2000/2003 or Unix/Linux systems to perform routing for your network.

Both Unix and Linux systems can be outfitted with multiple network adapters and configured to route network traffic. Many network administrators use Linux systems as part of a firewall. A lot of existing software, both free and commercial, can be used on these systems for this purpose.

Providing Security

When you think about how a router functions—it examines the header information of the network protocol portion of a packet so that it can make routing decisions—it also should become obvious that it is at the router that you can create a "chokepoint" for your network. That is, you can use router configuration rules to allow or deny network traffic based on information found in the network packet header. For example, when using a router as a first-defense mechanism in a firewall, you can enable or disable communication over specific TCP or UDP ports, to deny access to network traffic for selected applications. For example, this is how you could prevent someone from using Telnet to log in to a computer on your network—by blocking Telnet communications (port 23) at the router. You can also block certain network addresses from passing data through a router into your network (and vice versa). This is a very powerful capability used as part of a firewall.

A firewall, though, is usually composed of more than just a simple router, and includes things such as stateful-inspection techniques and application proxies. However, routers were the first devices used to create a "firewall" when it became obvious that the ever-expanding Internet no longer was the safe, academic environment it once was.

▶▶ You can learn more about routers and how they function in a firewall environment in Chapter 49, "Firewalls." Chapter 25, "Overview of the TCP/IP Protocol Suite," covers TCP and UDP ports.

Routers also provide logging facilities. You can use this data when trying to determine whether your network has been infiltrated. Although most serious hackers today are more sophisticated and would spoof IP addresses in a packet, newcomers who simply download the many free hacker utilities off the Internet can be found easily by checking log files on a router. To provide extra safety, some routers allow you to send log file information to the syslog daemon on the Unix/Linux host so that if the router itself is compromised, the log file data will still be available.

The Difference Between Routable Protocols and Routing Protocols

So far we've discussed routers and what they do, but we have not discussed the protocols involved. There are basic kinds of protocols that you need to understand when it comes to routers: *routable* protocols and *routing* protocols. For a protocol to be routable, it must make some provision for identifying a network as well as the host that's on a network. If a router had to keep track of every host on the Internet, it would be impossible to build a machine large enough to store all the routing table information. Instead, routable protocols specify network addresses as well as addresses of computers on those networks. Thus, routers only need to store a much smaller routing table that tells them where to forward packets based on the network address. After the packet reaches its destination network, it is delivered to the intended host using the host portion of the address field. TCP/IP (discussed in Chapter 25), for example, sets aside a portion of the IP address to use as a network ID. Other routable protocols include NetWare's IPX/SPX, DECnet, and AppleTalk. Each of these protocols can be used to create diverse network segments that can be tied together using a router. Many routers also support multiprotocol stacks and can route more than just TCP/IP. Examples of nonroutable protocols include Digital's (now HP) Local Area Transport (LAT) and NetBIOS (although NetBIOS over TCP/IP, or NBT, can overcome this limitation).

A *routing protocol*, on the other hand, is a protocol that routers use to communicate routing information among themselves. These protocols involve exchanging information about new routes, or old routes that no longer work, as well as *metrics* that describe the route (that is, the speed and hop count of the route). *Routes* are the path that a packet takes on its journey to its final network destination. At the local network, the host portion of the protocol address will be used to determine which computer on the local network the packet is destined for.

Routing protocols exchange information between routers so that routers gradually build up a view of the networks that can be reached. This information is dynamic because systems and routers can always experience downtime. When this happens, routers exchange information and, if a new route exists that can still reach the destination, the router may change its routing entries. When multiple routes to a destination exist, depending on the protocol, certain metrics (such as the number of hops between the source and destination) are used to determine what route a packet should take.

Note

Many kinds of routing protocols are in use today, each of which has its merits and shortcomings. Some are used for small internetworks, whereas others function on the Internet core routers. The most popular of these routing protocols are discussed in further detail in Chapter 37, "Routing Protocols."

When Do You Need to Use a Router?

Not every network needs a router. If you operate a small-office LAN, a simple switch-based LAN can provide all the file and print sharing your business needs within the LAN. However, if you have remote locations, or *if you connect to the Internet*, then you need a router because of the security features it can provide. One of these is called Network Address Translation (NAT). NAT allows you to use one or more IP addresses that are valid on the Internet, while using a reserved address space for the computers on the LAN. Although this might not seem important at first glance, keep in mind that it helps prevent computers outside your LAN from learning the addresses of computers inside your LAN. NAT is not the only technology used in a firewall, but it is a good start. For a small office, home office (SOHO) network, a router that performs NAT is a necessity when using a cable modem or DSL to connect to the Internet. As an added bonus, most SOHO routers that perform NAT also act as a DHCP server, preventing the requirement to configure another system on your network to run the DHCP service. Other features that NAT provides include expanding the address space so that you do not have to pay for additional IP addresses that are valid for use on the Internet. The reserved address space used inside the network is all yours to use.

There are several other situations in which a router might be needed:

- The size of your local LAN has grown rapidly and you are having problems with network congestion. You can divide your network into multiple subnets and connect them using a router. With this method, traffic local to a subnet doesn't have to pass through the router and use up bandwidth on other subnets.

- The size of your local LAN has grown rapidly and you would like to delegate authority for groups of users to individual departments, each on its own separate network segment.

- You want to connect to branch offices or other wide area networks, such as the Internet.

- You want to be able to filter the network traffic that passes between one LAN and the next, or between your network and the Internet. This use of a router generally is found as part of a firewall solution.

▶▶ For more information about NAT, as well as detailed information on using packet filtering techniques with a router as part of a firewall, see Chapter 49.

Growing LAN Sizes

As a business in today's market grows, so do the computing requirements. A company starting out with only a few computers, or even a few hundred, can easily get by using a LAN constructed with switches or older hubs. However, there comes a point when you reach the limits of either the traffic capacity of your LAN or the topological restrictions imposed by the type of LAN you create. When this happens, you can segment the network, using a router, thus preventing congestion or topology problems.

The IP address space provides a hierarchical addressing structure. Basically, there are different classes of IP addresses; for each type a certain number of bits are set aside to record a network address, and the remaining bits are used to specify the host on that network. By using the hierarchical nature of IP addressing, you can configure your IP subnets using routers, in a manner that reflects your business organization.

▶▶   For more information about the different address classes and other techniques, such as Classless Interdomain Routing (CIDR), see Chapter 25.

Using TCP/IP, each local network generally makes up both a physical and a logical subnet. The physical subnet consists of all the devices attached to the same broadcast domain, which includes all devices attached to the same hub and all hubs connected to that hub, if you are still using this older technology. Unless you've configured Virtual LANs (VLANs), the same goes for most switches, although the broadcast domain concept is limited when using a switch. For all nodes that exist on a particular physical subnet, it is a good idea to assign IP addresses that fall into the same network address or subnetwork address. Again, Chapter 25 explains how the network portion and subnet portion of the IP address work. The thing to remember here is that each separate physical subnet generally uses a separate IP network or subnetwork ID to identify all computers on that LAN segment. A separate host ID is used for each computer on each subnet.

VLANs allow you to configure the subnet that a port belongs to on a port-by-port basis. This is covered in the preceding chapter, "Virtual LANs."

In this situation, each computer on each segment is a peer to all other computers on the same segment. Communications take place on the local segments at the Ethernet frame level using hardware (MAC) addresses. In Figure 10.1, for example, workstation A and workstation B can send data frames back and forth, and the traffic they generate between them never passes through the router. The local hardware addresses are resolved using ARP (see Chapter 25 for more about ARP), and both nodes can talk directly to each other using Ethernet frames.

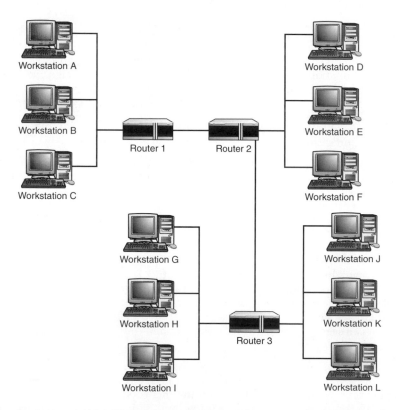

Figure 10.1   Routers are used to link different network segments to create a larger internetwork.

If workstation A needs to exchange data with workstation D or E, network traffic travels between the different subnets through routers 1 and 2. To carry the concept a step further, workstation A would have to send a data packet through three routers to exchange data with workstations G through L. As you can see, a router works much like a bridge in that it segregates traffic and passes it on to other segments only when the destination address of the packet isn't on the local segment. However, bridges work at layer 2 of the OSI model and use hardware MAC addresses. Routers switch traffic based on layer 3 addresses, such as IP.

A router is needed only when a packet needs to travel to a different logical IP subnet or network. Routers come in all sizes and combinations. Some have serial-line ports, Ethernet ports, twisted pair, and fiber-optic ports. If you have reached the limit on your LAN and don't want to add more workstations, consider installing a new LAN segment and connecting both your old and new LANs using a router.

Tip

Besides making it easy to organize your network layout by matching IP network and subnet addresses to your business organizational chart, you also can organize your Domain Name System (DNS) names to reflect the business organization. Remember that the host and domain names you assign to a particular network device or computer can, but do not have to, relate directly to the underlying IP address. Instead, these are assigned by the network administrator (or by using DHCP with certain scopes of addresses reserved for selected subnets). Thus, it is possible to use both IP addressing and DNS names to add some organization to the madness that typically makes up a large network. For more about using DNS and how fully qualified domain names are translated to IP and other network addresses, see Chapter 30, "Network Name Resolution."

Using this method, each subnet has its own unique subnet portion of the IP address space. The router is like all other devices on a traditional Ethernet network—it can see all traffic on the segments attached to it. In modern networks in which switches are used, each computer is configured to use a router (the default gateway) when it needs to send a packet to a network that is not on the same subnet. The router, however, has connections to more than one network segment and can transfer packets of information from one segment to another, based on their network address.

Figure 10.1 showed only a simplistic view of how routers can connect different network segments. In practice, you'll most likely have switches or hubs separating your client computers and servers from the hub. Figure 10.2 shows this view. The router is used to connect several LAN segments, each of which may have a switch (with attached workstations) or a powerful server. Additionally, a WAN port on the router is used to connect to the wide area network, such as the Internet.

As mentioned before, when you configure a client computer to use TCP/IP, you generally specify a *default gateway* (or this value can be supplied by DHCP when the client boots). The default gateway is the address of the router that attaches the local subnet to the larger network structure. Thus, when a client computer wants to send a packet, or series of packets, to a computer that is on a different logical IP subnet, it sends the packets instead to the default gateway—the router. The client computer can tell from its own address what subnet it is connected to. The client software knows to direct a packet to the default gateway when the network or subnet address of the packet differs from the sender's own network address.

A router makes decisions on where next to send the packet based on routing tables. Routing tables can be configured manually (static routing) by the network administrator, or they can be configured dynamically using various routing protocols. Simple routing protocols are useful for small internetworks, and complicated routing protocols are used by Internet core and border routers. However, the principle of routing is basically the same for all these protocols. Routers make decisions based on the

Network Access layer of the OSI model using logical IP addresses. Your local area network uses the ARP protocol to determine the actual hardware address (a flat address space) for communications within the local LAN segment.

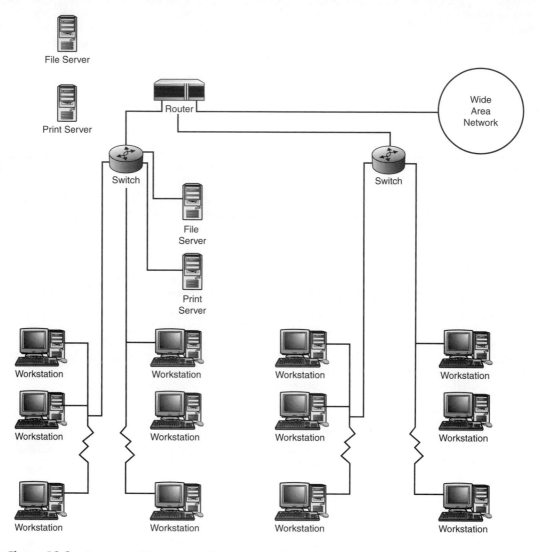

Figure 10.2 In a typical large network, switches or hubs separate individual workstations from the wide-area router connection.

When a client computer sends a packet to the default gateway router, it uses the source address in the frame header for the address of the router, even though that is not the eventual destination of the frame. The router is just the next hop for the frame. When the router notices a frame on a port that is addressed to it, it unpacks the frame to expose the IP header portion. Using the IP address, the router then decides on the next hop for the packet and reconstructs a frame to transmit the packet to the next hop. This might be another router or a host on another segment attached to the router. As you can see, routers actually change the packet (or frame) as it travels through an internetwork. For example, the Ethernet frame destination address is changed to indicate the next hop for the frame. Inside the IP header, the router changes the TTL (Time to Live) value. When this value reaches zero, the packet has traveled the maximum hops allowed and a router discards it. Because a router must change fields in the IP header, as well as the Ethernet frame header information, it also must recalculate any error-checking fields for these headers.

At each hop, a router also can be configured with a set of rules that filters out the packet. This capability provides for some security for your network, because you can prevent certain IP addresses or services from passing between your network and the Internet.

One very important concept to grasp is that routers only get a packet delivered to the router port that connects to the network that contains the destination of the packet. After the router determines that the packet should be output through a certain port, the MAC addresses of the networked computers and other devices come into play. That is, the IP address gets the data to the destination network. After the data has arrived, it is the MAC address that is used for the final leg of the journey.

On the local subnet the router sends out an ARP frame that contains the IP address of the packet. When a computer recognizes its IP address, it sends a frame back to the router telling the router what its MAC address is. From then on, the router can use the computer's MAC address to send additional packets. Routers keep a cache in memory of MAC addresses for a short period so that a continuous stream of data can be delivered after the router knows the MAC address of a computer on the local network.

Delegating Responsibility for Local Area Networks

Because routers can be used to separate one group of users from another, it makes delegation of administration at the local level much easier. Responsibility implies security. Routers can be programmed using a technique called Access Control Lists (ACLs), which are nothing more than rules that specify the following:

- What direction packets can travel—inbound to the LAN or outbound to another LAN
- Which IP addresses, both network and host addresses, can pass through the router (normally addresses can also be specified as wildcards)
- Which TCP or UDP ports can be allowed to pass through the router

This packet filtering capability lets a local administrator, who understands the router control, restrict access to the local LAN. For security reasons, this can be very important. Most people think of a firewall as a device that sits at the edge of a network and makes the connection to the Internet. That is only one use of a firewall.

A second use is to isolate departments within a particular network. For example, it's probably a good idea to isolate the accounting department from other sections of your company. You don't want employees probing around trying to break into your payroll records! With a router, you can configure rules that allow only selected users on other LANs (such as the one that services the executive suite) to pass through your router, while keeping others out.

By using controls within your network as well as at the edge, you also can help prevent the spread of any attack or infiltration that does occur.

Another important feature that many routers provide is logging. You usually can log both successes and failures to keep track of how your network is being used. If you find a particular workstation trying to Telnet or FTP to a prohibited LAN, you can use this evidence to discipline the employee. Many routers allow you to designate another system as the location for logging files. Typically, this is done using the Unix `syslog` daemon. This type of feature improves on security. If the router itself is compromised, you will have a record of the events leading up to it. If you regularly review your log files, you can take preventive measures if you suspect that suspicious activity is occurring.

Connecting Branch Offices

Many companies have offices in multiple locations. In the early days of computing, when 300 baud modems were the norm, sending data between two sites usually consisted of dial-up access. Today, you can lease lines between central headquarters and multiple branch offices. Additionally, other long-haul services, such as those provided by Frame Relay and Asynchronous Transfer Mode (ATM), can be used to enable you to connect securely to remote branch offices.

▶▶ For more information about using Frame Relay or ATM, as well as other high-speed network connections, see Chapter 16, "Dedicated Connections."

Routers come in all sizes and offer various features. You can use a router to connect branch offices easily. All you need to do is to provide a separate network ID—or more likely subnet ID—for each location and choose an appropriately sized router for each location. Some routers even allow you to use a dial-up line for a remote connection that is used only infrequently. This situation is ideal when all you need to do is poll remote computers after-hours to get sales totals and other information of that sort. Still other routers, usually at the low end of the line, allow you to connect to a cable modem or a digital subscriber line (DSL) modem and share that single IP address connection with several other computers. This kind of router/switch combination is ideal for a home office or a branch office that has only a few computers that need to be networked.

Using a Router to Protect Your Network—NAT and Packet Filtering

Chapter 49 demonstrates how routers fit into a well-designed firewall solution. However, this topic is important enough to deserve a brief mention here. When the Internet was first being commercialized, there were lots of IP addresses to go around. It was easy back then to get an ISP to assign you a group of IP addresses that were valid on the Internet. As the Internet has expanded year by year at a phenomenal rate, the IP address space has begun to run out.

Most routers provide a function called Network Address Translation (NAT). Briefly, NAT allows your network to use one, or a few, valid IP addresses on the Internet connection side of the router, and a private address space on your local network side of the router. When communications take place between a client on your network and a server on the Internet, the traffic passes through the router, which uses its own valid IP address to make contact with the outside server. Responses received from the server are repackaged and returned to the original client. Besides using IP address substitution, another version of NAT employs a technique of manipulating port addresses to keep track of multiple connections.

NAT helps keep your network secure because it helps prevent anyone outside your network from finding out any addressing information about servers or workstations inside your network. One of the most important security goals you can accomplish in network security is preventing outsiders from gaining any knowledge about your network, be it network addresses, hardware platforms, or operating systems and applications. The capability for a router to also block certain ports, as well as addresses, makes your local network even more secure. For example, although you might want to allow your users to browse the Web and possibly establish an FTP session with a remote server to download a new driver or software update, you might not want the reverse to be possible. By appropriately configuring your gateway router, you can pretty much block all but the most persistent hacker from getting into your network.

Router Ports and Connections

In a central headquarters, where network segments converge, a larger router with a greater capacity to handle large volumes of network traffic is used. A typical router found in many corporate environments, for example, is the Cisco 2505 series. This router comes in several models—to accommodate different network interfaces—and can provide for both Ethernet and Token-Ring support. The Cisco 2505 appears in Figure 10.3, from the rear, so that you can see the physical connections.

Figure 10.3   A router usually contains multiple interface connections to join different network segments.

In this figure, you can see that the 2505 model provides for eight Ethernet 10BASE-T connections on the left side that can be used to connect either individual computers or hubs (using crossover cables that swap the transmit and receive wires).

Tip

When configuring a router, you need to supply information about each port, or network interface, that is used. Typically, each port is named to indicate its use. For example, the Cisco IOS (Internetworking Operating System) software uses E0 to represent the first Ethernet port, E1 for the second, and so on. Serial ports are denoted using an "S" (S0, S1, and so on).

Other local area network interfaces you will find on other models in this series of routers include Token-Ring connectors (usually a DB-9 connector) and Attachment Unit Interface (AUI, usually a DB-15 connector) used to connect an Ethernet transceiver to the router.

Near the middle of Figure 10.3 are two 60-pin serial connections (DB-60 connectors) that can be used to connect to wide area networks. These connections usually are made to either a modem or a CSU/DSU that interfaces with the high-speed link. Like LAN ports, different models allow for other kinds of WAN connections. For example, the 2500 series includes support for Basic Rate ISDN to connect your office to a WAN.

In Figure 10.4, you can see a close-up of the serial ports, along with two RJ-45 ports.

Next to the WAN serial connections are two RJ-45 ports labeled CONSOLE and AUX. The console port is used to connect a terminal to the router for configuration and management purposes. The terminal you use can be either a dumb terminal (such as a VT-series terminal) or a terminal emulation program running on a PC. Either way, you'll probably also have to obtain an adapter to convert the RJ-45 connector to the type of serial port used on your terminal or PC serial port. Standard serial port converters might or might not be included with the router, so be sure to check the accessories list.

The AUX port can be used to connect a modem to the router. This can be handy for dial-on-demand routing, for infrequent connections to remote sites that don't need a full-time dedicated connection. Although you can connect a modem to the console port, this is not always a good idea. Some routers, such as the Cisco 2500 series we're discussing here, don't support RS232 modem controls. This means that when a user using this port logs out, the modem connection is not automatically dropped. If another call comes in shortly afterward, it's possible to access the router without knowing the administrative password, because the session is still in effect.

Figure 10.4   Serial connections allow you to connect a router to wide area connections while the console port allows you to configure and manage the router.

Configuring Routers

Most routers are similar to computers in that they run an "operating system." You can think of the router as a small computer that has only one basic function: Sort out where incoming packets need to go. To preserve your investment, most manufacturers store the router's operating system in non-volatile memory that can be reprogrammed when updates or fixes are released. When the router is first powered up, it runs a small bootstrap program that is used to locate and load the operating system. Most routers also allow you to load the router OS using a trivial FTP (tftp) server. This type of FTP server doesn't require a password and shouldn't be used in an insecure environment. However, within a LAN, using a tftp server to download router OS data can make it easier to keep track of different versions of the OS and the routers that are configured to use them.

Cisco's OS for its main router line is called IOS, and it has been updated many, many times over the years and adapted to the newest equipment. Cisco's Web site can tell you which versions are available for the different routers it manufactures. If you deal heavily in Cisco equipment, a good Web site for you to bookmark is the Cisco documentation Web site. Although Cisco routers do ship with a CD that contains most of this documentation, you'll find up-to-date copies at this Web site:

www.cisco.com/univercd/home/home.htm

Configuring a router usually begins after you take it out of the box and plug in everything. For each interface (that is, network connection), you need to configure the appropriate information. For example, for a 10BASE-T or Fast Ethernet port connecting to a LAN that uses TCP/IP, you must specify an IP address and subnet mask for the port.

There are also tasks you need to perform to configure the routing protocols that the router uses. The information you need for this depends, of course, on the routing protocols you plan to use.

Other configuration issues you need to address include access and security. If the router is being used as part of a firewall, or if there is a need within your network, you might have to set up access control lists to permit or deny network traffic from passing through any of the network interfaces.

One important thing to keep in mind is that the router's OS and the configuration information you enter are separate entities. Both the OS and the configuration file can be stored in nonvolatile memory (NVRAM), and both usually can be downloaded from a tftp server. However, the configuration file that is created when you initially set up a router should be saved in more than one place for backup purposes. Indeed, keeping a printed copy of the information contained in the configuration file can be a helpful troubleshooting tool.

Routers Come in All Sizes

Cisco manufactures a wide range of router products that spans the small home office to Internet core routers. After you get beyond a small basic router that would be useful in a small home office, routers tend to become more configurable—from a hardware perspective. That is, they are modular, and different models can be adapted to different environments by installing interface cards to match your needs. Additionally, all but the smallest routers come in rack-mounted versions so that you don't have to dedicate a large amount of valuable office space to them. No matter what size your LAN or network is, it's a bet that Cisco has a router solution for you.

At the high end of the market are routers capable of serving as Internet core routers. These are the high-bandwidth routers that your local ISP or other large-scale provider uses to connect to the Internet backbone. Such routers allow for line cards that allow them to connect to high-speed fiber-optic links, as well as cards that allow for connections to more typical 100BASE-T networks.

In addition to Cisco, other router vendors also offer a full range of products. At the high end of the market, however, the competition isn't so great. One vendor, Juniper Networks, markets only high-end routers. This company makes routers that are intended for very large networks and network backbone uses. For example, Juniper's M5 and M10 routers can route and forward network packets at 5 and 10Gbps (gigabits per second!). Juniper's routers can be configured with various physical interface cards (PICs), each of which contains different network interfaces, ranging from simple 10BASE-T Ethernet connections up to OC-192c/STM-64 optical fiber link connections. The high-end M160 router (shown in Figure 10.5) is intended to serve as either an Internet core router or a very flexible, configurable high-end router for a large network backbone.

In Figure 10.6, you can see one of the PIC modules you can use with the M160. This figure shows a simple Gigabit Ethernet module.

By carefully choosing the modules you configure into a high-end router, it is possible to aggregate smaller links, such as those provided by ISDN or T-carrier lines, into high-speed connections to the Internet. The fact that you can always change out modules to accommodate a changing network infrastructure helps justify the cost of these high-end routers.

The M160 isn't even the fastest or highest capacity router made by Juniper. In addition, Cisco and other manufacturers produce similar high-end routers. However, most users of this book will be dealing with low-end to medium-sized networks, and will find that they don't have to spend a lot of time configuring or managing a router if you set it up correctly in the first place. If you work with an ISP and use a high-end router, plan to spend a lot of time with the manuals.

For small offices, a multitude of vendors make router/switch/hub combinations that can be used to connect using dial-up or broadband (cable/DSL) to the Internet and other remote networks.

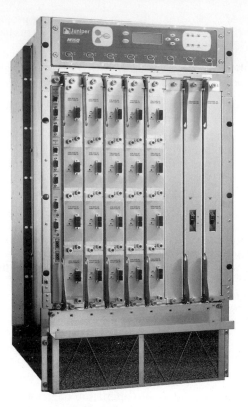

Figure 10.5 The Juniper M160 is a high-end Internet backbone router.

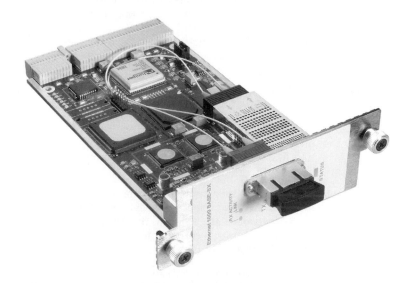

Figure 10.6 This PIC module enables the Juniper M160 router to connect to a Gigabit Ethernet link.

▶▶   Cable modems are discussed in Chapter 18, "Using a Cable Modem," and DSL devices are covered in
Chapter 17, "Digital Subscriber Lines (DSL) Technology."

Using Routers over Wide Area Networks (WANs)

You can create a wide area network (WAN) by purchasing your own set of leased lines—an expensive
proposition for many smaller companies—or you can connect your network to the Internet and take
your chances there. Using a good router that provides for packet filtering and Virtual Private Networks
(VPNs), you can effectively tunnel your network traffic through the Internet in encrypted form.
Connecting each branch office, you might find that using DSL technologies is much cheaper than
using a more expensive ISDN dial-up or T1 dedicated line. Instead, because you'll have a larger
amount of traffic bound to and from the company's headquarters, you can install a large pipe at that
point and use cheaper methods out in the field, spending the money for a large data pipe only where
it is needed: at the central headquarters.

If you choose to connect a business network to the Internet, you must be familiar with firewall technology. This means you must be familiar with the specific model of router used in your organization.
Cisco is perhaps the most widely known brand of routers, but for small offices there exist many viable
and inexpensive choices. Besides packet filtering and NAT that are generally supported by most
routers, you also should investigate using proxy servers to further isolate your network from the rest
of the world.

▶▶   Proxy servers are covered in more detail in Chapter 49.

Routers Make the Internet Possible

It should be obvious that without routers it would be almost impossible to consider the connection of
millions of computers such as has been accomplished with the proliferation of the Internet. In the
first place, the topological restrictions placed on Ethernet, Token-Ring, and other transport protocols
would limit the size to which the network could grow. Second, if routing were not done using a logical addressing scheme, any device that connects a network to another network would have to keep a
table in memory that consists of all nodes on all networks to which it is connected! Although computing power has been increasing at extremely fast rates in the past few years, it's doubtful that anyone could devise a machine that could keep track of all the computers in the world and efficiently
route a large number of packets to their correct destinations. The routing table would be so large that
it would take forever to route packets.

Instead, all a router must do is know the address of a network, or the address of another router that
knows how to deliver packets to the destination network. If you use the `tracert` command in
Windows (or `traceroute` in Unix and Linux) to trace the route a packet takes to a particular Web site,
you'll most likely see that it goes through many routers before it reaches its destination. For example:

```
G:\>tracert www.bd-studios.com

Tracing route to www.bd-studios.com [207.213.224.83]
over a maximum of 30 hops:

  1   140 ms   150 ms    150 ms  envlnjewsap01.bellatlantic.net
  ➥[192.168.125.173]

  2     *      140 ms      *     192.168.125.158
  3   140 ms   150 ms    151 ms  206.125.199.71
  4   140 ms   150 ms    150 ms  205.171.37.13
  5   140 ms   151 ms    150 ms  jfk-core-01.inet.qwest.net [205.171.30.85]
  6   150 ms     *        150 ms  wdc-core-02.inet.qwest.net [205.171.5.235]
```

```
 7    150 ms    160 ms    160 ms    wdc-core-03.inet.qwest.net [205.171.24.6]
 8    180 ms    180 ms    180 ms    hou-core-01.inet.qwest.net [205.171.5.187]
 9    180 ms    190 ms    191 ms    dal-core-02.inet.qwest.net [205.171.5.172]
10    180 ms    191 ms    190 ms    dal-brdr-02.inet.qwest.net [205.171.25.50]
11    180 ms    190 ms    190 ms    39.ATM1-0.BR1.DFW9.ALTER.NET [137.39.23.217]
12    180 ms    191 ms    190 ms    140.at-6-0-0.XR1.DFW9.ALTER.NET [152.63.98.126]

13    181 ms      *       180 ms    185.at-1-0-0.TR1.DFW9.ALTER.NET [152.63.98.26]
14    220 ms    231 ms    230 ms    128.at-5-1-0.TR1.LAX9.ALTER.NET [152.63.3.162]
15    221 ms    230 ms    220 ms    297.ATM7-0.XR1.LAX4.ALTER.NET [152.63.112.181]
16    220 ms    230 ms    231 ms    193.ATM6-0.GW4.LAX4.ALTER.NET [152.63.113.89]
17      *       220 ms    230 ms    savvis-lax2.customer.alter.net
➥[157.130.236.150]

18    390 ms    381 ms      *       affinity-2.uslsan.savvis.net [209.144.96.86]
19    431 ms    460 ms    501 ms    web33.ahnet.net [207.213.224.83]
```

Trace complete.

Clearly, connecting to another computer on the Internet isn't always such a simple thing! High-speed lines and fast, efficient core routers can make it seem (if you are using a fast, digital connection) as if all the servers you access are just around the corner from you. Instead, they could be on the opposite side of the world. Another interesting thing to note about routers is that packets that are part of the same original communication can take different routes to get to the eventual destination. Routing tables change constantly, and what might be a good route at one moment might not be the next. For this reason, higher-level protocols, such as TCP, take care of the mechanics involved in determining whether packets are received and reassembled into the correct order.

Network Attached
Storage and Storage
Area Networks

SOME OF THE MAIN TOPICS IN THIS CHAPTER ARE

CHAPTER 11

All the components that make up a computer, from the CPU to memory, the bus, and others, are rapidly expanding in capacity and probably will for many years to come. One area of the computer that is probably growing more slowly is directly attached storage devices, such as disk and tape drives. For desktop workstations that use limited storage, this is not really a problem. For server computers that offer file services to other computers, this is now a serious problem. As the need for storage continues to grow, it is pushing the limits of the most typical server storage interface today: the SCSI (Small Computer Systems Interface) interface. And because most large servers use RAID arrays, even more disks are needed to store data due to the mechanics of disk mirroring, striping, and so on.

The SCSI parallel architecture, using multiple wires and intricate clocking, can work only over short distances. The different levels of SCSI that exist today have different distance limitations as well as limitations as to the number of devices that can be attached to a SCSI cable. Because of these physical limitations, it is apparent that eventually you will run out of PCI slots to hold SCSI cards, and that all the storage you can fit within the limits of the current SCSI capabilities will be exhausted, as shown in Table 11.1.

Table 11.1   SCSI Types and Capabilities

Type	Bus Width	Speed	Max Number of Devices	Bus Length
SCSI-1	8 bits	5MBps	8	6–25 meters
Fast SCSI	8 bits	10MBps	8	3–25 meters
Ultra SCSI	8 bits	20MBps	8	1.5–25 meters
Ultra2 SCSI	8 bits	40MBps	8	12–25 meters
Fast Wide SCSI	16 bits	20MBps	16	3–25 meters
Wide Ultra SCSI	16 bits	40MBps	16	1.5–25 meters
Wide Ultra2 SCSI	16 bits	80MBps	16	12–25 meters
Ultra3 SCSI	16 bits	160MBps	16	12 meters

One practical solution would be to get another server and divide the chores. But for some very large servers (or clusters) that provide Internet services, or other applications that require a large amount of storage, the physical SCSI architecture is now seeing its last days. You can only connect so much storage to a server, given the distance limitations of SCSI technologies and higher disk capacities. Eventually, disk storage space that you can connect to a server will become finite, and a bottleneck. Thus, SCSI does have limitations.

Newer technologies will be needed in just a few years to satisfy the need for growing, reliable storage. One is the emerging InfiniBand technology (still in its infancy), and the other is the proliferation of Storage Area Networks (SANs).

As enterprise data begins to be measured in terabytes now instead of gigabytes, there simply must be a better way to make data available to one or more large network servers. Currently, that method—especially for large networks in which downtime is very rarely tolerated—is the Storage Area Network (SAN). Another method of expanding data storage by using networking technology—often used in small to mid-sized network environments—is the Network Attached Storage (NAS) device (sometimes called a network appliance), which you will also learn about in this chapter.

NAS devices are attached to a LAN along with client and server computers. SANs are usually connected to the larger servers using a separate network. There are exceptions to this rule, of course. Some enterprise networks still use NAS because it was "there first." There is no need to replace what works with a more expensive technology just because it exists. In this chapter you will find compelling reasons for using NAS, SANs, or possibly both in your network, depending on your requirements. Both of these technologies have specific features that make them useful in different environments. You will find that some networks can make use of both technologies, again, depending on the data requirements for the network.

First, let's examine the most widely used technology for attaching storage devices to a server: the Small Computer Systems Interface (SCSI). We'll also cover the limitations of this legacy technology in large enterprise networks.

Local Versus Networked Storage Devices

Both SCSI cards and network adapter cards connect to the PCI bus in your computer, but the similarity ends there. The network card uses a serial communications method (using two wires in most cases—for send and receive for modern Ethernet networks).

◄◄   You can learn more about traditional Ethernet network adapters by reading Chapter 7, "Network Interface Cards."

SCSI uses a parallel method, involving many wires (the number varies according to the SCSI specification). Serial communications techniques can be used to cover greater distances than parallel methods. That is why simple Ethernet networks can span much larger distances than can the locally attached SCSI devices for a server.

Many versions of SCSI exist today. The first started out with a limited bandwidth. Today, though, there are many versions of SCSI—more than the number of different cables used to make connections between SCSI devices (or controllers of these devices) and the PCI cards that provide the link between the server and storage. For more information on the different types of SCSI, check out *Upgrading and Repairing PCs, 15th Edition*.

Note

The SCSI parallel interface was first used by Apple Computers, and you will still find it in use for some Apple products. Just like FireWire (which was also developed by Apple), these advanced technologies have been adopted by the Intel community, and have also been adopted as specifications by the IEEE. Now Intel-based computers running Windows or Linux can easily support both of these protocols. Keep in mind, however, that these technologies do not provide the distance that Fibre Channel or IP SANs can provide, using their respective technologies.

Using fiber-optic cabling, serial communications can cover very large distances, and allow fast access to a network composed of many devices.

Just as a LAN can be used to allow a server to provide storage file shares to client workstations, there are two other major types of networked storage that can overcome the distance limitations imposed by SCSI devices: Network Attached Storage and Storage Area Networks.

Defining Network Attached Storage (NAS)

One way to attach additional storage is to place the storage itself on the network for the server or clients to access. This technique is called Network Attached Storage (NAS), because it shares the same network as the clients. When the storage device (such as a disk array or tape drive, or a mixture of both in the same box) is accessed, the data transfer occurs on the *same* LAN as your clients and servers. Thus, if your network is already experiencing heavy utilization, using NAS may further cause degradation in network performance. In a small network, such as in a SOHO setting or a small department that needs local access to a small number of files, a NAS device can be a perfect fit, especially if the majority of communications are between the NAS device and servers or clients of the local LAN segment. Yet if a large amount of network traffic is sent between servers or clients on the LAN, the NAS device can severely impact the bandwidth on the LAN. All of this is, of course, because the servers, clients, and NAS devices share the same network. This is one of the major differences between Network Attached Storage and Storage Area Networks. The latter option uses a separate network and does not cause any bandwidth degradation on the LAN.

For much larger networks, which use hundreds of servers and many thousands of clients, the choice between NAS and SANs is a little different. Because SANs reside on a network separate from the production network, data transfers between the server and storage can be greatly increased.

Defining a Storage Area Network (SAN)

Storage Area Networks (SANs) are similar to NAS in topology, with the exception that a SAN is made up of devices on a network that is not the same network used for the LAN. Figure 11.1 shows the basic difference between NAS and SANs.

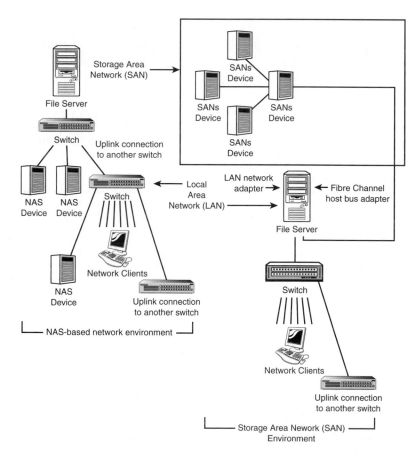

Figure 11.1 NAS and SANs use different network topologies.

The NAS-based network, shown on the left side of Figure 11.1, has network clients and servers as well as NAS devices attached to the LAN. The file server uses the same LAN to service client requests as it uses to get data from NAS devices. In many cases, it is possible to configure NAS devices to work as if they are servers, and the most popular disk formats are supported on the main players in this market. In a switched environment as shown in Figure 11.1, traffic will be minimized somewhat due to the switches involved. However, the single network adapter card on the file server is a bottleneck. You could put in another NIC and use it to attach to the NAS devices. This would be similar to the Storage Area Network (SAN) shown on the right side of Figure 11.1.

In the SAN, a typical NIC attaches the file server to the LAN. A separate card called a host bus adapter is used to connect the file server to a Fibre Channel–based SAN. Communications with devices on the SAN do not cause any traffic on the network's LAN. These examples are simplified explanations of most installed NAS and SAN networks, but however complex the design, the basics remain the same.

Network Attached Storage

NAS has some advantages over SAN technology. Consequently, in some situations it may be a better solution for your network storage needs:

- Your network traffic on the LAN is minimal and the impact of one or more NAS servers will not affect performance greatly. An example of this is using NAS to store data that is not used by the network clients frequently, such as reference material, software installation kits, or archived files.

- Your budget doesn't allow for the purchase of an expensive SAN. Some NAS devices sell for a few thousand dollars. Some SANs devices sell for a few hundred thousand dollars (and don't forget the maintenance costs), and some are over the million mark. You can always upgrade your NAS devices to newer technology in the future when your business can afford it. SANs are definitely not for the home or SOHO market.

- Your need for storage isn't as great as that which a SAN can provide. Smaller additions to storage can be done with NAS devices that can be shared among more than one server. If you need only a small amount of space, NAS devices might be cheaper to use. For larger storage needs (in the terabyte range) you'll probably do better with a SAN.

As you can see, NAS can be ideal for the small office environment, for a small departmental deployment that needs a large amount of storage, or even for home users with large storage demands.

Network Appliances

Many NAS solutions come as a packaged product. The "network appliance" will have its own operating system and network connection, and in many instances is pretty much a plug-and-play type of operation. Just connect it to the network and make some minor configuration tweaks, and you've got storage on the network that you can restrict to specific servers or other computers.

Note

Network NAS devices can be complex devices. They do not just offer simple file shares for the disk storage they provide. Instead, using management software for these devices, you can configure RAID sets, such as mirrored disks or stripe sets, that can be used to increase up-time by enabling a disk subsystem that can tolerate the loss of one or more disk drives. These functions are also performed by SANs. The point is that you don't have to pay more to obtain this level of data integrity. For more information, RAID is discussed later in this chapter.

You'll find many vendors of NAS, from HP to IBM to many other smaller firms. Check the specs first to be sure that the device you want to buy is one that will work on your network. For example, consider whether the device is expandable, or whether you'll have to buy additional NAS devices in the future to keep up with storage demands. You may want to make sure that the device has upgradable firmware to address future features and devices (such as newer tape drives). And you should be sure that any NAS device you purchase can be upgraded to incorporate additional storage so that you do not have to go through the process of adding yet more separate NAS devices to accommodate future needs. Except for the smallest network, a NAS device should provide an upgrade path to attach additional storage capabilities, be it disk or tape backup hardware.

Tip

Some NAS devices come with backup software that allows you to back up the NAS data directly to tape drives attached to the NAS device. This approach alleviates copying data across the network to a backup device and thus using a significant amount of the network bandwidth.

NAS Protocols

Most NAS devices support the major players in the file protocols just as they do the major disk file-system formats. Most NAS devices will support NetWare's now-legacy IPX/SPX protocols, Microsoft's NetBEUI, and Sun's Network File System (NFS). The SMB (now CIFS—Common Internet File System) protocol/name service is becoming increasingly popular, despite its age. The Storage Networking Industry Association has just published a document titled *Common Internet File System (CIFS) Technical Reference, Revision: 1.0*. You can download this from www.snia.org. Just use the search text "CIFS" and you should find this 150-plus–page PDF document!

The fact that SNIA (which is a trade association that supports both NAS and SAN) has published one of the few volumes that consolidate a lot of diverse CIFS information is indicative of the fact that CIFS—the overhauled Microsoft SMB—will still be a major player in networking protocols in the near future. Because NetBIOS support in future Windows operating systems is now in doubt, will this change if CIFS becomes an Internet or storage standard?

NAS Capacity Limitations—Bandwidth and Storage

The major trade-offs between SANs and NAS are storage capacity, response time, and the "backup window." Although it is quite possible to attach terabytes and terabytes of NAS storage to your LAN, there will come a time long before that when NAS begins to impede normal network response time for end users. Your network utilization will go through the roof and your NAS investment will give you no definite advantage. This assumes that the NAS devices are used by a large number of clients. If you have distributed data to the departmental level, and there is little interaction between those data stores and clients in other departments, then this may not impact your LAN performance.

For larger installations that tend to use higher-end storage solutions, the bandwidth factor divides NAS and SAN technologies. But this is just one of a few considerations you should think about before employing either in a production network.

If you have a need for a SAN to enable fast transfers of large amounts of data, it may be because you have a large number of client workstations to service with a high volume of file requests from a large data bank. Other situations in which you might use a SAN, when fast access to data is required, is workstations used in video and other mastering environments where speed is of the utmost importance. What would take hours or days to compute just five years ago would take only a few minutes today with modern processors. With the capability to process more data faster, workstations must have fast access to storage to prevent storage from becoming a bottleneck.

Or perhaps your environment is an industrial one that requires constant access to inventory, accounting, and other traditional computer resources, as well as manufacturing resource planning (MRP) software to help keep costs in control. Even instruments or computers used on the factory floor for data entry can generate voluminous amounts of information. Is a NAS sufficient? Or should you consider a SANs solution?

The other major reason that SANs are used in large network environments revolves around the backup window mentioned earlier. Only the more expensive NAS devices will be able to perform timely and efficient backups of data stored on their disks. Compare this to the capability of a large SAN device. Using both proprietary techniques and standards such as RAID technology, SAN devices can be enabled to take snapshots of their file systems and commit them to backup devices without involving the CPU of the computer systems that make use of SANs. The file server can continue offering resources to clients while a backup is being performed.

One of the techniques of this type of backup is to simply create mirror sets with three or more members and then break the mirror by removing a disk. Similar to a snapshot backup, a disk from a mirror set (all three disks contain the same data) is taken out of the mirror set and used for the backup. The remaining members of the mirror set provide redundancy (in case one of those disks fails!), so users can continue working. When the backup is completed, the third disk that was taken out of the mirror set is brought back in, and everything it "missed" while users had access to the others is updated so that within a short time all three disks are again complete copies of each other.

Another method of creating a snapshot of data is by using *checkpoints* in file systems so that the backup can proceed with copying data from a disk, and the operating system can keep track of changes that need to be applied to the disk (from the checkpoint onward) after the backup has completed.

In the next section you'll learn about the basics of a SAN, along with more differences between SAN and NAS.

Storage Area Networks

In Figure 11.1 you saw that a SAN operates as a file server on a separate network from the LAN. A SAN also has some advantages and benefits, based on its capabilities, when compared with NAS:

- SANs generally provide a faster response to a server than even some versions of locally connected SCSI devices. One version or another of SCSI technology is used in most standard servers/workstations today. SCSI has continued to be upgraded with newer versions, but the storage capacity that can be provided has reached its maximum in many environments.

- SANs can use bridges to existing SCSI equipment, thus preserving your existing investment in expensive devices. You don't have to throw out those older SCSI devices (or those you purchased yesterday...). Instead, a bridge can allow you to continue to use this hardware as long as it remains cost-effective.

- It would be difficult to limit the amount of storage a SAN can hold. Both Arbitrated Loops and Fabric Switched technologies (both of which are described later in this chapter) have their own methods of operation. Each of these solutions, or even a mixture of the two, can provide enough storage to meet nearly any computing environment today. Storage is practically unlimited for a SAN.

- Although it is possible to use copper cabling with many SANs, it is more common to use fiber-optic cabling. The term Fibre Channel was developed to separate the protocol from the fiber-optic cable; yet today it is associated more with fiber-optic cables than with copper cables.

- A very important feature of SANs is the capability of eliminating the backup window discussed earlier. NAS devices have their own CPU just as do SAN-enabled adapter cards. Yet if you have very large amounts of critical data that you want to back up, a SAN will definitely provide a better solution. SAN devices, in general, operate better at creating backups that don't impact the network. This is especially true because the SAN device can do the backup while continuing to offer file services to clients or servers, just as NAS does. However, the SAN Fibre Channel (or IP

SAN network) can satisfy the server's requests faster than local SCSI attached storage, often allowing a SAN to perform backup operations with very little or no noticeable impact on the clients.

■ The Fibre Channel protocol and associated hardware devices are the main choice for SANs implementers today. However, a newer technology, called IP SANs, promises to offer about the same performance as a Fibre Channel–based SAN. IP SANs will also offer minimal training (as opposed to Fibre Channel SANs) because employees will be using existing or similar devices such as IP switches and routers.

As you can see, SANs are fundamentally different from NAS storage. The main advantages that SANs based on Fibre Channel enjoy is the minimal overhead involved in Fibre Channel, the low-level error detection and correction techniques, and the fast fiber-optic transmission rates on a separate network. You can expect the Fibre Channel protocols to keep up with those of Ethernet (such as 10Gigabit Ethernet), because all use the same fiber-optic cabling.

SAN and NAS—Mix and Match

It is possible to use both NAS and SANs on the same network. For some departmental servers, where traffic is limited to the local LAN segment, using a file server with a NAS device for additional storage is an excellent choice, especially from an expense viewpoint. If your company has a large Internet presence, you may want to consider using a SAN to back up that important presence.

Most large networks consist of small departments as well as departments or applications that require huge amounts of mission-critical storage on demand. In this case a mix of NAS devices (for local departments) and SANs storage (for mission-critical storage support) may be your best solution.

The point to make is that NAS and SANs are not exclusive. Each has multiple functions to fulfill, and each performs using different techniques. The good news is that you can use both on your network at the same time.

Using Fibre Channel as a Network Transport

Most Storage Area Networks today use Fibre Channel to connect to a wide variety of SAN products. Fibre Channel is generally used across fiber-optic cables, although the specifications do allow for a short-distance copper-cable haul.

Fibre Channel uses a serial form of communications. Between any two devices, there are two connections: one to transmit data and one to receive data. The two cables are swapped so that the transmitter of one device is connected to the receiver of the other end of the connection.

With the use of two cables, it is also possible for information to be flowing in two directions at the same time—full-duplex communications. Many Fibre Channel functions are performed on the adapter itself (called a host bus adapter, although there are others), instead of those functions that a typical IP NIC passes up to software-based code to interpret and act on.

As if fiber-optic cabling were not fast enough, Fibre Channel also offers an encoding technique that has been around for years, used in other communication techniques used on both copper and fiber-optic cabling. This encoding is referred to as 8B/10B encoding. It was not selected by random from among the many choices. Instead it was selected because of its unique properties that provide a lot of error checking and long-distance serial communications.

Encoding Data on Fibre Channel Networks

Most network professionals think of a typical network packet, or datagram or frame, whatever level you are working at, to be a simple collection of bytes. However, if you are going to step into Fibre Channel, be aware that you won't find that convention used here. Instead, 8-bit characters are translated to 10-bit *transmission characters*. Although it may seem odd to convert 8 bits to 10 bits to achieve a high transmission rate, there are several good reasons for using this technique, discussed later in this chapter.

The main feature that distinguishes 8B/10B encoding from other standard LAN protocols is that it attempts to keep the number of zeros and ones transmitted on the network media to an equal number. This is called *neutral disparity*. Each transmission character to be used is chosen based on the current disparity (running disparity) of the serial communications. Only some of the transmission characters contain an equal number of zeros and ones. Others contain more zeros than ones, or vice versa. If a transmission character contains more ones than zeros, it is said to have positive disparity. If the transmission character has more zeros than ones, it is said to have negative disparity.

So if the last transmission character sent out onto the network media had a negative disparity, then the adapter card circuitry would choose a transmission character with positive disparity to keep the running disparity on the line neutral over a short time. Some 8-bit values translate into a transmission character with neutral disparity, whereas others translate into two characters: one with positive disparity and another with negative disparity. Those that translate to two values allow the adapter card to choose a character to help maintain neutral disparity.

What begins as a simple byte undergoes a transformation before being sent out on a Fibre Channel transmission. Fibre Channel uses a serial mechanism for sending bits out onto the network—one bit at a time, compared to a parallel environment (such as SCSI) in which several wires are used, each for a single bit, and a timing wire is used to inform the other end of the data transfer that a byte (or more) has been received.

Because serial data transfers occur only in one direction on a single cable (which is why you have send/receive cables on each host bus adapter), another method must be used to *recover the clock*. This is done by using special code, called a comma character, and by limiting the number of bits that can be transmitted in a row. The recipient of the data transfer can recover quickly if the correct number of bytes for a time period is not transmitted correctly, or if the comma character is sent through the communications channel.

The technique of 8B/10B encoding is beyond the scope of this book. However, as discussed previously, these are the important things about 8B/10B encoding:

- No more than four of the same bit (0 or 1) are ever sent in a row (other than for the comma character).

- Each 8-bit quantity can translate to either one or two 10-bit transmission characters. The character used depends on the *disparity* of the network.

- Disparity means that an equal number of zeros and ones are being transmitted within a short period. 8B/10B encoding chooses transmission characters that attempt to maintain *neutral* disparity, or an equal number of zeros and ones.

As you can see, the concept of *disparity* is crucial to the Fibre Channel protocol. There are several reasons for this. One reason is that lasers and fiber-optic transmitters can overheat. If the laser can be used only about 50% of the time, this can make equipment less expensive to produce. Thus, alternating between zeros and ones on a periodic basis can help keep heat to a minimum.

Another reason for guaranteeing a state change from more zeros to ones, and for using the special comma character, is to enable the receiver to recover the clock. Because there is no extra wire or signal to synch the timing between the two network adapters, another method must be used on the receiving end so that it can determine when it has received a transmission character. By forcing a change on the line within a guaranteed length of time, it is easy for the receiver to pick up after a garbled character and continue receiving data.

Pushing the Protocol Stack Down to the Adapter Level

The Host Bus Adapter (HBA) is the terminology given to the adapter card that connects a computer to a Fibre Channel SAN. The HBA differs from an Ethernet card in that the HBA performs more functions than the Ethernet card, which frees up CPU cycles for other duties. The Fibre Channel protocol elements are processed on the HBA. Fibre Channel can accept many different upper-level protocols, such as IP, SCSI, and HIPPI, and can transfer their frames as a payload of the Fibre Channel frame.

The Fibre Channel frame format also has a larger payload than a standard IP frame, as well as a lower header-to-payload ratio. In Fibre Channel the final frame is put together by the HBA and transmitted on the network media.

Much error recovery is done at the physical level, but the simplicity of the Fibre Channel protocols is such that errors occur at a very low rate. The running neutral disparity allows for a quick recovery in case of problems on the line.

Fibre Channel Over IP

Fibre Channel can cover distances measured in kilometers. When it is necessary to cover a larger distance, Fibre Channel frames can be encapsulated inside an IP packet and transmitted through an ordinary IP network. This does not imply a translation of the Fibre Channel frame to an IP frame. Instead, the Fibre Channel frame is stored in the payload of the IP frame, in the same manner that other protocol frames are carried as the payload of the Fibre Channel frame. This makes it possible to access data over long distances. It also enables you to create SANs that mirror each other in separate data centers for disaster recovery purposes.

Basic SANs: Arbitrated Loops

The earliest SAN technology, which is still around today, is the Arbitrated Loop. This is a simple physical ring topology (which can be wired as a star by using a hub) that bears some resemblance to Token-Ring technology. The word *arbitrated* indicates that a node on this SAN must contend for the network along with others connected to the ring. An arbitration process is used and, as with Token-Ring, only one node on the ring can exchange data with another node at the same time. The other nodes must wait to use the shared ring network media.

The Arbitrated Loop can be made up of up to 126 nodes, or 127 if you connect the loop to a fabric switch, which is discussed in the next section. The loop is self-addressing and uses a priority mechanism to access the SAN. Figure 11.2 shows an example of an Arbitrated Loop using a hub to centralize wiring of the SAN. In this figure note that the hub connects the transmitter of another node in the SAN, with the last transmitter connected back to the receiver on the first node plugged into the hub.

Unlike an Ethernet hub, in which a signal is broadcast to all other nodes on a segment, an Arbitrated Loop operates using a physical topology that resembles Token-Ring more than it does Ethernet. Because control and data frames must travel from one member of the loop to the next member physically wired to it, only two members of the loop can establish a link and exchange data at any single point in time. In the following sections you will learn how the Arbitrated Loop initializes itself to assign addressing and priority values to each member, and how members exchange data. Figure 11.3 shows the logical topology of how data flows around an Arbitrated Loop.

Whether you string cables through your computer-room floor to connect one loop member to another, or use a hub to centralize wiring, the result is the same: a physical loop. This loop must be initialized when it is powered up, or when another member joins the loop. A means for gaining access to the network media is also needed so that each member of the loop can send or receive data.

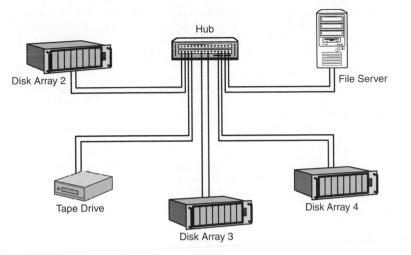

Figure 11.2   A hub is the simplest method for connecting members of an Arbitrated Loop SAN.

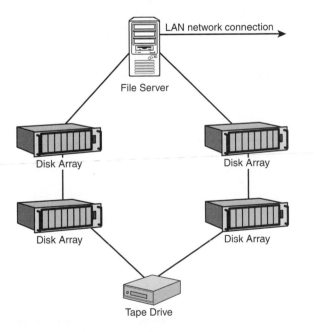

Figure 11.3   Data in an Arbitrated Loop uses a physical as well as logical loop topology.

Initializing the Loop

When a loop is powered up, or a new node joins the ring, a temporary loop master is elected and an initialization process takes place. The initialization process assigns addressing information to each member of the loop and sets the priorities of each member. The temporary loop master is chosen only for completing this initialization process, and it serves no function after that has been accomplished and the ring is functioning.

Each HBA, like an Ethernet card, has a hardware address burned into it by the manufacturer. This is a 64-bit number that is guaranteed (at least in newer equipment) to be unique throughout the world. The IEEE controls the range of numbers allocated to manufacturers. If an HBA has more than one port, each port also has its own unique hardware (or worldwide) address.

Note

Only newer SAN devices are likely to use worldwide names assigned by the IEEE. Older devices may have conflicting addresses, or require some configuration in order to assign this address.

These hardware addresses are used during the initialization process, and by some fabric switches. For the purpose of communicating on the ring, a separate address (24 bits) is used on the ring. This address is assigned or chosen during the initialization of the ring.

To begin the process, the temporary loop master must be chosen. A node begins the process by sending out a Loop Initialization Primitive (LIP). This LIP can be informative to the downstream neighbor if it does not yet know that the loop is being initialized. For example, a new device could have been added to the loop. Using this process, each node on the ring begins to transmit a LIP to its downstream partner in the ring.

This first LIP frame is called the Loop Initialization Select Master (LISM) frame. This frame contains information indicating its worldwide address and whether it is an NL_Port (node loop port) or an FL_Port (fabric loop port). The FL_Port can be used to connect an Arbitrated Loop to a larger fabric switched network.

If the LISM frame indicates that it was originated by an FL_Port, the receiving node stops transmitting its own LISM frame and instead repeats the FL_Port's frame. If it is just another NL_Port frame, the receiving node will compare its worldwide address with that of the received LISM frame. If the received frame has a higher priority (lower-numbered worldwide address), it is forwarded; otherwise, the receiver continues to forward its own LISM.

It takes only a few milliseconds before this technique notifies the node that either is connected to a fabric switch or has the lowest worldwide address on the loop that it is now elected the temporary loop master. Note that this designation can change as you add or remove hardware from the loop.

After the temporary loop master has been chosen (it has received back the LISM frame it sent out, so it knows that it must be the master of the loop), the temporary loop master sends out a frame informing the other members that it is assuming responsibilities as the loop master.

To finish the initialization process, it is necessary to assign values to the 24-bit IDs assigned to each member of the loop. This is accomplished by the temporary loop master sending around the loop four frames, each of which performs part of the process of assigning and recording the loop IDs of each node attached to the loop.

Note

The 24-bit address used as a port *identifier* is made up of two parts. The higher 2 bytes are assigned an identifier by a switch if the loop is attached to a switch. This is so that a switch can keep track of which nodes of an Arbitrated Loop are connected at what point. The lower 8 bits are used to assign one of 126 addresses to members of the loop (or 127 if a fabric attachment is used). This address, as a whole, is known as the AL_PA (Arbitrated Loop Physical Address). AL_PAs are used as sender and recipient addresses in Frame Relay communications.

Several of the next few initialization frames use a bitmap, in which each bit represents a numeric address that represents a byte address field. In other words, each bit in this sort of bitmap is used by the nodes that are part of the initialization process to represent an 8-bit (byte) field. In this manner, a single 256 range of bits can be used to represent a 256-byte address range. For example, bit 1 is used to indicate the first 8-byte address, bit 2 is used to indicate the second 8-byte address, and so on.

The first frame, called the Loop Initialization Fabric Address (LIFA), circles the loop and allows any member that remembers a switch assigned address to retain that address. This can easily occur when a new member has joined the loop and other nodes remember their previous addresses. Each node that remembers its previous address sets the bit in the bit map to indicate that the address has already been taken.

The second frame, called the Loop Initialization Previous Address (LIPA) frame, allows other nodes to claim an address if those nodes remember addresses assigned by some method other than by a switch. These nodes set the bit in the positional bit map to indicate that the address is already taken.

The third frame, called the Loop Initialization Hard Address (LIHA) frame, is used from older equipment. Such devices required that the administrator manually set an ID (worldwide address) for a device. Because these devices have a fixed address, this frame allows them to reserve it. Note that it may be necessary to change a hard address, and also that some newer equipment allows you to select the burned-in address or a manual address.

The last address selection frame is a catch-all frame called the Loop Initialization Soft Address (LISA) frame. Any node that does not yet have an address can select from those still available in the bit map. It is typical for servers and other important devices to select a higher-priority address, while other resources, such as disk arrays, select a lower-priority address.

After the temporary loop master has received this last frame, it can construct a map of all the nodes on the network as far as numeric addresses are concerned. The second matter to determine is to create a map showing the positions in the ring of those addresses. That is, the nodes around the ring do not have to have addresses that are in any order. The selection process lets each node, depending on circumstances, select an address.

So the Loop Initialization Report Position (LIRP) frame is next sent out to collect information about which addresses have been used, and in what order. Instead of a bitmap with each bit representing an address, this frame instead has a byte reserved for each address. As each node in the loop receives this frame, it fills in its address in the first available byte. Thus, when this frame arrives back at the temporary loop master, it has now an ordered listing of the topology of the loop.

The loop master then sends out a frame, called the Loop Initialization Loop Position (LILP) frame, that tells the other members of the loop about this physical location versus address information.

To finish the initialization process, the temporary loop master sends out a CLS (close) sequence. All nodes then enter an *idle* state and wait until a node in the loop wants to establish a connection with another node.

After this process has completed, it is necessary for a node on the Arbitrated Loop to gain access to the loop, log into a remote port, and then send or receive data.

Arbitrating for Loop Access

After the loop has started passing idles, a node on the loop can initiate a transfer of data to or from another node. This is accomplished by first logging into any ports that the node wants to establish a communications channel with. After the Port Login (PLOGI) sequence is completed, the two nodes can exchange information.

However, to gain access to the loop shared media (arbitrate for access), the node must send a frame around the loop requesting the access. This access is chosen by the priority set by the AL_PA. Similar to the method used to choose the temporary loop master, the frame circles the ring. If it arrives back at the node that sent it out onto the network, that node has permission to open a connection with another node and transfer one or more frames.

If another node that wants to begin a transmission receives this frame first, and notices that it has a higher priority than the incoming frame, the node will instead transmit its own. Again, if it receives this frame back, it has won the arbitration and can set up a session and transmit data to/from a Fibre Channel SANs device.

As you can see, as long as the bandwidth is sufficient (and Fibre Channel has progressed from speeds lower than 1Gbps to 10Gbps now), many devices can be accommodated in an Arbitrated Loop and satisfy many smaller clusters of servers, or single servers. If you have a much larger network, you'll probably need to upgrade to a fabric switched model so that you can add further capacity, and at the same time preserve your existing technology in Arbitrated Loops.

Using a Fabric Switched Topology for SANs

As you just learned, an Arbitrated Loop uses a physical ring topology and is usually wired by a hub. The hub simply maintains the physical loop topology, as with a Token-Ring network. A hub can, however, do such things as remove a misbehaving port from the physical ring, or insert a new device into the physical ring. A switch can perform similar functions, among many others. The main limitations of the Arbitrated Loop versus fabric switches is that the loop allows only one communication session to take place at a point in time between members of the loop, and is limited to 126 member nodes.

Note

It's not an all-or-nothing proposition. You can use both Arbitrated Loops and fabric switches at the same time. Remember that Arbitrated Loops can use that 127th connection to make contact with a fabric switch. You'll learn more about this subject later in this chapter.

However, the switch has now become an important player in the SAN environment, mainly due because the switch offers more features than an Arbitrated Loop, and by interconnecting switches you can create a much larger SAN network, and a much greater bandwidth. The 126-node limit is gone when it comes to switches—fabrics can support up to 15.5 million end nodes! To make a comparison with Ethernet again, consider switches to perform a similar function when switching data in one port and out the other. However, when it comes to how devices interact with switch ports, and perform login procedures with both switch ports and remote ports, things get more complicated.

The switch gets rid of having to pass data around a ring until one node decides it needs to send data frames. Instead, like Ethernet, Fibre Channel frames are sent out as needed. This means that switches keep some sort of routing table so that they know what the output port should be. In this way, they work like routers. The switch can transmit many frames at the same time, between various ports, or buffer those that can wait for a short period. Because a switch may be connected to another switch, and so on, you can see that some sort of setup is needed before this data transfer can begin. See Figure 11.4 for an example.

Figure 11.4 shows only two possible paths through the network between the file server and the disk array. In actual practice many switches can be interconnected, providing additional paths through the network, thus helping to keep downtime to a minimum.

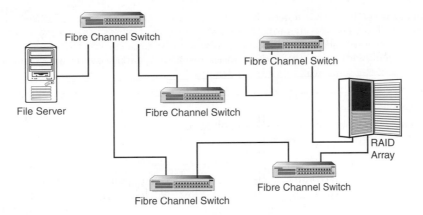

Figure 11.4   Fibre Channel fabric switches greatly expand the size of the SAN.

A connection must be made between the end points of the data transfer before the transfer through the switched network can begin.

Two forms of logins are used by Fibre Channel: Fiber Login (FLOGI) and Port Login (PLOGI). A port, if connected directly to a switch, must first log on to the switch. Then it can log on to ports on other devices it needs to make a connection with.

The FLOGI sequence is tried first, *because a device needs to know first if it is connected to a fabric switch* before it begins to log into ports it will interact with. If the FLOGI fails, the node will proceed with a port login and attempt to create a login exchange with other ports it will be exchanging data with. This is what happens on an Arbitrated Loop and the LIPs that initialize the loop.

If the FLOGI succeeds, the device or port knows that it has performed a login with a fabric switch port. In this case the PLOGI login sequence continues so that the switch can establish PLOGI logins with the ports (which may be several switches away), and the communication can proceed. Another factor to note is that there are several categories of service associated with Fibre Channel. The fastest connection, Class One, is set up by the intervening switches as a dedicated pathway. Other classes offer a lower service, but the technology is still faster than typical IP or other protocols for fast service.

Note

One important thing to note is that a port may be establishing connections to other ports, and each connection may be of a different class of service. All of these parameters are negotiated, depending on the capabilities of the ports, during FLOGI and PLOGI.

The classes of service for Fibre Channel are as listed here:

- **Class One**—A dedicated connection path is set up in advance by the switch(es) involved, and this service is thus guaranteed a certain bandwidth. This service provides acknowledgments for packets received and also ensures delivery of packets in the order in which they are sent.

- **Class Two**—This class provides a connection similar to Class One, but does not guarantee that packets will be delivered in the order sent. Acknowledgments are sent for packets received.

- **Class Three**—If you need a less reliable class of service, this one does not guarantee bandwidth and does not provide an acknowledgment mechanism. Yet this is a class that you will find supported by most products on the market. As long as your SAN is not overloaded with traffic, this is a reasonable class to use for such things as ordinary file-server accesses.

- **Class Four**—This class is a dedicated path, just like Class One, with the difference being that this class doesn't offer a guaranteed bandwidth. In other words, a single channel can be used by several devices to establish a connection that appears to be a Class One circuit. The exception is that the bandwidth required by the connection is not guaranteed, because multiple connections use parts of the same available bandwidth.

- **Class Six**—This class of service is used for multicasting, or sending the same data frames to multiple recipients.

- **Intermix**—To take advantage of the unused bandwidth that may exist in a Class One connection, Intermix allows the switch the capability of inserting Class Two and Class Three into a Class One connection.

A very important factor to consider when purchasing SANs equipment is what class of service you need, and whether the switch supports that class. Most switches do not support all the classes of service. It is more likely that you'll find only two or three classes of service. On lower-end switches, for example, Class One service may not be available, although Class Two and Class Three are.

Another interesting factor to note is that there is no Class Five. This is because this class was originally supposed to be used for a just-in-time isochronous service. This was intended to provide data at a continuous rate to a receiver so that no buffering at the receiver was needed. Compare this to the radio in your car. The radio station broadcasts at a specific rate, and your radio processes this incoming signal at the same rate.

For computer networks, an example of this would be an application such as video transmissions. However, as newer equipment was able to transfer data at faster rates, and as buffering technology improved, it was determined that this class of service was not needed.

A Mixed Topology of Loops and Switches

The interconnecting mesh topology created by a fibre switched network can be complex, but this complexity can provide redundancy should an emergency occur. Using multiple paths through the network helps keep any single device from becoming a single point of failure. If sufficient paths exist through the SAN network, the failure of more than one device can be bypassed with only minimal impact to the network.

Although switch technology is more expensive than that used for Arbitrated Loops, you don't have to throw out your existing loop technology to begin incorporating switches into the SAN.

Newer switches provide a large variety of features that can be used to connect Arbitrated Loops to the switch. You can connect multiple loops and allow communication paths to be established from a member of one loop to a member of another loop, or to a fabric-enabled device that is connected to a switch and is not part of a loop (see Figure 11.5). By allowing for this backward compatibility, switches can be introduced as you need them, and this will provide a minimal disruption of your existing SAN.

Tip

Because fabric switches can be used to connect more than one Arbitrated Loop, consider them to be a useful tool to join together multiple loop-based SANs. If you have several departmental Arbitrated Loop SANs, each requiring separate staff members to manage these networks, then by connecting all the separate loops to a switch you can centralize control of your SAN devices. In addition to hardware compatibility issues, it is important to select a management application that can be used for the hardware used on each loop that is connected to a switch.

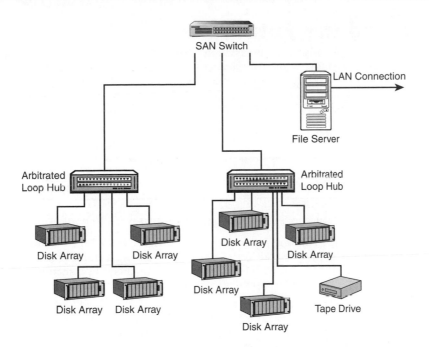

SAN Switch

LAN Connection

File Server

Arbitrated Loop Hub

Arbitrated Loop Hub

Disk Array

Disk Array

Disk Array

Disk Array

Disk Array

Disk Array

Disk Array

Disk Array

Tape Drive

Disk Array

Figure 11.5 Arbitrated Loops can be joined using one or more switches.

When using switches to connect Arbitrated Loops to a larger SAN, you should consider where to locate data on the SAN to minimize overall bandwidth. For example, if you have several loops that each serve a specific business unit, then the resources, such as file servers and tape drives, should be located on the same loop. In this manner the file server can make these resources available to its clients on the LAN.

At the same time, if you have data that needs to be available to a large number of clients spread out over a large network, put the file servers for that data on the same switch as the data, or use a series of high-speed interconnects between switches to make the data highly available to remote network nodes.

Using some SAN management applications, it is also possible to create duplicates of data (mirroring) so that more than one data storage unit stores the same data as another. This is a good method for providing a hot backup of data across a large geographical area, as well as making data that doesn't frequently change available to multiple destinations while reducing the overall bandwidth for the SAN. Remote copies also allow for redundancy in a disaster recovery plan. Backups are performed on data at frequent intervals. However, due to the time necessary to create a backup of a large amount of data, the data that is "exposed" to corruption between the backups might be considerable. If so, using a SAN that mirrors data with another SAN can provide you a backup that is 99.99% up-to-date with your production SAN. SANs separated by just a few kilometers can be connected using a fiber-optic network. To expand the distance between SANs (or between SANs and clients), you can tunnel Fibre Channel frames through other high-bandwidth technologies, such as ATM.

Switches enable your SAN to be stretched to its limits. You can connect Arbitrated Loops to more than a single switch in the SAN network, and thus enable communication between members of distant loops. The connections do not have to be made to the same switch. As you purchase new equipment, you can buy devices that can be connected directly to a switch, and provide an upgrade path for your SAN.

IP SANs and the Future

IP SANs use the Internet Protocol (IP), discussed in Chapter 25, "Overview of the TCP/IP Protocol Suite," instead of Fibre Channel frames to transmit data on a SAN. The difference between an IP SAN and NAS is pretty much the same as the difference between a Fibre Channel SAN and NAS. An IP SAN, like a Fibre Channel SAN, is placed on a separate network from the LAN that connects clients to the network. By offloading the SAN network traffic from the LAN, an IP SAN is similar in topology to a Fibre Channel SAN.

Tip

Don't confuse an IP SAN with tunneling Fibre Channel frames through an IP network, which was discussed earlier in this chapter. An IP SAN doesn't tunnel Fibre Channel frames. Instead, the IP frame is used *in place of* a Fibre Channel frame.

IP SANs definitely have a future in SAN technology. There are several important reasons for this:

- The differences in speed among the differing technologies, from Fibre Channel's newest incarnation to Gigabit Ethernet and 10Gigabit Ethernet, make this a limiting factor that doesn't matter as much as it used to. Even with frame overhead compared to payload ratio, at these speeds (and soon to come even faster speeds—it will never end!), speed will play less of a factor.

- IP is a technology that many network technologists and administrators are already trained on, *because* similar equipment is used for both types of networks. Standardized Fibre Channel equipment requires a new, challenging networking set of skills. IP SANs require only a few new features to learn, and much less investment in equipment.

- Fibre Channel is coming down in price at a drastic rate as economies of scale have reduced prices a lot. However, even having to train personnel on Fibre Channel technology can be costly. And you need to be sure that discounted hardware will interact with hardware from other vendors. Don't buy older technology because of its price, unless you are sure it's not older proprietary hardware that will be difficult to incorporate into your SAN.

These points apply to medium to largescale networks. However, for the very largescale network, the Fibre Channel network, with its increase in speed and low error rate, is often the choice to be made. Fibre Channel SANs aren't going to go away any time soon. Instead, IP SANs will probably develop to be a solution for an inexpensive SAN, while Fibre Channel SAN technology will continue to improve in speed, management software, and reliability.

Tip

The only downside to Fibre Channel and SAN equipment is that, although the technology has been around for about a decade in proprietary formats, it has been only the past few years that standards have been developed. Thus, if you decide to buy equipment from more than one manufacturer, be sure that it will first be tested with your existing equipment before the actual purchase. And check out your SAN management software to see whether it can be used with equipment from various vendors.

What Kind of NAS or SAN Solution Should You Use?

If you choose to use a NAS solution, you should map out the data requirements of your network. As mentioned earlier in this chapter, make sure you locate resources close to clients. Global data can be replicated to multiple sites, although this is more easily done using a SAN.

Most NAS devices are simple to install and manage. For all practical matters, to an experienced LAN technologist, it's just about plug-and-play. A few screens of installation and configuration information are all that are needed to get a simple NAS appliance up and running. If you are choosing between a NAS and a SAN solution, use NAS when your data resources can be compartmentalized for the most part, and use a SAN solution when more than one file server may need to access the same data at the same time. And if you need to keep up-to-date copies of data at different locations, SAN equipment performs this function faster and more reliably than NAS. In general, NAS is the choice for a small number of clients, whereas SAN is the choice for larger environments that use a much larger quantity of data, and have a requirement of almost 0% downtime.

Don't forget the budget when considering your need to add serverless-based storage to a network. It may be that NAS is a less expensive solution for now, although you project a data requirement available only by a SAN in the future. If your NAS solution involves SCSI devices, you can always use a SCSI-Fibre-Channel bridge to make use of these SCSI devices if you later install a SAN.

At this time it would be hard to justify committing to a SAN on a small scale, based on the prospect that later you will expand the SAN to encompass larger data requirements (or other features of a SAN such as RAID or serverless backups). This is because of the current environment that hasn't yet decided on precise standards that allow equipment from various vendors to work seamlessly together. NAS devices are similar to file servers and use protocols that are well defined.

Because many functions are implemented in hardware (the HBAs), SAN hardware devices may suffer from a lack of interoperability with hardware from other manufacturers. This situation is changing, and it will be some time before the adoption of the standards process is complete. The Bluefin initiative being advocated by the Storage Networking Industry Association (http://snia.org) is taking a good step in that direction, by providing a basis for creating a single management application that can be used with hardware from various manufacturers.

Lastly, if your need is not for expanded data storage, but instead for providing data availability for disaster recovery purposes, then a SAN might justify its expense in even the smallest of environments. As mentioned earlier in this chapter, the basic Fibre Channel SAN can cover several kilometers to connect two or more SANs. In a metropolitan geographical environment this may be sufficient. All you have to do is connect together several offices you have in a single local environment and create automatic data replication between each site.

For a business that is more geographically diverse, tunneling Fibre Channel frames through a long-distance protocol may be a better idea. By separating copies of your data by great distances, you can prevent a single local disaster from impacting all copies of your data.

In Figure 11.1 you saw that the topologies of NAS and SANs are much different. NAS devices operate similarly to a LAN client or server. As you can also see in Figure 11.1, a SAN uses its own network that is separate from the LAN used by clients of the servers that make use of the SAN.

In Figure 11.2 you saw that an Arbitrated Loop can be connected by a simple hub to centralize wiring. If all of your equipment is from the same vendor, an Arbitrated Loop is a great inexpensive introduction into a SANs environment. Switches, however, are more standardized and provide for a greater capability of exchanging data between SANs and management applications. NAS appliances also offer management applications, but incorporating the two technologies may offer an additional expense.

The main considerations for choosing between a NAS and a SAN solution mainly pertain to cost and data availability. Here are some other considerations:

- The size of your network and the amount of data that needs to be available to file servers or even high-end workstation clients. If the data requirements, as well as bandwidth requirements, are high, then the SAN is probably the best solution.

- If localized access for data is required (such as in a departmental LAN situation), and the data is generally localized to clients on the same LAN, then NAS may be a good solution.

- For data that changes frequently and is global to an enterprise, except for the smallest network, a SAN is a good choice. This provides multiple servers the capability to access the same data, and provide clients with a fast access to that data.

Tip

Both NAS and SAN devices offer the capability to map different file systems to selected devices. This is more prevalent in SAN equipment than in NAS devices, which generally offer one or more file systems, and usually one of those for each device attached to the different NAS devices on the LAN. SAN solutions, however, usually allow you to partition RAID sets into separate volumes, each of which can host a different file system.

Thus, using a SAN, you can more easily allow many different hardware/operating-system computers to access data on the SAN. And because many non-Windows operating systems (such as Unix/Linux) support reading FAT and FAT32 file systems used by older Windows systems, data interchange can be a simple affair. With the use of the Common Internet File System (CIFS), non-Windows clients, such as Unix/Linux platforms (especially those using SAMBA— www.samba.org), can be incorporated easily into a Windows environment.

Low-Level Network Protocols

SOME OF THE MAIN TOPICS FOR THIS PART ARE

The IEEE LAN/MAN Committee Networking Standards

The Oldest LAN Protocol Is Still Kicking: ARCnet

Ethernet: The Universal Standard

PART III

The IEEE LAN/MAN Committee Networking Standards

SOME OF THE MAIN TOPICS IN THIS CHAPTER ARE

CHAPTER 12

The key to enabling networking products from different manufacturers to work together is *standards*. For software products (including network protocols and applications), standards usually define functionality and the interfaces that expose the product to the world of interoperability. For hardware products (such as routers and switches), standards do pretty much the same, but they can also encompass physical components, such as how signaling is done on the wire and which types of network media can be used. In this chapter you will learn about standards established by the Institute of Electrical and Electronics Engineers, Inc. (IEEE). This nonprofit organization is responsible for many of the networking standards that are in use today on both local and wide area networks, as well the Internet. The IEEE uses committees to work on each area of standardization. The most relevant committees involved in networking are discussed in this chapter.

Note

The IEEE is responsible for a wide range of standards that cover not just computers and network products. The range of standards covers many areas from the electrical power lines that bring electricity to your house to consumer electronics. In this chapter only the important networking protocols are discussed. For more information about the IEEE and the vast range of activities it supports, visit its Web page at **www.ieee.org**.

At the time of this writing, there are almost 900 standards created (or refined) by the IEEE that are in widespread use. Approximately 700 others are in development. Note that although the IEEE is responsible for creating some standards from scratch, this organization has also been responsible for standardizing technology that was developed by other manufacturers. By taking input from existing de facto standards and casting the technology in print, the IEEE benefits both manufacturers and end users alike.

Several steps are taken to create a standard (or set of standards) within the IEEE:

- *Project Authorization Request (PAR)*—The PAR is the beginning of the standardization process. It defines the scope of the new standard as well as its purpose and contacts for individuals who will be responsible for the standard. There is an online form that can be used to begin the process that states the proposed name of the draft document as well as the type of project and contact information. A sponsor (which can be an individual or an organization) is set forth in the PAR.

- *Creating a Draft*—Using templates provided by the IEEE, a draft of the standard is first created. This draft is then submitted to a balloting process in which input is solicited to make changes to or approve the draft document. The draft is then submitted to the IEEE-SA Standards Board, which reviews the documentation and then publishes it for review by others. Note that a draft is just that—it is not a final standard. It is just the first iteration of the standards process.

- *Standards*—The next step is to submit the document to the IEEE Standards Department for approval. The procedures involved in this step are many, and it can take some time before the standard is officially approved. For example, the IEEE may send an application to the American National Standards Institute (ANSI) for its approval.

- *Publication*—After the standard has gone through these processes, it is published as a standard so that manufacturers (and other interested parties) can begin using it.

This is just a general explanation of the standards approval process. In fact, there are many forms to be filled out, many conditions that must be met. The process involves meetings of the working group and constant feedback to gather the information from the various parties to ensure that the final standard is a workable document. The important thing to remember from this is that standards are not created by just a single person or manufacturer. Instead, the proposed drafts are subject to intense scrutiny, and all aspects of the draft can be subject to modification before a final standard is produced. As if that were not enough, it is common to see many established standards modified to keep up with the ever-changing world of technology today.

What Is the LAN/MAN Committee?

This chapter discusses the important standards as defined by the Local Area Network/Metropolitan Area Network (LAN/MAN) Standards Committee (LMSC). This committee consists of various working groups, each of which is devoted to a particular technology. For example, one committee was responsible for the basic Ethernet standard, and another was in charge of developing the standard for the first Token-Ring networks. As if this division were not enough, there are other working groups that further divide the responsibility for a particular technology. For example, there are several working groups actively working on wireless standards at this time.

The focus of the 802.* working groups is trained at the two lowest layers of the OSI Reference Model—the *physical* and *data link layers*—and some aspects of higher layers relating to network management. The LMSC also coordinates its activities with other standards bodies, such as the International Organization for Standardization (ISO), and other standards groups outside of the U.S.

▶▶ The OSI Reference Model is discussed in Appendix A, "Overview of the OSI Seven-Layer Networking Reference Model."

The following sections cover important standards, some of which are mentioned for historical purposes, as well as newer standards that are still under development.

IEEE 802: Overview and Architecture

The IEEE 802 standards document sets forth the groundwork for the others that follow. It includes short descriptions of the types of networks that were to be considered by the committee, and a reference *model* for their development. The terms LAN and MAN are defined in this document:

- *LAN*—A local area network is typically part of a single organization. The LAN is a peer-to-peer network that allows nodes on the network to communicate with one or more nodes on the same LAN. In the original specification, the bus topology was used, though the document has been updated to include switching and other modern LAN techniques.

- *MAN*—A metropolitan area network is a collection of interconnected LANs that span a larger geographical area, such as a campus network or a city. MANs can also be owned and maintained by a single entity, but are more likely offered as services to multiple clients in order to provide a high-bandwidth connection to multiple client networks.

It is important to know that the OSI model is just that: a model. Very few protocols actually adhere strictly to this model. For example, TCP/IP was being developed before the OSI model was created, and thus the TCP/IP model differs from the OSI model.

Today, the OSI Data Link layer, for most network protocols, is usually divided into two sublayers. The Logical Link Control (LLC) and Media Access Control (MAC) sublayers are the result of this separation of the single OSI Data Link layer into two components (although in some standards the functionality provided by these sublayers becomes a little blurred).

The Media Access Control Sublayer

The Media Access Control sublayer provides a service to the LLC sublayers to get the data packets delivered to the destination node. At this sublayer the data to be transmitted are referred to as "frames." The MAC sublayer creates the frames to be transmitted on the physical network media, and includes some error checking to allow the receiving node to check the integrity of the data frame. The MAC address is an important concept when used in modern Ethernet networks. As you will learn in

Chapter 25, "Overview of the TCP/IP Protocol Suite," the IP protocol enables the hierarchical address space that is used on WANs and the Internet. At the LAN level a flat address space is used for communications between nodes on the same LAN.

There is an important distinction to be made between MAC and IP addresses. MAC addresses are simply addresses that are burned into a network card or other hardware by the manufacturer. Part of the address represents the manufacturer, and the remaining portion of the address is assigned in a serial fashion to each network card that the manufacturer produces. Because there is no "organization" using MAC addresses, this addressing technique is known as a flat address space. IP addresses, however, are divided into two parts: a network address and a host address. Thus, IP addresses (which are described in greater detail in Chapter 25) allow for routing and other functions. MAC addresses, however, are generally used only on the local LAN, which consists of a much smaller number of network nodes.

On a LAN, which is used when only a handful of network devices are connected (up to a few hundred or even a few thousand), a MAC address is sufficient for getting the data delivered to the appropriate node. The data frame is broadcast to all nodes—unless a switch is used. The switch learns the MAC addresses for attached devices and eliminates the "broadcast." When a node recognizes that a frame contains its MAC address, it responds by grabbing the frame, and from that point onward the MAC address is used to communicate between the two nodes. Many network devices have the capability of maintaining a table of MAC addresses to IP addresses. This information stays in the table for a short period in case additional communications take place. Eventually the entry is aged out of the table as new address pairs are added.

Tip

Distinguishing between MAC and IP addresses is simple. MAC addresses are used for any device on a LAN, whether it be a computer, printer, or router for exchanging data. IP addresses are used to exchange data between LANs. After the IP protocol has delivered the data to a router connected to a LAN, the MAC address is used to exchange data between the router and the destination device. And all communications on a LAN use the MAC address for communications.

The Physical Layer

At the bottom of the OSI model, you will find the physical components that perform the functions needed to transmit the data passed down from higher layers. These include the network adapter card and the network media—copper wire or fiber-optic cables, for example.

It is easy to understand the packet or frame that a higher-level protocol constructs, which you will learn about in following chapters. The actual signaling mechanism at the physical layer, however, can be different depending on the network media, and this mechanism can be different depending on the transmission protocol used for the network media. For example, 10BASE-T and 100BASE-T and Gigabit Ethernet transmissions across a copper network media use different methods to send bits of data across the network. Similarly, the mechanisms used to send data across a fiber-optic cable will depend on the protocol used.

Consider the process of sending single bits of information across a network cable. You might expect that each bit is represented by some kind of state change (electrical or photo-optic) on the cable. This is not always the case. Instead, at the physical level, various techniques are used. It may be as simple as varying the voltage on a copper wire or as involved as using statistical methods to vary the voltage and frequency of the signal. A good example of the physical method for transmitting bytes of information across a network is Fibre Channel, in which 10 bits are used to send 8 bits of data. In this case, for each byte of information there can be either one or two possible bit combinations used to transmit the same byte! This is because Fibre Channel, usually implemented using fiber-optic cables, tries to maintain a "running disparity" on the network media. This is for several reasons, which are covered in detail in Chapter 11, "Network Attached Storage and Storage Area Networks." Another example of this, Manchester Encoding, is described in Chapter 14, "Ethernet: The Universal Standard."

Other Physical Layer Components

The physical layer standards established by the 802.* committee involve many other concepts, such as bridges (see the chapter "Bridges, Repeaters, and Hubs," on the upgradingandrepairingpcs.com Web site) and the protocols associated with these devices, like the Spanning Tree Algorithm. After you get past the LAN/MAN specifications, the routing terrain is the next step. Because routing implies connecting various physical LANs, routing is beyond the scope of the LAN/MAN committee.

The most widely used LAN technology in use today is Ethernet. And this protocol and its associated technologies have been extended over time to allow for end-to-end Ethernet connections across MANs. The various 802.* standards for Ethernet, Token-Ring, and other networking technologies are explored in the following sections.

IEEE 802.1: Bridging and Management

The 802.1 standards concern bridging. Bridging involves connecting two or more networks using an intermediary network device that serves one or two purposes. First, a bridge can be used to connect several LAN segments so that traffic between nodes on the network is confined to that LAN segment. Second, a bridge can be used to translate between different protocols. For more information about bridges, see the chapter "Bridges, Repeaters, and Hubs" on the upgradingandrepairingpcs.com Web site.

Since the original publication of this standard, there have been several other standards that relate to the original 802.1. For example, IEEE 802.1Q discusses using bridges to create a virtual LAN. IEEE 802.1x provides for the use of a MAC bridge to create a virtual LAN. Both of these are discussed in further detail in Chapter 9, "Virtual LANs."

▶▶ Note that there are several standards groups that work on new technologies. For example, don't confuse 802.1 with 802.11, which is covered later in this chapter. Each letter following the "802." refers to different aspects of networking technology.

IEEE 802.2: Logical Link Control

As described earlier, the IEEE specifications divide the Data Link layer into two parts: the Logical Link Control (LLC) sublayer and the Media Access Control sublayer. The LLC sublayer provides services to the Network layer in the OSI model, independent of the underlying MAC sublayer.

This sublayer provides for three kinds of service. Type 1 defines an unacknowledged connectionless-mode link. Type 2 defines a connection-mode link. Type 3 defines an acknowledged connectionless-mode. It isn't important to understand exactly what these types of links really mean at this point. In Chapter 25, you will learn how TCP provides a connection-oriented link, whereas other protocols, such as UDP, provide a connectionless link. The important thing to remember here is that the IEEE 802 documentation defines the features and boundaries of these types of connections.

Type 1 services do not need any "setup" before communications can begin. This type of service provides no mechanisms for flow control or error detection.

Type 2 services dictate that a logical link must be established before data communications can begin. An example of this is the TCP protocol, which uses a "handshake" exchange of network packets to set up the link before the actual data exchange can begin. This type of service does provide for error detection and flow control.

Type 3 services provide for a connectionless link, in which no setup is required. However, acknowledgments are used to ensure that network packets are received intact and in the order in which they are sent.

IEEE 802.3: CSMA/CD Access Method

Until the development of full-duplex switches, the method used by nodes on an Ethernet network to gain access to the shared network media was called Carrier Sense Multiple Access/Collision Detect, or CSMA/CD. This simply means that before attempting to send data on a shared LAN segment, the computer (or other networked device) would first listen (carrier sense) to determine whether another device is already transmitting data (multiple access). If not, the node could begin to transmit data onto the network. If more than one node senses that the network media is not being used and both nodes begin to transmit data at about the same time, a "collision" occurs (collision detect). In that case, each node will stop transmitting for a semi-random interval before attempting to transmit again.

For small LANs this technique provides an inexpensive method to allow computers to use a shared network media. As networks have grown in size, switches have replaced hubs in most networks. Switches remove the "collision domain" so that communications take place between just the switch port and the computer connected to that port. If the switch operates in half-duplex mode, a collision can occur if the switch and the attached computer both try to transmit data at the same time. In full-duplex mode, which is the most widely used mode today, the switch port and the attached computer do not share the same wires, but instead each has a dedicated set of wires so that the switch can send data while the attached computer is sending data to the switch.

It is important to understand the CSMA/CD technique, however, so that you can see how Ethernet has evolved from a shared media networking technology to the switched environment used today. For more information about CSMA/CD, see Chapter 14.

IEEE 802.4: Token-Passing Bus Access Method and IEEE 802.5: Token-Ring Access Method

Token-Ring and Token-Bus technologies have a lot in common. They both assume a ring topology, and a token frame is passed from one node to another. When a node on the network needs to transmit data, it waits until it receives the token frame and then transmits a data frame. The data frame travels around the ring until the destination node receives it. Upon successfully receiving a data frame, the destination node sets a few bits in the frame to indicate that it was successfully received and retransmits the modified frame on the network. When the sending node receives the frame it originally sent, it can check the bits to see that the data was received, and it then transmits a token frame so that another node can use the network.

The major difference between the Token-Bus and the Token-Ring network is that the Token-Ring network is physically wired in a ring topology. That is, the transmitter of a node is connected to the receiver of the next node in the ring, until the last node in the ring connects back to the receiver of the first node in the ring. When a Token-Bus is used, a single network media is used that connects all nodes, similar to a bus topology in early Ethernet networks. However, the ring topology is maintained as a *logical ring*. Instead of using the CSMA/CD method to access the shared bus media, each node on a network passes the token frame from one node to another, in a predetermined order, and thus a ring formation is still used.

Token-Ring networks are still in use today, though their numbers are far outweighed by the installed base of Ethernet networks. Token-Bus networks were generally used in industrial situations, such as factory floors, where a guaranteed minimum access time was crucial. Development of Token-Bus topologies has now been discontinued. To quote the IEEE, "These standards were administratively withdrawn by the IEEE Standards Board." Although Token-Ring networks are still marketed today, the speeds at which Ethernet now operates has all but rendered Token-Ring to history.

For more information about Token-passing technologies, see the chapter "Token-Ring Networks," located on the upgradingandrepairingpcs.com Web site.

IEEE 802.7: Recommended Practices for Broadband Local Area Networks

This standard, first published in 1989, described various items that were pertinent to offering broadband communications at that time. These included a bus topology and amplifiers using coaxial cabling and frequency division multiplexing (FDM) that allows for communications in two directions, by using different frequencies for each direction of the link. This standard can be considered the grandfather of the standards used for cable and the xDSL modems that are so popular today. It is mentioned here so that you'll understand that broadband communications based on cable networks were envisioned many years ago, and are commonplace today.

IEEE 802.10: Security

First published in 1998, this standards document defines "IEEE Standards for Local and Metropolitan Area Networks: Standard for Interoperable LAN/MAN Security (SILS)." As the title implies, this standard discusses many aspects of security for both local area networks and metropolitan area networks. This document was updated in 1999, and it defines many concepts that have been adopted, or modified for use in networks today. For more information about current security standards, read Part VIII of this book, "System and Network Security," which contains several chapters devoted to this important topic.

IEEE 802.11: Wireless

Perhaps the most fascinating new development in the past few years is the widespread adoption of wireless networking technologies. From short-range technologies such as Bluetooth (see Chapter 23, "Bluetooth Wireless Technology") to the now popular Wi-Fi (802.11b) networks, wireless LANs have become commodity items as the price of hardware has dropped dramatically. The 802.11 standards are covered in several documents. For example, 802.11b is now available in your local discount electronics store, and the Wi-Fi branding enables you to choose equipment from different manufacturers with the guarantee that the equipment has been tested for interoperability.

As this book is being published, the 802.11a standard is rapidly coming into the marketplace. This standard uses a different frequency range than 802.11b and provides a larger bandwidth (that is, speed). Other 802.11 standards have been developed to encompass security measures, and other such items as virtual LANs, as discussed in Chapter 9.

Part V, "Wireless Networking Protocols," covers the implementation of wireless networking standards in greater detail.

Obtaining the IEEE 802 Standards Documents Free

Due to the technical nature of most of the IEEE standards documents, most are quite lengthy. If you are not an electrical engineer, you might find that reading these documents can be quite a chore. The same can be said for the Request for Comments (RFC) documents that are used to define Internet standards. However, for those who want to read the documents, the IEEE has made those mentioned in this chapter available online in Adobe Acrobat format. The most pertinent technologies are discussed in following chapters. However, if you are curious or just want to see how detailed the standards are, you can visit the IEEE Web site for the LAN/MAN standards at http://standards.ieee.org/getieee802.

The Oldest LAN Protocol Is Still Kicking: ARCnet

SOME OF THE MAIN TOPICS IN THIS CHAPTER ARE

Of the networking technologies still widely in use today, ARCnet is the oldest. It was created at Datapoint Corporation in the 1970s and is a token-passing system similar in many ways to Token-Ring. For small networks, ARCnet is a reliable technology that is easy to configure. However, also like Token-Ring, ARCnet equipment is produced by only a small number of manufacturers when compared to the huge number of manufacturers making Ethernet equipment. Along with its slow network speed (usually 2.5Mbs to 10Mbps), this makes ARCnet a prime candidate for an upgrade to newer technology for networking desktop systems. Although it was originally developed for the purpose of connecting minicomputers to create a local area network, you would be hard-pressed to find it used that way today.

All that said, ARCnet is still widely used for other purposes. For example, you can find this technology embedded in various controllers used for industrial automation on factory floors. The basic ARCnet standard is defined as ANSI/ATA 878.1, but extensions and other changes to the original standard have been developed over the years. This chapter gives you a good overview of the details of ARCnet operations and the hardware components involved. However, many vendors offer variations on the original standard, allowing for greater distances between nodes, for example. For those interested, the ARCnet Trade Association (ATA) keeps a Web page that contains links to many manufacturers of ARCnet hardware. You can visit their Web site at www.arcnet.com. There is also an ARCnet user group in Europe, which you can reach using the URL www.arcnet.de/.

As a matter of fact, you've probably encountered ARCnet at some point in your life and just didn't know it. For example, when you order at McDonald's or White Castle Hamburgers, the cash register (oh, I mean point-of-sale terminal) is probably linked to other similar systems through ARCnet. When you turn up the thermostat at work, there's a good chance that it's connected to a central computer for the building that uses ARCnet. You'll even find ARCnet used to connect medical devices, such as X-ray machines, at your doctor's office!

So although ARCnet is the oldest networking technology around today, its stability, simplicity, and low overhead make it a perfect solution for many different kinds of applications. Sometimes newer isn't always better! After all, would you want someone who says "Do you want fries with that?" at your favorite drive-through to be in charge of configuring a TCP/IP network?

Overview of ARCnet

ARCnet stands for Attached Resource Computer Network. Because it is a token-passing system, ARCnet is a deterministic network technology that is useful in situations where a predictable throughput is required. It was a very popular technology during the early 1980s, when Ethernet was still quite expensive and most local area networks were small. Its speed of 2.5Mbps was more than sufficient for implementing ARCnet in a small office network, given the relative power of PCs and minicomputers at that time. Now, it is most likely to be found in older departmental LANs (though I've never seen one) or in an industrial manufacturing plant or another similar setting. The basic ARCnet operates at a rate of 2.5Mbps and can be used to create a LAN of as many as 255 computers. Some network hardware vendors produce network adapters and hubs that allow for speeds up to 10Mbps.

Although ARCnet is no longer marketed primarily as a PC LAN solution, it does have many features that make it well suited for industrial applications. Factory floor automation requires that controllers and other devices have a communications network in place that allows for reliable, predictable throughput. The following are some of the reasons why ARCnet is still in use today, in environments such as this:

- It's deterministic. That is, because it uses a token-passing mechanism, it is possible to calculate the worst-case amount of time it takes to get a frame from one node to another. Using basic Ethernet, nodes on the network must contend for access to the shared network medium, and performance can suffer as network traffic increases.

- It's simplistic. Other than assigning an address to each ARCnet node, few software configuration or management tasks are needed. This makes ARCnet practically "invisible" to workers using devices that have embedded ARCnet adapters.

- Although ARCnet is similar to Token-Ring technology in that it uses a token frame to grant access to the network, no central computer or device is responsible for monitoring or managing the network. All nodes in the network are equal peers. Adding and removing devices from the network is a simple task.

- ARCnet can be wired using various cables—from coaxial to fiber optic. This makes connecting devices or adapters from multiple vendors easy.

- Although adapter cards for use in PCs and other computer are generally more expensive than Ethernet alternatives, chips used in embedded controllers are usually quite inexpensive.

In an environment such as factory automation, the fact that ARCnet requires little configuration and management makes it a good solution.

Although development was started before the OSI reference model was defined, ARCnet provides functions along the same lines as those defined in the physical and data link layers of the reference model. The ARCnet network adapter card, or the embedded chip in a factory device, takes care of the successful, reliable transmission of a message, relieving the software protocol of these functions.

▶▶ See "Overview of the OSI Seven-Layer Networking Reference Model," p. 1121.

Although Datapoint originally manufactured the chips used to create ARCnet network adapters, the primary manufacturer of chips used today is Standard Microsystems Corporation (SMSC). You can reach their Web site at www.smsc.com. This site contains specific technical documentation for the chips found in most ARCnet products today.

ARCnet Addressing and Message Transmission

The logical topology of the ARCnet network is always a token bus, although it can be physically arranged as a bus, a star, or a hierarchical star topology, which is a combination of the two (see "Bus and Star Topologies," later in this chapter). ARCnet is a *logical* token bus because no matter which physical topology is used, the *token frame*, which grants permission to a node to transmit data, is passed around in a sequential manner based on a numerical address from one node to the next. Thus, all nodes get an equal chance to access the network media within a maximum set time limit.

◀◀ See Chapter 2, "Overview of Network Topologies," p. 13.

▶▶ See the chapter "Token-Ring Networks," located on the upgradingandrepairingpcs.com Web site.

Note

ARCnet isn't restricted to the factory floor. For Linux users there is even a Linux How-To document, maintained by Avery Pennarun, that can guide you in choosing a card and a network driver so that you can link your Linux computers using ARCnet. You can find this How-To at www.worldvisions.ca/~apenwarr/arcnet/howto/index.html.

Each node on the LAN is configured with an address from within the range of 1–255. This is because the address fields in ARCnet frames are only 8 bits in length (one byte). Because the largest number you can store in a single byte is 255, this limits ARCnet LANs to small implementations. Of course, back in the 1970s, linking 255 computers was considered exceptional.

The token frame, called an Invitation to Transmit (ITT), is sequentially passed from one node to another based on the addresses assigned to devices in the network. When a node receives the ITT token, it can then transmit a message on the network, or it can pass the frame to the node that has the next highest numerical address in the network. The next node doesn't have to be the node that is located physically closest to the sending node; it can be anywhere on the network. The hierarchy of numerical addressing determines the order in which a node is granted permission to transmit on the network.

ARCnet Symbols and Frame Formats

Two different frame formats are used on an ARCnet LAN. The basic frame format consists of five types, each of which is used for a specific messaging purpose. The second frame format is the Reconfiguration Burst frame, which is the only frame of the five that is used in configuring the network. All frames, however, are made up using a set of basic symbols (see Figure 13.1):

- **Start Delimiter (SD)**—This symbol consists of six ones. All the basic frames use this symbol to indicate the beginning of a frame.

- **Reconfiguration Symbol Unit (RSU)**—This symbol is made up of eight ones followed by a zero. This symbol is used in a special frame, described later in this chapter. It is used to reconfigure the network when a node joins the network.

Besides these two symbols, a set of Information Symbol Units (ISU) is used. Each ISU consists of a bit pattern of 110 followed by an 8-bit value for each ISU. Thus, all ISUs are 11 bits in length. ISUs can serve to indicate the kind of frame that is being transmitted, network addresses, and the actual data that is transmitted inside a data packet frame. Most of the frames you will see on an ARCnet LAN consist of the SD symbol followed by one or more of the following ISUs:

- **Start of Header (SOH)**—This value indicates the beginning of a data packet. Note that the SOH should not be confused with the SD symbol, which precedes the SOH symbol. The SD symbol indicates the start of the frame, whereas the SOH symbol indicates that the frame contains a data packet. The value for this symbol is 0x01.

- **Enquiry (ENQ)**—This symbol is used in a frame that is sent to determine whether the destination node has enough buffer space in memory to receive a message. The value for this symbol is 0x85.

- **Acknowledgment (ACK)**—This symbol is used to send an acknowledgment. The value for this symbol is 0x86.

- **Negative Acknowledgment (NAK)**—This symbol is used as the opposite of an ACK. It is used in a frame to tell the sender that the destination node does not have free buffer space at this time. The value for this symbol is 0x15.

- **End of Transmission (EOT)**—This symbol is used in the token frame. The node that receives a frame containing this symbol can then begin to transmit a message on the network medium. The value for this symbol is 0x04.

- **Next Node Identification (NID)**—This symbol contains the address of the next logical node in the network and also is used in the token frame. This address is the node to which the token frame will be passed when the current holder releases it. The values of this symbol can range from 0x01 to 0xFF (1–255 decimal).

- **Source Node Identification (SID)**—This symbol contains the address of the sender of a data message packet. Like the NID, this symbol can have a value ranging from 0x01 to 0xFF.

- **Destination Node Identification (DID)**—This symbol contains the address of the node to which a request to send frame or a data packet frame is being sent. Like the NID and SID, this value can range from 0x01 to 0xFF.

- **Continuation Pointer (CP)**—This symbol indicates the length of the data packet. The value of this symbol can range from 0x03 to 0xFF. As explained later in this chapter, data packets come in two types: short and long. Short packets contain one CP symbol, whereas long packets contain two CP symbols.

- **System Code (SC)**—This symbol is assigned by the ARCnet Trade Association, mentioned earlier in this chapter, and is used to indicate a higher-level protocol. SC symbols are used in data packets. The value for this symbol can range from 0x00 to 0xFF. Using a symbol to specify the protocol allows more than one network protocol to be used on the same network. Note that the value of 0x80 is a reserved code and is used for diagnostic purposes only.

- **Frame Check Sequence (FCS)**—This symbol contains the value of the calculated cyclic redundancy check (CRC-16) used to verify that the contents of the data packet arrived intact and were not corrupted during transit. The value for this symbol can range from 0x00 to 0xFFFF. Because the value of 0xFFFF requires more than 8 bits in binary, two ISU symbols are used to create the FCS in a data packet.

- **Data**—The actual user data contained in a packet is composed of multiple ISUs, each 11 bits in length. Although you need only 8 bits to create a byte, remember that each ISU contains the 3-bit preamble of 110, so each byte of user data is actually represented by 11 bits inside the data portion of a data packet.

Using these basic symbols, it is now possible to define the kinds of frames that can be constructed so that nodes can communicate on the ARCnet LAN. The five basic frame types are listed here:

- **ITT**—Invitation to Transmit. This is the token frame that is passed around the logical network, giving the node that possesses the frame permission to send a data message on the network medium.

- **FBE**—Free Buffer Enquiry. This frame type is used by a node to determine whether the destination node has sufficient buffer space in memory to receive a message before it is sent.

- **ACK**—Acknowledgment. This frame is sent in response to the FBE frame if the destination is willing to receive the message.

- **NAK**—Negative Acknowledgment. This frame is sent in response to the FBE if the destination is not willing to receive the message at this time.

- **PAC**—Packet. This frame carries the actual message data. ARCnet uses two kinds of PAC frames: short and long. Obviously, the long version is meant for sending messages of a larger size.

Figure 13.1 shows the layout of the symbols used to construct the different frame types.

Note that in Figure 13.1, each frame type begins with the start delimiter (SD) symbol. Only the actual data packet frames (PAC) contain the frame check sequence that is used to verify the integrity of the data in the packet. Another interesting thing to note is that a short packet can contain as many as 2,772 bits in the data section, whereas the long packet type has a minimum of 2,816 bits for the data section. This is because data ISUs with values of 253, 254, or 255 are not allowed. If a message falls within these bounds, the message is sent in a long packet, with null padding (a string of zero bytes) added to adjust the length of the packet.

Note also that the number of bits includes the 3-bit preamble for each byte of data in the data portion of the packet. That is, although the data section in a short packet can be up to 2,772 bits long, that doesn't mean you can place 346.5 (2,772/8) bytes of actual data in the data section. Instead, you can place only a maximum of 252 (2,772/11) bytes of data. Each byte effectively is represented by 11 bits, with the first 3 bits being the constant value of 110. Likewise, the maximum number of bits in the data portion of a long data packet is 5,577, which means that the maximum number of bytes that a long packet can carry is 507 bytes (5,577/11).

6 bits SD	11 bits EOT	11 bits NID	11 bits NID

Invitation to Transmit (ITT)

6 bits SD	11 bits ENQ	11 bits DID	11 bits DID

Free Buffer Enquiry (FBE)

6 bits SD	11 bits ACK

Acknowledgment (ACK)

6 bits SD	11 bits NAK

Negative Acknowledgment (NAK)

Short Packet

6 bits SD	11 bits SOH	11 bits SID	11 bits DID	11 bits DID	11 bits CP	11 bits SC	0-2772 data bits	22 bits FCS

Long Packet

6 bits SD	11 bits SOH	11 bits SID	11 bits DID	11 bits DID	22 bits CP	11 bits SC	2816-5577 data bits	22 bits FCS

Figure 13.1   Frame types used on ARCnet LANs.

The following basic steps are involved in sending a message in an ARCnet network:

1. A node that has a message to send receives the token frame.

2. Before sending the message, the source node sends a Free Buffer Enquiry (FBE) frame to the node to which it wants to communicate. Looking back at Figure 13.1, you can see that this is a simple frame that doesn't even contain the source address of the computer or device making the request. Only the destination address is contained in the frame, and it is stored in the frame twice.

3. If the destination node has available buffer space to receive a message, it transmits an acknowledgment frame. If it does not have sufficient space in its memory to receive the message, it sends a negative acknowledgment. Again, this frame does not contain the source address of the device that originated the request.

4. When the sender sees the acknowledgment frame, it sends the message to the destination node. The message is sent in a packet that can range up to as many as 507 bytes of data. As with most network technologies, the message packet contains a header. Both the source and the destination addresses are included in this frame. This frame uses a CRC (cyclic redundancy check) value that the receiving node can use to ensure the accuracy of the message received.

5. When the receiving node checks the CRC value against the data and determines that the message was accurately received, it sends another acknowledgment frame around the network. If the message data fails the CRC test, the receiving node transmits nothing. A timer on the sending node eventually expires, so the sender knows that its message was not delivered correctly.

6. After a successful transmission (acknowledgment received) or unsuccessful transmission (timer expired), the sending node relinquishes the token by passing it to the network node that has the next higher address on the network.

In this sequence of events, the node that gains control of the token frame can make only one attempt at transmitting a data packet. If the data does not reach its intended destination—the timer expires before an acknowledgment is received—the sending node does not immediately try to resend the data packet. Instead, it passes the token frame (ITT) to the next logical member of the ring and waits until the token frame returns to it again before it attempts to send the data packet.

If the message that the sender wants to transmit is larger than 507 bytes, the sender divides the message into smaller units and must wait until it receives the token again to send each fragment. The receiving node reassembles the fragments to get the full message.

Note

ARCnet also supports a broadcast message, using zero as the destination address. When this type of message is sent, the acknowledgment procedure is not used. Additionally, only nodes that have been configured to respond to broadcast messages will process them.

This simple scheme shows that it is possible to calculate the minimum amount of time it can take to send a message from one node to another. It also shows that the worst-case scenario can be calculated by taking into account the number of nodes on the network, cable lengths, timer values, and other similar factors. Thus, for real-time applications in which network transmit time needs to be predictable, ARCnet can be a good solution. For example, the more nodes you add to the network, the greater the latency time before a node will be able to transmit. But it will, with some exceptions, be able to transmit within a specific time, which can increase as the number of connected nodes increases. This does not take into account the fact that not all nodes are waiting to transmit data. That depends on the type of network and the devices attached.

Network Configuration

ARCnet does not require that the network administrator assign addresses sequentially beginning with 1 and continuing through 255. In fact, as long as each node has a unique address assigned to it, it doesn't matter whether there are gaps in the address space. The ARCnet LAN uses a process that automatically lets each node discover its logical neighbor (the node with the next highest numerical address). When adding or removing nodes from the network, the network undergoes an automatic reconfiguration process.

The method by which a node joins the network uses the second frame format used by ARCnet: the Reconfiguration Burst frame format. This frame contains 765 RSU symbols (eight ones followed by a zero). When a node determines that it is not part of the logical LAN (that is, it doesn't receive the token within a short period) it uses the Reconfiguration Burst frame to effectively disrupt any current transmission or token passing that is in progress at the time. Other nodes on the network then begin a process of reconfiguration.

Each node backs off for a timeout period based on its numerical address. The node that has the highest address will be the first node to timeout. It then will attempt to locate its logical neighbor by incrementing its own address by one and transmitting a token frame. If a node with that address does not respond, the node increments the address again and continues to send a token frame until its neighbor is found. The remaining nodes on the network use this process so that, within a very short period, each node in the network knows its neighbor and normal communications can resume.

A node leaving the network is detected easily, and the network again undergoes a reconfiguration process. After a node sends a token frame to its neighbor, it continues to listen on the network to be sure that the neighbor will in turn pass on the token, or perhaps start the process of sending a message to another node. Remember that, although the ARCnet LAN can be laid out in bus and star formations, the address space (1–255) makes the network a logical ring so that a node can be sure that it will hear something on the network within certain time limits. In the original standard, the maximum time allowed for a frame to make the trip from one node to another is 32 microseconds. In actual applications, it is possible to extend this value by adjusting timers to allow for greater distances between nodes.

Thus, when a node determines that something has gone wrong with its current logical neighbor, it then starts to search for a new neighbor. It does this by taking the address of the neighbor that was removed from the network (or failed in some way) and incrementing it by one. It sends out a token based on this new address. This continues until some response is detected (that is, the token successfully passes around the net).

Hubs and Network Wiring

An ARCnet network can be wired using universal twisted-pair (UTP) cables, coaxial cables, or fiber-optic cables. For UTP, Category 3 cables or above should be used. Coaxial cables should be RG11U or RG-59U or RG-62. The distance between network nodes depends on the type of wiring used and the type of hubs used as wiring concentrators.

Two types of hubs can be used when creating an ARCnet network:

- **Active hubs**—Active hubs provide the longest distance capabilities for the ARCnet LAN. The active hub acts much like an Ethernet hub, and it is usually manufactured in 8- to 16-port units. The active hub takes the incoming signal and amplifies it before sending it back out on the other ports. Some active hubs perform other tasks, such as segmenting or blocking off a port that exhibits errors so that other segments are unaffected.

- **Passive hubs**—Passive hubs usually have only four ports and do no signal amplification. Instead, a passive hub acts as a simple signal-splitter, taking the incoming signal and dividing it among the other three ports. A passive hub can be used to create a very small LAN—that is, one with four nodes or fewer. The primary function of a passive hub in a larger LAN is to join individual workstations to an active hub. Unused ports on a passive hub usually should be terminated. Unused ports on active hubs, depending on the manufacturer, might or might not need to be terminated.

Bus and Star Topologies

Even though ARCnet is a token-passing technology, like a Token-Ring network, it can be wired in using several methods. Unlike with Token-Ring networks, no computer on the ARCnet LAN acts as a monitor to check for errors or otherwise manage the network. The reconfiguration process that ARCnet uses to form a logical ring is not directly related to the physical layout of the network.

Bus Topology

The simplest network topology that can be used for ARCnet is a bus using coaxial cables with BNC T-connectors. Up to eight nodes can be connected to any bus segment in a daisy-chain made up using the T-connectors. The total length of the segment is limited to 300 meters (1,000 feet). For such a small network, no hub would be necessary. However, as you can see in Figure 13.2, an active hub can be used to join multiple segments to create a larger LAN than can be created by using a single cable segment. A passive hub cannot be used to connect individual segments based on a bus topology; only active hubs can do this. Passive hubs can be used only to connect individual workstations.

You also can create a bus topology using UTP cables. The UTP ARCnet adapter has two connectors, usually RJ11 or RJ45. Stations are daisy-chained from one node to the next using both connectors. In some cases, the last node on each end of the bus will need to have a terminator inserted into the last connector. Some cards provide an auto-termination feature. When using UTP, you can have as many as 10 nodes on one segment, with any repeater counting toward that limit. Each node on the bus must be separated by a *minimum* of about 6 feet. The total segment length can be as much as 400 feet (120 meters).

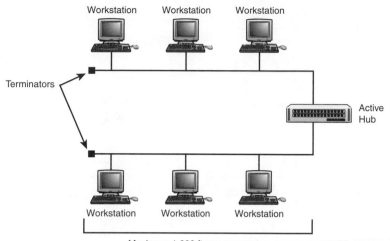

Figure 13.2 An active hub can be used to join multiple coaxial segments, and might need terminators.

Star Topology

You can create a physical star topology by using hubs. You can create a tree structure of multiple stars by cascading hubs. Figure 13.3 shows a small network that uses both active and passive hubs, and also has workstations that connect directly to an active hub.

The major difference you will notice in Figure 13.3 is that, when a station connects to an active hub, the distance can be as great as 2,000 feet (500 meters). When a station connects to a passive hub, the distance shrinks to only 100 feet (30 meters). These same rules apply when connecting hubs. The passive hub connected to an active hub cannot be farther away than 100 feet. Two active hubs can be separated by as much as 2,000 feet. The capability of the active hub to regenerate the signal accounts for the longer distances achieved. The overall size of the network should never exceed 20,000 feet (6,000 meters).

Note

You can use active hubs to reach the maximum distance of 6,000 meters. When a large LAN is constructed in this manner, remember that no loops can exist in the physical topology and the total number of network nodes is limited to 255 because of the 8-bit address used.

Many vendors sell hubs, cables, and other network devices that can be used to create ARCnet networks that vary from these topologies and their limitations. The best source for information about vendors who supply ARCnet hardware is the ARCnet Trade Association (www.arcnet.com).

ARCnet Network Adapter Cards

Because ARCnet has been around for so long, a lot of different network cards are still in use today. ARCnet cards are not interchangeable with Ethernet cards. During an upgrade, you will have to incur the cost of new NICs for each node on the network. Two main categories of cards are used in ARCnet networks: Bus NIC (high-impedance driver) and Star NIC (low-impedance driver). As their names imply, they are different in that the Bus NIC should be used on a bus topology and the Star NIC should be used on a star topology. Some newer cards can provide both options.

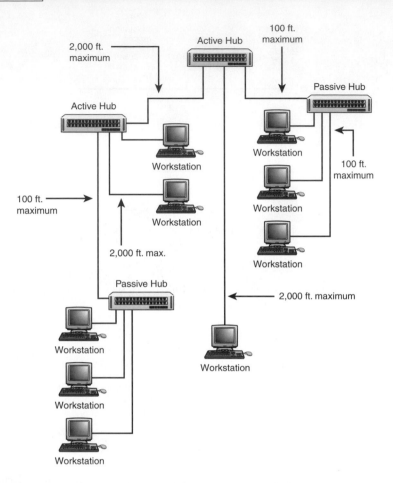

Figure 13.3   The star topology can be extended using additional hubs.

Tip

When you are choosing cards or devices with embedded adapters, it is important to pay attention to the cabling and connector supported by the adapter or device.

Connecting ARCnet LANs to Ethernet LANs

Because of the different signaling methods used and the different network access techniques, it should be obvious that you can't mix Ethernet and ARCnet nodes on the same cable. However, one of the advantages of ARCnet is that there are vendors who manufacture hubs and other devices that allow you to connect dissimilar cabled networks. For example, there are active hubs that allow for coaxial cable, twisted pair, and fiber-optic cabling. Conversion boxes are also available to bridge between an Ethernet network and an ARCnet LAN. Upper-level protocols, such as TCP/IP, can then be used to pass traffic between the two networks.

Troubleshooting ARCnet

Following are some items you should keep in mind when troubleshooting ARCnet:

- ARCnet active hubs will usually partition off a segment that exhibits problems that might interrupt other network activity. Thus, if a node fails, you should examine all the components between the hub and the network card.

- Network analyzers, including small, handheld models, can be used to check for cable problems.

- If a port on the hub is suspected to be the problem, terminate the port and insert the cable in another port.

- As with all network adapters, you can try inserting the card in a different slot in the computer or device, or swap out the card with one known to work, to determine whether the problem lies in the network card.

- When using a bus technology with coaxial cable, be sure that both ends of the segment are terminated properly, either by a terminator or by being plugged into a hub port.

- All BNC T-connectors on a coaxial cable should be examined to be sure that they are connected tightly to the network adapter, as well as to the two cable segments they connect.

- If using twisted-pair wiring, check the vendor's specifications to ensure that you are using the correct pin-out for the adapter or hub.

- Standard Ethernet twisted-pair cables will most likely not work, so be sure you're using the correct cable when installing a new node.

- As with any LAN networking technology, check to be sure that you've observed the distance and number of node limits imposed by the topology you choose. For example, when adding a hub to an existing network, be sure that the cables attached will not exceed the total network diameter and that the nodes attached to the hub will not exceed the 255-node limit for the LAN.

Ethernet: The Universal Standard

14

SOME OF THE MAIN TOPICS IN THIS CHAPTER ARE

CHAPTER 14

If you sit down at almost any PC or desktop workstation today, it is very likely that the computer will be linked to the local network by one form of Ethernet or another. Although other local area networking technologies, such as Token-Ring or Novell's legacy IPX/SPX, are still around, Ethernet-connected computers outnumber all other LAN technologies combined. You'll also find that, most likely, Ethernet is the underlying networking technology that connects servers, printers, and other devices on your network. Ethernet has become so pervasive that every major manufacturer of networking equipment sells equipment that is designed to work with or provide interconnectivity with Ethernet LANs.

So before we start talking about network transport protocols, services, and applications, it is important that you get a good understanding of what Ethernet is and how it functions. It's also important that you understand that there is more than one kind of Ethernet. What started out as a simple LAN technology has evolved to the point that it is now seriously considered a wide area networking technology. From the first commercial versions that operated at 10Mbps to the newest 10Gigabit Ethernet, you'll find that there's an Ethernet solution to most network problems you encounter. It's on the desktop. It's in the wiring closet. It's the backbone of your network.

In this chapter, we'll first look at how Ethernet got its start, and then describe the different versions that were standardized and marketed. After giving you a thorough lesson in Ethernet technology, we'll look at techniques that can be used to troubleshoot Ethernet networks.

A Short History of Ethernet

Ethernet was originally developed at Xerox PARC (Palo Alto Research Center) Laboratories in the 1970s. Robert Metcalfe was charged with the responsibility of networking a group of computers that could all use a new laser printer that Xerox had developed. Xerox also had just developed what was probably the first personal workstation, and had a need to network more than the usual two or three computers that you would find in a single building during that time.

The original Ethernet standard was developed over the next few years, and this resulted in a paper, "Ethernet: Distributed Packet-Switching for Local Computer Networks," written by Metcalfe and David Boggs (*Communications of the ACM*, Vol. 19, No. 5, July 1976, pp. 395–404). This paper gives credit to the ALOHA project that had been done in Hawaii with packet radio transmissions into the "ether," noting that scientists once thought that electromagnetic radio signals traveled through a substance known as "ether." In this first Ethernet experimental network described in the paper, the network covered a distance of 1 kilometer, ran at 3Mbps, and had 256 stations connected to it. For its time, this was an accomplishment.

Note

The Metcalfe and Boggs paper anticipated many other innovations that would appear in the next few years in the area of networking. They recognized the limits of a local area network using a shared medium. They also anticipated the use of bridges (repeaters with packet filters) and of higher-level protocols that would have an expanded address space that would allow for additional fields that could be used for routing purposes. Another interesting thing to note is that, similar to IBM when it created the now-famous personal computer that has become a standard, Metcalfe and Boggs also chose to use "off the shelf" parts for the network transmission medium: ordinary CATV coaxial cables and the taps and connectors used with them. This made it even cheaper to think about creating a commercial version of Ethernet. An online copy of this paper can be found at **www.acm.org/classics/apr96**.

Later, a consortium of three companies—Digital Equipment Corporation, Intel, and Xerox—further developed the Ethernet II standard, sometimes referred to in older literature as the DIX standard, based on the initials of the participating corporations. These companies used the technology to add networking capabilities to their product lines. For example, at one time Digital Equipment Corporation had the largest commercial network in the world, using DECnet protocols connecting Ethernet LANs. Today the dominant protocols used with Ethernet are TCP/IP and, to a smaller extent, IPX/SPX.

The idea of networking hundreds, and thousands, of PCs into a business LAN would have sounded pretty optimistic back when Ethernet was first developed. Yet, in part because of its simplicity and widespread support among manufacturers, Ethernet has adapted over the years to survive, running on newer devices and network media. You can now run an Ethernet network on coaxial cable, twisted-pair wiring (shielded and unshielded), and fiber-optic cabling.

Variations on a Theme: How Many Kinds of Ethernet Are There?

In 1985, the IEEE standard 802.3 "Carrier Sense Multiple Access with Collision Detection (CSMA/CD) Access Method and Physical Layer Specifications" was published. These specifications made it easy for vendors to create hardware, from cabling to LAN cards, which could interoperate. The many different Ethernet standards you will need to know about are all identified by a name that includes "IEEE 802." followed by a number and possibly a letter or two.

The IEEE 802 LAN/MAN Standards Committee is responsible for creating standards for local and wide area networking. This committee was formed in 1980 and was originally called the Local Network Standards Committee. The name has been changed to reflect the evolutionary development of some of the committee's standards to MAN (metropolitan area network) speeds. Chapter 12, "The IEEE LAN/MAN Committee Networking Standards," contains short descriptions of some of the more relevant standards that were defined for LAN/MAN networks.

Note

Anyone who knows anything about networking knows that LAN stands for *local area network*. Another popular acronym, WAN, stands for wide area network. So what, then, is a MAN? It's a metropolitan area network—smaller than a WAN but larger than a LAN—generally used to refer to a network that connects a group of smaller related networks within a city or regionalized geographic area.

Note

You can learn more about the activities of the IEEE 802 LAN/MAN Standards Committee and the different working groups that concentrate on specific network standards by visiting the Web site at `http://ieee802.org/`. You can also download many of the standards developed by the 802 LAN/MAN committee from this Web site, though printing all of them will require a lot of paper!

The committee is made up of various working groups and technical advisory groups. For example, IEEE 802.3 is the working group for standard Ethernet CSMA/CD technology, whereas IEEE 802.3z is the standard for Gigabit Ethernet, which is a faster version of the original 802.3.

▶▶ In the chapter "Token-Ring Networks" on the `upgradingandrepairingpcs.com` Web site, you'll read about Token-Ring networking, which is defined in standards documents produced by the IEEE 802.5 "Token Ring Working Group."

Different forms of Ethernet are also referred to using a naming scheme that links the network speed, the word "BASE" (for baseband signaling), and an alpha or numeric suffix that specifies the network media used. An example of this is 10BASE-T, which is broken down like this:

10 = Ethernet, running at a speed of 10Mbps

BASE = baseband signaling

T = over twisted-pair (T) wiring

Today there is a wide assortment of Ethernet solutions from which to choose. Originally, Ethernet used coaxial cable (10BASE-5) that was "tapped" into when a new workstation was added to the bus network. Later, thinnet (10BASE-2) was developed and allowed a smaller, more flexible cable to be used to connect the network. With thinnet, BNC connectors were introduced, making it unnecessary to "tap" into the coaxial cable. The most recent versions of Ethernet use twisted-pair wiring and fiber-optic cables and centralized wiring concentrators, such as hubs and switches.

The original Ethernet II network operated at a blazingly fast speed of 10Mbps. The most recent standard that is coming to market fast is Gigabit Ethernet, now that it has been standardized. And as if that weren't enough, the 10Gigabit Ethernet standard has been finished, and products are readily available for high-end networks.

These are the most common standards-based Ethernet solutions from the past to the present:

■ **10BASE-5**—Often called "thickwire" or "thicknet," this standard uses thick coaxial cable. The 10 in this name indicates the speed of the network, which is 10 megabits/second (Mbps). The number 5 in the name indicates that the maximum length allowed for any segment using this topology is 500 meters. 10BASE-5 networks used thick coaxial cable. To install a node on the network, it is necessary to use what is commonly referred to as a "vampire tap." That is, you attach a connector to the backbone thicknet coaxial cable by punching into the wire. A drop cable is then run to the workstation that is being added to the network. If you are still using this technology, it's time to upgrade!

■ **10BASE-2**—Often called "thinwire" or "thinnet," this Ethernet standard runs at the same speed as a 10BASE-5 network (10Mbps) but uses a smaller, more flexible cable. The number 2 in the name indicates a maximum segment length of 200 meters. This is a bit misleading, because it is actually rounded up from the true maximum segment length of 185 meters, but it sure was easier than calling it 10BASE-1.85. It is common to see older networks composed of multiport repeaters, with each port using thinnet cables to connect one or multiple computers. Each repeater is joined using a 10BASE-5 thicknet cable. Using a BNC T-connector, it is possible to create a simple daisy-chain bus using 10BASE-2. Again, if you are still using this technology, you are living in the past!

■ **10BASE-36**—This rarely used Ethernet specification uses broadband instead of baseband signaling. The coaxial cable for this technology uses a coaxial cable that has three sets of wires, each for a separate channel, and each channel operates at 10Mbps and can extend over a distance of about 3,600 meters.

■ **10BASE-T**—The network connection is made from workstations to a central hub or switch, using a physical star topology. The use of twisted-pair wiring (hence the "T" in the name), which is cheaper and much more flexible than earlier coaxial cables, makes routing cables through ceilings and walls a much simpler task. Centralized wiring also makes it easier to test for faults and isolate bad ports or move users from one area to another. Okay, if you are still using this technology, you can get by, but you'd find your job a lot easier if you upgraded to at least 100BASE-T.

◀◀ The topologies used by various forms of Ethernet are discussed in Chapter 2, "Overview of Network Topologies."

■ **10BASE-FL**—This version of Ethernet also operates at 10Mbps, but instead of using copper wires, fiber-optic cables (FL) are used—specifically, multimode fiber cable (MMF), with a 62.5 micron fiber-optic core and a 125 micron outer cladding. Separate strands of fiber are used for transmit and receive functions, allowing full-duplex to operate easily across this kind of link. This technology has also been relegated to history.

■ **100BASE-TX**—Uses Category 5 wiring (see Chapter 6, "Wiring the Network—Cables, Connectors, Concentrators, and Other Network Components") to allow a distance of up to 100 meters between the workstation and the hub. Four wires (two pairs) in the cable are used for communications. This technology is still used widely today, and will probably be around for a while until applications mandate the necessity of upgrading your network to use Gigabit Ethernet to the desktop.

■ **100BASE-T4**—Uses Category 3 or Category 5 wiring to allow for a distance of up to 100 meters between the workstation and the hub. Four wires (two pairs) in the cable are used for data communications. This is another 100Mbps technology that was used to provide an upgrade path for installations that had not yet upgraded to Category 5 cabling (or better). If you still use this technology, it's time to consider an upgrade if you find that network congestion and excessive errors are occurring.

■ **100BASE-FX**—Uses multimode fiber-optic cables to allow for a distance of up to 412 meters between the workstation and the hub. One strand of the cable is used for transmitting data while the other is used for receiving data.

■ **1000BASE-SX**—The 802.3z IEEE standards document, approved in 1998, defines several Gigabit Ethernet networking technologies. 1000BASE-SX is intended to operate over fiber links using multimode fiber, operating with lasers that produce light at approximately 850 nanometers (nm). The "S" in the name implies a short wavelength of light. The maximum length for a segment of 1000BASE-SX is 550 meters.

■ **1000BASE-LX**—This fiber-based standard defines Ethernet when used with single-mode or multimode fiber. The "L" in the name implies a longer wavelength of light, from 1,270 to 1,355 nanometers. The maximum length for a single segment of 10BASE-LX is 550 meters using multimode fiber, and up to 5,000 meters using single-mode fiber.

■ **1000BASE-CX**—This standard allows for Gigabit Ethernet across shielded copper wires. It is designed primarily for connecting devices that are only a short distance away—25 meters or less.

■ **1000BASE-T**—The IEEE standard 802.3ab added to the Physical layer of Gigabit Ethernet Category 5 unshielded twisted-pair wire cables. The maximum distance for any segment using 1000BASE-T is 100 meters.

Collisions: What Are CSMA/CA and CSMA/CD?

In the original PARC Ethernet, the method used to exchange data on the network media was called *Carrier Sense Multiple Access (CSMA)*. The Ethernet II specification added *Collision Detect (CSMA/CD)* to this technique. A collision occurs when two workstations on the network both sense that the network is idle and both start to send data at approximately the same time, resulting in a garbled transmission. The term *collision* itself seems to imply that something is wrong. In some technical literature, this kind of event is called a *stochastic arbitration event*, or *SAE*, which sounds much less like an error than does *collision*. However, collisions are expected in older Ethernet networks. Only when they become excessive is it time to search for the sources of the collisions and rearrange some workstations or network devices as appropriate.

Note

The collision domain has pretty much been relegated to history. Hubs and half-duplex connections still use CSMA/CD, but if your network uses Ethernet switches, in full-duplex mode, then CSMA/CD no longer comes into play. Instead, full-duplex switches use separate wire pairs in the cable so that the switch port can send data to the attached computer, while receiving data from that computer on another wire pair. When creating a new network today, the cost of network adapters and switches makes it a very inexpensive proposition to use full-duplex network adapter cards and switches. The CSMA/CD technology is discussed in this chapter to let you understand how Ethernet has evolved, and to provide information for those who still have legacy Ethernet equipment installed.

The Manchester encoding scheme that was used on early Ethernet implementations provided an electrical signal that varied from +0.85V to -0.85V. Collisions could be detected when this voltage varied by an amount considerably more than that allowed by this range.

So you can see that the rules used to create Ethernet networks are not simply arbitrary decisions made by some committee; they relate to the characteristics of the physical devices used to create the network. When using a collision detection mechanism to arbitrate access to the network, the transmitting device needs to know how long it will take, in the worst case, for its transmission to travel to the farthermost device that resides on the same segment.

Why is this? Consider what happens when a device starts transmitting. Because the signal moves through the wire at a non-instantaneous speed, it will take some amount of time before all devices on the same segment sense that the cable is being used. At the farthermost end of the cable, it is possible for another device that has not detected the first transmission to listen and then start signaling its own data onto the network, just before the first signal reaches it. The result is a collision. The first station that initiated a transmission will not detect that a collision has occurred until the corrupted signal travels back to it, hence the round-trip timer value.

A 10Mbps Ethernet network signals at a speed of 10 million bits per second. The standard says that the round-trip time can be no more than 51.2 milliseconds—this is the amount of time it takes to transmit about 64 bytes of data at 10Mbps. Thus, the rules state that a device must continue to transmit for the amount of time it would take for its signal to travel to the most distant point in the network and back—the round-trip time.

To put it another way, a workstation could not start to transmit yet another packet until enough time had elapsed for the two nodes farthest from each other in the particular topology of the Ethernet standard used to send a packet.

If the device does not continue transmitting for the duration of the round-trip time, it is not capable of detecting that a collision occurred with that frame before it began to transmit another frame.

If a frame that needs to be transmitted is less than 64 bytes in length, the sending node will pad it with zeros to bring it up to this minimum length.

A maximum size for the frame was also added by the Ethernet II specification, resulting in a frame size with a minimum of 64 bytes and a maximum size of 1,500 bytes.

Note

Actually, the term "byte" that is used in this chapter to specify the length of a field in an Ethernet frame is not the most specific term that can be used by those who designed these specifications. Instead, "octet," which means 8 bits, is the term you will see in most of the standards documentation. For purposes of clarity, the term "byte" is used here because most readers will be familiar with its meaning and less likely to be confused. However, if you are planning on obtaining certification for Cisco products, remember the word *octet*!

The method that a device uses to communicate on the network is described in the following steps:

1. Listen to the network to determine whether any other device is currently transmitting (Carrier Sense—CS).

2. If no other transmission is detected (the line is free), start transmitting.

3. If more than one device senses that no transmission is occurring, both can start transmitting at the same time. The network physical connection is a shared medium (Multiple Access—MA).

4. When two devices start transmitting at the same time, the signal becomes garbled and the devices detect this (Collision Detection—CD).

5. After transmitting data onto the network, the device again listens to the network to determine whether the transmission was successful or whether a collision has occurred. The first device that detects the collision sends out a jamming signal of a few bytes of arbitrary data to inform other devices on the network.

6. Each device that was involved in the collision then pauses for a short time (a few milliseconds), listens to the network to see whether it is in use, and then tries the transmission again. Each device that caused the collision uses a random backoff timer, reducing the chances of a subsequent collision. This assumes, of course, that the network segment is not highly populated, in which case excessive collisions can be a problem that needs troubleshooting and correction.

Note

Excessive collisions can reduce network throughput. Later in this chapter, we'll look at what you can do when network utilization starts to exceed 40%–50% of the capacity of the transport medium.

Because Ethernet enables more than one device to use the same transmission medium, with no central controller or token designating which network node can transmit, collisions not only can occur, but are indeed expected events. When this happens, as explained in the next section, each node "backs off" for a certain amount of time intended to prevent the possibility of another collision before attempting retransmission.

Note

In contrast, collisions don't occur on Token-Ring networks. Instead, access to the network is granted in a controlled manner by passing a certain frame (the token frame) from one station to another. A station that needs to transmit data does so after it receives the token frame. When it is finished transmitting, it sends the token frame to the next station on the network. Thus, Token-Ring is a deterministic network and guarantees each station on the ring the capability to transmit within a specified time. Ethernet, however, is a more competitive environment in which each station on the LAN must contend with any other station that wants to transmit on the same LAN. For more information on Token-Ring networks, see the chapter "Token-Ring Networks" on the **upgradingandrepairingpcs.com** Web site.

The Backoff Algorithm

Without a backoff algorithm, the device that detects a collision will stop and then try once again to transmit its data onto the network. If a collision occurs because two stations are trying to transmit at about the same time, they might continue to cause collisions because both will pause and then start transmitting at the same time again. This will occur unless a backoff algorithm is used.

The backoff algorithm is an essential component of CSMA/CD. Instead of waiting for a set amount of time when a device backs off and stops transmitting, a random value is calculated and is used to set the amount of time for which the device delays transmission.

The calculation used to determine this time value is called the *Truncated Binary Exponential Backoff Algorithm*. Each time a collision occurs for an attempted transmission for a particular frame, the device pauses for an amount of time that increases with each collision. The device tries up to 16 times to transmit the data. If it finds that it cannot put the information onto the network medium after 16 attempts, it drops the frame and notifies a higher-level component in the protocol stack, which is responsible for either retrying the transmission or reporting an error to the user or application.

Note

A method similar to CSMA/CD is *CSMA/CA*, in which the last two letters, *CA*, stand for *collision avoidance*. Networks that use this method access the physical medium—such as AppleTalk—and listen to the network just as an Ethernet device does. However, before sending out a frame on the network, networks using CSMA/CA first send out a small packet indicating to other stations that they are about to transmit. This method helps to greatly reduce collisions but is not widely used because of the overhead produced when its networks send out the informational packet. The IEEE 802.11 wireless networking standard also uses a form of CSMA/CA.

Defining the Collision Domain—Buses, Hubs, and Switches

In Chapter 8, "Network Switches," the concept of limiting the collision domain is discussed in depth. Because traditional Ethernet uses a shared network media, it is necessary to control access to that media and to detect and correct errors when excessive collisions happen.

For a small local network that connects only a few computers, a standard 10Mbps Ethernet hub can be purchased for well under $20, *if you can still find one*. A small 5- to 10-port switch can usually be purchased for around $20–$50, depending on the number of ports.

Using a small hub creates a collision domain that consists of usually 5 to 10 computers. Although the hub gives the appearance of a physical network star topology, the hub acts in that manner only as a wiring concentrator. All computers connected to the hub exist on a logical bus, and all communications pathways are shared. A frame transmitted by one workstation connected to the hub will be heard by all the other workstations attached to the hub.

Hubs were traditionally employed to connect smaller departments to a larger network. With switches now at about the same price as higher-end intelligent hubs, the choice is now obviously to purchase a switch. This is because the switch limits the collision domain to only two nodes: the switch itself and the computer attached to a particular port. If full-duplex mode is enabled, there is no collision domain. The switch acts to relay network frames only to another port so that it can be delivered. If most of your network traffic remains inside the departmental LAN, a switch can dramatically improve throughput for users.

If a substantial portion of the network traffic resides on servers outside the LAN, then using a switch that has a fast connection to the switch on which the server resides also can provide a faster connection for end users. By eliminating the collision domain, switches allow for greater throughput on an Ethernet network.

▶▶   For a more in-depth discussion of how hubs operate, see the chapter "Bridges, Repeaters, and Hubs" on the
upgradingandrepairingpcs.com Web site. For more about how switches function, check out Chapter 8.

The next few sections will acquaint you with the basics of early shared media Ethernet technology, from bus architectures to hubs. It is important that you understand these technologies in order to see the justification for upgrading to switched Ethernet technologies.

Restrictions on Legacy Ethernet Topologies

The topology of a *local area network (LAN)* can be described in two ways:

■ The first is the *physical topology*, which describes the physical layout of the network media and the devices that connect to it.

■ The second is the *logical topology*, which is not concerned with the actual physical connections, but with the logical path through the network that data can take from one place to another.

Several topologies are used with Ethernet, each with its own distance and other specifications. During the first few years of its development, Ethernet was run using a bus topology. When PCs caused corporate LANs to proliferate, new structured wiring standards led to the use of a star topology.

Limiting Factors of Ethernet Technologies

The two basic topologies that can be used to form an Ethernet local area network are the *bus* and the *star*. By using interconnecting devices, such as routers and switches, a larger network can be constructed, building on the bus and star to create a more complex network topology.

The restrictions that are imposed by a particular topology generally have to do with several factors:

■ **The network transmission media**—Imposes length and speed restrictions.

■ **Interconnecting devices**—Used to join different physical segments.

■ **The number of devices on the network**—Because Ethernet uses a broadcast method for data exchange, too many devices on the same network broadcast segment can cause congestion problems that can degrade performance.

■ **Media access mechanisms**—How the individual devices compete for or obtain access to the network media. In standard Ethernet networks, each workstation contends for access to the local media equally.

Interconnecting Devices and Cable Segment Length

Interconnecting devices and cable segment length are the most basic limiting factors for a local area network. As cables grow longer, the signal degrades (attenuation) until eventually it cannot be understood by another device attached to the same media. Even if you were to insert devices to strengthen or regenerate the signal at regular intervals, as is done with the public switched telephone network (PSTN), the length of the cable would be a problem because Ethernet networks rely on *round-trip timing* to determine whether a packet has been properly sent. The sending station can't wait forever to determine whether a collision has occurred or whether its data was successfully transmitted on the wire with no interference.

The length of a cable segment depends on the type of cable:

■ A segment of 10BASE-2, using coaxial cable (commonly called thinnet), can be as many as 185 meters, or 607 feet. With repeaters, the total diameter of the thinnet network is limited to 925 meters, or about 3,035 feet.

■ For 10BASE-T Ethernet, using twisted-pair wiring, the workstation must be within 100 meters (328 feet) of the hub or switch.

■ For Fast Ethernet environments, you can use different types of cable, from twisted-pair to fiber optic, and each of the Fast Ethernet specifications has different cable length limitations. For example, the 100-meter limit for any segment still applies for 100BASE-TX and 100BASE-T4 segments.

■ 100BASE-FX (fiber-optic cable) has a maximum segment distance of about 2 kilometers. The distance advantage the 100BASE-FX has over the other cabling methods makes it more suitable for use as a network backbone medium at these speeds. However, there are network cards available that allow you to go ahead and bring fiber to the desktop now, if you can afford it—and if you need the bandwidth. Fiber to the desktop today might be extreme unless you are supporting a high-end workstation, such as in a graphics development environment.

The 5-4-3 Rule

There is an easy way to remember what you can place between any two nodes on a legacy Ethernet LAN. The *5-4-3 rule* means that there can be

■ A maximum of five cable segments on the LAN

■ A maximum of four repeaters or concentrators

■ Only three segments containing cable with nodes attached

This is a general rule you should stick to when planning the network topology. Note, however, that the last part of the rule applies only to coaxial cable, such as 10BASE-2 or 10BASE-5. When nodes are connected using a hub or switch and twisted-pair wiring, each node has its own cable and can vary from a small workgroup of just a few computers to a much larger one supported by stacked hubs/switches.

Using a Bus Topology

The bus topology was used in the Ethernet networks. It is simply a series of workstations or devices connected to a single cable (see Figure 14.1). Connecting workstations along a single cable is commonly referred to as *daisy-chaining*. This is the topology used for networks that are composed of 10BASE-2 or 10BASE-5 coaxial cabling.

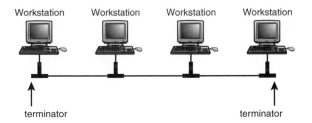

Figure 14.1 The bus topology consists of multiple devices connected to a single cable segment.

The bus topology, although simple to implement, has a few problems, including the following:

■ The cable itself is a single point of failure for the LAN. Each end of the bus must be terminated. One broken or loose terminator can disrupt the entire LAN.

■ Because all workstations or devices share a common cable, tracking down a node that is causing problems on the network can be very time-consuming. For example, a loose terminator or connector on a single workstation can disrupt the entire LAN, and you might spend hours going from one node to the next checking connections.

- Bus topologies for Ethernet are usually built using coaxial cable (10BASE-2 and 10BASE-5). Although less cable is used than in a star topology, these cables are more expensive than simple twisted-pair cables. In the case of 10BASE-5, the cable is not very flexible and can be difficult to route through wall or ceiling structures.

In spite of its limitations when used to connect individual workstations into a LAN, the bus is a method that has often been used to join smaller groups that are connected in star formation. For example, before Fast Ethernet and Gigabit Ethernet using fiber-optic cables were developed, connections between hubs or switches in a LAN were often done using coaxial cable.

Using a Star Topology

Instead of linking workstations in a linear fashion along a single cable, the hub acts as a wiring concentrator, providing a central point in the network where all nodes connect. Figure 14.2 shows a simple LAN connected to a hub in a star configuration.

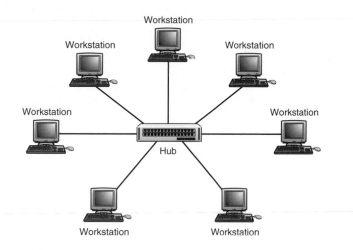

Figure 14.2 Workstations connect to a central hub in a star formation.

▶▶ The chapter "Bridges, Repeaters, and Hubs" on the **upgradingandrepairingpcs.com** Web site and Chapter 8 discuss the star topology, which was introduced after 10BASE-T was developed.

All data that travels from one node to another must pass through the hub. A simple hub merely repeats incoming transmissions on all other ports, whereas more complex hubs can perform functions that strengthen the signal or correct minor problems.

The star topology was continued when switches were developed. A central switch looks just about the same as a hub, but it limits the collisions in a LAN dramatically. Switches, which are covered in Chapter 8, do this because they don't rebroadcast a frame on every other port. They transmit the frame only onto the port that will get it delivered to its destination.

The star topology has only a few shortcomings when compared to the bus: More cabling is required, and the hub becomes a single point of failure. However, the benefits that the star topology has over the bus are many:

- Installing wiring for this type of network (twisted-pair cables, similar to telephone cables but of a higher quality) is easier than installing coaxial cabling used for the bus. Although more cable is required, the cables are also less expensive and more flexible for routing throughout a building.

- It is easier to detect errors in the LAN through LEDs on the hub/switch or by using a hub/switch that incorporates management software.

- One workstation or cabling segment that experiences problems does not disrupt the entire network.

- Adding and removing nodes from this type of LAN is a simple matter of plugging the cable into a free socket on the hub. Modern hubs don't require you to place terminators on unused ports.

- If a hub fails, it can be replaced quickly with a spare by simply unplugging cables and inserting them into the new hub/switch. Alternatively, in a wiring closet with multiple hubs/switches, you could simply move users from a disabled unit to free ports on other hubs/switches until repairs could be made.

Over the years, hubs became more intelligent, and finally switches were developed for use in local area networks. A switch works similarly to a hub, in that it centralizes the wiring of the LAN. The main difference, however, is that the switch doesn't broadcast every frame it receives on all the other ports after it learns where a particular computer is located. A switch is similar to putting multiple bridges into one device. After the switch learns the locations of all the computers attached to it, LAN traffic can be switched between ports at a very fast rate, eliminating the collisions that would occur in a high-traffic environment using a hub.

In a modern network, switches are the preferred wiring concentrator. If you have a small home or departmental network that doesn't generate a lot of network traffic, a cheap hub might have been a good solution a few years ago. However, you probably won't be able to find one today at your local computer store. Instead, switches are the wiring concentrator used today. Hubs are discussed in this chapter mainly to show you how Ethernet technology has advanced.

Hybrid LAN Topologies

Switches and hubs are simple methods for creating small workgroup LANs. By using structured wiring methods, it is easy to connect hubs and switches to create larger LANs. Two popular methods used to do this are the *tree* and the *hierarchical star*.

Tree

Figure 14.3 shows a combination topology that groups workstations in a star and joins the stars along a linear bus. Most of the problems of the bus are eliminated because a single workstation cannot bring the entire LAN to a halt. You can still add or change workstations by plugging them into different ports on the same hub/switch, or on another device. Intelligent hubs and switches are capable of isolating misbehaving ports. Some do this automatically, whereas others require management intervention.

This is an inexpensive method that can be used to join different work departments in a building. Each local workgroup can have an administrative person who is responsible for managing the connections on the local hub or switch. The network administrator can regulate when and where new wiring concentration devices are attached to the network.

The major problem with this type of hybrid topology, however, is that if there is a problem with the backbone bus cable, in a tree topology, the network becomes segmented into individual hubs or switches. Workstations on each local device can communicate with each other, but data transfers through the network to workstations on other hubs or switches will be disrupted until the cable problem is diagnosed and corrected.

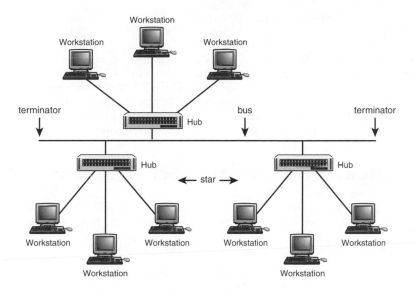

Figure 14.3 The tree topology connects star formations along a linear bus.

Hierarchical Star

Another method that can be used to connect hubs/switches is a hierarchical star. This method, shown in Figure 14.4, uses a central hub or switch to link other similar devices that have workstations attached.

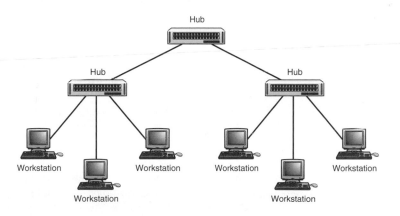

Figure 14.4 Hubs and switches can be used to form hierarchies of star networks.

This method can be used to attach up to 12 hubs to a central hub, creating a large LAN. Without using a bridge, you can connect as many as 1,024 workstations into a LAN using this method. Remembering the 5-4-3 rule, there can be up to five cable segments, connected by up to four repeaters in the path between any two nodes in the network. Only three of the five cable segments can be used for computers; the other two must be used to link repeaters.

Of course, if you are using switches instead of hubs, you can extend the size of your LAN to a much greater size. The 5-4-3 rule is a requirement of legacy hubs which create a collision domain that includes all the attached computers. Switches reduce the collision domain so that there is no contention for the network media on a particular LAN segment. Keep in mind, however, that communications between switches can be a limiting factor, because the link between two switches is shared by all ports on the connected switches. Computers attached to each switch can transfer data using the full bandwidth for the particular type of Ethernet used, such as 10Mbps or 100Mbps. However, when nodes are separated by two or more switches, the bandwidth through the switch interconnections is a limiting factor, because more than one communication session can be happening at the same time between the switches.

Using a Backbone to Connect the Enterprise

Up to this point, I have discussed how to connect individual workstations in an Ethernet LAN. The hub-based LAN is a broadcast domain in which all connected stations must be capable of receiving a data transmission from all other workstations in the LAN when using hubs. Switches allow for a huge reduction in the collisions on a network, provided either that LAN communications are mostly local or that the switch has a faster uplink to the rest of the LAN.

If other technologies were not available to connect these diverse broadcast domains called LANs, it would not be possible to have the Internet, which is nothing more than an interconnection of hundreds of thousands of smaller networks.

Chapter 10, "Routers," explains how routers work and how they can be used to create larger networks composed of multiple LANs. To put it succinctly, these devices can create a larger network because each segment joined by a router is a separate LAN in itself, subject to the limitations of individual cabling and protocol requirements. Broadcast domains operate at level 2 of the OSI network model. Routers operate at the Network layer (3) and allow for a hierarchical organization of all networks connected to the Internet. Routers make decisions about sending packets to other networks and can use many types of high-speed protocols on the LAN-to-LAN or LAN-to-WAN connections.

Ethernet Frames

When referring to the data that is transmitted through the network, it is a common practice to call the bundles of data "packets." However, the actual terminology for the containers of data exchanged between systems on a network varies, depending on which level of the OSI seven-layer reference model you are referring to (see Figure 14.5). For example, at the Network layer a unit of data is called a *packet* or *datagram*. The term *datagram* usually refers to a connectionless service, whereas *packet* usually indicates a connection-oriented service. You'll find that both terms are used in the literature when discussing the Internet Protocol (IP). At the Data Link layer these datagrams are usually referred to as *frames*. Each frame contains the information required for it to be transmitted successfully across the network media, as well as the data that is being exchanged. At the physical level, the frame is transmitted as a series of bits, depending on the particular technology used for encoding on the network medium.

▶▶ A good explanation of the different layers of the OSI network reference model can be found in Appendix A, "Overview of the OSI Seven-Layer Networking Reference Model."

The data portion of the frame usually consists of bytes of information that were packaged by a higher-level protocol and then delivered to the Data Link layer for transmission inside an Ethernet frame. For example, the IP protocol specifies the header information used by that protocol, as well as the data that is being carried by the IP datagram. When the IP datagram passes down to the Data Link layer, however, all this information is contained in the data portion of the Ethernet frame.

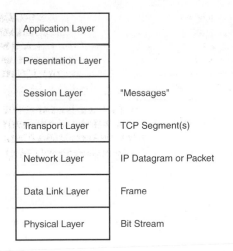

Figure 14.5   The name of the information unit changes as it passes up or down the OSI reference model stack.

The composition of the frame depends on the type of network. The original Ethernet frame format and Ethernet II format differ only a little from the IEEE 802.3 frame format, and the IEEE 802.5 (Token-Ring) standard defines a frame that is far different from these two. This is because Ethernet and Token-Ring have different methods for granting access to the network media and for exchanging data between network nodes.

In this chapter we will explore several frame types as they evolved with the technology. When heavy-duty troubleshooting is involved, you will need to get down to this nuts-and-bolts information to understand just what is happening on the wire.

XEROX PARC Ethernet and Ethernet II

The original Ethernet frame had defined several fields that were still used in the Ethernet II specification, including the following:

- **Preamble**—An 8-byte sequence of zeros and ones that is used to announce the start of a frame and to help synchronize the transmission.

- **Destination MAC (Media Access Control) address**—A 6-byte address usually expressed in hexadecimal format.

- **Senders MAC address**—Another 6-byte field specifying the address of the workstation that originates the frame.

- **Type field**—A 2-byte field used to indicate the client protocol (such as IPX, IP, and DECnet) that is to be found in the data field.

- **Data field**—A field of unspecified length that holds the actual data.

In this original frame it was left up to the higher-level protocol to determine the length of the frame. Because of this, the Type field was an important part of the frame.

Note

The term *MAC address* stands for Media Access Control address. This is a 48-bit address that is hardwired into the network adapter when it is manufactured. The MAC address (sometimes called the hardware address or the physical address) is usually expressed as a string of 12 hexadecimal digits, two for each byte, separated by dashes—for example,

08-00-2B-EA-77-AE. The first three hexadecimal pairs are unique to vendors that manufacture Ethernet equipment, and the last three pairs are a unique number assigned by the manufacturer. Knowing a manufacturer's three-pair MAC digits can be a useful tool when troubleshooting network problems.

A hardware address of FF-FF-FF-FF-FF-FF is used as a broadcast address, which is used to send a single message that all nodes on the network will read.

In Figure 14.6 you can see the layout used for the original Ethernet frame.

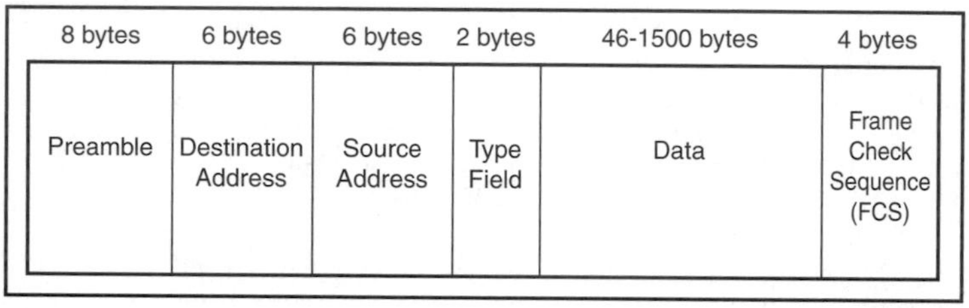

8 bytes	6 bytes	6 bytes	2 bytes	46-1500 bytes	4 bytes
Preamble	Destination Address	Source Address	Type Field	Data	Frame Check Sequence (FCS)

Figure 14.6   The layout of the original Ethernet II frame.

The 802.3 Standard

When the IEEE 802 project defined a frame format, it kept most of the features found in the Ethernet II frame. There are some important differences, however. In Figure 14.7, you can see the layout of the 802.3 Ethernet frame.

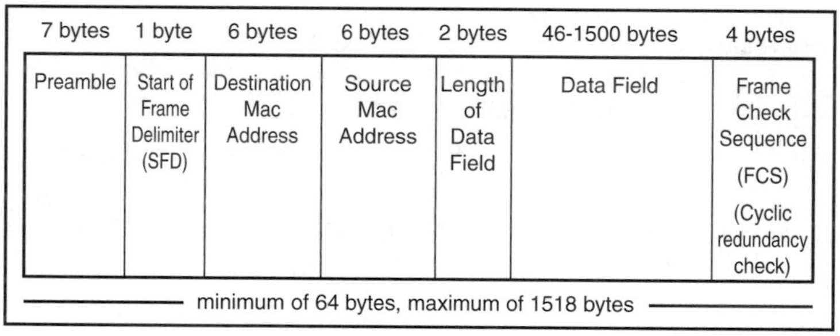

7 bytes	1 byte	6 bytes	6 bytes	2 bytes	46-1500 bytes	4 bytes
Preamble	Start of Frame Delimiter (SFD)	Destination Mac Address	Source Mac Address	Length of Data Field	Data Field	Frame Check Sequence (FCS) (Cyclic redundancy check)

minimum of 64 bytes, maximum of 1518 bytes

Figure 14.7   The IEEE 802.3 frame format.

The major changes included the replacement of the Type field with a new field. These 2 bytes were now used to specify the length of the data field that was to follow it. When the value in this field is 1,500 or less, you can tell it is being used as a Length field. If the value is 1,536 or larger, the frame is being used to define a protocol type.

Additionally, the preamble was reduced from 8 bytes to 7 bytes, and following it now is a 1-byte Start of Frame Delimiter (SFD). The SFD is composed of a bit configuration of 10101011 (the last byte of the earlier preamble has 10 for the last 2 bits).

The last part of the frame is a 4-byte frame check sequence (FCS). This is used to store a cyclic redundancy check value that is calculated on the frame. The transmitting station calculates this value based on the other bits in the frame. The receiving station calculates the CRC based on the frame's bits and compares it to this value. If they are not identical, the frame must have suffered some damage in transit and must be retransmitted.

The 802.2 Logical Link Control (LLC) Standard

In the OSI seven-layer reference model, the two lower layers are the Physical layer and the Data Link layer. When the IEEE designed its reference model, it took a slightly different approach. In Figure 14.8, you can see that the IEEE version includes a Logical Link Control sublayer and a Media Access Control sublayer on top of the Physical layer, with the Media Access Control layer straddling the boundary of the Physical and Data Link layers as defined by the OSI model.

▶▶ For more information about the OSI seven-layer network reference model, see Appendix A.

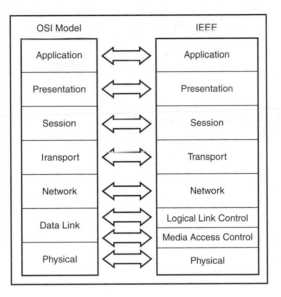

Figure 14.8 The IEEE model differs from the OSI Reference Model.

There is a rationale for incorporating some of the functionality of the OSI Physical layer in the Media Access Control layer and dividing up the Data Link layer to provide for a Logical Link Control sublayer: It is to allow different types of transmission media and methods of media access to exist on the same network.

The LLC Subheader

The Media Access Control sublayer is responsible for using the services provided by the Physical layer to get data transferred to and from remote stations on the network. This includes functions such as basic error checking and local addressing (physical, or MAC addresses).

The LLC sublayer offers services to the layers above it that can be classified into the following three types:

- **Unacknowledged connectionless service**—Some upper-level protocols (such as TCP) already provide flow control and acknowledgment functions that check on whether a packet was successfully sent. There is no need to duplicate those functions here.

- **Connection-oriented service**—This type of service keeps track of active connections and can be used by devices on the network that do not implement the full OSI layers in their protocols.

- **Acknowledged connectionless service**—This service is a mix of the other two. It provides acknowledgment of packets sent and received but does not keep track of links between network stations.

To implement these LLC functions, IEEE 802.2 specifies a subheader that is placed into the frame directly before the data field. This LLC subheader field consists of 3 bytes. The first is the destination service access point (DSAP), the second is the source service access point (SSAP), and the last is the Control field.

The LLC Ethernet Frame

In Figure 14.9, you can see that when the LLC subheader is combined with the standard 802.3 frame, the overall size of the frame doesn't change, but the amount of space remaining in the data portion of the frame does.

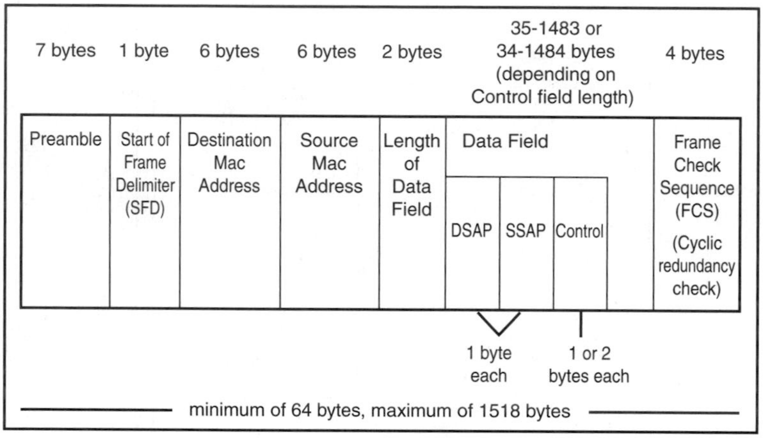

Figure 14.9 The 802.3 frame including the LLC subheader.

The 802.3 SNAP Frame

In the earlier Xerox PARC and Ethernet II frame formats, the 2-byte Type field was used to indicate the higher-level protocol for which the frame was being used. When the 802.3 frame was delineated, this field was replaced with the Length field that indicates the length of the data field.

To provide for backward compatibility with earlier networks that still needed to have something in the frame to identify the protocol that should be used, the SNAP subframe was introduced. The term SNAP stands for Sub-Network Access Protocol. It is constructed by adding additional fields to the LLC subheader, after the LLC fields:

- Organizationally Unique Identifier field (3 bytes)
- Protocol Type field (2 bytes)

The SNAP extensions must be used with the LLC subheader fields. There are no provisions for a SNAP subheader without the LLC subheader. Figure 14.10 shows the full 802.3 frame that includes the SNAP fields.

Note

The 802.5 specification defined the frame format used for Token-Ring networks. Token-Ring networks are fundamentally different from Ethernet networks not only in their frame formats but also in the methods used to grant access to the network media. For information on the format of the Token-Ring frame, see the chapter "Token-Ring Networks" on the **upgradingandrepairingpcs.com** Web site.

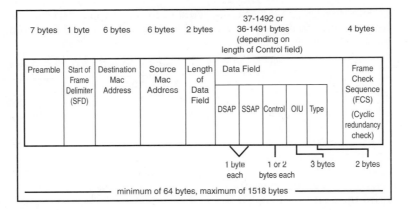

Figure 14.10   The 802.3 frame including the LLC subheader and SNAP extensions.

Fast Ethernet (IEEE 802.3u) and Gigabit Ethernet (IEEE 802.3z)

In the early 1990s, a faster version of Ethernet was developed, commonly referred to as Fast Ethernet. This standard (IEEE 802.3u) allows for Ethernet communications over both copper wire and optical fiber cables at a speed of 100Mbps. The different standards are named in the traditional way, as a concatenation of the speed, signaling method, and medium type, as described earlier in this chapter.

Fast Ethernet encompasses the 100BASE- class of Ethernet, whereas 1000BASE- denotes the Gigabit Ethernet standards. Gigabit Ethernet network cards and switches are already on the market today. The specification for 10Gigabit Ethernet was finished in July 2002, and some vendors, such as Cisco, are now marketing 10Gigabit hardware.

Fast Ethernet

Fast Ethernet was designed to be compatible with existing 10BASE-T networks. It uses the same frame format, and it still uses the CSMA/CD medium access method defined in the 802.3 standard. What makes it even nicer as an upgrade path for an existing network is that it can interoperate on the same wiring as 10BASE-T. That is, with an intelligent hub (or switch) that can detect the speed being used by a particular workstation's network adapter card (autosensing), you can use both types on the same network and they can talk to each other. The hub/switch takes care of buffering data to enable transfers between ports operating at different speeds. If your network still contains computers connected using 10BASE-T, it is time to upgrade to Fast Ethernet. You can do so gradually, as your schedule permits, because autosensing ports and network adapter cards allow for both 10BASE-T and 100BASE-T nodes on the same LAN.

100BASE-T

One of the nice things about migrating to 100BASE-T from older technology is that you can use existing wiring if the building has Category 3 cabling already in place. The 100BASE-T standard is defined for use with either twisted-pair wiring (100BASE-TX and 100BASE-T4) or optical fiber (100BASE-FX). 100BASE-T4 is the only standard that allows for the use of Category 3 wiring, so an upgrade path exists for those who cannot afford the expense of rewiring a building at this time. Running new cabling is one of the more expensive items when upgrading a network. Yet if you are still using anything less than Category 5 cabling, you should consider this expense something you should incur now, rather than later. A speed of 10Mbps is just too slow for most applications today in a large enter-prise network. Applications and data files continue to grow, and 100Mbps is now considered to be the minimum bandwidth for most wired LANs.

There is an important difference between 100BASE-T4 and 100BASE-TX: They do not use the same cable pairs to transmit and receive data. 100BASE-T4 uses all four cable pairs and a different signaling technique.

For sites that were forward-thinking and installed Category 5 cables when creating a 10BASE-T net-work, upgrading to a 100Mbps network will prove that the investment was worthwhile. This twisted-pair version of the 100BASE-T specification can be used on this cabling or on the shielded twisted-pair (STP) cables that are usually found on Token-Ring networks. The 100BASE-TX standard is based on the ANSI TP-PMD (Twisted-Pair Physical Medium Dependent) specification. The maximum segment length is 100 meters, but again you must remember to include the distance from where the horizontal wiring terminates at the work area faceplate to the workstation.

The total distance through the LAN can be as many as 200 meters, incorporating up to two hubs. There are two classes of hubs: Class I and Class II. Keep in mind that hubs are considered to be legacy devices today, and you will find this equipment only in older networks. You will probably not be able to purchase new devices of this sort. However, this information may prove useful if your network has not yet been upgraded to newer technology. Here's a rundown on the classes of hubs:

- **Class I hubs**—A standard 10BASE-T hub receives data from a segment and outputs the same signal on the other segments that are attached to its ports. Because three formats are used by 100BASE-T, a standard hub limits a particular LAN to having only one type of 100BASE-T seg-ment. A Class I hub solves this problem by translating the incoming signals from one format to another before sending the signal back out on the other ports. Because of the overhead involved in the signal processing, the standard limits a network to using only one Class I hub.

- **Class II hubs**—A Class II hub operates with only one media type—100BASE-TX. It performs no signal translation and acts as a simple multipoint repeater. There can be a maximum of two Class II hubs in the collision domain.

100BASE-T4

For those networks that have a heavily installed base of Category 3 or Category 4 cabling, this version of 100BASE-T provides an upgrade path. This standard uses half-duplex signaling on four pairs of wires, as opposed to the two pairs used by 10BASE-T and 100BASE-TX. Three of the wire pairs are used for actual data transmission, and the fourth pair is used for collision detection. The three pairs used in transmission each operate at only 33.3Mbps, for a total of 100Mbps (called the 4T+ signaling scheme). Additionally, a three-level encoding scheme is used on the wire instead of the two-level scheme used for most other media. Because 100BASE-T4 requires special hardware, such as network adapter cards and hubs, and because it operates only in half-duplex mode, it shouldn't be considered for a new installation, but only as a possible upgrade path when other options cannot be justified.

100BASE-FX

Fiber-optic cable provides the greatest distance for Fast Ethernet. 100BASE-FX, using a two-strand cable (one strand for transmission and one for receiving data and detecting collisions), can achieve a distance of up to 2 kilometers.

Fiber is a good choice for use as a backbone in the network. Unlike copper wire cables, which use elec-trical impulses for communications, fiber uses pulses of light. This also makes fiber cable a better choice in an environment with a lot of electrical interference. Because fiber-optic cable emits no elec-trical signals itself (which can be intercepted to eavesdrop on the network), it is also ideal in a situa-tion in which security is a great concern. Finally, optical fiber provides a built-in capability that will certainly be pushed to greater transmission speeds as new standards develop.

Gigabit Ethernet

In 1998, the 802.3z standard for Gigabit Ethernet was finished and includes the following:

- **1000BASE-SX**—Using multimode fiber for short distances. Up to 300 meters when using 50-micron multimode fiber, or 550 meters when using 62.5-micron multimode fiber.

- **1000BASE-LX**—Using single-mode fiber for distances up to 3,000 meters, or using multimode fiber for up to 550 meters.

- **1000BASE-CX**—Using twisted-pair copper cables rated for high performance for up to 25 meters. Intended for use in wiring closets.

- **1000BASE-T**—For use over Category 5 twisted-pair cables for a maximum distance of up to 100 meters.

Note

The UTP version of Gigabit Ethernet is known as the IEEE 802.3ab standard. Because of its short range (25 meters) it is intended mainly for use in connecting equipment in wiring closets.

Gigabit Ethernet is expected to mesh well with 10/100Mbps networks. It will use the same CSMA/CD medium access protocol and the same frame format and size. It will be ideally suited for use as a network backbone to connect routers and hubs or other types of repeaters, due to both its compatibility with existing technology and the speeds of transmission that can be accomplished. For example, another feature that will make Gigabit Ethernet a choice for the network backbone is the capability to run in full-duplex mode on nonshared connections. In this mode two connections—one for send, one for receive—are used to transmit data so that collision detection will not be needed. This will enable faster data transmissions between switches used to connect LANs.

The IEEE 802.3z standard for Gigabit Ethernet added another field to the basic 802.3 frame: the *Extension* field. This field is appended to the frame after the Frame Check Sequence field and is used to pad the frame so that its minimum size is 512 bytes instead of the 64 bytes used by slower standards. This increased size is needed only when operating Gigabit Ethernet in half-duplex mode when collision detection is still involved. This field is not needed in full-duplex mode.

Another method for making faster transmissions with Gigabit Ethernet is to reduce the overhead involved with using CSMA/CD for every single frame that is sent on the network. A mode of operation called *burst mode* was added in the 802.3z standard that provides for sending multiple frames, one after the other, after gaining access to the network media. This is accomplished by inserting special "extension bits" in the interframe gaps between normal frames. These extension bits keep the wire active so that other stations do not sense it as being idle and attempt to transmit.

Tip

Another proposal that is being considered by many companies is one called *jumbo frames*. This proposal, the work of Alteon Networks, Inc., raises the overall length of an Ethernet frame (on a full-duplex mode link) to 9,018 bytes. It is not practical to go much further past this 9,018-byte limit, because the CRC error detection/correction mechanism used by Ethernet cannot be as precise when frames get much larger than this. However, this is a dramatic increase over the standard 1,500-byte Ethernet frame.

Gigabit Ethernet is currently being widely deployed for use in local area network backbones to connect high-capacity servers or switches. This role was earlier played by Fast Ethernet (and, of course, before that by 10Mbps Ethernet). As one technology advances to the desktop, another replaces it in the backbone. As we get into the area of high-speed transport protocols, Gigabit Ethernet might now start competing in areas that were previously the domain of ATM and Frame Relay, which, in the past, were typically used to carry IP data. Although SONET is widely deployed as a metropolitan area network (MAN) solution, the faster Ethernet gets, the harder it is to justify carrying it by other transport protocols when used in a switched environment.

As IP approaches and passes the 10Gigabit speed limit, it will no doubt become an important player beyond network backbone usage. Because Ethernet is Ethernet (as long as you use the right interconnecting switches!), it's easier to manage a single transport protocol than to try to manage mapping one onto another. Gigabit Ethernet is definitely in your future, whether or not it is viable for you now, and 10Gigabit Ethernet products are already on the market, if you can justify the cost.

10Gigabit Ethernet (IEEE 802.3ae)

With other WAN protocols already in use on long-distance backbones for large networks and the Internet, you might not think that Ethernet, basically a LAN protocol, would need to be developed beyond what is required in a typical LAN. With switching, increasing speeds, and full-duplex connections, Ethernet has faired far better than other LAN technologies in the past 30 years. Just compare it to Token-Ring. However, there is no reason why Ethernet should not be pushed further, and there are advantages to doing so.

10Gigabit Ethernet keeps the standard 802.3 frame format and the same minimum/maximum frame sizes as previous versions of Ethernet. However, half-duplex operation will no longer be supported, and 10Gigabit Ethernet will not have any provisions for using a shared network media—you'll use switches, not hubs. By removing the half-duplex feature and removing the need for CSMA/CD, the distances that Ethernet can now cover are limited only by the physical network media and the signaling method used. Another important reason for dropping the half-duplex option is the fact that although Gigabit Ethernet supports half- and full-duplex modes, customers have almost unanimously chosen full-duplex products.

At the Physical layer, the 802.3ae specification provides for two Physical layer (PHY) types—the LAN PHY and the WAN PHY. The PHY layer is further subdivided into the Physical Media Dependent (PMD) part and the Physical Coding Sublayer (PCS). The PCS is concerned with how data is coded onto the physical network. The PMD represents the physical components, such as the laser or the light wavelength used.

The LAN PHY and the WAN PHY will both support the same PMDs. The PMDs for 10Gigabit Ethernet range from using an 850 nm laser on multimode optical fiber (50.0 microns) for short distances (up to 65 meters) to using a 1550 nm laser on single-mode fiber (9.0 microns) for up to 40 kilometers. The LAN PHY will be designed to operate with existing Gigabit Ethernet LAN encoding, but at a faster rate.

The WAN PHY is a separate physical interface that allows for longer distances, with an optional interface under consideration that would allow 10Gigabit Ethernet to use SONET/SDH as a transport. SONET OC-192 provides a payload that is close to the 10Gigabit speed offered by Gigabit Ethernet. All that is necessary to connect the two is to provide some simple buffering mechanisms in connecting network equipment. Because SONET/SDH is a widely deployed technology, this means that it will not require WAN providers to make a huge investment in new cables to carry 10Gigabit Ethernet traffic. Instead, it becomes a value-added service they can offer to their customers. End-to-end Ethernet connections for a wide area network without the time-consuming need to convert from one frame format will make managing WANs simpler because there will be fewer factors that can go wrong.

However, the current outlook is to use 10Gigabit Ethernet as the WAN protocol. It is estimated that it will be cheaper to implement 10Gigabit Ethernet services than to provide a similar T3 solution in a MAN or WAN environment.

Of course, there are critics who point out that Ethernet cannot provide the same guaranteed Quality of Service (QoS) that ATM does. And, when compared to SONET and other high-speed transmission protocols, Ethernet comes up lacking in the management tools area. However, the simplicity of Ethernet and the fact that it costs so much less than other WAN solutions make it very attractive for many markets.

Ethernet Problems

Because traditional Ethernet uses a shared network medium, tracking down problems can at times be difficult. Problems can arise from simple things such as bent or broken cables, to loose connectors, and faulty network adapters. The most common problem you will find, however, is in controlling collision rates as the network size increases.

Collision Rates

Keeping the network healthy requires that you be sure that all physical components are functioning normally and at optimal levels of performance. However, you still need to monitor the network to be sure that other factors are not limiting the amount of real data that can travel through the network.

Although collisions are a normal event in legacy Ethernet networks, and indeed are expected for a network based on Ethernet technology, it is always possible for excessive collisions to cause a significant degradation of performance that will be noticeable to end users.

Collisions and Network Utilization

When a device begins to experience collisions at a rate that is 1% of the total network traffic, you might have a problem. Another statistic to watch when monitoring the network is utilization. In theory, you might expect that a network operating at 10 million bits per second would actually be capable of transmitting that much data on a continuous basis. However, that is not the case. In most Ethernet networks, the actual utilization rate is only 40% before performance begins to degrade rapidly. As utilization rises, so do collisions.

Note

Keep in mind that in this section collisions are discussed, and collisions occur only on shared network media. If switches are used (in full-duplex mode), then collisions do not occur. If you are using hubs, it might be a simple solution to increase your network bandwidth utilization by simply replacing older hubs with newer switches.

If the network topology rules are followed and the network utilization is low, excessive collisions might be due to a faulty network card that is not listening to the network. You can find more information on this scenario later in this chapter in the section "Faulty Network Adapters."

Detecting Collisions

A simple method for determining how many collisions are occurring is to look at the LED lights on the hub or switch. Most hubs have an LED that lights up when a collision is detected. If you notice that this light is flashing continuously or very frequently, investigate further to determine whether the rate is excessive. If it is, take action to reduce it. Using network monitoring software, you can determine the utilization rate of the network. When you get above a 30%–40% utilization rate, it's time to start thinking of segmenting your LAN into smaller collision domains.

LAN analyzers and monitoring tools can aid you in counting the number of collisions that are occurring. Management consoles that employ SNMP and RMON probes can be useful for collecting statistical information used to localize segments in the network that experience high collision rates. The historical data maintained by RMON can be analyzed and stored for use in creating baseline data that you can use to judge network performance. If you are about to purchase a new switch or hub, check the documentation to see whether it supports telnet management sessions. This is a common feature on even low-end hubs now. In a small network with only a few switches, using built-in management software is a lot cheaper than investing in network management software like SMS or HP OpenView.

Collision Types

A good network analyzer gives you a lot of statistical information. When it comes to collisions, there will most likely be more than one kind of statistic to help point out the cause of the collision.

Local Collisions

A *local collision* (also called an *early collision*) is a collision that happens on the local segment during the transmission of the first 64 bytes of a frame. This is the most common type of collision you will see on a network segment, and usually does not indicate a hardware problem. This type of collision happens when two different stations on the LAN detect that nothing is being transmitted on the wire and both begin to transmit at about the same time. The result is a frame called a *runt*, named because only part of the frame was transmitted successfully before the collision event occurred. The Ethernet specifications take into consideration this expected event, and both stations use the backoff algorithm to delay transmission.

When high levels of early collisions are occurring, look to see whether the utilization on the segment is nearing or surpassing 40%. If this is the case on a regular basis, the segment is probably overloaded. Consider using a switch to limit collisions. If you can identify a particular node that is experiencing a high rate of local collisions, there might be a hardware problem. Check the connectors that join it to the network; if no fault is found there, try replacing the network adapter card to see whether that is the problem.

Late Collisions

A *late collision* occurs when two devices on the network start to transmit at the same time and do not detect the collision immediately. A network segment that is too long usually causes this kind of collision. If the time it takes to put the frame on the network is shorter than the amount of time it takes for the frame to travel to the node that is the greatest distance away, neither device will know that the other has started transmitting until after the first 64 bytes (the minimum frame size) have been put on the wire.

For example, suppose that workstation A begins to transmit a frame and finishes transmitting before the signal reaches workstation B, which has been cabled to the network at a distance that exceeds the specs. Workstation B, thinking that the wire is clear, begins to transmit its frame just before the signal from workstation A reaches it. Of course, because workstation B is closest to the collision event, it detects the collision. However, because workstation A has finished transmitting the frame, it has also stopped listening to detect whether a collision has occurred. The end result is that workstation A thinks it was able to successfully transmit the frame. It has no idea that a collision has occurred.

Late collisions do not cause a frame to be retransmitted, simply because the NIC does not know that a collision has occurred. It is up to a higher-level protocol to determine that something has caused an error and to request retransmission.

If the LAN is experiencing high levels of late collision events, check for topology problems. This includes not only excessive cable lengths, but also using too many repeaters or other devices. If no apparent problems are found and the network appears up to specifications, there is probably a hardware problem. Try to locate the offending NIC or cable by looking at the addressing information decoded by a LAN analyzer.

Sampling Intervals

When monitoring for collisions, don't jump to conclusions when you see only sporadic increases. Take samples several times during the workday, and try to correlate them with the functions being performed by users on the network at that time. Sometimes it is the actual day that matters, and not the time. For example, at the end of a month or a quarter, many business functions are performed—such as accounting reports—that generate large amounts of network use. It is a simple matter to determine which month-end tasks need to be done first and in what order. Sometimes scheduling is all that is necessary to solve a network congestion problem.

An overall average of the number of collisions that occur per second, along with the network utilization rate, is useful in determining whether the network is becoming saturated. Information about peak levels is useful for designing user work patterns so that the network is used more efficiently.

Reducing Collisions

There are several reasons why collisions will occur at excessive rates. Some of those reasons include ignoring topology rules, faulty hardware, and an overloaded segment (too many users).

Incorrect Network Topology

If you use segments that exceed the length permitted by your network topology, some devices on the network might not detect that the network is in use until a transmission by another node is well underway. Check your cable lengths and be sure they are within the standards. When it comes time to expand the LAN, you should never haphazardly add new segments by simply attaching a new repeater, hub, or bridge to the network. For this reason, it is important to keep an up-to-date map of the physical topology of the network so that you can plan additions before you implement them.

Remember that, for 10BASE-T, workstations can be no farther than 100 meters from the hub. In addition, the 5-4-3 rule states that there can be a maximum of five cable segments on the LAN, with a maximum of four repeaters or concentrators, and only three segments can have nodes attached. For Fast Ethernet and Gigabit Ethernet, be sure that you don't exceed the topological metrics imposed by the physical network media used.

Faulty Network Adapters

One particular problem is an adapter that does not sense the carrier signal due to faulty hardware, and begins to transmit whenever it wants to, thinking that the wire is available. In Chapter 7, "Network Interface Cards," you will find a more detailed discussion of troubleshooting NICs. However, a basic strategy to follow is to replace the suspect device and, if that does not solve the problem, try to use a different cable to connect the NIC to the network or try to reseat the NIC in another slot in the computer. When replacing the device, be sure to use a substitute that is known to be in good working order. The same goes for replacement cables. Another troubleshooting tactic is to use the diagnostic software provided by the network adapter's manufacturer.

Top Talkers

There are only so many devices you can place on a network in the same broadcast domain before performance begins to suffer. A small number of high-performance computers that generate a lot of network traffic can produce the same result. Remember that as utilization rises, so do collisions. So when you are experiencing a high collision rate and the network segment's utilization approaches or exceeds the 40% mark, it's time to consider segmenting the LAN using a switch or similar device. A switch, which can be used to give high-end servers a full-duplex connection, is an ideal choice when a local segment contains both end users and powerful servers that are "top talkers."

Ethernet Errors

Most of the problems addressed in the following sections can be remedied by making a simple change to your network. If you are still using hubs, consider upgrading to switches instead. Although it is possible to continue to use CSMA/CD-intensive Ethernet devices (and therefore have to worry about collisions), many new applications that rely on a large bandwidth to access multiple servers and other network resources will end up causing network traffic delays. It doesn't matter how good the new application is if it can't get data pushed through a slow network pipe. And the move today is toward centralizing servers rather than installing large applications or data on desktop computers.

However, if you are still using hubs and other equipment that enables collisions to occur, this section might help you in solving some problems that can come up.

Simple Error Detection

A lot of things can go wrong when you send hundreds of thousands of bits out on a copper wire, hoping they arrive at their destination in the proper order and with no changes. With the higher speeds that are being achieved with new technologies, detecting errors is becoming increasingly more important.

The simplest method for error detection is called a *parity check*. An example of this method is transmitting characters using the ASCII 7-bit character set with an eighth bit added. If *even parity* is being used, the eighth bit is set to zero or one, whichever makes the number of "1" bits an even number. If *odd parity* is being used, the eighth bit is selected to make the number of "1" bits an odd number. The receiving station can calculate what the parity bit should be by examining the first seven characters and making a simple calculation. This scheme easily breaks down, however, if more than one bit was transmitted in error.

Also, this type of error checking operates at the byte level and is not very useful for determining whether an error exists in a frame of data that is 1,518 bytes in length. Ethernet frames use the *frame check sequence (FCS)* to check the integrity of the frame. Higher-level protocols employ other methods to ensure that packets arrive intact and in the correct order. Besides errors involving corrupted frames that can be detected using the FCS, there are other types of common Ethernet errors. This chapter takes a quick look at the most common errors and their possible causes.

Bad FCS and Misaligned Frames

The most obvious place to start is the frame check sequence (FCS) error. The MAC layer computes a cyclic redundancy check (CRC) value, based on the contents of the frame, and places this value in the FCS field. The receive station can perform the same calculation and, by checking its result against that stored by the transmitting station, can determine whether the frame has been damaged in transit.

It is possible that this value was incorrectly computed by the sending station due to a hardware problem where this MAC layer function is performed. It also is possible that the adapter that is sending out this frame is experiencing some other kind of problem and is not correctly transmitting the bits on the wire. As with most errors, the problem might also lie with noise on the cables that are connecting the network.

When you monitor a level of bad FCS errors that exceeds 2% or 3% of the total utilization of bandwidth on the network, you should begin troubleshooting to find the offending device. Using a LAN analyzer, you can usually locate the source address of the faulty device and take corrective action.

To determine whether the suspected device is indeed the source of the error, first power it off and continue to monitor the network. If errors continue to occur but another address appears to be the source, there might be cabling problems on the network. If the errors disappear when the device is powered off, you can troubleshoot it further to locate the cause. You should look for the following:

- **Bad connector**—Check the connector that attaches the network cable to the workstation's adapter card.

- **Bad port**—If the workstation is connected to a hub or a switch, the port on that device might be causing the problem. Also, be sure to check the connector on that end of the cable segment.

- **Bad cable**—There's always the chance that a cable has been damaged or disconnected. If nothing you try solves the problem, use a diagnostic tool, such as a Time domain reflectometer, to search for problems in the network cabling.

- **Malfunctioning network card**—Finally, replace the network adapter card on the workstation to see whether this clears up the problem.

Because a frame is composed of bytes—units of 8 bits—the resulting frame should be evenly divisible by eight when it reaches its destination. If it's not, something has gone wrong. This type of error is called a *misaligned frame*, and the frame usually has a bad FCS as well. The most common reason for this type of error is electrical interference on the network or a collision. Another common cause is an incorrect network topology, in which more than two multiport repeaters are used in a cascaded fashion.

You can troubleshoot this type of problem using the same methods as for a bad FCS error. Of course, if you are aware of a topology problem, you already know where the problem is.

Short Frames (Runts)

A *runt* is an Ethernet frame that is smaller than the minimum size of 64 bytes. Remember that the transmitting NIC must transmit a packet for an amount of time that allows it to make a round trip in the local broadcast domain before it stops transmitting. Otherwise, the transmitting NIC cannot effectively detect a collision. The maximum propagation time for Ethernet segments is 51.2 microseconds, which is the amount of time it takes to transmit about 64 bytes. This minimum frame size does not include the preamble.

There are many reasons why short frame errors can occur on the network wire. Some of these short frames stem from the following:

- Collisions
- Faulty network adapters
- Topology errors

If a runt frame has a valid FCS value, which indicates that the frame appears to be internally valid, the problem is most likely in the network card that generated the frame. If the FCS value is not correct for the frame's contents, the problem most likely is due to collisions or topology.

Collisions are a normal event for Ethernet. Sometimes, however, the byproduct of a collision results in signals on the wire that are interpreted as a short frame. If you are experiencing a lot of errors that indicate short frames, check the utilization statistics for the segment. If the peak utilization is heavy, but ordinary overall utilization is acceptable, try to rearrange user workloads so that some tasks are delayed to a time when the network is less busy. Another option is to place high-end workstations that use a lot of bandwidth on a separate LAN segment, and thus free up bandwidth on the other segment. Connect these segments using a switch or router, and this might solve your problem.

If the utilization values for the segment are low, you might want to investigate further to determine the workstation or device that is originating the short frames, and subject the NIC to diagnostic testing to determine whether it is at fault. This can be a difficult task because a lot of errors of this type occur with frames so short that you cannot determine the source address.

Ignoring the topology rules of Ethernet also can produce short frames. A common error is to use more than four repeaters for a single collision domain, which can result in short frames appearing on the wire.

Giant Frames and Jabber

Sometimes, a network adapter produces frames that are larger than the maximum allowable size. The opposite of a short frame error is a *giant frame error*. According to the rules that govern Ethernet communications, the maximum size of a frame is 1,518 bytes, excluding the preamble bits. Reasons for oversized frame errors appearing on the wire include these:

- A defective NIC that is transmitting continuously.

- Bits indicating the length of the frame have been corrupted and indicate that the frame is larger than it actually is.

- There is noise on the wire. Random noise on a faltering cable can be interpreted as part of a frame, but this is not a very common reason why oversized frame errors occur.

Finding the location of a device that is malfunctioning might be simple if the LAN analyzer you are using is capable of detecting a source address. You can power off or disconnect the suspected node to determine whether it is the cause of the problem. It is possible that you will not be capable of detecting the address of the NIC if the malfunctioning card is repeatedly sending out meaningless signals. In that case, you need to look at each workstation on the segment, one by one, and try to remove them from the network to see whether the condition clears up.

The term *jabber* is sometimes used to refer to oversized frames, but it is really just a catch-all term used to indicate that a device on the network is not following the rules and is behaving improperly when it comes to signaling on the network. A defective NIC might be sending out frames that are larger than allowed, or it might be signaling continuously.

This type of error can literally bring down an entire segment because an adapter that continuously transmits does not give any other station a chance to use the wire. Because stations are supposed to check the network medium to see whether it is busy before transmitting, the workstations that are functioning normally simply wait until the network becomes available.

Multiple Errors

Depending on the tool used to monitor the network, the number of different error types you see might vary. For example, misaligned frame errors usually have a bad FCS field as well. Some analyzers record two errors for one event, whereas others might record the error as one type or the other.

Check the documentation for the product you use to determine whether this is true for your particular product.

Broadcast Storms

Broadcast storms usually occur when devices on the network generate traffic that causes even more traffic to be generated. Although this additional traffic might be due to physical problems in the network devices or the network media, it is usually caused by higher-level protocols. The problem with trying to detect the cause of this type of situation is that when it occurs, you are usually unable to access the network. Broadcast storms can slow down network access dramatically, and can sometimes bring it to a halt.

When monitoring the network for broadcast activity, you normally see a rate of 100 broadcast frames per second or less. When this value increases to more than 100 per second on an ongoing basis, there might be a problem with a network card, or you might need to segment the collision domain into smaller parts. You can use routers to do this because they do not pass broadcast frames unless they are configured to do so. Many bridges also can be configured to detect excessive broadcasts and to drop broadcast packets until the storm subsides.

Monitoring Errors

There are many tools you can use to monitor errors on the network. A *network analyzer*—for example, Network Sniffer from Network General—displays information about frames that contain errors, including runts, CRC, and alignment errors. Some software-based applications, such as the Network Monitor tool included in Windows NT Server or Microsoft's System Management Server, enable you to view statistics about frames dropped, CRC errors, and broadcasts. Simpler handheld tools also might provide functionality that enables you to detect when these errors are occurring.

For a network that requires centralized management and control, an SNMP management console application, using RMON, can be used both to monitor the network for Ethernet errors and to set up alerts that trigger notifications so that you can become aware of problems immediately. The history group of RMON objects allows you to record error counts over a period of time and use them for later analysis to assist in troubleshooting.

▶▶ You can find more information about SNMP, RMON, and network monitoring tools in Chapter 52, "Strategies for Troubleshooting Network Problems," and Chapter 53, "Network Testing and Analysis Tools." For more specific information on how to isolate Ethernet problems, see the chapters devoted to network cards, cables, hubs, switches, and routers.

Depending on the vendor, many internetworking devices—such as routers and intelligent hubs—are equipped with management software that can be tapped to display error statistics when you do not need a more extensive application (such as a management console). Checking statistical information on a regular basis and keeping a log of it is a good idea. When you keep track of error conditions on a regular basis, you can begin to solve problems more quickly because you can determine whether the current situation matches a previous problem.

Dedicated Connections and WAN Protocols

PART IV

Dial-Up Connections

SOME OF THE MAIN TOPICS IN THIS CHAPTER ARE

CHAPTER 15

If you operate a large corporate network, you might be tempted to skip this chapter. After all, you probably have one or more routers/firewalls and other devices connecting your corporate network to the Internet using a large dedicated data pipe, such as ATM (Asynchronous Transfer Mode) or Frame-Relay switch. However, if you have workers on the move, or employees who work from home, about the only way they can connect to your network is by using a dial-up modem or a broadband Internet connection. The former is more likely the case because broadband connections, which are discussed in following chapters, although quite popular, do not have nearly the user base of traditional dial-ups. So why are dial-up connections still important in a corporate setting? Keep in mind the following:

- As with any new technology, you should always have a backup procedure. What happens if the broadband connection fails? The broadband connection should not be a single point of failure in your network. A backup dial-up solution, while slower than broadband, might just satisfy your business need for the day or two that it takes to fix your higher bandwidth connection.

- What can you do if a mobile employee is staying overnight at a hotel that provides only dial-up access?

- Do you have personnel who work from home? Do they require the bandwidth provided by high-speed connections? If only a few keystrokes are needed to operate your applications, or if downloading a document or data file for processing is needed, then can you justify the cost of broadband against a single, inexpensive dial-up telephone line?

- For noncorporate users, there will come a time when you indeed need a broadband connection. You don't want to spend hours downloading a few files from the Internet. However, at this point in time, a simple dial-up connection may satisfy your needs.

Just as you can use Virtual Private Networks (VPNs), which are discussed in Chapter 50, "Virtual Private Networks (VPNs) and Tunneling," to create a secure path through the Internet, you can create VPNs using dial-up techniques and establish a server to handle incoming connections. Until the telcos and cable providers have finished wiring the world for broadband connections, you may have no choice other than dial-up access.

For those reasons, you should read this chapter to understand just how dial-up protocols (such as PPP) work.

Note

This chapter covers the basics of typical dial-up connection to the Internet. However, remember that in the case of a dial-up connection, the payload in your network packets is sent out on the Internet, where it is possible for someone to intercept your data. If you are dialing into the Internet instead of a server at your business, read Chapter 51, "Encryption Technology," so that you can use the latest techniques to keep others from viewing your data.

The Point-to Point Protocol and the Serial Line Internet Protocol

Communication on the Internet is based on the TCP/IP suite. TCP/IP is covered in detail in Chapter 25, "Overview of the TCP/IP Protocol Suite"; other services, applications, and tools designed to work with TCP/IP are discussed in Chapters 26, "Basic TCP/IP Services and Applications," 28, "Troubleshooting Tools for TCP/IP Networks," and 29, "BOOTP and Dynamic Host Configuration Protocol (DHCP)."

Although TCP/IP is a great LAN/WAN networking solution, it does not provide for dial-up connections. A *dial-up connection* is a point-to-point link using a phone line. Because of this, a router or server on the remote network will be your connection point to that network using a modem. The remote access server at the Internet service provider (ISP, or maybe your corporate dial-in modem bank) creates point-to-point connections with dial-in clients.

This connection needs a method for sending IP or other protocols across this point-to-point connection (where addressing doesn't matter because the conversation has only two parties) transparently to the actual network transport protocol. The Serial Line Internet Protocol (SLIP) was the first widely adopted protocol, and was initially found mainly on Unix systems. Many operating systems (including Unix, Linux, and Windows) still support SLIP today. However, far fewer use SLIP as compared to the Point-to-Point Protocol (PPP). PPP is more robust and has generally replaced SLIP in all but the most unique cases during the past few years.

PPP makes up for many of the shortcomings of SLIP. For example:

- PPP offers synchronous as well as asynchronous communications, whereas SLIP offers only synchronous.

- PPP includes error correction. SLIP relies on either the error-correction capabilities of the hardware used to make the connection or the error-correction capabilities of TCP/IP.

- PPP provides for automatic, dynamic address assignment. SLIP must be manually configured prior to dialing or during the initial session setup.

- PPP provides for compression. SLIP—for the most part—does not. There are variations of SLIP, such as Compressed SLIP, or CSLIP, that enable compression, but these are uncommon and often proprietary implementations.

- Multiple protocols can use the same PPP link (such as IP and IPX). With SLIP, you are limited to IP.

Both of these protocols are nonroutable, due to their point-to-point connection. There are only two parties to the connection, so there is no need for routing. Of course, this applies only to PPP or SLIP. Both can encapsulate *other* protocols that are then passed to routers or other devices. At the receiving end of a connection, the PPP or SLIP information is stripped off and the protocol (such as IP) that was sent across the serial link (such as a modem) is then transmitted through a network as if it were coming from a computer or another device attached to the network.

Note

Encapsulate is a networking term that means a particular protocol is carrying, in its payload section, another packet generated by a different protocol. SLIP is one of the simplest of the protocols developed for this purpose, using only two characters to successfully transmit other protocols across a point-to-point connection. PPP is more complicated, adding its own protocol header information to the packet (and stripping it off at the other endpoint), to make communications a little more flexible and reliable.

The Serial Line Internet Protocol (SLIP)

For some time, SLIP was a *de facto* standard in the Unix community as a means for establishing a point-to-point connection between two computers. It was finally documented in RFC 1055, "A Nonstandard for Transmission of IP Datagrams over Serial Lines: SLIP," in 1988. Yes, you read that right—a nonstandard. Although there are standards for IP, there is no standard for SLIP that concisely defines the protocol. For example, the last two characters of the acronym stand for Internet Protocol. Yet SLIP can be used for encapsulating and transmitting just about any kind of protocol packet across a point-to-point link. It is such a simple protocol that it's easy to send many higher-level protocols across a SLIP data connection. Even Microsoft supports SLIP, although in the past few years as a client, not as a SLIP server. Note that Microsoft Windows 2000/XP and 2003 Server no longer support a SLIP server (that is, for incoming connections). You can, though, use it for outbound connections—to Unix computers, for example. For outgoing SLIP connections on Windows systems today, you will need to use the serial port (or dial out via modem) on your computer instead of the network adapter card.

SLIP has been implemented in many ways, using different packet sizes, but the basic protocol consists of using two special characters:

- **END**—This character (decimal value of 192) is used to delineate the end of a packet.
- **ESC**—Not to be confused with the ASCII character set escape character, the SLIP ESC character (decimal value of 219) is used when a character in a packet is the same as the END character. In such a case, the character is "escaped" by prefixing the ESC character before the character that is the same as the END character. ESC just tells the receiving end that this is not the end of the packet, but an actual data byte in the packet. This is a common method used by many protocols to make it possible to use character sequences that otherwise would violate protocol rules.

Note

ASCII (American Standard Code for Information Interchange) was the standard method for representing alphanumeric characters in non-IBM systems, from early VT-style terminals to more modern enhanced terminal emulators. IBM used its own character coding scheme, EBCDIC (Extended Binary-Coded Decimal Interchange Code), for its mainframes and some other systems.

More recently, UNICODE has been adopted by systems such as Windows NT/2000/XP, and many other operating systems, including Unix. UNICODE can be used to represent not just the basic alphanumeric character set used for English, but also more than 34,168 characters, covering about 24 different languages. The coding scheme used by UNICODE is extensible, so in addition to historical and many modern language scripts, UNICODE can be adapted to include lesser-used languages as time goes by.

SLIP is a simple protocol. Just start sending the characters of a packet and send the END character at the end of each packet. Use the ESC character inside the packet if one of the data bytes is the same as the END character so that the receiving end can interpret the byte correctly. Now how much simpler could it be than that?

Although it was a good start, several problems can occur when using SLIP:

- No maximum packet size is defined, so it depends on the particular implementation. The Berkeley Unix SLIP drivers use a maximum of 1,066 bytes. For other implementations, check the documentation.
- No mechanism is used to configure the address of the sending or receiving end of the connection. Therefore, static addresses must be assigned in advance if the protocol encapsulated by SLIP is to be sent past the receiving computer or router to another host. In other words, before a SLIP connection can be set up, both sides must configure the link for the protocol to be used on the link. Because most dial-up connections today make use of the Dynamic Host Configuration Protocol (DHCP) to conserve the IP address space, SLIP won't work with an ISP or a dial-up server that uses DHCP.

■ SLIP just sends packets across the line. It doesn't prefix a header to the data like other protocols (such as TCP and IP) do. Thus, SLIP can't indicate to the receiving end of the connection what type of protocol is being used. Of course, the most common use for connecting to the Internet is TCP/IP, so IP packets generally are assumed for most connections. However, in the early days of SLIP, it often was used to connect one computer to another, and a separate connection was required if both computers used multiple protocols, such as IP, IPX/SPX (Internet Packet Exchange/Sequenced Packet Exchange), or DECnet.

■ No provisions are in the protocol for error detection or correction. This is left up to higher-level protocols. Because SLIP was developed for use over slow links, retransmission of packets found to have errors by higher-level protocols is an expensive proposition in terms of bandwidth.

■ SLIP provides no compression algorithm. So over the slow serial lines used for dial-up access, large amounts of the available bandwidth are wasted. For example, for a particular connection, most of the data in an IP header would not change from one packet to the next. Having to resend these unchanged bytes over and over again for each packet just wastes bandwidth.

Because SLIP was widely deployed when the Internet became available commercially, it was a common protocol used by many for an Internet connection early on. Windows 95 supported SLIP. You'll even find support for SLIP in Windows 2000 clients, so they can dial into older servers. However, as mentioned previously, more modern Windows clients or servers support SLIP only for *dial-in* clients.

All that said, you can probably understand why the Point-to-Point Protocol was developed. PPP replaces SLIP and provides a more robust method for sending and receiving data across serial connections, such as when dialing into a corporate modem bank or, more likely now, the Internet.

The Point-to-Point Protocol (PPP)

Like SLIP, PPP is a means for encapsulating packets from other protocols and transmitting them across a serial (or other point-to-point) link. Unlike SLIP, PPP provides a wide range of features that improve on the simple process of just sending data packets across the wire. PPP is documented in RFC 1662, "The Point-to-Point Protocol (PPP)." The pertinent features that PPP offers are listed here:

■ **High-Level Data Link Control (HDLC)**—You can use PPP not only for IP, but for a wide range of other protocols as well. PPP bases its frame format on the High-Level Data Link Control protocol, which is a standard method used for point-to-point connections.

■ **Link Control Protocol (LCP)**—This is an extensible protocol used to establish, configure, and test the data-link connection. Both sides of the link negotiate with the other side parameters that will be used for the connection, such as the maximum packet size.

■ **Network Control Protocols (NCPs)**—NCPs allow for different configuration options, depending on the protocol type of the packets being transported across the PPP link. NCPs enable specific network protocol sessions to be negotiated and set up after the link is established. Even better, PPP allows for multiplexing several different protocols on the same link.

For more information about PPP, extensions, and other specific details, many RFCs are available for you to examine. Table 15.1 lists several RFCs that might be relevant to your situation.

Tip

In Table 15.1 some of the RFCs listed are now standards, whereas others are *proposed standards*. Yet hardware vendors tend not to wait for a standard to become final before adopting the technology. For more information about RFCs, visit the Web site **www.rfc-editor.org**.

Table 15.1   RFCs Related to PPP

RFC Number	Title
1662	PPP in HDLC-like Framing
1552	The PPP Internetwork Packet Exchange Control Protocol (IPXCP)
1334	PPP Authentication Protocols
3241	Updates RFC 1332
2615	PPP Over SONET/SDH
2878	PPP Bridging Control Protocol (BCP)
1332	The PPP Internet Protocol Control Protocol (IPCP)
1661	Link Control Protocol (LCP)
1990	PPP Multilink Protocol
2484	PPP LCP Internationalization Configuration Option
2125	The PPP Bandwidth Allocation Protocol (BAP), the PPP Bandwidth Allocation Control Protocol (BACP)
2097	The PPP NetBIOS Frames Control Protocol (NBFCP)
1962	The PPP Compression Control Protocol (CCP)
1570	PPP LCP Extensions
2284	PPP Extensible Authentication Protocol (EAP)

PPP negotiates a link with a remote system, tests the link, sets up different protocol connections, and then sends your data from one computer to another. Because PPP is used across a point-to-point link, instead of a packet-switched network, it can be assumed that packets arrive at the destination in the same order in which they are transmitted. PPP also allows for sending more than one protocol packet type across the same link by multiplexing the various protocols. It also supports full-duplex communications (communications in both directions) on the same link. Additionally, PPP doesn't just use a special character to indicate the end of a packet (like SLIP does), but instead uses a frame header so that the data packet being transported across the link is fully encapsulated inside the PPP frame.

Figure 15.1 shows the basic layout of a PPP frame.

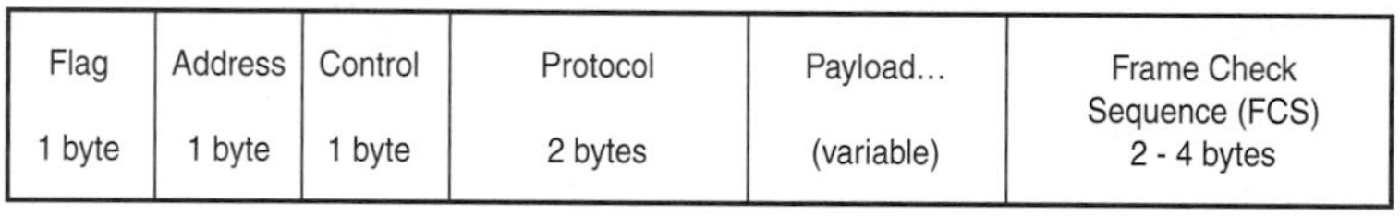

Flag	Address	Control	Protocol	Payload...	Frame Check Sequence (FCS)
1 byte	1 byte	1 byte	2 bytes	(variable)	2 - 4 bytes

Figure 15.1   The PPP frame consists of a simple header, the packet being transmitted as payload, and an error-detection field at the end of the frame.

The fields in Figure 15.1 are used in this way:

- **Flag**—This is used to indicate the start of a frame, and it consists of the binary value 01111110.

- **Address**—This field always contains a string of eight 1s, which is interpreted as a broadcast address by many protocols. Because PPP is a point-to-point link, no addressing is required.

- **Control**—This always contains the binary value 00000011. It is used in HDLC to indicate that this is an unsequenced information (UI) frame. PPP provides a connectionless service.

- **Protocol ID**—This 2-byte field is used to identify the protocol that is being transmitted inside the payload section of the PPP frame. Protocol ID numbers are assigned by Internet Corporation for Assigned Names and Numbers (ICANN). You can visit its Web site to learn more about protocol number assignment at www.icann.org.

- **Frame Check Sequence (FCS)**—This field can vary from 2 to 4 bytes in length, depending on the implementation. This provides the capability to store a 16- to 32-bit checksum calculation to ensure the integrity of the frame. This value is calculated by the sender based on the contents of the entire frame. The receiving end of the frame performs the same calculation. If the value does not match that stored in the FCS field, the packet is discarded.

The payload section of the PPP frame carries the packet of another protocol, as indicated by the Protocol ID field. The standard maximum length of a PPP frame, called the maximum receive unit (MRU), is defined in the standard as 1,500 bytes in length (which can accommodate a standard IP packet). However, this value can be increased or decreased during the original link negotiations.

Establishing a Link: The Link Control Protocol (LCP)

The process in which a PPP link is established is an orderly process. Each end of the connection first sends LCP frames that are used to test the data link and to configure the parameters that will be used on the link. Next, NCP packets are sent to configure any required options for the protocol(s) that will be encapsulated and sent across the link. After this, the data exchange can begin. When the link is no longer needed, LCP or NCP packets can be used to close the link. Alternatively, an external event, such as a timer, can be used to close an idle link. If you've ever been disconnected from a dial-up link to an ISP, you understand this process!

Figure 15.2 shows an example of the phases that a PPP link goes through for establishing and terminating a link.

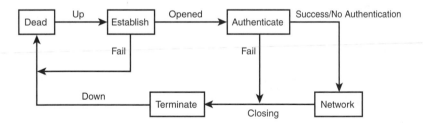

Figure 15.2 The PPP link must be established before data transfer occurs, and terminated when communications are finished.

The steps here are simple:

1. In the beginning, the link is "dead." No communications exist between the two nodes. This is also where you end up when the link is closed.

2. When some event (such as a modem dialing into a remote access server) occurs, LCP takes over to negotiate the link. When this task has finished successfully, the PPP link is in the Establish phase. The link is then Up. If the two endpoints of the communication cannot agree on a link, the attempt fails and, as you can see in the diagram, the PPP link is considered again to be in the Dead state.

3. If LCP is able to exchange configuration packets that both sides can agree on, the link is in the Opened state and, if required by the link, an Authenticate state must be reached. This can be

done using various methods, which are specified during the link establishment phase. If the authentication method fails, the link proceeds to the Closing state. If it succeeds, or if no authentication is required, then the Network phase is reached.

4. During the Network phase, NCP is used to configure one or more network protocols that will use the link. Remember that PPP can multiplex several protocols across the same link. After this is done, communication takes place using the protocols that are configured. Note that any network protocol can terminate its usage of the link at any time without causing the termination of the actual PPP link.

5. A link can be terminated due to an external event, such as the loss of the carrier signal or because of excessive noise on the line. However, an orderly termination can be done through the exchange of LCP packets. PPP is then considered to be in the Closing state. During the Closing state, PPP signals the network-layer protocols that are using the link so that they can gracefully close their connections.

6. PPP proceeds to the Terminate state, the link is then considered to be Down, and you end up back at the beginning of the model shown in the diagram, where it all started. The PPP link is dead.

LCP is used by both ends of the connection to negotiate the encapsulation options and packet size and then to terminate the link. Each side of the link sends information to the other about the configuration options it supports and which ones it wants to use. A large number of packet types are used by the LCP process to establish, manage, and tear down a link. They can be grouped into three general categories:

- **Link establishment frames**—These frames are used to set up a link and configure the parameters to be used for the link.

- **Link termination frames**—These frames are used to perform an orderly shutdown of the link.

- **Link maintenance frames**—These frames are used to manage the link and for debugging purposes.

An LCP packet can be identified by examining the Protocol ID field of the PPP frame. LCP packets use the protocol ID value of 0xC021. The rest of the LCP frame structure consists of a code that identifies the type of LCP message (one byte) and an identifier field (one byte) that is used to match up requests with replies during the exchange of LCP packets. A length field (2 bytes) is then used to indicate the size of the LCP packet. This is followed by the actual data used for the particular LCP message. The LCP packet rides in the payload section of the PPP frame, just like any other protocol.

LCP operates in a request/reply mode in which the LCP Configure-Request packet is first sent to open a link, and contains a list of options that the sender wants to use if they differ from the default values for the option. The Configure-Ack packet type is used for acknowledging that all the received options are acceptable to the other end of the connection.

The Configure-Nack message is used by the receiving end to indicate that it recognizes all the options that were sent, but is rejecting the configuration as a whole because one or more of the option values cannot be used on its side of the connection. This packet also contains a list of the options that are causing the negative acknowledgment along with values it would find okay to use.

The Configure-Reject message is similar to the Configure-Nack but is used when some of the options are not recognized by the receiver, or are nonnegotiable. Again, a list of these unrecognized or rejected options is returned in this rejection packet so that the sender can determine what the receiving end is trying to negotiate.

After receiving a Configure-Nack or Configure-Reject message, the sender can send additional Configure-Request packets, changing the values of options so that both sides can come to an agreement. Note that because this is a bidirectional communications path, the options negotiated for traffic going in one direction don't have to match the options used for traffic going in the opposite direction. Each side sends a Configure-Request to the other side to establish the options it is allowed to use to configure the link for sending to the other side.

After all options in a Configure-Request packet are acceptable to the receiving end, it sends the Configure-Ack message and the link setup is complete. After the link has been established using LCP, NCP packets are used to configure protocol-specific options that will be used on the PPP link.

During the time that the link is maintained, LCP uses maintenance packets for routine procedures to be sure that the link is still up and performing as it should. For example, the Echo-Request packet can be sent to determine whether the link is still operational after some time has passed with no transmissions. The Echo-Reply packet is returned in response to keep the link open.

Other maintenance LCP packets are used to indicate that the protocol the sender wants to negotiate is not supported by the receiver or that the LCP code is not understood by the receiver.

When either side of the connection wants to tear down the link, the Terminate-Request LCP packet is transmitted. The proper response is a Terminate-Ack packet. For a complete listing of LCP packets, and their particular formats, see the RFCs listed in Table 15.1.

Network Control Protocols (NCPs)

The most popular protocol used with PPP today is probably IP, because millions of people each day use PPP to dial in to the Internet. However, PPP allows for the use of multiple NCPs that further configure the protocols that are carried across the PPP link. For example, in the case of IP, the dial-in client must be provided with IP addressing information, which usually is done by a DHCP server.

The Internet Protocol Control Protocol (IPCP) is the NCP used to configure parameters for using the PPP link for transmitting IP packets. The Internetwork Packet Exchange Control Protocol (IPXCP) is used to set up IPX. Other protocols for which there are NCPs include AppleTalk, DECnet Phase IV (oh, the good old days!), and NetBIOS, among others.

The important thing to remember is that the PPP link parameters are negotiated before any actual network protocols are configured or are able to use the link. After the link is established, one or more NCPs use the link to configure the parameters for the protocol that will be carried in the payload section of PPP frames that use the link.

An Example: Configuring a Windows XP Professional Client

You can use a wizard to help configure Dial-Up Networking on a Windows client. The particular dialog boxes displayed vary from one version of Windows to another. This example uses Windows XP Professional to show how to configure a simple dial-up connection to the Internet. You can also set up more complex configurations using the wizard.

First, obtain from your ISP the telephone number that you'll need, your username and password that will be used to authenticate you on the ISP's server, and info on whether the ISP uses dynamic addressing (DHCP) or assigns you a static address.

To set up the client software on Windows XP Professional, carry out these steps:

1. Click on Start and select Control Panel and then Network Connections.

2. Under Network Tasks on the left pane on the window, select Create a New Connection. The New Connection Wizard pops up. Click Next to continue.

3. The next dialog box the wizard displays gives you the option of selecting the type of connection you want to create. In Figure 15.3, you can see these choices. For the purposes of this example, the radio button Connect to the Internet has been selected. Click Next to continue.

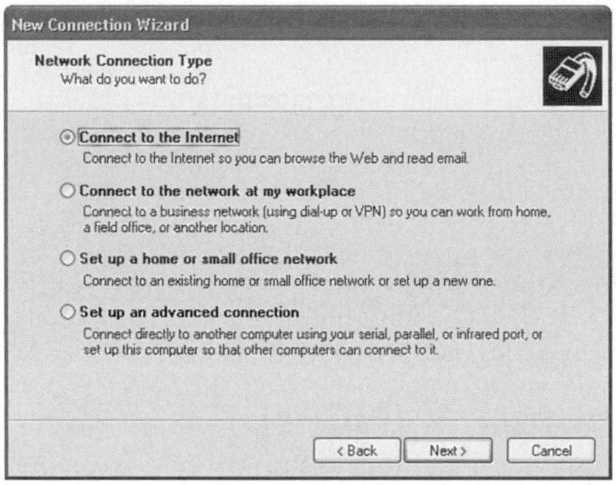

Figure 15.3 Select the type of connection you are creating. In this figure, Connect to the Internet is selected.

4. The next dialog box enables you to choose what kind of connection you want to create. You can choose from a list of ISPs, which will let you select Microsoft's MSN, or obtain a list of other ISPs. The last selection lets you use a CD from your ISP, such as AOL. For the purposes of this example, the radio button Set Up My Connection Manually has been selected to show the options available.

5. You next choose a type of Internet connection (dial-up broadband service that requires a password, or broadband that is always on). Select the first option, which is to use a dial-up modem connection.

6. You can enter a name for this connection in the next dialog box. This can be useful if you create multiple connections. For example, you might use a broadband connection to connect to your business network. Yet you can still use a dial-up phone-line connection as a backup should the broadband service become unavailable.

7. The Phone Number to Dial dialog box is used for just that purpose—enter the telephone number used to dial into your ISP's network.

8. Figure 15.4 shows the next dialog box: Internet Account Information. Use this to enter the username and password assigned to you by your ISP. You can also use the other dialog boxes to select other features, such as the Internet Connection Firewall that Windows XP provides.

9. The last dialog box lists the choices you made during the connection setup process. In addition, you can choose to add a shortcut to the desktop. Click Finish to exit the wizard.

After you have finished entering the configuration information for the dial-up connection, the Connect dial-up pop-up will appear. You can use this to test the dial-up connection you have just created.

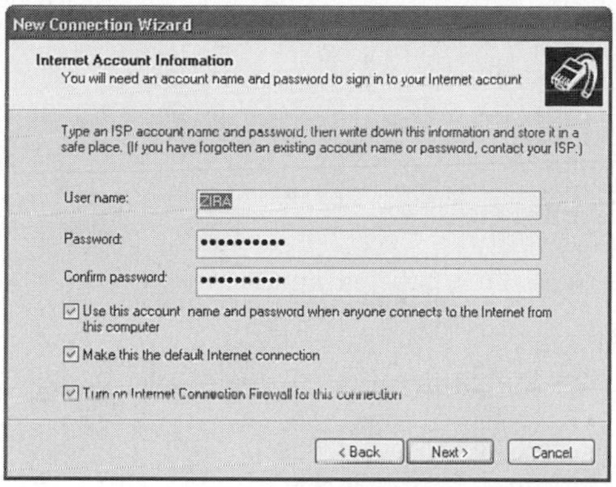

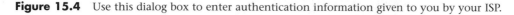

Figure 15.4 Use this dialog box to enter authentication information given to you by your ISP.

Note

The preceding example showed you how to set up a Windows XP Professional client for a basic dial-up Internet connection. If you're using Linux at home, I recommend that you check the documentation provided by your vendor, or possibly the Linux How-To documents available on the Internet.

When Dial-Up Isn't Fast Enough

This chapter discusses PPP and SLIP, the two main protocols used by dial-up users to make a connection to the Internet or another network, such as a company network or another WAN. For many users who don't use a lot of bandwidth, dial-up connections are inexpensive. And for mobile users, a dial-up connection is ubiquitous, whereas dedicated solutions—discussed in the next chapter—are not always easily accessed. Because a dial-up connection uses the public switched telephone network (PSTN), there are limits to the amount of information that can be carried across the link using a modem that translates digital signals to analog signals, and then reverses the process at the other end of the connection. Dial-up access should be used when you find that the cost of the service matches the user requirements or when you need a backup connection for when a broadband connection fails. It can also be used for users on the road where hotels offer only dial-up connections.

However, using digital connections, it's possible to get a much faster connection to the Internet or to connect one network to another. In Chapter 16, "Dedicated Connections," you'll learn about the methods used for dedicated connections. However, don't dismiss dial-up networking entirely, even if you are able to obtain a broadband or other fast connection. As slow as it might be, dial-up networking using a modem can serve as a backup when your other, faster connection fails!

Dedicated Connections

16

SOME OF THE MAIN TOPICS IN THIS CHAPTER ARE

CHAPTER 16

The preceding chapter covered some of the dial-up solutions you can use to connect your LAN to a wide area network (WAN), or to connect branch offices to your LAN. In this chapter you will learn about the dedicated techniques that have typically been used to connect business locations so that large data transfers can take place. Some are traditional approaches that still have a place in today's network environment. T1 lines (digital leased lines), ATM, and Frame Relay are not going to be relegated to history anytime soon. Indeed, ATM and Frame Relay have continued to adapt to today's networking environment by providing a fast transport for other better known protocols, such as IP. These types of connections are normally used in situations in which a large bandwidth and reliability of the connection are the most important considering factors.

Note

One technology that has been considered as a major contender for the past decade for access to the corporate network by a home user is ISDN (Integrated Services Digital Network). This technology was developed to offer up to 128Kbps (provided by two separate 64Kbps bearer channels, along with a separate control channel. This describes the Basic Rate Interface (BRI) ISDN service that is the most popular version. A higher-rate version called the Primary Rate Interface (PRI) offers 23 bearer channels to carry data. However, ISDN comes at a higher price than many of today's available options, and the conditioning, testing, and configuration for an ISDN line can be quite time-consuming. ISDN was developed a decade ago when the concept of high-rate transmissions across an analog telephone line was considered to be the high-tech solution at that time.

In the next two chapters you will learn about other technologies, such as digital subscriber lines (xDSL) and cable modems, that can be used to connect remote users to your network with a larger bandwidth than can be accomplished by using a dial-up modem and an ordinary telephone line. Although many network administrators consider these technologies to be targeted toward a home user, they can be employed inexpensively to allow you to connect low-volume traffic from home workers as well as branch offices.

Note

While ISDN seems to be falling by the wayside, DSL and cable modem access actually offer superior service in bandwidth compared to ISDN, in most instances. DSL service, if it is within the allowable distance from your phone company's office, provides a reliable service that can serve many branch office needs, at a fraction of the cost of a dedicated line. For users who work at home (which is now becoming realized as a boon for businesses), it is also much less expensive than ISDN. One important factor to remember is that most xDSL and cable modem connections offer a larger bandwidth for downloading than uploading. For xDSL customers, you will find that most telcos can offer a wide variety of services that are not geared toward home users, and can give you the same bandwidth for both uploads and downloads.

Leased Lines

Leased lines have been used by businesses for many years to establish point-to-point, dedicated connections. Leased lines provide a fixed bandwidth for a fixed cost. Connecting the telephone system from a branch office to the main office, for example, can be more cost-effective if you purchase a leased line from the telephone company and pay a flat fee for its use rather than using the normal long-distance network. Using leased lines to connect computer networks is a logical step up from using leased lines with telephone voice systems.

Basically, a leased line provides a permanent circuit between two points that you own and do not have to share with others. The leased line might consist of a physical line that traverses the entire length of the connection from end to end, or it might be composed of connections at both ends to the local exchange carrier, with the two exchanges connected by some other technology.

Because of the point-to-point topology of leased lines, no call setup is required at either end. The connection exists and you can use it whenever you need to—that's why it's often referred to as "always on" technology. The physical lines also are specially conditioned by the carrier to minimize errors as compared to an ordinary connection to the local exchange.

The first type of leased line was based on analog technology, just as the voice telephone network was, and often used modems at each end of the connection. Digital leased lines now provide connections of up to 56Kbps and use a *channel service unit (CSU)* device and a *data service unit (DSU)* device, which also are used on other digital lines, such as T1 and fractional T1 services. Both a CSU and a DSU are commonly implemented in the same device, and sometimes in combination with a router.

The CSU is used to provide the basic functions needed to transmit data across the line. Other basic functions provided by the CSU include the following:

- **An electrical barrier**—The CSU protects the T1 (or other line) and the user equipment from damage that can be caused by unexpected electrical interference, such as a lightning strike.

- **Keepalive signal**—The CSU transmits a signal on the line that is used to keep the connection up.

- **Loopback capabilities**—The telephone company can perform diagnostics on the line using loopback facilities provided by the CSU.

- **Statistical information**—Depending on the vendor and model, the CSU can provide statistical information useful to the network administrator. Some units have SNMP capabilities.

The DSU works with the CSU but also provides other functions. The DSU is responsible for translating between the data encoding used on the line, such as the time-division multiplexed (TDM) DSX frames that are used on a T1 line, and the serial data format used on the local network. A DSU usually has RS-232C or RS-449 connectors that can be used to connect to data terminal equipment (DTE), which then provides the actual physical connection to the LAN (see Figure 16.1). Each end of the line requires similar equipment.

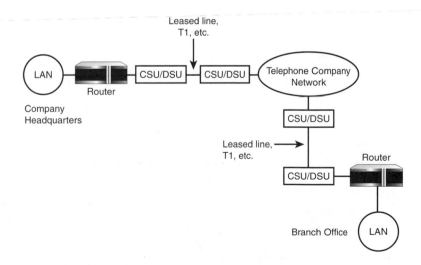

Figure 16.1 The CSU/DSU provides the connection to a leased line or other high-speed service from the local provider.

Other important functions that the DSU can perform include these:

■ Timing functions for user ports

■ Error correction

■ Handshaking across the line

Usually, the CSU and DSU are combined into one device. Typically, these functions also are incorporated directly into a router. If you use a router instead of a bridge (or another device), you can reduce the traffic that travels between the two connected LANs because only packets destined for the network on the other end are passed across the connection. In other words, you can save valuable bandwidth by routing only traffic destined for the far end of the network across the expensive leased line.

Analog leased lines are not as common as they once were. Most of the public switched telephone network (PSTN) between central offices has now been converted to digital lines because the service a digital line provides is much better than that of an analog line. Although an analog signal can be regenerated with amplifiers, noise on the line also is amplified, so the quality can deteriorate. Digital encoding with error correction techniques can deliver a signal over a long distance more accurately because the digital packets that are transferred can be corrected (in some cases where minor corruption has occurred) or retransmitted if the data cannot be recovered. Additionally, the conversion from digital to an analog signal and back again at the destination adds to the overhead of using an analog line. One of the disadvantages of a leased line is that it cannot be modified to give you a larger bandwidth. If you need additional capacity on the line, you must add another line or perhaps move up to another technology such as T1.

The T-Carrier System

In the past, leased lines usually would give you a bandwidth of up to 56Kbps. For larger bandwidth, you would need a larger data pipe, which is where the T-carrier or, if you are in Europe, the E-carrier system comes into play. Today, the term *leased line* can refer to various line speeds. The point is that the line is a dedicated link from one point to another, and you don't have to "dial" to set up the connection. The connection is dedicated and always on.

The T-carrier system was developed in the early 1960s by the Bell Telephone System in the United States and was used to digitally transmit voice communications. The first service offered was the T1, which can provide a transmission rate of up to 1.544Mbps. If you need more bandwidth than can be provided by a T1 line, you can contract for a higher level of service, such as a T3 line, which provides a 44.736Mbps connection. The range of transmission rates and number of channels for each kind of T-carrier service are listed in Table 16.1.

Table 16.1   T-Carrier Services in the North American Digital Hierarchy

Designation	Channels	Total Transmission Rate
FT-1/1	1	64Kbps
T1	24	1.544Mbps
T2	96	6.312Mbps
T3	672	44.736Mbps
T4	4,032	274.186Mbps

The T-carrier system is an all-digital transmission system. For voice systems that use a T1 line, the signal is sampled at a rate of 8,000 times per second, and the result is stored in 8 bits, or 1 byte. The T1 provides 24 separate channels that can be used to send voice or data from one place to another using two pairs of wires. Each of the 24 channels can transmit at a rate of 64Kbps.

Note

The European equivalent of the T1 line is called the E-1. Although the two use the same kind of technologies for transmission, the E-1 provides 30 channels and a total bandwidth of 2.045Mbps.

Time-division multiplexing, which allows each channel only a small amount of time to transmit (5.2 milliseconds), is used to combine all 24 channels into one signal. With each channel transmitting at 64Kbps, the total bandwidth on a T1 line is 64Kbps×24, or 1.536Mbps. The difference between the 1.536Mbps and the full bandwidth of the T1 pipe (1.544Mbps) is due to the overhead used for managing connections (8Kbps).

Fractional T1

In many cases, the full bandwidth provided by a T1 line is more than the end user requires. Yet a slower 56Kbps leased line might not provide enough bandwidth. To handle this situation, the communications provider allows several users to use the full T1 bandwidth by allocating each user one or more of the 24 channels that T1 provides. This is called *Fractional T1*.

Diagnosing Problems with T-Carrier Services

When purchasing a T1 or T3 service, the local provider must check out the actual physical line and provide "conditioning" to be sure that it can transmit data at the expected rate with minimal errors. *Conditioning* means making the line stable enough to provide the service you contract for. Bridge taps and load coils that are normally found on voice-grade lines can't be used because they can cause the electrical pulses to be slightly out of shape, which makes them unrecognizable by devices on each end of the line. Inadequate grounding of the copper cables and physically defective cables are other sources of problems.

Bridge Taps and Load Coils

Bridge taps are places along the copper wire that have been tapped previously to provide service. Unfortunately, when services are disconnected, the telephone company doesn't always go out and remove the tap. After all, when someone moves out of a house in a residential neighborhood, the line is used again shortly, so after it's tapped, the line usually stays in place. For voice-grade service, bridge taps don't distort the signal enough for you to really notice anything. However, because no telephone is connected to the bridge taps, they are unterminated and can cause all sorts of problems for digital signals that travel over the line.

Load coils are another animal altogether. Because copper wires on the PSTN were originally used for just voice communications, it wasn't necessary to use much of the bandwidth that copper wires provide. In fact, voice service is usually provided by just the first 4MHz of the total frequency bandwidth that can be used on a copper wire. Higher frequencies on a wire tend to leak out and interfere with other wires. To solve this problem, load coils, which are basically low-pass filters (they allow the lower voice frequencies to pass through), are used to attenuate, or block, higher frequencies on the line. For ordinary telephone service, this is important; however, these higher frequencies are becoming very important today for providing sufficient bandwidth for digital services.

As you can imagine, bridge taps and load coils can also cause problems for xDSL technology, discussed in the next chapter.

When you request a T-class of service from a local carrier, usually you must wait a few weeks to a few months before the service is operational. If the telephone cables in your area were put in place many years ago, the carrier might have to condition the line by finding and removing bridge taps. New wiring also might have to be run in places where the original cables have degraded over time. All these functions are labor and time intensive.

The distance from the central office to your site also is important when trying to condition a line for any digital service. For example, twisted-pair wiring is normally used in the "last mile" from the central office to your business or home. The farther you are from the central office, the more the electrical signal attenuates. Because of this, the farther you are from the central office, the less bandwidth the wire can provide by the time it reaches you. To solve this problem, many telephone companies have been running fiber-optic cabling out into the field and installing a digital-services box closer to homes and businesses. Because fiber-optic cabling can carry a signal much farther with less attenuation of the signal than can copper wire, this effectively lets the telephone company put a mini central office out in the field. From this digital-services box, ordinary copper wiring can be used to connect to your location.

The loopback capabilities provided by the CSU/DSU unit are used by the provider to check the signal quality on the line. One of the simplest methods for checking the line is the use of a bit error rate tester (BERT). This provides a simple test to determine whether specific bit patterns transmitted by the test equipment can be received back with no distortions. BERT usually is the first test performed and is used to qualify the line as functional after the physical cables have been installed.

When a T1 line is installed, usually it is checked to ensure that all circuits are correctly terminated, which includes checking the user's equipment (such as the CSU/DSU). Signal loss can indicate that the connection is broken somewhere along the line, the signal being transmitted is too weak, or a connector is faulty.

◄◄   For more information about BERT, attenuation, and other technical terms commonly used when discussing telephony, see Chapter 6, "Wiring the Network—Cables, Connectors, Concentrators, and Other Network Components," and Chapter 53, "Network Testing and Analysis Tools."

One problem that can occur is called timing jitter. As defined by the ITU-T (Telecommunication Standardization Sector of the International Telecommunications Union), *timing jitter* refers to "short-term variations of the significant instances of a digital signal from their ideal positions in time." The signal that is transmitted is a wave form; when viewed on an instrument such as an oscilloscope, you can see the rising and falling edges of the wave. If the wave form is slightly out of sync with the clocking mechanism, the signal might be interpreted by the receiving equipment incorrectly. All T1 circuits have a small degree of jitter, caused mainly by multiplexers or devices along the line that are used to regenerate the signal. Jitter also can be caused by electrical or atmospheric noise (as in the case of microwave transmissions).

Testing the line by using BERT or other instruments that depend on knowing the bit patterns that will be transmitted is called *out-of-service testing*. Obviously, this can be used only before the customer takes over the line for use. In-service testing, sometimes referred to as quality of service (QoS) testing, cannot make measurements based on expected bit patterns because the data transmitted by the customer can be roughly assumed to be random. Instead, tests performed when the line is already in service involve checking for things such as framing errors, parity errors, or checksum errors, depending on the kind of traffic carried by the line.

Asynchronous Transfer Mode (ATM)

Asynchronous Transfer Mode was developed by AT&T Bell Labs during the 1980s. It is a *connection-oriented* technology, much like the public telephone system, in which a connection is established between two endpoints before the actual data exchange can begin. ATM can be used in both LAN and WAN environments and provides for full-duplex communication. The fact that many kinds of traffic are being carried on electronic networks today influenced the design of ATM. The PSTN was originally designed to carry voice communications along with other simple services, such as telex. Today, electronic networks are used to transmit data, voice, and video, and to provide connections for other kinds of multimedia applications.

Note

The ATM Forum is a nonprofit organization that seeks to promote the use of ATM technology. You'll find technical specifications and other information about ATM at ATM Forum's Web site: **www.atmforum.com/**. Unlike organizations such as the IEEE (Institute of Electrical and Electronics Engineers), ATM Forum offers approved specifications for ATM free at its Web site.

In an attempt to design a one-size-fits-all network and provide for new kinds of traffic in the future, ATM uses a fixed packet size of 53 bytes (48 bytes for the payload and 5 bytes for the header) to transmit data. In referring to a packet of data in ATM networks, the term *cell* is normally used. The advantage to using a fixed-length cell as opposed to a variable-length packet such as that used by Frame Relay—discussed later in this chapter—is that hardware devices that switch network traffic usually can be designed to operate at higher speeds when switching fixed-length packets of information. The algorithm can be implemented with less complex code and hardware design because the switch that routes cells through an ATM network doesn't have to perform calculations to determine where one packet stops and another begins, which is the case in Frame Relay networks where packet size is not fixed.

The small header also means that the switch must process much less information for each packet. There are two kinds of ATM frame headers, but both are 5 bytes. During the development of ATM, some argued for a smaller cell size of 32 bytes, which would provide a better quality voice service. Others argued for a cell size of 64 bytes, which would provide more efficient data-delivery services. The 48-byte payload was finally chosen as a compromise. Add that to the 5-byte header, and you have a fixed-cell size of 53.

ATM Frames

ATM has two types of frame headers. The first is the User-Network Interface (UNI) header, which is used for ATM cells that travel between an endpoint in the connection—such as a standard network router or perhaps a PC or high-end workstation equipped with an ATM network card—and the ATM switch. This frame type, shown in Figure 16.2, consists of 5 bytes divided into eight fields.

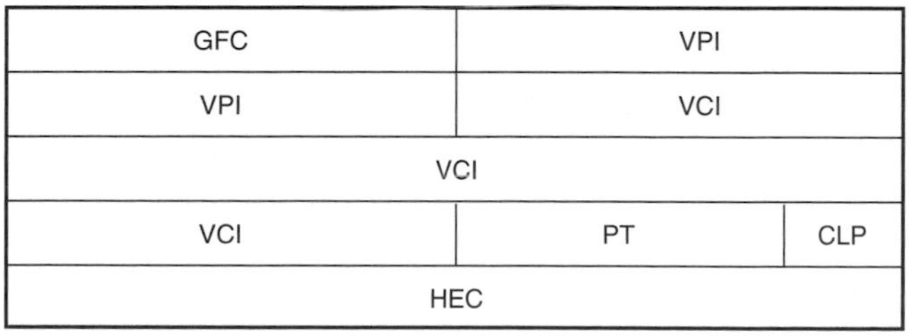

Figure 16.2   Note the contents of the ATM UNI cell header.

The fields of the UNI cell header are as listed here:

- **GFC (Generic Flow Control)**—This frame headers. The first is the 4-bit field isn't generally used any more, but you might find it used with local significance for identifying individual computers on the network or for traffic-control functions. The default value for this field is four 0 bits.

- **VPI (Virtual Path Identifier)**—This 8-bit field specifies a value that identifies the virtual path for a stream of cells. The VPI, used in conjunction with the next field, identifies a connection set up through the network of switches. A value of 0 in this VPI field means that the cell is being used for network administrative purposes, such as call setup or terminations.

- **VCI (Virtual Channel Identifier)**—This 16-bit field is used with the VPI to identify a path through the switched network. As explained later, many cells that have different values in the VCI field can have the same VPI value. Although up to 65,536 values can be stored in a 16-bit field, values 0–15 are reserved for use by the ITU, and values 16–32 are reserved by the ATM Forum for various signaling and management operations.

- **PT (Payload Type)**—The first bit in this 3-bit field indicates whether the packet contains user data (value = 0) in the payload section of the cell or whether the payload section contains control data (value = 1). If the cell contains user data, the second bit can be used to report network congestion. The second bit is set to 0 by the source and is set to 1 by a switch that is experiencing congestion. The destination endpoint then can use flow-control mechanisms to throttle back transmissions until it receives cells with a value of 0 in this bit. The third bit is used to indicate that this is the last cell in a series of cells that make up an AAL5 user frame. For nonuser cells, this value is used for administrative purposes.

- **CLP (Cell Loss Priority)**—When congestion in the network makes it necessary to drop cells, those with a value of 1 in this single-bit field are the primary candidates to be dropped as compared to those with a value of 0 in this field.

- **HEC (Header Error Control)**—This 8-bit field is used to store a CRC value that can be used to detect whether the cell becomes corrupted during transport.

The second kind of ATM cell header is the Network-Node Interface (NNI) format. NNI is used for transmissions between the switches that make up the ATM network, which, as you can see in Figure 16.3, is similar to the UNI cell header.

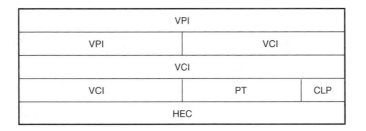

Figure 16.3   Note the contents of the ATM NNI cell header.

The main difference from the UNI header is that the NNI cell doesn't have the GFC field. The other fields are there; the VPI field has grown from 8 bits to 12 bits, which can provide for up to 4,096 virtual paths through the network.

ATM Connections

Connections created between endpoints in the ATM network can be either *permanent virtual connections (PVCs)* or *switched virtual connections (SVCs)*. Each switch in the ATM network keeps track of connections using routing tables, and decisions are made based on the information in the 5-byte header. Because the switch does not have to make any decisions based on the service data contained in the cell's payload section, hardware-based switches can quickly route and transport cells to their destinations.

ATM provides two kinds of transport connections: *virtual channels* and *virtual paths*. A virtual channel is used for an individual connection through the network. The *virtual channel identifier (VCI)* is used to identify cells in this connection. A virtual path is made up of multiple virtual channels that all share a common path through the network; it is identified in the cell header by a *virtual path identifier (VPI)*. When connections are grouped using VPIs, management and controlling functions must be performed only once for a group of individual connections (using the VPI), making the network operate more efficiently.

However, the values for the VPI/VCI fields do not remain the same when the cells travel through ATM switches. When a cell is received on one port of the switch, the VPI/VCI fields are used to perform a lookup in the routing table. When a match is found, the new VPI/VCI values are inserted into the cell and it is transmitted out on a port that gets it to its eventual destination, based on the path created during call setup (or as determined by the administrator for a PVC). To put it another way, VPI/VCI values have local significance only for the particular connection.

Before any data can be exchanged, the virtual connection path must be determined. Similar to the mechanism used in the telephone network, the path through the network from one switch to another switch is predetermined before any data exchange takes place. In determining the path that the connection will use, the quality of service for the traffic is taken into consideration to ensure that a path will be created that can provide the bandwidth needed by the service. Traffic is policed to ensure that a particular connection does not abuse the network by using resources to which it is not entitled.

The ATM Architecture Model (B-ISDN/ATM Model)

The basic architecture used for ATM involves three layers: Physical layer, ATM layer, and ATM Adaptation layer (see Figure 16.4).

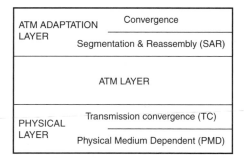

Figure 16.4   The ATM architecture model.

As you can see in this figure, the Physical layer is further subdivided into the Physical Medium Dependent (PMD) sublayer and the Transmission Convergence (TC) sublayer. The ATM Adaptation layer is further divided into the Segmentation and Reassembly (SAR) sublayer and the Convergence sublayer (CS).

The Physical Layer

The two components of the Physical layer are responsible for the actual transmission of cells across the network. Signal encoding and interfacing with the network transmission media (such as copper wire or fiber-optic cables) are performed by the PMD. By keeping the physical aspects of the protocol as a separate component, it is possible to define many kinds of PMDs for ATM. Thus, it's easy to create a PMD to allow ATM to operate over many types of physical networks.

The TC component of the physical layer interfaces with the ATM layer and is responsible for taking the stream of bits supplied by that layer and mapping the ATM cells onto the PMD-specific frame. For example, if the underlying network is SONET, the TC component maps the ATM fixed-length cells onto SONET frames and then passes these to the SONET PMD.

The ATM Layer

The VPI/VCI routing functions and flow control mechanisms are implemented on the ATM layer. Remember that the combination of VPI/VCI allows for multiplexing many connections across a common virtual circuit. The ATM layer is responsible for this multiplexing-demultiplexing functionality. This layer also can monitor connections and take corrective action if it finds that a connection is not performing within the boundaries that were negotiated during call setup. Routing functions use the VPI/VCI to ensure that the cells travel over the proper connection between the connection's endpoints. However, similar to the Internet Protocol (IP), the ATM layer does not provide for error control. If packets are dropped at a switch along the connection's path, it's up to higher-level protocols to recognize this and take the necessary actions to retransmit the data.

The ATM Adaptation Layer (AAL)

The AAL is responsible for packaging the data on the sending part of the connection into 48-byte payloads, and for unpacking the data and reassembling it into larger messages on the receiving end. For example, an IP datagram handed down by the IP protocol will be larger than the payload size that the ATM cell can handle. In the ATM Adaptation layer, this larger message is fragmented into smaller payloads and sent down to the Physical layer for transmission in ATM cells. At the receiving end of the connection, the individual payloads are reassembled back into the larger message and passed up to a higher-level network protocol.

In the Convergence sublayer (CS), a protocol data unit (PDU) from a higher-level protocol is encapsulated into a format so that it can be reassembled into that same format at the receiving end. In the Segmentation and Reassembly (SAR) sublayer, the data is divided into 48-byte payloads. These payloads then are passed to the ATM layer, which attaches the header to create the 53-byte cell.

Several ATM adaptation layers have been defined by the ITU-T:

- **AAL0**—This adaptation layer was created to provide for a user-defined layer. Basically, the 48-byte payloads are passed up and down the protocol stack when sending or receiving data.

- **AAL1**—This adaptation layer was created to provide for a time-dependent, constant bit-rate service for connection-oriented applications. AAL1 is usually found in voice or video applications and includes a higher amount of overhead when compared to other adaptation layers. For example, time stamps and error checking can be added to the payload section of the cell.

- **AAL2**—This adaptation layer was created to provide a variable bit-rate service for connection-oriented applications. AAL2 is used for compressed video and voice, for example.

- **AAL3/4**—These two adaptation layers offer a variable bit-rate service for connection-oriented (was AAL3) or nonconnection-oriented (was AAL4) applications, such as LAN traffic. Although originally defined as two separate adaptation layers, it is now a single entity. A small amount of overhead data (such as segment size and sequencing numbers) is added to the payload section of the ATM cell.

- **AAL5**—This adaptation layer gives a variable bit-rate service similar to AAL3/4 but has a lower overhead than AAL3/4. AAL5 is normally used for LAN traffic such as IP. AAL5 improves over AAL3/4 by adding a trailer to the data to be transferred that provides for error checking and specifies the size of the payload.

Of these layers, AAL5 was created specifically to make ATM an attractive choice for typical LAN applications. The AAL5 frame format is composed of several fields that are made up of the actual payload, followed by the AAL5 trailer fields:

- **Payload**—The payload field contains the actual application data and can range in size from 1 byte up to 65,535 bytes in length.

- **Pad**—This field, which can range from 0 to 47 bytes in length, is used for padding (adding zeros) to the frame to ensure that the total frame (or PDU) can be evenly divided into the 48-byte payloads created by the SAR sublayer.

- **User to User Indication**—This single-byte field is basically undefined and left up to the implementation.

- **Common Part Indicator**—This single-byte field is used for alignment processes to be sure that the AAL5 trailer is on a 64-bit boundary.

- **Length of Payload**—This 2-byte field specifies the length of the payload field. Length of Payload does not include any padding bytes, so it can be used by the receiving end to determine where the actual payload ends and padding begins.

- **CRC**—This 4-byte field is used to store a CRC value to ensure the integrity of the entire PDU being transmitted. It is not a calculation on the contents of any individual ATM cell, but applies to the message that is being broken into fragments for transmission in ATM's 48-byte payloads.

If you'll remember, the third bit of the Payload Type Indicator field of the ATM header is used to specify that the cell is the last cell of a message (or PDU) that was broken down into 48-byte payloads. Thus, larger messages from higher-level protocols (such as IP) can be identified and reassembled while passing through the ATM network of switches in simple, short, 48-byte payloads.

LAN Emulation (LANE)

ATM was originally designed to be a wide area networking protocol. However, local area networks have changed dramatically in the past few years. Whereas a simple 10BASE-T network might have provided sufficient bandwidth a few years back, you now see LANs composed of, or connected by, much faster links, such as Gigabit Ethernet and 10 Gigabit Ethernet.

Speed is not the only thing that's changed in the local area networking scene. The LAN that was used for simple file and print sharing now must support various applications. For example, videoconferencing is becoming a common application in the LAN. In a traditional LAN, however, you can't "reserve" or "guarantee" that the bandwidth needed to support such an application will always be available.

Using ATM in a LAN can help reduce congestion if the network consists of multiple kinds of traffic, such as one that supports workstations and file servers along with multimedia applications. If you use ATM as a backbone, you can interface it with your normal Ethernet or Token-Ring segments. The ATM Forum has published specifications for LANE to define the approach to be taken for using ATM in the LAN environment. LANE specifies how other traditional LAN protocols—such as Ethernet (IEEE 802.3) and Token-Ring (IEEE 802.5)—are to be carried over ATM.

The LANE protocol was developed to allow a LAN to be emulated using ATM. That is, LANE makes an ATM switched network look to the client computer just like a typical LAN. LANE consists of the following:

- **LAN Emulation Client**—This software interfaces between the traditional client's LAN software and ATM. To the client's LAN software, the LAN Emulation Client appears to operate just like the local LAN. To the ATM network to which the client is connected, the LAN Emulation Client performs the necessary ATM functions.

- **LANE Services**—This component of LANE provides for translating between traditional LAN addresses and ATM addresses.

LANE can be used with Ethernet and Token-Ring networks to provide a faster connection for your LAN because all traffic is sent through ATM switches. You can find many ATM switches that include support for LANE, or, as is the case with Windows 2000 or Windows Server 2003, the LAN Services component can reside on a Windows 2000/2003 Server.

IP over ATM

For most implementations, you'll find that AAL5 is used to send IP datagrams over ATM. The relevant RFC documents are RFC 1577, "Classical IP and ARP over ATM," and RFC 1626, "Default IP MTU for use over ATM AAL5." RFC 1577 doesn't define how ATM networks function, but provides instead a method for IP and address resolution mechanisms over an ATM network. RFC 1626 defines the value of 9,180 bytes as the *default* Maximum Transmission Unit (MTU) size for IP datagrams on an ATM network. It also discusses how, during call setup for a switched virtual circuit, the actual MTU size used for the connection can be negotiated.

When IP datagrams are sent over an ATM connection, the AAL5 trailer information is added to the end of the datagram and then passed to the SAR sublayer for division into the 48-byte payloads required for ATM. As explained in the preceding section, when the cell containing the last part of the IP datagram is created, the third bit of the PT (Payload Type) is set to 1 so that the endpoint recognizes that it now has all the information necessary to reassemble the smaller payloads into the original IP datagram.

IP over ATM has several advantages that make it a better choice for IP networks than LANE. First, LANE doesn't support the QoS capabilities of ATM, which you'll learn about in the next section. Second, IP over ATM has a lower overhead, so more bandwidth is available for transmitting actual data. Windows 2000 and Windows Server 2003 also support IP over ATM. Because of this, IP over ATM usually is faster than LANE.

Similar to LANE, the IP over ATM software interfaces between the TCP/IP protocol stack and the ATM network.

ATM Service Categories

Although early implementations of ATM use the technique of reserving a specified, fixed amount of bandwidth for a connection in advance, service categories now allow for several levels of service that can be matched to the needs of different types of traffic. Each level of service defines the network behavior for a different kind of network traffic that can be used to specify the QoS required for certain kinds of applications. For example, some network applications require precise timing and cannot tolerate excessive delays or reductions in bandwidth (such as video transmissions). Other applications tend to make bursty requests when bandwidth requirements vary widely in just a short time (such as file transfers).

The following service categories are presently defined by the ATM Forum:

- Constant Bit Rate (CBR)
- Real-Time Variable Bit Rate (rt-VBR)
- Non–Real-Time Variable Bit Rate (nrt-VBR)
- Available Bit Rate (ABR)
- Unspecified Bit Rate (UBR)

The CBR category is based on providing a constant maximum bandwidth allocation for the connection for time-sensitive applications. The application does not always have to use the maximum bandwidth, but the maximum is available if needed for this level of service. This service category is suitable for use by real-time applications, voice and video applications, videoconferencing, and other similar applications.

The rt-VBR service category also is meant to provide a high level of service for time-sensitive applications that do not always maintain a constant bit rate but are still time-sensitive applications.

The nrt-VBR service category is similar to the rt-VBR category in that the expected traffic will be bursty in nature, but the nature of the communications does not require that data be delivered without significant delays. Both VBR categories can be useful for applications such as voice, when compression techniques are used, and possibly transaction-based applications, such as reservation systems or for carrying Frame Relay traffic.

The ABR category is intended for applications that might increase or decrease their traffic level depending on network conditions. In other words, they can be satisfied by using whatever bandwidth is available. Connections of this type can specify a minimum required bandwidth level but then can use more bandwidth as the network makes it available. Typical uses for this kind of service are LAN connections, such as distributed file services.

The UBR service category represents a "best effort" connection and is intended for applications that really don't care about bandwidth or QoS. This bottom-of-the-barrel kind of service is useful for applications with traffic that needs to get from one place to another but is in no hurry; for example, file transfers that can be done in a batch mode and do not have users sitting at the keyboard waiting for completion. Messaging services, such as email, also might find this service level sufficient.

The Importance of Frame Relay and the X.25 Interface

The X.25 protocol defines an interface for delivering information to a packet-switched network and does not make any assumptions about the method used to carry the actual data from one place to another. Or, to put it another way, X.25 is not a transport protocol. It is an interface that can be adapted to different kinds of network transport protocols. X.25, which has been around for more than 20 years, was developed to allow connection to various public networks, such as CompuServe and Tymnet, and it provides for speeds of up to 56Kbps. Frame Relay is similar to X.25 except that it uses digital connections instead of the analog connections that X.25 was designed for. Although X.25 can be considered a "dying" technology, Frame Relay use continues to grow.

Frame Relay can operate at much higher speeds (up to 1.544Mbps) than X.25 because of the digital nature of Frame Relay, which is usually offered over a T1 or fractional T1 line. The digital nature of the line allows fewer errors than the analog system, and Frame Relay can operate faster than other technologies because it does not perform any actual error correction. When a frame error is detected, the frame is dropped. It is up to the endpoints to detect, through some higher-level protocol, that an error has occurred.

If an error is found in the frame, or if the network is too busy, the frame is dropped. This is similar to the way the IP functions. Frame Relay does its best to get the frame to its endpoint in the connection, but it does not notify the starting point of the connection if an error occurs. Because Frame Relay doesn't have to worry about reporting errors (which can occur anywhere along the path, at any switch) back to the sender, it can switch traffic at a faster rate. With today's fast CPUs and digital lines (which are less prone to errors than analog lines), it only makes sense to let higher-level protocols take care of detecting and remedying errors.

Because Frame Relay is a packet-switched technology, you must pay for only the bandwidth you expect to use. Instead of paying for the full cost of a T1 line between two geographically distant offices, you can use Frame-Relay services. The carrier mixes traffic from various sources and transmits it over the line so that Frame Relay represents a shared-medium technology. The downside is that it's always possible that the bandwidth you need might not be available when you need it. Just as you sometimes get a circuit-busy message when you try to place a telephone call during a peak holiday period, the same thing can happen if traffic from multiple users of a carrier's Frame-Relay service must transfer large amounts of data at the same time.

For this reason, when you purchase Frame-Relay services, you get a guarantee—called the *committed information rate (CIR)*—of the amount of available bandwidth that the carrier expects to be capable of providing. You might be able to get higher throughput rates than that guaranteed by the CIR, but there is always the possibility that, occasionally, you might not achieve rates that are guaranteed by the CIR. It is important to monitor your use in a high-traffic environment to be sure you are getting what you paid for.

Frame Relay also can reduce the number of physical connections you need at a site, which can make it a better choice than dedicated point-to-point lines. For example, if you have multiple branch offices, you could use a dedicated T1 (or Fractional T1) line to connect each office to the main head-quarters. Or you could use Frame Relay at each branch office, using only a single physical connection back at the main office. Traffic from all the branch offices is lumped together on this incoming Frame Relay line, so you don't need a separate physical dedicated line going to each branch office (see Figure 16.5).

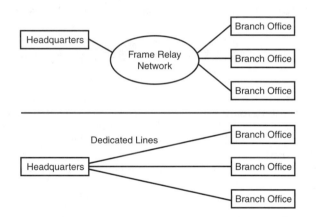

Figure 16.5   Using Frame Relay can reduce the number of physical connections required when compared to dedicated lines.

Frame Relay is similar to ATM in that it is a packet-switched technology. However, ATM uses a fixed sized for its cells, whereas Frame Relay packets are variable (similar to Ethernet frames). Packet switching in a Frame Relay network is done using virtual circuits, which are logical paths through the Frame Relay network.

Note

Some vendors of Frame-Relay services offer much faster capabilities, up to 45Mbps, using T3 lines.

The Frame Relay Header

Frame Relay also has a lower overhead than traditional network technologies, such as Ethernet. The Frame Relay header is only 2–5 bytes long. In Figure 16.6, you can see that the header doesn't contain a whole lot of information.

The following fields appear in Figure 16.6:

- **DLCI**—The Data Link Connection Identifier is used to identify the virtual circuit connection. Note that the DLCI is 10 bits long but is not stored contiguously in the header.

- **C/R**—The single-bit Command/Response field is application specific. Network switches do not modify this field.

- **FECN**—This single-bit field is the Forward Explicit Congestion Notification field.
- **BECN**—This single-bit field is the Backward Explicit Congestion Notification field.
- **DE**—This single-bit field is the Discard Eligibility Indicator field.
- **EA**—This single-bit field is the Extension Bit, which is used to indicate a 3- or 4-byte header.

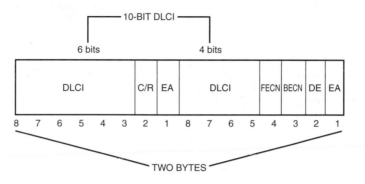

Figure 16.6   The Frame Relay header contains the DLCI (Data Link Connection Identifier) that identifies the connection.

The DLCI field is a 10-bit number used to specify the virtual circuit number for the connection. The DLCI identifies the particular port to which the local network is attached in the Frame Relay equipment. Throughout the network, this number is used to designate the endpoint of the connection.

When using a PVC, the network administrator must set up routing tables in the switches that make up the network. When a frame comes in one port, it is a simple matter to look up the DLCI in a table and then quickly switch the frame to an outgoing port that can take it to another switch, where the process is repeated, or to its eventual destination. Note that if a switch receives a frame that has a DLCI value that is not found in the switch's routing table, the frame is discarded.

If this sounds like a simple mechanism for getting a data frame from one point to another, it is. In addition to the short header, the Frame Relay packet also has a frame check sequence (FCS) value calculated to ensure the integrity of the packet, which is placed at the end of the frame. The switch can recalculate this value when it receives a frame and, if the newly calculated value does not match the value stored in this field, the frame is assumed to have become corrupted and is dropped.

Network congestion also can cause a packet to be dropped. After a switch's buffers are full, incoming frames are dropped until buffer space becomes available again. However, Frame Relay does provide some signaling mechanisms that can be used to help control network congestion. Frame Relay also provides for signaling to set up an SVC. Both of these signaling mechanisms, however, are optional components and vendors don't have to implement them. Remember that the higher-level protocol (such as TCP/IP) can detect when its data segments have not been acknowledged and retransmit any data that is dropped along the virtual circuit path.

Network Congestion Signaling

Three methods can be used to help prevent network congestion:

- Explicit Congestion Notification
- Discard Eligibility
- Implicit Congestion Notification

The Explicit Congestion Notification method uses 2 bits in the header: the FECN (Forward Explicit Congestion Notification) and BECN (Backward Explicit Congestion Notification) bits. The FECN bit is used to tell nodes farther along the path (forward) that congestion is occurring. Based on such things as the switch's buffer use and the length of frames waiting in a queue, a switch can detect that congestion probably is going to occur before it must start dropping packets. When this happens, the switch sets the FECN bit in a packet to 1 (the default is 0) and then sends the packet on to the next switch. In this manner, switches downstream from the switch approaching congestion are notified of the condition.

Similarly, the BECN bit is used to notify upstream sources that a network congestion condition is rapidly becoming a possibility. It does this not by returning packets sent from that source, but by watching for packets traveling in the opposite direction that are already addressed to that source. The BECN bit is set to 1 (again, the default is 0) in these packets. Thus, when a source sending out a lot of traffic starts to receive packets back from other switches, it can check this bit to determine whether packets are being transmitted too fast.

Implicit Congestion Notification is not performed by the Frame Relay switches. Instead, it means that the higher-level protocols, such as TCP, can detect that packets are not being acknowledged, take appropriate action to retransmit them, and, depending on the higher-level protocol, possibly slow down the transmission rate.

Referring to Figure 16.6, notice that another field, Discard Eligibility (DE), also can be present in a Frame Relay packet. This field is used to determine which packets should be dropped when a congestion condition occurs. Remember that the Frame Relay provider contracts to give you a CIR. Yet when the network is not busy, usually you can use more bandwidth. However, after you begin to send out data at a rate that is greater than the CIR you have contracted for, the DE bit is set to 1 (the default is 0).

When a switch needs to drop packets due to network congestion, those packets that have the DE field set to 1 are the first to go! If discarding those packets doesn't solve the problem, any packet can be dropped. When properly implemented, however, this mechanism lets a switch drop packets that probably are the source of the congestion in the first place: those that are sending at a rate above their contracted CIR.

The Local Management Interface Signal Mechanism

Another optional signaling mechanism that can be used in a Frame-Relay network is called the Local Management Interface (LMI) specification, of which there are several versions. However, the basic mechanism employed is to use nondata management frames to report the status of an interface or a virtual circuit. For example, a management frame can be used to send a keepalive signal, indicating that, although there isn't a lot of traffic flowing through the interface, the connection is still active. Another management frame can be used to report on the valid DLCIs for a particular interface. Finally, a management frame can be used to indicate the status of a virtual circuit (it's congested, for example).

Using Switched Virtual Circuits (SVCs)

Originally, most Frame Relay equipment was made to allow for the creation of PVCs. This requires that a network administrator of the Frame-Relay network set up routing tables so that a permanent connection exists between the two endpoints of a connection. This is a general principle, in that alternative routes can be used occasionally, but basically a PVC is an always-on, same-path type of connection.

An SVC is more like a telephone call; it's an on-demand path created for the duration of the data-transfer session. After it has been used, the virtual circuit is torn down and doesn't stay in a switch's routing table like the DLCI entries for a PVC. When an SVC needs to be created, the destination is notified of the need, and, if it is willing to accept the circuit, a path is created through the Frame-Relay network for the SVC (call setup). When the circuit is no longer needed, either side of the connection can notify the network to terminate the circuit.

The advantage of using an SVC is that you have to pay only for what you use. It's less expensive than maintaining a PVC that doesn't have a constant rate of traffic. SVCs also can be used in conjunction with PVCs. You can use PVCs for your basic network traffic that flows at a predictable rate, and create or tear down SVCs as needed to handle additional traffic.

Note

The Frame Relay Forum organization was formed to promote the use of Frame-Relay technology and to help create standards for the technology. You can visit its Web site at **www.frforum.com**.

The methods used for signaling to set up and terminate SVCs is beyond the scope of this book, and this is a subject that should be pursued if you are an administrator of a Frame-Relay network. For the end user, however, the mechanisms used for call setup and termination aren't that important. You might want to visit the Frame Relay Forum's Web site, which contains a wealth of information on the technical details involved in signaling, as well as documents about proposed new methods and features for Frame-Relay networks.

Possible Problems Using Frame Relay

You might encounter the following problems when using Frame Relay:

- **Bandwidth use**—As you grow, you might find that the amount of bandwidth you purchased is inadequate for your needs.
- **Bursting**—When you try to send a large burst of traffic that is in excess of the contracted rate, the switch might discard packets it receives that are above the allowable rate, forcing retransmissions and increased response times.
- **Network congestion**—Although the vendor might give you a guarantee of the available bandwidth (the CIR), when many customers use the network at the same time, network congestion can result.

The Frame Relay Forum defined several metrics that can be used to determine the quality of service in a Frame-Relay network. These metrics, which can be found in the forum's FRF.13 Service Level Definitions Implementation Agreement, are listed here:

- **Frame Transfer Delay**—The time required to transfer a frame through the network.
- **Frame Delivery Ratio**—The ratio of frames received (frames delivered) to the number of frames sent (frames offered) in one direction across a single virtual connection.
- **Data Delivery Ratio**—Similar to the Frame Delivery Ratio, but measures the ratio of payload octets received to those sent.
- **Service Availability**—Outages resulting from faults in the network (called Fault Outage) as well as those beyond the control of the network, including scheduled maintenance (called Excluded Outage).

When reviewing the Service Level Agreement (SLA) that your Frame-Relay provider offers, use these metrics to help you understand what kind of commitment the vendor is making. With these metrics, the vendor might further qualify them based on the CIR as opposed to bursts allowed by the agreement. For example, it would be unreasonable to expect to receive the same kind of delivery ratio for bursts of high-volume traffic that you receive for traffic that flows through the network at the rate guaranteed by the CIR.

When you review the SLA, be sure you understand how each metric will be measured. Does the vendor use statistics provided by its own switch (and will the vendor allow you access to these statistics?), or does the vendor use an RMON probe or SNMP MIB to define the metrics? What portion of the connection is to be measured for metrics: end-to-end or switch to switch?

Digital Subscriber Lines (DSL) Technology

SOME OF THE MAIN TOPICS IN THIS CHAPTER ARE

DSL and cable modems are the fastest technology available today for accessing the Internet for home or small-office users. Although both of these technologies offer a very fast download speed, and a variable upload speed (depending on the service agreement), they are not a substitute for the T-carrier dedication connections, ATM, or even Frame Relay. Those technologies are for high-speed networks that require service-level agreements for bandwidth commitments or dedicated connections, whereas DSL and cable modems are for home workers, small offices, and home users who just want to have fun. Just because DSL and cable modems aren't a substitute for a T-carrier line doesn't mean that they are not a good solution for a small business, or a small business unit that is separated geographically from the main office. However, not a lot of businesses I know of have cable TV at work!

For example, DSL and cable modems are perfect for branch offices, where the cost of a dedicated service (or the slowness of a dial-up service) aren't appropriate. DSL can enable a small office to upload and download significant amounts of information from a central network, or to other branch offices. Employing Virtual Private Networks (VPNs) can provide for security on an Internet connection.

Although DSL technologies (usually called xDSL because you can get different bandwidths and so on depending on the prices charged) are a good solution for a small business, there can be problems. First, DSL is not available in as many locations geographically as cable technology. Cable modems are easier to install—most of the time you only need to put a T-connector on your cable connection and run one cable to your television set (or set-top box) and use the other side of the T-connector to run a cable to your cable modem. For DSL, where it is available, you can experience disruptions when other lines are added or removed from the local loop. Some DSL flavors require you to use special devices to connect other phones at your location to the phone lines, or otherwise the voice channel can become degraded. In general, cable modems are simple to install, whereas DSL technologies can be more complicated. If you don't understand the technology, it can be difficult to do a self-install.

▶▶   See Chapter 50, "Virtual Private Networks (VPNs) and Tunneling," for detailed information on VPNs.

DSL comes in many flavors (described later in this chapter). If your telephone company can reach you within the limits imposed by DSL technology, you can be sure there will be more than one offer you can choose from. Some companies offer DSL service in a faster direction (upload/download) than other service categories. Others offer a standard home user package that gives a faster download time, with a slower upload time. The difference should reflect your own needs.

Tip

Just about every new technology mentioned in this book has an industry/vendor group association associated with advancement of the technology, definition of standards, or the setting of requirements for testing. This is also true for DSL. The Web site **www.dslforum.org** is a good reference if you want to keep up with current DSL technology and other developments. Another Web site, **www.dsl.com** (a commercial one), will let you enter information pertinent to your location and then show you different DSL offerings. When deciding whether to use DSL for your office or home, check out all the providers in your neighborhood. Choose a vendor based on price and service capabilities.

There are other things to think about when using DSL. For example, do you have a small network, and do you want to enable each node to access the Internet through this single connection? Do you have any policies set up for creating a firewall between your company network and the Internet? We'll explore these topics, along with others, in this chapter.

DSL and Cable Modems

The next chapter is devoted to using cable modems for Internet access. Both DSL and cable modems offer a larger bandwidth connection than you will ever get with a dial-up modem. However, it is important to understand the main difference between cable and DSL technology.

As mentioned earlier, most home users can't afford to spend the several hundreds or thousands of dollars a month it would cost to put in a T-class of service. For many years, ISDN (discussed in the preceding chapter, "Dedicated Connections") was the primary digital method for connecting home offices or those who have large bandwidth requirements to the Internet or to a company's remote access servers. ISDN, however, has become almost outdated for most of today's remote users for several reasons. One reason is that if you can get DSL or cable access in your area, you will probably pay less for those than for ISDN service.

However, sometimes ISDN is a good choice for a connection, but it does have some drawbacks:

- ISDN is a dial-up technology. To connect to the Internet or a remote site, you must place a call, just like you do with a telephone.

- ISDN BRI (Basic Rate Interface service), with two 64Kbps channels you can use for data transmission, although cheaper than a T-class of service, is still priced beyond the reach of most typical home users or small businesses. This pricing discrepancy will drive away most customers who can get DSL or cable modem access. And although DSL/cable providers have pretty much stabilized to offer services in a small range of prices, the same cannot be said for ISDN—or for the T-carrier lines either. You will find that the cost of ISDN service varies widely from one location to another.

- Newer technologies have been developed over the past 10 years that are not only faster than ISDN, but also much cheaper to provide. These digital services are provided by either your local cable television company through a cable modem, or by one or more providers in your area using the same twisted-pair telephone wires that connect your telephone to the local central office. This is, of course, the topic of this chapter: DSL technology.

With the advent of faster modems, the price that telephone companies charge for ISDN's basic maximum of 128Kbps (two 64Kbps lines) service isn't really justifiable for most users when you consider that current modem technology (with multilink capabilities, as you'll find in Windows operating systems) can easily come close to this speed. However, in such a situation the cost of multiple phone lines coupled with the difficulty of finding a service provider that supports multilink would probably be prohibitive factors when compared to DSL.

Topological Differences Between Cable and DSL

Both cable modems and DSL are digital *broadband* technologies, but that's about all they have in common. The first major difference is the physical connection. DSL provides a direct point-to-point connection to a termination point in the telephone company's central office using the same twisted-pair wiring used for telephone services. Because DSL uses copper wires and the signal attenuates (weakens and degrades) the farther you get from the central office, DSL has a limited distance, usually a maximum of 18,000 feet of cable. Another thing to keep in mind is that the farther you get from the central office, the slower the speed you will be able to get from a DSL line.

Note

The term *broadband* has many definitions. The most basic definition is that broadband connections (DSL, cable, and ISDN, for example) use more than one frequency for data transmissions, and can thus multiplex data streams across multiple frequencies at the same time. Compared to a "nonbroadband" or "narrowband" connection (such as your 4MHz telephone channel), the multiple frequencies allow a larger data pipe. Some definitions rely on the actual bandwidth achieved, no matter what the method.

Because most people don't live next door to a central office, and because most telephone companies have been trying to extend profitable service offerings to more and more of their customer bases, a solution that creates a "mini" central office in the field is being rapidly deployed in many areas. This involves using high-capacity lines (usually fiber optic) from the central office to connect a digital concentrator out in the field. The fiber-optic cable enables digital communications back to the central office from your neighborhood. Using this method, it's easy to deliver digital services in the "last mile" by moving the digital equipment out of the central office and closer to subscribers. Building out this fiber network is to the benefit of telephone companies, because the fiber can be used for many services, such as telephone service, cable TV, and DSL.

Back at the central office, the data portion of the signal is split off and sent directly to a high-speed digital connection to the Internet. The voice portion of the signal (the first 4Mhz) is directed to the public switched telephone network (PSTN). See Figure 17.1 for an example. This means that your connection is shared by no one and, after the service has been provisioned and installed, you can expect to get the same speed no matter what time of day from your connection to the telephone company's central office. Cable systems work in a similar manner, separating Internet traffic from television data at the cable company's front end.

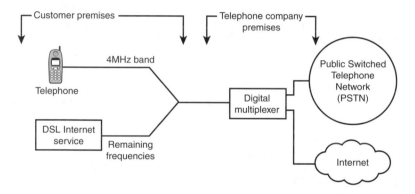

Figure 17.1 DSL uses frequencies that are left unused on a typical voice-grade copper cable.

The communication path for cable modems is a shared access medium, similar to an Ethernet network. The coaxial cable that snakes through your neighborhood delivering cable television services is used for both television and cable-modem communications. When you get DSL advocates and cable-modem aficionados in the same room arguing, the DSL guys will tell you that the shared access coaxial cable is a choke point that can limit the speeds you can obtain. This argument is based on the notion that as more homes in your neighborhood begin to use the cable-modem service, the shared coaxial cable can become saturated. Although most cable modems, when working at top speed, can easily surpass a DSL connection, your actual speed using a cable modem will vary from the maximum capacity depending on how many other users are using the same cable at the same time. In practice, however, cable systems offer a higher bandwidth than many DSL systems, especially if you don't live close to a central office or there isn't a digital connection sitting in a box somewhere in your neighborhood. And, as cable segments become heavily populated, cable companies can split the cable into different segments and run a line back to a router that connects to the Internet. Because DSL tends to be the most flexible service, in that you can choose from various speeds for upload and download capabilities, it is probably the choice for a business. Cable modems typically offer only one or two types of service—which are probably due to their physical capabilities—and cable service providers won't generally allow you to do such things as maintain a Web site and keep a static IP address. DSL business class, however, can give you these features.

If you have only a small office that uses another provider to offer your Web page, and you just need a fast connection to the Internet to check email and so on, then a cable modem connection can serve you very well, and usually at a much less expensive price than a DSL connection. The next chapter covers cable modem technology in more detail. However, after you read that chapter, another question you must ask yourself when making a decision about using a cable modem or DSL is which company provides you better service now? When you call your local telephone company or cable company, which is the quickest to respond? Which company provides better service? How important is that Internet connection to your business or for recreational use? Today, access to the Internet is becoming a business necessity. Before choosing an access method (or a backup method), be sure to evaluate how important this access is to your business.

DSL Services

Just as you can obtain phone service from more than one company, using the same telephone lines, the same goes for DSL services. Although your local telco might not offer the service, other providers in the same area might. Many telephone companies invested heavily in the equipment needed to provide ISDN services several years ago, charged a lot for the service, and found few customers. Some are hesitant to invest in the DSL Access Multiplexer (DSLAM) and other equipment needed to provide DSL services. However, that doesn't stop third parties from co-locating their own DSL equipment at the local telco office and offering you the service. Today DSL service is booming, due in part to the demand from both home users and businesses that cannot afford T-carrier and other networking services.

Keep in mind that for both cable modems and DSL connections the high-speed capacity they both provide is only on the link from your computer to the ISP Internet connection. This is very important to consider. Both cable and DSL modems *will do nothing to make the Internet itself or Web servers work faster*. So if your favorite Web site is being swamped with a large number of hits, you may not notice any difference between a dial-up connection and a digital connection. And if a large number of your customers are trying to connect to your Web site, it is not just your bandwidth between your network and the local ISP that matters. When it comes down to it, the lowest common denominator is the speed of the Internet itself. If everyone is downloading the newest update to a popular software product, you can expect to experience slower transfer rates and lower bandwidth availability due to circumstances beyond your local connection to the telco or cable modem provider.

For these reasons, don't expect DSL to be the absolute solution to bandwidth on the Internet. The Internet is far too complex for such a simple solution.

A Quick Primer on the PSTN

Before you can understand why DSL technology and cable modems are revolutionizing high-speed access to the Internet, it is important that you understand how your ordinary telephone line works. Given that knowledge, you can understand how DSL takes advantage of the remaining capacity inherent in the telephone voice cabling, and why cable modems can offer a service using another type of cabling.

Ordinary voice-grade service, called plain old telephone service (POTS), has its roots back in the 1930s when it was discovered that human beings can hear frequencies of up to about 20,000KHz but normally talk in frequencies that range up to only about 3,500KHz. Because of this, the original telephone network was designed to transmit in channels of only 4,000KHz. However, those ordinary copper wires used in the last mile to the home can transmit signals using much higher frequencies. The problem with using the PSTN to provide high-speed data communications comes from the fact that although the copper wiring *can handle* transmission at greater frequencies, the techniques used at the central office to digitize voice-grade traffic cannot. The incoming analog voice signal is sampled 8,000 times per second and coded into 8 bits for transmission on the digital portions of the PSTN.

This means that the effective data throughput is limited to 64Kbps. Because most telephone circuits use one of the bits for network-management purposes, the actual data throughput shrinks to only 56Kbps.

Communications between central offices and long-distance lines make use of more modern techniques, stacking multiple voice circuits on top of each other in 4KHz segments and sending them across high-capacity fiber-optic lines. The Internet backbone is composed of similar high-capacity lines capable of extremely fast transmission of large amounts of data. The limiting factor for dial-up modems is the old, switched telephone network that sets the ceiling at 8,000 samples per second.

The maximum speed of today's dial-up modems is achieved by using sophisticated coding techniques on the wire on which data is transmitted as symbols, coupled with other compression algorithms. Yet *analog modems* are limited to using only that first 4KHz of bandwidth on the copper wire (the voice channel—which is why you can hear the squealing and clicking of modem communications if you pick up a voice line while a data connection is active). Because the twisted-pair telephone wire can support higher frequencies, it's only natural to assume that there would be a digital solution to the speed roadblock that the voice-grade telephone circuit forces you to use.

And ordinary analog modems on a voice circuit may not achieve the highest rate for that modem. Because of noisy lines, and other interference, it is often the case that a modem connects to an ISP or another modem at a rate lower than the highest rated speed.

xDSL

The term xDSL is usually mentioned when discussing DSL because there isn't just one type of DSL; instead, you can choose from an assortment of similar technologies, depending on your needs. For example, perhaps the most popular xDSL technology is ADSL (Asymmetric Digital Subscriber Line). This service provides a fast download speed to your computer or network, but you'll have a much smaller data path back to the provider of this service.

One thing to keep in mind about xDSL technologies is that their usability is limited by the distance from the telephone company's central office. This is due to several factors, including attenuation of the signal as it travels down the copper wire and interference caused by signals from wires in a cable bundle interfering with other wires in the same bundle. Because telephone cables were initially laid down with no thought for offering digital services, it's possible in many locations that you won't be able to get any kind of xDSL connection until local lines are upgraded.

Tip

One factor that may help you make a decision on which vendor to select is the availability of email accounts and USENET access. When you obtain a DSL connection, there is an associated ISP that connects your digital line to the Internet. Newsgroup access (USENET) may not be important to many companies (but it can be a very useful research tool), and if it isn't available, there are various Web-based solutions (such as `http://groups.google.com`) providing access to most of the nonbinary newsgroup postings. However, email is usually a very important factor, and one that may be a deciding factor when it comes to making a decision about connecting to the Internet. Check the number of email accounts your DSL ISP provides. If it is not sufficient to support your business users, don't panic. You can always use another service on the Internet (such as `www.activewebhosting.com`) that will provide you a Web page, FTP storage, and a number of email mailboxes. If your ISP limits you on email, consider using a third-party provider instead, and your own domain name. The last feature, your own domain name, is an attractive feature if you really want to project a presence on the Internet.

These are some of the more common offerings you'll find in the xDSL world:

- **ADSL**—Suited best for a home user or a small office where data requires a large download speed (1,500Kbps to 8,000Kbps) and a slower upload speed (32Kbps to 1,088Kbps). ADSL can potentially reach up to 18,000 feet from the central office.

- **RADSL**—Rate-Adaptive Digital Subscriber Line is a variation of ADSL. The modems on this type of connection can test the line to determine what speed it will support. RADSL usually provides for a longer distance from the central office (about 21,000 feet) but provides for slower speeds. Expect download speeds from 600Kbps to 7,000Kbps. Typical upload speeds are from 128Kbps to 1,000Kbps.

- **SDSL**—This Single-line Digital Subscriber Line allows for symmetric bidirectional communications. Unlike ADSL, SDSL gives you the same bandwidth in either direction. Generally, you must be within 10,000 feet of the central office. Transmission rates (depending, of course, on distance) range from 160Kbps to 2,084Kbps.

- **HDSL**—High bit-rate DSL is an early entry into the xDSL market. HDSL also gives you the same bandwidth for both directions.

- **G.Lite (also called Universal ADSL)**—This form of ADSL is easier to install than the traditional ADSL. Traditional ADSL requires installing a splitter at the consumer premises, which effectively splits the lower voice-frequency channel from the higher frequencies used for digital transmission. G.Lite operates at a lower speed than ADSL (1,544Kbps downstream, 384Kbps upstream) but does so without using a splitter.

There are still other xDSL technologies, but some are proprietary and the solution you end up choosing will depend on what your local provider offers. There's even a version called IDSL, which offers an ISDN service using xDSL technology. Of course, the higher-rate services are going to cost more. For most small offices or home users, the advent of cheap ADSL and G.Lite services can be an ideal solution for remote connections.

DSLAMs, CAP, and DMT

Implementing ADSL services in a central office is not nearly as costly as implementing ISDN. Using ADSL, the network traffic never actually enters the PSTN like dial-up modem analog connections do. At the central office, the incoming signal is split, sending the voice-grade frequencies (the first 4KHz channel) to the normal telephone switch, and the higher frequencies used by DSL to a device called a DSL Access Multiplexer (DSLAM). The DSLAM is responsible for concentrating traffic it receives and passing it to the Internet by using higher-capacity technologies, such as T1–T3 lines, or to an ATM switched network, for example. Lucent and Nortel make telephone line cards that can be used in the central office which combine digital and voice functions. If these cards are used, it isn't even necessary to rewire your phone line at the central office when DSL is provisioned, making it even easier for telephone companies to offer the service. One of the first drawbacks of getting DSL service is how it will be supported by the local telephone company. No matter who the "provider" of this service might be, much depends on how the telephone company handles the digital signal after it's split off from the voice signal.

And it does get just a little more complicated. For ADSL, two basic methods use those higher frequencies on copper wires: Carrierless Amplitude Phase (CAP) and Discrete MultiTone (DMT). Both of these methods use frequencies that are well past the 4KHz voice channel, and because of this are called *passband* technologies. Both voice and data can be carried on the same twisted-pair wires at the same time, operating in full-duplex mode. The voice-grade frequency range is *not* used for data (it is "passed by"), and there is a small amount of separation of frequencies before the ADSL upstream channel starts and another separation before the downstream channel starts, depending on whether your DSL is implemented using CAP or DMT. This separation helps to reduce the probability of one channel interfering with another.

The main difference between CAP and DMT is the way in which they use the higher frequencies on the ordinary copper wire pair. CAP uses two different carriers, a smaller frequency range for the upstream data and a larger frequency range for the downstream data path, as you can see in Figure 17.2. CAP uses a small part of the frequencies above the voice channel for uploading data to the Internet, and a much larger range of frequencies for the downstream data path.

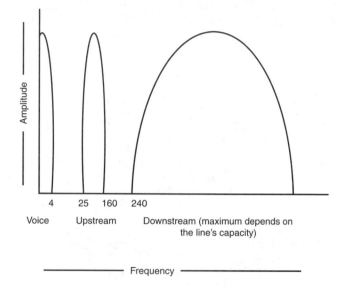

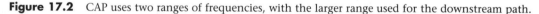

Figure 17.2 CAP uses two ranges of frequencies, with the larger range used for the downstream path.

However, a drawback of CAP is that any noise on the line can easily cause the signal to become corrupted. This can be caused by wiring that has degraded, interference from other wires in a cable bundle, or bridge taps that haven't been removed. To overcome this, CAP-based modems usually try to measure the line when they start up to determine the defects inherent in it. The modems then try to use equalizers to create mirror images of the line distortion that can be used to clean up the signal.

DMT uses channels above the voice channel just like CAP does. However, as you can see in Figure 17.3, DMT divides the upper frequencies into many discrete, separate 4KHz channels, and assigns some for upstream communications and others for downstream data flows. Each channel is called a *bin*.

DMT can monitor each channel to determine which ones are having problems with interference, and not use those small segments of the available frequency range, or use the troublesome bins for a lower rate of data transmission. Bins in the lower frequency range are used for the upstream data path, and those in the higher frequency ranges are used for the downstream data path. DMT constantly monitors each bin and adjusts their use depending on performance. Bins in the lower frequency range also can be used as bidirectional communication channels. If this is done, echo-canceling circuitry is necessary, making DMT a more expensive technology.

CAP was originally deployed by ADSL vendors early in the game, and much of the equipment is proprietary. That is, a modem you get from one provider might not work with another provider's system. This really shouldn't matter, however, if you intend to keep the same provider for a while.

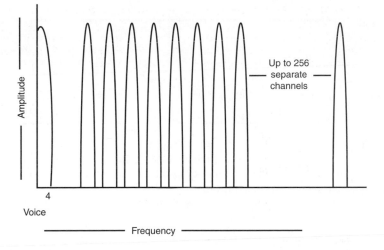

Figure 17.3 DMT creates multiple channels in the upper-frequency range and assigns them for upstream or downstream communication.

The ITU selected DMT as the standard method to be employed for ADSL. However, a lot of equipment using CAP has been installed in the past and can continue to have a useful life for some years to come. When it comes to choosing a provider, you might not have many choices in your area. You might have to take what you can get—if you can get it. You might be located too far from the central office to make DSL a solution for your home or small-business connection. Or the building in which you are located might have been wired years ago and contain a lot of bridge taps and deteriorating cables.

However, it is important to know the difference between CAP and DMT. Because DMT is a standard now, most new equipment that will be produced is likely to use DMT. Of course, your best protection against changing standards is to use service providers that include the DSL equipment with the DSL service.

ADSL

ADSL is ideal for home users for Internet surfing because it's usually priced reasonably, and the bandwidth use for home users is generally asymmetrical. That is, you click the mouse button on a link and then wait for a large download of data to your computer. Most Internet Web page communication for the home user involves a minor amount of data being sent *upstream* to the Internet, with a large amount of data being sent downstream to the computer in response to the request. With multimedia applications, such as streaming audio and video, the large data pipe that ADSL provides will make the Internet appear to be lightning fast to a home user, or a business user performing research.

However, the opposite is not true. If you operate a Web server from your house or business, keep in mind that ADSL provides a much *smaller* data pipe back to your ISP. And many DSL providers will try to prevent you from using your connection for a Web server by using DHCP to assign your address. If you are a business customer, you may be able to get a business class of service that includes a faster upstream link and a static IP address. Otherwise, expect to be treated as a "home" customer. If you want to place a server on the Web, and you expect to send out large volumes of data to the Internet (or receive a very large number of hits), you'll probably have to settle for another xDSL technology and pay the telco a little more for the dedicated address.

Note

The Dynamic Host Configuration Protocol—see Chapter 29, "BOOTP and Dynamic Host Configuration Protocol (DHCP)"—is used to dynamically assign network information, such as an address, to clients of the network. Because of its dynamic nature, a client may acquire a different address if it disconnects and then reconnects later. This is because the DHCP server may have reused the older address and it has been assigned to another client. This is why you shouldn't consider using a DSL or cable modem service that uses DHCP if you want to create a Web presence from a computer on your network. Instead, use a service provider to host your Web page, and use your DSL link to manage the Web site.

If a business has users who work from home, ADSL might be a good way to establish connectivity back to the main office through the Internet. For example, a help-desk technician can use the voice channel on the telephone line to take customer help calls. To assist the worker in his job, the ADSL connection can be used to allow the technician to search Web site pages or a database residing on a server back at the business's main office. As long as it isn't necessary for the worker to send large amounts of information back to the office, ADSL can be a good fit here.

Another aspect to examine for this type of service is a work-from-home user who needs to download larger amounts of data to work with, and then upload the changes. Using the fast download provided by ADSL, graphic files, programming files, and so on can be obtained quickly. Then, using a slower upload path, the home worker can send the files back to the main network.

A practical example of the use of ADSL is the food service industry. When branch office managers need to consult the headquarter's database to obtain data about price quotes or discounts, or to simply download a listing of company products, the capacity provided by ADSL can prove very beneficial. This assumes, of course, that the headquarter's site also uses the bandwidth necessary to communicate with a large number of branch offices. Yet because each branch office will probably upload much less data to produce the reports necessary for headquarters to make delivery computations, this can be an expensive service.

Think here about which direction your data flows. Do you have more incoming or outgoing traffic when connecting to the Internet (or another intranet)?

G.Lite DSL

Concerns over putting too many wires in a cable bundle to use for high-frequency DSL services spurred the development of a version of DSL called G.Lite. This version of DSL doesn't require a splitter (to separate the voice channel from the ADSL channels) and operates at lower frequencies. Lower frequencies allow for downstream data flows of only about 1Mbps to 1.5Mbps. Upstream capacity usually runs at 100Kbps to 300Kbps. However, download capacity can range up to 6Mbps and upload speeds to 384Kbps. By using a lower range of frequencies, it's possible for telephone companies to offer a more reliable service, over a longer distance, because attenuation of the higher frequencies (and the cross-talk they can cause) is less of a factor. The speeds provided by G.Lite recognize that the Internet itself, like the PSTN, can be a limiting factor when it comes to speed. It doesn't matter how fast your particular connection to the Internet is if the Web site you're trying to access is on a slow server, or connected by a slow link. Most users won't notice the difference between 1.5Mbps and 8Mbps that can be attained with more expensive DSL technologies.

G.Lite was developed by the Universal ADSL Working Group (UAWG). Its mission was to develop a lower-cost version of ADSL, based on standards, that could be easily installed. The ITU approved G.Lite as a standard in 1999 (no. G-992.2). G.Lite is a good solution to a technological problem. G.Lite doesn't require a "truck roll," which means that the phone company can mail you the package and you can install it without the company's help. Each time a telco truck has to visit a customer, the expense is a serious cost to the telephone company.

Note

Note, however, that for those versions of DSL that don't require a splitter on the home end of the connection, it might be necessary to plug in inexpensive filters for every telephone in the house. This helps reduce the noise that telephones can introduce into the wire, when you take them off the hook, for example. In addition, these filters remove the higher-frequency signals used by the DSL connection before they reach the telephone, because some users are otherwise able to hear a very high-pitched whine resulting from the high-frequency data communication. Without filters, you might find that a previous modem dial-up line no longer works after you've installed a DSL modem. In this case, installing a filter between the modem and the telephone faceplate should also solve this problem.

The Future of DSL

For telephone companies to remain competitive in the telecommunications industry, they must innovate and seek new revenue streams from new technology. Upgrading of the old PSTN infrastructure is going on right now. It will take many years to upgrade the majority of the current copper cable capacity to fiber-optic cabling. Yet the higher bandwidth offered by fiber-optic cables will enable telcos to provide a wider range of services.

DSL is likely to remain a driving force for Internet connections for some time to come. Because it maximizes the otherwise-wasted frequency range of ordinary copper cables, DSL is a technology that can adapt to the current cabling of the PSTN, although it can provide that service only to a qualifying set of customers. As the fiber network grows farther out into the neighborhoods, you can expect to find that DSL technologies will become more widely available. As older copper segments of the PSTN are removed, so are obstacles that cause errors in DSL communications.

And with the improvement of the physical infrastructure of the PSTN, you should expect to see improvements and new types of xDSL technologies in the near future.

Using a Cable Modem

18

SOME OF THE MAIN TOPICS IN THIS CHAPTER ARE

CHAPTER 18

The two most popular methods for connecting home users and many small businesses to the Internet are DSL and cable modems. Both have their advantages as well as disadvantages. The preceding chapter explained how DSL works, and in this chapter you will learn about how cable modems work, as well as how they differ in many respects from DSL.

Although a cable modem connection might work for a home user or a small business, you must again think of the service provider before committing your network's connectivity to the Internet. Some cable companies are just great, providing quick resolution to problems, and others are not so great. Again, if you're not getting a good response (or better yet, response time) from your cable company at home, you might want to consider other options before using the same company as a link for your small business.

Note

Depending on where you live, you might not be able to get Internet access using a cable modem. Not all cable companies have the equipment necessary to provide this service. In that case you should consider using xDSL for a high-speed connection to the Net. Or you may live in a metropolitan area that offers both services. If that is the case, I suggest you read this chapter and Chapter 17, "Digital Subscriber Lines (DSL) Technology," and make your decision based on the topics covered. If you live in an area where neither service is available, you are out of luck, because "two tin cans and a string" uses amplitude modulation instead of digital signaling. Just seeing whether you're paying attention!

Another factor you might think about is the actual cost for cable modem services. Because many cable companies are now trying to maximize their revenues, since the cable TV market is pretty much saturated, you might find that you can get a special deal when subscribing to both cable TV and Internet access. If anything, you may be able to get a few months of cable-modem access at a reduced price.

How Cable Modems Work

By their very nature, cable television networks are not constrained by the problems caused when data needs to pass through the PSTN. Cable television networks don't use the PSTN. Instead, they use a shielded coaxial cable (and some high-speed fiber links to get closer to your house) to deliver quality TV signals, usually using 6MHz bands for each digital channel. To provide for cable modem service, all that is necessary is to set aside one or more of these frequency bands and use them as delivery channels for Internet access. Again, the offering is usually asymmetrical, just like ADSL. By using a high-bandwidth channel for downstream communications, cable can offer a larger bandwidth (for all subscribers on a shared segment) to send data from the Internet to your home. By using time slots (some dedicated to each subscriber, and some called contention slots that anyone can try to use), cable companies offer a smaller upstream data communications path. Because most Internet access involves a larger amount of data transfer in the download direction, this makes sense. If you want to operate a Web site—and need a higher upload bandwidth—then residential cable modem service is not for you. Instead, some companies offer xDSL with varying up- and download bandwidths. These services are generally for business users and are more expensive than the service provided by the telcos and other DSL providers.

Cable modems aren't really modems at all. The term *modem* used to be spelled MODEM because it's an acronym (MODulation/DEModulation), and a true modem is a device that converts digital signals to analog signals for transmission over an analog telephone line. The receiving modem does the opposite, converting the analog signal back to a digital signal your computer can understand. The term *cable modem* is just a convenient way of indicating that you're getting a fast connection from the cable company. No "analog" signal is involved in the connection whatsoever.

Tip

If you subscribe to both cable TV service and cable Internet access, you might be able to make the most of your cable access. Use a splitter. This is a simple device that plugs the incoming cable into one side, and on the other side there are two outlets. You can plug in one coax cable and run it to your cable modem, and run a line from the other outlet to the graphics card on your computer. If the software that came with your graphics card supports a TV tuner, you can then watch television on your computer's monitor while surfing the Web at the same time. In some cases you might also have to use a digital filter with the cable segment that attaches to your computer's graphics card.

Providing IP Addresses to Cable Modems

Most cable companies won't allocate a static IP address because (1) it's easier to use DHCP to dynamically assign addresses, just like most network administrators do in a typical LAN situation, and (2) there just aren't that many addresses available to grant a unique address to each node on the large network that the cable company operates. Using DHCP, which is discussed in Chapter 29, "BOOTP and Dynamic Host Configuration Protocol (DHCP)," the cable company doesn't have to perform the manual task of assigning IP addresses for each customer. The DHCP server (on the cable company's end) performs this task automatically by interacting with DHCP client software on your computer. Figure 18.1 diagrams the address translations involved in connecting a single computer to a cable modem.

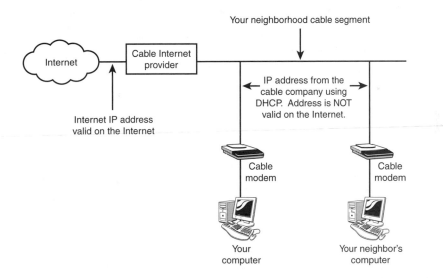

Figure 18.1 IP addresses using a cable modem.

Note

DHCP can be used to supply IP addresses that are not valid on the Internet, as described previously. However, you can also use DHCP to configure clients using a range of addresses that are valid on the Internet. In a business situation, a cable company can supply a static IP address to your connection so that you can run a Web server or another Internet application that requires the address to stay the same. This can be done by editing the networking information on your computer to manually configure a static IP address given to you by the installer. It is also easy to reserve IP addresses using DHCP so that they are allocated to just selected clients that need them.

In the figure you can see that each cable drop goes to a single cable modem, and then is used by just one computer—one for you and one for your neighbor. This is exactly how the cable company (as well as xDSL companies) wants the system to operate. The less traffic on the line, the less bandwidth that needs to be aggregated by the cable provider where it connects to the Internet.

However, DHCP can be cascaded so that more than one device is providing addresses to computers (and other network devices) for your home network. This is accomplished by attaching the cable connection to a switch/router instead of directly to your computer. The switch/router does the same thing that the router at the cable company does: provide addresses that are not valid on the Internet to computers attached to the switch/router. In Figure 18.2 you can see the way this cascading of addresses works.

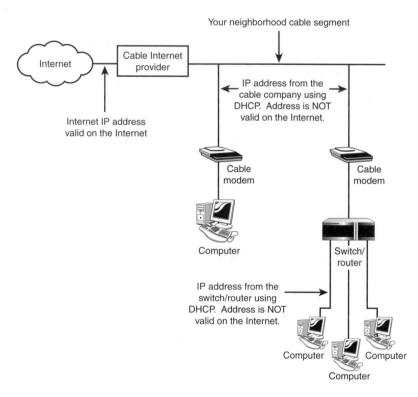

Figure 18.2 IP cascading IP addresses using a router and a cable modem.

Here the cable company provides you with an address that is not valid on the Internet. The switch/router uses this address to communicate with your cable provider. The switch/router then uses DHCP to assign addresses to your computer(s), each of which is not valid on the Internet. By using DHCP, communications eventually flow through the IP addresses that the cable company owns that *are* valid on the Internet. Of course, with a large number of subscribers, the cable company will have more than one valid IP address, and use multiple routers to connect various segments of its network to the Internet. Again, Chapter 29 will give you an understanding of how DHCP operates and keeps track of which computer is sending/receiving data from another computer on the Internet. The important thing to keep in mind here is that you can connect more than one computer to the Internet using a cable modem (or xDSL). If all computers are accessing the Internet at the same time (as in an office setting), they must share the bandwidth provided by the cable modem. If only one computer is using the network at any point in time, it should be able to achieve the full bandwidth that the cable provider can offer at that time. Note that this does not, however, help you overcome any bottlenecks that are inherit in the Internet itself. For example, if you are trying to access a busy Web site, you will find that the bandwidth of your ISP doesn't make any difference. The access wait-time will be dependent on the Web site's capabilities.

First-Generation Cable Modem Systems

Early implementations used a separate, ordinary telephone modem connection for the upstream data channel. If you still have this kind of service, you might as well consider using that single telephone twisted-pair wiring for ADSL (see Chapter 17). This is because DSL will provide voice and data circuits, whereas using the phone line for an upload to the Internet eliminates the voice circuit. If you can get only the cable modem service, then a second phone line for the upload traffic is a good idea if you are running a home business, or if you work at times when the home telephone is frequently used. Again, note that this is an old technology. That investment must be recouped by small cable companies before they can outfit their cable networks with more modern technologies, such as the newest version of DOCSIS (Data Over Cable Service Interface Specification). This is discussed briefly later in this chapter.

How Cable Modems Differ from xDSL Broadband Access

DSL is a dedicated connection from your location to the telco's central office using your existing phone line. A cable modem gives you access to a *shared network media*, similar to the older Ethernet technology. This shared network media is nothing more than a part of the signal that travels through the coaxial cables used by cable companies to deliver service to your home or business. Just as the bandwidth of ordinary twisted-pair copper cables is actually used for voice transmissions, an almost-similar situation exists for coaxial cabling from your cable company. Digital cable signals use channels, which are basically time slots in which each channel is sent in a channel of usually 6MHz. Cable companies need only set aside some of these slots for cable service instead of for channels that no one ever watches anyway.

Cable modems also give you a higher bandwidth for downloading from the Internet, when compared to DSL solutions. As cable segments become overpopulated, your performance may vary, depending on other users' habits and the capacity provided to your local neighborhood. Performance may vary from hour to hour, depending on when the service is being used by your neighbors. This is because—and this is important to remember—cable segments are shared media. If you are the only person in your neighborhood using a coaxial cable that terminates at the cable company, you'll have the best cable service possible! If you have several dozen other cable modems on your segment, all must share the available bandwidth on the shared coaxial cable. Don't worry, however—your TV channels will still work just as well as ever!

Note

Don't forget that if you use a switch/router to connect more than one computer to a cable modem, you may also see a decrease in speed if all of your computers are accessing the Internet at one time.

For now, cable modems are a welcome solution for many who have phone lines that cannot be provisioned for DSL service. Almost everyone within even a small city can obtain cable TV services, whether or not the local telco can provide DSL service. By offering Internet access over existing equipment, a cable company can add a router and connect cable segments to a large Internet pipeline and generate extra revenue from existing customers. Offering cable Internet service also is a good selling point for attracting new customers. Because the cable TV market is now pretty much saturated, cable companies need a new technology to offer in order to keep growing.

For some small-business access, and especially for many home users, cable modem access is a great solution. Whereas DSL requires that the telephone company provision the line (remove bridge taps, voice coils, and so on) and test it to determine the bandwidth that can be supported, cable modems can be purchased in an electronics store and self-installed. Or you can have someone from your cable company install the cable modem. After you have cable TV installed, adding a cable modem is simple.

No matter which technology you want to use, it really comes down to the simple matter of what is available in your location. In some places you may be able to get DSL access, and in others cable modem access. Yet in more competitive environments you might have a choice between the two.

The Data Over Cable Service Interface Specification (DOCSIS)

Newer cable systems, however, based on the DOCSIS (Data Over Cable Service Interface Specification) standards allow for bidirectional, asymmetrical communications. Version 1.1 and 2.0 of DOCSIS include the necessary authentication and encryption features that make cable modem access as secure as DSL. In general, if you can see other computers in your Network Neighborhood, your cable provider is using an older system and you might want to take steps to protect yourself, such as using a firewall appliance.

DOCSIS specifications can be found at the URL www.cablemodem.com/. This is the Web site of an organization responsible for establishing specifications and testing hardware to ensure that it meets the standards for cable television—Cable Television Laboratories, Inc. (CableLabs). This testing ensures that a cable company can buy hardware from different manufacturers and be assured that the system that is installed will work. For example, the router may come from one company, and the cable modems used at customer sites may come from another manufacturer.

DOCSIS version 2.0 is the most recent standard. This version has been adopted by the International Telecommunications Union–Telecommunication Sector (ITU-T) as a worldwide standard.

DOCSIS 2.0 specifications (developed by both CableLabs and Cable Television Laboratories, Inc.) cover many aspects of using a cable system for Internet access:

- **Radio Frequency Interface Specification:** This document describes the physical media specification, including items from signal processing to a scrambler for the upload channel. This specification also defines parameters, such as the protocol used for downloading as well as other specs to Media Access Control mechanisms, and quality of service. This specifications document is more than 500 pages long and can make quite interesting reading for electrical engineers, like the following specifications.

- **Operations System Support Interface Specification:** This specification document covers networking subjects such as the Simple Network Management Protocol (see Chapter 53, "Network Testing and Analysis Tools"). This specification also provides the documentation for the Management Interface Base used by SNMP to collect data about the network. You will also find here such things as how subscriber billing should work and fault management. This specification is relevant to most users as the one that defines the interface between the cable system and the user's cable modem.

- **Baseline Privacy Plus Interface Specification:** Encryption and key management are covered in this document, including the use of X.509 certificates.

- **Cable Modem to Customer Premises Equipment Interface Specification:** This document covers the "last few feet" to the user's cable modem. Here you'll find information about the Ethernet interface, as well as other information about the end-user equipment and how it interfaces with the cable network.

- **Cable Modem Termination System Network Side Interface Specification:** Here you will find out the specifications concerning connections from the cable company's service and high-speed connections such as Asynchronous Transmission Mode (ATM, covered in Chapter 16, "Dedicated Connections").

- **Acceptance Test Plan:** This document defines the tests that cable modem technology must meet to be certified by CableLabs.

This list of specifications can be read in more detail by developers by visiting the DOCSIS Web site (www.cablemodem.com). For most end users it will not matter at all if you get the service you expect. For network and application developers, reading the specs is the only way you'll be informed of the technologies being used by most cable Internet providers today.

Which Should You Choose—Cable or DSL?

The first consideration is whether both services are offered at your location. If not, you are stuck with a single broadband solution. And it goes without saying that any broadband solution is better than a dial-up modem (whether 28Kbps or 56Kbps).

Wireless Networking Protocols

SOME OF THE MAIN TOPICS FOR THIS PART ARE

Introduction to Wireless Networking

IEEE 802.11b: It's Here and It's Inexpensive

Faster Service: IEEE 802.11a

The IEEE 802.11g Standard

Bluetooth Wireless Technology

Other Wireless Technologies

PART V

Introduction to Wireless Networking

SOME OF THE MAIN TOPICS IN THIS CHAPTER ARE

CHAPTER 19

Although the installed base of networked computers today is mainly made up of technologies using copper wire and fiber-optic cable, the growing market for wireless technologies should not be underestimated. The popularity and rapid growth of the cellular telephone market, for both personal and business applications, attests to this fact. Just 10 years or so ago, cellular telephones were high-priced items used mainly by business executives. Today, they are sold in shopping malls, and it is common to see teenagers walking around with them stuck to their heads (no offense intended!). You can even rent a prepaid cell phone now and pay as you go. The fact that several states have passed laws that prevent use of a cell phone (unless it's "hands free") by the driver of a car can attest to the wide acceptance, and use—or misuse—of the cell phone.

Other than the CB (Citizens' Band) radio craze that peaked a few decades ago, it was not until cell phones became inexpensive that wireless networking became a hot issue. And now wireless networking of many kinds of devices is working its way into everyday life.

Today's wireless phones and other wireless devices now have uses that probably were never envisioned by the creators of this technology. Use your cell phone to report an automobile accident. Put up a wireless camera to monitor a child. Access the Internet through your cell phone. I could go on...

Note

It's hard to write this chapter without discussing the first wireless network: radio! (Hey, we're talking electronic technology here, not the village crier.) Broadcast commercial radio is a one-way technique, but there are many variants of two-way radios, from those used by police and fire departments, to the CB radios that were a hot item years ago. However, today we're discussing wireless communications between computers, consumer electronic devices—the sky is the limit.

Many mobile phones today are already equipped to handle text messaging, Internet email, and some limited Web-browsing capabilities. This chapter will introduce you to just a few of the many problems that wireless networking can solve, and introduce you to some of the technologies basic to many of the wireless technologies. Other networking solutions are found in Chapter 24, "Other Wireless Technologies," and Bluetooth is covered in Chapter 23, "Bluetooth Wireless Technology." Although Bluetooth is a wireless technology, its original purpose is not as far reaching as the IEEE 802.11b, 802.11g, or 802.11a technologies (covered in Chapters 20, 21, and 22). Instead, Bluetooth was initially designed to replace cables that span only a very short distance. Yet new profiles, which are discussed in Chapter 23, do indeed enable you to create a small LAN using Bluetooth. Because of distance limitations, however, it still is not the wireless LAN technology of choice for anything but a small LAN that requires a small bandwidth.

You can now use Bluetooth to exchange data between a mobile phone and a PC. For example, properly configured, a Bluetooth-enabled wireless phone can be used for a modem connection to a PDA or laptop similarly equipped. Or you can use a Bluetooth keyboard and mouse with a Bluetooth receiver attached to your computer. This short-distance communication capability does not address the much larger distances that the specifications 802.11a, 802.11b, and 801.11g can cover. But it is important to keep in mind that although you can create a small LAN using Bluetooth, it was not developed to create a LAN or WAN. It works best for short-distance transmissions between peripheral devices and consumer electronic devices. Because it uses a radio spectrum, it is possible to create many devices, such as a TV remote, using Bluetooth, because current devices require a line-of-sight. If your cable box is in the living room and you're in the bedroom, you could use a Bluetooth-enabled cable box/remote to change the channel, all while staying in bed!

Despite my predictions in previous versions of this book, Bluetooth devices have started finally to make it to the low-cost marketplace, and you can expect to see more of this technology.

More than a few users like the portability of their keyboard and mouse, as well as the convenience of wireless synchronization with a PDA or downloading from a digital camera. Bluetooth has a few major competitors in the consumer market though—IEEE 802.11b, 802.11a, and, more especially, 802.11g (see Chapter 22, "The IEEE 802.11g Standard").

▶▶ In Chapter 24, you'll find that myriad other devices, such as PDAs and tablet PCs, can also be used with wireless technologies, enabling you to "carry it with you" yet still be able to communicate with consumer devices, or your desktop/laptop computer.

Why Wireless Networks Are Inevitable

If the previous considerations did not convince you that wireless is going to play an important part in your future, consider some of the more useful applications that wireless can be used for. As with a typical purchase of computer/network equipment, it's the applications that drive the purchases, especially in a business environment. As more hardware is created and security is improved, wireless technology will become as commonplace as the standard 100Mbps switched LAN is today.

Laptop computers provided the first true mobility for computer users. Linking these powerful platforms to a computer network can be accomplished easily by means of either a PC-card network adapter or a docking station. By using DHCP to assign network configuration information, it's easy to move a portable computer from one location to another, and still provide a simple connection to the network. However, until the advent of wireless network connectivity, this kind of mobility still depended on a wired connection of some sort. If your network takes advantage of wireless networking, the mobility and usefulness of the notebook computer are increased dramatically.

For a technology to grow, it must solve some kind of problem. That is, it must be useful in some way. As described previously in the discussion of the types of devices that now use wireless networking, the most obvious benefit this kind of networking provides is mobility. Wireless LANs are now quickly becoming a mainstay networking infrastructure for many SOHO networks as well as home networks where multiple computers may share a single Internet connection. Other benefits that you might get from wireless networking include the following:

- Faster installation when compared to cabled networks. Just configure the network adapter (and Access Point if you have one) and start networking with others.

- Adaptability in a dynamic environment.

- The capability of sharing an Internet or other WAN connection.

- The continuing development of new electronic devices (or newer versions) that use wireless technology, such as PDAs.

- With the widespread deployment of wireless Access Points that are being constructed in public places, you will soon be able to access the Internet from most any place that has a sizable population.

- Reduced costs in many situations—for example, to avoid having to install cabling throughout a building.

One caveat to keep in mind is that with wireless networking, security is a big issue. You'll find out more about the standard Wired Equivalent Privacy (WEP) security that was first developed for IEEE 802.11b networks, as well as newer security techniques that have been recently developed, in Chapter 24.

In a typical LAN setup, it is necessary to install and configure the networking software on the client computer and provide the wiring from the network switch to the user's work area. With a wireless LAN, you only need to install the wireless NIC and configure the computer's networking software.

You don't have to string cables through the building for each user. In an environment that changes rapidly, this can be an advantage. For example, point-of-sale terminals in a large store can be reconfigured easily for seasonal adjustments, such as the end-of-the-year Christmas buying spree. In a warehouse, the floor layout might change during the year for similar kinds of reasons. Relocating computers is much easier when there are no cabling issues to deal with. After the initial investment is made in wireless LAN devices, the capability to reconfigure the physical network topology can result, in many cases, in reduced costs over time.

An ad hoc network or temporary setup (see the following list) is another important aspect. For example, if you are in the consulting business and need to have several consultants exchange information, you can use wireless networking to set up your own local network and bypass your customer's wired network. Knowing this allows your client to worry less about security than if the client has to go through the typical paperwork and other management functions to get your consulting team connected to the company network.

In addition to these kinds of environments, you will find wireless LANs increasingly being used in situations such as the following:

- **Hospitals**—Patient information can be obtained easily using a laptop computer or, more likely today, a specialized terminal made just for that kind of job. Instead of having to return to a central location, such as the nurse's station on the hospital floor, doctors and nurses can get information quickly as they make their patient rounds.

- **Older buildings**—In some cases, it can be difficult to wire the premises for a traditional network. Some older buildings that do not have plenum areas in the ceiling can be difficult to adapt. Using wireless communications makes networking in this kind of environment an easy task.

- **Temporary setups**—This feature was mentioned in the introductory paragraph to this list. You can extend it further to such situations as a trade show, where the network usually is set up for only a few days; the computers can be configured ahead of time so that the only thing your company representative has to do is turn them on.

- **Warehouse and factory floors**—Laptop computers and handheld bar-code scanners that use wireless LAN technology can quickly return the investment needed for their implementation. In this kind of situation, however, it is important to test the equipment first to ensure that no other machines or devices in the area can interfere with the wireless transmissions.

Caution

In a discussion of the applications of wireless networking, the dialogue should not be limited to computers. As data collection devices, such as bar-code scanners, or handheld data-entry terminals, such as cash registers, are equipped with wireless networking connections, many more practical uses for wireless communications will develop in the next few years.

However, you should consider that when making a transaction at this type of service, you can't be sure of what kind of security is in place. If simple WEP security is used (see Chapter 24), with a small key (40 bits), then it is a simple matter for a hacker to use tools freely available on the Internet to intercept these communications.

Before you give your credit card to a cashier, you might want to find out from the store manager what kind of wireless technology is being used to ensure your privacy. You should also check your credit (or debit) card statement each month to be sure your information has not been compromised!

Access Points and Ad Hoc Networks

Before getting into the specifics about IEEE standards and how data is transmitted on radio frequencies, you first should look at the topology a wireless network can take. In Chapter 2, "Overview of Network Topologies," you learned that a wireless network doesn't use a bus topology. Instead, because in some situations all nodes can hear all other nodes (within a specific area), one wireless topology can be considered a mesh topology. That is, in the simplest wireless network, all stations participating in the network can hear and talk to all other stations in the network. In a traditional wired network, this is equivalent to having a network card make a cabled connection to every other node in the network.

Another topology used in wireless networks involves using an Access Point (AP) that operates much like a hub or switch but incorporates a few extra features, such as provisions for some security issues.

Ad Hoc Networks

A simple peer-to-peer network, composed of computers that have compatible wireless network adapter cards, can be used to quickly set up a small network on-the-fly. This kind of workgroup LAN can be useful when only a few stations need to communicate in a small geographical area (see Figure 19.1). You can set up your own individual network at a trade show, in a conference room, or even for an entire small-business enterprise. Wireless bridges, which you'll learn about in Chapter 24, can extend the distance between wireless Access Points so that in a business you can create a network without having to pull cables at all. For a home office, where you probably don't want to drill holes in your walls and pull cables, wireless products can be the best solution possible.

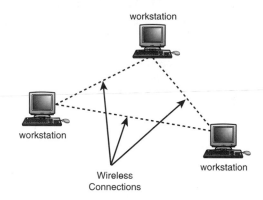

Figure 19.1   All you need to create a network on-the-fly are a few computers, each with a wireless network adapter.

This network is referred to as an *ad hoc* network because it involves simple peer-to-peer connections in a wireless environment. No central hub or switch coordinates the communications that occur. Instead, any computer equipped with a compatible wireless adapter can join the ad hoc network, provided that the appropriate security mechanisms have been implemented. For example, if you are using a Windows operating system and a simple workgroup setup for network communications, any computer that uses that same workgroup name can join your small ad hoc network. If any file or print shares are offered by members of this ad hoc network, you can protect them by using a password. This is not a great way to protect files, because anyone who needs to map to a resource share will use the same password.

Tip

In a very small network, using simple file shares is a good compromise considering the administrative overhead involved in managing a more sophisticated security system, such as that offered by the NTFS file system used by Windows NT/2000/Server 2003/XP. If you need to segregate users who need access to some, but not all, of the same files, then divide those files into a directory (and share it on the network), and then create separate file shares for other files needed by different groups of users.

If you use more secure methods, such as a Unix system with each workstation requiring a username/password, you can create a more secure wireless ad hoc network. The same goes for using a Windows domain. The only difference is that the network is wireless—there are no cables—and the same security mechanisms you'd use for a wired network should be used for this simple peer-to-peer network.

Tip

Although the term *ad hoc network* usually is used for a quick setup of wireless stations, another term you'll hear when reading the literature is *Basic Service Set (BSS)*. A BSS is nothing more than two or more wireless computers that have established communications among themselves. The simplest BSS, consisting of just wireless computers described in this section, also is called an Independent Basic Service Set (IBSS) because it doesn't have an AP to coordinate the communications between the wireless computers.

Using an Access Point to Mediate Wireless Communications

You also can use a wireless AP to create a small wireless network. This device can also be attached to a wired network, which is discussed next, or as a standalone device that can effectively double the distance of the wireless network. As you can see in Figure 19.2, if the Access Point device is placed in the center of the network, each computer equipped with a wireless network adapter can be placed farther away from other computers. This is because each computer only needs to be able to communicate with the AP, which in turn relays the signals to other computers that participate in the wireless LAN.

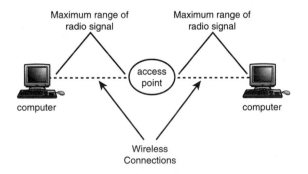

Figure 19.2   As you can see, an AP can double the range of a wireless network.

You can add APs to a traditional wired network as well; the APs will serve the same purpose that hubs or switches do for your wired clients. The AP coordinates communications to and from the wireless computers and the rest of the network, whether the destination resides on copper or fiber-optic cables (see Figure 19.3) or within the range of another wireless Access Point.

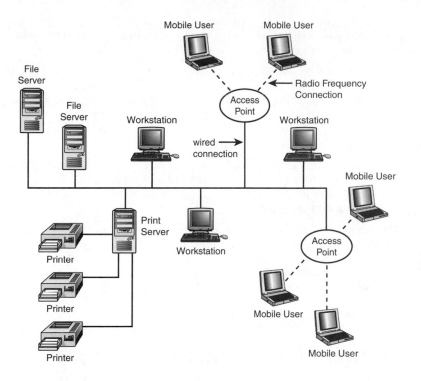

Figure 19.3 APs provide the connection to the wired network for mobile users.

Because multiple APs can be placed throughout the network, this topology allows for a wider geographical range for mobile users. An AP is a simple and very inexpensive device that can connect to the wired network and provide a transmitter/receiver that can be used to communicate with mobile users' workstations. In addition to providing the wireless communications service, an AP typically is responsible for buffering data between the wireless clients and the wired network. Unlike an ad hoc wireless setup, the AP also is responsible for mediating communications between wireless clients that operate within range of the same AP.

Note

Wireless Access Points are used for devices based on the 802.11a, 802.11b, and 802.11g (and other) standards. Some work with only one particular technology, whereas others operate in a "dual mode" and can operate with two or all three standards. Of course, such an Access Point will *not* increase the bandwidth for a computer that uses a lower-bandwidth wireless network card. The AP will, however, buffer data between that laptop and other faster devices, such as those based on 802.11a or 802.11g.

Most of the consumer devices on the market today support 11–60 wireless clients on a single AP at any given time. However, your mileage can vary depending on the manufacturer. For example, Cisco offers APs that can scale up to 200 or more wireless devices. Many tests by magazine labs, as well as others, indicate that you will not get the full bandwidth, much less close to it, when using wireless transmissions. The ballpark figure, based on several examples, is about one-third to one-half of the bandwidth the technology specifies. You may indeed get close to 90% throughput under ideal conditions. However, all wireless technologies suffer from the fact that barriers (such as large buildings) do exist. Keep this in mind when deciding what kind of network traffic to use in the wireless part of your network. In an outdoor environment, you will probably get a much greater distance between client and AP before the bandwidth begins to degrade.

APs come in all sizes and shapes. For example, D-Link (www.d-link.com) offers Access Points (called wireless routers) that can connect IEEE 802.11b, as well as 802.11a through 802.11g products. Thus you don't have to worry about your previous investments in 802.11b equipment (or sooner, 802.11a devices). If all can work together, your replacement policy can concentrate on such things as the actual client's bandwidth requirements. Another vendor for consumers or SOHO clients is NETGEAR (www.netgear.com).

For enterprise networks where a large number of APs will be needed, and for which greater security is required, networking hardware is generally purchased from an existing vendor. This may result in using one vendor for all networking products, or several. For example, Cisco and Apple both offer their wireless networking options, from network cards to APs to special antennas.

Cisco's main offering is a line of products named Aironet. There are many products in the different Aironet series. Apple was one of the first computer companies to bring wireless networking to market with its AirPort product line. The newest product, the 54Mbps AirPort Extreme, is based on IEEE 802.11g (see Chapter 22), supporting both 802.11b and 802.11g (11Mbps to 54Mbps). Shop around and you will find that many wireless products are now commodity items. With trade associations doing their best to nail down specifications for each new technology, you can expect to see even better hardware in the near future, and for a much lower cost than today. Someday soon you'll have that Dick Tracy watch, if you know what I mean, but it will be connected to a Star Trek computer.

Physical Transmission Technologies

The next few sections will familiarize you with the details involved in the actual transmission for wireless devices. Two major types of technology are used here: *frequency hopping* and *spread spectrum*. Both have been around for quite a few years. And each can be adapted to an environment where their techniques can be useful.

Frequency Hopping Versus Spread Spectrum

The most popular method for providing a communications medium for a wireless LAN is typical radio wave transmissions. Another method for sending data from one device to another without using copper or fiber-optic cabling is the infrared spectrum. However, this technology is primarily used in line-of-sight applications.

As stated earlier, the Federal Communications Commission (FCC) allocated a radio spectrum in 1985 that is called the Industrial, Scientific and Medical (ISM) band. It operates in the 2.400GHz–2.483GHz range and does not require the end user to obtain any kind of license. Similar agencies in other countries have followed suit and set aside this range for the same use. In the development of products for wireless networking using this range, a technique called spread-spectrum broadcasting is used.

For faster wireless services, such as those provided by IEEE 802.11a and 802.11g, the 5MHz band is used.

Spread-Spectrum Technology

During World War II, the military began developing a radio transmission technology called *spread spectrum*. Normal radio signals, such as those you pick up on your car radio, are called *narrowband* because they concentrate all their transmitting power on a single frequency. Spread-spectrum technology uses a much larger bandwidth instead and can be deployed using two basic methods: DSSS or FHSS. Spread-spectrum techniques are attractive to manufacturers of wireless equipment for many reasons. One of the more important reasons is that they can be difficult to detect or intercept. Additionally, from a security standpoint, spread-spectrum techniques are difficult to "jam" or interfere with.

Hedy Lamarr

Hedy Lamarr (also known as Hedwig Kiesler Markey) is most often remembered as a sultry screen actress from the early part of the twentieth century. Few people realize, however, that she and a composer named George Antheil received a patent in 1941 (U.S. Patent no. 2,292,387) for an invention that allowed for ultra-secret communications. What was this invention? It was a primitive form of what today is called spread-spectrum technology. Using a system of paper tapes that contained codes, transmitters and receivers could be synchronized to send and receive bits of a communication by alternating between seemingly random radio frequencies. Unfortunately, it took many years for the microchip to come along and make this technique easy and inexpensive to implement in environments other than military. Thus, poor Hedy never made a lot on this invention.

These are the two main aspects of any spread-spectrum technique:

- The signal that is transmitted is of a greater bandwidth than the actual transmitted information's bandwidth. In other words, more data is transmitted than the actual data the user intends to send.
- The resulting bandwidth is determined by some method other than the information being transmitted.

For commercial systems, the actual bandwidth used might be from 20 to 200 times the bandwidth of the actual information that is being transmitted, perhaps even larger. Some systems use a bandwidth that is up to 1,000 times larger than the information. Because the signal is spread out over a larger bandwidth, it can occupy the same bands as ordinary narrowband transmissions with little interference. A narrowband transmission can interfere with only a small portion of the signal being sent using spread-spectrum technology, and error-correction techniques can be used to compensate for this.

DSSS systems use a signal that is a combination of a pseudo-noise signal and the actual information modulated on an RF (radio frequency) carrier. By mixing two different signals to produce only one for transmission, the data is masked by the seemingly random signal it is combined with. That is, this results in a signal with a wide bandwidth that appears to be noise. At the receiving end, the pseudo-noise signal is used as a mask so that the actual data part of the signal can be recovered. The pseudo-noise signal is not truly a random signal, but instead is an agreed-upon method for generating a signal that both ends use.

FHSS employs a much simpler technique. It uses a narrowband carrier that continually changes frequencies. For this to work, the transmitter and receiver must both be synchronized to know which frequencies are used and in what order. The FCC dictates that at least 75 or more frequencies must be used for this technique, and any single frequency cannot be used for a burst of data longer than 400ms. Some methods of FHSS employ a simple pattern of switching from one frequency to the next. Others use a technique in which certain frequencies are skipped or in which frequency changes appear to be random.

The IEEE 802.11 Wireless Standard

The main standard for wireless LANs is the IEEE 802.11 group of standards, which were in definition as early as 1990 and have gone through several drafts since then. This standard includes definitions for the Physical layer (PHY) and the Media Access Control (MAC) layer protocols for wireless networking—both of which are covered later in this chapter. If you are familiar with Ethernet, you know that the MAC address, which is a unique address burned into a network adapter when it is manufactured, is used on a local area network to communicate with other members of the same LAN.

The standard envisions two kinds of clients: ad hoc and client/server. The ad hoc client method involves a peer-to-peer network between clients located close to each other. The client/server method uses an AP device to mediate network communications and possibly provide a connection to a wired network. Note that the first draft of the IEEE 802.11 standard provided for only transmission rates of 1Mbps and 2Mbps, but the newest standards (802.11a, b, and g) provide for much faster data transmission rates. The next few chapters discuss the three main wireless technologies. Before getting into those, however, let's take a look at the PHY and MAC portions that are the basics of these standards.

The Physical Layer

The Physical layer of a network involves the mechanisms used to actually transmit the signal on the network medium. In this case, the medium is infrared, Frequency Hopping Spread Spectrum (FHSS), or Direct Sequence Spread Spectrum (DSSS). In the original IEEE 802.11 standard using FHSS, the data rate is 1Mbps. For DSSS, the original standard defines both 1Mbps and 2Mbps techniques. Infrared communications (it's really wireless, after all) also is supported at both 1Mbps and 2Mbps data rates. Because few, if any, infrared devices are on the market today, they aren't discussed in this chapter. The most important devices are those using radio frequencies (FHSS and DSSS), which you'll find for sale by many vendors.

Note

Although the standard defines both spread-spectrum and infrared methods at the Physical layer, wireless clients using different Physical layer components may or may not interoperate. In other words, an infrared-equipped client can't communicate with another computer that uses the radio frequency spectrum for transmissions. Yet there are Access Points that can handle a combination of 802.11a, 802.11b, and 802.11g at the same time. These specifications all involve similar technologies, but operate in different frequencies or use different transmission techniques.

The MAC Layer

For the MAC layer, the standard is similar to the 802.3 standard for traditional Ethernet networks. Before a network node (or station, as they're usually called in the wireless world) can transmit, it must first determine whether the radio frequency channel is available, and a mechanism must be used to determine whether a transmission was successfully received by the destination station.

Carrier Sense Multiple Access/Collision Avoidance

Chapter 14, "Ethernet: The Universal Standard," explains the mechanism Ethernet network adapters use to gain access to the network medium (a copper wire, for example): Carrier Sense Multiple Access/Collision Detection (CSMA/CD). The network adapter that wants to transmit a frame of data first listens to the wire. If the wire is silent, the card transmits a frame. It then listens to make sure that no other network adapter tried to transmit at the same time (a collision). If a collision occurs, each of the nodes that caused the collision backs off for a random interval before attempting another transmission. This random back-off mechanism is intended to keep multiple network adapters from trying to transmit at the same time again.

This works well when you have a network adapter card that transmits and receives at the same time, which is exactly how Ethernet network adapters operate. However, when you're dealing with the airwaves, a wireless adapter can either transmit or receive, but not both at the same time. So another method for gaining access to the medium (the radio frequency on which the network is based) is used. It's called Carrier Sense Multiple Access/Collision Avoidance, or CSMA/CA for short.

Using this principle, the wireless network adapter card first listens to determine whether any other station is transmitting, just like a traditional Ethernet card does. If the frequency is not being used, the station can transmit a frame. However, because it can't listen at the same time to determine whether a collision has occurred, another method is used. If the destination of the transmission receives the frame intact, it sends back an acknowledgment packet (ACK). The standard provides for a higher priority for transmission of ACK packets so that they are transmitted before other stations can transmit.

After a wireless adapter has transmitted a frame, it waits to see whether an ACK is sent back. If some other station also has transmitted a frame during the same time, then the receiving end of both communications attempts will not receive an intact frame, no ACKs will be sent back, and thus both stations know they must retransmit the frame. Just as with traditional Ethernet cards, the stations that do not receive an ACK in response to a transmission assume that a collision has occurred, and wait for a random time interval before again listening to the airwaves to determine whether they can retransmit.

Another term used in the specifications for this media access method is Distributed Coordination Function (DCF); all stations based on IEEE 802.11 must implement this method.

Virtual Carrier Sense—RTS/CTS

As stated earlier in this chapter, it's always possible that two wireless-equipped computers can begin to transmit at the same time. However, what happens when you use an AP and two stations that are so far apart they can't hear the transmission of the other computer? This is referred to as the *hidden node* problem. In this situation, another means must be employed to ensure that only one station on the wireless network is transmitting at a given time.

To solve this problem, wireless computers that want to transmit a frame must first make a request for air time. Instead of just listening to the radio frequency and starting a frame transmission if the frequency is not being used, the network adapter instead transmits an RTS (request to send) frame to the AP. This frame contains information that identifies the station that wants to transmit, as well as the duration of time it wants to reserve for the transmission.

If the RTS frame is received by the AP (that is, no collision occurred due to another station also trying to transmit an RTS frame), the AP transmits a CTS (clear to send) frame that grants permission to the original computer to begin its transmission. This frame also contains the ID field of the computer that is being given permission to transmit, as well as the amount of time granted to it. Because all stations participating in the wireless network controlled by the AP can hear the CTS frame, they know they can't begin a transmission and they also know how long they must wait before making an attempt to send an RTS frame.

This method of accessing the transmission media also is referred to as Point Coordination Function (PCF). Although DCF is required by the IEEE 802.11 standard, PCF is not. It can be implemented but is optional according to the standards.

Other Services Performed at the MAC Layer

The MAC layer also provides other services, such as *association* and *reassociation*. Remember that an AP and its clients make up a BSS in the network. A client is associated with a particular BSS. When a client moves from one BSS to another, reassociation takes place. Although the 802.11 standard provides for the concept of reassociation, the actual mechanism for this function is not specified in the standard.

Sources of Interference for Wireless Networks

Because wireless network products use radio waves for the "physical" transmission medium, you need to consider other devices that produce radio waves in the same spectrum that IEEE 802.11b devices use. For example, the most common device, which is present in the home, many offices, and many public places, is the microwave oven. Yes, these devices use radio waves to heat your food, and they have a metal grating surrounding them that is supposed to prevent microwave transmission from emanating outside the box. However, if that were true you wouldn't see those warnings saying you shouldn't be close to one if you have a pacemaker and there wouldn't be a market for inexpensive devices you can purchase to measure leakage from a microwave oven. Microwave ovens *do* leak microwave signals and these can interfere with IEEE 802.11 devices.

Even the new wireless telephones that operate in the ISM frequency range can interfere with wireless network devices.

The good news is that microwave ovens aren't typically operating continuously. However, you still should consider them a source of interference that can dramatically slow wireless communications. Another source of interruption to wireless networks operating in the 2.4GHz radio spectrum is other consumer devices, such as those 2.4GHz portable telephones, as well as camera devices that can be used to transmit video back to your PC. Consider this when deciding whether to use a wireless network that uses the same radio spectrum.

Wireless devices based on these two main standards can interfere with each other. It is beyond the scope of this chapter to discuss the heated debate going on about which technology is better adapted to avoid interference from another wireless device, be it 802.11a, b, g, or even Bluetooth. Each group of supporters can make arguments about the capability of their products to recover from interference, but at this point, there isn't enough data or testing to prove it one way or the other.

In a business environment, however, other sources of interference must be considered. For example, some companies use microwave lighting. In military installations, radar can cause interference. Magnetic resonance imaging (MRI) devices used in hospitals can interfere with wireless network products. When you get down to it, microwave technology is used in many industrial applications, so you might want to perform testing beforehand, instead of just choosing a solution that appears on the surface to solve your networking problem. Interference can be mitigated, in some cases, by simply placing additional APs so that mobile devices are closer to an AP. The farther away from an AP or a home base unit, the weaker the signal and, thus, the greater the chance for interference.

IEEE 802.11b: It's Here and It's Inexpensive

SOME OF THE MAIN TOPICS IN THIS CHAPTER ARE

This chapter is intended to give you a brief introduction to the IEEE 802.11b standard. As discussed in the preceding chapter, the 2.4GHz radio frequency band (the Industrial, Scientific and Medical—ISM—band) has been set aside as a worldwide (for the most part) radio frequency to be used for specific purposes, and this frequency range doesn't require a radio operator's license for you to use it. This is the frequency range that was chosen to use for wireless networking based on the IEEE 802.11b standard. The 802.11a standard, which uses the 5GHz band, is covered in the next chapter.

Why Wi-Fi?

The Wireless Ethernet Compatibility Alliance (WECA) was formed specifically to test products from different manufacturers that are subjected to stringent testing to ensure interoperability. The brand name chosen by WECA that will be used for these products is Wi-Fi ("Wireless Fidelity"). You can access the organization's Web site at www.weca.net. There you'll see that the new name of the organization is the Wi-Fi Alliance.

Although the original Wi-Fi organization was created to encourage testing for interoperability for 802.11b products, the scope of the organization has continued to expand to include new wireless products. This organization now tests 802.11a products, as well as 802.11b. For example, in the following chapter you'll learn that 802.11a products are now called Wi-Fi 5. Note that Wi-Fi and Wi-Fi 5 are *not* names assigned by the IEEE, but are instead names used to signify that the products have passed tests for interoperability and can use the Wi-Fi designation to make it easier for consumers to purchase equipment.

Thus, when you hear a product advertised as Wi-Fi, you can be assured that it's based on IEEE 802.11b and that it should work with other products that have the Wi-Fi logo. At this time IEEE 802.11b is the most popular wireless networking technology, and the hardware is very inexpensive. This is because the technology has been around for a few years, and as manufacturing ramps up, costs come down. If you want a wireless network for your home, a few IEEE 802.11b network cards and, if needed, one or more Access Points are all you need. You can buy all the parts separately, though some manufacturers sell kits that contain two or more adapters and an AP, at computer stores. If you aren't in a hurry, a quick search on the Internet can point you to vendors that sell the same equipment at discounted rates. After you've obtained the parts, you can have a network up and running in an hour or two—all for about $150 (depending on the number of computers in your home network that will need a wireless network adapter card).

While the IEEE was still debating (seemingly endlessly) about the specifications for the IEEE 802.11a standard, the working group for the 802.11b standard got to the finish line first. For this reason, don't get confused now that the newer 802.11a products are starting to hit the shelves at higher prices. Prices will continue to drop as did those for 802.11b hardware. You can also decide to use 802.g hardware, as discussed in Chapter 22, "The IEEE 802.11g Standard." This standard can operate in both the 2.4GHz and the 5GHz spectrums, and even in a mixed-mode with computers using either frequency. IEEE 802.11g can also serve as an upgrade path for your network. You can replace older, slower 802.11b devices with 802.11g hardware as your budget allows.

This scenario seems familiar, doesn't it? When the prices for both 10Mbps and 100Mbps wired Ethernet began to penetrate the home or small office, these technologies became commodity items. Hubs and switches that used to cost thousands of dollars dropped tenfold or more. Wired switches followed the same path as hubs, and they are now the main wired network connectivity hardware used to centralize wiring in a wired network. The same thing has happened for wireless networks. Other wireless networking will follow this path, as 802.11b products already have.

What to Look For When Using 802.11b Networking

Because they are so common now, Access Points are sometimes called broadband wireless routers. This is because most of the APs on the market today include a port that can be used to connect to a broadband Internet connection, such as a cable/DSL modem. Things to look for when purchasing an AP include the following:

- Broadband support, as mentioned previously
- Dynamic Host Configuration Protocol service (DHCP)
- Network Address Translation (NAT)
- RJ-45 ports

If you are going to use the Access Point only in a closed network, the broadband connection won't be necessary. However, you will be hard-pressed to find an Access Point that doesn't have this port. DHCP enables clients to obtain IP configuration from the Access Point. A DHCP server uses a private address range (one that is not valid for use on the Internet). When making a connection to the Internet, the Access Point substitutes its IP address in packets the client sends out onto the Internet. When packets for the client are returned to the Access Point, it removes its own address and replaces the client's address. This technique is known as Network Address Translation. Using NAT and a private address range enables you to use a single Internet connection and share it with two or more computers. A second benefit of NAT is that it helps keep other computers on the Internet from gaining addressing information about the computers on your local network. Although not a perfect firewall solution, NAT can prevent simple attempts at intrusion.

DHCP is usually employed by Internet service providers (ISPs). This is because the IP address space used on the Internet is finite, and there aren't enough addresses to go around for all the computers that connect to the Internet. Thus, if you have a broadband connection for your Access Point, network packets going to and from the Internet are going through two levels of NAT! The first level is between the ISP and your wireless Accent Point. The second is between the Accent Point and a client computer on the wireless network.

For more information about Network Address Translation, see Chapter 49, "Firewalls." DHCP is covered in Chapter 29, "BOOTP and Dynamic Host Configuration Protocol (DHCP)."

An Access Point that also has a few RJ-45 ports enables you to connect computers to the Access Point using a wired connection. This feature is useful when you only need to use wireless networking for a few computers (such as laptops that you move around the home or office), while other wired computers (such as a desktop workstation or server) are located in a fixed location. Another reason for using an Access Point that provides both wired ports and wireless networking is that 802.11b operates at speeds ranging from 1Mbps to 11Mbps. Although these rates may be sufficient for some computers, servers and other client computers that transfer large amounts of data are candidates for a wired 100Mbps connection. Thus, you get the best of both types of networking. This also enables you to add wireless capabilities to computers over time, allowing you to spread out your expenses when buying wireless network cards.

Note

802.11a wireless networks operate at rates up to 54Mbps. Although this is less than 100Mbps you can achieve using a wired connection, it might be sufficient for servers and some clients in your network, especially laptop computers.

Distance Limitations

In general, 802.11b networks can span a distance up to 100 meters indoors and up to 300 meters outdoors. However, such seemingly trivial things as buildings, trees (as well as the weather), and other similar barriers can dramatically reduce this distance. When planning for the installation of a wireless network that will require more than one Access Point, because of distance limitations, start with just one Access Point, and test using it at different parts of the building. Using this method, you can determine how many Access Points will be needed. Don't count on the distances provided for in the 802.11b specifications. Additionally, if you are going to use more than one type of network adapter card—such as one for laptop computers and another for desktop computers—or cards from different manufacturers, then be sure to perform the same tests using each type of adapter.

Firewalls

In addition to NAT, some Access Points come with minimal firewall capabilities. For example, you can use port blocking and packet filtering to help protect your LAN. Although not a necessity, a firewall, along with a good antivirus program, will help to protect your wireless network from many of the malicious attacks that periodically occur on the Internet. Even if the Access Point does provide a simple firewall, you should probably go the extra mile and buy a software-based firewall for each computer in your network that uses other firewall techniques. The costs for these programs is minimal (usually around $50). When you consider the time it takes to restore data from backups when a virus, a worm, or another similar program invades your computer, $50 is not much to pay for the extra security that a firewall and an antivirus program can give you.

Note

NAT and firewalls are covered in greater detail in Chapter 49. This is recommended reading for anyone who is thinking about connecting any LAN to the Internet. In addition, all chapters in Part VIII, "System and Network Security," should be required reading material for anyone who operates a network in which a high degree of security is desired.

Do You Need a Wireless Network?

After comparing wireless 802.11b networking to cabled network technologies, how do you decide which is best for you? A number of factors should be considered.

A large enterprise with hundreds, or perhaps thousands, of computers will obviously need a large wired network, with LANs connected by ATM, Frame Relay, and other switched network technologies. Deciding where to use Access Points at some locations is a choice to be made by

- The need for wireless networking at that point
- Distance limitations
- The security considerations associated with the placement of the Access Point

In Chapter 24, "Other Wireless Technologies," you will find a discussion of the security implications of using a wireless network, and how encryption and authorization mechanisms can be used to make the network secure.

Some small businesses will get along just fine with an ad hoc wireless network, or one that uses an Access Point. Some will require the most stringent security requirements, using other technologies that are discussed in Chapter 24, as well as virtual private networks, covered in Chapter 50, "Virtual Private Networks (VPNs) and Tunneling."

Connecting the Wireless Network to a Wired LAN

In Chapter 19, "Introduction to Wireless Networking," you learned that you can create an *ad hoc* wireless network by using a collection of computers, or by using an Accent Point to mediate communications between the wireless clients. When you're using a few laptop computers in a temporary location, an ad hoc wireless configuration may suffice.

However, if you are going to connect your LAN to the Internet, an Access Point will be required to connect the LAN to the cable/DSL modem or another Internet connection.

If the wired network or broadband connection operates at a faster bandwidth (and most do today, with 100Mbps being the lowest common denominator for wired networks), then the Accent Point can buffer between the 11Mbps wireless network and the 100Mbps wired network.

Dual-Mode Access Points

The next chapter covers 802.11a. This standard enables data rates up to 54Mbps. A dual-mode Accent Point operates using both technologies, and can buffer data between the lower and higher data rates. Dual-mode Accent Points cost more than an Accent Point that works with just one technology.

A dual-mode Accent Point can be useful in several situations:

- In expanding an existing 802.11b network. For example, if you have already invested in 802.11b devices, but want to use the faster 802.11a technology when you add newer devices to the network, a dual-mode Accent Point can enable all devices to interact with each other.

- In providing an upgrade path for your wireless network. Again, if you have already invested in 802.11b equipment, a dual-mode Accent Point can enable you to slowly replace these devices with 802.11a as your budget permits. In a large network, it can be expensive to change out all of your network adapters, as well as Accent Points, at the same time.

- In providing access to temporary network clients. If a business client, a consultant, or another person visits your site and brings his own wireless computer (such as a laptop), then a dual-mode Accent Point enables that person to make a connection to your network no matter whether he uses 802.11a or 802.11b.

The next chapter will give you an overview of 802.11a networking, and Chapter 22 covers a newer standard, 802.11g.

Faster Service: IEEE 802.11a

SOME OF THE MAIN TOPICS IN THIS CHAPTER ARE

IEEE 802.11a is a wireless networking specification that has a future, but what that future will be is not yet known. You can expect in the future to see additional radio frequency bandwidths devoted to wireless networking, so the frequencies used by 802.11a may soon be superceded by other frequencies. Today the two main radio frequencies used for wireless LAN devices are the 2.4GHz and 5GHz frequencies. In the future, as wireless networking becomes an essential factor in everyday use, you will see newer encoding techniques in these bandwidths, as well as re-allocation of some current frequencies. Wireless networking has a great future, and I can only begin to speculate about the possibilities. The addition of the 2.4GHz spectrum to the 5GHz for wireless networks is indicative of this progress. Future expansion will depend on the addition of more radio frequencies, as well as new methods for modulating data on the available frequencies so that as time goes by, faster data rates are inevitable.

IEEE 802.11b devices, which were the first to market (before the IEEE 802.11a standard was complete) are very popular, but they are limited for the most part to about 11Mbps bandwidth using radio frequencies in the 2.4GHz bandwidth. And, as with the subject of this chapter, you may not get the full bandwidth that the standards define. This can depend on many factors, from barriers to the radio frequencies (because these are at the lower radio frequency spectrum). That is one advantage that the 5GHz spectrum gives you over the 2.4GHz spectrum. The 5GHz spectrum offers a larger bandwidth for wireless communications, and it uses a modulation technique that is superior to those used in the 2.4GHz bandwidth.

Note

The term *wireless networking*, used in this chapter as well as in Chapters 20, 22, and 23, refers to wireless methods for exchanging data over small distances to form a LAN. For transmitting data over longer distances (to create a WAN), another form of wireless networking is used: microwaves. This form of transmission has been in use for years by telephone companies, and more recently in campus networks where it is too costly to use copper or fiber-optic cables.

If it were not for a newer specification, IEEE 802.11g (which you will read about in the next chapter), one would think that as prices begin to drop over time, IEEE 802.11a would overtake the now-inexpensive 802.11b hardware. The increased bandwidth and declining costs should be a driving factor. 802.11a uses radio frequencies in the 5GHz band, and this enables it to provide a data rate of up to 54Mbps. That is almost five times the speed of 802.11b. There are a few other reasons why 802.11a might not get off to a speedy start, and these are discussed later in this chapter.

Note

You might wonder, then, why IEEE 802.11b (Wi-Fi) devices are so prevalent, and inexpensive, when compared to IEEE 802.11a (also known now as Wi-Fi 5 by a trade industry association). What was the reason that 802.11b-compatible hardware was the first to market?

The answer is simple. It took longer to develop the "a" standard than the "b" standard (people on a committee shouldn't argue so much). While the IEEE working group was still working on the 802.11a standard, 802.11b was finished, and manufacturers were anxious to start producing hardware for a new market: wireless networking.

Overview of the IEEE 802.11a Standard

Because IEEE 802.11b operates in the 2.4GHz bandwidth, it is subject to more interference because this bandwidth is basically a "free for all" (see the preceding chapter), meaning that many kinds of devices contend for the frequencies in the 2.4GHz spectrum. Spread spectrum techniques are used in 802.11a and 802.11b wireless radios to help minimize interference, and they are effective to some extent. For more information about spread spectrum techniques, see Chapter 19, "Introduction to Wireless Networking."

Interference from Consumer Devices

IEEE 802.11a uses frequencies in the 5GHz radio spectrum. This spectrum does not suffer from as much interference from consumer devices, such as microwave ovens, newer cordless telephones, and other devices that produce radio waves. Additionally, hardware using the 5GHz spectrum will not interfere with the previously mentioned consumer devices. Given the larger bandwidth provided by the 5GHz radio spectrum, there will be less interference, and the capability to support more channels than you can get from IEEE 802.11b. One thing to note, however, is that mobile phones that operate in the 5GHz bandwidth are becoming more popular, and this may become a problem for 802.11a in the near future.

Because 802.11a radio devices today suffer less interference by other devices, it might be a good choice if you are just starting to use wireless networking. One caveat is that the 802.11g standard, discussed in the next chapter, offers the same data rate but operates in the 2.4GHz spectrum and can easily interoperate with 802.11b.

If you choose a product based on the 5GHz spectrum (which is the subject of this chapter), you can forget that microwave oven in the break room or that cordless telephone that causes problems in an 802.11b network.

Note

There has recently been some discussion about U.S. military usage of this spectrum, but the outcome of that situation is unknown at this time. You should take this information into consideration when making a decision to use 802.11a.

Increased Bandwidth in the 5.4GHz Band

It may not seem like a lot—going from the 2.4GHz range of radio frequencies to the 5GHz range. However, the larger bandwidth is capable of transmission of data at faster rates.

Note

The 802.11g standard provides the same data rate as 802.11a. With 802.11g using the 2.4GHz radio frequency spectrum, how is this possible? Just as twisted-pair cables in a wired network can be used to transfer data at 10Mbps or 100Mbps, new methods for modulating data on a particular network media make this possible. 802.11g technology can operate at the same data rate as 802.11a because it uses a different method for modulating data. However, that doesn't mean that the 5GHz spectrum has already been pushed to its maximum throughput. Just as newer technology has enabled faster data rates in the 2.4GHz spectrum (802.11g), it is inevitable that advances in technology will enable faster data rates in the 5GHz band sometime in the future.

The 5.4GHz range will give you about 54Mbps throughput using the 802.11a standard. And as with other wireless technologies, you will not always achieve the maximum speed defined by the standard. Which technology makes more sense for you when it comes to purchasing equipment should be determined based on budget and need. If you are still operating a network that uses 10BASE-T networking (10Mbps), then when adding 802.11b wireless components you won't notice much difference in response time when a wireless client exchanges data with a computer on the wired network. This assumes that the Access Points (APs) are placed close to the clients in order to maximize data throughput. If you were to use 802.11a devices that operate at a faster speed than 10Mbps then a 10BASE-T wired network is a bottleneck. A wireless client communicating with a client on the wired network would not utilize the throughput that it is capable of, because the wired network cannot operate at that higher speed. Keep in mind, however, that all the wireless technologies discussed in this section of the book will probably not operate at the upper limit that the standards specify, due to environmental factors and such.

Note

By adding additional Access Points at strategic points in your network, you can reduce congestion in the *wireless* portion of your network. And this might just also accomplish diminishing other bottlenecks in your network by moving some departmental clients to wireless, leaving the backbone of the wired network to handle the larger network traffic.

802.11a wireless clients, however, will still be able to transfer data at faster rates among themselves.

The opposite is true when using 802.11a clients with a 100Mbps wired network, because 100Mbps is faster than 54Mbps, and the wireless network then becomes a bottleneck.

To put it another way, if you choose 802.11a hardware, you will benefit from this increased bandwidth only if your other network components can work at this speed (or faster). Because most enterprise networks, as well as SOHO networks, now operate using Fast Ethernet (100Mbps), IEEE 802.11a is a good fit. Though not as fast as Fast Ethernet, 802.11a does offer (depending on the manufacturer) over a five-fold increase in bandwidth over 802.11b, just over one-half of the bandwidth that Fast Ethernet will give you. In comparison, 802.11b, the current widespread wireless standard, will give you only about 11Mbps, which is almost a tenth of what Fast Ethernet can attain. These are performance statistics under perfect conditions, however. Have you ever been driving late at night and that great radio station just fades away, and then you have to look for another one? With wireless, including 802.11a, other factors, such as distance, buildings, and electrical devices, can also limit the actual bandwidth you will achieve.

Using Wireless Networking in Public Places

Wireless can be used for so many situations in which wired-network components would not be a good fit. As mentioned in previous chapters, just being able to sit in an airport or a shopping mall (waiting on that other shopper), and connect directly to the Internet while you are waiting, is going to be where wireless networking succeeds with the ordinary consumer as well as computer enthusiasts. Today several large telecommunications companies are beginning to lay the groundwork for this capability by creating a large network of 802.11b APs in public places where computers are likely to be used.

For example, in many airports there are rooms set aside for business travelers who need access to computer services, the Internet, faxing, and so on. These services aren't necessarily cheap. Yet if an Internet provider can offer its services over a network that spans most of the country, the price for an Internet connection will continue to drop, and you will be able to use your laptop computer pretty much anywhere in a public place. The main drawback to this for the next few years is that it will take time to create a large network, and builders will concentrate on the larger metropolitan areas first because that's where revenues from the service will be larger. Such a network will have to be built-out over the long run, just as the telephone network was when that technology was first introduced over a hundred years ago.

This type of network will not be entirely wireless. Instead, the wireless APs will be connected to backbone cabling in a similar way that wireless APs are used in a corporate LAN. For the long haul, this backbone cabling will be joined to the WAN using existing high-speed technologies such as ATM and Frame Relay. This is also the way that the Internet operates. Your connection to the local ISP can be accomplished using a telephone line (DSL service) or a cable modem. Whichever method is used, your line terminates back at the ISP's central office, and from there it is connected to the Internet using high-speed connections.

The only problem with this technology is that because it has already been adopted by so many current users, this type of network will initially consist of 802.11b technology. The reason it is mentioned here is that competition will eventually drive this type of network to use faster technology, such as 802.11a. Internet communications are becoming more bandwidth-intensive, and a mere 11Mbps (if you can get that maximum speed) won't suffice for many users in the near future. Uploading a large spreadsheet or graphics file using 802.11b probably won't suffice as applications begin to generate more data, and larger files. For email and other applications that don't need a lot of bandwidth, 802.11b will work well. The transition from 802.11b to 802.11a will probably be accomplished by using dual-mode APs, which were discussed in Chapter 20, "IEEE 802.11b: It's Here and It's Inexpensive."

If you can afford it, 802.11a is a good start for an enterprise network, again because applications that transfer larger amounts of data are typical in this type of network. For those who do not require the larger bandwidth, 802.11b is ideal—for example, in a SOHO or home network.

Security Concerns

The 802.11b standard suffers from a weak security link: the Wireless Equivalent Privacy (WEP). The first version of WEP used a key size that made it easy to penetrate a network. IEEE 802.11a also uses WEP, with much larger keys, ranging from 64 to 152 bits. Service Set Identification (SSID) is another method that offers additional security for wireless networks. Administrators can manage their wireless clients more efficiently today than a few years ago. You can read more about wireless security mechanisms, such as WAP (Wireless Application Protocol) in Chapter 24, "Other Wireless Technologies."

The IEEE 802.11g Standard

22

SOME OF THE MAIN TOPICS IN THIS CHAPTER ARE

CHAPTER 22

The preceding two chapters discussed two wireless protocol standards that are on the market today at very inexpensive prices. IEEE 802.11b hardware is quickly reaching the status of a commodity item (just check the prices at your local computer or electronics discount store). You can buy network cards for under $50 if you get them on sale or with a rebate. You can purchase wireless Access Points for less than $100—again if you watch for the sales and rebates. At those prices, IEEE 802.11b is a bargain—approaching the lower costs of 100Mbps Ethernet equipment. Because 10/100Mbps network adapters for a wired network can now be purchased at some chain stores for around $15, you need to evaluate your network to decide whether wireless networking will enable you to further your business requirements.

For example, if you already have an installed base of network cables for users in a wired environment, do you really need wireless networking? Conversely, there are a few scenarios that make wireless networking the best solution. If wireless is for you, the question of which standard to choose arises. Although some variants of wireless networking hardware are now very inexpensive, there are a few relevant considerations you need to think about, such as these:

- Major vendors are now shipping IEEE 802.11b hardware. Yet this is a slower specification and may not suffice for your network bandwidth needs beyond a few years (depending on the applications used in your network). However, in a SOHO environment, where you are the boss, 802.11b may be an excellent choice for your applications. For many word processing and other office applications, this bandwidth should suffice for your needs.

- IEEE 802.11b provides for a data rate of 11Mbps. IEEE 802.11a increases this to 54Mbps, as does IEEE 802.11g.

- The newer standard, 802.11g, can interoperate with both 802.11g and 802.11b. Thus, you can obtain a network bandwidth of 54Mbps in the 2.4GHz bandwidth, and use both 11Mbps and 54Mbps in the same network. The 802.11g devices can be used as an upgrade path for 802.11b hardware. Pay as you go, so-to-speak. Do you really need to use 802.11a if you can achieve the same bandwidth using 802.11g? And 802.11g lets you start replacing older hardware as you can afford it, because it can also work with your legacy 802.11b hardware.

- Cost, of course. However, this is not much of a factor today unless you have a very large wireless network in which replacing several hundred network cards (as well as Access Points) can add up to a large amount of cash.

The 802.11g standard was approved in 2003. Even though devices based on the draft specifications work quite well, you should probably make sure that future hardware purchases of 802.11g hardware are based on the final standard. The first-to-market hardware devices are not necessarily a good solution unless upgrades to firmware are available from the manufacturer to meet the final specifications.

Note

In the past few chapters have you noticed that the letters used for wireless networking don't seem to be in the correct order? IEEE 802.11b hardware came to market first, and then IEEE 802.11a suddenly appeared. Then along comes IEEE 802.11g—now where did that come from?

The truth is that the IEEE 802.11a standard was developed over a longer period, with different participants having to wrangle and compromise over the 802.11a standard. Before they finished, however, the IEEE 802.11b standard was completed and hardware is now readily available. Because "b" was the first to market, enough time has passed to make the hardware very inexpensive. Keep in mind that "a" and "b" are backward if you look at the standards from a time and bandwidth viewpoint. IEEE 802.11a, as you learned in Chapter 21, "Faster Service: IEEE 802.11a," is faster than the "b" version. IEEE 802.11g tries to incorporate the best of all the wireless protocols and may come out the winner in this new race for a standard. This is the standard that is covered in this chapter. And just as the 802.11g standard now offers the same bandwidth as 802.11a, you can expect that in the next few years newer standards will be developed that make even 802.11g outdated! However, for today, 802.11g or 802.11a are the standards you should choose if you want the 54Mbps bandwidth.

Overview of the 802.11g Standard

The fact that IEEE 802.11a and 802.11b manufacturers are now selling hardware that will work with either standard indicates that the same should be true for 802.11g.

Note

The IEEE 803.11a standard uses the 5GHz spectrum. This is the most significant difference between 802.11a and 802.11g. Hardware based on the 802.11g standard suffers from the same limitations as the 802.11b standard—interference from microwave ovens and some portable telephone devices, as well as from other electrical devices. Thus, for some environments, the 802.11a standard may be more appropriate. However, you can locate interfering devices so that they do not impact your 802.11g network.

Increasing Bandwidth in the 2.4GHz Spectrum

The newer 802.11g specification increases the bandwidth from 11Mbps (802.11b) in the 2.4GHz radio spectrum to 54Mbps. With backward compatibility built into most new hardware, you can preserve your investment in IEEE 802.11b equipment when you begin to incorporate 802.11g hardware into your wireless network.

But does 802.11b provide for your bandwidth needs? Consider that the basic bandwidth of 11Mbps is about the same speed you could obtain with a 10Mbps switched Ethernet wired network. A wired network consisting of 10Mbps (also known as 10BASE-T), if already installed, is already considered legacy hardware. You should probably have already increased your network bandwidth by upgrading the wired network to 100Mbps (100BASE-T). In this situation you need to consider whether you really need wireless networking in your enterprise (or your SOHO). Because *most* users don't actually make full use of the 100Mbps that 100BASE-T enables, using wireless connectivity, with its lower bandwidth, may be a cost-effective solution. This is especially true for mobile users.

Newer Gigabit and 10Gigabit Ethernet wired specifications are generally used for network backbone cabling, and have not reached the desktop except in a few instances. For example, if your office only uses word processing, email, and spreadsheet software, then 10Mbps (or 11Mbps provided by 802.11b) will probably suffice.

However, if you are using newer applications that require a larger bandwidth to satisfy users, such as graphic or other similar software, then the difference between 54Mbps and 100Mbps is not that great. Although 100Mbps is twice as fast as 54Mbps, you needn't consider 100Mbps unless your clients actually use the entire bandwidth! Even when transferring large amounts of data, 54Mbps (wireless) versus 100Mbps will probably not be noticed by your users.

In the rest of this chapter, I'll show you examples for installing a wireless Access Point (AP), as well as a wireless network adapter card.

Installing Linksys Wireless-G Broadband Router (Model Number WRT54G)

This section covers the steps needed to get your network up and running using a wireless Access Point and also how to install a wireless network adapter.

Note

A wireless Access Point is a device that acts much like a switch in a wired network. Wireless clients send and receive data by sending it through the Access Point. The Access Point can also be connected to a wired network, and thus provide wireless clients to communicate with clients on the wired network. Contrast this with an ad-hoc network, where no Access Point is used. Instead, wireless clients in this type of small network simply establish direct links with each other.

Not all manufacturers use the same interface, or support the same functionality. However, this section will give you a good overview of a typical installation and configuration of an AP. The steps are listed here:

1. Turn off all devices that will be used in the wireless network, including your PC, and the cable or DSL modem. *Do not* connect the power cable to the Wireless-G router yet. Power off every device that will be connected to any of the four Ethernet ports on the router, as well as any PCs that are going to use a wireless network card.

2. If you are going to use the router only for wireless data transfers, skip this step; otherwise you can connect any other PCs or network devices that are located near the router by connecting them to one of the four switch ports. Standard Category 5 UTP cabling is all that you need.

3. Use the leftmost port on the back of the router (it's labeled "WAN") to connect an Ethernet cable to your broadband connection (cable or DSL modem). Note that you should use only this port for connecting to the modem. The other four ports should be used only for connecting devices that do not make use of the router's wireless features.

4. To configure the wireless router, you must use a wired connection. This is because you can't use a "wireless" connection for the configuration because you have not yet configured the AP to use wireless networking, much less a client computer. This means you need to connect a computer to one of the four Ethernet ports to continue this configuration.

5. Power on the devices in your network in the following order: first the cable or DSL modem, then the wireless router, and finally any PCs that are directly connected to the router.

6. On the front panel of the router, check to see that the Internet Link and Activity LEDs are green. Note that when you first power up the router, the red Diag (diagnose) LED will light up for a short time while the router performs its diagnostic checks. If the red LED does *not* turn off, a problem exists.

7. Check the configuration for PCs that are connected to the wired switch ports to ensure that each is set up to automatically configure IP addressing information. This feature tells your computer to automatically obtain all necessary addressing information using DHCP—the Dynamic Host Configuration Protocol. For example, for Windows XP, select Start, Control Panel, and then in the Control Panel double-click on the Network Connections icon. In Figure 22.1 you can see an example of this showing a connection to a local area network (LAN). Remember that these steps, and those following, are for configuring the computers that connect via a cable to the switch ports that the wireless router provides. In the next section you will learn about how to use a wireless network adapter with the wireless Access Point. One of these computers that use a wired connection will also be used to configure the wireless Access Point.

Note

If you are using Windows 2000, use Start, Settings and then click on the Control Panel. Double-click on the Network and Dial-up Connections icon. Double-click on the LAN connection you want to use to configure the router.

Also, if you prefer the Category view of the Control Panel that is the default for Windows XP, you will have to use the menu this interface provides to get to the LAN connections window. From the Pick a Category menu, select Network and Internet Connections. The Pick a Task menu will pop up, and you should select Network Connections, which appears at the bottom of the menu under the heading Or Pick a Control Panel Icon. Click on Network Connections. You will then see the Network Connections window and can continue to configure your computer as described in these steps.

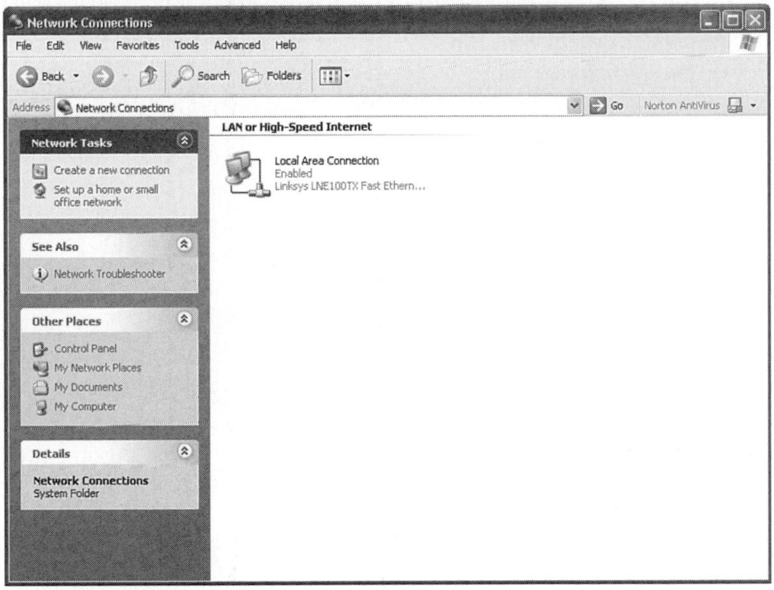

Figure 22.1   In Windows XP the Network Connections window allows you to view and make modifications to your computer's network configuration.

8. For Windows XP, right-click on the Local Area Connection icon to bring up the Properties dialog box for this connection. In Figure 22.2 you can see the General tab, which lists the protocols, services, and other network components used by this connection. If the Internet Protocol (TCP/IP) check box is not selected, click on the check box.

Tip

If you have not yet set up a LAN connection, use the Create a New Connection option, located on the left side of the Network Connections window under the Network Tasks section for Windows XP. Windows 2000 users will see an icon labeled Make a New Connection that can be used for the same purpose. A wizard will walk you through the process step-by-step.

9. After the check box for TCP/IP has been selected, you can click once on the TCP/IP entry in the dialog box, and then click on the Properties button. The properties for the TCP/IP protocol will pop up, as shown in Figure 22.3. If the radio button labeled Obtain an IP Address Automatically is not selected, click on it. Next click the OK button to dismiss the dialog box.

10. If the TCP/IP properties dialog box already has been set up to use DHCP to automatically configure the IP information, simply click OK on the dialog boxes as you back out of the LAN configuration. This means your computer has already been set up to use DHCP. This is usually the case when you have a computer already connected directly to a cable/DSL modem. If you changed the configuration by choosing the automatic configuration option, any static addressing information entered previously will not be used. Also, if you had to change the configuration to use DHCP, restart your computer.

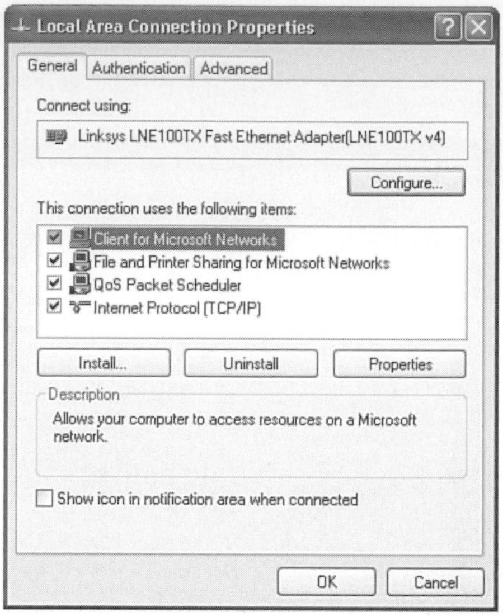

Figure 22.2   Make sure that the Internet Protocol (TCP/IP) check box is selected.

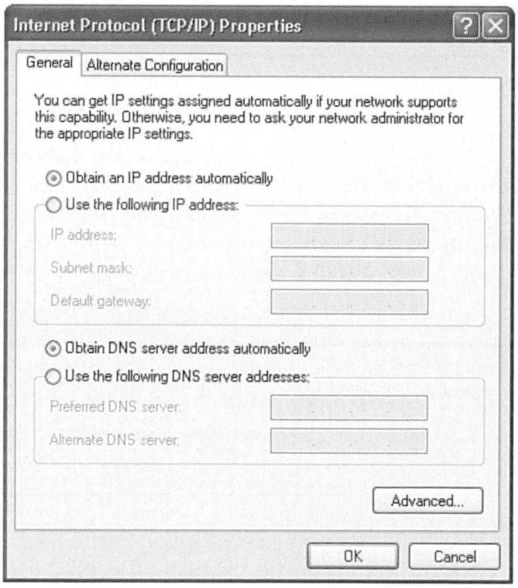

Figure 22.3   Select the radio button labeled Obtain an IP Address Automatically.

After you have configured the PCs that are attached using cables to the ports on the router, you can configure the wireless access port. Keep in mind that you will need to use a wired connection in order to configure the Access Point, because no wireless adapter has yet been configured!

1. Using the PC that you just configured to use automatic addressing, launch an Internet browser (Internet Explorer, Netscape, Opera, and so on). Enter the URL necessary to work with your Access Point in your browser's Address field. (For example, the URL needed to work with my Access Point is http://192.168.1.1. Check the documentation of the Access Point you purchase to determine the addresses it uses.)

2. A dialog box will pop up asking you for a username and password. Because no username has yet been configured, use the default password. For this Linksys router, the username should be left blank, and the password is admin, in lowercase letters. Click the OK button.

3. After you enter the default password, the PC will establish contact with the wireless router and display a page similar to that shown in Figure 22.4.

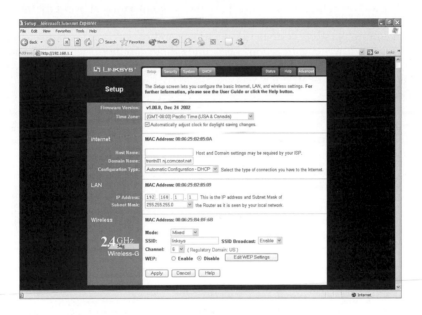

Figure 22.4   The router will send an HTML page to the PC you are using to configure the wireless router.

4. If your ISP requires a hostname for your computer, enter it in the field shown in Figure 22.4. In many cases, you will not have to put anything in this field. However, the Domain Name field will probably need to be filled in. Note that the HTML page here is usually capable of obtaining the Domain Name information if you are connected to the Internet (via your ISP) during this configuration process. If you are not sure whether this info is required by your ISP, give it a call, or check any documentation it may have provided.

Tip

You can get the hostname for your computer by entering the command **hostname** at the command prompt. Similarly, if the HTML page that the router displays on the computer you are using to configure the router does not display the domain name, use the **ipconfig** command from the command prompt to find out the hostname and domain name of your computer.

Note that for many cable modems you can leave both of these fields blank.

If you are not sure about these fields, check any documentation that was included when you established your broadband connection. As a last resort, you can always check with your ISP's technical support line.

5. The Configuration Type field shown in Figure 22.4 allows you to specify the method your ISP uses to connect you to the Internet. This information is based on protocols that your ISP uses. This field uses a drop-down menu to show you the options available. These are the most prominent:

- **Automatic Configuration - DHCP**—This is most like the case, as described previously, for most users.

- **Static IP**—Although it is unlikely that an ISP will have enough IP addresses that are valid on the Internet to use static IP addresses for all customers, some business-class customers may be assigned a static address. If so, your ISP should give you the address, or as described in the preceding tip, you can use the `ipconfig` command to get this information.

- **PPPoE**—This abbreviation stands for Point-to-Point Protocol over Ethernet. This protocol is generally used in buildings (such as hotels, office buildings, or apartment buildings) where more than one customer uses a broadband connection to connect to the Internet. Because an Internet connection is becoming more commonplace, and in many instances a necessary requirement for doing business, you can expect to see this protocol used more extensively over the next few years.

Tip

PPP is a protocol that has traditionally been used for dial-up connections. Data that is usually sent through a PPP connection is instead placed into the data portion of an Ethernet frame. (See Chapter 14, "Ethernet: The Universal Standard.") PPPoE allows multiple users to use a LAN to access the broadband connection. PPP is just what it says—a point-to-point connection. That is, only two devices are part of the configuration: the dial-up modem and the modem at the ISP's end of the connection. Because Ethernet frames contain the IP address of the sender and recipient of the frame, this allows for multiple users to use the same connection, and the Ethernet frame is used to identify each individual user. The main reason this protocol is used is for identifying each individual using a single broadband connection. This allows the ISP to charge individual users according to their usage of the connection.

- **PPTP**—The Point-to-Point Tunneling Protocol provides the best of both worlds—the LAN and the WAN. Although this standard is mostly found in Europe at this time, it may become widely adopted in other parts of the world in a few years. This is because PPTP basically operates much like a VPN when it comes to a secure "tunnel" through the Internet. Companies that have more than one location can use PPTP (if offered by their ISPs at each location) to get a secure "tunnel" through the public Internet.

6. Looking at Figure 22.4, you can also see other information about your connection, such as the MAC address, which is used for the network adapter on your computer, as well as the router to identify each computer or network device on a LAN. IP addresses are used to route data through the Internet. MAC addresses are used to send data to and from nodes on the same LAN, such as your computer and the router. This information is for display and troubleshooting purposes only. You can't modify these fields. This is because the MAC address is burned into the network adapter by the manufacturer to uniquely identify the adapter.

Note

In addition to the fields discussed in this chapter, you can see from Figure 22.4 that you can change other fields, such as the Time Zone, among others, as appropriate for your locale.

7. The field labeled Mode lets you select the bandwidth the wireless router will use. You can select Mixed, which supports the earlier 802.11b protocol, or you can select G-Only, which gives you a faster network speed. Or you can select Disabled to keep users from using the wireless AP. This is useful during maintenance times or if you want to shut off access for specific times, such as nighttime when no employees are using the network.

8. The SSID field is *very* important. This is similar to a "workgroup" in older Windows operating systems. *You should change this from the default value to something that will not be easy to guess.* Consider this a "password" that allows *only* the computers you want to use your network to establish a connection to the AP. Change this from the default or you will be subject to hackers (and they can usually pick up your signal from outside of your office/building). You should also be sure to select the Disable selection in the SSID Broadcast field, because these signals can be picked up by hackers who use tools freely available on the Internet to locate wireless access zones.

9. The Channel field allows you to use different frequencies. If you are having problems (such as a slow bandwidth), try changing this to a different channel. It may be that other APs are using the same channel, decreasing your bandwidth.

10. The WEP (Wireless Equivalent Privacy) field is used for encrypting the data sent over the wireless connection. The basic WEP that was originally used by the IEEE 802.11b standard used a key-length that could easily be hacked. To use WEP on your wireless network, click on the radio button labeled Enable for WEP, and then Edit WEP Settings. You can see this in Figure 22.5.

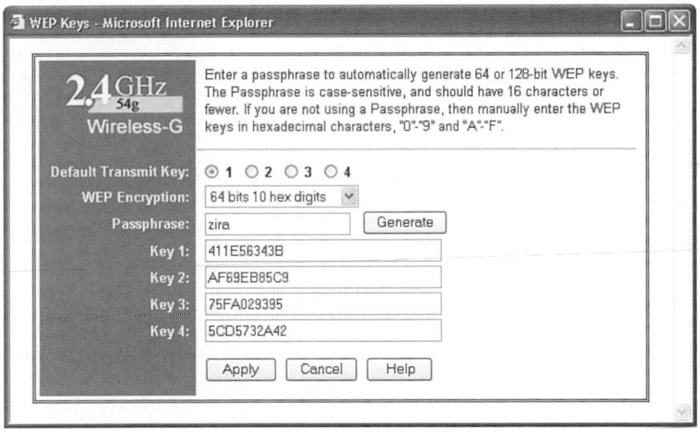

Figure 22.5 Use this dialog box to configure the encryption security used by your wireless AP.

11. In this dialog box you can specify the length of the encryption key (64 bits or 128 bits). To create the keys, enter a value in the Passphrase field, and then click the Generate button. The router will use the value in the Passphrase field to create keys that will be used for encryption. You can also simply make up your own keys by entering them in the fields provided. Click Apply to save these settings.

12. After entering the WEP information, click on the Apply button and close this dialog box. If you have successfully entered the appropriate information, a pop-up will tell you that the settings are successful. That's all you need to do for a basic configuration. You can now close the browser and restart the computer.

Note

In the preceding example, configuring the AP was done manually using a browser. With most APs there will be a setup CD you can use to perform the same functions in a simpler manner. By using the manual method, however, you can see all the features you can configure. If you decide to make changes to the AP's configuration, you can use the manual method (via a browser) and use the appropriate property sheet to make changes.

There are other tabs on this properties sheet. Although it is not absolutely necessary to use the other tabs, it is important to know what you can accomplish using them. With the exception of the Security property sheet, in most circumstances you will not need to use these property sheets. The following list describes the functions that can be accomplished using the other property sheets:

- **Setup**—This is the property sheet that has been described in the previous steps to initially set up the router.

- **Security**—This tab brings up a dialog box that allows you to configure several security items. For example, you can specify a password for the wireless router. This password will be required in order to *make changes to the router's configuration*. It is not a password that is used for clients to connect to the AP. For this brand of router, the default password is *admin. You should change this at once!* Otherwise, someone familiar with this technology will probably have already obtained a list of default passwords for many types of wireless routers and other networking components. *Change this password!* You can also configure VPN, DMZ (demilitarized zones, used for firewall protection), and other security parameters.

Caution

For any networking equipment (or any software) that requires a password for any type of access, you should *always* change the default password. Computer hackers can easily obtain default passwords for just about anything by searching the Internet. In addition, it is important to use passwords that are not easy to guess, such as words that can be found in a dictionary. Hackers can typically cross-reference standard terms found in a dictionary in a matter of minutes with programs available on the Internet. Ideally, you'll want to create passwords that are difficult to discover using a traditional dictionary attack. Chapter 46, "Basic Security Measures Every Network Administrator Needs to Know," can assist you in determining a password policy for your network.

- **System**—This tab allows you to restore router settings to their factory default values. This will, of course, replace any other configuration information you have already set up. Use this if you are having problems and need to start over from scratch! You can also enable/disable other features, as well as view a log of incoming and outgoing links to/from the router. You can also use this tab to upgrade your router's firmware by downloading it from the Linksys Web site. It's a good idea to visit Linksys's site (www.linksys.com) to ensure that the firmware upgrade is one that is needed by your network.

- **DHCP**—This property sheet lets you enable/disable the DHCP feature that the router provides. Unless you have a good reason to change this, do not change the default, which is to use DHCP. If you already have a DHCP server on your network such as those provided with Windows servers, Linux-based systems, and others, then use this property sheet to *disable* the router's DHCP feature. It doesn't matter what device on your network is used for DHCP. If you are using another computer for this service, use the DHCP Server field on this property sheet and set it to Disable. There are other features that can be configured here, such as the length of time a computer can use an IP address provided by DHCP before it has to be renewed, and you can also view a table of IP addresses that have already been leased to clients. You can also configure the address range used by the router when it allocates addressing information to client computers.

The address ranges reserved for "private" networks by the Internet Engineering Task Force (IETF) are 10.0.0.0 to 10.255.255.255.255, 172.16.0.0 to 172.31.255.255, and 192.168.0.0 to 192.168.255.255.

These addresses are *not valid on the Internet*, but instead are used by Network Address Translation (NAT) to distinguish computers on your LAN from computers on the Internet that use valid IP addresses. You can specify here a private address range that the router-provided DHCP service will use. Keep in mind that it is a good idea to use an address range separate from the one used by your ISP. Although there is only a small chance that NAT will fail if you use the same address range, it's best to use one of the two address ranges that the IETF has set aside for private networks.

- **Status**—This property sheet lets the administrator view the current network configuration for the router. You can also use this property sheet to release or renew DHCP configuration data for the wireless router. This is not the IP address that the router can provide to clients on your network, but instead is the IP address the router may have obtained from your broadband provider.

- **Help**—The Help tab can be used to connect to the Linksys Web site for more information, or use a PDF document for viewing help topics.

Tip

You need Adobe Acrobat Reader to view .PDF documents. Although the .PDF application that creates these documents is a product that must be purchased, the reader is free. You can download this application using the hyperlink in the Help tab, or visit the Web site **www.adobe.com**. This application is used for many vendors to produce documentation. Whether or not you need to use it to view information in this Help tab, I recommend that you download the latest version and install it, because you will find that many other applications also use it to read their documentation.

- **Advanced**—The Advanced tab is used to configure options for the wireless router that you will most likely not need to change, such as entering MAC addresses for only those computers that will be able to access the AP. You can also create a list of MAC addresses that will specifically be *excluded* from access. In a large enterprise network, you may find items here to modify. However, for most large networks, as well as SOHO networks, you will probably never need to use this tab.

Note

At this point you only need to configure one PC to use automatic IP addressing configuration. This PC will be used to configure the router, and you can then follow the instructions for wireless network interface cards. After you have configured the AP, you can proceed to configure the remaining client computers so that they can use the AP. This subject is discussed later in this chapter.

Now that you have installed the Access Point and set up Windows to use automatic addressing, it's time to adjust the router's software settings.

Installing and Configuring a Wireless Network Adapter

The next step you will have to complete is to install wireless network adapters for the computer(s) you want to enable to use this wireless LAN. A wireless network is perfect for a small office where all the clients are in close proximity to each other. Perhaps the best use you will put wireless networking to is for laptop computers. If this is the case, you can go out into your back yard and relax in the sun and establish and maintain a connection to the network.

The network card installation described in this section is based on the Linksys Wireless-G Notebook Adapter, model WPC54G, and should be considered only an example. As always, use the documentation for the particular network adapter that you purchase. Additionally, the example details the steps to install and configure the adapter card on a computer using Windows 98SE through Windows Server 2003.

When configuring the AP in the previous section, a browser was used to configure *settings stored on the AP*. When configuring a network adapter, you need to install a driver on the computer, and then configure the card so that it can interact with the AP. Because of this, most manufacturers provide a CD that contains the driver, documentation, and other software. The following configuration example *is not going to make any changes to the AP*. Instead, these steps will configure your computer so that it can make use of the network adapter.

Do not insert the wireless adapter into the PCMCIA/CardBus slot on your laptop computer.

1. Place the setup CD in the computer's CD-ROM drive. After a few seconds, a wizard dialog box (see Figure 22.6) will pop up. You can choose to read the user's guide, begin the installation, or exit the wizard. Click on the Install button.

Figure 22.6   Click the Install button to begin the network adapter setup.

2. Click the Next button when the License Agreement dialog box appears. Of course, as always, be sure to read the license agreement text first. If you do not agree with the terms of the license, click the Back button and then exit the wizard. You can then return the adapter to the place of purchase.

3. The Wireless Mode dialog box, shown in Figure 22.7, will allow you to decide whether you want to use the adapter in an infrastructure mode or in ad-hoc mode. In either case you will need to enter text into the SSID (Service Set Identifier) field. Each computer in the network will use the same value. If an AP is used, it also must use the same SSID. Click Next to continue.

Tip

Ad-hoc mode is used when no AP is available. Instead, each computer that is part of the wireless network will communicate directly with the others, similar to the legacy Windows workgroup network. Infrastructure mode means that the adapter will exchange data with other computers via an AP. The AP can be standalone if it will be used only to provide connectivity between a selection of associated wireless clients, or the AP can be connected to a wired network if you will be providing access to services available on the wired network. Depending on the brand of your network card, the term

SSID could possibly be Network Name, Preferred Network, or other terms. Whatever term is used, be sure to change it from the default value! For the adapter used in this example installation, the default SSID is Linksys. Using the default value makes it easier for others to tap into your network.

Figure 22.7 Use the Infrastructure Mode radio button if the adapter will coordinate data transfers via an Access Point.

4. If you are going to operate in ad-hoc mode, a dialog box will pop up enabling you to select a channel to be used for the particular network. The default is channel 6. This is to prevent different ad-hoc networks in close proximity from communicating with each other. Use different channel numbers for each separate ad-hoc network if you set up more than one. Also, you must select what mode the ad-hoc network will operate in: Mixed Mode (both IEEE 802.11g and 802.11b) or G-Only Mode (802.11g).

5. As shown in Figure 22.8, a dialog box lets you view the choices you have made. Click Next to continue, if you are satisfied with the configuration. Otherwise, use the Back button to back up through the wizard screens to make any changes you want.

Figure 22.8 Review the configuration you have created.

6. The setup program will copy the files necessary for your configuration to the computer's hard drive. When it's finished, another dialog box will tell you whether you were successful in setting up the card's configuration. Click Exit to finish the installation.

After you have finished with the setup wizard, you can physically install the network adapter. First, *power off* the computer. If you do not, it is possible that the card could be damaged, or the setup configuration may not work. Insert the adapter into a PCMCIA or CardBus slot on the computer and restart the computer. When Windows has finished booting, it will start to copy the adapter card's driver software. After the driver files have been copied, you are finished with the network card installation.

If you are using Windows XP (or Windows Server 2003), use the following steps:

1. Power off the computer.

2. Insert the network adapter.

3. Power up the computer.

4. The Windows XP Found New Hardware Wizard will pop up after the computer has finished the boot process. When the wizard appears, place the setup CD into the computer's CD-ROM drive.

5. Click the Install the Software Automatically radio button, and then click Next. The Windows XP Wireless Zero Configuration icon will be placed in the system tray. Double-click on that icon.

Windows XP will then prompt you for the same information used in the previous example, with one exception. Windows XP doesn't use a Passphrase, so you will have to enter an encryption key (which you can get from your AP). This will be necessary only if you select to use WEP. In any case, after the required files are copied to your computer, click the OK button. If your configuration was successful, a balloon will pop up from the system tray telling you that you are connected to the network.

Which Wireless Protocol Should You Use?

This chapter, as well as the preceding three chapters, was written to introduce you to the current wireless network standards. This chapter includes examples of 802.11g hardware installations, because new wireless networks will most likely use the latest standard. This is because the cost difference is not going to be much among 802.11a, b, and g in the near future. Although the price differences for hardware for all of these standards are diminishing, even a small difference in price can be a large expense if you want to create a large network. The small difference in price adds up as your network scales to up to 100 or more users.

Because Wireless 802.11g can work with both 802.11b and 802.11g, it might make sense that you should now purchase 802.11g hardware. Think of what your network bandwidth requirements are first. If you already have an installed base of 802.11b, and the bandwidth it provides (11Mbps) is sufficient for your needs, then you can use 802.11g as an upgrade path because it interoperates with both standards. Or you can continue to use 802.11b if 11Mbps is all you need. In this case when you need to add clients to the network, you will find that the hardware will be less expensive than 802.11g at this time. What should you consider in making this judgment? Consider the applications you are currently using, as well as those you see as possibilities in your future. If you expect to upgrade software applications, and forecast uploading or downloading large amounts of data, then start upgrading to 802.11g as you add new computers to your wireless network.

The difference in bandwidth (11Mbps–54Mbps) is the main deciding factor. If 11Mpbs (about the same offered by now-legacy 10BASE-T networks) is all you need, and you operate in an environment where software upgrades will not be necessary in the near future, then stay with what you already have! After all, although the Microsoft Office suite of programs continues to be updated year after year, there are a large number of users who are still using Office 97. Why upgrade to newer versions if the applications you are using already provide all the features you need?

The following questions offer some things to consider:

- Are users of your 802.11b network complaining about response time?

- Do you contemplate upgrading to software applications that require a large bandwidth, such as graphics, video, or other similar software?

- Is your decision based on creating new wireless network(s)? If a large number of computers are involved, then why begin the process with a lower bandwidth specification?

- If you already have an 802.11a network, which also can operate at 54Mbps, do you want to reinvest in hardware for your network just to keep up with the neighbors and use the latest standards?

- Do you really need a wireless network at all? See Chapter 19, "Introduction to Wireless Networking."

23

Bluetooth Wireless Technology

SOME OF THE MAIN TOPICS IN THIS CHAPTER ARE

The preceding few chapters have covered IEEE 802.11b (Wi-Fi) and IEEE 802.11a, which are the two major contenders for the wireless networking market. Both of these technologies have trade organizations whose purpose is to advance their technology for the markets they target. The 802.11 wireless protocols aim for a market ranging from the home to the workplace to public spaces such as airports, malls, and just about anywhere you can use a cell phone today. The goal of the 802.11 protocols is to provide a worldwide standard that enables you to use a single wireless network adapter card in many different environments.

Bluetooth is another matter altogether. Bluetooth technology was originally designed to replace wires, and for only short distances. The original expectations for Bluetooth were that it would be used to connect such things as a keyboard, mouse, computer, and possibly mobile phone. It was not designed, from the start, to be a wireless networking solution that would span any great distance. Other technologies, such as Wi-Fi and 802.11a, were expected to cover that territory, giving mobile clients easy access to a network. In the home arena, this means that a single Internet connection can be shared by numerous wireless clients (computers, printers, gaming devices). In the work environment, Access Points can allow a mobile user to quickly connect to the corporate cabled network anywhere that a wireless Access Point has been placed. For the business and residential user, it's possible that one or the other of these standards will allow you to open your laptop in a coffee shop, an airport, or some other public space and instantly connect to an Internet provider.

Note

The name Bluetooth comes from the legacy of an ancient king named *Harald Blátand* (940–985 A.D.). The legend has it that he was able to unite the countries of Norway and Denmark. Yet, the word *Blátand* can be translated to "Blue tooth." Some say that this name was given to him because he didn't have much time to visit a dentist, and he had blue teeth due to his fondness for blueberries. The adoption of this name is probably, however, based on the fact that he was able to unite the two countries. The Bluetooth technology does the same thing—it enables different devices to work together, bringing together a wide range of manufacturers.

Bluetooth has been in development for several years. When the second edition of this book was written, it was expected to be the hottest new technology of the year. However, there were still parts of the specifications that needed to be refined, and very few manufacturers decided to create devices based on Bluetooth. Over the next few years the specifications were further defined, and short-distance networking became part of Bluetooth. Other profiles (which are discussed later in this chapter) were added so that Bluetooth became a practical solution for short-distance networking for many types of consumer and computer devices today. One might say that Bluetooth has finally arrived.

There are two good reasons to consider using Bluetooth to create a small wireless network although 802.11b and 802.11a are now readily available. First, as was the original intent, Bluetooth enabled devices, ranging from keyboards and mice to cellular telephones. But now you can also use this technology for networking computers (such as laptops) over short distances. This is the same capability that 802.11b (Wi-Fi) gives you.

Second, Bluetooth radio chips are inexpensive to manufacture, so you can expect to see them in many other devices in the next few years. And this includes not just computers and communications between computers and computer peripherals, but also many other consumer devices. At this time wireless networking based on the 802.11 specifications are pretty much limited to computers. You can't plug a PCI or CardBus network adapter into your cell phone yet. But you can do this with Bluetooth.

The Bluetooth wireless technology is

- A short-range, lower-power wireless technology
- A means to replace cables, such as those that connect your keyboard, mouse, printer, and other standard computer peripherals
- A protocol that uses a very inexpensive radio transmitter compared to other wireless protocols
- A method to allow data communications between diverse devices such as computers, mobile phones, network appliances, handheld devices, digital cameras, and other consumer devices

This chapter takes a quick look at Bluetooth because some major vendors still back this technology. For more than three years, promises have been made that *this year* will be the year of Bluetooth. That didn't happen last year, but now these kinds of devices are starting to make it into the consumer marketplace. Just check your local computer store and you are likely to find several different Bluetooth-enabled devices. The same could not be said a few years ago.

You might be wondering what the problem is. The actual radio devices are very inexpensive when used in more expensive peripherals, such as printers and laptop computers. Replacing a mouse or keyboard with a Bluetooth product is now feasible, because a simple mouse or keyboard can easily be had for less than $25, and usually much less—but the addition of a Bluetooth transmitter adds little to the cost. If customers are satisfied with a $10 mouse, they probably won't pay the extra few dollars it costs to add a Bluetooth radio to a mouse. However, they might pay for other uses, such as a keyboard. Although IrDA (infrared) equipped devices can be used to place some distance between a keyboard and a computer, this technology is a line-of-sight technology. Bluetooth communicates via radio waves, so you don't have to try to get your keyboard pointed in just the right direction for it to work. Just think of what it would be like to put Bluetooth into your television's remote control. But for most of the market today, Bluetooth is an inexpensive chipset to add to more expensive devices, such as mobile phones, printers, and laptop computers, without significantly impacting the prices of these devices.

The Bluetooth Special Interest Group (SIG)

Bluetooth technology was originally developed by the Swedish company Ericsson, which now licenses the Bluetooth trademark to the special interest group (SIG) of manufacturers that want to market products based on this technology. You used to be able to visit the Web site at www.bluetooth.com to find more information about the group and the vendors that are members. However, recently the SIG has incorporated, and you need to sign up as a member to view the contents of the site, such as the standards documents.

The IEEE has also licensed Bluetooth technology from the Bluetooth SIG and given it the name of IEEE 802.15.1 to establish a standard. You can view an abstract (in PDF format) of the version of the IEEE standards document using the URL http://standards.ieee.org/getieee802/new.html. You can also purchase the proposed standards documents for just under $200!

Bluetooth-enabled devices, which are based on a set of standards called *profiles*, should make it easy to interconnect and exchange voice and data between almost any kind of electronic devices you can think of.

General Overview of Bluetooth

The original Bluetooth version 1 specifications were modified somewhat, and version 1b was released. Since then, version 1.1 has been the current standard, and it addresses many problems that were uncovered during compatibility testing of Bluetooth devices from different manufacturers. Version 2.0 of the specification is still under development, but most of the functionality of version 1.x is expected to be compatible with version 2.x devices. Version 2.0 is also expected to offer transmission rates between 4Mbps and 12Mbps, which is faster than the current standard offers.

Bluetooth technology uses lower-power transmissions and therefore is limited in the distance it can cover—up to about 10 meters. A more powerful version of Bluetooth allows for higher-power transmissions that can range up to 100 meters. Instead of creating a new technology from scratch, some parts of the Bluetooth specification were borrowed from existing technologies. Some of the more important ones include the following:

- **Frequency-hopping spread spectrum (FHSS)**—Bluetooth hops at 1,600 hops per second, using 79 frequencies each separated by 1MHz, over the total spectrum allowed in the 2.4GHz range. Both asynchronous communication (at 721Kbps) and synchronous communication (at 432.6Kbps) are supported to provide for both voice and data transmissions.

- **Motorola's Piano**—This technology allows the formation of small ad hoc networks, sometimes referred to as personal area networks (PANs). Although ad hoc networks are also used by other wireless technologies, Bluetooth forms ad hoc networks within just a small area, usually up to 10 meters.

- **Digital Enhanced Cordless Telecommunications (DECT)**—This specification was adopted for the voice and telephony applications that Bluetooth can provide.

- **Object Exchange Protocol (OBEX)**—This technology was borrowed from the IrDA (Infrared Data Association). It allows for data exchanges such as synchronizing address books between a Bluetooth-enabled PDA and a PC, for example, or for exchanging electronic business cards.

Bluetooth uses a frequency-hopping technique in which each transmission lasts for only 625μ. This means that data is sent over one radio frequency for just this short time. After that, the radio frequency changes and another small amount of data is transmitted. Because of this small allocation of time for each transmission, a transmission of just a simple message is sent over the air by dividing it into many smaller bits of information, and sending these small discrete units over a preset pattern of ever-changing radio frequencies (see Figure 23.1).

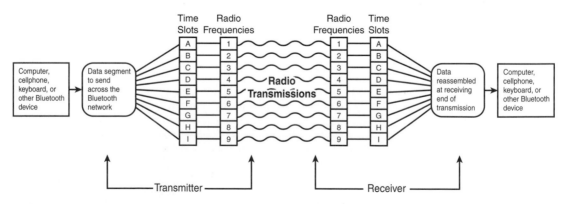

Figure 23.1 Data is sent in smaller units, each of which uses a different radio frequency.

In Figure 23.1 you can see that a Bluetooth device delivers data that needs to be sent to the radio transmitter. The radio transmitter breaks the message into many smaller units of information. Each of these units (A, B, C, and so on) is sent using a small window of time, each using a different radio frequency (1, 2, 3, and so on). At the receiving end of the transmission, each unit of data sent on different frequencies is combined back into the original data and passed on to the receiving device.

This is, however, a simplistic illustration. In a typical situation, more than one device is transmitting or receiving at the same time. Thus, the time slots (A, B, C) may not be contiguous, but are shared by all devices. So in reality a transmitter might send data using one time slot, and then wait for a few time slots before sending the next unit of data. Each unit of data, however, is sent using a different radio frequency, hence the term *frequency hopping*.

At the receiving end of the transmission, each small unit of data is received on a separate radio frequency, and each unit of data for each time slot is reassembled into the full message of data that was transmitted before it is passed to the receiving device. Because both the transmitting end and the receiving end of the communications know in advance what time slots will be allocated, and what frequencies will be used, it is a simple matter to keep track of multiple devices transmitting/receiving at the same time. This is because each device will be allocated different time slots, and thus different frequencies, for each data transmission.

A simple Bluetooth network consists of a single master and up to seven slaves. Transmissions take place based on a frequency-hopping scheme decided on by the master, and all members of a *piconet* (discussed in further detail in the next section) use the same frequency-hopping pattern. Thus, it's possible to have multiple piconets within close proximity of each other because each piconet uses a different *hopping pattern* among the 79 available frequencies. When a device joins a piconet, the address of the master device is sent to the slave in a special packet called a frequency-hop synchronization packet (FHS packet). The hopping pattern is calculated based on the address of the master node. The master device's clock is used to determine which particular point in the hopping sequence is the current one, and all slaves keep track of the difference between their own clocks and the master's so that they can all hop along together.

Communications can take place in both directions, between master and slave, with each time slot numbered. The range of time slot numbers is from 0 to $2^{27}-1$. The master device can start transmissions in even-numbered time slots, whereas slaves can start transmissions in odd-numbered slots. To provide for larger data transfers, up to five consecutive slots can be used. However, for these five slot transmissions, the data is transmitted on the same frequency, determined by the frequency to which the hopping pattern is set when the first packet is transmitted.

Piconets and Scatternets

The ad hoc nature of Bluetooth networking minimizes the need for management or administrative functions for networks made up of Bluetooth-enabled devices. In Chapter 19, "Introduction to Wireless Networking," you learned that an ad hoc network consists of multiple wireless devices that communicate with each other, without a central controlling device. This is basically the method used by Bluetooth. Contrast this with using an Access Point with 802.11 wireless networks. 802.11 wireless networks can be used to create an ad hoc network, but usually a controlling Access Point is used to coordinate communications between members of the wireless network. To put it quite simply, an ad hoc network consists of multiple wireless devices that communicate with each other. In the case of Bluetooth, as described next, there is no dedicated Access Point to control data transmissions. Instead, the first Bluetooth device that initiates a transmission becomes a temporary "master" of the small network, and other devices are "slaves" that receive permission to transmit/receive from this master. The master is not a dedicated device like an Access Point.

In PANs, devices in close proximity can discover each other and form a small network (called a piconet) without user intervention. This enables users to transfer data between a cellular phone and a laptop computer, for example, by coming within range and instructing the cellular phone or computer what action to perform.

Piconets

A *piconet* is formed when two or more devices discover each other and begin to communicate. A piconet can have up to eight devices, with one device acting as a master and the rest acting as slaves. The first device to initiate transmission becomes the master, although the specification provides for a master and slave unit to exchange roles. A specific frequency-hopping sequence is used by all devices within each piconet. Figure 23.2 shows the simplest example of a piconet: A cell phone is downloading address-book and telephone-number information to the user's laptop.

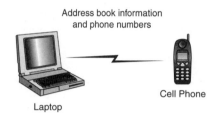

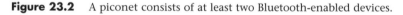

Address book information
and phone numbers

Cell Phone

Laptop

Figure 23.2   A piconet consists of at least two Bluetooth-enabled devices.

In this example, the laptop acts as a master. The application software running on the laptop contacts the cell phone when it is within range, and requests that it synchronize its database with the one stored on the laptop.

As stated earlier, a single piconet can have up to eight devices. The reason for this limit is simple: The address is only 3 bits long. This means that in binary, only the values of 0–7 can be stored in the address field. The master has no address, but 0 is reserved for broadcast messages; so the only addresses remaining for use by slaves are 1–7. However, a device can participate in two different piconets (called a *scatternet*), which is covered in the next section. Figure 23.3 shows an example of a larger piconet, in which one master controls multiple slaves in a piconet.

You can see that it's possible to link various devices in a piconet. You can download digital images from your digital camera to the laptop, use more than one Bluetooth-enabled cell phone to place voice calls, and even connect a personal digital assistant (PDA) to the laptop to exchange information. Another interesting thing to note in this figure is that you also can use a single connection to the Internet without having to have a direct cable connection to the modem or broadband connection.

The master device in Figure 23.3 is the laptop computer. It controls the other devices, which are called slaves.

Scatternets

A device can be a master of only one piconet. The device can, at the same time, also be a slave in another piconet that is within range. A slave can also participate in two different piconets that are within its range. However, because the master device determines the hopping pattern used for a piconet, a device cannot be a master of more than one piconet. An example of a simple scatternet is shown in Figure 23.4.

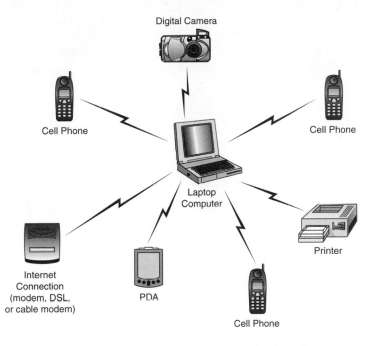

Figure 23.3 A piconet can have only one master and up to seven slave devices.

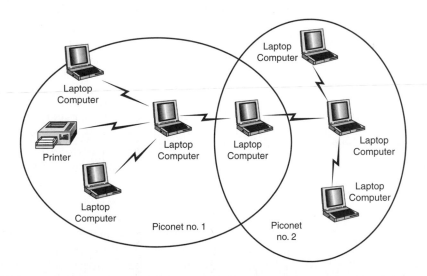

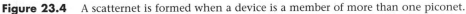

Figure 23.4 A scatternet is formed when a device is a member of more than one piconet.

In this example, a laptop computer communicates with devices in both piconets. Note that the laptop is a slave in both piconets. It is possible, however, for the laptop to be a master in one piconet and a slave in another, as shown in Figure 23.5.

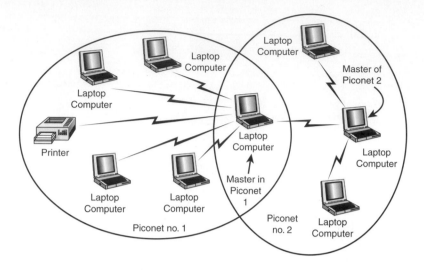

Figure 23.5   This Bluetooth-enabled laptop computer is a master in one piconet and a slave in another.

When a device is a member of two piconets, it keeps track of both frequency-hopping patterns and occasionally listens in on the correct frequency on each of the two piconets so that it can stay in touch with both piconets. A master device transmits a packet to its slaves occasionally to maintain the link, based on negotiations between the master and its slave devices. Thus, a device that is a member of two piconets must listen for these transmissions (or make them if it's the master in one piconet) within the timeframe negotiated for each of the piconets of which it is a member.

Bluetooth Device Modes

Although you can incorporate Bluetooth radios in ordinary PCs, they were originally designed to be used for low-power devices. Because of this, it isn't necessary for the Bluetooth device to be in an active state—consuming power—all the time. Before a piconet is formed, a device is in *standby* mode, in which a device will listen for messages every 1.28 seconds. To initiate a connection with another device, an *inquiry* message is sent, which is used to find other Bluetooth devices within the transmission range. If the address of the device to which a connection is desired is already known, a *page* message is used instead to begin the communication session.

In addition to being involved in active communications (the *active* mode), a device can be put into three other modes:

■ **Hold**—A master unit can put a slave unit into hold mode, or the slave unit can request that it be placed into this mode. This is a power-saving mode in which the unit no longer actively exchanges data with other devices.

■ **Sniff**—In this mode, the device does not actively participate in communications with other devices. Instead, the device "wakes up" and listens for messages frequently. How often this occurs depends on the particular application for which the device is used, and the frequency is programmed into the device by the manufacturer. A master device can request that a slave device be put into sniff mode, but cannot force it to.

■ **Park**—In this low-power mode, the device is still considered to be part of a piconet, but no longer has an Active Mode Address (AM_ADDR) associated with it. The device listens for broadcast messages and resynchronizes its clock with the master, but does not actively communicate. Before a device enters Park mode, the master will assign a Park Mode Address (PM_ADDR) to the device, easing the process of re-establishing active communications in the future.

These different modes are mainly designed to allow for different levels of low-power consumption for a Bluetooth-enabled device.

SCO and ACL Links

Two kinds of links can be established between master/slave devices in the network: the synchronous connection-oriented (SCO) link and the asynchronous connectionless (ACL) link.

SCO Links

The SCO link is established between the master and a particular slave in the network. Reserved time slots are set aside for these links, and up to three SCO links can be used for communication between the master and one or more slaves. SCO links are suitable for voice communications because the reserved slot nature of the link makes it easy to provide a steady stream of data instead of a variable rate that could cause a voice signal to degrade.

SCO links are considered switched-circuit links and must be set up before they can be used. The frequency of the dedicated time slots and other setup information is first established before an SCO link can be used.

ACL Links

ACL links are packet-switched connections between the master and one or more slaves, and can use any time slots *that are not currently being used for SCO links*. However, only one ACL link can exist at any one time between the master in the network and a particular slave.

Bluetooth Packets

Most Bluetooth packets use a standard format that consist of three basic fields:

- **Access Code**—This is a fixed-length field of either 68 or 72 bits.
- **Header**—This is a fixed-length field of 54 bits.
- **Payload**—The payload field can range from 0 to 2,745 bits in length and contains the actual data portion of the packet.

The Access Code field is used for synchronization purposes and to identify a particular channel in a piconet. If the Access Code field is followed by a header field, the Access Code is 72 bits in length; otherwise, it's 68 bits long. Three kinds of Access Codes are used:

- **Channel Access Code (CAC)**—The CAC is used to identify a particular piconet. That is, all devices in the same piconet use the same value in the Access Code field.
- **Device Access Code (DAC)**—The DAC is used during certain signaling procedures, such as paging and responses to pages.
- **Inquiry Access Code (IAC)**—The IAC consists of two other kinds of access codes: the General Inquiry Access Code (GIAC) and the Dedicated Inquiry Access Code (DIAC). GIAC is used to discover other Bluetooth devices that are within range, whereas the DIAC is used by Bluetooth devices that share some common characteristic.

The Packet Header field consists of several components:

- **AM_ADDR**—This is the active member address, and it is only 3 bits in length. This is why only 7 slaves can be in a single piconet, because 3 bits can be used to express an address range from 0 to 7 in binary notation. The address of 0 is used to broadcast packets to all slaves in a piconet. The slave's 3-bit address is used in packets that travel to and from the master/slave. The master doesn't need an address, because Bluetooth uses a point-to-point messaging service and there is only one master in the piconet.

- **PM_ADDR**—This is used to put a device into park mode, making it easier to re-establish active communications in the future when the device needs to transmit or receive data.

- **Type**—This is a 4-bit field, so up to 16 packet types can be specified for either an ACL or an SCO link.

- **Flow**—This is a single-bit field used for flow control purposes on an ACL link. A value of 0 indicates that data transmissions should be stopped. When the receiving end of the communication has sufficient buffer space to begin receiving ACL packets, it sets this bit to a value of 1.

- **ARQN**—This acknowledgment indication is a 1-bit field used to acknowledge (value = 0) that a packet was received successfully (that it passed the CRC check), or that it was not (value = 1).

- **SEQN**—This 1-bit field is used to determine that packets are received in the correct order (sequence number), and alternates between 0 and 1.

- **HEC**—The Header Error Check field consists of an 8-bit word calculated based on a polynomial. This error checking covers only the header information.

The address field is important because it limits the number of devices that can participate actively in a piconet at any given time. The master can reuse any address when a slave goes into park mode so that a large number of devices can be used in a piconet. However, only seven can be assigned active addresses and are allowed to communicate at any point in time.

The Type field has different values depending on whether the packet is an SCO or an ACL packet. It is beyond the scope of this chapter to define all the packet types, and indeed some are still undefined in the specification and reserved for future use. However, five packet types are commonly used:

- **ID packet**—This type of packet is used for paging, inquiry, and responses to paging and inquiries, and the packet contains the DAC or IAC value.

- **Null packet**—This packet type is made up of only the HAC and the CAC, and no payload. It is generally used to return the status of a previous transmission (the ARQN field), and the Null packet does not have to be acknowledged.

- **Poll packet**—The master can use this packet to poll slaves in the network. This packet is similar to the Null packet in that it has no payload, but slaves are required to respond to this packet even if they have no data to send at the time.

- **FHS packet**—This is the packet type discussed earlier that a slave device uses to obtain the frequency-hopping sequence of the piconet, along with other information about the piconet. This packet also contains the address the slave will use if it is joining the piconet.

- **DM1 packet**—This type of packet is used for control messages for both the SCO and the ACL link types.

Various packet types are defined in the Bluetooth 1.1 specification for ACL and SCO links. Refer to the documentation available at the SIG Web site for further information. The details of these packets and the ways they are used depend on the kind of Bluetooth device being considered. One of the ways Bluetooth differs from other wireless technologies—such as Wi-Fi (IEEE 802.11b)—is that in addition to defining the mechanisms to grant access to the media (air waves) and provide transport (packet types), Bluetooth also defines *profiles*, which describe basic functionality for many devices that are expected to adopt this technology.

What Are Bluetooth Profiles?

Profiles are an important concept in Bluetooth technology. A *profile* is a set of specifications for how end-user functionality should be implemented. The International Organization for Standardization

(OSI) developed the idea of profiles many years ago, which makes sense because OSI is, after all, in the business of standardizing technology worldwide. Many profiles exist for Bluetooth because it has a large number of possible uses. A profile defines minimal parameters for particular Bluetooth product types, but also allows vendors to enhance their products so that they can differentiate it in the marketplace. Also, if a Bluetooth device implements a feature that is described by a profile, it must do so in the way the profile dictates. Because of this, the capability of Bluetooth devices that implement the same function(s) can be achieved across different vendor platforms. This doesn't mean that all features described by a profile need to be implemented by all vendors—just that they must be implemented in the same way if a particular feature is used.

Profiles aren't entirely separate entities. Instead, a layered approach is taken. The Generic Access Profile gives a basic starting point for designing Bluetooth devices. It is composed of the Service Discovery Application Profile and three other basic profiles used by other profiles:

- **The Serial Port Profile Group**—This group of profiles uses the RFCOMM for serial port emulation.

- **The Generic Object Exchange Profile Group**—The OBEX protocol is used by all profiles in this group.

- **The Telephony Control Protocol Specification Group**—The name of this profile should make its use obvious—for profiles for telephone (and intercom) devices.

The Generic Access Profile is examined first, and then the other profiles defined in the current standard are discussed briefly.

The Generic Access Profile

All Bluetooth devices must implement the Generic Access Profile. This profile can be considered a base on which the other profiles are built because it specifies functionality common to all Bluetooth devices. To summarize, this profile provides for the methods that devices use to discover other Bluetooth devices, specifies link-management techniques for establishing connections, and also provides some common formats for the user interface. This profile also defines the methods used to initially establish security mechanisms for the device, if desired and selected by the user.

The protocols used to establish and maintain links between Bluetooth devices—the Link Controller (LC) and the Link Manager Protocol (LMP)—are at the lower levels of the protocol stack. Also included are higher-level protocol elements, relating to services and security. The Logical Link Control and Adaptation Protocol (L2CAP) is above the LC portion of the protocol.

Finally, sitting above these protocols are several other protocols used by various profiles:

- Telephony Control Protocol (TCS)
- RFCOMM
- Service Discovery Protocol (SDP)

Discovery, Security, and Bonding

The LC and LMP components of the protocol stack describe how Bluetooth-enabled devices are to behave when in standby mode (anything other than the active mode), and how they operate when trying to discover other Bluetooth devices and establish connections.

Bluetooth devices can operate in various modes, described in the Generic Access Profile. Bonding occurs when devices that allow connections establish a link. However, a device does not have to automatically respond to requests from another device. A Bluetooth device can be in a discoverable or nondiscoverable mode. If the device is set to nondiscoverable mode, it won't respond to inquiries from other devices. The profile describes several types of discoverable and nondiscoverable modes, such as limited discoverable mode and general discovery mode. Basically, these terms define the length of time a device will respond or will not respond to inquiry messages from other devices.

During the discovery process, the initiator of the discovery obtains the address, clock, and class of the discovered device, as well as the name of the device.

The important thing to remember is that just because a Bluetooth device comes within range of another similarly enabled device, a connection does not automatically happen. This can be controlled by the user or the application. In addition to discoverability modes, this profile also defines bonding and pairing modes, which establish whether a connection can be made after a device is in a discoverable mode.

During the bonding procedure, the Bluetooth devices establish a link between each other and exchange a key that is stored in the device to identify the link for future data exchanges.

If a device is discoverable, and if it allows a link to be established, security mechanisms come into play. This profile defines several levels of security:

- **Security Mode 1 (nonsecure)**—This mode means that the device will not initiate any security mechanisms, such as authentication.

- **Security Mode 2 (service level enforced security)**—In this security mode, the device will not initiate any security mechanisms until after a channel-establishment procedure or request has been initiated. The service for which the device is used determines whether security mechanisms (authentication, authorization, or encryption) are used.

- **Security Mode 3 (link level enforced security)**—This mode requires the device to initiate security mechanisms before the LMP link setup procedure has completed.

Creating Connections

After devices have discovered each other and established a link, they create a channel through which applications can create a connection. Additionally, multiple applications can establish more than one connection using the same channel, or a separate channel that is created between the two. A channel is a specific radio frequency hopping sequence. As you learned earlier in this chapter, a device can be a member of one or two piconets, and thus can establish a channel on each. Applications can establish connections using the channels created between devices to exchange data.

The Service Discovery Application Profile

This profile describes the methods used by an application to discover the services of another Bluetooth device, and to obtain information about those services. This profile uses the SDP to find out what services another device offers. SDP can search for services based on the service class or service attributes. SDP also supports browsing for services to determine what is available.

The SDP process generally consists of the exchange of a series of messages defined by SDP in a connectionless mode. That is, SDP is a connectionless datagram service. Instead, SDP makes use of the Logical Link Control and Adaptation Protocol portion of the protocol stack for any link establishment, as well as for tearing down the connections that might be used during an exchange of SDP Protocol Data Units (PDUs).

The Cordless Telephony Profile and the Intercom Profile

This profile is used for Bluetooth devices that implement cordless telephony services to communicate with a base station, which is connected to a telephone network, as well as for voice connections between two Bluetooth telephone devices. Two roles are defined in this profile: gateway and terminal. A *gateway role* implies that the device acts as a base station to connect to an external telephone network. In most cases, this is a unit connected to the public switched telephone network (PSTN). However, support also is provided for other telephony connections, such as ISDN (Integrated Services Digital Network) and satellite connections that offer telephone services.

A *terminal role* describes the unit that communicates with a gateway device, or perhaps another terminal (acting more like an intercom). Because Bluetooth devices can communicate directly with each other in this role, you can eliminate cellular phone charges if you are using a Bluetooth-enabled cordless phone that is within range of another. This intercom capability is also described by the Intercom Profile, which must be supported by the Bluetooth device for this functionality to be implemented.

The L2CAP layer of the protocol stack is used to establish a connection between a terminal and a gateway when they come within range of each other. When a terminal unit is within range of a gateway device, the terminal unit is normally put into park mode, discussed earlier in this chapter. When a call needs to be sent or received, the terminal is put into active mode. The L2CAP connection does not need to be re-established each time a call is made.

This profile also describes how services such as call setup, termination, and caller ID are performed.

The Serial Port Profile

This profile defines the use of Bluetooth devices that emulate serial port communications—such as RS232 cable connections. Most PCs have several kinds of ports you can use to connect external devices, ranging from serial ports to USB (universal serial bus) ports and FireWire ports. This profile deals with the decades-old serial port type of connection. This type of port was commonly used for such things as connecting to a modem or another device to establish a communications session. For example, you can use a serial cable to create a quick connection between two PCs and exchange files using products such as LapLink or other similar programs.

The Headset Profile

The Headset Profile describes how headsets are to be implemented using Bluetooth. A headset can be used for telephone audio use, for listening to music, and in various other similar cases. Headsets can even be used with voice-recognition software to provide input/output capabilities for a PC.

Similar to the Cordless Telephony Profile, the Headset Profile defines a gateway and a Headset device. The gateway can be a cordless telephone, a PC, or another similar device that is equipped with Bluetooth for audio communications. The Headset is the actual headset device that the user wears to provide the earphone and microphone hardware.

The profile provides for the initiation of a session by the gateway (as in the case of an incoming telephone call) or by the end user (by pressing a button on the device, for example). The connection can be terminated by either side of the connection. Provisions are also made for controlling the volume of the transmitted or received audio signal.

The Dial-Up Networking Profile

Bluetooth devices can act as an "Internet bridge" to allow you to use a cellular phone (or another device that can connect to an ISP) so that you can use a laptop or another device to communicate on the Internet. This profile also allows a computer to use a cellular phone to accept incoming digital calls. Like the Headset Profile and the Cordless Telephony Profile, this profile defines a gateway device, which is the cellular phone or possibly a modem with a cabled connection to the Internet. A Data Terminal (DT) is the device that makes use of the gateway to connect to the Internet. This profile provides for speeds up to 128Kbps, but higher speeds are optional.

The profile specifies a subset of the AT modem command set that is employed for this type of service; only one call can be established between the gateway device and a DT. That is, the DT cannot be used to establish more than one call with a gateway device at any point in time. Just as you'd need more than one telephone line if you had two modems in your computer, the DT is capable of placing only a single call through a gateway.

Other Bluetooth Profiles

In addition to the profiles discussed in this chapter, Bluetooth 1.1 and 2.0 specifications provide for several others. More profiles are expected to be added if the technology is accepted by the marketplace as a solution for short-distance cable replacement. Many of the following profiles are still in draft format and are not yet considered to be standards that all Bluetooth vendors will adopt. When you purchase a Bluetooth device that supports the following profiles, be sure to check the description of the device to determine whether it supports an established standard, or whether it is based on a draft standard. For example, devices supporting 802.11g wireless networking (see Chapter 22, "The IEEE 802.11g Standard") were originally released based on the draft of this protocol, assuming that there would be very few changes from the drafts to the adopted standards.

Tip

Some of the following drafts may become standards in a short time. Thus, the reader is again cautioned to check the description of any device that claims to support the profiles described in this section. And you can expect that additional profiles will be added as Bluetooth devices continue to make inroads into the consumer marketplace.

For those who want to find out what may be in store for Bluetooth devices, the draft profiles include the following:

- **Fax Profile**—This profile allows for wireless fax services.

- **LAN Access Profile**—This profile provides for a connection to a LAN. This is similar to the functions that Wi-Fi provides using Access Points. The Point-to-Point protocol (PPP) is used. This profile also can be used to create a LAN consisting of only Bluetooth devices.

- **Generic Object Exchange Profile (GOEP)**—This profile borrows from the OBEX protocol and allows for the exchange of data between devices—between a cordless telephone, a PDA, and a PC. It is used by the other profiles in this list.

- **Object Push Profile**—This profile uses GOEP for the exchange of simple objects, such as electronic business cards or appointment data. This profile can be used to "pull" objects, as well as to push them to another device.

- **File Transfer Profile**—This profile uses GOEP to browse a file system on a remote device, as well as transfer files between devices, delete files, or create new folders (directories).

- **The Synchronization Profile**—This profile uses GOEP to provide a service for synchronizing data in various kinds of databases, for example, calendars, address books, and Personal Information Managers (PIMs).

- **The Audio/Video Remote Control Profile (AVCP)**—This profile describes features used for Bluetooth devices that support audio and/or video exchanges. The command set used for this type of exchange is defined by this profile. Streaming audio or video is not defined in this profile, however.

- **The Generic Audio/Video Distribution Profile (GAVDP)**—Based on AVCP (and other previous profiles, such as the Generic Access Protocol), this profile describes the techniques necessary to support streaming audio and video between Bluetooth devices.

- **The Advanced Audio/Video Remote Control Profile (AVRCP)**—This profile is designed to enhance AVCP and GAVDP by providing for remote control functionality, for example, the features usually found on an audio or video remote control, such as volume settings, pause, play, and so on.

- **The Basic Imaging Profile (BIP)**—Standard network protocols such as FTP can be used to transfer graphic imaging files, as well as other types of files. With FTP, however, there is no guarantee that a receiving device can correctly display the images it receives. This profile provides the mechanisms needed to provide interoperability between devices, by requiring that Bluetooth devices be able to transmit/receive imaging files in JPEG thumbnail formats, regardless of the imaging format stored on the sender. This profile also enables the device to download the characteristics of other imaging file formats, and transfer them to printers, as well as offering the capability of controlling an imaging device, such as a digital camera.

- **Basic Printing Profile (BPP)**—The Generic Object Exchange Profile and Generic Access Profile are combined with the specifications of this profile to provide simple printing capabilities for Bluetooth. This profile addresses printing simple files, such as emails, and some formatted documents, such as calendars.

- **The Bluetooth Extended Service Discovery Profile (ESDP)**—This profile describes how Bluetooth devices can make use of Bluetooth's Service Discovery Protocol (SDP) to discover devices that use the Universal Plug and Play (UPnP) service.

- **The Hands-Free Profile (HFP)**—A minimum set of functions necessary for a mobile phone that uses hands-free devices is described by this profile. The Bluetooth device will be able to provide voice communications as well as remote control for the hands-free device.

Bluetooth Is More Than a Wireless Communication Protocol

As you can see, Bluetooth is not just a protocol used to exchange data between devices. The use of profiles further delineates the different kinds of applications that can be used with Bluetooth radio transmitters and thus makes it easier for manufacturers to produce portable devices that have applications built in and ready for use. You can contrast this with Wi-Fi, which simply provides the communications link just as traditional LAN or WAN protocols provide. Bluetooth provides both the radio frequency transport mechanisms and application-specific solutions that make interoperability between devices easy to implement.

Other Wireless Technologies

24

SOME OF THE MAIN TOPICS IN THIS CHAPTER ARE

The previous chapters on wireless technology were devoted to examining wireless devices that are currently available. No doubt the wireless world will change rapidly as the market grows and wireless technologies become saturated and are no longer able to satisfy the customer or operate an acceptable rate that will be required by larger applications and data files. In that case, additional radio frequency spectrum will have to be allocated, because wireless is definitely the future for many consumer and business devices. This chapter covers a few wireless technologies, but not future standards for wireless networking that are still in the planning stages. Additionally, other topics, such as security, can be found in this chapter.

Instant Messaging and Consumer Devices

Probably the first thing that would come to mind if you asked a typical consumer about wireless networking would be a cell phone, or perhaps a PDA-like device. These are wireless devices, and newer devices can do everything from accessing email to browsing the Web, in addition to providing voice communications. Technically, even satellite phones are wireless devices.

Personal Digital Assistants (PDAs)

These are some of the more popular PDAs:

- **Blackberry** (www.blackberry.net)—The Blackberry PDAs use Java applications and are produced by a company called Research In Motion (RIM).

- **Palm** (www.palm.com)—Palm uses an operating system developed in-house for the PDAs it manufactures. The OS has also been adopted by many other manufacturers, such as HandEra (formerly TRGPro) and Sony. Perhaps the most unique port for the Palm operating system is a wristwatch-size device available from Fossil Tech (www.fossil.com).

- **Pocket PC** (www.microsoft.com)—Developed by Microsoft, you can get Pocket PCs from a large number of manufacturers, such as HP, Toshiba, and Dell. Microsoft's Pocket PC operating system commands the largest number of manufacturers at this time.

The Blackberry line is produced by Research In Motion (RIM) and uses industry partners to give you to many Internet services in addition to its standard PDA capabilities. Typical PDAs usually include a calendar, an address book, to-do items, a small notepad word processor, and other applications. Both Palm and Blackberry devices also work with third-party applications, so you can customize your device. Blackberry uses Java applications, whereas Palm uses its own operating system. These devices even have software applications for playing games.

The Palm PDAs come in several varieties (don't forget that wristwatch mentioned previously), and you will find a lot of third-party developers that produce applications for Palm devices. Although Microsoft's Pocket PC operating system has the largest number of manufacturers that use the OS at this time, competition is growing, especially with respect to Palm.

Microsoft's Pocket PC OS can be found on devices from a large number of manufacturers, and also commands a large contingent of followers who create software applications and programming environments. Because Pocket PC applications can easily interact with Microsoft's other operating systems, it is a natural fit for many users. However, that doesn't mean that it will continue to dominate the market.

Third-Generation Mobile Phones

The term 3G has been often talked about in the computer press, and it stands for third-generation mobile phones. This new generation of mobile phones incorporates many of the features found in today's PDAs. Indeed, depending on the phone you purchase, you might find it hard to distinguish between such a phone and a PDA. Beyond using typical wireless phone technology, 3G phones also enable Internet access, include a high-resolution screen, and, in some cases, include an MP3 player so that you can listen to your favorite music. To enable the multimedia aspects of a 3G phone, the International Telecommunications Union (ITU) has defined a 3G phone as one that operates at 144Kbps or faster.

Because security is one of the most important topics when it comes to networking today, a desirable feature of a 3G phone is GPS (global positioning satellite) capabilities. Using GPS, it is a simple matter to locate the phone if it is stolen. This is an important feature because this type of phone can be used to store personal information (such as your credit-card numbers). Some 3G phones require you to enter a PIN in order to use them, further increasing security. Another important reason to employ a phone that includes GPS is that it can be very valuable in case of an emergency. If you call 911, for example, for whatever reason, the GPS functionality will make locating you a simple matter.

The investment required to build a 3G network, however, is quite expensive, so this technology is not widespread. Its future depends on increasing developing standards that are better than the current ones, because the target is for 3G phones to work worldwide. Another factor is that, as with the typical cell-phone market, it will be quite expensive to set up a network that covers large geographical distances. Cell phones still lack complete coverage, and the network they use is not compatible with 3G phones.

I don't want to sound too pessimistic. Any new technology that offers a lot of features over its predecessors usually takes time before it becomes widely accepted. Exceptions to this are Wi-Fi products, discussed in previous chapters. Yet Wi-Fi (802.11 standards) devices do not operate worldwide, and are now used to connect to other similar wireless devices, or to a wired network.

Wireless Security

Several years ago proponents of 802.11b wireless networks maintained that their products were secure, because the Wired Equivalent Privacy (WEP) security mechanism would keep intruders from intercepting and decoding wireless communications. In addition to eavesdropping on your wireless network, WEP was supposed to keep intruders from joining your wireless network. However, because WEP uses only a shared 40-bit encryption key, it is very easy to break. It is important to point out that the Wireless Ethernet Compatibility Alliance (WECA), now called the Wi-Fi Alliance, has stated that WEP was never meant to be a single solution for securing a wireless network. Instead, other technologies, such as VPNs (see Chapter 50, "Virtual Private Networks [VPNs] and Tunneling"), as well as other mechanisms (such as secure authentication) typically found on a wired network, were meant to fill this gap.

WEP

Because the first version of WEP uses a simple 40-bit encryption key, and the same key is used on both the Access Point (AP) and the wireless client, it is a simple matter to break this security. For example, there are several utilities on the Internet you can use to determine whether WEP is protecting your network adequately.

Caution

One of the most important reasons you need to take extra steps to secure a wireless network as compared to a wired one is that in a wired network you can physically secure the computers, the network cabling, and even a connection to a WAN (such as the Internet—by using a firewall). Wireless networks, on the other hand, do not offer a physical barrier. Instead, the distance that your wireless network can cover will usually include a range that is accessible outside your building(s). And because the signal cannot easily be controlled using the same physical methods you use for a wired network, interception of transmissions, much less intrusions into your network, becomes a simple matter when relying solely on WEP. WEP was part of the original 802.11 specification, developed in 1997. A lot of time has passed since then—enough time to break the encryption using simple techniques available today.

You can visit the following Web sites to gain access to software that can be used by both you and hackers, to determine whether your network is secure:

- **WEPCrack**—This open-source tool is available to everyone, so you might as well use it yourself to determine whether your network is secure. For more information, see `http://wepcrack.sourceforge.net`.

- **AirSnort**—This tool simply listens, and saves, 5 to 10 million packets from a wireless network (and that is really not a large number of packets if you have more than just a few clients). When the program determines that enough packets have been intercepted, it can take a second or two to decrypt the shared encryption key. AirSnort runs on Linux platforms, so you will need a Linux system in order to use this application. For more information, see `http://airsnort.shmoo.com`.

At this time it is *not illegal* to use devices to listen to wireless network transmissions. It would be great if such laws were enacted worldwide. Yet, because these tools are available to everyone, *you should probably use them to see whether your network is as secure as you think it is*. This is not meant to encourage hackers to use these tools; the tools previously listed are meant for you to use them so that at least both sides can have access to the same intrusion applications.

This goes along with the benefits touted by the open-source community. While the source code and applications are available to everyone (a glass house, so to speak), they enable hackers to search for vulnerabilities, and they also enable users to create solutions to prevent these attacks. This is an argument that is often used to compare proprietary operating systems and applications and open-source ones. I guess it all depends on your perspective. If you want to use proprietary applications, you will have to depend on your vendor to fix security problems. If you use open-source applications, there are many programmers worldwide who can develop a solution.

Whom do you trust? This is a difficult decision to make. But, at the very least, you should have access to the same programs that hackers use to determine whether your network is vulnerable, whether or not you use other open-source applications. And if you search the Internet, you will find many other programs used by hackers in addition to those listed previously. A good search, on a regular basis, is recommended by this author.

Second-Generation WEP: Using a 128-Bit Key

Even a newer version of WEP that uses a 128-bit key is easily detected and broken. Because of this, it is recommended that you separate a wireless network from the wired network using a firewall (see Chapter 49, "Firewalls"). At least this will assist in keeping intruders from accessing the entire corporate network, though the wireless portion is still vulnerable. And you should incorporate techniques such as VPNs, as suggested by the Wi-Fi Alliance, to further enhance security on the wireless portions of the network.

Many consumers who purchase inexpensive devices for home networks may think that the SSID (service set identifier) that you enter when installing the network card and Access Point provide security for the wireless network, but this is not the case. Instead, the SSID is simply used to separate wireless networks. The SSID is easily discovered, especially if you do not choose to use additional security mechanisms. The SSID is *not* a security mechanism! It is simply a method used to associate wireless devices with an AP. Without using some form of encryption, the SSID is easily discovered by broadcast messages from the AP. When discovered by an eavesdropper, all that is necessary for the intruder is to reset his wireless adapter to use the same SSID, and then join your network.

A good Web site to visit if you are interested in the latest developments in wireless security is `www.netstumbler.com`. Here you'll find various articles about wireless security, as well as downloads that can help you enhance your current wireless device and check out security lapses.

Tip

If you operate a home or SOHO network, you might be satisfied using WEP technology (but make sure you use a 128-bit version). If your SOHO network contains very sensitive information, consider other techniques as mentioned in the main text of this chapter. If you use a broadband connection to access the Internet, all you really need to worry about is having neighbors intrude on your wireless network and also use your broadband connection. This type of invasion has received a lot of attention in the press lately. Yet, because it is typical that a home user does not store sensitive information on a computer (unless using a credit card online), and because most users do not continuously use the entire bandwidth provided by broadband services, you probably won't notice much difference in performance. Indeed, you might want to enable a neighbor to use your wireless network and split the cost. Check the agreement you have with your broadband provider, however, before making a decision like this. Otherwise, there may be legal ramifications, or you may just lose your broadband connection.

Yet, as criticism of WEP continued to grow, and made some potential customers think twice about using 802.11b Wi-Fi technology, work has been done to create newer wireless security standards.

Tip

There is one situation in which you might want to ensure that your wireless network is secure in a home network. Because the distances of the current technologies can range from about 100 to 300 meters, it's quite possible for someone in the house next door to use your wireless Access Point and tap into your broadband Internet connection! If you don't want to have neighbors sharing your bandwidth, it is a must that you use whatever security measures your particular technology provides. This should also be a factor when choosing hardware devices.

Wired Protected Access (WPA) and 802.11i

In response to the vulnerability and criticism of WEP, the Wi-Fi Alliance has created the Wired Protected Access (WPA) standard, which should be considered as an interim protocol until something better comes along. WPA will most likely be a thing of the past when the IEEE finishes work on 802.11i, which is a security protocol intended to provide a better solution to security for wireless networks.

One of the main complaints about WEP, besides its limited-length keys, is the fact that the same key is used by both sides of the transmission. And the key does not change during a session. That is why it is easy to examine network traffic on a wireless network and eventually crack the encryption key.

The 802.11i standard is still under development, but it is mentioned in this chapter because vendors are beginning to adopt the features that have already been published in draft form. As the old Roman saying goes, *caveat emptor*—let the buyer beware. If you purchase hardware based on draft standards, don't expect it to necessarily work when the final standard is published.

WPA solves two problems associated with the earlier WEP security mechanisms. First, it uses encrypted techniques for authentication, which should assist in preventing unauthorized clients from becoming part of the wireless network. Second, it uses a constantly changing key instead of the single shared key used for encryption by WEP. By changing in the encryption key at frequent intervals, WPA can be much more difficult to crack. Yet this all remains to be seen after the IEEE has finished work on the 802.11i standard.

The constant changing of encryption keys is known as the Temporal Key Integrity Protocol (TKIP). This key-changing method will make it very difficult for intruders to decipher keys used by your wireless network, especially when compared to the static keys known by both sides of the communications link used by the simple WEP standards.

WPA also includes an integrity check that is basically a check sum based on the network packet that can detect whether a packet is originating from a valid network user or an intruder who is attempting to crack the key used by your network. Thus, if an unauthorized user uses the standard techniques to attempt to determine a fixed key, you can detect these intrusion attempts, and then deal with them.

How Well Do You Know Your Users?

One of the main concerns of network administrators in the 1980s was that any person in the company network could easily install a modem in her computer and connect to computers outside the network. For digital telephone systems, this was not a problem. But for small businesses using an analogue telephone system, this could present a major security headache.

The equivalent today is known as rogue Access Points, and these are difficult to detect with modern network analysis tools. Because APs are so inexpensive, what can you do to stop a user, or a department in your company, from installing an AP and enabling wireless access? In large corporate environments where it can be a complicated process, what is to stop a user from simply connecting an AP to her own network connection, and thus enabling a larger number of computers to connect to the network? Because APs generally use DHCP to assign addresses to clients, and use the single valid address on your network to exchange data for these clients, just how secure is your network?

This is yet another reason to use wireless detection programs on a regular basis, even if you do not authorize wireless networking, to determine whether some user has enabled this access on your wired network.

In Chapter 46, "Basic Security Measures Every Network Administrator Needs to Know," the importance of establishing corporate security policies and procedures was discussed. If you ensure that each and every employee, contractor, and vendor signs off on these policies (which should include wireless access), then you will at least have grounds to dismiss those who violate the procedures, and possibly to pursue legal action. There's not a lot you can do about rogue users, and this problem is more common than many administrators think. If a user is stymied by corporate procedures and paperwork, it is not a difficult thing to justify implementing a solution on his own. Again, because these types of security breaches can easily occur, especially in a large network, you should use wireless sniffing programs to determine whether users are bypassing your policies and procedures that are employed in your network.

Although you may indeed use wireless networking at certain junctions in your network, you should regularly test to see whether unauthorized wireless networks are being created by users. When you consider the low cost of an AP today, it is very feasible to install a wireless network anywhere in your large network. And many of the users who have been caught using this method say that the reason they did so is that it would take too long to get permission from the network administrator, or whatever body you use to authorize such connections.

I guess the best thing to say about this topic is "trust no one."

Personal Area Networks (PANs)

A personal area network (PAN) is a short-range wireless network that can span from a few feet to a few hundred feet. This covers many different short-range wireless standards.

As weird as it may sound, a recent PAN solution may enable you to exchange data (such as an electronic business card, or other similar information) by simply shaking hands with another person. How is this possible? IBM is currently developing a PAN solution that involves passing a very small amount of electrical current through the human body. The amount of current used is much smaller than that already passing naturally through your body. Using a PAN, it would also be possible to create devices that connect your Dick Tracy wristwatch to other larger computing devices simply by walking past them, transmitting a signal through your shoes. This may sound far-fetched, but development is underway at this time, and standards for PANs are still being developed. For more information about the ongoing development of PANs and the use to which they can be put, check out the Web site www.IEEE.org.

Another sort of PAN is the Bluetooth technology discussed in Chapter 23, "Bluetooth Wireless Technology." Although) not as succinct as the PAN previously described, Bluetooth provides communications between devices over a very short range. However, if Bluetooth continues down the development path that currently appears to be competitive with the IEEE 802.11 standards, then it may not be considered a PAN alternative in the future.

Bluetooth can be used to create a wireless environment for PCs so that you don't have to have all those cables connecting your keyboard, printer, mouse, and other peripheral devices. Bluetooth has undergone a long, rough ride to get to the consumer marketplace. When the third edition of this book was published, you would have been hard-pressed to find any Bluetooth device at a computer or consumer electronics store. Today, the technology is now widely available. Today Bluetooth devices are just as common in your consumer electronics store as Wi-Fi devices.

Yet, because most of this chapter is devoted to security issues, it is worth noting that you should probably limit the use of Bluetooth in large networks. Because so many consumer devices can be used to associate with a computer or another device, and because the security mechanisms used by Bluetooth at this time are not entirely secure, Bluetooth should be usually used only in a nonsecure network, such as a SOHO network where security is not a great issue.

The IEEE approved the 802.15.1 standard for personal area networks (PANs), adopting much of the technology from Bluetooth standards.

The basics of a PAN is a network limited to just 255 devices, and a connection to a wired network is not generally allowed. Only one device is enabled to control the PAN, and it is responsible for controlling traffic between other similar devices. The controlling device allocates time slots for each device that makes a request to transmit data.

The IEEE is also working on other versions of this standard, which involve higher data rates as well as reducing the power requirements for PANs.

In the future you might expect various consumer devices (as well as computers) to interact using PAN technology. For example, it might just be that in the future you can use your watch to instruct the thermostat in your house what temperature you want it to be set at. Or you might have a stove that incorporates both heating and refrigeration capabilities to)defrost and have dinner waiting for you at the time you request!

LAN and WAN Network, Service, and Application Protocols

SOME OF THE MAIN TOPICS FOR THIS PART ARE

Overview of the TCP/IP Protocol Suite

Basic TCP/IP Services and Applications

Internet Mail Protocols: POP3, SMTP, and IMAP

Troubleshooting Tools for TCP/IP Networks

BOOTP and Dynamic Host Configuration Protocol (DHCP)

Network Name Resolution

Using the Active Directory

Overview of Novell NetWare IPX/SPX

Overview of the Novell Bindery and Novell Directory Services

Expanding and Enhancing NDS: NetWare's eDirectory

File Server Protocols

The Hypertext Transfer Protocol

Routing Protocols

The Secure Sockets Layer (SSL) Protocol

Introduction to the IPv6 Protocol

PART VI

Overview of the TCP/IP Protocol Suite

SOME OF THE MAIN TOPICS IN THIS CHAPTER ARE

CHAPTER 25

TCP/IP is the primary network protocol used on the Internet. Unlike many earlier network protocols—such as ARCnet and DECnet—TCP/IP was not developed by a single vendor as a proprietary solution. TCP/IP was created to provide a network link between computer hardware and software platforms from various vendors (such as IBM and Digital Equipment Corporation at the high end, as well as personal computers at the low end). By standardizing on a single set of protocols, each of which serves a specific function, TCP/IP can be used to create a network, no matter what underlying hardware is used. During the early years of TCP/IP, universities, businesses, and government organizations were able to exchange information on the ARPANET—the Internet's predecessor—because TCP/IP could be implemented on just about any kind of computer. It is easy to implement TCP/IP on a wide variety of operating systems because TCP/IP was developed with a layered approach, which means that network functionality was compartmentalized into layers instead of the traditional approach of writing network drivers as single programs tied to specific hardware.

Using this layered approach means that a vendor need only write a low-level driver for their hardware to work with the upper layers of the TCP/IP code (which provides a standard interface). By freeing the development of the protocol(s) from the hands of particular manufacturers, TCP/IP has been developed to satisfy the needs of the many, instead of the needs of a single vendor's proprietary hardware. TCP/IP has evolved over time, using a process in which many individuals have had the opportunity to supply input into its development. The Request for Comments (RFCs) documents that you hear about all through this book are the documents that allow suggestions for protocol enhancements and new protocols to be reviewed by a diverse group of individuals who specialize in the particular topic at hand. Although many projects created by a committee turn out to be unwieldy, cumbersome works, this is not the case with TCP/IP. Instead, the RFC process allows for a great deal of input when creating standards, often resulting in a higher quality standard after scrutiny by experts in the field.

Note

Request for Comments documents can be useful when you are learning new technology. Over the years newer documents have superceded older standards documents as TCP/IP (and other related protocols used on the Internet) has matured. If you have difficulty understanding how a protocol works, or why it was developed the way it was, you can read the documents online at **www.rfc-editor.org**. This site contains all the RFC documents—both new and those that have been replaced. Some of these documents are difficult to read at first but can prove valuable guides for readers who want to understand the minute details of any particular protocol.

In this chapter, we will look at all the major protocols that make up the TCP/IP suite and show how they work together. In addition to the protocols you will read about here, the TCP/IP suite includes some standard applications, such as FTP and Telnet. These are discussed in Chapter 26, "Basic TCP/IP Services and Applications." Finally, in Chapter 28, "Troubleshooting Tools for TCP/IP Networks," you will find useful information about programs that were written to help diagnose problems when this complex suite of protocols and applications doesn't appear to be working as it should.

To begin, it is important to understand the basic protocols on which the entire TCP/IP suite is built.

TCP/IP and the OSI Reference Model

As discussed earlier, TCP/IP was built using a layered approach. You may have heard about the OSI (Open Systems Interconnect or Open Systems Interconnection) Reference model that is used mostly as a framework around which a discussion of network protocols can be discussed. Developed in 1984 by the International Organization for Standardization (ISO), this model defines a protocol stack in a modular fashion, specifying what functions are performed by each module.

▶▶ For further discussion of the OSI reference model, see Appendix A, "Overview of the OSI Seven-Layer Networking Reference Model."

For the purposes of this chapter, it should be noted that development of TCP/IP began long before the OSI model, and, as can be expected, TCP/IP protocols don't always neatly match up to the seven layers of the OSI model.

Note

There is one bit of Internet trivia that is perpetuated about the ISO "acronym" that you might find interesting. You'll find that many writers say that ISO stands for the International Standards Organization. Sounds right, doesn't it? Well, it's not true. In the first place, *ISO* is not an acronym, it's a name. And it's not the International Standards Organization, it's the International Organization for Standardization (which would be IOS if one were to create an acronym). The name ISO was chosen for a very specific reason. "ISO" is derived from the Greek word isos, which can be translated as "equal." In the English language you'll find the prefix iso- quite frequently with this meaning; for example, the word "isometric." Established in 1947, the ISO wanted a name that could be used worldwide, without having to take into account translations of their name, which would result in different acronyms depending on the language or translation. Thus, OSI is an acronym, but ISO is a name and is used to refer to this standards organization worldwide. You can find out more about the wide range of standards promulgated by this organization at its Web site: **www.iso.ch**.

The ISO used this model to develop a set of open network protocols, but these were never widely adopted. This was due to several factors. First, at that time many computer vendors held market share by keeping customers locked into proprietary hardware/software solutions. Second, the OSI protocols required a considerable amount of system resources, so it was impractical to try to implement them on smaller computers, such as minicomputers, much less the now-standard PC. However, the OSI networking model is still used today when discussing network protocols, and it is a good idea to become familiar with it if you will be working in this field. TCP/IP was developed based on a similar, though less modular, reference model, the DOD (Department of Defense) or DARPA model.

In Figure 25.1, you can see the four layers that make up the TCP/IP-DOD model, and how each layer relates to the OSI model.

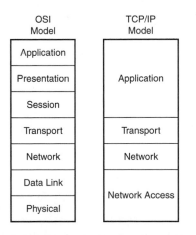

Figure 25.1 Comparison of the TCP/IP and OSI networking models.

As you can see, TCP/IP doesn't exactly fit into the OSI model, but it is still possible to refer to the model when discussing certain aspects of the protocols and services that TCP/IP provides.

TCP/IP Is a Collection of Protocols, Services, and Applications

The acronym TCP/IP stands for Transmission Control Protocol/Internet Protocol. In addition to these two important protocols, many other related protocols and utilities are commonly grouped together and called the TCP/IP protocol suite. This "suite" of protocols includes such things as the User Datagram Protocol (UDP) and the Internet Control Message Protocol (ICMP), and others discussed in this chapter and in several other chapters in this book.

Note

The terms *protocol stack* and *protocol suite* often are used to mean the same thing. Although it is convenient to think of TCP/IP as a single software entity, that is not the case. The protocols discussed in this chapter are called a "suite" because they work together, some providing services to others. For example, IP is the transport protocol that TCP uses when it wants to send data on the network. UDP likewise uses IP when it communicates on the network. At the bottom of the stack, ARP functions to associate hard-coded network card addresses with IP addresses. And when you get to the physical layer of any protocol, many methods can be used to transmit bits of information from one place to another. For LANs the most prevalent "wire" protocol is Ethernet. You may also encounter Token-Ring networks, though this protocol commands only a very small portion of the marketplace today.

Thus, when we talk about TCP/IP protocol suite (or stack), we are talking about a group of protocols, applications, and services.

TCP/IP, IP, and UDP

The main workhorses of this protocol suite are IP, TCP, and UDP:

- **IP**—The Internet Protocol is an unreliable, connectionless protocol that provides the means to get a datagram from one computer or device to another and for internetwork addressing.

- **TCP**—The Transmission Control Protocol uses IP but provides a higher-level functionality that checks to be sure that the packets that IP manages actually get to and from their intended destinations. TCP is a reliable, connection-oriented protocol, requiring that a session be established to manage communications between two points in the network so that errors can be detected and, if possible, corrected.

- **UDP**—The User Datagram Protocol also uses IP to move data through a network. Whereas TCP uses an acknowledgment mechanism to ensure reliable delivery, UDP does not. UDP is intended for use in applications that don't necessarily need the guaranteed delivery service provided by TCP. The Domain Name System (DNS) service is an example of an application that uses UDP. Applications that make use of UDP are responsible for taking on the functions of checking for reliable delivery that is provided by TCP.

As you can see in Figure 25.2, IP is the basic protocol used in the TCP/IP suite to get datagrams delivered.

This figure shows that TCP/IP and its related protocols work above the physical components of the network. Therefore, it is easy to adapt TCP/IP to different types of networks, such as Ethernet and Token-Ring. When you talk about using TCP/IP on the network, what it all boils down to is that you're packaging your data into an IP packet that is passed down to the actual network hardware for delivery. Because IP is the common denominator of the TCP/IP suite, this chapter covers it first, and after that shows how the remaining protocols build on the functions provided by IP.

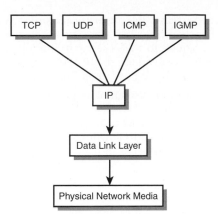

Figure 25.2 IP is used by many other protocols as the mechanism by which their data is routed and delivered through the network.

Note

The terms *datagram*, *packet*, and *frame* are often misunderstood and used interchangeably. Starting with the TCP protocol, the data to be sent is actually called a *segment*. TCP passes segments to IP, which creates packets (or datagrams if the data comes from UDP) from these segments. IP passes the data farther down the protocol stack, and when it reaches the wire, it's called a *frame*. For all practical purposes, however, you can consider a packet and a datagram to be the same thing.

Other Miscellaneous Protocols

In addition to TCP and IP, many other protocols are part of the TCP/IP suite. Back in Figure 25.2 you can see that the IGMP and ICMP protocols are included. IGMP is the Internet Group Management Protocol, which is used to manage groups of systems that are members of multicast groups. *Multicasting* is a technique that allows a datagram to be delivered to more than one destination. Figure 25.2 also shows the Internet Control Message Protocol (ICMP), which performs many functions to help control traffic on a network. In addition to these protocols, which are discussed later in this chapter, other protocols usually considered as part of or associated with the TCP/IP protocol suite include the following:

- ■ **ARP**—The Address Resolution Protocol. ARP (discussed along with RARP later in this chapter) is used by a computer to determine what hardware address is associated with an IP address. This is necessary because IP addresses are used to route data between networks, while communications on the local network segment are done using the burned-in hardware address of the network cards.

- ■ **RARP**—The Reverse Address Resolution Protocol is similar to ARP but works in reverse. This is an older protocol that was developed to allow a computer to find out what IP address it should use, based on a table stored on a device such as a router. This functionality has generally been replaced by other protocols, such as BOOTP and DHCP. However, you can still find this protocol in use on many networks that contain older legacy equipment that has yet to reach the end of its useful life, such as diskless X-Windows terminals.

- **DNS**—The Domain Name System is the hierarchical naming system used by the Internet and most TCP/IP networks. For example, when you type `http://www.twoinc.com` into a browser, your TCP/IP stack sends a request to a DNS server to find out the IP address associated with that name. From then on, the browser can use the IP address to send requests to the Web site. More information about DNS can be found in Chapter 30, "Network Name Resolution."

- **BOOTP**—The Bootstrap Protocol is also an older protocol that has generally been replaced by DHCP. In fact, most DHCP servers can act as BOOTP servers as well. BOOTP was created to allow a diskless workstation to download configuration information, such as an IP address and the name of a server that can be used to download an operating system. Because the diskless workstation has no local storage (other than memory), it can't store this information itself between boots.

- **DHCP**—The Dynamic Host Configuration Protocol relieves the network administrator of the task of having to manually configure each computer on the network with addressing and other information. Chapter 29, "BOOTP and Dynamic Host Configuration Protocol (DHCP)," covers this topic in great detail.

- **SNMP**—The Simple Network Management Protocol was developed to make managing network devices and computers from a central location easy. You can find out more about SNMP in Chapter 53, "Network Testing and Analysis Tools."

- **RMON**—The Remote Monitoring protocol was developed to further enhance the administrator's ability to manage computers and network devices remotely. This protocol is also covered in greater detail in Chapter 53.

- **SMTP**—The Simple Mail Transfer Protocol is the protocol that gets your email from here to there. Chapter 27, "Internet Mail Protocols: POP3, SMTP, and IMAP," can give you more information about how this protocol functions, along with other email protocols.

The Internet Protocol (IP)

Although the Internet protocol is the second component of the TCP/IP acronym, it is perhaps the more important of the two. IP is the basic protocol in the suite that provides the information used for getting packets from one place to another. IP provides a connectionless, unacknowledged network service, and also provides the addressing mechanism used by TCP/IP. The following main features distinguish IP from other protocols:

- IP is a connectionless protocol. No setup is required for IP to send a packet of information to another computer. Each IP packet is a complete entity and, as far as the network is concerned, has no relation with any other IP packet that traverses the network.

- IP is an unacknowledged protocol. IP doesn't check to see that a datagram or packet actually arrives intact at its destination. However, the Internet Control Message Protocol does assist IP so that some conditions can be corrected. For example, although IP doesn't receive an acknowledgment from the destination of an IP packet, it will receive ICMP messages telling it to slow down if it is sending packets faster than the destination can process them.

- IP is unreliable. This is easy to see based on the first two items in this list. IP lacks a mechanism for determining whether packets are delivered, and thus packets can be dropped by routers or other network devices. This can happen, for example, when the network traffic exceeds the bandwidth that a network device can handle.

- IP provides the address space for TCP/IP. This is perhaps the most important feature of the IP protocol. The hierarchical nature of IP addressing is what makes it possible to connect millions of computers on the Internet without requiring each computer to know all the addresses on the network.

IP Is a Connectionless Transport Protocol

IP is connectionless—each packet is separate from the others. From the IP standpoint, each packet is unrelated to any other packet. IP does not contact the destination computer or network device and set up a route that will be used to send a stream of data. Instead, it just accepts data from a higher-level protocol, such as TCP or UDP, formats a package that contains addressing information, and sends the packet on its way using the underlying physical network architecture. The information found in the IP datagram header is used on a hop-by-hop basis to route the datagram to its destination. When a higher-level protocol uses IP to deliver a series of information packets, there is no guarantee that each packet created by the IP layer will take the same route to get to the eventual destination. It is quite possible for a series of packets created by a higher-level protocol to reach the destination in a sequence out of order from how they were transmitted. IP doesn't even care whether packets arrive at their destination. That function is left to the protocol that uses IP for delivery. This doesn't mean that IP is a useless protocol, however—it just means that the higher-level protocols (such as TCP) that use IP need to provide for some kind of error checking, packet sequencing, and acknowledgment. You'll learn more about this subject in the section "The Transmission Control Protocol (TCP)," later in the chapter, when we talk about how TCP sets up a connection and acknowledges sent and received packets.

IP Is an Unacknowledged Protocol

IP does not check to see whether the datagrams it sends out ever make it to their destination. It just formats the information into a packet and sends it out on the wire. Thus, it is considered to be an unacknowledged protocol. The overhead involved in acknowledging receipt of a datagram can be significant. Leaving out an acknowledgment mechanism enables IP to be used by other protocols and applications that do not require this functionality, and thus eliminates the overhead associated with acknowledgments. Applications and protocols that do need to know that a datagram has been successfully delivered will not use the IP protocol. Instead, they can implement the acknowledgment mechanism found in the TCP protocol.

One way of thinking about this relationship between IP and upper-level protocols is to consider how the postal service works. If you send a letter through the mail, you have no way to know when—or even whether—the letter was correctly delivered. Unless you pay the extra money to get a signed receipt of delivery returned to you, you can't be sure that the letter ever reached its destination.

IP Is an Unreliable Protocol

Because IP is connectionless and because it does not check to see whether packets arrive at their destination, and because packets may arrive out of order, IP is considered an unreliable protocol. Or, to put it another way, it's a best-effort delivery service. IP doesn't perform routing functions (that task is left up to routers and routing protocols), and IP can't guarantee what route a datagram will take through the network. Another reason it is considered unreliable is that IP implements a Time to Live (TTL) value that limits the number of network routers or host computers through which a datagram can travel. When this limit is reached, the datagram is simply discarded. Because no acknowledgment mechanism is built into IP, it is unaware of this kind of situation. The reason for this is to solve problems associated with routing. For example, it's quite possible for an administrator to configure a router incorrectly, causing an endless loop to be created in a network. If it were not for the TTL value, the packet could continue to pass from one router to another, and another, forever. The TTL value is used mainly to prevent just this type of situation from occurring.

IP Provides the Address Space for the Network

Addressing is one of the most important functions implemented in the IP layer. In earlier chapters you learned that network adapter cards use a burned-in address, usually called a Media Access Control (MAC) address. These addresses are determined by the manufacturer of the network card, and the address space created is considered to be a "flat" address space. That is, there is no organization provided by MAC addresses that can be used to efficiently route datagrams from one system or network to another. On an Ethernet card, for example, a MAC address is composed of two parts. The first part of the MAC address identifies the manufacturer of the network card. The remaining octets (or bytes) are assigned, usually in a serial fashion, to the cards the manufacturer produces. The MAC address assigned to each adapter is unique and is made up of a 6-byte address (48 bits), which is usually expressed in hexadecimal notation to make it easier to write. For example, 00-80-C8-EA-AA-7E is much easier to write than trying to express the same address in binary, which would be a string of zeros and ones 48 bits long (in this example, 0000000010000000110010001110101010101001110011).

IP addresses are also made up of two components: a *network* address and a *host* address. By allowing a network address, it is possible to create a hierarchy that allows for an efficient routing mechanism when sending data to other networks. Whereas a particular network might consist of systems that have network adapters from multiple vendors, and thus have MAC addresses that are seemingly random numbers, IP addresses are organized into networks. Because of this, routers don't have to keep hundreds of millions of MAC addresses in a memory cache to deliver datagrams. Instead, they just need a table of addresses that tells them how to best route a datagram to the network on which the host system resides.

Just What Does IP Do?

IP takes the data from the Host-to-Host layer (as shown earlier in Figure 25.1) and fragments the data into smaller packets (or datagrams) that can be transferred through the network. On the receiving end, IP then reassembles these packets and passes them up the protocol stack to the higher-level protocol that is using IP. To get each packet delivered, IP places the source and destination IP addresses into the packet headers. IP also performs a checksum calculation on the header information to ensure its validity. Note, however, that IP does not perform this function on the data portion of the packet.

Note

The term *checksum* is used to refer to a mathematical calculation performed at the source and destination of a collection of bits to ensure that the information arrives uncorrupted. For example, the cyclic redundancy check (CRC) method, which is used by many network protocols, uses a polynomial calculation for this purpose. Some error detection methods work better than others. CRC not only can detect that an error has occurred during transmission, but can, to some degree, determine which bits are in error and fix the problem.

As already noted, TCP/IP allows for networks made up of different underlying technologies to interoperate. While one network might use the Ethernet 802 frame format, another might use FDDI. Each of these lower-level frames has its own particular header that contains information needed by that technology to send frames through the physical network media. At this lower level in the protocol stack, the IP packet rides in the data portion of the frame. After IP adds its header information to the message it receives from a higher-level protocol, and creates a packet of the appropriate size, it passes the packet to the Network Access layer, which wraps the IP packet into an Ethernet frame, for example. At the receiving end the Ethernet frame header information is stripped off, and the IP datagram is passed up the stack to be handled by the IP protocol. Similarly, the IP header information is stripped off by the higher-level protocols that use IP, such as TCP or UDP.

Examining IP Datagram Header Information

In Figure 25.3 you can see the format of an IP packet. In the IP header you will find the addressing information that is used by routers and other network devices to deliver the packet to its eventual destination.

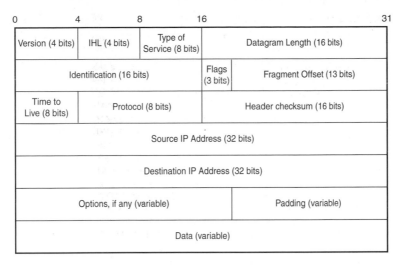

Figure 25.3   The IP header contains information concerning addressing and routing the packet.

These are the header fields of the IP packet:

- **Version**—IP comes in different versions. This 4-bit field is used to store the version of the packet. Currently, IP version 4 is the most widely used version of IP. The "next generation" IP is called IPv6, which stands for version 6. Because different versions of IP use different formats for header information, if the IP layer on the receiving end is a lower version than that found in this field, it will reject the packet. Because most versions of IP at this time are version 4, this is a rare event. Don't worry about this field until you upgrade your network to IPv6.

- **Internet Header Length (IHL)**—This 4-bit field contains the length of the *header* for the packet and can be used by the IP layer to calculate where in the packet the *data* actually starts. The numerical value found in this field is the number of 32-bit *words* in the header, not the number of bits or bytes in the header.

- **Type of Service**—This 8-bit field is intended to implement a prioritization of IP packets. Until recently, however, no major implementation of IP version 4 has used the bits in this field, so these bits are usually set to zeros. With Gigabit Ethernet and 10 Gigabit Ethernet, this is changing. Because these faster versions of Ethernet can compete with other protocols such as ATM, which do provide a type of service function, you can expect to see this field used in faster versions of Ethernet. IPv6 also provides mechanisms that allow this functionality.

- **Datagram Length**—This field is 16 bits long and is used to specify the length of the entire packet. It contains the number of 8-bit octets (or bytes). The largest value that can be stored in 16 bits is 65,535 bytes. Subtracting the IHL field from this value, IP will yield the length of the *data* portion of the packet.

- **Identification**—IP often must break a message it receives from a higher-level protocol into smaller packets, depending on the maximum size of the frame supported by the underlying network technology. On the receiving end, these packets need to be reassembled. The sending computer places a unique number for each message fragment into this field, and each packet for a particular message will have the same value in this 16-bit field. Thus, the receiving computer can take all the parts and re-create the original message.

- **Flags**—This field contains several flag bits. Bit 0 is reserved and should always have a value of zero. Bit 1 is the *Don't Fragment* (DF) field (0 = fragmentation is allowed, 1 = fragmentation is not allowed). If a computer finds that it needs to fragment a packet to send it through the next hop in the physical network, and this DF field is set to 1, then it will discard the packet (remember that IP is an unreliable protocol). If this field is set to 0, it will divide the packet into multiple packets so that they can be sent onward in their journey. Bit 2 is the *More Fragments* (MF) flag and is used to indicate the fragmentation status of the packet. If this bit is set to 1, there are more fragments to come. The last fragment of the original message that was fragmented will have a value of zero in this field. These two fields (Identification and Flags), along with the next field, control the fragmentation process.

- **Fragment Offset**—When the MF flag is set to 1 (the message was fragmented), this field is used to indicate the position of this fragment in the original message so that it can be reassembled correctly. This field is 13 bits in length and expresses the offset value of this fragment in units of 8 bytes.

- **Time to Live (TTL)**—Were it not for TTL, a packet could travel forever on the network because it is possible for loops to exist in the routing structure (due to an administrator's error, or the failure of a routing protocol to update routing tables in a timely manner). The TTL value is used to prevent these endless loops. Each time a packet passes through a router, the value in this field is decremented by at least one. The value is supposed to represent seconds, and in some cases in which a router is processing packets slowly, this field can be decremented by more than one. It all depends on the vendor's implementation. When the value of the TTL field reaches zero, the packet is discarded. Because IP is a best-effort, unreliable protocol, the higher-level protocol that is using IP must detect that the packet did not reach its destination and resend the packet.

- **Protocol**—This field is 8 bits long and is used to specify a number that represents the network protocol for the data contained in this packet. The Internet Corporation for Assigned Names and Numbers (ICANN) decides the numbers used in this field to identify specific protocols. For example, a value of 6 is used to specify the TCP protocol.

- **Header Checksum**—This 16-bit field contains a computed value used to ensure the integrity of the header information of the packet. When information in the header is changed, this value is recalculated. Because the TTL value is decremented by each system that a packet passes through, this value is recalculated at each hop as the packet travels through the network.

- **Source IP Address**—The IP address of the source of the packet. This is a 32-bit-long field. The format of IP addresses is discussed in greater detail later in this chapter.

- **Destination IP Address**—The IP address of the destination of the packet. This also is a 32-bit-long field.

- **Options**—This is an optional variable-length field that can contain a list of options. The option classes include control, reserved, debugging, and measurement. Source routing can be implemented using this field and is of particular importance when configuring a firewall. Table 25.1 lists the option classes and option numbers that can be found in this field.

- **Padding**—This field is used to pad the header so that it ends on a 32-bit boundary. The padding consists of zeros. Different machines and different operating systems work based on different sizes for bytes, words, quadwords (all of which are multiples of 8), and so on. Padding makes it easier to handle a known quantity of data (that is, to pad the header to a known length) than for the system to have to find some other method for determining where a data structure ends. For example, a router must operate quickly. It must perform calculations, look up information in the routing table, and so on. Extracting the header information from a packet can be implemented in hardware or software to make the router work faster by using known quantities of bits.

The Options Field and Source Routing

The Options field is optional. Source routing (which is discussed in Chapter 49, "Firewalls"), for example, can be implemented using this field. Although IP usually lets other protocols make routing decisions (that is, the path the packet takes through the network), in most cases it is possible to specify a list of devices for the route instead. As shown in Table 25.1, IP can use two options for routing purposes. These are *loose source routing* (option number 3) and *strict source routing* (option number 9).

Table 25.1   Option Classes and Option Numbers

Option Class	Option Number	Use
0	0	Indicates end of option list
0	1	No options
0	2	Security options for military use
0	3	Loose source routing
0	7	Activates routing records
0	9	Strict source routing
2	4	Timestamping active

Hackers can use source routing to force a packet to return to their computer, using a predefined route. Using source routing with TCP/IP should be discouraged. For more information, see Chapter 49.

Each of these techniques for source routing provides a list of addresses that the packet must pass through. Loose source routing uses this list but doesn't necessarily use it in all cases—other routes can be used to get to each machine addressed in the list. When strict source routing is used, however, the list must be followed exactly; if it cannot, the packet will be discarded.

IP Addressing

Although most people think of IP as the transport protocol used by higher-level protocols, one of its more important functions is to provide the address space used by the TCP/IP suite. Earlier in this chapter we discussed the difficulty of having to create a routing table that consists of hundreds of millions of actual hardware addresses, providing for no built-in organization capability.

IP addresses are used for just this purpose: to provide a hierarchical address space for networks. Each network adapter has a hard-coded network address that is 48 bits long. When data packets are sent out on the wire of the local area network (LAN) segment, this MAC address is used for the source and destination addresses that are embedded in the Ethernet frame, which encapsulates the actual IP packet. After an IP packet reaches the destination network, the router sends the packet out onto the network segment that contains the destination. The MAC address is used from there on to deliver the data. On a LAN segment, MAC addresses can be used efficiently because most LAN segments consist of just a few hundred or a few thousand host computers. This number of addresses can easily be stored in network devices, such as bridges or switches.

IP Addresses Make Routing Possible

Because the IP address is composed of two components, the network address and the host computer address, it is a simple matter to construct routers that use the network portion of the address to route packets to their destination networks. After the packet has arrived at a router on the destination network, the *host* portion of the address is used to locate the destination computer. Without the capability to designate a network address, as well as a host address, the hierarchical address space could not exist, and routing would require routing tables that literally would have to store every address of every computer or device on the network. In such a scenario the IP address would have no advantage over the MAC address. As it stands, IP gets a packet to the destination network by limiting routing tables to storing only network addresses allowing routing to be a simple and more efficient process.

IP addresses allow you to organize a collection of networks in a logical hierarchical fashion. There are three kinds of IP addresses:

- **Unicast**—This kind of address is the most common type of IP address. It uniquely identifies a single host on the network.

- **Broadcast**—Not to be confused with an Ethernet frame broadcast, IP also provides this capability by setting aside a set of addresses that can be used for broadcasting to send data to every host system on a particular network.

- **Multicast**—Similar to broadcast addresses, multicasting addresses send data to multiple destinations. The difference between a multicast address and a broadcast address is that a multicast address can send data to multiple networks to be received by hosts that are configured to receive the data instead of every host on the network.

Additionally, there are address classes, which are used mainly to define the size of the network and host portions of the IP address.

IP Address Classes

The Internet is a collection of networks that are all joined together by routers to create a larger network. The name itself says it all. The Internet Protocol (IP) makes this possible because it allows for addressing each network that is attached to the Internet, as well as identifying the host computers that reside on each network. When packets are routed through the Internet (or through a private corporate network that uses TCP/IP—an intranet), the IP address is used to get the data to the destination network. When the data packet is delivered to a router on the destination network, the actual hardware address (MAC address) of the computer is used to deliver the packet to the correct computer. This is done by taking the host portion of the IP address and consulting a table that maps hardware addresses to IP host addresses for the local network. If no match is found, the Address Resolution Protocol (ARP) is used on the local wire to find out the hardware address, and it is added to the table.

The important factor here is that it's possible to assign an address both to networks and to the individual hosts.

Note

IP Address classes were first defined in RFC 791. Although this class system has served its purpose for many years, routing on the Internet today actually is much more complicated than these simple address classes allow for. However, it is essential to understand address classes on a local LAN or a corporate network. For more information on how the IP address is used for routing purposes on the Internet, see Chapter 37, "Routing Protocols."

An IP address is 4 bytes long (32 bits). Whereas MAC addresses usually are expressed in hexadecimal notation, IP addresses usually are written using dotted-decimal notation. Each byte of the entire address is converted to its decimal representation, and then the 4 bytes of the address are separated by periods to make it easier to remember. As you can see in Table 25.2, the decimal values are much easier to remember than their binary equivalents.

Table 25.2   IP Addresses Are Expressed in Decimal Notation

Decimal Value	Binary Value
150	10010110
204	11001100
200	11001000
27	00011011

As you can see, it is much easier to write the address in dotted-decimal notation (150.204.200.27) than to use the binary equivalent (10010110110011001100100000011011).

Note

If you have problems converting between binary and decimal, or even hexadecimal and octal numbering systems, don't worry. There's a simple way to do this using the Windows Calculator accessory. When you bring up the calculator, select the View menu and then select Scientific. You'll get a larger display for the calculator that allows you to enter a number in any of the supported numbering systems. You can then simply click on another numbering base system to automatically convert the value you entered to the value you want to see in another numerical base system. If you don't use Windows, affordable calculators that will perform the same function are widely available. If all else fails, use a pencil and paper and think back to your high-school math class.

Because IP addresses are used to route a packet through a collection of separate networks, it is important to know what part of the IP address is used as the network address and what part is used for the host computer's address.

IP addresses are divided into three major classes (A, B, and C) and two less familiar ones (D and E). Each class uses a different portion of the IP address bits to identify the network. There is a need for classifying networks because there is a need to be able to create networks of different sizes. Whereas a small LAN might have only a few computers or a few hundred, larger networks can have thousands or more networked computers. The class system of IP addresses is accomplished by using a different number of bits of the total address to identify the network and host portions of the IP address. Additionally, the first few bits of the binary address are used to indicate which class an IP address belongs to.

The total number of bits available for addressing is always the same: 32 bits. Because the number of bits used to identify the network varies from one class to another, it should be obvious that the number of bits remaining to use for the host computer part of the address will vary from one class to another also. This means that some classes will have the capability to identify more networks than others. Conversely, some will have the capability to identify more computers on each network.

The first 4 bits of the address tell you what class an address is a member of. In Table 25.3, you can see the IP address classes along with the bit values for the first 4 bits. The bit positions that are marked with an "x" in this table indicate that this value makes no difference in the determination of IP address class.

Table 25.3   The First 4 Bits of the IP Address Determine the Class of the Address

Address Class	Bit Values
Class A	0xxx
Class B	10xx
Class C	110x
Class D	111x
Class E	1111

Class A Addresses

As shown in Table 25.3, any IP address that has a zero in the first bit position is a Class A address. The values for the remaining bits make no difference. Also, you can see that any address that has 10 for the first 2 bits of the address is a Class B address, and so on. Remember that these are bit values, and as such are expressed in binary. These are not the decimal values of the IP address when it is expressed in dotted-decimal notation.

Class A addresses range from all zeros (binary) to a binary value of 0 in the first position followed by seven 1 bits. Converting each byte of the address into decimal shows that Class A addresses range from 0.0.0.0 to 127.255.255.255, when expressed in the standard dotted-decimal notation.

Note

It is not possible to have an IP address expressed in dotted-decimal notation that exceeds 255 for any of the four values. The decimal value of a byte with all 1s (11111111) is 255. Take the address 140.176.123.256, for example. This address is not valid because the last byte is larger than 255 decimal. When planning how to distribute IP addresses for your network, keep this fact in mind. It is not possible to express a value larger than 255 in binary when using only 8 bits.

Keeping in mind that the class system for IP addresses uses a different number of bits for the network portion of the address, the Class A range of networks is the smallest. That is because Class A addresses use only the first byte of the address to identify the network. The rest of the address bits are used to identify a computer on a Class A network. Because the first bit of the first byte of the address is always zero, this leaves only 7 bits that can be used to create a network address. Because only 7 bits are available, there can be only 127 network addresses (binary 01111111 = 127 decimal) in a Class A network. It is not possible to have 128 network addresses in this class because, to express 128 in binary, the value would be 10000000, which would indicate a Class B address.

However, Class A networks can contain the largest number of host computers or devices on each network, because they use the remaining 3 bytes to create the host portion of the IP address. Three bytes can store a value, in decimal, of up to 16,777,215 (that's 24 bits all set to 1 in binary). Counting zero as a possibility (0–16,777,215), this means that a total of 16,777,216 (2 to the 24th power) addresses can be expressed using 3 bytes.

To summarize, there can be a total of 127 Class A networks, and each network can have up to 16,777,216 unique addresses for computers on the network. The range of addresses for Class A networks is from 0.0.0.0 to 127.255.255.255. When you see an address that falls in this range, you can be sure that it is a Class A address.

Class B Addresses

The first 2 bits of an IP address need to be examined to determine whether it is a Class B address. If the first 2 bits of the address are set to 10, the address belongs in this class. Class B addresses range from 1 followed by 31 zeros to 10 followed by 30 ones. If you convert this to the standard dotted-decimal notation, this is 128.0.0.0 to 191.255.255.255. In binary, the decimal value of 128 decimal is 10000000. The decimal value of 191 translates to 10111111 in binary. Both of these values in binary have 10 as the first two digits, which places them in the Class B IP address space.

Because the first 2 bytes of the Class B address are used to address the network, only 2 remaining bytes can be used for host computer addresses. If you do the calculations, you'll find that there can be up to 16,384 possible network addresses in this class, ranging from 128.0 to 191.255 in the first 2 bytes. There can be 65,536 (2 to the 16th power) individual computers on each Class B network.

You might wonder why the number of network addresses and the number of host addresses aren't the same in the Class B address range, because they both use 2 bytes. It's simple: Just remember that the network portion of the Class B address always has 1 for the first bit position and 0 for the second bit position. That zero in the second position is what keeps the number of network addresses less than the number of host computer addresses. In other words, the largest host address you can have in a Class B network, expressed in binary, is 10111111, which is 191 in decimal. Because there is no restriction on the value of the first two digits of the *host* portion of the address, it is possible to have the host portion set to all ones, giving a string of 16 ones, which would be 255.255 in dotted-decimal notation.

Class C Addresses

The Class C address range always has the first 3 bits set to 110. If you convert this to decimal, this means that a Class C network address can range from 192.0.0.0 to 223.255.255.255. In this class the first 3 bytes are used for the network part of the address, and only a single byte is left to create host addresses.

Again, doing the math (use that Windows calculator!), you can see that there can be up to 2,097,152 Class C networks. Each Class C network can have up to 256 host computers (0–255). This allows for a large number of Class C networks, each with only a small number of computers.

Other Address Classes

The first three address classes are those used for standard IP addresses. Class D and E addresses are used for different purposes. The Class D address range is reserved for multicast group use. *Multicasting* is the process of sending a network packet to more than one host computer. The Class D address range, in decimal, is from 224.0.0.0 to 239.255.255.255. No specific bytes in a Class D address are used to identify the network or host portion of the address. This means that a total of 268,435,456 possible unique Class D addresses can be created.

Finally, Class E addresses can be identified by looking at the first 4 bits of the IP address. If you see four 1s at the start of the address (in binary), you can be sure you have a Class E address. This class ranges from 240.0.0.0 to 255.255.255.255, which is the maximum value you can specify in binary when using only 32 bits. Class E addresses are reserved for future use and are not normally seen on most networks that interconnect through the Internet.

Note

It became apparent during the early 1990s that the IPv4 address space would become exhausted a lot sooner than had been previously thought. Actually, this forecast has proved to be a little overstated. Network Address Translation (NAT) can be used with routers so that you can use any address space on your internal network, while the router that connects to the Internet is assigned one or more actual registered addresses. The router, using NAT, can manipulate IP addresses and ports to act as a proxy for clients on the internal network when they communicate with the outside world.

Request For Comments 1918, "Address Allocation for Private Internets," discusses using several IP address ranges for private networks that do not need to directly communicate on the Internet. These are the ranges:

```
10.0.0.0 to 10.255.255.255
172.16.0.0 to 172.31.255.255
192.168.0.0 to 192.168.255.255
```

Because these addresses now are *not* valid on the Internet, they can be used by more than one private network. To connect the private network to the Internet, you can use one or more proxy servers that use NAT. If you have a DSL or cable modem and want to use the broadband connection for more than one computer, you can purchase an inexpensive router (around $100, less with rebates) to perform this very function. See Chapter 49 for more about how this is done. Windows operating systems (2000, Millennium, and XP) also use the 192.168.0.0 address space when computers are configured to get addressing information from a DHCP server and no DHCP server is present. This procedure is known as Automatic Private IP Addressing (APIPA). You can learn more about how APIPA works by reading Chapter 29.

Up to this point we have identified the possible ranges that could be used to create IP addresses in the various IP address classes. There are, however, some exceptions that should be noted. As previously discussed, an address used to uniquely identify a computer on the Internet is known as a unicast address.

Several exceptions take away from the total number of addresses that are possible in any of the address classes. For example, any address that begins with 127 for the first byte is not a valid address outside the local host computer. The address 127.0.0.1 (which falls in the Class A address range) is commonly called a *loopback* address and is normally used for testing the local TCP/IP stack to determine whether it is configured and functioning correctly. If you use the ping command, for example, with this address, the packet never actually leaves the local network adapter to be transmitted on the network. The packet simply travels down through the protocol stack and back up again to verify that the local computer is properly configured.

You can use this address to test other programs. For example, you can Telnet to the loopback address to find out whether the Telnet program is working on your computer. This assumes that you have a Telnet server running on the computer.

Other exceptions include the values of 0 and 255. When used in the network portion of an address, zeros imply the current network. For example, the address 140.176.0 is the address of a Class B network, and the value of 193.120.111.0 is the address of a Class C address.

The number 255 is used in an address to specify a broadcast message. A broadcast message is sent out only once but doesn't address a single host as the destination. Instead, such a packet can be received by more than one host, hence the name "broadcast." Broadcasts can be used to send a packet to all computers on a particular network or subnet. The address 140.176.255.255 would be received by all hosts in the network defined by 140.176.0.

After subtracting these special cases, you can see in Table 25.4 the actual number of addresses for Classes A through C that are available for network addressing purposes.

Table 25.4   IP Addresses Available for Use

Class	Number of Networks	Number of Hosts
A	126	16,777,214
B	16,384	65,534
C	2,097,152	254

There is another exception to usable addresses that fall within the IP address space. This is not dictated by an RFC or enforced by TCP/IP software. Instead, it is a *convention* followed by many network administrators to make it easy to identify routers. Typically you will find that an IP address that has as its last octet the value of 254 is a router. When you stick to this convention, it is easy to remember the default gateway when you are setting up a computer. It's the computer's address, with 254 used as the last octet.

Subnetting Made Simple!

The IP address space, although large, is still limited when you think of the number of networked computers on the Internet today. For a business entity (or an Internet service provider) to create more than one network, it would appear that more than one range of addresses would be needed. A method of addressing called subnetting was devised that allows a single contiguous address space to be further divided into smaller units called *subnets*. If you take a Class B address, for example, you can have as many as 65,534 host computers on one network. That's a lot of host computers! There aren't many companies or other entities in the world today that need to have that many hosts on a single network.

Subnetting is a technique that can be used to divide a larger address space into several smaller networks called subnets. So far, you've learned about using part of the IP address to identify the network and using part of the address to identify a host computer. By applying what is called a subnet mask, it is possible to "borrow" bits from the host portion of the IP address and create subnets.

A subnet mask is also a 32-bit binary value, just like an IP address. However, it's not an address, but instead is a string of bits used to identify which part of the total IP address is to be used to identify the network and the subnet.

The subnet mask is expressed in dotted-decimal format just like an IP address. Its purpose is to "mask out" the portion of the IP address that specifies the network and subnet parts of the address.

Note

The technique of using subnetting was first discussed in RFC 950, "Internet Standard Subnetting Procedure."

Because subnet masks are now required for all IP addresses, the A, B, and C address classes that were just described all have a specific mask associated with them. The Class A address mask is 255.0.0.0. When expressed as a binary value, 255 is equal to a string of eight 1s. Thus, 255.0.0.0 would be 11111111000000000000000000000000. Using Boolean logic, this binary subnet mask can be used with the AND operator to *mask out* (or identify) the network and subnet portion of the IP address. Using the AND operator, the TRUE result will be obtained only when both arguments are TRUE.

If you use the number 1 to represent TRUE and use 0 to represent FALSE, it's easy for a computer or a router to apply the mask to the IP address to obtain the network portion of the address. Table 25.5 shows how the final values are obtained.

Table 25.5   Boolean Logic Is Used for the Subnet Mask

IP Address Value	Mask Value	Result
1	1	1
1	0	0
0	1	0
0	0	0

A Class A address, as you can see, will have a subnet mask of 255.0.0.0. The only portion of the IP address that is used with this mask to be the network address is those bits contained in the first byte (11111111 in binary). Similarly, a subnet mask for a Class B address would be 255.255.0.0 (1111111111111110000000000000000 in binary), and for a Class C address it would be 255.255.255.0 (a lot of ones!).

Because we've already set aside certain values at the beginning of an IP address to identify what class the address belongs to, what value can be gained by using subnet masks? Each subnet mask just discussed blocks out only the portion of the IP address that the particular class has already set aside to be used as a network address.

The value comes by using part of the host component of the IP address to create a longer network address that consists of the classful network address plus a subnet address. By modifying the subnet mask value, we can mask out additional bits that make up part of the host portion of the address, and thus we can break a large address space into smaller components.

To put it simply, subnetting becomes useful when you use it to take a network address space and further divide it into separate subnets.

Note

One of the benefits of subnetting is that, before the advent of switches, it allowed you to take a large address space and divide it using routers. A large number of computers on a single subnet would create a large amount of traffic in an Ethernet environment. In this kind of situation, you would eventually get to a point where the broadcast traffic on the segment would result in too many collisions and network performance would slow to a crawl. By taking a large address space and subnetting it into smaller broadcast domains, and connecting them using a router, you can increase network performance dramatically.

If you use a subnet mask of 255.255.255.128, for example, and convert it to binary, you can see that a Class C address can be divided into two subnets. In binary, the decimal value of 128 is 10000000. This means that a *single bit* is used to create two distinct subnets. If you were to use this mask with a network address of 192.113.255, you would end up with one subnet with host addresses ranging from 192.113.255.1 to 192.113.255.128 and a second subnet with host addresses ranging from 192.113.255.129 to 192.113.255.254. (In this example, addresses that end in all zeros or all ones are not shown because those addresses are special cases and are generally not allowed as host addresses—192.113.255.0, for example.)

To take subnetting one step further, let's use a mask of 255.255.255.192. If you take the decimal value of 192 and convert it to binary, you get 11000000. Applying this subnet mask to a Class C network address space yields four subnets. Each subnet using the remaining bits of the host address can have up to 62 host computers. The reason you have four subnets is that the first 2 bits of the last byte of the subnet mask are 11. Because the first 2 bits are ones, there are four possible subnet values you can express using these two digits (11 in binary equals 3—if you count zero, you have four values that can be expressed using 2 bits). When this mask is applied to a byte, there are only 6 bits remaining to be used for host addresses. Because you cannot use a host address of all ones or all zeros, this means that although the largest number you can store in 6 bits is 63, you must subtract 2 from this value. This leaves only 1–62 for host addresses on these subnets.

Note

If you don't want to go through the trouble of calculating subnet values yourself, you'll find a handy table on the inside front cover of this book. This discussion is intended to help you understand the mechanics working behind the scenes in routers and protocol stacks that make subnetting possible.

In Figure 25.4, you can see that the IP address now consists of three parts: the network address, the subnet address, and the host address.

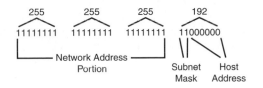

Figure 25.4 A subnet mask can be used to identify the network address, subnet address, and host portions of the IP address.

The first thing you should do when preparing to subnet an address space is decide how many host addresses will be needed on each subnet. Then convert this number to its binary value. Looking at the binary value, you can see how many bits you will need for the host portion of the address space. If you then subtract that value from the number of bits available (which is 8 if you're subnetting the last byte of a Class C address), you can calculate what the decimal equivalent would be for a binary number that contains that number of leftmost bits set to one.

Suppose you wanted to create subnets that would allow you to put up to 30 computers on each subnet. First, determine what 30 is when converted to binary: 11110. You can see that it takes 5 bits to represent the decimal value of 30 in binary. After you subtract this from 8, you have left only 3 bits that can be "borrowed" from the Class C host part of the address (8 – 5 = 3). In binary, this mask would be 11100000. If you convert this value to decimal, you get 224.

The next question to ask is how many subnets can you create using this mask? Because only 3 bits are left, just figure out the largest number you can express using 3 bits in binary. You'll come up with a value of all 1s (111), which translates to 7 in decimal. Therefore, you can have seven possible subnets, or eight if you include zero as a possibility.

After you've calculated what your subnet mask needs to be, you'll need to calculate what the actual host addresses must be for each subnet. The first subnet address would be 000. Because the IP address is expressed in dotted decimal notation, calculate how many addresses you can store in an 8-bit binary value that always begins with 000, and then translate that to decimal: 00000001 to 00011110, which is 1–30 in decimal.

Note

Remember that the addresses of 00000000 and 00011111 are not valid because they result in a host address of all zeros or all ones. If this mask were applied to a Class C network address of 192.113.255.0, hosts in the first subnet would range from 192.113.255.1 to 192.113.255.30.

Continuing the process, the *second* subnet address would be 001, and the third would be 011. The range of host addresses that could be created for a subnet value of 001 is 00100001 to 00111110, which is 33–62 in decimal.

The range of hosts on the second subnet would be from 192.113.255.33 to 192.113.255.62.

Simply continue this process and you'll be able to figure out the correct subnet addresses, based on the mask you've chosen.

It's possible to further divide the Class C address space by using up to 6 bits for the subnet mask, but this would leave only two usable host addresses and is not very practical. However, it can be done!

Note

In the examples given in this book for creating subnets, and in the charts you'll find on the inside front cover, subnets consisting of all zeros or all ones are included. In the original RFC on subnetting (RFC 950), these values were specifically excluded from use. However, when this is done, a large number of subnets, and thus host addresses, are excluded. RFC 1812 allows for the use of all zeros or all ones in the subnet mask. However, you should check to be sure that the routers on your network support this before using these subnet addresses. Older routers most likely will not support them. Newer ones probably will require that you configure them to operate one way or the other.

Classless Interdomain Routing Notation and Supernetting

As we discussed earlier in this chapter, the system of classifying IP addresses (A, B, C) worked well when the Internet was much smaller. The class system and subnetting is still widely used on local network routers. However, on the Internet backbone routers, a system called Classless Interdomain Routing (CIDR) is the method used to determine where to route a packet. This technique is also referred to as *supernetting*. CIDR can be considered a technique that uses a subnet mask that ignores the traditional IP class categories.

Why is CIDR needed? When the IP address class system was introduced, it was simple for routers to use the first byte of the IP address to figure out the network number, and thus make routing an easy task. For example, for an IP address of 140.176.232.333, the router would recognize that 140 falls in the Class B address range, so the network number would be 140.176.0. A quick glance at the routing table was all that was necessary to determine the next hop to which a packet should be routed to get to its network.

As the Internet continued to grow (or explode, as some might say), the huge number of Class B and Class C networks that were being added meant that routing tables on Internet backbone routers were also growing at a fast rate. Eventually, there would come a point where it would be impossible to efficiently route packets if routing tables continued to grow.

CIDR allows for address aggregation. That is, a single entry in a routing table can represent many lower-level network addresses.

Another reason why CIDR was needed is that much of the classful address space is wasted. This happens at both ends of the spectrum. Consider a small network at the low end, with a total of 254 usable addresses in a Class C address block. If the owner of that address space has a network with only 50 or 100 computers, that means that more than half of the available host addresses are essentially lost to the Internet. At the high end, a Class A network has a total of 16,777,216 possible host addresses. How many organizations need 16 million host addresses?

By dropping the address class constraints, and instead using a subnet mask to specify any number of contiguous bits of the IP address as the network address, it is possible to carve up the total 32-bit address space into finer blocks that can be allocated more efficiently.

Note

CIDR was widely implemented on the Internet beginning in 1994. For specific details about CIDR, see RFCs 1517, "Applicability Statement for the Implementation of CIDR"; 1518, "An Architecture for IP Address Allocation with CIDR"; 1519, "CIDR: An Address Assignment and Aggregation Strategy"; and 1520, "Exchanging Routing Information Across Provider Boundaries in the CIDR Environment."

CIDR uses a specific notation to indicate which part of the IP address is the network portion and which is the host portion. The CIDR notation syntax is the network address followed by /#, where # is a number indicating how many bits of the address represent the network address. This /# is commonly called the *network prefix*. Table 25.6 shows the network prefix values for A, B, and C network classes.

Table 25.6   CIDR Network Prefix Notation for A, B, and C IP Address Classes

Address Class	Binary Subnet Mask	Network Prefix
A	11111111 00000000 00000000 00000000	/8
B	11111111 11111111 00000000 00000000	/16
C	11111111 11111111 11111111 00000000	/24

However, because CIDR no longer recognizes classes, it's quite possible to have a network address like 140.176.123.0/24. Thus, while 140 would indicate that only 16 bits are used as the network portion of the address when using classful addressing, the /24 notation would specify that the first 24 bits are used, and the remaining 8 bits would be used for host addressing. Using the /24 notation allows the former class B address space to be allocated in smaller blocks than the class system allows.

In Table 25.7 you can see how this system allows for networks that range in size from 32 hosts to more than 500,000 hosts. The middle column shows the equivalent of a Class C network address space that the CIDR prefix creates, and the last column shows the number of hosts that would exist in the network.

Table 25.7   Use of CIDR Network Prefix Notations

CIDR Prefix	Class C Equivalent	Number of Hosts
/27	1/8 of a Class C	32
/26	1/4 of a Class C	64
/25	1/2 of a Class C	128
/24	1 Class C	256
/23	2 Class Cs	512
/22	4 Class Cs	1,024
/21	8 Class Cs	2,048
/20	16 Class Cs	4,096
/19	32 Class Cs	8,192
/18	64 Class Cs	16,384
/17	128 Class Cs	32,768
/16	256 Class Cs	65,536
/15	512 Class Cs	131,072
/14	1,024 Class Cs	262,144
/13	2,048 Class Cs	524,288

In Table 25.7, note that I've expressed the Class C equivalent networks that can be created. However, when using the /16 prefix, you get 256 Class C size networks, which is the same thing as a single Class B network. To continue this train of thought, a /15 prefix will allow you to create two Class B–sized networks, and so on.

Using CIDR, blocks of addresses can be allocated to ISPs that in turn subdivide the address space efficiently when they create address spaces for clients. One drawback is that a network that is composed completely of CIDR routing would require, in order to operate most efficiently, that addresses remain with the ISP under which a particular block is owned. This means that if your company decides to move to a different ISP, you would most likely have to obtain a new address block and therefore have to reconfigure your network addresses. If you use Network Address Translation and a private address space on your internal corporate network, this would be only a minimal problem.

Another problem with CIDR is that some host clients might not support it. That is, if the TCP/IP stack recognizes the different classes, it might not operate if you try to configure it using a subnet mask that does not match the traditional Class A, B, or C values. Again, because most routers do support this capability, you can solve this problem by using the CIDR addresses for your routers and using NAT and a private address space for the internal network.

Note

Because of the limited number of Class A networks, and because there are practically no business or governmental entities that require the large number of hosts that can be accommodated by that class, many of the original holders of those addresses have begun to return portions of their address range so that these addresses can be used for other networks. CIDR makes it possible to subdivide these large address spaces and distribute them in a more equitable fashion.

The Address Resolution Protocol—Resolving IP Addresses to Hardware Addresses

As just discussed, IP provides a logical hierarchical address space that makes routing data from one network to another a simple task. When the datagram arrives at the local subnet, however, another protocol comes into play. The Address Resolution Protocol (ARP) is used to resolve the IP address to the hardware, to the address of the workstation, or to another network device that is the target destination of the datagram. Whereas IP addresses are used to allow for routing between networks or network segments, ARP is used at the end of the road for the final delivery.

It is important to understand that when devices communicate directly on the local network segment (on the wire, so to speak), the actual address used to communicate between two devices, whether they are computers, routers, or whatever, is the built-in Media Access Control (MAC) address. In the case of two hosts on the same subnet, ARP can quickly resolve the correct address translations, and communications take place quickly and efficiently. When a router stands between two computers, the actual hardware address that the computer communicates with is the MAC address of the router, not of the computer that lies at the end of the connection. Using Ethernet as an example, when a datagram needs to be routed to another network or subnet, the computer sends the datagram to the default route, sometimes called the default gateway, which is the router that connects the network segment to the rest of the world (or the rest of the corporate network).

Note

In the context of a default route or default gateway, it is not always the case that the address sends the data to a dedicated "hardware" router. Many operating systems, from Unix to Windows 2000/Sever 2003, are quite capable of acting as routers as well as application platforms. A typical scenario is running firewall software on these computers. Even hardware routers implement part of their functionality in an operating system that is routinely updated.

The router then consults its routing tables and decides on the next device that the packet needs to get to on its way to its destination. Sometimes this is simply a computer that is connected on another segment that is also connected to the router. Sometimes it is several more routers that the packet must pass through. However, when the packet finally reaches the network segment on which the target computer is located, ARP is used by the router to find out the MAC address of the computer that is configured with the IP address found inside the packet.

To get this MAC address, a computer or router will first send out a broadcast message that every computer on the local segment can see. This ARP message contains the sending computer's own MAC address and also the IP address of the computer to which it wants to talk. When a computer recognizes its IP address in this broadcast packet, it sends a packet that contains its own MAC address back to the computer that originated the ARP message. After that, both computers know the MAC address of the other, and further transmissions take place using these hardware addresses.

The actual fields in the ARP broadcast frame are listed here:

- **Hardware Type**—This is a 2-byte field that identifies the kind of hardware used at the data-link layer of the sending computer. For diagnostic purposes, Table 25.8 contains a list of the most common hardware types.

- **Protocol Type**—This is a 2-byte field that specifies the protocol type of the address that the computer wants to translate to a hardware address.

- **Hardware Address Length**—This is a 1-byte field that specifies the length of the source and destination hardware address fields that will follow.

- **Protocol Address Length**—Similarly, this 1-byte field specifies the length of the source and destination protocol address fields that will follow in this packet.

- **Opcode**—This 1-byte field is used to determine the type of ARP frame. Frame types are listed in Table 25.9.

- **Sender Hardware Address**—This variable-length field (as defined by the Hardware Address Length field) contains the sending computer's hardware (MAC) address.

- **Sender Protocol Address**—This variable-length field (as defined by the Protocol Address Length field) contains the sender's protocol address—an IP address, for example.

- **Target Hardware Address**—This variable-length field (as defined by the Hardware Address Length field) contains the destination computer's hardware (MAC) address.

- **Target Protocol Address**—This variable-length field (as defined by the Protocol Address Length field) contains the protocol address that the sender wants to resolve to a hardware address.

Table 25.8　Hardware Type Field Values

Type Field Value	Data Link Layer Type
1	Ethernet (10MB)
2	Experimental Ethernet (3MB)
3	Amateur Radio AX.25
4	Proteon ProNET Token Ring
5	Chaos
6	IEEE 802 Networks
7	ARCnet
8	Hyperchannel
9	Lanstar
10	Autonet Short Address

Table 25.8   Continued

Type Field Value	Data Link Layer Type
11	LocalTalk
12	LocalNet (IBM PCNet or SYTEK LocalNET)
13	Ultra Link
14	SMDS
15	Frame Relay
16	Asynchronous Transmission Mode (ATM)
17	HDLC
18	Fibre Channel
19	Asynchronous Transmission Mode (ATM)
20	Serial Line
21	Asynchronous Transmission Mode (ATM)
22	MIL-STD-188-220
23	Metricom
24	IEEE 1394.1995
25	MAPOS
26	Twinaxial
27	EUI-64
28	HIPARP
29	IP and ARP over ISO 7816-3
30	ARPSec
31	IPsec Tunnel
32	Infiniband

As you can see from this table, the Address Resolution Protocol is not limited to just resolving IP addresses on a standard Ethernet network. It has been extended over time to accommodate many kinds of networking technologies. Some of the entries in Table 25.8 are dinosaurs—extinct protocols that no longer are being marketed. This list will probably continue to grow, however, as newer technologies are developed.

Table 25.9 shows that the Opcode field also has a large number of values, some of which might at first appear quite strange. For example, the MARS entries are not used for resolving addresses for strange spacecraft that appear in the sky now and then. They are used for address resolution on ATM networks where multicasting is being used.

◄◄ For more information about ATM, see Chapter 16, "Dedicated Connections." For more information about MARS, see RFC 2022, "Support for Multicast Over UNI 3.0/3.1 Based ATM Networks."

The InARP entries in Table 25.9 are used for Inverse ARP. This form of ARP is used when the underlying network technology is a nonbroadcast multiple access (NBMA) type, such as an X.25, ATM, or Frame Relay network. In these types of networks, a virtual circuit identifier is used instead of a hardware address. RFC 2390 contains the details about InARP and how it is used in a Frame Relay network to find out the IP address when only the virtual circuit identifier is known. Finally, you will also see entries in the table that correspond to Reverse ARP, which is discussed in the next section.

Table 25.9   Opcodes for ARP Frames

Opcode Value	Description
1	ARP Request
2	ARP Reply
3	Reverse ARP Request
4	Reverse ARP Reply
5	DRARP Request
6	DRARP Reply
7	DRARP Error
8	InARP Request
9	InARP Reply
10	ARP NAK
11	MARS Request
12	MARS Multi
13	MARS Mserv
14	MARS Join
15	MARS Leave
16	MARS NAK
17	MARS Unserv
18	MARS SJoin
19	MARS SLeave
20	MARS Grouplist Request
21	MARS Grouplist Reply
22	MARS Redirect Map
23	MAPOS UNARP

To prevent a storm of broadcast messages that would result if this were done for each packet that needed to be delivered on the local network segment, each host keeps a table, or cache, of MAC addresses in memory for a short time. When it becomes necessary to communicate with another computer, this ARP cache is first checked. If the destination address is not found in the ARP cache, the ARP broadcast method is used.

Note

Host and domain names (such as www.microsoft.com and www.twoinc.com) and IP addresses are used for the convenience of humans to make it easier to configure and manage a network in an orderly manner. At the lowest level, though, it is the hardware address that network cards use when they talk to each other. Imagine what the Internet would be like if we all had to memorize hardware addresses instead. Because the MAC address is simply a series of numbers that are "burned into" the network adapter when it is manufactured, it bears no relation to the actual *location* of a computer or other device in the network. Thus, to route messages throughout the Internet using only these hard-coded MAC addresses, it would be necessary for a router to keep an enormous table in memory that contained the MAC address for every other computer that exists on the Internet. An impossible task, of course!

Figure 25.5 demonstrates how IP addresses are used during the routing process, while hardware addresses are used for the actual device-to-device communications.

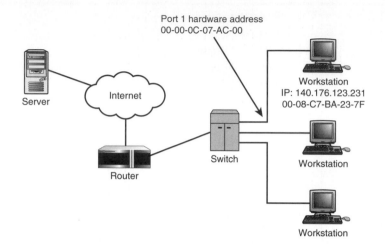

Figure 25.5   The IP address routes the datagram through the network, while the hardware addresses are used between individual workstations and devices on the network.

If the server in this figure wants to send a packet to the workstation with the IP address 140.176.123.231, it will quickly realize that this address is not on the local subnet and will send the IP packet, perhaps encapsulated in an Ethernet frame, to its default gateway. The gateway, which is connected to the Internet, uses the IP address to route the packet to the local router for the workstation. When the router receives the packet, it consults its routing tables and finds the switch (or hub) that is connected to the network segment by comparing the network portion of the IP address to entries in the routing table. When the packet finally arrives at the switch, the switch consults a table of MAC hardware addresses to look up the hardware address of the destination computer. From then on, communications between the workstation and the switch use these hardware addresses for actual communication.

In fact, every device, from the server shown later in Figure 25.6 to the router to the switch, and all the devices that lie in between on the Internet, uses the MAC address for communications. The IP address information is used by routers to deliver the packet to the next hop the packet must take to get to the final destination local segment. The MAC addresses are used for device-to-device communication. The ARP protocol is used to find out the hardware address at each hop, unless it's already stored in the ARP cache.

The arp command (which is found in both Unix and Windows NT, 2000, XP, and Server 2003 operating systems) lets you view the ARP table. It also can be used to add or delete entries in the table. Although the syntax varies between different systems, the following should work for most:

- **arp -a**—Displays the current contents of the arp table.
- **arp -d *IP_address***—Deletes the entry for the specified host.
- **arp -s *IP_address ethernet_address***—Adds an entry to the table.

Note

If you are using Unix or Linux, use the command **man arp** to find out the syntax for your machine. If using a Windows operating system, simply type **arp** at the command prompt with no command-line parameters and you'll see the syntax for that particular version of Windows.

For example, to add an entry use the following syntax:

```
arp -s 192.113.121.88    08-00-2b-34-c1-01
```

Using the few commands in this list will help you become more familiar with how ARP works. Examine the contents of your local table. Then, try pinging several other systems and examine the table again to see whether entries for those systems have been added to the table. Wait a few minutes and check the table again to see whether the entries have timed out.

Proxy ARP

Sometimes, different network segments both use the same network ID and are connected by a router or another device. Because ARP uses broadcast packets to resolve IP addresses to hardware addresses, it would appear that computers on different network segments that use the same network ID would never be able to communicate.

Proxy ARP allows for just such a situation. The router or other device that connects the physical network segments is configured to provide the proxy ARP service. When a host broadcasts an ARP packet to learn the hardware address of a device that is on a different physical segment, the ARP proxy device recognizes this situation and acts as a go-between. The proxy device responds to the ARP broadcast and sends the originating computer a datagram that contains the proxy device's IP address instead of the actual target computer's IP address. From that point on, the host that originated the ARP request will communicate with the host on the other segment by sending packets to the proxy device, which will know to forward them to the computer on the other subnet.

Another use of proxy ARP comes into play for remote access servers. For example, when users dial into a computer that is acting as a remote access server, they are communicating with software on the remote access server and are not actually physically connected to the subnet. The remote access server recognizes this and will intercept any ARP broadcast packets that are trying to resolve the dial-in computer's IP address. Communications then take place between the host on the local subnet and the remote computer through the remote access server. The host on the local subnet sends unicast packets to the remote access server, which forwards them to the remote client.

Yet another use for proxy ARP is to support older systems that use a TCP/IP stack that doesn't understand subnetting or those that use the older method for broadcast packets—a host address of all zeros instead of the current standard of all ones. Although this is not really much of a problem today, you might still find older legacy systems that cannot be abandoned, yet they cannot properly interact with newer systems when you subnet your network. The solution for this is to place the older systems on a separate network segment and let the proxy ARP device take care of resolving protocol addresses.

RARP—The Reverse Address Resolution Protocol

The Reverse Address Resolution Protocol (RARP) does just what it sounds like it would do. It performs the opposite function of ARP. It is most commonly used by diskless workstations that need to discover what their IP address is when they boot. Because the diskless workstation already knows its hardware address (because the address is burned into the network card), the workstation uses RARP to send a broadcast packet requesting that a server respond to its request by sending it an ARP frame containing an IP address it can use.

Note that the same packet format is used for ARP and RARP. The Opcode field is used to indicate what kind of operation is being performed.

The Transmission Control Protocol (TCP)

As we have discussed so far, the IP protocol is a protocol that can be used to make a best-effort attempt to get a packet from one host to another, even when the hosts are on different networks. The Transmission Control Protocol uses IP but adds functionality that makes TCP a *reliable*, connection-oriented protocol. Whereas IP doesn't require any acknowledgment that a packet is ever received, TCP does. Whereas IP does no preliminary communication with the target system to set up any kind of session, TCP does. TCP builds on the functions that IP provides to create a session that can be used by applications for a reliable exchange of data. As stated earlier in this chapter, IP is similar to sending a letter in the mail. TCP can be compared to the "return receipt requested" function which acknowledges that the letter was received by someone at the destination address. One interesting difference, however, is that TCP doesn't necessarily need an acknowledgment for each packet sent. Instead, it is possible for a single acknowledgment to be sent in response to more than one IP packet.

TCP Provides a Reliable Connection-Oriented Session

Whereas IP provides a checksum mechanism in its header to ensure that the IP header is not corrupted during transit, the TCP protocol provides checksums on the data that is transmitted. TCP also has mechanisms that regulate the flow of data to avoid problems associated with congestion. TCP also uses sequence numbers in the TCP header so that IP packets can be reassembled in the correct order on the receiving end of the communication.

Examining TCP Header Information

Each layer in the TCP/IP protocol stack adds information to the data it receives from a layer above it. This process is usually called *encapsulation*, and the added data is usually called a *header*. The header information is significant only to the layer that adds it, and it is added as a message is passed down the stack and stripped off at the destination as the packet is passed back up the protocol stack. Some layers also add data at the end of the packet. This is called a *trailer*.

Earlier we looked at the makeup of the IP header. In Figure 25.6 you can see the layout of the TCP header. This header information is sometimes referred to as the *TCP Protocol Data Unit*.

Remember that TCP is responsible for establishing a reliable connection-oriented session between two applications across a network. TCP receives data (called messages) from layers above it in the protocol stack, adds its own header information, and then passes it to the IP layer, which then adds its own header information. The messages sent to TCP from applications up the stack are usually called a *stream* of data, because the amount of data can vary and is not limited to a set number of bytes. TCP takes these messages and, if they are too large to fit into a packet, breaks them into smaller segments and sends each segment in a separate packet. The TCP layer at the receiving end reassembles these messages before passing them up to an application.

Note

Don't confuse the fact that TCP can break up large messages into smaller units before it passes them to IP with the process of IP fragmentation. These are *not* the same thing. TCP processes messages from applications that use it and breaks up these messages into an appropriate size for the IP layer. The IP layer, on the local computer or on another device that is in the path the packet takes to reach its destination, can further fragment the IP packets. At the end, the IP packets are reassembled before being given to the TCP layer, which then reassembles any messages it might have chopped up before passing them up to the application.

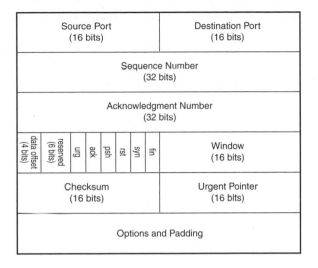

Figure 25.6 The TCP protocol header fields also can be used for filtering packets.

Whereas most of the header information we looked at in the IP header was used for routing the packet through the Internet, the information in the TCP header is concerned with other issues, such as reliability of the connection and ordering of the messages being sent. The header fields for TCP include these:

- **Source port**—This 16-bit field is used to identify the port being used by the application that is sending the data. Ports are discussed in more detail later in this chapter.

- **Destination port**—This 16-bit field is used to identify the port to which the packet will be delivered on the receiving end of the connection.

- **Sequence number**—This 32-bit field is used to identify where a segment fits in the larger message when a message is broken into fragments for transmission.

- **Acknowledgment number**—This 32-bit field is used to indicate what the next sequence number should be. That is, this value is the next byte in the data stream that the receiver expects to receive from the sender.

- **Data offset**—This 4-bit field is used to specify the number of 32-bit words that make up the header. This field is used to calculate the start of the data portion of the packet.

- **Reserved**—These 6 bits were reserved for future use and, because they were never generally used, are supposed to be set to zeros.

- **URG flag**—When this bit is set to 1, the field titled Urgent Pointer will point to a section of the data portion of the packet that is flagged as "urgent."

- **ACK flag**—This is the acknowledgment bit. If it's set to 1, the packet is an acknowledgment. If it's set to 0, the packet is not an acknowledgment.

- **PSH flag**—If this bit is set to 1, it indicates a push function; otherwise, it is set to 0.

- **RST flag**—If this bit is set to 1, it is a signal that the connection is to be reset; otherwise, it is set to 0.

- **SYN flag**—If this bit is set to 1, it indicates that the sequence numbers are to be synchronized. If it's set to 0, the sequence numbers are not to be synchronized.

- **FIN flag**—If this bit is set to 1, it specifies that the sender is finished sending information; otherwise, it is set to 0.

- **Window**—This 16-bit field is used to specify how many blocks of data the receiving computer is able to accept at this time.

- **Checksum**—This 16-bit field is a calculated value used to verify the integrity of both the header and the data portions of the packet.

- **Urgent pointer**—If the URG flag is set, this 16-bit field points to the offset from the sequence number field into the data portion of the packet where the urgent data is stored. TCP does not use this field itself, but applications above TCP in the stack might do so.

- **Options**—This field can be of variable length and is similar to the Options field in the IP header. One function this field is used for is to specify the maximum segment size.

Because the Options field can vary, the header is padded with extra bits so that it will be a multiple of 32 bits.

The amount of information stored in the TCP header makes it possible to use the protocol for complex communications. TCP can implement error checking, flow control, and other necessary mechanisms to ensure reliable delivery of data throughout the network. However, because of the complexity of this header, hackers can use many different methods to manipulate the TCP protocol when trying to gain access to your network or otherwise cause you problems.

One interesting thing to note about the checksum field is that it is calculated based on three things:

- The TCP header fields
- The TCP data
- Pseudo header information

The pseudo header information consists of the source and destination IP addresses, one byte set to all zeros, an 8-bit protocol field, and a 16-bit field that contains the length of the TCP segment. The address and protocol fields are duplicated from the IP packet, and the length field is redundant because it also is contained in the TCP header. Because the algorithm used to calculate the checksum is based on 16-bit words, the TCP packet may be padded with a zero byte for calculation purposes only. If the checksum field contains a value of zero, this indicates that no checksum was calculated by the sender. If by some chance the value of the checksum results in a value of zero, the checksum field is set to all 1s (65,535 decimal).

TCP Sessions

Because TCP is a connection-oriented protocol, the computers that want to communicate must first establish the conditions that will govern the session and set up the connection. TCP allows for two-way communication—that is, it's a bidirectional, full-duplex connection. Both sides can send and receive data at the same time. To set up a connection, each side must "open" its side of the connection. On the server side this is called a *passive open*. The server application runs as a process on the server computer and listens for connection requests coming in for a certain port. For example, the Telnet server process typically listens for connections on port 23. By using both the IP address and a port number, the server process can uniquely identify each client that makes a connection request. Ports are discussed in more detail later in this chapter.

When a client computer wants to establish a connection to a server, it goes through a process known as an *active open*. The server is already listening for connection requests (passive open), but the client must initiate the actual connection process by sending a request to the port number of the server application it wants to use.

In Figure 25.7 (shown in the next section), the single-bit field named SYN is the "synchronization" bit. You also can see in Figure 25.7 another field titled ACK, for the acknowledgment bit. These 2 bits are very important and are used during the process of setting up a TCP/IP session so that a reliable connection can be established between two computers on the network.

Setting Up a TCP Session

A TCP/IP connection is made between two computers, using their addresses and, depending on the application using TCP, port numbers. The SYN and ACK bits in the TCP header are important components used to establish this initial connection.

The steps involved in setting up a TCP/IP connection appear in Figure 25.7 and are listed here:

1. The client sends a TCP segment to the server with which it wants to establish a connection. The TCP header SYN field ("synchronize") is set indicating that it wants to synchronize sequence numbers so that further exchanges can be identified as belonging to this particular connection and so that the segments sent can be reassembled into the correct order and acknowledged. This first initial sequence number in the TCP header is set to an initial value chosen by the TCP software on the client computer. Additionally, the port-number field in the TCP header is set to a value of the port on the server to which the client wants to connect. Port numbers can be thought of as representing the application to which the computer wants to connect.

2. When the server receives this segment, it returns a segment to the client with the SYN field set. The server's segment also contains an initial sequence number, which is chosen by its TCP software implementation. To show the client that it received the initial connection segment, the ACK bit is also set, and the acknowledgment field contains the *client's* initial sequence number, incremented by 1.

3. The client, upon receiving this acknowledgment from the server, sends another segment to the server, acknowledging the server's initial sequence number. This is done in the same manner in which the server acknowledges the client's initial sequence number. The acknowledgment field contains the server's initial sequence number incremented by a value of 1.

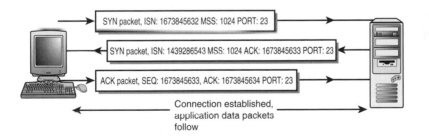

SYN packet, ISN: 1673845632 MSS: 1024 PORT: 23

SYN packet, ISN: 1439286543 MSS: 1024 ACK: 1673845633 PORT: 23

ACK packet, SEQ: 1673845633, ACK: 1673845634 PORT: 23

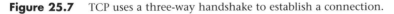

Connection established, application data packets follow

Figure 25.7 TCP uses a three-way handshake to establish a connection.

During this exchange, the 16-bit acknowledgment field is incremented by 1. You might wonder why the acknowledging computer doesn't just send back the same sequence number it received from the sending computer. It increments the sequence number that it received to indicate the next sequence number it expects to receive from the sending computer. Thus, during each exchange of TCP segments, each side is telling the other side what it is expecting to get from the other side during the next transmission. The sequence numbers are used to indicate the next byte in the data stream that the receiving end of the connection expects to receive. Thus, when the actual data exchange begins to take place, the sequence numbers are not simply incremented by a value of 1, but instead they are set to the actual number of bytes received (offset from the initial sequence number chosen for the connection) plus 1.

Because three segments are used in this process, the connection setup is often referred to as a *three-way handshake*. In the last of these three steps the SYN bit is not set, because the segment is simply acknowledging the server's initial sequence number. Note also that port numbers are used to indicate the application for which the connection is being set up. TCP headers don't need to contain the source and destination IP addresses because that information is already stored in the IP datagram that encapsulates the TCP message.

The method used to choose values for the initial sequence number can vary from one implementation of TCP to another. However, there are two important points to understand about the sequence numbers:

1. For each connection a client makes to another computer, the initial sequence number for each connection must be unique. If the same initial sequence number were used for every connection the client made to a single server, it would be impossible to differentiate between different connections of the same application (that is, port number) between the two machines. Although the IP address and port number can uniquely identify a computer, they can't uniquely identify multiple applications of the same process running on the same computer.

2. Sequence numbers are incremented for each segment exchanged and are acknowledged by the receiver so that both sides can determine that segments are being delivered reliably and not getting lost in the network. However, it is not necessary that each and every segment be acknowledged with another segment. Using a technique called *sliding windows* (which we'll get to in a moment), TCP allows for a single acknowledgment of a number of segments.

In Figure 25.7 another field is also shown in the first two packets that are exchanged. The Maximum Segment Size (MSS) field in the TCP header indicates the maximum number of bytes of data that the sender wants to receive in each TCP segment. This value is used to help prevent fragmentation of the TCP segment as it travels through various network devices that might have different transmission frame sizes. This value applies only to the size of the data that the TCP segment carries, and does not include the bytes that make up the TCP and IP headers. You will see this field only during the connection setup. After the application data exchange begins, this field is not used. If the client or server does not put a value into this field during the connection setup, a default value, usually 536, is used.

Not shown in this figure is the TCP field that stores the window size. This field is used to help manage the connection after the application data exchange begins.

Managing the Session Connection

After a TCP session has been established between two computers, the application that uses TCP can begin to communicate with its counterpart on the other computer. TCP receives a stream of bytes (called a *message*) from an application and stores them in a buffer. When the buffer is full, or when the application indicates that it wants TCP to send the message to the destination computer, the bytes are assembled into a TCP segment with the necessary TCP header information, and the segment is passed to IP for transmission on the network.

Note

Although it is more efficient to send a large number of data bytes in a single TCP segment, some applications do not work well in this manner. For example, when Telnet is used, each keystroke the user enters must be sent to the remote Telnet server, acknowledged, and echoed back to the sender. This means that a TCP segment, and thus an IP datagram, can actually be sent for every single keystroke! When you consider the overhead involved in sending each datagram, this is a waste of valuable bandwidth. To help solve this problem, the Nagle Algorithm (as described in RFC 896) allows for small amounts of data (that is, single keystrokes) to accumulate in a buffer and not be sent until an acknowledgment is received for data previously sent. This means that, in practice, multiple keystrokes can be sent in a single packet instead of having to use a separate packet for each one. Because the speed (or bandwidth) of networks is increasing every year, the delay of buffering a few characters is usually unnoticeable by the user of the application.

Each transmission was acknowledged during the initial connection setup. This is not always the case when the actual exchange of data begins between two computers. Instead, there are several important mechanisms that TCP uses to manage a connection after it has been established. These include

- TCP timers
- Sliding windows
- Retransmissions

When a segment is passed to the IP layer for transmission, a timer is set and a countdown starts. When this retransmission timer reaches zero with no acknowledgment, the sending computer assumes that the segment did not make it to its destination and retransmits the segment. This function requires that TCP keep data in a memory buffer until it is acknowledged.

During the connection setup, each side of the connection indicates to the other side the maximum amount of data it can buffer in memory. This is the *window size*. This value indicates how many TCP segments the computer can receive before an acknowledgment is required. For example, on a Windows 2000 client the default value for this field when using Ethernet for transmission is 12 segments.

Note

Because many applications used on networks are interactive, often a connection will not be a continuous exchange of data. Instead, as users interact with the client application, there are times when no data exchange is performed. To ensure that the connection is still valid—that is, that both sides are still up and running—TCP uses a *keepalive* segment exchange to indicate that the connection is still being used. This segment consists of a TCP segment with the ACK bit set, but the segment contains no data. The sequence number field in the TCP header is set to a value of the current sequence number minus 1. The other end of the connection returns a segment that also has the ACK bit set, but in the acknowledgment number field the value is the next byte of data that the receiver expects from the sender. The *keepalive* timer is used to determine when a keepalive segment should be sent.

This keepalive function is not used by all TCP implementations. For example, in Windows 2000 it is disabled by default. However, an API (application programming interface) function can be used by programmers to activate this feature.

Another feature of TCP that helps to reduce the number of packets transmitted is the fact that the acknowledgment of received data does not have to travel in a packet separate from those that hold data. In other words, when sending data in a TCP segment to the remote computer, the sending computer also can use the ACK bit and the sequence number fields to acknowledge data that it has received from the remote computer. This is sometimes called a *piggyback* ACK because both data and an acknowledgment of data received travels in the same packet.

Having sliding windows also helps to reduce the number of packets transmitted by allowing a single acknowledgment to be sent for multiple segments. Instead of acknowledging every single segment that it receives, the receiver can send an acknowledgment that indicates the last byte received when it receives several contiguous segments in a short time. That is, the acknowledgment can be cumulative. Each end of the connection uses a send and receive buffer to store data received or waiting for transmission.

Remember that the application which uses TCP passes a stream of bytes to TCP or receives a stream of bytes from TCP, depending on the direction in which data is flowing at any particular point in time. The term *sliding window* refers to the fact that the receiving buffer can hold only so much data (the window size advertised by the receiving end). The amount of space available in the buffer can change over time, depending on the amount of time it takes for the application to accept the bytes from TCP and thus make more room in the buffer. The receiving end can use the window size TCP header field to tell the sender the number of bytes it can currently receive and store in its buffer. This window size is called the *offered window* size. That doesn't mean that the sender must send that amount of data, just that the receiver is ready to accept any number of data bytes, up to that size.

As you can see in Figure 25.8, the sender can calculate the amount of data it can send by comparing the window size offered, the bytes already sent and acknowledged, and the bytes that have been sent but not acknowledged. In this figure the window size offered by the receiver is 4 bytes. Because 2 bytes have already been sent and the window size is four, the sender can transmit 2 more bytes at this time. As bytes are acknowledged by the receiver, the left edge of the window slides toward the right, as shown in this figure. Depending on how well the receiving end of the connection is able to process incoming bytes, the offered window size can change, which in turn can affect the number of bytes that the sending end can transmit. As the buffer empties at the receiving end, a larger window size can be advertised and the right edge of the window slides toward the right.

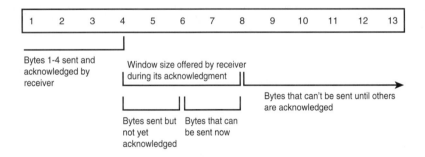

Figure 25.8   The window size advertised by the receiver of TCP segments determines which bytes in the data stream the sender can transmit.

It also is possible that the buffer at the receiving end becomes full, and the sender is sent a window size that is now zero. The sender will not send any more segments until the window size is offered again at a value greater than zero.

Using this scheme, there are several things to keep in mind. First, the sender does not have to send an amount of data that is equal to the size of the offered window. It can send less. Second, the receiver does not have to wait until it has received data in the amount of the offered window before it sends an acknowledgment. Third, the window size is controlled, under most circumstances, by the receiving end of the connection.

In this example we have used a transmission that consists of only a few bytes at a time. For most TCP communications the amount of data, and the window size, is much larger.

Sliding windows tell the sender when and how much data it can transmit. When a connection is initially established, a technique called *slow start* is used to govern the amount of data that is sent, allowing it to increase to a point that the particular network will tolerate. When a connection has been in use for some time, congestion can occur and it might be necessary to slow down the rate at which segments are transmitted, by using a technique called the *congestion avoidance algorithm*. These two methods work together to control the flow of data during the connection.

Slow start means that when the transmitting side of a connection first transmits data, it does so by observing how fast it receives acknowledgments of data from the receiving end. A variable in the TCP software keeps track of the *congestion window* (cwnd), which is initially set to one segment. For each segment that is acknowledged, the cwnd variable is incremented. Then, the sender is allowed to send an amount of data up to the value of cwnd or the size of the offered window, whichever is the lower value. As you can see, the faster the receiving end acknowledges segments, the larger the cwnd variable becomes, and thus the more segments that the sender will be able to transmit (up to the offered window size). The offered window size enables the receiving end to control the amount of data that can be sent. The congestion window gives the sending end of the transmission control over how much data can be transmitted. Thus, both sides work together to throttle up data transmissions, starting off slowly, until the receiver is unable to buffer data at a faster rate or until network congestion forces the connection to operate at a slower rate.

The term *slow start* isn't actually an accurate way to describe what happens. In reality, the receiving end might acknowledge several segments, thus increasing the size of cwnd by more than one when it sends a single acknowledgment to account for multiple segments. This means that, instead of being incremented by one for each acknowledgment, cwnd can be incremented at a much faster rate. However, this method does allow for TCP to "test the waters," so to speak, to determine the rate at which data can be sent, up to the receiving end's capacity to buffer data and pass it up to the application on its end of the connection.

As packets make their way through the network, however, another problem can arise. In today's world, communications often take place between computers that reside on different networks that are connected by routers, and we find that, just like the freeway system, congestion can occur when too many computers are trying to send and receive data at the same time. When a router or another network connection device becomes a bottleneck, it can simply drop IP packets—remember that IP is an unreliable protocol. It is up to TCP to realize what is happening and to compensate for it by retransmitting unacknowledged segments.

The retransmission timer that we discussed earlier is used by the transmitting end of the connection to determine when a segment should be retransmitted. This value is recalculated over time, depending on the round-trip time it takes for a transmission to make it to the receiving end and an acknowledgment to get back to the transmitting side of the connection. The round-trip time can change over time, depending on the amount of data flowing through the network. Round-trip time also can change when the routes chosen by routers change, thus sending packets through a different path in the network that can take more or less time than previous transmissions.

Note

It is beyond the scope of this book to get into all the details of the calculations used to determine the round-trip time and thus the value of the retransmission timer. For more information, the reader is encouraged to read the RFCs that pertain to TCP/IP. A quick search on the Internet will give you a large list of RFCs that can provide some great nighttime reading if you have a hard time going to sleep. As mentioned earlier in this chapter, a good source for RFCs is www. rfc-editor.org.

The *congestion avoidance algorithm* is used to take care of situations in which the network becomes congested and packets are dropped—that is, they are not being acknowledged by the receiver. Although this algorithm is separate from the slow start technique, in practice they work together. In addition to the cwnd variable, another variable called the slow start threshold size (ssthresh) comes into play. This variable is initially set to 65,535 bytes when a connection is established. When congestion is detected, the value of this variable is set to half the currently offered window size, and the variable cwnd is set to the value of one maximum segment size (MSS)—though this can vary from one implementation to another. In recent Microsoft operating systems including Windows 2000 and Windows XP, cwnd is set to the value of two times the MSS. The send window value then is set to the lower of the cwnd and the offered receive window size.

Based on which value is chosen, TCP segments are then sent. If the segments are acknowledged, cwnd is incremented. If the value of cwnd is lower than the value of ssthresh, a slow start is used. When the value of cwnd is equal to half the current offered window size from the receiving end of the transmission, congestion avoidance is used. Remember that the value of ssthresh can be used to determine this because it recorded the value of the offered window size (divided by two) that was in effect when congestion started.

During congestion avoidance, the value of cwnd is incremented by one cwnd for each acknowledgment received—again, this value might be different according to your particular TCP implementation. Thus, instead of a possible exponential increase that a slow start method would allow, congestion avoidance allows for a smaller increase in the value of cwnd. After all, if congestion is occurring, the last thing you want to do is quickly increase the rate of transmission. Instead, you want to throttle it up more slowly. So although slow start will increment cwnd by the number of segments acknowledged by a single acknowledgment, the congestion avoidance algorithm will increment cwnd by only one segment for each acknowledgment received, no matter how many segments are being acknowledged by the acknowledgment.

Other mechanisms are used for flow control in TCP, such as the fast recovery algorithm and the fast retransmit algorithm. Discussing these topics is beyond the scope of this book. The important thing to understand is that TCP does monitor and adjust its transmissions, from both sides of the connection, to try to get the maximum amount of data flowing without causing problems. It's a self-regulating protocol, you might say.

Ending a TCP Session

When the party's over—the application is finished sending data to another computer—it tells TCP to close the connection from its side. Because the connection must be closed from each end, this is called a half-close. To fully close a TCP connection, four steps are required, as opposed to the three-way handshake method used to set up the connection. Four steps are required because TCP operates as a full-duplex connection—that is, data can flow in both directions. Thus, each side needs to tell the other side of the connection that it has finished sending data and wants to close the connection.

For example, when the client application, such as Telnet, wants to close a connection, TCP sends a segment that has the FIN bit set in the TCP header to the remote computer. The remote computer must first acknowledge this FIN segment, and does so by sending a segment to the client that has the ACK bit set. Because the connection is full-duplex, the server TCP software informs the Telnet server application that the user application on the other end of the connection is finished. It then sends its own FIN segment to the client, which, as you can probably guess, sends an acknowledgment segment back to the server.

Although this is the general method used to close a TCP connection, another technique can be used in which one side sends a FIN segment, closing its data pipe, but the other side of the connection does not. Instead, it is possible for the other side to continue sending data until it is finished, at which time it sends the FIN segment and waits for an acknowledgment, which effectively closes the connection.

A good example of this method is the Unix rsh (remote shell) utility. This utility allows a user to execute a command on a remote server. Because Unix allows for the capability to redirect input (using the < operator), a user can use rsh to execute a command on a remote server, and use the < operator on the command line to redirect the input for the command from the command line to a file. In such a situation, the client's side of the connection sends the command to be executed to the remote server and then starts sending the data that is in the file. After the client's side of the connection finishes sending the data contained in the file to the remote server, it instructs TCP to close its side of the connection. Yet, at the other side of the connection, the data needs to be processed by the program invoked by the rsh command. When finished, the program on the remote server sends the data back to the client and then instructs TCP to close its side of the connection.

TCP Session Security Issues

Calling TCP a reliable protocol means that it uses an acknowledgment mechanism to ensure that the data is received at the remote computer intact. Reliable does not mean that TCP is a secure protocol. If that were so, there would be no need for firewalls! Although the connection setup and termination methods used to create a connection create a virtual circuit between the two computers, there are many ways to exploit TCP (and IP) to break into a computer. For example, every time a new connection is requested on a server (the receipt of a TCP segment with the SYN bit set), the computer sets aside data structures in memory to store information about the connection it is setting up. This requires a few CPU cycles and memory on the computer.

It should be obvious that an easy way to cause a "denial of service" attack against a computer is to simply send a large number of SYN segments to it in a short period. If the number of SYN segments and the rate at which they are sent exceed the capacity of the CPU or memory of the server, then, depending on the operating system and how the TCP/IP stack is implemented, the system might slow to a crawl or crash.

For more information about how the inner workings of TCP/IP and related protocols can be used maliciously, see Chapter 48, "Security Issues for Wide Area Networks." For information on how to protect yourself against these sorts of attacks, see Chapter 49.

The User Datagram Protocol (UDP)

Although TCP uses an acknowledgment mechanism to ensure that data is actually delivered to another computer, the User Datagram Protocol (UDP) does not. Both use IP as a transport protocol, but UDP is a much simpler protocol that doesn't require the overhead that TCP does. If an application does not need the benefits that a TCP connection provides, UDP can be used. Because UDP does no session setup, and all UDP datagrams are independent entities on the network, it can be considered an *unreliable*, *connectionless* protocol.

An example of this is the Domain Name Service (DNS). Most implementations of DNS use UDP packets in order to efficiently exchange information with other computers. If a client doesn't receive a response back from a simple DNS request, it can try again, or simply use another DNS server if it is configured to do so.

Examining UDP Header Information

Compared to the TCP header, the UPD header is much smaller because it doesn't require fields for sequence or acknowledgment numbers. UDP also doesn't need the connection setup flags, window size fields, and other information required for a connection-oriented protocol. In Figure 25.9 you can see that UDP has only four fields.

The following are the purposes of the UDP header fields:

- **Source port**—This 16-bit field is used to identify the port being used by the application that is sending the data.

- **Destination port**—This 16-bit field is used to identify the port to which the packet will be delivered on the receiving end of the connection.

■ **Length**—This 16-bit field is used to store the length of the entire UDP datagram, which includes both the header and data portions.

■ **Checksum**—This 16-bit field is used to ensure that the contents of the UDP datagram are not corrupted in transit.

Source Port (16 bits)	Destination Port (16 bits)
Length (16 bits)	Checksum (16 bits)

Figure 25.9   The UPD protocol uses a smaller header.

Although the length field in the UDP header can store a value of up to 65,535, in actual practice the size of a datagram is usually limited to a much smaller value. For example, the application programming interface (API) of a particular operating system might use smaller fields to specify the length of a datagram.

The checksum field is calculated on the UDP header information and its data, along with pseudo header information, just as is done with TCP. Using this method, UDP can determine whether the IP layer has passed to it a datagram that was not intended for this computer. If the checksum calculated on the receiving end does not match the value stored in this field, the UDP datagram is discarded. Similar to IP, no message is sent back to the sender of the datagram if this happens. For a reliable connection an application should use TCP, not UDP.

Note

The User Datagram Protocol is defined in RFC 768, "User Datagram Protocol."

Interaction Between UDP and ICMP

Whereas UDP has no built-in mechanisms for guaranteeing delivery of the information carried in its datagrams, the Internet Control Message Protocol (ICMP) is used to report conditions back to the sending computer. For example, if a UDP datagram is sent to a computer with a destination port that is not being used (that is, that service is not running on the destination computer), then the ICMP port unreachable message (subcode value 3 of the destination unreachable message) is returned to the sender.

ICMP messages also can be used with UDP to find out the maximum transmission unit (MTU) size—that is, the largest size a datagram can be in order to be sent through the network without being fragmented. Remember that on a network that uses different routers, or perhaps on an internetwork that is made up of different types of equipment or network media, the maximum size of a frame can change from one device to another. To discover the maximum size of a datagram that can be sent through the network, another subcode of the ICMP unreachable message (subcode 4) can be used along with UDP.

To create a utility that can be used to discover the MTU of a network connection, the IP Don't Fragment field can be set in the IP header information. When the UDP datagram reaches a router or other device that can't forward the datagram without fragmenting it, it will return the ICMP unreachable message "fragmentation needed, don't fragment bit set."

Finally, in some implementations a router or host will return the ICMP "source quench" error if a system is sending UDP datagrams at a rate that is too fast for the system receiving them. In this case, the application using UDP should be coded to take this into account, because the datagrams will be discarded by the system that generates the "source quench" ICMP messages.

Ports, Services, and Applications

If all applications that used the network only identified the destination for their data exchange as a single IP address, the information would arrive at the destination computer, but it would be almost impossible for the targeted system to figure out which process to give the data to.

Both the TCP and the UDP protocols use port numbers to solve this problem. Each application that communicates on the network using TCP/IP also specifies a port number on the target computer. The port numbers are endpoints for the communications path so that two applications communicating across the network can identify each other. Think of a street address for a business. If all the mail arrived simply addressed with the street address, how would you determine who should get each letter? A person's name or the suite or room number is used so that the endpoint of the communication becomes more fully defined. This is how ports work.

For example, suppose you've established a Telnet session with a remote computer and decide you want to download a file to that computer. Telnet doesn't transfer files, so you would have to open an FTP connection. Because the source and destination addresses would be the same in the IP packet for both of these sessions, port numbers are used to indicate the application.

When you combine an address with a port number, you have an identifier that can uniquely identify both endpoints of a communication. The name used for this combination of numbers is a *socket*. This is illustrated in Figure 25.10, in which two computers have established two communication sessions, one for Telnet (port 23) and one for FTP (port 20). FTP actually uses two ports—port 20 for sending data and port 21 for exchanging command information.

Figure 25.10 A socket is composed of an address and port number, and uniquely identifies an endpoint of a network connection.

It should quickly become apparent to you why a packet filter would find these port numbers useful. Instead of having to permit or deny packets based only on their source or destination address—and thereby allow or disallow *all* communications—it is possible to selectively allow or disallow individual *services*. Although you might not want your users to Telnet to a remote host computer (or vice versa), you might not care if they exchange files through anonymous FTP sessions. By using port numbers in packet filtering rules, you can enable or disable network services one at a time.

Well-Known Ports

The Internet Corporation for Assigned Names and Numbers (ICANN) is the organization that controls the first range of port numbers that are available (0–1023), and these are usually called "well-known ports." The use for these ports has been defined in several RFCs, most recently RFC 1700. However, in

January 2002, RFC 3232, "Assigned Numbers: RFC 1700 Is Replaced by an On-line Database," made RFC 1700 obsolete. Instead, RFC 3232 is a simple memo which states that port numbers will be maintained in an online database that you can access via the IANA Web site.

Note

In the original BSD implementation of TCP/IP, port numbers from 0 to 1023 were called *privileged* ports. That is, programs that run as root (or "superuser") on the Unix machine use them. These "programs" are usually just the server program for a particular application. Following this convention, client programs would choose a port number that was greater than 1023.

Note

The Internet Corporation for Assigned Names and Numbers (ICANN) was created in 1998 as a technical coordination body for the Internet. ICANN assumed most of the functions that were previously performed by the Internet Assigned Numbers Authority (IANA). In addition to taking responsibility for port numbers, ICANN also is responsible for managing how Internet domain names, IP addresses, and protocol parameters are managed and assigned. At this time IANA is still responsible for some of these functions, such as managing registered port numbers, among other tasks. You can learn more about ICANN by visiting its home page at **www.icann.org**. You can learn more about IANA by visiting its site at **www.iana.org**.

Well-known ports are usually accessible on a given system by a privileged process or privileged users. For example, the FTP utility uses ports 20 and 21, whereas the Telnet utility uses port 23. In most cases the User Datagram Protocol (UDP) and Transmission Control Protocol (TCP) make the same use of a particular port. This is not required, however. Understanding the application that a port is used for can be useful when deciding which ports to block when building a firewall. Some of these applications will never be used by your system, and because of that, there exists no good reason to allow network traffic through the firewall that uses these ports.

Registered Ports

Ports numbered from 1024 to 65535 also can be used but are not reserved by IANA. These ports are called registered ports and can be used by most any user process on the system.

The Internet Control Message Protocol (ICMP)

The Internet Control Message Protocol is a required part of any TCP/IP implementation, and the functions it performs are very important to routers and other network devices that communicate through TCP/IP. Like TCP and UPD, this protocol also uses the IP protocol to send its messages through the network. If you have used the `ping` or `traceroute` commands, you have used ICMP. ICMP was first defined in RFC 792.

Whereas TCP can usually recover from dropped datagrams simply by requesting that IP retransmit them, ICMP is used as a reporting mechanism that can be used by IP (and thus the protocols that use IP).

There are many kinds of ICMP messages, but all share a similar format. These are the fields of an ICMP message:

- **Type**—This 1-byte field is used to indicate the kind of ICMP message (see Table 25.10).
- **Code**—This 1-byte field is used as a subcode to further identify a message. This field is set to zero if the particular message type does not need to be further delineated.

- **Checksum**—This 2-byte field is used to provide an error-checking code for the entire ICMP message.

- **Type-Specific Data**—This field can vary in length and is used to provide further data specific to the ICMP message type.

ICMP Message Types

Table 25.10 shows the different types of messages that make up ICMP. The numbers listed in the Message Type field are what will be found in the Type field of the ICMP message.

Table 25.10   ICMP Message Types

Message Type	Description
0	Echo Reply
3	Destination Unreachable
4	Source Quench
5	Redirect Message
6	Alternate Host Address
8	Echo Request
9	Router Advertisement
10	Router Solicitation
11	Time Exceeded
12	Parameter Problem
13	Timestamp Request
14	Timestamp Reply
15	Information Request (no longer used)
16	Information Reply (no longer used)
17	Address Mask Request
18	Address Mask Reply
19	Reserved for Security
20–29	Reserved for Robustness Experiment
30	Traceroute
31	Datagram Conversion Error
32	Mobile Host Redirect
33	IPv6 Where-Are-You
34	IPv6 I-Am-Here
35	Mobile Registration Request
36	Mobile Registration Reply
37	Domain Name Request
38	Domain Name Reply
39	SKIP
40	Photuris
41–255	Reserved

The ping command uses the echo request and echo reply messages to determine whether a physical connection exists between systems. Another important function on the Internet is traffic control, and the source quench message can be sent to tell a sending host that the destination host cannot keep up with the speed at which it is sending packets. The transmitting computer can keep sending these quench messages until the sender scales back its transmissions to an acceptable rate.

A router uses another valuable function ICMP (the Redirect Message) to tell another router that it knows of a better path to a destination. Routers also can use the time-exceeded messages to report to another device as to why a packet was discarded.

Routers are not the only devices that use ICMP. Host computers can use ICMP. For example, when a computer boots and does not know what the network mask is for the local LAN, it can generate an address mask request message. Another device on the network can reply to assist the computer.

Note

The Information Request and Information Reply message types are shown in Table 25.10 only for completeness. Their functionality was originally developed to allow a host to obtain an IP address. This function is now supplied by the BOOTP protocol and by the Dynamic Host Configuration Protocol (DHCP). For more information about these protocols, see Chapter 29.

The Code field in the ICMP message is used for only some of the ICMP message types. The Destination Unreachable message has the largest number of code types. Table 25.11 lists these codes.

Table 25.11   ICMP Message Codes

Message Type	Code Field	Description
3	0	Network unreachable
	1	Host unreachable
	2	Protocol unreachable
	3	Port unreachable
	4	Fragmentation needed but the Don't Fragment bit is set
	5	Source route failed
	6	Destination network unknown
	7	Destination host unknown
	8	Source host isolated (no longer used)
	9	Destination network administratively prohibited
	10	Destination host administratively prohibited
	11	Network unreachable for TOS
	12	Host unreachable for TOS
	13	Communication administratively prohibited by filtering
	14	Host precedence violation
	15	Precedence cutoff in effect
5	0	Redirect for network
	1	Redirect for host
	2	Redirect for type of service and network
	3	Redirect for type of service and host

Table 25.11 Continued

Message Type	Code Field	Description
11	0	TTL equals zero during transit
	1	TTL equals zero during reassembly
12	0	IP header bad
	1	Required option missing

As you can see, ICMP can be used to compose quite detailed messages to indicate error conditions, offer advice on routing possibilities, and perform other functions that help make the Internet easier to manage.

Some situations will cause an ICMP message to not be generated. For example, ICMP messages are never created in response to an error in another ICMP message. That doesn't mean that ICMP messages can't be created in response to other ICMP messages, however. For example, the echo request and echo reply messages work together in a query/response format. Other instances that usually don't generate ICMP messages include these:

- IP broadcast and multicast messages
- Link-layer broadcast messages (that is, Ethernet frame broadcast messages)
- Datagrams that have a source address that is not for a unique host, such as the loopback address
- Messages that have been fragmented, except for the first fragment

If ICMP messages were allowed to correct problems with multicast or broadcast messages, a large number could be generated, causing the problem to become worse. This is the reason for most of the preceding conditions limiting the use of ICMP.

For the most part, the use of ICMP is described in other sections of this book where their use is employed. For example, Chapter 28 discusses using ICMP to implement the traceroute and ping commands. Some of these messages are not discussed in this book, either because they are no longer used (as indicated in the table) or because their use is trivial or rare.

Basic TCP/IP Services and Applications

SOME OF THE MAIN TOPICS IN THIS CHAPTER ARE

In the preceding chapter, it was mentioned that TCP/IP usually refers not just to the two protocols represented by its acronym (the Transmission Control Protocol and the Internet Protocol), but also to other related protocols, services, and applications that were developed to work together. These are referred to as the TCP/IP protocol suite. A wide range of services and applications have been developed to work with TCP/IP, and most implementations contain a standard set of these, which are the subject of this chapter. In addition to services and applications, other protocols have evolved along the way as the Internet has grown, such as the Simple Mail Transfer Protocol (SMTP), discussed in the next chapter, which makes global email possible.

This chapter deals with the TCP/IP suite of utilities that are generally used by end users, and the protocols that these utilities use to communicate.

▶▶ Troubleshooting utilities, such as Ping and Traceroute, among others, are covered in Chapter 28, "Troubleshooting Tools for TCP/IP Networks."

Because you've already read about how the basic TCP/IP protocols get data from one point to another using TCP or UDP along with IP, it's time to look at some of the protocols and applications you can use on a network. In this chapter you will see examples from various operating systems, including Unix, Linux, and Windows.

For some of the more important applications, such as FTP and telnet, we'll look closely at the protocol itself and the messages that are exchanged between client and server. These are the actual protocol commands that a particular utility uses to communicate with its counterpart. These low-level message or command exchanges can be useful when you are troubleshooting these applications using a protocol analyzer.

The sample syntaxes for commands found in this chapter are meant to show you that it's a good thing help files (or man pages) were invented. The difference in a command from one system to another can vary greatly.

The File Transfer Protocol (FTP)

FTP is used to transfer files between computers. It is a complex protocol that enables the exchange of data files using different methods of data representation and file storage. In its simplest form, FTP uses clear-text username and password exchanges and is not considered to be a very secure utility. FTP was originally created when the Internet was still composed mostly of large business, government, and educational institutions, and a breach of security wasn't considered that big of a threat. When used on the Internet, however, most every legacy TCP/IP utility is best used in a secure environment. The commands in this chapter show you how to use FTP. To ensure a secure exchange of information, be sure to read the chapters in Part VIII, "System and Network Security."

The syntax for FTP varies from one vendor's implementation to another. However, the simplest format, used to initiate a connection, is

`ftp` *hostname*

in which you simply follow the `ftp` command with a hostname—for example, `ftp ftp.archive.org`. You also can use the dotted-decimal address instead of the DNS name of the system with which you want to establish a connection. Alternatively, you can enter **ftp** at the command prompt and then, from the `ftp>` prompt, enter the commands needed to accomplish a particular task.

Tip

The Web site **ftp.archive.org** is a great place to practice using ftp commands, and is also a great place to obtain a lot of free files if you are interested in historical films. At this site you can set your default directory to **pub\movies** and will find several thousand "ephemeral" films that have been encoded in several different digital formats (take your pick).

These films include everything from home movies to corporate films, as well as TV commercials and—for us old folks—those flicks you used to see in high school way-back-when, telling you how to behave on a date! This site is a treasure trove of files that you should investigate if you have any interest in twentieth-century life.

A lot has changed in the past 20 to 30 years. More secure forms of authentication and data exchange have been added to create more secure forms of FTP. Before we look at a few common FTP clients and their syntaxes, let's look at the basic FTP protocol and get a feel for how it works.

Note

The File Transfer Protocol can be found in a large number of RFC documents that were created over the years. The main RFC that most documents point you to is RFC 959, "File Transfer Protocol (FTP)." RFC 2151, "A Primer on Internet and TCP/IP Tools and Utilities," is also a nice read and covers many of the utilities in this chapter. RFC 2228, "FTP Security Extensions," deals with the inherent security problems found in the FTP protocol. This last RFC discusses extensions that can be used to provide for secure authentication and encryption for the FTP protocol. In addition, there are several proposed RFCs that are on the path toward becoming a standard. RFC 2640, "Internationalization of the File Transfer Protocol," and RFC 2428, "FTP Extensions for IPv6 and NATs," provide insight into the future of FTP.

FTP is based on a client/server architecture. An FTP server (called a *daemon* on Unix or Linux systems and a *service* on Windows systems) manages a file system (anything from a single directory to a disk farm). FTP servers authenticate the client user using a username and password, and then work with the client to transfer files between the client and server computers. The basic protocol is a simple exchange of *messages*. Traditional FTP uses a simple command-line interface. Today, many shareware and commercial GUI versions of FTP are available. For example, if you are already using a favorite FTP site, try using a URL such as ftp://ftp.archive.org to see whether your browser supports a GUI interface for FTP. Either way, command line or GUI, it is an extremely useful utility because it allows the transfer of many types of files between two hosts on the network.

Note

FTP clients come in many forms. As mentioned in the text of this chapter, you can use a command-line interface using a computer running Unix/Linux or any Windows operating system. Most browsers support the prefix "ftp" just as they do the "www" prefix when browsing Internet sites. You can also download GUI FTP applications that operate outside the command line or browser interface. Use a search engine and you will find many of these applications. Most differentiate themselves from others by providing additional features, such as an easy-to-use interface or integration with other applications, such as Windows Explorer.

FTP Ports and Processes

The FTP server daemon listens in the background for FTP requests on TCP port 21. In the literature, the server is composed of two components, though they are often combined into a single program. The first is the Server-PI, which stands for "server protocol interpreter." This is the component that listens to TCP port 21 and interacts with its client counterpart, the User-PI. The user protocol interpreter initiates an FTP session by sending a request to the server. The client's request can include a port that the client wants the server to use when it opens a data channel.

The second component of the server is the Server-DTP, which stands for "server data transfer process." This is the code that interacts with its counterpart, the User-DTP, to perform the actual file data transfers. An overview of this process appears in Figure 26.1. The important thing to notice in this figure is that two channels of communication are used for FTP—one for commands and one for the actual exchange of data—and that both of these channels work in both directions.

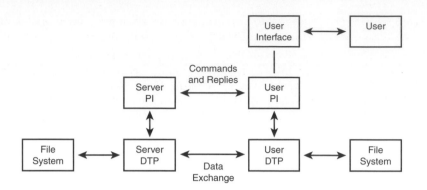

Figure 26.1   The FTP session consists of both a command and a data channel.

The client's User-PI should be listening on the specified port for incoming data transmissions before it has issued the commands necessary to start a data transfer from a remote server. The actual commands used on the control connection are in the same format used for the telnet utility (NVT-ASCII), which is discussed later in this chapter.

Data Transfers

All FTP data transfers take place using bytes (8 bits), independent of the size of the actual data being transferred. That is, if the local file system uses a different size for storage, such as a word or a floating-point numerical representation, FTP just sends 8 bits at a time. The data is reconstructed on the receiving end into its original format. The client and server applications are responsible for making sure that conversions are done on their end to make data usable on their respective systems.

When you're using an FTP client, it is important that you know what type of file you are sending or receiving. The default for most clients is to send/receive ASCII text files. If you want to send or receive an executable program, most clients use the command "binary" to inform the server you interact with that this is not an ASCII text file.

Additionally, there are three modes that are used for transfers:

- **Stream mode**—This is a simple transmission of a stream of bytes. To represent record and file structures using this mode, End of Record (EOR) and End of File (EOF) control bytes can be used. Control bytes consist of 2 bytes. The first byte is set to all ones (which is the escape character), and the second byte is the control character. A value of 1 for this byte indicates that it is the EOR character. A value of 2 indicates that it is the EOF character. A value of 3 indicates both characters (EOR and EOF). Note that if an actual byte of all ones is in the data stream, it is transmitted as a 2-byte sequence also, with both bytes being set to all ones.

- **Block mode**—This transmission mode sends a series of data blocks, each of which has a header. The header information consists of 3 bytes of information. The 16 lower-order bits indicate the byte count, which is the total length of the block (expressed in bytes). The remaining high-order byte is used for a descriptor code. A descriptor code value of 128 indicates that the end of a data block is the end of a record (EOR). A value of 64 indicates that the end of a data block is the end of a block of data (EOF). A value of 32 is used to indicate that there is reason to suspect errors in the data stream.

- **Compressed mode**—In this mode, data can be sent using various compression mechanisms.

All transfers are done in 8-bit bytes, regardless of the way the bits are interpreted on the receiving system. The data types that FTP allows are very basic. The ASCII type consists of standard 8-bit NVT-ASCII characters. In this format, the carriage-return and line-feed characters are used to indicate the end of a line. Some systems, such as many Unix systems, do not use this combination of characters, and the receiving side converts the received stream of bytes to its own format.

The EBCDIC type (Extended Binary-Coded Decimal Interchange Code) is a method of character representation used mainly on IBM mainframe computers, which were quite popular back when development on FTP (and its predecessors) first started. The EBCDIC and ASCII transfers are sent as 8-bit characters and are similar, with just the character representations of the numerical values differing.

The IMAGE mode of transfer sends data as a simple stream of bits, which are stored in the usual 8-bit transfer byte used by FTP. At the receiving end, the bits are stored in a contiguous manner, with padding added to the end of a file or record as necessary. The method used must ensure that the process of this padding can be reversed if the file is transferred to another system that does not use that method.

The LOCAL type allows the user to set a logical size for the bytes to be sent. All data is still sent as a byte, but on the receiving end this command allows the receiver to know how to reassemble the bits into the correctly sized bytes for that operating system.

FTP Protocol Commands

This section looks at some of the more useful commands that the protocol uses to control an FTP session. This is not an exhaustive discussion of all possible protocol commands, however. The next section looks at examples of the syntax for FTP for several implementations so that you can see how various FTP applications work, and how their command structure matches up user commands to the commands actually used by the FTP protocol processes.

Note that these "protocol commands" are the commands exchanged by client and server applications on the network. Commands entered by an end user are a different matter altogether. Many end-user commands involve a sequence of protocol commands to accomplish the desired function. Here we examine the commands exchanged between the server and client applications, not the command entered by a user.

FTP protocol commands start with the command code itself and are usually followed by one or more arguments. All FTP protocol commands are four characters or fewer and can be grouped into a few categories:

- **Access Control Commands (ACT)**—These are used to authenticate the user, change directories, and so on.
- **Transfer Parameter Commands (TPC)**—These commands control the actual data transfer process, such as the port used and the file structure.
- **FTP Service Commands (FSC)**—These commands indicate the function the user wants to perform, such as sending or receiving a file, or perhaps renaming or deleting a file.

Table 26.1 is a list of commonly used commands along with a description of their use.

Table 26.1   FTP Protocol Commands

Command	Type	Description
USER	ACT	This command is followed by a username valid on the remote system.
PASS	ACT	This command is followed by the password associated with the remote user account.
ACCT	ACT	Some implementations require a text string identifying a user account, which is sent with this command.
CWD	ACT	Change working directory on the remote system.

Table 26.1   Continued

Command	Type	Description
CDUP	ACT	Change to parent directory.
SMNT	ACT	Used to mount a different file system.
REIN	ACT	Reinitialize. This flushes all user account and I/O data and reinitializes the connection. Typically, another USER command is then used to start a new session.
QUIT	ACT	This is the logout command to end a session.
PORT	TPC	Used to specify a host data port other than the default.
PASV	TPC	Communicate in Passive mode. This command causes the server to listen on a specified port other than the default.
TYPE	TPC	The data representation type (that is, ASCII, IMAGE, and so on). A numerical value is used for each type.
STRU	TPC	File structure. F = file (no record structure), R = record structure, P = page structure. The default is file.
MODE	TPC	Transfer mode. S = stream, B = block, C = compressed.
RETR	FSC	Retrieve. Instructs the server to send a file.
STOR	FSC	Store. Instructs the server to receive and store a file.
STOU	FSC	Similar to STOR but creates a unique filename on the server.
APPE	FSC	Append with create. If the file exists on the server, data is appended. If not, a file is created.
ALLO	FSC	Used to allocate space before file transfer.
REST	FSC	Restart. Restarts the file transfer at a specified checkpoint.
RNFR	FSC	Rename from. The old pathname of a file that is being renamed. Followed by an RNTO command.
RNTO	FSC	Rename to. Specifies the new pathname of a renamed file.
ABOR	FSC	Instructs the server to abort the previous command and/or data transfer.
DELE	FSC	Deletes a file on the server.
RMD	FSC	Remove directory. Removes a directory on the server.
MKD	FSC	Make directory. Creates a directory on the server.
PWD	FSC	Displays the name of the current directory (print working directory).
LIST	FSC	Lists information about a file or lists files in a directory.
NLIST	FSC	Name list. Sends the client a list of just the names in a directory.
SITE	FSC	Site parameters. Implementation dependent.
SYST	FSC	Sends the client a reply indicating the operating system of the server.
STAT	FSC	Causes the server to return a status response.
HELP	FSC	What it says!
NOOP	FSC	No-operation. Causes the server to send an OK reply.

As you can see from this table, there are many commands that the client side can use to control file transfers. In the next section we will look at the replies that the FTP server can send in response to these commands. Remember, these are the commands used in the protocol exchange. The replies in the next section are not manually entered by a user at a keyboard. They are the replies sent by the FTP server in answer to the protocol commands of the FTP client.

Server Replies to FTP Commands

In the FTP protocol, every command must be followed by a reply from the server. In some cases, more than one reply will be sent to the client. The actual reply is a three-digit number, but it is transmitted as text characters. Following this number is usually some variable-length text. The numerical value is used by the program, and the text is intended for the user of the FTP client. Because some of the text is configurable, you can expect to see different text for the same numerical reply from one implementation to another. For example, you can usually specify the text that is displayed on the client when the user first logs in to your server.

To reply to the client, the three characters representing the numeric reply code are sent, followed by a minus sign (–) or space character and then the reply text. A simple convention is used for multiline text messages. The first line contains the three-letter numerical code followed by the – character and then the text. The last line replaces the – character with the space character. By matching up the two three-digit codes, the client can determine the beginning and ending of a particular multiline message.

Reply Codes

Each of the actual digits that make up the reply code is significant. If you've ever wondered why all those text lines start with numbers, you'll find their meaning in this section. The text displayed will vary from one vendor to another, but the codes should still be implemented for the same general reply condition.

The first digit indicates success or failure:

- A value of 1 indicates a Positive Preliminary reply, which means that the function requested by the client has been started.
- A value of 2 is the Positive Completion reply, which means that the requested function was successfully performed.
- A value of 3 is the Positive Intermediate reply, indicating that the command was received by the server but has not been executed. The server might be waiting for further information.
- A value of 4 indicates a Transient Negative Completion reply. This means that a temporary error situation has prevented the function requested by the client from being performed.
- A value of 5 in the first position is the Permanent Negative Completion reply. This indicates that the requested action was not performed. Unlike the Transient message code, the user is not encouraged to retry the command.

The second digit is used to place message types into groups:

- A value of 0 refers to a syntax error.
- A value of 1 is an informational message.
- A value of 2 indicates that the reply refers to either the control or the data connection.
- A value of 3 is used for replies regarding authentication and accounting, such as during the initial logon process.
- A value of 4 is unspecified at this time.
- A value of 5 means that the reply refers to the status of the file server's file system as it relates to the user request.

The third digit in the response code is used to further divide the replies based on the categories indicated by the second digit.

In Table 26.2, you can see the recommended reply codes, in numerical order, as specified in RFC 959.

Table 26.2 FTP Numerical Reply Codes

Code	Description
110	Restart marker reply.
120	Service ready in *nnn* minutes.
125	Data connection is already open, the transfer is starting.
150	File status okay—about to open data connection.
200	Command okay.
202	Command not implemented.
211	System status or a help reply text.
212	Directory status.
213	File status.
214	Help message.
215	System type.
220	Service is ready for new user.
221	Service closing the control connection.
225	Data connection is open but no transfer is in progress.
226	Closing the data connection, and the requested function (such as file transfer) is complete.
227	Entering passive mode.
230	User logged in.
250	Requested file action is okay and has been completed.
257	The requested pathname has been created.
331	Username is okay but password is needed.
332	An account name is required to complete the logon.
350	The requested file action is waiting for further information.
421	Service is not available. The control connection is being closed.
425	Unable open data connection.
426	Connection closed—transfer aborted.
450	Requested file action was not taken.
451	Requested action aborted due to local processing error.
452	Requested action not taken due to insufficient storage space.
500	Syntax error. The command was not recognized (or line too long).
501	Syntax error in parameters or arguments to command.
502	Command not implemented.
503	Incorrect sequence of commands.
504	Command not implemented for a particular parameter.
530	User not logged in.
532	Need account for storing files.
550	Requested action not taken. Usually file not found or access denied.

Table 26.2   Continued

Code	Description
551	Requested action aborted: page type unknown.
552	Requested file action aborted due to storage allocation exceeded.
553	Requested action not taken. Filename not allowed.

Using a Windows FTP Command-Line Client

Client implementations can vary from simple command-line interfaces to programs that enable you to drag and drop using a graphical interface. All Windows client operating systems, from 98 to XP, provide a default FTP client that works from the command line. The syntax for the Windows XP Professional FTP client is simply the command FTP followed by the server to which you want to connect. The complete syntax for the command is

```
ftp [-v] [-n] [-i] [-d] [-g] [-s: filename] [-a]
➥[-A] [-w:windowsize] [hostname]
```

where

- **-v**—This parameter suppresses responses from the remote server.

- **-n**—The Windows FTP client automatically prompts you for a username and password. This option suppresses these prompts. You are presented with the ftp> prompt and allowed to use the USER command to specify your logon username.

- **-i**—This turns off prompting that occurs when transferring multiple files with the MGET or MPUT command. This is the same function performed by the PROMPT command when you're at the ftp> prompt.

- **-d**—Enables debugging the FTP session. All commands (the actual protocol commands) sent between the client and server are displayed.

- **-g**—Disables filename globbing. When globbing is turned on, you can use wildcards (asterisk and question mark) in filenames. This option forces you to use the exact path and filename.

- **-s:filename**—The commands found in the file named filename are executed after the FTP command line is entered.

- **-a**—Indicates that any local interface can be used when binding the data connection.

- **-A**—Performs an anonymous logon to the FTP server.

- **-w:windowsize**—Specifies the transfer buffer size. The default is 4,096 bytes.

- **hostname**—The hostname or IP address of the remote server.

You can also just enter the command **ftp** and enter a state called interactive mode. During interactive mode, you will see the prompt ftp> at which you can enter commands. These include some of the same options you can enter on the command line and additional commands that can be used to transfer files, list directories, and so on. The following commands are available with the Windows XP client:

- **!** *command*—Yes, it's an exclamation point. Used with no command, this causes you to exit to the "shell," which on a Windows system is the command prompt. After you have performed any tasks that you need to, you can type **exit** to return to the current FTP session. This command enables you to escape temporarily to check execute commands on the local system without being forced to terminate the FTP program. Alternatively, you can enter a command (separated by a space from the exclamation character) and the program will execute the command on the local system and remain the FTP client program.

- **? or help**—Typing **?** prints a list of commands available. The word `help` followed by a command gives you local help text for that command.

- **append** *filename filename*—Appends data to an existing file.

- **ascii**—Sets the transfer type to ASCII (default).

- **bell**—Toggles on or off a bell that sounds after each file transfer. The default is off.

- **binary**—Sets the file transfer type to binary for image files.

- **bye**—Exits the client and ends the current FTP connections.

- **cd** *directory*—Changes the working directory on the remote FTP server.

- **close**—Closes the current connection and leaves you in the `ftp>` interpreter prompt so that you can continue to perform other actions, such as open another server.

- **debug**—Similar to the `-d` command-line option; causes the protocol messages exchanged between client and server to be displayed, prefixed with the characters `- - - >`.

- **delete** *filename*—Deletes a file on the remote server.

- **dir**—Lists files and directories on the remote server. You can follow this command with a wildcard to narrow your listing, provided that globbing is turned on.

- **disconnect**—Disconnects the session with the current server, leaving you in the FTP interpreter prompt to continue working.

- **get** *filename*—Is used to get a single file from the remote server.

- **glob**—Toggles (as does the `-g` command-line option) for globbing filenames. This is a simple way to say that you can use wildcards in local filenames and pathnames, and it is the default.

- **hash**—What you used to eat in the Army. Actually, this command causes a hash mark (more correctly called the number-sign character) to be printed for every 2,048 bytes transferred. This is helpful in a long transfer because you can watch the progress and determine whether it has stalled or stopped.

- **lcd** *pathname*—Changes the working directory on the client's local system. Compare to CD, which changes the working directory on the remote server's system.

- **literal** *text*—Sends text, verbatim, to the server. A single response is expected back.

- **ls**—Displays an abbreviated listing of the files or directories on the remote server system. Similar to the `dir` command.

- **mdelete** *filenames*—Is used to delete more than one filename on a remote server. You can use wildcards for this if needed (check that globbing).

- **mdir**—Displays a listing of files and directories that exist on the remote sever.

- **mkdir** *directoryname*—Creates a new directory (or subdirectory) on the remote server.

- **mls**—Displays an abbreviated listing of the files and directories that exist on the remote server.

- **mput** *filenames*—Performs multiple file transfers from the client to the server, using only one command. Wildcards can be used.

- **open** *hostname*—Is used to connect to a specific server after the FTP interpreter prompt has been issued.

- **prompt**—Is used to toggle on or off prompting during multiple file transfers. The default is on. This means that if you use mget, mdel, or mput to work with files, you'll get prompted for each file. Toggle this off if you want to work with a large number of files and let it just run without having to answer Y or N to each prompt for each file.

- **put** *filename*—Transfers a single file to the remote FTP server from the client.

- **pwd**—Stands for Print Working Directory. This displays the current directory on the remote FTP server.

- **quit**—Exits the FTP client and ends any outstanding connections.

- **quote**—Same function as the literal command.

- **recv**—Same as the get command.

- **remotehelp**—Displays help from the remote server.

- **rename** *filename filename*—Renames a file on the remote FTP server.

- **rmdir** *directory*—Removes a directory on the remote FTP server.

- **send** *filename*—Same as the put command.

- **status**—Toggles on or off a status display.

- **trace**—Toggles on or off a display showing the routes taken by each packet.

- **type** *type*—Sets the current transfer type. Examples: type ascii (for text files) or type binary (for program files).

- **user** *username*—Is used to specify a username during the logon process.

- **verbose**—Toggles on or off verbose mode. The default is on, so all replies sent by remote server are displayed.

As you can see, many commands duplicate functions performed by others. Over the years, commands have been added that are easier to remember. For example, you'll find that some of the commands supported by Linux are different than Windows FTP clients.

Note that there are usually two commands to perform file functions, depending on whether you are operating on one or multiple files. For example, use GET *filename* to get a single file, but to get multiple files, use MGET *filename* in a format such as MGET REPORTS*.*. Don't forget that, when using the "M" (multiple) commands, you might want to first issue the PROMPT command to turn interactive mode off. Otherwise, you will be prompted before downloading each file and have to enter Y or N. Conversely, you can leave prompting turned on if you know you want to retrieve most of the files that match your file specification but want to exclude a few by answering no to the prompts.

In the following listing, you can see how the command is invoked to connect to the remote server, the reply messages received from the server, and a directory listing produced by using the DIR command. Next, the ls command is used to show the difference in the output. Finally, the session is set to show hash marks (hash) and then set to do a binary download (binary). You can see the results of using the HASH command and then the GET command to retrieve a file from the remote server.

```
J:\>ftp ftp.twoinc.com
Connected to ftp.twoinc.com.
220-ArGoSoft FTP Server for WinNT/2000, Version 1.2 (1.2.1.1)
220-Welcome to Active Web Hosting
220-For more information on our
220-services please call
220 (800) 946-7764 or (702) 451-1577.
User (ftp.twoinc.com:(none)): twoinc.com
```

```
331 User name OK, need password
Password:
230 User twoinc.com logged in successfully **
ftp> dir
200 Port command successful
150 Opening binary data connection
drw-r--r--  1 user    group         0 Mar 06 00:00 ..
-rw-r--r--  1 user    group       436 Feb 24 13:36 cnt.htm
-rw-r--r--  1 user    group       455 Feb 24 13:36 default.htm
-rw-r--r--  1 user    group       949 Feb 24 13:36 default.html
-rw-r--r--  1 user    group       807 Feb 24 13:36 emp.htm
-rw-r--r--  1 user    group   1729597 Mar 06 09:52 hiroshimamontage.mp3
-rw-r--r--  1 user    group       268 Feb 24 13:36 lnk.htm
drw-r--r--  1 user    group         0 Jan 26 12:56 logs
-rw-r--r--  1 user    group      1969 Feb 24 13:36 pub.htm
-rw-r--r--  1 user    group      1317 Feb 24 13:36 who.htm
226 Transfer complete
ftp: 807 bytes received in 0.15Seconds 5.38Kbytes/sec.
ftp> ls
200 Port command successful
150 Opening binary data connection
..
cnt.htm
default.htm
default.html
emp.htm
hiroshimamontage.mp3
lnk.htm
logs
pub.htm
who.htm
226 Transfer complete
ftp: 147 bytes received in 0.05Seconds 2.94Kbytes/sec.
ftp> hash
Hash mark printing On ftp: (2048 bytes/hash mark) .
ftp> binary
200 Type set to Image (binary)
ftp> get hiroshimamontage.mp3
200 Port command successful
150 Opening binary data connection
##############################################################################
##############################################################################
##############################################################################
##############################################################################
##########################################
226 Transfer complete
ftp: 1729597 bytes received in 573.14Seconds 3.02Kbytes/sec.
ftp>
```

As you can see, using the FTP utility is an easy way to examine directory information on remote systems or to exchange files.

Using Red Hat Linux FTP

Red Hat Linux Version 8.0 offers both a GUI FTP client and a command-line client. If you choose to install the server version of Red Hat Linux, you will also find an FTP server. In Figure 26.2 you can see an example of the GUI version. To start up the GUI FTP client, click on the Red Hat symbol (it's in the same place as the Start button on Windows systems), Extras, Internet, and then gFTP.

Figure 26.2 Red Hat Linux offers a GUI FTP client.

From Figure 26.2 you can see that the GUI FTP client allows you to enter the destination location (Host = ftp.archive.org) and also lets you use the CD (change directory) command to get to the target directory (/pub/movies/mpeg2). From this directory you simply double-click on the file to download. The lower portion of the window shows the progress being made (the number of total bytes for the file, and the number of bytes transferred so far). At the very bottom of the window, you can see the actual FTP commands that are used during this session. These can be just as useful as those from a command-line client when you're trying to determine what has gone wrong during troubleshooting efforts. Also notice that on the right side of the window you can see the files available in the local directory (in this case the root directory, which you shouldn't use unless you know what you are doing!).

Tip

Because this GUI client is so easy to use, it is the preferred method for those who are just now learning how to use Linux. One important thing to note here is that, unlike with Windows, there are several graphical user interfaces, usually referred to as desktops in the Unix/Linux community. In the example shown in Figure 26.2, you are seeing the Gnome desktop. Another popular desktop is the KDE desktop. Depending on the company from which you obtain your Linux system, you may find one of these, both of these, or other desktops. Some even allow you to use one desktop while listing accessories from the other desktops installed on the system! Additionally, Linux itself is just an operating system. The applications, such as the GUI FTP client described here, are open-source applications that Red Hat decided to ship with its version of Linux. With other Linux vendors, your mileage may vary, as the saying goes.

Using the Red Hat Linux Command-Line FTP Client

Just about every operating system in existence today offers, just as Windows does, a command-line version of the FTP client. Although a GUI version is usually easier to use, the command-line version offers specific capabilities (as you learned earlier about the Windows version) that can be incorporated into script files. For those who are used to using a command-line version, you'll find it in Linux also. If you are trying to automate the transfer of a file (such as a report or data file created by an application) to another system, then the command-line version is the choice to make. You could manually use the GUI version, but if you use the command-line version, the process can be automated. Simply check the log file to ensure that the file has successfully been transferred to (or from) the other system.

Note

In the FTP syntax listing for Linux, keep in mind that unlike some other operating systems, Linux is case-sensitive. That is, a –a is not the same as a –A. And the command ftp is to be entered, not FTP. Other commands, such as quit, will not work if capitalized. You will find that many Unix/Linux utilities use the same alphabetic characters in the same utility, and it is the case of the character that makes the difference. And don't forget filenames! If you attempt to send a file from a Unix/Linux system that is named myfile, you'll get an error (file not found) when trying to send MYFILE or MyFile.

The syntax of the Red Hat Linux command-line version of the FTP client is

ftp [-v] [-d] [-i] [-n] [-g] [-k *realm*] [-f] [-x] [-u] [-t] *hostname*

where

- **-v**—Invokes the verbose option, which makes the FTP client show all responses that the remote server sends. Also displays the statistics of the session.

- **-d**—Displays debugging for troubleshooting purposes.

- **-i**—For multiple file transfers, such as filenames specified with a wildcard, this option will prevent the ftp utility from prompting you (Y or N) for each file.

- **-n**—This command prevents ftp from attempting an autologin to the remote server. The file named .netrc in the user's home directory is checked to see whether authentication is necessary. Otherwise, you will be prompted for authentication credentials when logging in to a remote server.

- **-g**—As described in the previous syntax for Windows, prevents globbing.

- **-k** *realm*—This is used when Kerberos authentication is used. This command will obtain the authentication tickets valid for the Kerberos realm.

- **-f**—This option causes authentication credentials to be forwarded to the remote computer.

- **-x**—The encryption procedures will be negotiated with the remote host after a successful authenticated login.

- **-u**—Causes the client to negotiate authentication methods with the remote system. The AUTH command, as described earlier in this chapter, is used instead.

- **-t**—This option enables packet tracing for the session.

- *hostname*—This is the DNS hostname, or the IP address that you want to connect to using ftp.

Similar to the Windows version, if you simply enter **ftp** for the Red Hat command utility, you will enter a command-line interpreter mode in which you can issue commands interactively. Most of the commands you can enter in interactive mode are the same as the Windows versions. Following is a list of additional commands provided by the Red Hat ftp command-line utility in interactive mode.

- **account** *[password]*—Used to enter a second password after the initial logon if the server computer requires it. If you just enter **account**, you will be prompted for the password.

- **case**—This command toggles on/off filename case mapping. When off, which is the default, filenames from remote systems that use uppercase letters are converted to lowercase letters when a file is transferred to the client.

- **cdup**—Similar to cd, this command changes the current directory on the remote server. The working directory is set to the parent directory of the current working directory.

- **chmod** *mode* *filename*—This change mode command is used to alter the permissions (*mode*) of the remote *filename*, provided you have the right to do so.

- **cr**—For ASCII file transfers, this command toggles on/off the stripping of carriage-return (CR) characters. Some operating systems, such as Windows, use a CR/LF (linefeed) character to denote the end of a text record. Unix and Linux use just the LF character. When toggled on, the CR character is removed. Otherwise, both CR and LF are left in the file retrieved from the server.

- **debug**—Toggles debug mode on/off. When on, commands sent to the remote server are printed, preceded by the ---> text string.

- **help** *command*—Provides a short help text message for *command*.

- **idle** *seconds*—Sets the inactivity timer on the server (after which a disconnection can occur). When it's used without *seconds* being specified, the current inactivity timer value is displayed.

- **macdef** *macroname*—Used to define a macro, which is a set of commands to be executed. See help text for information on defining macros in FTP.

- **mode** *modename*—Sets the default transfer mode to *modename*. The default is stream mode.

- **modtime** *filename*—Displays the time a file on the remote server was last modified.

- **newer** *filename*—If the modification time on a remote file is newer than a file of the same name on the client, the newer file is retrieved from the server. If the file does not exist on the client, the remote file is retrieved.

- **reget**—Similar to the get command, this command will check to see whether a file with the same filename exists on the local machine. If so, and if the file is smaller than the same file on the remote server, then it is assumed that a previous file transfer was interrupted, and the reget command restarts the transfer from the point where it stopped. Useful for transferring large files.

- **restart** *marker*—Similar to reget, this restarts an interrupted transmission. For most Unix/Linux systems, *marker* is a byte offset into the file indicating where the file transfer should be resumed.

- **runique**—Useful when retrieving files that have the same names as existing files on the client. Instead of replacing the file, a number in the format of ".1" is attached to the filename, with a possible total of 99 versions of the file. runique toggles this behavior on/off.

- **size** *filename*—Gets the size of a remote file.

- **sunique**—Similar to the runique command, causes unique filenames to be used on a remote system when the name of the file being sent already exists on the remote server. The remote server must support this command.

- **system**—Returns the operating system running on the remote server.

- **tenex**—Sets the file transfer to a type used to exchange data with a TENEX machine.

There are other commands available in interactive mode, such as those related to security. Use the help command interactively to learn about these and other commands that are not often used.

The Trivial File Transfer Protocol (TFTP)

This protocol was developed to be a "lite" version of FTP, where security and elaborate mechanisms for error control were not needed. Generally, TFTP is used to download operating systems, firmware upgrades, and other files to network devices or diskless workstations. For example, a diskless workstation can use BOOTP (or DHCP) to obtain IP configuration information and the location of a TFTP server, along with the name of the file to download. For more information about BOOTP and DHCP and how they allow diskless workstations to obtain the information they need in order to boot, see Chapter 29, "BOOTP and Dynamic Host Configuration Protocol (DHCP)."

No authentication is used, so this is a service that should be used only where it is absolutely needed. The syntax for the TFTP command is

```
tftp [-i] host [get | put] source [destination]
```

The command-line option -i specifies a binary image transfer, which is precisely the kind of transfer for which this utility is usually used. If you omit this option, an ASCII file transfer is done by default.

The get command specifies that the source file is to be transferred from *source* to *destination*. The put command works, just as in FTP, in the opposite direction to send a file from the client to the TFTP server.

The following are other important differences between FTP and TFTP:

- FTP uses TCP, whereas TFTP uses UDP.
- Only file transfers are supported. Directory listings, file deletions, and other features of FTP are not implemented in TFTP.
- TFTP was designed to be simple and compact so that its code could be stored in a small amount of read-only memory, making it an ideal solution for implementation in device firmware.

The official specification for TFTP can be found in RFC 1350, "The TFTP Protocol (Revision 2)." It uses a simple set of messages to establish the file exchange. In each message, the first 2 bytes are reserved for use as an opcode. Five message types are used:

- **1**—This opcode (RRQ) is used to initiate a read request to download a file from the TFTP server to the client. After the first 2-byte opcode, a variable number of bytes specifying the filename follows and is terminated with a zero byte. Following this is the *mode* used for the transfer. This can be the text netascii, which means that the transfer will consist of ASCII text lines terminated by the carriage-return/line-feed combination. The text octet in the mode field indicates that the data transfer will be a simple transfer of 8-bit octets of data.
- **2**—This opcode (WRQ) is similar to the first one, except that the file transfer will be made from the client to the TFTP server.
- **3**—This opcode (data) is used to send a block of data. The 2-byte opcode is followed by a 2-byte field that contains a block number. Following this is from 0 to 512 bytes of actual data.
- **4**—This opcode (ACK) acknowledges the block transferred. Each block is acknowledged. The format for this packet is the 2-byte opcode followed by the 2-byte block number being acknowledged by the receiver.
- **5**—This opcode (error) is reserved for reporting errors. The 2-byte opcode is followed by a 2-byte error code and a variable-length error message terminated by a zero byte. Note that, for most error types, the connection is aborted and must be tried again.

The interoperation of this protocol is quite simple. For each block sent, an acknowledgment is sent back to the sender. This is sometimes called a stop-and-wait protocol. Remember that TCP uses an acknowledgment mechanism in which one ACK can acknowledge multiple segments of data. In TFTP, each block is acknowledged.

Block numbers are numbered starting at 1. However, for a write request, the acknowledgment number returned to the sender is a zero because a data block has not yet been exchanged.

Termination of the file transfer is also simply done. When a block that has less than 512 bytes of data in it is received, the file transfer has finished. Because UDP is used instead of TCP, the TFTP client/server software must implement its own retransmission technique for blocks that get lost or damaged in the network. Again, to make the protocol as simple as possible, no checksum is calculated on the TFTP messages. Instead, the simpler methods used by UDP are depended on to catch any errors.

Ports used by TFTP are allocated on a client-by-client basis. When the TFTP server receives the first client request message on its well-known TFTP port of 69, the server then allocates another port for use and communicates this back to the client. The client can continue to use a port on its side of the connection. However, from that point on it uses the newly assigned port it received from the TFTP server as the server host port. This feature allows a TFTP server to service multiple requests from different clients. The well-known port of 69 is used only for the initial communication.

The Telnet Protocol

Telnet is another of the most useful tools that make up the TCP/IP protocol suite. The "remote terminal" telnet application enables you to establish an interactive logon session with a remote computer and execute commands as if you were logged directly into that remote computer. Telnet not only can be used to establish sessions with other computers, but also is embedded in many network devices, such as print servers (or HP Jet-Direct Cards), hubs, switches, and routers. Using telnet is an easy way to manage multiple network nodes—computer or network devices—from a central location.

However, basic implementations of telnet suffer from a similar problem that plagues FTP. It uses a clear-text method for passing user authentication information and the remaining data transfers.

The main RFC that defines basic telnet operation is RFC 854, "Telnet Protocol Specification." In addition, many additional RFC documents have been issued to add security, provide additional functionality, or further clarify the Telnet protocol.

The protocol is based on three basic concepts:

- The Network Virtual Terminal (NVT)
- Options negotiation
- A symmetric view of terminals and processes

This protocol was designed to allow interactive sessions with terminals of many types. A basic Network Virtual Terminal is defined by the telnet protocol, but clients and servers can negotiate additional parameters using options. Because either side can initiate options negotiations, the protocol is called symmetric.

What Is a Network Virtual Terminal and NVT ASCII?

Each end of the telnet connection is called a Network Virtual Terminal. It is simply a data construct that keeps track of the current state of the terminal, keeping both ends in sync. The virtual terminal operates in a bidirectional manner, sending and receiving data from another remote NVT. The basic NVT uses a 7-bit ASCII code, stored in an 8-bit byte. The high-order bit is set to zero. Carriage-return and line-feed characters are transmitted to indicate the end of a line. The method of representing characters and delineating lines is known as *NVT ASCII*. You'll find that many different TCP/IP utilities use this to communicate commands to and from the client and server.

Conversion to other codes can be done at each client's end. The NVT has both a virtual terminal (or printer, as it's called in the RFC) and a keyboard.

Characters that are entered on the keyboard at one end of the connection are locally echoed, and do not have to be echoed back from the remote terminal. Usually, a buffer is set aside in the host's memory to store a line of characters for transmission. The characters are transmitted when a line is complete or until some other signal (from the user, for example) causes the line to be sent.

The basic NVT is designed to be the lowest common denominator for telnet sessions. Options can be negotiated, usually more so at the beginning of a session, that change the characteristics of the basic NVT. By a process of negotiation, both sides will always have the NVT default to fall back on if the other side of the connection does not support certain options. Thus, the NVT is the basic telnet terminal, without any extra options enabled.

Upon the initial connection, both sides are basic NVTs. Usually, options will be negotiated by both sides before the user has time to begin typing. Occasionally, option changes will be requested during the later data exchanges, but the basic setup for the session is done at the beginning.

Telnet Protocol Commands and Option Negotiations

Commands for the telnet protocol are 2 or 3 bytes in length, with the first character being the *interpret as command (IAC)* character. This character has the ASCII value of 255. If it is necessary to actually send this character as part of the data stream, it is sent as two successive bytes of 255. Following the IAC character, another command character usually is sent. For option negotiations, a third byte is used to indicate the option code being negotiated. In Table 26.3 you can see a list of the basic telnet protocol commands, along with descriptions of their functions.

Table 26.3 Telnet Protocol Commands

Code #	Code Name	Description
240	SE	End of subnegotiation parameters.
241	NOP	No operation.
242	Data Mark	The data stream portion of a Sync. This code should be accompanied by a TCP Urgent notification.
243	BREAK	NVT character for BREAK.
244	Interrupt Process	The IP function.
245	Abort Output	The AO function.
246	Are You There	The AYT function.
247	Erase Character	The EC function.
248	Erase Line	The EL function.
249	Go Ahead	The GA signal.
250	SB	Signals that what follows is a subnegotiation of the indicated option.
251	WILL (option code)	Indicates the desire to start performing or to continue performing an option.
252	WON'T (option code)	Nonacceptance of an option or discontinuance of an option.
253	DO (option code)	Requests that the other side perform an option.
254	DON'T (option code)	Requests that the other side stop performing an option.
255	IAC	When following an initial IAC, a second character of 255 is interpreted as a data byte instead of a command.

This simple command structure is used to establish a telnet session, negotiate the optional parameters, if any, and end the session. Telnet, like FTP and other client/server protocols, requires that a telnet server process listen on a well-known port, which in this case is port number 23. The server listens for incoming telnet commands from telnet clients.

Following is a short description of some of the protocol commands:

- **Are You There**—This command is used as sort of a "keep-alive" signal. It is intended to be sent after the connection has been idle for an amount of time. The remote end should respond with some visible response.

- **Erase Character**—Most operating systems have the capability to backspace and erase a character. Again, telnet uses a common command for this function, because not all operating systems support it or use the same numerical code for this function.

- **Erase Line**—This is similar to the Erase Character command, but it instead maps the local keyboard's command sequence or key used to erase a line to a command that can be passed to the remote side of a connection.

- **Interrupt Process**—This command is used to map to the typical Ctrl+C or other character sequence used on a local machine to interrupt a process. This can differ from one computer operating system to another, hence the need for a common code to pass this condition to the other end of the connection.

- **Data Mark**—This command is sent as part of a TCP Urgent segment and is notice to the receiving end that it should look for "interesting" characters (such as IP, AO, and AYT) in the data stream. This causes an immediate action. The TCP Urgent message followed by a DM also is called a telnet sync operation. This allows out-of-band communications for important events—for example, an IP that results from a user entering Ctrl+C.

Options and Negotiations

The standard NVT described in RFC 854 might not be sufficient for all situations, and thus the telnet protocol allows for a process of negotiation of options. This allows for additional capabilities and services to be provided using telnet. For example, an option could be used to provide for a different character set than the standard. Either side of the telnet session can send a request to the other side for an option. The receiving end can then reply with either an acceptance or a rejection of the option. If an option is accepted, it takes effect at once.

The following are some basic rules of the negotiation process:

- Option requests are sent only to change an option. If the option is already in effect, sending out a request for the option simply to announce that it is being used is not permitted.

- Similar to the preceding rule, an option request for an option that is already in effect should not be acknowledged.

- In addition, if one side sends a request to *disable* an option, that request must be honored.

In Table 26.3, the DO, DON'T, WILL, and WON'T operations are used when one side of the connection wants to do something and inform the other side, or when one side wants the other side to perform an action. For example, when an NVT receives a WILL command followed by an option code, it means that the sender will start, or has started, using this option. The receiver of this message can reply with a DO if the option is acceptable or a DON'T if it doesn't support the option. If the sender sends a DO command, followed by an option, then the sender is telling the receiver that it would like for it to use a particular option. The receiver can respond with a WILL command if it does support the option, or a WON'T command if it does not.

In addition, a sender can send a WON'T command, which indicates that a particular option is disabled. The receiver should respond with a DON'T command. The sender also can send a DON'T command to indicate that it wants the receiver to disable an option. The response to this command must be a WON'T. Remember that an option cannot be used unless both sides agree to it. Instead, the basic NVT is used with any options that were negotiated.

Finally, some options will lead to subnegotiations to further identify parameters of a particular option. These are beyond the scope of this chapter—refer to the appropriate RFCs.

In Table 26.4, you can see a summary of RFCs that describe some of the more useful options for use with telnet.

Table 26.4   Additional Option Code Definitions

RFC	Option Code #	RFC Name
856	0	Telnet Binary Transmission
857	1	Telnet Echo Option
858	3	Telnet Suppress Go Ahead
859	5	Telnet Status Option
860	6	Telnet Timing Mark Option
726	7	Remote-Controlled Transmission and Echo
652	10	Telnet Output Carriage-Return Disposition
653	11	Telnet Output Horizontal Tabstops Options
654	12	Telnet Output Horizontal Tab Disposition
655	13	Telnet Output Formfeed Disposition
656	14	Telnet Output Vertical Tabstops Option
657	15	Telnet Output Vertical Tab Disposition
658	16	Telnet Output Linefeed Disposition
698	17	Telnet Extended ASCII Option
727	18	Telnet Logout Option
735	19	Revised Telnet Byte Macro Option
732, 1043	20	Telnet Data Entry Terminal Option: (DODIIS Implementation)
734, 736	21	Telnet SUDUP Option
749	22	Telnet SUDUP-Output Option
779	23	Telnet Send-Location
1091	24	Telnet Terminal Type Option
885	25	Telnet End of Record Option
927	26	TACACS User Identification Telnet Option
933	27	Output Marking Telnet Option
946	28	Telnet Terminal Location Number Option
1041	29	Telnet 3270 Regime Option
1053	30	Telnet X.3 PAD Option
1073	31	Telnet Window Size Option
1079	32	Telnet Terminal Speed Option
1372	33	Telnet Remote Flow Control Option

Table 26.4   Continued

RFC	Option Code #	RFC Name
1184	34	Telnet Linemode Option
1096	35	Telnet X Display Location Option
1416	37	Telnet Authentication Option
1572	39	Telnet Environment Option
2066	42	TELNET CHARSET Option
861	255	Telnet Extended Options: List Option

In addition to this summary of options, others exist that are defined in documents other than RFCs. In addition to the basic telnet commands, telnet recognizes some, but not all, of the special ASCII control code characters. Table 26.5 lists these characters.

Table 26.5   ASCII Control Characters Recognized by Telnet's NVT

Value	Name	Description
0	NULL	No operation.
10	LF	Line feed. Moves the NVT printer to the next line. Does not change horizontal position.
13	CR	Carriage return. Moves the printer to the left margin. Does not change vertical position.
7	BELL	Optional code. Rings a bell. Does not advance the print head by a character.
8	BS	Optional code. Backspace. Moves print head one position to the left.
9	HT	Optional code. Horizontal tab. Moves print head to the next tab stop.
11	VT	Optional code. Vertical tab. Moves print head to the next vertical tab stop.
12	FF	Optional code. Form feed. Moves printer to the top of the next page.

Telnet and Authentication

One of the problems with applications that were developed during the early years of TCP/IP is that Internet (or ARPANET, depending on how far back you want to go) security wasn't as big an issue as it is today. Because of this, many protocols and utilities have been exploited over the past few years by hackers who know how to take advantage of this lack of foresight. Telnet is just such an application. However, with the use of options, it is possible to perform authentication using other than the traditional clear-text method.

In RFC 2941, "Telnet Authentication Option," an option to allow for more secure authentication methods, is set forth. This specification is intended to provide a mechanism that can be used by many authentication methods. The code number used for the AUTHENTICATION option is defined as 37. In Table 26.6 you can see some of the codes used to specify different types of authentication.

Table 26.6   RFC 2941 Telnet Authentication Methods

Value	Description
0	NULL
1	Kerberos V4
2	Kerberos V5
3	SPX

Table 26.6   Continued

Value	Description
4	MINK
5	SRP
6	RSA and SRA
7	SSL
8–9	Unassigned
10	LOKI
11	SSA
12	KEA_SJ
13	KEA_SJ_INTEG
14	DSS
15	NTLM

The RFC specifies that IANA will be responsible for maintaining the numbers associated with authentication types in the future. In addition, not all of those in the table were submitted to the Internet Engineering Task Force (IETF) as a standard, so some of the values may change.

Using Telnet and FTP with a Firewall

FTP and telnet are very useful utilities. They are also very powerful utilities. For this reason, you should be careful when configuring a firewall to ensure that FTP and telnet are not used to compromise your system or network.

Firewalls employ many techniques to protect your network. However, one of the basic functions you will find in all firewalls is the capability to enable or disable ports, for both incoming and outgoing traffic. Consider the case of telnet. It may be a good idea, if your environment requires it, to allow users on your network the capability to establish a telnet session on a remote server outside of your network. The reverse, though, is not always a good idea. Because telnet allows the user to interact with the computer and issue commands at the operating-system level, it is possible that telnet could be used to (1) gather information about your systems and (2) make changes to your systems, depending on the "privileges" granted to the user account associated with the telnet session.

Yet there may be situations in which you need to allow telnet sessions from computers outside of your network. In such a case, it is a better idea to place the computer that will be the target of incoming telnet sessions in a "demilitarized zone" using a firewall. This limits telnet access to just that computer, while blocking access to other computers in your network.

The same principle applies to FTP. You might want to enable ports that allow users on your network to download files from Internet sites. For example, FTP can be used to download device driver or software updates from a vendor's site. However, it isn't always a good idea to allow users on your network to upload files to computers outside of your network. Confidential information could easily be transferred this way, and go undetected. For the same reasons, you should not always allow incoming FTP sessions. If you have a business need to let customers upload files to your network, consider using a dedicated server in a demilitarized zone in the same manner you would provide a telnet service. Decide whether you want to allow both uploads and downloads, or one but not the other.

Chapter 49, "Firewalls," explains the concept of a demilitarized zone in detail. You will also find information in that chapter about using "anonymous FTP" and some considerations for configuring servers to allow users outside your network to gain access to data as your business requires it, without compromising the rest of the network.

The R-Utilities

This famous set of network utilities was originally developed at the University of California at Berkeley and included in its versions of Unix that followed. Because all these utilities start with the letter R, which stands for remote, they often are lumped together and called the R-utilities. These utilities share more than just a common first letter. They also use an authentication scheme that most network administrators consider to be very insecure. These files will be discussed first, and then we'll look at some of these utilities, showing the syntax examples from Solaris 8 and FreeBSD for comparisons.

How the Traditional R-Utilities Authorize Access to Your Network's Resources

Newer versions of these utilities use authentication schemes using such methods as Kerberos tickets, as you will see in some of the syntax examples for the FreeBSD commands. However, because these tools were developed to make it simple to perform basic network functions, having to enter a username and password each time you used a utility was considered too much of a hassle. Those were the days, you should remember, before security was considered an issue.

To overcome this username/password obstacle, the R-utilities can use two files to perform authorization without having to send a password across the network. These are the hosts.equiv and .rhosts files.

The System's `hosts.equiv` and `.rhosts` Files

The hosts.equiv file is a global file that is managed by the system administrator for a computer. It contains a list of remote computers that are to be trusted on this computer. When a user executes one of the R-utilities, this file can be consulted to see whether the host computer of that user is a trusted one. If so, the user is allowed to perform the same actions and is given the same access as a local account of the same name. This file also can have one or more usernames associated with a remote host, restricting access to just those usernames.

The file .rhosts is a local file that can be created in any user's home directory. It performs the same function as the systemwide hosts.equiv file. The format for basic entries into either of these files is

```
hostname [username]
```

If you enter only a hostname on a line by itself, all users from that host who have accounts on this computer will be allowed access. If you place a username after the hostname (with a space or tab to separate them), that particular user will have access. To make it easier to restrict access with these files, most Unix systems allow you to use a few other methods to create entries in these files:

- **+ *username*—**Allows access for this username.
- **- *username*—**Specifically prohibits access for this username.
- **_hostname_ +—**Allows all users from _hostname_ to access the system using a local user account.
- **- _hostname_—**Specifically prohibits users from _hostname_ from access.

For example, the entry

```
hostname -username
```

prohibits the user indicated by *username* coming from the host *hostname* from gaining access to the local computer using the hosts.equiv or .rhosts file.

To make matters even more complicated, you must consider the search order and how the entries in these files are evaluated. The hosts.equiv file is searched, and then the .rhosts file is searched. When a positive entry is found, granting access, the process stops. When a negative entry is found that denies access, the process stops. If no entries are found that grant or deny access, then access is denied.

The use of these files, and indeed of any insecure earlier versions of the R-utilities, is highly discouraged. For more information about how these can be abused, see Chapter 46, "Basic Security Measures Every Network Administrator Needs to Know."

The *rlogin* Utility

This utility uses TCP (port 513) and enables you to establish an interactive session with another computer, similar to telnet. However, the rlogin command uses a much simpler protocol. It was introduced in version 4.2 of BSD Unix and is defined in RFC 1282, "BSD Rlogin." Unlike telnet, rlogin does not use option negotiation. Instead, it allows a simple exchange of commands between the two systems.

The protocol is a simple one. The client software sends a string of text to the server. This string consists of a zero byte, the login name of the user on the client, another zero byte, the login name to be used on the server, another zero byte, the terminal type, the slash character, the speed of the terminal, and, finally, another zero byte.

The rlogin server will respond to this string with a zero byte. Then, if a password is required on the server (that is, the user is not found in the hosts.equiv or .rhosts files), the server will send a prompt string to the client. If the user sends the correct password back, the session can continue. Note again here the security problem with another TCP/IP utility. The username and the password are not encrypted in most versions of this utility. They go over the network as ordinary clear text that any network sniffer can detect. Newer forms of this utility use more secure authentication methods, but the basic protocol does not define this.

Finally, the server sends a request to the client to find out the client's window size. After the session has been established, communication from the client to the server takes place using only one character at a time. When you consider that the server then echoes back the character to the client, you can start to see that rlogin isn't as efficient as some other protocols. To help prevent this, the Nagle algorithm normally is used, enabling the buffering of several characters into a single TCP segment.

The only command that the client can send to the server is the window size, and the client can send this only in response to a query from the server. The server can send various commands to the client, and it uses TCP's Urgent Data pointer to indicate the control command byte in the data stream. A client receiving a TCP segment with the Urgent Data pointer will immediately buffer all data up to the command byte and then interpret the command byte. There are only four possible commands:

- **0x02**—This causes the client to discard all buffered data that hasn't yet been displayed on the client.

- **0x10**—This switches the client to "raw" mode, in which the ASCII STOP and START characters (Ctrl+S and Ctrl+Q) are ignored by the client and passed as data to the server to deal with.

- **0x20**—This switches the client back to its normal mode of interpreting the ASCII START and STOP characters.

- **0x80**—This is the window size request the server can send to the client.

The control byte pointed to by the Urgent Data pointer is not displayed on the client's display, and all values other than those listed are ignored.

Using the `rlogin` Command

The syntax for this command will, as with most Unix commands, vary from system to system. Here we'll look at the syntax for Solaris 8 and then the syntax for FreeBSD Unix.

The syntax for the `rlogin` command for Solaris 8 is

```
rlogin [ -8EL ] [-ec ] [ -l] username | hostname
```

where

- **-8**—Indicates that 8-bit data should be used for the connection instead of 7-bit data representations.
- **-ec**—Is used to specify a different escape character. Substitute the escape character for *c*.
- **-E**—Means that no character will be recognized as the escape character.
- **-l** *username*—Is used to specify a different username for the logon procedure. The default is to use the same username you used to log on to your local system.
- *hostname*—Specifies the name of the remote host to which you want to log on.

Solaris also enables the user to enter escape characters during the `rlogin` session. The tilde character (~) starts the escape sequence. The sequence of characters ~. causes the computer to immediately disconnect from the remote host. ~susp suspends the login session if you are using a shell with Job Control.

The syntax for the `rlogin` command for FreeBSD is

```
rlogin [-468DEKLdx] [-e char] [-i localname] [-k realm] [-l username] host
```

where

- **-4 (-6)**—Specifies to use IPv4 or IPv6 addresses only.
- **-8**—Allows for 8-bit data transmissions.
- **-D**—Sets the TCP-NODELAY socket option. This can improve interactive responses, but also increases the load on the network.
- **-E**—Means that no character is recognized as the escape character.
- **-K**—Turns off all Kerberos authentication.
- **-L**—Lets the `rlogin` session run in "litout" mode.
- **-d**—Turns on socket debugging.
- **-x**—Turns on DES encryption for the data stream passed between client and server. Because the original implementation of `rlogin` uses clear-text, this is a very good option to use.
- **-e** *char*—Is used to specify a different escape character. Substitute the escape character for *char*. The default escape character is the tilde.
- **-i**—Lets the sender specify a different local name to be used for authorization purposes. Processes must have the UID of zero to use this feature.
- **-k** *realm*—Requests that `rlogin` obtain Kerberos tickets in the host *realm* instead of the host's currently defined realm.
- **-l** *username*—Is used to specify a different username for the logon procedure. The default is to use the same username that you are logged in under on your local system.
- *host*—Specifies the host with which you want to establish a remote session.

As you can see, the FreeBSD's latest version of rlogin provides more security than the basic version of this program. By adding authentication schemes other than clear-text, and by allowing the data stream to be encrypted, this utility can be used in an environment requiring a medium amount of security.

Using *rsh*

The Remote Shell (rsh) utility enables you to execute a single command on the remote node. This utility first makes a connection to the remote computer and then executes the command specified by the user. It copies standard input to the remote command, and the standard output resulting from the remote command, if any, is copied back to the local standard output. Likewise, the remote standard error stream is copied back to the local standard error stream.

This utility is not meant for use when you need to execute a lot of commands or use an interactive program, such as the vi editor, that is screen-oriented. Instead, it is a quick way to execute a single command on another network node that supports the protocol.

The rsh utility has been implemented, like most of the other R-utilities, differently on various Unix flavors.

The syntax for the rsh command on Solaris 8 is

```
rsh [ -n] [ -l username] hostname command
rsh hostname [ -n ] [ -l username ] command
rmesh [ -n ] [ -l username ] hostname command
rmesh hostname [ -n ] [ -l username ] command
hostname [ -n ] [ -l username ] command
```

This command makes a connection with the remote *hostname* system. The *command* you enter on the command line will be executed. Standard Unix inputs and outputs will be manipulated to display the results of the command on your display. Note that if you don't include a command in the syntax, you will enter an rlogin session for this command on Solaris. See the preceding section for information about using rlogin.

Command-line parameters for this command include the following:

- **-l *username***—Substitute this username on the remote system instead of using the local username.
- ***hostname***—The name of the remote host on which the command will be executed.
- ***command***—The command to be executed on the remote computer.
- **-n**—Redirects the input of rsh to /dev/null.

Remember that this utility runs just one command on the remote system. For example, you can use it to rename a file or copy a file on a remote system. To edit the file, however, you would have to use telnet or rlogin, both of which allow for interaction with a program running on a remote system.

The syntax for this command on FreeBSD is

rsh [**-46Kdnx**] [**-t** *timeout*] [**-k** *realm*] [**-l** *username*] *host* [*command*]

where

- **-4 (-6)**—Specifies to use IPv4 or IPv6 addresses only.
- **-K**—Disables Kerberos authentication.
- **-d**—Turns on socket debugging.

- **-n**—Redirects input to the special device /dev/null.

- **-x**—Turns on DES encryption for data exchanges, possibly causing a delay in response time due to the encryption overhead.

- **-t** *timeout*—If no data is sent across the connection established by rsh for *timeout* seconds, the rsh program will exit.

- **-k** *realm*—The rsh utility tries to get Kerberos tickets from the host in *realm* instead of the remote host's realm.

- **-l** *username*—Is used to specify a username on the remote system to use for authentication. The default is to use the same name as the local username.

Like the Solaris version of rsh, if you choose to omit a command from the command line when you invoke rsh, the rlogin program will run instead.

In both cases (Solaris and FreeBSD), metacharacters recognized by your shell must be enclosed in quotation marks for them to be included as part of the remote command.

You can also obtain a version of RSH and many other Unix commands and utilities by purchasing Microsoft's Services for Unix (see www.microsoft.com).

Using *rcp*

The Remote Copy (rcp) command is used to copy files between two computers on the network. You also could use FTP for this, but the rcp utility enables you to do the same thing with a more simplified syntax, and allows for authentication using .rhosts and hosts.equiv files. Another thing you can do with rcp that you can't do easily using a standard FTP client is to recursively copy directories and subdirectories.

The syntax for the rcp command for Solaris 8 is

```
rcp [ -p ] filename1 filename2
rcp [-pr ] filename ... directory
```

where

- **-p**—If possible, this option causes the copied file to have the same modification and access times as the original, as well as the same mode an any ACLs that were applied to the original file. Note that rcp will not work correctly if you try to copy ACLs to a system that doesn't support them.

- **-r**—This option is used when the destination is a directory. It indicates that each subtree that is rooted at *filename* (a directory) is copied.

In the first line of the preceding syntax, *filename1* and *filename2* are the source and destination filenames. In the second example, *filename* is a starting point for a set of subdirectories that will be copied to a directory *directory* on the remote system. Also note that you can use the rcp command to copy files between computers other than your own (third-party computers). In this case, you must specify the *filename* variables on the command line to include *hostname:path*. If you want to use a different username for authentication purposes, use the format *username@hostname:filename* instead. For third-party copies, the host that is the source of the file to be copied must have permission to access the target computer.

The FreeBSD syntax for this command is

```
rcp [-Kpx] [-k realm] file1 file2 rcp [-Kprx] [-k realm] file ... directory
```

where

- **-K**—Disables all Kerberos authentication.

- **-k *realm***—The rcp utility tries to get Kerberos tickets from the host in *realm* instead of the remote host's realm.

- **-p**—Makes rcp attempt to keep the same modification times and modes of the source files when making copies.

- **-r**—Is used when the destination is a directory. It indicates that each subtree that is rooted at *filename* (a directory) is to be copied.

- **-x**—Turns on DES encryption for data that is sent between the two computers, at the expense of a slower copy time.

This version of rcp also enables you to perform third-party copying. The addition of Kerberos authentication and DES encryption are welcome improvements over the original rcp.

Using *rwho*

The rwho command is used to show information about users on the network. It works similar to the who command, but gets information from computers on the network instead of just local users.

Both Solaris 8 and FreeBSD versions of this command assume that a computer is down if they don't receive any data from it for five minutes. If a user is logged in but does not interact with the computer for more than an hour, the user will not be included in the display by default. The syntax for this command is

```
rwho [ -a ]
```

The -a option causes the report to include all users and ignore the one-hour idle timeout.

The file /var/rwho/whod.* path is used to store data files containing the hosts on the network about which the command reports (/var/spool/rwho/rwhd.* for Solaris 8). Each computer on the network that can show up in the display produced by rwho must be running the rwhod daemon process. This background process sends out a broadcast packet of information on a periodic basis. Other servers store this information and use it when producing a display.

Using *ruptime*

For each machine on the network, the command ruptime reports a status line showing how long the system has been booted. Again, the file /var/rwho/whod.* (/var/spool/rwho/rwhd.* for Solaris 8) path is used to store data files containing the hosts on the network about which the command reports. Each system must be running the rwhod daemon. Note that this background process sends out informational packets that remote systems collect for use with both the rwho and the ruptime commands.

For this command, both Solaris 8 and FreeBSD use the same syntax:

```
ruptime [ -alrtu ]
```

where

- **-a**—Causes the utility to report on the number of users on remote machines even if they have been idle for more than one hour.

- **-l**—Causes the display to be sorted by load average.

- **-r**—Reverses the sorting order for the displayed information.

- **-t**—Causes the display to be sorted by the amount of uptime for the systems shown.
- **-u**—Causes the display to be sorted by the number of users on the systems shown.

As you can see, ruptime can be a very handy utility to use to quickly survey selected nodes on your network.

The Finger Utility

The finger utility is a more complex utility that gives the administrator a lot of information, with a syntax that allows for selective reporting. You can use finger to get information about local users or users on remote hosts on the network. RFC 1288, "The Finger User Information Protocol," is the most recent RFC in a series to define this protocol.

The finger protocol uses TCP, port 79. The `finger` command opens a TCP connection with a finger server daemon on a system and sends a line of text that makes up the query. The server responds and then closes the TCP connection. The RFC goes on to define different types of queries and how they can be forwarded from one machine to another. If you think that people who write these RFCs don't have a sense of humor, ponder the following paragraph taken from RFC 1288:

> 2.5.5. Vending Machines
>
> "Vending machines SHOULD respond to a {C} request with a list of all items currently available for purchase and possible consumption. Vending machines SHOULD respond to a {U}{C} request with a detailed count or list of the particular product or product slot. Vending machines should NEVER NEVER NEVER eat money."

Now, with a sense of humor like that, is it any wonder that they name a user information protocol "finger"? However, you should note that as the Internet continues to infiltrate almost every type of electronic appliance, there are already "snack machines" that are part of a network. Recently, beverage machines have been developed that charge a different price depending on the current temperature! The capability to inventory such machines from a remote site can greatly reduce labor costs associated with visiting each machine on a regular basis.

The syntax for the `finger` command on Solaris 8 is

```
finger [ -bfhilmpqsw ] [ username ... ]
finger [ -l ] [ username@hostname 1 ] [@hostname 2 ...@hostname n ... ] ]
finger [ -l] [ @hostname 1 [ @hostname 2 ...@hostname n ... ] ]
```

where

- **-b**—Suppresses listing the user's home directory and the shell used when using the long format output.
- **-f**—Suppresses listing the header that is displayed in the non-long format output.
- **-h**—Suppresses printing the contents of the .project file when using the long format.
- **-i**—Displays "idle" format showing only the login name, terminal, login time, and idle time.
- **-l**—Causes a long display format. More data is shown.
- **-m**—Causes matches to be made on the user's username, not on the first or last name.
- **-p**—Suppresses displaying the contents of the .plan file when using the long format.
- **-q**—Produces a quick format output. This is almost the same as the short format, but the only items displayed are the login name, terminal, and login time.

- **-s**—Causes a short form of the user information to be displayed. Less data is shown.

- **-w**—Suppresses the display of the user's full name in a short format output.

The default information displayed about each user is the username, the user's full name, the terminal type, the amount of idle time, the login time, and the hostname if the user is logged in to the system remotely. If you provide a username on the command line, more information will be displayed. When using this method, you can specify more than one username and the user does not have to be logged in to the system for finger to display information about the user. However, this is limited to just users on the machine on which you are executing the finger command.

Additional information you'll see if you specify one or more usernames includes the user's home directory and login shell, the time the user logged in (or last logged in), the last time the user received any email, and the last time the user read his email. If the plain-text files .project and .plan exist in the user's home directory, their contents will be displayed.

In the syntax that uses the *username@hostname1* [@hostname2 ... @hostnamen] or @hostname1 [@hostname2 ...@hostnamen], the finger request is sent first to the last hostname in the list (*hostnamen*), which sends it to the next-most previous host in the list, until the request reaches *hostname1*. Note also that the *username@hostname* syntax allows only the -l command-line option.

The FreeBSD syntax for this command is a little simpler. The syntax is

finger [**-lmpshoT**] [*user* ...] [*user@host* ...]

where

- **-l**—Produces a display of several lines. All the items that the -s option outputs are displayed, along with the user's home directory, home phone number, login shell, mail status, and the contents of the files .forward, .plan, .project, and .pubkey, if these files are found in the user's home directory.

- **-m**—Suppresses matching of usernames. By default, finger tries to match a login username and users' real names. This option forces finger to use only the login username.

- **-p**—When used with -l, suppresses the listing of the contents of the .forward, .plan, .project, and .pubkey files.

- **-s**—Displays the user's login name, full name, terminal, idle time, login time, and either the office location and office phone number or the remote host, depending on which of the remaining options are used.

- **-h**—Causes the -s option to display the remote host instead of the office information.

- **-o**—Causes the -s option to display the office information instead of the remote host. This is the default.

- **-T**—Is used to disable "piggybacking" data on the initial TCP connection request with some finger implementations.

This version of finger also enables you to view information about hosts on other computers. Use the format *user* for users on the local machine and *user@hostname* for remote users.

Other Services and Applications Built on the TCP/IP Suite

You'll find many services in older RFC documents referring to protocols or utilities that once served an important purpose—for example, the ARCHIE and WAIS utilities. However, as the Internet has made obsolete many older protocols and utilities, it has provided a hotbed for the development of new utilities, services, and applications. Many of these services are no longer needed or used, or are used in limited locations because more improved methods have generally replaced them.

Other protocols, such as the Simple Mail Transfer Protocol (SMTP) and the Simple Network Management Protocol (SNMP), are also very popular and useful protocols for providing application support on the network. However, these protocols are not as limited in their scope as the "utilities" discussed in this chapter. SNMP is discussed in Chapter 53, "Network Testing and Analysis Tools." SMTP and other Internet email protocols are covered in Chapter 27, "Internet Mail Protocols: POP3, SMTP, and IMAP."

Secure Network Services

As pointed out several times in this chapter, using some of the standard TCP/IP utilities that have been developed over many years can have security implications, especially now that most businesses are connecting to the Internet. The matters of user authentication and data encryption become more important when you expose your network to the world. Fortunately, as with most security issues, a need generally leads to someone coming up with a solution. In this section, we'll look at some more utilities that perform tasks similar to those already discussed, but in a more secure manner.

The Secure Shell (SSH) is the name given to a protocol that enables you to replace rsh, rlogin, rcp, telnet, rexec, rcp, and ftp with a more secure application. You can visit a Web site devoted to these utilities at www.ssh.org. Here you can find out about the specifications for the protocols, mailing lists, patches, and places to download the utilities for your system. Although there are no Request for Comments documents yet for SSH, several Internet drafts are available at the Web site that describe everything from authentication to transport protocols.

SSH provides you with complementary commands for the utilities listed in the preceding paragraph. For example, instead of using the `ftp` command, you would use the `sftp` command. The same goes for the other utilities.

Secure Shell utilities can use various encryption methods for both authentication and encryption of the data sent across the network. Because different software houses may implement the SSH protocol a little differently, you might want to consider checking which ciphers are used by a particular product.

Internet Mail Protocols: POP3, SMTP, and IMAP

SOME OF THE MAIN TOPICS IN THIS CHAPTER ARE

Although protocols such as IP are responsible for transporting and routing traffic on the Internet, application protocols such as SMTP, IMAP, and POP3 provide the message exchanges needed to make client/server applications available over the network. The following list briefly explains these protocols:

- The Simple Mail Transfer Protocol (SMTP) is used to transfer mail messages from a client to an SMTP server, and to transfer those messages from one SMTP server to another.

- The Post Office Protocol (POP3) is a client mail application used to retrieve messages from an SMTP server. This protocol is often referred to as POP3 because it is the third version of the protocol.

- The Internet Message Access Protocol (IMAP) is used to store email messages on a server. A client that supports IMAP can view the headers of email messages and decide to download messages, or just read them and leave them on the server. IMAP also enables the user to create folders on the server that can be used to store messages. This protocol is often referred to as IMAP4, because it is the fourth version of the protocol.

In this chapter, you'll learn about the basic functions provided by these three protocols.

Note

In addition to the mail protocols discussed in this chapter, you can use an HTML interface with most email providers. This enables you to check email without using a mail client, such as Outlook Express. Instead, you can enter the URL for your mail server (such as `mail.twoinc.com`), and examine, read, reply, and delete mail using Web pages generated dynamically by the server. For more information about HTML (and HTTP), see Chapter 36, "The Hypertext Transfer Protocol."

How SMTP Works

As an application protocol, SMTP relies on the error-detection and correction mechanisms of the underlying transport protocols and does not implement these sorts of functions in the SMTP protocol. For example, TCP uses sequence numbers to keep track of TCP segments sent and acknowledged. Those that are not acknowledged within a timely fashion are retransmitted. Thus, SMTP, using TCP as a transport protocol, doesn't have to worry about this sort of thing. SMTP has also been implemented using other transfer protocols, including NCP, NITS, and X.25. For purposes of this text, I will be focusing on SMTP using the TCP Transport service, because that is the most common model you are likely to see. Because SMTP is an application protocol, it's associated with a port number just like FTP, Telnet, and other applications that make up the TCP/IP suite. The port generally used for SMTP is TCP port 25.

Note

SMTP was first defined by RFC 821, but it has been superceded by RFC 2821, "Simple Mail Transfer Protocol." Additional RFC documents have added functionality to the protocol. For example, RFC 3207, "SMTP Service Extensions for Secure SMTP over Transport Layer Security." This RFC provides for both authentication and encryption for the transfer of email, based on TLS. TLS is basically an upgrade to the Secure Sockets Layer (SSL) security used by many Web browsers. For more information on these security protocols, see Chapter 51, "Encryption Technology."

SMTP is used to send email from a client to an SMTP server and for SMTP servers to exchange mail. Other protocols, such as POP3 and IMAP, are used by clients to retrieve mail from mailboxes that reside on SMTP servers. SMTP is not used for that purpose, as you can see in Figure 27.1.

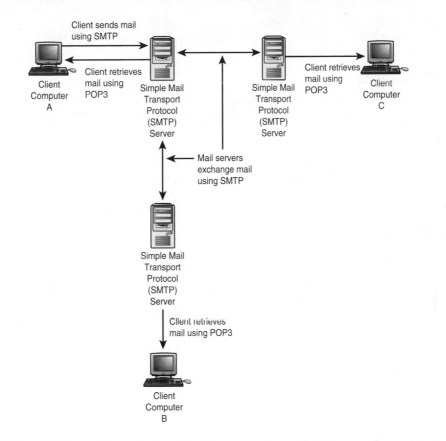

Figure 27.1   SMTP is used to upload email to the server, whereas POP3 is generally used to download mail.

In this figure, you can see that Computer A sends outgoing email to its local SMTP server operated by the Internet Service Provider (ISP). Computer A uses the POP3 protocol (Post Office Protocol) to check for and retrieve messages stored on the server. If Computer A needs to send an email to Computer B, the message travels first through SMTP to the local SMTP server. This server looks up the mail server for the domain in which the recipient on Computer B resides and sends the message, again using SMTP, to Computer B's SMTP server. When Computer B decides to check messages, it uses POP3 and gets the email sent by Computer A. Note that if either computer wants to send email to Computer C, then still another SMTP server becomes involved.

Note, however, that there isn't real centralization. SMTP servers communicate among themselves directly and do not go through any central clearinghouse. It's possible that a mail message will take a route through several SMTP servers to reach the eventual mailbox that is the destination of the email. When a client initially starts a session with an SMTP server, it can give the server a source-route (list of hosts) through which the message should travel to get to its destination. This is called a *forward-path*. In addition, the client can give the server a *reverse-path*, which is a source-route to return error messages to the client if something happens during the transmission of the email message.

Because it is a decentralized system, the operation is simplified. The failure of an SMTP server, here and there, doesn't affect the entire Internet. The only people who get to complain are those who use the downed SMTP servers for their email.

When mail is downloaded from an SMTP server using POP3, the messages are deleted from the SMTP server's database and stored locally on the user's computer. If you delete the email messages stored locally on your computer, they are gone forever!

The SMTP Model

RFC 2821 recognizes that an SMTP server would have to service both local clients and relay mail messages to other SMTP servers when the destination is not a client of the original server. In the original RFC, names were given for the different processes involved, depending on who is doing what to whom. For example, SMTP applications can act as either of the following, depending on the direction of the flow of information:

- **Sender-SMTP**—The client establishes a two-way (full-duplex) session with the local SMTP sever.

- **Receiver-SMTP**—The SMTP server receives commands from the Sender-SMTP. The Receiver-SMTP process can be an SMTP server that can deliver the message to its recipient's mailbox or to another SMTP server.

To bring these definitions up-to-date using more modern terminology, the Sender-SMTP is now referred to in the RFCs as the SMTP Client (Sender-SMTP) and the SMTP Server (Receiver-SMTP).

Note that when a message passes through several SMTP servers, one server becomes the SMTP Client and the server to which the message is being sent becomes the SMTP Server. The SMTP Client process does not always indicate the original client that created the email message in the first place.

In fact, there are four types of SMTP server roles that are dependent on the services provided:

- **Originator**—A server that originates an email message and sends it out onto the Internet (or an intranet).

- **Delivery**—A server that receives email messages and stores them for the client to retrieve.

- **Relay**—An SMTP server that relays an email message from one SMTP server to another, and is not the originator or delivery SMTP server.

- **Gateway**—A server that acts as a go-between SMTP and another messaging system. The gateway may modify the contents of the SMTP message to accommodate the other messaging system.

Most of the original definition of SMTP from RFC 821 remains intact. A few other RFCs over the years have added minor changes to the protocol, but it has remained basically a system for request/reply messages, or in the words of the RFC, a lock-step method. A request is made and a reply is sent. In the original version, a client sends a command to the server and the server responds with a single reply. The connection between the client and the SMTP server is a simple two-way channel (using the single TCP port 25).

SMTP Service Extensions

SMTP was developed more than a decade ago. Over time it has been necessary to provide additional functionality to the protocol, called service extensions. These were first added to SMTP by RFC 1425, "SMTP Service Extensions." Further RFCs added to these additional services, which are now covered by RFC 2821. An additional extension has been added by RFC 2920, "SMTP Service Extension for Command Pipelining."

Service extensions are negotiated between SMTP servers to find out which extensions are supported by each server. There are four basic categories of service extensions:

- Delivery
- Authentication and Security
- Command Pipelining
- Enhanced Status Codes

The Internet Assigned Numbers Authority (IANA) is responsible for maintaining a list of SMTP extensions. You can consult the IANA at www.iana.org.

SMTP Commands and Response Codes

The first command that the Sender-SMTP client sends is either the HELO command or the EHLO command. EHLO is now the preferred command and is part of the basic service extensions. If an SMTP server does not support additional service extensions, it will respond with an error message indicating a syntax error.

This is the basic syntax for SMTP commands:

`<command> <arguments> <CRLF>`

In this syntax, <CRLF> indicates that a carriage-return followed by a line-feed character is used to signal the end of the command line.

In the following commands, the term *forward-path* is a list of hosts the message travels through to reach its destination. The term *reverse-path* is used to indicate how to get back to the sender of the email, which can be helpful when returning error or other informational messages.

Note

One important thing to note about SMTP commands is that they are not case-sensitive. The client or server code must accept both upper- and lowercase text for commands and not differentiate between the two. Commands can even be a mixture of upper- and lowercase letters. This is *not* true, however, of user mailbox names, although hostnames (that is, the portion of the email address following the "@" sign) also are not case-sensitive. Because SMTP allows mailbox names to be case-sensitive, the actual user's mailbox name may be limited to a particular case on some servers and should be preserved by the server and transmitted exactly as received.

The basic SMTP commands include the following:

- **HELO**—This command (or the next one in this list) is sent by the Sender-SMTP client to the SMTP server to begin the mail transfer session. The argument to this command is the hostname of the Sender-SMTP computer.

- **EHLO**—This is now the preferred command that replaces the HELO command and indicates that the Sender-SMTP client wants to use SMTP extensions. If the SMTP server supports SMTP extensions, it returns a code of 250 to the client. If the server does not support the extensions, it returns a code of 500.

- **AUTH**—This stands for *authenticate*. The user provides a username/password to the SMTP server to authenticate the client before mail can be sent.

- **ATRN**—This stands for authenticated TURN. After a client has been authenticated to the SMTP server, this command instructs the Receiver-SMTP to return an OK response. In that case, the SMTP server must assume the function as the sender of the mail. Otherwise, the SMTP server can return a Bad Gateway message (reply number 502) and remain in the role as Receiver-SMTP.

- **DATA**—This command is followed by actual data that makes up the email message. This includes both the body text and such things as the subject line.

- **EXPN**—This stands for *expand*. This command requests the SMTP server to tell the client whether the argument included with the command is a mailing list. If so, the server returns a list of the members of the mailing list to the client.

- **HELP**—This command instructs the SMTP server to return help information to the sender. The HELP command might or might not contain arguments.

- **MAIL**—This command includes the *reverse path* as its argument. This is the name of the sender, but it also can be a list of hosts that were used to relay the mail message from its original Sender-SMTP. In a list of hosts, the first host is the current Receiving-SMTP server. The last is the destination of the email.

- **NOOP**—This is the "no operation" command. The server responds with OK.

- **QUIT**—The Sender-SMTP sends this command when it is finished. The server should return an OK message and then close down the transmission channel (that is, TCP connection).

- **RCPT**—This stands for recipient. The argument for this command is a single recipient, specified by using a forward-path list preceded by the letters TO:. If a mail message is being sent to more than one recipient, a separate RCPT command must be issued for every recipient.

- **RSET**—This aborts the current email transaction. The SMTP server should respond with an OK message.

- **SAML**—This stands for Send and Mail. Mail is the typical use today with SMTP. The send method is meant to be used when the SMTP server has been implemented to deliver mail directly to a recipient that is actively connected. The argument for this command, again, is a reverse-path showing the path to the destination of the email. The reverse-path text is preceded by the text FROM:.

- **SEND**—This command, not often implemented, specifies that the mail message be delivered directly to the destination, if it's actively connected. If this cannot be done, the server returns a message code of 450 (the mailbox is not available). Similar to the SAML command, the argument for this command is the text FROM: followed by the reverse-path to the destination mailbox.

- **SIZE**—This command lets the Sender-SMTP inform the server of the size of the mail message it wants to send. This is supported only by SMTP implementations that use the SMTP Service Extensions. The server can return a message indicating that it cannot handle mail of the size requested, or it can accept the message.

- **SOML**—This stands for Send or Mail. Similar to SAML, this command requests that the mail be "sent" (for example, directly to the actively connected recipient) or mailed. The server tries the Send method first, and if that fails, the server attempts to deliver the message to the destination mailbox.

- **TURN**—This command instructs the Receiver-SMTP to assume the role of the sender of the mail (in which an OK response is returned). The server can refuse (with a code 502) and remain in the role of Receiver-SMTP.

- **VRFY**—This command asks the Receiver-SMTP to verify that the username that is passed as an argument with the command be checked to determine whether it's valid. If the username is a valid one, the full name and mailbox of the user are returned.

Because SMTP allows for sending a single message to multiple recipients, a large mailing list could generate a lot of network traffic. Thus, the original SMTP RFC 821 recommends that only one copy of the actual email be sent to the server in this sort of situation. The SEND command (and its associated commands) was intended originally to send a message directly to a user's terminal. In today's world of PCs and workstations, it isn't typical to find a user sitting at a terminal. It also usually is not desirable to have mail pop up suddenly on a user's terminal if this function is still supported in your network. Instead, the MAIL command and its other associated commands are usually used.

The DATA portion of the mail message is terminated using the period (.) character by itself on a single line—which is followed by the line terminating characters (CRLF). Typically this will be <CRLF>.<CRLF>, because the first <CRLF> terminates the last line of actual data.

Note

SMTP commands are sent as single lines of commands or data terminated with **<CRLF>**. However, the term *mail object* is used to describe an email message. A mail object consists of an *envelope* and the content of the mail message. The envelope contains such information as the sender and recipient addresses and protocol extensions. The content consists of the data sent by the message.

SMTP Response Codes

Remember that for each command issued by the Sender-SMTP, a single response is expected from the Receiver-SMTP. This simple lock-step method keeps things synchronized so that both sides of the connection are aware of the current state of the transaction. The three-digit response codes that the Receiver-SMTP can use are similar in format to those returned by FTP servers. The first digit indicates the general meaning (or category) of the response.

These are the first digits for SMTP response codes:

- **1**—This is a positive response. The command has been accepted by the SMTP server and the server is waiting for further information to determine whether it should continue or abort processing. At this time, no SMTP commands allow this kind of reply message.

- **2**—This is a positive response. The function requested by the client-SMTP has been completed, and the server is ready for another command.

- **3**—This is a positive response. This is similar to category 2 but indicates that the action requested is being held up, waiting for further information or commands from the Sender-SMTP.

- **4**—This is a negative response. It indicates that something went wrong and the command could not be completely processed. The Sender-SMTP should retry the command, or sequence of commands, that led up to this response.

- **5**—This is a negative response. Unlike the "4" response code category, this one indicates that an error has occurred that prevents the command from being executed, such as a misspelling. The command can be tried again, but not unless the Sender-SMTP can determine the problem and correct it before trying again.

The second digit of the response code provides a further subdivision within that category to further indicate the response. The second digit can have the following values:

- **0**—This indicates a syntax error or that the particular command is not supported by the server. For example, if the Sender-SMTP client supports the SMTP service extensions but the Receiver-SMTP server does not, it returns this value.

- **1**—This is used in replies that return help messages to the client.

- **2**—This is used for replies that refer to the transmission channel.

- **5**—This is used in replies that are reporting the status of the mail system, as it pertains to the requested mail transfer or the current command.

Note in the preceding list that numbers 3 and 4 are omitted. They are undefined at this time.

The third digit further delineates the response indicated by the first two digits, and the list of possible codes that result from this combination is much too long to list here. Table 27.1 lists just a few of the more common numeric responses that are used in most SMTP implementations today.

Table 27.1   Typical Reply Codes Used by SMTP

Reply Code	Definition
500	Syntax error or unrecognized command.
501	Syntax error in parameters or arguments.
502	Command not implemented.
503	Bad sequence of commands.
504	Command parameter not implemented.
211	System status or system help reply.
214	Help message (useful only for the user).
250	The requested mail action is okay or completed.
251	The user is not a local user, so the email will be forwarded.
252	Cannot VRFY (see preceding commands), but will attempt delivery.
450	Mailbox unavailable (that is, busy), so requested action not taken.
550	Mailbox not found, not accessible, or rejected due to policy.
451	Action aborted due to error in processing.
551	User is not local, followed by a possible forward-path to use.
452	Action not taken due to insufficient system storage.
552	Action aborted because it will exceed the storage allocation.
553	Action not taken because mailbox syntax is incorrect.
354	Start mail input and end with <CRLF>.<CRLF>.
554	Transaction failed or reply that there is SMTP service available.

Putting It All Together

Now that you've seen the simple command set that is used by SMTP, and the simple response code mechanism, you can put it all together and see an example of how a particular mail transaction might occur:

1. First, the Sender-SMTP sends a HELO or an EHLO command to the SMTP server.

2. The MAIL command is used, with the reverse-path information. At this state, the SMTP server knows who wants to send the mail message and a return path to send back error messages should anything go awry. The server clears the necessary buffers and sends the "250 OK" message back to the sender.

3. The RCPT command is issued by the client giving a forward-path of exactly one recipient of the mail message. If more than one recipient is the target of the message, multiple RCPT commands must be used. The "250 OK" response is sent if the server thinks it can get the message delivered. If not, the SMTP server returns a code of 550, which is a failure code.

4. The DATA command is sent to the server. The server will return an intermediate reply code, 354, indicating that the remaining lines it receives from the sender will be interpreted as part of the email message.

5. The client sends each line of text, and the server responds with "250 OK" for each line received. When the client is finished sending the message, a line with a single period character (".") is sent (with the appropriate \<CRLF\> that ends every line of text in SMTP).

6. After receiving a final OK from the server, the client issues the QUIT command to terminate the session.

In these steps, information typically found in an email message—the subject, date, and so on—are included as part of the email message data that is transmitted following the DATA command. Also, this is a simple message exchange. It can get more complicated. For example, the server can return a reply code of "251 - User not local; will forward to..." followed by the forward-path information. This happens when the Receiver-SMTP knows the correct host on which a destination user's mailbox is located, but it differs from the one sent by the client. Another message of a similar type leaves the process of sending mail to another destination up to the client. This message, "551 - User not local..." supplies the client with the forward-path that the client can use to deliver the message. In this case, however, the server does not forward the message but lets the client take further action.

The Post Office Protocol (POP3)

Mail clients use SMTP to send outgoing mail to an SMTP server. To retrieve mail messages, however, the Post Office Protocol (currently version 3) generally is used. POP3 is a stateful protocol, progressing from one state to another, depending on the results of the transaction in progress and the commands that are issued. The states are listed here:

- **AUTHORIZATION**—In this state, the user supplies a username and password to authenticate the client to the mail server. In its original implementation, the protocol supports clear-text for username and password transmissions. This, of course, can be a security problem, and other techniques should be used in a secure environment.

- **TRANSACTION**—In this state, the client issues commands and receives responses from the server.

- **UPDATE**—In this state, the client has finished its commands (by issuing the QUIT command), and the server can then delete messages that were marked for deletion and close the TCP connection.

In the following sections, you'll see what happens during each state and the POP3 commands that can be used in each state. Similar to SMTP, commands are not case-sensitive and are either 3 or 4 characters long. The total length of arguments allowed for a command is 40 characters. Responses, however, can be up to 512 characters in length.

Finally, the status indicators that the POP3 server can return to the client are limited to only two:

- **+OK**—A positive response.
- **-ERR**—A negative response.

Each of these status indicators can be followed by text that describes the response. In many cases, the response consists of multiple lines. Both the +OK and the -ERR status indicators must be sent by the server in uppercase only. When multiple lines are sent as part of a response, the same method used by SMTP to mark the end of the response is used: the period character on a line by itself.

The AUTHORIZATION State

A POP3 server typically listens on TCP port number 110 for incoming requests from POP3 clients. After a TCP connection is established between the client and the POP3 server, the POP3 server sends a greeting to the client. At this point, the process is said to be in the AUTHORIZATION state. During this state, the client uses some authentication method to identify itself to the POP3 server. This can be clear-text username and password combinations, or it can be a more secure authorization method. For more information about secure forms of authentication when using POP3, see RFC 1734, "POP3 AUTHentication command." This RFC defines the AUTH command that can be used to negotiate an authentication mechanism between the client and the server.

After the client has been authenticated to the POP3 server, the server attempts to gain an exclusive lock on the client's mailbox files. This lock prevents changes to the mailbox during the session so that the current collection of messages remains the same through the UPDATE state. Failure to lock the mailbox could allow new messages to arrive. As you'll find out in the next section, the server uses message numbers to identify each message in the mailbox. If new messages were allowed to enter the mailbox while the users were accessing it, it would be possible for confusion to exist during the UPDATE state, especially if messages are to be deleted. Thus, the mailbox is locked so that it will remain consistent for the current session.

The TRANSACTION State

After authentication has been performed successfully, the process enters into the TRANSACTION state, in which the client can send commands to the POP3 server. When finished issuing commands to the server, the client uses the QUIT command to terminate the session. At this point, the server enters the UPDATE state.

The POP3 server assigns a unique message number, beginning with 1, to each message in the mailbox. During this TRANSACTION state, the client can use the following commands to communicate with the POP3 server:

- **STAT**—This "status" command results in the server returning information about the mailbox to the client. This is called a *drop listing*. The format is the +OK status indicator followed by a single space and then the number of messages currently in the mailbox. The drop listing also contains the size of the messages contained in the mailbox in octets (bytes).

- **LIST**—This command can be optionally followed by a message number. If a message number is included, the POP3 server returns a "scan listing" for the specified message. If no message number is specified, the server responds with the +OK status indicator and then lists, line by line, a scan listing for each message in the mailbox. The scan listing consists of the message number followed by one single space and then the size of the message in octets.

- **RETR**—This is the retrieve command used to pull copies of messages from the server. A message number must follow the RETR command. The server responds with the +OK status indicator, followed by a multiline response that consists of the actual text of the mail message itself. The message is terminated with the period character.

- **DELE**—This command allows the client to request that a message be deleted from the POP3 server. Again, a specific message number is required. The message will be marked as deleted, but it still exists in the mailbox until the session enters the UPDATE state.

- **NOOP**—Again, the no operation command does nothing, but the POP3 server responds with the +OK status indicator.

- **RSET**—This "reset" command causes any messages that have been marked as deleted to be reset to a nondelete state.

After the client has finished issuing commands to the server and processing the responses the POP3 server returns, the client issues the QUIT command to indicate that it is finished. This ends the TRANSACTION state.

The UPDATE State

After the QUIT command has been received by the POP3 server, the session enters the UPDATE state. In this state, the POP3 server can delete the mail messages that were previously marked for deletion by the client. Again, if the session is terminated (by a network failure, for example) before the client can issue the QUIT command, messages that were marked for deletion are not deleted because the session never makes it to the UPDATE state.

When the POP3 server deletes messages during this state, it sends the +OK status indicator back to the client. If an error occurs trying to delete any of the messages, the -ERR status indicator is returned to the client.

After deleting the messages, the server performs other housekeeping chores, such as removing its lock on the mailbox, and then terminates the TCP connection.

The Internet Message Access Protocol Version 4 (IMAP4)

This Internet email protocol was also developed many years ago, but has been gaining wide adoption only in the past five years. Like POP3, users can download email messages from an IMAP server. However, it is also possible to leave the messages on the server. You can download a list of header information (such as the sender, subject line, and date of the email) and decide which messages you want to read. The messages still reside on the server. You do not have to download them to your workstation. Similar to the way in which POP3 email clients function, you can also create folders on the IMAP server so that you can organize your email. When using POP3 or IMAP, you can also create local folders that are stored on your computer's hard drive.

Storing email messages on a central server enables a system administrator to create backups of the email database—reducing the worry of accidentally deleting a message after you download it from an SMTP server. Provided that the message was put to backup before you deleted it on an IMAP server, it can be restored from the backup. Another benefit for the network administrator is that it is easy to enforce limits on the number of messages that can accumulate in a user's mailbox, and automatically delete older messages. Of course, a good administrator will first send out an email to users approaching their limit to inform them.

Perhaps a more important feature that is useful to the end user is that you can access your email from more than one location. For example, you can read email at work or from home, and it will appear the same. This can be useful for mobile users who are away from the office. Using POP3, messages that are downloaded to your workstation may no longer be available on the SMTP server. IMAP will store the messages on a central server so that you can access them from any location that allows a connection to your network, such as through a VPN or an authenticated Web-based client. You can read messages while on the road and still have them to download to your mail client back at your office when you return. The alternative, when using a POP3 client, is that you have to extract the messages from your client software on your laptop and then import them into the client software on your desktop computer.

Note

Although most POP3 clients adhere to the RFC standard, there is a loophole in the standard that can be used to leave messages on the server, in a manner similar to IMAP. This is not the intention of the design of POP3 clients, however.

Of course, the end user can also delete messages from the IMAP server via client software if they are no longer needed.

Note

IMAP is a client protocol, like POP3. When IMAP is used, the SMTP protocol is still used to send email messages. IMAP is used only to view, delete, rename, or download messages from the central IMAP server.

Transport Protocols

IMAP is an application protocol. As with POP3 and SMTP, the underlying transport protocol is TCP/IP. The IMAP server listens on port 143 for requests from IMAP clients. The mechanism for receiving data is also similar to SMTP. Lines of data (text or other data) are used, and each line is terminated by the <CRLF> sequence.

Client Commands

Each command sent by the client application begins with a *tag*. Each tag consists of a string of characters followed by the line of text. A tag consists of the unique identifier of the command or the message sequence number. This allows the client and server to keep track of which requests and responses are being sent or acknowledged. Either of the following may be part of the tag:

- **Unique Identifiers (UIDs)**—These usually exist across sessions between the client and the IMAP server. Thus, these numbers are not assigned in a sequential manner; however, they should be assigned in an ascending order should they change.

- **Message Sequence Number**—Each message in the user's mailbox is assigned a message sequence number, starting with the number one, so that each message is uniquely identified in the mailbox of that user by this number. When messages are deleted, the message sequence number for those messages that follow the deleted message are reassigned to maintain a contiguous numerical ascending order.

Note

There are two exceptions to the rule that a client command code is not followed by text that consists of a complete command. The first is one that sends an *octet* count. An octet is just another way of saying a *byte* of information.

The second situation involves authentication. In this case, a response is required from the server before the command sequence can be completed.

System Flags

The IMAP server also maintains a set of flags that tell it the status of each email message. All system flags begin with a backslash (\). These are the common system flags:

- **\Seen**—The message has been read by the client software application.
- **\Answered**—The message has been sent an answer by the client software.
- **\Flagged**—The message has been marked for some type of action, such as deletion, urgency, or special attention.
- **\Deleted**—The message has been marked for deletion by the function called expunge.
- **\Draft**—The message has not been finished and is flagged as a "draft" message so that you can save it and complete it later.
- **\Recent**—The message is new to the current session. If more than one session is opened by client software, this flag may not be seen by all client software applications.

Retrieving the Message Header and Body of the Message

Because IMAP must interact with SMTP, it recognizes the SMTP *envelope*, which consists of the header information and data stored in the email message. There are several states that the protocol goes through when interacting with the IMAP server.

The *selected state* means that a mailbox has been selected. The *logout state* indicates that the connection is to be terminated by either the client or the server.

Data Formatting

Although all transfers occur in text format, similar to SMTP, there are several forms of data that can be used with commands/responses that are exchanged between the client and the server of the IMAP computers:

- **Atom**—One or more special characters.
- **Number**—One or more numerical digits.
- **String**—Two versions of this type are used:
  - A *literal string* consists of a sequence of zero or more string ASCII characters. The literal string is prefixed with a number (enclosed in braces {}) that indicate the number of characters to follow. The literal string includes the <CRLF> characters. An empty literal string is represented as {0}<CRLF>.
  - A *quoted string* is a string of characters made up of zero or more 7-bit characters, not including the <CRLF> characters. The string of characters contains a quote character (") at the start and end of the string as a delimiter of the string. Thus, no count of characters is required. An empty quoted string is represented as "".
- **8-bit binary text**—This type of data uses MIME (Multi-Purpose Internet Mail Extensions) that transfers encoding using 8-bit encoding.
- **Parenthesized list**—A sequence of data structures, each delimited by a space character, and surrounded by the parentheses characters (and). An empty list is represented as ().

In addition, the *NIL* data type is a special type of the *atom* data type which indicates that a data type is nonexistent. This is used to differentiate between the null string "" and the null parenthesized list ().

The User's Inbox and Other Mailbox Naming

Most mailbox names used by IMAP4 depend on the particular IMAP implementation. The *Inbox* is a reserved term used to designate the incoming mail (inbox) of a user.

Other mailbox names start with the pound (#) character.

Note

Other characters than # are used for foreign implementations of the mailbox character.

Universal Commands

Clients may also send the following commands:

- **Capability**—This command starts with the AUTH command to determine whether the server can use a particular authentication method.

- **NOOP (No Operation)**—Generally does nothing. This command can be used to poll the server to update the client's listing to see whether any new messages are available, or to reset a time after which the client will be logged off the server. In other words, it's an "I'm still here" type of command.

- **LOGOUT**—This tells the server that the client software is finished and the connection should be closed.

Other IMAP Commands
Non-Authenticated Commands

In addition to the commands listed earlier in this chapter concerning IMAP, the following commands are used before the user has been authenticated to the server. These are the commands that are indeed used during the initial authentication process.

- **AUTHENTICATE**—Is followed by the name of an authentication mechanism, and the server can ask for additional data for the authentication. The server can then accept or reject the client's logon. The server can also reject this command if it does not support the method of authentication requested by the server. Subsequent communications between the client and the server depend on the method of authentication chosen.

- **LOGIN**—Sends the user's name and password in clear text without using any encryption mechanism, such as LOGON OGLETREE ZIRA. In an environment where security is important, the AUTHENTICATION command should be used to select a more secure mechanism.

Authenticated Commands

These commands can be used after the client has authenticated itself to the server:

- **SELECT**—Is used to select the mailbox. The server can respond that the mailbox exists and, if so, can indicate the number of recent messages, and any flags defined in the mailbox (such as urgent).

- **EXAMINE**—Is nearly identical to the SELECT command, except that the mailbox is available for read-only access.

- **CREATE**—Is used to create a new mailbox.

- **DELETE**—Is used to delete a mailbox.

- **RENAME**—Renames an existing mailbox.

- **SUBSCRIBE**—Is used to subscribe to a newsgroup, such as pets.cats.zira.

- **UNSUBSCRIBE**—You guessed it—is used to unsubscribe from a newsgroup.

- **LIST**—Lists the contents of a mailbox (mail or newsgroup).

- **LSUB**—Returns a list of names for newsgroup lists the user has subscribed to, even if they no longer exist.

- **STATUS**—Obtains the status of the mailbox. Replies can include MESSAGES (number of messages in the mailbox), RECENT (number of messages in the mailbox with the \Recent flag set), UIDNEXT (the value of the unique identifier, UID, that will be assigned to the next message received), or UIDVALIDITY (the unique identifier validity value of the mailbox).

- **APPEND**—Adds a new message to another mailbox.

- **CLOSE**—Removes messages that have the /Deleted flag set, unless the mailbox was opened with EXAMINE or is in a read-only state.

- **EXPUNGE**—Permanently removes messages with the /Deleted flag set.
- **SEARCH**—Searches a mailbox for messages per criteria set by the client. A large number of criteria can be used, which can be obtained by reading RFC 2060.
- **FETCH**—Obtains all or part of a message (such as the header or body of text of the message) for the client to read.
- **STORE**—Alters data that is part of a message in a mailbox.
- **COPY**—Copies a message to the end of a destination mailbox.

The responses sent by the server to the client will depend on the particular command in this list, and the list is quite lengthy. As with the SEARCH command, the reader is encouraged to read RFC 2060. This chapter was designed to give you an idea of how a client interacts with the server to get or manipulate messages stored on the server.

Troubleshooting Tools for TCP/IP Networks

28

SOME OF THE MAIN TOPICS IN THIS CHAPTER ARE

CHAPTER 28

Because TCP/IP allows for decentralized management—many separately managed networks are interconnected through the Internet or an intranet—tools have been developed for troubleshooting connection and configuration problems dealing with the TCP/IP protocols and services. These tools can be used for troubleshooting problems within your local network, as well as for attempting to isolate Internet-related problems. In Chapter 25, "Overview of the TCP/IP Protocol Suite," you learned about the Internet Control Message Protocol (ICMP) and the User Datagram Protocol (UDP). These two components of the TCP/IP suite are put to use in this chapter to build tools that are helpful for diagnosing simple problems. In addition, in this chapter you will learn some other utilities that are not part of the standard TCP/IP implementation.

Checking the Host System's Configuration First

Before you start to check the cables, network adapters, hubs, and other physical components of the network, you should check to see whether there is a problem with a computer's TCP/IP configuration. You can do this by using the tools provided with the operating system. Information about Windows configurations can be found in Chapter 25. Linux or Unix users should check their specific documentation and man (manual) pages for information on how to configure networking on a system. This configuration information can usually be entered during the installation of the operating system, but you may find it necessary to change it. For example, if you move the computer to a different subnet, you will have to make changes. Check to be sure that the system has an IP address that uses the same network number as the other computers on the local subnet. Also check to be sure that the correct subnet mask and default gateway are used. If you are using DHCP to assign configuration information, check to see that there is a DHCP server on the subnet, or a DHCP relay agent operating on the subnet. If everything checks out okay, it is time to start using the basic troubleshooting tools that are available with most versions of TCP/IP.

▶▶ The Dynamic Host Configuration Protocol (DHCP) is covered in Chapter 29, "BOOTP and Dynamic Host Configuration Protocol (DHCP)."

Using *hostname* and Related Commands

The hostname command is perhaps the simplest command you can use to begin checking the configuration of a host computer. On Windows systems, this command prints the name of the host computer on which it is executed. Just enter the command in the Command Prompt window.

Why would you want to use the hostname command? Because the hostname is translated into an IP address, you can use the system's hostname to ensure that the correct IP address is associated with that name. If a Domain Name System (DNS) server shows a different IP address, you will know that you cannot reach this particular host by using its hostname. If this is the case, check to see whether the IP address is in use by another system. If not, you can change the DNS record so that the hostname and IP address are related. Other methods can also be used to translate hostnames to IP addresses. See Chapter 30, "Network Name Resolution," for more information about this topic.

The hostname command can be used on Unix and Linux. Depending on the operating system, and how your network is configured, and the command-line parameters used, you may get just the name assigned to your computer, or the fully qualified DNS name, as well as other Unix/Linux-specific information. You will find several other *related commands* discussed here that can be used to return information about the name of the system, as well as network information. Whereas this command on Windows NT/2000/XP systems outputs the name of the host to the command line, the Linux version offers you many options for viewing the hostname for the system. Following is the syntax for using hostname (and a few variants that return similar information) for Linux Version 8.0:

```
hostname [-v] [-a] [--alias] [-d] [--domain] [-f] [--fqdn]
         [-i] [--ip-address] [--long] [-s] [--short] [-y] [--yp]
         [--nis] [-n] [--node]
```

```
hostname [-v] [-F filename] [--file filename] [hostname]
domainname [-v] [-F filename] [--file filename] [name]
nodename [-v] [-F filename] [-file filename] [name]

dnsdomainname [?-v]
nisdomainname [?-v]
ypdomainname [?-v]
```

- **[-a] [--alias]**—Displays the alias name of the host if one is being used. The alias name should be found in your Domain Name System (DNS) server database.

- **[-d] [--domain]**—Displays the name of the DNS domain.

- **[-F] [--file filename]**—Reads the hostname from the specified file *filename*. Note that the hostname file is now considered a relic of the past, but it still serves a useful purpose for some specific situations, as discussed in Chapter 30.

- **[-f] [--fqdn] [--long]**—Displays the FQDN (fully qualified domain name). A FQDN consists of a short hostname and the DNS domain name found in the /etc/hosts file.

- **[-h] [--help]**—Prints a usage message and exits. This is all you have to remember if you don't carry this book around with you!

- **[-I] [--ip-address]**—Displays the IP address(es) of the host.

- **[-s] [--short]**—Displays the short hostname. That is, instead of the FQDN, only the first part of the hostname (before the first period character) is displayed.

- **[-V] [--version]**—Prints version information on standard output and exits.

- **[-v] [--verbose]**—Causes the command to produce additional output.

- **[-y] [--yp] [--nis]**—Displays the NIS (or the older YP) domain name. If a parameter is given (or --filename), then root also can set a new NIS domain.

As you can see, the Linux command is a little more complex than the Windows version. The following related commands can also be used: domainname, nisdomainname, and ypdomainname. Each will give you the hostname that is stored in the NIS (Network Information System) database.

Note

YP stands for Yellow Pages, which is now called Network Information System, or NIS. The name was changed due to a trademark dispute. For more information on managing users with YP and NIS, see Chapter 42, "Managing Unix and Linux Users."

Using *ipconfig* and *ifconfig* to Check Host Configurations

The ipconfig command is useful for checking the TCP/IP configuration of Windows workstations or servers. A similar command on Unix and Linux workstations is ifconfig. On Windows 95/98 or Windows Me systems, you can use the winipcfg command.

ipconfig for Windows

Simply enter the ipconfig command at the command prompt.

Using the ipconfig command with no parameters displays network configuration information about each adapter on the system, as well as for PPP (dialup or VPN) connections. The basic information includes the following:

- IP address
- Subnet mask
- Default gateway
- DNS server information
- Windows domain

With the /all parameter, you also can obtain the hardware (MAC) address and DHCP information. You also can use this command to renew or release DHCP configuration information to attempt to reconfigure the computer with updated information.

The syntax for Windows is

```
ipconfig [/? | /all | /release [adapter] | /renew [adapter]
         | /flushdns | displaydns | /registerdns
         | /showclassid adapter
         | /setclassid adapter [classidtoset] ]
```

- **/all**—Causes a verbose display of all the configuration information that the `ipconfig` utility has access to, including multiple adapters.
- **/release [adapter]**—Releases an IP address that was configured using DHCP. If you use just the /release qualifier by itself, the system will attempt to release IP configuration for all adapters on the computer. Otherwise, you can use the syntax of /release *name* to release the IP configuration for a specific adapter with the specified name. Note that you can use wildcards, such as /release "wireless*" to release all wireless addresses.

Note

You can see the adapter names with the unqualified **ipconfig** command. For example, if an adapter is listed as "Ethernet adapter Local Area Connection," you could use **ipconfig /release "Local*"**. Note that under Windows 2000/XP/2003, you can also view the adapter names by right-clicking Network Neighborhood and selecting Properties from the pop-up menu. The adapter names are the names of the icons. If you use the Details view, the name is conveniently listed under the Name column.

- **/renew [adapter]**—Renews an IP address that was configured using DHCP. If you use just the /renew qualifier by itself, the system will attempt to renew IP configuration for all adapters on the computer. Otherwise, you can use the syntax of /renew *name* to renew the IP configuration for an adapter with the specified name. As with /release, you can use wildcards, such as /renew "wireless*" to renew all wireless addresses.
- **/flushdns**—Purges the DNS resolver cache.
- **/registerdns**—Refreshes all leases granted by DHCP for the adapter and reregisters DNS names.
- **/displaydns**—Shows the contents of the DNS resolver cache.
- **/showclassid [adapter]**—Displays all the DHCP class IDs allowed for *adapter*.
- **/setclassid [adapter] [classidtoset]**—Modifies the DHCP class ID. DHCP class IDs are covered in more detail in Chapter 29.

Tip

When a Windows system obtains a translation (hostname to IP address) from a DNS server, it stores the record in a cache for a short period. When the name is used again, the TCP/IP stack will first consult the cache to see whether the record exists, thus providing a quicker response than if a DNS server is queried. To keep the cache set to a reasonable size, each record is flushed from the cache after a Time to Live (TTL) value for the record expires. If you have made a change to a DNS record, you can use the `ipconfig /flushdns` command to remove all records from the cache so that the DNS server will again be consulted, and the cache will begin to store new records. The `ipconfig / displaydns` command will show you the contents of the cache, which can be helpful when you are not sure whether the cache or DNS server is being consulted for the name translation.

Obviously, this command is extremely useful when you are trying to solve problems related to DNS and DHCP functions. For example, you can use /release and /renew to see whether you are having problems obtaining configuration information from a DHCP server. You can use the DNS qualifiers when you've made configuration changes and want to keep the local cache updated or register the new configuration information with a DNS server. The /all qualifier shows all the output to which the command has access and is frequently used to scan for problems. To see all the output without having it scroll off the screen, use the command in the form of ipconfig /all | more. You can also use the command ipconfig /all > *filename* to send the information to a file so that you can print it, or save the information for use in the future.

The quantity of information you can show is useful when constructing a spreadsheet or other document for help-desk use. One method that will help you keep up with current configuration information is placing the following command in a login script or startup file:

ipconfig /all > *network drive*%computername%.config

The %computername% environment variable is replaced with the computer name that is assigned to the system and a text file is created. By placing the output file on a network drive, you can have it available for use by administrative or help-desk staff. The server that provides the file share *network drive* can use a script file appropriate for that operating system to parse the information and store it in a database.

Tip

A common method for importing information into a spreadsheet is to create a comma-delimited file. If you use Windows, Unix, Linux, or some other operating system, it is easy to take the information provided by the `ipconfig` command and parse it, and separate the important information by inserting commas. Your script file can then be used to load the information into a spreadsheet on a periodic basis.

ifconfig for Unix and Linux

On Unix and Linux systems, `ifconfig` is a *very powerful command*. You can use it to display IP configuration information, and also to make changes to the configuration. This command is used in startup files to enable network adapters or provide addressing information, among other items. Online you can use this command to make changes to the configuration.

Some versions of Unix allow you to use this command to view statistics or configuration information for each network adapter. Others simply print a short list of the same, and are mainly used to configure the adapters.

Although the `ifconfig` command is used during the boot sequence to perform the initial configuration for network adapters, after the system is up and running, only the root account can use this command to *change* the configuration. For troubleshooting, it is a quick way to get the information you need in order to determine whether the system was properly configured. For those unfamiliar with Unix, the superuser is just another term for the user account that has full system privileges and can perform all tasks. For Unix/Linux this account is named root.

Tip

The root account on Unix/Linux machines is a powerful account. Consider it to be the same thing as the Administrator account on Windows computers. It is a good idea to use this account only when absolutely necessary, because it's possible to make a mistake if you use the account as your everyday login. Instead, for Unix/Linux systems, an ordinary user account should be used. When you need to gain the privileges that the root account provides, use the **su** command. This command will prompt you for the password to the root account and allow you to make changes on an as-needed basis. To exit back to your normal account, use Control-D (for Solaris Unix). Check the documentation for your Unix/Linux system to see whether another character combination is used to exit the root environment. You can also specify other command-line options for the **su** command, such as another user account to use, and the shell to use, but these are beyond the scope of this book, and will vary from one version of Unix/Linux to another.

To simply display the current configuration information, you can execute the command followed by the network interface name. For example:

```
ifconfig -le0
```

This command will show less information than the Windows `ipconfig` command, but other commands described later in this chapter (such as `netstat`) will enable you to obtain additional configuration information. The output from this command will typically show you the following:

- The IP address assigned to the interface
- Whether the interface is up and running
- The mtu—maximum transmission unit (usually 1,500 bytes because this is the maximum for Ethernet transmissions)
- The network subnet mask (in hexadecimal format)
- The broadcast address

To display information about all network adapters in a computer that uses multiple adapters, use this command:

```
ifconfig -a
```

You do not need to specify the adapter names using this form of the command.

Note

Keep in mind that Unix and Linux are case-sensitive. Enter all commands discussed in this chapter in lowercase. If you use uppercase for a command, you will get an error. You can, however, use upper- or lowercase commands for such things as filenames. When you use a command that uses the filename, though, you must specify the filename exactly as you created it.

As always, check the documentation for your Unix/Linux system (the man pages) to ensure that you have the correct syntax, because it may vary from that shown previously. The capability to set routing metrics and mark an adapter as either up or down can be useful when the Unix or Linux box is being used for routing functions or is part of a proxy firewall solution.

Using *ping* and *tracert* to Check Connectivity

Two of the most basic commands that can be used to test connectivity on a TCP/IP network are the `ping` command and the `tracert` command. In this section we'll look at how these commands work and the kind of troubleshooting information you can gain from their use.

The *ping* Command

The ping command is a good place to start your troubleshooting efforts. The name of this command might not make a whole lot of sense at first glance. This utility is used to test connectivity between two systems on the network. ping uses the ICMP protocol (which, you'll remember, uses UDP packets for transport) to exchange packets with the remote system. This utility was originally developed by Mike Muuss and operates in a simple manner. It uses the ICMP protocol to send UDP messages to an address (ECHO REQUEST) and waits to hear for a reply (ECHO REPLY). The remote system sends the reply packets back to their source, and the round-trip is determined. Thus, ping is used to "grope" around trying to find out whether it can communicate with another system on the network. You also can think of ping as a sonar type of mechanism.

◄◄ ICMP uses UDP datagrams. UDP stands for the User Datagram Protocol, and you can learn more about this protocol (as well as ICMP) in Chapter 25, "Overview of the TCP/IP Protocol Suite."

Figure 28.1 shows the layout of the ICMP ECHO REQUEST and ECHO REPLY packets. If the message type is an ECHO REQUEST, the first field of the ICMP (message type) packet will have a value of 8. If the message type is an ECHO REPLY, this field will contain a zero.

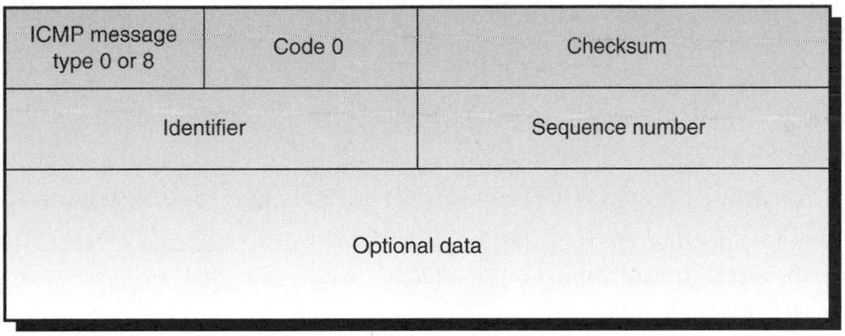

ICMP message type 0 or 8	Code 0	Checksum
Identifier		Sequence number
Optional data		

Figure 28.1 Layout of the ICMP ECHO REQUEST and ECHO REPLY packets.

Using *ping*

The way that ping functions is quite simple. The sequence number field is first set to zero, and then incremented for each packet sent. On most Unix and Linux implementations, the identification field is set to the process ID of the process sending the ping ECHO REQUEST message. This can vary with other operating systems, but the identifier is important and is used to uniquely identify the returned packets in case more than one user on a machine is using the utility at the same time. When the receiving computer gets the ECHO REQUEST message, it sends back a reply, containing the identifier and the sequence number. In this way the receiving machine can tell whether all packets are returned and also, more important, tell you if packets are being dropped or returned out of order. These conditions can indicate problems on the network. Another possibility is that the remote system is working at a high capacity and cannot respond to all the ECHO REQUEST messages in a timely manner.

The ping utility tells you how long (in milliseconds) the round-trip took, and it tells you when packets do not make it back successfully. To determine the round-trip time, the utility stores the time that it sends the initial request packet in the optional data portion of the packet and compares it to the current time when the reply packet is received. The basic program also prints a Time to Live (TTL) value, which is typically decremented by at least one second for each host or router through which the packet passes.

Occasionally you will notice that the round-trip time value declines for subsequent ping requests. This is because the destination machine (or the gateway router) isn't currently in the local ARP table, and it takes a few milliseconds for arp to determine the hardware address for sending out the first packet. If you ping by using a hostname instead of a TCP/IP address, it might take a few seconds for the ping utility to contact a DNS server and resolve the hostname to the IP address.

When you're using ping, it's best to first use it to ping the local interface, or the loopback address (127.0.0.1, or 120.0.0.1 on some older systems). The loopback address is used in TCP/IP stacks to enable you to test whether the local stack is functioning correctly. This is a reserved IP address that cannot be used on the Internet. If you can't ping the local system's own IP address, you might have a configuration problem. If you can't ping the loopback address, you might have a problem with the TCP/IP stack or perhaps the network adapter.

In RFC 2151, "A Primer on Internet and TCP/IP Tools and Utilities," the basic ping syntax is defined as follows:

ping [-q] [-v] [-R] [-c *Count*] [-i *Wait*] [-s *PacketSize*] *Host*

- **-q**—Quiet output; nothing is displayed except summary lines at startup and completion.
- **-v**—Verbose output. Lists ICMP packets that are received in addition to echo responses.
- **-R**—Record route option; includes the RECORD_ROUTE option in the ECHO REQUEST packet and displays the route buffer on returned packets.
- **-c *Count***—Specifies the number of ECHO REQUESTs to be sent before the concluding test (default is to run until interrupted with a Ctrl+C).
- **-i *Wait***—Indicates the number of seconds to wait between sending each packet (default = 1).
- **-s *PacketSize***—Specifies the number of data bytes to be sent; the total ICMP packet size will be PacketSize + 8 bytes due to the ICMP header (default = 56, or a 64-byte packet).
- ***Host***—Host IP address or hostname of target system.

An older syntax for ping that you might find is

ping [-s] {*IP_address*|*hostname*} [*PacketSize*] [*Count*]

When using the -s option, the ping command will send a message to the target every second. This can be helpful when you are monitoring an intermittent problem and want to be able to watch in real time whether a connection can be made.

The syntax for ping can vary depending on the operating system, and even among different variants of Unix. However, its basic use is simply ping *hostname* or ping *address*. The syntax for a Linux ping follows:

ping [-R] [-c *number*] [-d] [-I *seconds*] host

The options include the following:

- **-c *number***—Specifies the number of ICMP ECHO_REQUESTs that are sent.
- **-d**—Causes ping to send packets as fast as they are echoed back from the remote system, or up to 100 times per second. Exercise caution when using this option regularly to avoid generating high volumes of traffic on a busy network.
- **-I *seconds***—Enables you to specify the number of seconds between each packet sent; the default is 1 second. This option cannot be used with the -R option.
- **-R**—Records the route taken by the packet.

Using *ping* on Windows Systems

The *ping* command has a much different syntax when used with the Windows operating systems (both servers and clients):

```
ping [-t] [-a] [-n count] [-l size] [-f] [-i TTL] [-v TOS]
       [-r count] [-s count] [[-j host-list] | [-k host-list]
       [-w timeout] destination-list
```

The options include the following:

- **-t**—Continues pinging until explicitly stopped by Ctrl+C. Statistics are displayed after you stop the command.

- **-a**—Resolves addresses to hostnames.

- **-n *count***—Specifies the number of ICMP ECHO REQUEST packets to send.

- **-l *size***—Sends buffer size.

- **-f**—Sets the don't fragment flag in the packet. Useful to determine whether a device is changing the packet size between nodes.

- **-i *TTL***—Time to Live value.

- **-v *TOS***—Type of Service.

- **-r *count***—Displays route for count hops.

- **-s *count***—Displays a timestamp for each hop.

- **-j *host-list***—Loose source route along *host-list*.

- **-k *host-list***—Strict source route along *host-list*.

- **-w *timeout***—Timeout value to wait for each reply (in milliseconds).

As you can see, the syntax can vary widely between implementations, as can the usefulness of *ping* as a diagnostic tool.

Following is an example of a simple use of the *ping* command:

```
C:\>ping www.activewebhosting.com

Pinging www.activewebhosting.com [24.120.30.50] with 32 bytes of data:

Reply from 24.120.30.50: bytes=32 time=97ms TTL=105
Reply from 24.120.30.50: bytes=32 time=95ms TTL=105
Reply from 24.120.30.50: bytes=32 time=90ms TTL=105
Reply from 24.120.30.50: bytes=32 time=89ms TTL=105

Ping statistics for 24.120.30.50:
    Packets: Sent = 4, Received = 4, Lost = 0 (0% loss),
Approximate round trip times in milli-seconds:
    Minimum = 89ms, Maximum = 97ms, Average = 92ms
```

In this example, the computer is responding well. There was 0% packet loss in the transmissions, and the reply time was about 100 milliseconds. The size of the packet sent was 32 bytes. This simple usage of the *ping* command can tell you right away if there is a problem between two nodes on the network. It might be a broken cable, possibly a router configuration issue, or some other problem. But if you start with *ping* you'll find out right away whether there is an IP pathway between the two network nodes. If there is, you can begin to use other tools to explore why certain applications are not functioning.

Note

An inability to ping a remote node is not a guarantee that the node is disconnected physically from the network. In other words, you cannot simply assume that a `ping` failure indicates a wiring problem. It might be that an intermediary device, such as a switch, router, or gateway, is malfunctioning. This is one of the reasons you need to keep a detailed map of your network. When you have to troubleshoot, you can check not just the end nodes, but also every device and cable along the path between them.

Troubleshooting a Network Connection with the `ping` Command

For basic connectivity troubleshooting, use the following steps:

1. Ping the local system's own numeric IP address.

2. Ping the system's hostname. The `ping` command resolves the hostname to an address before attempting to send packets to the hostname. If the address that `ping` resolves isn't the address you think it should be for your computer, you might need to check with your computer's configuration. You might have configured the local computer with one IP address, yet the entry in the DNS (Domain Name System) server has your hostname associated with a different address. For more information about checking the DNS server, see "Using the `nslookup` Command to Troubleshoot Name Resolution Issues," later in this chapter. You could also check the local `hosts` file for the computer to see whether you've defined your hostname in that file with an incorrect address. However, with only a few exceptions, most computers today use DNS for name resolution, and the `hosts` file is becoming a relic of the past.

3. Ping another system that you know is on the local subnet. If that works, you know you can communicate with members of the local broadcast domain.

4. Ping the default gateway (also called the default route). This is the router or other device that connects your subnet to other networks. If you can't ping the default gateway, there are two possibilities to consider. First, you might have a wrong address for the subnet you are attached to. Check the computer's configuration to be sure you have used the correct address for the router or other host acting to forward packets for the local subnet. Second, you might have a problem with the actual gateway itself. Try pinging it from another computer to see whether that works. Of course, if the router or host that provides the default route is in close physical proximity, you can check it to see whether there is a problem. For more information about checking router problems, see Chapter 10, "Routers," and Chapter 37, "Routing Protocols."

5. Ping a system on a remote subnet. If this action is successful, your connectivity works through the default gateway to the target system, and your issue may be with the original target system, with the routing to a particular subnet, or with equipment on the other side of your local connection.

As you can see from these steps, it is possible to use `ping` to help track down various problems that can occur, from simple connectivity to name resolution. Using `ping` as your first step can help point you in the right direction should other tools need to be used to continue the troubleshooting effort. For example, if you can ping the local broadcast domain members, and if you can ping the default gateway, the next step is to attempt to ping hosts outside your network, perhaps on the Internet. Note that the network administrator may disable this functionality if your company institutes a good firewall security policy. Many times the administrator for the firewall will prevent outgoing ICMP ECHO REPLY messages to keep intruders from outside the network from finding out information about computers protected by the firewall. For more information about allowing the ping utility to work through firewalls, see Chapter 49, "Firewalls."

Note

The ping utility serves an important function in troubleshooting TCP/IP network connectivity. However, the Ping of Death, which you've probably heard about, does not. This attack method uses a program that creates ICMP packets that are larger in size than is allowed. If the software on the receiving end is not patched, or is a new version, it might accept this larger-than-life packet, causing part of the program memory to be overwritten as the data is stored in the allocated buffer and, then, beyond. For more information about allowing the use of **ping** in a secure environment, see Chapter 48, "Security Issues for Wide Area Networks."

The *traceroute* Command

If you find that you cannot successfully ping a host that lies past your default gateway router, try using the traceroute (tracert for some operating systems, such as Windows) command. This command enables you to see every host that a packet passes through to get to the destination. Eventually you will find that the traceroute program cannot get past one of the routers in the path, and it is from there you should start investigating the problem. You can use this information to locate a troublesome router or other device along the network path.

If you've established the fact that you can't get here from there, or that the response time is bad when using ping, try using the tracert command to determine the path that is being taken from your system to the target system. This diagnostic command is similar to ping in that it uses ICMP messages to try to locate each device through which a packet passes to reach its destination. This can provide useful information if you are not sure about the route being taken when you are trying to diagnose a sluggish response from ping. It also can help you find where along the network path the network is failing by showing each hop up until it fails if you can't get to the target system.

For most Unix and Linux operating systems, the command to trace a route through the network is traceroute. From Windows 98 to Windows 2003, a version of this command is called tracert. No matter what the actual command name, this utility can determine each route through the network by setting the TTL (Time to Live) value in the packet, hoping to receive an ICMP TIME_EXCEEDED message from each hop the data packet takes on its path. Remember that the TTL value is the *allowable* number of hops a packet can take before it is discarded by IP. Thus, by setting this value, starting with one and incrementing by one for each pass, traceroute (or tracert) can get the TIME_EXCEEDED ICMP message from each router or other device through which the packet must pass. For each attempt, three packets are sent to average the time that it takes to get to that point in the network. The basic function of this utility appears in Figure 28.2.

In this figure, you can see that Computer A generates a series of ICMP ECHO REQUEST messages and sends them to Computer D. When the first packet is sent out, the TTL value is set to 1. It is decremented to zero at the first router, and an ICMP TIME EXCEEDED ICMP message is sent back to Computer A. Computer A then sends out another ICMP ECHO REQUEST packet, but this time sets the TTL value to 2. Thus, the first router passes the packet to the next router after decrementing the TTL value from 2 to 1. The second router looks at the TTL value of 1 and decrements it to zero, and once again an ICMP TIME EXCEEDED message is sent back to Computer A.

As you can see, intermediate routers drop packets when the TTL value expires. An ICMP TIME_EXCEEDED message is sent back to Host A, *until the TTL value has been set to a value sufficient to reach the destination Computer D*. Thus, Computer A can determine the number of hops it took to reach Computer D, assuming that it is successful in getting there.

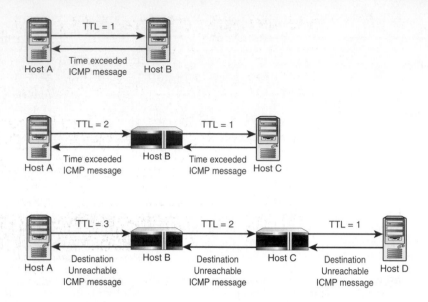

Figure 28.2   The tracert utility manipulates the TTL value to discover host systems along a particular route.

The original traceroute utility sets the port in the UDP header to an "unreachable" port. Thus, when the TTL value is finally incremented enough so that the ICMP packet actually reaches the target system, it will return the ICMP DESTINATION UNREACHABLE message, as you can see in Figure 28.2. If the last hop you see in the traceroute output is the destination, the program has displayed all the hops between your system and the destination system. This can vary depending on the implementation of the utility.

If the last hop that is returned by this command is *not* the target system, you should begin investigating the system that does show up as the last hop.

Note

Various implementations of the traceroute utility might function differently than the method just described here. Some use the function of the **Record-Route** option in IP to attempt to trace the route. However, because the amount of space to record routes is limited, and because the Internet is much larger than it was a few years ago, the UDP method that manipulates the TTL value is probably a more reliable way to implement this utility.

The basic syntax for the traceroute command as given in RFC 2151 is

traceroute [-m #] [-q #] [-w #] [-p #] {IP_address|host_name}

- **-m**—The maximum allowable TTL value, measured as the number of hops allowed before the program terminates (default = 30).
- **-q**—The number of UDP packets that will be sent with each Time to Live setting (default = 3).
- **-w**—The amount of time, in seconds, to wait for an answer from a particular router before giving up (default = 5).
- **-p**—The invalid port address at the remote host (default = 33434).

The syntax for using `tracert` in Windows NT/2000/XP and Windows 2003 Servers is

`tracert [-d] [-h *maximum_hops*] [-j *host-list*] [-w *timeout*] *target_name*`

The more useful options include the following:

- **-d**—Do not resolve hostnames to addresses.

- **-h *maximum_hops***—Maximum number of hops to search for target.

- **-j *host-list***—Loose source route along *host-list*.

- **-w *timeout***—Wait *timeout* milliseconds for each reply.

Of course, *target name* is the host computer that you are executing the `tracert` command for.

The following is an example of the output from executing the Windows version of `tracert`:

```
D:> tracert www.bellsouth.net
Tracing route to www.bellsouth.net [205.152.0.46]
over a maximum of 30 hops:
  1    231 ms    200 ms    220 ms    envlnjewsap02.bellatlantic.net.
➥[192.168.125.189]
  2    261 ms    160 ms    160 ms    192.168.125.158
  3    180 ms    200 ms    181 ms    206.125.199.71
  4    181 ms    160 ms    180 ms    Hssi4-1-0.border2.teb1.IConNet.NET.
➥[209.3.188.201]
  5    241 ms    180 ms    180 ms    POS10-0-0.core2.teb1.IConNet.NET.
➥[204.245.71.221]
  6    180 ms    181 ms    280 ms    Hssi0-0-0.peer1.psk1.IConNet.NET.
➥[204.245.69.174]
  7    180 ms    181 ms    180 ms    BR1.PSK1.Alter.net. [192.157.69.60]
  8    180 ms    181 ms    240 ms    Hssi0-1-0.hr1.nyc1.alter.net.
➥[137.39.100.2]
  9    180 ms    181 ms    200 ms    101.ATM2-0.XR2.NYC1.ALTER.NET.
➥[146.188.177.90]
 10    240 ms    181 ms    200 ms    194.ATM3-0.TR2.EWR1.ALTER.NET.
➥[146.188.178.230]
 11    301 ms    200 ms    200 ms    105.ATM6-0.TR2.ATL1.ALTER.NET.
➥[146.188.136.37]
 12    241 ms    220 ms    180 ms    198.ATM7-0.XR2.ATL1.ALTER.NET.
➥[146.188.232.101]
 13    201 ms    200 ms    220 ms    194.ATM11-0-0.GW2.ATL1.ALTER.NET.
➥[146.188.232.69]
 14    321 ms    200 ms    220 ms    bs2-atl-gw.customer.alter.net. [157.130.69.106]
 15    220 ms    220 ms    221 ms    205.152.2.178
 16    200 ms    281 ms    200 ms    205.152.3.74
 17    220 ms    220 ms    201 ms    www.bellsouth.net. [205.152.0.46]
Trace complete.
```

As you can see, you can gain a lot of information about how your network functions by using this command. The three columns show how long it took each of the three attempts to reach the particular node for that hop. An asterisk character that is displayed in any of these time columns indicates that the ICMP packet was not returned. The hostname and address are displayed by default. If the command fails at any point, you can start tracing the network fault at the last successful hop to determine where the fault lies.

If you are using a Linux system, the following syntax may prove a useful reference. Because this is a Linux system, the command is not `tracert`, but instead is `traceroute`.

```
traceroute [ -dFInrvx ] [ -f first_ttl ] [ -g gateway ]
           [ -i iface ] [ -m max_ttl ] [ -p port ]
           [ -q nqueries ] [ -s src_addr ] [ -t tos ]
           [ -w waittime ] [ -z pausemsecs ]
           host [ packetlen ]
```

Options for the preceding commands are listed here:

- -d—Starts debugging at the socket level.
- -f *first_ttl*—Sets the TTL value for the first outgoing ICMP packet.
- -F—Suppresses setting the "don't fragment" bit.
- -g—Specifies a loose source route gateway (8 maximum hops).
- -i *iface*—For a computer with more than one network adapter, specify the network interface to obtain the source IP address for outgoing probe packets.
- -m—Use this option to set the maximum TTL value used by outgoing packets. By combining this option with the option –f, you can specify numeric boundaries when trying to pinpoint a specific area of failure.
- -n—Display address of each hop in numerical format instead of looking up hostnames. This can save a little time, especially when you first use the command to determine that there is a problem. Next you can allow for printing of hostnames (limiting output by possibly using other options to limit the range of routers involved) to locate a specific network node that may be causing a problem.
- -P *port*—Use this to set the *port* number to use. The default is 33434.
- -r—This option will bypass routing tables and send packets directly to a host on a network directly attached to the current network.
- -s *src_addr*—Sets the source address for the outgoing ICMP packet.
- -t—The type-of-service value for the ICMP packets can be set using this option. The value is a decimal number from zero to 255 (the default is zero). This might be useful in trying to determine which type of service would best handle network traffic. However, this functionality may be of lesser importance today, because of not only the new IP services offered on client and server operating systems, but also new features offered by routers, broadband modems, and so on.
- -v—You guessed it. As with most other Unix/Linux commands, this causes additional text to be output during the execution of this command. Useful when debugging. Annoying when doing a quick exam!
- -w—This option sets the number of seconds waiting for a response to a traceroute probe packet. The default is 5 seconds.
- -z—Use this to set the time to pause between sending out ICMP packets (in milliseconds).

If you have a map of your network, you can check to determine whether the best path is being followed when using the traceroute utility—maybe a primary router is not up and running, and a backup path with a lower bandwidth is sending the packet on a different route through the network. If you use this command on a regular basis and keep an output of the information you see, you can learn to notice when a particular router used by your ISP (or possibly in your own network) is having problems.

By using both ping and tracert, you can usually discover problem areas in your network and then plan steps to remedy the problem. If the problem lies outside your network, that is, with your ISP or some other router on the Internet, resolving the situation can be more problematic. However, for troubleshooting the internal corporate network, these commands should prove very useful for basic configuration and connectivity problems.

The *netstat* and *route* Commands

On Unix, Linux, and Windows systems, the netstat command is used to obtain statistics about the TCP/IP protocols that are in use on the computer. This command is most useful when you are trying to debug network problems. The route command is also useful, because it can be used to view or manipulate the routing table on a computer.

Using the netstat Command on Windows Operating Systems

The syntax for netstat for Windows NT/2000/XP and Windows 2000 Servers is

netstat [-a] [-e] [-n] [-s] [-p *protocol*] [-r] [*interval*]

- **-a**—Displays all connections and listening ports.
- **-e**—Displays Ethernet statistics. This can be combined with the -s option.
- **-n**—Displays addresses and port numbers in numerical form.
- **-s**—Displays per-protocol statistics. By default, statistics are shown for TCP, UDP, and IP. The -p option can be used to specify a subset of the default.
- **-p *protocol***—Shows connections for the protocol specified by *protocol*; *protocol* can be TCP or UDP. If used with the -s option to display per-protocol statistics, *protocol* can be TCP, UDP, or IP.
- **-r**—Displays the routing table.
- ***interval***—Redisplays selected statistics, pausing *interval* seconds between each display. Press Ctrl+C to stop redisplaying statistics. If this is omitted, netstat will print the current configuration information once.

You can investigate a lot about the protocols operating on your system by using the netstat command, as you can see from the preceding syntax options. For example, the command

netstat -r

displays the routing table that is maintained on the current host. (Note that you can also use the command route print to display the routing table information. See Chapter 37 for more information about using the route command and its command-line options.) Following is an example of the routing table as shown using netstat -r and an explanation of the data that is shown using the Windows 2003 Server version of this command:

```
IPv4 Route Table
===========================================================================
Interface List
0x1 ........................... MS TCP Loopback interface
0x10003 ..00 04 5a 42 53 99 ..LNE100TX Fast Ethernet Adapter(LNE100TX v4)
===========================================================================
===========================================================================
Active Routes:
Network Destination        Netmask          Gateway       Interface  Metric
          0.0.0.0          0.0.0.0      192.168.1.1   192.168.1.201      20
        127.0.0.0        255.0.0.0        127.0.0.1       127.0.0.1       1
      192.168.1.0    255.255.255.0    192.168.1.201   192.168.1.201      20
    192.168.1.201  255.255.255.255        127.0.0.1       127.0.0.1      20
```

```
        192.168.1.255  255.255.255.255    192.168.1.201    192.168.1.201    20
            224.0.0.0        240.0.0.0    192.168.1.201    192.168.1.201    20
      255.255.255.255  255.255.255.255    192.168.1.201    192.168.1.201     1
Default Gateway:            192.168.1.1
===========================================================================
Persistent Routes:
  None
```

In this listing you can see the basic routing table used by this computer when you issue this command. If you become familiar with what the routing table should look like, this command might help you focus troubleshooting efforts and quickly spot a problem due to an incorrect routing table entry. Another important thing to remember is that there are many virus programs that manipulate the local host's routing table. On servers, check this table often.

Note

Another **netstat** option available on many Linux computers is **-o**. This command-line option lets you specify the owner of each process associated with each connection.

Each line in this display starts with a destination address. When a decision is being made as to where to send a packet, this table is consulted to see whether one of these destination addresses matches the destination address of the packet in question. In the first line, the address of 0.0.0.0 might not seem to make sense. This is the entry, or the *default gateway*. That is, if a packet cannot be routed to its destination using any of the remaining entries in the route table, it will be sent to this address.

The second column shows the netmask for this route entry. Like a subnet mask, this mask is used to mask out portions of the destination address when a routing decision is to be made. The netmask is converted to binary. When the decision is being made as to whether a packet matches the destination address, the portions of the destination address that are in the same position as a 1 must match the packet's destination address exactly. A netmask of 255.255.255.255 is a string of 32 ones in binary. This is used for a host address, and the packet must match the address exactly to be routed by this entry.

The next column shows the gateway. Packets that match this entry will be sent to this address. The next column—Interface—is the address of the network card or PPP adapter that the packet will be sent through. The last column—Metric—shows the number of hops the packet will take to reach its final destination.

The output for the Windows 2000/Server 2003 command is similar, but presented in a different format:

```
C:\>netstat -r

Route Table
===========================================================================
Interface List
0x1 ......................... MS TCP Loopback interface
0x2 ...00 08 c7 ba 23 7f ...... Compaq Ethernet/FastEthernet or Gigabit NIC
===========================================================================
===========================================================================
Active Routes:
Network Destination        Netmask          Gateway       Interface  Metric
        0.0.0.0          0.0.0.0  140.176.187.254  140.176.187.185       1
      127.0.0.0        255.0.0.0        127.0.0.1        127.0.0.1       1
    140.176.187.0  255.255.255.0  140.176.187.185  140.176.187.185       1
```

```
140.176.187.185  255.255.255.255        127.0.0.1        127.0.0.1    1
140.176.255.255  255.255.255.255  140.176.187.185  140.176.187.185    1
      224.0.0.0        224.0.0.0  140.176.187.185  140.176.187.185    1
255.255.255.255  255.255.255.255  140.176.187.185  140.176.187.185    1
Default Gateway:     140.176.187.254
===========================================================================
Persistent Routes:
  None
```

Other uses for the `netstat` command include showing the current state of TCP/IP ports and sockets (netstat -a) or showing the ARP table (use `netstat -p` on Unix or the `arp` command on Windows NT).

To see statistics about the specific protocols—UDP, ICMP, TCP, or IP—use the `netstat -s` command. This is especially helpful when you are trying to diagnose connectivity problems that are intermittent or might be due to network congestion. The output is quite lengthy, so you might want to pipe the results to a text file (netstat -s > stats.txt). What follows is an example of the data you can obtain by using the -s option with this command on a Windows NT or Windows 2000/XP or Windows 2003 Server system:

```
netstat -s
IP Statistics
  Packets Received                = 19942
  Received Header Errors          = 0
  Received Address Errors         = 2
  Datagrams Forwarded             = 0
  Unknown Protocols Received      = 0
  Received Packets Discarded      = 0
  Received Packets Delivered      = 19942
  Output Requests                 = 19682
  Routing Discards                = 0
  Discarded Output Packets        = 0
  Output Packet No Route          = 0
  Reassembly Required             = 0
  Reassembly Successful           = 0
  Reassembly Failures             = 0
  Datagrams Successfully Fragmented = 0
  Datagrams Failing Fragmentation = 0
  Fragments Created               = 0

ICMP Statistics
                         Received    Sent
  Messages               341         257
  Errors                 0           0
  Destination Unreachable 30         16
  Time Exceeded          142         0
  Parameter Problems     0           0
  Source Quenchs         0           0
  Redirects              91          0
  Echos                  34          189
  Echo Replies           44          34
  Timestamps             0           0
  Timestamp Replies      0           0
  Address Masks          0           0
  Address Mask Replies   0           0
TCP Statistics
```

```
Active Opens                    = 454
Passive Opens                   = 0
Failed Connection Attempts      = 4
Reset Connections               = 33
Current Connections             = 0
Segments Received               = 6399
Segments Sent                   = 6359
Segments Retransmitted          = 14

UDP Statistics
  Datagrams Received    = 13184
  No Ports              = 325
  Receive Errors        = 0
  Datagrams Sent        = 13048
```

Again, the valuable information you get using this command can be very handy when troubleshooting networking problems. For example, you can check to see whether the number of errors or dropped packets is excessive when compared to your ordinary operating environment. To understand and make good use of this type of information, you should be familiar with the protocols that are displayed, such as IP and UDP. For more information about these protocols, see Chapter 25.

Using the `netstat` Command on Unix or Linux Systems

The syntax for the `netstat` command varies depending on which Unix or Linux implementation you are using; however, you will see similar information, and it will be mostly the formatting that changes. For example, the syntax for `netstat` for the FreeBSD Unix operating system is

```
netstat [-AaLln] [-f address_family] [-M core] [-N system]
netstat [-bdghilmnrs] [-f address_family] [-M core] [-N system]
netstat [-bdn] [-I interface] [-M core] [-N system] [-w wait]
netstat [-p protocol] [-M core] [-N system]
netstat [-p protocol] [-i] [-I Interface]
netstat [-s] [-f address_family] [-i] [-I Interface]
```

where

- **-A**—Shows the address of any protocol control blocks associated with sockets. This generally is used for debugging purposes.

- **-a**—Shows the state of all sockets. By default, sockets used by server processes are not shown.

- **-b**—When used with the `-i` (interface) option, shows the number of bytes in and out.

- **-d**—With the `-i` option (interface), shows the number of packets dropped.

- **-f** *address_family*—Use this to narrow down the statistics displayed to specific protocols. The values you can use here include `inet`, `inet6`, `ipx`, `atalk`, `netgraph`, `ng`, or `unix`.

- **-g**—Displays multicast routing tables and interfaces. With the `-s` option, also shows statistics.

- **-h**—Obsolete. Was used to show the IMP host table.

- **-I** *interface*—Displays information about the specified interface *interface*. Can be used with the `-f`, `-s`, and `-p` options to narrow down the information displayed.

- **-i**—Displays the status of interfaces that are statically configured and not located at boot time. Used with `-a`, multicast addresses that are in use are shown for each Ethernet and IP interface. If used with `-f` or the `-p` options, statistics are shown for the address families or protocols indicated.

- **-L**—Displays the size of listen queues. Displays the number of unaccepted connections and the number of unaccepted incomplete connections. Also shows the number of queued connections.
- **-l**—Causes the display to print the full IPv6 address.
- **-M**—Uses values from a name list instead of the default file /dev/kmem.
- **-m**—Displays statistics about memory management routines.
- **-N**—Extracts the name list from the specified system instead of the default /kernel.
- **-n**—Displays network addresses as numbers instead of names.
- **-p** *protocol*—Specifies a protocol for which information is displayed. Protocol names are listed in the /etc/protocols file.
- **-s**—Causes the display to show per-protocol statistical information.
- **-r**—Displays the routing tables.
- **-w** *wait*—Causes the interface statistics to be updated at intervals of *wait* seconds.

For Linux the capabilities of this command grow to encompass a larger number of functions. Most of the command options previously listed will work in the same manner for Linux. To find out about more complex commands that can be used with this utility to troubleshoot network problems, see the man page man netstat.

The *arp* Command

IP addresses and hostnames are used for the convenience of humans so that we can configure and manage a network in an orderly manner. At the lowest level, however, network cards use the hardware MAC address when they talk to each other. Remember that a computer finds out the hardware address of another computer on the local segment by using the Address Resolution Protocol (ARP). Just as a host computer keeps a table of routing information, it also keeps a cache of MAC-to-IP address translations known as the *ARP table*.

The arp command enables you to view the ARP table and to add or delete entries within it. Again, the syntax varies among different systems.

To show the differences you might encounter, let's look at the Windows 2000/XP and Windows 2003 Servers and then Linux versions of this command. For Windows 2000/XP and Windows 2003 Servers the syntax is

```
ARP -s inet_addr eth_addr [if_addr]
ARP -d inet_addr [if_addr]
ARP -a [inet_addr] [-N if_addr]
```

- **-a** *inet_addr*—Displays current ARP cache entries. If you specify a specific host (*inet_addr*), the display is restricted to information about that host.
- **-g**—Same usage as -a.
- **-N** *if_addr*—Shows ARP information about the network interface, *if_addr*.
- **-d** *inet_addr* or **-d** *if_addr*—Deletes a host *inet_addr* (IP address) or *if_addr* (interface name) from the ARP table. Use the wildcard * (asterisk) to clear the ARP table of all host information.
- **-s** *inet_addr, eth_addr*—Associates an IP address (*inet_addr*) with a MAC address (*eth_addr*).

For example, to add an address pair to the ARP table, you might use this:

```
arp -s 192.123.111.2   08-00-2b-34-c1-01
```

For Linux systems the syntax is

```
arp [-evn] [-H type] [i if] a [hostname]
```

```
arp [-v] [-i if] -d hostname [pub]
```

```
arp [-v] [-H type] [-i if] s hostname hw_addr [temp]
```

```
arp [-v] [-H type] [-i if] s hostname hw_addr [netmask nm] pub
```

```
arp [-v] [-H type] [-i if] Ds hostname ifa [netmask nm] pub
```

```
arp [-vnD] [-H type] [i if] f [filename]
```

where the command-line options are

- -v—As always, this is the *verbose* option, which causes more information to be displayed when you enter a command.
- -n, --numeric—Causes the command to show only numerical addresses instead of host, port, or user names.
- -H *type*, --hwtype *type*, or –t *type*—Used when reading or modifying the ARP cache. This option is used to specify the underlying network hardware code (Ethernet, ARCnet, and so on).
- -a [*hostname*], --display [*hostname*]—If *hostname* is supplied, all entries for that host are shown. If just the –a option or --display option is entered, all entries in the ARP cache table are displayed.
- -d *hostname*, --delete *hostname*—Deletes records for *hostname*.
- -D, --usedevice—The command uses the interface's hardware address.
- -i *If*, --device *If*—Selects which interface (*If*) to use when executing the command.
- -s *hostname hw_addr*, --set *hostname*—Use this to create a manual entry for a hostname to address records in the ARP table.
- -f *filename*, --file *filename*—Adds a record, like the –s option, but gets addressing information from *filename*. If no filename is used, /etc/ethers is used as a default.

As you can see, the arp command can be quite powerful. It should be used carefully when adding or deleting entries in the ARP table. However, for display purposes it can be easily used to determine problems of resolving hardware addresses on the local subnet or network segment.

The tcpdump Utility

If you are extremely knowledgeable about TCP/IP and are capable of understanding the bits and bytes of IP frames, you can use the tcpdump utility to capture header information from packets as they pass through the network. Because there can be a potential security problem with being able to view this information, it is not a utility that the ordinary Unix user can use. It is generally restricted to the root user or must be installed with setuid to root.

Note

When a file has "setuid to root bit" enabled, it means that the program will run with the privileges of the owner of the file, and not the privileges of the user who is running the program. In Unix or Linux systems, this feature allows the administrator to let users execute programs that perform specific tasks that require more privileges than the user has. However, the user is able to use the privileges only to run the program to accomplish a specific task. The user does not inherit the rights or privileges of the program after running it.

Because the tcpdump utility can be used to examine network packets (and thus "snoop" on network traffic), it must run with the privileges granted to the root (or superuser) account.

Many command-line parameters are associated with this utility, and you can create complex expressions that are used to evaluate which packets to intercept. You can also supply no selection criteria, and all packets will be dumped.

Some of the more useful options for the tcpdump command are listed here:

- **-a**—Tries to convert network and broadcast addresses to names.
- **-c** *count*—Exits after receiving *count* number of packets.
- **-d**—Dumps the compiled packet-matching code in a human-readable form to standard output and stop.
- **-dd**—Dumps packet-matching code as a C program fragment.
- **-ddd**—Dumps packet-matching code as decimal numbers (preceded by a count).
- **-e**—Displays the link level header information on each line (the Ethernet header information).
- **-F** *file*—Uses the text found in *file* for the selection expression. If you use this option, any expression given on the command line is ignored.
- **-f**—Prints "foreign" Internet addresses numerically rather than symbolically.
- **-i** *interface*—Specifies the interface to monitor. If you do not specify this, tcpdump will select the lowest numbered configured interface, excluding loopback.
- **-n**—Doesn't convert host addresses, port numbers, and so on to names.
- **-nn**—Suppresses printing of port or protocol names, and shows numbers instead.
- **-N**—Doesn't display domain name qualification of names.
- **-p**—Doesn't put network interface into promiscuous mode.
- **-q**—Limits the amount of information displayed for a shorter listing.
- **-r**—Reads packets from *file* (which was created with the -w option). Standard input is used if *file* is "-".
- **-s**—Snarfs *snaplen* bytes of data from each packet rather than the default of 68, which is adequate for IP, ICMP, TCP, and UDP but may truncate protocol information from name server and NFS packets.
- **-S**—Prints absolute TCP sequence numbers.
- **-t**—Doesn't print a timestamp on each line.
- **-tt**—Puts a timestamp on each line. -ttt prints a delta time between the previous and current lines.
- **-u**—Displays undecoded NFS handles.
- **-U**—Drops root privileges.
- **-v or -vv or -vvv**—Gives additional information from each packet. Each of these causes the output to be more verbose.
- **-x**—Prints each packet in hexadecimal format.
- **-X**—Prints ASCII as well as hexadecimal format.

There are additional advanced options, but the preceding options are the basic ones. The selection expression criteria can be quite complex, and you should consult the extensive man pages for tcp-dump to get the full listing of other options, expressions, and examples. The scope of the capabilities of this program is beyond this book. A couple of simple uses follow:

```
tcpdump host hercules
```

This command shows packets that are going to or coming from the system named `hercules`.

```
tcpdump ip host venus and not hercules
```

This command shows packets going to or coming from the system named `venus`, unless they are coming from or going to `hercules`. The output displayed by this command depends on the protocol of the packet that is intercepted.

You can download the most recent version and patches for this utility at `www.tcpdump.org/`. In addition, you can sign up for mailing lists that relate to this utility. Join the first list by sending an email message to the address `tcpdump-announce@tcpdump.org`. This mailing list is used for announcements about the utility. The second mailing list is used for both announcements and discussions concerning the code of tcpdump. To subscribe to this mailing list, send an email to `tcpdump-workers@tcpdump.org`.

The source code for this program is also available for compilation on many different Unix and Linux platforms. Although it's not a tool for a novice, tcpdump can be used by a skilled administrator to diagnose network problems. This section has given you only a brief overview of the capabilities of this simple network capture utility. After installing the software, be sure to review any readme files for up-to-date information.

The WinDump Utility

The tcpdump utility has been ported to the Windows environment and is known as WinDump. Like the tcpdump program, this program was developed by the Network Research Group of the Information and Computing Sciences Division of the Lawrence Berkeley National Laboratory. More recent versions and patches for the utility are maintained at `http://netgroup-serv.polito.it/windump/`. There are also several sites you can find using a quick Internet search engine that enable you to download WinDump. Currently, Windows NT through 2000/XP are supported. By using WinDump, you can gain a lot of information by examining network packets to troubleshoot network problems. The interface, however, is different than the command-line version of tcpdump. The WinDump utility, like tcpdump, is covered under a Berkeley-style license.

Note

A Berkeley-style license means that you can share software with others as long as you include a copy of the license. You cannot use the code to create commercial products to sell, however.

To install WinDump you first must download the drivers appropriate to your version of the Windows operating system. Drivers are available for Windows 95/98, Windows NT, and Windows 2000. Drivers for Windows Server 2003 should be available shortly. After you've installed the driver, you can install the WinDump components. To install the driver (filename `Packet2k.exe` for Windows 2000), simply execute the file. It prompts you for a temporary directory to which to extract files. Accept the default or enter a directory name of your choosing, and then proceed to unzip the files. To install the driver, follow these steps:

1. Launch the Control Panel (Start, Settings, Control Panel) and double-click the Network and Dial Up Connections icon.
2. Double-click the Local Area Connection icon that appears. Click the Properties button.

3. Click the Install button. In the Select Network Component Type dialog box, click Protocol, and then click the Add button.

4. Click the Have Disk button, and when the next dialog box appears, enter the pathname to the place where you unzipped the driver files. Click OK.

5. In the Select Network Protocol dialog box, highlight Packet Capture Driver v2.01 and click OK.

6. When the Local Area Connection dialog box appears again, click OK to close the dialog box. The packet capture driver should now be installed. You must reboot the machine before the driver is loaded.

Next, you need to download the WinDump program. Just click the WinDump link on the download page and the executable file will be downloaded to the directory you specify. After that, set your working directory to the same directory and you are ready to execute WinDump commands.

The command syntax for WinDump is almost exactly the same as that for the tcpdump utility; consult the syntax listed earlier in this chapter for more help. Or visit the WinDump home page and follow the link to the extensive man page found there.

Again, remember that examining network packets is not a job for a novice. You should first have a good understanding of the frame types seen on your network, and a good understanding of the types of datagrams sent by applications and services you use. Some of the standard packets you should familiarize yourself with include DNS, ICMP, and TCP session setup and close. Depending on the services your network uses, you can quickly become familiar with the type of expected network traffic and then use this tool to look for exceptions when troubleshooting.

Using the *nslookup* Command to Troubleshoot Name Resolution Issues

This command is another simple command that is available with all TCP/IP implementations. Its purpose is to query a DNS name server to find out the name registration information for a particular host. By using nslookup, you can find out whether the address that is associated with the computer's hostname is accurate. This can be handy for troubleshooting if you are trying to use one of the TCP/IP utilities, such as FTP or Telnet, to reach a particular host by name, yet find that you cannot establish a connection or that the remote system is not the one you thought it would be.

This utility can be run in two different modes. First, you can specify all the commands on a command line and get a result returned from a DNS name server (noninteractive mode). Second, you can enter "batch" mode (called interactive mode by Microsoft) and issue several commands in a row to the server. The basic syntax for the command in Windows operating systems is

```
nslookup [-option ...] [computer-to-find | - [server]]
```

Options you can use with the command are

- **computer-to-find**—Specifies the name of the computer whose name you want to look up.

- **server**—Specifies a DNS name server other than the default server configured on the client.

For example:

```
C:> nslookup www.twoinc.com
```

This command sends an inquiry to the default DNS server. If information is received, it will print the name of the server that the information is from, and then print the IP address of the server you inquired about. For example:

```
C:\>nslookup www.twoinc.com
Server:  home8-qwest.bellatlantic.net
Address:  151.204.0.84

Non-authoritative answer:
Name:    www.twoinc.com
Address:  216.65.33.219
```

In this example you can also see that the server that gave the response indicates that it is a non-authoritative answer. This means that the server is not the server that actually holds the domain name record for this domain, but has cached the name locally. The record for the domain is located elsewhere in the DNS hierarchy.

The nslookup command also enables you to enter several options on the command line or to use these features from within the interactive environment. When it's used on the command line, precede each option with a minus sign (–). The options and values that can be used with Windows NT through Windows 2003 Servers are listed here:

- **help**—Displays help text.
- **exit**—Exits nslookup when in interactive mode.
- **finger [*username*] [> *filename*] | [>> *filename*]**—Connects to the current finger server and looks up a *username*. You can specify a *filename* for the output.
- **ls [*option*] *dnsdomain* [> *filename*] | [>> *filename*]**—Lists information about a domain. Generally this includes computer names and addresses. Suboptions to this command allow you to get other information.
- **lserver *dnsdomain***—Uses the initial server to retrieve information about *dnsdomain*.
- **root**—Sets the current default server to be the root server.
- **server *dnsdomain***—Uses the current server to retrieve information about dnsdomain.
- **set *keyword=[value]***—Changes configuration settings about how nslookup works. See the help text for more information.
- **set all**—Displays current configuration settings for the nslookup utility and shows information about the default server.

There are many set commands you can use to customize the way nslookup works. For more information, check the help text that comes with the version you are using. Using nslookup in interactive mode enables you to perform multiple hostname lookups without having to retype the nslookup command. Use the exit command to exit the interactive mode.

Other Useful Commands

The TCP/IP suite consists of several protocols and utilities that have been developed over the years. Other commands can be useful for troubleshooting. For example, the telnet command is used to establish a remote terminal session on another computer. If you are having trouble with a workstation, you can always telnet to it and perform diagnostic functions directly. This is convenient when the network is dispersed geographically. It is also possible to telnet to many networked devices, from printers to routers. This feature can enable you to resolve many remote problems without having to leave your office. Just telnet into a system and use the commands provided by that system.

Telnet also can be useful when you're trying to resolve connectivity problems with a particular server. If you can't ping or otherwise connect to a system, try using telnet to get to another system and try your diagnostic commands from that location in the network. Using this method to attempt to connect to a remote system by using other remote systems can help you locate the spot in the network where potential trouble lies.

Advanced users can use telnet to connect directly to ports used by specific services to enable troubleshooting for the service. For example, by using telnet to connect to a Web server on port 80, you can manually enter commands that would be sent by an Internet browser and examine the responses sent by the server. To see how this works from a Windows 2000/XP client, issue this command:

```
telnet www.google.com 80
```

This connects you to Google. After you have connected, there will be no response until you type a command. To request the index page, use the following command:

```
GET /index.html HTTP/1.0
```

Note that you must complete the command before the Web server drops your connection. This time varies on each server, but it can be rather quick. If you beat the timeout, the first part of the response will be the header. The first line is the HTTP Response code. Two common responses are 200, which means you were successful, and 404, which means the page was not found. The rest of the header information is fairly self-explanatory.

Following is an example of this:

```
HTTP/1.0 200 OK
Content-Length: 2532
Connection: Close
Server: GWS/2.0
Date: Mon, 06 Jan 2003 23:09:11 GMT
Content-Type: text/html
Cache-control: private
Set-Cookie: PREF=ID=67734bf5226e142a:TM=1041894551:LM=1041894551:S=E_cwh20x6SQGp
kqD; expires=Sun, 17-Jan-2038 19:14:07 GMT; path=/; domain=.google.com
```

◄◄ Response codes for Telnet are covered in detail in Chapter 26, "Basic TCP/IP Services and Applications."

Next, the HTML content—the bits that would normally be rendered by the browser—of the page that you requested are displayed. I've trimmed the content of this section, because the details are not important.

```
<html><head><meta http-equiv="content-type" content="text/html; charset=ISO-8859
-1"><title>Google</title>
..
..
..
&copy;2003 Google</font><font size=-2> - Searching 3,083,32
4,652 web pages</font></center></body></html>
```

And then you will be disconnected:

```
Connection to host lost.
```

The ftp command can be used to move files to and from a remote system. This can be useful to retrieve the output of a diagnostic command, a log file, or perhaps a configuration file so that you can examine or edit it locally.

Depending on the importance of the server, you should consider the capabilities of both Unix/Linux and Windows operating systems to audit activities on the system. The syslog daemon on Unix/Linux computers can be configured to capture a lot of data from many sources. If troubleshooting becomes nonproductive, consider increasing the events logged by the operating system so that you might find important data that can help assist in solving the problem.

BOOTP and Dynamic Host Configuration Protocol (DHCP)

SOME OF THE MAIN TOPICS IN THIS CHAPTER ARE

You should read this chapter and Chapter 30, "Network Name Resolution," as though they were one, because they cover both sides of the coin when talking about how computers are uniquely identified on a network. This chapter deals with the specifics of how computers can be set up to automatically receive addressing and other information when they boot. This relieves the system administrator from having to manually configure each computer individually every time a global change is made. Chapter 30, discusses how other computers on the network go about determining the particular address of another computer on the network by registering themselves and querying the Domain Name System (DNS) database.

BOOTP is an old protocol. DHCP also has been around awhile. However, DHCP basically is a protocol that builds on and expands the capabilities that were first provided by BOOTP. For this historical reason, and the fact that BOOTP still is in use in many networks, both are examined in this chapter. Most modern DHCP servers, including the Windows 2000 and 2003 servers, and the Unix/Linux family of operating systems, still support BOOTP.

What Is BOOTP?

BOOTP stands for the Bootstrap or BOOT Protocol. The standard method for booting a computer is to locate a boot block on a local drive and then go from there, so why are we discussing booting in a book that is supposed to be about networks? During the 1980s, BOOTP was developed to allow *diskless* workstations to boot by downloading the operating system from another network node. Many operating systems at that time used this protocol because it allowed the use of cheaper desktop workstations on the network—long before PCs became a standard desktop item. At the time, the X-Windows workstation was popular in Unix and OpenVMS networks. BOOTP was an economical way to provide an X-Windows desktop with an operating system, without the need to equip the machine with disk drives and other devices not necessary for a simple client. Other types of network clients adopted the BOOTP protocol, allowing network devices to also be suitably configured by use of the protocol.

Note

The BOOTP protocol was originally defined in RFC 951, "Bootstrap Protocol," in 1985, and further details were provided by RFC 1542, "Clarifications and Extensions for the Bootstrap Protocol," in 1993. That RFC was made obsolete by several other RFCs, of which the most current is the proposed standard of the same name (RFC 2132). Another important proposed standard is RFC 1534, "Interoperation Between DHCP and BOOTP."

Downloading an operating system is only one of the functions performed by BOOTP. In addition, the diskless workstation (or other client) can also obtain network addressing information. This is because the lowest-level BOOTP client is presumed to be "diskless." It has no method to store configurable IP addressing information between power cycles.

The BOOTP protocol is not complex. Indeed, it is a simple protocol that is small and easy to implement in programmable read-only memory (PROM) chips. The following are some important features of BOOTP:

- A simple request/reply mechanism is used. The same packet format is used for both requests and replies.
- The UDP protocol is used to carry messages (ports 67 and 68, the same as are used by DHCP).
- Using relay agents, BOOTP exchanges can occur across routers.
- BOOTP can supply the client with an IP address, a subnet mask, and a default gateway. A BOOTP server also can give the client name of a trivial FTP server (TFTP) and a filename that can be used to download an operating system. This TFTP server is especially important for

diskless workstations, as well as network devices that need to download an operating system. The trivial FTP server, which is a stripped-down simple version of FTP, is covered in Chapter 26, "Basic TCP/IP Services and Applications."

◄◄ Another protocol, the Reverse Address Resolution Protocol (RARP), operates at the second layer of the OSI network model and also is capable of providing an IP address to another node that is booting on the network. However, RARP is very limited. For more information about RARP, see Chapter 25, "Overview of the TCP/IP Protocol Suite."

Format of the BOOTP Packet

The client and server share a common packet format. This packet is passed to UDP (the User Datagram Protocol) and encapsulated inside a UDP packet. The UDP and IP headers are added, and the information finally is passed to the Data Link and Physical layers for transmission on the network medium.

◄◄ The IP and UDP protocols are also discussed in greater detail in Chapter 25.

The fields of the BOOTP packet are used for the following purposes:

- **Opcode**—This 1-byte field has a value of either zero or one. If set to a value of one, the packet is a request from a client to a BOOTP server (or a DHCP server, as explained later). If the value is zero, the packet is a reply from a server to the client.

- **Hardware Type**—Values in this 1-byte field are used to designate different kinds of hardware, or different computer types or network device types, for example. A value of one in this field indicates that the underlying hardware type of the network is 10Mb Ethernet, whereas the value of 32 is used for the emerging technology known as InfiniBand. You can find the full list of values at www.iana.org/assignments/arp-parameters.

- **Hardware Address Length**—This 1-byte field indicates the number of bytes that the client hardware address field contains. For Ethernet, this value is six, because it takes 6 bytes to represent the 48-bit Media Access Control (MAC) address used by Ethernet network cards.

- **Hop Count**—This 1-byte field is always set to zero by the client, though the BOOTP server uses this field when relaying BOOTP requests across routers.

- **Transaction ID**—This is a 4-byte field that is a unique 32-bit integer the client sets so that it can match up replies from the server to the requests the client has sent.

- **Seconds**—This 2-byte field is expressed in seconds and is filled in by the client with a value indicating the time that has elapsed since the client started the boot process. This value can be used by secondary servers to recognize that the client's primary server is not responding. In that case, a secondary BOOTP server can make an attempt to satisfy the request.

- **Flags**—In the original specifications for BOOTP, this 2-byte field was not used. However, in RFC 1542 this field was set aside to store flag bits. Only one has been defined so far. The most significant bit in this field is used as a Broadcast flag. The remaining bits are not yet defined and should be set to zeros.

- **Client IP Address (ciaddr)**—If the client already knows its own address (which is explained shortly), it will fill in that address in this 4-byte field. In most cases, the client does not know its own IP address (because that's one of the main things BOOTP is used to supply to the client), and in that case the value for this field should be zero.

- **Your IP Address (yiaddr)**—This field is used by the BOOTP server to supply an IP address to a client requesting one. It also is a 4-byte field, the number of bytes needed to store an IP address. Although the client can fill in the ciaddr field with a requested address, this field contains the address the DHCP server returns to the client to use.

- **Server IP Address (siaddr)**—The BOOTP server fills in this field, usually placing its own address here.

- **Gateway IP Address (giaddr)**—If a BOOTP proxy server is being used, the address in this 4-byte field is the address of the router or other device performing the proxy function. Proxy BOOTP services are discussed later in this chapter. Note that this *is not* the address the client should use as a default gateway for TCP/IP configuration (though it could be the same). This field is used only to relay BOOTP requests across routers to and from the actual BOOTP server. The default gateway information is supplied in BOOTP options, described later in this chapter (see the section "Enabling the DHCP Relay Agent").

- **Client's Hardware Address (chaddr)**—If the client already knows its own IP address, it will place the IP address into this 4-byte field. The client must fill in this required field because the typical BOOTP server uses it in an index of values it keeps track of for its clients.

- **Server Hostname (sname)**—This field can be up to 64 bytes in length and contains a null-terminated ASCII string of characters that represent the server's hostname on the network. This hostname can be a simple hostname or a fully qualified domain name (FQDN). This is an optional field.

- **Boot Filename (file)**—This field can be up to 128 characters in length and is used to supply the client with the filename it can download and use to boot. The value here is also a null-terminated string and includes the full path the client needs in order to locate the file.

- **Vendor-Specific Area**—These 64 bytes are set aside to store vendor-specific optional information. The items are listed in Table 29.1 in the section "BOOTP Vendor-Specific Information Options." The first four octets in this field will be a "magic cookie." The last octet is the "End" tag, the value 255.

The client's hardware address (technically called the Media Access Control address, or MAC address) that is placed in the BOOTP packet is the same hardware address that will be found in the Ethernet frame that delivers the packet. However, after the Ethernet frame is received, the lower-level header information (such as the client's hardware address) is stripped off before the remaining packet is passed up through the IP and UDP layers. At the point where the BOOTP protocol begins to examine the packet, the Ethernet frame header information is not available in most TCP/IP stacks. For this reason, *the hardware address is duplicated inside the BOOTP packet.* Remember that the RARP protocol is a link-layer protocol, so it can retrieve the client's hardware address from the Ethernet frame, something most implementations of BOOTP cannot do.

Note

For those who are interested in the nitty-gritty details, the packets discussed here are transmitted on the wire in the order shown in the figures in this chapter. Additionally, the individual bytes are sent with the leftmost bit being the most significant. For multi-octet values, the most significant octet is transmitted first. This information might help you when diagnosing problems on the network using a LAN analyzer or other methods to intercept and interpret network packets.

The BOOTP Request/Reply Mechanism

Because it usually is implemented in a read-only memory (ROM) chip, the BOOTP protocol client is a simple, concise bit of code. The exchange of UDP messages between the client and the BOOTP server consists of a series of requests and replies. The same packet format is used for both types of messages, with an Opcode field used to indicate whether the message is a request from the client or a reply from the server.

The following basic steps are involved in obtaining information from a BOOTP server:

1. The client sends a broadcast message at the link-layer level because the client at this point is unaware of its own IP address or that of any BOOTP server that might be on the network. In the IP header information for the request, the client usually sets the source IP Address field to 0.0.0.0 and the destination address to 255.255.255.255. Because this is a UDP packet being sent through IP, the client sets the destination UDP port number to 68 (the BOOTP server port) so that a listening server will know to intercept the packet. The Transaction ID field that the client places in the BOOTP request packet is used by clients to sort out which replies are meant for them. The first 4 bytes of the vendor-specific information area should be set to a magic cookie.

Note

A *magic cookie* is a method used by BOOTP to tell the server what kind of format to use when creating a reply for a client's request. The magic cookie usually is the value 99.130.83.99 but can be a vendor-supplied value. The magic cookie usually is used to indicate that the vendor-specific area contains information for the server to examine. The remaining information in the 64-byte vendor-specific information is defined as a series of tags followed by a length field and then, in most cases, a variable-length field of information.

2. If the broadcast flag is set, the server next broadcasts a reply that contains the client's IP address, the server's own IP address, and other requested information.

3. If the broadcast flag is not set, the server can send a unicast address using the client's IP address to the address supplied by the client. The server should always check the Client IP Address (from Client) field set by the client to be sure it is not the default value of 0.0.0.0. If it is not, then, depending on the implementation, the server will set the Client IP Address (from Server) field to the same value and send a directed (unicast) packet back to the client. However, note that this can vary from one implementation to the next, and the server might decide to override the client's requested IP address and substitute another.

4. Another possibility that occurs when using a router or other host to act as a proxy relay agent is that the Default-Gateway server field will be filled in. In this case, the server knows to use this field to send a directed (unicast) packet to the router or other device that is relaying the message, instead of trying to broadcast or send the packet directly to the client using the client's address.

In step 2, even though the client might be capable of determining what it thinks its own IP address should be—by saving it to a disk file in the case of a workstation that does have that capability, for example—the server can choose to return a different IP address to the client. In that case, the client should stop using its previous IP address and accept the new one from the server. There is some disagreement in the literature about this situation, and you might find that it varies from one implementation to another. For example, some vendors allow the client to specify the address it wants to use, ignoring the one supplied by the server. In this type of situation, the client usually is using the BOOTP server to obtain other configuration information, such as a boot filename or vendor-specific items, when it already knows what its own IP address should be.

BOOTP Vendor-Specific Information Options

In addition to supplying a network node with an IP address and a boot filename (and the server from which the file can be retrieved), 64 bytes are reserved in the BOOTP Reply/Request packet that can be used to supply additional configuration information to the client. The client can also use the options fields to request certain information from the server.

The options used by BOOTP are a subset of those now incorporated into DHCP. Those listed in this section apply, therefore, to both BOOTP and DHCP. These options are defined (and discussed in greater detail) in RFC 2132, "DHCP Options and BOOTP Vendor Extensions."

The format for data in the options field is standard:

- **Option Code**—This 1-byte field contains a code that identifies the particular option. The value of 0 is used for padding and the value of 255 is used as an end marker. Note that Option Code values from 128 to 254 are reserved for site-specific options.

- **Length Octet**—This 1-byte value specifies the length of the option data to follow. This length *does not* include the Option Code or the Length Octets.

- **Variable-length optional configuration data**—This data depends on what kind of information the option supplies.

As noted earlier, the value of 255 marks the end of an options list in the packet.

RFC 2132 defines a large number of options that can be used. Table 29.1 lists those that apply to both BOOTP and DHCP.

Table 29.1   Definition of BOOTP Vendor Extension Opcodes

Opcode	Name	Description
0	Pad	Used to align following entries on a word boundary.
255	End	Marks end of options.
1	Subnet Mask	Subnet mask for client to use.
2	Time Offset	UTC time offset value.
3	Router	List of IP address of routers on the client's subnet.
4	Time Server	List of time servers.
5	Name Server	List of IEN 116 name servers.
6	Domain Name Server	List of DNS servers (RFC 1035).
7	Log Server	List of MIT-LCS UDP log servers.
8	Cookie Server	List of cookie servers (RFC 865).
9	LPR Server	List of LPR printers (RFC 1179).
10	Impress Server	List of Imagen Impress servers.
11	Resource Location Server	List of resource location servers (RFC 887).
12	Host Name	Client's hostname.
13	Boot File Size	Size in 512-byte blocks of the default boot image file for the client.
14	Merit Dump File	Path of file that client can use for a memory dump.
15	Domain Name	Name of DNS domain of client.
16	Swap Server	IP address of client's swap server.
17	Root Path	Pathname for client's root disk.
18	Extensions Path	Specifies a file that contains information similar to this vendor-specific information area.
19	IP Forwarding	0 = Disable IP forwarding, 1 = enable IP forwarding on client.
20	Non-Local Source Routing	0 = Disallow forwarding, 1 = allow forwarding of nonlocal source-routed datagrams.

Table 29.1   Continued

Opcode	Name	Description
21	Policy Filter	A list of IP addresses and subnet masks to use to filter incoming source routes.
22	Maximum Datagram Reassembly Size	The maximum size datagram that the client should be able to reassemble.
23	Default IP TTL	Default value client should set the TTL field for outgoing datagrams.
24	Path MTU Aging Timeout	Seconds to use when aging path MTU values (as discovered via RFC 1191).
25	Path MTU Plateau Table	Table of sizes to use for path MTU discovery (RFC 1191).
26	Interface MTU	MTU for this interface (per interface).
27	All Subnets	0 = Subnets can have smaller MTU, 1 = Subnets have same MTU.
28	Broadcast Address	Broadcast address for client to use.
29	Perform Mask Discovery	0 = Do not perform mask discovery, 1 = Perform mask discovery using ICMP.
30	Mask Supplier	0 = Client should not respond to subnet mask request using ICMP, 1 = Client should respond.
31	Perform Router Discovery	0 = Do not use router discovery, 1 = Use router discovery (RFC 1256).
32	Router Solicitation Address	Address for router solicitation requests.
33	Static Route	List of static routes (destination address + router address) to be inserted into client's routing cache.
34	Trailer Encapsulation	0 = Do not use trailers, 1 = Attempt to use trailers.
35	ARP Cache Timeout	Seconds for ARP cache timeout.
36	Ethernet Encapsulation	0 = Use Ethernet Version 2 (RFC 894), 1 = Use IEEE 802.3 (RFC 1042).
37	TCP Default TTL	Default TTL for client to use when sending out TCP segments.
38	TCP Keepalive Interval	Seconds to wait before sending TCP keepalive messages. Zero indicates no messages to be sent, unless requested by application.
39	TCP Keepalive Garbage	0 = Do not send octet of garbage for compatibility with older versions, 1 = Send garbage octet.
40	NIS Service Domain	Network Information System (NIS) domain of client.
41	NIS Servers	List of IP address of NIS servers.
42	NTP Servers	List of IP addresses of NTP time servers.
43	Vendor Specific Information	Vendor-specific information, as defined by vendor.
44	NetBIOS over TCP/IP Name Server	List of NBNS servers (RFC 1001/1002).
45	NetBIOS over TCP/IP Datagram Distribution Server	List of NBDD servers (RFC 1001/1002).
46	NetBIOS over TCP/IP Node Type	NetBIOS node type (RFC 1001/1002).
47	NetBIOS over TCP/IP Scope	NBT Scope parameter (RFC 1001/1002).
48	X Window System Font Server	List of X Window System Font servers.

Table 29.1   Continued

Opcode	Name	Description
49	X Window System Display Manager	List of IP addresses of systems running the X Window System Display Manager.
64	NIS+ Domain	Name of NIS+ domain.
65	NIS+ Server	List of IP addresses of NIS+ servers.
68	Mobile IP Home Agent	IP addresses of mobile IP home agents.
69	SMTP Server	List of Simple Mail Transport Protocol (SMTP) servers.
70	POP3 Server	List of POP3 servers.
71	NNTP Server	List of Network News Transfer Protocol (NNTP) servers.
72	Default WWW Server	List of WWW servers.
73	Default Finger Server	List of Finger servers.
74	Default IRC Server	List of default Internet Relay Chat (IRC) servers.
75	StreetTalk Server	List of StreetTalk servers.
76	StreetTalk Directory Assistance	List of STDA servers.

Downloading an Operating System

After a client has obtained the data needed to configure itself for network access, it can use the boot file information supplied by the BOOTP server to locate and download an operating system. The BOOTP protocol only gives the name and path that can be used to locate the file. BOOTP does not perform any other functions to assist the client in obtaining a copy of the file. Instead, the client uses the Trivial File Transfer Protocol (TFTP) to retrieve the file.

◀◀   The Trivial File Transfer Protocol is discussed more fully in Chapter 26.

TFTP, like BOOTP, is a simple protocol to implement, making it easy to create client code that can be stored on a chip or embedded in a device's firmware. There is no exchange of authentication information, such as a username and password, between the client and the TFTP server. Instead, the client simply requests a copy of the file and it is sent to the client on a packet-by-packet basis, with the client acknowledging each packet. This start-stop, single-packet exchange method is slower than that which could be accomplished using TCP, but it is not intended for everyday file transfers. TFTP is more than adequate for downloading operating-system code during the boot process.

After the file has been downloaded to the client, it is executed and the client boots to become a full-fledged member of the network.

Taking BOOTP One Step Further: DHCP

Even though diskless workstations are a small percentage of the total number of network nodes in the world today, the concept of receiving configuration information from a central server has not gone away. The Dynamic Host Configuration Protocol (DHCP) was developed after BOOTP as a means for providing a workstation (or any other network device) not only with basic configuration information, but also with a lot of other configuration information, including the capability to add vendor-specific items to the networked computer. DHCP is an extension of the BOOTP protocol, and the relevant RFCs require that a DHCP server be backward compatible with BOOTP clients. This means that you can use a DHCP server on a network that contains newer clients that understand this protocol, as well as older clients that still use BOOTP. Like BOOTP, DHCP uses UDP. Messages are sent to port 67 on the DHCP server. Messages from the server are sent to the DHCP client's UDP port 68.

Note

The Dynamic Host Configuration Protocol is discussed in several RFCs. RFC 1541, "Dynamic Host Configuration Protocol," was an early document, and RFC 2131, also titled "Dynamic Host Configuration Protocol," further clarified the protocol. RFC 2131 added a new message type ("DHCPINFORM"), extended the classing mechanism to include vendor-specific classes, and removed the requirement for a minimum lease time. In addition, RFC 1533, "DHCP Options and BOOTP Vendor Extensions," provides for various options to be included in either BOOTP or DHCP packets. RFC 1533 was updated by RFC 2132, which has the same title. You might notice that some of these RFCs were mentioned earlier in this chapter. This shows the close relationship between BOOTP and DHCP.

DHCP supports various configuration message options that a server can offer as a resource to a booting network node. This includes all the standard IP configuration information, such as IP address, subnet mask, and default gateway. The original BOOTP did not include all the options that were listed earlier in Table 29.1. BOOTP (and DHCP as well) has been augmented over the years to allow for more flexibility and to allow for a larger exchange of configuration data between the client and the server. RFC 1533, "DHCP Options and BOOTP Vendor Extensions," added to the options that were first described in RFC 1497 and includes options for both BOOTP and DHCP. RFC 2132 superceded RFC 1533.

Note

If you want to find out about late-breaking developments with regard to DHCP, you might want to look at the Web site **www.dhcp.org**. This unofficial site contains links to recent developments, as well as links to the RFC documents that relate to DHCP.

Unix users also can use another Web site to download a free version of DHCP. The Internet Software Consortium has developed reference model implementations of DHCP and DNS (BIND) that you can compile on your local system. Visit the consortium's Web site at **www.isc.org**. This site also sponsors an email mailing list for DHCP topics. You can subscribe or unsubscribe from the main page. The latest version of DHCP available at this Web site at the time of this writing is version 3.0p1, which was released on May 8, 2002. This version fixes a serious vulnerability that was part of the original 3.x version.

RFC 2131 provides for three mechanisms that DHCP servers can use to provide addressing information to clients:

- **Automatic allocation**—DHCP simply assigns a client a permanent address.

- **Dynamic allocation**—The most widely used mechanism, this method leases the address to the client for a certain amount of time, until the client wants to abandon the lease (that is, the workstation shuts down), or until the lease time expires and is not renewed by the client.

- **Manual allocation**—Typically used by the administrator to manually enter addresses into the DHCP server's database for computers or other devices.

The dynamic method is the most useful in a network consisting of a large number of client computers that do not require a static address assignment. Using the dynamic method, the administrator can set the time limit for leases. Before a lease expires, the client will attempt to contact the server to renew the lease. If that fails, the client will seek another server from which it can obtain an IP address lease. This mechanism allows for IP addresses to be conserved when the network topology changes frequently. If an address is not being used because a workstation is down or has been moved to another subnet, the lease will eventually expire and the address can be reused.

Note

So what happens when there is no DHCP server when a client attempts to attain configuration information? Automatic Private IP Addressing (APIPA) can solve this problem for Windows XP and Server 2003. The computer sends out the standard DHCP packet. If no response is received, the computer will assign its own configuration information automatically. The address range used is 169.254.0.1 through 169.254.255.254. The subnet mask is set to 255.255.0.0. Note that this range of IP addresses is *not* valid on the Internet, and is intended for use only on a LAN. If you connect to the Internet using a router (or a cable or xDSL modem for a SOHO office), then you will need to configure your router to use Network Address Translation (NAT) so that the router can translate between this private address space and the IP address used on the Internet. Most SOHO routers are already configured to use NAT, so you won't have to do anything. For more information about NAT, see Chapter 49, "Firewalls."

APIPA is ideal for a small network. Just set your network configuration to automatically obtain IP configuration information and forget it. For more information about APIPA, see the section near the end of this chapter titled "What Is APIPA?"

These three methods are not exclusive. For example, for most situations it is easy to configure a desktop client to obtain network configuration information automatically using DHCP and then simply boot the client. Yet, for servers that need a static address, such as file/print servers, DNS servers, or Web servers, the administrator can place a manual entry in the server's database so that the DHCP server will always provide the same address when the server boots.

Alternatively, it's still perfectly okay to configure the server manually with static information and then mark the address as allocated (or reserved) on the DHCP server so that it won't try to use the address. When using a small SOHO router with a cable/DSL modem, you can usually specify the range of addresses to be used, or excluded. One instance in which you might want to do this is when using a Windows domain, whether it be Windows NT/2000 or Server 2003. A domain controller needs to have a static address, whereas the clients do not. Simply assign the static addressing information for the domain controllers, and exclude these addresses from being assigned by NAT. Configure the clients to use automatic configuration (NAT), and the domain controllers to use static information.

Another note of interest is that cable/DSL providers also often turn to NAT. There are simply not enough IP addresses to assign every single computer and networking device in the world a unique address any more. So the Internet provider you use has a set of valid IP addresses, which are used to provide a connection to the Internet for the ISP's clients. The clients are then assigned addresses by the ISP via NAT. And then if you use a cable/DSL modem router, a second layer of NAT is used.

Note

A lease from a DHCP server is not as transient as it might seem at first. For example, when a client shuts down for a short period and then reboots, it is not automatically assigned a different IP address than it acquired during its previous lease. Instead, most DHCP servers keep track of IP addresses and the lease time. When a client reboots, it is reassigned the same IP address as long as no other client is using the address. Likewise, when the DHCP server itself is rebooted, all information should be retained in its database so that on reboot it will be able to continue to track existing leases or issue new ones.

However, keep in mind that if you move the client computer to a subnet that is served by a different DHCP server, the computer will be assigned an address from the pool of addresses available to that server and valid on the new subnet, and will thus obtain a new address that is valid on that particular subnet. On the same topic, if you have a server (such as a domain controller) that uses static configuration information, you'll have to change that when moving the server to a different subnet.

The DHCP Packet Format and Additional Options

Similar to BOOTP, DHCP uses a request/reply mechanism, and the packet format is almost the same for both, to provide for backward compatibility. The layout of the packet used by DHCP looks very much like the layout of the BOOTP packet, with a few exceptions. The first 11 fields are the same. However, the last field, which is called the Vendor Extensions area in the BOOTP packet, is called the Options field in the DHCP packet. The format of the options is the same as it was for BOOTP. However, some of the options that are defined in RFC 2132 are specific only to DHCP. The options available for use with BOOTP clients are a subset of those available for use with DHCP clients. Although this field was limited to 64 bytes in the BOOTP packet, it now is a variable-length field that has a minimum of 312 bytes for DHCP options.

Additional Options Available for DHCP Servers

Following is a listing of the options that can be used for both types of clients. This list includes additional options defined in RFC 2132 that can be used, in addition to those found in Table 29.1, with DHCP servers and clients. The options listed here are not for use with BOOTP clients.

- **Requested IP Address (Opcode=50)**—The client can use this field to request a specific IP address.

- **IP Address Lease Time (Opcode=51)**—The client can use this field to request a particular lease time. The server can use this field to fill in the lease time it is willing to offer. The value used in this field is expressed in seconds.

- **Option Overload (Opcode=52)**—This option enables the server to use the fields originally allocated in the DHCP packet for the server name and filename fields to store options. This can be done when there are a large number of options to convey to the client. A value of 1 flags the filename field as holding options. A value of 2 flags the server name field as holding options. A value of 3 indicates that both fields hold options.

- **TFTP Server Name (Opcode=66)**—This field is used to specify the TFTP server when Option Overloading has used the field previously reserved for this.

- **Bootfile Name (Opcode=67)**—This field is used to identify the boot filename when Option Overloading has used the field previously reserved for this.

- **Server Identifier (Opcode=54)**—DHCP servers use this field so that clients can distinguish between multiple DHCP servers answering a request. Clients then will use this address when they need to send unicast messages to the server chosen from the offers received. DHCP clients also use this option when they accept an offer from a server. The value for Server Identifier is simply the IP address of the server.

- **Parameter Request List (Opcode=55)**—This option enables the client to request certain configuration values. A list of option codes follows this option.

- **Message (Opcode=56)**—The DHCP server uses this field to send an error message to the client, including it in the DHCPNAK message. The client can also use this field to specify a reason why it has declined to use certain parameters offered by the server. The client uses the DHCPDECLINE message type for this. Both of these message types are discussed shortly.

- **Maximum DHCP Message Size (Opcode=57)**—This value is the maximum length for a DHCP message that the client can accept. It is used in the DHCPDISCOVER or DHCPREQUEST messages, described later.

- **Renewal (T1) Time Value (Opcode=58)**—This value is the number of seconds that elapse before a client holding an IP address transitions to the renewing state, at which time it will try to renew an existing IP address lease.

■ **Rebinding (T2) Time Value (Opcode=59)**—This value is the number of seconds that elapse before a client holding an IP address transitions to the rebinding state.

■ **Vendor Class Identifier (Opcode=60)**—This parameter can be used by clients to identify the vendor type and configuration of the client. The DHCP server should respond to this option by using Option 43 to return to the client vendor-specific information. Servers that do not support this option should ignore it.

■ **Client Identifier (Opcode=61)**—Clients can use this to specify a unique identifier. The server can use this value to search its database for addressing information for the client. The identifiers chosen by administrators should be unique on the subnet.

Remember that two option values don't have a data component. These are option zero (Pad option) and option 255 (which marks the end of the options list).

Option Overloading

When the Options Overload option is used in addition to the variable-length option field that is typically used for options, two other fields can be used to store options. This can be useful when a client or server has a maximum size for the total DHCP packet that is not large enough to store all the options the client/server needs to negotiate.

The Options Overload option data field can be 1, 2, or 3. As explained earlier, a value of 1 means that the server name field (sname) contains options. A value of 2 means that the boot filename field (file) contains options. A value of 3 means that both fields contain options.

In this case, other options can be used to store the values that are normally placed into these fields, if necessary. The following must also be done:

■ The actual options field must still be terminated with the 255 end option field. The Pad option (zero) can be used to pad the options field.

■ An option cannot be split across the options field, the sname field, or the file field. Each option tag and its value must be contained in the same field in the packet.

■ The order of precedence for interpreting options is to read them first from the options field, then the sname field, and then the file field (depending on whether the Options Overload field is set to 1, 2, or 3).

■ Some options can be used more than once in a packet, and if so, are concatenated by the client.

The DHCP Client/Server Exchange

Although based on the simple BOOTP protocol, the DHCP protocol client/server exchange is a little more complicated. Both sides communicate using a set of messages, as listed here:

■ **DHCPDISCOVER**—The client broadcasts this message to locate DHCP servers.

■ **DHCPOFFER**—The server uses this message type to offer a set of configuration parameters to the client.

■ **DHCPREQUEST**—A client can use this message type to explicitly accept an offer from one server while implicitly implying that it is not going to use the offers made by other servers. This message type also can be used to confirm the configuration data when the client reboots or when it is attempting to extend a lease.

■ **DHCPACK**—The client sends this acknowledgment to the server, including the configuration parameters that were accepted.

- **DHCPNAK**—The server sends this negative acknowledgment to the client to inform the client that the address it has requested is not correct. For example, when a client is moved to a new subnet and attempts to renew an old IP address, the server can use this message to inform it that it needs a different one.

- **DHCPDECLINE**—The client can send this message to a server to indicate that a particular IP address is already in use.

- **DHCPRELEASE**—The client can give up an IP address and use this message to tell the server that the address can be recycled.

- **DHCPINFORM**—The client can use this message to request local configuration information from the server when the client has already been configured with an IP address by some other means.

The order in which these messages are exchanged appears in Figure 29.1.

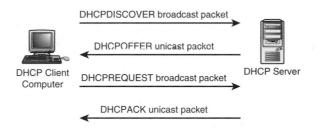

DHCPDISCOVER broadcast packet

DHCPOFFER unicast packet

DHCP Client
Computer

DHCPREQUEST broadcast packet

DHCP Server

DHCPACK unicast packet

Figure 29.1   The DHCP client/server message exchange is a simple process.

Requesting Configuration Information from the DHCP Server

The communication process between the DHCP client and server is simple. The client initially broadcasts a DHCPDISCOVER message on the local subnet to which it is attached. If known, the client can insert configuration options in this discover packet, such as the IP address and a requested lease time.

All DHCP servers that receive the DHCPDISCOVER request can respond with a DHCPOFFER message, including a suggested IP address and any other options it can offer. Because more than one server can respond to a DHCP request (remember that DHCP packets can be relayed across routers using BOOTP relay agents), it then must decide which offer to accept.

Note that in Figure 29.1 the DHCPOFFER packet is sent as a unicast packet instead of a broadcast packet. The DHCP server can unicast or broadcast messages, which is determined in this way:

- If the Gateway IP Address (giaddr) field in the client's packet is a nonzero value, the server assumes that this is the address of an intermediary router and unicasts the packet to this address, using the DHCP server port (67).

- If the Gateway IP Address field is zero but the Client's IP Address (ciaddr) field is not, the server unicasts the packet to this address that the client has filled in.

- If both of these fields are zero and the broadcast flag bit is set in the client's packet, the server broadcasts the packet to the client.

- If both of these fields are zero and the broadcast flag bit is not set, the server unicasts the packet to the client's hardware address and the Client's IP Address (yiaddr) field.

When a selection has been made, the client broadcasts another packet that contains a DHCPREQUEST message. This packet must include the server identification option, indicating from which server the client has chosen to accept the offer.

When the servers see this broadcast packet, those not chosen by the client use it as a flag that their offer was not accepted, and no further communications need to take place between the client and these servers. The chosen server binds the client to the addressing configuration information, and then sends the client a DHCPACK acknowledgment message. This packet also contains the set of agreed-upon options and parameters. If the server cannot grant the request—the IP address requested by the client is already in use, for example—the server responds with a DHCPNAK negative acknowledgment message.

After the client receives an acknowledgment packet indicating that it can use the configuration information, it still must perform some checks to be sure that the information is correct and will allow the client to function on the network. A few simple checks are performed. For example, the client can use ARP to check that the IP address it is about to use is not already in use on the network. This can happen when a DHCP server has been configured incorrectly. If there are no challenges, the client has the information it needs and the configuration of its protocol stack is performed. The client now can participate in the network.

◀◀ The Address Resolution Protocol (ARP) is covered in more detail in Chapter 25.

If this last-minute test informs the client that the address is already in use, the client sends the DHCP server a DHCPDECLINE message. In this case, or if the client has received a DHCPNAK message from the server, the process backs off for a few seconds and begins again.

If the client does not receive either the DHCPACK or the DHCPNAK message within a set amount of time, it also restarts the configuration process.

Implicitly Releasing Configuration Information

In a DHCP environment, configuration information usually is granted for a set amount of time, called a *lease*. When the lease expires and the client has made no attempt to renew it, the configuration information can be used for another client. This can happen if a computer is moved from one subnet to another. Eventually, the original address it had obtained on the previous subnet will expire.

A client also can choose to implicitly release the addressing information. For example, a client that is gracefully shutting down can send a DHCPRELEASE message to the DHCP server, telling it that the lease is no longer needed.

The `ipconfig` command can be used by Windows XP Professional/2000 Client and Windows 2003 servers to release or renew a lease obtained from a DHCP server. To release an address lease, use the following syntax:

```
ipconfig /release
ipconfig /renew
```

If more than one network adapter is installed in the system, you can also specify the name of the adapter on the command line. This command releases the bindings obtained from DHCP servers for all adapters. If you are unsure of the adapter name, use the following command to display the current IP configuration for your computer:

```
ipconfig /all | more
```

The `ifconfig` command can be used on Unix/Linux systems to perform configuration tasks related to IP. The syntax of this command varies from one implementation of Unix to another. However, this command on a Unix system performs a wider variety of tasks than the Windows `ipconfig` command, so use caution when using `ifconfig`. This `ifconfig` command can be used to configure each network interface on the Unix system, including address, subnet mask, and other important parameters. A general version of the command to release an IP address leased from a DHCP server for Unix is

```
/sbin/ifconfig interface release
```

Note that not all versions of Unix use the `ifconfig` command to manage DHCP, either the server or the client. As always with Unix, check the printed documentation and the manual (man) pages.

For example, Red Hat Linux uses the command `dhclient` to obtain a lease (`dhclient -l`) or release an address (`dhclient -r`).

Reusing an Address After Reboot

When a client is rebooted, it does not have to obtain a new IP address. Instead, it can request that the address assignment made from a previous exchange with a DHCP server be used. In this case, when the client reboots, it broadcasts a DHCPREQUEST packet that contains the requested IP address option. Servers that know about this configuration information should respond with a DHCPACK message to the client. However, if the information is invalid—the client is now on a new subnet, for example—the servers should respond with a DHCPNAK message to force the client into beginning the lease process again.

The client also makes its own checks, again using ARP to find out whether the address is in use by another client. If so, it sends a DHCPDECLINE message back to the server and starts the process over.

Using the DHCPINFORM Message

It is quite acceptable for the network administrator to configure some of the IP configuration information on a client and then let DHCP be used for the remaining data. For example, a client can be manually configured with an IP address and subnet mask by the administrator, and then set to get the remaining information from a DHCP server. In this case, the client will broadcast a DHCPINFORM packet that contains the manually configured information. The server then responds to this message with a DHCPACK message. However, the server should not fill in the fields telling the client what its IP address should be and should not include any lease time values. Additionally, the server should not check its own database to see whether a binding for this address already exists.

Because the DHCP server knows the client's address, the DHCPACK message is sent as a unicast packet instead of a broadcast one.

Lease Expiration and Renewal

If a client is using a lease and the lease time expires, the client must immediately stop using the IP address granted by the lease. There are two timers that the client uses to keep track of when and how to renew a lease. These are called T1 and T2. After the time value specified by T1 expires, the client begins trying to renew the existing lease. The client makes attempts to contact the DHCP server from which the lease was obtained to get this extension. At this point, the client is said to be in the RENEWING state.

If no response is received from the DHCP server when the time stored in T2 has expired, the client enters a REBINDING state and attempts to communicate with any other DHCP server so that it can obtain a new IP address.

Obviously, T1 is a value that is less than the lease time, because a lease must be renewed before it expires. The value for T2, likewise, must be longer than that for T1.

If a client is unable to renew or acquire a lease before the expiration of the current lease, the client must stop using the information acquired through the lease and enter into an INIT state to start the process of acquiring configuration information all over again.

After a client has successfully renewed a lease or acquired a new one, it is said to be in the BOUND state. This is the normal state at which configuration is complete and the client computer is functional on the network.

In addition, an administrator usually can renew a release manually. The Windows command `ipconfig` can be used for this:

```
ipconfig /renew
```

As with the `/release` option, you optionally can place an adapter name on the command line to specify an adapter for this operation. If none is specified and more than one adapter is installed and configured using DHCP, all adapters will undergo the renew process.

Overview of How a DHCP Server Chooses the Client's IP Address

RFC 2131 summarizes the process that a DHCP server goes through to decide what IP address to return to a client:

- Use the client's current address as recorded in the client's current address binding, or
- Use the client's previous address recorded in a previous binding that has already expired or has been released, as long as it's not already in use, or
- Use the address found in the Requested IP Address option if specified and if not already in use, or
- Use a new address from the pool of available addresses

In the last case, an address is selected to match the client's subnet or the subnet of the relay agent that forwarded the DHCP request.

An Example: Installing and Configuring a DHCP Server on Windows 2000/2003

Installing a DHCP server on Windows 2000 or Windows 2003 Servers is just as simple as most application installs. However, you'll need to have some information ready before you begin the installation. You will need to know the range of addresses that the server will administer and lease to clients. If you have any servers on the network that need static addresses, you'll need to know those if they fall within the scope of the DHCP managed addresses. For example, DNS and WINS servers must have static IP addresses, and most DHCP servers do also. In a large network, you also should consider using multiple DHCP servers and enabling routers so that they can forward DHCP packets.

Installing the DHCP Server Service on Windows 2000 or Server 2003

In this section you will learn about installing DHCP on both Windows 2000 and Windows Server 2003 server platforms. To install the server, follow these steps:

1. From the Control Panel, select Add/Remove Programs (Add or Remove Programs for 2003).
2. Click on Add/Remove Windows Components. For Windows 2000, click the Components button at the top of the Add/Remove Programs dialog box.
3. When the Windows Components Wizard appears, select Networking Services and then click Details.
4. From the Networking Services dialog box, select the Dynamic Host Configuration Protocol (DHCP) check box, and then click OK to close this dialog box. Click Next when the Windows Components Wizard reappears. A dialog box displays the progress of the installation.
5. The last dialog box tells you that you have successfully completed the Components Wizard. Click Finish.

Tip

If you know from the start that a particular server will be used as a DHCP server, you can select the DHCP network component during installation of the operating system and skip the preceding steps.

You won't have to restart the computer to begin configuring the DHCP server.

Tip

You can check to see that the DHCP service and other services are running by using the Component Services administrative tool. From the MMC tree, select Services (local) to view the services running on the local server. In the list of services that show up in the right pane of the MMC console, look for DHCP Server. Its status should be "started."

Before the server can begin managing IP addresses on the network, you will have to authorize the server in the Active Directory and then configure a *scope* of addresses that the server can administer.

Authorizing the Server

The DHCP manager snap-in for the Microsoft Management Console utility is used to manage the DHCP service on the Windows server. For Windows 2000 click Start, Programs, Administrative Tools, DHCP. For Windows 2003 click Start, Administrative Tools, DHCP. The MMC utility pops up with the DHCP Management snap-in ready for you to use, as shown in Figure 29.2.

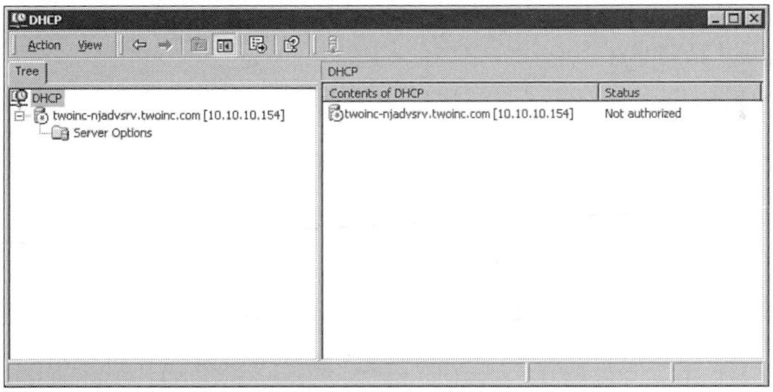

Figure 29.2   The MMC DHCP snap-in is used to manage the DHCP service on the Windows 2000 Server.

On the left side of the management console is a tree structure that can be used to manage one or more DHCP servers from a central location. Click on the server that falls under DHCP and you'll see the Server Options folder for this particular DHCP server.

After you click on the server, you'll notice that the icon to the left of the server name will change and a red arrow (pointing downward) will appear on top of the icon. This is a reminder that this server has not yet been authorized in the Active Directory. Windows 2000/2003 DHCP servers perform a process called *rogue server detection*. When a Windows 2000/2003 server boots and the DHCP service is started, it sends out a DHCPINFORM packet. Other DHCP servers, if any are configured on the network, reply with the DHCPACK message. Next, the service checks to see whether it is registered in the Active Directory. If it is not, it will not begin answering client requests. Figure 29.3 shows an example of the event log entry that the server makes when this occurs.

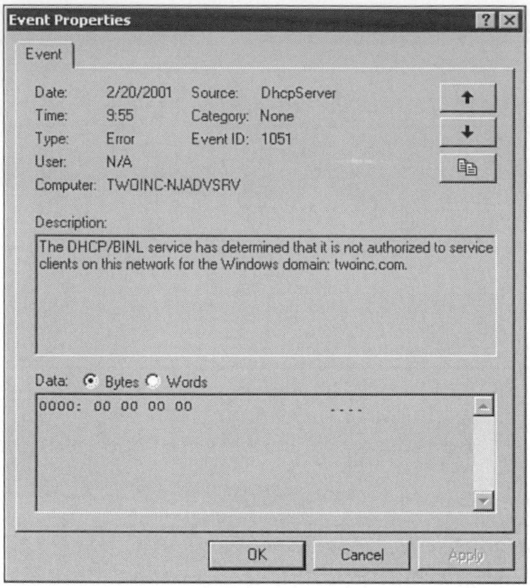

Figure 29.3   The DHCP server will log an error in the system event log file if it is not authorized to run on your network.

The DHCP server undergoes this rogue server detection process once each hour. Thus, each DHCP server can keep track of other authorized DHCP servers on the network.

Authorizing a server is simple:

1. Log on to the server using an administrator-level account.

2. Run the DHCP MMC snap-in by selecting it from the Administrative Tools folder.

3. Click once on the server you want to administer.

4. From the Action menu, select Authorize. It might take up to a minute or two before the process completes.

Use the Refresh option from the Action menu to determine when the process has finished. The red arrow is replaced with a green arrow pointing upward.

Using the MMC Action Menu

To configure a server, click once to highlight it, and then click the Action menu. The Action menu allows you to perform the following tasks if you select a particular DHCP server object:

- **Display Statistics**—This shows statistical information about the selected server, such as the time the server started, the number of requests and offers, and the number (and percentage) of addresses in use, among other things.

- **New Scope**—Use this to create a new scope of IP addresses that the server can offer to clients. After the server is authorized in the Active Directory, this will be the first action you take to set up an address space the DHCP server can use.

- **New Multicast Scope**—Use this to set up a group of IP multicast addresses that can be distributed to computers on the network. You can use this to define multicast scopes for selected network computers.

- **Reconcile All Scopes**—This menu option compares information in the DHCP database about address scopes with that stored in the Registry, and reconciles any differences. Although it's not a substitute for better disaster recovery operations (such as making backups), this can be used to recover a DHCP server and be sure that the scope of addresses it is allowed to use is valid.

- **Authorize/Unauthorize**—As explained in the preceding section, this action item allows you to authorize a server to function on the network by registering it in the Active Directory. This option is presented as Unauthorize if you've highlighted a server that is already authorized.

- **Define User Classes**—Use this to create classes of options. Clients can be assigned to a class to gain access to options not defined by their scope.

- **Define Vendor Classes**—This option enables you to create vendor-specific option classes.

- **Set Predefined Options**—This enables you to set up predefined option classes. These include DHCP standard options (as defined in the RFCs), Microsoft options, Microsoft Windows 2000 options, and Microsoft Windows 98 options.

- **All Tasks**—This gives you access to the Stop/Start/Pause/Resume/Restart tasks.

- **Delete**—This menu option deletes the selected entry in the MMC console tree.

- **Refresh**—This refreshes the current display.

- **Properties**—This option brings up the properties page for the selected entry.

When you first install the service, the first thing you need to do is create a scope of IP addresses that the DHCP server can use to allocate leases to its clients. After that, other options in the Action menu can be used to further configure the server.

Creating an Address Scope

After you have authorized a server on the network, you can create a scope of addresses that the DHCP server can administer to clients. From the MMC utility, click once on the server you want to administer, and then select New Scope from the Action menu. The New Scope Wizard pops up. Alternatively, you can right click the server and select New Scope. Click Next to dismiss the introductory dialog box and continue creating an address scope. The wizard then prompts you through the following steps:

1. A dialog box pops up that you can use to give the scope a name and description. The description is optional, but you must at least supply a name for the scope so that it can be differentiated from other scopes you might create. Enter the name and, if you want, a description and click Next.

2. The next dialog box, shown in Figure 29.4, prompts you to enter the range of IP addresses for this scope. Enter a starting address and an ending address. You also should enter a subnet mask associated with this address range. The subnet mask can be entered in the traditional way using dotted-decimal notation, or you can specify the mask by indicating the number of bits in the Length field (as in CIDR notation). When finished, click Next.

3. The next dialog box (shown in Figure 29.5) enables you to specify any addresses that fall within the range you have entered that you want to exclude from the scope. You can enter a single address and click the Add button, or you can enter a range of addresses (starting and ending addresses) and click the Add button. If you change your mind about an address, highlight it and click the Remove button. When finished adding addresses to be excluded, click Next. You should exclude the DHCP server's own address if it falls within the range of addresses you defined in the preceding step.

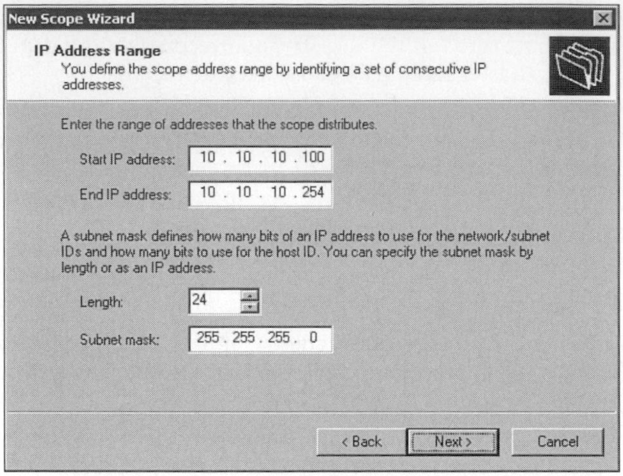

Figure 29.4 The wizard prompts you to enter the address range and specify the subnet mask for the scope.

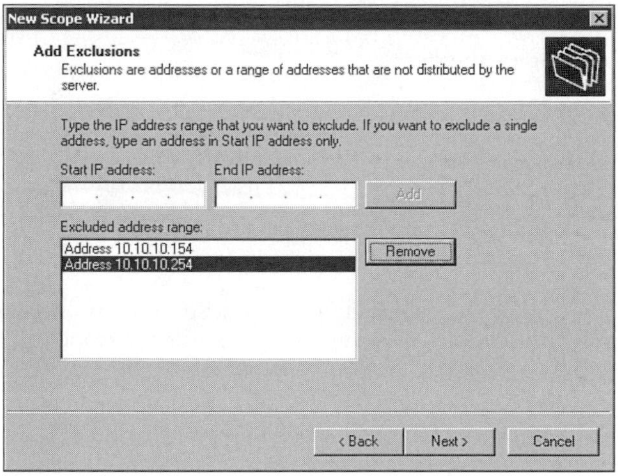

Figure 29.5 Enter the address range to be excluded from use by the DHCP server, and an appropriate subnet mask for the address range.

4. Next, you are prompted to enter the amount of time to lease the addresses in this scope. In Figure 29.6 you can see that this dialog box defaults to 8 days. As it suggests, you should consider creating scopes that have lease values relevant to your network. For example, mobile computers that frequently move from one place to another can be given a shorter lease time, thus keeping your address pool from becoming populated by unexpired, unused leases. This dialog box also enables you to specify the lease in hours, minutes, and seconds.

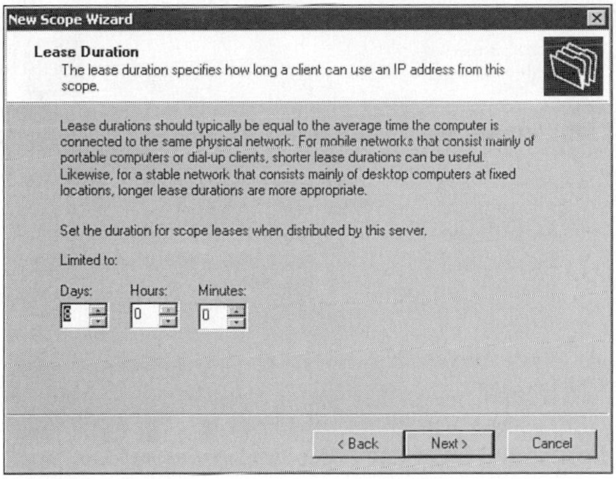

Figure 29.6   This dialog box enables you to customize the lease period for this scope of addresses.

5. As discussed earlier in this chapter, the DHCP packet can contain various options. The dialog box shown in Figure 29.7 prompts you to enter options valid for this scope or to put it off until another time. For this example, go ahead and configure the options. Leave the Yes, I Want to Configure These Options Now radio button selected, and click Next.

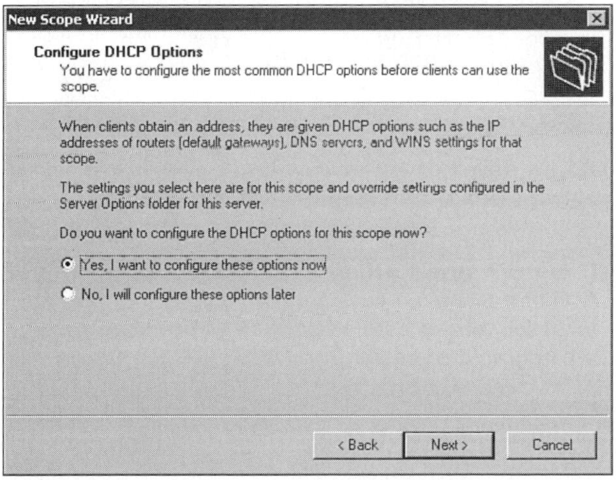

Figure 29.7   You can set up options for this scope now or later.

6. The first option, shown in Figure 29.8, prompts you to enter the default gateway for the subnet covered by this range of addresses. Enter one or more IP addresses for the routers you want to use, clicking the Add button to add each one. Note that here you are entering the default gateway to which clients will send IP datagrams when the destination is not on the local subnet. This is *not* the gateway computer discussed earlier in this chapter that serves as a BOOTP or DHCP Relay Agent. Again, if you change your mind, you can highlight any router address and click the Remove button to delete it from this list. Click Next when you have finished adding routers.

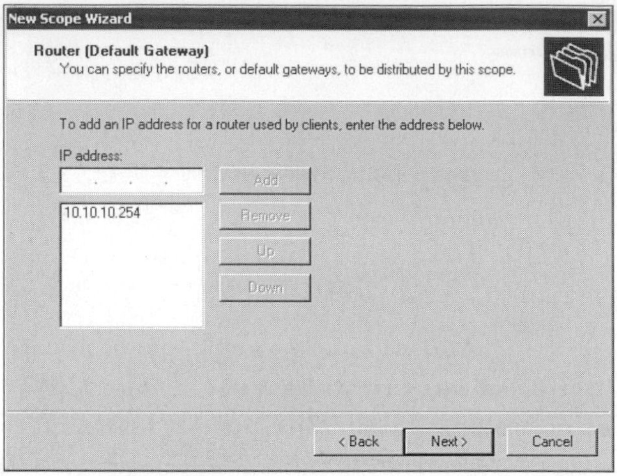

Figure 29.8 Enter one or more routers that will operate as default gateways for the LAN segment served by this scope of IP addresses.

7. Next, a dialog box prompts you to enter the parent name of your network. This is the name of the domain that client computers are configured to use for DNS name resolution. In Figure 29.9 you can see that you also can enter the names or addresses of domain name servers the client is configured to use. If you enter a server name, click Resolve to have the wizard look up the address, or enter an address and click Add to add it to the list. Use the Remove button if you change your mind. Place the order of DNS servers in the same order in which you want clients to access them. You can highlight a server in the list and use the Up and Down buttons to change the order.

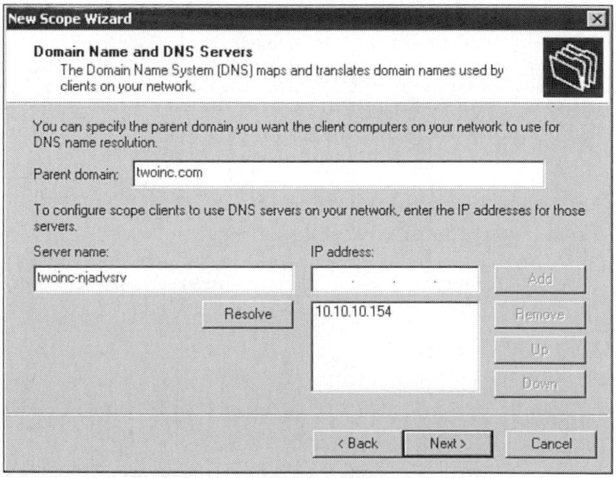

Figure 29.9 Enter the client computer's domain name and then the domain name servers for the domain.

8. If you still are using Microsoft's Windows Internet Naming Service (WINS), you can use the next dialog box, shown in Figure 29.10, to enter the names or addresses of the WINS servers. If you enter the name, use the Resolve button again to have the server translate the WINS server's name to an IP address.

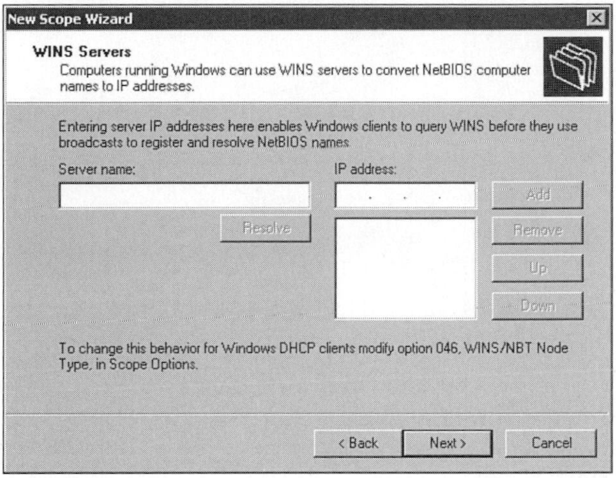

Figure 29.10   Enter the name or IP address of each WINS server that clients can use.

9. Finally, a dialog box asks whether you want to activate the scope now or later (see Figure 29.11). The server does not begin allocating addresses in the scope to clients until the scope is activated. After making your choice, click Next. A final dialog box notifies you that the wizard is finished creating the scope. Click the Finish button.

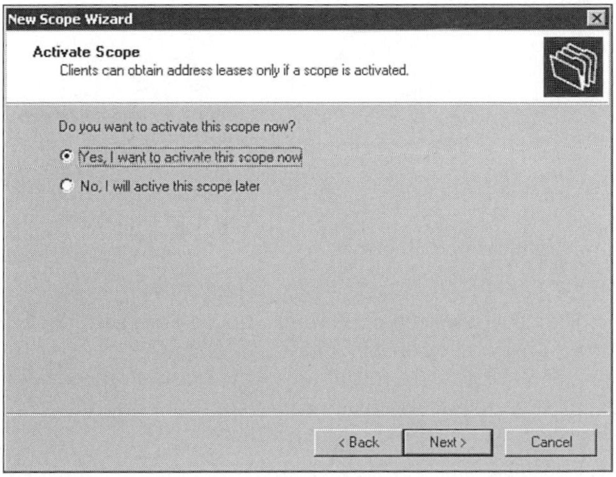

Figure 29.11   You can choose to activate the scope right after you create it or later.

If you did not choose to activate the scope, you can do so later by right-clicking on the scope and selecting Activate. Alternatively, click once on the scope and select Activate from the Action menu.

In Figure 29.12 you can see the DHCP MMC snap-in after a scope has been created and activated.

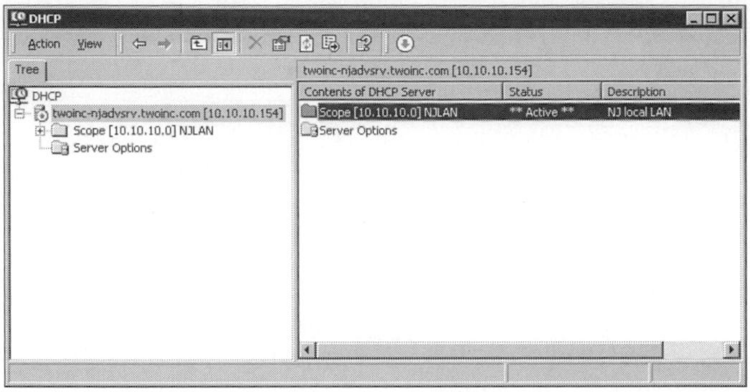

Figure 29.12   The new scope shows up in the right pane of the DHCP MMC snap-in utility.

The Status field in this display tells you whether the scope is active, and the Description field can be useful when you create multiple scopes and need a reminder of their use. After the scope has been activated, clients that boot on the network and that have been configured to use a DHCP server can now receive configuration information from this DHCP server. If you expand the scope by clicking on the plus sign in the left pane, you can see that there are four other objects that can be managed. Figure 29.13 shows the new scope with the Address Pool object selected.

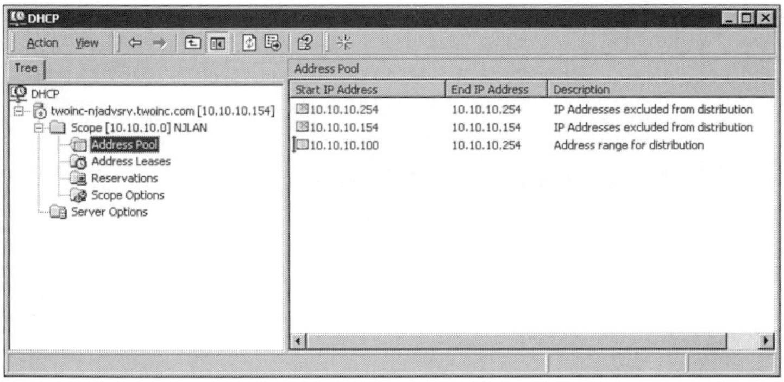

Figure 29.13   You can manage addresses, leases, reservations, and options offered by the scope using the DHCP MMC snap-in.

You can click on any of the other objects to see information. For example, if you want to see what options are enabled in this scope, click Scope Options. The option number (from the RFCs), name, and values for the options are displayed. In the case of this initial setup using the wizard, you would see options for the default router (gateway), DNS server, and domain name. If you entered an address for a WINS server, that option would also be displayed.

Reserving a Client Address

You can choose to exclude certain addresses from a scope that you know are configured manually, such as routers. However, you might want to use the Reservation method to reserve an address for a DHCP client that might need to keep the same IP address, but obtain other information from the DHCP server at times. A DNS server is a good example of a server that should have a reserved address.

To reserve an address within a scope, expand the scope in the MMC console and open up the Reservation dialog box either by highlighting the Reservation object and selecting New Reservation from the Action menu, or by right-clicking the Reservations object and making the same selection. In Figure 29.14, you can see the simple dialog box used to create a reservation.

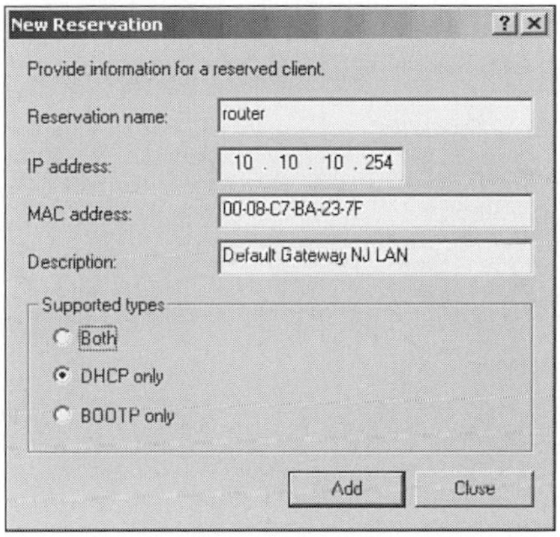

Figure 29.14 You can identify specific computers that will have a reserved IP address on the DHCP server.

As discussed later in this chapter, assigning options to a reserved IP address gives the administrator the best method for fine-tuning what options the client will end up being offered by the DHCP server. Options associated with a reservation override all other options defined for the server, the scope, or any option class to which the computer might belong.

Configuring the DHCP Server and Scope Options

Earlier in this chapter, many options that can be used for BOOTP and DHCP clients were discussed. The Windows 2000/2003 DHCP service enables you to configure which options will be offered to clients of the service. To configure the options, expand the MMC tree of DHCP servers to locate the server you want to manage. Click that server to get to the Options Folder for that server. After you have highlighted the Options Folder, click the Action menu.

Note

Although the RFCs support option overloading, as described earlier in this chapter, note that the Microsoft DHCP server does not support this function. Additionally, the maximum number of bytes stored in the DHCP packet options field is 312 bytes.

From the Action menu, select Configure Options. In Figure 29.15, you can see the default dialog box used for configuring options. Note that this dialog box has a General and an Advanced tab. Figure 29.16 shows the Advanced tab.

Because the server enables you to specify options for several levels, it is important to understand the precedence used to decide which options apply to a client. Options can be set for the following, and in this order:

- **Global Options**—These are the server's global options. These options apply to all scopes, unless superceded by the following options.

- **Scope Options**—These apply to a scope the client uses. Options in this class that conflict with server global options will supercede them.

■ **Class Options**—These apply to clients that are members of the class. Options in a class will supercede server global options and class options.

■ **Reserved Client Options**—By assigning options to a particular client for which an IP address reservation has been created, you are given the finest granularity of control. Options defined for a reserved client address override all other options.

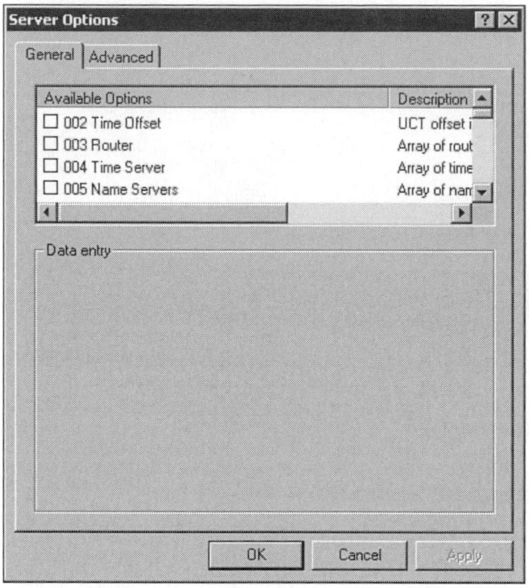

Figure 29.15 You can configure the options that the server can present to clients using this dialog box.

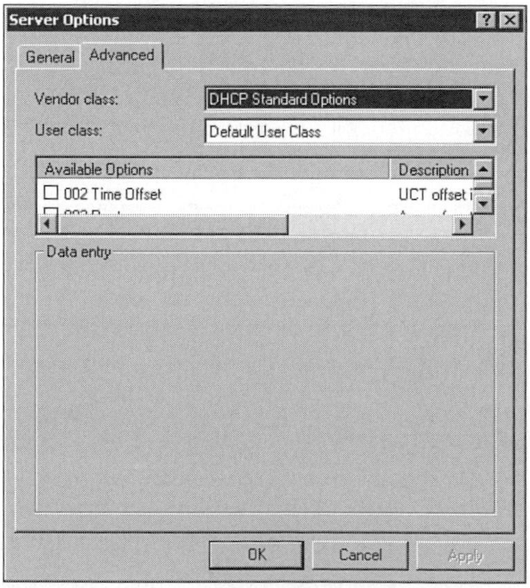

Figure 29.16 The Advanced tab enables you to more precisely control the options that are offered to clients.

Similarly, you can configure options for a scope if you did not do so during the initial creation of the scope. You also can use these same steps to change or add options to the scope. To change the options for a scope, expand the scope and select the Scope Options folder.

Option Classes

In Figure 29.15, the list of Available Options is the list of options that are defined for the current DHCP server, and they are mostly the same options you'll find in RFC 2132. Note that although the server can offer all these options, not all Microsoft clients can use this entire set of options, which is why the wizard prompted you for only a few options when it allowed you to select options for the newly created scope.

The Advanced tab shown previously in Figure 29.17 enables you to look at the different classes of objects. You'll see a *vendor class* and a *user class*. Vendor classes are groupings of options that are useful for a particular vendor's client, such as Microsoft 98 or Windows NT clients. User classes are for grouping options that a particular class of users has in common; for example, BOOTP clients or Remote Access users.

If you define options for the server, the scopes you create will inherit them. A good place to start is to define the basic subset of options that all clients will need, if you have such a list, and configure these options for the server. Next, you can expand the particular scope and select the Scope Options folder to add or remove options that apply to a particular scope.

Superscopes

In the earlier example, only one scope of addresses was created on the DHCP server. The server is capable of handling additional address scopes, however, to provide for other clients that might be physically accessible to the DHCP server but use a different logical subnet address. To create a superscope, you first must create the scopes to be included in it. Use the same procedures as before to create the new scope, specifying its address range, options, and so on. Next, select New Superscope from the Action menu. A wizard pops up and again prompts you through the process:

1. Click the Next button to dismiss the wizard's opening dialog box.
2. In the next dialog box, give your superscope a name and click Next.
3. Figure 29.17 displays the current list of scopes defined on the server. Select the scopes that will fall under this superscope. Use Shift+click and Ctrl+click to select one or more scopes from the list. Click Next.
4. Finally, the wizard shows you a summary of your superscope, including the name and the names of the scopes that make it up (see Figure 29.18). Click the Finish button.

Providing Support for BOOTP Clients

The Windows 2000/2003 DHCP servers provide support for BOOTP clients. The Default BOOTP user class of options is used to configure the information that is supplied to these clients. Although standard BOOTP servers require that the server be configured in advance with a table of client hardware addresses and corresponding IP addresses, Windows 2000/Server 2003 DHCP servers instead select the next available address to give to a BOOTP client. This matches the method the DHCP server uses when granting IP address leases to its DHCP clients.

Enabling the DHCP Relay Agent

RFC 1542, "Clarifications and Extensions for the Bootstrap Protocol," defined support for a BOOTP relay agent. That agent now is supported by almost every router. The relay agent function enables you to support clients on different subnets, using a single BOOTP or DHCP server. DHCP requests are forwarded by the router to the DHCP server, and the server's responses are returned to the client. Because BOOTP and DHCP use almost the same frame format and the same UDP ports, you'll also find that most BOOTP relay agents will perform this duty for DHCP clients.

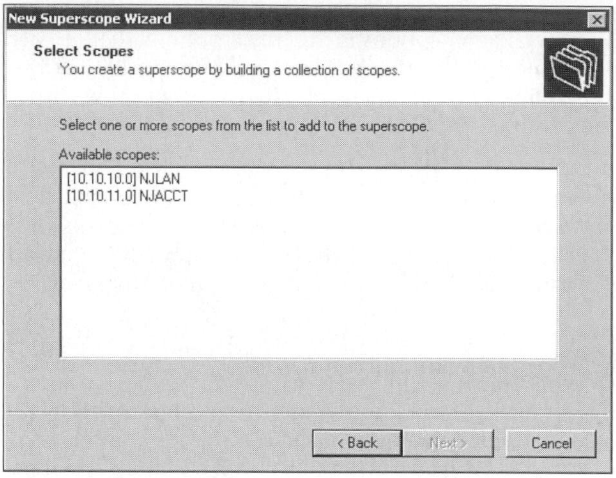

Figure 29.17   Select the scopes to include in the superscope.

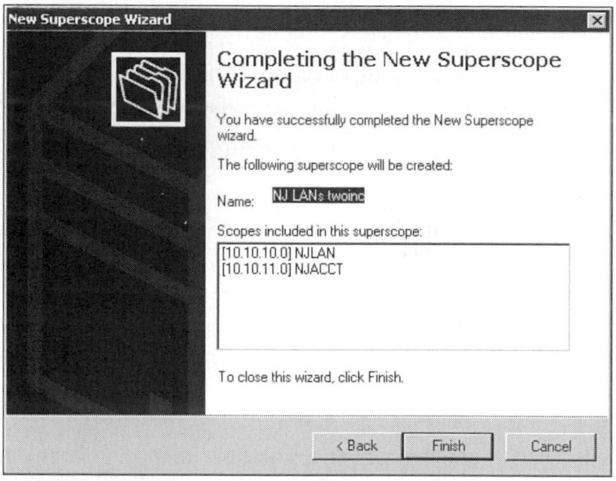

Figure 29.18   Confirm your selections before exiting the Superscope Wizard.

However, on a small network, you might not have a router. Instead, you might be using the Routing and Remote Access services available in Windows 2000/2003 Servers. In that case, you'll need to add the DHCP Relay Agent protocol. Follow these steps to enable the DHCP Relay Agent:

1. Click Start, Programs, Administrative Tools (Start, Administrative Tools for 2003), and then Routing and Remote Access (for Windows Server 2003, Start, Administrative Tools, Routing and Remote Access).

2. In the left pane of the MMC console utility, click the plus sign to expand the server's list of objects.

3. Click the plus sign for IP Routing to expand the list of objects it contains.

4. Right-click on General, and from the menu that pops up select New Routing Protocol.

5. In Figure 29.19, you can see the New Routing Protocol dialog box displaying a list of available protocols. Select DHCP Relay Agent, and click OK to dismiss the dialog box. The DHCP Relay Agent protocol now shows up as an object under IP Routing.

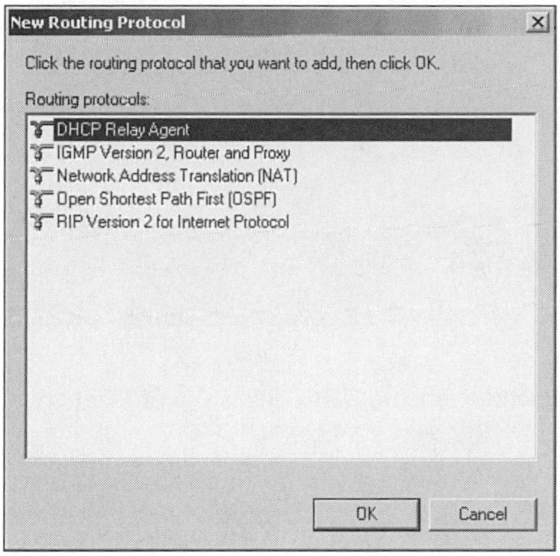

Figure 29.19   The New Routing Protocol dialog box enables you to install the DHCP Relay Agent service.

6. Right-click on this new object and select Properties. In the Properties sheet for the DHCP Relay Agent, you can add the addresses of one or more DHCP servers to which BOOTP and DHCP messages will be relayed (see Figure 29.20).

When the relay agent receives a DHCP or BOOTP broadcast message on one of its network interfaces, which it can recognize because the packet is addressed to port 67, it will forward the message to a DHCP server. You can see an example of this in Figure 29.21. The DHCP server resides on Subnet 1, along with other servers. This subnet is connected to Subnet 2 using a router—or possibly a Windows 2000 server running the DHCP Relay Agent service.

When Workstation A on Subnet 2 boots, it broadcasts a DHCPDISCOVER message using UDP. When the router sees this broadcast, it looks at the Gateway Address field (discussed earlier in this chapter, and not to be confused with a default gateway on a TCP/IP LAN). If the value for this field is all zeros (0.0.0.0), the relay agent service on the router will place its own address in this field. This enables the DHCP server to reply directly to the router when it replies to the DHCP or BOOTP request.

The DHCP server looks at the Gateway Address field. It then consults its list of scopes to determine an appropriate address based on the value of the Gateway Address field and sends a DHCPOFFER packet back to the router, which then broadcasts the packet on Subnet 2. Remember that a broadcast is necessary in this case because at this time Workstation A knows its hardware address but doesn't yet have an IP address. If the client decides to accept the address offer, it sends a DHCPREQUEST message to the server, and the server responds with a DHCPACK acknowledgment granting the workstation the lease.

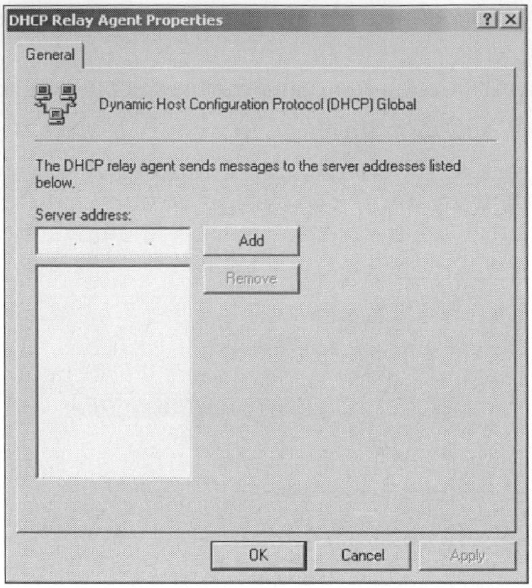

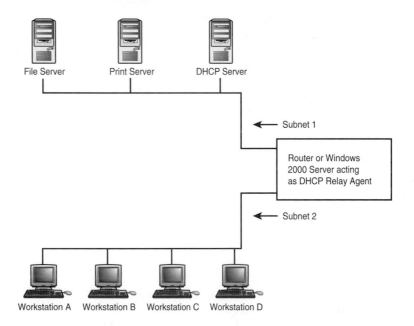

Figure 29.20 The Properties sheet for the DHCP Relay Agent is where you specify the DHCP servers that will handle requests forwarded by the relay service.

Figure 29.21 The DHCP Relay Agent can support clients on another subnet.

What Is a DHCP Cluster?

If you are using Windows 2000 Advanced Server or Windows Server 2003 Enterprise or Datacenter servers, you can use the clustering feature for DHCP. This allows two separate DHCP servers to be administered as a single DHCP server. Windows 2000/2003 clustering supports a failover mode in which a service running on one computer can be monitored. If the node that is supplying a DHCP service supported by the clustering software fails, another node that runs the same service can be activated to take over for the failed node. By clustering DHCP services between two nodes, you will make the network less prone to downtime due to problems with your DHCP server.

The alternative to clustering is to use two separate DHCP servers, each responsible for a portion of the address scope. This allows all your clients to get an address from one or the other server. Because leases usually are measured in days or weeks on a stable network, the loss of a single DHCP server for a few hours or a day or so might not cause you any problems unless someone decides to reboot every PC on the network. A secondary server, configured with a smaller portion of the address space, can continue to handle DHCP traffic while the main server is repaired.

In a larger network, however, where computers are frequently moved, a more stable DHCP service can be provided by hosting the DHCP service on a cluster.

Keep the following points in mind when using a Windows cluster for the DHCP service:

- The DHCP service should be installed before the clustering service is installed on the computers.

- As with most cluster installs, one server should be configured first, with the DHCP service and the clustering service, while the other cluster member-to-be is powered off.

- When you're finished with the installation on the first member, power up the second and install the DHCP service and then the cluster service.

In addition, keep in mind that the cluster itself must have a unique IP address, which can't be delegated to it by a DHCP server. Additionally, you'll need to create a domain security group and make both servers members. To this group, assign Full Control permissions for the DNS zone object in the Active Directory where DHCP A and PTR records are stored for the servers' clients.

Using Windows clusters is the subject of many books. Before you decide to use a cluster on your network, I would recommend that you become intimately familiar with Windows clusters. There are many aspects of clustering (such as the utilities used to start/stop and otherwise manage the cluster) that you need to learn before you try to set DHCP and the clustering software.

Considerations for Using DHCP in Large or Routed Environments

In a large network you need to provide for redundancy for DHCP servers. Because a larger network typically is connected using routes to join a diverse set of network segments, you will need to enable BOOTP and DHCP forwarding on any routers in the network. Each DHCP server will need to be carefully planned, and the address scopes, reservations, and exclusions will need to be carefully thought through in advance. You don't want, for example, a DHCP server to allocate an address to a client when that address should have been reserved and already is in use by another server! This is exactly the kind of thing automatic dispensing of IP addresses is supposed to solve.

Of course, when you're planning the placement of DHCP servers in a large, routed environment, it's easiest to place a single DHCP server on each subnet. In many cases, though, this is not practical. And with the forwarding capabilities it is not necessarily needed. Also, don't yield to the temptation of placing all your DHCP servers on the same subnet, allowing them to receive forwarded replies from other network segments. If the single subnet becomes unavailable, all your DHCP servers become unavailable. This applies to any major server. Don't place all your eggs in one basket, so to speak.

How DHCP Interacts with Microsoft's Dynamic Domain Name Service (DNS)

Microsoft's version of DNS supports dynamic updates, as specified in RFC 2136, "Dynamic Updates in the Domain Name System (DNS UPDATE)." Windows 2000 clients can send dynamic updates after having received configuration information from a DHCP server. When a DHCP lease expires, the client will send an update to deregister the addressing information.

To register with DNS, the client first contacts a name server. If the name server is just a local server and is not authoritative for the zone, it will return the address of the authoritative server to the client. The client then will contact the primary authoritative server to send it the updated addressing information. If it's successful, a reply is sent back to the client.

The DHCP server also can be used to send dynamic updates to DNS. This is useful for pre–Windows 2000 clients that do not understand the dynamic update process. This also can be negotiated between the DHCP server and a Windows 2000 client during the initial DHCP process. This is done using a special FQDN (fully qualified domain name) DHCPREQUEST packet (using Option number 81). This packet has three possible flags that can be set:

- **0**—This flag specifies that the client wants to be responsible for updating the A resource record on the DNS server, but would like for the DHCP server to update the PTR resource record.

- **1**—This flag specifies that the client wants to perform both updates.

- **3**—If this flag is set, the DHCP server will register both records, regardless of the client's wishes. If the server sends a packet to the client with this flag set, the client does not attempt any updates.

▶▶ For more information about A and PTR records that are used in the DNS database, see Chapter 30.

These flags are not all that controls the process of which computer performs which updates. Instead, both the client and the server can be configured to perform (or not perform) this function.

Configuring Dynamic Updates on the DHCP Server

On the server side, you can specify in the properties page for the server how it will respond to dynamic update requests, and whether it will perform dynamic updates for clients that do not support this function (that is, pre–Windows 2000 clients). To configure the service for this functionality, follow these steps:

1. Click Start, Programs, Administrative Tools, DHCP (or Start, Administrative Tools, DHCP for Windows Server 2003).

2. In the left pane, expand the tree structure by clicking the plus sign next to the server's name to expand the tree to show the scopes that belong to the server.

3. Right-click the scope you want to modify, and select Properties.

4. When the Properties page appears, click the DNS tab. In Figure 29.22 you can see the properties found on this tab.

5. The first check box, Automatically Update DHCP Client Information in DNS, enables you to specify this function using two options. Click either the Update DNS Only If DHCP Client Requests radio button or the Always Update DNS radio button. If you select the second button, the server will always make updates for clients, ignoring their requests.

6. To enable the server to handle dynamic updates for clients that do not support dynamic DNS update, select the check box Enable Updates for DNS Clients That Do Not Support Dynamic Update.

7. Click the Apply button, and then click the OK button to dismiss the dialog box.

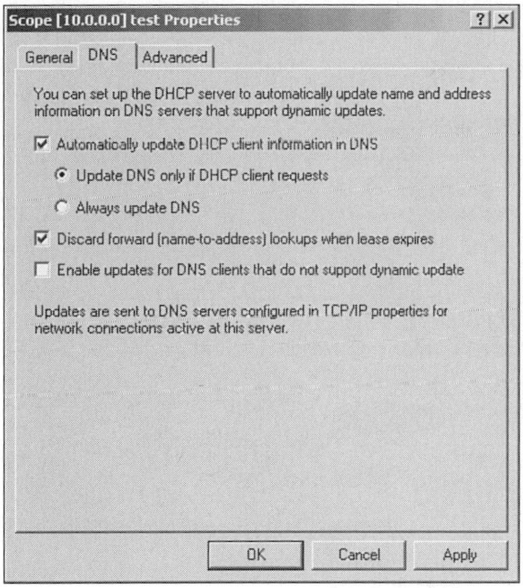

Figure 29.22   The DNS tab enables you to configure DHCP server behavior in regard to DNS dynamic updates.

Configuring Dynamic Updates on the Client

You also can control how the client handles the dynamic DNS update function if you are using Windows 2000 clients. Remember from the preceding section that the server can override a client's request if the appropriate selection is made on the scope's DNS properties page.

Windows 2000 clients and servers, as well as Windows XP and Windows Server 2003, are already configured, by default, to send the FQDN packet with the Flags field set to zero. This means the client wants to update the A resource record and wants the server to update the PTR record. You can change this behavior by doing the following:

1. Right-click the My Network Places icon (or double-click the Network icon in the Control Panel). For Windows Server 2003, click on Start, Control Panel, Network Connections.

2. Right-click the icon for the network connection you want to configure. From the menu that pops up, select Properties.

3. Highlight Internet Protocol (TCP/IP) and click the Properties button.

4. Click the Advanced button, and then select the DNS tab. A properties page similar to that shown in Figure 29.23 pops up. At the bottom of the properties page, you'll notice that Register This Connection's Addresses in DNS is selected, and Use This Connection's DNS Suffix in DNS Registration is not. The second option is the default.

5. To disable the client from performing DNS updates, deselect the check box labeled Register This Connection's Addresses in DNS.

6. When finished, dismiss the properties page by clicking OK in each dialog box.

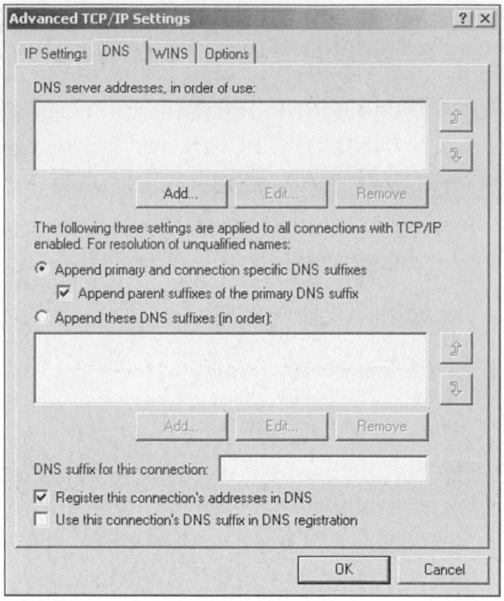

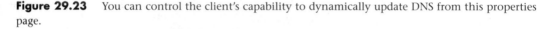

Figure 29.23   You can control the client's capability to dynamically update DNS from this properties page.

Reservations and Exclusions

Some computers or other networked devices, such as routers or printers, might need to keep the same IP address all the time. For example, Microsoft very strongly suggests you be sure that your DHCP server has a static, unchanging address. There are two ways you can be sure a particular computer or device keeps the same static address. The first method is to manually configure the client using the client's software. For example, when you configure a Microsoft Windows 2000 Professional client or a Windows XP client, you can specify a static IP address (along with other network information) using the TCP/IP properties page for the client.

If you use the first method, you'll need to exclude the address you use from the address pool that you assign to a scope. If you forget this step and the address does fall within the range of a scope, eventually it will be issued to a client, causing a duplicate address error on the LAN.

A reservation is similar to an exclusion but is used for computers or devices that do support DHCP but still require a constant, static address. You can enter a reservation for an address that falls within the address pool for a scope. The reservation is linked to the computer or device's hardware address so that when it boots and begins the process of obtaining configuration information via DHCP, it will always receive the same address.

Exclusions are created when you create the address pool, as explained earlier in this chapter. To create a reservation, carry out these steps:

1. Bring up the DHCP MMC console by clicking Start, Programs, Administrative Tools, DHCP. Expand the tree in the left pane to get to the scope in which the reservation will be created.

2. Expand the scope and right-click Reservations.

3. From the menu that pops up, select New Reservation.

4. The New Reservation dialog box appears. Enter a descriptive name you want to use for this reservation.

5. Next, enter the IP address that falls within the scope but that is to be reserved.

6. Enter the hardware address of the computer for which this address will be reserved. For Windows NT/2000 clients, use the IPCONFIG/ALL command at the command prompt to get this address. For routers or other computers, consult your documentation.

7. Select whether the reservation will be used for a BOOTP request or a DHCP request, or both.

8. Click OK to dismiss the dialog box. The reservation is complete. The address is handed out only to the device that uses the hardware address (also called the MAC address) you defined for the reservation.

Note in this example the reservation was made for a router. Other types of devices for which you might want to reserve addresses (or exclude if the computers are statically configured) are important servers that are mapped to specific addresses in your DNS system. Also, if you have non-Windows clients, such as Linux or Unix desktops or servers, you might want to reserve an address for them if they cannot use DHCP.

What Is APIPA?

If a client is configured to use DHCP, what happens if no DHCP server is available on the network? In that case, Microsoft Windows 2000 clients can use Automatic Private IP Addressing (APIPA). This is not a solution for a large network. It is for use on small LANs, such as a home office with 25 or fewer network nodes.

Simply configure each client computer to use DHCP in the properties page for TCP/IP, and reboot. When the client computer realizes that no DHCP server is on the network (because it's not receiving any replies from its broadcasts), it will timeout and begin to use APIPA. The scheme in which addresses are allocated is not that complicated.

The network of addresses reserved for use by APIPA is 169.254.0.1 to 169.254.255.254, with a subnet mask of 255.255.0.0. When the client does not receive an answer from any DHCP server after a short time, it will select an address randomly from this network. It then will test to see whether this address is already in use.

Note

The only information that APIPA will configure for the client computer is an IP address and a subnet mask. It does not allow the client to configure other items that could be offered as options by a DHCP server. One important item to note is that APIPA does not provide the capability for the client computer to detect a default gateway. Thus, communication is limited to computers on the local LAN that all share the same 169.254.0.0 network address space. If you plan to connect your small LAN to the Internet, or to any other network using a router, you'll need to either manually configure IP addressing information on each client or configure a DHCP server that can perform this function for you.

Note that a Microsoft client that is using APIPA will periodically check the network (about every five minutes) to see whether a DHCP server has become available. If one does come online, the client will perform as any other DHCP client and obtain configuration information from the DHCP server it discovers.

Because clients randomly choose IP addresses, it is always quite possible that one computer will choose an address already in use. To solve this problem, each computer first chooses an address and then broadcasts a packet containing that IP address and waits to see whether another computer replies that the address is already in use. This is referred to as gratuitous ARP. When this occurs, a client will attempt to select an IP address up to 10 times before ending the process.

Troubleshooting Microsoft DHCP

Troubleshooting DHCP can be a complicated process. Perhaps you've forgotten to authorize the server on the network or activate a scope. Clients might be unable to locate the server. In any case, there are several things you can do to troubleshoot DHCP problems. With the client, start by using the `ipconfig /all` command at the command prompt to view IP configuration data. If the client shows either no address or an address of 0.0.0.0, a problem exists between the client and the server. It might be a network card, a misconfigured router, or another network component. Use the standard TCP/IP tools (that is, ping or tracert) from another client on the same subnet to the DHCP server to see whether connectivity exists. If you can't reach the DHCP server from that client, try the same tests from other clients on other subnets to help localize where in the network the problem lies.

Two other useful tools for troubleshooting are the Windows 2000 Event Logs and the DHCP server's own audit log file. Earlier in this chapter you saw an example of an event log entry. In the next section you'll learn how to enable the DHCP server's own logging capabilities.

Managing Logging

Besides the records that the DHCP server records in the event log, you also can enable logging by the server to its own log file. For troubleshooting purposes, both the event log and the server's own log file can be very useful.

To manage the server's log file, follow these steps:

1. Start the DHCP MMC console.

2. Click once on the server you want to modify, and select Properties from the Action menu. Alternatively, right-click on the server and select Properties.

3. In the General tab for the properties page for the server, select the check box labeled Enable DHCP Audit Logging.

4. Click the Advanced tab. Here you will find two fields. You can use the first field to enter the location where you want the log files to be created. The default is `%systemroot%\System32\dhcp`.

5. The second field can be used to enter the path for the location of the DHCP database files. The default for this is the same as that for the log files.

6. Click OK to dismiss the properties page when you have finished viewing or modifying these fields.

When you enable audit logging, a new log file is created at midnight each day. Header information is written to the file and significant events are logged. The format for the filename used for log files is `DhcpSrvLog.day of week`. For example, a log file created on Monday morning would be named `DhcpSrvLog.Mon`.

Because the day of the week is used as the file extension for the log file, it should be obvious that in a week you'll have to overwrite an existing file. Indeed, this is what happens, unless the file has been modified within the past 24 hours. If this happens, logging will be suspended until the file is removed or renamed.

The log file is a simple ASCII text file using comma-delimited fields. Each event is recorded as a single line in the file, using the fields

`ID, Date, Time, Description, IP Address, Host Name, MAC Address` which are as described here:

- *ID*—An event code to indicate the kind of event logged.
- *Date*—The date of the event.
- *Time*—The time of the event.
- *Description*—A short description of the event.
- *IP Address*—The IP address of the client.
- *Host Name*—The hostname of the client.
- *MAC Address*—The hardware (MAC) address of the client.

The standard event IDs are as listed here:

- **00**—The log was started.
- **01**—The log was stopped.
- **02**—Because of a low-disk-space condition, logging was suspended.
- **10**—A new IP address lease was granted to a client.
- **11**—A client renewed its lease.
- **12**—A client released its lease.
- **13**—An address was found to be already in use on the network.
- **14**—The address pool has been completely used, so the server was unable to grant a lease to a client.
- **15**—A lease was denied to a client.
- **20**—An address was given to a BOOTP client.

As you can see, a significant amount of information is stored in the log files. Start your troubleshooting efforts here if you are experiencing problems with the server itself or with multiple clients. You can follow the trail of events leading up to the current problem. Again, if you are having problems with a single client, examine the event log file on the client to look for any indication that the client was unable to locate or interact with the DHCP server.

Using DHCP with Red Hat Linux

During the installation of Red Hat Linux, you will be prompted for the network components to install, just as you are with Windows. You can specify at that time to use DHCP for a client workstation, or you can assign a static address. If you elect to use DHCP, you will be able to access a DHCP server to obtain IP configuration information from a DHCP server. You can also choose to install a DHCP server when you install Linux so that you can service other client computers.

The client configuration information is stored in several files for Red Hat Linux:

- dhclient.conf—This file stores information about all network devices attached to the computer, such as the amount of time the client will wait before attempting to contact a DHCP server when no response has been received. If you have a DNS server that supports dynamic updates, you can list the fully qualified name of those servers in this file.
- dhclient.leases—This file records leases previously obtained so that the client can request them again after a reboot. More than one address can be listed in this file because the computer can have more than one network interface.
- dhcpd.options—This file lists options requested by the client, as described earlier in this chapter.

You probably won't have to make any edits to the previously listed files—the default values created when you elect to use DHCP on the client are usually sufficient in all but the most extreme circumstances. If you do need to tweak some of the data contained in the configuration or options files, use the man pages for the DHCP client to obtain more detailed information.

The DHCP Server Daemon

The server portion of DHCP for a Red Hat Linux system is a background process (called a daemon) that is also started at boot time. The name of this daemon is dhcpd. Several important files used by the server daemon include the following:

- dhcpd.conf—This is the configuration file for the daemon that contains, among other things, the range of IP addresses the server can lease to clients.

- dhcpd.leases—The leases that have been allocated to clients are stored in this file. New leases are appended to the end of the file. Periodically, the server examines the file and removes addresses (or other information stored here) that is no longer valid, and rewrites the file so that it will be available if the server or the daemon is restarted. The old file is not deleted but instead is renamed dhcpd.leases~.

Although the actual command to start the DHCP server on the computer is contained in a startup file that is executed when the computer is booted, you can execute commands online to restart the server. This capability can be useful when you are debugging a problem with the server, for example, and want to run it as a foreground application instead of a background daemon.

The syntax for the DHCP daemon is

```
dhcpd [-p port] [-f] [-d] [-q] [-t | -T] [-cf configfile] [-lf leasefile] [-tf tracefile]
 [-play tracefile] [if0 [... ifN]]
```

where

- -p port—The standard port that the server listens to for DHCP requests is port 67. Use this to specify a different port number.

- -f—Causes the server to be run as a foreground process instead of a background (daemon) process. This is useful when using a debugger to diagnose problems with the server.

- -d—This option causes the server to output the DHCP log to the standard error descriptor instead of the syslog file.

- -q—Suppresses printing the copyright notice when the daemon is started.

- -t | -T—When the system is booted, the configuration file and lease file are read. The -t option will examine the configuration file to ensure that the syntax is correct, but won't connect to the network. Similarly, the -T option will examine the lease database. When using the -play option (listed in the following text), use an alternate lease file because the playback option might overwrite your lease file with test data.

- -cf configfile—Use this to specify a filename for the configuration file if you don't want to use the default filename.

- -lf leasefile—Use this to specify a filename for the lease file if you don't want to use the default filename.

- -tf tracefile—Use this to specify the filename that will log the startup of the server. Useful for debugging.

- -play tracefile—Use this to "playback" the tracefile.

- if0 [...ifN]—Specify the network interface on which the server will be used.

The DHCP Relay Agent

DHCP and BOOTP messages can be exchanged with clients and servers that are not on the same subnet. This is done by running the `dhcrelay` daemon on the subnet where the client resides. This daemon is responsible for intercepting the requests and forwarding them to a DHCP server and, likewise, returning the responses to the client.

The syntax for the agent can be found using the command `man dhcrelay` if you need to use this capability.

Network Name Resolution

30

SOME OF THE MAIN TOPICS IN THIS CHAPTER ARE

CHAPTER 30

Computers use hardware addresses when exchanging data on the local subnet. These addresses are burned into the network adapter and are often referred to as MAC (Media Access Control) addresses. MAC addresses produce a flat address space, so network protocols, such as IP, are typically used to create a hierarchical address space. However, for humans, both MAC and IP addresses (or IPX/SPX addresses, for that matter) are difficult to remember. Names are convenient for use by humans who have to operate computers. So, besides identifying a computer or network device using a protocol address, it's also important to be able to give a name to a computer, a network device, or a service, and then have that name resolved to the address so that data communications can take place on the network.

Understanding how name resolution works on your network will better prepare you to troubleshoot the problems users encounter when trying to locate resources.

This chapter deals with standard name resolution techniques ranging from the simple LMHOSTS files to the Windows Internet Name Service (WINS) for NetBIOS names and HOSTS files and the Domain Name System (DNS) service for IP names. For most networks, such as those that have Unix, Linux, or Windows computers, the name resolution methods described in this chapter will suffice. However, Windows 2000, Windows XP, or Windows Server 2003—when deployed using the Active Directory—adds a whole new dimension to name resolution. The Active Directory stores objects that can represent everything from a user account to a resource on the network, such as a computer or a printer. In a similar fashion, Novell Directory Service—NDS, now called the eDirectory—is a directory-based solution for locating resources on the network. If you employ Windows 2000 Servers in your network, you might find the next chapter, "Using the Active Directory," to be an important resource. If your network is NetWare-based, Chapter 33, "Overview of the Novell Bindery and Novell Directory Services," and Chapter 34, "Expanding and Enhancing NDS: NetWare's eDirectory," will provide more detailed coverage of these technologies.

Note

The Active Directory and the eDirectory can be used to quickly locate resources on the network. They take the concept of name resolution farther down the road, however, in that you can locate a resource by using its name as well as by specifying attributes of the resource you need to use. For example, if you don't know the name of a printer, directory servers enable you to specify search criteria to locate a resource. For a printer, for example, you can specify that it be a color printer, be located in a particular location, and even such things as whether it prints in duplex mode or has three-hole paper installed.

Another important factor to consider when using a directory service is that *it is not a replacement for the name resolution techniques described in this chapter*. This is easy to understand when you consider that that, in a Windows 2000/.NET environment, a client computer uses a DNS entry to locate a domain controller so that it can authenticate itself to the network before it can even begin to use the Active Directory.

For Unix/Linux systems, the upgrade path from the older HOSTS file was Sun's Network Information System (NIS), which was formerly called Yellow Pages, until trademark issues forced a name change. Therefore, you'll find both NIS commands as well as commands that start with the letters yp on some Unix systems. Today there is a growing movement to move authentication and other information to an LDAP-based directory server. A number of LDAP-enabled directory servers can be used with different operating system platforms, and a quick search on the Internet can reveal a lot of information. In addition, there's an open source version of an LDAP server that you can review at http://www.openldap.org. For a basic overview of LDAP, see Appendix D, "The Lightweight Directory Access Protocol."

When working in a multiprotocol environment, there are several ways in which you can create a single namespace using an LDAP-enabled directory to provide a single directory service for Windows,

Unix, Linux, and NetWare clients. You'll find a discussion of these topics and the utilities that can help you get there in Part XI, "Migration and Integration," later in this book.

Hardware Versus Protocol Addresses

When communicating on the same network segment, a computer can communicate directly by sending directed datagrams to another computer and specifying the unique MAC address that's burned into the network card when it's manufactured. In TCP/IP networks, the Address Resolution Protocol (ARP) is used in a local broadcast domain to determine the hardware address of another computer by sending out a broadcast packet that contains the computer's IP address. When a computer recognizes an ARP packet that has its IP address, it responds to the ARP request with another packet that tells the original computer what the destination computer's MAC address is. For more information about hardware addresses and ARP, see Chapter 25, "Overview of the TCP/IP Protocol Suite."

The TCP/IP protocol is pretty much the standard today for local area networks. NetBIOS has been adapted to run over IP, and beginning with NetWare 5, IP is now the preferred protocol used in NetWare LANs. To begin, however, let's look at the older NetBIOS namespace and NetBEUI protocol that were used on Microsoft's first offerings in the LAN environment.

NetBIOS

The NetBIOS and NetBEUI protocols are described in "NetBIOS and NetBEUI," which is on the upgradingandrepairingpcs.com Web site. Although the original specifications were sufficient for use on only very small LANs (fewer than 200 nodes), NetBIOS has been a mainstay in most Microsoft network products. Until Windows 2000, NetBIOS names were integral to the Windows operating systems' management functions. For example, domain names and host names are made up of NetBIOS names. The Server Message Block (SMB) protocol that's used for resource access and administrative duties in LAN Manager and the Windows operating systems' networking software modules are based on NetBIOS names.

Note

The Server Message Block protocol is now called the Common Internet File System (CIFS), which is discussed later in this chapter. To provide for interoperability with Windows networks, many vendors created SMB/CIFS products. Even the Linux and other communities have ventured into this territory with Samba. Samba is an SMB/CIFS client/server system that you can install on non-Windows clients and use to access typical Windows NetBIOS-based resources. You can read up on the latest version of Samba or download the software using the URL http://www.samba.org.

The *LMHOSTS* File

In the %systemroot%\SYSTEM32\DRIVERS\ETC directory on Windows NT 4.0, Windows 2000, and Windows Server 2003 computers is a file named LMHOSTS.SAM. For Windows 95 and Windows 98 clients, this file is found in the \WINDOWS directory. It's used to map NetBIOS names to IP addresses. The .SAM filename extension indicates that this is a *sample* file. If you're going to use the file, you have to copy it or rename it LMHOSTS *with no file extension*. Because it's always a good idea to keep the original copy in case things become confused along the line, making a copy is a good choice.

To rename the file from the command line, set your working directory to the directory in which the file resides and enter

```
ren lmhosts.sam lmhosts
```

To copy the file (and preserve the original sample file), enter

```
copy lmhosts.sam lmhosts
```

The Windows files are basically the same for all versions of Windows, except for a few of the comment lines. The following is the version you'll find in Windows Server 2003:

```
# Copyright (c) 1993-1999 Microsoft Corp.
#
# This is a sample LMHOSTS file used by the Microsoft TCP/IP for Windows.
#
# This file contains the mappings of IP addresses to computernames
# (NetBIOS) names.  Each entry should be kept on an individual line.
# The IP address should be placed in the first column followed by the
# corresponding computername. The address and the computername
# should be separated by at least one space or tab. The "#" character
# is generally used to denote the start of a comment (see the exceptions
# below).
#
# This file is compatible with Microsoft LAN Manager 2.x TCP/IP lmhosts
# files and offers the following extensions:
#
#      #PRE
#      #DOM:<domain>
#      #INCLUDE <filename>
#      #BEGIN_ALTERNATE
#      #END_ALTERNATE
#      \0xnn (non-printing character support)
#
# Following any entry in the file with the characters "#PRE" will cause
# the entry to be preloaded into the name cache. By default, entries are
# not preloaded, but are parsed only after dynamic name resolution fails.
#
# Following an entry with the "#DOM:<domain>" tag will associate the
# entry with the domain specified by <domain>. This affects how the
# browser and logon services behave in TCP/IP environments. To preload
# the host name associated with #DOM entry, it is necessary to also add a
# #PRE to the line. The <domain> is always preloaded although it will not
# be shown when the name cache is viewed.
#
# Specifying "#INCLUDE <filename>" will force the RFC NetBIOS (NBT)
# software to seek the specified <filename> and parse it as if it were
# local. <filename> is generally a UNC-based name, allowing a
# centralized lmhosts file to be maintained on a server.
# It is ALWAYS necessary to provide a mapping for the IP address of the
# server prior to the #INCLUDE. This mapping must use the #PRE directive.
# In addition the share "public" in the example below must be in the
# LanManServer list of "NullSessionShares" in order for client machines to
# be able to read the lmhosts file successfully. This key is under
# \machine\system\currentcontrolset\services\lanmanserver\parameters\nullsessionshares
# in the registry. Simply add "public" to the list found there.
#
# The #BEGIN_ and #END_ALTERNATE keywords allow multiple #INCLUDE
# statements to be grouped together. Any single successful include
# will cause the group to succeed.
#
# Finally, non-printing characters can be embedded in mappings by
# first surrounding the NetBIOS name in quotations, then using the
# \0xnn notation to specify a hex value for a non-printing character.
#
# The following example illustrates all of these extensions:
#
```

```
# 102.54.94.97     rhino          #PRE #DOM:networking  #net group's DC
# 102.54.94.102    "appname  \0x14"                     #special app server
# 102.54.94.123    popular        #PRE                  #source server
# 102.54.94.117    localsrv       #PRE                  #needed for the include
#
# #BEGIN_ALTERNATE
# #INCLUDE \\localsrv\public\lmhosts
# #INCLUDE \\rhino\public\lmhosts
# #END_ALTERNATE
#
# In the above example, the "appname" server contains a special
# character in its name, the "popular" and "localsrv" server names are
# preloaded, and the "rhino" server name is specified so it can be used
# to later #INCLUDE a centrally maintained lmhosts file if the "localsrv"
# system is unavailable.
#
# Note that the whole file is parsed including comments on each lookup,
# so keeping the number of comments to a minimum will improve performance.
# Therefore it is not advisable to simply add lmhosts file entries onto the
# end of this file.
```

As you can see from the sample file, you can place comments anywhere on a line by using the # character. Using comments aids in managing the file when there are multiple administrators. However, as the last bit of text explains, the entire file is parsed (read) each time it's consulted for a name lookup. For this reason, when you copy the file to create your LMHOSTS file, you should delete all the default introductory comments, populating the file with only hostnames and comments applicable to your needs. If the number of entries in this file becomes quite large and full of both name translations and comments, it has probably outgrown its usefulness and you need to look to another means of name resolution, such as WINS or DNS.

Note

WINS can perform name translation for NetBIOS names to IP addresses. The **LMHOSTS** file is considered to be a legacy holdover from earlier Microsoft LANs—for example, those using Windows 95/98 or Windows NT 4.0. The **LMHOSTS** file can be used to override entries stored on a WINS server, or can be used in a very small network that doesn't use a WINS server. This chapter describes this file for historical purposes, as well as to point out that if you're still using it, it's time to upgrade. The exception to this advice is a network based on those older operating systems where the software application still works and there is no upgrade path.

In addition to serving as the comment character, the # character can be used to specify several keywords that have specific functions when used in this file. The keywords are

- **#PRE**—Load this entry into the NetBIOS name cache.
- **#DOM**—This entry is a domain controller.
- **#INCLUDE**—Use the filename following this keyword to get name-to-address mappings.
- **#BEGIN_ALTERNATE** and **#END_ALTERNATE**—The #INCLUDE commands within this block are to be processed in order until one of them succeeds in performing the name translation.

For small networks that have several subnets separated by a router, using the #DOM keyword for an entry can enable a client to locate a domain controller on another subnet. Although it's preferable to have a backup domain controller on each subnet (for Windows NT 4.0 and earlier versions of Microsoft's operating systems), this workaround can be helpful for special conditions.

In Figure 30.1, you can see the logical steps that a b-node goes through when trying to resolve a name to an IP address. The NetBIOS name cache is consulted first, followed by broadcasting. Finally, if those two methods fail, the LMHOSTS file is checked.

▶▶ You can find more information about b-nodes and other node designations that are used with NetBIOS names by reading "NetBIOS and NetBEUI" on the **upgradingandrepairingpcs.com** Web site.

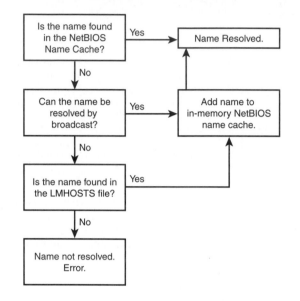

Figure 30.1   In Microsoft networks, a b-node consults the LMHOSTS file when other methods fail.

The in-memory NetBIOS name cache is always consulted first. This cache can hold up to 100 entries. When a name is successfully resolved by the broadcast method or by a lookup in the LMHOSTS file, it's added to the name cache and can be resolved there from that point onward.

You can ensure that an entry will be placed in the name cache when the workstation boots by using the #PRE keyword for that entry in the LMHOSTS file:

```
175.110.32.31      yoko.ono.com      #PRE
```

This can be useful for ensuring that servers that are accessed often by clients are resident in the memory cache, eliminating the need to perform a disk access to look up the entry in the LMHOSTS file.

Tip

You can force an update to the NetBIOS cache by using the command **nbtstat -R** to reload the cache from the LMHOSTS file. This is useful if you've just made edits to the file. Also note that if an identical name exists in both the HOSTS file and LMHOSTS file, the definition in the LMHOSTS file will be used.

Windows Internet Name Service

WINS is Microsoft's NetBIOS Name Server (NBNS) developed according to the details set forth in RFCs 1001 and 1002, and is based on a client/server architecture. Only Windows server operating systems can run the WINS service, and the server does not have to be a domain controller. In the traditional DNS server that originated on Unix systems, an administrator is responsible for manually editing files to maintain address-to-name mappings. WINS is a dynamic database. Name registrations are performed by unicast messages (direct contact) between the server and the WINS client. Because the WINS server does not have to be on the same network segment as the client, and because no broadcast messages clutter up network medium, WINS is a more efficient method of name resolution when compared to b-node functionality.

Note

If your network contains clients or applications that need a WINS server for name resolution, and they won't work with DNS, consider upgrading the clients or keeping a WINS server. More likely, consider replacing the client or NetBIOS applications.

The following are some of the important benefits of using WINS:

- **Ease of administration**—Updates to the database are dynamic. When a computer is moved to a different location and acquires a new address, it updates the WINS server when it boots. If DHCP is used on the network, moving the client computer requires nothing more than hooking it up to the network and booting the computer, provided the client has been configured to use Dynamic Host Configuration Protocol (DHCP) and WINS.

Tip

WINS was developed to provide name resolutions services for NetBIOS names. WINS is a dynamic database, so clients can obtain configuration information from a DHCP server and register this information in one or more WINS servers. Modern implementations of DNS servers also support dynamic updates. Therefore, this first benefit that WINS provides is no longer as important as it once was. In an all-TCP/IP network, you shouldn't have to use WINS unless you have older applications that require it.

- **Interaction with DNS**—Beginning with Windows NT 4.0, WINS has the capability to interact with Microsoft's DNS server, provided that you configure the client to do so. If properly configured, a non-Windows client can query the DNS server, which can then query the WINS server to obtain the address of a NetBIOS client if the DNS server does not find a name translation in its own database.
- **Static mappings**—If WINS is not set up to interact with the DNS server, you can place static mappings in the database for clients that do not have WINS client functionality. In a network composed of different operating systems, static mappings can help to integrate them into the Windows environment, making it easy for WINS clients to locate these computers.
- **Replication**—Although not specified in the RFCs, WINS servers are typically set up with replication partners. This means that over a given convergence time, all WINS servers in the network are updated with changes made on any one of them.
- **Fault tolerance**—Clients are typically configured to locate a primary WINS server and a secondary WINS server. Because the database is replicated at intervals, the secondary WINS server can continue to service all clients until the primary server is brought back online.

When to Use WINS

WINS was a good solution for resolving names before Windows 2000 came along. Beginning with Windows 2000, you don't necessarily need to install a WINS server on the network. This is because Windows 2000 clients can use DNS and the Active Directory to find out about other hosts on the network. However, if you have a network that's composed of multiple operating systems, such as Windows 98 or Windows NT computers, WINS can still be useful because all versions of Windows prior to Windows 2000 require NetBIOS name support. Some applications, such as SMS, might require NetBIOS.

Of course, NetBIOS name support doesn't mean that you need to install WINS. It depends on the topology of your network. On a small office LAN with only one physical cable segment (or a hub/switch) and just a few computers, NetBIOS broadcasts are probably sufficient for name resolution for these older clients and will not use up a large amount of bandwidth. However, if you operate a larger network that contains many segments and a large number of computers, or if you're just starting to introduce Windows 2000 or Windows Server 2003 servers into a network that already has older legacy clients or applications that use NetBIOS names, WINS is a good interim solution until you can plan an upgrade to remove these older clients and applications.

Configuring WINS Clients

To use WINS, a client must first be configured with the address of a WINS server. This can be done in one of two ways. First, you could configure the client manually, using a network properties page for the particular Windows operating system. Second, you could configure a DHCP server to provide the name of one or more WINS servers to a client if you use DHCP in your network. For more information about configuring WINS options using a DHCP server, see Chapter 29, "BOOTP and the Dynamic Host Configuration Protocol (DHCP)."

If your network consists of nothing but Windows 2000, Windows XP, or Windows Server 2003 computers, you won't need the WINS service. The Active Directory combined with DHCP and a dynamic DNS server provide all the name registration and resolution functionality you need. However, Windows 2000 clients can still be configured to use WINS. This might be necessary if you have a mixed network using clients from Windows 98, Windows NT, or even Unix or Linux clients that have Samba installed.

To configure a Windows 2000 client to use WINS, follow these steps:

1. Click Start, Settings, Network and Dialup Connections.

2. Right-click on the network connection you want to set up to use WINS and select Properties from the menu that appears.

3. Click once on Internet Protocol (TCP/IP) and click the Properties button.

4. Click the Advanced button at the bottom of the Properties page. The Advanced TCP/IP Settings Properties page is displayed. Click the WINS tab (shown in Figure 30.2).

5. Click the Add button. A dialog box pops up that you can use to enter the IP address of a WINS server. Enter the address and click OK. Continue using the Add button to add more WINS servers, if they're present on your network for backup purposes.

You'll also notice in Figure 30.2 that you can use the Edit and Remove buttons. To remove a WINS server, simply highlight the server you want to remove by clicking on it once and then click the Remove button. The Edit button can be used to change an entry. Highlight the entry and click the Edit button, and the same dialog box used for adding WINS servers pops up. The WINS server you've selected to edit appears in the fields on this dialog box. You can change any part of the IP address and click OK.

One final note about Windows 2000 clients that network administrators will appreciate: You don't have to perform a reboot of the computer after you add, edit, or remove WINS servers.

Client Name Registration and Release

For a client computer to register a name with the WINS server, it sends a name registration request to the server. This is a directed message, not a broadcast message—that's why you have to configure the client to know the address of one or more WINS servers. If the name is not found in the database, the WINS server returns a positive name registration response to the client. The record is given a timestamp, and a renewal interval is also recorded in the record. The record is given an owner ID as well, which identifies the WINS server that originated (or in other words, owns) the record. When the record is replicated to other WINS servers, they use this ID to identify the original server.

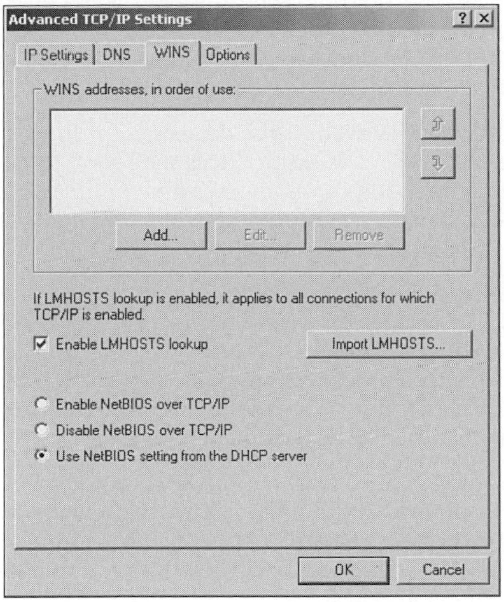

Figure 30.2   Use the Advanced TCP/IP Settings Properties page to configure Windows 2000 clients to use WINS.

After half of the renewal period has elapsed, a Windows client attempts to reregister its ownership of the name by sending the server a name refresh request. The re-registration process functions the same as the initial registration. By setting a time-to-live (TTL) value on each record, the WINS database can eventually be purged of records that are no longer valid.

Note

The term *time to live* is used by many protocols and services. Don't confuse the TTL value described here with the TTL field used in the IP packet header, for example. For IP packets, the TTL field is used to prevent a packet from getting stuck in a routing loop. Each time the IP packet passes through a router, this field is decremented by at least one and the packet is dropped when the TTL value reaches zero. WINS uses a TTL value to determine when to begin the process of getting rid of records that appear to no longer be in use because the client has not renewed the record registration. Later in this chapter, you'll see that DNS servers also use a TTL value.

The state of the name record changes over time depending on the status of the client. At any time, a record is either in the *active state* or it can be marked as *released* or *extinct*. At each state, a TTL is marked on the record and is used to determine when to change it to the next state.

A name can be released in two ways:

- The name can be released explicitly if the client computer is shut down in a proper manner. The client sends a message to the server telling it to release the name.
- The name is set to a released state by the WINS server if it does not receive a name refresh request before the renewal period expires.

When the name is released, the WINS server does not yet delete the record from the database. Instead, it marks the record as released, adds another timestamp (showing the time of the release), and then adds an extinction interval to the record. If the WINS server that receives the release is the original owner of the record, it does not propagate a record update to other WINS servers, which reduces replication traffic. If another WINS server that still has a record showing the name is active receives a request from another computer to use the name, it tries to contact the original owner and find out whether the name can be reused.

At certain intervals, the WINS server scavenges the database. If it finds a record whose extinction interval has expired, it marks the record as extinct. This state is often referred to as the *tombstone state*. When a record is marked as extinct, it receives another timestamp and an extinction time-out value. If a record has not been re-registered by the end of this final time-out interval, the scavenge process will finally remove it from the database.

If a WINS server receives an explicit release request from a client and the server is not the original owner of the record, it makes itself the new owner of the record. Instead of placing the record into the released state, it proceeds directly to the extinct state. Unlike records in the released state, records in the extinct state do get replicated at replication time. The reason that a WINS server immediately marks a record it does not own as extinct is so that the record will be replicated quickly and will get back to the WINS server that originated the record.

If a name is already in the database, the client can still be awarded ownership of it, depending on certain factors. If the name is in the released or extinct state, the server knows that it can reassign the name because the previous owner has released it. If the name is in the active state, the WINS server tries to contact the original owner. If the original owner does not respond, the WINS server reassigns the name to the node that's requesting it.

Note

In general, static entries made to the WINS database aren't subject to the scavenge process and remain in the database. However, the administrator can configure the server to operate differently by setting the Migrate On switch in the WINS Administrator Utility. If this switch is set, the static entry can be overwritten by a new name request if the original owner does not answer a challenge from the WINS server. The Migrate On switch is meant to be used when migrating a network from static entries to dynamic entries. This might be the case when you're upgrading your network with new client software, for example, and relieves the administrator of the burden of having to remove the static entries manually.

When a client workstation is moved to a new subnet and receives a new address, it sends a name registration request to the WINS server. The WINS server queries the old IP address, determines that the name is no longer in use, and then grants the name to the new IP address.

Tip

Not sure whether your workstation is using NetBIOS names? Use the **NBTSTAT** command at the Command Prompt. **NBTSTAT** -n will list the NetBIOS names in the workstation's local cache.

Static Name Entries

You can enter static entries into the WINS database using the WINS Manager utility. This is usually done for non-WINS clients, such as Unix workstations. Although you can configure the Windows client to use DNS to resolve these names, a static entry into the WINS database does two things. It makes name resolution faster because the client only has to query the WINS server. It also helps to prevent errors by preventing a WINS client from registering a name that's already in use by a non-WINS enabled client.

Name Queries

In Figure 30.3, you can see the process that a client computer goes through when trying to resolve a name using WINS servers. The steps it takes depend on whether it has one or two WINS servers in its configuration (primary and secondary WINS servers) and whether the node is configured as a p-node or an h-node.

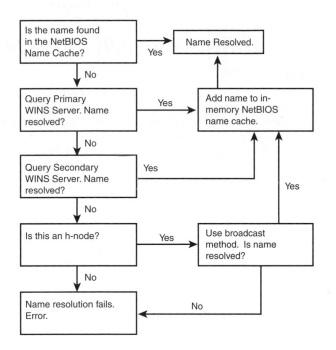

Figure 30.3   Name resolution using WINS servers for p-node and h-node clients.

When a WINS server receives a name query request from a node, it returns a positive name response with one or more IP addresses associated with the NetBIOS name to the requestor via a UDP packet. If the WINS server does not have a record for the name, it sends a negative name response. If the client is configured with the address of a secondary WINS server, it attempts to resolve the name by contacting that server.

If the secondary server also returns a negative name response, the client either fails to resolve the name (if it's a p-node) or it uses a broadcast message as a last resort (if it's an h-node). If the computer that the client wants to contact is on the local network segment, the broadcast can succeed. If not, the client is unable to resolve the name to an IP address and will be unable to contact the other computer.

What Is the WINS Proxy Agent?

To provide access to the WINS server information for b-nodes that cannot query the WINS server directly, the concept of a proxy server was created. A *proxy server* listens to broadcast messages issued by a b-node on the local network segment and if the name being sought is in the proxy server's name cache, it returns a response to the b-node. If the name isn't in the proxy server's cache, it queries the WINS servers it knows.

When a proxy server is also configured to monitor name registration broadcast messages, it listens for these messages and sends a negative response to a b-node that attempts to register a name that exists in the WINS database. However, the proxy server does not make name registrations into the WINS database for a b-node. It merely responds to name registrations that conflict with the database.

To resolve names for b-nodes, the proxy server examines the subnet address of the b-node that's performing the name query. This is done so that the proxy server does not respond to name queries for nodes that are on the local subnet and can respond for themselves.

Installing and Configuring WINS on Windows 2000/2003 Servers

If you're running a network that has Windows NT 4.0 and earlier versions of Microsoft operating systems, you can continue to use the WINS servers you've already installed. However, you can also set up Windows 2000 Server or Windows Server 2003 to offer the WINS service to your network. Installing the WINS service is a simple matter. You can choose to install the WINS service during the initial installation of Windows 2000 Server, as you would with other networking services. You can also install the WINS service after you've completed the operating system installation by using the following steps:

1. Click Start, Programs (All Programs for Server 2003), Control Panel.
2. From the Control Panel, double-click the Add/Remove Programs icon.
3. When the Add Remove Programs window pops up, click Add/Remove Windows Components that you'll see on the left part of the window. The Add Remove Programs window now displays a Components button in the upper-right side of the window. Click the Components button, and the Windows Components Wizard dialog box pops up.
4. Scroll down until you find Networking Services and highlight it by clicking on it once. Then click the Details button (see Figure 30.4).

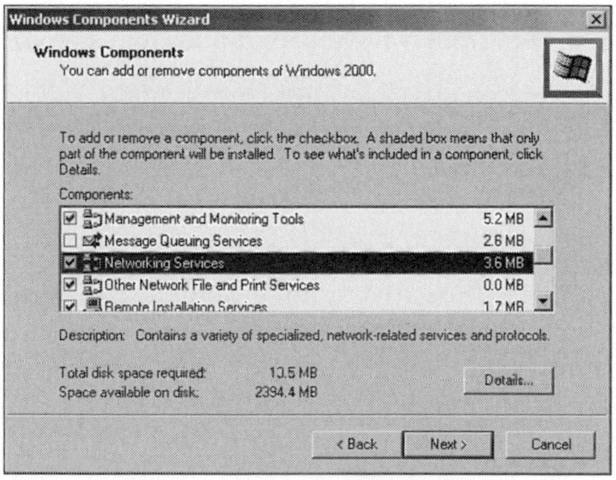

Figure 30.4 Highlight Networking Services and click Details.

5. When the Networking Services dialog box appears, scroll down until you find Windows Internet Name Services (WINS). Click the check box next to the component and click the OK button, as shown in Figure 30.5.

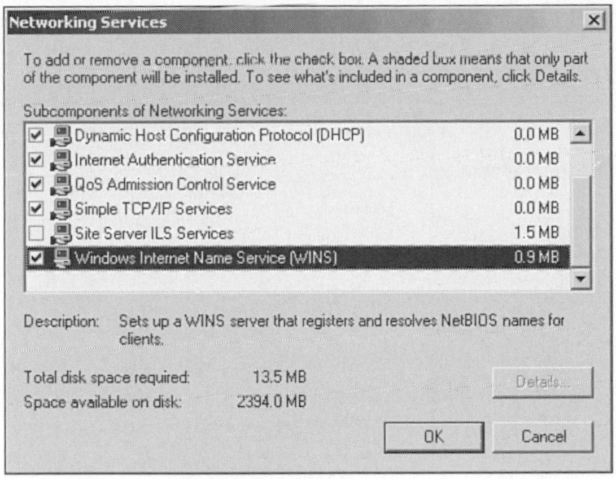

Figure 30.5 Select the WINS service from this dialog box and click OK to install the service.

6. When prompted, insert the Windows 2000 or Server 2003 source CD into your CD-ROM drive and then wait a minute or so while files are copied to your hard drive. When the Windows Components Wizard window reappears, click Next.

7. Another window, titled Completing the Windows Components Wizard appears. Click the Finish button.

8. When the Add Remove Programs window reappears, click OK.

After you've installed the service, you won't have to reboot the computer. Instead, you can start managing the WINS service immediately.

Managing the Windows 2000 WINS Server

The Microsoft Management Console (MMC)—discussed throughout this book because it's Microsoft's newest innovation in management interfaces introduced with Windows 2000—is used to manage the WINS server, and you'll find a new utility in the Administrative Tools folder. Simply click Start, Programs/Administrative Tools and then select WINS from the available tools.

When the MMC console appears, you'll see your server name and IP address listed in the tree in the left pane of the console. Click the server name and it will expand to show you two additional folders: Active Registrations and Replication Partners (see Figure 30.6).

To see a list of computers and group names in the WINS database, simply click the Active Registrations folder. Similarly, to see any other servers you've configured to be a replication partner, just click the Replication Partners folder.

Of course, you'll first have to set up clients and reboot them before you'll see any computers registered in the database. And you'll have to set up replication partners before anything will show up in that folder.

Adding Servers and Replication Partners

Most of the management capabilities for WINS servers can be accomplished through either the Action menu or by using properties pages. For example, to start or stop the WINS service, click the server once to highlight it and from the Action menu select Start or Stop. You can also use the Pause and Restart functions found there. These options work just as they did in the Windows NT 4.0 WINS server.

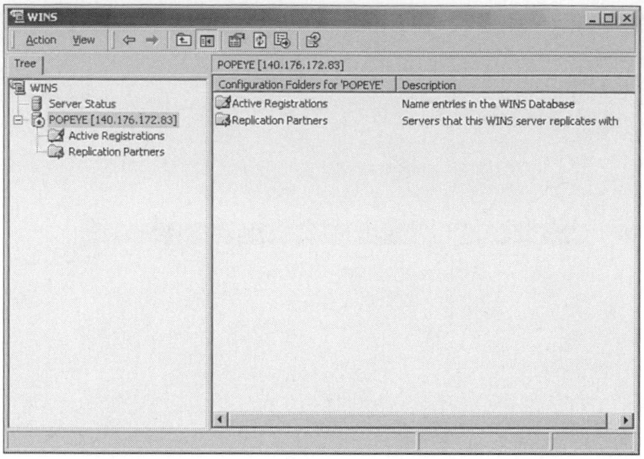

Figure 30.6   WINS is managed on a Windows 2000 server using the MMC console.

The MMC console enables you to manage multiple WINS servers from a single console. Simply click the WINS entry in the left pane (refer to Figure 30.6) and then, from the Action menu, select Add Server. The Add Server dialog box pops up and prompts you to enter the NetBIOS name or IP address of the server you want to add to the management console. Once it's added, you can select which server you want to manage by simply clicking it once in the left pane tree of servers.

To add a replication partner, open the Replication Partners folder found under the server you want to set up for replication and, from the Action menu, select New Replication partner. A dialog box again prompts you for the name or IP address of the server with which you want to enable replication.

Using the Action Menu to Configure MMC Properties

The first entry in the tree structure found in the left pane of the MMC console is WINS. Click WINS and, from the Action menu, select Properties. Or you can right-click WINS and select Properties from the menu that pops up. In Figure 30.7, you can see the general properties page for the MMC WINS console.

From this properties page, you can select to have WINS servers in the console tree be displayed using either their NetBIOS name or the IP address of the server. You can also select to show a DNS-style name for the server. Finally, you can configure the server to validate its cache of WINS servers when the server starts up to ensure that they're still online and that the list is accurate. Because this involves sending a message to each server, this can take some time if you manage a lot of servers or if they're connected by slow links.

Using the Action Menu to Manage Individual WINS Servers

You can perform most of the basic management tasks associated with WINS servers by selecting the WINS server from those you've added to the tree structure in the left pane and then using options from the Action menu. Alternatively, you can right-click on a server and select the same options from the menu that pops up. The things you can manage from the Action menu for any server are

- **Display Server Statistics**—This option enables you to see when the server was started, statistics about replication, name registrations, releases, and so on.
- **Scavenge Database**—This starts the scavenging process, as described earlier in this chapter. You can determine when this process has finished by looking in the event log.

■ **Verify Database Consistency**—This function pulls records from other WINS servers by examining records in the local database to determine the owner of each record. If the record still exists on the owner-WINS server and is identical to the local record, the timestamp for the record is updated. Otherwise, if the record pulled from the owner-server has a higher version ID than that of the local record, the local record is marked for deletion and the new record is added to the local database.

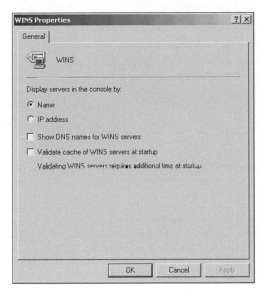

Figure 30.7   Use the WINS server's properties page to configure general properties for the server.

Caution

Using the Verify Database Consistency option should be done during nonpeak hours on your network because it can produce a large amount of network traffic, depending on the number of records in the database and the number of WINS servers on the network. Don't do this during rush hour at work! Note that you can schedule this operation for another time by using the properties page for the server.

■ **Verify Version ID Consistency**—This is similar to the previous function, but the server checks to see that, for the records it owns, the local record has the highest version ID among other WINS servers on the network. This operation can take some time to complete.

■ **Start Push Replication**—Use this to start an immediate replication, pushing records to a replication partner. This can be useful if you've made changes to the database (such as adding static records) and you don't want to wait for the next scheduled replication interval. A dialog box prompts you for the server to which you want to push records.

■ **Start Pull Replication**—Similar to the previous menu item, but you use this to force another server to immediately begin the replication process by sending records to your server.

■ **Back Up Database**—Use this to back up the database. A dialog box prompts you to enter the location that you want to use to store the database file backup. When the process is finished, another dialog box pops up to inform you.

- **Restore Database**—Use this to restore a WINS database that you have previously backed up. Again, you'll be prompted to enter the location of the backup files and will be informed when the process has finished.

- **All Tasks**—Start, stop, pause, resume, or restart the WINS server.

- **Delete**—Use this to delete a WINS server from the MMC console list. Note that this does not delete any data on that WINS server, but merely removes it from the list of servers you manage using MMC on the local computer.

- **Refresh**—Use this to refresh data displayed on the MMC console.

- **Export List**—This menu item enables you to export a list of records stored in the WINS database. You're prompted for the location in which the file will be created. You can create ASCII text files or Unicode files, and can select that the file be either tab or comma delimited. This function is useful for exporting the WINS database records for use in another application, such as a spreadsheet.

- **Properties**—This displays the properties sheet for the selected server.

- **Help**—Use this when all else fails!

The properties page for a server (which can be displayed using the Action menu as just described) can be used to further configure the server. The properties page has four tabs:

- **General**—Here you can select the time interval used to automatically refresh the statistics shown on the MMC Console for the WINS server. You can also specify a location to store the database during a backup, and use a check box to enable backing up the database automatically when the server is shut down.

- **Intervals**—This tab allows you to set the time intervals used for record renewals, deletions, and verification.

- **Database Verification**—Use this tab to set a time for scheduling database verification. You can specify that it be done every so many hours or you can set a specific time for verification to begin. This function performs the database consistency check described earlier. If you have a large database, a field on this tab enables you to enter the maximum number of records to be verified during each interval.

- **Advanced**—This tab (shown in Figure 30.8) enables you to perform many functions.

The Advanced tab is singled out here for special mention because it contains some important configuration items. For example, you can specify the path to use for the database files. You can decide to enable logging detailed events to the event log for troubleshooting purposes. This is not a feature you should leave enabled unless you're having problems with WINS.

The Enable Burst Handling check box enables you to customize (low, medium, high, or specify a number) the number of client registrations and renewals that the server can handle at a single time. This can be useful if you have a server that you want to use mainly as a backup for your primary WINS server. You can set its burst mode to low and then change this property to high on the server you want to handle the most requests.

You can enter a starting version ID in a field at the bottom of this dialog box. Finally, you can use a check box to enable the use of computer names that are compatible with LAN Manager if you have older Microsoft clients on your network.

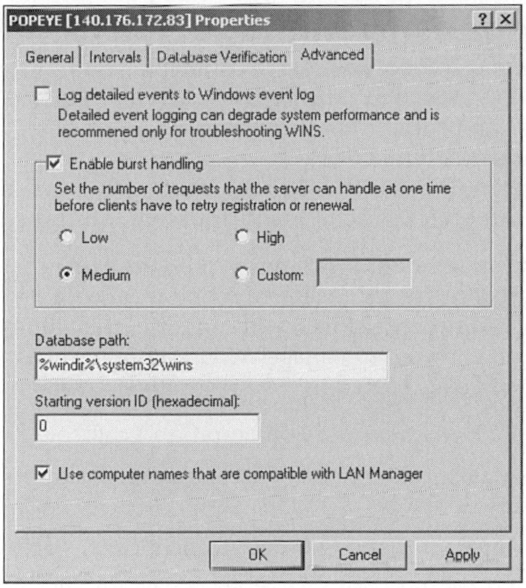

Figure 30.8 The Advanced tab of the server's properties page enables you to configure important server properties, such as the location of the database.

Managing the Windows Server 2003 WINS Service

Open the WINS MMC management console by selecting it from the Administrative Tools folder (Start, Administrative Tools, WINS). In Figure 30.9, you can see that the MMC console looks the same as that used for Windows 2000. You can use this MMC snap-in to manage WINS just as you did in Windows 2000.

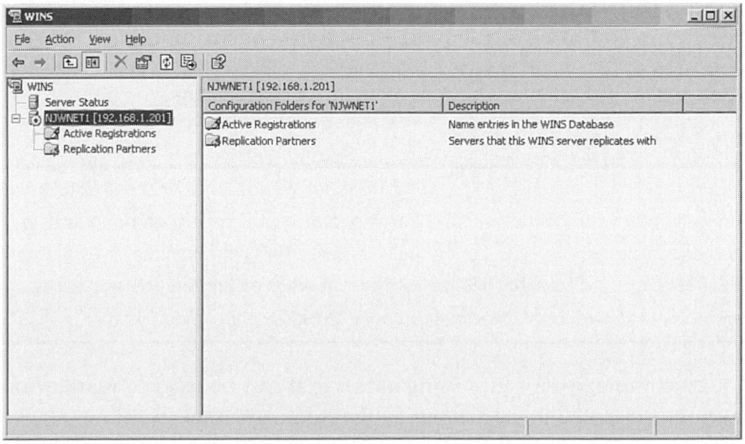

Figure 30.9 The WINS MMC Console application looks the same in Windows Server 2003 as in Windows 2000.

Using the MMC interface to manage WINS servers on Windows Server 2003 is, for all practical matters, the same as discussed in the previous section about Windows 2000. However, if you're still managing WINS in a network running Windows Server 2003, it might be time to consider an upgrade to the client systems or applications that still rely on the WINS infrastructure.

Using *netsh* Commands to Manage WINS

Both Windows 2000 Server and Windows Server 2003 enable you to use the `netsh` command (Netshell) set to manage WINS as well as other network services, such as DHCP and other network configuration utilities. This can be useful for those who are accustomed to using a command-line interface (such as the Command Prompt), or when you want to include commands in a batch file or other scripting file to manage WINS servers. The `netsh` commands can be used to manage a wide variety of other utilities. They can even be useful when troubleshooting a server via a Telnet link.

The `netsh` command is not limited to use with just WINS. Instead, `netsh` can serve to manage many other network services. Each different management scope is called a *context*. For example, after you enter the `netsh>` command prompt interpreter, you can enter the command WINS to set the Netshell command environment to enable you to manage WINS components. A selection of other contexts (which are discussed in much greater detail in their respective chapters) are

- **DHCP**—To manage the Dynamic Host Configuration Protocol
- **DIAG**—To execute diagnostic commands that are useful for troubleshooting operating system or application problems
- **IP**—An interface into managing the Internet Protocol configuration
- **RAS**—To manage any Remote Access Servers on your network

In this section, you learn about some simple tasks you can perform using `netsh` for WINS. However, it's important to understand that the command-line interface, which greatly expands on the simple DOS and newer commands available in the Command Prompt, means that many of you can continue to write script files to control logins, network functions, and so forth.

Tip

netsh commands can also be useful when you're administering a server across a wide area network link. In many instances, **netsh** commands can be accomplished more quickly than when using the GUI MMC interface.

The following list shows you some of the more important `netsh` commands for Windows Server 2003 that relate to WINS. To enter an interactive command session using commands available using the WINS context, use `netsh` and then at the `netsh>` prompt, enter **wins**.

Note

The syntax listed here for **netsh** is almost identical to that used for Windows 2000. You can check to be sure by entering the command **netsh** **/?** at the Windows 2000 Command Prompt. For help on an individual command, use **netsh** **<command>** **/?** instead. This second syntax can be useful in determining the commands available for a certain context, for example. From the help topics displayed, you can further drill down to find out more specifics of this well-implemented addition to the standard command-line utilities offered in early Windows operating systems.

You can create quite complex script files using `netsh` that can be used to manage many different aspects of a computer. Here you'll learn about some of the commands used with WINS. For example, the two following commands select a WINS server that will be the target of the `netsh` commands:

- **server**—This shows the name of the current WINS server as well as your access (read/write) for the server.
- **server \\<servername>**—This syntax enables you to specify the remote WINS server that subsequent commands will be executed on. Use this to change the context to another WINS server other than the local host. You can use either a hostname or an IP address for *servername*.

After you enter `server` or a remote server name, the prompt will change to `netsh <wins server>` prompt (to reflect the server you're now managing). From this prompt you can enter commands specific to this context, which are

- **Add**—Use to add a filter, add a name to the WINS database, add a replication partner, add a pgserver (Persona Grata servers), add a pngserver (Persona Non Grata server), or add another server to the WINS console utility. Persona Non Grata servers are those to block from sending records, and Persona Grata servers are ones to accept records from.

- **Check**—Check the WINS database for consistency, check a list of name records with a set of WINS servers, and check the version ID numbers for record owners in the database.

- **Delete**—Delete a name from the WINS database, delete records for particular owner from the database, delete replication partners, delete pgservers and pngservers, delete records from the database or mark them as in the tombstone state, or delete a WINS server from the MMC console interface.

- **Init**—This command has many uses, from initiating a backup of the WINS database to starting other functions, such as scavaging, searching, and pulling and pushing records.

- **Reset**—Reset the statistics counter for the local WINS server.

- **Set**—Use this command to set many options for WINS, from the default log parameters to a backup path for the database.

- **Show**—Similar to `Set`, this command will display a great deal of information about the current WINS server.

The complete syntax of the commands available is too vast to cover in a single chapter. The topic of the `netsh` command syntax could very well be a good reference book on its own because it can be used in other contexts to control other utilities, such as DHCP, and to perform diagnostics on the system.

TCP/IP Names

The address space for IP addresses is a hierarchical one that allows computers to be grouped into networks and subnetworks. The flat address spaces created by MAC addresses don't allow for any kind of grouping because they only provide an address for the host physical adapter and do not provide any sort of organization that can be used outside a LAN. In a small LAN, it doesn't matter that MAC addresses are not ordered. Each node can recognize a packet that's destined for it by examining the MAC address for every packet that passes on the LAN. This concept would not work on a larger network because every packet would have to be forwarded to every node for examination. Imagine having every packet on the Internet sent to every node! It's also possible to create a hierarchical namespace for nodes on a TCP/IP network by concatenating the hostname with a domain name. For example, the host computer named zira in the domain named nirvana.com is zira.nirvana.com as a fully qualified name.

Names are more convenient for humans than the numerical address format implemented in the TCP/IP suite. Just as the numerical address space is a hierarchical one, so is the namespace. However, it's important to understand that the two do not have to be directly related on a one-to-one basis. For example, suppose that a computer named printserver.ono.com has an address of 193.220.113.10. This is a class C IP address, so the network portion of the address is 193.220.113. You might be inclined to think, then, that a computer with a name of fileserver.ono.com is also located in the same network and has an address that begins with 193.220.113. However, there is no direct relation between the two.

Not that there can't be. It might be very convenient to set up a small network with a few subnets and create host computer names that all match up to a particular network address or subnet. In practical terms, however, this is hard to maintain as the network grows and changes.

Instead, use the TCP/IP namespace to create a logical arrangement of computers that matches some kind of business layout or other type of function. It makes sense to use names such as the following:

```
susan.accounting.zira.com
```

```
heather.accounting.zira.com
```

```
holly.shipping.zira.com
```

```
penny.research.zira.com
```

```
foster.research.zira.com
```

It's clear from these names that the company or organization is called Zira and that there are computers in the accounting, shipping, and research departments. In this case, however, it might be that Susan works out of the company's office located in the heart of downtown, whereas Heather works in a suburban office. Their TCP/IP hostnames reflect the business organizational unit in which they work. However, their IP addresses can be on completely different subnets or networks, depending on the physical location or other factors.

The rules for creating a hostname are not as carefree as those used for NetBIOS names. You cannot use spaces in a TCP/IP name, for example. The following rules must be followed when creating a hostname:

- You can use alphabetical characters (a–z) or numeric characters (0–9), and the first character of the name *must* be a letter or a digit.

- You can use the minus sign (dash), but this cannot be the last character in the name.

- Periods are allowed, but are used to separate hostnames from domain or subdomain portions of the name. This is covered in RFC 921, "Domain Name System Implementation Schedule." Because the period is used to separate components, it cannot be the last character in the name either.

- Names are not case sensitive. An uppercase A is the same as a lowercase a.

- The host portion of the name should not be longer than 24 characters. In practice, you can exceed this limit most of the time, but doing so is not a good idea if you're connected to the Internet where there are other computers and devices that do stick to the strict limit.

Note

These restrictions apply to names you enter in the HOSTS file. When using a DNS server, the restrictions are a little different, as is explained in the following sections.

Although you can use names in the TCP/IP networking environment to conveniently organize your host computers, there must again be a mechanism for resolving these names to the actual IP addresses that are associated with the computer. TCP/IP provides the HOSTS file, which was originally a central file maintained by a central authority and periodically distributed to nodes throughout the Internet. You can probably guess that this method—as with the LMHOSTS file used on NetBIOS networks—has been outgrown by the rapid growth of the Internet, and is now used only on small networks or for special cases.

The Domain Name System is now the primary means for resolving IP addresses to hostnames on the Internet. In some Unix shops, the Network Information System (NIS) is used. NIS was originally called Yellow Pages, but had to change its name due to a trademark infringement.

The *HOSTS* File

On Unix systems, the HOSTS file is usually found in the /etc or /etc/inet directory. Like the LMHOSTS file, it has no filename extension. It is a text file that contains IP addresses followed by the hostname or names associated with the address. The # character is used to denote comments. Each line should have only one IP address, followed by a space or tab character, and then the hostname. You can place more than one name on the line (each separated by a space or tab character) to provide multiple names for a host (sometimes called *nicknames*). For example:

```
#This is the HOSTS file
#
127.0.0.1       localhost
10.1.22.13      pkd.ubik.com            # Server at Atlanta office.
10.1.22.46      psi.ubik.ocm            # Joe's workstation.
192.208.46.158 www.compaq.com           # Compaq's homepage.
```

Note that the first entry in the file is the loopback address for the local adapter. You will find this in many HOSTS files, but it isn't a requirement.

The HOSTS file has the same limitations as the LMHOSTS file. Mainly, it doesn't scale very well. Each time a change is made in the network, you need to update the file on each machine to reflect the change. This makes it easy to get different copies out-of-sync on a larger network.

In a very small TCP/IP network that doesn't change very often and doesn't use NetBIOS names, using the HOSTS file might be preferable to using DNS. You can get a decent DNS server from everyone from Microsoft to Novell to any Unix/Linux server. But if it means that you have to purchase a server operating system to provide for a small number of clients, you might be better off using a simple LAN without a DNS server. For a growing network or one in a fast-paced business environment where employees are always on the move, DNS or NIS should be used.

However, even in a SOHO office, there should be little need to keep using this legacy HOSTS file. If you're connected to the Internet, network names can be translated using a DNS server provided by your Internet provider. Names on the local LAN can be resolved using NetBEUI.

Domain Name System

When TCP/IP became the standard protocol used on ARPAnet (which evolved into the Internet), the HOSTS file was maintained by SRI-NIC at a central location. Changes were periodically made to the file as administrators emailed requests to SRI-NIC. The updated HOSTS file then had to be distributed to every node, making the maintenance of this file a major administrative chore. For a few thousand computers in the beginning, this was a difficult enough task. But just imagine trying to coordinate the distribution of text files containing IP to name translation files in today's Internet environment, where there are many millions of users all over the world.

In 1984, the Domain Name System (DNS) was adopted for the Internet. DNS is not only a hierarchical database, but also a distributed one. WINS servers use replication with partners to keep a full copy of the WINS database on each WINS server. On the Internet, each registered domain (for example, zira.com or microsoft.com) has a DNS server, which is responsible for managing the database of hostnames within that domain or subdomains. This distribution of the database makes it easier to scale to a larger size than with the WINS model. Administration can also be delegated so that no central management of the entire database is needed.

Tip

One of the first implementations of DNS was developed at Berkeley for its BSD Unix (version 4.3) operating system. Therefore, you'll often see the term BIND (Berkeley Internet Name Domain) used in place of DNS on many Unix and Linux systems.

The topmost entry in the DNS hierarchy is called the root domain and is represented by the period character (.). Underneath this root domain are the top-level directories that fall into two groups: geographical and organizational. Geographical domains are used to specify specific countries. For example, .au for Australia and .uk for the United Kingdom. Under each of the geographical domains, you might find organizational domains. Organizational domains include

- **com**—Used for commercial organizations
- **edu**—Used for educational institutions
- **gov**—Used for U.S. government entities
- **mil**—Used for U.S. military organizations
- **int**—Used for international organizations
- **net**—Used for network organizations such as Internet service providers
- **org**—Used for nonprofit organizations
- **arpa**—Used for inverse address lookups

The structure of the Domain Name System is similar to an inverted tree. In Figure 30.10, you can see that at the top is the root domain with the com through arpa domains underneath. Under the com domain are individual business organizations that each have their own domain. Under any particular domain there can be subdomains.

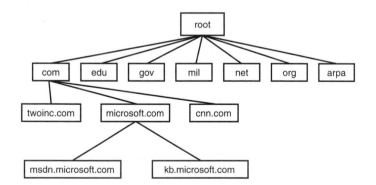

Figure 30.10   The Domain Name System is a distributed hierarchical structure.

At each level, a fully qualified domain name (FQDN) is created by concatenating the local name with the names of the entities above it in the hierarchy. Thus, msdn.microsoft.com is used to name the msdn subdomain in the microsoft.com domain that falls under the com domain. By using the FQDN, it's possible for a hostname to be used multiple times, as long as it produces a unique FQDN. For example, fileserver.twoinc.com names a host called fileserver. This host cannot become confused with another host of the same name that resides in a different domain such as fileserver.acme.com.

There are a number of restrictions to the names you can use in the DNS system:

- The maximum length of a domain name or a host label is 63 characters.
- The maximum length for the FQDN is 255 characters.
- There can be up to 127 subdomains.
- Text is not case sensitive.

New Top-Level Domains

Since ICANN took over responsibilities for handling names and numbers used on the Internet, several new top-level domains have been created. Over the next few years, you can expect to see additional top-level domains added to this list. The most recent additions were made in 2000. These are

- **aero**—Intended for use by the air-transport industry
- **biz**—For use by businesses
- **coop**—For use by cooperatives
- **info**—Anything you want
- **museum**—Guess?
- **name**—For registration of individual names
- **pro**—Accountants, lawyers, and physicians

Note

In 2003, NeuStar, Inc. was asked by the U.S. congress to set up a new domain name called `.kids.us`. All content on any Web site registered for a domain name in `.kids.us` will be screened to ensure that it contains no adult or other information that might be harmful to kids.

Of these domains, some are unsponsored (biz, info, name, and pro), which means that they will be governed by the global Internet community through ICANN, whereas the others (aero, coop, and museum) are sponsored domains. That means they'll be governed by specific entities. For example, the coop domain is sponsored by the National Cooperative Business Association.

Note

You might have noticed recently that there are other domains that appear to be new, such as the popular **tv** domain. However, note that the `.tv` domain is *not* a new top-level domain. Instead, **tv** is the country code domain for the country of Tuvalu (a small island in the Pacific Ocean), which has allowed an enterprising company to use its country-style domain name for a fee. The company can market the **tv** domain to register domains that are associated with, of course, television. However, remember that this is just a country code domain. It isn't one of the *new* top-level domains that ICANN has authorized. There is nothing that requires a particular country to use its own domain designation for just its use. Whoever thought up this method for establishing what appears to be a new domain should be named Capitalist of the Year!

To stay up-to-date on what the current top-level domains are, visit the ICANN Web site at www.icann.org. You'll also find a lot of other valuable information at this site if you administer a network that makes heavy use of the Internet. If you want to use the Internet to increase your business, it's important that the networking staff understand who is responsible for the network numbers, protocols, and so forth on the Internet. Therefore, as many others mentioned in this book, the previous URL should be something you put in your bookmarks or favorites folder.

Primary, Secondary, and Caching-Only Name Servers

For each domain on the Internet, there must be a primary server and a secondary server. The primary DNS server for the domain contains a collection of *resource records* that contain the address mappings for hostnames in the domain. The primary DNS server is the final authority for these mappings. The secondary DNS server contains a copy of the database maintained by the primary server and can continue to resolve names when the primary server is offline. It's important to note that the primary DNS server is where changes are made to the database. Through the use of the zone transfer mechanism, the data is copied to secondary servers.

In many cases, a DNS server answers name queries for domains for which it isn't the authority. In that case, the DNS server contacts a DNS server further up the hierarchy until one is found that can resolve the name or that can point to another DNS server that is the authority for the name. The DNS server maintains a cache of names that have been resolved by this method so that it doesn't have to continually poll other servers for names that are frequently queried.

A third type of DNS server is a caching-only server. This type of server does not maintain a database for a particular zone. To put it in other terms, a caching-only server isn't authoritative for any zone or domain and does not use the zone transfer mechanism to keep a current copy of the entire database. Instead, a caching-only name server has to contact another DNS server to initially resolve a name, but like the other servers it maintains a cache of names it has resolved so that it doesn't have to keep forwarding the query to another server. This type of server is normally used on a network segment that's connected to the rest of the network by a slower link (or a more expensive one) and is used to reduce network traffic.

Zones

In many cases, it isn't efficient to have a single server maintain the database for an entire domain. Instead, a primary DNS server can be authoritative for only a zone in the domain. A *zone* is a partition of the domain into subdomains. For example, one DNS server might be the authority for the zone zira.twoinc.com, whereas another might serve as the authority for the zone research.twoinc.com. Both subdomains exist within the same domain: twoinc.com. However, by dividing the domain into subdomains, it becomes easier to manage not only the DNS servers but also the individual business or organizational units that the domain services.

A *zone transfer* occurs when a secondary DNS server contacts a server that is primary for the zone and finds that it needs to obtain changes to the database. This is accomplished by using serial numbers contained in the database. If the secondary server has a lower serial number, a new copy of the database is copied to it.

Standard DNS Database Files

There are three basic types of files used by DNS servers. In most DNS implementations, you need to use a text editor to make changes to these files. Most newer DNS servers, such as Microsoft's DNS server, provide a graphical interface that can be used for adding or changing information in the DNS files. The basic files are

- **Database File**—This is the file that stores the resource records for the zones for which the DNS server is responsible. The first record in this file is the Start of Authority (SOA) record.

- **Cache File**—This file contains information for other name servers that can be used to resolve queries that are outside the zone or domain for which the server is responsible.

- **Reverse Lookup File**—This file is used to provide a hostname when the client only knows the IP address. This can be useful for security purposes. For example, a Web server that receives a request from a client can query the DNS with the name of the client to find out whether the hostname associated with the IP address is correct.

Resource Records

Until recently, most DNS databases were usually composed of ASCII text files containing records that could be used to translate a name to an IP address. Several types of records can be used in the database, with each representing a specific type of resource, such as a computer hostname or a mailserver name. Today, many fast DNS servers maintain a database with far greater capabilities than those that used a flat-file format. Therefore, newer DNS servers also contain many newer capabilities, such as dynamic updates.

When representing a domain name in DNS, a specific syntax is used. The term *label* is used in RFC 1035, "Domain Names—Implementation and Specification," when describing this syntax. A *label* is a one-byte length field followed by a data field. The length field indicates the number of characters in the data field. A domain name is represented by a series of labels and the entire domain name string is terminated with a length field of zero. For example, Figure 30.11 shows the layout of a series of labels that would be used to define the domain name zira.twoinc.com.

Tip

You can find other RFCs, both standards and proposed standards, by entering **DNS** as a keyword in the search capability offered on the Web's own archive for RFCs: `http://www.rfc-editor.org`.

Figure 30.11 The domain name is represented by a series of labels in DNS.

Although the string is only 13 bytes long, excluding the periods, it takes 17 bytes to represent it in the database because of the length fields and the terminator field. To avoid repetition for domain names that are used a lot in the database, a pointer record can be used.

The general format used for a resource record contains the following fields:

- **Name**—The owner name. This is the name of the domain to which this record belongs.
- **Type**—A 2-byte field that specifies the resource record type code.
- **Class**—A 2-byte field that specifies the resource record class code.
- **TTL**—A 32-bit signed integer that specifies the time-to-live value. The TTL value specifies the amount of time a record can be cached before its value needs to be refreshed from the authoritative source. 0 indicates that the record cannot be cached.
- **RDLENGTH**—An unsigned 16-bit integer that indicates the length of the data field that follows.
- **RDATA**—The data field. This part of the record describes the resource. The contents depend on the values of the type and class fields.

The Type field indicates the type of resource record. Table 30.1 contains a list of the standard record types used in most DNS implementations, along with a description of their use.

Table 30.1 DNS Resource Records

Record Type	Description
A	Host IP address
AAAA	Host IP address (Ipv6)
NS	Name server record
PTR	Pointer to another domain name record
SOA	Start of a zone of authority
WKS	Well-known service
HINFO	Host information
MX	"Mail exchanger" for the domain
MINFO	Mailbox or mail list information
TXT	Text entry for miscellaneous information
CNAME	Canonical name for an alias

In earlier implementations of DNS, other record types were also used. For instance, MD and MF were used to specify mail destination and mail forwarder records. RFC 1035 made obsolete three other RFCs: 882, 883, and 973. Four other record types that are considered experimental are

- **MB**—Mailbox domain name
- **MG**—Mail group member
- **MR**—Mail rename domain name
- **NULL**—Null resource record

In addition, RFC 2782, "A DNS RR for Specifying the Location of Services (DNS SRV)," added a new record type that figures *heavily* into a Windows 2000/.NET network: the SRV or *service record*. This type of record is used to store records in a DNS database that clients can use to look up services. For example, Windows servers use this type of record to enable clients to use DNS to locate domain controllers and other services. We'll get into more details about that in the next chapter.

The Start of Authority (SOA) record is used at the beginning of the database and is used to describe the database. It's used mostly by secondary DNS servers to get zone information. The fields in this record are

- **Domain name**—Name of the domain for which this database is the authority.
- **IN**—The class type of Internet.
- **SOA**—The Start of Authority record type indicator.
- **Primary server**—The FQDN of the primary DNS server for this domain.
- **Email address**—The email address of a person who is responsible for this domain.
- **Serial number**—A 32-bit value that shows the revision number of the database file. It is incremented each time a change is made to the database so that secondary servers can detect the change.
- **Refresh rate**—A 32-bit value used by secondary servers. After this interval has elapsed, the data for a record needs to be checked again in the primary server database.
- **Retry rate**—A 32-bit value indicating the amount of time to wait before retrying to refresh data after a failed attempt.

- **Expire rate**—A 32-bit value indicating the maximum amount of time a secondary server is to try to refresh data before it stops processing DNS data for this zone.
- **Minimum TTL**—The minimum amount of time for a resource record's TTL. This value can be overridden by the TTL value specified in the record itself.

All time values in the SOA record are in seconds.

The NS record type can be used to indicate that another name server is authoritative for this subdomain. For example, the record

```
zork.twoinc.com     IN     NS     zira.twoinc.com
```

indicates that the name server whose FQDN host name is zira.twoinc.com is the authoritative name server from which to get information about the subdomain zork.twoinc.com. To get the address of the name server zira.twoinc.com, an A type record is needed:

```
zira.twoinc.com     IN     A     216.65.33.219
```

The CNAME record is used to specify aliases or nicknames that can be used in addition to a hostname; for example:

```
ftp.zira.twoinc.com     IN     CNAME     zira.twoinc.com
```

Pointer records (PTR class) are used to get the name that's associated with an IP address—a reverse translation. For example

```
219.33.65.216     IN     PTR     zira.twoinc.com
```

can be used to perform a query to get the name of this host when only the IP address is known. However, notice that *the IP address has been reversed* in this record. It is represented in a pointer record as 219.33.65.216 instead of 216.65.33.219. The reverse format is used to make a key lookup in the database function properly. The special domain IN-ADDR.ARPA contains the data used when a server needs to look up the hostname for an address in the domain.

The Class field is generally IN, which stands for *Internet*. The numeric value for this code is 1. In addition to this class type, you might see references to CS, which stands for the obsolete CSNET class. The CH class stands for the CHAOS class and the HS class code stands for the Hesiod class.

Configuring a Unix DNS Server

On most Unix systems, configuring a DNS server involves editing ASCII text files and making the appropriate entries. The actual files to edit depend on the brand of Unix you're using. The most common is the Berkeley Internet Name Domain (BIND) implementation. This server uses a daemon called in.named.

In addition to the actual zone database files, you also have to edit

- **/etc/named.boot**—This file provides information for the in.named daemon when it starts up. The Directory directive specifies the directory that holds the zone database files (usually /var/named). The Cache directive tells the server to load a cache of initial hostnames. The Primary directive tells the server that it will function as the primary DNS server for the zone and the Secondary directive tells the server that it will function as the secondary DNS server for the zone.
- **/var/named/db.cache**—This is the usual name for the cache file.

To start the BIND service daemon after you've edited all the appropriate files, you only need to enter the command `in.named` at the system command prompt (or in a startup file). If you've edited the `/etc/named/boot` file or its equivalent on your Unix/Linux variant, the server automatically starts the next time the system is booted.

The most time-consuming task is the editing of the zone database files and making entries for the hosts in the domain.

Configuring DNS Clients

Unix/Linux clients usually get their information about name servers from the `/etc/resolv.conf` file. (Note that this might be different for your variant of the "universal" Unix operating system. Check the manual pages.) To configure the client, edit this file. To place comments in this file, you can use the semicolon (;) character. The three directives that you configure in this file are

■ **Domain**—The default domain name. This name is appended to any names that are partially qualified.

■ **Search**—This is a search list of domains used to look up names that are not fully qualified. You can specify up to six domain names with a total of 256 characters for this directive.

■ **Nameserver**—You can specify up to three DNS servers by IP address with this directive. Note that if you don't specify a nameserver address, the default is the local domain.

For example:

```
;This is the /etc/resolv.conf file for local workstations
domain twoinc.com
; Name servers
nameserver 199.45.32.38
nameserver 151.197.0.39
nameserver 216.645.33.219
; search lists
search twoinc.com biznesnet.com
; end of file
```

A client using this file to try to resolve the name of a host named `zira` would first search the domain `twoinc.com` and then the domain `biznesnet.com`. The first match found is the one that will be used to resolve the name to an IP address.

To configure a Microsoft client to use a DNS server, you only need to enter the IP addresses of the DNS servers when you perform the initial client network setup (or set your DHCP server to provide this information to the client).

Using *nslookup*

The `nslookup` utility is generally employed to find the IP address associated with a name. However, the utility can be used to interrogate the DNS database to find not only IP addresses, but also information stored in other records in the database. The utility can be used either in interactive mode, where the user can continue to issue commands, or in a one-shot, non-interactive mode where a single query is executed. The basic syntax for the command is

```
nslookup [[-option ...] [hostname to locate]] - [server]
```

If you omit the last item in this syntax (- *server*), the local DNS server is queried. However, when you have multiple servers or if you want to query a server outside your organization, specify it with this parameter.

A simple example of the command is `nslookup twoinc.com`, which returns the following information:

```
Name:    twoinc.com
Address:  216.65.33.219
```

If you want to retrieve more information about the server, you can use options and specify the info records:

```
nslookup -query=hinfo -timeout=10 www.twoinc.com

twoinc.com
        primary name server = ns1.tentex.com
        responsible mail addr = hostmaster.twoinc.com
        serial  = 1342
        refresh = 3600 (1 hour)
        retry   = 600 (10 mins)
        expire  = 86400 (1 day)
        default TTL = 3600 (1 hour)
```

As you can see, this tool is useful for looking up addresses, but can also be used to query the DNS database and help you debug configuration problems. With this simple query, you can see the serial number of the current database along with other information stored in the SOA record. The syntax for the options of this command varies depending on your operating system.

Dynamic DNS

Earlier in this chapter, I discussed Microsoft's WINS servers. These NetBIOS name servers can be used to dynamically accept information from clients so that the network administrator does not have to make edits to the database each time a node is added to the network or a workstation is moved to a new location. The Dynamic Host Configuration Protocol (DHCP) has eliminated the necessity of manually configuring each computer host with network information. Microsoft's DNS server can be configured to query the WINS server when it needs to resolve a name it cannot find in its own databases.

This solution does not help if you have a multivendor network with workstations running different operating systems. There are several relevant RFCs that address these problems associated with standard DNS implementations, such as

- **RFC 2136, "Dynamic Updates in the Domain Name System (DNS UPDATE)"**—This RFC describes a method that can be used for dynamic updates to DNS. It provides for an atomic (all-or-nothing) update mechanism that can be used to add, delete, or modify one or more resource records in a zone file. This RFC was updated by a proposed standard, RFC 3007, "Secure Domain Name System (DNS) Dynamic Update," among others.

- **RFC 1995, "Incremental Zone Transfer in DNS"**—Incremental zone transfer means that only portions of the zone database file that have been modified need to be transferred from primary DNS servers to secondary servers. This process conserves network bandwidth and decreases the latency time for changes to be distributed throughout the Internet.

- **RFC 1996, "A Mechanism for Prompt Notification of Zone Changes (DNS NOTIFY)"**—The third piece of the solution enables the primary DNS server to notify the secondary servers that changes have been made to the zone database. Currently, zone transfers can occur only after a refresh interval has passed.

Offerings for a DNS server that's truly dynamic and a corresponding DHCP server capable of making updates are becoming more widespread at this time. Portions of the technology are implemented here and there, while some vendors offer both and DNS and DHCP solutions that work well together. For example, The Internet Software Consortium (ISC), which maintains BIND, released—on March 4, 2003—version 9.2.2 of BIND, which supports RFC 2136. You can download documentation or the kit files from the ISC Web site at `http://www.isc.org`.

At the same site, you will also find a version of DHCP, along with a list of products developed by other developers that are based on or can work with these products.

For network administrators who already have DNS servers running on the network but are concerned about whether these servers can be used in conjunction to the Windows 2000 version of DNS, please note that Windows 2000 DNS server also supports the following RFCs in addition to the dynamic update RFCs listed previously:

- **RFC 1034, "Domain Names—Concepts and Facilities"**
- **RFC 1035, "Domain Names—Implementation and Specification"**
- **RFC 1123, "Requirements for Internet Hosts—Application and Support"**
- **RFC 1886, "DNS Extensions to Support IP Version 6"**
- **RFC 2181, "Clarifications to the DNS Specification"**
- **RFC 2308, "Negative Caching of DNS Queries (DNS NCACHE)"**

Check the documentation for your BIND or DNS server to see which RFCs it supports. You might be surprised to find that this new and improved DNS server from Microsoft might be as good as, or perhaps better than, your current version.

Installing DNS on a Windows 2000 or 2003 Server

Because it's so closely tied to the Active Directory and Windows 2000, installing and managing the DNS server for Windows 2000 and Server 2003 when using the Active Directory is covered in greater detail in the next chapter. Windows clients in the network use DNS to locate domain controllers, which hold the Active Directory database. When you decide to promote a Windows 2000 or 2003 server to become a domain controller, you'll be prompted to install a DNS server as well, unless another DNS server already exists on the network. After the domain controller has been properly configured, it will register records in DNS that enable clients to find the domain controllers in the domain.

However, you can always install a DNS server on the Windows 2000 or 2003 Server whether or not you decide to use the Active Directory. For example, you might have a few Windows servers in a Unix network and decide to use Microsoft's version of DNS because you find the graphical interface easy to use (tired of editing those text files and making a mistake?). Or you might want to install additional DNS servers to provide a backup for a primary DNS server. You don't have to install the DNS service on just a domain controller, but the system must be a Windows 2000 or 2003 Server.

Installing the service is just as simple as installing the WINS service:

1. Click Start, Programs, Control Panel (Start/Control Panel for 2003).
2. From the Control Panel, double-click the Add/Remove Programs icon.
3. When the Add Remove Programs window pops up, click Add/Remove Windows Components (on the left part of the window). The Add Remove Programs window now displays a Components button in the upper-right side of the window. Click the Components button, and the Windows Components Wizard dialog box pops up.

4. Scroll down until you find Networking Services and highlight it by clicking it once. Then click the Details button.

5. When the Networking Services dialog box appears, scroll down until you find Domain Name System (DNS). Click the check box next to the component and click OK.

6. When prompted, insert the Windows 2000 or 2003 source CD into your CD-ROM drive and then wait a minute or so while files are copied to your hard drive. When the Windows Components Wizard window reappears, click Next.

7. Another window appears, titled Completing the Windows Components Wizard. Click Finish.

8. When the Add Remove Programs window reappears, click OK or Close.

Chapter 31, "Using the Active Directory," looks more closely at how managing DNS on a Windows 2000/2003 server is done using the MMC console, as well as how DNS can be installed at the same time, and integrated into the Active Directory.

Network Information Service

As mentioned earlier, Sun developed a product that was originally called Yellow Pages, but the name was later changed due to a trademark owned by British Telecom. Sun's product was Network Information Service (NIS), a client/server system that allows for the sharing of information on a network that includes not only hostnames and addresses, but also other information, such as password files. The goal of NIS is to reduce administrative overhead problems associated with having multiple copies of files on hosts throughout the network.

NIS is based on a flat namespace design. Sun has now released NIS+, which resembles the Domain Name System in its hierarchical structure. NIS+ uses a concept of NIS domains, which might or might not be paired with DNS domains. NIS uses a concept called *maps* for storing data. Maps use a simple keyword/data concept. NIS+ uses a more traditional database format with tables containing multi-columned rows of data.

NIS is mentioned in this chapter not because it is a name resolution mechanism, but because on many Unix networks, NIS is responsible for keeping synchronized other files that perform name resolution. If you use NIS (or NIS+), I recommend you become familiar with its installation and configuration. Security on Unix systems can be a difficult task if you just install NIS and forget about it. You need to understand how it works, and you should consider the security implications of keeping important information on different servers throughout the network.

Using the Active Directory

31

SOME OF THE MAIN TOPICS IN THIS CHAPTER ARE

CHAPTER 31

In Chapter 41, "Windows 2000 and Windows Server 2003 User and Computer Management Utilities," you will find a lengthy overview of using the Active Directory for basic functions, as the title of that chapter suggests. In this chapter you will learn more about how the Active Directory is structured, and how to manage the directory itself. The Active Directory, especially in Windows Server 2003, can play an important role in a Windows-based network.

▶▶   If you have a heterogeneous network composed of Windows and other operating systems, see Part XI, "Migration and Integration," to learn how the Active Directory can be used in this type of network.

The Active Directory was introduced by Microsoft with Windows 2000. The Active Directory is an LDAP-based directory service that enables you to store information about user accounts, domains, and resource objects in the same place for easy management. And because LDAP (see Appendix D, "The Lightweight Directory Access Protocol") is a standard embraced by a large number of vendors, from Novell to Netscape, it is possible to enable networks that use different directory services to interact with each other. This can be an important factor when integrating two networks, or when migrating from one type of network to another.

The Active Directory can be installed on a Windows network when you migrate from Windows NT 4.0 to Windows 2000, or Windows Server 2003. The examples in this chapter are based on Windows Server 2003, which incorporates many new features. However, the concepts are basically the same, though the windows and dialog boxes may look a little different if you are using an earlier version of Windows.

When you upgrade from Windows NT, domains become container units within the directory. Additionally, the nature of trust relationships between domains changes. There are many other subtle differences you will notice, but for the most part you will find it easier to manage network users and resources using the Microsoft Management Console (MMC) snap-ins to perform routine tasks. Other snap-ins can be installed in the MMC to allow you to perform more complicated functions, such as modifying the schema.

Note

You can create a small workgroup-style network using Windows 2000 Professional and Server. If you want to maintain an environment where security and administrative tasks can be centralized and controlled, as in the previous Windows NT domain models, you'll have to use the Active Directory, or perhaps another directory service, such as the eDirectory from Novell (see Chapter 33, "Overview of the Novell Bindery and Novell Directory Services," and Chapter 34, "Expanding and Enhancing NDS: NetWare's eDirectory").

The only information stored in the Windows NT 4.0 SAM (security accounts manager) database is user and computer accounts, along with some security information, such as trust relationships between domains. Information about printers, file shares, and other resources is scattered here and there in separate databases and is managed by separate utilities. Administering network resources using multiple utilities with disjointed interfaces can become quite a nightmare in a large network. This disjointed method of administration has created a situation in which many upgraded their networks to Windows NT 4.0, but also adopted Novell Directory Services on the same network. Adding NDS to a Windows NT 4.0 network can solve a lot of problems by giving you a single place to administer many kinds of resources. The Active Directory consolidates information from these different sources into a single database, and provides you with a simpler management interface.

Early Directories

The first directory that comes to mind when you think of early computer systems is the file system directory. The organization of data files and programs into a structure of directories and subdirectories became more important as the size of the available storage grew. When networking PCs became a necessity, the capability to organize users and secure data from inappropriate access led to the concept of logging in to the computer or network, just as had been done with multiuser, mini, and mainframe computers for many years. This made it necessary to create another database (that is, a directory) to keep track of users and security information.

For network administrators and users alike, there is a great need today to quickly locate resources that, in a modern distributed computing environment, can be anywhere from the computer on the user's desk to a file server halfway around the world. So when you're deciding what kinds of information to store in a directory service database, the needs of both the users and the administrators of the system must be taken into consideration.

The Difference Between the Directory and the Directory Service

The first thing you will need to understand about the Active Directory is that it is composed of a database and many different programs that can be used to operate on the database. The term *directory* is used to describe the underlying database that holds all the information managed by the directory service. The actual information store, the directory, is stored in the Extensible Storage Engine (ESE)—ESE is a derivative of Microsoft's oft-used JET engine—and a variant of this same technology is also used by Microsoft Exchange Server.

The term *directory service* refers to the programs that manage the database and allow users and programs to access its data in a meaningful way. After you've created a domain controller in a Windows 2000 or 2003 network, you'll find several new utilities in the Administrative Tools folder, such as the Active Directory Sites and Services Manager and the Active Directory Users and Computers tools. You'll find other tools in this folder, depending on the components you selected when installing the operating system. The Event Viewer application is still present, but now it uses the MMC interface, as do most of the other system management tools.

The directory service consists of the programs and application programming interfaces—the Active Directory Service Interfaces (ADSI) and the LDAP C lower-level API. These can be used to create additional tools for use with the directory. The directory service offers the network a *namespace* that can be used to locate objects throughout the network by querying by the object's name or one of its attributes.

The *Directory System Agent (DSA)* provides the service responsible for performing actual queries and updates to the database. Because applications and APIs make requests to the DSA in a defined fashion, the functions they perform are separated from the actual underlying format of data storage.

Interesting Objects

The Active Directory provides the capability to query a large database that can be used to locate any object, or information about any object, stored in the directory database. To understand how important the Active Directory is in Windows 2000/Server 2003, you should first understand the kinds of data that will be stored in the objects that the directory organizes.

Knowing what kind of data should be a candidate for management by a directory service is not easy. Here, the definition of a directory service gets kind of fuzzy.

It is common to compare directory services to the white and yellow pages of the traditional phone directory. White pages are specific queries in which the input is a person's name and the output is the person's telephone number. Yellow pages have a more general "browsing" capability, with more general input about a subject or concept. This results in a specific output selected by the user from the information found. The Active Directory provides the best of both. You can search for a specific object if you know the name you are looking for (such as a username or computer name), or you can browse for objects by using the data stored in the many attributes that objects can possess. Looking up a username in the Active Directory is sort of like using the white pages of the telephone book.

However, suppose you are a mobile employee. You have just walked into the Atlanta office and you need to print a document. You quickly search the directory to find an object that

- Is a printer
- Is located in the Atlanta branch on the third floor
- Supports color printing

This situation shows that directory services also can be used in a manner similar to the telephone book's Yellow Pages service. You can specify the attributes for an object you want to find, and perform a search of the directory to see whether there are any matches. Or, if you know the name of an object, you can query the database to find that object and then view its properties. This method of querying the database enables you to find something you know a little about, or to find the attributes of an object you already know about. In the latter example, you might know the name of a printer located down the hallway but not be aware of whether it supports duplex-printing. The Active Directory can tell you that, as long as the information has been put into the directory database.

As you can see, the Active Directory stores the traditional kind of information that usually is found on a network computer operating system. What other kinds of objects can you store in the directory? Well, just about anything you can think of, as long as you can express it as a collection of attributes (or features of the object). If you want, it's possible to create objects that represent your stamp collection. You can create objects that represent just about anything. The Active Directory comes with a large number of built-in objects. These are defined in the *schema*, a concept that is discussed later in this chapter. You can extend the schema to add objects (and attributes) that are particularly useful for your business or situation. However, almost everyone agrees that the information stored in the directory should be interesting or of some practical use.

What Active Directory Delivers

Because the Active Directory is based on industry standards, it can offer many services to a network. The Active Directory provides some very important features to a Windows network, or a heterogeneous network made up of computers using different operating systems:

- A single logon for the entire network. This was present, more or less, in previous versions of Windows, but it can be extended today to incorporate NetWare, Unix, Linux, and other operating systems. For examples, see Part XI.

- A hierarchical structure that organizes objects and tasks into a logical format so that you can quickly and easily locate the information you need. The X.500 hierarchical format has been adopted in the Active Directory.

- An extensible format that enables the directory to encompass new objects as operating systems and management functions evolve. This means that the schema of the directory should be easy to modify. Using MMC snap-ins, this can be a simple chore with the Active Directory. Note, though, that Microsoft has created a schema for the Active Directory that should suffice for most networks, and you should modify the schema only after you become aware of the possible consequences of your changes. Changes to the Active Directory schema are permanent and cannot be undone by any means short of recovering all domain controllers from backups made prior to extending the schema.

- Fault tolerance and a distributed database. You don't need to create numerous domains with primary domain controllers to receive updates and back up domain controllers to "hold the fort" when a PDC isn't available, as was the case with NT. Instead, all domain controllers in a native-mode Active Directory network are peers, and each domain controller in the domain holds a copy of that domain's portion of the Active Directory database. There is no need to "promote" a backup domain controller if a primary one fails, because all domain controllers in a domain are considered to be the same.

- Scalability. Management tasks can now be centralized or distributed as your administrative needs dictate. You can delegate authority over parts of the database (such as a domain or part of a domain) as you see fit.

- Programmability. Application developers and script writers can use many tools to interface with the database.

- Manageable security mechanisms. From the small desktop system to the worldwide enterprise, you can grow the network to one that consists of millions of users.

One of the most important features that large enterprises would like to see is a *standards-based implementation* so that you do not get locked into a single vendor for all your software needs. Migration tools, both to and from the directory database, are needed until the standards issues settle down and products from different vendors work together as seamlessly as they do in the telephone network.

From X.500 and DAP to the Lightweight Directory Access Protocol

When you think of standards, the name International Organization for Standardization (ISO) probably comes to mind. After all, the ISO has been involved in efforts for many years to help make the interchange of data between computers less of a proprietary chore and more of a free flow of information. The ISO, along with the International Telecommunications Union (ITU), developed the X.500 group of standards to promulgate a global white pages directory service. Under the umbrella of X.500 there are many standards, which include naming conventions and networking protocols (OSI—the Open Systems Interconnection protocols).

Note

Although many books state that the letters ISO are an abbreviation for International Standards Organization, that is not the case. Instead, the actual name of the organization, in English, was originally International Organization for Standardization. The term ISO was eventually selected by this group because of its root meaning from the original Greek word isos, which translates generally to "equal." This name was chosen because it pretty much indicates standardization, without having to use a particular language to create an acronym. Thus, the ISO works with standards bodies from many different countries, attempting to make technological things "equal" so that they will work together. You can find out more about ISO and its member organizations by visiting **www.iso.ch/**.

However, the OSI networking protocol never did take off as expected, although some vendors implemented parts of it. Digital Equipment Corporation (DEC was absorbed by Compaq Computer Corporation, and Compaq was of course recently acquired by HP) tried for years to get OSI standards adopted by evolving its own proprietary networking protocol—DECnet—into an OSI-compliant protocol and by releasing an operating system (OSF) based on OSI standards. Even today the venerable operating system once called VMS (for Virtual Memory System) has been called OpenVMS for many years because of this attempt to adopt open standards.

While all this discussion of standards was going on in committees and protocols were being discussed, debated, and refined, the Internet took off. And as everyone now knows, it is TCP/IP that glues together the Internet, not OSI. It's funny in a way that standardization came about ad hoc instead of through an orderly process.

But it was not just the lack of interest in OSI network protocols that stifled the acceptance of X.500 proposals. Several other important factors were involved, such as the overhead associated with implementing many of the X.500 protocols. Although X.500 (et. al) does a good job defining protocols, it does not attempt to define standard programming interfaces (APIs, which make it easy for different vendors to write applications that implement the protocols).

Another reason you won't find X.500 standards implemented in many places is its complicated naming scheme. The hierarchical organization of the directory, which can be seen in its naming format, is a good idea, but the long-winded name is not. For example, which of the following would you rather try to remember when sending someone an email message: the X.500 format or the RFC 822 name?

- X.500

    `CN=Ono,OU=Studio One,OU=New York,O=mydomain,C=US`

- RFC 822

    `Ono@mydomain.com`

The X.500 name, in this example, reveals the organization structure of the directory, whereas the RFC 822 name does not. But every user shouldn't have to be fully cognizant of the directory structure in order to use it. If you want to send Ono a message via email, you should not have to know that she works in Studio One (organizational unit=Studio One) and that she is in the company's New York division (organizational unit=New York). You shouldn't have to specify that she is in the United States because you already indicated that she is in New York. And because you can have additional organizational units (OU=) in the directory, the X.500 address actually could have been much, much longer. Note that in the preceding example one container object can contain other container objects before you eventually get to the "leaf" object that is the object containing the attributes you wanted to locate in the first place.

Directory services should make things easier, not more difficult. Microsoft's Active Directory (as well as other LDAP-based directories) uses the hierarchical treelike organization as spelled out by the X.500 standards, but the Active Directory also adapts the Windows NT domain system, by using DNS as a locator service, to the structure. That is, in addition to the standard container types such as OU for organizational unit, and so on, the Active Directory has a DC, or *domain component*, container object which is defined in the schema that can be used to house domains in the directory. By incorporating domains into the directory, rather than simply discarding the domain concept, Microsoft has made it easier for users of Windows NT 4.0 to interact with or make the migration to Windows 2000, Server 2003, and future versions of Windows. Domains can be imported into the directory when migrating existing Windows NT networks. You can learn more about this in Chapter 62, "Migrating from Windows NT 4.0 to Windows 2000, Windows 2003, and Windows XP."

The overhead associated with other X.500 recommendations also needs to be overcome. Four "wire" (or communication) protocols were defined:

- Directory Access Protocol (DAP)
- Directory System Protocol (DSP)
- Directory Information Shadowing Protocol (DISP)
- Directory Operational Binding Management Protocol (DOP)

These protocols were developed during a time in which PCs did not have sufficient computing power to host such complex protocols and still be capable of performing adequately as a desktop workstation. And mini-computers and mainframe computers used proprietary operating systems that were not easily adaptable to these protocols, nor did it provide a benefit to vendors to adopt an open protocol when the whole purpose of marketing their products was to keep the customer "satisfied" with a single source. The exception of course, mentioned earlier, was Digital Equipment Corporation.

▶▶ For more information about the history of the X.500 protocols and the development of LDAP, see Appendix D.

To reduce the overhead associated with the X.500 directory structure, a new set of Request for Comments (RFCs) was developed to define the Lightweight Directory Access Protocol (LDAP). LDAP is the protocol that Microsoft and many other vendors have chosen to implement to create directory services. LDAP has gone through several refinements via the RFC process, and the Active Directory has been designed to be compatible with both version 2.0 and the newer standard, LDAP version 3.0.

Note

For those interested in some very boring reading, version 2.0 of the Lightweight Directory Access Protocol (LDAP) is defined by RFC 1777.

If that doesn't put you to sleep, try reading up on version 3.0. It has been adopted by most LDAP products, including Microsoft. LDAP version 3 is defined by RFC 2251, "Lightweight Access Directory Protocol V 3," by Wahl, Howes, and Kille. In Appendix D, you'll find a list of additional RFCs that further define aspects of the LDAP protocol.

By using a standard that is being implemented by many other vendors, including Netscape and Novell, the Active Directory can exchange data and queries with other directory service implementations; thus, you won't get stuck in yet another proprietary solution. Of course, this all depends on how Microsoft and other vendors choose to interpret and implement LDAP features as they are standardized and refined.

The Active Directory Schema

If you are familiar with databases that are manipulated using the Structured Query Language (SQL), you might already understand what a schema is. Put simply, it is the definition of the types of things, or objects, you can store in the directory structure. The directory contains many types of objects, such as user accounts, printers, and computer accounts. Each object is made up of attributes that contain the specific data for the object. The schema is the definition of these objects, their attributes. Technically, these templates of objects are called classes. A particular object in the directory is derived from one or more classes defined by the schema, and perhaps tweaked a bit by the addition of new attributes by the network administrator. For C programmers, this is like using a header file to define certain programming objects, creating instances of these objects as needed for your application.

In some directory implementations, the schema is stored as an ordinary ASCII text file, similar to the way some DNS servers store their information. Each time the software that runs the directory is booted up, the schema file is read into memory. One of the drawbacks of using this method is that if you want to make changes to the schema, you usually have to edit the text file and then reload it into the application. The Active Directory avoids this problem by defining the schema of the directory in the directory itself. You can add to the schema just as you do other objects in the directory, and you can disable attributes and most objects in the AD.

Note

The abbreviation ASCII stands for American Standard Code for Information Interchange. This 7-bit code allows for up to 128 character definitions, including alphabetic, numeric, and punctuation and other characters. Unicode and other computer numeric representations have been developed in the past few years to extend a computer's recognition of characters involving languages other than English. For example, see Unicode (which is supported by most modern operating systems) in Appendix B, "Networking Glossary."

Specifically, the Active Directory schema is made up of four types of objects that are used to define the schema:

■ **Schema container object**—Each directory instance has at least one schema container object, which is a direct child of the directory root object. The schema container holds the other objects, which describe the object classes and attributes of the directory.

■ **Class container object**—This container object holds the object classes that define what kind of objects can be stored in the directory. Class objects define objects that store the actual properties, or attributes, of an object class. You create instances of objects by using the definitions of an object class.

■ **Property object**—This type of object is used by the schema to define a particular attribute or property of the object. It references the syntax object.

■ **Syntax object**—This object describes a particular syntax that is applied to one or more properties defined by property objects.

Note

An object in a directory database is made up of a number of attributes. Think of this like an address used for a postal letter. An address is made up of a name, street address, state, postal code, and so on, depending on the country. Each of these subcomponents of the "address" object is called a property of the address object. Additionally, the terms *property* and *attribute* are used interchangeably throughout this chapter. An attribute or a property of an object is merely a component that makes up the object.

Objects and Attributes

For the most part, an *object* is nothing more than a collection of specific pieces of information about the object. For example, an object that represents a user account contains attributes that hold information about the particular user. When you create user accounts in the Active Directory, you supply the same information that you did when you created user accounts using the User Manager for Domains in previous Windows versions, as well as a great deal of other information. Chapter 41 details the information you can store about a user, for instance. The Active Directory contains objects that can be used to store information about everything from user accounts to printers to the actual schema of the Active Directory itself.

However, the Active Directory can be used to store almost any kind of information you want. It's just a matter of finding the correct object (or creating a new object class) and then entering the data for instances of the object.

From the discussion of X.500 names earlier in this chapter, remember the term "organizational unit (OU)," as it is represented in the X.500 naming scheme. An *organizational unit* is an object in the directory that holds or contains other objects. For example, in the Active Directory, a domain is a container object. It holds other objects, some of which are container objects also, such as the Users object. The Users object holds the actual individual user accounts. It is in these *instances* of the User object that the attributes will be found that contain the data for each user in the domain.

Attributes are simply the fine-grained details of the data stored in an object. Each attribute for an object holds a specific kind of data, and thus has a specific syntax associated with it. An attribute that is used to hold a person's name would have a syntax that requires a text string. The syntax would define a minimum and maximum length for the string. An attribute that represents a numeric value would have a syntax that specifies the minimum and maximum value of the number that can be stored in the object.

When a new class of objects is defined, you have the capability to create two particular types of attributes: *required* or *optional*. If an attribute is of the required type, each object you create of the particular object class *must* have some value defined for the required attribute. However, there can be other attributes you might want to define for the User object class that do not apply to all users. For example, you might want to keep a list of the names of the user's spouse and children. However, not all users will necessarily have a spouse or offspring, so this kind of attribute could be created as an optional attribute.

Standard Objects in the Active Directory

The Active Directory comes with two sets of standard objects: *container* and *leaf*. Container objects hold other objects in the directory. Leaf objects are the endpoints in a directory tree that contain specific attributes about a directory object entry. In other words, the leaf objects contain the actual data (attributes) that the Active Directory stores, whereas container objects group these leaf objects, such as individual users or printers, into meaningful groups.

Note that a container object also can contain other container objects, as well as leaf objects. This makes it possible to create subdivisions in the directory that model your business or administrative needs. Using the uniform Microsoft Management Console (MMC) interface, container objects appear as folders in a tree.

What Objects Are Included in the Active Directory?

These are the standard container objects you are most likely to encounter during day-to-day system management chores:

- Namespaces
- Country
- Locality
- Organization
- Organizational Unit
- Domain
- Computer

And these are the standard leaf objects that are provided:

- User
- Group
- Alias
- Service
- Print Queue
- Print Device
- Print Job
- File Service
- File Share
- Session
- Resource

These built-in object classes provide most of the functionality a network will need when using the Active Directory to manage users, computers, and resources. This is not a complete listing, however, of all the objects you'll find in the Active Directory. There are many, many more. And if you need the capability to store still other types of objects, you can modify the schema by using the Active Directory Schema Manager Snap-In.

The Directory Namespace

Two types of names can be used to identify an object in the directory. The first is called the *distinguished name (DN)* and the second is the *relative distinguished name (RDN)*. The relative distinguished name is just a value of a particular attribute of the object. For example, for user objects, the RDN is the common name (CN) of the object. So for the user object that holds account information for user Luke Kurtis, the RDN for the object would be Luke Kurtis. In the Active Directory there can be more than one Luke Kurtis, so there needs to be a method for telling them apart. The distinguished name is that method.

A distinguished name consists of the RDN of the object, *plus all the RDNs of every object* that precedes it in the directory. Referring to the X.500 address format, it quickly becomes apparent that the DN of an object not only uniquely identifies the object in the directory, but also reveals its location in the hierarchy.

The example given earlier showing how X.500 defines an object name shows the structure of a distinguished name:

```
CN=Ono,OU=Studio One,OU=New York,O=mydomain,C=US
```

Here the RDN of the user object is the common name Ono. But the object Ono is located in the container object named Studio One, which is located in the container object called New York, which is located in the container object called mydomain, and so on. Although there can be more than one Ono object in the directory, there can be only one object with the RDN of Ono that is located in the Studio One department in New York for this domain in the United States. If another Ono comes to work in that department, she will have to use a different name! There is an easier way around this, of course. When assigning usernames to employees, many companies already use a combination of letters rather than an employee's full name. For example, John Doe might be assigned a username of doej, using the last name plus the first letter of the first name. If another John Doe is hired, a variation on this can be performed by assigning the new employee the username doej2.

However, another distinct Ono might work in the manufacturing department in the same organization. For example,

```
CN=Ono,OU=Manufacturing,OU=New York,O=mydomain,C=US
```

is a perfectly legal distinguished name and can reside in the same directory database as the first Ono.

What Is a Domain Tree? What Is a Forest?

The Active Directory gives you one single enterprise-wide namespace. This namespace is used for user accounts, resource objects, application configuration information, and so on. What you decide to store in the directory, beyond the default objects set up by the installation process, is up to you. The namespace can be global, provided you organize your domains into a domain tree.

A domain tree is nothing more than a method of organizing the domains in your enterprise into a structure so that they all share a common directory schema and a *contiguous* namespace. Although a domain tree is a structure formed by a collection of domains, a forest is a collection of domain trees. *The namespace in the forest does not have to be contiguous*, as it does in the tree, so a forest can be used to link disparate domain trees in the organization so that trust relationships still can be used to allow a single user logon in the network.

To understand what a domain tree or a forest is, you must know what it is replacing in the Windows NT networking scheme.

Domain Models—May They Rest in Peace

In Windows NT, the domain was used to group users and resources with a common security policy to simplify administrative tasks. In large organizations, a single domain was not sufficient to hold all the users and resources, and was not an efficient method of administering user rights and privileges or resource protections. Because of this, multiple domains were created and linked in what is termed a *trust relationship*. This trust relationship allowed users from one domain to be granted access rights to resources in another trusting domain.

A trust relationship in earlier versions of Windows NT could be a one-way or a two-way relationship. In a one-way trust relationship, one domain would trust the users that had been authenticated by another domain. The administrator in the trusting domain could grant users (or groups of users) from the trusted domain access rights in the local trusting domain. In a two-way trust relationship, the relationship existed in both directions. The trust relationship is not transitive. That is, if domain A has a trust relationship that allows its users to be assigned rights in domain B, and if domain B has a trust relationship that allows its users to be assigned rights to resources in domain C, a user in domain A cannot be granted rights in domain C by use of these trust relationships. That would require that domain A establish a separate trust relationship with domain C.

The way domains were organized into user or resource domains, and how the trust relationships were set up, led to the development of several domain models that could be used, depending on the size of your enterprise and the methods used to administer them. These were the single domain, multiple domain, master domain, and multiple-master domain models.

Because the domain essentially was the boundary for the security accounts manager (SAM) database, you had two basic choices. You could put all your user accounts into a single master domain, and then grant them access rights to objects in *resource* domains, or you could put users into separate domains, depending on your organization, and maintain a complicated set of trust relationships and administrative policies.

The headache associated with managing multiple trust relationships—and moving users to and fro when reorganizations occurred—is one of the major drawbacks of the SAM-based domain models.

Partitioning the Active Directory into Domains

When you install Windows 2000/Server 2003 and create a new domain, you are given several choices that decide how the domain will fit into an Active Directory tree. You can create a new forest or become part of an existing forest and create a new tree, making this new domain the first domain in the new tree. Or you can make the new domain a child domain in a domain tree that already exists in the forest.

Each domain in the domain tree is a *security boundary* in the Active Directory, just as it is in previous versions of Windows NT. However, you no longer have to create one- or two-way trust relationships between domains for users to be granted access rights and privileges in other domains that are in the same domain tree.

When a Windows domain joins a domain tree, a *two-way transitive trust relationship*, based on the Kerberos security authentication method, is automatically established between the child domain and its parent domain in the tree. Because the trust relationship is *transitive* (two-way), there is no need to manually configure additional trust relationships with other domains that exist in the domain tree. This means that after your domain is created and joined to a domain tree, your users can be granted access rights to resources in any other domain in the tree without the need to further create a complicated set of trust relationships with other domains.

Note

The MIT Kerberos (version 5) authentication method is defined in RFC 1510, "The Kerberos Network Authentication Service (V5)," by Kohl and Neuman.

Each domain in the tree holds the portion of the Active Directory database that represents the objects found in that domain. However, the namespace is contiguous throughout the tree. Each domain controller in the domain holds a complete replica of the directory for that domain. And, to help reduce network traffic and administrative overhead, you can create additional replicas of the domain's portion of the directory and place it close to users in other domains that frequently access the resources in your domain. You only need to create an additional domain controller. This may seem similar to the primary domain controller/backup domain controller mechanism that Windows NT 4.0 uses. However, you no longer have to promote a backup domain controller (a BDC) to become a primary domain controller should the PDC fail. Instead, any peer domain controller can handle all authentication requests, and other Active Directory requests, within a domain, without operator intervention.

A Domain Is Still a Domain

The domain in Windows 2000/Server 2003 is still a security boundary, just like it was in Windows NT. Domain administrators can still take command and exert their authority over all users and resources in the domain. From that perspective, nothing has changed.

However, the management of your relationships with other domains is now much easier. The two-way transitive trust relationships are set up automatically, so you don't have to coordinate managing this with other administrators throughout the network. If you upgrade from a previous version of Windows NT, all your groups and users are migrated into the Active Directory under your same domain. You can manage them as you always have, although there are new tools (using the MMC interface) that are used instead.

▶▶ For more information about how to manage users (and computers) in the Active Directory, see Chapter 41.

Active Directory Trees and Forests

As discussed earlier in this section, a domain tree is a collection of domains that have a contiguous namespace, whereas trees in a forest can have a noncontiguous namespace. Contiguous namespace means that the object in each child domain in the tree has the name of its parent domains prefixed to its distinguished name. This also means that the names used to identify each child domain will have the names of the parents prefixed. Figure 31.1 shows an example of a domain tree. The domain tree starts at the top and flows down the tree, rather than from the bottom up.

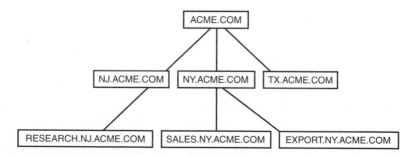

Figure 31.1 A domain tree is a contiguous namespace.

In this domain tree, the most senior parent in the tree is the acme.com domain. Beneath that are three child domains, nj.acme.com, ny.acme.com, and tx.acme.com. Under the New York child domain, you can see a sales domain (sales.ny.acme.com) and another domain called export.ny.acme.com. This tree could be further expanded by adding additional child domains to any of the domains in the tree. The way you construct the fully qualified domain name for a domain positions it in the tree structure.

In the best of all possible worlds, each enterprise would have exactly one domain tree and one large contiguous namespace. However, in this rapid-paced business world, nothing remains the same for long, including business organizational units. Corporate mergers and acquisitions, for example, can bring in large numbers of users and resources that must be incorporated quickly into the network structure. In this situation, it might not be possible to easily include the acquired assets into the naming structure.

However, you can still join two disparate domain trees. You can't put them into the same tree because the naming for all objects would not be contiguous. You can, however, join domain trees into a structure called a forest.

A forest is like a domain tree, but the namespace does not have to be contiguous throughout the forest. The directory schema is still common for all domains, and you can establish trust relationships between the trees. Users can still use a single logon to access resources in domains that reside in different domain trees (see Figure 31.2).

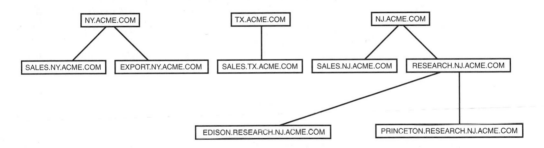

Figure 31.2 Domain trees with disjointed namespaces can exist in a forest.

The Active Directory and Dynamic DNS

DNS, or the Domain Name System, is the most widely used network address/name translation service in the world, and is used on the Internet. This service was created many years ago when the first DARPA network, the predecessor of today's Internet, experienced rapid growing pains and needed a distributed naming service that could be used to locate the address of any server in the network.

◀◀   You can read more about the Domain Name System (DNS) in Chapter 30, "Network Name Resolution."

The Internet has grown so large in the past years that, without a distributed naming service, it would be almost impossible to keep track of all nodes in the network, much less the services they offer. DNS has evolved to contain many types of records that can be used to translate names to addresses. These include not only names of servers or workstations on the Net, but also services, such as the World Wide Web and email.

Dynamic DNS

Administering a large number of computers in a network can be quite a chore. Moving a computer from one network subnet to another used to require that the administrator manually reconfigure the DNS servers in the enterprise so that he or she could accurately translate the computer's name to its correct address. With the advent of mobile computing and the proliferation of laptops that are here today, gone tomorrow, reconfiguring network addresses can become a full-time job on a large network.

The Dynamic Host Configuration Protocol (DHCP) solves part of this problem by allowing a computer to request a network address, along with other configuration information, when it boots into the network. However, this doesn't completely solve the problems that arise as the result of mobile computing. After the client computer has obtained network address and configuration information, how does it communicate that information to other computers so that they can locate it on the network?

◄◄ You can read more about DHCP in Chapter 29, "BOOTP and Dynamic Host Configuration Protocol (DHCP)."

In early versions of Windows NT, the Windows Internet Naming Service (WINS) was the answer to this problem. After a computer boots, it can contact a WINS server, which acts very much like a dynamic DNS server. It accepts registrations from clients and stores or updates their information so that other computers can query the database to find the client's network address.

In Windows 2000/Server 2003, you still can use the WINS service, which might be helpful for legacy Windows clients if you have a mixed network of Windows 2000 and earlier Windows NT computers. However, Windows 2000 and Windows Server 2003 come with an updated version of Microsoft's DNS, which includes the capability to dynamically update the DNS database. In fact, using DNS is the method that clients in an all Windows 2000/Server 2003 network use to locate domain controllers in the network.

Note

Dynamic updates to the DNS database are defined in RFC 2136. This RFC defines the UPDATE opcode and a format to be used as the update message, along with procedures that can be used to implement dynamic DNS. Dynamic DNS has been gaining acceptance with vendors of other operating systems. Thus, you might be able to use a DNS server from another operating system within your Windows network.

How the Active Directory Uses DNS

The Active Directory uses DNS to keep track of domain controllers. DNS is used as a locator service as well as a name/address translation service. Remember that the Active Directory provides a service to its users through the LDAP protocol. Services can be recorded in DNS through Service Resource Records (SRV RRs), and this is how the Active Directory uses DNS.

Note

SRV Service Resource Records are defined by RFC 2052, "A DNS RR for Specifying the Location of Services (DNS SRV)," by Gulbrandsen and Vixie.

An SRV RR record consists of data in this format:

`service name.protocol.domain`

Because the Active Directory uses LDAP, a resource record for this service would look like this:

`LDAP.TCP.twoinc.com`

Because the DNS that is provided with Windows is a dynamic DNS, there is no associated administrative work when you add domain controllers to your network. Each domain controller automatically contacts a DNS server and provides it with the necessary information to register its name, its address, and the services it offers. Each domain controller also checks back at frequent intervals to be sure that the information is accurate and will make changes to the DNS information as changes are made on the server.

One thing to note about the use of DNS as a locator service is that you do not have to use Microsoft's own DNS server to have an Active Directory–enabled network. The DNS product you use, however, *must* support SRV records, because this is how domain controllers advertise themselves to the network. The DNS server you use does not have to use dynamic DNS functions, however. This just makes the DNS administrator's life a lot easier in a rapidly changing environment.

Using Sites to Manage Large Enterprises

In Windows 2000/2003 a site is nothing more than a collection of well-connected computers that exist on an IP subnet, and that usually are located close to each other geographically. The grouping of computers into sites is done to make replication fast and efficient. It is not a concept that relates to managing or administering users, resources, or network security. The following are two important things to remember about a site, as used by Windows:

- A domain can have computers in more than one site.
- A site can contain computers from more than one domain.

Windows 2000/2003 uses only domain controllers to hold the Active Directory database. *There is no longer a primary domain controller that controls writing or modifying directory information and backup domain controllers that provide a read-only service to users and computers.* In Windows, all domain controllers can receive updates to the database, and the changes then are replicated to all other domain controllers that participate in the directory tree.

The Knowledge Consistency Checker service is run on every domain controller, and it is this service that establishes connections with other domain controllers within the site to be sure that directory replication can occur. Although the administrator can configure connections manually, the consistency checker will automatically establish new connections when it determines that there is a hole in the replication topology within a site.

The administrative tool that is used to control how servers participate in directory replication is the Active Directory Sites and Services Manager. This MMC snap-in allows you to

- Add new sites and subnets and associate a site name with a subnet
- Show all the sites that exist throughout the enterprise
- Show all the servers that are contained in each site
- Create and display the links between servers and the links between sites, including the protocols that are used for replication
- Show the timing values used to schedule replication
- Manage subnets

Note

Sites are represented in the Active Directory database and are defined by the site object. Although all computers in the directory have a computer object, domain controllers also have a server object. This server object is a child object of the site object that represents the site to which the domain controller is assigned.

Directory Replication

LDAP v3.0 is the current LDAP Internet standard. For the Windows implementation of directory services, Microsoft uses a proprietary method called multimaster replication, because there is not yet a standard method for replication between LDAP directory servers. However, RFC 3384 is an informational RFC that does specify requirements for replication of LDAP information. Time will tell whether an Internet standard is developed, and whether Microsoft adopts it.

In Windows NT, *primary domain controllers (PDCs)* were responsible for updates to the directory database (the old SAM). Additions or modifications to the database were made on the PDC and at regular intervals replicated to backup domain controllers throughout the network. The most obvious disadvantage this system has is that without a PDC, no changes can be made to the database. When a PDC becomes unavailable, because of its own failure or possible network link failure, users still can log on because they can be authenticated by a BDC. However, if you have a large enterprise, perhaps a global one, it is almost necessary to have a PDC at every geographical site where frequent changes occur, or to have an extremely good network infrastructure.

Using the Active Directory, any domain controller can receive updates or additions to the Active Directory database. These changes are propagated to other domain controllers based on *update sequence numbers (USNs)*. The USN is a 64-bit number used by the Active Directory to determine which updates are the most recent. In addition to the server's USN, each property (or attribute) in the database has its own property version number. These two numbers are used by multimaster replication to ensure that updates are correctly applied throughout the enterprise.

Because all replicas of the directory database can be written to, it is possible that a change can be made before a previous change has been fully replicated throughout the enterprise. Some directory databases use timestamps to determine which update is the most recent. This method requires that every server be tightly synchronized with all other servers with respect to the correct time. Windows 2000 does provide a time service that can be used to synchronize servers, but with one exception: The timestamp is not the method used to determine which is the correct update to apply to a directory update message.

Each server in a network has its own USN, which it advances when it makes an update to the directory. Each server also stores a table of USNs—the highest USN it has received during previous replications from each server in the network. When replication starts, a server requests from other servers only those changes that have a higher USN than the one it has stored for each server during previous replication sessions. This minimizes the amount of information that needs to be exchanged between servers during the replication procedure. Because each server knows exactly which changes it has received from every other server in the network, replication between servers is efficient.

This method also allows a server to recover quickly when it crashes or some other failure, such as a network failure, occurs. All it must do is request updates that are greater than the USN it has stored for the other servers in the network. This means that a full replication between servers is not necessary in the event of a catastrophe.

Property version numbers come into play when a specific attribute is modified on more than one replica of the database within a short period, before the replication service can update the change on all nodes. Remember that with the Active Directory's distributed nature, each domain controller holds a writable copy of the directory database. A property version number is incremented only on the server on which the change is actually made. It is not incremented on a server that is receiving it as an update.

The only time a timestamp is used during multimaster replication is when a collision occurs. This happens when a server receives an update message from another server, and although the property version numbers are the same, the contents of the attribute are not. In this case, and only in this case, the timestamp on the update is used. If the update message has a timestamp later than the value stored with the property, the update is applied to the data; otherwise, it is discarded.

Summarizing the Directory Data Using the Global Catalog

The Active Directory is scalable to millions of objects. The directory is partitioned into domains, because it would be very difficult to store a complete copy of the entire directory database on a single server. Of course, with the advances being made in CPU speed and storage capabilities, this might be possible in the future, but for now it is not practical.

One of the assumptions behind the partitioning of the directory is the fact that most queries that are made to the directory are for local information. Users generally want to locate a printer or another resource that is near them. Occasionally, it might be desirable to locate a printer that resides in a different geographical location, but for the most part, queries are for local resources.

To satisfy a query for information that cannot be found in the local portion of the Active Directory, it is necessary to query every other partition of the directory until the information is found. This too can be an impractical method. In a large enterprise, moderate use of this type of query, whereby the entire database is searched, could cause significant network and CPU resource consumption.

The *global catalog* is the answer that Microsoft has implemented to solve this problem. The global catalog is a *subset* of the entire directory. It holds entries for every object that exists in all partitions of the directory, but it contains only *selected attributes* for each object. If your query cannot be satisfied by querying the global catalog, the query will have to be resolved by searching a portion of, or possibly the entire, directory database.

Active Directory Service Interfaces (ADSI)

To make it easy to directory-enable any application, Microsoft has provided Active Directory Service Interfaces (ADSI). ADSI is a collection of several interfaces that can be used to access the Active Directory from within executable application programs. Programmers might want to use ADSI instead of the LDAP C API because ADSI makes it possible to write an application that can access directory services from multiple providers. If the directory service provider has designed its directory service product to be compliant with at least version 2.0 of LDAP, ADSI should be capable of providing an interface into the directory. The current version of ADSI is 2.5, and it is included with Windows 2000/2003.

In addition to providing access to Microsoft directory products, such as Exchange Server 5.5, ADSI has been tested by Microsoft against the following:

- Netscape Directory Server 1.0
- University of Michigan's SLAPD Server
- Novell's LDAP-enabled NDS product

ADSI provides an interface that allows all the functionality of the LDAP C API, but does so in a manner that is easier to understand and write code for. Another reason for using ADSI in application development is that ADSI can be used by many higher-level programming languages, including Microsoft Visual BASIC, Perl, Rexx, and C or C++.

ADSI uses the Component Object Model (COM) interface to allow programmers to access and manipulate the underlying directory objects found in multiple directory services. A program written using ADSI should function correctly with any directory service for which ADSI has a provider interface.

Directory-Aware Application Programming

ADSI is one of the features of Microsoft's development of Active Directory Services that might benefit large enterprises the greatest. If the Active Directory were limited to specific types of objects or attributes that could be stored in the directory, and if only programs supplied by Microsoft were able to access and manipulate the directory store, there wouldn't be much to say about Active Directory beyond its being a major improvement in the administration of Windows servers and clients.

However, if it's properly employed, using ADSI to incorporate application program configuration information into the directory database along with other types of data can produce real cost benefits in a large network. For example:

- Many applications use similar configuration information that is duplicated in each application's specific configuration data file (or, possibly Registry entries). Information about computers and locales can be stored in the directory, along with other configuration information, and shared by many applications.

- Shared information that already is stored in the directory can be shared by ADSI-aware applications. User information already is stored in user objects in the Active Directory. By extending this object and adding attributes, you can create a customized user object that can be used by applications unique to your environment. Eliminating redundant resources of information also can help ensure a greater accuracy in your database because data must be updated only once in a single location.

- Applications that depend on central configuration databases found on servers in the network can benefit from reduced downtime. If a server that contains configuration data files goes offline, clients must wait for the server to return to working order. If the clients use the Active Directory, replicas of the directory can be configured so that the loss of a server no longer is a point of failure.

- Applications can "publish" themselves in the Active Directory, listing the services that they can give to clients and the information needed to use the service. In a volatile network in which users move frequently, reconfiguring applications can be simplified by having the application programmed to locate the information it needs for the new locale.

Many types of applications can benefit from using the Active Directory. Human resource departments and security departments can share a common user database resource by storing information in the directory. System management products can be written to access the information already contained in directory user and computer objects.

Now It's Just Domain Controllers and Member Servers

When you create a domain controller for a Windows 2000/2003 Server, you are no longer required to do so during the installation of the operating system, which was the case with Windows NT. And to make things even easier, you no longer must create primary and backup domain controllers. In Windows 2000/Server 2003, no distinction is made as to primary or backup domain controllers. Instead, each domain controller in a domain (and there can be as many as you need) holds a complete copy of the domain's partition of the Active Directory. Updates can be made at any domain controller, and updates are propagated using multimaster replication to all other domain controllers in the domain.

Remember that in the Active Directory domain, names are expressed as DNS-style names. That is, instead of naming a domain acme, for example, it is now named acme.com, which is a DNS-style name. When you create a tree of domains in the Active Directory, you must use a hierarchical DNS naming scheme so that you maintain a contiguous namespace.

Each domain in the tree is a subdomain of the topmost domain. The domain tree provides a two-way transitive trust relationship between all domains that exist in the tree. Inheritance of security rights flows downward from the top of the tree, so you can assign users administrative access rights and permissions at a single point in the tree, and therefore grant them the same rights for child objects farther down the tree.

When you have a network that is composed of disparate namespaces, you can create separate trees and group them into a forest. Recall that a forest is a collection of domain trees. In this type of organization, each domain tree represents a contiguous namespace, but other disjointed namespaces are in the network. A domain forest is used in a similar manner to a domain tree, in that users can still be granted access rights in domains that are contained in other domain trees. The main difference between a domain tree and a forest is the disjointed namespaces.

The Active Directory Schema

The schema in the Active Directory is stored in the directory. The schema comes preconfigured with the types of objects that you need in order to set up the Windows 2000/2003 Server and manage a network of computers. However, the Active Directory is flexible and extensible in that you can modify the existing objects to use new attributes, or you can create new object classes that contain almost any kind of information.

In addition to the typical objects that you will use to manage the directory and user and network resources, the directory contains hundreds of other objects that are used for many of the applications that interact with it.

The directory should not be thought of as simply a glorified user database. You can create objects that are used by application programs. Sharing information between different applications can become much easier if the same configuration database is being used. Rather than having a conversion utility of some sort to transfer information between different applications, they now can be written, using the application programming interfaces provided for the Active Directory, to store that information in the directory database.

Modifying the Active Directory Schema

You can add objects or attributes to store data in the directory that is shared by different applications so that you do not need duplicate databases scattered around that get out of sync with constant updating. Extending the schema to include additional employee information, such as vacation schedules, sick time, and pay rates, can allow payroll applications to share the same data with other employee management software. The accounting and legal departments always can be sure they are working with the same set of data if there are no duplicate databases being used that can become unsynchronized because of an application failure or a simple user error.

The MMC snap-in that you use to examine or modify the schema is called the Active Directory Schema Snap-In. Unlike other MMC snap-in tools, such as the Active Directory Computers and Users Management Snap-Ins, this one is not found under the Administrative Tools option in the Start menu, by default. The reasoning behind that is simple: Tools that are used to add or modify user or computer accounts probably will be used frequently by the network administrator. Making changes to the schema probably will be performed only on rare occasions, such as when a new object or attribute is needed by the development of a new directory-aware application.

In just about every book or article you read about modifying the Windows Registry, you are cautioned that making changes can be a dangerous thing. One little mistake in a Registry edit can render a server unbootable. You should take editing the Active Directory Schema just as seriously. First, look through the directory to see whether an object class already exists that you can use before you begin creating new object classes (or attributes for that matter) on-the-fly.

Installing the Windows 2000 Administration Tools

After you've installed Windows 2000 Server (or Advanced Server), or versions of Windows Server 2003, you can install, using the same source CD, the Windows Administration Tools. To install these additional tools, you must be logged in to the server as an administrator.

Note

Before you can install the Windows 2000/Server 2003 Administration Tools, you first must exit any other tools that are included in the Administrative Tools folder. For example, if you are running the MMC Snap-In Active Directory Computers and Users Management, exit the application before beginning to install these additional tools. If you do not, the results of the installation will be unpredictable. The installation might succeed, or it might not. If it does, the tools might not work correctly after you've finished the installation. As with any application installation, it's also a good idea to exit any other programs that are running on the computer before you begin to install these additional administration tools.

You can use the same source and steps described in the following text to install the administrative tools on Windows 2000 Professional (though there a few differences in the dialog boxes). And if you're running Windows XP, you can download from **www.microsoft.com** the **adminpak.msi**, or install the tools from the Server 2003 CD. Note, however, that the admin pak may not run on Windows XP. If this is the case with your version of XP, search the Microsoft Web site (**www.microsoft.com**) and download the patch named **q329357_WXP_SP1_x86_ENU.exe**. For more information about this, see the Knowledge Base article 329357.

When you are ready to install the additional tools from the Windows Server 2003 CD, follow these steps:

1. Insert the Windows Server 2003 source CD into your computer's CD-ROM drive. When the autorun Microsoft Windows Server 2004 CD window appears onscreen, click Perform Additional Tasks and then Browse This CD.

2. In the next window, you will see a list of folders that exist on the CD. Double-click the I386 folder.

3. In the I386 folder, double-click `Adminpak.msi`. The Windows 2003 Administration Tools Setup Wizard appears. Click Next.

4. The wizard copies the required files to your hard drive, and then displays an informational window telling you that the tools were successfully installed. Click Finish.

After you've installed the additional tools, you can run the Microsoft Management Console and add the Active Directory Schema Snap-In.

Adding the Active Directory Schema Snap-In to the MMC

Adding snap-ins to the MMC is simple. For Windows 2000 and Windows Server 2003, simply click Start, Run, and then enter `mmc /a` in the Open: field. Note that there is a space after `mmc` before the `/a` switch. Click OK.

When the MMC Console screen appears (shown in Figure 31.3), with only the Console Root in the left pane, use the following steps:

1. Click once on the File menu at the top of the MMC. From the menu that appears, select Add/Remove Snap-In. The Add/Remove Snap-In dialog box appears.

2. Click the Add button in this dialog box and the Add Standalone Snap-In dialog box (see Figure 31.4) appears, listing all the types of snap-ins available for your use.

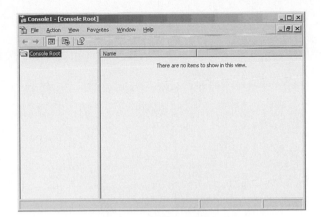

Figure 31.3   You'll need to add a snap-in to the empty MMC.

Figure 31.4   Select the Active Directory Schema Snap-In to add to the console.

3. Select Active Directory Schema and click the Add button.

4. The Add/Remove Snap-In dialog box reappears, but now you'll see that the Active Directory Schema Snap-In appears in the dialog box. Click the Close button. When the MMC reappears, you'll see that the Active Directory Schema Snap-In is now available under the Console Root, ready for you to use (see Figure 31.5).

You can now start using the snap-in. However, if you think you might want to use it again soon, click on File and then Save. This saves the console as a tool in the Administrative Tools folder so that you won't have to go through all this trouble again. Note that the default filename is Console1.msc. It would probably be more helpful to choose a name such as Modify Schema.msc so that you will recognize this new MMC snap-in utility in the future.

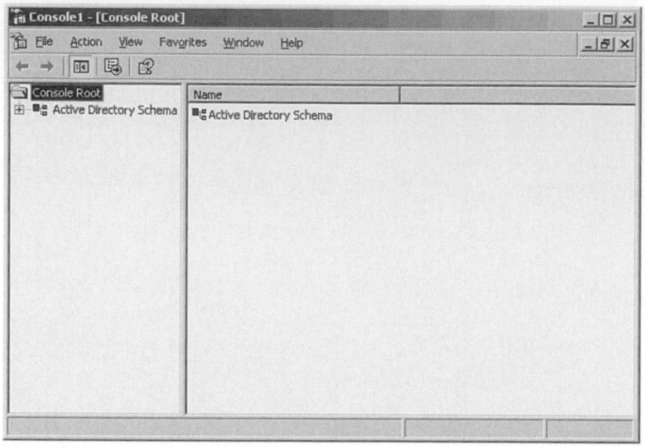

Figure 31.5 The MMC console now has the Active Directory Snap-In installed and ready to use.

Before You Use the Active Directory Schema Master

Before you begin to use the Active Directory Schema Snap-In, you should be aware of two important concepts. First, remember that a domain tree exists in a forest. The forest can contain a single domain tree, which is a single contiguous namespace, or it can contain multiple domain trees. Throughout a forest, however, a single domain controller is in charge of making changes to the schema that is shared by the forest. This domain controller is known as the Schema master domain controller. You can connect to this domain controller to make changes to the schema, or you can enable any domain controller to be the schema master.

Second, each object in the schema is uniquely identified by an object identifier, which is nothing more than a dotted-decimal number issued by some naming authority. Each attribute in the directory also is uniquely identified by an identifier. If you are operating in an environment where you will only use the Active Directory for internal network use and will never need to interact with any other LDAP/X.500 directory, you can more or less create your own object identifiers. However, consider what happens if your business acquires another business and you both use directory-based networking systems. To import or export information from one directory to another, or simply to join a domain tree from another business you've acquired, all your object IDs must be unique, and you should obtain them from a responsible source.

In the United States, the registration authority for this is the American National Standards Institute (ANSI). Other countries have an equivalent registration authority. The national registration authority issues the root object IDs for an enterprise. To obtain unique object IDs from Microsoft, refer to `http://msdn.microsoft.com/library/en-us/netdir/ad/obtaining_an_object_identifier_from_microsoft.asp?frame=true`.

Using the Active Directory Schema Snap-In

Using the Active Directory Schema Snap-In is not complicated. Being sure that you know how objects and attributes are related to each other—and the organization of your domain tree and the forest in which it resides—can, however, be quite complicated. You'll probably remember that in the movie *The Wizard of Oz*, there's a sign on the Yellow Brick Road that says "I'd go back if I were you." Don't proceed unless you fully understand the changes you are about to make. Because the schema applies to the entire forest—that is, to every domain tree and every domain in every domain tree—you can potentially not only render a single computer nonfunctional, but make the entire network unusable if you are not sure about the changes you are going to make.

Note

This section is intended to demonstrate how an administrator can use the Active Directory Schema Snap-In to modify the directory schema. You also can modify the schema by using LDAP Data Interchange Format (LDIF) scripts and by writing programs using tools supplied by Microsoft. Both of these methods are beyond the scope of this chapter. However, you can find out more about them by visiting the Microsoft Developer's Network Web site at `http://msdn.microsoft.com`.

When you are ready to make modifications to the schema, you must be logged in using an account that is a member of the Schema Admins group.

▶▶ For more information about how to place a user account into a group, see Chapter 41.

To begin, right-click Active Directory Schema in the MMC console that you created. From the menu that appears, click The Schema May Be Modified on This Domain Controller. This makes this domain controller the schema master.

Double-click on Active Directory Schema in the left pane of the MMC and you'll see that the schema has two folders under it: Classes and Attributes (see Figure 31.6).

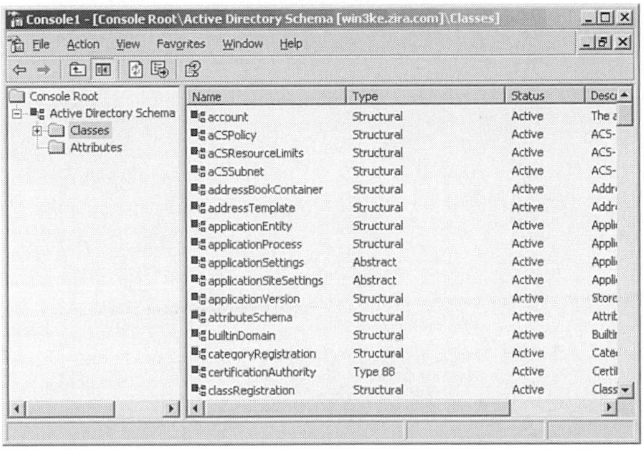

Figure 31.6 You can expand the tree structure to show the classes that currently exist in the Active Directory.

If you double-click on Classes, the tree structure will expand to show you the classes that already exist in the Active Directory (also shown in Figure 31.6). Many of these have unfamiliar names and should be an indication to you of how complex the Active Directory really is and why you should educate yourself thoroughly before making any changes to it.

Likewise, if you double-click on the Attributes folder, you'll get a display of all the attributes available in the Active Directory (see Figure 31.7). In this figure, you can see that the attribute named accountExpires, which can be used, for example, in a user account object, has a syntax of Large Integer. Other attributes have different syntaxes, as shown in this figure.

You can view the details about a particular object or attribute by double-clicking on it or by right-clicking and selecting Properties from the pop-up menu. For example, Figure 31.8 shows the Properties sheet for the OrganizationalPerson object class. This is the object type that is used to store user accounts in the Active Directory. Notice that there are no mandatory attributes for this object, but there are a large number of optional attributes.

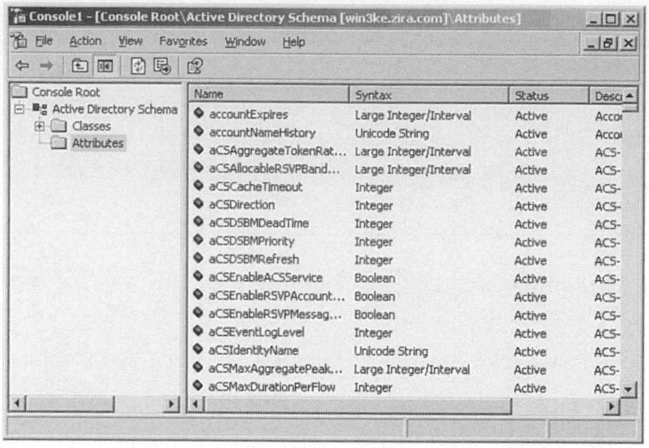

Figure 31.7   The list of attributes that make up objects can be displayed using this snap-in.

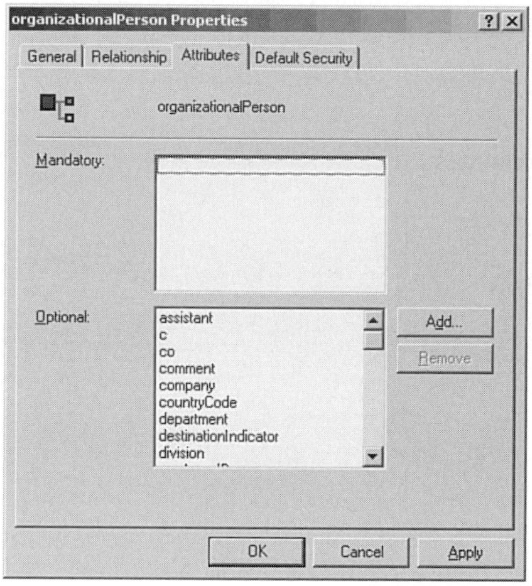

Figure 31.8   The Properties sheet shows the attributes for this object.

In Figure 31.8, you can see that for each object you can have attributes that are either optional or mandatory. All objects in the directory of a particular class must each have values for all the attributes required by the object class. The optional attributes can be used if you need them.

In the case of the OrganizationalPerson class, there are no required attributes. This is not the case with all classes, however. For example, in Figure 31.9, you can see that the PrintQueue class has five mandatory attributes that will be created for any object you create using this class. Additionally, there are various optional attributes you can also add to an object you create using this class. Keep in mind that classes and their attributes are merely templates. When you create an object in the Active Directory, you choose what class to use, and an object is created. The class that the object is derived from is not changed.

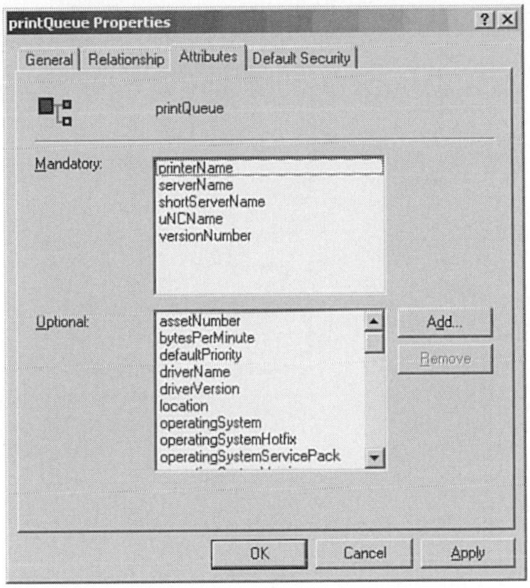

Figure 31.9 The PrintQueue object contains both mandatory and additional attributes.

In Figure 31.7, you saw a partial list of the attributes that are defined in the directory. You can use the scrollbar to scroll through the entire list to locate attributes. When you modify or create a new object in the schema, you can select from these attributes or create a new attribute. To create a new attribute, right-click on the Attributes folder in the left pane of the MMC and select New and then Attribute. A warning will pop up letting you know that adding an attribute is permanent, and you will not be able to delete it later. However, you will be able to "disable" the attribute if you no longer want to use it. Each attribute has a particular syntax associated with it, which defines the type of data that the attribute can hold. Figure 31.10 shows the dialog box associated with creating a new attribute with the syntax field expanded. As you can probably determine from this, modifying the schema requires that you fully understand what you are doing.

Caution

Even though I said it earlier in this chapter, it bears repeating: Modifying the schema is not a task that should be delegated to an uninformed employee or done simply for convenience. It is easy to add new objects and attributes whenever you want. However, if you are not intimately familiar with the directory, you might find that over time, you have added superfluous duplicate entries. If the same information can be stored in more than one attribute, it makes searching the directory much more difficult because you have to know all the duplicate attributes to search.

Disabling an object or attribute from the directory is also not something that should be done casually. If your organization creates internal application programs that are written to use ADSI to interface with the directory, you should be sure to implement a program that tracks changes to the schema so that you can always quickly ascertain the uses of a particular customized object or attribute.

As when editing the Registry, you should be extremely careful when making changes to the Active Directory schema. Plan your changes in advance, create a checklist of what you want to do, and then perform the steps methodically. If another class or attribute can be used to store the data you need to place into the Active Directory, consider that choice instead of creating additional classes or attributes.

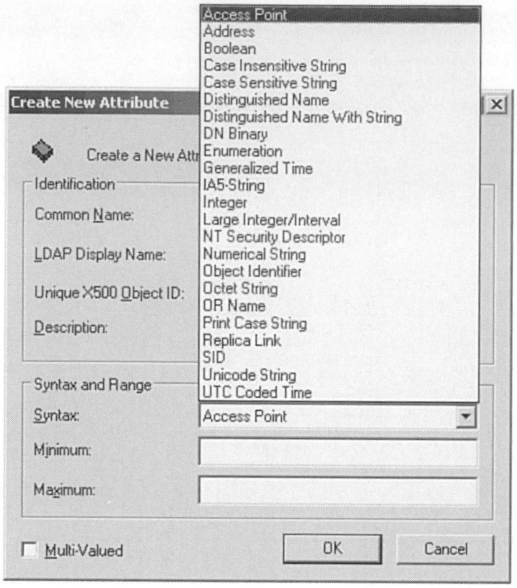

Figure 31.10   It's easy to add new attributes using the Schema Manager.

You can add a new Schema object class almost as easily as you can modify an existing class. To add a new class, right-click the Classes folder in the left pane of the MMC Active Directory Schema Snap-In, right-click on Classes, and select New and then Class. After a similar warning message appears, click Continue. The Create New Schema Class dialog box appears (see Figure 31.11).

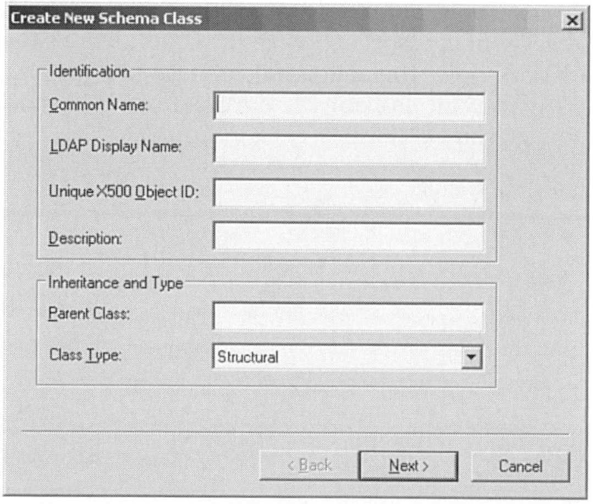

Figure 31.11   You can create a new object class in the Active Directory using this dialog box.

As you can see, you'll have to supply a common name (CN), an LDAP display name, and a unique object ID for the class. If you want to create a class that is similar to an existing class, you can use the Parent Class field under the Inheritance and Type section of the dialog box to specify the class from which your new class will inherit a set of attributes that have already been defined. You can use the Class Type drop-down menu to specify the type of class you are creating.

The next dialog box allows you to enter the mandatory (required) and optional attributes for the class you are creating. When you've finished selecting these attributes, click the Finish button.

Finding Objects in the Active Directory

If you've gotten this far into this chapter without falling asleep, it's time to put your knowledge to work. That is to say, it's time to get practical and look at a few things you can accomplish using the Active Directory.

When viewing the property pages for a user account in the directory, you see that you can add much more information than was possible before. There are eight tabs on the properties page for a user object.

If you select each tab and look at the different fields, you can see that the user object now contains a wealth of information that can be quickly accessed by searching the directory, including the following:

- **Who Is This User?**—The user's full name, the user's logon name, and a description of the user. The user's title, department, company, manager, and reporting information.
- **Address**—The office in which the user can be found, the user's address.
- **Telephone**—Phone numbers, fax numbers, pagers, mobile phone, IP phone, email addresses, and home page URLs.
- **Logon**—Which servers the user can log on to, during which hours, password information, and expiration and account information. The user's profile, logon path, and home directory.
- **Dial-In**—Whether this user can log on using remote access, and from where. Callback options and addressing information.
- **Groups**—User groups to which this user belongs.

Note

The Active Directory schema, which defines the objects and their attributes, can be extended. For example, if you install a product such as the newest version of Microsoft Exchange Server, you might see additional attributes in the user, as well as other objects.

The main benefit of having this information available in the directory might not become apparent at first. Most of this information could have been found in the old User Manager utility, in the Remote Access Administration utility, or in the human resources department. But now it all can be centrally located in a global, searchable directory. With the proper rights and permissions, the administrator or user can search the directory for any of the attributes associated with users. And because the Active Directory schema can be extended, you can add additional attributes that contain information specific to your business.

Finding a User Account

For example, instead of being limited to queries such as "Show me everything about user John Doe," you now can execute queries such as "Show me all users that work in the accounting department in Florida" or "Show me all users who work in the accounting department in Florida that are in the Administrators group and have dial-in access."

If you look at the total number of attributes associated with the user object, it's quite large. For example, suppose you want to "find" a user in the Active Directory. It's a simple thing to do by using the Active Directory Users and Computers MMC Snap-In in the Administrative Tools Folder. For example:

1. Click Start, Administrative Tools, and then click Active Directory Users and Computers.

2. In the left pane of the MMC console, highlight the domain you want to search and select Find. In Figure 31.12, you can see the Find Users, Contacts, and Groups dialog box that is used to search the directory for these sorts of objects.

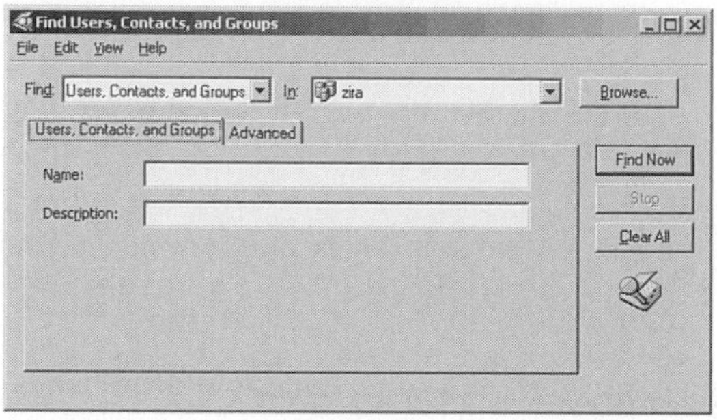

Figure 31.12   You can easily search the entire directory for a user or user group using this dialog box.

3. To find a user, simply enter the name or a description. If you want to narrow the search, use the In field. Here, you can select to perform the search throughout the entire directory, or a specific container object, such as a domain. Then, simply click the Find Now button.

If that all seems too simple, it is. This simple search function on the User, Contacts, and Groups tab enables you to perform a search by specifying just a little information.

Even though we've invoked the "find" dialog box in the Active Directory Users and Computers tool, you still can search for other objects in the directory. After we finish going over how to search for a user object, we'll use a similar dialog box, for example, to search for a printer. As you can see, other objects you can search for include the following:

- Users, contacts, and groups
- Computers
- Printers
- Shared folders
- Organizational units
- Custom search

The next field (named In) is also a drop-down menu, which enables you to further specify the container object, such as a domain, that you want to search. If you already know in what domain a user account exists, narrowing the search using this field will save time. Finally, when you've entered a user's name, and/or a description, and narrowed the search to the container object in which you want to look, click the Find Now button.

However, to show you the power of the search capability in the Active Directory, let's use the Advanced tab. In Figure 31.13, you can see the same dialog box, with the Advanced tab selected. Here, the Field drop-down menu enables you to refine your search criteria to a user, a group, or a contact.

Notice in Figure 31.13, however, that when you click on User in the Field menu, a whole range of attributes is displayed that you can use to specify the search criteria. The number of attributes is so large that it won't fit on my computer screen, so there's a down arrow at the bottom that can be used to select even more attributes. There are actually more than 60 attributes you can use to specify search criteria, from the simple username, telephone number (and mobile telephone number), to the Web page address for a user or the manager of the user. Of course, the search will succeed only if you actually use these fields when you create user accounts. You don't have to fill in every attribute when you create a new user. However, the more information you store in the directory about a user, the easier it's going to be to locate that user when you have only a little information to go on.

Figure 31.13 The Field menu enables you to search for a user, group, or contact using the Advanced tab.

After you specify an attribute, you can enter a value that will be used for the search in the Value field. Use the Condition field to specify how this value will be evaluated in the search. These are the conditions you can set for this attribute's value in the search:

- Starts with
- Ends with
- Is (exactly)
- Is not
- Present
- Not present

As you add search criteria (an attribute, a selection condition, and a value to use for comparison in the search), they appear in the pane at the bottom of the dialog box.

After you have specified values for the attributes to be used for the advanced search, click the Find Now button. Next the dialog box expands to add another pane, which displays the results of the search.

One or more entries can show up in the results pane, depending on the search conditions you used. To view the detailed attributes for objects in the results pane, simply double-click an entry and a property sheet appears for the object.

Finding a Printer in the Active Directory

The directory doesn't just contain information about users; it holds information about many resource types in the network. An object that represents a printer resource might contain the name of the printer, the type of hardware associated with it, and its location. With directory services you do not even have to know the name of a printer. You can execute a query such as "Show me all printers located on the third floor of the accounting department in the Florida office," and then pick the printer you want to use, based on the information returned from the query.

For example, in a Windows Server 2003 network that has the Active Directory enabled, you'll find that there's a button (Find) on the Print dialog box that wasn't there in previous versions of Windows NT. This button first appeared in Windows 2000.

Note

To locate a printer in the Active Directory, you must first "publish" the printer (which basically means to put the information about the printer into the directory). Windows XP and Windows Server 2003 make this a simple process. After you create a printer, select its properties pages. On the Sharing tab select List in the directory.

When you click Find Printer, a dialog box similar to the one used to search for users pops up. This should be an indication to you that the Active Directory is tightly integrated into the Windows 2000 and Server 2003 operating systems.

At the top of this dialog box, use the In drop-down menu to narrow your search. For example, you can use the default to search the entire directory, or you can use this menu to specify a particular domain or other container object.

There are three tabs on the Find Printers dialog box that you can use for a search:

- **Printers**—If you know the name, location, or model of the printer you want to find, you can specify it on this tab and click Find Now.

- **Features**—This tab enables you to specify attributes the printer must have, such as whether it can print double-sided (duplex printing) or whether it is a color printer. You also can select the resolution, the printer speed, and whether the printer can staple the document after it's printed, among other features, depending on the capabilities of the particular printer.

- **Advanced**—This tab works in the same way that the Find Users dialog box worked. You can use the Field drop-down menu to specify any of the attributes associated with the Printer object, and then specify a condition and a value to be used for the search.

After you've specified the search criteria using any of these tabs, click the Find Now button and you'll get a listing of the printers that match your search. You then can select which printer to use.

After you've found the printer you want to use, it's a simple matter to make a connection to the printer. In the search Results pane, just right-click on the printer and select Connect. Or, if you're in a real hurry, just double-click on the printer in the Results pane.

The Active Directory is accessible from within many other applications in Windows 2000. You can search for file shares and objects that you create yourself. The important thing to remember about the Active Directory is that, after you begin to use it in your network, it is not something to be taken lightly. Use caution when making modifications to the directory.

Using Start/Search

In the previous examples, we searched for users by using an Administrative Tool—the Active Directory Users and Computers Snap-In. To search for a printer, we used the Find Printer button on the print dialog box. However, there is a simpler way to find almost anything in the directory, provided that your logon account has the necessary access permissions to locate the object. Simply click Start and then Search.

The Search function in Windows 2000 Server and Professional is found from the Windows Start menu and allows you to

- Search for files or folders
- Search the Internet
- Search for printers
- Search using Microsoft Outlook
- Search for people

If you use the For Printers or the For People options in the menu, you'll get dialog boxes similar to the ones used in the examples earlier in this chapter.

Thus, the Active Directory is not just a tool that can be used by administrative personnel to administer the network, but it also is something that can be used by everyday users to locate objects or information they need to perform their jobs.

Windows Server 2003: New Active Directory Features

The examples in this chapter were based on the Active Directory installed on a Windows 2003 computer. With the release of Windows Server 2003, there are some new features that will make administration of the directory a simpler task. Some of these include the following:

- The Active Directory Migration Tool (ADMT) now copies passwords for user accounts when upgrading from Windows NT 4.0 (with Service Pack 2) and Windows 2000 Servers.
- You can now rename domains (except for the root domain in a tree) in the Active Directory.
- Although you can't delete system classes or attributes, you can now deactivate classes or attributes.
- The Microsoft Group Policy Management Console (GPMC) makes it easier to manage group policies by giving you a single MMC tool that includes capabilities that were previously contained in several other tools.
- You can create queries to the database and save them for use later.
- The MMC interface lets you select multiple objects at the same time to make editing objects an easier task.
- A user account can exist in one forest, with the computer account created in another forest. The user needs only to log on once to gain access, preserving the single sign-on. This is called Cross-Forest Authentication.
- Cross-Forest Authentication enables the administrator to select users and groups from a trusted forest and place them into a local group.
- If you have a domain controller located at a branch office, and the data link to the main office becomes unavailable, cached data at the remote office can be used to authenticate users and access resources until the link is restored.

You can learn more about these new features at www.microsoft.com, by searching for Windows Server 2003. The preceding list contains only a few of the additions to the Active Directory, and a brief description of what they do. If you operate an enterprise-wide network, these new features can be of great importance when managing multiple domains, trees, sites, and forests.

For a smaller network, in which a single forest is used, these tools may prove useful, but the standard MMC tools should be sufficient.

Installing the Active Directory on a Windows Server 2003 Computer

The previous sections of this chapter enabled you to understand how the Active Directory works with Windows Server 2003 (and in a similar manner, to the AD that comes with Windows 2000). Now that you understand the principles behind the Active Directory, you can choose whether to install it. This section gives you an example of how to install the Active Directory on a Windows Server 2003 operating system. The example here is based on the Enterprise edition, but it should be the same or similar for all other Windows 2003 servers (other than the Web edition).

To install the Active Directory on Windows Server 2003, follow these steps:

1. In Figure 31.14 you can see the first window that the Configure Your Server Wizard pops up after the installation is finished and you have logged on using the Administrator account.

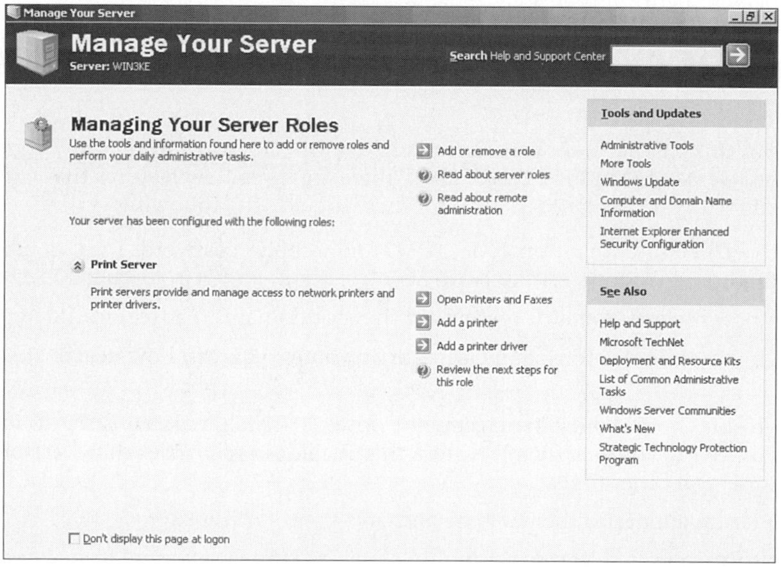

Figure 31.14   In Windows Server 2003 you can select one or more roles that the computer will be used for in the network.

Tip

If the current server is using DHCP to obtain an IP address, you should change this to a static address before continuing. The Active Directory computer is also a domain controller, and this requires a static address. If you do not assign a static address, you will be prompted to do so later in the Active Directory installation process.

2. When you click on the Add or Remove a Role button, the next window lists preliminary steps you should perform before continuing to select a role (see Figure 31.15). For example, if you will use a modem or another peripheral device, they should be installed. Because this computer will host the Active Directory, and provide AD services to clients on a network, you need to be sure that you have one or more network cards installed.

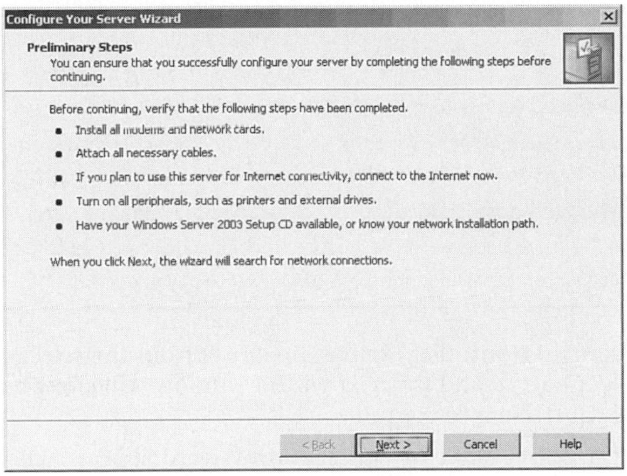

Figure 31.15 These steps should be performed before you select a role for your Windows Server 2003 computer.

At this point you will need to have a connection to the Internet and have the Windows 2003 CD available—or know the network path that holds the Windows 2003 setup files. This is necessary because some roles, such as the Domain Name System (DNS) or the Active Directory will require copying additional files to your computer.

3. When you click the Next button, the wizard makes sure that you are connected to a local network or the Internet. If this is the case, the next window the wizard displays is the one shown in Figure 31.16.

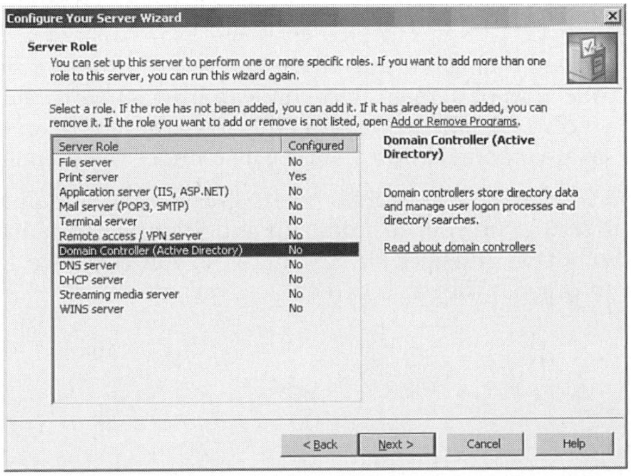

Figure 31.16 This wizard page enables you to install the Active Directory.

The Active Directory must be installed on a Domain Controller. In both Windows 2000 and Windows Server 2003, all domain controllers within a domain are equals, more or less. The distinction between Primary Domain Controllers (PDCs) and Backup Domain Controllers (BDCs) has been removed. There are still some details about which domain controller in a domain controls the global catalog, for example, but these are outside the scope of this chapter.

Note

In Figure 31.16 you can see that there are other roles your computer can be used for. For example, the computer can be used as a DHCP server (see Chapter 29). You can execute this wizard more than once to add roles to the computer. This chapter concentrates on the Active Directory (and the Domain Name System server) required for the Active Directory. You can also use another computer on your network as the DNS server, if you want—however, the DNS server you use must support dynamic updates. In a large network, you will probably need more than one DNS server (and on the Internet two are required if you have a registered domain name), and Active Directory computers can still use these other servers for DNS. Yet, in a small network, using a single server to host both DNS and the Active Directory is a good idea, because it gives you a single computer you can use to manage both services.

4. After you select Domain Controller (Active Directory) from the selections displayed in Figure 31.16, click the Next button and the next wizard window will show you a summary of what you have selected. Click Next to continue.

5. The Welcome to the Active Directory Installation Wizard appears. Click Next and the wizard displays information such as earlier versions of Windows (Windows 95 and Windows NT 4.0 with service pack 3 or earlier). Those earlier computers will *not* be able to log on to the Windows Server 2003 version of the Active Directory. Click Next to continue.

Note

You can, however, install an Active Directory client software application on Windows 95. For Windows NT 4.0, you need to install Service Pack 4.

6. In Figure 31.17 the next dialog box presented by the wizard is shown. Here you need to make a selection based on your current AD setup. You can choose to create a domain controller for a new domain, or install the AD on a domain controller in a domain that already has the Active Directory installed on another computer. For purposes of this example, a new domain controller will be used.

7. Likewise, the next wizard dialog box asks whether this will be a new domain in a new forest. A forest is simply a collection of domain trees that can interact with each other. In Figure 31.18 you can see that it is also possible to create a child domain within an existing domain. For example, you can create a domain called art.by.ono under the domain by.ono.

8. The third selection in Figure 31.18 enables you to create another domain in an existing forest of AD trees. If you are setting up your first domain and your first instance of the Active Directory, select the first radio button and click Next. Otherwise, you will have already done this and should be cognizant of what the other two choices mean!

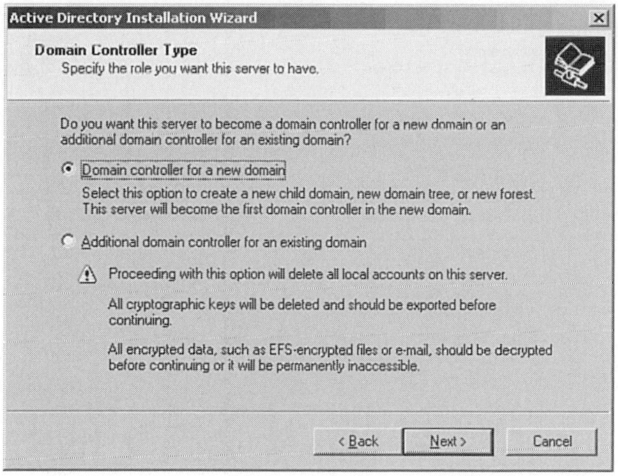

Figure 31.17 Select to install a new domain controller for a new domain, or to install the Active Directory in a domain that already has the Active Directory installed on another server.

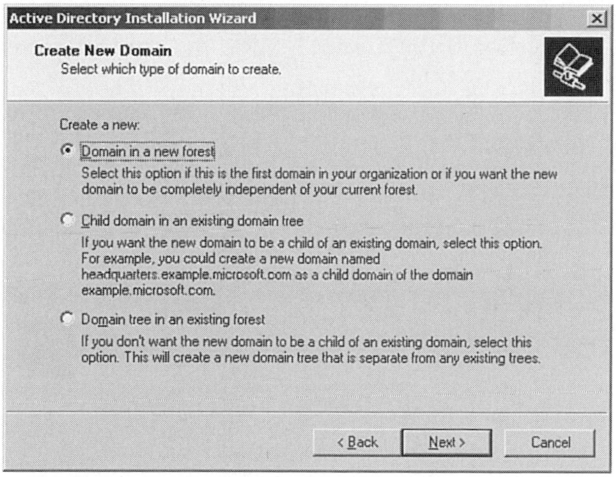

Figure 31.18 You can create a new domain in a new forest, a child domain, or a domain tree in an existing forest.

9. The next wizard (see Figure 31.19) dialog box asks you to enter the fully qualified domain name for the domain (that is, include the .com, .net, or other qualifier). After entering the domain name, click the Next button.

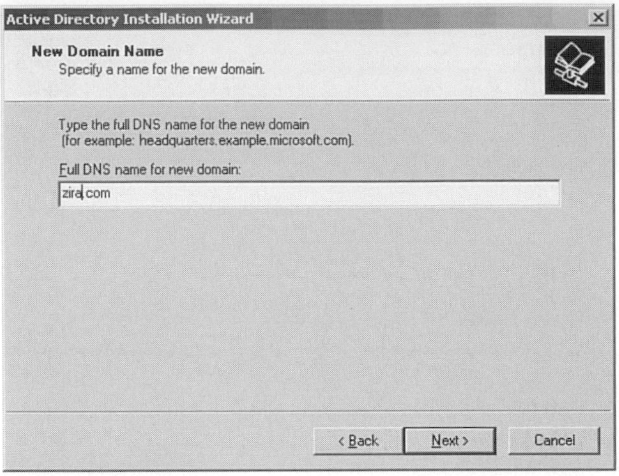

Figure 31.19 Here you should enter the fully qualified domain name.

10. The next wizard screen enables you to enter a NetBIOS name that can be used by older Windows operating systems to access the directory. It is suggested that you use something similar to the domain name you entered in Figure 31.19. For example, the domain in Figure 31.19 was zira.com. The suggested NetBIOS name is ZIRA. You can change this NetBIOS name or take the default. Click Next to continue.

11. Next the wizard asks you where the database files for the Active Directory should be stored (see Figure 31.20). It is suggested that you put these files on a disk other than the one that holds the operating system. This increases performance, because both the operating system and the Active Directory, in a larger network, will probably be accessed frequently. By placing the files on a separate disk, you can improve performance.

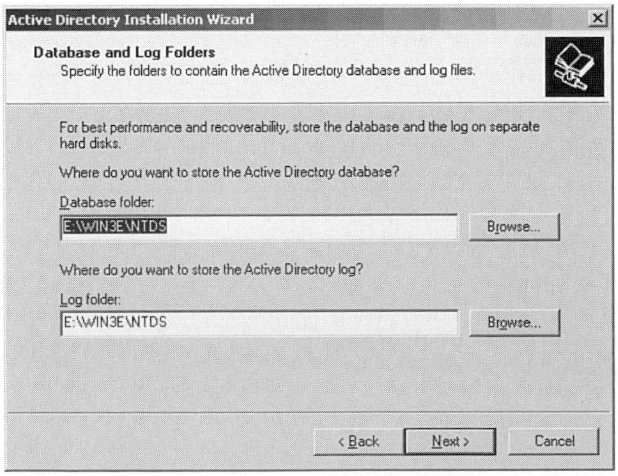

Figure 31.20 Specify the location that will be used on your server to store the Active Directory data files.

If you don't want to use the default disk drive or directories that the wizard suggests, use the Browse buttons for both the Database folder and the Log folder to change them to a location more suitable for your system.

12. The next wizard dialog box asks you to specify a location for the SYSVOL directory. This directory (or folder) contains public information that is replicated to all domain controllers in the domain. This is the situation when you create more than one domain controller, which is a good idea for the fault tolerance it provides. Again, you can take the default or use the Browse button to select a location that best fits your environment. Click Next after making your choice.

13. The Domain Name System server had not been installed on this computer, and Windows Server 2003 cannot find a domain controller that can resolve the name you have chosen for your domain. It is at this point that you can choose to create a DNS server on the same computer used by the Active Directory. If you want, you can fix the problem—is the DNS server for your network offline for some reason? Or you can choose to configure a DNS server after the Active Directory installation. For the purposes of this example, the default action (create the DNS server on the same server) is used.

14. You must now select what kind of permissions you will use on the server. If you are operating a mixed-mode network, which contains Windows operating systems that were marketed before Windows 2000, then select the first radio button (Permissions Compatible with pre-Windows 2000 Server Operating Systems).

Note also that this radio button should be used if your Windows Server 2003 system participates in a mixed-mode network that also has domain controllers prior to Windows 2000. For example, if you still have a mixed-mode Windows 2000 network that contains Windows NT 4.0 networks, select this option.

The second radio button on this Wizard dialog box lets you enable permissions to the Active Directory for just Windows 2000/2003 clients. If you've upgraded your network to these servers (and in the case of Windows 2000, the Professional Edition), then make this selection. This will provide a more secure network than one using earlier clients or servers.

15. Finally, the wizard asks you to enter a password that can be used if you find a need to restart the server in Directory Services Restore Mode. This is not the same password used for the Administrator account on the computer. It is used only when you need to restore the Active Directory in case of a problem.

16. The Summary dialog box enables you to view the selections you have made before proceeding to create the Active Directory. Read these carefully to ensure that you are about to install the AD using selections compatible with your network. You can make changes using the Back button. When you are satisfied with your selections, click the Next button. An information dialog box will let you know that the Active Directory is being configured on your server. It will take a few minutes if you are installing on a high-end server, or longer if you are using a server based on the minimum requirements for Windows Server 2003.

17. The last Wizard dialog box lets you know that the Active Directory installation has finished. Click the Finish button. You will then have to restart the server to continue. When the system reboots, you can view the log file of what has been changed. See the location for this log file described earlier in this chapter.

If you chose to install the DNS server on the same server as the Active Directory, you will see a Manage the DNS Server selection on the Manage Your Server window that appears after the reboot. For instructions on how to manage a DNS server, see Chapter 29. Because DHCP is used to provide IP addressing configuration information to clients on your network, it is important that you understand the implications of setting the scope of IP addresses that the DHCP server can allocate. Inside a private intranet (or on a SOHO cable/DSL router), be sure to assign addresses for this scope that do not interfere with another DHCP range of addresses, such as those provided by your ISP. If you already have a range of IP addresses that are valid on the Internet, you should probably still use a private address range within your intranet to add a bit of security to your network.

The Manage Your Server window reappears after you have completed the installation of the Windows 2003 Active Directory.

You can continue to add roles to the server, such as Manage Users and Computers in Active Directory. However, the management functions listed here can also be found in the Administrative Tools folder. You can go ahead and choose to continue setting up your server using this window, or use the Administrative Tools later.

If you want, you can now create additional roles for this server, or you can use other servers to set up other roles. Your decision should depend on what role you choose, and the capacity of the servers you will use. In a small to moderate-sized network, you might be able to use a single server to perform the roles you select. However, in an Enterprise network, you should carefully plan to install many servers to use for separate roles in your network. Indeed, if you use multiple subnets, you will have to consider how network traffic affects your network, and probably use servers on each subnet that are set up to perform specific roles.

Overview of Novell NetWare IPX/SPX

32

SOME OF THE MAIN TOPICS IN THIS CHAPTER ARE

In addition to an extensive discussion of Novell's IPX, SPX, and NCP protocols, this chapter highlights the most important of the other Novell proprietary protocols.

Although Novell has been making a shift to IP since Version 5.x, NetWare can still use IPX/SPX. In addition to backward compatibility, IPX/SPX is used for the RCONSOLE utility. The primary reason to use IPX/SPX is for compatibility with older network components and for other applications that use only the IPX/SPX protocol. This chapter is intended to give you an overview of these protocols to enable you to better make your case to upper management as to why it is time to upgrade. And, for those stuck with an older Novell network, the information found in this chapter might prove useful to help you in troubleshooting and solving problems until you can upgrade to a newer version of NetWare (or another operating system).

An interesting note to consider is that NetWare was once king of the PC networking industry. Even as Microsoft introduced its LAN Manager product, among others, it was not until Windows NT was marketed that Windows operating systems began to incorporate built-in networking functionality. NetWare provides both an application server and a network protocol. If you can find the same functionality in another less expensive product, where does Novell fit in today? For more about the current version of NetWare, just look at the next chapter to see where Novell has positioned the product today.

Note

If you don't realize what a threat NetWare was to Microsoft many years ago, consider this: Windows NT 3.51 provided support for several network protocols. The default protocol was Microsoft's own version of the IPX/SPX protocols, called NWLink. When Version 4 of Windows NT was released, the default network protocol was TCP/IP. Enough said!

Using the Novell Proprietary Protocols

The workstations and other machines and resources on your network communicate with the NetWare server by using communications protocols. A *protocol* is a set of rules that specifies how resources move data across the network. In a sense, the protocol is the language that the network and machines on the network use to communicate with each other. It's important that the client and the server speak the same language. Novell has several protocols designed specifically for use on Novell NetWare networks. These proprietary protocols include the following:

- Internetwork Packet Exchange (IPX) that operates on the Network layer
- Sequenced Packet Exchange (SPX) that operates on the Transport layer
- Packet Exchange Protocol (PXP) that operates on the Transport layer
- Novell Core Protocol (NCP) that operates on the Transport, Session, Presentation, and Application layers
- IPX Routing Information Protocol (IPX RIP) that operates on the Network layer
- NetWare Link Services Protocol (NLSP) that operates on the Network layer
- Service Advertising Protocol (SAP) that operates on the Network, Transport, Session, Presentation, and Application layers

Although the following sections overview all the previously listed protocols, this chapter contains detailed discussion on IPX, SPX, and NCP. Most of the protocols that the following sections discuss are routing protocols. However, neither SPX nor NCP plays a direct role in routing.

When designing the IPX, PXP, and SPX subnet protocols, Novell used the Xerox Network System (XNS) as its springboard because the design of the XNS protocol lends itself readily to LAN (local area network) environments. The XNS design does not lend itself well to WAN (wide area network) environments or their large time delays; neither does its progeny—the Novell subnet protocols—work as efficiently as a WAN environment needs. Although the Novell protocols do overcome some of these limitations, they still work best in a LAN environment.

Both IP and IPX use the Routing Information Protocol (RIP), which is a distance vector routing protocol, but the implementations are slightly different. IP RIP and IPX RIP use similar processes for discovering, maintaining, and prioritizing routes. In addition, they both send route requests for obtaining routing information and send periodic route updates to synchronize the routing information tables. IP RIP and IPX RIP differ by virtue of the protocols with which they are associated, the way in which they prioritize routes, and their routing table update intervals.

Note

RIP is considered by the Internet Engineering Task Force (IETF) to be an "interior" routing protocol suitable for use within a specific business entity that uses routers to connect many different LAN segments. These protocols are referred to in the literature as Interior Gateway Protocols (IGP). Another commonly used IGP is the Open Shortest Path First (OSPF) Protocol. When it becomes necessary to connect this network to a larger internetwork, such as the Internet, other routing protocols called Exterior Gateway Protocols (EGP) are used. For more information about routing protocols and how they relate to each other and exchange information, see Chapter 37, "Routing Protocols."

NLSP is an IPX link state routing protocol that Novell developed to overcome limitations of using IPX RIP and SAP in larger internetworks, particularly over WAN links. Link state routers and servers exchange information about their routes to other devices on the network. Using this information, each router can construct the topology of the internetwork and derive routing information. NLSP converges router information tables faster, uses firsthand routing information, and generates less traffic than IPX RIP does. Because of these attributes, network managers can use NLSP to interconnect small or large IPX networks without routing inefficiencies.

SAP extends over the Transport, Session, Presentation, and Application layers. SAP allows file, print, and gateway servers to advertise their services and addresses. The Novell routers keep these services in a Server Information Table (SIT). The server address field includes the full internetwork address, network number, node address, and socket number of the server.

The NetWare Protocol Suite

A protocol suite is a group of protocols that have evolved together—regardless of whether the same company created them—or are used in the same environment. Protocol suites have definitions for the interface between protocols that occur at adjacent layers of the OSI (Open Systems Interconnection) model. One such relationship exists in the NetWare protocol suite between IPX in the Network layer and SPX in the Transport layer. The NetWare IPX/SPX protocol suite provides file, print, message, and application services.

▶▶ For more information about the OSI Networking Reference Model, see Appendix A, "Overview of the OSI Seven-Layer Networking Reference Model."

IPX and SPX compose the Novell NetWare protocol suite. SPX resides in the Transport layer. When compared to the TCP/IP protocol suite, IPX provides routing and internetwork services similar to IP, and SPX provides Transport layer services similar to TCP. IPX and IP are connectionless datagram protocols, whereas SPX and TCP are connection-oriented protocols.

If you are running a mixed NetWare/Windows environment, you will most likely use Microsoft's NWLink implementation of the IPX/SPX protocols. NWLink is an IPX/SPX-based, routable transport protocol that you can use to establish connections between computers running any Windows operating systems. NWLink enables NetWare servers and Windows NT computers to send Novell NetBIOS packets to each other.

Note

NWLink is a useful tool to use when you are migrating an older Windows-based network that uses NetWare's IPX/SPX to a modern network based on TCP/IP. NWLink enables you to keep existing legacy servers that do not understand the IP protocol (such as NetWare 3.x systems) in your network until you can upgrade those servers to a newer version of NetWare, or dispose of the NetWare software entirely, and upgrade your Windows systems to use TCP/IP. In Part XI, "Migration and Integration," you will find that Microsoft has other packages, such as Services for NetWare, that can assist you in making these transitions.

Connectionless Service and Protocols

A connectionless service does not require the sender and receiver to establish a session before sending packets to the destination. Networks can implement this service in the Network layer or the Transport layer of the OSI model.

The following are characteristics of connectionless service:

- Packets can arrive at the destination out of sequence, but the receiving station must reassemble them in sequence.
- No time is required to establish a session—indeed, there is no session setup because a session is not used—and data can be sent immediately.
- It does not use acknowledgments to check for packet delivery.

Note

Another connectionless protocol that you should already be aware of is the Internet Protocol (IP). IP is used by the Transmission Control Protocol (TCP) to establish sessions that must be set up before the data exchange can begin, and torn down in an orderly manner when the session ends.

The Internet is the largest connectionless network in the world, and it uses the Internet Protocol (IP) to deliver the packets to their destinations. IPX is the connectionless-oriented protocol that Novell systems use to deliver packets, and it operates at the OSI Network layer. A connectionless protocol is similar to a radio broadcast or letter delivery. The sender receives no acknowledgment for receipt of the letter delivery or radio broadcast.

This connectionless protocol is best used for disseminating information that is time sensitive and does not need retransmission, such as real-time video and audio. If a packet is not received, it's pointless to retransmit the packet after the remaining packets in that sequence have been sent to the video/audio processing software.

Connectionless protocols at the Transport layer take advantage of the port structure already in place. For example, say you have two hosts, one transmitting real-time audio, and the other connecting to the first host to receive the transmission. The second host receives the transmission on a UDP (User Datagram Protocol) port identified by the software that is receiving the real-time audio transmission. No error correction or packet acknowledgment is coordinated between the two hosts, but both use the same port for the transmission and receipt of the data. In effect, connectionless protocols, such as IP, IPX, and UDP, are similar to sending a letter or a radio broadcast because the sender is not concerned whether the recipient actually received the packet.

Connection-Oriented Service and Protocols

Connection-oriented service provides reliable data delivery by establishing a virtual circuit between the sending host and the receiving host. Some characteristics of connection-oriented service are the following:

- The initial request for a session involves some setup time between the hosts.
- The server considers the connection as a virtual circuit.
- The server uses acknowledgments of data receipt to guarantee data delivery.
- Long transmissions are common.

Both TCP and SPX are connection-oriented protocols. SPX is the NetWare protocol for providing connection-oriented service. TCP uses ports between hosts to create a virtual circuit between two host computers on an IP network. TCP is not concerned with the process of routing through the network but is concerned with the data delivery in the datagram.

For example, if two host computers want to transfer Simple Mail Transfer Protocol (SMTP) traffic between them, the sending host requests a session with the receiving host on TCP port 25. After the initial protocol negotiation is complete, the virtual circuit is established, and the two hosts can guarantee data delivery. TCP and SPX are connection-oriented protocols, which are similar to a certified letter because the sender ensures that the recipient received the packet.

Internetwork Packet Exchange (IPX)

Novell originally developed IPX as the native protocol for the NetWare 3.x and 4.x operating systems. In 1998, NetWare 5 changed the IPX legacy by making IP the native NetWare protocol; however, it still uses IPX. The IPX design has as its basis the Internet Datagram Protocol (IDP) of the XNS protocol.

Although Novell recommends pure IP on your network, small networks might benefit from using IPX only because IPX requires no special address resolution protocols (it can assign addresses dynamically). IP is better suited for large IP-based networks attached to the Internet, to WAN links, or where IP is the exclusively required protocol. If you don't require IP for any of these reasons, and you can use an IPX network, you might find that an IPX implementation is easier to administer. Because IPX automatically distributes subnet addresses, whereas you must manually configure IP, IPX is easier to manage than IP.

Note

NetWare 6.x networks now use TCP as well as IP, and NetWare has adopted many other industry standard protocols, such as HTTP/HTML and SUN's Network File System (NFS). By shedding itself of older proprietary protocols (though maintaining backward compatibility), newer versions of NetWare provide an upgrade path for existing customers. The focus of the company today is to develop applications—not protocols—that can be used to solve users' business needs and interact with other vendors' products.

In contrast to the Microsoft NetBEUI (NetBIOS Extended User Interface) protocol, IPX/SPX is routable. It should be noted, however, that Microsoft provides for sending NetBEUI over TCP/IP, which is a routable protocol. IPX was a good solution for small and mid-sized networks for many years. Several major network operating systems and most desktop operating systems support the IPX protocol, mostly to accommodate legacy clients and servers. If you want to connect a Windows server and a NetWare server, you can use either IPX (and Microsoft's NWLink) or TCP/IP. Several other network operating systems, from Windows NT and Windows 2000 to Windows 2003 servers, include the NWLink protocol to provide interoperability with NetWare and NetWare-compatible applications and devices.

Although older NetWare networks (specifically NetWare 3.x) still use IPX as an internetwork protocol, Microsoft uses IPX differently than Novell due to NetBIOS naming. In a Windows NT network using IPX, you must configure all routers to broadcast NetBIOS on all segments if you want services to be locatable. Novell isolates traffic per segment and uses IPX RIP/SAP or NDS to find its resources. Because of this difference, Microsoft's use of IPX is inefficient as a routed protocol. Yet you must consider that Microsoft provides NWLink only (1) to enable data exchanges between older NetWare systems, which may indeed reside on a single network segment, and (2) to provide an upgrade path so that you can migrate your older NetWare servers (and the data they hold) to more modern Windows platforms.

The IPX protocol uses the ODI (Open Data-link Interface) specification for DOS and Windows workstations on the network. ODI allows workstations or servers to use multiple protocols on the same network. Each workstation can use a combination of protocols on the same network card. This allows your workstation to communicate with the NetWare network and other systems, such as a mainframe computer or an Internet connection, concurrently. In addition, the ODI specification provides a modular way of installing network drivers so that when you replace a network adapter, you need change only the LAN card driver.

Note

In contrast to NetWare's ODI, Microsoft, along with 3COM, created the Network Driver Interface Specification (NDIS) to solve the same problems addressed by ODI. Today, NDIS drivers are generally the interface of choice, with the capability of using network adapter cards from all the major NIC vendors. The support for ODI is slowly going away as the market for these devices continues to decline.

Similar to IP, IPX is an internetworking protocol that provides datagram services. IPX is a connectionless datagram service, which means after the computer sends a datagram, there are no guarantees that it was delivered. One application for which you might use simple IPX is that of broadcast messages, such as error notifications and time synchronization. IPX performs dynamic route selections based on tables of network reachability information compiled by RIP.

IPX Packet Communications

The IPX protocol divides data into packets to send across the network. Packets are a specific size and contain a certain amount of information. A packet contains the data designated for transmission, in addition to the necessary addressing information. NetWare uses three main types of addressing:

- IPX external network numbers are set for all servers in a single network, and multiple servers in the same network use the same number. You use this number to transmit data across multiple networks.

- IPX internal network numbers are unique and must be set at each server to locate specific servers on the network.

- Each workstation has a network address to locate a specific workstation on the network. Network addresses, also called MAC (Media Access Control) addresses, are usually set in hardware in the network card.

IPX also can send groups of packets, called *bursts*, without requiring the recipient to acknowledge each packet. NetWare added burst-mode technology to enhance the IPX protocol when used over

WAN links. Burst mode lets a workstation make one request for a file. After it receives the request, the server responds with a continuous stream of packets and then requires only a single acknowledge response from the recipient after it has received the packet burst. Burst mode improves network throughput and greatly reduces the amount of traffic on the network, two important factors for improving performance over WAN links. Burst mode improves performance in these environments:

- LAN segments that typically transmit large files
- WANs with slow asynchronous links
- Internetworks linked with bridges and routers
- WANs using X.25 packet switching or T1 and satellite links

IPX Packet Structure

The Transport Control Field contains 8 bits, the last field of which (0) is the packet type. It identifies the data contents of the data portion of the IPX packet. Field 8 provides for protocol multiplexing, which enables other protocols to reside on top of IPX and helps IPX determine which of the client protocols to send the packet to. Table 32.1 defines the Packet Type Assignments for IPX.

Table 32.1 IPX Packet Type Assignments

Packet Type	Protocol
0	Regular IPX packet type
1	Routing Information Protocol (RIP) packet or NLSP packet
2	Echo packet
3	Error packet
4	Packet Exchange Protocol (PXP) packet or diagnostic
5	Sequenced Packet Exchange (SPX)
17	NetWare Core Protocol (NCP) or NDS
20	NetBIOS name packet

An IPX protocol packet can be 30 to 65,535 bytes long. Table 32.2 outlines the packet structure for the IPX protocol. Ethernet networks have a default packet size of 1,500 bytes, and Token-Ring networks have a default packet size of 4,202 bytes.

Table 32.2 IPX Protocol Packet Structure

Field	Contents	Size
Checksum	Provides integrity checking	2 bytes
Packet length	Length in bytes of the packet	2 bytes
Transport control	Number of routers a packet can traverse before it is discarded	1 byte
Packet type	Defines the service that created the packet (NCP, NetBIOS, NLSP, RIP, SAP, or SPX)	1 byte
Destination network	Network address of the destination network	4 bytes
Destination node	MAC address of the destination node	6 bytes
Destination socket	Address of the process running in the destination node	2 bytes
Source network	The network address of the source network	4 bytes

Table 32.2   Continued

Field	Contents	Size
Source node	MAC address of the source node	6 bytes
Source socket	Address of the process running in the source node	2 bytes
Data	Information that the packet surrounds	Variable; determined by server or router

The IPX datagram structure includes a network address and a node address. You normally assign the network address to the network when you install the first NetWare server or router on a segment. Each of the four frame types can be installed and bound to the same Network Interface Card (NIC) in a server, establishing a different network address for each frame type. All subsequent NetWare server installations on that network must correspond to the network address of each frame type assigned by the first server. A router that is set up to route IPX also must have a corresponding network address for each frame type that it uses. The node address is the MAC address assigned to the NIC. A socket address is included to identify a running process in a computer. An example of an IPX address is 1AB47E3F 0080D4287DE1 0121.

IPX Frame Types

The IPX protocol has four Ethernet frame types and two Token-Ring frame types. The default frame type for NetWare 4.x on an Ethernet network is IEEE_802.2, more commonly known as Ethernet 802.2. Table 32.3 identifies the frame types for both Ethernet and Token-Ring networks.

Table 32.3   Ethernet and Token-Ring Frame Types

Frame Type	Description
Ethernet	
Ethernet_802.2	A data-link protocol that controls the link between stations; also known as IEEE 802.2 LLC (Logical Link Control).
Ethernet_802.3 RAW	The Novell proprietary frame type.
Ethernet_II	Used to bind TCP/IP on a NetWare server.
Ethernet_SNAP (Sub-Network Address Protocol)	Includes an organization code field and a type field that indicates the upper-level protocol that is using the packet. It is the frame type for AppleTalk environments.
Token-Ring	
Token_Ring	Conforms to the IEEE 802.5 and IEEE 802.2 standards. The SAP fields indicate the protocol type, and Novell networks set it to 0xe0 to indicate that the upper-layer protocol is IPX.
Token_Ring_Snap	Allows network protocol stacks to use Ethernet II frames.

Sequenced Packet Exchange (SPX)

Novell developed SPX as a Transport layer protocol to provide end-to-end data transport and to add reliability to IPX deliveries within NetWare networks. In designing SPX, Novell used the Xerox Packet Protocol (XPP) as the foundation for this protocol. The SPX layer (layer 4) sits on top of the IPX layer (layer 3) to provide connection-oriented services between two nodes on the network. SPX and SAP are the two most important protocols that operate in the Transport layer.

Client/server applications, such as print servers, are the primary users of SPX. Most communications on a network, such as workstation connections and the NetWare print server and Remote Console (RCONSOLE), use the SPX protocol.

SPX Packet Communications

SPX is concerned with addressing, segment development (division and combination), and connection services (segment sequencing, error control, and end-to-end flow control). SPX provides guaranteed packet delivery and delivers the packets in their proper sequence by locating the SPX message within the IPX packet, and then transporting it using the IPX datagram delivery service.

When a user or resource on the network sends a transmission, SPX first sends a control packet to establish a connection, and then associates a connection ID for that virtual circuit. After the packet transmission, SPX requests verification from the destination that it received the data. The packet destination must correctly acknowledge receipt of the packet(s). If an acknowledgment request brings no response within a specified time, SPX retransmits the packet. After a reasonable number of retransmissions fail to return a receipt acknowledgment, SPX assumes that the connection has failed and warns the operator of the failure.

If SPX determines that packets were lost en route, SPX resends lost packets and uses the sequencing numbers to ensure that the packets arrive in the proper order without duplication. SPX uses a timeout algorithm to decide when it should retransmit a packet. SPX dynamically adjusts the timeout based on the delay experienced in packet transmission. If a packet times out too early, SPX increases its value by 50%. This process can continue until it reaches a maximum timeout value or the timeout value stabilizes. To verify that a session is still active when there is no data activity, SPX sends probe packets to verify the connection.

The number of available listen buffers determines and provides the flow control. SPX can send messages in a given direction only until the number of unacknowledged messages is equal to the number of listen buffers available on the receiving side. As the number of buffers varies, SPX is able to also vary the number of messages that it will send before receiving an acknowledgment. This ensures that the incoming data does not arrive too rapidly and thus overrun the destination node buffers.

If the destination source acknowledges receipt of the packet, the SPX verification must include a value that matches the value calculated from the data before transmission. By comparing these values, SPX ensures not only that the data packet arrived at the destination, but also that it arrived intact. The values include the sequencing numbers of the packet, which the receiving side uses to check for missing, duplicate, or out-of-sequence messages. If the recipient received the packets successfully, it acknowledges by returning the next expected sequence number in the Acknowledgment Number field of a message that is sent back to the sender. At the end of data transmission, SPX sends an explicit control packet to break the connection.

One disadvantage of using a connection-oriented protocol such as SPX is in the handling of broadcast packets. In this instance, the protocol must establish a connection with every destination before it can send the packet, which can amount to a time- and resource-consuming process. To avoid this situation, you can use higher-level NetWare protocols, such as NCP, to bypass SPX and communicate with IPX.

SPX Packet Structure

Although SPX guarantees delivery of every packet it sends, it is slower than IPX alone. This is because the SPX header includes the IPX header and adds an additional 12 bytes of sequencing, flow control, connection, and acknowledgment information.

SPX packets contain the same header fields that IPX packets contain, but add a 12-byte SPX header in the Data field at the end of the header. The SPX header can contain at the most 534 bytes of data, whereas the normal IPX packet format allows 576 bytes. Table 32.4 outlines the packet structure for an SPX packet header.

Table 32.4   SPX Packet Structure

Packet Field	Contents	Size
IPX Packet Header	See Table 32.2.	30 bytes
SPX Header	(As defined in the remainder of this table.)	12 bytes
Connection Control	Regulates flow of data across the connection.	1 byte
Data Stream Type	Indicates whether SPX data field contains data or a packet, and identifies the upper-layer protocol to which the SPX data must be delivered.	1 byte
Source Connection Identifier	Identifies the number assigned to the connection on the source socket end.	2 bytes
Destination Connection Identifier	Identifies the number assigned to the connection on the destination socket end.	2 bytes
Sequence Number	Numbers each packet in a message as the packet is sent; SPX uses it to detect lost and out-of-sequence packets.	2 bytes
Acknowledge Number	Indicates the next packet that the receiver expects. The sequence and acknowledgment fields apprise both the sending and the receiving computers of which packets have been sent and which have been received. This value implicitly acknowledges any unacknowledged packets with lower sequence numbers.	2 bytes
Allocation Number	Indicates how many free buffers the receiver has available on a connection. The sender uses this value to pace data transmission.	2 bytes
Data	Contains higher-level information being passed up or down in the protocol-layer hierarchy.	534 bytes

Sequenced Packet Exchange II (SPXII)

Novell 4.0 and later includes SPXII as a backward-compatible enhancement to SPX, and features a true sliding-window flow-control mechanism. With this mechanism, the sender and receiver can initially negotiate in the window without receiving any acknowledgments. Each sent packet decreases the window, and each acknowledged packet increases the window. In this way, the receiver can acknowledge groups of packets simultaneously.

Note

The concept of *sliding windows* is not specific to SPX. TCP/IP has included this concept from the earliest days to allow for delayed acknowledgments so that multiple network packets can be sent before an acknowledgment is received. Using a slow-start algorithm, TCP/IP can begin to scale up the communications link to allow for more unacknowledged packets, depending on the quality of the network link. When congestion or other network problems result in dropped network packets, TCP/IP can adjust and slow down the transmission and later begin to increase the "sliding window."

SPXII also improves the negative acknowledgment (NAK) capability. A NAK speeds up the recovery process by allowing the sender to retransmit missing or erroneous packets immediately instead of waiting until the end of the transmission. In addition, SPXII does away with the 576-byte limitation and allows for a packet size as large as is supported on a system. SPXII also provides new option-management functions such as permitting the application to negotiate network transport options and allowing for future expansion for the protocol.

NetWare Core Protocol (NCP)

Novell clients use the NCP to access resources, such as NDS, the file systems, and the printer services. If you have NetWare 5.0 or above, you can use NCP over IP as opposed to or in addition to NCP over IPX. However, the NCP packet signature function can consume CPU resources and slow performance, for both the client workstation and the NetWare server.

The NCP packet signature is more of a security feature than a protocol, in the sense that the term *protocol* is normally used. This feature protects servers and clients that are using the NCP services. The NCP packet signature prevents packet forgery by requiring the server and the client to sign each NCP packet using the RSA (Rivest-Shamir-Adleman) public- and private-key encryption. The RSA algorithm is the standard for data encryption, especially for data sent over the Internet. The packet signature changes with every packet.

By using NCP, NetWare workstations and file servers can communicate by defining the connection control and service request encoding aspects of their interaction. NCP maintains its own connection control and packet-level error checking instead of relying on other protocols for those functions. NetWare workstations issue NCP requests to a server to establish and terminate connections, and to retrieve the following types of information:

- File access and transfers (with the NCOPY command)
- Virtual drive mappings (with the MAP command)
- Directory searches (with the FILER utility)
- Print queue status (with the PCONSOLE utility)

NetWare servers then respond to these requests with NCP replies. When the server has processed and complied with the request, the workstation terminates the connection by sending a Destroy Service Connection request to the server.

If the server discovers any NCP packets that have incorrect signatures, it discards them without breaking the client workstation's connection with the server. In addition, the server sends an alert message about the source of the invalid packet to the error log, the affected client workstation, and the NetWare server console.

If you do not install NCP packet signature on your system, a network intruder could pose as a more privileged user and send a forged NCP request to a NetWare server. By forging the proper NCP request packet, an intruder could gain the Supervisor object right and access to all network resources. If you install NCP packet signature on the server and all the network client workstations, it is virtually impossible for an intruder to forge an NCP packet that would appear valid.

NCP Packet Signature Options

When you use NCP, several signature options are available, ranging from never signing NCP packets to always signing NCP packets. NetWare servers and NetWare clients each have four signature levels you can set. The signature options for servers and client workstations combine to determine the level of NCP packet signature on the network. You can choose the packet signature level that is most suitable for your system performance needs and network security requirements to include packet signatures and job servers. You should install NCP packet signature if you have any of these security risks:

- An untrusted user at a workstation on the network
- Easy physical access to the network cabling system
- An unattended, publicly accessible workstation

However, some combinations of server and client packet-signature levels can slow performance, but low-CPU-demand systems might not show any performance degradation. NCP packet signature is not necessary for every installation. You might choose not to use NCP packet signature if you can tolerate security risks, such as in these situations:

- Only executable programs reside on the server.
- You know and trust all network users.
- Data on the NetWare server is not sensitive and loss or corruption of this data would not affect operations.

The default NCP packet signature level is 1 for clients and 1 for servers. This setting provides the most flexibility while still offering protection from forged packets. Table 32.5 provides some examples of situations requiring different signature levels.

Table 32.5   Setting NCP Signature Levels

Situation	Security Concern	Recommendation
All information on the server is sensitive.	Intruders can gain access to information on the NetWare server that could compromise the company.	Set the server to level 3 and all clients to level 3 for maximum protection.
Sensitive and nonsensitive information resides on the same server.	The NetWare server has a directory for executable programs and a separate directory for corporate finances.	Set the server to level 2 and clients that need access to company finances to level 3. Set all other clients to level 1.
Users often change locations and workstations.	You are unsure which employees use which workstations, and the NetWare server contains sensitive data.	Set the server to level 3 and all client workstations to level 1.
A workstation is publicly accessible.	You have an unattended workstation that is set up for public access to nonsensitive information, but another server on the network contains sensitive information.	Set the sensitive server to level 3, the unattended workstation to level 0, and the nonsensitive server to level 1.

Server Signature Levels

Before you set a new signature level on the server, you need to determine the server's current signature level, which you do by typing the following console command:

```
SET NCP Packet Signature Option
```

You can use the SET console command to change the signature level from a lower to a higher level, but you cannot change from a higher to a lower level unless you reboot the server. Before you use the SET console command, you must add

```
SET NCP Packet Signature Option = 1
```

to the `startup.ncf` file, and then restart the server. Then, each time you bring up the server, you can set the Signature level for that server by typing

`SET NCP Packet Signature Option = `*`desired signature level`*

The default level is 1. Following is a description of the server signature levels:

- **0**—Server does not sign packets (regardless of the client level).
- **1**—Server signs packets only if the client requests it and the client level is 2 or higher.
- **2**—Server signs packets if the client is capable of signing (client level is 1 or higher).
- **3**—Server signs packets and requires all clients to sign packets or logging in fails.

Client Signature Levels

To set DOS or MS Windows 3.x client signature levels, add this parameter to the workstation `net.cfg` file:

`signature level = `*`number`*

To set Windows 9x, Windows NT, or Windows 2000 client signature levels for individual workstations, you can change the parameter settings with the Advanced Settings tab of Novell NetWare Client Properties, by following these steps:

1. From the system tray, right-click the Novell symbol *N*.

2. Click Novell Client Properties.

3. Click Advanced Settings, and then select Signature Level from the scrollable list. You can set client signature levels to 0, 1, 2, or 3; the default is 1. Increasing the value increases security but decreases performance.

You can set the signature level for multiple clients at once by adding the signature level to the configuration file when you install the clients. The following list describes the client/workstation packet signature levels:

- **0**—Disabled. Client does not sign packets.
- **1**—Enabled, but not preferred. Client signs packets only if the server requests it, and the server level is 2 or higher.
- **2**—Preferred. Client signs packets if the server is capable of signing (server level is 1 or higher).
- **3**—Required. Client signs packets and requires the server to sign packets or logging in will fail.

Packet Signature and Job Servers

A *job server* is a server that performs a task and then returns the completed task. Job servers can serve as database servers, Web servers, file servers, proxy servers, or a firewall. You should be aware that some job servers do not support NCP packet signature. A job server might produce unsigned sessions if any of the following conditions exists:

- It does not operate on top of DOS.
- It does not use standard Novell clients.
- It is not an NLM (NetWare Loadable Module).
- It uses its own implementation of the NCP engine (such as embedded print servers in printers).

To minimize security risks associated with job servers, you can install queues only on servers that carry a packet signature level of 3. After that, do not allow privileged users to put jobs in queues on servers with signature levels less than 3. In addition, you should make sure that the job server's account is unprivileged, verifying that the job server cannot change client rights. If it has that permission, you can disable it and prevent the job server from assuming the rights of a client by adding the following SET command to the server's startup.ncf file:

```
SET Allow Change to Client Rights = OFF
```

The default is ON, because certain job servers and third-party applications cannot function without changing to client rights. Refer to the server's vendor documentation to determine whether the job server can function without client rights.

Effective Packet Signature Levels

The signature levels for the server and the client workstations combine to determine the overall level of NCP packet signature on the network—called the effective packet signature level. Some combinations of server and client packet signature levels might slow performance. However, low-CPU-demand systems might not show any performance degradation. You can choose the packet signature level that meets the performance needs and security requirements of the system. Table 32.6 shows the interactive relationship between the server packet signature levels and the client workstation signature levels.

Table 32.6   **Effective Server/Client Signature Combinations**

Client Level	Server = 0	Server = 1	Server = 2	Server = 3
Client = 0	No Packet Signature	No Packet Signature	No Packet Signature	No Login Access
Client = 1	No Packet Signature	No Packet Signature	Packet Signature	Packet Signature
Client = 2	No Packet Signature	Packet Signature	Packet Signature	Packet Signature
Client = 3	No Login Access	Packet Signature	Packet Signature	Packet Signature

Troubleshooting Packet Signature Conflicts

If the client workstations are not signing packets, you should ensure that the signature level on the client workstation is not set to 0. SECURITY.VLM loads by default when the client signature level is set to 1, 2, or 3. Use the virtual loadable module (VLM) /V4 command-line parameter when loading the VLM software to display load-time information.

If the client workstations cannot log in, make sure the packet signature levels on the server and the client workstation are correct and do not conflict. If any of the following signature combinations exists, clients will not be able to log in:

- Server packet signature = 3 and the client workstation signature = 0.
- Server packet signature = 0 and the client workstation signature = 3.
- The LOGIN utility is an older version that doesn't support packet signature.
- The NetWare DOS Requester or the shell is an older version that doesn't support packet signature.

If you get the Error Receiving from the Network error message, the client workstation is using a version of LOGIN.EXE file that doesn't include NCP packet signature. To remedy this situation, you can install a version of LOGIN.EXE, and its applicable utility files, that is compatible with packet signatures on all NetWare servers on the network.

NetWare Security Guidelines

In addition to installing NCP packet signature, you can use other NetWare security features and protective measures to keep client workstations secure. The following security guidelines are suggested for client workstations:

- Use only the most current versions of system software, NetWare Client software, and patches.
- Check for viruses regularly.
- Use the SECURITY utility to detect vulnerable access points to the server.
- Enable intruder detection and lockout.
- Advise users to log out when they leave their client workstations unattended.
- Enable NCP packet signature level 3 on all unattended client workstations.
- Require unique passwords of at least five characters on all accounts, and establish forced password changes at least every three months.
- Limit the number of grace logins.
- Limit the number of concurrent connections.
- Enforce login time restrictions and station restrictions.

NCP Protocol Independence

The NetWare 5 operating system is NCP protocol independent, which means that internal to NetWare, the NCPs can make and receive specific requests for services that are handled by IP, IPX, UDP, or a combination of these protocols.

To see which protocols NetWare loads and in what order it loads them, you can use several NetWare 5 console commands and SET parameters. The server console commands that are NCP-specific include these commands:

- NCP STATS
- NCP ADDRESSES
- NCP TRACE
- NCP DUMP

To see which IPX, TCP, and UDP addresses are loading and in which order, you can go to the server prompt, type **NCP ADDRESSES**, and press Enter. The resulting list shows the order that the AUTOEXEC.NCF or the NetWare Configuration file loaded the protocols. For instance, maybe you thought you were loading the IP address before IPX but you see that IPX is loading before IP. You can use the SET parameter to change their designated order, regardless of which protocol you bind first through the AUTOEXEC.NCF file or through the NetWare Configuration file. To do this, follow these steps:

1. In the MONITOR utility, select the Server Parameters option from the Available Options window.
2. Select the NCP option, highlight the NCP Protocol Preferences, and press the Enter key.
3. Use the SET command to specify the order in which you want the incoming service requests to use these protocols. After you save this configuration, the NetWare Configuration file contains this information and uses it each time you bring up the server. The syntax for the SET parameters is as follows:

```
SET NCP EXCLUDE IP ADDRESSES = decimal IP address
```

and

```
SET NCP INCLUDE IP ADDRESSES = decimal IP address
```

You should note that the exclusions take precedence over the inclusions. That means if you have the same address as both an exclude and an include, the server will exclude it, regardless of the order in which you entered the parameters. However, you do not need to both include the NCP interface and exclude the non-NCP interface. One or the other will work. You can enter the parameters at the server console, in AUTOEXEC.NCF, or in Monitor under Server Parameters, NCP.

As a practical example of the preceding steps, say you have a server with IP bound to two interfaces and one of them goes to the Internet. You might want to disable NCP traffic over the Internet interface for security reasons. The fictional IP address for the public interface is 200.100.50.25 and the internal interface is 10.20.30.40. To disable NCP on the Internet interface, you can use either of the following SET parameters:

```
SET NCP EXCLUDE IP ADDRESSES = 200.100.50.25
```

or

```
SET NCP INCLUDE IP ADDRESSES = 10.20.30.40.
```

NCP chooses the first protocol bound as the preferred protocol it uses. If both IP and IPX are bound—currently without any default value inserted—and both are installed on a server, NCP defaults to use IPX because IPX loads first. The set parameter—NCP Protocol Preferences—needs to be set to "NCP Protocol Preferences = TCPIP" so that IP is the preferred protocol used by NetWare 5.

Overview of the Novell Bindery and Novell Directory Services

Throughout NetWare's lifetime, it has used two distinctly different types of database management and directory structures: bindery services and NetWare Directory Services (NDS). In this chapter, you will learn the differences between the two, as well as the advantages and disadvantages of each. In addition, you will learn how to use the NetWare Administrator and the NDS Manager, two of the most important utilities for managing a NetWare network.

In the next chapter you will learn about the new eDirectory and how it interacts with NetWare 6.x.

Understanding NetWare Directory Structures

A database's architecture determines the naming and organization of network resources and dictates the kinds of features the directory or domain service offers. The architectural foundation of a directory or domain service is the namespace structure, which determines how the database is organized. Namespaces have one of two types of organizational structures: hierarchical or flat.

Within the Novell family are representatives of each of these structures. The bindery database of NetWare 3.x and earlier used a flat structure, whereas the NDS database of NetWare 4.x (and later versions) uses a hierarchical structure. In the following sections, you will learn about each of these structures.

Reviewing the Bindery Structure

The bindery is a flat network database that the early versions of NetWare 3.x and NetWare 2.x used for the primary purpose of security and access control. When we say that the bindery files are *flat*, that means the entries in the bindery do not have an explicit relationship to any of the other entries. Although you could add users to groups, unless you looked up each specific user, the relationship was not apparent. The bindery is server-centric, which means that each file server contains and maintains a unique bindery that contains settings for the printers, usernames, object IDs, passwords, and security. In this structure, if a user needs access to two bindery servers, that same user must have one account on each server, because different servers do not communicate with each other to exchange security information. The NetWare Name Service (NSS) utility synchronizes user account and user security information between multiple servers to try to create a semblance of a hierarchical structure prior to the release of NDS.

In a bindery structure, each entity on the network, such as a user, printer, or workgroup, constitutes a single object definition in the database. Each object connects directly to the root directory of the server, keeping in mind that the root does not branch beyond itself and the list of objects it contains. Figure 33.1 provides graphical representation of the bindery structure. In the bindery, the network supervisor can design, organize, and secure the network environment based on each entity's requirements. The following three components make up the bindery:

- **Objects**—These represent any physical or logical entities, such as users, user groups, workgroups, file servers, print servers, or any other entity that has an assigned name in the database.

- **Properties**—The characteristics of each bindery object. This includes passwords, account restrictions, account balances, internetwork addresses, lists of authorized clients, and group members.

- **Property data sets**—These represent the type of data stored in the bindery. The data type can be text, number, table, date/time, network address, and stream.

Reviewing the NetWare Directory Service Structure

Like the bindery, NDS is an informational directory of objects that represent the resources on the network. These objects, just as in the bindery, are users, groups, printers, servers, and other organizational units. However, unlike the bindery, the objects are represented in a hierarchical structure, meaning that you have one root structure and then branches from the root that contain other branches and leaves. Compare this to the flat file structure of the bindery. NDS shows you the relationships among different objects in the directory.

Figure 33.1 The Novell bindery has a flat structure.

Note

Chapter 31, "Using the Active Directory," covers Microsoft's implementation of directory services based on LDAP, and Chapter 34, "Expanding and Enhancing NDS: NetWare's eDirectory," explores the newest version of NetWare's directory, as well as some of the new features found in NetWare 6 that are integrated with the eDirectory.

NDS uses a hierarchical tree structure that organizes objects in a multilevel, object-oriented, directory tree, loosely based on the X.500 standard developed by ISO. An X.500-standard directory structure looks like an upside-down tree (thus the nomenclature *directory tree*), with the trunk at the top and the branches extending below it. X.500 defines users and resources as objects and uniquely identifies them by their locations and a distinguished name. Figure 33.2 illustrates the NDS structure.

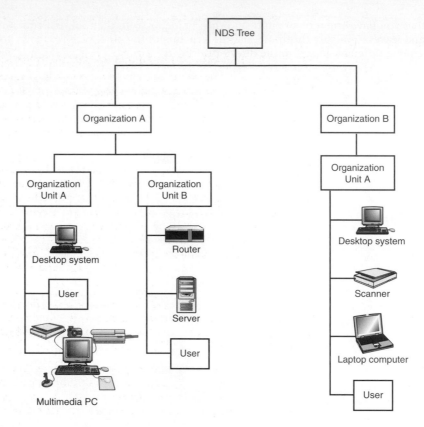

Figure 33.2 The Novell Directory Service is a hierarchical structure based upon the X.500 standard.

▶▶ For more on the X.500 standard protocols and its replacements, see Appendix D, "The Lightweight Directory Access Protocol."

However, the directory does not force you to conform to a hierarchical structure. Underneath a single organization (O), you can define all objects into a flat structure, something like a super-bindery. The directory hierarchy enables you to take advantage of the natural organization of information.

Most of the time, an organization will configure its directory tree according to the way users access and use company resources. In this way, NDS acts as a repository of information based on the specific needs of the organization. Because this method makes resources easy to locate, use, and manage, network administrators can log in as the Admin user from any workstation on the network and manage the entire directory tree.

In addition, whether your NDS servers are running NetWare, Unix, or Windows, NDS can keep all resources in the same directory tree. That means you do not need to access a specific server or domain to create objects, grant rights, change passwords, or manage applications. This open access is available due, in large part, to a Novell product that allows a single network login across multiple platforms.

NDS maintains information about every resource on the network and stores this information in a single, logical database that lets the users see a global view of all services and resources on the network. In an NDS environment, users log in to a multiserver network and view it as a single system instead of as a collection of individual servers. The most important benefit of this scenario is that users can access network services and resources through a single login, regardless of where the user or the resource is located on the network. This access also is conditional on whether the user has the requisite rights to use that resource.

Objects in the NDS Directory Tree

Resources you will see in an NDS environment include users, groups, printers, volumes, applications, fax servers, computers, and nearly any other device or application that attaches to the network. When you log in, you will see one global view of the entire network and all its resources, as opposed to seeing a group of servers, as you would with the bindery.

The network resources appear in the NDS directory tree as one of several types of objects, called object classes, which have distinct properties. The schema defines the containment rules for object classes and their properties. The main types are leaf objects and container objects. Table 33.1 defines what each type of directory structure can contain.

Table 33.1   NDS Object Composition

Directory Object	Object Composition
[Root]	Contains Country, Organization, and Alias objects.
Country	Contains Organization, Application, and Alias objects.
Organization	Contains Organizational Units and Leaf objects.
Organizational Unit	Contains other Organizational Units and Leaf objects.
Leaf	Cannot contain any other objects.

Figure 33.3 shows you the NDS object containment. The following are the container objects you will see in NDS:

- **[Root]**—Located at the topmost level of the directory tree, which allows trustee assignments that grant rights to the entire directory tree.

- **Country objects**—Enable you to perform one task on one container object, and those changes will apply to all objects within that container.

- **Organization objects**—Usually are the first container class under [Root] and typically bear your company name. Small companies can simplify management by having all other objects directly under the Organization object.

- **Organizational Units**—Fall under the Organization to represent separate geographic or functional divisions. You also can create organizational units under other organizational units to further subdivide the tree.

Leaf objects represent actual network resources, such as users, groups, file servers, printers, and network applications. The following are the Leaf object classes:

- **Alias objects**—Provide a quick way to access objects in another context. Alias objects do not contain any other objects, but point to other permitted objects in another context besides the user's own.

- **Bindery objects**—Represent objects that an upgrade or migration utility has placed in the directory. NDS uses them only to provide backward compatibility with bindery-oriented utilities.

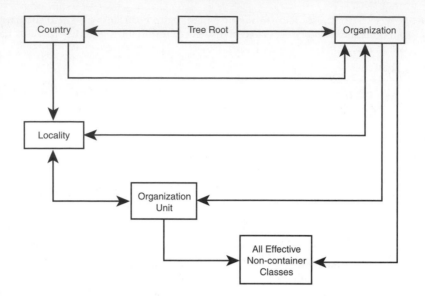

Figure 33.3 NDS object containers can be the root, as well as Country objects, Organization objects, and Organizational Units.

- **Bindery Queue objects**—Represent a queue that an upgrade or migration utility has placed in the directory tree. NDS uses them only to provide backward compatibility with bindery-oriented utilities.

- **Computer objects**—Represent a nonserver computer on the network, such as a client workstation or a router. This object stores information about the computer, such as its network address, serial number, or the person to whom you have assigned the computer.

- **Directory Map objects**—Represent a particular directory in the file system. They can be useful in login scripts by pointing to directories that contain applications or other frequently used files. If you want to avoid making changes to many login scripts as application locations change, you can create a Directory Map object, reference it in the login script, and change it when the application location changes.

- **Group objects**—Assign a name to a list of User objects that are located anywhere in the directory tree. Use a Group object to assign rights to a group rather than to individual users. The individuals that belong to a group will inherit the rights that you assign to that Group object, no matter their location in the directory tree.

- **NetWare Server objects**—Represent a network server running NetWare. Whenever you install a NetWare server in the tree, NDS automatically creates a NetWare Server object. This object stores information about the server, including the following: the server's location on the wire, the server's physical location, and the different services that the server provides.

- **Organizational Role objects**—Define a position or role within an organization, such as a department manager or vice president of sales. You can assign any User object as an occupant of the Organizational Role object, and the occupants inherit the same rights granted to the Organizational Role object.

- **Print Queue objects**—Represent a print queue on the network. You must create a Print Queue object for every print queue on the network.

- **Print Server objects**—Represent a network print server. You must create a Print Server object for every print server on the network.

- **Printer objects**—Represent a physical printing device on the network. You must create a Printer object for every printer on the network.

- **Profile objects**—Contain a profile script (a type of login script) that appears as part of the User object properties and executes whenever a User object logs in to the network. The Profile object executes after the system login script, but before the user login script. You can create a Profile object for any set of users who need to share common login script commands but who are not located in the same directory container. In addition, Profile objects will suit any users who are a subset of users in the same container.

- **Unknown objects**—Represent an NDS object that has been invalidated and cannot be identified as belonging to any other object class.

- **User objects**—Represent a person who logs in and uses the network. You must create a User object for every network user. When you create a User object, you can create a file-system home directory for that user that includes default rights assignments. You also can determine which default rights you want the User object to have, and customize a USER_TEMPLATE object, which you will assign to new users.

- **Volume objects**—Represent a physical volume on the network. The INSTALL program automatically creates a Volume object for every physical volume on a server at installation time. The properties of the Volume object store information about the NetWare server where the physical volume is located. It also specifies which name the operating system gave the server after initializing the volume during installation (such as SYS). If you create a Volume object during installation, NDS places this information in the properties of the Volume object by default. NDS also uses Volume object properties to map drives.

- **Container objects**—Organize network resources into branches and can contain Leaf objects and other Container objects in the directory tree. Container objects enable you to manage other objects in sets, rather than individually.

Bindery Services

The dilemma for many administrators, after they upgrade to an NDS operating system, is how they can tie in their legacy bindery system. For this express purpose, Novell provides bindery services, which enable NDS to emulate a bindery database.

Bindery services provide NDS-based networks (NetWare 4.x and NetWare 5.x) with backward compatibility to NetWare versions that used the bindery. This enables clients that are using older software to access the network. In addition, when you have enabled bindery services, NDS objects, bindery-based servers, and client workstations can access all objects within the specified container's bindery context.

Bindery services do this by simulating a flat (nonhierarchical) structure for the objects within a set of Organization (O) and Organizational Unit (OU) objects, representing only the leaf objects of the container. Consequently, bindery service users have limitations that other NDS users do not have.

Bindery Context

The bindery context is the Container object in which bindery services are set. It appears as a branch of the NDS tree that serves as a simulated bindery and allows bindery-based servers, clients, and utilities to coexist on an NDS network.

In early versions of NetWare, you could set the bindery context in only one container (Organization or Organizational Unit) within the directory tree, and all bindery objects had to be located in that container. However, later NetWare versions have a bindery context path that allows multiple containers to contain bindery objects—as many as 16 bindery contexts for each server. In addition, recent NetWare versions support NetWare Loadable Module (NLM) programs that rely on bindery services to access objects in multiple containers.

However, you might experience problems when you use a bindery context path. Although you cannot have more than one object of the same name in the same container, you can have objects with the same name in the different containers of a bindery context path. The problem is that users see only the objects in the first container of a path. The visible name overrides other objects of the same name in the other containers, regardless of whether these objects are of the same type. The only way to prevent this is to avoid having objects of the same name in different containers if these containers are in the same bindery context path.

When you install any NetWare server into the directory tree, the operating system automatically creates a NetWare Server object in the Container object. Figure 33.4 illustrates a bindery context in an NDS structure. By default, NetWare activates bindery services and sets the bindery context for that container object.

Bindery Emulation Drawbacks

Because bindery emulation is necessary in some networks, you must understand how it affects overall network use and performance on an NDS directory.

For every NetWare server that must perform bindery emulation, you must have a replica of the NDS partition that contains the network entities that are requesting bindery access. In this case, servers that normally would not have required a replica now must have one to maintain the server-centric bindery database.

Because this means that the replica ring is larger than it would have otherwise been, your network now has more traffic as these servers synchronize. Additionally, events such as user login cause servers to verify authentication with other servers in the replica ring, which can cause significant delays. This is especially true when many users are doing the same tasks at once, such as initial login first thing in the morning.

Bindery emulation also leaves less bandwidth available for data transmission. This means that the server can delay user requests while the servers perform functions they otherwise could have avoided if the network was strictly NDS.

In addition, server processor use is a factor where bindery use is prevalent. Although bindery is single-threaded, NDS is multithreaded. This means that every time an application, or the operating system, initiates an execution path, it must wait in a queue until the CPU can process that command. Because bindery is single-threaded, only one thread handles all the bindery requests made to a server. While the CPU handles another thread, it puts all bindery requests on hold. When the CPU does address the bindery thread, it may monopolize the CPU while other vital functions are on hold. In comparison, each NDS request creates its own thread that the CPU can handle separately with less risk of CPU monopoly.

Contrasting and Comparing Bindery and NDS

Although Novell had a step in the right direction with its bindery database, the bindery structure had a lot of room for improvement. In this section the attributes of the bindery will be compared to the new and improved attributes of NDS. Additionally, you'll see how NDS picks up where bindery left off to form a more complete and efficient database structure.

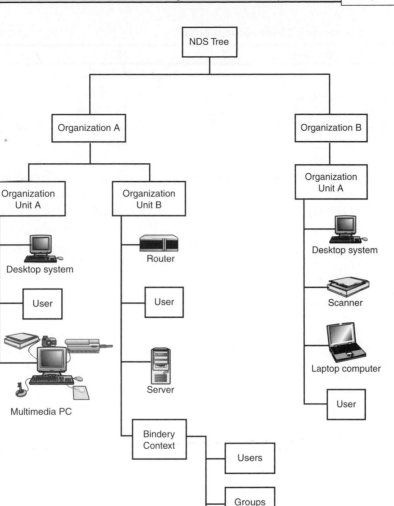

Figure 33.4 Bindery services let you establish a bindery context within an NDS structure.

Most modern networks contain multiple servers. This makes managing the network on a server-by-server basis time-consuming, often redundant, and not very efficient, especially when it comes to fault tolerance, network security, and data synchronization. In addition to the administration work-load, network performance also suffers. Table 33.2 outlines the most important differences between the bindery and NDS, and the following sections provide details on those differences.

Table 33.2   Comparing Bindery and NDS

Feature	Bindery	NDS
Group Accounts	Users must be assigned on each server	Group assignments are networkwide
Logical Structure	Flat	Hierarchical
Network Printing	Has no friendly printer map	Provides user-friendly access to network printers
Network Volumes	On the local server only	Volumes extend across the network as global objects
Partitions	None	Distributed database
Queues	Only local objects will queue	Queues form for systemwide objects
Replication	Does not replicate	Replicates partitions
Synchronization	No replicas to synchronize	Synchronizes replicas
Trustees	On the local server only	Global objects
User Accounts	Users must have separate accounts on each server	Users have one global account for the network
User Login and Authentication	Users must have one password per server	Sponsors networkwide authentication

Administration

In a bindery environment, the administrator must maintain separate servers that are, in effect, their own complete network environment. This includes setting up specific user accounts on specific servers so that the user could access the resources there. Therefore, if a user needs access to resources on five file servers, the administrator must create an account for that user on each of the five file servers. In addition, the administrator also must synchronize individual files and relationships between the servers.

NDS eliminates this redundant administration by requiring only one user account per user for the entire network. In addition, NDS also does away with the redundant administration that is typical in multiserver, non-NDS environments.

Centralized Login

In a bindery environment, users log in to their own context and must access new contexts on other servers by signing in to those servers as well. This means that each user must have a distinct account on each server. In addition, the bindery maintains Login scripts separately on each server, instead of centrally, meaning that the administrator must update and maintain those scripts separately.

NDS requires only one user account per user for the entire network. This simplifies life for ordinary users, because they need only one login, and one password, for all subsequent security authentications during the network session.

Directory Structure

The most distinctive difference between bindery and NDS is the directory structure. In the bindery, you could see only the main organization and then all the individual components of that organization, which branched directly off from the root directory. If you looked at the directory tree in this scenario, you could not tell the vice president of the company from the printer, except by name.

Whereas the bindery was very limited in how it could represent divisions, departments, and groups, an NDS tree can encompass an entire network. In so doing, it can closely resemble the corporate structure, wherein a top-level root branches into various functional or geographic departments or groupings.

As a corporation grows, the number and size of its departments grow and are further subdivided, in addition to the number of network resources (that is, users, printers, and servers) and the relative entries in the NDS database. NDS can represent this growth by adding and expanding the administrative designators, such as organization and organizational unit containers corresponding to the actual organizational charting.

Object Recognition

In addition to a limited organization structure, the bindery recognizes only the following object types:

- User
- Group
- Queue
- Print Server
- Bindery objects

This limits the way clients can use the directory service because they are limited to those objects, and administrators are limited in their ability to alter and improve user access to network resources. Administrators are so limited because the bindery objects are limited to the server on which they are located, as opposed to the NDS security structure of network access. In addition, administrators cannot use any new features and products by Novell or third-party companies that leverage the directory to create new objects or add new attributes to existing ones.

In contrast, NDS can recognize a full range of directory objects, which the structure breaks down into logical sequence and division. Divisions in an NDS tree increase the efficiency and responsiveness of NDS—particularly for users in branch offices—as well as decreasing server load and making the tree more manageable. NDS, therefore, is a distributable database that the administrator can place where he or she sees fit.

Access to Resources

In a non-NDS environment, users must know on which specific server the desired resource resides. Even after yet another login, that user must also have access rights to both the server and the resource. The bindery resources are server-centric and NDS resources are network-centric. The bindery resource is made available to NDS users by setting a bindery context so that the resource can be accessed from the NDS. You can log in totally as a bindery user and you will have access only to the resources in the bindery context and can use only bindery tools such as SYSCON and PCONSOLE.

NDS allows users to access a more global view in which objects exist individually and can access other entities, regardless of physical or logical location. The NDS database resides on a server, or servers, that users can access from anywhere on the network without having to know on which specific server the resource resides.

Partitions

Although the bindery does not support partitions, NDS can break the database into separate pieces at the container level to manage large numbers of network resources. When the operating system originally creates a directory tree, that tree has one partition. In this case, the NDS database exists in its entirety wherever it physically resides. However, network administrators can divide the tree into any number of smaller pieces to give logical structure to the partitions. One reason to partition the tree is to place that portion of the tree closer to the user. You would want to partition the NDS tree on a WAN and place the NDS objects closest to the users.

Replicas, Synchronization, and Fault Tolerance

Another feature that bindery does not support is replicas. You can set NDS to copy one server's partition of the directory database to other NetWare servers in the tree—a process called *replication*. In this manner, NDS creates a distributed database system, employing a concept that is similar to disk mirroring.

Replication reduces possible data loss if the server holding the database fails. You can copy any partition onto any other server for fault tolerance. Three replicas of an NDS partition on the network should provide enough fault tolerance for almost any server failure scenario. However, you do not need to put replicas on all your NDS servers, because the servers on the network know which servers have replicas and which do not. If a client requests a server's resources, the network can check with the other servers that have replicas to authorize access. In this way, servers can be more efficient with their resources and do their specific, assigned tasks with less overhead.

NetWare 4.x servers with replicas participate in a replica ring, which should be no more than 10 servers and no fewer than 3 servers. All the servers in a replica ring automatically synchronize changes to the NDS database and update the partitions. The smaller the replica ring, the less time the servers spend synchronizing.

With NetWare 5, server replication no longer occurs within a replica ring or list as it has in the past. Transitive synchronization works through a migration agent server that checks the replica list and each target server's ReplicaUpto vector. If the source server's ReplicaUpto vector is more recent than a target server's vector, the source server does not need to synchronize with that target server. This procedure uses both the IPX and the IP protocols and reduces synchronization traffic to free up bandwidth.

Using Novell Directory Services

NDS automatically installs on your server whenever you install any of the NetWare products that provide it, which are intraNetWare, NetWare 4.x, and NetWare 5.x. That means that you have no additional installation procedures specifically for NDS. However, you can configure NDS, which means that you also are configuring your network. Now that the principles of the NDS structure have been covered, it's time to configure NDS so that it best suits your organization. You can accomplish your administrative tasks through the NWADMN32 and NDS Manager. If you are running NetWare 5.x, you will run these utilities as snap-ins through the ConsoleOne Management framework.

Novell has designed several products so that NDS will work with third-party products. The following are some examples of these products:

- Novell NDS Corporate Edition works with Microsoft's Windows 2000 Active Directory. This product replaces NDS for NT, which worked with Microsoft's NT File System (NTFS) to provide network security.

- NDS eDirectory allows NetWare's NDS to work in a mixed Unix-NT environment.

- MacNDS allows Macintosh (Apple) computers to work with the NDS Directory structure.

- NetWare NFS allows Unix NFS to work with NDS.

Using NWADMN32

The NWADMN32 utility merges all the network administrative functions into a single, intuitive interface. With it, you can see the availability and location of network resources. If you have NetWare releases prior to NetWare 5, the network administrator is NWAdmin. The NWADMN32 utility is the management console for the entire network, through which you can do the following:

- Create and delete NDS objects
- Move and rename NDS objects
- Assign rights and permissions in the NDS tree and in the NetWare file system
- Set up print services
- Set up licensing services

You can browse the directory tree through NWADMN32, and then double-click a selected object to see all the information and properties associated with that resource. You also can set property values for multiple objects simultaneously. With drag-and-drop functions, you can assign access rights to any NDS object and move objects within the directory tree. In addition, NWADMN32 has a configurable toolbar that has shortcuts to menu options and a configurable status bar. With it, you can hide and sort property pages for individual NDS objects. NWADMN32 also has other network administration tools through which you can manage directory trees, subtrees, and containers.

Because NWADMN32 is the location from which you will make most of your network changes, start NWADMN32 by following these steps:

1. Log on to the network as the administrator by typing **admin** or by typing **admin.dept.company**, depending on whether you have set up the network for contextless login. You should be sure that you are running the current client software and that you have an administrator account for the network.

2. Normally, when you log in, the operating system automatically provides you with a path to the SYS:PUBLIC directory, after which you should go to the \WIN32 subdirectory. If NetWare did not automatically send you to the SYS:PUBLIC directory, you need to map a drive to it. To do this, open the NetWare administration program, which is loaded into the SYS:PUBLIC\WIN32 directory on the NetWare server.

3. Next, use the RUN command to execute the NWADM32.

Tip

After you access NWADMN32, the easiest way to use this application is to create a shortcut on your desktop, although you can always continue to use the RUN command to execute it.

As soon as you log in as the network administrator, the operating system will display the NetWare Administrator window, as Figure 33.5 shows. The NetWare Administrator window shows you the entire network directory.

Creating and Deleting Objects

If you need to create a new object, you should determine what kind of object you want to create (object classes were discussed earlier in this chapter). After that, follow these steps:

1. At the NetWare Administrator window, highlight the container where you want to place the new object. If you will be deleting an object, be sure you open the container where the object is located, and then highlight the object. (Don't worry, NDS will not let you delete a container unless you first delete everything in that container.)

2. From the toolbar, click Object to display the Object menu.

3. If you are going to delete an object, select Delete. If you are going to add an object, select Create to display the New Object screen.

4. Choose the type of object you want to create, and click OK. The next window you will see depends on the type of object you are creating. Regardless of the type of window you see, you will need to fill in some specific properties for the object type you have chosen.

5. When you have filled in the necessary information, click Create.

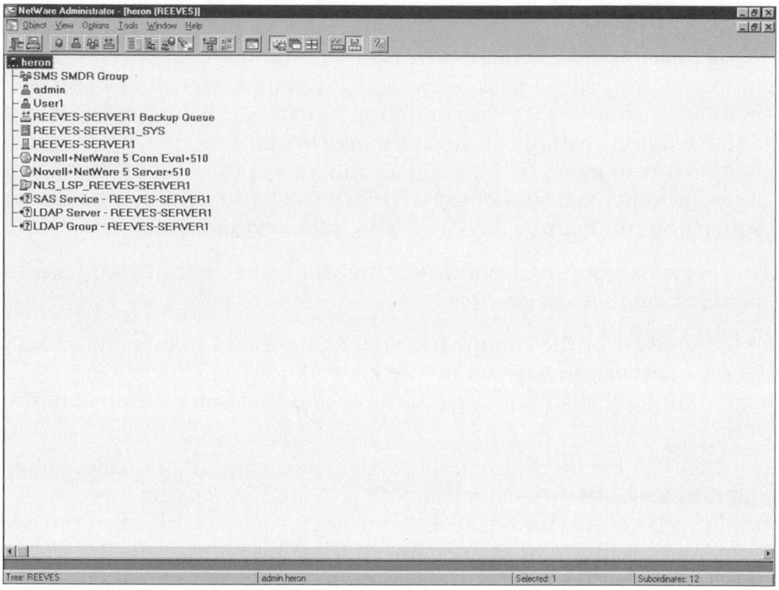

Figure 33.5 You will see the NetWare Administrator window when you log in as the administrator.

Context and Naming

To understand where an object fits in the NDS structure, you must understand how the NDS naming system works. The context of an object implies its position in the NDS tree. Specify the context as a list of containers separated by periods, between the specified object and the [Root]. Normally, NDS automatically assigns a new object a context based on where you put it in the directory tree. The context can be represented as described here:

- The *complete name*, also called the *distinguished name*, of an object is its object name with the context appended. An example would be *username.departmentname.divisionname.companyname*. A complete name does not have a leading period. A complete name can be either typeful or typeless.

- A *fully distinguished* name is a complete name with a leading period, so that the name appears as such: *.username.departmentname.divisionname.companyname*. The leading period means that NDS will resolve the name from the root, regardless of the current context. A fully distinguished name also can be either typeful or typeless.

- You also might see the *typeful name* displayed in some NDS utilities. In creating a typeful name, NDS uses the type abbreviation, an equal sign, and then the name of the object. You can use typeful names interchangeably with typeless names in NDS utilities. A *typeless* name is essentially a typeful name without an object type. Typeful names include the object type abbreviations shown in Table 33.3.

Table 33.3   Typeful Name Abbreviations

Object Class/Type	Abbreviation
All leaf object/Common Name	CN
Organization	O
Organizational Unit	OU
Country	C

- *Name resolution* is the process that NDS uses to find the location of an object within the directory tree. When you use object names in NDS utilities, NDS resolves the names relative to either the current context or the [Root].

- *Current (workstation) context* is set when the networking software runs, and it's key to understanding the use of leading periods, relative naming, and trailing periods.

- *Leading periods* resolve the name from [Root], no matter where the current context was previously set.

- *Relative naming* means that NDS resolves names relative to the workstation's current context, rather than [Root]. Relative naming never involves a leading period because a leading period indicates resolution from [Root]. For example, if the workstation's current context is accounting.yourcompany and the user's relative name is joeuser.accounting, NDS reads the name as joeuser in accounting in the current context.

- *Trailing periods* can be used only in relative naming, and you cannot use both leading periods and trailing periods. A trailing period changes the container from which NDS has resolved the name. Each trailing period changes the resolution point one container toward the [Root].

The NetWare 5 catalog services and simplified login make it easy for you to create NDS-enabled applications, improve directory access performance, and allow users to log on from any computer in any location without requiring directory knowledge. You can customize directory information that is stored in catalog or index format to enable you to search, sort, and report against the directory entries. Distribution and replication of these indexes allows administrators to quickly access a "snapshot" of the complete network directory as opposed to performing a query across the entire network. NetWare 5 has contextless login, which leverages the NDS catalog to enable users to authenticate from any point on the network by typing their login names and passwords. This type of login removes the need for the user to specify his exact user object location in the NDS tree.

Moving and Renaming Objects

The capability to move and rename objects comes in handy for things such as interdepartmental transfers. To move a Leaf object from one container to another, follow these steps:

1. At the NetWare Administrator window, browse to the Leaf object you want to move, and click it.

2. From the Object menu, click Move to display the Move dialog box.

3. Browse to the destination container object and click OK.

The procedure for renaming an object is simple: Follow step 1, but click Rename at the Object menu. Type in the new name for the object, and click OK.

Assigning Rights and Setting Permissions

When you create an NDS tree, the default rights assignments give your network and its objects generalized access and security. Some of the default assignments are as shown here:

- User Admin has Supervisor rights to [Root] for complete control over the entire directory. Admin also has Supervisor rights to the NetWare Server object for complete control over the volumes on that server. [Public] retains the Browse right to [Root] so that any user can view any objects in the NDS tree.

- Objects created through an upgrade process or migration receive NDS trustee assignments appropriate for most situations.

NDS security controls access to directory objects such as users, groups, printers, and organizations. You can control a user's ability to modify or add objects and to view or modify their properties. When you understand NDS security, you can assign users the necessary directory and object rights while you maintain a secure network. However, before setting rights and privileges, reviewing some basic principles that relate to NDS security is in order.

Trustees

NDS security assigns rights to objects by using object *trustees*. The Access Control List (ACL) for each object contains the list of trustees for that object. An object trustee is any user (or other object) to whom you have assigned rights to the object. These object types often have trustee rights such as these:

- The [Root] object
- Organization objects
- Organizational Unit objects
- Organizational Role and Group objects
- User objects
- The [Public] trustee

To view the trustees of an object, follow these steps:

1. At the NetWare Administrator window, highlight File System Object, then click Object, and then click Details to display the Details window for that object.
2. Click the Trustees of This File System button to display the list of trustees for the object.
3. If you want to see the other objects for which a certain trustee has rights, click on the trustee's name. If you want to remove a trustee, highlight the trustee's name and click the Delete Trustee button.
4. To add a trustee, click Add Trustee to display the Select Object dialog box. In this dialog box, you can select a user, a group, or another object.
5. After you add the trustee, you can assign rights by clicking the desired check boxes. By default, NDS assigns the Read and File Scan rights.
6. Click OK to save your changes.

To view the objects for which a specific trustee has rights, follow these steps:

1. At the NWADMN32 window, browse to the desired object (or user), highlight the object name, and then click Object, and click Details to display the Details window for that object.
2. Click Rights to Files and Directories.

3. Click the Find button to find the volumes you want to display, and then click the volumes you want to see. NWADMN32 shows you all the directories and files to which the user has rights.

4. If you want to add rights for that user/object to another file or directory, click the Add button.

5. In the Select Object box, browse to the desired object and highlight it, and click OK to add the user to the list of trustees for that object. You can specify which rights the user/object has, for which Read and File Scan are the defaults.

Access Control List (ACL)

The Access Control List is an attribute of NDS objects, and every object in the NDS tree has an ACL attribute. The ACL contains information such as which trustees have access to the object (entry rights), which trustees have access to the object properties, and which users or groups are denied access to that object. This information is stored as the following:

- The trustee name
- The affected attribute—[Entry Rights], [All Attributes Rights], or specific attributes
- The privileges

The base schema defines a default ACL template that provides minimum access security for new objects. Because the Top object class defines the properties for a default ACL template, all object classes will inherit a default ACL template. This gives objects that create other objects the right to supervise the created object, which ensures that every new NDS object has a supervisor. When you create an object in an NDS tree, the creation process can set the object's ACLs to any value, including one that changes a value that comes from a default ACL template.

Object Rights

Object *rights* are the tasks that a trustee can perform on an object. When a trustee receives rights for an object, any child objects of that container inherit those rights. Subsequently, the trustee receives rights for these child objects also, unless the rights are blocked. There are five types of object rights:

- **Supervisor**—The trustee receives all rights of the object, which are Browse, Create, Delete, and Rename. Unlike the Supervisor right in the file system, you can block the NDS Supervisor right through the Inherited Rights Filter (IRF).
- **Browse**—The trustee can see the object in the directory tree. If an object/user does not have the Browse right, NDS will not show the object in the list.
- **Create**—The trustee can create child objects under the object. This right is available only for Container objects.
- **Delete**—The trustee can delete the object from the directory. To delete an object, you also must have the Write right for All Properties of the object.
- **Rename**—The trustee can change the name of the object.

Property Rights

Property rights are the tasks that a trustee can perform on an object's properties. This enables the trustee to read or modify the property values. Trustees can inherit property rights in the same manner as object rights, except that they can inherit only those rights given with the All Properties option. If a trustee receives rights to selected properties of an object, child objects cannot inherit those rights because each of the types of objects, such as Users and Organizational Units, has a different list of properties. Note that although some property rights have the same name as the object rights, the two sets of values are not the same. There are five types of property rights, as listed here:

- **Supervisor**—The trustee receives all property rights, which are Compare, Read, Write, and Add Self. Again, the IRF can block this right. Trustees with Supervisor object rights automatically receive Supervisor rights to All Properties of the object.

- **Compare**—The trustee can compare the property's values to a given value. This enables the trustee to search for a certain value but not to look at the value itself.

- **Read**—The trustee can read the values of the property. Any trustee who has the Read property right automatically receives the Compare right.

- **Write**—The trustee can modify, add, or remove values of the property.

- **Add Self**—The trustee object can add or remove itself as a value of the property. For example, a user who has the Add Self right for a group could add himself to the group. The Write right is automatically granted to a trustee who is granted the Add Self property.

Inherited Rights

When an object trustee receives rights to a Container object, that same trustee also receives the same rights for all children of the object. Inheritance affects both object rights and property rights. When a trustee receives rights to a Container object, those rights flow down the directory tree until they are blocked. You can block inherited rights in two ways: with a new (explicit) trustee assignment or with the Inherited Rights Filter (IRF). Figure 33.6 shows you how inherited rights work within the NDS structure and how NDS can block those rights.

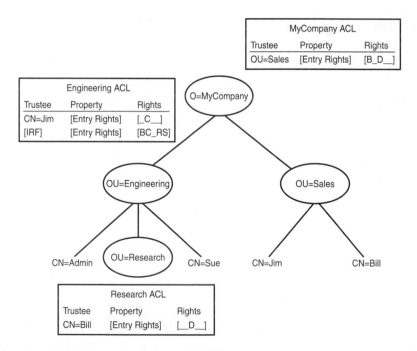

Figure 33.6 Inherited rights can allow rights or block them.

Through the *Inherited Rights Filter*, you can control which trustee rights an object can inherit for its parent object. You cannot use the IRF to grant rights, but can only block or permit rights that the object receives from a parent directory. If the IRF includes a right, the child objects can inherit that right. If the IRF omits a right, no trustee can inherit that right for that object.

Each NDS object has an IRF for object rights, and each object has an IRF for property rights. As with the rights themselves, you can set the IRF for All Properties or Selected Properties. You also can set an IRF for all properties, and then set different IRFs for certain selected properties.

Through *explicit assignments*, you can block the rights that a trustee can inherit for a particular object by giving the trustee new explicit assignments to the object. You can use new trustee assignments to block inherited rights or to add rights. The new trustee assignment replaces the rights that an object would have otherwise inherited. Because explicit assignment blocks inherited rights, you do not need to consider inherited rights if you are granting an explicit assignment.

To set the IRF, follow these steps:

1. From the NWADMN32 window, browse through the directory tree to find the desired object. Highlight the object, click Object, and then select Trustees of This Object.

2. Click the Inherited Rights Filter button to display the Inherited Rights Filter window.

3. You can block/allow both object rights and property rights. Check the boxes to permit inheritance of that right, or uncheck them to block that right. In addition, you can set the IRF for selected properties of that object or for all properties.

4. When you have specified all the desired rights, click OK to apply the rights filter.

Security Equivalence

Under some conditions, a trustee can automatically receive all the rights that you or NDS has assigned to another trustee. This practice is called *security equivalence*, of which there are two types: implied security equivalence and explicit security equivalence. Security equivalence also includes instances in which you assign rights to a container object, and all other objects within the container will receive the same rights. If one of these objects is also a container object, the objects in that second-level container will receive the same rights of the first-level container. This is referred to as *implied security equivalence* or *container security equivalence*.

Although this process might seem very much like inheritance, it is different. With inheritance, any trustee rights you assign to a container object also will be given to the objects composing the container object. To further define the difference, remember that an object inherits the trustees assigned to its parent object, and the IRF *can* block these rights. On the other hand, a trustee is security equivalent to its parent objects, and the IRF cannot block those rights.

The other kind of security equivalence that an object can have is *explicit security equivalence*. The user's Security Equal To property lists all explicit security equivalences. You specifically assign explicit security equivalence to a user by any of these three means:

■ Through the Security Equal To property that each user has. You can add users or other objects to this list, and the user receives the rights given to those objects.

■ If you assign a user to the membership list of a Group object, the user becomes security equivalent to the Group object, and the Security Equal To property will reflect that equivalence.

■ If a user is an occupant of the Organizational Role object, the user becomes security equivalent to the Organizational Unit object, which also is reflected in the Security Equal To property.

Effective Rights

Many factors affect a user's rights to Directory objects, such as the following:

■ Rights given directly to the object/user

■ The object's inherited rights from parent objects

- Limitations specified by the Inherited Rights Filter or an explicit assignment
- Rights received from containers in which the user resides through implied security equivalence
- Security equivalences to Group or Organizational Role objects

So how can you determine what users can do and what they cannot? First, you could calculate them manually—not a very attractive option. On the other hand, you can take advantage of the nifty little tool that NWADMN32 provides to automatically calculate the user's actual rights. The rights that a user can perform on an object are their *effective rights*. You can go to either the Trustees of This Object or the Rights to Other Objects properties and see the Effective Rights button. The Effective Rights window shows the current effective rights. Rights that you have granted to the user appear darkened, but those rights that the user does not have are muted. If you have made changes to the trustee rights, you must save the changes before Effective Rights will reflect those changes.

Login Security

Because users log in to a global directory, you don't need to manage multiple server or domain accounts for each user. It also means that you don't need to manage trust relationships or pass-through authentication among domains. Although a workstation connects to the network, the user has virtually no access to the network resources until they successfully log in. Before a user logs in, the administrator must create a User object in the directory for that user. The User object has a name and password, as well as other properties.

When the user logs in, he or she enters a username and password. NetWare does not send the password across the network for authentication; this would be a security risk. Instead, network login security encrypts the username, password, workstation, and other vital details to form a unique user code. The login security performs the same process at the authenticating server, and if the codes match, the user receives network access.

Through NWADMN32, you can define several types of user access and login restrictions, as listed here:

- Login restrictions enable you to disable the account entirely, make it expire on a certain date, or limit the number of concurrent logins for the user.
- Password restrictions include various options dealing with passwords. You can specify whether the user can change passwords, how often the user will be required to change the password, and how many grace logins are allowed with the old password after a change is required.
- Login Time restrictions control the times and days the user is allowed access to the network.
- Network Address restrictions enable you to create a list of workstation addresses from which the user can access the network. This lets you limit the user to a single workstation or a particular group of workstations.

In addition to these login security types, you can define intruder detection so that you can specify a number of login attempts that the system will allow before it locks the account. You also can specify a reset interval, which unlocks the account after a certain time elapses following intruder detection. If the system locks a user's account and does not reset automatically, you can unlock it from the Intruder Lockout property of the User object.

Default Rights for a New NetWare Server

When you install a new NetWare Server object into an NDS tree, Novell has designed the operating system so that it will make the NDS trustee assignments outlined in Table 33.4 by default.

Table 33.4   Default Rights for New Servers

Default Trustees	Default Rights
Admin (first NDS server in the tree)	Supervisor object right to [Root].
[Public] (first NDS server in the tree)	Browse object right to [Root].
NetWare Server	Admin has the Supervisor object right to the NetWare Server object, which means that Admin also has the Supervisor right to the root directory of the file system of any NetWare volumes on the server.
Volumes (if created)	[Root] has Read property right to the Host Server Name and Host Resource properties on all Volume objects. This gives all objects access to the physical volume name and physical server name. Admin has the Supervisor right to the root directory of the file systems on the volume. For volume SYS, the container object has Read and File Scan rights to the \PUBLIC directory of the volume. This allows User objects under the container to access NetWare utilities in \PUBLIC.
User	If you set the system to automatically create home directories for users, they have the Supervisor right to those directories.

Delegated Administration

NDS enables you to delegate your administration rights of an NDS tree branch, and thus revokes your own management rights to that branch. This attribute is useful if special security requirements require a different administrator to take over your responsibilities with complete control over that branch. You can delegate administration either by granting the Supervisor object right to a container or by creating an IRF at the container that filters the Supervisor and any other rights you want blocked.

Network Printing

NDS represents print servers, print queues, and printers as individual NDS objects that you can create and manage independently. NDS users can easily locate and capture printers and queues.

The PCONSOLE bindery utility has a Quick Setup option that makes it easy to define and link printers, print servers, and print queues. However, because you will find PCONSOLE only on bindery systems, you will most likely not have an occasion to use this utility.

NWADMN32 integrates the Print management utilities and gives you a graphical view of NDS resources to make it easy for you to administer network print services. In addition, a layout page shows all the printers attached to the print server, the queues serviced by those printers, and the print jobs in the queue.

Using NDS Manager

The NDS Manager is an NDS database administrative tool that lets you manage partitions and replicas. The Schema Manager utility of the NDS Manager enables you to manage and modify the NDS schema and distribute updated NDS versions to NetWare servers. Execute SYS:PUBLIC\WIN32\ NDSMGR32.EXE to display the NDS Manager window (see Figure 33.7).

Partitioning

A *partition* is a logical division of the NDS directory database that forms a distinct unit of data in the NDS tree to store directory information. Each partition contains a set of container objects, the objects in the container, and the object properties. Keep in mind that NDS partitions contain only NDS directory information, and not any information about the file system, where your data is stored.

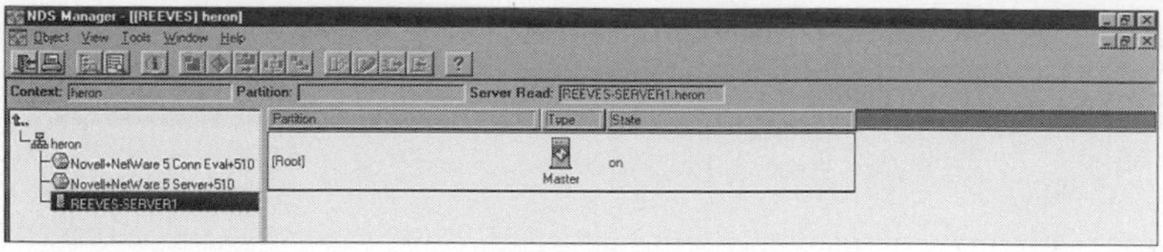

Figure 33.7 The NDS Manager window lets you manage partitions and replicas.

The NetWare default is to keep the entire directory in one partition. That being the case, how do you know whether you should partition your NDS directory? If you have in excess of 1,000 objects in your NDS tree, your server might be overwhelmed and access to NDS could be slow. A new partition allows you to divide the NDS directory and move the objects in the specified branch to a different server.

A slow WAN link is another indication that partitioning might be for you. You can make NDS perform faster and more reliably if the directory is divided into two partitions. If you left your NDS structure with only one partition, NetWare will do one of two things. It will either keep the replicas of the single partition at one site (discussed in the next section), or distribute the single partition between the servers on either side of the WAN link.

You have the option of partitioning the NDS or leaving it as one big database. The deciding factor should be slow NDS response. The two major factors that affect NDS response are size and network speed.

The problems that might arise from the first scenario are that users at the other side of the WAN link experience login and resource accessing delays. In addition, if the WAN link fails, those users cannot log in or access resources at all.

The second scenario, too, has problems: If NDS distributes the replica of the single partition between the two sites on either side of the WAN link, users can access the directory locally. However, the WAN link is the conduit for the server-to-server synchronization of replicas. This means that if the WAN link is unreliable, there might be NDS errors, not to mention that directory changes are slow to reproduce across the WAN link.

So now that you understand the benefits of partitions, let's get to the business of actually creating a partition. At the NDSMGR window, highlight the container object that will be the root of the new partition, click Object, and then click Create Partition to display the Create Partition dialog box. If you are certain that you have chosen the correct object, click the Yes button to initiate the new partition. Repeat these steps as many times as needed. Before you start creating partitions, however, you should think about why you want to create each partition, and what benefit it will serve on the network. Reasons for creating partitions include, as mentioned earlier, putting that part of the database in close proximity to the users. Another good reason to create partitions would be to divide up the workload among several other servers in a network where the directory is frequently accessed.

Creating Replicas

Replicas, as previously indicated, allow for the creation of a distributed database system within NDS. Here are a few more details so that you will know how to institute them on your NetWare network. If your network consists of at least three NDS servers, you can create replicas of the NDS directory. Replicas provide a measure of fault tolerance if a server or network link fails, which means that you will not lose your directory structure and the information about your NDS objects.

Replicas are simply a copy of the entire directory, or a copy of a partition of the directory. Each replica contains the same directory information as other replicas for that partition or the entire directory, depending on whether you use partitions. Changes to the directory or partition are replicated to the other replicas.

However, NDS replication does not provide fault tolerance for the file system (that means your data). You can establish fault tolerance for file systems through any of the most commonly used fault tolerance methods, such as disk mirroring and disk duplexing (RAID Level 1), Stripe sets with Parity (RAID 5), or Novell Replication Services (NRS). If your network provides bindery services, you must create a master or read/write replica of the directory structure.

Replication also decreases access time for users who access NDS information across a LAN or WAN link. To reduce access time, you can place a replica of the needed information on a local server (that is, on the other side of the WAN or LAN link). You can create four types of replicas, as shown here:

- **Master replica**—By default, the first NDS server on your network holds the master replica. There is only one master replica for each partition at a time. If you create other replicas, they will be read/write replicas by default. If you plan to bring down the server that holds a master replica, you can promote one of the read/write replicas to the master. Then, the original master replica automatically becomes read/write. A master replica must be available on the network for NDS to perform operations such as creating a new replica or creating a new partition.

- **Read/write replica**—NDS can access and change object information in the master and any read/write replicas. Any changes you make automatically replicate to all the other replicas. If NDS responds slowly to users because of delays in the network infrastructure (such as slow WAN links or busy routers), you can create a read/write replica closer to the users who need it. You can have as many read/write replicas as you have servers to hold them, although more replicas cause more traffic to keep them synchronized with each other.

- **Read-only replica**—Novell created this type of replica in anticipation of capabilities that future implementations of NDS might offer. Read-only replicas receive synchronization updates from master and read/write replicas but don't receive changes directly from clients.

- **Subordinate reference replica**—Subordinate reference replicas are special, system-generated replicas that don't contain all the object data of a master or a read/write replica, and therefore do not provide fault tolerance. They contain only enough information for NDS to resolve names across partition boundaries. You cannot delete a subordinate reference replica because NDS deletes it automatically when it no longer is needed. NDS creates subordinate reference replicas only on servers that hold a replica of a parent partition but that have no replicas of its child partitions. If NDS copies a replica of the child partition to a server holding the replica of the parent, the subordinate reference replica is deleted automatically.

Synchronizing Servers

When multiple servers in the network hold replicas of the same partition, those servers create a replica ring. NDS automatically keeps those servers synchronized, so the object data is consistent on all replicas. By default, the synchronization process, sometimes referred to as *NDS heartbeat* or *skulking*, takes place every 30 minutes for NetWare 4, or every 60 minutes for NetWare 5. The following NDS processes work to synchronize the servers in the replica ring:

- Replica synchronization
- Replica Purger
- Schema synchronization

- Limber
- Janitor
- Flat Cleaner
- Database Initialization
- Backlinker

In a single-server environment, the server's internal clock can maintain a common and consistent time source for the network. However, for multiserver networks, NDS requires that all the servers agree on time. Time synchronization does these things for your network:

- Applications that run on your server provide accurate timestamps to events. Messaging and collaboration applications and databases all benefit from synchronized time.

- You can configure workstations to get their time from the servers, taking synchronized time benefits to locally run applications.

- NDS applies correct timestamps to NDS events.

Whenever you make changes to NDS objects, you can specify that the operating system make those changes to different replicas on different servers, and these changes must be enacted in the order in which they were requested. NDS records the time of each event with a timestamp. The timestamp ensures that when NDS actually modifies the database, events appear on the replicas in the time and order in which they happened. NDS also uses timestamps to record time values for the network and set expiration dates.

Setting Up Bindery Services

You still might find applications, such as print servers and backup software, that were written for NetWare 2.x and 3.x. These applications used the NetWare bindery instead of NDS for network access and object manipulation. As discussed before, the bindery is a flat database of objects such as users, groups, and volumes known to a given server. The bindery is server-specific and server-centric.

In addition, older NetWare client software used a bindery login procedure in which a user logged in to a specific server only. Access to multiple servers required multiple logins using multiple user accounts.

NDS allows applications written for a bindery to function using bindery services. Bindery services enable you to set a context or several contexts as a server's virtual bindery. The context you set for the server is the server's bindery context. Whenever you institute bindery services, you should keep the following in mind:

- To use bindery services, you must set a bindery context for the server.

- Not all NDS objects map to bindery objects. Many NDS objects, such as Alias objects, do not have a bindery equivalent.

- Most bindery applications have been upgraded to work with NDS. Check with your application vendor to get the newest version.

- Each server (before NetWare 5) with a bindery context must hold a master or read/write replica of the partition that includes the bindery context.

Expanding and Enhancing NDS: NetWare's eDirectory

SOME OF THE MAIN TOPICS IN THIS CHAPTER ARE

CHAPTER 34

Long before Microsoft released its first version of the Active Directory, many other directory service products had been around for many years. These include Banyan's StreetTalk, as well as Novell Directory Services (NDS). After NetWare version 6.x was released, NDS was renamed the eDirectory. One of the benefits of the eDirectory when compared to the Active directory is that the eDirectory has been ported to platforms other than NetWare. Many of the utilities and applications that interact with the eDirectory are also available as products separate from NetWare. This means that you do not have to purchase the entire NetWare package in order to make use of the eDirectory. Much of the eDirectory operates in the same manner as NDS, discussed in the preceding chapter. However, in this chapter you will learn about the new eDirectory and how it can be put to use in your network.

Note

This chapter is not intended to be an introduction to NetWare 6.x. Instead, it will help you understand how the eDirectory has evolved from NDS, and it covers some of the newer applications that can be used with the eDirectory, such as iPrint and iFolder.

This does not preclude using the Active Directory, because there are tools that can be used to create a network that uses both of these directories. For more information about this subject, see Part XI, "Migration and Integration." And there are many *metadirectory* products offered by third-party software developers that can let both directories interact.

Basics of the eDirectory

In Chapter 33, "Overview of the Novell Bindery and Novell Directory Services," you learned a great deal about managing Novell Directory Services. However, with the release of NetWare 6, there have been changes to the eDirectory. The name itself should tell you that NDS is now considered to be an "enterprise" solution to directory services. These are the main differences between NDS and the eDirectory:

- Additional interface applications you can use to manage the eDirectory.
- New applications that make use of the eDirectory.
- A new backup utility, support for SNMP, and TLS/SSL, among others.
- Support for additional operating systems, as described in the next section.

The eDirectory has been ported to various operating systems. Contrast this with the Active Directory, which now runs only on Windows server platforms.

The eDirectory Can Be Installed on Many Different Operating Systems

Another feature of the eDirectory (which was also available during the past few versions) is that the eDirectory can be installed on more than one operating system. You don't have to use a Novell-only network in order to use the eDirectory. Instead, you can install the eDirectory on the following platforms:

- Windows NT 4.0
- Windows 2000
- Windows Server 2003
- Solaris Unix

- AIX Unix
- Linux

Compared to the Active Directory, that's quite a lot of options for a network administrator. Because you can also use products that can be used to coordinate information between different directories (metadirectories), you can use the eDirectory in the same network in which you use the Active Directory. Both of these platforms also have software and migration tools that enable you to interoperate, or migrate from one to another. Thus, you can use more than one directory in the same network, or you can migrate one to another, if you are changing your network to a single operating-system platform, for example.

▶▶ You can read more about migrating from one directory to another, or about using both directories in the same network, in Part XI.

Options to Consider for Installing the eDirectory

Before you can use the eDirectory, you must decide what operating system you want to use. Because the eDirectory can be hosted by many operating systems, this choice will depend on the major operating systems used in your network. For example, if you are a windows shop, you might want to install the eDirectory on a Windows platform. If your network is based primarily on Unix or Linux, you may prefer to install the directory on one of those platforms. The choice of which platform to use for the installation should be made by considering which operating system your IT department is most familiar with.

Hardware Requirements

Depending on the number of objects and attributes you will store in the eDirectory, as well as the operating-system platform you will use, the hardware requirements will vary. In the following sections that describe installing the eDirectory on different operating systems, you will find a table that describes several situations that show the hardware requirements, depending on the size of the eDirectory you want to create. If you anticipate using the eDirectory for more than the minimal number of objects, you should also plan to use a hardware platform that is more powerful, as shown in these tables. If you decide to add objects or attributes that are not part of the generic eDirectory installation, you need to consider using values larger than those shown in these tables. For example, if you operate a specialized business that requires you to create objects specific to your business requirements, and the default objects in the eDirectory cannot be used for your purposes, then use these tables to estimate the hardware you will need.

Novell suggests the following basic hardware requirements for installing any version of the eDirectory:

- Java 1.3.
- Video graphics card supporting 8 bits, 256 colors (which all modern systems support).
- If installing on NetWare, the video card should at least be compliant with VESA (a 32-bit bus operating at 50MHz, which operates at approximately the speed of the microprocessor). However, for NetWare 6.x, this may not be necessary. Obviously, with all current systems supporting both PCI and AGP, this requirement should not be much of a roadblock.

Although the preceding video settings are basic to the installation of the eDirectory, you should probably consider upgrading your video card. It is quite possible that you will end up viewing distortions on your monitor that might hang the installation. So, for most installs, consider upgrading your video card to a higher specification than the minimal specifications described.

Hardware Requirements for NetWare 6.x, Windows NT/2000/Server 2003, and Linux

You can install the eDirectory on NetWare 6.x. For backward compatibility you can also install the directory on 5.x servers, but you should check the Web site www.novell.com to ensure that your 5.1 NetWare system has been patched and upgraded to the newest requirements for the eDirectory. For NetWare 5.1 this includes Support Pack 5, as well as other requirements. The hardware and software requirements described in the remainder of this chapter are based on the eDirectory, version 8.7. In some cases you may be required to update your 5.x NetWare installation to NetWare 6 to use the eDirectory.

Note

Upgrading from NetWare 5.0 to the eDirectory version 8.7 or greater is not supported.

For installing the eDirectory on NetWare 6.x, Table 34.1 describes the hardware requirements, depending on the minimal number of basic objects and attributes (included with the eDirectory) you will require. This table can also be used to judge the minimal requirements necessary for installing the eDirectory on Windows NT/2000/2003 servers.

Table 34.1   Minimal Hardware Requirements for NetWare 6.x

# of Objects	# of Processors	System Memory	Disk Space
100,000	Pentium III 400–700MHz (one CPU)	384MB	144MB
1,000,000	Pentium III 450–700MHz (2 CPUs)	2GB	1.5GB
10,000,000	Pentium III 450–700MHz (2–4 CPUs)	2GB (or more)	15GB

Hardware Requirements for Solaris Unix

Another popular operating system you can use to install the eDirectory is the Solaris operating system from Sun Microsystems. Table 34.2 shows the hardware requirements you will need to meet in order to install the directory on this platform. Again, these are minimal requirements, and you need to take into consideration additional requirements if you plan to use additional objects or attributes. In the Unix environment this will probably be an important factor due to the nature of Unix versus NetWare, Linux, and Windows systems. This is due to the dissimilarity of these operating systems, and the types of objects you will need to access using the eDirectory.

Additionally, if you plan to use multiple authentication methods or encryption, or other services, such as security certificates, which will use additional CPU resources, then consider increasing your hardware from these minimal requirements. And if you choose to create additional indices in addition to those offered by the directory, again consider increasing both disk space and CPU capacity to provide for acceptable performance.

Table 34.2   Minimal Hardware Requirements for Solaris Unix

# of Objects	# of Processors	System Memory	Disk Space
100,000	Sun Enterprise 220	384MB	144MB
1,000,000	Sun Enterprise 450	2GB	1.5GB
10,000,000	Sun Enterprise 4500 using more than one CPU	2GB (or more)	15GB

Hardware Requirements for Solaris AIX Unix

IBM's version of Unix is called AIX. This version of Unix was designed to run on large mainframes as well as minicomputers and now typical network servers. The requirements for this platform are described in Table 34.3.

Table 34.3   Minimal Hardware Requirements for Solaris Unix

# of Objects	# of Processors	System Memory	Disk Space
100,000	RS/6000	384MB	144MB
1,000,000	RS/6000	2GB	1.5GB
10,000,000	RS/6000	2GB (or more)	15GB

Installing the eDirectory for Supported Platforms

If you have met the hardware requirements described previously for the platform that will host the eDirectory, you can begin the installation. Because the steps involved are vastly different for each of the supported operating systems, see the NetWare documentation for specific instructions on how to install the eDirectory, provided that you have met the minimum hardware requirements listed in the preceding section.

New Features the eDirectory Delivers

Besides the new name, the eDirectory comes with a few features not found in Novell Directory Services (NDS). Some of these are listed here:

- **Transport Layer Security (TLS)**—This is an enhancement of the Secure Sockets Layer protocol and is used to set up a secure connection across the network. Support for SSL is also included, and both TLS and SSL are implementations based on the OpenSSL version.

- **iMonitor Version 2**—This feature enables you to monitor eDirectory functions using a Web browser.

- **The Simple Network Management Protocol (SNMP)**—You can now monitor eDirectory events using the standard SNMP protocol.

- **Extensible Match**—A method of searching a directory database, defined in RFC 2251, "Lightweight Directory Access Protocol (v3)."

- **Backup and Restore**—A new tool, Backup eMTool, enables hot backups. Cold backups can also be performed. Unlike the older TSA backup utility, which can back up an entire NDS tree, the Backup eMTool is used to back up partitions on a single server.

TLS/SSL

These protocols are placed between the Application layer and the TCP/IP layer in the protocol stack. Applications (such as HTTP) are sent through TCP/IP sessions encrypted using TLS or SSL. These two protocols use a public/private (asymmetric encryption) key technique to set up an initial connection, and then create a single key (symmetric encryption) that is used for the data transfers that follow.

TLS/SSL can use many types of symmetric encryption, which is negotiated during the setup phase. SSL can also be found in your typical browser/Web server environment, where it is used to create secure connections for exchanging sensitive data, such as credit-card numbers.

iMonitor

This utility complements, and can work with, the NetWare Remote Manager used for NetWare 5.x networks. You can use a browser from a remote location in your network to examine statistical and diagnostic information about eDirectory replicas, partitions, and servers. iMonitor can replace traditional tools used to gather information about directory services, such as DSBrowse, DSTrace, and DSDiag. Additionally, some of the features of DSRepair can be found in iMonitor.

Note

To use the iMonitor utility, you must have an account that grants you the rights to view specific information. Depending on your account, some of the features that iMonitor offers may not be available to you.

Some of the information you can view using iMonitor include the following:

■ The health of the eDirectory on a server, replica, or partition. The Agent Synchronization Summary shows the information about synchronization between the current server and other replicas and partitions, such as errors and the time since the last synchronization. You can also set up filters so that only specific information fields are displayed.

■ The Agent Information Page enables you to see data about connections made by the server. You can see addresses that can be used to access the server and timing information, among other data.

■ The Known Servers List shows the names of servers that are known by the server you are monitoring, including which servers are part of a replica ring. You can also see which servers are up and running, and those that are offline. The time at which the current server last communicated with another server is displayed; the state of a server is set to unknown if the current server has never communicated with a remote server.

■ The Partitions page shows data about replicas on the *current server* that you are monitoring. This information includes information about both replicas and partitions, showing the last time data was written to the replica as well as information about the synchronization status for partitions and replicas on the server.

■ The Agent Activity page displays information about network traffic and can be used to identify system bottlenecks, and gives some information about background processes, among other items.

■ The Error Index page displays errors on eDirectory servers. This includes errors specific to the eDirectory as well as other errors, with links to Novell documentation about the errors when available.

iMonitor can perform other functions in addition to those covered in the preceding list. For example, you can run several reports that come with iMonitor or create customized reports. You can use the Schema page to examine class and attribute definitions in the schema. You can also search for specific objects based on the schema definitions.

The Simple Network Management Protocol (SNMP)

For many years SNMP has been an industry standard used to monitor network devices. Items that are monitored are stored in a Management Information Base, usually referred to as an MIB. As new hardware is developed, it is necessary to create a new MIB that contains information about what can be monitored.

▶▶   You can learn more about SNMP in Chapter 53, "Network Testing and Analysis Tools."

The MIB for the eDirectory contains four types of managed objects. The Cache Database Statistics Table is used to monitor statistical information about entries cached on each eDirectory server. The Config Database Statistics Table collects similar information about entries on the server, not cached entries. The Protocol Statistics Table is used to monitor access and operations for the eDirectory server, as well as errors.

The eDirectory MIB contains 119 traps, which are beyond the scope of this chapter. You can find a description of each trap in the eDirectory documentation.

Extensible Match

This version of the eDirectory supports partial functionality of an extensible match. Basically, an extensible match is the capability of using a filter to search an LDAP directory by using matching rules and the values that are to be searched for, including which attributes are to be searched. At this time eDirectory (version 8.7) supports only matching for the Distinguished Name (DN) of an object.

Note

RFC 2251, "Lightweight Directory Access Protocol (v3)," contains a full description of the functionality provided by using an extensible match.

Because this version of the eDirectory does not support user-specified matching rules, only an exact match is performed.

Backup and Restore

Previous versions of NDS used TSA for making backups of the directory database. You can still use this utility with the eDirectory. However, a new tool has been created that you might find more beneficial if your network is accessed around the clock: the eDirectory Backup eMTool. Backup eMTool is a component of the eMBox set of tools, so you will need to install the eMBox service on the server that you want to back up using Backup eMTool. There are several differences between TSA and Backup eMTool. The older TSA is used to back up an entire directory tree. Backup eMTool is used to back up that portion of the directory stored on a server. Thus, if you have only a small LAN that uses a single server to hold the entire directory tree, using TSA might be a good solution for the time being. Yet, as the directory continues to be enhanced, you may find that changing to the new backup tool is a good idea at this time.

This new backup utility can be used on all operating-system platforms that can host the eDirectory, and it has several new features:

- You can easily restore the backup to an individual server.
- The backup process is capable of backing up the eDirectory as it scales to larger capacities over time. The only bottleneck is the speed of the connection between the server hosting the directory database and the backup device.
- When used with the DSMASTER (disaster recovery) servers, you can quickly restore the directory tree.
- You can back up files other than just the directory database files, such as security files and other files you specify.
- You can remotely administer the backup process using a browser, or create a batch file to automatically perform the backup process.
- You can create a "hot" backup that creates a backup of the entire database, without having to take the database offline. Or you can perform a cold backup.

Note

The eDirectory Backup eMTool can be used to create a backup of a partition of the database and files stored on a server. It cannot be used to back up or restore portions of the database partition. Additionally, you can create a backup of the databases and associated files only onto a disk. You must then use another backup utility to put the backup to tape.

If you choose to use a batch file to perform the backup, don't forget to check the log file produced to make sure that the backup was successful. Before using the new backup utility, you should upgrade all servers holding replicas to at least version 8.5 of the eDirectory, or later if possible.

For remote backups, install the eMBox client on the server. You can also use iManager with this backup utility, but a cold backup, among other features, is not supported using iManager.

Note

For those unfamiliar with NetWare 6.x, eMBox is a Java client that enables command-line interaction with Backup eMTool, as well as other NetWare utilities. When you install the eDirectory, the eMBox client is automatically installed. You can copy the file (**eMBoxClient.jar**) to other servers if you want to use those servers to perform the backup remotely. eMBox requires Sun's Java Virtual Machine, version 1.3.1.

Although Backup eMTool is faster than TSA, TSA can write backups directly to tape. Because Backup eMTool simply creates a backup on the file system of the server, you could lose the data should the server encounter an unrecoverable hardware problem, such as a disk failure. Because of this, you should always schedule a backup to tape immediately following the backup created by Backup eMTool. The main benefits you get from using Backup eMTool are that you can back up just a partition, and not the entire tree, and you can perform a hot backup. The tape backup can be scheduled to run on a server that has additional hardware capacity so that the tape backup does not degrade the server's main goal of providing directory services for users on the network.

File Server Protocols

35

SOME OF THE MAIN TOPICS IN THIS CHAPTER ARE

The first thing that comes to mind when you think "network" is probably file and print servers. When an addition is made to the network for a new business unit, or when existing units are shuffled around and users and resources must be regrouped, it is usually the files that users access and the printing capacity they require that need to be given special consideration. Plan for the necessary bandwidth, and check the logical and physical topology of the LAN to be sure that you have the necessary capacity, either in bandwidth or in storage. In this chapter, the protocols that are used for file services are detailed.

▶▶ Chapter 44, "Network Printing Protocols," covers print services for the LAN.

Why Should You Read This Chapter?

Understanding how a particular protocol functions will better enable you to troubleshoot network problems that prevent users from timely access to file resources. For example, using a LAN analyzer to review network traffic during a troubleshooting session will be of little use unless you know what types of frames you are looking for and understand their function in the file-sharing process. You also can use the knowledge gained from this chapter to assist in making decisions about future additions to the network.

There are many ways you can share files. You can copy them to a floppy disk or tape cartridge (or more likely today, a CD you just burned) and pass them around the office (a la *sneaker-net*). This is not a very efficient method when your volume of data grows and you find yourself trying to keep track of multiple versions of a file.

When TCP/IP was developed, several handy utilities were created to work with the protocol to provide clients some useful file- and system-sharing functionality. One of these, the *File Transfer Protocol (FTP)*, enables a user to copy a file to or from a remote computer to his own so that manipulation of the data can be done locally, and then the file can be transferred back onto the original server.

FTP is an ideal mechanism when you want to distribute multiple copies of a file to multiple people. When used in an environment where the goal is to allow multiple users to modify a file, however, FTP doesn't really improve much on the floppy method, except that the network can often handle a larger number of files over a greater distance more quickly. However, because users end up with more than one copy of the file, there is always the potential of creating mismatched versions when trying to coordinate multiple access to a file by making many copies of it. For example, if the user forgets to copy the file back to its original location after making changes, the next user who makes a copy of the file will find herself working on a file that does not contain these changes. Another problem with the copying method is that the network bandwidth (or lack of it) can become a problem for very large files, though this is less of a problem in today's faster networks. It may be a hindrance, however, in slow dial-up connections to the network.

◀◀ FTP, telnet, and a host of other useful network utilities are covered in Chapter 26, "Basic TCP/IP Services and Applications."

Other TCP/IP utilities can be used to access files remotely. For example, you can establish a telnet session to a remote computer and then issue commands locally to manipulate data.

Using telnet, the user's PC or workstation acts as nothing more than a terminal emulator, and a rather expensive one at that. All applications that are needed to manipulate the data must be installed on the remote computer. This is probably a better method to use than copying from an FTP site or floppy disk when trying to share a single file among many users, because it maintains only one copy of the file. However, it is still not a very convenient method for several reasons. If you want to access files on more than one remote system, you need a separate telnet session for each one. This means it is not possible for an application, such as a word processor or database, to access files or remote systems at the same time (because the word processor or other application is running on the target system and not the client workstation). When using a telnet client, the user must have a user account set up on each remote system so that the logon can be validated. This can be overcome by using a single sign-on technology such as the Active Directory. But using telnet is not as transparent a process as simply running an application on the user's workstation and accessing files in the local file system.

The *Network File System (NFS)* protocol was developed by Sun Microsystems to make remote file access as simple a process for the user as local file access. NFS enables a user to access a remote file system while making it appear to the user to be a local file system. There is no need to copy files back and forth from servers. Using NFS, a file system (or a portion of it) residing on a remote system can be made to appear to the client as though it were simply part of the local file system. Early on, NFS was found only on Unix boxes. However, its popularity spread, and you can now find NFS server applications and client applications for most major operating systems. A minor disadvantage to using NFS is that network problems can interfere with file access. However, this is true for any kind of network file-sharing protocol.

Note

Microsoft's Services for Unix (version 3.0) provides various Unix-like utilities and commands to Windows 2000 and 2003 server. These include an NFS client as well as an NFS server. You can learn more about Services for Unix 3.0 in Chapter 61, "Migration and Integration Issues: Windows NT, Windows 2000, Windows 2003, Unix, and Linux."

Microsoft operating systems have long used the *Server Message Block (SMB)* protocol to provide file and printer access to networked clients. This protocol has developed over the years and has been adopted into Windows NT and Windows 2000. Whereas NFS is built on top of several other complex protocols and is used to provide only file-sharing capabilities, SMB is a more basic protocol that can be used across a network to provide network access to files and print sharing to interprocess communication, and other resources such as named pipes and mailboxes. The latest incarnation of SMB is called the Common Internet File System (CIFS) protocol.

In this chapter, you will briefly look at these protocols that enable you to share files on a network.

Server Message Block (SMB) and the Common Internet File System (CIFS)

A common protocol you will find on almost any computer running a Windows operating system, from early LAN Manager products to Windows Server 2003, is the Server Message Block protocol. This is a protocol used for basic file sharing and printer sharing, and for locating other network resources. It is a basic client/server protocol that uses request and response messages.

SMB has also been used by many vendors other than Microsoft to provide file and print services, including IBM (OS/2) and Digital Equipment Corporation (now HP) in its Pathworks products.

SMB has been around for awhile and has been modified to support new functions as PC networks have evolved. Each new version of the protocol is called a *dialect*. Table 35.1 shows the dialects in order from the earliest to the latest, and any server implementing a particular dialect must also support interaction with clients of any earlier dialect in this table. This allows for backward compatibility for older clients when parts of the network, such as servers, are upgraded.

Table 35.1 SMB Protocol Dialects

SMB Dialect	Description
PC NETWORK PROGRAM 1.0	Original MSNET SMB protocol, sometimes called the *core protocol*.
PCLAN1.0	Alternative name for the core protocol.
MICROSOFT NETWORKS 1.03	MS-NET 1.03. Lock&Read and Write&Unlock added to the protocol and defined a special version of raw read and raw write.
MICROSOFT NETWORKS 3.0	LANMAN 1.0 protocol for the DOS operating system. Same as LANMAN1.0 except that the server must map errors from OS/2 errors to a DOS error.
LANMAN1.0	First complete version of LANMAN 1.0.
LM1.2X002	First complete version of LANMAN 2.0.
DOS LM1.2X002	Same as LM1.2X002 (LANMAN 2.0), except that the server maps errors to DOS errors.
DOS LANMAN2.1	DOS LANMAN 2.1 protocol.
LANMAN2.1	OS/2 version of the LANMAN 2.1 protocol.
Windows for Workgroups 3.1a	Windows for Workgroups version 1.0 of the protocol.
NT LM 0.12	SMB for Windows NT. Added special SMBs for NT.

SMB Message Types

SMB is a message-oriented protocol in which the client makes a request of the server using a message formatted according to a specific SMB message type. The server responds to the client's request using a specific SMB format. There are many types of messages, which are listed in Table 35.2. Note that not all message types are supported by all clients. The table is subdivided into sections showing at what point in the development of SMB-based networks a particular message type was introduced.

Table 35.2 SMB Message Types

PC NETWORK PROGRAM 1.0	
SMB_COM_NEGOTIATE	SMB_COM_CLOSE_PRINT_FILE
SMB_COM_CREATE_DIRECTORY	SMB_COM_DELETE_DIRECTORY
SMB_COM_OPEN	SMB_COM_CREATE
SMB_COM_CLOSE	SMB_COM_FLUSH
SMB_COM_DELETE	SMB_COM_RENAME
SMB_COM_QUERY_INFORMATION	SMB_COM_SET_INFORMATION
SMB_COM_READ	SMB_COM_WRITE
SMB_COM_LOCK_BYTE_RANGE	SMB_COM_UNLOCK_BYTE_RANGE
SMB_COM_CREATE_TEMPORARY	SMB_COM_CREATE_NEW
SMB_COM_CHECK_DIRECTORY	SMB_COM_PROCESS_EXIT
SMB_COM_SEEK	SMB_COM_TREE_CONNECT
SMB_COM_TREE_DISCONNECT	SMB_COM_SEARCH
SMB_COM_QUERY_INFORMATION_DISK	SMB_COM_WRITE_PRINT_FILE
SMB_COM_OPEN_PRINT_FILE	SMB_COM_GET_PRINT_QUEUE

Table 35.2   Continued

LANMAN 1.0

SMB_COM_LOCK_AND_READ	SMB_COM_WRITE_AND_UNLOCK
SMB_COM_READ_RAW	SMB_COM_READ_MPX
SMB_COM_WRITE_MPX	SMB_COM_WRITE_RAW
SMB_COM_WRITE_COMPLETE	SMB_COM_WRITE_MPX_SECONDARY
SMB_COM_SET_INFORMATION2	SMB_COM_QUERY_INFORMATION2
SMB_COM_LOCKING_ANDX	SMB_COM_TRANSACTION
SMB_COM_TRANSACTION_SECONDARY	SMB_COM_IOCTL
SMB_COM_IOCTL_SECONDARY	SMB_COM_COPY
SMB_COM_MOVE	SMB_COM_ECHO
SMB_COM_WRITE_AND_CLOSE	SMB_COM_OPEN_ANDX
SMB_COM_READ_ANDX	SMB_COM_WRITE_ANDX
SMB_COM_SESSION_SETUP_ANDX	SMB_COM_TREE_CONNECT_ANDX
SMB_COM_FIND	SMB_COM_FIND_UNIQUE
SMB_COM_FIND_CLOSE	

LM1.2X002

SMB_COM_TRANSACTION2	SMB_COM_TRANSACTION2_SECONDARY
SMB_COM_FIND_CLOSE2	SMB_COM_LOGOFF_ANDX

NT LM 0.12

SMB_COM_NT_TRANSACT	SMB_COM_NT_TRANSACT_SECONDARY
SMB_COM_NT_CREATE_ANDX	SMB_COM_NT_CANCEL

From the list in Table 35.2, it is easy to see that SMB has evolved over the years and has a specific command set that provides detailed functionality while maintaining simplicity by using a simple message exchange format. Most LAN analyzers have the capability to decode SMB packets, and you can troubleshoot SMB client/server sessions to observe the interaction of the commands shown in the table.

SMB Security Provisions

SMB has the capability to provide for two kinds of security for file sharing:

- Share level
- User level

The most basic level of security that can be used on an SMB network is *share-level* security. This approach offers a disk or directory as an available resource on the network, protecting it with a password. Users who want to access a resource that is protected at the share level need only know the name of the resource, the server that offers it, and the password for it to make a connection. This kind of file sharing is usually employed by Windows 9x/Me computers configured as a workgroup, in which using domains and the Active Directory would require too much administrative overhead—not to mention expense. In a small LAN in which there is not a great need for a high degree of security among users, it is simple to set up and maintain a network based on this model.

A superior method that is more likely to be found in the business environment involves making users accountable for accessing resources. A *user-level* security model dictates that each user should log in using a unique identifier, called a *username*, which is associated with a password for the user account. After logging in to the network, users are granted access to resources based on the rights accorded their accounts (what the user can do) and the resource protections placed on files or directories (what the user can do with the resource). This user-level method enables you to assign different kinds of access based on username and resource.

Note

In addition to a username/password model commonly used for computer access, there has been a rapid increase in the marketplace for more secure authorization mechanisms, such as using smartcards with assigned PIN numbers to each employee. As recognition software continues to increase at the top edge, you can use it in your network also. It won't be long (the technology is available now, at quite some expense) before you'll use technologies of recognition software such as one now used by super-secure organizations—a retinal scan. Just as computer hardware gets less expensive every year as production ramps up to higher levels, you can expect the same from recognition devices in the very near future.

In the share-level security model, access to a share enables the user to access any files in the top-level directory of the share and all the files in all the subdirectories that might fall under the top-level directory. In the user-level security model, the administrator can place different access limitations on every directory, subdirectory, and file that exists in the share.

The earliest SMB clients do not have the capability to exchange an account name and password with a server and are thus limited in what they can do in a more modern environment. SMB servers will generally provide some functionality for user-level security. For example, if the client computer's computer name matches an account name that is known to the server, and if the password that the client passes as a "share" password matches that of the account, the SMB server can perform a logon for the user and grant access to the resource.

Protocol Negotiation and Session Setup

SMB has a built-in mechanism that is used by the client and server to determine the other's capabilities so that a common protocol version can be established that the two will use for the network connection. The first SMB message that the client sends to the server is one of the SMB_COM_NEGOTIATE type. The client uses this message to send the server a list of the dialects it understands. The server selects the most recent dialect it understands from the client's list and returns a message to it.

The response the server returns depends on the type of client. The information includes the dialect selected and can include additional information, such as buffer sizes, supported access modes, time and date values, and security information. After the client receives this response, it can continue to set up the session by using the SESSION_SETUP_ANDX message type.

If the initial server response indicates that user-level security is being used, this message type can be used to perform a user logon. The client sets a value in the message header called the *UID (user ID)* for the account it wants to use. It also supplies the account name and password to the server by using this message type. If these values are validated by the server, the user can continue to use the UID to make subsequent accesses.

Other setup functions that are performed by using SESSION_SETUP_ANDX include the following:

- Set the maximum values for the size of buffers that will be used in the message exchange.
- Set the maximum number of client requests that can be outstanding at the server.
- Set the virtual circuit (VC) number.

If the VC passed to the server is zero and the server has other circuits open for the client, it will abort those services, assuming that the client has rebooted without freeing those services first. To properly close a session, the client uses the message type LOGOFF_ANDX, which causes the server to close all files associated with the user's UID.

Accessing Files

Other SMB message types are used to traverse the resource directory and to open, read, write, and close files. First, the user must connect to the resource by using the TREE_CONNECT message. The message includes the name of the resource (server and share name) and, for earlier clients that do not perform logons, a shared password. The server responds by sending the user a value called the *TID (Tree ID)*, which will be used in SMBs exchanged for this connection.

After the connection has been established, several basic SMB command formats can be used to manipulate files and directories that reside on the share. For example, the CREATE_DIRECTORY message is used to create a new directory in the file share's directory structure. The client passes the pathname for the new directory, and the server creates the directory, provided that the client has the appropriate access rights or permissions. The DELETE_DIRECTORY SMB message can be used to remove a directory, again based on the functions allowed for the username.

Opening and Closing Files

The OPEN message is used by a client to open a file. The path for the file is given, relative to the file share root. The client specifies the access that is desired, such as read, write, or share. If the file is successfully opened, the server returns a *File ID (FID)* to the client, which is used to further access the file using other SMB message types; it is similar to a file handle, which most programmers will recognize.

The server also returns data to the client indicating the actual access that was granted, which is read-only, write-only, or read/write.

The CLOSE message is sent by the client to tell the server to release any locks held on the resource file held by the client. After this message, the client can no longer use the FID to access the file, but it must instead reopen the file and obtain a new value.

When a client does not know the exact name of a file that it wants to open, the SEARCH message can be used to perform a directory lookup. This function enables wildcards to be used, and the server response can include more than one filename that matches the request.

Reading and Writing

The SMB protocol uses the READ and WRITE message types to perform I/O operations on a file for the client. Using the READ request, a client can request that the server return information from the file by specifying a number of bytes and an offset into the file. The server returns the data, indicating the actual number of bytes returned, which can be less than requested if the user tries to read past the end of a file.

The WRITE command updates a file in a similar manner. The client sends in the data that will be written, indicating the number of bytes to write and an offset into the file where the write operation will begin. If the request causes a write past the end of the file, the file is extended to make it larger. The server sends a response telling the client the number of bytes that were written. If the number is less than the requested value, an error has occurred.

To increase read/write performance, the READ_RAW and WRITE_RAW message types can be used to exchange much larger blocks of information between the client and the server. When these are used, the client must have only one request issued to the server. In one send, the server will respond with data that can be as many as 65,535 bytes in length. The WRITE command works in the opposite direction, allowing the client to send a large buffer of raw data to the server for a write operation.

Locking Mechanisms

Locking allows a particular client exclusive access to a file or a part of a file when it is shared on the network. In SMB, the capability to create a lock is called an opportunistic lock, or *oplock* for short. This is better explained by looking at the way in which it works. A client can create a lock on a resource using three kinds of locks. The first is an *exclusive* lock, in which the client has exclusive access to the data held by the lock. A *batch* oplock is one that is kept open by the server when the client process has already closed the file. A *Level II* oplock is one in which there can be multiple readers of the same file.

The locking process consists of the client requesting the type of lock it wants when it opens the file. The server replies to the client with the type of lock that was granted when it responds to the open request.

A lock gives the client the capability to efficiently manage buffer space it uses when accessing a file over the network. For example, if a client has exclusive access to a file and is performing writes to it, it can buffer a lot of the newly written information before having to send it to the server to update the file. This can provide a reduced number of network packets when updating a file. A client that has an exclusive lock on a file can also buffer read-ahead data to make reading a file much faster.

These locks are called opportunistic locks for a reason. A client can be granted exclusive access to a file if no other client has it open at the time of the request. What happens when another client needs to read the file? The server notifies the first client that it needs to break the exclusive lock. The client then flushes its buffers so that any data that has not been written to the file is processed. The client then sends an acknowledgment to the server that it recognizes that the exclusive lock has been broken. In Figure 35.1, you can see the interaction between two clients and a server as these messages are exchanged.

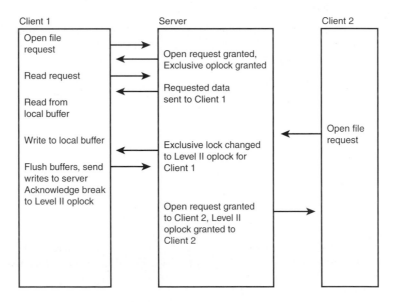

Figure 35.1 Exclusive oplocks are changed to Level II oplocks when a second client wants to open a file.

Batch oplocks are used to reduce the amount of traffic on the network when some programs require continual reopening of a file to obtain commands, as when a batch command procedure is executed.

For example, a batch procedure executed by the command processor usually opens a file, locates the next line to be executed, reads that line, closes the file, and then executes the command. The problem with this is that these steps are taken for each command line in the procedure, resulting in multiple file open/closes that are not really necessary.

This procedure for reading individual lines from a file is done by using a batch oplock whereby the client can read the data from its local read-ahead cache instead of reopening the file on the remote server to get each line.

Level II oplocks were new with the NT changes to SMB. This kind of lock allows more than one client to have a file opened for reading. When a client must read from a file that is opened by another exclusively, the server informs the current client that its exclusive lock has been broken and is now a Level II oplock. No client that has a Level II oplock will buffer data to or from the file. Thus, after the lock has changed to a Level II oplock (and the first client has flushed any data in its buffers), both clients can continue reading the file.

Using *NET* Commands

The set of NET commands form the basis for a command-line interface that the client can use to access SMB-based file services. For server functions, the NET commands allow you to create and configure shares, manage users and groups, and more. This command, with its many command-line parameters, can be used to make a directory available for sharing, to connect or disconnect a resource, or to view resources available on a server, among other functions. Clients using operating systems such as Windows 98/Me or Windows NT/2000/XP/2003 can also use Microsoft Windows Explorer to connect to file resource shares on the network. However, the NET command provides a simple interface that also can be incorporated into command procedures, such as user login script files. You can also use these commands during troubleshooting. For example, you can establish a telnet session with a remote client who is having problems with a file share and execute the NET commands directly via the Command Prompt window. When present at the actual computer that is experiencing a problem, you will probably get more information by using commands than by using the GUI interface. The exception to this is the Event Viewer, which can give you valuable guidance by narrowing down the problem that generated an error. Reading the Event Viewer records can be confusing, and they are often easily interpreted only by experienced personnel. Yet, using the Event Viewer, you can at least determine such basic conditions as a bad password, a nonexistent user account (create it), and other simple items that often show up in day-to-day network activities.

Note

More information about using the Event Viewer on Windows systems can be found in Chapter 47, "Auditing and Other Monitoring Measures." By setting up the correct items to be audited, and using the Event Viewer to check for messages, you can quickly debug many problems.

Because the NET command can be a useful tool both for setting up users to connect to resources and for troubleshooting clients, it is worth looking at the basic functions you can perform using this command.

There are several command parameters you can use with NET. For file sharing, these are the most basic commands:

- SHARE
- USE
- VIEW

NET SHARE

The NET SHARE command enables you to offer a disk or directory structure for sharing on the network. If used by itself with no other parameters, the command will show you the current shares that are being offered by the workstation or server, as in the following example:

```
C:\>net share
Share name   Resource                        Remark
-------------------------------------------------------------------------------
IPC$                                         Remote IPC
D$           D:\                             Default share
print$       F:\WINNT\System32\spool\drivers Printer Drivers
E$           E:\                             Default share
C$           C:\                             Default share
F$           F:\                             Default share
ADMIN$       F:\WINNT                        Remote Admin
documents    d:\
HPLaserJ     LPT1:              Spooled  HP LaserJet 6L
The command completed successfully.
```

Note

In the listing of file shares, note that some end with a dollar sign, such as **C$** and **F$**. An administrative drive share for each unique local drive volume on nonremovable media is automatically created using this syntax. However, unless you have administrator privileges, you won't see these when using the **NET** command to view shares on another computer. The dollar sign can be added to any new file share that you create as well. Any share that ends in a dollar sign is a "hidden" share. Hidden shares other than the previously mentioned root drive shares can be accessed by any user who has permissions to the share and who knows the hidden share name. Administrative drive shares cannot be accessed by anyone other than administrators, and these permissions cannot be modified.

In this example, you can see that SMB is used not only to provide network communications for file sharing, but also to provide shared printing (HPLaserJ LPT1:) and interprocess communications (IPC$).

The basic syntax for sharing is as follows:

NET SHARE *sharename*

Entering just this command will return an error message, because you haven't specified what is to be shared. To make a directory available for sharing, specify the name you want the file share to use on the network, and follow it with the path to the directory to be shared:

NET SHARE *sharename=drive:path*

You can further configure the share by using the following qualifiers:

- **/Users:*number* or /UNLIMITED**—You can specify the maximum number of users that are allowed to simultaneously connect to the share.
- **/REMARK:*text***—You can display text to describe the share.
- **/CACHE:**—You can specify manual, automatic, or no.

See the following example:

```
F:\>NET SHARE ACTFIL=D:\ACCTPAY /USERS:5
ACTFIL was shared successfully.
```

This code offers the file share `actfil` on the network. It allows as many as five concurrent connections to the files contained in the directory `D:\ACCTPAY` and all subdirectories that fall under it.

Deleting a file share on the server is also a simple matter:

```
F:\>NET SHARE ACTFIL /DELETE
ACTFIL was deleted successfully.
```

In this example, you can also specify the pathname that is being shared:

```
F:\>NET SHARE D:\ACCTPAY /DELETE
ACTFIL was deleted successfully.

D:\ACCTPAY was deleted successfully
```

In both of these instances, the actual directory that was offered for sharing is not deleted. Only the file share is deleted.

Troubleshooting Using NET VIEW and NET USE

These two commands enable you to view the resources available on the network and then make connections to them. `NET VIEW` returns a list of the servers it knows about on the local network. You can use `NET VIEW \\servername` to get a list of services offered by any server in the list, as in the following example:

```
F:\>NET VIEW \\bcanjs1
Shared resources at \\bcanjs1

Share name   Type        Used as   Comment
-------------------------------------------------------------------------------
acct         Disk                  Accounting
cdrom        Disk                  CD Drive on BCANJS1
documents    Disk
dvdrom       Disk                  DVD Drive on BCANJS1
HPLaserJ     Print                 IIP LaserJet 6L
Rschlz       Disk                  Restricted
The command completed successfully.
```

It is easy to get confused when trying to troubleshoot problems with users connecting to shared resources. If you are using a Microsoft-based network that provides file sharing through SMB mechanisms, the `NET VIEW` command can be extremely useful. You can determine from this command whether the remote resource server is even seen in the browsing list by the client computer. If it is, you can display the resources offered. To connect to a resource manually, you can use the `NET USE` command. When executed by itself with no other command-line parameters, this command displays a list of your current connections.

To make a new connection, the syntax is very basic, though it has variations:

```
NET USE device sharename
```

Here, *device* can be an actual drive letter (such as `D:` or `E:`), a device name for a printer (`LPT1:`), or the wildcard `*`, in which case the next available drive letter will be chosen automatically when the connection is made. Observe the following example:

```
NET USE X: \\BCANJ1\DOCUMENTS
```

Tip

If you use an asterisk (*) instead of a drive letter with the **NET USE** command, the system will assign drive letters starting with the end of the alphabet (Z, unless it is already in use). Then, for each subsequent **NET USE** command that uses the asterisk, the next lower alphabetic character will be used.

This attaches the drive letter X: to the resource documents on the server BCANJ1.

You can also specify a username that can be used to evaluate your access rights to the remote resource:

```
NET USE X: \\BCANJ1\DOCUMENTS /USER:[domainname\]username
```

Here, you would specify a valid username and, if it is a domain account, the name of the Windows domain. To delete a connection to a remote resource, use the /DELETE qualifier:

```
NET USE X: /DELETE
```

The NET USE command is most often associated with creating user logon scripts or other batch-oriented procedures that are used to interact with files offered as resources on a network. It can also be a very handy command to remember when performing a new installation or upgrading a user. For example, when installing a new application or troubleshooting a misbehaving one, you can quickly connect to a remote resource to download configuration or driver files.

Monitoring and Troubleshooting SMB Communications

You can use the NET STATISTICS command to obtain a quick view about statistics related to the SMB protocol.

Use either WORKSTATION or SERVER as a keyword to indicate which set of statistics you would like to see, as in the following example:

```
F:> NET STASTICS SERVER

Server Statistics for \\BCA-NJ-S1
Statistics since 11/09/02 05:45 PM
Sessions accepted               1
Sessions timed-out              0
Sessions errored-out            0

Kilobytes sent                  3
Kilobytes received              3

Mean response time (msec)       0

System errors                   0
Permission violations           0
Password violations             0

Files accessed                  7
Communication devices accessed  0
Print jobs spooled              0

Times buffers exhausted
```

```
Big buffers                        0
Request buffers                    0
```

The command completed successfully.

From this display, you can quickly see whether a server is having problems with a recent password change—password violations will probably be excessive. A high value for permission violations can indicate that an access control list on a file or directory might have recently been changed. The other statistics shown here also can be used for many different troubleshooting scenarios.

The NET command has the capability of showing you a lot of information. For example, in addition to giving SMB statistics, the NET command can be used to show the services currently running on an NT/2000 or Windows 2003 family of operating systems. Using the NET START command with other parameters on the line displays a list of the services currently running. If you are troubleshooting a client and see, for example, that the Workstation service is not running, you can use the NET START WORKSTATION command to start it. The NET command enables you to view, start, and stop services without having to use the graphical interface and can be a great help when performing remote diagnosis.

When you upgrade a network or make repairs, it is often useful to send a message to users to let them know what is happening. For example, replacing a network card might require that a server be out of commission for a short time. Changing a network cable might disrupt network access for users. You might have established a telnet session with a user's workstation and want to send him a message on the screen to let him know that you are working. You can use the NET SEND command, using the following syntax, to send a message to users:

NET SEND {*name* | * | /DOMAIN[:*domainname*] | /USERS} *message*

Here, you can see that you can send a message to a single user or use the wildcard * character to send the message to all users. You can use the /DOMAIN:*domainname* variation to send the message to all users in a particular domain, for example. See the following command:

NET SEND * I am monitoring your workstation right now. Will call when finished.

When logged in to a server, this command produced the pop-up message on the terminal of the logged-in user shown in Figure 35.2.

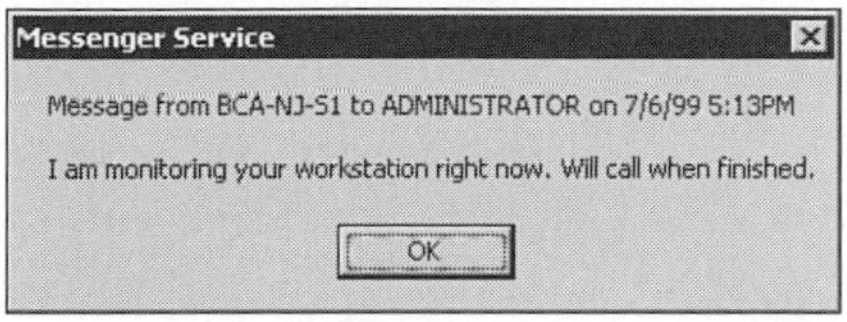

Figure 35.2   The NET SEND command can be used to send a message to users when you are logged in to their workstations.

To carry problem diagnosis any further when using SMB for file sharing, you need to resort to a LAN analyzer of some kind. You can use this to verify that the correct SMB messages are being exchanged between the client and the server. In Figure 35.3, you can see the Microsoft Network Monitor being used for this purpose.

You can step from one packet to the next to discover where a problem might be occurring. For example, is a password required? Are there problems with opening a file? You can watch the sequence of commands that are used to connect to a tree, open a file, and make an attempt to read or write.

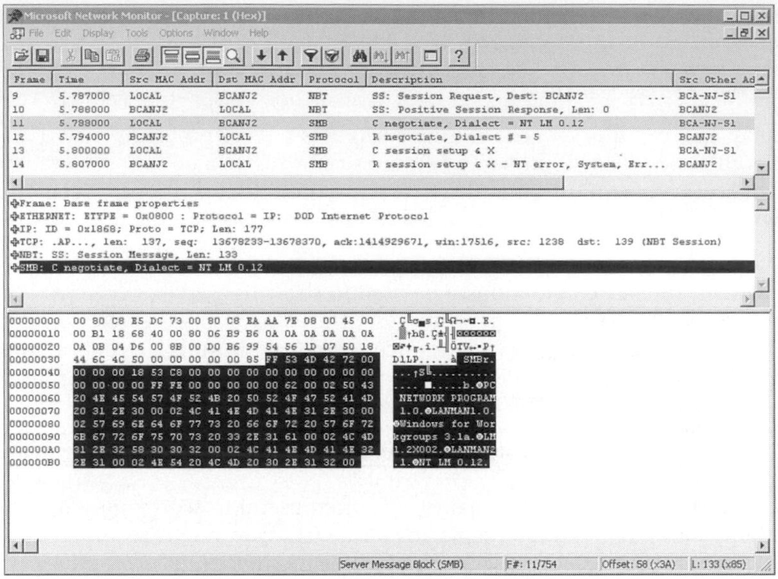

Figure 35.3 Using Microsoft Network Monitor, or a similar LAN analyzer, you can examine the exchange of SMB packets between the client and the server.

The Windows 2003 family of servers offers a slightly different view of the Microsoft Network Monitor, as shown in Figure 35.4.

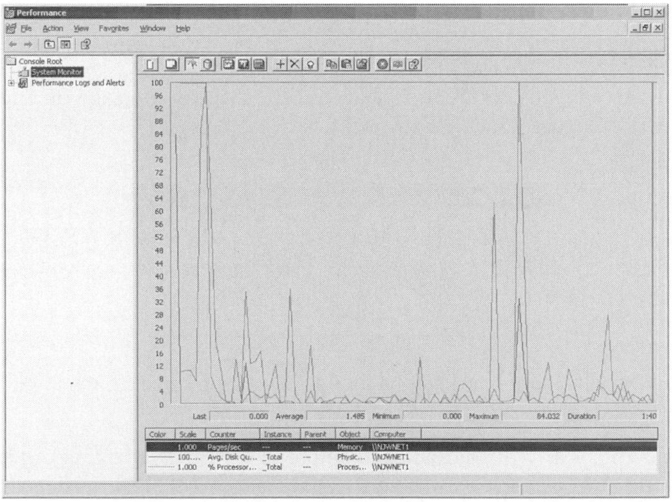

Figure 35.4 The Windows 2003 family of servers' Network Monitor has an updated interface.

In Figure 35.4 you can see a simple example of tracking network performance. You can customize this tool to further capture and display network packets just as you can in Windows 2000.

Although it would be necessary to have more detailed information about the format of SMB packets to make a detailed diagnosis at this level, it is still very helpful to be able to see the types of messages being exchanged, regardless of whether you can understand every byte in the packet. Viewing the data at this level can be used to troubleshoot most problems with this protocol. You also can use the event-logging capabilities of Windows NT/2000 and the Windows 2003 family of servers (the Event Viewer) to look for problems. For example, if you have a password failure and have set the server to audit failed resource accesses, the Event Viewer will have a record showing you the failed attempt, and you can quickly resolve the problem by giving the user the correct password or by changing it. The Event Viewer can also let you know whether the network services installed on your server were started correctly, or encountered problems.

▶▶ The Microsoft Network Analyzer is covered in more detail in Chapter 53, "Network Testing and Analysis Tools." Using the Event Viewer is covered in Chapter 47.

Using the SMB/CIFS Protocol on Non-Microsoft Clients: Samba

SMB/CIFS is a protocol that is highly entrenched in the Microsoft world of operating systems and networking products. It makes sense, then, that there would be a way in which these workstations and servers could be integrated into a Unix/Linux environment without a lot of difficulty. The answer to this problem is called Samba, which is a set of products that provide for SMB conversations between SMB servers, such as Microsoft Windows operating systems, and those that do not use it natively, such as many different variants of Unix or Linux systems. In addition, Samba has been ported to several other popular operating systems, including OpenVMS.

Tip

You might not have to download Samba from the Web. Some Unix or Linux vendors include it as part of the installation package. For example, Samba is included with Red Hat Linux, which is one of the more popular Linux distributions.

Samba was originally developed by Andrew Tridgell and is now maintained by him and other developers (the "Samba Team") on the Internet. You can go to the home page for the Samba effort by using the URL www.samba.org.

From this Web site you can choose a mirror Web site for your country, and then you can view the documentation for Samba and download the most recent version. The software is freely distributed under the GNU public license.

You can configure Samba servers on your Unix boxes to enable high-performance machines to be used as file servers on the Windows network. You can still manage the servers using Unix file administration procedures, and yet to the client computers, the shares appear no different than those offered by other Windows-based file servers.

Troubleshooting a Samba server can be made easier by starting the Samba server software using the -d parameter to specify a debug level (from 1 to 100), which will cause more output messages, depending on the level you specify.

You can also use a LAN analyzer to view the sequence of exchange of SMB messages between server and client. Available as a download from the Samba home page is an extension to the tcpdump utility, called tcpdump-smb. You can use this to capture smb packets and decode the header information.

The Common Internet File System (CIFS)

CIFS is intended to be a replacement, or an upgrade, of the SMB protocol. Design considerations include making it platform-independent. While SMB resides in the NetBIOS legacy environment, CIFS runs on top of TCP. Other improvements over SMB include the following:

- Unicode filenames are used. Because the Internet is global, it's helpful to be able to encode characters that support multiple languages.

- Service is automatically restored after a network disruption.

- CIFS is not proprietary to Microsoft. It is an Open Group standard (X/Open CAE Specification C209). It has also been proposed as an Internet standard to the Internet Engineering Task Force (IETF). This is an improvement over the earlier SMB protocol.

- DNS is used to translate between computer hostnames and IP addresses.

- Both share-level authentication and user-level authentication are supported. With user-level authentication, the user must be authenticated (using a username/password valid on the server) before access is granted. This is much more secure than share-level access, discussed earlier in this chapter. Authentication is done using DES encryption.

- CIFS has been optimized to make communications across a slow link—such as a dial-up modem—possible.

Tip

CIFS (or SMB) is not going to be dying out anytime soon. The Storage Networking Industry Association (**www.snia.org**) has a 150-page PDF file discussing the use of CIFS in both Storage Area Networks (SANs) and Network Attached Storage (NAS)—both among the hottest networking technologies coming to market today. You can find out more about SANs and NAS in Chapter 11, "Network Attached Storage and Storage Area Networks."

CIFS is basically an enhanced version of SMB and still uses server message block messaging. Better security and the use of DNS are necessary additions if the protocol is to be used on the Internet.

NetWare Core Protocol (NCP)

NetWare is composed of several protocols. *IPX* is a connectionless delivery service that can be used by higher-level protocols (such as NCP or SPX) to create a connection-oriented, reliable transport service. Two other important protocols used in NetWare are the *Service Advertising Protocol (SAP)* and the *Routing Information Protocol (RIP)*. It is through SAP that servers announce their presence periodically and clients can make requests to locate resources. RIP is used to locate servers on the network.

Another protocol, called *NetWare Core Protocol (NCP)*, is used for communications exchange between a client and a server when file reads, file writes, or other file-related activities are being performed. It provides connection control and defines the methods used to encode requests and replies. NCP is a simple request-response protocol, similar to SMB in that respect. NCP requests are encapsulated in IPX packets. The NCP header information, which follows the IPX header information, consists of five fields. The first indicates the request type, which provides the function of the packet.

The client can make a request using four request types in this field, and the server can use this field to indicate a type of reply:

- Create a service connection (1111)
- General service request (2222)
- General service replies (3333)
- Terminate a service (destroy) connection (5555)
- Request burst-mode transfer (7777)
- Request being processed (9999)

These services can be further qualified by function and subfunction codes contained in the request packet. Other fields in the NCP header include the following:

- Sequence Number field, which is used to track the sequencing information for the connection.
- Connection Number Low field, which is a service connection number that is assigned to the client when it logs on to the server.
- Task Number field, which is a value that identifies the client that is making an NCP request.
- Connection Number High field, which is currently not used and should always have the value of 00 hex.

The header information for the response packet that the server sends back to the client will contain these same fields, but it will also add to additional fields. The first is a Completion Code field, which will be set to 0 if the request was successfully completed or to 1 if an error was encountered in processing the request. The Connection Status field might have values indicating an error condition between the client and server connection.

When the client initiates a connection request with a server, it will create a service connection (1111) request type. The server gives the client a connection number in its response. This connection number is used by the client when it submits its remaining requests. Each time a request is sent on the particular connection, the sequence number is incremented. The response to a request contains the same sequence number, making it easy for the client to match up responses to pending requests.

General Requests and Responses

Most of the exchanges between client and server are usually the result of requests made by the client (type 2222) and the replies sent by the server (type 3333). These requests can be used to search directories or to open, read, and write to files.

The server uses the connection ID number and the sequence number when it sends a reply to a request. The Completion Code field is filled in to indicate success or failure, and other data might follow in the packet that is used to fulfill the request (such as data read from the file).

Burst Mode

NCP provides commands that can be used to read and write blocks of information in files that reside on the network. However, when larger files must be transferred, a special NCP request (Request Type value=7777), using burst mode, allows the server to send a larger, single burst of data to the client at one time—much larger than the amount allowed by the regular read and write requests (up to 64K).

Burst mode capabilities can be found on NetWare 3.0 and later servers.

The actual mechanics of burst mode involve more than just sending larger amounts of data in a single operation. The client first performs testing to determine a value that will be used for the Interpacket Gap Time (IPG) and the size of the data request (the burst windows size). The window size might vary during the history of the connection, based on how successful communications are. When data is lost during a transmission, the client can send a request to the server to transmit only fragments of the original data stream, those that were not correctly received.

An error condition such as this causes the window size to be reduced. As communications continue with no problems, the window size gradually increases.

Request Being Processed Response

When a client does not receive a response to a request after a timeout period, it will send in a duplicate request. If the server is heavily loaded, it might send back a request that has a request type value of 9999, which is the Request Being Processed type. This is an indication to the client that the request has been received, but that the server is just too busy to do anything about at it the time. This reply does not guarantee the client that the request ever will get answered, however. It only lets the client know that it can reset its timer and wait longer if need be.

When the client's timer expires, it can send another request to the server, which might respond to the request or which might send another message telling the client to wait. This response type is used to help reduce congestion in a busy network by reducing the number of requests transmitted on the network.

Terminating Connections

This request type is used to end a connection between the client and the server. The only information needed in this packet, other than the request type (5555), is the sequence number of the request and the connection ID number. The server will respond with a standard response packet (3333) with a completion code of zero to indicate that the connection has been successfully brought to a close.

Unix Network File System (NFS)

The Network File Systems (NFS) protocol consists of several protocols that perform specific functions. Sun Microsystems has published the specifications for NFS so that other vendors can easily implement these protocols to allow for remote mounting of file systems independent of the operating system of the computers. RFC 1094 defines the most widely used version of NFS (version 2). RFC 1813 documents version 3, which adds better support for wide area networking. If you think you will be involved in troubleshooting NFS on the network, you should find out on which version your NFS software is based and become familiar with these documents.

Note

A newer *proposed standard* is possibly going to replace RFCs 1094 and 1813. RFC 3010, "NFS Version 4 Protocol," discusses a newer version of the protocol. The newer version includes more detailed support for locking and the mount protocol (discussed earlier in this chapter), as well as stronger security and internalization issues.

NFS is built on routines made up of *remote procedure calls (RPC)*. XDR is used as the data format so that data from different systems can be represented in a common format for interchange. In addition, the *Mount* protocol is used to make the initial connection to a remote file system. Because NFS is built in this layered fashion, and problems can occur at any level, you will need to understand not only how the NFS protocol functions, but also RPC, XDR, and the Mount protocol.

Protocol Components: Remote Procedure Call (RPC) Protocol

RPC is a simple client/server protocol application. RPC defines the interaction between a client, which formats a request for execution by the server, and the server, which executes the client's request on the local system. The server performs whatever processing is required and returns the data and control of the procedure to the client. Sun developed RPC for use in NFS, but it has since been employed quite usefully by many other client/server-based products.

The rpcbind daemon (a process that runs in the background waiting for requests) runs on both the client and the server and is responsible for implementing RPC protocol exchanges between hosts on the network.

A service is a group of RPC procedures that have been grouped together into programs. A unique number is used to identify each service, which means that more than one service can operate at any given time. An application that needs to use a service can use the different programs that make up the service to perform specific actions. For example, when designing an NFS service, one program might be responsible for determining a file's attributes, and another program might be responsible for the actual transfer of data between the client and server computers.

The unique service number is used to identify different network services that run on a particular system, and the mapping for this is usually found in the file /etc/rpc. The RFC that defines RPC sets forth numbers used for many common services, and these are shown in Table 35.3.

Table 35.3   Numbers Used to Identify RPC Services

Unique Service Number	Name of Service
100000	portmapper
100001	rstat_svc
100002	rusersd
100003	nfs
100004	ypserv
100005	mountd
100007	ypbind
100008	walld
100009	yppasswdd
100010	etherstatd
100011	rquotad
100012	sprayd
100013	3270_mapper
100014	rje_mapper
100015	selection_svc
100016	database_svc
100017	rexd
100018	alis
100019	sched
100020	llockmgr
100021	nlockmgr
100022	x25.inr
100023	statmon
100024	status
100026	bootparam
100028	ypupdated
100029	keyserv
100069	ypxfrd
150001	pcnfsd

The portmapper service (using port 111 for UDP or TCP) manages the port numbers used in TCP/IP communications. Because there can be more than one open connection between a client and a server, a *port number* is used to identify each connection.

Don't confuse port numbers with the numbers assigned to services. Service numbers are used to identify a particular RPC service. *Port numbers* identify connections between two computers that use a service.

External Data Representation (XDR)

A common format is used when exchanging data between computer systems that are running different operating systems. Some use ASCII code for text, whereas others use Unicode. Some use big-endian encoding techniques, whereas others use little-endian, which determines the order in which bytes are used to represent data (left to right or right to left). It is even more complicated when you look at how different computer systems represent numeric data in memory or storage. When using a multiple-byte value to represent a floating-point number, for example, you need to know which bits are used for the exponent and which are used for the mantissa.

NFS uses the External Data Representation (XDR) standard for data exchange. The details of XDR are covered in RFC 1014. It is a C-like notation for representing data, not a programming language itself. An item, such as a character or numeric value, is represented in XDR by using 4 bytes (32 bits), with the lower bytes being the most significant.

Other encoding features of XDR include the following:

- Signed integers are stored using "twos" complement notation and range in value from –2,147,483,648 to +2,147,483,647.
- Unsigned integers can range from 0 to 4,294,967,295.
- Hyper integers and unsigned hyper integers are 8 bytes in size and can be used to represent larger integers.
- Floating-point formats are also defined, and so are the enum type (familiar to C programmers) and a Boolean type.
- Structures, arrays, constants, and many other data types are also defined.

XDR provides an extensible data description format that makes implementing NFS on multiple hardware and software platforms much easier.

The NFS Protocol and Mount Protocol

The NFS protocol is a set of procedures (called *primitives*) that are executed via RPC to allow an action to be performed on a remote computer. NFS is a *stateless* protocol, which means that the server does not have to maintain information about the state of each client. If the server (or the network) fails, the client needs only to repeat the operation. The server doesn't have to rebuild any data tables or other structures to recover the state of a client after a failure.

Note

Certain operations, such as file or record locking, do require a *stateful* protocol of some sort, and many implementations of NFS accomplish this by using another protocol to handle the specific function. NFS itself is composed of a set of procedures that deal only with file access.

The RPC procedures that make up the NFS protocol are the following:

- **Null**—The "do nothing" routine. It is provided in all RPC services and is used for testing and timing operations.
- **Get File Attributes**—Gets the file attributes of a file on a remote system.
- **Set File Attributes**—Sets the file attributes of a file on the remote server.
- **Get File System Root**—No longer used. Instead, the Mount protocol performs this function.

- **Look Up a Filename**—Returns a file handle used to access a file.
- **Read From Symbolic Link**—Returns information about symbolic links to a file on the remote server.
- **Read From File**—Procedure to read data from a file on a remote system.
- **Write to Cache**—Cache feature to be included in version 3 of the protocol.
- **Write to File**—Used to write data to a file on a remote server.
- **Create File**—Creates a file on the remote server.
- **Remove File**—Deletes a file on the remote server.
- **Rename File**—Renames a file on the remote server.
- **Create Link to File**—Creates a hard link (in the same file system) to a file.
- **Create Symbolic Link**—Creates a symbolic link (can be used to link a file across file systems). A symbolic link is a pointer to a file.
- **Create Directory**—Creates a directory on the remote server.
- **Remove Directory**—Deletes an empty directory on the remote server.
- **Read From Directory**—Obtains a list of files from a directory on the server.
- **Get File System Attributes**—Returns information about the file system on the remote server, such as the total size and available free space.

There is no provision in these procedures to open or close a file. Because NFS is a stateless protocol, it doesn't handle file opens or closes. The Mount protocol performs this function and returns a file handle to NFS. The mountd daemon runs on both the client and the server computer and is responsible for maintaining a list of current connections. Most implementations of NFS recover from client crashes by having the client send a message to the NFS server when it boots, telling it to unmount all its previous connections to the client.

When compared to the NFS protocol, the Mount protocol consists of only a very few procedures:

- **Null**—The "do nothing" procedure, just like the one listed under the NFS protocol.
- **MNT**—Mounts a file system and returns to the client a file handle and the name of the remote file system.
- **UNMT**—The opposite of the MNT procedure. It unmounts a file system and removes from its table the reference to it.
- **UMNTALL**—Similar to the UNMT procedure, but this one unmounts all remote file systems that are being used by the NFS client.
- **EXPORT**—Displays a list of exported file systems.
- **DUMP**—Displays a list of file systems on a server that are currently mounted by a client.

Configuring NFS Servers and Clients

The biod daemon runs on the client system and communicates with the remote NFS server. The daemon also processes the data that is transferred between the NFS client and the NFS server. The RPC daemon must also be running, and either UDP or TCP needs to be running, depending on which one your version of NFS uses as a transport. Users can mount a file system offered by an NFS server, provided that they are not prevented from mounting the file system by the server, by using the mount command.

Note

The commands shown in the following sections might differ from one version of Unix to another. As always with Unix or Linux, consult the man pages to determine the exact syntax for commands and the locations of files mentioned in relation to the commands.

NFS Client Daemons

On the client side of the NFS process, there are actually three daemon processes that are used. The first is biod, which stands for block input/output daemon. This daemon processes the input/output with the NFS server on behalf of the user process that is making requests of the remote file system. If you use NFS heavily on a client, you can improve performance by starting up more than one biod daemon. The syntax used to start the daemon is as follows:

```
/etc/biod [number of daemon processes]
```

This daemon is usually started in the /etc/rc.local startup file. Modify this file if you want to permanently change the number of daemons running on the client system. You can first test by executing the command online to determine how many daemons you need to start and then place the necessary commands in the startup file.

When deciding performance issues, remember that on a heavily loaded client, making a change in one place might result in poorer performance from another part of the system. So don't assume that you need a lot of extra daemons running unless you can first show that they are needed and do improve performance. Each daemon process is like any other process running on the system, and it uses up system resources, especially memory. Begin by using one or two daemons if you are using a workstation dedicated to one user. For a multiple-user computer, test your performance by increasing the number of daemons until NFS performance is satisfactory (all the time checking, of course, other performance indicators to be sure that the overall system impact is justified).

Although having multiple daemons means that NFS requests can be processed in parallel, remember that the network itself might be a bottleneck. Additional biod daemons will not increase throughput when the network itself is the limiting factor.

Also note that the biod daemon is a client process. You should not run it on an NFS server unless that server is also a client of another NFS server.

In addition to the biod daemon, the lockd and statd daemons also run on the client. For more information on these, see the section "Server-Side Daemons," later in this chapter.

The mount Command

The mount command is used to mount a local file system, and you can also use the command to mount a remote NFS file system. The syntax for using mount to make available a file system being exported by an NFS server is as follows:

```
mount -F nfs -o options machine:filesystem mountpoint
```

In some versions of Unix, the syntax for mounting a remote NFS file system is a little different. For example, in SCO Unix you use a lowercase f and an uppercase NFS:

```
mount -f NFS -o options machine:filesystem mountpoint
```

In BSD Unix, there is a command called mountnfs, which uses the system call mount to perform most of its functions. This version of the mount command comes with a lot of additional parameters, including the capability to specify on the mount command line whether to use UPD or TCP as the underlying transport mechanism.

The value you supply for *machine:filesystem* should be the hostname of the remote server that is exporting the file system you want to mount for *machine*. Substitute the name of the file system for *filesystem*. The following example causes the remote file system on host zira, called /usr/projectx/docs, to be made accessible in the local file system hierarchy at the /usr/docs directory:

```
mount -F nfs -o ro zira:usr/projectx/docs /usr/docs
```

This is the same way you mount other local file systems into the local hierarchy. Under the /usr/docs directory, you can access any other subdirectories that exist on host zira under the /usr/projectx/docs directory.

The -o parameter can be used to specify options for the mount command. In the preceding example, the letters ro for the option were used to make the remote file system *read-only* by users on the local computer.

Other options that can be used when mounting a remote file system include the following:

- **rw**—Mounts the file system for local read-write access, which is the default.
- **ro**—Mounts the file system for local read-only access.
- **suid**—Allows setuid execution.
- **nosuid**—Disallows setuid execution.
- **timeo=x**—Specifies a timeout value (in tenths of a second). The mount command will fail if it cannot mount the remote file system within this time limit.
- **retry=x**—The mount command will attempt to mount the remote file system *x* number of times, with each attempt lasting for the length of time specified by the timeo parameter.
- **soft**—Causes an error to be returned if the mount is unsuccessful. Opposite of the hard option.
- **hard**—Causes the mount attempt to continue until it succeeds. Opposite of the soft option.

For more command-line parameters and options, see the man page for the mount command for your particular system.

Caution

A computer can be an NFS server, an NFS client, or perhaps both a server and a client. However, you should not try to mount an exported file system on the same server that is exporting it. This can lead to looping problems, causing unpredictable behavior.

The *mountpoint* is the path to the location in the local file system where the remote NFS file system will appear, and this path must exist before the mount command is issued. Any files existing in the mountpoint directory will no longer be accessible to users after a remote file system is attached to the directory with the mount command, so do not use just any directory. Note that the files are not lost. They reappear when the remote file system is unmounted.

Using the fstab File to Mount File Systems at Boot Time

When you have file systems that need to be remounted each time the system reboots, you can use the file /etc/fstab to do this. This file is also used to mount local file systems, so be careful when making edits. The format for a record is as follows:

```
filesystem  directoryname  type  options  frequency  pass
```

The *filesystem* field for a record used to mount a remote file system includes the server hostname and the pathname of the remote file system separated by a colon (*hostname:path*). The second field, *directoryname*, is the path for the mountpoint on the local system, which indicates where the remote system is mounted and made available for access. The next field, *type*, is used to specify the filesystem type, which can be any of the following:

- **ufs**—A typical local Unix file system.
- **mfs**—The memory file system.
- **nfs**—An NFS remote file system.
- **swap**—A disk partition used for swapping by the virtual memory system.
- **msdos**—An MS-DOS–compatible file system.
- **cd9660**—A CD-ROM file system as defined by ISO 9660.
- **procfs**—A *filesystem* structure used to access data about processes.
- **kernfs**—A *filesystem* structure used to access kernel parameters.

The *options* field is used for a comma-delimited list of mounting options (rw, ro, and so on). The *frequency* is used in determining when a file system will be "dumped" for backup purposes. This can usually be set to zero for NFS systems mounted on a client because it is usually the NFS server that is responsible for making backups of local data. The final field, *pass*, can also be set to zero most of the time for an NFS file system mounted on a client. This field is used by the fsck utility to determine on which pass it is to check this file system.

Caution

The order in which you place entries in this file can be important. For example, do not place a command in this file to mount a remote NFS file system on a mountpoint unless the file system that contains the local mount has been mounted earlier in the file!

Server-Side Daemons

The nfsd daemon process handles requests from NFS clients for the server. The nfsd daemon interprets requests and sends them to the I/O system to perform the requests' actual functions. The daemon communicates with the biod daemon on the client, processing requests and returning data to the requestor's daemon.

An NFS server will usually be set up to serve multiple clients. You can set up multiple copies of the nfsd daemon on the server so that the server can handle multiple client requests in a timely manner.

The syntax for the command to start the daemon is as follows:

```
/etc/nfsd [number of nfs daemons to start]
```

For example, to start up five copies of the nfsd daemon at boot time, modify your startup scripts to include the following command:

```
/etc/nfsd 5
```

Unix systems and the utilities that are closely associated with them are continually being updated or improved. Some new versions include using the concept of threads to make it possible for a daemon to be implemented as a multithreaded process, capable of handling many requests at one time. Digital Unix 4.0 (now HP True64 Unix) is an operating system that provides a multithreaded NFS server daemon.

Other daemons the NFS server runs include the lockd daemon to handle file locking and the statd daemon to help coordinate the status of current file locks.

Configuring Server Daemons

For an NFS server, choose a computer that has the hardware capabilities needed to support your network clients. If the NFS server will be used to allow clients to view seldom-used documentation, a less-powerful hardware configuration might be all you need. If the server is going to be used to export a large number of directories, say from a powerful disk storage subsystem, the hardware requirements become much more important. You will have to make capacity judgments concerning the CPU power, disk subsystems, and network adapter card performance.

Setting up an NFS server is a simple task. Create a list of the directories that are to be exported, and place entries for these in the /etc/exports file on the server. At boot time the exportfs program starts and obtains information from this file. The exportfs program uses this data to make exported directories available to clients that make requests.

Sharing File Systems: The exportfs Command

At system boot time, the exportfs program is usually started by the /sbin/init.d/nfs.server script file, but this can vary, depending on the particular implementation of Unix you are using. The exportfs program reads the information in the /etc/exports configuration file.

The syntax for this command varies, depending on what actions you want to perform:

```
/usr/sbin/exportfs [-auv]
/usr/sbin/exportfs [-uv] [dir ...]
/usr/sbin/exportfs -i [-o options] [-v] [dir ...]
```

The parameters and options you can use with this command are listed here:

- **a**—Causes exportfs to read the /etc/exports file and export all directories for which it finds an entry. When used with the -u parameter, it causes all directories to be unexported.
- **i**—Specifies options in the /etc/exports file to be associated with each directory to be exported. It is used to tell exportfs to ignore the options you placed in this file.
- **u**—Used to stop exporting a directory (or all directories if used with the -a option).
- **v**—Tells exportfs to operate in "verbose" mode, giving you additional feedback in response to your commands.

The options you can specify after the -o qualifier are the same as you use in the /etc/exports file (see the following section, "Configuration Files").

To export or unexport (stop sharing) all entries found in the /etc/exports file, use the -a or -u option. This is probably the most-often-used form because you can specify the other options you need on a per-directory basis in the /etc/exports file. This example causes all directories listed in /etc/exports to be available for use by remote clients:

```
exportfs -a
```

The following example causes your NFS server to stop sharing all the directories listed for export in the /etc/exports file:

```
exportfs -au
```

The second form can be used to export or unexport (stop exporting) a particular directory (or directories) instead of all directories. You specify the directories on the command line. You can use this form if you want to stop sharing a particular directory because of system problems or maintenance, for example. Using the following syntax causes the NFS server to stop sharing the /etc/user/accounting directory with remote users:

```
exportfs -u /etc/users/accounting
```

The next form of the command can be used to ignore the options found in the /etc/exports file. Instead, you can supply them (using the -o parameter) on the command line. You will probably use this in special cases because you could just as easily change the options in the /etc/exports file if the change were a permanent one. If, for example, you decided that you wanted to make an exported directory that is currently set to be read-write to be read-only, you could use the following command:

```
exportfs -o ro /etc/users/purch
```

You can also dismount and mount remote file systems using different options when troubleshooting or when researching the commands you will need when preparing to upgrade a network segment where connections need to change.

If changes are made to the /etc/exports file while the system is running, use the exportfs command (with the -a parameter) to make the changes take effect. To get a list of directories that are currently being exported, you can execute the command with no options, and it will show you a list.

Of course, it is not necessarily a good idea to make changes on-the-fly without keeping track of the connections. When you decide to perform online testing to mount or dismount file systems, be sure that you are not going to impact any users who are currently making productive use of the resources. To make testing more foolproof and to provide a quick back-out procedure, try copying the /etc/exports file to keep a safe starting copy and making changes to the copied file, loading it by using the exportfs -a command. When you determine that something has been done incorrectly, you can simply use the backup copy of the file you have made to restore the status quo.

Configuration Files

To make a file system or a directory in a file system available for export, add the pathnames to the /etc/exports file. The format for an entry in this file is as follows:

```
directory [-option, ...]
```

The term *directory* is a pathname for the directory you want to share with other systems. The options you can include are the following:

- **ro**—This makes the directory available to remote users in a read-only mode. The default is read-write, and remote users can change data in files on your system if you do not specify ro here.

- **rw=*hostnames***—This specifies a specific host or hosts that you want to have read-write access. If a host is not included in *hostnames*, it will have only read access to the exported file system.

- **anon=*uid***—Use this parameter to set the *uid* (user ID) that will be used for anonymous users, if allowed.

- **root=*hostnames***—Users who have root access on a system listed in *hostnames* can gain root access on the exported file system.

- **access=*client***—This specifies a client that can have mount access to this file system.

For example:

```
/etc/users/acctpay -access=acct
/etc/users/docs -ro
/etc/users/reports/monthend -rw=ono
```

In this file, the first directory, /etc/users/acctpay, which stores accounts payable files, will be shared with a group called acct—the accounting department. The /docs directory can be accessed by anyone in read-only mode. The /reports/monthend directory can be accessed in read-only mode by most users, but users on the computer whose hostname is ono will have read-write access.

Caution

You should give considerable thought to the matter before using NFS to export sensitive or critical data. If the information could cause great harm if it were to be altered or exposed, you should not treat it lightly and make it available on the network via NFS. NFS is better suited for ordinary user data files and programs, directories, or other resources that are shared by a large number of users. There are not enough security mechanisms in place when using many implementations of NFS to make it a candidate for a high-security environment.

Automounting File Systems

The Mount protocol takes care of the details of making a connection for the NFS client to the NFS server. This means that it is necessary to use the mount command to make the remote file system available at a mountpoint in the local file system. To make this process even easier, the automountd daemon has been created. This daemon listens for NFS requests and mounts a remote file system locally on an as-needed basis. The mounted condition usually persists for a specified number of minutes (the default is usually five minutes) in order to satisfy any further requests.

As with other daemons, the automountd daemon is started at boot time in the /etc/rc.local file. You can enter it as a command after the system is up and running, if needed. When a client computer tries to access a file that is referenced in an automount map, the automountd daemon checks to see whether the file system for that directory is currently mounted. The daemon temporarily mounts the file system so that the user's request can be fulfilled, if needed.

The *automount map* is a file that tells the daemon where the file system to be mounted is located and where it should be mounted in the local file system. Options can also be included for the mount process, for example, to make it is read-write or read-only. The automountd daemon mounts a file system under the mountpoint /tmp_mnt. It then creates a symbolic link that appears to the user as part of his file system.

Mounting File Systems Using the automount Command

The /etc/rc.local file usually contains the command used to start the automountd daemon. This daemon is responsible for processing NFS mount requests as they are defined in special files called *map files*.

The syntax for the automount command is as follows:

```
automount [-mnTv] [-D name=value] [-f master-file]
[-M mount-directory] [-tl duration] [-tm interval]
[-tw interval][directory mapname [- mount-options]]
```

The options you can use are the following:

- **m**—Ignores directory-mapname pairs that are listed in the master map file.
- **n**—Dynamic mounts are to be disabled. If a directory is already mounted, the user's request will succeed, but no further file systems will be mounted.
- **T**—Causes the daemon to provide trace information about each request. The output is sent to standard output.

- **v**—Verbose; causes the daemon to send status messages to the console.

- **D** *name=value*—Defines automount environment variables. The text associated with *value* is assigned to the variable name.

- **f** *master map file name*—Provides the name of the master map file to the automount daemon.

- **M** *mountpoint directory*—Specifies a directory to use for the temporary mountpoint (one other than */tmp_mnt*).

- **tl** *time value*—Specifies how long a file system should stay mounted after the last user request before automount automatically dismounts it. The default is usually five minutes.

- **tm** *time value*—The amount of time (in seconds) that should elapse between attempts to mount a file system (the default is 30 seconds).

- **tw** *time value*—The amount of time (in seconds) between attempts to unmount a file system that has exceeded its cached time. The default is usually one minute.

- **mount_options**—Options to be applied to all the directories listed in the map file. Any options listed in a map file override those listed here on the command line.

Master Maps

The automount daemon uses the master map to obtain a list of maps. The master map also contains mount options for those maps. The master map file is usually named `/etc/auto.master`. The syntax for the entries in this file is as follows:

```
mount-point map [mount-options]
```

mount-point is the pathname of the local directory for an indirect map specified in the map field. If the map specified in the map column is a direct map, the mountpoint is usually `/-`.

The data listed under the *map* field is used to find the map that contains the actual mountpoints and the locations of the remote file systems. Any data you supply for *mount-options* will be used when mounting directories in the map file associated with it.

Following is an example of a master map file (lines that begin with # are comments):

```
#mount-point   map                options
/etc/users     /etc/auto.usr      -ro
/-             /etc/auto.direct    -rw
```

When the automount daemon determines that access is needed for files found in the `/etc/users` directory, it will look for another map file, named `auto.usr`, to get the rest of the information. The `-ro` options are specified for this entry and will be applied to the file system designated in the `auto.usr` map file.

The argument `/-` is used to specify that a map file it points to, in this case `auto.direct`, is a direct map file or one that contains the mountpoints and the remote file-system information needed to complete the mounts.

Direct Maps

The remote file systems can be mounted into the local file system, and the mountpoint should be information you will find in a direct map. The construction of this file is very direct. The syntax for an entry is as follows:

```
key [mount-options] location
```

The *key* field is the mountpoint to be used for this entry. *mount-options* are the options used with the mountd daemon discussed earlier in this chapter. The *location* field should be in the format of *machine:pathname*, where *machine* is the hostname of the remote system that the file system actually resides on and *pathname* is the path to the directory on that file system. You can specify multiple locations to provide for redundancy. The automount daemon queries all locations in this case and takes the first one to respond to its requests.

Indirect Maps

In an indirect map file, most fields are the same as in a direct map file, except that the first field (*key*) is not a full pathname. It is a pointer to an entry in the master map file. You can list multiple directories in an indirect map file, and each of these remote file-system directories will be mounted under the mountpoint designated in the master map file that contains a reference to the indirect map.

Check the man pages on your system to be sure of the syntax for options used in map files because they might vary just like options do for the mount command among different Unix systems.

Troubleshooting NFS Problems

Many of the TCP/IP utilities that are used for troubleshooting can be employed when trying to diagnose and fix problems having to do with NFS. For example, if a remote file system suddenly becomes unavailable, it only makes sense to first determine whether the remote server is still functioning. You can do this quickly by using the ping command to establish basic network connectivity. A failure to communicate using this small utility indicates that there is a server problem at the other end or perhaps a network malfunction that is preventing communications with the remote system. When you're troubleshooting, this tells you that the problem is most likely not one to be found in the NFS subsystem.

◄◄ You can find detailed information about using various TCP/IP utilities for troubleshooting purposes in Chapter 28, "Troubleshooting Tools for TCP/IP Networks."

The tracert utility also can be used when ping fails to determine how far along the network route the packet is getting on its trip to the remote system. Use this when trying to isolate the particular point of failure in the network.

There is a useful command specific to NFS that can be used to display statistical information about NFS. It is nfsstat. This command shows you statistics about NFS and RPC. The syntax for nfsstat is as follows:

```
nfsstat [-cnrsz] [vmunix.n] [core.n]
```

These are the options you can use:

- **c**—Shows only client-side information.
- **n**—Shows only statistics for NFS, both client- and server-side.
- **r**—Shows only statistics for RPC, both client- and server-side.
- **s**—Shows only server-side information.
- **z**—Is used to zero out the statistics. You can combine it with other options to zero out statistics referred to by those options (for example, -zc to zero client size information). Write access to /dev/mem is required to zero statistics.
- **vmunix.n**—The name of the kernel image.
- **core.n**—The name of the system's core image.

All statistics are shown if you do not supply any parameters when executing the command. The statistical data that will be displayed depends on the options you choose. For an example of the detailed data you can obtain using this command, see the man page for nfsstat for your particular Unix or Linux system.

Examining the output from the nfsstat command can be useful on an ongoing basis to help you establish a baseline for performance evaluations you will need to make later when thinking about upgrading. You can easily selectively store data output by this command in a text file or spreadsheet. You can also create a simple script file that can be used to gather statistics using this command on a periodic basis, storing the results in a temporary directory for your later review.

For example, the command nfsstat -s displays statistics for the NFS server as shown here:

```
# nfsstat -s

Server RPC:
calls       badcalls    nullrecv    badlen
23951       0           0           0

Server NFS:
calls       badcalls
23164       0
null          getattr       setattr       root          lookup        readlink
1  0%         64   0%        0   0%         0   0%         121    0%      0   0%
read          wrcache       write         create        remove        rename
22951 99%     0   0%         0   0%         0   0%         0   0%        0   0%
link          symlink       mkdir         rmdir         readdir       fsstat
0  0%         0   0%         0   0%         0   0%         25   0%       2   0%
```

In this display you can see statistics for the total number of remote procedure calls, along with information about those RPC calls that relate to NFS. In addition to the total number of calls, you can see statistics concerning the following items for RPC:

- **badcalls**—Number of calls that were rejected by the server.
- **nullrecv**—Number of times that there was no RPC packet available when the server was trying to receive.
- **badlen**—Number of packets that were too short.

In addition, some implementations might show additional RPC fields. For the NFS server, there are many columns of information displayed, showing you the number of reads and writes, along with other useful information. For example, you can examine cache usage (wrcache), or determine when other file commands are used to create or remove directories.

If the number of badcalls begins to become significant when compared to the overall number of calls, a problem obviously exists. If the value displayed for badlen is consistently a higher percentage of the overall number of calls, a client might be incorrectly configured or a network problem might be causing packets to become corrupted. Again, you may see different or additional fields of information in the display, depending on the Unix/Linux and NFS implementation you are using. A careful review of the documentation for your system will give you a good idea of the performance to be expected from your server and the kinds of events to look for.

Microsoft Distributed File System (DFS): Windows 2000 and Windows Server 2003

Like NFS, DFS employs a tree structure for file systems. A directory that is being imported by a client is attached at a point somewhere in the local file system, where it is then made available to applications as if the directory and its files were local.

Windows 2000 and the family of Windows 2003 servers include DFS as an integral part of the operating system. The interface is written as a snap-in to the Microsoft Management Console (MMC) tool, making administration a simpler process. A wizard prompts you through setting up a DFS root, and from there on out you can add, modify, or remove directory paths from the DFS tree. Paths represented in the DFS tree can come from one or more servers on the network. A tree is not bound by a single host.

In Windows NT 4.0, directory replication allowed you to create copies of directories on multiple systems, keeping them in sync. This functionality was replaced in Windows 2000 with Distributed File System (though it is also possible to download DFS for Windows NT 4.0). DFS is now included as a part of modern Windows operating systems. DFS allows you to move away from the *server*\ *sharename* concept to one based on the domain. Instead of having to remember (or browse and find) on which server a particular file share is hosted, you can use DFS to create shares that are global to the domain. That is, if you're a member of the domain, you can specify the share as *domainname*\ *share*. DFS also allows for replication. This means that you can have more than one copy of the data being shared, but only have to use the global domain-wide share name to connect. This provides for some fault tolerance. If a server goes down that happens to host a replica of a share, then the other servers that contain copies of the share can be connected to by users. Note that this does *not* provide any kind of failover if a server crashes. The user can, however, restart her work by reconnecting to the share. The connection will be made to another replica of the file share.

Tip

Although DFS does not come with Windows NT 4.0 Server, you can obtain it from Microsoft (www.microsoft.com). The downloadable version can be installed on Microsoft Windows NT Server 4.0 systems and can be used to provide a service to clients similar to that offered by NFS. At the main Web site, click on Downloads and look for it under Downloads for Windows NT 4.0.

Important terms to understand when dealing with DFS are listed here:

- **Root**—A server can have only one root installed. It is just about the same thing as a file share, with a few differences, which will become apparent shortly.

- **DFS link**—Under the root you create DFS links. These are links to file shares that will be available under the root you have created. This means you can create a single root yet place multiple shared directories under the root so that only one file share connection is necessary. If not, users would have to connect to each directory as a separate file share.

- **Replica**—You can create shares that replicate the data in other shares. This can be done to provide for both load balancing and a degree of fault tolerance.

Creating a DFS Root

Creating a DFS tree is not a complicated task when using a graphical interface such as the one provided by the MMC and by the wizards that walk you through setting up your file system. To create a new DFS root, use the following steps:

1. Click Start, Programs (All Programs for the Windows 2003 family of servers), Administrative Tools, Distributed File System.

2. When the management console appears, select New Root from the Action menu. A wizard pops up. Click Next.

3. You can select to create a file system that makes use of the Active Directory for storing the DFS configuration information. You can also select to not use the Active Directory. For the purposes of this example, I've chosen to not use the Active Directory. After making the selection, click Next.

4. The next dialog box prompts you to enter the name of the server that will host the distributed file system. The default is usually the server on which you are running the wizard. Use the default or enter another server. Click Next to continue.

5. The wizard next prompts you to enter the name of the new root DFS file system. Note that what you enter here shows up in the field Share to Be Used at the bottom of the dialog box. You can use the name of an existing share in the Root Name field, or create the share to be used after you complete this wizard.

6. If you entered a share that does not yet exist, you can now choose the folder to share by entering it in the field or by using the Browse button.

7. Finally, the wizard displays a summary of the information you have entered. Click the Finish button to complete the process of creating the new DFS root.

When you're finished, your DFS root will show up in the tree structure in the left pane of the MMC, as you can see in Figure 35.5.

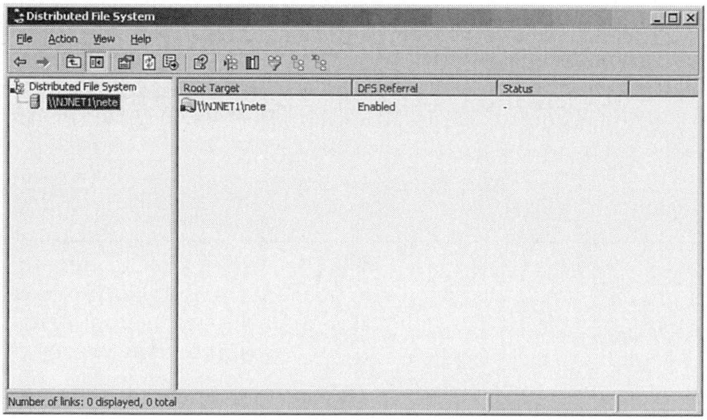

Figure 35.5   The new DFS root is now displayed in the MMC.

Adding Links to the DFS Root

After you've created the initial root for your file system, you can add one or more links. Links, as you will recall, are actual directories (or folders, depending on which terminology you prefer) that will be accessible from your DFS root.

To create a link, right-click on the root in the left pane of the console. From the menu, select New DFS Link. In Figure 35.6 you can see the dialog box used to input the information about the link.

First you need to enter a name that will be used as a logical association for the link. That is, when the user connects to the share, this name will show up as a folder he can use. You can see that in the next field you are asked to fill in the actual pathname for the folder being offered as part of the DFS share.

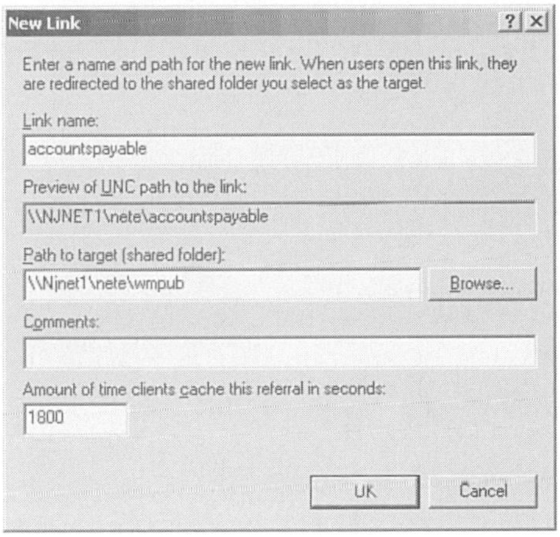

Figure 35.6 You can specify a logical name that users will see so that they don't have to remember the actual directory path.

In the example in Figure 35.6, the folder that users will see is called `accountspayable`. The shared directory that contains the actual files is `\\Njnet1\wmpub`. Note that there is also a comment field in this dialog box. In a large network with many resources, you'll appreciate this information when managing your network. Finally, the last field allows you to specify how long a client will cache the link. When the client makes the initial connection, the connection will be made to the actual directory. However, the user's computer will check back with the DFS server when the cache timer expires.

DFS is a domain-wide file system. In the dialog box shown in Figure 35.6, you can easily browse a file share located on another server in the domain. Thus, you can hide the physical location of files from users. Instead of having to remember servers and share names, the user only has to remember the share name. Because the share name is domain-wide, you can't use the same share name on one server that you do on another. Users can then simply connect to the share `\\domainname\share`. They don't need to know the server names on which the actual folders in this share are located.

You can use the Action menu to add or delete a DFS root. You can also use the Action menu to manage links and replication.

DFS does not add any additional security features to the file system. Instead, the usual rights and permissions that are already in place on the server are used when evaluating a client's access to a file or directory in the DFS tree.

One major difference between NFS and DFS is that DFS is built using SMB messaging techniques for the most part and is not compatible with all NFS servers. If you have a mixed-environment network in which most of your data files are offered via NFS on Unix servers, it would be more economical to acquire PC-based NFS client software than it would be to replace all your existing servers with NT DFS servers.

The Hypertext Transfer Protocol

36

SOME OF THE MAIN TOPICS IN THIS CHAPTER ARE

The Internet is certainly familiar to readers of this book. Web pages are coded using the Hypertext Markup Language (HTML), as well as Java, ASP, and other technologies. Underlying all of these technologies is an application protocol—the Hypertext Transfer Protocol (HTTP). HTTP is the underlying application protocol that is used to deliver Web pages to your browser. Like other protocols (FTP, Telnet, and others) the transport protocol for HTTP is usually the TCP/IP suite of protocols, using port 80. HTTP can be sent over other network protocols, but that option is rarely used today. Port 80 is not a requirement for HTTP. Other ports can be used, and often are. To specify a different port, use a colon character (:) at the end of the URL, followed by the port number. However, in the original RFC specification for HTTP, port 80 was used.

◄◄ To learn about the basics of TCP/IP, ports, and related protocols and applications, see Chapter 25, "Overview of the TCP/IP Protocol Suite."

The protocols TCP and IP were developed long before HTTP was created. HTTP, like other application protocols, is transmitted on the network using TCP/IP as the underlying protocol to ensure a timely, reliable transport.

Yet HTTP is the protocol that is placed between HTML and TCP/IP. Keep in mind that HTML is just a language used for creating Web pages. HTTP is used to transfer these pages to end users, and HTTP is transported across the Internet using TCP/IP.

This chapter is not going to help you learn the many versions of HTML, or other programming languages (such as Java and C#). Instead, you will learn about HTTP.

Note

HTTP is currently defined by version 1.1. In this chapter you will learn about some of the history of HTTP, including the concepts presented by the original version as well as HTTP v.1.1.

It All Started with the World Wide Web Consortium (W3C) at CERN

The W3C is a vendor-supported consortium, and although it was responsible for the creation of many Internet Web standards, the most prominent are the Hypertext Transfer Protocol and other Internet standards. In 1989, CERN (the High Energy Particle Physics Laboratory in Geneva, Switzerland) scientist Dr. Tim Berners-Lee developed the first version of HTTP, which was to help the World Wide Web gain popularity and grow dramatically. Instead of the usual email, FTP, and other utilities that the Internet was using at that time, the new HTTP allowed an easier way to share information quickly.

Because of the time involved in ongoing development of HTTP, CERN partnered with INRIA (the French National Institute of Research for Computer Science and Control). Today, many other organizations are involved in continuing the development of HTTP, such as the Massachusetts Institute of Technology (MIT) Laboratory for Computer Science, and the Internet Engineering Task Force (IETF). Thus, you can find RFC (Request for Comments) documents on the Web about current and future development of the protocol.

Note

The W3C is not a government organization. It is an industry-supported consortium whose purpose is to promote standards for the Web, including interoperability among Web protocols and software. W3C does help to establish standards to achieve this goal.

Current proposed, informational, and standards RFCs include the following:

- RFC 1945, "Hypertext Transfer Protocol – HTTP/1.0." Written in 1996 by Berners-Lee, R. Fielding, and H. Frystyk, this informational RFC was the beginning of the standardization process within the Internet community.

- RFC 2145, "Use and Interpretation of HTTP Version Numbers." This is also an informational RFC that further specifies how version numbers of the HTTP protocol should be used.

- RFC 2519, "HTTP Extensions for Distributed Authoring – WEBDAV." This is a proposed standard.

- RFC 2831, "Using Digest Authentication as a SASL Mechanism." This RFC is also a proposed standard, and it discusses using SASL (Simple Authentication and Security Layer) to provide support for connection-based protocols, such as HTTP.

- RFC 2935, "Internet Open Trading Protocol (IOTP) HTTP Supplement." IOTP messages are transported as XML (Extensible Markup Language) documents. The goal of this RFC is to ensure that XML documents are successfully exchanged between the parties involved in the communication.

- RFC 3229, "Delta Encoding in HTTP." This RFC proposes a method for conserving valuable bandwidth on the Net by downloading only changes to cached Web pages. Rather than sending the entire data transported by HTTP, only changes, called delta encoding, are sent.

- RFC 3230, "Instance Digests in HTTP." This is another proposed standard for HTTP version 1.1 that describes the use of MD5 (Message Digest v. 5) to ensure reliable transport of data carried by HTTP. MD5, created by Ronald L. Rivest of MIT, is the third version of this encryption technique. The previous versions were MD2 and MD4.

- RFC 3310, "Hypertext Transfer Protocol (HTTP) Digest Authentication Using Authentication and Key Agreement (AKA)." This is another informational RFC discussing authentication for use with HTTP.

The preceding RFCs (and others referenced in these RFCs) are recommended reading for those who want to pursue newer developments that may become part of the HTTP protocol in the near future.

What Is HTTP?

HTTP was created to enable HTTP to transport *hypertext* through the Internet. *Hypertext technology* was first developed by Ted Nelson—and was officially known then as the Xanadu system. Xanadu was a method of creating documents on the Web, using one or more authors. One of the main features was the use of hyperlinks. Although Nelson's original ideas never caught on, they were instrumental in the development of HTML as well as HTTP.

HTTP is basically a protocol that enables the transfer of text, images, and other data between computers on the Web. Although HTML might seem to be a protocol, it is not. Without HTTP, or a similar protocol, there would be no HTML pages on the Internet. HTTP relies on the underlying TCP/IP protocols for transport through the Internet, and thus HTTP can be considered an *application protocol*.

Although HTTP has been in use on the Net since 1990, in RFC 1945, first published in 1996, the Hypertext Transfer Protocol (version 1, commonly referred to as HTML/1) was described by Berners-Lee and other authors. HTTP is a *stateless* protocol, similar to IP. It is also an application protocol because it uses TCP/IP as a transport mechanism. The term *stateless* means that there is no requirement for a session, such as with a TCP session in which parameters are exchanged between the endpoints of a connection (the setup phase) before data exchanges can occur. Instead, a request is sent to a server via the Net, and provided that no errors occur, a response is sent back.

HTTP Mechanics

As previously indicated, HTTP is a client/server protocol. The client application (such as a browser) sends a request to the server that hosts the information the user needs (typically a Web page). The server sends back a response. The data object the client requests is identified by a Uniform Resource Identifier (URI), such as a Uniform Resource Locator (URL). Both of these are described later in this chapter.

The data object is encapsulated by HTTP and returned to the requestor. Although HTTP commands are terminated using the combination of <CR><LF> (carriage return/line feed), the object encapsulated in HTTP (the payload) does not have to adhere to this rule. Instead, the payload (referred to as the entity-body in HTTP terminology) is determined by the type of information being transferred. For example, plain ASCII text may use the <CR><LF> combination to mark the end of a record, whereas Unix/Linux systems use just the <LF> character. And graphics files can be composed in many different formats, from GIF to JPEG, among others. The important thing to remember is that the entity-body carried by HTTP is independent of the HTTP protocol.

Most all browsers today also maintain a cache, which stores recently requested pages. At the top of your browser, there should be a button you can use to refresh a page—send a request to the server to get the most up-to-date version of a page instead of one stored in the cache. Some pages are marked by the server so that they will not be stored in the requestor's cache. These pages are refreshed from the HTTP server each time you reference the data source.

HTTP Header Fields

HTTP header fields (not to be confused with headers that may exist in the entity-body, or payload being carried by HTTP) can vary depending on the version of HTTP, as well as the content being carried. Each HTTP header field is made up of a name followed by the colon character (:), then a space, and finally the value for the particular header. Names for fields are case insensitive.

Some examples of HTTP headers include a content type field to identify the entity-body, as well as the length of the data. Another example, which can affect the time the content from a request is cached, is the Expires field. Browsers that recommend this field will not display Web pages/data to the user from the cache after the information has expired. Instead, a new request will be sent to the HTTP server.

Many other header fields are also defined, and you can find out about them by reading the RFCs listed at the beginning of this chapter. Here, just the basics are presented, as well as the syntax for forming header fields.

Although most users are familiar with using the Address field in a browser to enter a URL, most do not know what a URL is.

URLs, URIs, and URNs

Most any user of the Internet understands that you need to put a URL (Uniform Resource Locator) in the Address field of a browser to send a request to a Web server. However, the URL is only one of many URIs (Uniform Resource Identifiers—although in the original HTTP RFC, URL was termed *Universal* Resource Identifier). You specify a URL by using the prefix http:// in the address space of your browser. However, other URIs (*identifiers*) can be used, such as ftp:// if you want to use a browser to download files from a remote server.

The important thing to remember here is that URLs are just a subset of URIs, and there are many URIs. However, URLs are probably the most widely used URIs.

RFC 1630, written by Berners-Lee, also discusses URNs (Uniform Resource Names), which refer to a namespace that is more persistent than objects that refer to URLs.

Although this definition is not considered to be a standard, Berners-Lee describes the URI syntax this way:

- It should be extensible so that new naming schemes can be added later as determined by how the Web evolves.
- The syntax should be complete so that any naming scheme can be encoded in a URI.
- The URI should be "printable," meaning that any URI should be able to be described using 7-bit ASCII characters.

To provide for the extensible characteristic of the syntax, this RFC assumed that new URI prefixes (http://, ftp://, and so on) can be an arbitrary string of characters, but also should be registered by some authority to ensure uniformity on the Web. The text that follows the prefixed URI designator is dependent on the prefix. For example, http:// would assume that a Web server address follows the prefix. For ftp://, the text following this prefix should be in conformance with FTP conventions, in order to specify an address and file to be downloaded.

This RFC also requires that a colon character (:) follow the prefix. The use of slashes (//) is used to indicate a hierarchy of some sort, such as a path through a naming convention that leads to the eventual location of information, or the object sought by the prefix.

Note

The use of the slash character should not be confused with the character used in some operating systems as a directory hierarchy specification. There is no relationship between the text following a URI and the text that follows, even if it contains the slash character.

Because some characters (such as the space character) can cause conflicts (especially when URIs are used in email messages, and are so long that the text is wrapped), an escape character is used. The *percent sign* (%) is used as the *escape character*. This character should be used for only this purpose, and nothing else.

Other characters, such as the hash character (#) and the question mark (?), also serve a particular purpose. The # character is used to separate the object of a URI from an identifier related to the specific URI. The ? character is used to separate the URI from an object that can be queried. In other words, the ? means that the text that follows it is used to pass data to a query based on the original object that is referenced by the URI. You will see this character appear in many URLs when you reference a Web site. This character is used in many URLs after you enter text (in a search engine, for example) to create the final URL that is used to apply the syntax of your query to the object you referenced in the URL that you entered. You can try this by visiting just about any major Web site, such as Microsoft, or a search engine. Watch the Address field on your browser and you will see a longer string of what *appears* to be a meaningless string of characters. It is, however, the syntax that the search engine (or other Web site) uses to apply your query to find the information you are looking for.

Note

Although the use of spaces in a URL or URI is discouraged, the plus sign (+) is used to indicate a space. If you want to use + in the URI or URL, it must be escaped (in other words, the text that follows the escape character should be interpreted literally). The escape, as explained in the main text, is the percent character (%). To identify a specific character, you would first use the escape character followed by the ASCII hex value for the character. A literal plus sign (ASCII code 2B) would therefore be represented as %2B.

Other reserved characters, which can be used by any URI and which apply to the syntax of those URIs, are the asterisk (*) character and the exclamation mark (!). In other words, these characters do not mean the same thing for all URIs. Each URI can use these characters for a meaning specific to the particular URI.

If this sounds confusing, just go to a search engine and look at the string of characters that follows your query. In Figure 36.1 you can see that entering the URL **www.google.com** brings up the initial query page for this search engine.

Figure 36.1   You can enter a URL to bring up a particular Web page, such as a search engine.

Yet when you enter text into this search engine's Search field, and click on the Search button, the URL in the Address field of your browser is translated to a query that the search engine uses to locate resources related to your query, as shown in Figure 36.2.

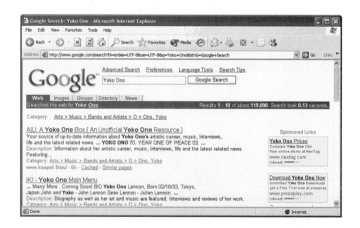

Figure 36.2   Your query can change after you enter text in a search engine.

In Figure 36.2, notice the long string that was created by the search engine to satisfy your search request. Also notice that the Web site for Yoko Ono is the first result to show up. This Web site is the premier site for all information related to Yoko Ono, and is the first Web site to show up on the search engine.

Note

Because some characters are not allowed by the 7-bit URI scheme described in this chapter, you can escape them using the % character, followed by the hexadecimal equivalent of the character you want to use.

Tip

Whereas binary notation uses just two numbers, 0 and 1 (also called base 2), and the octal numbering scheme uses numbers 0–7 (base 8), hexadecimal (base 16) is a numbering system that uses the numbers 0–9, and then the alphabetic characters A–F (in decimal, the numbers 10–15). In decimal notation (base 10), the value after the numerical representation 9 is 10. The number 9 is the upper limit of representing numbers in a decimal scheme. Binary uses just two characters, zero and one, so the equivalent of ten in binary is 1010. Because only zeros and ones are allowed in binary, a longer string of numbers is needed to represent the same two-digit representation of ten in decimal. Hexadecimal is another thing altogether. Instead of being a subset of base 10, Hexadecimal (hex) expands on base 10, by adding the alphabetic characters needed to denote base 16. So decimal value 10 is represented in hexadecimal as the letter A.

The RFC goes on to explain URIs for specific applications, such as gopher, news, and mail. Some of these have been superceded by other RFCs. However, RFC 1630 should serve as a beginning document for those readers who want to study the details of URIs and URLs. URIs and URLs are also discussed in other RFCs than those discussed in this chapter. However, URLs are the most common when you consider the intense growth of the Web. There are even "hidden" URLs that don't appear until you click on an embedded link in a Web page. Each link (or hyperlink in some RFCs) in a Web page that refers to another Web page simply provides, using HTML syntax, another URL request that will be sent to the server defined in that link.

Routing Protocols

SOME OF THE MAIN TOPICS IN THIS CHAPTER ARE

CHAPTER 37

Routers are devices that examine Network layer protocol addresses and make decisions based on those addresses on how best to send a network packet on its way to its destination. Routers can be used in a corporate network to interconnect various LAN segments, to connect to a wide area network—for connecting branch offices to the headquarters, for example—or, more commonly, to connect the local network to the Internet.

▶▶ Routers also play an important part in firewalls, which are covered in Chapter 49, "Firewalls."

However, to make decisions on the best path a packet needs to take as it travels through the network, a router must keep a table in memory that it can use to locate the destination network for each packet that passes through it. Because routers generally are used to connect many different networks, and because networks usually undergo changes frequently, there must be a method for keeping the routing table up-to-date. Network transport protocols (such as TCP/IP) are used to transfer data across a network. Routing protocols are used by routers to communicate with other routers to exchange information, such as routes or routes that no longer exist.

◀◀ Chapter 25, "Overview of the TCP/IP Protocol Suite," not only gives you a detailed overview of TCP/IP, but also contains a great deal of information about address classes, subnet masks, subnetting, and the Classless Interdomain Routing (CIDR), among other basic TCP/IP topics. I strongly recommend that you read Chapter 25 before this one to make it easier for you to comprehend the topics covered here.

For example, suppose that an important router suddenly fails. All other routers that have this router in their routing table need to know this so that they can discover another route, if there is one, that can be used to bypass this failed device. Routing protocols come in all sizes and shapes, but all generally perform the same function: keeping routing tables up-to-date.

Basic Types of Routing Protocols

There are two general types of routing protocols: interior and exterior protocols. *Interior* protocols perform routing functions for autonomous networks. *Exterior* routing protocols handle the routing functions between these autonomous networks and glue the Internet together. These routing types are more commonly referred to as Interior Gateway Protocols (IGP) and Exterior Gateway Protocols (EGP). The network you manage for your business is an independent domain that functions internally as a unit. It is an *autonomous system* within which you can make decisions about which hosts use a particular address and how routing is done. When you connect your network to the Internet, the ISP or other provider manages routers that allow your autonomous system to exchange information with other routers connected to other autonomous systems throughout the Internet.

For the most part, the network administrator is concerned with IGP protocols. Two are used most often: RIP and OSPF.

Note

Another IGP you might hear about occasionally is the HELLO protocol. This protocol is mentioned here mostly for historical purposes because it is not employed as much these days. HELLO, used during the early days of the NFSNET backbone, uses a round-trip, or delay, time to calculate routes.

The Routing Information Protocol (RIP)

RIP is an acronym that stands for Routing Information Protocol. It is the most common routing protocol for autonomous systems in use today, though that doesn't mean it's the best. There are newer IGP protocols that give additional functionality, but RIP, due to its low overhead, is still in widespread use.

RIP is a distance-vector protocol, which means that it judges the best route to a destination based on a table of information that contains the distance (in hops) and vector (direction) to the destination. A hop is simply another router along the route that the packet will take. There is a limit to the number of hops a packet can take, and this is defined by which routing protocol is used. This value limits the number of routers a packet can pass through before it is dropped. Without this value, it would be possible for a packet to continue to travel through the Internet endlessly if the routers were not correctly configured.

Figure 37.1 shows two company sites that are connected through two links that have routers between them. The user on Workstation A wants to connect to a resource in the remote network that resides on Server A.

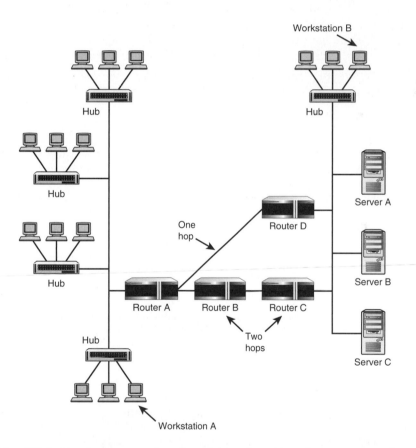

Figure 37.1   RIP decides the best route based on the number of hops between two nodes.

When Router A sees the first packet from workstation A and realizes that it cannot be delivered on the local network, it consults its routing tables to first determine whether it can find a path that will get the data to its destination. If more than one path exists, as it does here, it then makes a decision on which path to take. A simplified version of the routing table information would look like this:

```
Destination   Next Hop   Metric
Server A      Router D    1
Server A      Router B    2
```

Router A has two paths it can use to get the packet delivered. The routing table it keeps in memory doesn't tell it the actual names of the servers, as is shown here. Instead, it uses network addresses. It also doesn't show every single router through which the packet will pass on its route to its destination. It shows only the next router to send the packet to and the total number of routers through which it will have to pass.

Note

There are actually two versions of the RIP routing protocol. Version 1 of RIP is defined in RFC 1058, "Routing Information Protocol." Version 2 of the protocol is defined in RFC 2453, "RIP Version 2." Version 2 adds some security mechanisms to the protocol, and also provides for additional information to be exchanged between routers than what was provided for in RIP version 1. There are many other RFCs you can read that pertain to proposed standards and informational documents that discuss certain aspects of the RIP protocols. Visit the Web site `http://rfc-editor.org` and perform a search if you would like to view the history of how RFCs for RIP were developed over many years.

Earlier versions of RIP routing made simple decisions based solely on the metric called a *hop count*. In this case, RIP would decide to send the packet to Router D, because that route indicates that the packet has to pass through only one additional router to reach its destination network. If it were to route the packet through Router B, it would take two hops.

The number of hops to a destination cannot be infinite. In RIP routing, the maximum number of hops that will be considered is 15. If a destination lies more than 15 hops away from the router, it is considered to be an unreachable destination and the router will not attempt to send a packet. When this happens, the router will send an `ICMP Destination Unreachable` message back to the source of the network packet. Because RIP is considered an IGP, most packets should never have to pass through more than 15 hops.

◀◀   For more information about ICMP (the Internet Control Message Protocol), see Chapter 25.

Another situation that needs to be taken into account is that a network administrator can configure a router to use up more than a single hop or *metric* value. Because of this, it is possible that a network packet may be dropped before it passes through 15 actual routers.

Note

The term *router* is not limited to a dedicated hardware device that is used as a router. Indeed, many server operating systems can also serve as routers on a LAN. You can see this by using the appropriate commands to view the routing table on this kind of server. Additionally, such a computer can usually both operate as a router and provide other services to the LAN, such as a file or print server.

As simple and straightforward as this might seem, it might not be the best route to take. One of the problems that RIP routing has is that it never takes into consideration the bandwidth of the route. The path from Router A to Router C might be made up of high-speed T1 links, and the line between Router A and Router D might be a slower connection. For small simple packets, such as an email delivery, this might not make a great deal of difference to the end user, because a few seconds or a minute or two won't make much difference for this type of application. For a large amount of traffic, though, this can make a significant difference. Routing a lot of traffic over slow links can significantly impact performance.

Another problem with RIP is that it doesn't load balance. If a lot of users are trying to get to the remote system, it will not use both of the available routes and divide up the traffic. RIP continues to select what it considers the best route and just sends the packets on their way.

You can also manipulate the metric value used in the routing table to make it appear that one route—usually a slower link—is farther away than a faster route simply by modifying the routing table to change the hop count of the slow route to a number larger than that of the faster route link. Thus, although a faster link might actually send packets through more routers than the slower link, you can "fool" RIP into using the faster link.

Updating Routers

RIP routers periodically exchange data with each other (through the User Datagram Protocol, or UDP, using port 520) so that each router can maintain a table of routing information that is more or less up-to-date. In earlier versions of RIP, a router would broadcast its entire routing table. Newer versions allow a router to send only changes or to respond to routing requests from other routers (called triggered RIP updates).

The format of the RIP message for version 1 appears in Figure 37.2. For version 1 of the protocol, the largest RIP message that can be sent in a UDP datagram is 504 bytes. When you combine this with the 8-byte UDP header, the maximum size of the datagram is 512 bytes.

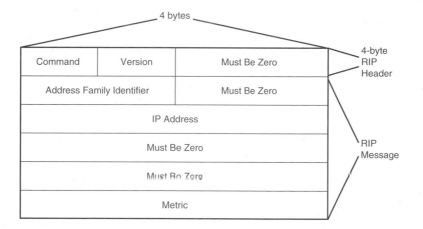

Figure 37.2 The format of the RIP message for version 1 of the protocol.

In Figure 37.2, the portion following the first 4 bytes can be repeated as many as 25 times, depending on the number of routes that are being sent in a single message. The fields labeled Must Be Zero should contain all zero bits. The first field, Command, can have the following values, which indicate the purpose of the message:

- **1 Request**—This message requests that the recipient of the message send all or part of its routing table to the sender of this message.

- **2 Response**—This message is a response to a request, and contains all or part of the sender's routing table to the requestor. Additionally, this message can be sent as an update message that does not correspond with any particular request.

- **3 Traceon**—This is an obsolete command that should be ignored.

- **4 Traceoff**—This is an obsolete command that should be ignored.

- **5**—This is a value reserved by Sun Microsystems for its own use. Implementations of RIP might or might not ignore this type of command.

Note

Why would anyone create a message type with so many fields that contain only zeros? The reason is simple. The creators of RIP version 1 anticipated that enhancements would be made to the protocol (hence the Version field), and they wanted to create a message that could be used for the current version 1 as well as for future versions of the protocol. In RFC 1058 (the original RFC for RIP version 1), rules for RIP routing specify that all messages that have a version number of zero are to be discarded. If the version number is 1, the message is to be discarded if any of the Must Be Zero fields contains a nonzero value. If the Version field contains a value greater than 1, the message is not discarded. In this way, it is possible for RIP version 1 to interact with RIP version 2. Version 1 of the protocol can ignore the Must Be Zero fields when it receives a message from a router that uses RIP version 2 and still garner information from the packet that can be used to update its routing table.

Of course, this doesn't provide for fully functional backward compatibility. If you mix RIP version 1 and version 2 routers in the same network, you should avoid using variable-length subnet masks because the IP address field would then be difficult for the RIP 1 router to understand. For more information about subnetting, see Chapter 25.

The Version field denotes the version of the RIP protocol. For version 1 this field contains, of course, a value of 1. The Address Family Identifier field was defined in RFC 1058, but only one address type (the IP address) was defined, and the value for this field should be 2. The IP Address field is 4 bytes long and is used to store a network address or a host address. For most request messages, this value is set to the default route of 0.0.0.0.

The final field is used to store the hop count, or metric, for the route. This field can contain a value ranging from 1 to 16. A value of 16 indicates that the destination is unreachable, or to put it in other words, "you can't get there from here."

Because RIP version 1 was created before Classless Interdomain Routing (CIDR), and before the concept of subnetting was introduced, there is no subnet field in the message. Because of this, a RIP version 1 router must determine the network ID by examining the first 3 bits of the IP address, which determine to which *class* (A, B, or C) the network address belongs. From this it can apply the appropriate subnet mask for the class. If the address does not fall into one of these classes, the router will use the subnet mask associated with the interface on which it received the message and apply it to the address to determine whether it is a valid network address. If that subnet mask does not match up to create a network address, the mask of all 1s (255.255.255.255) is applied, and the address is assumed to be a host address instead of a network address.

The message traffic generated by RIP routers can be significant in a large network. RIP routers update their routing tables every 30 seconds by requesting information from neighboring routers. They also announce their existence every 180 seconds—hey, you have to allow for network latency and other network problems, so the 180 seconds value was chosen to give more than 30 seconds for another router to respond when changes are being sent or received. If a router fails to announce itself within this time, other routers will consider it to be down and will *modify their routing tables*. The router itself might have been taken offline by the network administrator, or it could have simply gone offline due to hardware failure. It's also quite possible that the network link between the router and the rest of the network has been broken. The thing to remember is that RIP routers dynamically update routing tables so that packets don't get sent out into the ether and just disappear!

RIP Version 2

Although other protocols, such as OSPF (described later in this chapter) were developed after the original version of RIP and contain more features, you might wonder why RIP version 2 was developed. The reasons are simple: RIP has a large installed base, and it's easy to implement and configure. And, for small to medium-sized networks, you don't necessarily need a more complex routing protocol when RIP will do the job just as well.

Version 2 of the protocol uses a slightly different message format, as shown in Figure 37.3.

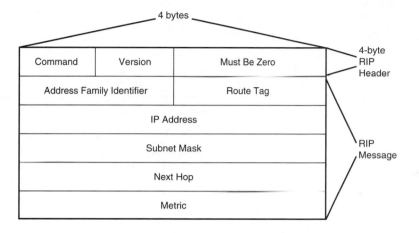

4 bytes

Command	Version	Must Be Zero
Address Family Identifier		Route Tag
IP Address		
Subnet Mask		
Next Hop		
Metric		

4-byte RIP Header

RIP Message

Figure 37.3 Format of the RIP message for version 2 of the protocol.

As you can see, the message format is the same size, but some of the fields that were previously reserved for all zeros have been put to use in version 2 of the protocol. Specifically, they contain Route Tag, Subnet Mask, and Next Hop fields.

Note

You probably can guess that the Version field for version 2 of the RIP protocol contains a value of 2. By using the Version field, routers can determine whether a RIP message is from the newer version or whether it is coming from an older router still using RIP version 1.

The Route Tag field is an administrative field used to mark certain routes. This field was introduced in RFC 1723 so that routers that support multiple routing protocols could distinguish between RIP-based routes and routes imported from other routing protocols. The Subnet Mask field is used to implicitly store a subnet mask associated with the IP address field so that the router does not have to try to determine the network or host address. Applying the mask can yield this result.

The Next Hop field is used to indicate the IP address to send packets for the destination advertised by this route message. If this field is not set to 0.0.0.0, the address in this Next Hop field must be reachable on the logical subnet from which the routing advertisement originates.

Disadvantages of RIP

RIP is a good routing protocol to use in small networks, but it doesn't scale very well to very large networks. It became quite popular early on because it was distributed as part of the Berkeley version of Unix, in the form of the routed daemon. The following are the major disadvantages of RIP:

- The broadcast messages used to update routing tables can use a significant amount of network bandwidth.
- There is no general method to prevent routing loops from occurring.

- For larger networks, 15 hops might not be a large enough figure for determining whether a destination is unreachable.

- Update messages propagate across the network slowly from one router to the next, hop by hop (called slow convergence), so inconsistencies in routing tables can cause a router to send a packet using a route that no longer exists.

OSPF (Open Shortest Path First)

RIP is a vector-distance protocol, whereas OSPF uses a link-state algorithm. OSPF routers maintain a routing table in memory just as RIP routers do, but instead of sending out the entire routing table in a broadcast every 30 seconds, OSPF routers exchange link-state information every 30 minutes. In between that interval, very short Link State Advertisements (LSAs) are used to send changes to other routers.

▶▶ The Open Shortest Path First (OSPF) routing protocol (version 2) is defined in RFC 2328, "OSPF Version 2."

OSPF was developed by the Internet Engineering Task Force and was meant to solve most of the problems associated with RIP. Instead of using a simple hop count metric, OSPF also takes into consideration other cost metrics, such as the speed of a route, the traffic on the route, and the reliability of the route. Also, OSPF does not suffer from the 15-hop limitation that RIP employs. You can place as many routers between end nodes as required by your network topology. Another difference between RIP and OSPF is that OSPF provided for the use of subnet masks at a time when version 1 of RIP did not.

Although OSPF functions more efficiently than RIP, in a large network the exchange of information between many routers still can consume a lot of bandwidth. The time spent recalculating routes can add to network delay. Because of this, OSPF incorporates a concept called an *area*, which is used to divide up the network. Routers within a specific area (usually a geographical area, such as a building or campus environment) exchange LSAs about routing information within their area.

The Link State Database (LSDB) and Areas

Each router maintains a Link State Database (LSDB), in which it stores the information it receives through LSAs from neighboring routers. Thus, over time, each OSPF router essentially has an LSDB that is identical to other routers with which it communicates. Each router is assigned a router ID, which is simply a 32-bit dotted decimal number that is unique within the autonomous network. This number is used to identify LSAs in the LSDB. This is not to be confused with the actual IP addresses of the router's interfaces, but is merely a number used to identify the router to other routers. However, most implementations of OSPF will use either the largest or the smallest IP address of a router's interfaces for this value. Because IP addresses are unique within the autonomous network, Router IDs also will be unique.

A router that is used to connect these areas with a backbone of other routers is called a *border router*. A hierarchy of routing information is built using this method so that every router does not have to maintain a huge database showing the route to every possible destination. Instead, a border router will advertise a range of addresses that exist within its area instead of each address. Other border routers store this information and therefore have to process only a portion of an address instead of the entire address when making a routing decision. Border routers store this higher level of routing information and the information for routes in their area.

In Figure 37.4, you can see a network that has four major areas, each of which has routers that maintain a database of information about its specific area. These routers exchange information with each other that keeps them updated. Each area has a border router that is part of the area and also part of the backbone area. These border routers exchange summary information about their respective areas with other border routers that are part of the backbone area.

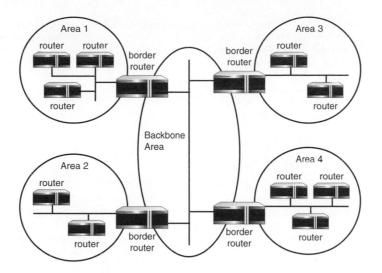

Figure 37.4 OSPF routers are responsible for their areas.

OSPF has the drawback of administrative overhead. Also, low-end routers might not be capable of coping with the amount of information a border router needs to manage.

OSPF Route Calculations

I'll leave the exact explanation of how OSPF calculates the best route to the mathematicians. However, for those who are interested, the algorithm used is called the Dijkstra algorithm, and it is used to create a shortest path tree (SPF tree) for each router. This tree contains information that is valid only from a particular router's point of view. That is, each router builds its own tree, with itself as the root of the tree, while the branches of the tree are other routers that participate in the network. Thus, each OSPF router has a different tree than other routers in the network. From this tree, the router can build a routing table that is used for the actual lookup that is performed when deciding which interface a packet should be sent out on.

Multi-Protocol Label Switching

Today the division between routers and switches is a fine line. Whereas switches were initially designed to help segment a LAN into multiple collision domains, and thereby allow you to extend the reach of a particular LAN topology, switches have moved higher up the ladder in the network in the past few years. When switching is used in a LAN to connect individual client and server computers, the process is known as *microsegmentation*, because the broadcast domain has been reduced to just the switch and the computer attached to a port. Switches at this level generally work using the hardware (MAC) addresses of the attached computers.

Layer 3 switching moves switching up the ladder by one rung by switching network frames based on the OSI Network layer address—an IP address, for example. But wait, that's what a router does, isn't it? Of course. A layer 3 switch is basically a router, but it implements most of its functions in application-specific integrated chips (ASICS) and performs its packet processing much faster than does a traditional router, which uses a microprocessor (much like a computer CPU) for this function.

◀◀ Details on layer 3 switching can be found in Chapter 8, "Network Switches."

When you get to the top of the ladder, where large volumes of data need to be routed through a large corporate network—or the Internet, for that matter—even the fastest traditional routers or layer 3 switches easily can become bogged down by the volume of traffic. Because of this, the core of a large network traditionally has been built using ATM or Frame Relay switches, and IP traffic is sent over these switched networks.

To speed up the processing of routing packets at high-volume rates, a newer technology has been developing over the past few years and goes by the name of Multi-Protocol Label Switching (MPLS).

So just what is MPLS anyway, and why is it becoming so popular?

Combining Routing and Switching

Traditional routers have a large amount of overhead processing they must perform to get a packet to its destination. Each router along the packet's path must open up and examine the layer 3 header information before it can decide on which port to output the packet to send it to its next hop on its journey. If a packet passes through more than just a few routers, that's a lot of processing time. Remember that IP is a connectionless protocol. Decisions must be made about a packet's travel plans at each stage of its journey through the network. The solution to this problem lies in newer technology—high-speed switching. Specifically, Multi-Protocol Label Switching, which is discussed in the next section, combines the best of routing techniques with switching techniques.

When you look at concepts such as ATM or Frame Relay, which are connection-oriented protocols, this isn't the case. Instead, virtual circuits (either permanent or switched) are set up to connect to endpoints of a communication path so that all cells (as in the case of ATM) or frames (as in the case of Frame Relay) usually take the same path through the switched network.

◄◄   For more information about ATM and Frame Relay and how these connection-oriented switched networks function, see Chapter 16, "Dedicated Connections."

Adding a Label

MPLS is a method that takes the best of both worlds and creates a concept that allows IP packets to travel through the network as if IP were a connection-oriented protocol (which it isn't). Using special routers called Label Switching Routers (LSRs) does this. These routers connect a traditional IP network to an MPLS network. A packet enters the MPLS network through an *ingress LSR*, which attaches a label to the packet, and exits the MPLS switched network through an *egress LSR*. The ingress LSR is the router that performs the necessary processing to determine the path a packet will need to take through the switched network. This can be done using traditional routing protocols such as OSPF. The path is identified by the label that the ingress router attaches to the packet. As you can see, the ingress router must perform the traditional role that a router fills. It must perform a lookup in the routing table and decide to which network the packet needs to be sent for eventual delivery to the host computer.

However, as the packet passes through the switched network, it is only necessary for the switch to take a quick look at the label to make a decision on which port to output the packet. A table called the Label Information Base (LIB) is used in a manner similar to a routing table to determine the correct port based on the packet's label information. The switch doesn't perform IP header processing, looking at the IP address, the TTL value, and so on. It just spends a small amount of time doing a lookup of the label in the table and outputting the packet on the correct port.

Note

Similar to ATM and Frame Relay networks, the label attached in an MPLS network doesn't stay the same as the packet travels through the network of switches. Labels are significant locally and only identify links between individual switches. Depending on the MPLS implementation, labels can be set up manually (like permanent virtual circuits) or can be created on-the-fly (like switched virtual circuits). However, after a path (or circuit) through the switched network has been created, label processing takes only a small amount of time and is much faster than traditional IP routing. Each switch simply looks up the label, finds the correct port to output the packet, replaces the label with one that is significant to the output port, and sends it on its way.

When the packet reaches the egress LSR, the label is removed by the router, and then the IP packet is processed in the normal manner by traditional routers on the destination network.

If this sounds like a simple concept, that's because it is. MPLS still is in the development stages, so you'll find that different vendors implement it in different ways. Several Internet draft documents attempt to create a standard for MPLS. Other features, such as Quality of Service (QoS) and traffic management techniques, are being developed to make MPLS a long-term solution.

Using Frame Relay and ATM with MPLS

One of the best features about the current design of MPLS is that it separates the label-switching concept from the underlying technology. That is, you don't have to build special switches that are meant for just MPLS networks. MPLS doesn't care what the underlying transport is. It is concerned only with setting up a path and reducing the amount of processing a packet takes as it travels through the circuit.

Because of this, it's a simple matter for an ATM or Frame Relay switch vendor to reprogram or upgrade its product line to use MPLS. For ATM switches, the VPI (virtual path identifier) and VCI (virtual channel identifier) fields in the ATM cell are used for the Label field. In Frame Relay switches, an extra field is added to the IP header to store the label. However, don't get confused and think that an MPLS network is an ATM network or a Frame Relay network. These switches must be reprogrammed to understand the label concept. It's even possible, for example, for an ATM switch to switch both ATM and MPLS traffic at the same time. By allowing for the continued use of existing equipment (and these switches are not inexpensive items), large ISPs or network providers can leverage their current investment, while preparing to install newer MPLS equipment when the standards evolve to a stage that makes it a good investment.

For the long term it's most likely that MPLS will be implemented using technology similar to Frame Relay instead of ATM. This is because of the small cell size of the ATM cell (53 bytes) combined with a high overhead (the 5-byte cell header). In a small network with little traffic, this 5-byte cell header seems insignificant. However, when you scale this to large bandwidth network pipes, this amount of overhead consumes a large amount of bandwidth given the small amount of data carried in the 53-byte cell. Thus, variable-length frames are most likely to become the basis for MPLS networks in the next few years.

The Secure Sockets Layer (SSL) Protocol

SOME OF THE MAIN TOPICS IN THIS CHAPTER ARE

Sending important information across the Internet, such as your credit-card numbers, can be a problem when using a clear-text method. Using clear-text is just about as bad as giving your credit-card number to a telephone solicitor. If you don't know who's on the other side of the transaction, can you be sure that your information will be kept secret?

In the case of Internet transactions, you should first be sure that you are dealing with a reputable vendor that has adopted a good privacy policy—and that the vendor is not a fly-by-night Web site. This may be difficult at times, because there are so many Web sites that will sell you everything you can imagine. As always, if it's too good to be true, then it probably isn't. Yet if you are making a purchase from a reliable vendor, you need to further be sure that your credit-card information (as well as other privacy information, such as your name and address) are kept confidential between you and the vendor.

Determining whether a vendor is reliable is beyond the scope of this book. But the subject of this chapter, the Secure Sockets Layer (SSL) protocol, still plays an important role in ensuring secure data transfers across the Internet. SSL provides the means of authentication, proving that the server is who it says it is, and possibly vice versa. To facilitate this authentication, SSL implements a key exchange that is used to encrypt data transfers.

Just as a clear-text transaction is not acceptable on a small network, or a large intranet, the same applies to the Internet. And indeed, with the many millions of Web sites on the Internet, the security problems are exponentially greater than on a company network or small LAN.

The Secure Sockets Layer protocol was developed to address just that kind of situation. Any information you exchange between your computer and a vendor on the Internet can be encrypted and offer you a great deal of security. Note that this does not prevent a hacker from infiltrating a Web site and stealing credit card or other personal information if that information is not encrypted or otherwise securely stored. SSL just protects the transactions that occur between you and the Internet vendor. This is another reason you should choose carefully the dealers you interact with on the Interact.

Note

The Secure Sockets Layer was originally developed by Netscape. It was adopted by both Netscape Navigator and Microsoft's Internet Explorer, as well as many other browsers. SSL is a common method today for exchanging secure transactions on the Internet. An Internet draft, "The SSL Protocol Version 3.0," was published in 1996. It is not yet an Internet standard, however.

SSL can be used to authenticate Web servers and clients and to provide a means to encrypt data that flows between them.

Symmetric and Asymmetric Encryption

SSL is based on encrypting data between your browser and a Web server. There are other uses for SSL, but this is perhaps the most widespread use. There are two basic methods for encrypting data transactions on a network:

- **Symmetric**—A single key known by both sides of the communication is used to encrypt the data.

- **Asymmetric**—Two keys, called the public key and private key, are used to establish an encrypted data transfer.

When you're using symmetric encryption, there is the problem of exchanging the single key so that both sides can use it to encrypt and decrypt the data. How do you send a secret key to the other party to a transaction? Use snail mail, place a telephone call, or send it as plain-text across the Internet? Obviously, none of these methods is truly secure. Sending the key via the postal service can take a few days or more, and using a telephone conversation for each Web server you want to contact can take more time than it would be worth. And, a plain-text transfer, like the previous two methods, is open to interception by a third party. Letters can be opened and resealed. Telephone conversations can be tapped. Plain-text is easily intercepted on the Internet.

Although this may sound paranoid for a casual user, a large business might think otherwise. It is not uncommon for corporate spies to go through the trash of a company looking for important data. Certain newspapers usually found at the grocery store check-out lane often use this method to get information about public figures, such as movie stars! You can protect sensitive data stored on paper by simply shredding (or burning) it. Protecting data transferred on the Internet is another thing altogether.

▶▶ Chapter 51, "Encryption Technology," gives a broad overview of technologies used to protect information using encryption techniques, including symmetric and asymmetric encryption, as well as digital certificates discussed in this chapter.

A better method for exchanging the symmetric key is to use public/private (asymmetric) key encryption. This type of exchange can set up an encrypted data path that can then be used to exchange the symmetric key for the remainder of the session.

Asymmetric encryption uses both private and public keys, and enables your browser and the Internet server to exchange data without having to first exchange a single encryption key.

Digital Certificates

SSL depends on a private and public key pair for the initial exchange of the symmetric key, as well as for authentication using digital certificates. Public keys are readily available on the Internet from companies that provide digital certificate services. There are several major providers of these sorts of keys, such as VeriSign (www.verisign.com) and Entrust (www.entrust.com), among many others. Digital certificates are used so that your browser can ensure that the Web server being contacted is indeed who it says it is.

The SSL Handshake Procedure

The SSL handshake procedure uses public/private keys to accomplish the following:

- Determination of the SSL version to be used
- Deciding what type of symmetric encryption will be used
- Server authentication
- Client authentication (optional)
- Exchange of a symmetric key

The exact details of the messages exchanged and the syntax used are a little complicated, but the basic method is as follows:

1. The client sends a request to a server that supports SSL. This message contains such things as encryption techniques and the version of SSL supported by the client, as well as some randomly generated data.

2. The server returns similar information to the client and, if authentication is to be used, the Web server's digital certificate.

3. The client uses the public key obtained from the Web server to encrypt some data and sends this encrypted data to the Web server. If the client wants to authenticate the Web server (to determine that the digital certificate is valid), it can contact the issuer of the certificate (certificate authority, or CA) and compare the data for the copy of the server's certificate. The client uses the public key of the CA to determine whether the CA's copy of the Web server's certificate is valid. If any data does not match the certificate sent to the client by the Web server, the server is not authenticated and the client ends the exchange between it and the Web server.

4. Assuming that the Web server has been authenticated, the client proceeds to encrypt (using the public key found on the Web server's digital certificate) some secret data and sends the message to the Web server. The Web server uses its own secret key to decrypt the secret data sent by the client.

5. Both the client and the Web server then go through several steps, depending on the method chosen for symmetric encryption, to come up with a symmetric session key.

6. The client sends a message (encrypted using the newly created symmetric key) to the Web server. From then on, messages between the client and the Web server will use this key. The server replies using the same method, and both sides of the connection send messages indicating that the handshake process is finished.

The preceding steps describe the basic method used to set up an SSL session. Other steps can also be involved. For example, in these steps the client first authenticated the Web server's certificate by contacting the CA to check the validity of the certificate the client received from the server. The opposite can also be performed: The Web server may need to authenticate the client. This will depend on which way sensitive data is being exchanged. If you are placing an order on a Web site and need to send credit-card information, your browser will definitely want to authenticate the Web server. If the Web server is sending sensitive data to the client (such as when you send confidential data to a customer), the Web server should also authenticate the client so that the server knows that the client is who it appears to be.

Using Information in the Digital Certificate to Prevent Interception Attacks

The preceding section described the basics of SSL. Although the techniques used may appear to be all that is necessary to ensure secure communications, because both sides of the session can authenticate with each other, that is not always the case. In Chapter 51 you will learn about a "man in the middle" attack that is used by hackers for many different protocols. The concept is to place an application between both of the parties to the secure session during the setup phase, and impersonate the server to the client, and the client to the server.

Some of the typical information that is found on a digital certificate includes the following:

- The public key of the CA used by the Web server. This is used to ensure that the certificate issued to the Web server is a valid one, and that the information has not been altered.

- A serial number that uniquely identifies the certificate.

- The time period during which the certificate is valid.

- The server's domain name.

The last item, the server's domain name, is not actually part of the SSL protocol. However, it is used by many browsers. The first three items must match those of the certificate presented by the Web server (or the client in the case of client authentication). The server's domain name, however, is very important.

For example, if the first three items listed are correct (the certificates have not been altered, and the certificate has not yet expired), does that guarantee that the Web server's certificate has not been stolen and is being used by another Web server to impersonate the server that was originally issued the certificate?

The application used to intercept communications between the Web server and the client performs two functions to satisfy both sides of the data exchange, and gain access to the encrypted data that will be sent using SSL:

- It uses its own public or private key to perform the handshake between the Web server and the client so that each side thinks it is talking to the other side of the communication.

- It establishes one symmetric key for communicating with the Web server, and another for communicating with the client.

Using this method is not an easy task. It usually is done by an insider of an organization because intercepting and impersonating clients and the Web sites with which they will establish important sessions is not very profitable, considering the huge amount of traffic on the Internet.

Worse yet is the fact that such a compromise in security can produce bad publicity for your company. Would you want to trust an Internet site with your credit-card number if that site had been hacked recently?

Yet, when this type of attack succeeds, the application that stands between the client and the server can intercept all data from either side. Worse yet, it can modify the data to serve some other purpose. No matter what the reasoning for using this type of attack, and the fact that it is difficult to implement, this threat can be practically eliminated by using the domain name of the client or Web server's digital certificate.

The domain name can be resolved to an IP address. The application that stands between the client and the Web server will have to use a different IP address. Looking up the domain name and checking to see whether the IP address that each side is talking to is accurate usually prevents this kind of attack from occurring.

What Are *http://* and *https://*?

When you are using a browser to access a typical Web page, the address field usually begins with http://, followed by the Web site. When using SSL, you'll notice that this text has an extra character added to it: https://. The "s" that is attached to the URL lets you know that SSL is being used. Watch that field. You might start out on a Web page that uses http://. Then when you decide to make a purchase, or conduct some other transaction involving sensitive information, you will usually have to click on a button. The next page that appears should have https:// in the address field. If it doesn't, don't trust that page. Many browsers will also display a padlock icon on the status bar to indicate that you are connected to a secure site.

Adding Another Layer to the Network Protocol Stack

Now that you have a good understanding of how SSL works, you'll want to know where it fits into the protocol stack on your computer. SSL can work with many protocols other than just HTTP. So it needs to be below the Application layer. Yet, because TCP/IP (at the Network layer) is used to ensure reliable communication sessions, SSL needs to be above TCP/IP in the protocol stack. As you can see in Figure 38.1, that is exactly the case. SSL is stuck neatly between these two layers.

Another important distinction is that the typical port used for HTTP communications is port 80. For SSL that port is usually 443. Both of these settings can be changed by altering the syntax of the URL in the address fields, but it's best to just use the defaults to ensure compatibility with some Web servers that don't let you use another port.

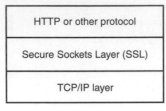

Figure 38.1 SSL resides between the Application layer and the Network layer.

Does SSL Provide Enough Security for Internet Transactions?

For the most part, SSL is a very secure mechanism for most data transfers on the Internet. Although SSL is still a proposed standard for the Internet Engineering Task Force (IETF), the IEEE has adopted SSL, and in addition, a successor called Transport Layer Security (TLS), which is also an IETF proposed standard. TLS is built on the SSL protocol, and you can find out more about it by searching at the Web site www.rfc-editor.org.

Before January 2000, the U.S. government prohibited the export of encryption technologies that used keys longer than 40–56 bits. That restriction has been lifted, so applications using 128-bit keys can now be exported, with the exception of countries that the U.S. places trade restrictions on (such as Libya and Cuba). Thus, it is now possible to ensure a great deal of security when transacting with Web sites in various countries. Keep in mind, however, that securing a session is one thing. Trusting the Web site to be a reliable vendor is another.

OpenSource SSL

Major Web servers today (such as Microsoft IIS, Apache, and Netscape) all provide SSL. However, for those that do not, you can find several places on the Internet that you can use to download source code for SSL.

Introduction to the IPv6 Protocol

SOME OF THE MAIN TOPICS IN THIS CHAPTER ARE

The first Request for Comments (RFC) to define the next generation of the Internet Protocol (IP) was RFC 1883, "Internet Protocol, Version 6 (IPv6) Specification," published as a "standards track" RFC in 1995. When you consider that the Internet was expanding at a very rapid rate at that time (as it continues to do), it seemed a natural thing to develop a new version of IP to accommodate a larger address space, and to patch some holes in the current version of IP. Many other RFCs have been created since this original one. Specifically, RFC 2460 has updated RFC 1883. Other RFCs apply to very specific aspects of IPv6, such as changes to the Internet Control Message Protocol (ICMP) and other standard TCP/IP protocols and utilities. These RFCs are too numerous to be discussed in this chapter. You can, however, do a quick search at www.rfc-editor.org to get a list of all the RFCs related to IPv6.

During the years since, other technologies such as Network Address Translation (NAT) and Classless Interdomain Routing (CIDR) have enabled the current IPv4 address space to remain viable for the current Internet. Yet IPv6 encompasses many other capabilities. Currently, IPv6 is used only in very large enterprise networks, and in many routers at the Internet's core. The hardware to route and use IPv6 exists today. Indeed, in Windows XP and Windows Server 2003, you'll find that you can use IPv6.

◀◀ Both NAT and CIDR are covered in greater detail in Chapter 25, "Overview of the TCP/IP Protocol Suite."

However, besides the increased address space, IPv6 offers many other features that will make it the ideal replacement for IPv4 (down to the desktop) in a few years.

This chapter is not meant to be as comprehensive as Chapters 25 through 29, which cover the current TCP/IP protocols, applications, and utilities. However, this chapter provides a good overview of what IPv6 has to offer. Some of the capabilities of IPv6 (such as security) have already been implemented in IPv4 technologies (especially in Virtual Private Networks, or VPNs). The fact that some IPv6 features are already being backward implemented for IPv4 applications should give you an idea of the revolution that this newer IP version will bring.

What's the Difference Between IPv4 and IPv6?

The IP protocol is a connectionless, unreliable protocol. TCP uses IP to establish sessions with remote computers and provides the reliability of the data transactions. IP, however, provides the hierarchical address space used by IPv4. Yet this address space is limited to fields in the IP datagram that are only 32 bits in length. When first created, it seemed like this address space would provide enough IP addresses to last for decades or more. After all, only government, educational facilities, and a few other institutions used what was then the ARPANET (the predecessor of the Internet). The address classes' original part of the IPv4 address space has pretty much been displaced by CIDR, to prevent wasting large ranges of addresses allocated to a single entity (such as class A networks).

Note

TCP (the Transmission Control Protocol) is not the only protocol that uses IP for sending datagrams across a network. There are many other protocols, such as the User Datagram Protocol (UDP) and the Internet Control Message Protocol (ICMP), that also use IP. The point to be made is that when it comes to the Internet and most modern networks, IP is the workhorse that other protocols rely on to get data from one point to another. It is up to the upper-level protocols to ensure that the data is delivered in a reliable fashion.

IPv6 increases this 32-bit address space to 128 bits. At first glance, 32 bits versus 128 bits doesn't seem to be a big difference. When you consider the number of possible addresses that each of these bit ranges can provide, however, there is a tremendous difference. Fill a 32-bit field with all ones and you end up with a number just over 4 billion. A 128-bit field can provide a much larger number of possible addresses. The actual number of addresses, of course, depends on which bits are used to identify a network and which are used to identify a host on a network.

The address space that IPv4 enables can give us enough addresses to satisfy the demand today, especially when using NAT for LANs and using CIDR to reclaim wasted address space that was created by the original address classes. Yet the world of electronics today has changed the playing field. It's not just computers that need an IP address. Handheld devices, mobile phones, and other consumer devices will likely require an IP address in the near future. NAT might work well in a LAN or a small enterprise network, but when you consider that many wireless devices will roam from one provider to another, an assigned IP address becomes more important. NAT is performed at a local level, not a national or global one.

Expanding the IP address space is not the only feature that IPv6 gives to the Internet and your LAN or WAN. Other important features include the following:

- A simpler header format for the IP datagram, which makes it possible to create faster routing techniques implemented in hardware designs.

- Support for new extensions to the IP header, as well as a means to include future expansion for additional headers that may be created later.

- The replacement of certain options left over from the IPv4 specification, as well as new options, and, again, room for expansion of additional options as required in the future.

- The capability to specify which datagrams require special handling when it comes to flow control. This capability can enable real-time handling of a stream of IP datagrams (needed, for example, for real-time voice or video communication over an IP network), a feature usually accomplished by other protocols tunneling IP.

- Authentication and encryption capabilities to provide for a secure connection.

As you can see, there are many differences between the capabilities of IPv4 and those of IPv6. The remainder of this chapter will give you an idea of how this new functionality is accomplished.

The IPv6 Headers

In Chapter 25 you learned about the simple IPv4 header format. Headers are used by protocols to provide information about source and destination addresses, protocols, or the payload encapsulated by the datagram. It is typical that one protocol's packet is sent as the payload of another protocol. For example, the IP datagram is usually sent across most LANs encapsulated in an Ethernet frame. At the destination, the Ethernet portion of the frame is stripped off and the IP packet information is revealed. The IP information is then removed by the protocol stack, and the TCP (or other protocol) information is then removed before the actual data is reassembled and sent to an application.

A few of the IPv4 fields were never put to any practical use. And some of those fields no longer exist in the IPv6 header. In Figure 39.1 you can see the fields that make up the IPv6 header.

The fields for IPv6, as shown in Figure 39.1, are as listed here:

- **Version**—This 4-bit field is the version of the Internet Protocol. The value for IPv4 was 4. The version for IPv6 in this field is 6. Routers and other devices use this value to determine what type of datagram is being processed.

- **Traffic Class**—Similar to the Flow Label field, this field enables nodes to specify a particular "traffic class," the definition of which is still being defined by many RFC documents. This field should be supported by any intervening device (such as a router) that understands this field (as it exists today), and ignored by those that do not.

- **Flow Label**—This 20-bit field is used to request that devices that stand between the source and the destination give special preference to this datagram. This can be compared to the Quality of Service field of IPv4 headers.

- **Payload Length**—This 16-bit field is used to indicate the length of the payload section of the datagram. This does not include the original header of the IP datagram, but it does include any additional headers, as well as the actual payload of the datagram.

- **Next Header**—One of the most useful features that IPv6 provides is that additional headers can be included in a datagram, in addition to the main IPv6 header itself. There are many types of headers (discussed later in this chapter), and they can be useful depending on the type of payload, or the treatment of the current datagram (such as routing techniques).

- **Hop Limit**—This 8-bit field is similar to a Time to Live (TTL) field used by many other protocols. It is decremented by 1 at each router the datagram passes through. When the value reaches 0, the datagram can be discarded.

- **Source Address**—A 128-bit address used to describe the IP source of the datagram.

- **Destination Address**—A 128-bit address used to describe the IP destination address of the datagram.

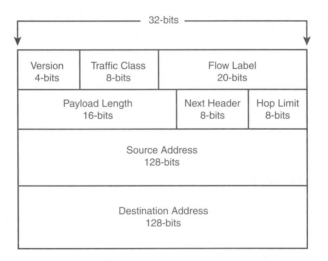

Figure 39.1   The IPv6 header is vastly different from the IPv4 header.

This section describes just the initial IPv6 header format. In the next section you will learn about how IPv6 can include additional headers that extend the traditional header to provide information about additional services for the IP protocol.

IPv6 Extension Headers

In general, most protocols have header information followed by a payload that contains the actual data to be transmitted from one point to another. Some protocols include a trailer that usually is used to provide some type of integrity check, such as CRC, to ensure that the frame or datagram has arrived at the destination without corruption.

Still other protocols, and we're talking about IPv6 here, allow for additional headers to follow the initial IPv6 header, to describe certain aspects of the datagram. These headers are not required, but one or more can be placed into the datagram. These additional extension headers are placed directly after the IPv6 header, where the payload section is usually located. The payload that follows the IPv6 header, or the extension headers, will be a header for the encapsulated upper-layer protocol being transported by the IPv6 datagram. It is interesting to note that among the following headers, if the hop-by-hop header is used, it must follow the IPv6 header as the first additional header. Other extension headers don't have to be in any particular order, but the RFCs do suggest that certain headers be placed in a certain order.

Note

Although the extension headers don't necessarily have to be placed in any particular order (except for the hop-by-hop header, described in the following text), any node that needs to look at the extension headers is required to do so in the order in which they appear in the datagram. A node cannot simply look through the headers trying to find a specific header.

The field Next Header is used to indicate whether another header follows the current header, after the initial IPv6 header. Yet if the next header is not one that the receiving node recognizes, the node should discard the datagram and send an ICMP message to the source indicating that there was a problem with the packet. In IPv6, the ICMP code for this is 1, which in text format means "unrecognized Next Header Field Header type encountered." This ICMP message is used in many of the IPv6 procedures.

It is important to note that an IPv6 datagram doesn't have to have any extension headers. They are used only when the feature is implemented in the IPv6 hardware (or software) routing mechanism.

The extension headers that can follow the IPv6 header include these:

- **Hop-by-Hop**—If present, this is the only header that must be examined by every node (read that as *router*, whether an actual router device or a computer acting as a router). This header, as described previously, must be placed directly after the IPv6 header. If you look back at the Next Header field of the IPv6 header shown in Figure 39.1, a value of zero indicates that the Hop-by-Hop header is the next header, and must be examined. The IPv6 header is the only header that can use a value of zero in the Next Header field. If any other extension header contains this value, an ICMP message value of 1 will be sent back to the source. This value indicates "unrecognized Next Header type encountered." This option type can be of variable length.

- **Destination Options**—This header can also be of variable length, and is used only by the destination of the packet. This extension header is used to carry additional information, which is to be defined by other RFCs.

- **Routing**—This field specifies specific network nodes that a packet should be passed through (a route) to reach its destination. Routers usually decide the route a packet will take depending on the routing protocol. Using this option, IPv6 routers can specify a route. The nodes listed in this option are not guaranteed, however, because there is always the possibility that a particular node might not be online. Or the Maximum Transmission Unit (MTU) of a router listed here might not accept the size of the packet, and thus the packet can't be sent through that router.

- **Fragment**—This option enables the source node to fragment a packet so that it will be able to reach its destination based on the MTU of the routers between the source and the destination. However, because this value is set by the source node, and it cannot be certain of the MTU value of intervening nodes, packets can still be dropped. A field called the M flag field can be set to one if more fragments of the original message are to be sent, or zero if the packet contains the last fragment of the original message. An Identification field is used to identify which fragmented packets should be considered as a group to be reassembled at the destination node. At the destination, fragments are identified by the source address + destination address + Identification field.

Note

IPv6 assumes a minimum MTU of 1,280 bytes. If the MTU of any link (router) that lies between the source and the destination of the packet uses a smaller MTU, then the packet will be fragmented by the router that lies between the source and the destination, not by IPv6 itself.

- **Authentication**—This extension header is described in detail in Chapter 50, "Virtual Private Networks (VPNs) and Tunneling."

- **Encapsulating Security Payload**—This extension header is described in detail in Chapter 50.

- **Upper-layer header**—This header follows the other headers, as in an IPv4 packet, and describes the data contained in the remainder of the payload section of the packet.

The preceding list is described in the recommended order suggested by the RFC. This can change depending on a few circumstances. For example, if the Destination Options header should be read not just by the node specified by the destination address found in the initial IPv6 header, but also by the other destinations listed in the Routing header, then the Destination Options header should be placed immediately after the Hop-by-Hop header, followed by the Routing header.

The Options Type Field for Hop-by-Hop and Destination Options

If the Destination Options header should be examined only by the final destination node, it should be placed just before the upper-layer header. The Options Type field for Hop-by-Hop and Destination Options is an 8-bit field. However, it should be interpreted by bit values, not by byte values.

Table 39.1 lists the first two highest-order options type bits. These bits specify what should be done if a node does not understand the option.

Table 39.1 High-Order 2-Bit Option Type Values

Value	Action
00	Ignore this header and continue to process the remaining headers, if any.
01	Drop this packet.
10	Drop this packet and send the source address an ICMP packet indicating that option type was not recognized for this packet, and indicating the header that was not recognized.
11	Similar to 10, but not applicable for multicast packets.

The third-highest-ordered bit used is either zero or one. If the bit has a value of zero, the data contained in the option cannot be changed by a node it passes through on the way to its eventual destination. If the bit has a value of one, a node can change data in the extension header.

The Next Header field is used by all options. It simply specifies what the next option (following the current option) will be. These option type numbers are based on those described for IPv4. These numbers were originally defined in RFC 1700, and later RFCs. However, the RFC process was not sufficient to keep up with newer protocols and services that were being developed, so an online database now exists at the Web site www.iana.org. You can use this database to determine what type of protocol or option the Next Header field indicates.

Other IPv6 Considerations

Although IPv6 contains a field that defines the maximum number of hops (the Hop-to-Hop field), it is not required that all nodes support this function, though they can if desired. Instead, upper-layer protocols (such as TCP) are generally delegated this responsibility.

In addition, upper-level protocols should be aware that the maximum payload space has been reduced if IPv6 headers are to be added to the packet. Again, this is a modification that will require that upper-layer protocols be modified, or that the source use fragmentation to deliver packets to their destination.

The Future of IPv6

IPv4 has been in use for over 10 years now. Although most of the address-space issues have been resolved—for the time being—other features that IPv6 enables are very useful and will only enhance the capabilities of the Internet Protocol in the future. If not this year or the next, you can expect to see IPv6 on your network in the near future.

Network User and Resource Management

PART VII

Windows NT Domains

40

SOME OF THE MAIN TOPICS IN THIS CHAPTER ARE

The Windows NT domain is a collection of users and resources. It is the primary unit of user and resource administration. Administrators in any particular domain can control the addition or modification of user accounts in their domain and can control which resources any user can access, along with the type of access. To begin to understand the logon process under Windows NT, you should first become cognizant of how users and security information is organized into user groups and domains and how these interact. Understanding how domains operate in the Windows NT environment makes it easier for you to plan an integration with, or upgrade to, Windows 2000. When you upgrade your network to include only Windows 2000 computers, you'll find that instead of primary and backup domain controllers, you'll have only domain controllers (that are neither primary nor backup), which are essentially peers on the network. It is important to understand how primary and backup domain controllers work if you plan to keep both Windows NT and Windows 2000 computers in the same network.

In this chapter we examine the tools an administrator can use to manage users of a Windows NT 4.0 server. In the next chapter we look at managing users of Windows 2000/Windows 2003 servers using the Microsoft Management Console utility. As a prerequisite to the next chapter, you might want to first read Chapter 31, "Using the Active Directory."

Note

Windows Server 2003 servers are now coming to market, and Windows XP Professional has been available as a replacement for Windows NT 4.0 Workstation as well as Windows 2000 Professional. However, the basic concepts of the Windows domain are important to understand, whether or not your network contains Windows NT servers. These domains were incorporated into the Windows 2000 Active Directory as container objects. The trust relationships that you have to establish manually, as described in this chapter, are now transitive and automatic in the Active Directory. Yet, for those still using Windows NT 4.0, as well as those who have upgraded to Windows 2000 or Windows Server 2003, the concepts covered in this chapter can be useful. If you are still using Windows NT 4.0 domains, consider this chapter to be a guide to managing those domains. If you have already upgraded to the Active Directory, you should read this chapter to understand how domains have changed in the Active Directory, as well as to understand how to manage Windows NT 4.0 domains in your directory if you have a mixed-mode network that contains both Windows NT 4.0 domains and Windows 2000/Windows Server 2003 domain container objects.

Windows NT 4.0 has had several years to settle down. With the latest service packs that Microsoft and other third parties have provided, you can expect to see NT 4.0 used in networks for a few more years, despite the advent of Windows 2000 and Windows Server 2003 and their implementation of Active Directory. Windows NT 4.0 is a stable platform, and you needn't upgrade your systems as long as you can still support the applications important to your users. For example, there have been several releases of Microsoft Office since Office 97, but these newer products have been slow to be adopted because Office 97 provides most of the functionality that many businesses need today. If you do have a need to upgrade to newer software applications, you might want to consider Windows 2000 or Windows Server 2003.

Tip

If you are not yet considering a move away from Windows NT 4.0 Server domains, you might want to review the availability and support schedule published at `www.microsoft.com/ntserver/ProductInfo/Availability/Retiring.asp`.

Upgrading to Windows 2000 can be expensive from both a hardware and a software point of view. Planning the namespace for the Active Directory, used in Windows 2000 and Windows Server 2003, can be a complex task as well. A carefully managed Windows NT 4.0 network can continue to serve you for a few more years, but availability and support are dwindling. It would be a good idea to start planning your migration strategy early, because an adequate Active Directory model is much harder to design and implement than an adequate Windows NT 4.0 domain.

This chapter will walk you through the Windows NT 4.0 domain management utilities. The next chapter, Chapter 41, "Windows 2000 and Windows Server 2003 User and Computer Management Utilities," will introduce you to the new Microsoft Management Console (MMC), which is a consistent interface used to manage many aspects of Windows 2000/2003 (as well as the client operating system Windows XP Professional). You will also learn in that chapter how to manage users and user groups under Windows 2000.

Before you read that chapter, however, explore the concepts in this chapter so that you will better understand what a domain is. In Chapter 41, you will then find it easier to understand how these domains are incorporated into the Active Directory.

Workgroups and Domains

Let's step back even farther in time to find out how earlier versions of Windows provided for authentication and access controls before the concept of the domain was created.

In many ways, a domain is similar to a Windows 3.1 workgroup, but with one major exception: The domain has a single, centralized security accounts manager (SAM) database that holds all security information for the domain. In a workgroup, each computer in the network has its own security database, and the user of that computer can set passwords on resources that the computer provides to the network. Whereas a domain provides for centralized administration of the network's resources and users, the workgroup provides a highly decentralized, peer-to-peer networking model.

The disadvantages to the workgroup method include not only the decentralized management functions, but also the ways in which the workgroup method impacts the end user. For example, to access a resource on another computer in a workgroup, the user needs to know the password associated with that share-level resource. Because a different person can potentially manage each computer or workstation, you often need to know as many different passwords as you have resources to which you need to connect. Keeping track of multiple passwords usually leads to lax security because you must write them all down so that you don't forget them.

In a domain the administrator is in charge of the security policy for the entire domain. Users need only a single username and password to log on to the network and access resources throughout the domain. There are limits, however, to what a single domain can do in a network. As the network grows in size, whether it is in users, resources, or geographical size, using a single security database can have some drawbacks. Specific computers are designated to be domain controllers. These computers are the repositories of the security database—the SAM. This database contains data for four types of security objects, or accounts:

- User accounts
- Computer accounts
- Global group accounts
- Local group accounts

As you can see, in addition to keeping track of usernames, passwords, and other information about the users on the network, the SAM also keeps track of which computers have joined the domain and which user groups have been defined, along with the members of each group. Note that only Windows NT computers are tracked in the database. Users on other platforms, such as Windows

95/98/Me, can log on to a Windows NT domain, but their computers will not have computer accounts in the domain. Windows NT computers actually join the domain when the administrator creates a computer account for that workstation in the SAM.

The number of accounts that a single Windows NT 4.0 domain can accommodate, according to Microsoft figures, is around 40,000 due mostly to the maximum size to which the SAM database can grow. This figure can vary, depending on the information you store in the SAM. For example, you might have a lot of computer and user accounts but only a few trust relationships stored in the SAM. Or you might have a large number of trust relationships stored in the SAM, and this would mean you would have less room for computer and user accounts. You would need more than one domain for a larger network.

Note

There are actually two places where you can find the SAM for Windows NT. The domain controllers hold copies of the domain database, and this is used to validate domain logons and grant users the ability to access resources in the domain. However, any Windows NT Server or Windows NT Workstation computer that is not a domain controller also has its own local security database, much like a Windows for Workgroups computer. The local user can create individual user accounts on the local computer and can grant access to resources on the computer to these users. However, users who are validated by a computer's local database cannot use this logon to access domain resources, unless their username/password on the local computer matches one on the Windows NT computer, as long as the administrator creates an account on the Windows NT computer with the same name/password. This is called *pass-through authentication*. Additionally, when a Windows NT computer joins a domain, the domain administrator's global group is, by default, placed into the local domain administrator's group, giving the domain administrators the ability to control security functions on the local computer.

Of course, it will probably be a rare thing to find a domain that actually has 40,000 user or computer accounts. When a network grows this large, a solution needs to be found that provides a convenient method of managing users and controlling access to network resources.

The solution is to create multiple domains in the network and allow them to interact with each other so that users can access resources anywhere on the network, while still using only a single username and password to log on. In Windows NT this is done using a concept called a *trust relationship between domains*.

Interdomain Trust Relationships

To support the concept of one username and one password throughout a collection of domains, the trust relationship is used to allow domains to share information contained in the security database. Without a trust relationship you would have to create a new user account in the database of each domain to which a user would need to have access. This would be sort of like the workgroup model, only on a larger scale using domains instead of individual computers.

When a user account is created in a domain, it is assigned a unique identifier, called an *SID*, which stands for *security identification descriptor*. If you create several accounts in different domains for a user, with the same logon username and password, the SID will not be the same from one domain to another. The user's logon name is ordinary text, which is used for the convenience of humans who must remember it. The SID is the actual method that the network uses when identifying a particular user (and to identify the domain, which holds the user account) and deciphering what access that user is allowed, based on Access Control Lists (ACLs).

▶▶ For more information on ACLs, see Chapter 43, "Rights and Permissions."

Because there should be only one username and password for any user throughout the network, no matter how many domains are created, a method is needed to allow a domain to recognize that a user has already been validated in another domain. If this can be communicated between domains, it becomes possible to simply trust a user if a domain trusts the domain from which the user comes.

A trust relationship is created when an administrator from one domain uses the User Manager for Domains utility to create a specific relationship with another domain. For example, if domain A has a trust relationship whereby it trusts the users in domain B, then the administrator of domain A can grant access to resources in domain A to users who reside in domain B. A trust relationship, however, is a one-way street. So this example does not give users in domain A access to resources in domain B.

Note

A trust relationship does not automatically give users in one domain access to resources in another domain. Just as users in a domain are granted access to resources by their domain administrators, users from *trusted* domains must be granted the necessary access rights and privileges in a trusting domain before they can access resources. The trust relationship that is set up between two domains is merely the prerequisite that allows users to be *granted* access to resources in another domain.

A trust relationship enables the Windows NT LSA (local security authority) to use *pass-through authentication* to validate a user. When a user from a trusted domain tries to access a resource, the netlogon service contacts the domain in which the user account resides to confirm that the user account is valid. The LSA receives copies of the user's SIDs (the account SID and the SIDs for any global groups of which the account is a member). After this pass-through authentication process, the LSA has all the information it needs in order to evaluate the user against the Access Control List entries that might be present in an ACL for a particular resource.

For users in both domains to have access to resources in both domains, the administrators of each domain must create two trust relationships.

Creating a Trust Relationship

The domain administrator uses the User Manager for Domains utility to create trust relationships. To start the utility, select Start, Programs, Administrative Tools, and finally User Manager for Domains. In Figure 40.1 you can see the utility as it looks when it is first started, showing a list of user accounts in the domain at the top and a list of user groups at the bottom.

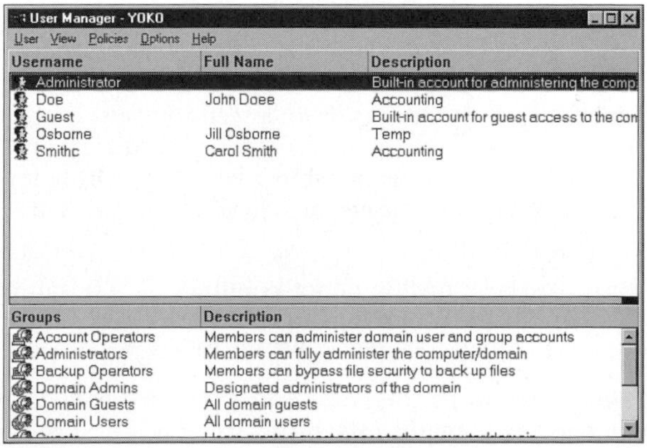

Figure 40.1   The User Manager for Domains is used to create a trust relationship.

To create a trust relationship the administrator in both domains will have to run the utility and enter the other domain's name into the list of domains it trusts or is trusted by. To bring up the dialog box that is used to accomplish this task, select the Policies menu at the top of the utility and select Trust Relationships (see Figure 40.2).

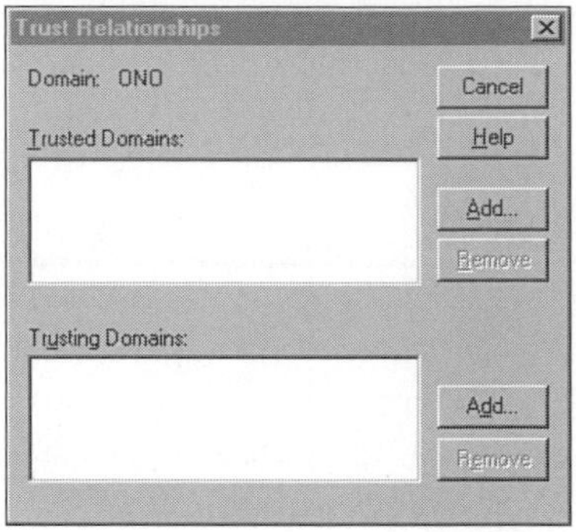

Figure 40.2   The Trust Relationships dialog box is used to create a trust relationship with another domain.

The order in which a trust relationship is established is important. The administrator of the domain that will be trusted should run the utility first to add the name of the domain that will trust his domain. To do this, click the Add button next to the Trusting Domains list. The Add Trusted Domain dialog box appears. Here you enter the name of the domain that will trust your domain, and an optional password, and click OK.

The administrator of the domain that will trust this domain must perform the same function, this time clicking the Add button next to the Trusted Domains list. In the Add Trusted Domain dialog box, the administrator will put the name of the domain it will trust and then the same password that was entered by the administrator of the trusted domain.

Although the password is optional, you should always use one. The password is not used later by domain controllers that are performing pass-through authentication. It is used only to verify both ends of this process of creating the trust relationship. After the trust relationship has been established, the domain controllers will use SID information to validate each other.

After the trusting domain has entered the correct password, a message is displayed indicating that the trust relationship was set up. Each administrator then sees the other domain listed in the trusted or trusting section of the Trust Relationships dialog box. If you have a network that has multiple domains and a large number of administrators, from a security viewpoint, it is a good idea to regularly check this dialog box to be sure that the trusts you expect to exist are there and that no others have been added. Remember that a trust relationship gives a user with administrative privileges the capability to grant rights and privileges to users outside your domain. This is a very powerful capability.

Again, remember that each trust relationship under Windows NT 4.0 is unidirectional. If you want both domains to allow users from the other domain to access resources in each domain, you will have to repeat the process and create two trust relationships between the two domains.

When it becomes necessary to remove a trust relationship, all you have to do is select the domain from either the trusted or trusting domains lists in the dialog box and click the Remove button.

Domain Controllers

The domain controller is a computer that holds a copy of the SAM. Domain controllers authenticate users when they log on to the network. In Windows NT there are two kinds of domain controllers:

- **Primary Domain Controller (PDC)**—This type of domain controller is where the master copy of the SAM resides for the domain. Updates to the SAM can be made only on the PDC, which then propagates the changes to the other domain controllers. Because there can be only one master copy of the domain's SAM, there can be only one PDC in any given domain.

- **Backup Domain Controller (BDC)**—This domain controller holds a copy of the SAM and receives updates to this copy via replication from the PDC. A BDC can authenticate users, but changes to the SAM must be done on the PDC. Because the BDC holds a copy of the SAM, there can be multiple BDCs in the network. BDCs are usually used to offload processing from a busy PDC, provide quick network access to the SAM in network segments that are distanced from the PDC, or provide for fault-tolerance so that users can still log on to the network when the PDC becomes unavailable.

Only a Windows NT Server computer can be used to create a domain controller, and this must be done during the initial installation of the operating system. Without a complete reinstallation of the operating system, Windows NT Servers that are installed as ordinary "member servers" cannot be upgraded later to become a PDC. Nor can a domain controller be downgraded to a standard member server without a complete reinstall. Windows NT Workstation computers cannot be used as domain controllers in any fashion. However, a Windows NT Workstation has its own local SAM database that can be used to allow users to log on to the local workstation, but not the network. This can be useful in small networks in which a domain controller is not necessary. However, in such a situation, if a user needs to access resources on more than one workstation, the user must have a user account on each workstation to which it needs access.

Note

Windows 2000 Server does not use the concept of primary and backup domain controllers. Instead, all domain controllers are the same, and they exchange information among themselves. The way in which Windows 2000 enables you to "promote" a server to be a domain controller is discussed in Chapter 41.

All Windows NT computers that participate in a network run a service called the netlogon service. You can see it listed in the Services applet found in the Control Panel. This service is responsible for taking a user's logon request and communicating with a domain controller to process the logon. It also is the entity that handles synchronization between the PDC and the BDC copies of the SAM database.

Windows NT Domain Models

The single logon principle that is so important in Microsoft networking is enhanced by allowing domains to trust each other's user base by using trust relationships. However, in a network that contains a large number of domains, it is important to decide on a model to use when establishing trust relationships to make them easy to manage for the particular needs of your environment. Although it would be very easy to create trust relationships among all domains in a large network, that is not the way it's usually done. Instead, four basic models are often used:

- Single domain model
- Master domain model

- Multiple master domain model
- Complete trust domain

Deciding on which domain model to use depends on many factors, but the basic things to consider are the size of the network (in users) and the organization of the business, along with management and geographical factors.

The Single Domain Model

For a small organization that has a centralized management team for its network, a single domain might be sufficient. In this model, all the user accounts are created in a single domain, along with all the network resources, such as file and print services. There are no interdomain trust relationships to worry about because there is only one domain.

In this model there is only one PDC, but one or more BDCs are typically created for fault-tolerance purposes. If users are located at different sites geographically, you can use this model and put a BDC at each site to reduce network traffic associated with logons, allowing users to be validated by the local BDC. Having a BDC at each site also enables users to continue working if the network link between them and the site that has the PDC goes down.

The Master Domain Model

In a large enterprise it might be desirable to have one central database that contains all the user accounts, while maintaining other departmentalized databases that hold security information about resources in the network. In the master domain model one domain is designated to be the master domain, and all user accounts are created in this domain. Additional *resource domains* are then created, which do not have to contain any user accounts other than those used for the local administrators to manage resources. Because of the concept of trust relationships, you don't even have to create accounts for these administrators in their own domains. By using global and local groups, it is possible to give a user account from the master domain the capability to administer another domain by placing that user account in a special Domain Admins user group.

In the resource domains, file and print shares are created and can be managed locally in the resource domain by the domain's administrators. User accounts can be managed from a central location—by administrators in the master domain. In this model each resource domain has a one-way trust relationship with the master domain whereby it trusts the users in the master domain, as shown in Figure 40.3.

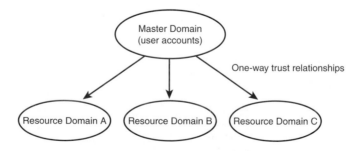

Figure 40.3   Resource domains trust the users validated by the master domain in this model.

This type of domain model is ideal if you need a central place to manage user accounts but want to let local administrators take responsibility for managing resources in their area of the network. In a large company you might want the personnel or human resources department to be responsible for creating accounts for new employees and deleting accounts when users leave the company. The accounting department then can take charge of managing printers and other resources in their own domain, while those in charge of the warehouse can similarly be responsible for granting access to resources in their domain.

The Multiple Master Domain Model

The multiple master domain model is similar to the master domain model, but in this case there can be more than one master domain. Resource management is still decentralized by allowing resource domain administrators to control local resources, but instead of one master domain to hold all user accounts, there are several. In Figure 40.4 you can see an example of this model in which users in the United States are managed by one domain, while users in the United Kingdom are managed by a separate master domain.

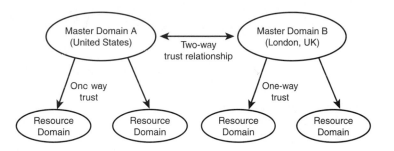

Figure 40.4 In the multiple master domain model there can be more than one master domain to hold user accounts.

This model is the most scalable domain mode because you can just add another master domain if you need to add more users when the existing master domains become highly populated, or when a new geographical area is brought into the company. In fact, if you have a large network that already has more than 40,000 user accounts and you want some degree of centralized user administration, then the multiple master domain model is the best method to use. It provides for local administration of resources but also allows you to separate users into large administrative groups for management purposes.

In an enterprise that has a global network, this model can be used to allow large divisions of a company to control users located in their area. User account management is still centralized, but into several large groups that each division manages. If trust relationships are set up correctly, a user still needs only one logon to be granted access to resources that exist anywhere throughout a worldwide global network.

Another reason you might choose the multiple master domain model over the master domain model is to minimize network replication traffic. Remember that updates to the SAM are made to the database residing on the PDC, and are then sent to BDCs during the replication process. If you have a user base that experiences frequent changes, replication traffic on a global scale can consume valuable network bandwidth. By having several master domains, one for each location, you reduce the bandwidth consumption because replication occurs only within each domain.

The Complete Trust Model

This domain model provides for decentralized user account management and decentralized resource management. Each domain in the network has a two-way trust relationship with every other domain in the network, as shown in Figure 40.5. Administrators can still manage their own local resources but also can manage their own user database. This method requires good communication skills among domain administrators to make sure that users are properly granted access to the resources in other domains.

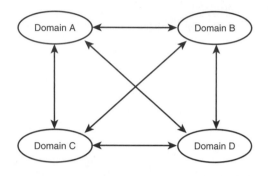

Figure 40.5   The complete trust model provides the highest degree of decentralized management in a large network.

Although this model has the greatest chance of causing confusion when one is trying to troubleshoot logon or resource access problems, it can be a good method to choose under some circumstances. For example, in the highly competitive business environment of the past decade, in which growth is achieved by acquisition, this model can be used to quickly join networks when companies merge. This assumes, of course, that both business entities are using a Microsoft Windows NT network.

Windows NT User Groups

To make assigning access rights and privileges easier to manage, Windows NT enables you to group users together. Rather than spending an inordinate amount of time granting each user the right to access a particular file share, for example, you can simply put multiple users into a user group and grant or revoke the right from the group. User groups can be either a local group that exists on a particular computer, or domain-wide local or global groups.

Local groups in a particular server are used to allow the local administrator of a member server to control access to local resources. For example, when a member server (a Windows NT Server computer that is not a domain controller) joins a domain, the domain's global group called Domain Admins is placed into the server's local group called Administrators. It is through this mechanism that the domain administrators are granted the capability to administer the local server. Of course, it is also quite possible for the user of the member server to use the server's built-in Administrator account to remove the Domain Admins global group from the local administrators group, and thereby deny the domain administrators their access to administer resources on the member server.

Local domain groups function in much the same way, but on a domain-wide scale. When a trust relationship is created between two domains, users in one domain do not automatically gain access rights to resources in the trusting domain. Instead, the administrator in the trusting domain needs to grant each user the needed access privilege. Because granting access rights on a user-by-user basis can be quite tedious in a large network, groups can be used for that purpose as well.

Local domain groups can contain users from the domain in which the group is created, and users or global groups from other trusted domains. Domain administrators can grant or deny access to domain resources by granting or denying access to the local domain groups.

Global user groups contain only users or groups from a single domain. Global user groups are used to "export" users to another trusting domain as a single unit. For example, the domain administrator of a trusting domain can place global groups from trusted domains into a local domain group and grant or deny access to domain resources by the local domain group.

Built-In User Groups

To make things easier when you first set up a Windows NT computer, several local and global groups are created by default. If the computer is a Windows NT Server computer operating as a domain controller, you will find these domain local groups:

- Administrators
- Backup Operators
- Account Operators
- Guests
- Print Operators
- Replicator
- Server Operators
- Users

The functions of most of these groups are fairly obvious at first glance. The Administrators group is a local group that is granted rights to manage the domain. The Backup Operators group can be used to enable users to perform backups, bypassing normal security restrictions for this purpose. The Print Operators group has the necessary privileges to manage printers and print queues for the domain, and so on. The Users local group is used to group users on the particular server, whereas the Domain Users group usually contains all users in the domain. If you look at the membership of the server's Users group, you can see that the Domain Users global group is a member of the group, which is how ordinary domain users are able to get limited access rights to the server.

If the server is a domain controller, you also will see three built-in *global* groups:

- Domain Admins
- Domain Guests
- Domain Users

Windows NT Workstation computers, along with Windows NT Server computers that are operating as a non-domain controller computer (called a member server) have the following built-in local groups:

- Administrators
- Backup Operators
- Power Users
- Guests
- Replicator
- Users

Note

The rights associated with built-in user groups are what give them their functionality. For an in-depth discussion of user rights and the functions that a member of a built-in user group can perform, see Chapter 43.

Creating User Groups

These built-in groups make it easy to set up initial groups of users that can perform standard server or network management tasks. For more specific functions you can create your own groups. To do so, use the User Manager for Domains utility.

First make a list of the functional groups you want to create, based on the resources or type of access you think each group will need. For example, if your domain supports several different business units, such as an accounting department, a research department, and a warehouse, you might want to create three user groups, one for each of these departments. If one group of users, such as the accounting users, needs to be further subdivided into groups with some having more access to confidential data than others, you can create several user groups for that department instead of a single group.

The important point to remember is that by creating groups you will make the job of granting or revoking access rights easier as resources or users on the network change.

To create a group, you need to activate the User menu in the User Manager for Domains, and select either Create New Local Group or Create New Global Group. In Figure 40.6 you can see the dialog box used to create a new local group.

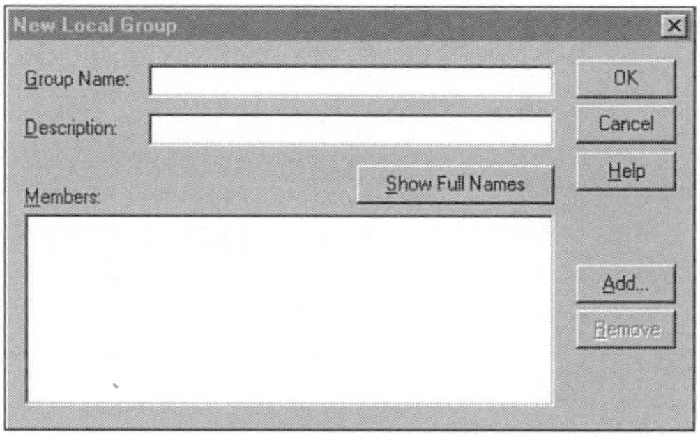

Figure 40.6 To create a new local group, specify the group name and then add members.

After you enter the name of the new group and an optional description, you can click the Add button to bring up the Add Users and Groups dialog box. This dialog box is used for many different functions in the User Manager for Domains when selecting users is required. In Figure 40.7 you can see that all you have to do is select a username or a group name, and then click the Add button to move that name to the Add Names display at the bottom of the dialog box. You can use the Search button to locate names if the list for your network is very large and you don't want to scroll through the entire list to find the correct name.

After you have finished selecting users or groups to add to this local group, click the OK button. You are returned to the New Local Group dialog box, and the users or group names that were selected now appear in the Members list at the bottom of the dialog box. Click OK to dismiss this dialog box when you are finished.

If you need to modify group membership later, all you need to do is select the user group from the display on the main window of the User Manager for Domains and then, from the User menu, select Properties. Alternatively, you can simply double-click the group name to bring up the Properties sheet. This display is exactly like the one used when creating the new group except for its title. You can use the Add and Remove buttons to modify group membership.

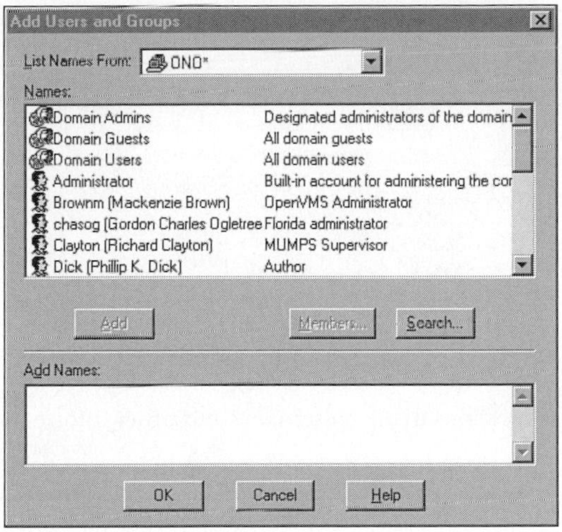

Figure 40.7 Select user or other groups to place into the new local group.

Special User Groups

Besides the local and global built-in groups that were just described, there are several user groups whose memberships are not assigned by the administrator. These groups are not seen when looking in the list of user groups in the User Manager for Domains. They are, however, seen when you use other utilities, such as the Windows NT Explorer, to grant access to files and directories. These are the groups:

- **Interactive**—Users who are currently logged on locally to the computer.
- **Network**—Users who are currently logged on to the computer through the network.
- **Everyone**—Just what it says: any interactive or network user on the computer.
- **System**—The operating system itself.
- **Creator owner**—The user who creates an object, such as a file or directory.

Managing User Accounts

On Windows NT Server member servers and Windows NT Workstation computers, the User Manager utility is used to manage the local SAM. In a domain, the utility is similar but is called the User Manager for Domains. This is the tool you use for most user account management in Windows NT. To start the User Manager for Domains, select it from the Administrative Tools folder in the Programs folder.

The User menu in this utility can be used to add, delete, or modify user accounts. To modify an existing account, simply double-click the account name and the Properties dialog box appears (you also can highlight the account and select Properties from the User menu).

To add a new user, select New User from the User menu. The New User dialog box (shown in Figure 40.8) appears. You can enter the user's logon username here (as many as 20 characters), along with other useful information such as the user's full name and a description of what the account is used for.

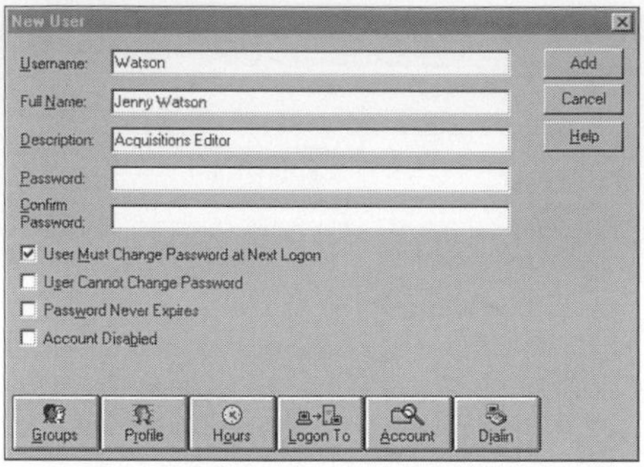

Figure 40.8 Add a new user by specifying a username and other information for the account.

When you enter the password for the user account, you must enter it twice to confirm what you have typed. You can select from the check boxes any of the password options you want to use. If you select User Must Change Password at Next Logon, users will be prompted when they first use the account to create a new password known only to them. You can use this same check box on an existing user's Properties dialog box when resetting a user password that the user has forgotten. This allows you to reset the password to a new value you can give the user, but still force the user to change the password when using it for the first time.

If you select User Cannot Change Password, the user will be locked out of this function. This function is useful for service accounts, such as for SQL Server, because it precludes anyone from changing the password, which would cause the service to not start on boot.

If you select Password Never Expires, this bypasses the password policy you can set for the domain, which would usually force the user to change the password to a new value on a periodic basis. Finally, you can use the Account Disabled check box to temporarily disable logons for an account when you do not want the account to be accessible but also do not want to delete it.

After you have finished filling in the information for this dialog box, you can click the Add button to add the account, or you can use the buttons at the bottom of the dialog box to bring up additional prompts.

Adding a User to a Group

If you click the Groups button in the New User dialog box, you get the Group Memberships dialog box, shown in Figure 40.9. When an account is first created, it is, by default, a member of the Domain Users local group. You can select other groups from those shown and use the Add button to add the user to the group. You can select a group of which the user is already a member and use the Remove button to remove the user from that group. To specify the primary group to which a user will belong, highlight that group under the Member Of box and click the Set button. When you have finished selecting user groups for this user, click the OK button.

User Profiles

You can use the Profile button in the New User dialog box to bring up the User Environment Profile dialog box. Here you can specify a path to the location of the file that contains the user's profile (desktop and environment settings), as well as the name of a logon script that is executed each time the user logs on to the domain. In Figure 40.10 you can see that this also is where you specify the path to the user's home directory.

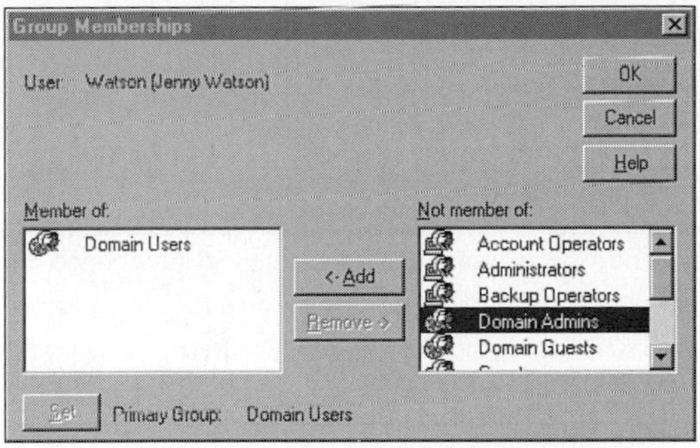

Figure 40.9 The Group Memberships dialog box allows you to control to which groups a user belongs.

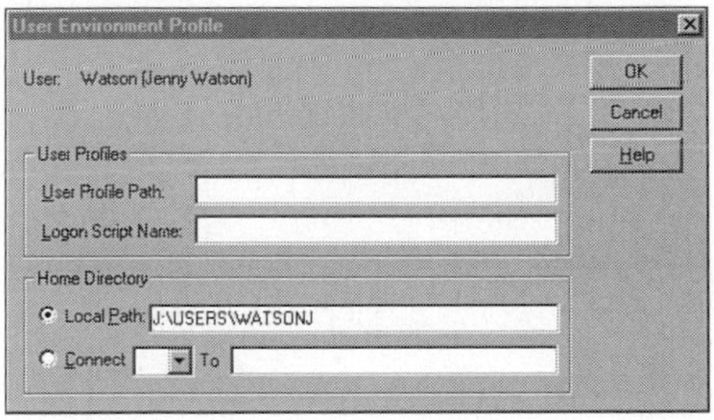

Figure 40.10 The User Environment Profile dialog box allows you to set the user's profile and home directory.

You also can specify drive letters in the Connect box and then specify a pathname. This will cause the user to be automatically connected to the file shares you specify when the user logs on to the system.

Limiting the Time a User Can Log On

The Hours button in the New User dialog box brings up the Logon Hours dialog box (see Figure 40.11), where you can select the days and hours that a user account can be used.

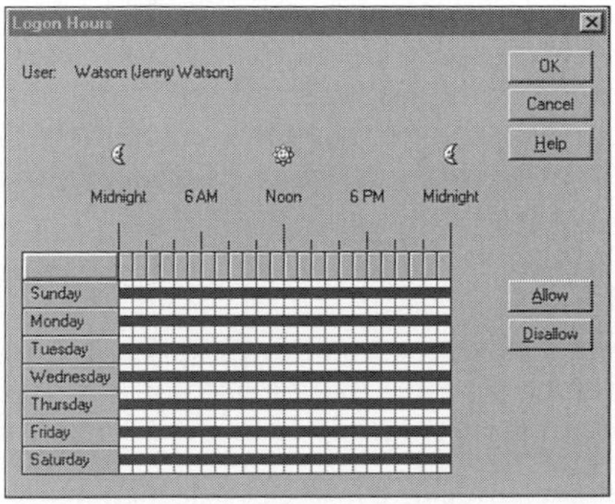

Figure 40.11 In this dialog box specify the hours an account can be used.

In this display you can select one-hour periods by clicking on one or more of them and then using the Allow or Disallow button to specify whether the user can log on during that period. By default, all the boxes representing hours for all days are filled in with a blue color indicating that the user can log on at that time.

Tip

What happens when a user is already logged on and the time changes to a period when they are disallowed? This depends on the settings you make in the Accounts Policy for the domain. You can allow the user to continue working but not make any new network connections, or you can set the policy to force the user off the server when the time changes to a disallowed period.

Limiting Which Workstations a User Can Log On To

The Logon To button in the New User dialog box will bring up the Logon Workstations dialog box (see Figure 40.12), which you can use to specify up to eight workstations to which the user is allowed to log on using this domain account.

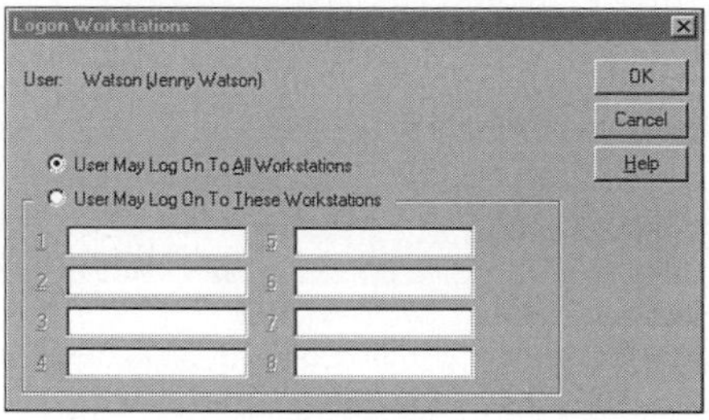

Figure 40.12   The Logon Workstations dialog box can be used to limit the workstations a user can use to log on to the domain.

If you want the user to be able to log on by using any workstation in the domain (the default selection), select the appropriate radio button in this dialog box.

This dialog box can be useful for situations in which security is a high priority. For user accounts that have been given advanced rights and are able to access sensitive data, you might want to restrict their use to computers that are in a particular physical location that can be monitored. For example, the payroll process is usually a very sensitive function in an organization. Not only do you want to prevent unauthorized users from modifying information here, but you also want to keep prying eyes out of information that might cause user embarrassment or discomfort. By limiting the payroll applications to specific user logon accounts and by restricting those accounts to selected workstations, you can make the monitoring process easier and more defined.

Account Information

The Account button in the New User dialog box brings up the Account Information dialog box, shown in Figure 40.13. Here you can specify that an account will never expire, or you can set a date at which time the account will no longer be able to be used for a domain logon.

There are two types of domain accounts, and you can select the type for this account in this dialog box. A global account is the default account for a user in that user's own home domain. This account can be placed into a global group and exported to another domain to be granted access to resources.

Local groups are more limited. They are used to provide access for a user who is *not* a member of a trusted domain. This can be used by a user in another Windows NT domain or by a user from another operating-system type. The local account cannot be used to log on locally to a Windows NT computer and is provided so that you can give access through the network. Because the local account is provided so that you can give access to your domain to special-case users, you cannot place local accounts into a global group and export them to another domain.

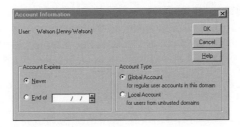

Figure 40.13   The Account Information dialog box can be used to specify the type of account and limit its use.

Allowing Dial-Up Access

If you want the user to be able to dial into the network using the remote access service (RAS), click the Dialin button in the New User dialog box to bring up the Dialin Information dialog box (see Figure 40.14). Here you can select the callback option. Callback means that after a user dials into the network, the server will disconnect the phone and then dial the user's computer back. This can be used for security purposes or for cost savings.

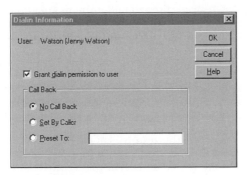

Figure 40.14   The Dialin Information dialog box can be used to control dial-up access to the network for this account.

These are the Call Back options:

- **No Call Back**—This is the most common form, which enables a user to log in using a modem and, after validation, begin working.

- **Set By Caller**—The caller can specify the telephone number that the server will use to perform the callback function.

- **Preset To**—The administrator can set the telephone number that will be used for the callback.

If security is not a great issue for this user's account, you can select the No Call Back option. If the user is a mobile user and you want the long-distance charges to be paid by the server's end of the telephone line, use the function to allow the caller to specify the callback number. If security is an important issue for this account, use the third option so that you can specify the number that will always be called back. This prevents users from other locations from using this account to dial in to your system and establish an RAS session.

Replication Between Domain Controllers

Modifications to the SAM database are always made on the primary domain controller. Periodically, the PDC will check the database to determine whether any changes have been made. The default value for this time interval is 5 minutes. When changes to the database are detected, the PDC will send a message to each BDC informing the BDC that it holds changes that need to be applied to the BDC's copy of the database. The BDC can then poll the PDC to get the updates. The process is called directory synchronization.

To prevent a large number of BDCs from making synchronization requests at the same time, the PDC staggers the messages it sends out when there are multiple BDCs. By default, the PDC sends the message to only 10 BDCs. When the first 10 BDCs have finished the synchronization process, the PDC sends the message to the next 10 BDCs that need to be informed, and so on.

Full and Partial Synchronization

There are two types of synchronization: full and partial. When a BDC is created during a Windows NT Server installation, one of the first tasks it must perform is to download a copy of the full SAM database. This is an example of full synchronization. When it's complete, the BDC is able to respond to logon requests from clients.

When changes are made on the PDC, they are not immediately propagated to the domain's BDCs. Instead, a change log file 64KB in size is used to buffer the modifications. Each change record is stamped with a serial number and a version number. The change log is a circular file. That means that when it becomes full, it simply wraps back on itself, overwriting the oldest record in the file.

When the PDC sends out notifications that changes exist in the database, it does so only to those BDCs that it knows do not have the most recent data. The PDC can do this because it keeps track of the serial numbers of the most recent records updated to each BDC. This partial synchronization prevents unnecessary replication traffic. When a BDC polls the PDC for the changes it needs, it receives only those changes that it has not already gotten during a previous poll, based on the serial number.

A full replication can still occur under this process. For example, a BDC can be taken offline for an extended period. Or the network link between the BDC and the PDC might be unavailable due to a network problem. Again, using the serial numbers of the records it already has, the BDC can determine whether any changes have been overwritten in the PDC's change log, and it can then request a full synchronization so that it will have a complete copy of the database.

Logon Failures Related to Synchronization

One common function administrators or help-desk personnel perform is that of adding a new user account or changing the password for an account when the user cannot log on. As simple a matter as this might seem, the role played by backup domain controllers can be an issue when this is done in a Windows NT network.

When a password is changed or an account added, it is done on the master copy of the database that resides on the PDC. Remember that the BDC does not immediately receive updates that are made on the SAM. If you add a new account or if you modify a user account, whether it be to change the password or remove a lockout condition, the user who is validated at a remote location by a backup domain controller might not be able to immediately log on because the BDC might not be aware of the change.

You could just tell the user to wait and try again, but this is not the kind of response that builds up trust between users and the help-desk personnel or the administrator. Instead, Windows NT allows you to force the synchronization process to begin. To do this, you must invoke the Server Manager, which is found in the Administrative Tools folder. From the Computer menu select Synchronize Entire Domain. A pop-up dialog box informs you that this process can take a few minutes. Click the Yes button to proceed. The PDC then begins sending out messages to the BDCs, informing them that it is time to synchronize. Windows displays a message informing you that the synchronization process has begun.

After a few minutes, you can check the Event Viewer to find out whether the synchronization process has completed. You should check both the BDC and the PDC for these messages. The Event Viewer utility enables you to connect to another computer to check messages in its log files, so this can be done from one location by the administrator. When synchronization has finished, you can instruct the user to try the new password or account again.

Passwords and Policies

Windows NT enables the administrator to set certain parameters that control passwords and accounts. This is called the account policy for the domain. To view the defaults or make changes, select Account from the Policies menu in the User Manager for Domains utility. The Account Policy dialog box (see Figure 40.15) is displayed.

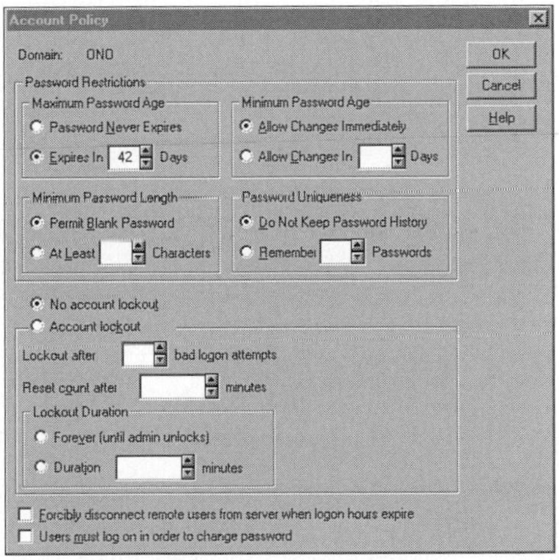

Figure 40.15 The Account Policy dialog box.

As you can see, you can configure various settings here. The values you choose for these parameters should reflect the degree of security you want to enforce at your site. At the same time, you need to balance your concerns with the abilities of your users. For example, if you set a large minimum password size and a low value for the number of days it can be used, users might end up writing down passwords just to keep track of them.

These are the parameters you can configure here:

- **Minimum Password Age and Maximum Password Age**—The Minimum Password Age specifies the number of days that must elapse before a user is allowed to change a password. The Maximum Password Age is the number of days that a password can be used, after which the system will force the user to change it. Both of these parameters can be set to a value ranging from 1 to 999 days.

- **Minimum Password Length**—This is the minimum number of characters that must be used for a password. Too small a value will make it easy for hacker programs to guess a password. Too large a value will make it difficult for users to think up new passwords. This parameter can be set to a value ranging from 1 to 14, or you can permit a blank password (no password), although it is hard to imagine a network where you might want to allow, as a policy for every user in the domain, a blank password.

- **Password Uniqueness**—The system will keep a history list of passwords used by each user and will not allow them to reset their password to one that is still in the list. This prevents users from constantly reusing a few easy-to-remember passwords, which can be bad for security purposes. Set this parameter to a value from 1 to 24. Selecting not to keep a history list is probably not a good idea because many users will take advantage of this option, and eventually someone else will find out what their usual password is.

- **Account Lockout**—You can set up the system so that a user account is "locked out" after a number of failed login attempts. This can be used to prevent an unauthorized user from trying to guess a password for an account, as is done in the brute-force method by many hacker programs that simply go through a dictionary, trying every word until they crack an account. If you set a value for bad logon attempts, you also can use the Reset Count After field to a time value (in minutes). This field specifies the period of time during which the failed logon attempts are counted. The Lockout Duration fields can be used to permanently lock the account until an administrator intervenes, or to set a time in minutes that the account will be disabled. A good idea is to set a small value for the Lockout After parameter (3 to 5 is a good choice), while using a long lockout value. Thirty minutes to an hour will usually suffice to deter unauthorized users.

At the bottom of this dialog box, you can see two other check boxes. The Forcibly Disconnect Remote Users check box must be checked in order for the user to be disconnected from the server when he stays logged on past the authorized period specified in the Hours button of the user's Account Properties dialog box. If the second check box, User Must Log On in Order to Change Password, is checked, users will not be able to log on after their password expires and change it. The administrator will have to perform this function instead. If this box is not checked, after a user password expires the user still will be allowed to log on but will be required to change the password before performing any other function.

Detecting Failed Logon Attempts

User logon failures occur for many reasons. The most common reason is that users forget passwords or type them incorrectly enough times to trigger the account lockout mechanism. Because Windows NT allows you to create a single username and password logon for each user, the problem of multiple passwords is usually not a problem as it is some other networks.

The Windows NT Event Viewer utility, found in the Administrative Tools section along with the User Manager for Domains, can be used to check for failed logon attempts. This is the first place you should look when a user is having problems logging on to the domain or connecting to a resource on a remote server. The user might not be providing the correct password or might be trying a username for which there is no account. The Event Viewer keeps three log files: Application, System, and Security. It is in the Security log file that you will find messages that relate to logon attempts.

Some of the more common logon attempt–related messages found in the Event Viewer are listed in Table 40.1.

Table 40.1   Common Logon Errors You Can See Using the Event Viewer

Event ID	Description
528	Successful logon
529	Invalid username or password
530	Violation of logon time restrictions
531	Account disabled
532	Account expired
533	Logon not allowed on this computer
534	Invalid logon type (network or interactive)
535	Expired password
536	Netlogon service not running
537	Unexpected error
538	Successful logout
539	Account currently locked out

As you can see, successful logon and logout events can be tracked. These types of messages can be useful when you are trying to determine who was on the system, perhaps during off hours, when you are trying to troubleshoot security problems. The other messages can be helpful in quickly identifying what the problem is when a user cannot log on to a server or connect to a resource.

The security log file you can examine using the Event Viewer can be configured to track all successful and unsuccessful logon attempts. This includes users who log on locally at the computer, connections made through network access, and logons by special accounts that you set up to run services.

Windows NT does not automatically track events such as these. You must enable the types of events you want to audit before they will be recorded in the security log file. See Chapter 47, "Auditing and Other Monitoring Measures," for information on how to set up the events to audit for Windows NT computers.

Strategies to Minimize Logon Problems

The best way to solve a problem is to take all necessary measures to ensure that the problem doesn't happen in the first place. Although it is not possible to completely eliminate every source of failed logon problems, you can do a lot to keep your network users happy by taking a few precautions:

- **Place a backup domain controller on every physical subnet**—If a network link goes down, users can still be validated by the local BDC and continue to work with resources to which they can still connect. A BDC with enough available resources can simultaneously perform the same functions as any other Windows NT Server, so if you have a server on a subnet that is offering resources and it is not already overloaded, consider replacing it with a BDC and let it serve two roles. Remember, if the server is not already a domain controller, you will have to re-install the OS and select that option during setup.

- **Enforce reasonable password policies**—Some operating systems allow you to computer-generate random passwords that are very difficult to remember. If a user cannot remember a password, most of the time the user will just write it down somewhere, which can compromise security. If you force users to change passwords too frequently, they will most likely have a hard time remembering what the recent password is, unless they write it down somewhere. If you set the account policy lockout values too low, you will find that users get locked out because of simple typing errors, and the help desk will spend a lot of time unlocking these accounts.

- **Keep track of user accounts**—You can use a paper method or an electronic one such as a spreadsheet or database. Delete accounts for users who leave the company and create new ones for new employees. Getting rid of the dead wood will help avoid confusion when troubleshooting and will help keep the SAM databases down to a reasonable size.

- **Never use generic accounts where more than one user logs in under the same username**—Though this is a tempting idea because you have fewer user accounts to manage, it can be a security nightmare if something goes wrong and you are unable to use auditing measures to figure out the who, what, and when of the matter. Also, when more than one person is using the same account to log on, it takes only one person with fumble-fingers to incorrectly type a password a few times and lock an account, also preventing others who use the same account from logging in.

To fully understand how to troubleshoot problems with logons, you should make yourself knowledgeable about the Windows NT Event Viewer administrative tool. You can find out more about this valuable utility in Chapter 47.

Windows 2000 and Windows Server 2003 User and Computer Management Utilities

SOME OF THE MAIN TOPICS IN THIS CHAPTER ARE

In Windows NT Server 4.0, every basic management task required you to use a different program: the User Manager, the Server Manager, and others. In Windows 2000 and Windows 2003 servers, the Microsoft Management Console (MMC) is the main interface for most all administrative tools. By using a common interface, MMC makes it easy to learn new utilities, because they all operate about the same.

The Microsoft Management Console

MMC is intended to provide a common interface into various administrative tools used with Windows 2000/XP/2003. Utilities are created as *snap-ins* that are loaded into the MMC application and presented to the user. Each console consists of a left pane with a tree of objects you can manage using the particular snap-in. This tree can contain things such as folders and other containers, or administrative objects. Some objects in the tree can be expanded by clicking on the plus sign (+) next to them, to reveal a further nesting of objects. Hence the treelike structure, which is similar to a set of directories and subdirectories.

Note

The MMC interface is not limited to Microsoft management applications. Many third-party applications also have designed snap-ins that can be used with MMC. The goal of this effort is to provide a consistent interface to manage not just the operating system and layered products, but also applications and utilities created for Windows platforms.

The right pane is usually used to display data or other information based on choices made in the left pane. For example, in the Computer Management administrative tool, you select Disk Defragmenter from the tree of options in the left pane, and the disk defragmenter displays disks that you can defragment, as well as the progress of the fragmentation process, in the pane on the right.

Note

For the most common system management tasks, you don't have to worry about setting up a snap-in for MMC. Use Start, Programs, Administrative Tools for Windows 2000, and you will see that the familiar utilities are already set up, along with some others you might not recognize. For Windows Server 2003, use Start, Administrative Tools.

User Management

The Active Directory Users and Computers MMC snap-in is used to manage both users and computers in the domain. Most of the functions that were done using the User Manager for Domains have been moved into this MMC snap-in. The main difference is the interface—the MMC console—and the amount of information you can keep track of using the Active Directory as compared to the limited amount of data that could be stored in the old security accounts manager (SAM) database of previous versions of Windows NT.

This chapter first covers the basic functions of this utility: adding users and computers to the domain. Then you'll learn about built-in user groups and how you can create your own user groups to help make administrative duties for large numbers of users an easier task.

Creating a New User Domain in the Active Directory

This common task is simplified by the use of a few dialog boxes to create the account. After the user account has been created, you can go back and use the properties page for the account to add more information.

◄◄ For Windows domains beginning with Windows 2000 domain controllers, information—from user accounts to computer accounts, resource records, and so forth—is now stored in the Active Directory. You can learn more about the Active Directory and the objects it stores in Chapter 31, "Using the Active Directory."

To create a new user account in a domain in the Active Directory, follow these steps:

1. Click Start, Administrative Tools, Active Directory Users and Computers. For Windows 2000, use Server, Start, Administrative Tools, and then Active Directory Users and Computers.

2. The MMC console pops up. In the left pane there is a domain with a tree of objects under it. In Figure 41.1 you can see the opening screen and the folders you can use to manage users and computers.

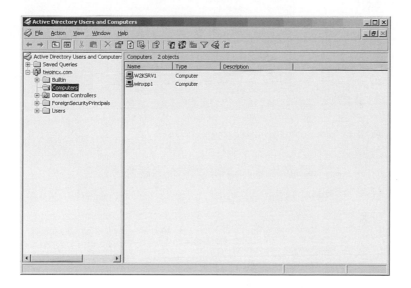

Figure 41.1   The Active Directory Users and Computers MMC snap-in is used to administer users in the domain.

3. Click the Users folder in the left pane, and a list of user groups and individual users is displayed as shown in Figure 41.2.

4. Right-click on the Users folder and select New and then User. The New Object-User dialog box pops up. Here you can fill in information such as the username; the user's first, last, and full names; initials; and other information. Figure 41.3 shows an example, adding a new user named Yoko Ono.

5. The next dialog box (see Figure 41.4) enables you to enter a password for the user and to use one of several password options. For most new users, it's easiest to use the first check box (User Must Change Password at Next Login) so that the user can enter his own unique password, unknown to anyone else, even the administrator who created the account. If you are creating an account to use for running a service or some other similar use, you might want to use the Password Never Expires option so that you don't have to change the password periodically. Finally, you can disable a user account with the Account Is Disabled check box. This is useful when creating new accounts so that they are all initially disabled. When users are contacted about a new account, the administrator can deselect this property and give the user the first password needed to log in to the account.

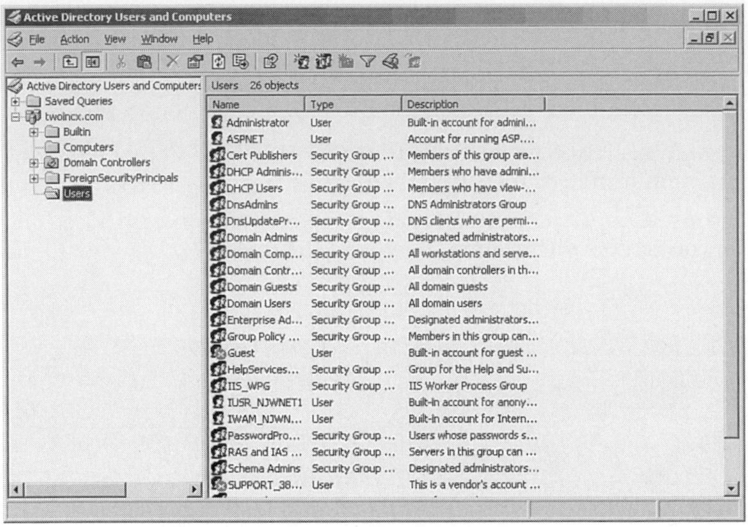

Figure 41.2 The Users folder contains user groups and users.

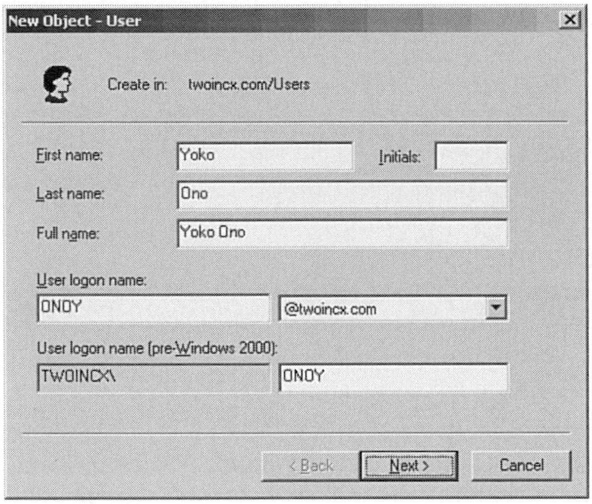

Figure 41.3 The New Object-User dialog box enables you to input basic information about the new user account.

6. Finally, a summary screen pops up showing the data you've entered for the new account. Click the Finish button to complete the process of creating the new account.

After creating a new user account, you might want to log in yourself before informing the user. This way you can avoid mistakes, such as having entered the wrong password for the account. Note that if you elected the option that the user must change the password at the next logon, you will also be forced to do that. An easy method for creating a large number of accounts is to enter a password you can remember and, when you log in to check the account, set the new password to one that matches the password policy for your organization.

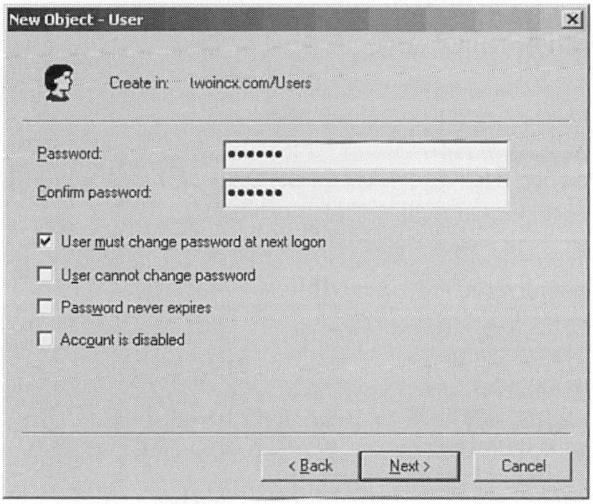

Figure 41.4   You can manage password administration using this dialog box.

Managing Other User Account Information

When you enter a new user account, you are prompted for only the minimal information needed to create the account in the Active Directory. After the account is created, you can use the properties page for the user account to add or modify other information. Simply right-click on the username in the right pane of the MMC console, and select Properties from the menu that appears. In Figure 41.5 you can see that, despite the minimal input used to create the account, there are several tabs that enable you to track all sorts of useful information about the user.

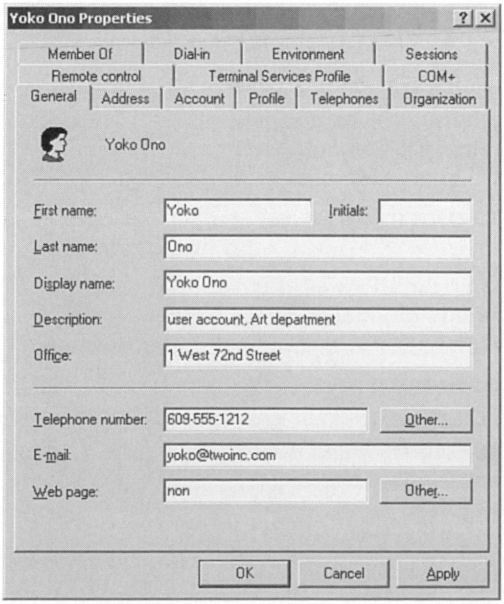

Figure 41.5   The properties page for a user account enables you to administer a lot more information than was input during account creation.

Rather than try to show all the tabs for this properties page (because there are so many), all the user attributes that are part of the default user object are listed for reference in Table 41.1. This summary listing should make it easy to locate the data you want to look at or modify, and go straight to that properties page tab.

Table 41.1   Attributes of the User Account Object

Attribute	Tab on the Properties Dialog Box	Description
First Name	General	User's first name.
Initials	General	User's initial(s).
Last Name	General	User's last name.
Display Name	General	Defaults to show first three fields, although you can modify it.
Description	General	Text field, anything you want.
Office	General	Office location for this user.
Telephone Number	General	User's telephone number.
Email	General	User's email address.
Web Page	General	User's Web page.
Street	Address	Multiline street address field.
P.O. Box	Address	Post office box.
City	Address	City.
State/Province	Address	State or province.
Zip/Postal Code	Address	ZIP code or postal code.
Country/Region	Address	Country or region.
User Logon Name	Account	User account logon username.
(Pre-Windows 2000)	Account	Logon for pre-Windows 2000 users.
Logon Hours	Account	Brings up dialog box to enter time restrictions for the account.
Log On To	Account	Brings up dialog box to enter which computers a user can log on to.
Account Options	Account	Options for logons, such as password policies.
Account Expires	Account	Enter **Never** or set account expiration date.
Profile Path	Profile	Path for user profile.
Logon Script	Profile	Path for logon script.
Home Folder	Profile	Local path or remote file share.
Connect	Profile	Use this to specify a drive letter that contains the user's home folder if it is not on the local computer's hard drive.
Home	Telephones	User's home number. Use the Other button to add additional numbers (this button works for all the phone number fields).
Pager	Telephones	User's pager number.
Mobile	Telephones	User's mobile phone number.
Fax	Telephones	User's fax number.
IP Phone	Telephones	User's IP telephone number.
Notes	Telephones	Add notes here, such as a PIN number for the user's pager.
Title	Organization	User's job title.

Table 41.1   Continued

Attribute	Tab on the Properties Dialog Box	Description
Department	Organization	Business department for this user.
Company	Organization	Use this to record a company name. This can be useful when using a single network for multiple corporate entities, or when creating accounts for outside vendors.
Manager	Organization	The user's supervisor.
Direct Reports	Organization	Multiline text field.
Member Of	Member Of	List of user groups a user is a member of. Use the Add and Remove buttons to change group memberships for the user.
Primary Group	Member Of	Use this button to specify the user's primary group. This is used by Macintosh users, or users running Posix applications. You should not change this field otherwise.
Remote Access Permission	Dial-in	Allow or deny dial-in access here.
Verify Caller-ID	Dial-in	Use to verify caller ID for incoming calls.
Callback Options	Dial-in	Set to No Callback, Set by Caller, or Always Callback To if you want to supply a telephone number for Callback.
Assign a Static IP Address	Dial-in	Use the same address each dial-in. Not available in a mixed-mode network.
Apply Static Routes	Dial-in	You can define static routes for this client's dial-in session.
Starting Program	Environment	Used to specify a program to run at logon for Terminal Services clients.
Client Devices	Environment	Check boxes allow you to connect drives, printers, and a default printer at logon time.
End a Disconnection Session	Sessions	Set time (or never) to end Terminal Services idle session.
Active Session Limit	Sessions	The maximum amount of time before an active Terminal Services session is disconnected (or never).
Idle Session limit	Sessions	The maximum time before an idle Terminal Services client is disconnected (or never).
Session Limits	Sessions	You can specify that a session be ended or disconnected when a timer expires.
Allow Reconnection	Sessions	Permit disconnected client to reconnect.

In addition to these fields, there are two other tabs (for Windows 2000). The Remote Control tab enables you to remotely control or view a user's session when using Terminal Services. The Terminal Services Profile tab enables you to set a path for a home directory and user profile for Terminal Services users. This also is where you use a check box (Allow Logon to Terminal Server) to enable the user account for Terminal Services. Generally, terminal services are not heavily deployed in most networking environments and are not detailed any further here.

For Windows Server 2003, there is an additional tab labeled COM+. This tab can be used to designate the partition set for the user. Partition sets are made up of one or more COM+ partitions to enable users to access COM+ applications.

As you can see, you can keep a lot more information about a user on your network than was possible under Windows NT 4.0 Server's simple User Manager for Domains and the Security Accounts Manager (SAM) database. And if that isn't enough data to keep about a user, you can always *extend the schema*, which is the definition of all the classes of objects (and attributes) in the Active Directory. You can add new attributes and then add them to this user class of objects. You can also create a new user object (with a different name) if your business has a need to create objects for users who differ radically in the attributes associated with them. For example, in a factory environment you might want to use attributes that define the method used to pay the employee, or perhaps an attribute to store the skills the employee possesses. Although extending the schema should be done only when absolutely necessary, there are times when it is a good idea.

Caution

Never extend the schema unless you are absolutely certain of your decision. You cannot roll back an extension to the schema—your changes will be permanent! Always keep this in mind when evaluating third-party software that requires extending the AD schema.

Note

For more information about the Active Directory and the schema, see Chapter 31. As indicated in that chapter, the kinds of objects and attributes that can be stored in the directory database are extensible. That is, you can create new attributes and objects. If you've installed Microsoft Exchange Server, for example, or a third-party product that is integrated with the Active Directory, you might find additional tabs or fields in the properties sheets for a particular object.

Using the Action Menu

In the preceding section you brought up the properties page by right-clicking on the user account and selecting Properties from the menu that popped up. You also can reach this menu, called the Action menu, by highlighting a user or group and then clicking on the Action menu at the top of the MMC console. Use this menu to do the following:

- **Delegate Control**—Brings up a wizard that enables you to delegate control of folders and objects by groups or by users.

- **Find**—Brings up a search dialog box you can use to search the directory.

- **New**—Brings up a submenu you can use to add a new computer, contact, group, InetOrgPerson, MSMQ Queue Alias, printer, user, or shared folder.

- **All Tasks**—Enables you to delegate control or use the Find search function. The Find Users, Contacts, and Groups dialog box is shown in Figure 41.6. Click on the Advanced tab if you want to refine your search more precisely.

- **Refresh**—Refreshes the display with current information.

- **Export list**—Enables you to export a list of users and groups to various file types, such as comma-delimited or tab-delimited ASCII and Unicode files. You can use this to import listings into other applications, such as Microsoft Excel.

- **Properties**—Accesses all those user attributes covered in the preceding section. This is an alternative way to bring up the user's properties page.

- **Help**—Provides help for using this utility.

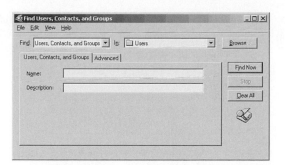

Figure 41.6 Use the Find dialog box to locate information in the Active Directory.

There are many useful items on this Action menu. The Export List capability is especially useful in large environments where it is necessary to produce reports on users or the user database. The New menu item enables you to manage not just users, but also other objects, such as computers, which is the topic of the next section, and user groups, which is discussed later in this chapter.

Computer Management

Again, you use the Active Directory Users and Computers MMC snap-in to manage computers in the domain. Click the Computers folder in the left pane, and the right pane displays a list of computers in your domain, as you can see in Figure 41.7.

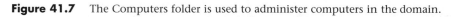

Figure 41.7 The Computers folder is used to administer computers in the domain.

The Action menu for managing computers is similar to that for managing users. The first thing to do is add a computer to the domain. This should be done when you are setting up new computers on the network. In addition to creating user accounts, computers must have an entry in the Active Directory database.

Adding a Computer to the Domain

To add a new computer, you can use the Action menu and select New and then Computer. Alternatively, you can right-click on the Computers folder and select the same items. The New

Object-Computer dialog box, shown in Figure 41.8, enables you to input basic information about the computer, such as the hostname.

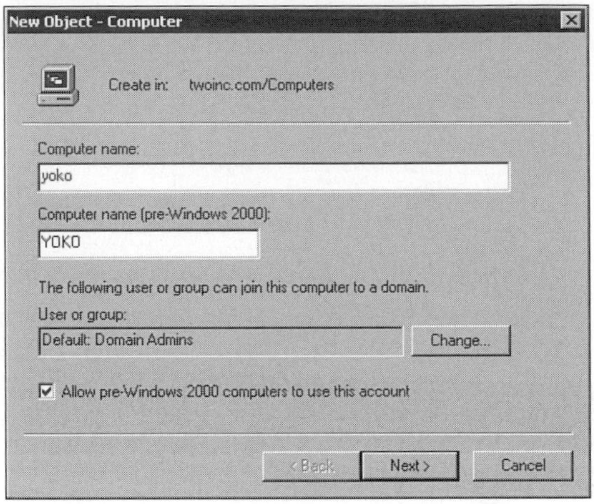

Figure 41.8 You enter basic computer information in this dialog box when adding a computer to the domain.

What TCP/IP users typically call a hostname goes in the Computer Name field. There is also a field to enter a pre-Windows 2000 computer name that can be recognized by older computers. Another field enables you to specify the users or groups that can add computers to the domain. The default is the Domain Admins group. If the user who will be joining the computer to the domain is not a member of the Domain Admins group, you should change this value to either the user's name or a group to which the user belongs. If you are uncertain who will be adding a particular computer account to the domain, you can specify the Everyone group. Finally, if the computer is not a Windows 2000 or Windows XP client, select the check box labeled Allow Pre-Windows 2000 Computers to Use This Account. You would want to check this box for Windows NT and Windows 98 computers, for example. Click the Next button to continue the process of adding the new computer.

The next dialog box prompts you to specify whether this is a managed computer and, if so, the GUID/UUID for the computer. These values are usually found in the computer's BIOS or on a label attached to the computer. Click the Next button to continue adding the computer.

Finally, a dialog box displays a summary view of the information you've entered. Click Finish to create the computer account. After you've done this, the computer should be able to boot and join the domain. Users who have accounts on the domain should be able to log in to the domain using the computer.

Managing Other Computer Account Information

Just like the user objects you create, the computer objects have a lot more attributes than you are prompted for when creating the initial computer account in the Active Directory. You can get to the properties page for a computer by right-clicking on the computer in the left pane and selecting Properties, or by highlighting the computer and selecting Properties from the Action menu. In Figure 41.9 you can see an example of a computer object properties page.

There are six tabs for this properties sheet: General, Operating System, Member Of, Location, Managed By, and Dial-In.

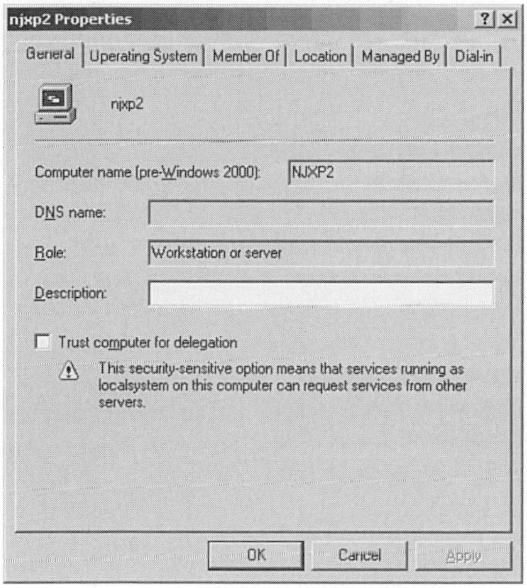

Figure 41.9 The properties of a computer account enable you to manage a large amount of information about the computer.

The General Tab

This tab shows you the fully qualified domain name of a computer, as well as its pre-Windows 2000 name. You also can see what role the computer plays in the network (workstation or server). The Description field enables you to enter useful information that will help you identify this computer or its use (or perhaps its location), depending on the information you want to enter. Finally, you can select the check box labeled Trust Computer for Delegation. This allows services running on the computer to request services from other computers as long as the service is running under the localsystem special account.

The Operating System Tab

This tab has only a few fields. Here you can see the operating system running on the computer, the version, and the highest level service pack installed.

The Member Of Tab

This tab enables you to add the computer to a group. For example, a domain controller computer is a member of the Domain Computers group, and this is its primary group. However, you can use other built-in groups or create new groups to assist you in managing computers that are similarly configured or used.

Use the Add button to add a new group. A list of groups is displayed in another dialog box, and you can select the groups from there. You also can remove group membership by using the Remove button. The Advanced button on the Select Groups dialog box that pops up from the Add button enables you to search for groups based on search criteria you enter so that you can refine your group selection to the greatest degree. The search function allows you to specify a term and then choose from these options:

- Starts with
- Is exactly

Another button on this page, Location, allows you to select the location from which the search should be executed, such as the domain, the built-in groups, and other computers such as domain controllers.

The Location Tab

This tab has only one field: Location. Use it to specify the particular office, or perhaps building, in which a computer is located. This information can be very useful when you get a call from a user and need to visit the computer for maintenance purposes. The Browse button enables you to select from other locations that have been entered previously.

The Managed By Tab

This tab enables you to select the user that manages this computer. Use the Change button to bring up a dialog box to select the user. After a user has been selected, the fields on this tab show the following information:

- The user's name
- The user's office
- The user's street address
- The user's city, state/province, country/region data
- The user's telephone number
- The user's fax number

Again, you can see that this kind of information can be valuable when trying to locate the person responsible for managing this computer in a large network. When this detailed information is kept in the Active Directory, it is accessible by computers throughout the domain, provided that the user has the access rights.

The Dial-In Tab

This tab allows you to specify values that allow dial-in access for *this computer*. You can use two radio buttons to either allow or deny dial-in access. If you choose to allow dial-in access, you can select to control the access using a Remote Access Policy (another topic entirely, and beyond the scope of this book). You can also specify callback options, specify a callback number set by the user, and specify to always call back. These fields are the same as those used for a user account, and they allow you to add a static IP address and static route to be used for dial-in access.

Windows 2000 User Groups

You need to understand several concepts about user groups in Windows 2000/.NET before you begin to create them. Groups are helpful because they simplify administrative tasks when you have groups of users that must be treated similarly when it comes to rights and permissions. Second, because groups can be limited in scope, they can be useful for security purposes, limiting the computers or domains in which a user can be granted access.

Choosing a Group Based on the Group's Scope

Groups each have a scope, which is basically the area of the domain or global forest that the group covers. By having several types of groups, each with its own particular kind of membership and scope, you can put together combinations that should solve most of your administrative needs for managing users with similar needs. The types of groups, and the scope implied by each, are as listed here:

- **Domain local group**—These groups are limited to just the domain in which they are created. Users can be placed into these groups for local domain management purposes.

- **Global group**—These groups are made up of users or groups from a single domain but are used to grant access for the members of the group in other trusted domains. Think of this as a way to "export" users to allow them access to resources in other domains.

- **Universal group**—This type of group can contain user accounts and global group accounts from any trusted domain that exists in the Active Directory forest. This is similar to a global group but allows members of the group to be granted permission to resources in domains throughout the entire forest.

As described previously, groups can be members of other groups just like users, and this is where things can become a little complicated. For example, a domain local scope group can have the following as members:

- **Groups that have global scope**—You place the global group into a local group and then manage the local group when granting rights and permissions.

- **Groups that have universal scope**—Again, you can place universal scope groups into a local group and then use the local group for management purposes.

- **Groups with domain local scope**—Other domain local scope groups can be placed in a domain local scope group.

- **User accounts**—You can put individual users into a group with domain local scope.

Note that the domain local group does not have to have just one of the preceding groups (or users) as its members. You can combine any of the preceding and place them into a single domain local scope group, and then use the group to manage the members of these other groups locally in your domain.

A domain local group is a very useful management tool. For example, if you have a particular resource that several users share, place the users in the group and grant the group the necessary access to the resource. The resource can be a folder or a file, or perhaps a printer. If the resource changes in the future (for example, you decide to use a new file server for a particular set of files), you have to change permissions only on the group to let the group members access the new resource. Otherwise, you'd have to modify the permissions for each individual user, which in a large environment can be an almost impossible task if your network changes frequently.

Unlike domain local groups, global groups can have as members only users or other groups from within a single domain. Yet global groups can be granted access to resources in other trusted domains. This enables you to package a group of users that need similar treatment in other domains when it comes to resource permissions.

Universal groups also can be used to grant permissions in multiple domains—throughout the forest of domain trees. Note that these groups are available only if you have an Active Directory structure that is part of a multidomain forest. They serve no purpose in a single-domain tree because domain local groups and global groups provide the necessary functions in a single-domain tree.

The membership of a universal group should not change on a frequent basis. This is because when a universal scope group's membership changes, the entire list of members is replicated to every global catalog in the forest of trees. Use universal groups for grouping users and other groups that are more stable in membership. Although global groups enable you to create groups of users and other groups that can be granted access in trusted domains, their membership must come from a single domain. To make managing a universal group easier, first place users into global groups in their own domains, and then place these global groups into a universal group. Thus, when the membership of a global group changes, there is no need to replicate the universal group membership to every other global catalog. Only the global group has changed. The universal group has as its member the global group, not the individual users who come and go from the global group.

Built-In Groups

There are several kinds of built-in groups, depending on where you look in the directory structure. For example, in Figure 41.10 you can see the list of groups found under the Builtin folder. Simply click the Builtin folder and you'll see the list of built-in domain local groups. As the name implies, each group was designed to give the access permissions to perform specific types of administrative jobs.

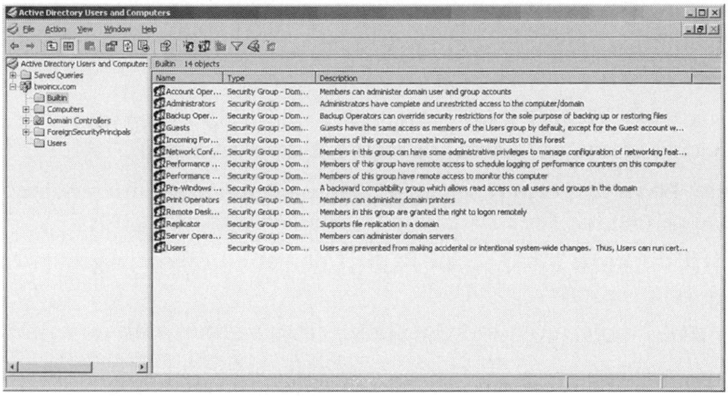

Figure 41.10   The Builtin folder contains a collection of domain local scope groups you can use.

The domain local scope built-in groups can include the following:

- **Account Operators**—Users placed into this group can perform account management duties, such as creating new users.

- **Administrators**—This is the most powerful group. Members of this group can do just about anything they want in the domain, including taking ownership of files and creating user accounts.

- **Backup Operators**—Members of this group get the access rights needed to perform backups on computers in the domain.

- **Guests**—A guest group, which can be used to grant very limited access to users from other domains.

- **Incoming Forest Trust Builders**—Users in this group can create incoming trust relationships from other forests. Keep in mind that trust relations in the Active Directory are transitive but must be established manually between Active Directory trees in the forest.

- **Network Configuration Operators**—This group allows users to manage *some* aspects of network configuration.

- **Performance Log Users**—Members of this group can schedule logging of performance monitors on this computer, from a remote computer.

- **Performance Monitor Users**—This user group can monitor performance on this computer from a remote computer.

- **Pre–Windows 2000 Compatible Access**—This group is meant for pre–Windows 2000 users to enable them to have read access for users and groups in the domain stored in the Active Directory.

- **Print Operators**—You guessed it: Members of this group can control printers and print jobs.
- **Remote Desktop Users**—Users in this group can log in to this computer from a remote computer.
- **Replicator**—Used by services responsible for replication.
- **Server Operators**—Members of this group can perform tasks on specific servers.
- **Users**—A built-in group for ordinary users in the domain, which can run applications, but not make systemwide configuration changes.

In addition to these built-in groups, you can click on the Users folder and see a list of predefined groups, which also can be used to organize users. These are global scope groups, so you can use them to organize users and computers, and then place them in domain scope groups in the current domain or in other domains. If none of the following group names fits your needs, you can create your own groups, which we'll look at next.

The Predefined groups found in the Users folder are listed here:

- **Cert Publishers**—Users can publish certificates to the Active Directory.
- **DHCP Administrator**—Members can administer the DHCP service.
- **DHCP Users**—Members of this group have view-only access to the DHCP service.
- **DnsAdmins**—The DNS Administrators group who can manage the DNS service.
- **DnsUpdateProxy**—This group allows members to update the Domain Name System (DNS) service for other clients, such as a DHCP server.
- **Domain Admins**—Users who administer the domain.
- **Domain Computers**—All workstations and servers joined to the domain.
- **Domain Controllers**—Every domain controller in this domain is a member of this group.
- **Domain Guests**—Members are guests in the domain, with limited access.
- **Domain Users**—All members of the domain.
- **Enterprise Admins**—Members can administer the entire enterprise.
- **Group Policy Creator Owners**—These users can modify the group policy for a domain.
- **HelpServicesGroup**—Users that provide help via the Help and Support Center.
- **IIS_WPG**—Members who manage the Internet Information Server.
- **PasswordPropDeny**—Members of this group should not have their password synchronized.
- **RAS and IAS Servers**—Servers that are members of this group can access the remote access properties of users.
- **Schema Admins**—Administrators of the Active Directory schema.
- **Terminal Server Computers**—Computers that can communicate with the Terminal Services License server.
- **WINS Users**—Members of this group have view-only access to the WINS server.

In general, the groups you'll use most in the list will probably be the Domain Computers and Domain Users groups. By default, when you create a user account, the new account is placed automatically into the Domain Users group. Likewise, when you add a computer to the domain, the computer is automatically placed into the Domain Computers group. Looking at the domain from an overall picture, you can use these two groups when you want to make changes that apply to all users or all computers in a domain. The Domain Admins group can be used to give selected individuals administrator-level rights in a domain. It is always a good idea to not use the actual built-in Administrator account for a domain. Instead, create individual accounts for each user, and then place the user into one or more groups that give him the access he needs. If you need to grant a user administrator-level rights, just place him into the Domain Admins groups.

The other groups will depend on the services you have installed. Some may not appear if you have not installed that service (such as DHCP).

A few notes about these predefined groups in the Users folder:

- The Domain Users group is a member of the domain's Users group (the one located in the Builtin folder).
- The Domain Admins group is automatically a member of the Administrator's group in the Builtin folder.
- The Domain Guests group is automatically placed into the Guests group in the Builtin folder.

Note

User Profiles are never cached locally on any system for members of any out-of-the-box Guest groups.

Some of the other groups listed here also can be used to organize users and grant them access to resources on a group basis. However, you can always create your own group and tailor the rights and permissions for the group to match your exact needs.

Creating a New User Group

To start the process, click Action, New, Group. In Figure 41.11, you can see the dialog box that pops up to allow you to enter basic information about the group, such as the new group's name, the scope (Domain Local or Global), and the type (Security or Distribution).

Figure 41.11   The New Object-Group dialog box prompts you for basic group information.

These are the differences between these two types of groups:

- Security groups are used to manage user access and permissions. Users and other groups can be members of a security group. This is the sort of group discussed so far in this chapter.

- Distribution groups are used for functions such as grouping users for other purposes, such as email. These groups cannot be used to grant access to resources.

You can probably guess that after you fill in the basic information and click OK, the group is immediately created. In the example, a group was in the Users folder. Just as with User objects and Computer objects in the Active Directory, you can now bring up a properties page for the group and from there configure additional attributes for the group.

Right-click on the group and select Properties. You also can highlight the group and select Properties from the Action menu. In Figure 41.12 you can see an example of the properties page for the group we just created.

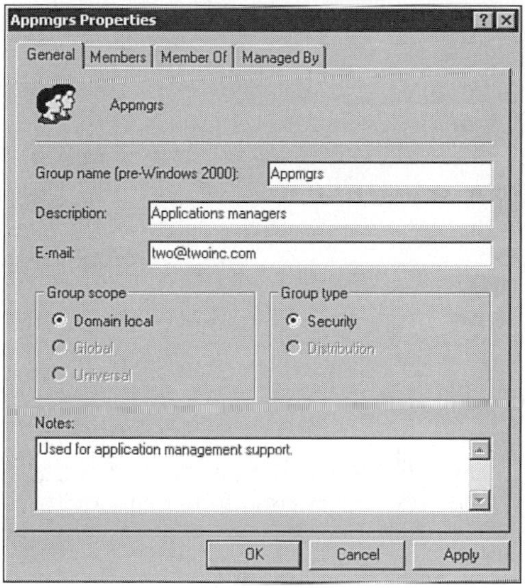

Figure 41.12   You can configure and view additional attributes by using the properties page for the new group.

Here you can see fields that allow you to input a description of what the group is used for, as well as an email address that can be used to send email to members of the group. Additionally, you can put in notes about the group that might be helpful in the future. For example, you might create a group to be used only for a short period. You can put notes here to remind yourself to remove the group later.

Two other tabs relate to group membership. The first tab, Members, lists current members of the group. On this tab you can click the Add button to bring up a dialog box to use for adding other users or groups to the group. The Member Of tab displays groups of which this particular group itself is a member. You also can use the Add button on this property sheet tab to add the group to other groups.

Finally, the Managed By tab is similar to that discussed earlier, and is used to define a responsible contact person for this group.

Other Things You Can Do with the Active Directory Computers and Users Snap-In

This utility is not as simple as the User Manager for Domains that was included in previous versions of Windows NT. However, most of the additional functions for which you can use this utility don't directly relate to user or computer management, so it's not relatively important to go into the nitty-gritty details. For example, you can create organizational units and use them to further subdivide the objects managed in your domain.

◄◄   For more information, see Chapter 31 as well as the help files that accompany Windows 2000 and Server 2003.

There are other tools you'll find in the Administrative Tools folder that again don't relate directly to user or computer management, but you should be aware of them in case they are used at your site. Some of these utilities won't show up in your Administrative Tools folder unless you've already installed the prerequisite software. For example, the DHCP manager MMC snap-in won't be there if you haven't installed a DHCP service on the server.

Some of the more popular tools include the following:

- **Active Directory Domains and Trusts**—This utility manages trust relationships. The User Manager for Domains formerly handled that job.

- **Component Services**—This selection allows you to configure COM+ applications.

- **Event Viewer**—Use this standard utility to review the system, security, and application log files. It's similar to its Windows NT 4.0 predecessor but uses the MMC console instead.

- **DHCP**—This snap-in enables you to manage the DHCP service on the local server. If a user's computer is having problems communicating on the network, you can check the DHCP logs to see whether the client has obtained a valid IP address.

- **DNS**—This snap-in will be present if the server is running the DNS service. This service is used by computers on the network to locate both domain controllers (for authentication purposes) and other resources on the network.

- **Computer Management**—Use this tool to manage services and other aspects of your server. You can defragment disk drives, see system information, and use the Event Viewer, among other things.

- **Distributed File System**—This will show up if you've installed the Distributed File System.

- **Internet Services Manager**—IIS can be installed on Windows 2000/2003 servers. This tool can be used to manage the IIS services, as well as to set up printers for the Internet Printing Protocol (IPP). You can also choose to install IIS later if you want to put it off until you have installed the operating system and then want to choose which servers to use for IIS.

◄◄   For more on DFS, see Chapter 35, "File Server Protocols." IPP is covered in detail in Chapter 44, "Network Printing Protocols."

There are many other administrative tools you can use, from the Performance Monitor (and Network Monitor) to utilities used to manage Terminal Services. If you are using components that are not part of the default installation, be sure to examine the administrative tools to find an MMC snap-in utility for those components.

Managing Unix and Linux Users

SOME OF THE MAIN TOPICS IN THIS CHAPTER ARE

Unix is not generally considered an office desktop operating system. The Windows OS family has pretty much taken over the desktop, along with other minor players such as Apple's Macintosh operating system and, to some degree, Linux. However, Unix is a dominant player in the server market, and many large networks are made up of a collection of Unix servers, X-Window Systems clients, and, usually, some Windows clients. Unix becomes much more prevalent when you get past the office desktop environment and into the workstation or server region. Establishing a network connection or an interactive session on a Unix server requires, in most cases, that the user provide some form of authentication (that is, username and password).

This chapter covers the files typically used for user authentication purposes on Unix and Linux systems and some of the problems commonly associated with the logon process.

In addition, you'll learn a bit about Network Information Service (NIS). This set of client/server programs can be used to manage many important files on multiple computers, keeping all computers within an NIS domain in sync. These files include those used for user management, as well as others, depending on the implementation, such as network configuration files. Although it is impossible to cover all the various things you can do with NIS in only one chapter, you'll get a good overview of the kinds of tasks associated with setting up and managing multiple servers using NIS.

User Administration

Several files are generally associated with the user logon process for Unix systems. These files can be located in different directories, and the fields within some of these files can vary from one implementation to another. However, the following two files are generally used:

- **/etc/passwd**—This is the password file. It is used to store the username, the password (in encrypted format), and other information specific to the user account. This file has its file protection value set to be world-readable so that anyone can access the file when logging in to the system. It also means that when someone gets into your system, he or she can usually copy this file and then begin to crack the passwords it contains.

- **/etc/groups**—This file contains a list of user groups and a numerical value associated with each group. A field in the /etc/passwd file references a group in this file using this value.

The **/etc/passwd** File

The Unix operating system usually authenticates users by comparing their credentials with those stored in one or more files on the server. This is similar to the method used for Novell's bindery, in which users must authenticate to each server they want to access. The typical username/password exchange is used, and the /etc/passwd file is the standard file used to store most user information. It is a simple text file that stores data using ASCII characters, and it's world-readable because access to the file is required during the logon process.

The fields in this file store information such as the username, the home directory, the default shell, and an encrypted password, among other things. This file is one of the most vulnerable and sought-after files by hackers. You might think that it's a safe file because the password field in this file is encrypted. Not true! After a hacker has access to this file, a large number of utilities can be downloaded from the Internet to run against a password file to decrypt the password. Many hackers just use a dictionary and known encryption techniques and then compare the result with the value found in your /etc/password file. When a match is found, the hacker knows your password for that account.

Keep in mind that this file is world-readable. That means after someone has broken into even the most restricted account, if they can get to a shell command prompt, they can most likely copy this file and use it to further compromise accounts that have been granted much greater access rights to the system.

Note

This chapter covers files used to secure individual or groups of Unix servers and workstations in a network. It should be obvious that managing a large number of workstations, even using things such as NIS, can be a difficult task from a security standpoint. For this reason, every network that connects to another outside network, or the Internet, needs a good firewall. The authentication files discussed in this chapter help protect an individual Unix system. A firewall can help protect the entire network from outsiders. Chapter 49, "Firewalls," contains more information on this important topic.

After the root password is discovered, or the password to any account that has administrator-equivalent privileges is discovered, your system is wide open to attack. This is just one of many reasons why it is very important to use a long, meaningless, and complex password consisting of a mix of letters, numbers, and symbols. Password complexity makes it more difficult to use either dictionary or brute-force attacks to break a password. However, don't make your password so difficult to remember that you have to write it down.

This is the format for the /etc/passwd file, on most systems:

`username:password:uid:gid:GECOS:homedir:shell`

Note that the colon character (:) is used to separate fields. If a field is to be left blank, you'll see two colons in a row. The fields in this file are detailed here:

- **username**—The account name used to log in to the account.

- **password**—The encrypted password for the user account. An asterisk character (*) in this field means that the account is disabled. If this field is left blank, no password is required for the account. Unless you have a very good reason, you should not have any account with a blank password on a networked computer. Any access can usually lead to further access by a clever user. An x character in this field generally means that a shadow password file, discussed later, should be used.

- **UID**—A numerical value that the system gives to the account to identify the user when running processes or evaluating access to files and other system resources. A value of zero for this field is used to indicate the *superuser*, or a user who has the same privileges as root. On some systems values from 1 to 99 are reserved for use for system processes, such as background daemons.

- **GID**—A numerical value that identifies a user group to which the account belongs. The file /etc/group contains a listing of user groups and the numbers associated with them. Group membership can be used to make managing access to system resources, such as files and directories, an easier task. Access to a resource can be granted to the group. The alternative method is to grant access individually, which is a time-consuming process when you have a large number of users who have similar computing needs.

- **GECOS**—Yet another computer acronym! GECOS stands for General Electric Comprehensive Operating System. However, it is used to hold comments about the user, such as office and telephone number. This field can also be used to hold text that is used by certain applications, such as the finger utility. If more than one item is included in this field, commas should separate the items. It is common to store the user's full name in this field.

- **homedir**—This text field specifies the user's home directory. When the user logs in to the system, he or she is initially placed in this location in the file system. As with most operating systems, a separate home directory is maintained for each user for storing his or her own files. Home directories also can contain subdirectories to make organizing one's files a simple task.

- **shell**—The user on a Unix system interacts with the system using one of the many shell applications available for Unix today. This field in the /etc/passwd file is used to specify the shell program that will be invoked when the user logs in to the system.

A typical entry in the /etc/passwd file looks like this:

```
jdoe:Gfjhjo9Uia$jpo2dYtaGGdsh:223:100:John Doe:/home/jdoe:bash
rsmith:HuiTytsm$ld34tTbd9Saa2:119:110:Rob Smith:/home/rsmith:bash
```

Note that the second field, the password field, appears to have nonsense characters. This is the encrypted password that is highly prized by network intruders.

Using a Shadow Password File

To plug the password security hole presented by the /etc/passwd file, a technique called a *shadow password file* is usually used. This file contains the actual passwords, also in encrypted format. However, the shadow password file is not world-readable, and permissions are set so that only the root account can access this file.

On many systems, the name of the shadow password file is /etc/shadow. Check your documentation to determine the exact path on your system. Also note that on some older systems (and a few current ones), you'll have to load an extra component to install the shadow password file capabilities. Keep up-to-date by consulting your vendor's Web site.

The contents of this file also can vary from one system to another. However, the following format contains the fields used in most implementations:

username:password:last:may:must:warn:expire:disable:reserved

The following list describes these fields:

- *username*—This field is used for the same purpose as it is in the /etc/passwd file. It is the login name for this user's account.

- *password*—The user account password stored in encrypted format.

- *last*—The number of days, since January 1, 1970, that the password for this account was changed.

- *may*—The number of days that must pass before the password for this account can be changed.

- *must*—The number of days after which the password for this account must be changed.

- *warn*—The number of days before the password expires to warn the user about the upcoming password expiration.

- *expire*—The number of days that must pass before the account password expires and the account becomes disabled.

- *disable*—The number of days, since January 1, 1970, that the account has been disabled.

- *reserved*—This field is reserved for future use.

As you can see, using a shadow password file gives you additional control over accounts, such as setting password expiration values. It also gives you informational fields (such as last and disable that can be used when managing user accounts.

The /etc/groups File

This file contains a list of user groups and a numerical value used to identify the group. The syntax for entries in this file is as follows:

groupname:grouppassword:groupID:username1,username2 ...

- *groupname*—A name associated with the group. Using a meaningful name can help you simplify user administration.

- ■ *grouppassword*—Yes, you can place a password on a group, but this is generally not done. Instead, this field is usually left blank.

- ■ *groupID*—This is the group's ID number, which is used by the operating system to identify the group. It is often referred to as the GID. This number can range from 0 to 32,767, and the numbers 0 to 10 are generally reserved for system groups. For example, in most Unix implementations, the root user has a GID of zero.

- ■ *username1,username2 ...*—This is a comma-delimited list of members of the group. Separate each using a comma.

Users can be members of more than one group. If this is the case, the first group is the user's primary group, and the GID of this group is used when files are created or saved. Users can use the groups command to view the group(s) of which they are a member. The command chgrp can be used to change the current default group.

Adding or Removing User Accounts

To add or remove a user from a Unix/Linux box, you can edit the password and group files. However, whenever you make an edit to such an important file, there is always the chance that something will go wrong and you'll end up rendering an account, or possibly a system, unusable. It's advisable to always make a backup of an important file before making any edits.

After making entries in the /etc/passwd and /etc/groups files, you'll have to create the user's home directory and install any files that are part of your standard distribution, such as shell files.

However, on most systems you won't have to go through all this trouble. Instead, most versions of Unix or Linux provide a program that can be used to perform all the functions needed to add or remove a user. On FreeBSD Unix, for example, the adduser command can be used. The syntax for this command is as follows:

```
adduser [-dDv] [-c changetime] [-C class] [-e expiretime] [-g primarygroup]
   ➡[-G gecos] [-h homedirectorybasedir] [-H homedirectory]
   ➡[-m homedirectorymode] [-p passwd] [-P encryptedpasswd] [-s shell]
   ➡[-S skeletondir] [-u uid] [username...]
```

- ■ **-v**—This is the typical Unix/Linux "verbose" option. It causes the adduser command to output more information about its operations. Good to use if you're new at this.

- ■ **-d**—This is equivalent to the rmuser command (remove user) described later in this section.

- ■ **-D**—If you use the uppercase "D" character, the adduser command does not actually add a user. Instead, it sets defaults to use the next time adduser is invoked.

- ■ **-C** *class*—This specifies a login class for the user. FreeBSD Unix provides a file called /etc/login.conf that stores class definitions for users. Classes can be used to customize authentication methods and the user environment.

- ■ **-e** *expiretime*—This field is not generally used. It is intended to set an expiration time for the password.

- ■ **-g** *primarygroup*—This sets the user's default group value. If you do not include this on the command line, adduser will prompt you for it.

- ■ **-G** *gecos*—This is the GECOS comment field. You'll be prompted for this value if it is not included on the command line. Substitute text after the -G command that you want to appear in the GECOS field.

- ■ **-h** *homedirectorybasedirectory*—Use this to specify the home directory for the user. The value of *homedirectory* is the base directory under which the user's directory is created using the username.

- **-H** *homedirectory*—This version of the home directory option lets you specify the complete path of the user's home directory.

- **-m** *homedirectorymode*—Use this to specify the mode for the user's home directory. The default is 0775.

- **-p** *passwd*—This option enables you to enter, in clear text, a password for the user account.

- **-P** *encryptedpasswd*—This option enables you to enter, in encrypted format, a password for the user account. You must use either -p or -P. If neither is used, you will be prompted for a value.

- **-S** *skeletondir*—You can set up a "skeleton" directory to serve as a template to use when creating user home directories. This option enables you to specify the name of the template to use for this user's home directory and possible subdirectories.

- **-u** *uid*—Enter the user's ID (UID) with this option. FreeBSD starts ordinary users' UID at 100 and increments the value. Other flavors of Unix/Linux may use different starting values.

- *username* ...—You can enter one or more user account names separated by spaces.

If you enter the adduser command with no command-line arguments, the command will prompt you for the information it needs (such as a username) to create the new account. You can use the large number of options available with the command to construct your own command to add users. If you need to add a large number of users at a time, or if you use the same command-line options frequently, create script files that can be used to invoke the adduser command for your customized requirements.

By using this command, you not only make the necessary entries into the /etc/passwd and /etc/groups files, but also create the user's home directory.

The rmuser command can be used to remove a user. Simply follow the command with the username that is to be removed. The -v option is the only other command-line option available with this command.

The addgroup command works similar to the adduser command and helps automate the process of managing entries in the /etc/groups file. The syntax for this command is much simpler because there are fewer fields in the groups file, and no directories or other data structures need to be created. The syntax for this command is as follows:

addgroup [**-vd**] [**-g** *gid*] [**-m** *members*] [*groupname...*]

- **-v**—Again, this causes more output to be displayed during the execution of the command. Useful when you are first learning to use the system.

- **-d**—Similar to the adduser -d command, this command is the equivalent of using the rmgroup command that is used to remove a group. For example, addgroup –d *groupname* will remove that groupname from the /etc/groups file.

- **-g** *gid*—This is used to specify the group ID (GID) for the group you are adding. If you omit this, the next available (unused) group number will be used.

- **-m** *members*—Use this to specify the initial members of the group, separating each by a space when more than one member is entered.

- *groupname*—This is the name you want to give to the group.

Other versions of Unix/Linux have similar programs. For example, Compaq's True64Unix uses the useradd command. The syntax is similar to that of the adduser command, but a few other options are available. For example, the -x option enables you to further specify options relating to NIS, password expiration times, and so on. Red Hat's Linux distribution enables you to use a similar useradd command. However, it also offers a more complex tool called linuxconf, which can be used in text mode, and also in a GUI mode using an X Window Systems interface or a Web browser. This tool goes far beyond simple user configuration tasks, including options for managing groups, file systems, system services, and many other objects.

Check the documentation of your Unix or Linux version to determine the commands and exact syntax for any script files or other utilities that can be used to automate user management.

Tip

In addition to any printed documentation you get with the Unix or Linux product you purchase, you can get online help. The command MAN followed by a topic will display text for the command you specify. The term *MAN* comes from Manual Pages. Consider this as a first resort when you need help with command syntax, and so on.

Using a Linux GUI Utility to Manage Users

Both Unix and Linux systems come with a graphical interface that can be used to perform many of the functions you can do at the command line. Some of these utilities provide all the functionality of the command-line version, whereas others offer a subset. For example, in Figure 42.1 you can see an example from Linux—the Red Hat User Manager.

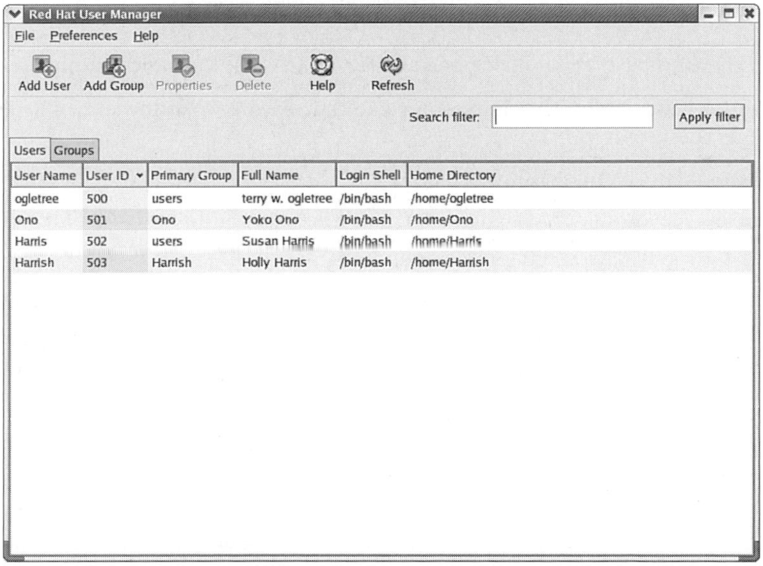

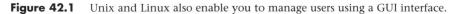

Figure 42.1   Unix and Linux also enable you to manage users using a GUI interface.

To bring up this utility, click on the Red Hat (the equivalent of the Windows Start button), and then from the menu click on System Settings and finally Users and Groups.

The only account that exists on this computer now is the root account, which exists on the computer when it is first booted. It was set up during the operating-system installation. As the "superuser" account, this has the rights and privileges to do anything on the computer, depending on what mode the Linux box is booted into. You can also enter user accounts during the installation and use the user manager utility to add or modify accounts later.

To add users, use the Add User button at the top of the window. Similarly, to add a new group that you can use to categorize users, use the Add Group button. In Figure 42.2 you can see an example of the Create New User dialog box.

Figure 42.2 The Create New User dialog box allows you to enter the basic information about a new user.

Here you can enter information that looks a lot like that used in Windows NT 4.0. There are just a few fields such as these:

■ **User Name**—This is the logon username.

■ **Full Name**—As you may have guessed, this is the user's full name—useful in large networks.

■ **Password**—You'll have to guess this one.

■ **Confirm Password**—Okay, if you got the last one right, then you might just get this one right, too.

■ **Login Shell**—Unix/Linux operating systems have different "shells," which are basically command environments that wrap around the Unix kernel, and each shell has its own set of commands. Different users prefer different command environments. The default is the "bash" shell, located in /bin/bash, as the figure shows. However, if you click the down arrow on the Login Shell field, you'll see a lot of options you or your users can use instead of the default bash shell.

Note

As mentioned in the main text, shells in Unix/Linux are basically command environments, similar to the commands you can enter in a DOS system (a DOS shell implemented by the program **COMMAND.COM** or **CMD.EXE** and other program files). Every operating system has a command interface of some sort. Another thing to consider when deciding which shell to use in your network is that each shell has its own commands, and thus, it's own syntax and command structure for creating script files. Script files are a valuable part of most operating systems because they group together commands to perform one or more functions. This saves the network administrator the chore of having to enter voluminous commands on many workstations. Script files are also used to perform setup duties for users when they log in to the system. So when choosing which shell to use, evaluate the commands and their flexibility and find out from seasoned Unix/Linux employees which is the one they prefer. If an administrator or programmer has to learn a new shell syntax from scratch, you might lose their years of experience using another shell. And you can let each user account use a different shell.

- **Create Home Directory**—If you want to give this user his own home directory, select the Create Home Directory check box and use the default shown in the Home Directory field, or change it to suit the specifications in your LAN. This is the default directory in which a user's files will be stored. Unless this is a special account, such as one used only by an in-house written application, each user will most likely need a home directory. Note that due to the capability of the Unix/Linux operating systems to mount file systems from another computer, you can specify here a home directory on another computer by specifying the full pathname to the directory.

Note

You can learn more about mounting file systems in Unix/Linux using the Network File System protocols that were first developed by Sun Microsystems, and later ported to most modern operating systems, by reading Chapter 44, "Network Printing Protocols."

- **Create a Private Group for the User**—Generally it is a good idea to plan your network based on some business organization and create user groups to gather together users who perform similar functions. However, sometimes you get a new user for which there is no match for your existing groups. Use this check box to later enable you to create a new group for the user.
- **Specify User ID Manually**—In general, when you are adding a lot of users, selecting a user ID is not that important, except that each user should have a unique ID. The group ID and the user ID can uniquely identify a particular user on the system. If you don't want to use the default user ID displayed in this window, click on the Specify User ID Manually check box and enter a new value.

When you are finished entering information for a new user, click the Cancel button if you've changed your mind (or any time when you are entering information and are not sure of what data needs to be entered). If the information is correct, click on the OK button. The new user account then shows up in the window shown earlier in this chapter, in Figure 42.1.

As you enter information in this dialog box, you'll notice that other fields are filled in automatically with default information. For instance, when you enter the username, the Home Directory field expands from /home/ to /home/<username>, where *username* is the name you chose for the login username. If you like this method for naming home directories for clients, this utility will save you a lot of time.

When you want to review a user's account properties, you can click on the user in the main Red Hat Users Manager and use the Properties button. Figure 42.3 shows the basic information entered in the Create New User dialog box. Note that you can use this dialog box after the account has been created to change the user's password, something the Help Desk has to do often in many networks. You can also update additional information by using the tabs at the top of the dialog box.

These are the tabs you can use:

- User Data
- Account Info
- Password Info
- Groups

The first tab (User Data) enables you to change the basic information you entered when creating the account, such as changing the password.

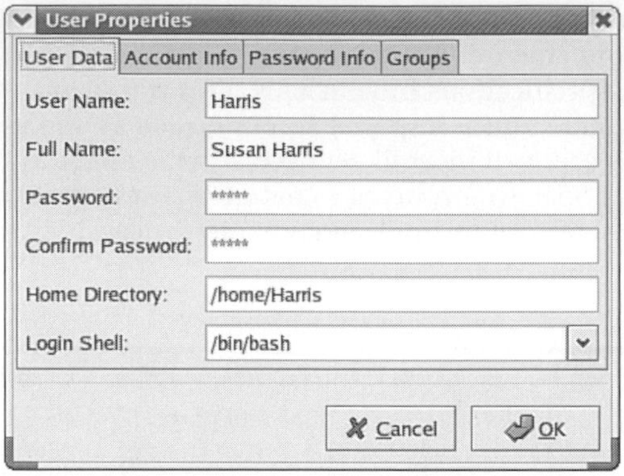

Figure 42.3 The Properties button on the Red Hat User Manager utility allows you to review a user account, and make changes.

You can use the Account Info tab to enforce an account expiration date or lock the account. The Password Info tab lets you find out the last date that the password was changed, and enable a password change policy. These are the items that make up this policy:

■ **Days Before Change Allowed**—Use this to restrict arbitrary changes in a very short length of time, which can indicate intruder attempts.

■ **Days Before Change Required**—All good things must come to an end, or be re-created. A good password must be changed to something else after this value expires. You should keep this to 30–90 days, depending on the value you place on the date hosted by your network.

■ **Days Warning Before Change**—This is the number of days before the expiration of a password that users will begin to get notices that the password is about to expire.

■ **Days Before Account Inactive**—Those who don't change their password, or use their account, will no longer be able to access the account after this number of days.

■ **The Groups tab**—As shown in Figure 42.4, this allows you to use check boxes to select (or view) the groups that the user is a member of. The groups that the user is a member of may determine some of the capabilities the user has on the system.

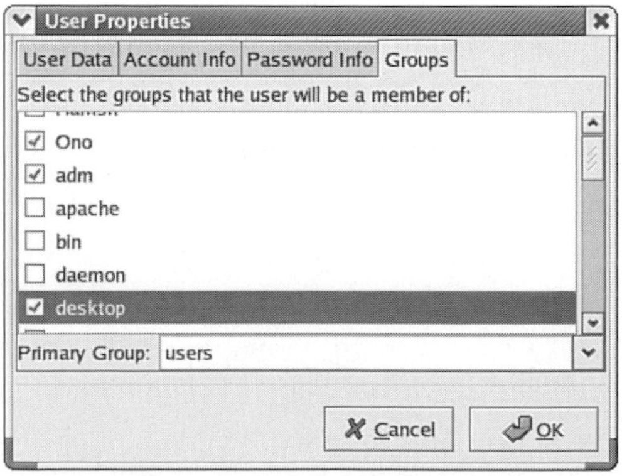

Figure 42.4 The Groups tab allows you to view user groups, including membership.

This simple graphical interface allows you to perform a number of functions that would require many command-line interface commands. As the fast pace of computer and software development continues, it's possible, and very likely, that Linux may become a competitor for the desktop. The main driving forces for the desktop are cost, ease of use, and the applications. Windows operating systems can be more complex. In many cases Linux can be implemented more easily and at a much lower cost.

In the main window (shown in Figure 42.1), there is another tab right next to the Users tab: the Groups tab. Selecting this tab enables you to manage the groups of users on your network. If you simply click on the Groups tab, you will see a name for the group(s) on the computer, the group ID (GID), and the members of each group. You can use tabs at the top of this window to change this data. In Figure 42.5 you can see the Group Members window, which lets you see the members of each group.

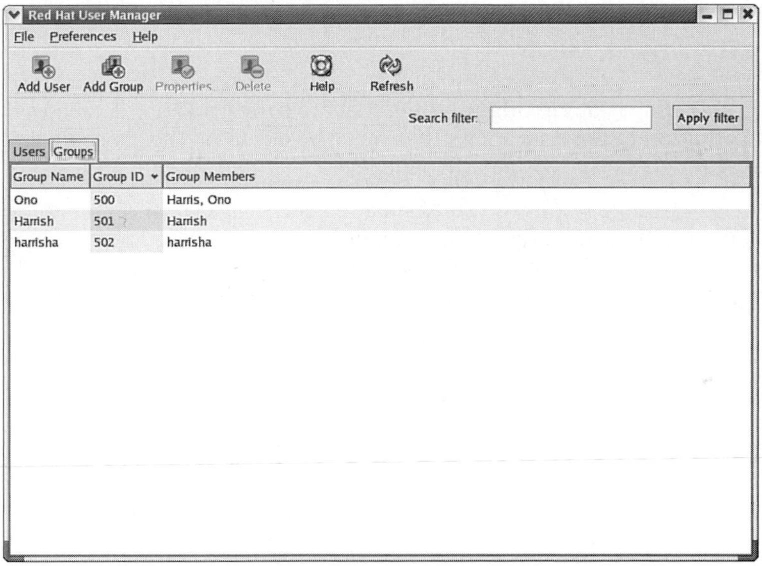

Figure 42.5   This tab enables you to see the name of each group, its GID, and the members of the group.

You can also click on any group to select it and then use the Properties button at the top of the window to see a dialog box showing the group name and the members of the group, should the member accounts not fit on the main display.

Lastly, the Delete button (in Figure 42.1) can be used to remove a user account from the system.

Network Information Service (NIS)

One of the main problems inherent in storing logon information on each computer on a network is managing user accounts on multiple machines. Every time a change is made for a user, the change must be propagated to other computers on the network that the user logs in to. Instead of visiting each Unix box to make changes to the appropriate files, you can use Network Information Service (NIS). This application was developed by Sun Microsystems and was originally called Yellow Pages (or YP for short). You still might see references to Yellow Pages in older documentation. However, due to trademark infringement, the application is now known as NIS.

Master and Slave NIS Servers

NIS stores important information for servers on a network in a central database. When important information is stored in a central location, management of the data becomes much easier. The network administrator can make the necessary changes to the maps on an NIS *master server* and let NIS take care of informing the affected *slave servers* on the network about the change. The NIS master server also works to authenticate users against its database. However, to provide a backup, slave servers on the network also keep copies of the same files maintained by the NIS master server. This redundancy enables users to keep working if an NIS master server is offline for a short period. The master/slave method also can be used to provide for load balancing so that the master NIS server does not become overloaded on a large network.

The kind of data that NIS can manage for Unix servers includes the standard /etc/password and /etc/group files. It also includes other important files containing data about remote file systems, other hosts on the network, and so on.

NIS Maps

When you initially set up NIS, important system files are converted into databases that are referred to as NIS *maps*. In addition to the typical files that we've talked about in this chapter so far, the following files also are candidates for NIS management:

- **/etc/ethers**—This file results in two NIS maps: ethers.byaddr and ethers.byname. The Reverse Address Resolution (RARP) uses this information when resolving Ethernet hardware (MAC) addresses to IP addresses. Typically, this is used by diskless workstations that need to discover their assigned IP address (which might not be stored locally) during the boot sequence.

Note

The concept of a master and slave in the NIS structure does not apply to a server as a whole. For example, one NIS server might be the master server for a particular map or set of maps, while it is also the slave server for other maps controlled by other master servers. The terms *master* and *slave* relate to whether the NIS server holds the master map (where changes are made and then propagated to slave servers) or whether the server holds a duplicate copy that is regularly updated by the master map's server. Each map contains information that tells it what its master server host is.

Note that, unless you have good reasons to distribute master copies among different servers, the whole point in using NIS is to centralize information updates. In general, it's a good idea to use one master server in a typical domain and several slave servers (if needed) to help provide for load balancing and redundancy.

- **/etc/networks**—This file also results in the creation of two NIS maps: networks.byname and networks.byaddr. You probably can guess that these maps store information used to associate network names with IP network addresses.

- **/etc/services**—Only one NIS map is created from this file. It contains a list of network services and the TCP and UDP ports associated with these service port numbers.

- **/etc/protocols**—Two NIS maps result from this file. The first is called protocols.byname and the second is called protocols.byaddr. These maps work similarly to the services maps, in that they act to cross-reference protocol numbers with the names of the protocols.

- **/etc/netmasks**—The NIS map created by this file is called netmasks.byaddr, and it is used to store the subnet masks for the network.

- **/etc/hosts**—This field also results in two NIS maps, hosts.byname and hosts.byaddr. The standard hosts file used in TCP/IP is almost an antique today but still has a few uses. These maps can be used to translate hostnames to IP addresses for computers. The Domain Name System (DNS) servers typically perform this function on most networks today.

- **/etc/aliases**—This file also results in two NIS maps. They are `mail.aliases` and `mail.byaddr`. These maps are used to define alias email addresses.

The ypserve daemon runs on a central server and manages the NIS maps created from the standard systems files. The ypbind daemon runs on workstations and is responsible for interacting with the ypserve daemon to satisfy user requests and information interchange.

Note

NIS works in a fashion similar to DNS. Both provide information to clients from a database that stores all kinds of network information. To help you distinguish the difference between NIS and DNS, think of NIS as a local client/server mechanism that helps keep information sorted on and made available to local clients. DNS is part of a global, hierarchical system for managing IP addresses, domain names, services, and other data used for wide area communications, as well as functioning perfectly well on a local area network to satisfy requests for the data it manages. Note that DNS and NIS do not keep identical information. For example, DNS does not store usernames and passwords. This is a local function of the LAN.

Also note that NIS uses the concept of domains, like DNS. However, although it is typical to create domains that use the same name and cover the same network territory, this does not necessarily have to be the case. So when thinking about NIS domain names, don't confuse them with DNS domain names. They might be the same for the affected portion of the network, but the administrator can choose to use different names for the different domains. For more information about DNS, see Chapter 30, "Network Name Resolution."

In addition to these files, other files that can be used on most NIS implementations include the following:

- Shadow password files—As discussed earlier in this chapter, a user authorization file that is not world-readable like the /etc/passwd file. Instead, only root can manage this file.
- bootparams—Specific parameters for booting computers on the network.
- netgroup—Used to define networkwide groups (as opposed to the /etc/group groups). This makes managing groups of users on the network a simpler task.

The NIS Server *ypserve* Daemon and Maps Location

On the NIS server, the NIS maps can be found in a subdirectory that falls under the /var/yp directory. Names for the subdirectories are created by using the NIS domain name you have chosen. To use the old venerable acme.com name, the resulting file path for this domain would be /var/yp/acme.com.

The ypserve daemon is the background server process that is responsible for finding the information in its maps to satisfy client requests. When NIS is set up, you must have at least one master server that runs this daemon in order for NIS to function on the network.

Setting the NIS Domain Name Using the Command *domainname*

After you've decided on a name to use for the NIS domain, you'll need to issue the domainname command to set that name on the Unix system.

To set the NIS default domain name, use the following command:

```
# domainname acme.com
```

You also can place a similar command (substituting your NIS domain name in the example for *acme.com*, of course), in a startup file to automate the process during system boot.

You also can enter the command domainname from the command line, without any command-line parameters. This syntax of the command displays the current NIS domain name so that you can check it for accuracy when making changes or performing troubleshooting efforts.

Starting NIS: *ypinit, ypserve,* and *ypxfrd*

Installing NIS on Unix and Linux platforms is not the same for all platforms. See the usual README.TXT and installation and release notes files for your platform to install the necessary files that are used to configure NIS on the server or client system.

The ypinit command creates the /var/yp/*domainname* directory (where *domainname* is the name you've chosen for your NIS domain) and reads the files in the /etc directory and creates the NIS maps. The NIS maps are then saved in the *domainname* subdirectory. When the ypinit program is finished, you can use the command ypserv to start the NIS server. When the server is up and running, you'll need to start the map transfer daemon if you have configured other NIS servers in the network. Type **ypxfrd** at the command line. You also could add the command to the /etc/rc.local file to have it start automatically at startup.

After you've finished the initial installation, use the following commands to configure and set up NIS:

- **ypinit**—This command is used to create the map directory and subdirectories (that is, /var/yp/acme.com) on the server. This command also runs through the various /etc files and creates the maps needed for the domain. This command also can be used to set up the /var/ypbinding/*domainname*/ypservers file on client computers, where *domainname* is the name of the NIS domain.

- **ypserv**—After you've used ypinit to create the necessary NIS databases, use the ypserv command to start the server on the NIS server. The format for this command is ypserv -m. You can enter this at the command line or put it into a startup file if you want the server daemon to start each time the system is booted.

Note

By default, the domain name and hostname used by NIS are taken from the files /etc/nodename and /etc/defaultdomain. During the system boot process, these files are consulted and used with the appropriate NIS commands (that is, the domainname command).

To use ypinit, you should be logged in as root. Next, make edits to the /etc/hosts file and be sure that it contains all the IP addresses of each NIS server. Start the process of building the maps by using the following command:

```
/user/sbin/ypinit -m
```

The command (actually a script file) prompts you for the names of other host computers that you want to make into NIS servers. Be sure to include the server you are working on as well as the names of other NIS server candidates you've created. Next, you'll be asked whether you want to terminate the operation if a nonfatal error occurs. Generally, you should enter **yes** to this prompt so that you can fix any problems that crop up. After fixing any problem, you can reinvoke ypinit to start over again.

Next, ypinit asks whether you want to delete any currently existing files that are in the /var/yp/*domainname* directories. If you are reinstalling NIS, you are prompted to delete the files created by the previous installation.

After this, ypinit uses make to process instructions contained in the makefile. The script file uses makedbm to create the maps and places the name of the master server for each map in a location in the map so that it will know its master server.

The Default Makefile Used by ypinit

When the ypinit command is invoked to begin configuring your server, it calls the make(1) command to process information in a makefile that is usually located in the /var/yp directory. You can make modifications to this file if required for your environment. The makefile is used to convert the input files discussed earlier into the ndbm(3) format, which is beyond the scope of this discussion. The makefile then creates the appropriate maps that NIS uses.

NIS Slaves

NIS slaves hold exact duplicates of NIS maps as the master server. The slave also runs the same ypserv daemon. The only difference between the two servers is that only the slave answers client requests; the slave doesn't make any changes to the NIS maps. Only the master server can update the NIS maps. When the master server makes a change to the maps, it then propagates the changes to all the slave servers in the NIS domain.

Setting Up Slaves

Creating a slave server is similar to creating the master server. First, set the NIS domain name by typing **domainname** at the command line. After setting the NIS domain name, start the ypbind server process by entering this:

ypbind

And then enter the following on the slave server-to-be:

ypinit -s *NISmaster*

The -s option specifies that you are setting up a slave server, followed by the NIS domain master server name. After the slave server is initialized, the master server transfers all the NIS domain information to the slave. During the setup of the slave server, it does not look at its local /etc files to create the NIS maps. The slave server has only the information that is stored in the maps on the master server.

Deciding when to create a slave server should be done during the initial planning phase of setting up the NIS network. Although growing networks don't exactly grow according to plan, it is possible to add slave servers later. If you add a slave server after the initial setup of the master server, you'll need to add the new slave's hostname to the ypservers map file.

Starting and Stopping the NIS Service on Slave Servers

Starting and stopping all YP processes is a simple task. These commands may be used online to start or stop the services. The following line will cause the YP processes to all stop running:

/etc/init.d/yp stop

To start all YP processes, use the following command:

/etc init.d/yp start

Now it can't be simpler than that, after all you've gone through to get this system up and running!

Changing NIS Maps

You can make changes to the normal system files (that is, /etc/passwd) on the NIS master server. After you make these kinds of changes, set your default directory to be /var/yp, and then execute the command make *mapname*, where *mapname* is the name of the map being modified.

To update the system after making changes to the makefile, you'll need to stop the YP processes, make the changes, and restart NIS. You can make changes to the makefile to add or remove maps. Use the same start/stop commands described in the preceding section for this purpose.

Pushing Modifications to NIS Slave Servers

After you've made modifications on the master NIS server, the changes must be sent to all other slave servers so that the databases can be kept in sync. The makefile utility uses the yppush command to send these map changes to the affected servers. The process is accomplished by sending a message to the ypserve daemon. The ypserve daemon that resides on the slave server then starts up another process using the ypxfr utility. This utility establishes communication with the ypsfrd daemon that runs on the master NIS server to see whether any changes need to be made. If so, the yppush program sends the map changes. If they are successfully applied to the slave server, it returns a successful status message to yppush.

Note that yppush sends only maps that have changed and that already exist on the slave servers. If you create new maps on the master NIS server that don't yet exist on the slave NIS servers, use the command ypxfr by itself on the command line to do this. For troubleshooting purposes you can check the results of the command by viewing the log file named /var/yp/ypxfr.log.

Other Useful NIS YP Commands

Although the documentation for your system contains a lot of other tasks you can perform using NIS, this chapter has only touched on the basics. However, a few other useful commands that you'll find in most implementations of NIS include the following:

- **ypcat** *mapfilename*—This command lists the values stored in a map file. If you want to list the keys for the map file values, use the option -k in this syntax directly after the ypcat command.

- **ypwhich** -m—This command lists all the available maps on the server and their masters. If you want to list only the master server for a particular map, include the map name following the -m option.

NIS Clients

Starting the NIS client is simple. First, set the NIS domain on the local machine using the domainname command, and then start the ypbind service by entering **ypbind** at the command line. To have ypbind start every time the machine boots, ensure that the ypbind script exists in the /etc/rc.local file and that it is not commented out.

The following is a sample boot script to launch ypbind in the correct NIS domain:

```
domainname acme.com
. . .
if [ -d /var/yp ] ; then
 ypbind; echo -n ' ypbind'
fi
```

Common Login Problems

The most common problem users encounter when logging in to a Unix system is summed up by the following error message:

```
login incorrect
```

This message doesn't convey a great deal of information to the user, but it usually indicates one of the following conditions:

- There is no user account in the /etc/passwd file for this username.
- The password entered by the user is not correct.
- The home directory for the user (as specified in the password file) does not exist.

In the first instance, the administrator might not have gotten around to creating a record for the user in the /etc/passwd file. It is more likely that the user entered the username incorrectly. Remember that, in the Unix operating system, usernames and passwords are case sensitive. For example, if your username is LukeKurtis, entering lukekurtis or LUKEKURTIS will not work.

When you're choosing passwords, it is a good idea to choose one that is not easy for others to guess. Unfortunately, this sometimes means that it is also easy for a user to forget. Choosing a text string that contains both uppercase and lowercase letters, along with numeric and alphabetic characters, is a good idea. When you receive the login incorrect error message, check to be sure that you are really entering the password as it was originally set up.

In all cases, one of the first things to check is that the Caps Lock key is not on. On a notebook, you may also need to double-check the settings of your Num Lock key, because the right half of the keyboard often acts as a 10-key when Num Lock is enabled.

If the account is new, it is possible that the user's home directory has not been created or the administrator has not set the correct permissions on the directory to allow the user access to it. Using a script file to create new user accounts can help prevent this problem. Coding all the necessary commands by a script file will prevent the problems caused when an administrator creates a new account in a hurry and forgets a step or two.

Rights and Permissions

43

SOME OF THE MAIN TOPICS IN THIS CHAPTER ARE

CHAPTER 43

Controlling access to system and network resources is a very important topic for the network administrator to understand. In a homogeneous network where all file servers and clients are of one particular brand, it can still be difficult to keep track of all file and print shares and which users need access to these resources. When you begin to add a mixture of network nodes consisting of more than one operating system to create a more diverse network, you can end up with the requirement to understand the access restrictions imposed by more than one operating system.

Note

A network composed of more than one operating system is generally referred to as a heterogeneous network. Part XI, "Migration and Integration," can help you learn the similarities and differences between different operating systems, and the utilities and add-on products that can enable them to coexist and share data on the same network. However, this chapter is one you should read first, because you will learn the importance of protecting important resources when operating a heterogeneous network.

Two kinds of identifying values are used to decide on access. The first is an identifier that uniquely specifies the user who is logged on to the system and the specific rights (or privileges) defined by an operating system. Rights are definitions of the types of actions that can be performed on the system by the users. For Windows 2003, the terms *rights* and *permissions* are used interchangeably when granting rights to a user account. The term *permissions* is also used, as described in the next paragraph, to define access and restrictions to files, directories, and other objects.

Permissions placed on each resource usually are granular, giving permission separately to read, write, execute, or delete a file or directory. Depending on the operating system, the names used for these permissions can vary, and other types of permissions and combinations of these basic types can be found.

The important point to remember when setting up new users or resources, or when troubleshooting existing connections, is that you might need to look at both ends: What rights does the user possess and what access controls (permissions) exist on the resource? Both of these factors determine what users can do on the network. This chapter takes a quick look at the concepts of rights and permissions in several major operating systems and discusses some of the methods used to solve problems related to them.

Tip

Rights and permissions are just one side of the coin. You can't ensure that security measures are working as they should unless you also use the operating system's auditing facility. In Windows, this is accomplished using the Event Viewer to examine security violations. For Unix/Linux systems, the `syslog` daemon is generally used for this purpose. You can find out more about the Windows Event Viewer, and how to set up which security events to audit, as well as how to set up the configuration files used by the Unix/Linux syslog daemon, in Chapter 47, "Auditing and Other Monitoring Measures."

User-Level and Share-Level Security

There are two basic means for protecting resources offered on a network. Each method strives to make the protected resources available only to users who have been authorized access to these resources. They do so in different ways, however, and grant different kinds of access.

Share-level security involves securing connections to a network share point by a password. Users who know the name of the share point and the password can connect to the share point. All subdirectories and files found under the share point are accessible by using only the single password.

User-level security involves using access controls in the file system and does not stop at placing a single password on an entire tree of resources (although you can do it that way if you want). Instead, access permissions can be placed on any directory or file in a directory, or subdirectories. When a user connects to a resource protected by user-level security mechanisms, the user must first authenticate himself (log on to the server). The user then is granted access rights to each file or directory on the resource, either by the access control restrictions implicitly placed on the resource or by inheritance of access rights.

Obviously, the user level of security permissions provides the administrator a finer granularity of detail when making resource access decisions. A combination of both share-level security and user-level security mechanisms can enable you to create resources on the network that are more secure than using just one of these methods.

When a logon username is employed to identify the user who is accessing a resource, an audit trail with more specific details can also be kept for troubleshooting purposes.

Tip

An audit trail can show you who did what, and when they did it. In Windows, Unix/Linux, and NetWare, you can decide which types of events to log, thus creating an audit trail that matches the level of security required in your network. One mistake often made by administrators of all three of these operating systems is to use the Administrator account (Windows), the root account (Unix/Linux), and the superuser account (NetWare) for administrative tasks.

In this type of situation—if you have more than one administrator—your audit trail can be useless for the capabilities these accounts enable. An audit trail should tell you the event that was logged, as well as *what user* performed the action. If all administrative users make use of a single built-in administrative account, you will not be able to easily track down the person who performed an event. For security reasons you should not use these accounts. Instead you should create separate accounts for each administrative user and grant the rights needed and give these accounts the same permissions (or a subset) that the highly privileged accounts use. This approach will allow you to delegate authority to selected users (such as network administrators), while maintaining an audit trail—by username—that you can use to determine what user performed a particular action on the network or computer.

Microsoft networks allow for both share-level and user-level permissions on network resources. Windows 95/98 operating systems allow each computer in the network to offer a directory (or subdirectory) as a file share on the LAN and protect it with a password. For example, you don't have to use a Windows 2000/2003 server to offer file shares on the LAN; you can also do so with Windows 2000 Professional or Windows XP.

In this type of scenario, each computer has its own security database that stores the share-level password. That means that a user might need to learn several passwords, depending on the number of share connections required in order to get their job done. A simple solution to this would be to use the same password for each share, on each computer. However, the drawback to this is that anyone who knows the password for one file share would know the password for all file shares. So, when all is taken into account, using share-level security is not really a good idea in a large network.

For Windows operating systems, starting with Windows NT 4.0, you need to have both a valid username (for the server you want to connect to, or a domain account) and a password valid for that account in order to connect to a resource share.

Tip

In a small network, such as a SOHO network, you might not need to worry about security problems when you have a small LAN consisting of just a few client computers. For this kind of LAN, you probably don't even need a server-class computer, because share-level security can be implemented by the clients, including Unix or Linux computers.

If you have a firewall of some sort protecting your small LAN from intruders from the Internet (as well as a good virus prevention program), then you might want to use a single password for all file shares to make your job easier. You don't have to be an advanced network administrator to operate a LAN that is under your control, in which only you or a few others use the LAN resources. Keep in mind, however, that if sensitive information (such as payroll information) needs to be viewed by only yourself, you should not offer that as a file share, and instead should manage those resources yourself.

Microsoft Windows Share-Level Security

Earlier versions of Windows operating systems used the FAT (File Allocation Table) and FAT32 (similar to FAT, but for larger disk volumes, as well as other features) file systems. Beginning with Windows NT, the NTFS file system enabled a more secure file system. FAT and FAT32 don't provide the mechanisms to store security attributes, such as access control lists (ACLs), for files or directories, as NTFS does.

The main benefit of using NTFS is that it does allow you to store a lot more information about a file or a directory. When you use the NTFS file system to format a disk, you can apply *user-level* security permissions on individual files or directories. You can still create file shares using Windows sever operating systems, but NTFS allows you to further define which files/directories a user can access when using the file share. For an environment that requires a high degree of security, the NTFS partition is the choice to make. Additionally, the Windows 2000/2003 operating systems allow for other features that make NTFS a more secure choice, including the capability to encrypt and decrypt data on-the-fly when storing or retrieving it from disk. You can also choose to compress data on files so that less disk space is used to store files.

For either of these options, just right-click on a folder and select the properties page from the menu that appears. You'll see an Advanced button on the General tab. After clicking that button, you'll see two important check boxes. The first is Compress Contents to Save Disk Space. The second is Encrypt Contents to Secure Data. Select either or both of these check boxes to enable that feature for the folder.

The only reason to format a disk using FAT or FAT32 is if you are going to dual-boot the computer, and one of the earlier operating systems (such as Windows 95/98) will be used. This is because Windows 95/98 systems are not capable of using an NTFS partition. You can create one partition and format it using FAT, and create additional partitions using NTFS for Windows NT and later operating systems, such as Windows 2000/2003/XP. However, this sort of dual-boot setup should be used only in an environment where security is not an important issue, such as a standalone computer (one not connected to a network). This is because a FAT partition does not let you set file or directory partitions and does not support encryption.

Another example is in your home, where you don't have such strict security requirements. For example, you might need to use an older software application that will not run under newer Windows operating systems. Even then, if you are connected to the Internet, you should consider the implications of using FAT or FAT32 on a home computer because many hackers regularly scan IP addresses looking for vulnerable systems. If you stay online for extended periods browsing the Internet—or if you're online all the time using a broadband connection such as a cable or DSL modem, then a FAT-based disk is wide open for planting a Trojan horse and other malicious programs. If you use NTFS instead, and set up your user accounts correctly, you can potentially head off this sort of problem. This is because on NTFS partitions you can set permissions for every file or directory on a one-by-one basis.

Single computers and small LANs typically use an out-of-the-box firewall solution, such as a DSL/cable router, which can offer some degree of protection, such as Network Address Translation (NAT). However, by applying permissions on an NTFS formatted disk, you can further enhance your security.

▶▶ For more information about NAT, see Chapter 49, "Firewalls."

Assigning User Rights for Windows 2000, Server 2003, and XP

Users who are logged in to a Windows 2000/Server 2003/XP computer can be granted rights by the administrator of the computer. If the user logs in to a domain account instead of the local computer, a domain administrator can manage these rights. Rights granted to an account that resides on an individual Windows 2000/Server 2003/XP computer protect access to resources on *that* computer only. The security information for the computer is stored *locally*, in the Security Accounts Manager (SAM) database, and applies only to resources on that local system.

Accounts that are created on a domain controller can be used when assigning user rights to resources on computers throughout the domain. And, by placing users into groups, you can easily manage a number of users who need the same access to resources or the same rights. This is done by granting the rights to the group, instead of individual users. If a user needs access to resources that are not granted by the group membership, you can place the user in more than one group. Because groups enable you to simplify granting rights to users, the following discussion will concentrate on those rights. User groups are discussed later in this chapter.

Starting with Windows 2000, most Administrative Tools are snap-ins for the Microsoft Management Console (MMC). By using the MMC to create management tools, you'll find it easy to switch from one MMC console to the next, without having to relearn the mechanics of the particular utility. For example, when using MMC you'll find two panes on the screen. The left pane contains a tree of objects that can be managed. An Action menu presents you with functions you can perform. The right pane is used to display different kinds of information, based on the particular utility and the actions you take. The MMC allows you to create new utilities by installing a snap-in that is appropriate for the functions you need to perform. However, most of the tasks you will use to manage the computer or domain have already been set up as an MMC application. Other snap-ins, which are used for more sensitive operations, such as altering the Active Directory schema, must be created by installing the snap-in.

◀◀ For more information about using MMC snap-ins, see Chapter 31, "Using the Active Directory."

In Figure 43.1, you can see the MMC with the snap-in for managing domain users and computers loaded. Although the User Manager or User Manager for Domains was used by Windows NT 4.0 computers, the MMC snap-in is used with Windows 2000 and 2003 to manage users and computers in the domain. After you've created a domain controller in a Windows 2000 or 2003 network, this utility is already set up. The example used in this section is based on Windows 2003. For Windows 2000 computers, the MMC is pretty much the same for the tasks that are described in the text that follows.

Tip

If you are not logged in to an account that grants administrator privileges, you can simply hold down the Shift key and then right-click on the desktop. Select Run As and a dialog box will pop up and enable you to enter another username and password for an account that does have the necessary rights to run Administrative Tool utilities.

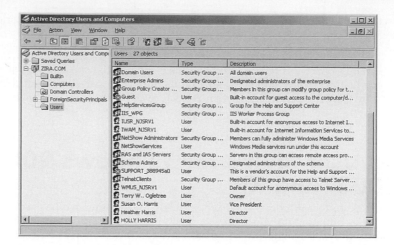

Figure 43.1 Windows 2003 uses the Active Directory Users and Computers MMC snap-in to manage users.

To begin, click Start, All Programs, Administrative Tools, and then Active Directory Users and Computers. In Figure 43.1 you can see the MMC with the Users folder selected. The Users folder has been expanded in the left pane, and in the right pane you can see user groups and users for the domain.

Note

You still can use the MMC snap-in for managing users and computers to manage other domains. In Windows NT 4.0, you needed to have a *trust* relationship set up with other domains you wanted to manage from a central location. The Active Directory automatically creates transitive (two-way) trust relationships between all domains that are in the same domain tree. You can simply use the first entry in the left pane shown in Figure 43.1 (Active Directory Users and Computers), and then select Connect to Domain from the Action menu to connect the utility to another domain whose users or computers you want to manage. Essentially, you can use this MMC snap-in to manage all the users and computers throughout the domain tree. See Chapter 31 for more information about the Active Directory tree structure (as well as the concept of a forest of trees).

Windows NT defined certain basic rights you could grant to a user account, as well as a set of rights that were granular. The basic rights were simply combinations of these granular rights. In Windows 2003, rights have been divided into two categories. These are logon rights and privileges. Logon rights are few in number, and can generally be used to manage most users or groups.

Tip

The Administrators user account cannot be deleted or removed from the Administrators group. However, because many hackers know that this account exists on Windows servers, you can, and should, rename it. You can also disable this account, while giving other accounts the same rights and privileges. Think about this in a high-security environment. Lastly, as discussed elsewhere in this chapter, creating an individual account for each user who requires administrative rights and permissions can help you to determine the source of any changes, using the Event Viewer. If every administrator uses the same account, your audit trail becomes meaningless, because you cannot determine which administrative user has made changes to the operating system.

These logon rights are listed here:

- **Allow log on through Terminal Services**—Enables a user of a computer to log on using Microsoft Terminal Services. Essentially, a Terminal Services client runs programs on a server designated to supply this service, and the Terminal Server client computer displays the GUI interface for the application. This enables you to use older computers with fewer resources (such as memory or processor speed) to be used in your network.

- **Allow log on locally**—Enables a user to log on locally at a workstation or server; that is, to log on sitting at the workstation or computer, not using a network connection. Generally, administrators are the only users who can log on locally at a server.

- **Access this computer from a network**—Enables a user to log on to the computer from the network. In other words, this gives the capability to make a network connection, such as to access a file share on the computer.

- **Log on as a batch job**—Allows a user to submit a batch job (using the task scheduler) that will run under the user's account. Unless you deny this right, the default allows users to submit batch jobs to run in the background. Batch jobs are used to perform specific functions at a certain time, unlike services that run in the background and respond to certain system or user events.

- **Log on as a service**—This right allows the user to start a service using his or her account. A service is a process that runs in the background continuously.

- **Deny log on as a batch job**—Prevents an account from running a batch job on the computer.

- **Deny log on as a service**—Prevents an account from being used to run a service (a background process that runs without a GUI interface).

- **Deny log on locally**—Is the opposite of the Allow log on locally right. This right overrides the Allow log on locally right.

- **Deny access to this computer from network**—Is the opposite of the Access this computer from the network right. This right overrides the Access this computer from a network right.

- **Deny log on through Terminal Services**—Is the opposite of the Allow log on through Terminal Services right.

If you are familiar with the complete list of rights used by Windows NT, you'll see that the privileges that Windows 2003 uses are similar to those, with a few additions. These are the privileges you can use with Windows 2003:

- **Act as part of the operating system**—This right is usually granted to subsystems of the operating system, and for running services. It allows the holder to act as a secure, trusted part of the operating system. This is not a right you would normally need to grant to a user. The LocalSystem account possesses this privilege by default. You won't see this account, however, when you list user accounts in the Active Directory.

- **Add workstations to a domain**—Users or groups granted this privilege and logged in at a domain controller can add client computers (but not domain controller computers) to the domain. This privilege is granted by default to users that are authenticated and are logged in to a domain controller, in which case the user holding this privilege can add up to 10 other computers to the domain.

- **Adjust memory quotas for a process**—If an account is granted this privilege, the user can make changes for the amount of memory a process can use.

- **Bypass traverse checking**—The user holding this right can read through a directory tree, even though she might not have access to all directories in the tree. Thus the user can be granted access to a file that exists in a directory (or subdirectory) for which the user is denied access. The user account granted this privilege, however, cannot list (view) the contents of directories that are bypassed to get to the file or directory for which access is granted.

- **Create a pagefile**—This right is usually granted to just the Administrators group. It allows the user to create additional page files using the System applet in the Control Panel. By creating page files on disks other than those used for the operating system or for applications, you can usually increase performance on the system. Note that a partition of a disk is not the same thing as a separate disk. Using separate partitions on the same disk will not give you the increased performance.

- **Create a token object**—This is the right to create a user logon token and is usually not granted to an individual user, but instead only to the local security authority (LSA) on the Windows computer.

- **Create permanent shared objects**—This is the right to create special resource structures, such as a directory, that are used internally by the operating system. Again, this is not a right generally needed by, or granted to, users.

- **Debug programs**—This right allows a programmer to do low-level debugging. It is helpful for applications developers and administrators. However, as in most networks, this right should be granted *only on laboratory or development systems*, and not on a *production server*. It is not a good idea to allow application development to be performed on the same computer that is a production server that network users make use of. The reason for this is obvious. The application being tested or created on a development system can potentially cause the server to crash, or corrupt data.

- **Enable computer and user accounts to be trusted for delegation**—The Trusted for Delegation right for a user or computer can be performed by accounts that hold this right. The holder of this right can access resources on another computer—unless that computer has the Account Cannot Be Delegated control flag set. The account holding this right can use the authentication credentials of the client computer.

- **Force shutdown from a remote source**—This is a right you should grant sparingly. It allows a user to shut down another computer on the same network. If a computer or user's account becomes compromised because of security problems, this right can be used to shut down other computers, and thus be used to deny other computers access to those computers, resulting in a denial-of-service attack. A denial-of-service attack is an attack that attempts to overwhelm a computer by overloading it with resource requests. For example, a continuous stream of TCP connection attempts can quickly use up the memory data structures a computer can offer. By shutting down a computer that is undergoing a denial-of-service attack, you can begin to protect your network, especially if more than one computer is experiencing this type of attack.

- **Generate security audits**—This right is needed to create security audit log entries. This right generally is assigned not to a user, but instead to the operating system or applications.

- **Increase scheduling priorities**—This gives the capability to boost the scheduling priority of a process. Administrators have this right by default. However, increasing the priority of one process can potentially allow a process that is making heavy use of system resources to dramatically slow down or lock out other processes. To use this right, the Task Manager utility is used. Do not give this right to typical users who do not understand that raising the priority for their session can potentially severely impact other users of the computer. For all practical purposes, Windows server operating systems can adjust priorities as needed. The administrator can also use the System Applet in the Control panel to grant priorities to foreground (applications) or network services, without having to modify process priorities on a process-by-process basis.

- **Load and unload device drivers**—This gives the capability to load and unload device drivers (as well as other kernel mode code). Because kernel processes are the heart of the operating system, you should not grant this right to ordinary users. This right, instead, is granted to Administrators by default.

- **Lock pages in memory**—This right gives the capability to lock pages into physical memory so that users do not get swapped out to the pagefile during normal virtual memory operations. This is useful for a process running a real-time application, but this right is not generally given to ordinary users.

- **Manage auditing and security log**—This right lets the user determine those objects and resources that will be recorded in the security log file, and view the events produced by the auditing.

- **Modify firmware environment variables**—A user granted this right can modify firmware values stored in nonvolatile RAM of computers that are non-X86 computers (such as Intel or AMD). For example, on X86 computers, the user holding this right can modify *only* the Last Known Good Configuration setting. For Itanium computers, users granted this right can run the bootcfg.exe application and manage the Startup and Recovery properties for the computer.

- **Profile a single process**—This allows the user to set the collection information about a non-system process, used for measuring performance. The user who has this right can use the Performance Monitor to view the performance of non-system processes running on the computer. Administrators have this right by default.

- **Profile system performance**—Similar to the preceding right, users who hold this right can perform the same functions, including the right to set or view system processes.

- **Remove computer from docking station**—This right enables a user account to gracefully remove a computer from a docking station without having to first log on to the computer. By default, this right is not granted to any user.

- **Replace a process-level token**—This right is usually restricted to the operating system, which gives the user the capability to modify a process's security access token.

- **Restore files and directories**—A user with this right can traverse directories and restore files and directories, or similar objects. This means that the user can restore files or entire directories, whether or not the user has permissions to access those files or directories when performing duties other than backup or restore functions. The user holding this right cannot access files or directories using this right to examine or change the contents of those files or directories. This right applies only to the restoring files or directories.

- **Shut down the system**—Users holding this right can shut down the system. The user must be logged on to the system locally to perform this function.

- **Synchronize directory service data**—This gives the capability to synchronize all directory services. There is no account that possesses this right by default.

- **Take ownership of files or other objects**—Creators of files, directories, and other objects are in most cases the owners of these objects. Users holding this right can take ownership from the owner. This is useful when a user has left the company, and access is needed to the files, directories, or other objects.

Each of the previous privileges can be enabled for specific user accounts or groups. Some of these rights, however, are granted to groups by default. For example, the Backup Operators group can use the backup utility to back up files to offline storage, despite the protections that are in place for these files. This does not, however, give the Backup Operators group the capability of viewing or modifying files. Members of this group can just use the backup utility to save files to another media, such as a tape.

The Active Directory can be used to delegate management for selected objects that are contained in the directory.

The MMC interface for Windows XP is much the same as that for Windows 2003. To view the rights you can assign on a client Windows XP Professional computer, use the Local Security Settings. Click on Start, Control Panel (and then switch to Classic View), Administrative Tools, and then Local Security Policy (see Figure 43.2). Under the Security Settings tree shown in Figure 43.2, click on Local Policies and then User Rights Assignment.

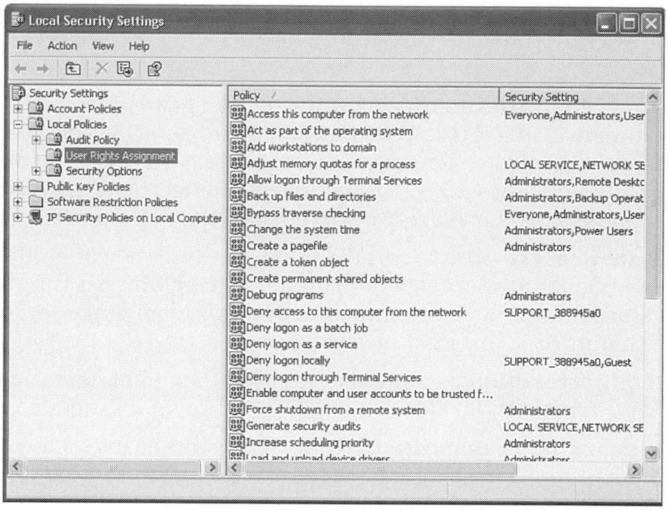

Figure 43.2   You can manage user rights for a Windows XP computer using the Local Security Policy.

In the right pane of this window, you will then see the rights that can be granted to users, as well as the current assignments to existing users or groups. Most of the rights you will see in the right pane are the same as or similar to those described earlier in this chapter. Because Windows XP is a client operating system, many of the rights listed here can be pre-empted by the Default Domain Controller Group Policy object (GPO) if the XP computer is part of a domain. However, if not restricted by the GPO, or if your Windows XP computer is not part of a domain, you can make changes to the rights granted to a user. Note that the rights and privileges for the Windows XP computer are similar to those described earlier for Windows 2003.

Managing User Password Policies

This chapter uses several examples to demonstrate the protections you can use to secure your network. In the preceding section you learned about the rights and privileges you can grant a user (or a group). In this section you will find that these user rights are similar for Windows XP Professional, which you can use as a client in a large network, or as a computer in a SOHO network where a computer using a server operating system is needed.

However, here it's time to look at other security settings that you can use to control user access to a computer. For example, under Account Policies, you can see (in Figure 43.3) that the Password Policy and Account Lockout Policy can be found.

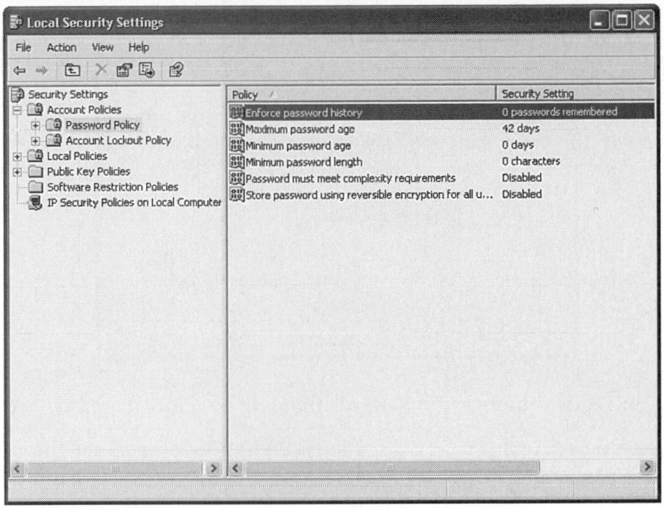

Figure 43.3   You can manage password policies for a Windows XP computer using the Local Security Policy.

Note

Although this example uses Windows XP Professional, the same password policies are applicable to Windows 2003, and most are also the same for Windows 2000.

Password policies enable the user of the Windows XP computer to enforce several aspects that relate to the use of passwords on this computer. For example:

- **Enforce password history**—You can set a value here that controls the length of time a password is stored in a history file to prevent the same password from being used within this time frame. This is a very useful password policy, because you can use this to ensure that the user chooses a different password when the current one expires. I suggest that you set the value for this item to a number larger than the default. Preventing a user from using the same password over and over again will likely make your system more vulnerable than if the user is required to choose a password that has not been used frequently. If you double-click on the Enforce Password History entry, you will see the dialog box that enables you to set the number of passwords that will be remembered (see Figure 43.4).

- **Maximum password age**—This policy defines the length of time a password can be used before the user is required to change the password. A dialog box similar to that shown in Figure 43.4 is used. However, this dialog box allows you to set the number of days a password can be used. In combination with the Enforce password history entry, you can further enhance security as it applies to user passwords.

- **Minimum password age**—This entry enables you to set the minimum number of days that a password must be used before it can be changed. Although it may seem that the default of zero days is a good one, consider that if someone other than the user gains access to the account, he can change the password easily (and thus lock out the original user). Because of this, it's a good idea to set this to another value to keep an intruder from changing the password. The value you set here should be less than or equal to the Maximum password age value.

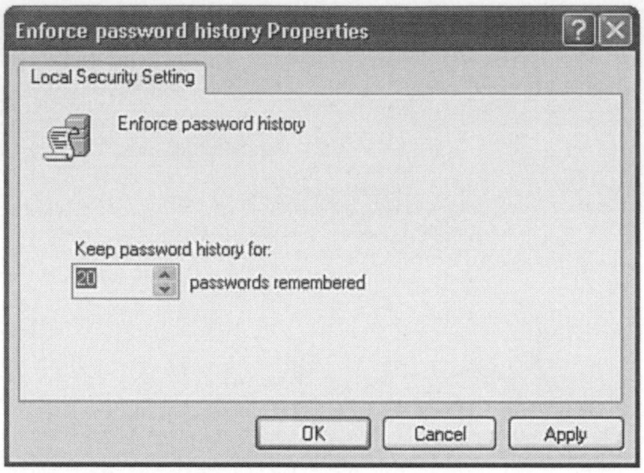

Figure 43.4 You can set the number of passwords that will be remembered by Windows XP.

- **Minimum password length**—This value is obvious—you can set the minimum number of characters (both alpha and numeric) that the user needs to choose for a password. Short passwords are much easier to discover using many password cracker programs available on the Internet. A recommended value for this field is 10 characters. The next item is also useful to prevent an outsider from guessing a password.

- **Password must meet complexity requirements**—This policy is a very important one. Although setting the minimum and maximum password policies are important, this still leaves your user accounts open to a dictionary attack. This sort of attack simply uses a dictionary of ordinary words to attempt to break into your system after a user account name is known. This type of attack is generally used against the Administrator account, because it is a known account for Windows systems. This policy requires that passwords meet certain requirements, such as including numeric as well as alphabetic characters.

Note

The Password must meet complexity requirements option should be used on networks that contain a large number of computers (an Enterprise network, for example) as well as for simple SOHO network LANs. Both types of networks are vulnerable to password attacks. As described in Chapter 46, "Basic Security Measures Every Network Administrator Needs to Know," and Chapter 48, "Security Issues for Wide Area Networks," one of the main attacks used by malicious persons is based on many single computers. By planting programs on a large number of computers that have been hacked, a Distributed Denial-of-Service attack can be launched from all the computers that the user has gained entry to. Thus, when a signal is sent to the many hundreds (or even thousands) of computers, a large volume of network traffic can be simultaneously directed to a targeted computer. This means that your local computer can participate in an attack without your knowledge.

- **Store password using reversible encryption for all users in the domain**—If this is enabled, Administrator as well as other accounts that hold administrative privileges can recover the encrypted password. This is not necessary if an Administrator account possesses the right to take ownership of another user's files. Yet it can be useful if a user forgets his password.

As you can see from the previous password policies, you can set policies that can help protect your network from compromise for both internal and external users. Don't think that all security breaches are from external users. Can you be certain that all users inside your LAN are happy users? If so, why is it necessary to let some users go? And remember that when someone is let go, it can take some time for the human resources department to deactivate user accounts (or another entity in your business).

If a Windows XP computer is part of a domain, you can manage user accounts on a domain controller so that the user can be granted access to other computers in the domain instead of just the local workstation. The rights on a Windows XP Professional computer in a domain setting are controlled by a Group Policy Object (GPO), which can be used to set a large number of security and other settings for computers in the network. For a SOHO network, you probably won't need to assign rights to any user account, but can instead add the user account to a user group that possesses the rights needed to perform the tasks necessary.

◄◄ To learn about how you grant rights to a user or group, see Chapter 41, "Windows 2000 and Windows Server 2003 User and Computer Management Utilities."

Windows NT/2000/2003 NTFS Standard Permissions and Special Permissions

When a disk partition is formatted using NTFS, you can grant permissions that control which directories and files can be accessed by users, and what kind of actions the user can take on a file or directory. Whereas *rights* grant a user the capability to perform some function, *permissions* specify which users (or groups) can access a particular object, such as a file, directory, or printer, for example. Some rights, such as Backup of files and directories, *can override permissions applied to files or directories*. Without this capability, a user who is responsible for performing backups would have to be granted access to every file and directory. Don't worry, however. That right only allows the user to back up the files, not to read or access the files in any other way.

Tip

If you don't see the Sharing or Security tabs, you are not using an NTFS partition, but a FAT or FAT32 partition instead. Those file systems do not support the same sharing and security features offered by NTFS. If you are not dual-booting Windows 95/98 on your computer with Windows NT 4.0/2000/Server 2003, there isn't really a good reason for using a file system other than NTFS.

In the following example Using Windows 2003, the Windows Explorer utility (found under the Accessories folder) can be used to add or change permissions on files and directories. To view or modify the permissions on a directory using Windows Explorer, simply right-click on the file or directory and select Properties. From the File Properties sheet, select the Security tab and from this tab click the Permissions button. In Figure 43.5 you can see the Security tab selected for a directory.

In Figure 43.5 you can see that members of the Administrators group of the Zira domain are allowed full access to this directory. Note the Allow and Deny check boxes in the lower pane of this properties sheet.

Using the top pane, you can select other users or groups to see what access has been granted (or denied) them. To add a user or group, click on the Add button, and the Select Users, Computers, or Groups dialog box will allow you to enter one or more usernames or groups (see Figure 43.6). If you know the username, enter it. To see more information about that user (such as the person's entire name as stored in the Active Directory), click on Check Names after entering the username. In Figure 43.6 this has been done so that I can be sure I have the right person associated with the username I entered.

Tip

The dialog boxes shown in Figure 43.6 and Figure 43.7 are standard dialog boxes used by many utilities to locate users, computers, and other objects in the Active Directory. You can use the Object Types button to select a specific object.

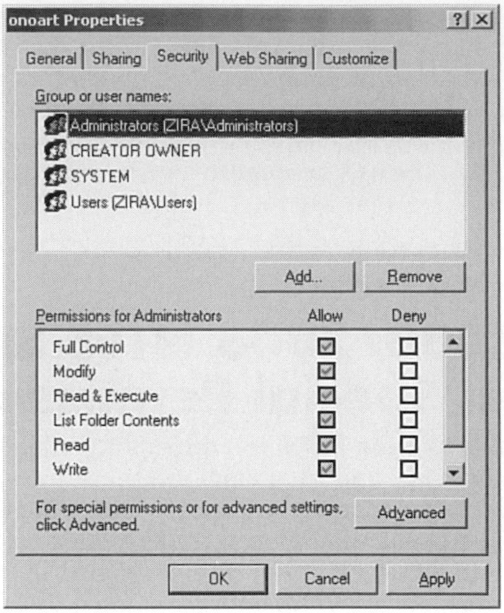

Figure 43.5 Use the Security tab to set permissions on files or directories for NTFS partitions.

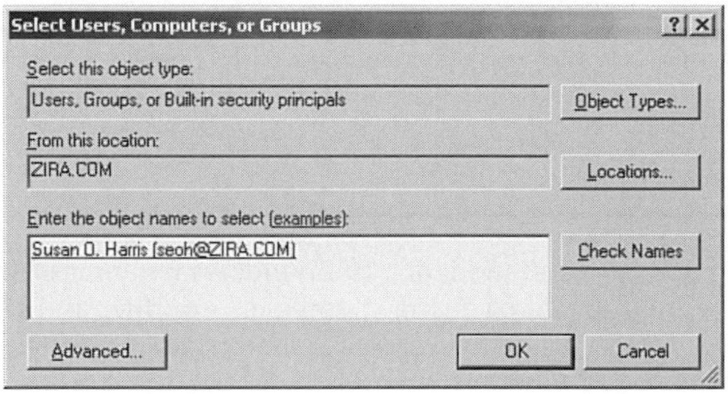

Figure 43.6 This dialog box enables you to select a user or group.

In Figure 43.6 you'll see that there is also an Advanced button. If you click on this button, you can search the Active Directory to find a username. This expanded dialog box is shown in Figure 43.7.

After you have selected the user for which you want to manage access to a file or folder, click the OK button on the Select Users, Computers, or Groups dialog box, and you will be returned to the Security tab of the object's properties sheets. The user you have added will appear in the top pane. Select the user by clicking on the name once. Then you can select which permissions to allow or deny. The basic permissions for a resource are the following:

- **Full Control**—Gives the user full control over the object.
- **Modify**—Enables the user to make changes to the object.
- **Read & Execute**—Just what it says: lets the user read files and execute applications in the directory.
- **List Folder Contents**—Lets the user see the files contained in the folder.

- **Read**—Grants the user read access to the folder or file.
- **Write**—Lets the user write to the file or folder.
- **Special Permissions**—This last entry is scrolled off of the pane in Figure 43.5. This check box will be selected if you have granted the user any of the special permissions by using the Advanced button.

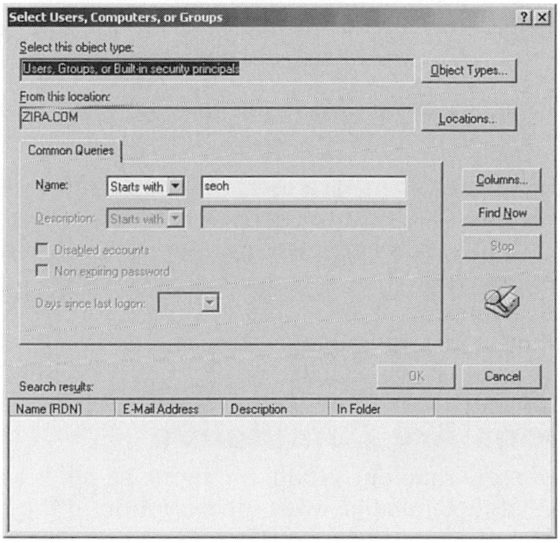

Figure 43.7   You can use the advanced search feature to locate users in the Active Directory.

The Advanced button will let you further refine the permissions, auditing, and other features, including how permissions can be inherited by subfolders that are created under the folder you are currently managing. Although it is beyond the scope of this chapter to list all the possibilities that the Advanced button offers, Figure 43.8 shows the Advanced Security Settings for a folder, and the tabs that can be used to further customize permissions and other features applied to the folder.

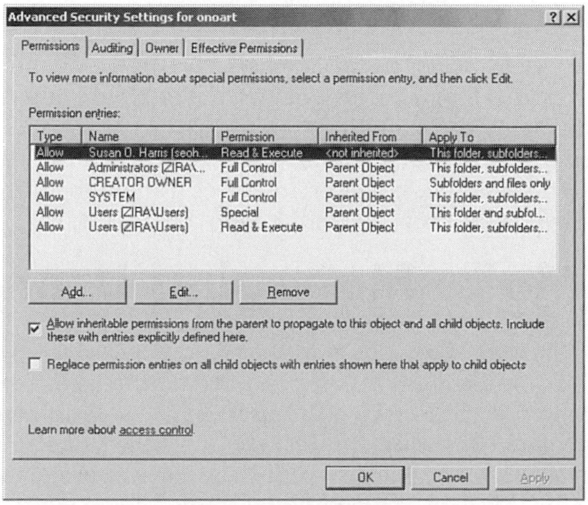

Figure 43.8   The Advanced button enables you to micromanage permissions, auditing, ownership, and other features.

One important thing you can see in this figure is the check box labeled Allow Inheritable Permissions from the Parent to Propagate to This Object and All Child Objects. If it's selected, then if you are modifying permissions for a subfolder, it will also inherit access controls from parent folders above it. Similarly, new subfolders created under this one will inherit the access controls you have just created. If you want to apply your access control modifications to existing subfolders, use the second check box, labeled Replace Permission Entries on All Child Objects with Entries Shown Here That Apply to Child Objects.

Is that complicated or what? Yet, this just shows that you can fine-tune permissions on objects (such as files, folders, and printers) that are in a domain that uses the Active Directory.

When you are finished making changes to the permissions (access controls) for a folder or file, click the Apply button and then the OK button shown back in Figure 43.8.

Whereas rights and privileges can be granted to users or groups, and enable them to perform certain actions on a computer, permissions are used to restrict which resources a user can access. The NTFS file system enables you to assign granular permissions to every file or directory on your computer, as well as other objects. You can override these permissions, as described previously. For example, the administrator's right to take ownership of a file or directory can override *any* permissions you place on a file or directory. Yet, for the majority of your users who do not possess this type of right, permissions on files or directories can serve as a valuable protection that can keep your data safe.

Windows Permissions Are Cumulative

When a user is a member of more than one group, the rights he holds are cumulative. In addition, *permissions* on a resource are also cumulative, with the exception of the No Access permission. Take, for example, a user who has been granted the Read permission to a directory because of his membership in a group (such as "world"). However, if the user is also a member of another group called "accountants," the user's permissions are calculated using permissions granted to that group as well. If the accountants user group has been granted the Change permission for the directory, the user has both the Read and Change permissions when he is evaluated for access to the directory.

The only exception to this rule is the No Access right. This right *specifically denies* all other access. Thus, if a user is a member of one group that has been granted Full Control over a directory, but is also a member of another group that has been granted the No Access permission for the directory, the user will not be able to access the directory. The No Access permission overrides other access permissions.

The capability to selectively deny access to specific users can be a useful tool when setting up or managing user accounts. It is easier to grant access to everyone in a large user group and then to deny access to a few select individuals who should not be allowed to use the resource. The alternative is to create a more finely tuned user group that eliminates those who do not need access and then grant access to this new group. This method, however, increases the number of user groups you have to manage and, thus, its use becomes less effective the more you use it.

User Groups Make Managing User Rights Easier

Granting rights to a user can be a tedious task if you have hundreds or thousands of users on your network. The easiest method for granting rights to users in an environment where you have a large user base is to create *user groups* consisting of users who need the same kind of access to the same resources. You can then grant rights to the groups instead of each user. Users of a group inherit the rights assigned to the group, as well as any additional rights you assign to the user. A user can be a member of more than one group, and thus inherit the rights assigned to each of the groups of which the user is a member. This is an important concept, because many users do not fit neatly into a single group.

Tip

In addition to placing users into one or more groups to facilitate assigning rights and permissions to the users, you can still assign rights for the individual user in addition to those provided by group membership.

Windows NT enables you to use two basic kinds of groups: local groups and global groups. Local groups can be local to a particular computer or can be domain local groups. Global groups are used for grouping users from one domain so that they can be *managed as a unit* in another domain where the administrator can place the global group into a local group created on that computer for administrative purposes. This is a very important distinction to make. You can literally "export" a global group from one computer to a local group on another computer. This capability again makes an administrator's chore easier. For users who are members of a global group, the administrator of the other computer does not have to grant access to that computer on a one-by-one basis for each user. Instead, a group of users from one computer to another can be imported as a local group, and the administrator of that computer can manage the group when making decisions about rights and permissions.

Windows NT computers come with several built-in user groups, which vary depending on the role of the computer in the network. What is important to understand here is that, although NT allows a large number of specific rights to be assigned to users, you can do this on a group basis rather than for individual user accounts if you want to make user management tasks easier.

User Groups in Windows 2000 and 2003

There are a few differences between user groups in standalone Windows computers—those not part of a domain—and those created in the Active Directory. The following groups are available on a local server whether it is part of a domain or a standalone server:

- **Administrators**—Members of this group have full control over the local server. As recommended earlier in this chapter, it is a good idea from a security standpoint to rename the Administrator account. Then you can create individual accounts for administrative-level users and grant them the same rights by adding them to this group.

- **Backup Operators**—This group lets you specify which users can perform backup and restore operations.

- **DHCP Administrators**—If you have installed a DHCP server on the computer, this group will be created automatically. Place members into this group if you want them to be able to manage the DHCP service.

- **DHCP Users**—This group simply lets members view information about the DHCP database. They cannot make changes to it, however.

- **Domain Administrators**—This group grants members the rights that the Administrator account possesses. It is a good idea to create accounts with a name other than Administrator and put them in this group, and then change the name of the Administrator account. This will enable you to track in the event log which Domain Administrators user has made changes to the system, and protect you from simple attacks that target the known Administrator account.

- **Guests**—This group is disabled by default and is used to let members log on using a temporary user profile. No rights are granted by default to this group. You should probably leave this group disabled for security reasons.

- **HelpServicesGroup**—This group also does not possess any default rights. If you do grant rights to this group (which you should not!), then they will apply to all Microsoft help applications, such as Remote assistance. Because this group is used by applications, you should not place user accounts into this group.

- **Network Configuration Operators**—This group enables its members to make changes to network protocols, such as TCP/IP.

- **Performance Monitor Users**—This group enables its members to use performance monitor counters to evaluate the operation of the local server.

- **Performance Log Users**—This group is a superset of the preceding group, in that its members can also manage which performance counters are enabled, and enable logs and alerts on the local server.

- **Power Users**—This group is granted the following rights, and should be used only for users who understand what these rights can do: Access this computer from the network; Allow log on locally; Bypass traverse checking; Change the system time; Profile single process; Remove computer from docking station; and Shut down the system.

- **Print Operators**—This group's members can manage printer resources on the local computer.

- **Remote Desktop Users**—This group holds the right Allow log on through Terminal Services. Its members can log on to a server remotely.

- **Replicator**—No user accounts should be added to this group. It is used by several replication functions, specifically those used to access replication services on a domain controller.

- **Terminal Server Users**—This group is made up of users who are currently logged on as Terminal Services users. It is generally used to run older applications, such as those created for Windows NT 4.0.

- **Users**—This group contains any user account currently logged on to the computer, as well as the Domain Users group, if the computer is joined to a domain. Members can perform everyday functions such as running applications and using resources such as printers attached to the computer.

- **WINS Users**—If you are still using the Windows Internet Naming Service (WINS) this late in the game, this group will be present if WINS is installed and running. Members of this group can only read information from the WINS database, but cannot change it.

Active Directory Groups

When you use the Active Directory in your network, a number of other groups can be used. The Active Directory controls many aspects that grant or deny access to resources throughout the network, including other domains, and possibly other Active Directory trees in a forest of AD trees. Following is a list of these default groups:

- **Account Operators**—This group's members can create user accounts and groups in their domain in the Active Directory, as well as modify or delete them. The exception is that members cannot access the Domain Controllers organizational unit. They cannot make changes to Administrator accounts in the domain, or accounts that are members of the Domain Admins group. However, members of this group can shut down a domain controller, so be careful when selecting users to add to this group.

- **Administrators**—This group, of course, can do anything on any domain controller for a particular domain. The groups Domain Admins and Enterprise Admins (for Windows 2003 Enterprise Edition) are automatically placed into this group. This group can perform all functions in a domain, so choose its members very carefully. For example, if only a subset of the administrative functions are required, choose another built-in group that matches the job specifications, or create a new group and grant it the rights to perform those functions.

- **Enterprise Administrators**—There is very little this group cannot do. Enterprise Administrators have full control permissions, enabling them to have Read permissions throughout the enterprise. And, you can consider the group Enterprise Administrators to have the same capabilities as Domain Administrators or the local Administrators group.

- **Backup Operators**—As discussed earlier in this chapter, members of this group can perform backup and restore functions. In addition, however, note that this group's members can log on to a domain controller and shut it down.

Caution

Placing a user account into any group that can shut down a domain controller should be done with great caution. For example, if you have just one domain controller in your domain, shutting it down can have a severe impact on your domain. Even if you have multiple domain controllers (which is highly recommended for fault-tolerance), that will not prevent a user who has the right to shut down one domain controller from doing the same to others.

- **Guests**—See the previous entry for the Guests group for the local computer.

- **Incoming Forest Trust Builders**—This group will be present only in the forest root domain. A forest is a collection of domain trees. This group can create incoming trust relationships between trees in a forest. This is a powerful right, so be sure to understand the implications before adding members to this group. By default, there are no members in this group.

- **Network Configuration Operators**—This group can modify the TCP/IP configuration, and release/renew DHCP configurations for the same, on domain controllers.

- **Performance Monitor Users**—This group's members can monitor the performance on a domain controller.

- **Performance Log Users**—This group, as you can probably guess from the local group definitions, can manage the items that are set up as counters, alerts, and logs for performance monitoring—but this group can do so on domain controllers.

- **Pre-Windows 2000 Compatible Access**—This group is used to provide backward compatibility for Windows NT users, as well as earlier operating systems. If your network is composed of Windows 2000 and later editions of the operating system, this group will not be present, or needed.

- **Print Operators**—This is another group that is similar in function to the local group for a particular server. Yet this group can manage printers on a domain controller. More important is the fact that members of this group can make changes in the Active Directory for printer objects, and can also shut down domain controllers. Choose members for this group carefully!

- **Remote Desktop Users**—This is the same as the local group, but this Active Directory group can also log on to domain controllers in your network.

- **Replicator**—This is another group that is similar to the local group of the same name. This group can also be used to enable file replication between domain controllers.

- **Server Operators**—Members of this group can log on locally to a domain controller. They can perform many other functions in addition, such as create/delete shared resources (such as file or print shares), start/stop most services, shut down the server, and also back up/restore files on the server. Members can also change the system time.

- **Users**—Members of this group, as with the same local group, can run applications and perform other functions. Any domain account you create becomes a member of this group.

As if that were not enough, there are additional groups contained in the Users container in the Active Directory. These groups are many, and you should investigate their use after becoming familiar with the Active directory. These groups can contain both users and computers.

Tip

Earlier in this chapter you learned that you can disable or rename the Administrator account. However, an important fact you need to remember is that if you boot the computer in Safe Mode, the administrator account will be enabled, to help you recover the system. This is an example of why you need to protect important servers using not only the safeguards built into the operating system, but also the physical constraints used to access the server. In other words, unless the server is located in a secure computer room, there is always the possibility that it can be compromised.

NetWare

When a user logs in to a NetWare 4.x or 5.x, a three-level tiered mechanism is at work to decide how access of resources is to be granted. The first level of security is logon security. The user must be authenticated against a user object in the NDS tree. The second level of security is NDS security, in which access can be controlled by granting or denying the user access to an object or its properties. The third level of security is NetWare file systems security, which involves the permissions on files and directories contained in the NetWare file system. Four types or categories of rights are used in Novell Networking. Versions prior to NetWare 4 and 5 used only the first two of these:

- File system directory rights
- File system file rights
- NDS object rights
- NDS property rights

The first two rights are those you normally would associate with an operating system and its file system. These are rights that control access to directories and files in those directories on the disks for which the operating system (or network operating system) is responsible. The last two of these categories are used for rights that apply to accessing objects that reside in the Novell Directory Services (NDS) database.

◄◄   Chapter 33, "Overview of the Novell Bindery and Novell Directory Services," is recommended reading if you want to understand how NDS can be used to implement security in a NetWare environment.

Trustees

In NetWare networks, a user or group of users who have a right granted to them for a file or a directory are called a *trustee* of the directory. These rights sometimes are referred to as *trustee assignments*. A trustee assignment includes all the applicable rights, including a No Rights declaration. For NetWare 4.x and 5.x, other NDS leaf objects and container objects also can be granted a trustee assignment.

Trustee rights can be granted by an administrator using a program such as RIGHTS or FILER. You also can grant trustee rights using the NetWare Administrator. These trustee rights relationships also can be inherited. When discussing how rights are granted in a NetWare environment, remember that when a user or group is made a trustee of a file or directory, the user or group has been granted some kind of access permission right.

File-System Rights

File-system rights are those that control how a user can list the contents of a directory, add to a directory, or remove files or directories from a file system. Table 43.1 lists the terms used for the rights permissions that can be placed on files and directories, along with a short description of their functions.

Table 43.1   NetWare File and Directory Rights

Right	Description
Read	Grants the trustee the right to read the contents of files existing in a directory and to execute applications.
Write	Enables the trustee to add to or modify the contents of existing files.
Create	Allows the trustee to create a file or a subdirectory.
Erase	Gives the right to erase a file or directory.
Access Control	Enables a user holding this right to grant rights to the directory or files to other users, and to modify the Inherited Rights Filter (IRF). Similar to the Active Directory, a NetWare trustee inherits rights granted to container objects that are farther up the directory tree. Yet you can also deny specific rights that would be inherited, by modifying the IRF.
Modify	Enables the trustee to rename a file or directory and gives him the right to change attributes of the file or directory.
File Scan	Enables the user to list the files that are contained in a directory.
Supervisor	Gives the holder all other rights to this directory and to its subdirectories—this is the most powerful right.

Creators/owners of files and directories usually have the access control right over files they create. This means that they can assign permissions to other users on the system who might need to access their files. The user who has Supervisor access can do as much or more than the owner of a file or directory can do. The File Scan right gives the user the capability to scan the directory and see its contents when searching for a file.

Object and Property Rights

The NDS database is a hierarchical tree structure. Rights in this tree flow from top to bottom, such that an object in the directory can possibly inherit the rights values from all parent objects above it in the tree. Two basic kinds of rights are associated with NDS: Object rights and Property rights. The first, Object rights, defines the kinds of actions a trustee can perform on an object in the NDS tree. These rights do not necessarily give the trustee access to any of the information stored in the object's properties, just access to the mechanisms used to manipulate objects.

Property rights define access to the information stored in the properties of an object. These rights apply to the properties of an object and not to the object itself. For example, an administrator might choose to grant users the ability to change certain properties of their own user object in the directory. This would allow users to change their own telephone-number properties, email account properties, and so on, relieving the administrator or another resource of this chore.

Table 43.2 shows the object rights and Table 43.3 shows the property rights, along with descriptions of their use.

Table 43.2   NDS Object Rights

Right	Description
Supervisor	The most powerful object right grants the trustee all rights to the object as well as its properties. Note that in the case of the other object rights, only the Supervisor right can also grant access to property values.
Browse	Enables the user to see the object in the NDS tree and to search for it based on the base class of the object or the relative distinguished name (RDN) of the object.

Table 43.2   Continued

Right	Description
Create	Applies to container objects, and gives the trustee the right to create a new object in the NDS tree. This right cannot be assigned to leaf objects, because by definition they cannot contain any other objects. This right can be granted only to container objects and gives the trustee the right to create new objects in the container.
Delete	Gives the right to delete an object in the NDS tree. Note that a container object can be deleted only if there are no other objects beneath it. If there are, you must first delete any existing objects within the container before you can delete the container. The Write right (property right) for all properties is also needed to delete an object.
Rename	Gives the right to change the name (RDN) of an object.
Inheritable	Is used to specify whether the rights assignment for the object is inherited by the trustee to subordinate objects in the NDS tree, and this right can be assigned only to a container object.

Table 43.3   NDS Property Rights

Property Right	Description
Add Self	Enables you to add or remove yourself as a value of a property. You cannot use this right to change other property values, however. This right applies only to properties that contain a list of other object names, such as a membership list.
Compare	Gives the right to make a comparison of a value to the value of a property. This right does not enable you to see the actual value of the property. Instead, the compare operation returns a value of true or false.
Read	Is the right needed to see the value of the property of an object. This right includes the Compare right.
Supervisor	Gives you all rights to the property. This right can, however, be blocked by an Inherited Rights Filter.
Write	Gives the right to add, change, or delete values of a property. This right includes the Add Self right.
Inheritable	Specifies whether the rights assignment will be inherited by the trustee for objects subordinate to this one in the NDS tree. This right can be used only on container objects.

Differences Between NDS and File-System and Directory Rights

NDS rights are used to assign access capabilities to objects and their properties that are contained in the NDS directory database. File-system rights are used to assign access capabilities to directories and files stored in the file system. The first difference you will notice between the two is that the NDS rights consist of two other kinds of rights: Object and Property rights. This concept does not exist in the file-system rights.

Finally, trustee assignments in NetWare 3.x could be made only for a user account or a user group. In NetWare 4.x and 5.x, the trustee can be any NDS object, leaf, or container, anywhere in the NDS tree. Because the NDS tree is a distributed database, objects located on different servers can be made trustees to files on other servers.

Inheritance of Rights

Inheritance of rights in the NDS tree is the process by which an object acquires some of the rights granted to objects superior to it in the tree. Rights are inherited starting at the top of the tree, where objects underneath the [root] object inherit some of the rights granted to [root]. The two methods used to block an object from inheriting rights from a superior object are the inherited rights filter (IRF) and direct trustee assignments by an administrator. Direct trustee assignments made anywhere in the path from the [root] object to the object in question can change the rights flowing down the tree.

The Inherited Rights Filter

The Inherited Rights Filter (IRF) can be used to stop one or more rights from being acquired in this fashion. The filter is used to block an object from receiving selected kinds of trustee assignments that it would otherwise inherit. When displaying the IRF, you will see a string of characters enclosed in square brackets. Each letter is the first letter of one of the rights that can be inherited by the object or potentially blocked by the filter. The values for directory and file rights can be read, write, create, erase, modify, file scan, and access control.

To make modifications to an IRF, you can use the utilities RIGHTS, FILER, NetAdmin, or NWADMIN.

Note that an IRF can block the Supervisor right from being inherited in the NDS tree to block access to an object in the tree. However, an IRF cannot block inheritance of the Supervisor right for file-system rights inheritance. Also, if a right is blocked by an IRF at a higher level, you can always grant the right to a child object specifically. The IRF only blocks rights from being inherited from above, and does not block a right at the level which it is assigned.

Security Equivalence

Security equivalence is another method of granting trustee access rights in NetWare. Using this method, one User object is made equivalent to another object and thus takes on the same trustee assignments. Security equivalence is a property of the User object. Trustee rights gained by this equivalence method are in addition to any other rights the User object might possess. Also, a user might be granted rights that are granted to a group of which the user is a member.

This concept is helpful when it becomes necessary to allow one user to have access to objects in a manner similar to another user—for example, when a user is temporarily out of work and another is brought in to fill in.

Tip

It is not a good idea to grant a user the right to change the Security Equivalent property of their own User object. If the user also has the Write property right to the ACL property of an Admin User object, the user could potentially acquire all the rights associated with the Admin User object.

Effective Rights

When looking at the various means that are used to grant trustee rights to an object in NetWare, it quickly becomes apparent that trying to figure out the actual rights a user possesses might become confusing. The actual rights that a user will end up with are called the effective rights to the object. A few simple rules can be used to deduce effective rights:

- If no trustee rights are granted to the directory, the effective rights are computed by a logical AND operation of the parent directory's effective rights and the Inherited Rights Filter.

- An explicit assignment of trustee rights to a directory overrides an Inherited Rights Filter.

- If the Supervisor right is granted to a directory, the trustee will have all rights for all files and subdirectories underneath the directory. Remember that an IRF cannot block the Supervisor right in the file system.

Rights are additive in this computation. Inherited rights are masked by the Inherited Rights Filter, and any rights not masked out are added to any direct assignments made to the object, as well as any rights acquired by security equivalence. If the access granted from one source is less than that granted by another source, the higher-level right is used.

The Everyone Group and the [Public] Group

In NetWare 3.x a group called Everyone was usually assigned the Read and the File Scan right to SYS:PUBLIC. This user group allowed the administrator to assign rights to all users in a convenient method. The Everyone group consists of all users on a NetWare 3.x server. In NetWare 4.x and 5.x, there is no Everyone group, by default.

Note

By default, NetWare 4.x and 5.x do not contain an Everyone group. However, the migration process from NetWare 3.x to NetWare 4.x or 5.x can cause the Everyone group to be migrated as a user group.

Novell Directory Services allows for the creation of user groups. The hierarchical nature of the NDS database enables you to place user objects into container objects. Using this method, you can group users who share the same level of access permissions, for example, so that you have to modify the permissions only at the container level instead of at the individual user object level. However, a user object (or any object in the NDS tree) can be associated with only one container object. Of course, the container object itself can be encompassed by another container object, but it is not possible to just take a single user object and place it into multiple containers at the same time. Instead, you can create a Group object. This kind of object has a property that lists members of the group, which consists of user objects that reside elsewhere in the NDS tree.

The *implicit* group [Public] exists by default and is made up of all users who have a network connection. This includes users who have not been authenticated by NDS. This means that you can effectively assign rights to objects in the database for workstations that do not have to use a username/password to connect to the database. This enables you to assign the Browse right to all users, by creating a trustee assignment for the [Public] group on the root object in the tree. Sometimes, though, letting unauthenticated users even see (browse) the database can be a security problem. In this case you would not want to grant this right to [Public], or you might want to consider removing the browse right using an IRF for sections of the tree.

Unix and Linux

Under Unix and Linux, users will fall into one of the three following camps:

- User
- Group
- Superuser

Every user on a Unix system must be identified by a username, just as in all Windows operating systems, as well as NetWare. The user also can belong to one or more groups, one of which is considered to be the user's primary group. User groups provide a method for assigning access permissions to directories and files based on groups of users with similar needs. Finally, there is a special user called a superuser, whose capabilities on the system are superior to those of ordinary users.

The superuser or root user account is all powerful. The root account, as it is usually called, is represented by the user ID (UID) of zero. This UID can access any file on a local file system and can access information about any process on the system. Some functions that only the superuser can perform on most Unix systems include these:

- Mount or unmount a file system
- Create device special files
- Change another user's password
- Change the date or time on the system clock
- Modify the local network interfaces
- Shut down the system

In Windows it was possible to choose from a large number of specific rights to assign to a user or a group so that different users could perform functions requiring different degrees of access. In the Unix environment, the root user account is the one that possesses the super-powers, so to speak, and to perform these functions you must log in as or become the root user.

File permissions are assigned to each file or directory in the following three categories.

- Owner permissions
- Group permissions
- Other permissions

The first category defines permissions that apply to the owner of the file. Group permissions apply to users who are in a group to which the file belongs. The last category is the permissions that will be applied to all other users who try to access the file. The access permissions that can be granted to each of these categories are as listed here:

- **Read**—This permission enables the user to read the contents of the file. When applied to a directory, this permission enables the user to list the files stored in the directory along with their attributes.

- **Write**—This permission enables the user to change the contents of the file. This right enables a user to add or delete files in a directory.

- **Execute**—For a program file, this right enables the user to execute, or run, the program. For a directory, this right enables the user to access the directory.

Viewing File Permissions

The ls command can be used to show a listing of files along with information about the permissions applied to the files. There are many command-line parameters you can use with this command, but the simple usage shown here is sufficient to view the ownership and permission information about a file:

```
ls -l /usr/bin/two
dr-xr-xr-x  1 two  biz        0 Jul 12 2001 html
dr-xr-xr-x  1 two  biz        0 Feb 13 2001 invoices
-r-xr-xr-x  1 two  biz     1624 Jun 20 2001 notices.txt
-r-xr-xr-x  1 two  biz     1624 Jun 20 2001 appt.dat
```

The first entry in the directory listing shows a directory file named html. You can tell it is a directory because the first character on the line is a d. The next file is also a directory, named invoices. Both of these directories are owned by the user listed in the third column, two. The group the file belongs to is found in the next column and, in these examples, is biz for all entries. The remaining items on each line show the size and date of the file and its name. Note that Unix is case sensitive when it comes to filenames. Keep this in mind when using the ls command with wildcards when hoping to locate a file.

In this listing, the first thing you notice on each line is a string of letters separated by dashes. This string contains the access permissions for the entry. It is sometimes called the *permissions array*. This is followed by other information, separated into columns. Each line represents either a directory or a file in the current directory. The permissions array can be easily deciphered. The first character indicates whether the file is a directory (d) or a user file (-), and the remaining three groups of letters indicate the access permissions for the file's or directory's owner, the file's group, and then a group called "other."

Note that the dashes in the permissions array are not separators. Each position in the array is a fixed place that can either contain a permission for the file or directory or represent the absence of the permission, using the dash (hyphen) character. In the previous listing this means that the owner, group, and world permissions for each of the directories and files listed is Read and Execute (r-x).

Granting permissions to "other" gives the permission to all users on the system. It is important to remember that, in Unix, if you grant access using the world permissions fields, denying access by owner or group fields will not work. Thus, use the world access permissions on files to set values that you would like to apply to all users. For example, if all users will be allowed to read the file, set the Read permission in the world permissions. Use the owner and group fields to grant more restricted access to smaller groups of users.

SUID and SGID File Permissions

In addition to the ordinary permissions that exist to control which users can access a file or directory, two other permissions are used on Unix and Linux systems to give special privileges to executable files. These are called the Set User ID (SUID) and Set Group ID (SGID) permissions. When an executable image is run that has the SUID permission set on it, the image will take on the permissions that are equivalent to those of the owner of the executable file.

The permissions available to a user can also be acquired from group membership. When an executable image is run, it usually runs under the permissions of the user who executes the file and the permissions available to the group to which the user belongs. When the SGID permission is set on an executable, it will inherit permissions from the group of the owner of the file and not the permissions of the user who executes the file.

These two permissions can be very useful. There are times when it is necessary to run a program that must have more access rights than the user who is executing the program. For example, when a user needs to change his password, he needs to be able to make edits to the password file. Because this file is normally protected against writing by most ordinary users, the program that changes your password can get the necessary permission to modify the file. This is a simple example of a process that occurs at many levels in an operating system. Other programs use permissions elevated above the ordinary user to accomplish such tasks as managing print queues and allowing basic system management tasks.

When used on a directory instead of a file, the SUID permission, placed in the group field, indicates that all files created in the directory will take on the ownership of the group that owns the directory.

You can tell from a directory listing (using the ls command) whether the SUID or SGID permission has been set for a file. In the permissions array, the letter s will appear in the position normally used to indicate the owner's execute access. If the s character is lowercase, the Execute permission for the owner is not set. If it is an uppercase S, the Execute permission is also set for the owner.

In a directory file the s character will appear in the character position that normally indicates a group's execute access.

Using the *chmod* and *chown* Commands

When moving files around on the network, it frequently is necessary to change their ownership or the access permissions so that a new set of users can gain the appropriate access. For example, when a user leaves a company, it is usually customary for someone else to take over managing files and important directories for which the user had been responsible. The two commands you can use to modify ownership and access for files are the chmod (change permission mode) and chown (change owner) commands.

The chown command is a simple one. If you are the owner of a file or if you are the superuser, you can use this command to assign a new owner and/or group to a file. The basic syntax is

```
chown [ -fhR ] owner [ : group ] file ...
```

Here, *owner* is the new user or group ID that will be assigned to the file or files represented by *file* .... The -f parameter suppresses error reporting. The -h parameter is used to cause an ownership change to be effective on a symbolic link to a file instead of the actual file the link references. Without this parameter, the ownership is changed on the actual file that is referenced by the symbolic link. The -R parameter causes the command to operate recursively, changing the owner ID for files and subdirectories under the current specification.

You can use chown to easily change the ownership of one or more directories when a new user takes responsibility for them. The chmod command can be used by users and administrators to change the access permissions on files or directories.

The chmod command can be used to change access permissions for the owner, group, or others by specifying the rights by either a numeric or a character format. The numeric format for the chmod command specifies rights as a numeric value, totaling each right as described in the following list:

- **0**—No access
- **1**—Execute file (or search a directory)
- **2**—Write
- **4**—Read

Using this format, you would change the access permissions on a file in a manner similar to this:

```
chmod 666 myfile1
chmod 664 myfile2
chmod 640 myfile3
```

Here the filename myfile1 has its access permissions set to Read + Write (4 + 2 = 6) for the owner, group, and world fields. The file myfile2 is set to Read + Write for the owner and group fields, but to only Read (4) for the other or world field. Finally, myfile3 is set to give the owner Read and Write permissions. The group permission is set to Read only and the other field is set to No Access (0).

Using the other syntax format for the chmod command enables you to change the permission fields without having to memorize numerical values. Instead, you use the letters r (read), w (write), and x (execute) to specify the permissions, and the letters u (user), g (group), o (other), or a (all, indicates user, group, and other) to specify the user field for which a permission will be modified. For example:

```
chmod u+rw myfile1
chmod g+rwx myfile1
chmod o+rw myfile1
```

Here it is easy to see that the user field (user owner, group, or other) is appended to the letter identifying a right (rw, rwx) by the plus sign. This indicates that the right is to be added to the user field indicated for the file myfile1. To remove a right using chmod, use the minus sign:

```
chmod g-x personalfile
chmod o-w specialfile
```

Here the command is used to remove the Execute right from the group for the file named personalfile. For the file named specialfile, the owner has used chmod to remove his own right to write to the file. This is not done for security purposes, but because the owner wants to be sure he doesn't alter the contents of the file by mistake. Because he is the owner, he can always set the mode back to write if it becomes necessary.

Using the *su* Command

To perform some important system management tasks on a Unix or Linux system, only the privileges granted to the root account can be used. Although it would be easy to let multiple system administrators log in to the root account to perform administrative functions, this is not a very good thing to do from the viewpoint of security. If only one account is used, it is difficult to construct an audit trail to determine which administrator performed a specific function.

To get over this limitation, the su command enables you to log in using your normal user account and then become the root user or another user. The log file /var/adm/sulog tracks attempts to become another user using the su command, and so an audit trail is kept to help when troubleshooting. You can use the su command by itself to become the root superuser, or you can use it in the form of su *username* to become another user. In all cases you will be prompted for the password for the user account you want to become, unless you are already logged in to the root account.

The power held by the password to a root account can be seen by how it can be used with this command. As a standard security matter, you should regularly review the /var/adm/sulog log file to keep track of how the command is being used.

Network Printing Protocols

44

SOME OF THE MAIN TOPICS IN THIS CHAPTER ARE

CHAPTER 44

The most basic functions provided by a LAN are the file and print services. A *print server* is a computer or a networked device that has one or more physical printers attached and that accepts data for printing from other computers. You can learn more about print servers in the next chapter.

A parallel port, USB port, or even FireWire (IEEE 1394, also called iLink) port can be used to directly connect a printer to a single computer. The parallel port provides a high-speed connection on a set of wires used exclusively by the printer and the computer for this communication path. USB and FireWire provide much faster communication links between the computer and the printer. Most small-scale printers today support both parallel connections and USB connections. Larger printers intended for enterprise environments also include network adapters, so you can access them from multiple clients on the network without having to send a print job through a server that is directly connected to the printer. Instead, the printer is just like another member of the network.

Tip

When you have a few hundred or thousand (or many more) employees, it is just not economically feasible to give each user a printer. In these large environments, a server is often dedicated to the sole task of processing print jobs. You could audit the print jobs to determine who was making use of the printer, among other features. Now, configuring a client to use a printer directly connected to the network is often a better, less expensive way of providing print services to clients. This doesn't mean that you have to choose one or the other. You can have networked printers, as well as printers connected to computers on the network at the same time.

Most networked printers also support logging their activity to a syslog daemon. That is, they can send their operational and auditing information to a syslog daemon running on another Unix/Linux computer, and thus provide you, to some degree, an audit trail as well as report errors. Windows servers can record printing events in the system error log files for printers that are connected to the server, which you can view using the Event Viewer. You can also use Windows server computers to make a connection to networked printers, acting as a gateway for clients. In this manner, the Windows error logs can also record information about print jobs for the networked printers they manage.

In anything but a very small network, you will also find that it is *more efficient* to connect a printer to the network, instead of a computer. This can be done in two ways: purchase a printer that comes with a network connection (such as the HP JetDirect), or use a small print server device that connects one or more printers to the network.

In this chapter, we'll look primarily at the protocols used to communicate with a printer, or a print server, to exchange data and command information.

Printing Protocols and Printing Languages

A printer language is not the same as a printer protocol. For example, PostScript and PCL (Printer Control Language) are languages that describe how a document is to be rendered into the final printed product by the printer. When a printer is directly connected to a printer port on a computer, the printer language is important and is used by the software driver to format the information being sent to the printer.

A network protocol, however, is used to send the formatted job, both data and instructions compiled using the printer language, to the printer. A few protocols will be detailed here that are more specific in their use and implementation; that is, they generally are used for communicating with a printer.

Several protocols are used for network printing. Some are proprietary protocols used by only one computer or network operating system (NOS). Others, such as lpr/lpd—which was first developed for use on Unix networks—have been implemented in many environments. Data Link Control (DLC) is an

IBM protocol that has been adapted for use on many printers although it is not used much today. This chapter covers the basics of these major protocols, with examples from Unix, Windows Servers, and NetWare systems.

Also covered is the newest printing protocol: the Internet Printing Protocol (IPP), which was created by a working committee of the Internet Engineering Task Force (IETF). Development is underway for standards to further define this new protocol. You will find, however, that both Windows 2000/2003/XP and NetWare 6.x already support IPP. Novell even sells its iPrint as a separate product that can be used in a non-NetWare environment.

Note

The abbreviation IPP is also used in some books to mean Internet Presence Provider. If you are studying for a certification exam, be sure to interpret the usage of this term by the context in which it is used.

Using lpr/lpd and the TCP Stream Protocols

TCP/IP was originally developed for the Unix operating system (OS), of which there are several flavors. Depending on the version of Unix (as well as Linux) running on a workstation or server, you will find that TCP/IP printing falls into one of two major types:

- BSD (Berkeley System Distribution) Spooling System
- SVR4 (System V, Release 4) Printing System

The BSD system uses the lpr (line printer remote) program to send files to printers. The printers can be connected to a network, or to a computer. Whichever way, the lpd (line printer daemon) receives these print requests and interacts with the lpr to send the print job to the printer. The /etc/printcap text file is used to set up characteristics for each printer. The SVR4 Unix system uses the lp (line printer) program and the lpsched daemon (printer scheduler) to print files. Although the SVR4 system is considered more sophisticated because it has several utility commands for managing the system, the BSD system probably is easier to manage in a networked environment.

When using either of these methods, the actual print commands and data are sent to the printer in the payload section of a TCP/IP packet.

Although all Unix and Linux systems support TCP/IP printing, many support other protocols as well. For example, Red Hat Linux can also be configured to use SMB (Server Message Block) to connect to a Windows server (or a Unix/Linux computer configured to offer printing services using SMB).

The lpr/lpd protocols work well, but are mostly used by older operating systems. In the next chapter, "Print Servers," you can learn about how to configure lpr/lpd printing on Unix/Linux servers, as well as Windows systems.

TCP/IP stream sockets the Unix provide yet another way to use TCP/IP to connect to a printer. Streams are a two-way communication TCP/IP session between the computer (or print server). When using TCP/IP streams, you need to specify a port (also known as a socket in Windows terminology). Thus the address of the networked printer, paired with a port number, provides a unique address so that the data exchange can be accomplished.

Note

The TCP/IP suite includes protocols (such as TCP, UDP, and IP) and a set of services and utilities based on them. For more information about TCP/IP, see Chapter 25, "Overview of the TCP/IP Protocol Suite."

Data Link Control Protocol (DLC)

For all practical)purposes, DLC is rarely found anymore in the network. This IBM protocol was widely used during the early days of networked printing, as well as for other applications. However, more robust protocols, such as TCP/IP, have made this protocol a less desirable solution for network printing.

The DLC protocol was developed by IBM primarily for use in connecting to mainframe computers as part of its Systems Network Architecture (SNA) specifications. DLC can also be used to establish terminal sessions with AS/400 computers. In addition to the HP Jet Direct card, you will find that other vendors also make network cards for printers that can use DLC. For example, the Brother NC-600X and NC-2010h network cards both can be used for this purpose. However, you'll find that DLC no longer is present in Windows systems starting with Windows) XP.

Internet Printing Protocol (IPP)

The Internet Printing Protocol (IPP) has gained high visibility as more computers become dependent on LAN as well as Internet resources. Although most network servers and clients can be configured to use the lpr/lpd, Telnet, or DLC protocols, there are still many other protocols that can be used to send data to printers, such as SPX/IPX. The driving force of the Internet is making many vendors conscious of the need for more unified standards for basic functions, such as file and print sharing, and new protocols are being developed to meet those needs.

In 1996, several groups were developing a new standard. Novell and Xerox were working on a protocol that was titled Lightweight Document Printing Application (LDPA), IBM was developing the Hypertext Printing Protocol (HTPP), and Microsoft and HP were working on still another new protocol. Finally, a working group was formed under the auspices of the Internet Engineering Task Force (IETF) to work on a new standard. IPP uses the Hypertext Transfer Protocol (v. 1.1) as the underlying transport protocol.

Note

When an important new network protocol is developed, it is usually the case that the Institute of Electrical and Electronics Engineers (IEEE) will create a working committee and establish a standard for that protocol. Keep in mind that Request for Comments (RFC) documents—discussed throughout this book—are issued under the auspices of the IETF, and many of these RFCs are used, along with other input, to develop an IEEE standard. To continue this process, other international standards organizations usually cooperate to produce standards that are used worldwide.

If you want to keep up-to-date with the latest developments of the IEEE in regard to IPP, visit the IEEE Printer Working Group (PWG) at its Web site, `www.pwg.org/ipp`.

The goals of the first) efforts of the project were to develop a protocol that defines the user end of the printing process and includes the following capabilities, as well as a few other features:

- Allow the user to discover the capabilities of a particular printer.
- Allow the user to submit jobs to the printer.
- Allow the user to get the status of the printer or a print job.
- Allow the user to cancel a print job.
- Define a set of directory attributes that make it easy to find a printer in a directory database.

All these are standard items incorporated into the first version of the standard (1.0).

Security and authentication mechanisms are also being created for IPP—just as for many other protocols that access the Internet.

The newest version of this protocol is 1.1. It is being developed by the RFC process, as well as the IEEE standards process. Following is a list of RFCs that have been written (as either a draft or an established standard) for version 1.2 of IPP:

The work of the original IPP group so far was defined by several RFCs. Version 1.0 RFCs include the following

- RFC 2565, "Internet Printing Protocol/1.0: Encoding and Transport"
- RFC 2566, "Internet Printing Protocol/1.0: Model and Semantics"
- RFC 2567, "Design Goals for an Internet Printing Protocol"
- RFC 2568, "Rationale for the Structure of the Model and Protocol for the Internet Printing Protocol"
- RFC 2569, "Mapping Between LPD and IPP Protocols"
- RFC 2639, "Internet Printing Protocol/1.0: Implementers Guide"

Version 1.1 of IPP is defined (at this time) by the following RFCs:

- RFC 2910, "IPP/1.1: Encoding and Transport"
- RFC 2911, "IPP/1.1: Model and Semantics"
- RFC 3196, "Internet Printing Protocol/1.1: Implementer's Guide"

Additional Internet Draft documents are still in the review stage and will add additional functionality to the protocol. For example, see also the following RFCs:

- RFC 3239, "IPP Requirements for Job, Printer, and Device Administrative Operations"
- RFC 3380, "IPP: Job and Printer Set Operations"
- RFC 3381, "IPP: Job Progress Attributes"
- RFC 3382, "IPP: The 'collection' Attribute Syntax"

Although standards bodies continue to refine and add new functionality to IPP, that has not stopped software vendors from using the protocol. If you want to keep abreast of newer developments in the IPP standards process, search for IPP at www.rfc-editor.org, as well as the previously mentioned Web site of the IEEE working committee.

IPP Object Types

In the first version of this protocol, two basic object types are defined: *printer* and *print job*. The printer object encompasses the functions that are accomplished by the actual physical printer, rendering the printed page, as well as some of the functions that are traditionally performed by the print server, such as spooling the print file and handling scheduling procedures. The functions of the printer object can be implemented in a print server or on the printer itself. The printer object can be used to send output to a single physical printer or to more than one device.

When a user sends a document to a printer, the printer object creates a new object called a print job. The print job object contains the document to be printed and can contain more than one document per job. The printer object manipulates the print job and handles how it is sent to the physical printer.

IPP Operations

The protocol defines several operations, which consist of a request and a response. The operation allows the client to communicate with the object.

These are the operations defined in the first version of the protocol that can be used with the printer object:

- Print-Job
- Print-URI
- Validate-Job
- Create-Job
- Get-Printer-Attributes
- Get-Jobs

The operations that can be used with the print job object are as defined here:

- Send-Document
- Send-URI
- Cancel-Job
- Get-Job-Attributes

Note

The term URI used in these operations refers to Uniform Resource Identifier, which is described in RFC 2396. URIs are used to unambiguously identify an object. You might be familiar with the term URL, which stands for Uniform Resource Locator, another standardized term that can unambiguously identify a location for a resource. The concept here is similar in that a unique identifier is assigned to the print job.

A client submits a document to print by using the Print-Job request. Using this operation, the client "pushes" or sends the text to be printed. A client also can submit a job using the Print-URI operation, in which the client sends only the URI reference for the data to be printed and the printer object "pulls" the data itself. To send multiple documents to be printed, the client uses the Create-Job operation followed by multiple Send-Document or Send-URI operations, which also operate in a push-pull fashion.

The printer object responds to Validate-Job requests from the client depending on the current state of the printing job (pending, processing, and so on). For example, the printer object might return a message to the client indicating that the URI is no longer valid. Or the printer object might return error messages to the client.

Other operations are fairly self-explanatory. The Get-Printer-Attributes and Get-Job-Attributes operations return information about the printer or the print job. The Get-Jobs operation allows the client to get a list of job objects that are being processed by the particular Printer object. The Cancel-Job operation is used by the client to remove a job from the Printer object, basically just stopping a job from printing.

The RFCs also go into detail describing the attributes of each object, some of which are required and some of which are optional. These attributes include information about the job, such as its name, time stamps for different parts of the printing process, and the output device assigned to print the job. Attributes for the printer object include the name of the printer, its location, the location of the printer driver for the printer, and other information, such as the make and model of the printer.

What's in Store for Version 1.1?

Version 1.1 of IPP has added more functionality to the protocol. Several new operations have been defined:

- Pause-Printer
- Resume-Printer
- Purge-Printer

In addition, Version 1.1 suggests the order in which steps should be taken by an IPP 1.1 implementation. In general, these are as listed here:

1. Validate the protocol version.
2. Validate the requested operation.
3. Validate the presence of operation attributes.
4. Validate the values of operation attributes.
5. Validate the attribute values against the object's supported values.
6. Validate any optional operation attributes.

For each request or response, the protocol version number must be included. This value and its semantics are kept in the same place in the packet for future versions to provide for backward compatibility. Next, the operation identifier must be validated against the printer object's operations-supported attribute. The presence of operation attributes and their values are then evaluated, followed by the validation of optional attributes.

If the IPP object receives from a client a request message that is missing a required attribute, or the attribute groups are presented out of order, the object rejects the request.

The IPP protocol has already been widely adopted by major operating vendors, such as Microsoft and Novell NetWare. It will solve a lot of problems for both end users and vendors of printing equipment. Many companies are beginning to use the Internet to create virtual private networks (VPNs) instead of creating WANs using leased lines and other dedicated links. As the Internet continues to weave itself into every nook and cranny of the modern business world, standards such as IPP will generate new types of services. It is easy to foresee a business segment that will take over handling some, or all, of the aspects of printing for a large organization. Standards such as IPP will make implementation of these sorts of services much easier because it won't rely on multiple proprietary protocols and skill sets.

In addition to helping you manage printing across your own private network, IPP might provide some promising business opportunities for those who are clever enough to take advantage of them. For example, using IPP, you could set up a printer to allow your clients to send purchase orders and other documents straight to your desktop. Or you could use IPP to "publish" your product sales literature, catalogs, and documentation, directly to a customer's printer.

Where Can You Find IPP?

A large number of vendors have adopted the IPP protocol, most notably Windows 2000 (Server and Workstation), Windows 2003 and XP Professional, and NetWare 6.x (iPrint). You can submit a job to a printer on the Internet by specifying the URL for the printer.

In the next chapter are a few examples of how to configure, manage, and use IPP.

Print Servers

CHAPTER 45

In the preceding chapter, several protocols that typically are used for printing on a network were discussed. In this chapter, you'll examine some of the ways in which printers can be configured, deployed on the network, and made available to users. This function traditionally has been accomplished by using a computer that has a printer directly attached to it. It is now commonplace in large networks to connect printers directly to the network so that any computer can access the printer. You should be sure to determine the mechanisms that your operating system uses to grant/deny access to networked printers.

It is also easy to attach multiple printers to a network directly, yet still manage them from a central *print server* computer. A print server can take the load off of individual workstations by storing local copies of the files to be printed, as well as giving the network administrator a central point for administrating printing services. By routing the print traffic through a computer that acts as a print server (or hardware print server device), the network administrator is better able to control access to these printers and gather statistics that can be used to improve network performance. In addition, small network devices (usually described as network printer appliances) are small hublike devices that attach to the network. These devices provide several ports, such as the traditional parallel and serial ports and Ethernet ports (for printers that come network ready), as well as newer ports, such as USB and FireWire, so you can connect multiple printers to the network using a single connection.

This chapter looks at managing print servers using Unix/Linux, Windows NT/XP/2000/2003, and NetWare operating systems, and it takes a quick look at network print server appliances.

Unix/Linux Printing

There are two ways of setting up a print server on Unix or Linux computers. This is because there are two major types of Unix, which is where TCP/IP printing was first used. In the following sections you will learn about how to configure printers for Unix/Linux computers, using

- The BSD Spooling System: lpr and lpd
- The SVR4 Printing System

The BSD Spooling System: lpr and lpd

In BSD printing, the user sends files to print by using the line printer remote (lpr) utility; the line printer daemon (lpd) handles the details needed to get the data in the file formatted and sent to the physical output print device.

To set up a printer on a Unix/Linux system that uses lpr/lpd, you need to do several things. How you accomplish them depends on your particular brand of Unix (or Linux) and whether the vendor has supplied script files or applications to help automate the process. These are the basic actions you need to take to configure a print server that will use lpr/lpd:

- Physically connect the printer to a port on the server computer or print server or, alternatively, configure a network printer with a TCP/IP address so that you can direct print jobs to it.
- Create a special device file that Unix (and most Linux OSs) use to reference devices if the printer is connected physically to the computer.
- Create entries in the printer configuration file (/etc/printcap) that describe the characteristics of this printer, along with management items such as accounting or log files.
- Create the directories that will be used to store files while they are waiting to print (spooling directory).
- Place commands in the appropriate Unix startup file (rc file) to start the lpd daemon when the system boots.

Tip

The steps described to set up lpr/lpd printing are given here so that you can understand how to configure Unix/Linux systems to interact with printers. However, as Unix and Linux are becoming more popular alternatives to Windows and other operating systems, setting up printers has also become a much easier process. For example, Red Hat Linux (as well as other flavors of Linux) can usually detect when a new printer has been connected to the system and load the appropriate drivers and configure the printer automatically—just as most Windows operating systems can. Yet if you are a network administrator, trying to solve a printing problem, you should be familiar with the files, devices, and other configurable aspects of printing under Unix/Linux.

To create the special device file, use the command /dev/makedev *port*. The *port* should be the port on the server to which the printer is attached. Typically, the parallel ports are named lpt*n* (that is, lpt1, lpt2...). If the printer is connected to a serial port, the name of the port probably will be in the form of tty*nn* (that is, tty01, tty02...). Check your system documentation to make sure you have the correct port name. Depending on the system, you might also have to make further adjustments to configure the port, such as setting the speed.

Tip

After you have attached a printer and configured the port, you can use the **lptest** command to send a simple stream of ASCII characters to the port. This confirms whether you have been successful up to this point. You also can use this command when a printer suddenly stops printing to test simple connectivity. If the printer had been functioning normally but stops unexpectedly, and **lptest** does not succeed, you might want to check the cabling or fault lights on the printer itself.

To create the spool directory, use the mkdir command. The spooling directory usually is created under the /var/spool/lpd directory. After you create a directory for the printer, use the chmod, chgrp, and chown commands to set the proper ownership and permission mode (for the lpd daemon). For example:

```
# cd /var/spool/lpd
# mkdir laser1
# chmod 775 laser1
# chgrp daemon laser1
# chown daemon laser1
```

The lpr command is used for printing files in the BSD system. The syntax for this command is

```
lpr [-parameters][filename...]
```

Everything but the command itself is optional. You can specify one or more files, but if you do not specify a filename, the text to be printed comes from *standard input*. Depending on how your particular Unix vendor has implemented the command, you have a lot of options to choose from, including these:

- #—Specifies the number of copies to print.
- c—The date file(s) to be printed were created by the cifplot filter.
- C—Text following the C ("Job Classification") character is printed on the *burst page* for the print job.
- d—Indicates that the data file(s) to be printed contain data created by the tex command.
- f—Printing FORTRAN files. The first character in each line is interpreted as a FORTRAN carriage control character.

- **g**—The data file(s) to be printed contain data created by a program using the standard plot routines.

- **h**—Suppresses printing the burst page.

- **i** *Indent value*—If a job is printed with an indent of 8 spaces by default, you can change it with this parameter. This value is passed to the Unix input filter, which does the actual formatting of the data to be printed.

- **J** *Job*—Text following the J character is printed on the burst page for the print job. If this parameter is not used, the name of the first file on the print command line is used on the burst page.

- **l**—Control characters are printed and page breaks suppressed.

- **m**—Send a mail message after the job is printed.

- **n**—The data file(s) to be printed contain data created by the ditroff command.

- **p**—Uses the pr command as the filter to process the print job.

- **P**—Name of the destination printer.

- **r**—Removes the file when spooling (or printing using the -s parameter).

- **s**—Indicates that the file should not be spooled. Instead, a symbolic link is used. This is a good option to use when printing large files, or a large number of files, to minimize consumption of disk space.

- **T** *Title*—Used with the -p option, which causes the pr command to be used to format the file to be printed. Text specified with this parameter is passed to pr. If blank spaces or special characters are used, the text should be enclosed by single quotes (' ').

- **t**—Indicates that the data file(s) to be printed contain binary data created by the troff command.

- **v**—The data file(s) to be printed are in raster image format.

- **w**—Number of columns. This parameter specifies the number of characters on the page (width).

Tip

A *burst page* or *banner page*, sometimes called a separator page, refers to a page that is printed at the beginning or end of a print job and is used to separate one user's print job from the next. In a high-volume printing environment, these pages make it easier to identify print jobs so that they can be distributed to the appropriate user.

This extensive list of parameters is shown here to make the point that the lpr/lpd printing system is highly configurable from the network administrator's point of view. It might look more complex at first glance than it actually is. For example, the command

```
lpr -Phplj1 letter01.txt report.txt
```

is all you need to use to send the files letter01.txt and report.txt to a printer named hplj1. In most circumstances, the user will not use a large subset of these parameters, but only a smaller combination that fits his work environment. Many of these parameters have default values. For example, if the printer is not specified by using the -P parameter, the Unix environment variable PRINTER will be evaluated and used for the destination of the print job.

After the lpr command has determined the printer to which the data will be sent, it scans the /etc/printcap file to get information about the printer, such as the spooling directory path. It then creates several temporary files and notifies the lpd daemon that the file is ready to print.

The lpd Daemon Controls the Printing Process

The `lpr` command creates a data file in the spooling directory associated with the printer and a control file that contains information telling the lpd daemon how the file should be printed. This daemon process usually starts up when the system boots by commands found in one of the rc files. However, when troubleshooting printing problems, it's often necessary to kill the lpd daemon process and restart it. The syntax for restarting the daemon is

```
lpd [-l] [-Llogfile] [port#]
```

The `-l` parameter tells the daemon to record valid network requests in a log file. The uppercase parameter `-L` is used to specify the name of the logfile. The *port#* parameter is used to specify the Internet port number the daemon will use for process-to-process communications.

When the daemon first starts, it reads the `/etc/printcap` file to obtain information about the printers it can use. If any print jobs are outstanding from the time it was last running, the daemon begins to print them after it reads the `printcap` file.

When it needs to actually print a file, the lpd daemon first checks to see whether another lpd daemon process is currently processing print jobs for that particular printer. If so, it passes the print job to that daemon. If not, the lpd daemon spawns a copy of itself for the printer destination, and that process continues to process jobs for the printer. The original lpd daemon that starts at boot time continues to listen for print requests and spawn new copies of itself when needed. A spawned copy of the daemon continues to run until there are no more files to print on the printer it was invoked to handle.

The lpd daemon and its spawned copies control the printing process but do not perform the mechanics needed to get the data to the printer. Instead, the lpd daemon runs a filter program that sends the data to the printer, and optionally does some formatting that is needed to make the data compatible with the specific printer.

Caution

In a multiuser environment a locking mechanism can be used to prevent multiple processes from trying to access the same resource at the same time. When a new lpd daemon is spawned to perform print-processing functions, it creates a lock file (by using the Unix system call **flock**) in the spooling directory. This lock file remains in the directory while this particular lpd daemon processes files to prevent other lpd daemons from being spawned for the particular directory. The lock file is a simple ASCII file that contains the process ID (PID) of the current lpd daemon and the name of the control file for the current print job.

When troubleshooting lpd daemons, you can examine the lock file to determine whether the daemon listed there is still running. In some versions of Unix, the second line of the lock file also shows the status of the current job as the daemon believes it to be. In some other versions, a file named **status** is used for this purpose.

The /etc/printcap Configuration File

When you set up printing on a Unix computer that uses lpr/lpd, you must create the `/etc/printcap` file. Keep a written log listing changes as you make them to this file so that if something suddenly goes wrong with a printer that has been working just fine, you can check the log to determine whether anyone has recently made a change to the entry in the `printcap` file for the troublesome printer. This file is not a user-friendly file. In many cases, the syntax for each entry is just a few lines, but for complicated setups, editing this file can become confusing if you make changes infrequently.

Tip

Because the `printcap` file is itself a simple ASCII text file, you can make recovering from configuration issues easier by simply printing the file itself each time you make a change (or copying to a different filename, such as `printcap.sav`). In this manner, you can keep track of modifications to the file and have a back-out plan. And, if you ever have a problem, you can look at the changes that have been made and then make the appropriate corrections to the `printcap` file.

Entries in this file specify the name used for a printer along with two-character symbol/value pairs (*symbol=value*) that define the characteristics for the printer. The printer can have multiple names (aliases), which are separated by a vertical-bar character. For example, an entry for a printer named laser could be as simple as this:

```
laser|laser1|lp|lp0|HP Laser Jet Accounting:\
   :sd=/var/spool/lpd/laser:\
   :lp=/dev/tty01:
```

The first line contains the name of the printer (`laser`), followed by several alias names that users can use to access the printer. The last alias on the first line shows a common technique used by many administrators: Describe the printer and/or its location. You also can put comments into the /etc/printcap file by using the pound-sign character (#) as the first character in the line. In this example, you also can see that the colon character (:) is used to separate the symbol/value pairs from each other. Although only one colon character is needed between each pair, it's customary to put one at the beginning of a line and one at the end of the line when the entry spans multiple lines. The following two entries are equivalent:

```
:sd=/var/spool/lpd/laser1:br#9600:
```

```
:sd=/var/spool/lpd/laser1:\
:br#9600:
```

Note that the backslash character (\) is used to indicate continuation of the entry across multiple lines. Also, some entries in the file do not have a value. For example, some are Boolean entries that have no associated value and are activated by their presence in the file.

In these examples, the sd symbol is followed by a directory path. This specifies the spooling directory that lpd will use to store files that are waiting to be printed. Multiple users can send files to the printer using the lpr command. Copies of the files to be printed are created by the lpd daemon in the spooling directory and remain there until they are printed. After a file has been printed, the lpd daemon deletes the control and data files used for it.

The lp symbol is used to indicate the special device file for the printer. In Unix, device files are used as a link to a physical device. The makdev command is used to create the device file just as for any other device attached to the computer. However, in the case of a remote printer, use the hostname/queue name on the remote system for this value instead of a device filename. Entries can be much more complex than in this simple example. Table 45.1 lists the symbols you can use to customize a printer.

Table 45.1   Symbols Used in the */etc/printcap* File

Symbol	Type	Default Value	Description
af	string	NULL	Name of accounting file.
br	numeric	no default	Baud rate if lp is a tty.
cf	string	NULL	The cifplot data filter.
df	string	NULL	The TeX data filter (DVI format).

Table 45.1 **Continued**

Symbol	Type	Default Value	Description
du	string	no default	Used to specify a nonstandard user ID for the daemon.
fc	numeric	0	If lp is a tty, clear flag bits.
ff	string	/f	String to send to printer for form feed.
fo	Boolean	false	Print a form feed when device is opened.
fs	numeric	0	If lp is a tty, set flag bits.
gf	string	NULL	Graph data filter (plot format).
hl	Boolean	false	Print the burst header page last.
ic	Boolean	false	Driver supports (nonstandard) ioctl to indent on printout.
if	string	NULL	Accounting text filter.
lf	string	/dev/console	Name of error logging file.
lo	string	lock	Name of lock file.
lp	string	/dev/lp	Output device.
mc	numeric	0	Maximum number of copies allowed.
mx	numeric	1000	Maximum file size (in BUFSIZ blocks)—zero means unlimited.
nf	string	NULL	The ditroff data filter (device independent troff).
of	string	NULL	Output filtering program.
pc	numeric	200	Price per foot or page (in hundredths of cents).
pl	numeric	66	Page length in lines.
pw	numeric	132	Page width in characters.
px	numeric	0	Page width in pixels (horizontal).
py	numeric	0	Page length in pixels (vertical).
rf	string	NULL	The FORTRAN-style text file filter.
rg	string	NULL	Restricted group. Only members of this group are allowed access to the printer.
rm	string	NULL	Machine name for remote printer.
rp	string	lp	Remote printer name argument.
rs	Boolean	false	Restrict remote users to only those who have local accounts.
rw	Boolean	false	Open the print device for read/write.
sb	Boolean	false	Short (one-line) banner.
sc	Boolean	false	Suppress multiple copies.
sd	string	/usr/spool/lpd or /var/spool/lpd	Spooling directory.
sf	Boolean	false	Suppress form feeds.
sh	Boolean	false	Suppress printing of burst page header.
st	string	status	Name of status file.
tf	string	NULL	Name of troff data filter (cat phototypesetter).

Table 45.1   Continued

Symbol	Type	Default Value	Description
tr	string	NULL	Trailer string to print when queue is emptied (that is, form feeds or escape characters).
vf	string	NULL	Raster image filter.
xc	numeric	0	If lp is a tty, clear local mode bits.
xs	numeric	0	If lp is a tty, set local mode bits.

Following is an example of a more complicated entry:

```
lp|lp0|Color Laser: \
   :af=/usr/adm/printer/clp.acct:\
   :br#9600:\
   :lf=/usr/adm/lpterror:\
   :lp=/dev/tty05:\
   :mx#0:\
   :sd=/var/spool/lpd:\
```

This example defines the spooling directory for a printer, as well as the logfile and accounting file. The mx#0 entry means there is no maximum size limit for files that can print on this printer.

When specifying a printer device, you also can tell the lpd daemon to use a print queue that resides on another system. For example:

```
xprint|laser2|Manufacturing printer:\
   :lp=:\
   :rm=mfgunix:\
   :rp=lp:\
   :sd=/var/spool/lpd/xprint:\
   :mx#0:\
```

In this example, the lp symbol is set to null. This indicates that the print device is not on this system. You still have to include the lp symbol so that the default value for it will not be substituted by the lpd daemon. The rm symbol is used to indicate the hostname of the remote computer, and the rp symbol is used to define the name of the printer on that system. Also, even though the actual printing is done on the remote computer, you must specify a spooling directory because files submitted to the queue still need to be temporarily stored before they are copied to the remote system.

Useful Commands: *lpq, lprm, and lpc*

From the user's perspective, printing is a simple task. Just use the lpr command and wait for the paper to come out of the printer. As the administrator, you need commands that can help you manage print queues and track usage.

The lpq command shows information about jobs waiting in the print queue. The information this command shows you includes the following:

■ The order of print jobs in the queue

■ The name of the user who submitted the job to print

■ The job identification number

■ The names of files waiting to print

■ The size of the print job (in bytes)

For example:

```
Rank  Owner      Job Files          Total Size
active ogletree   133 prm0d1x        31540 bytes
1st   heywood    141 letter1        3423 bytes
2nd   chasog     216 jandata        98465 bytes
3rd   peter      323 twoinchtml      2342 bytes
4th   menton     122 queulst        55432 bytes
```

You can use the -P parameter to specify the printer just like you can with the lpr command. Similarly, the Unix environment variable PRINTER determines the printer to display if you do not specify one. The syntax for the lpq command is as follows:

```
lpq [-Pprinter][-1][+[interval]][job#...][username...]
```

The -1 parameter causes a "long" listing (more output, additional information) to be displayed. The plus sign (+) can be used by itself or with a numeric value, and it causes the command to continuously display the status until the print queue empties. If you follow the plus sign with a numeric value, it is used as the number of seconds between each refresh interval.

Use the job ID numbers or the user's username when troubleshooting specific print jobs so that you won't have to look through a long listing of all print jobs. The job ID number also can be used by other print-queue management commands, so it is common to use lpq to get a job's ID number before executing other commands.

To remove a print job from the queue, you can use the lprm command. Its syntax is similar to the lpq command:

```
lprm [-Pprinter][-][job#...][username...]
```

Although any user can remove her own files that are pending in a print queue, only the superuser (root account) can remove other users' files. You can specify the job ID number associated with a specific file, or you can specify a username to remove all print jobs currently pending in the queue for that user.

Note

To remove jobs from a print queue, the **lprm** command actually kills the current lpd daemon that is processing files for that queue. It then deletes the specific files from the print queue and restarts a new daemon process to continue processing the remaining files.

Examining a print queue and removing pending jobs can be useful for troubleshooting simple problems. For more control over the BSD printing system, you can use the lpc (line printer control) command. The syntax for this command is more complicated than that of the lpq and lprm commands because of the more complex functions it can perform. The syntax for lpc is as follows:

```
lpc [command [parameters...]]
```

These are the commands you can use with lpc:

- **abort [all | *printer*...]**—Kills the active lpd daemon and then disables printing for the specified printers. Stops the print job that is currently printing. After this, lpr will not be able to create a new lpd daemon for the specified printers. Use this option when you need to quickly disable a printer.

- **clean [all | *printer*...]**—Removes temporary files (including control and data files) from the specified printer's spooling directory when the files do not form a complete print job. Useful for "cleaning up" a spool directory when something has gone wrong.

- **disable [all | *printer*...]**—Prevents lpr from submitting new print jobs to this print queue. This command turns off printing for the specified queue.

- **down [all | *printer*...] *message*...**—Turns off the print queue and disables printing. *Message...* text is entered into the status file for the printer so that lpq can report it.

- **enable [all | *printer*...]**—Enables spooling on the printer(s) so that users can begin to use the lpr command to submit print jobs.

- **restart [all | *printer*...]**—Starts a new daemon for the queue. When a printer daemon dies unexpectedly, you can use this command. The jobs currently existing in the queue are printed by the new daemon. You should perform this command when the lpq command gives you the no daemon present message.

- **start [all | *printer*...]**—Enables printing and starts a spooling daemon for the printers specified. Changes the owner's execute permission on the lock file to accomplish their tasks.

- **status [all | *printer*...]**—Gets the status of printer daemons and queues. Shows whether the queue is enabled or disabled, or whether printing is enabled or disabled. Also shows the number of entries in the queue and the status of the printer's lpd daemon.

- **stop [all | *printer*...]**—Stops a spooling daemon and disables printing. The daemon stops after it finishes the current print job. Use the abort command if you want to stop the daemon and kill the current job that is printing.

- **topq *printer* [*job#.. .*][*username*...]**—Moves print jobs to the top of the queue. Use this to bypass the normal first-in, first-out (FIFO) order of printing. Specify one or more job numbers as an argument to this command. Specify a username as the argument to move all jobs pending for that user to the top of the queue.

- **up [all | *printer*...]**—Enables all printing and starts a new printer daemon. Opposite of the down command.

- **exit or quit**—Causes the lpc program to exit (when in interactive mode).

- **? [*command*] or help [*command*]**—Displays a short help text for each *command*. If no command is specified after the help command, a list of all commands that the lpc program recognizes is displayed.

Although the lpc program usually is used by an administrator (the root user account, sometimes referred to as the superuser account), ordinary users can use the restart and status commands.

The following is an example of using the lpc command to get the status of a printer named laser1. In this example, the queue is enabled and printing. Only one job is in the queue. When you use the command without command-line parameters, it prompts you in interactive mode:

```
% /usr/sbin/lpc
lpc> status laser2
laser1:
    printer is on device '/dev/tty03' speed 9600
    queuing is enabled
    printing is enabled
    1 entry in spool area
lpc>quit
```

In this next example, the lpd daemon for this queue has exited unexpectedly. Using the lpc command, you can detect this condition and fix the problem:

```
% /usr/sbin/lpc
lpc> status laser2
```

```
laser2:
    printer is on device '/dev/tty03' speed 9600
    queuing is enabled
    printing is enabled
    7 entries in spool area
    no daemon present
lpc> restart laser2
lpc>quit
```

Examining Printing Statistics

Part of managing a network is gathering statistics. This is done for several reasons. First, historical data is nice to have when you are trying to determine the circumstances leading up to a problem. Second, statistical data can help you plan for enough capacity when you are deciding on expansion or reorganization. Another use for the information is user or department accountability. In environments where costs are charged back to a department, you can use the pac command to gather the data you need.

The syntax for this command is

```
pac [-Pprinter][-cmrs][-pprice][username]
```

As is the custom with other printing commands, the -P parameter allows you to specify a printer. If you do not, the value of PRINTER is used; otherwise, the system default printer is assumed. These are the other parameters you can use:

- **c**—Sorts the report by cost instead of machine/username.
- **m**—Groups charges by username with no regard to the hostname of the computer from which the job(s) were submitted.
- **r**—Reverses the sort order for the report.
- **s**—Summarizes the accounting data and writes it to a summary file. The summary file is usually in the form of *printer*.acct_sum.
- **pprice**—Allows you to specify the cost per unit (foot or page) for print jobs. The default is two cents per unit.
- **username**—If you supply usernames at the end of the command, only statistics for print jobs for those users are included in the report.

Tip

You can include the **pac** command in script files to create automated procedures to produce accounting reports. For example, you could use a script file to produce reports by user or department, and then email a copy of the report to a responsible person.

The following output shows the type of information you can get by using the pac command. The costs for each print job are just simple calculations based on the unit and the cost you supply to the command, as the following illustrates:

```
Login           pages/feet    runs   price
atlunix1:harris   14.00         1     $ 0.28
atlunix1:brown    3.00          2     $ 0.06
pluto:ogletree    21.00         3     $ 0.42
```

The SVR4 Printing System

Another major type of Unix variant is the System V, Version 4 (SVR4) system. The SVR4 printing system uses the `lp` command and `lpsched` command to print and manage printer queues. Although an `/etc/printcap` file also is used, it doesn't have to be edited manually. The lpadmin utility will do this for you.

Using `lp`, `cancel`, and `lpstat`

The `lp` command is used just like the `lpr` command. However, the `lp` command does more than just send files to a printer; it also can be used to modify print jobs. The `cancel` command is used to remove a job from the print queue. The syntax for the `lp` command comes in two different forms:

```
lp [-c][-m][-p][-s][-w][-d dest]
  [-f form-name [-d any]][-H special-handling]
  [-n number][-o option][-P page-list]
  [-q priority-level][-S character-set][-d any]]
  [-S print-wheel[-d any]][-t title]
  [-T content-type][-r]][-y mode-list]
  [filename...]

lp -i request-id ... [-c][-m][-p][-s][-w]
  [-d dest][-f form-name[-d any]]
  [-H special-handling][-n number][-o option]
  [-P page-list][-q priority-level]
  [-S character-set[-d any]]]
  [-t title][-T content-type[-r]]
  [-y mode-list]
```

The first version of this command is used to send files to print. The second version is used to modify a print request that is already pending. If you use the second version to modify a job that is already printing, it stops the job and restarts it with the changes you have made.

These are the parameters you can use with the `lp` command:

- **c**—A copy of the file to be made before it is printed. The default action is to create a link to the file. If you use the `-c` parameter, you should not remove (delete) the file before it is printed. Any changes you make to the file after submitting the print request will not be reflected in the output if you use this parameter to create a copy of the file.

- **d** *dest*—Specifies the destination printer or class for the print job.

- **f** *form-name*—Specifies a form to be mounted on the printer to process the print request. If the printer does not support the form, the request is rejected. Note that if you use the `-d any` parameter with this one, the print request can be sent to any printer that supports the form.

- **H** *special-handling*—Puts the print request on hold or resumes requests that are holding. If you are an LP administrator, this command causes the request to be the next one to print. The terms you use for *special-handling* are hold, resume, and immediate, respectively.

- **m**—Send mail after the print job has finished.

- **n** *number*—The number of copies to print.

- **o** *option*—Specifies printer-dependent options. You can specify more than one option by using the `-o` parameter more than once. You also can include multiple options by enclosing them in quotes—for example, `-o "option1 option2 ..."`.

Terms you can use for the *option* are listed here:

- **nobanner**—Do not print banner page.

- **nofilebreak**—Do not insert a form-feed character between files when multiple files are printed.

- **length=*scaled-decimal-number***—Specifies the page length. You can specify lines, inches, or centimeters. Length=66 specifies 66 lines per page, and length=11I specifies 11 inches per page, for example.

- **width=*scaled-decimal-number***—Similar to the length option. Use this format to specify page width in columns, inches, or centimeters.

- **lpi=*scaled-decimal-number***—Like length and width. Use this to specify line pitch (lines per inch).

- **cpi=*scaled-decimal-number***—Like length and width. Use this to specify characters per inch. You also can use the terms pica (10 characters per inch), elite (12 characters per inch), or compressed (to allow the printer to fit as many characters on a line as it can).

- **stty='*stty-option-list*'**—Specifies options for the stty command. Enclose the list with single quotes if it contains blank characters.

- **P *page-list***—If the filter can handle it, this causes only the pages specified by *page-list* to be printed. You can specify single pages or a range of pages.

- **p**—Enable notification on completion of the print request.

- **q *priority-level***—Priority levels range from 0 (highest) to 39 (lowest). This parameter changes the print priority of a print request. Giving a request a lower priority causes it to print before requests with a higher priority.

- **s**—Suppress messages from lp.

- **S *character-set* or S *print-wheel***—Used to select a character set or print wheel to be used on the printer for the request. If the character set or print wheel is not available, the request is rejected.

- **t *title***—Prints *title* on the banner page. Use quotes around the text if it contains blank spaces.

- **T *content-type***—Causes the request to be printed on a printer that supports *content-type* if available, or to use a filter to convert the content to the appropriate type. If you specify -r with this option, a filter will not be used. The request is rejected if no printer for this type is available and/or a filter cannot be used.

- **w**—Sends a message to the user's terminal after the print request completes. If the user is not currently logged in, a mail message is sent.

- **y *mode-list***—Use *mode-list* options to print. The allowed values for *mode-list* are locally defined and the job is rejected if there is no filter to handle the request.

If you need to simply stop a job from printing, you can use the cancel command. These are the syntax alternatives for the cancel command:

```
cancel [request-id...][printer...]
```

```
cancel -u login-ID-list [printer...]
```

The first syntax example can be used to remove a specific print job by specifying its ID number. The second example shows how to remove all print jobs for a particular user (or users). If you list multiple users on the command line, enclose the list in quotes and use a space between each ID name. Ordinary users can cancel only their own print requests. Administrators can cancel any print job.

To get the request-id of a print job, you need to use the lpstat command. This command can be used by ordinary users with no parameters and will return information about only their print jobs. However, the administrator can use this command to see data about the entire printing system. The syntax for lpstat is as follows:

```
lpstat [-d] [-r] [-R] [-s] [-t] [-a [list]]
   [-c [list]] [-o [list]]
   [-p [list]] [-P] [-s [list] [-l]]
   [-u [login-ID-list]] [-v [list]]
```

In this example, *list* can be a comma-delimited list or a series of items separated by spaces and enclosed in quotes. You can omit a list or use the keyword all in most instances to get the status of all the requested objects. These are the parameters for this command:

- **a [*list*]**—Shows whether print destinations (printers or printer classes) are accepting print requests.

- **c [*list*]**—Displays the names of all classes and members of the class. You can identify specific classes using *list*.

- **d**—Displays the system's default print destination.

- **o [*list*]**—Displays the status of output requests. The *list* value can specify either printers, class names, or request-ids.

- **p [*list*]**—Displays the status of printers. Use *list* to specify printer names.

- **r**—Displays the status of the print scheduler daemon (lpsched).

- **s**—Displays summary information about the printing system.

- **t**—Displays all the available status information about the printing system.

- **u [*login-ID-list*]**—Displays the status of print requests for the users listed in *login-ID-list*.

- **v [*list*]**—Displays pathnames of the output device files for printers indicated by *list*. For remote printers, this displays the name of the remote system.

Administering the System: lpadmin, lpsched, and lpshut

The lpadmin command performs a wide range of functions necessary to set up a printer on a Unix system. The command adds, removes, or modifies printers, and creates the necessary text files in the spooling directory for you so that you don't have to edit them manually. This command also can be used to set up "alerts" when the printer experiences a fault condition. The syntax for this administrative command is

```
lpadmin -p printer-options
lpadmin -x dest
lpadmin -d [dest]
lpadmin -S print-wheel -A alert-type [-W minutes]
     [-Q requests]
lpadmin -M -f form-name [-a [-o filebreak]
   [-t tray-number]
```

The first line of this syntax example shows how to add a new printer. Use the -p option on the command line to specify the printer's name and then list the printer's characteristics. For example:

```
lpadmin –phplj5 –v/dev/tty03 –mdumb -cpr
```

This command performs the functions needed to create a printer named hplj5. Following the printer name, the options here indicate that the actual printer device is connected to a serial port that can be accessed through the Unix device file /dev/tty03. This printer uses a dumb interface (-m option) and is a member of a class of printers named pr (the -c option). As explained later, the –m option is used to specify an interface program used to interact with a particular printer model. In the preceding example, dumb refers to a generic line printer. The file /usr/spool/lp/model contains other model interface programs, and you can view this file to see which printer models are supported on your system.

Tip

After you set up a printer using lpadmin, it does not automatically allow users to print. Use the **accept** *printer* command to enable printing.

The man pages for your system give you a full list of the options you can use on the command line, and they vary depending on the flavor of Unix you have. However, the following list shows some of the more useful ones you'll find on most systems:

- **A** *alert-type* **[-W** *minutes***]**—Sets up an alert action that is invoked when a printer fault occurs. The *alert-type* can be mail (sends an email) or write (puts a message on an administrator's terminal). You also can use quiet to suppress alerts, showfault to execute a fault-handling procedure, or none to remove alerts. You also can specify a shell command to be executed.

- **c** *class*—Specifies a class to which the printer will belong. If *class* does not exist, it will be created. The -r parameter can be used to remove a printer from a specific class.

- **D** *comment*—Sets the text (*comment*) that is displayed when the user requests a full description of the printer.

- **e** *printername*—Copies the interface program used by an existing printer (*printername*) for use with the printer you are creating. You quickly can clone entries when adding a printer of a type you already have, or when you are setting up a network that has many printers of the same type at the same time.

- **i** *interface*—Specifies the interface program for the printer. See -e earlier in this list to copy an interface from an existing printer.

- **m** *model*—Selects the *model* interface program that comes with the lp print service. You cannot use -e or -i with this option.

- **s** *system-name* **[!***printer-name***]**—Creates a remote printer. A remote printer is a printer on another system that you want your users to be able to use as if it were local. The *system-name* is the name of the computer on which the printer resides, and !*printer-name* is the name the printer uses on the remote system. You can use a different printer name on your system than the name on the remote system.

Tip

Unix and Linux commands can be complex and difficult to remember. Both of these operating systems use "man" pages (which stands for *manual*) that are basically help files. You can consult them when you need help for a particular topic. For example, the command **man lpadmin** can be used to get the help text for the **lpadmin** command on the system so that you can see a full list of the options supported.

To remove a printer from the LP printing system, use the -x command-line parameter:

```
lpadmin -xhplj5
```

This command removes the hplj5 printer from the system. If this is the last printer in its class of printers, the printer class also is deleted.

In the /etc/init.d/lp file, you will find commands that can be used to start the print scheduler daemon at boot time. The syntax, in case you want to change the boot-time command, is

```
lpsched [-nofork][-debug][-nobsd]
```

You also can use this command to restart the daemon if you find it necessary to kill it when you are troubleshooting printer problems. The lpsched daemon works sort of like the lpr daemon—it creates a new copy of itself to handle print jobs. The original daemon remains free to respond to additional user requests.

Note

The -nofork parameter can be used to suppress the creation of a separate daemon process. This is recommended to be used during debugging. You also can use the -debug parameter to put the daemon into "verbose" mode. In this mode, more messages are displayed that can be useful when trying to solve printer problems.

The -nobsd parameter can be used to tell lpsched to ignore the BSD spooler's well-known port. If you also are running an lpd daemon on the system and it is using the default port, use this option to change the port used by lpsched.

Tip

"Well-known ports" are IP port numbers from 0 to 1024. These are generally assigned to system processes that operate using privileges that the ordinary user does not have. A port is used by TCP and UDP to specify an endpoint that an application can use, along with an IP address. This combination of IP address and port number can uniquely identify both endpoints for exchanging data using the TCP/IP protocol suite. In essence, the IP address gets the network packets to the correct computer (or other hardware device), and the port number specifies a process (such as a background daemon process) that is listening for incoming requests that use the port number assigned to the process or daemon.

For example, the basic FTP protocol uses ports 20 and 21, and the basic Telnet daemon uses ports 23 and 24. Ports above 1024 have been assigned to various applications, many of which are now extinct. However, it is important that you understand that port numbers 1024 and below should be used only by applications or utilities that can perform actions an ordinary user cannot.

You can use several commands to shut down a printer, depending on just what you need to do:

- **lpshut**—This command stops all printers. Jobs that are currently printing are stopped, but they are reprinted in their entirety when the printers are again started, as are other print jobs waiting in the spooler directory. The user can continue to submit to a printer that has been stopped using this command. Use lpsched when you want to start printers again.

- **reject [-r reason] printer**—This command stops a printer from printing, but users cannot continue to submit jobs to the printer for later printing. If you want the users to know what is happening with the printer, use the -r command and specify the text you want them to see. If the text contains blank characters (it's more than one word), enclose the text in quotes. To restart the printer, use the accept printer command.

- **disable[-c | -W] [-r [reason]] printer**—This command can be used to disable a printer temporarily while still allowing users to submit jobs to the spooling directory that will print when the queue is restored to service. The -c and -W options are exclusive. Use -c to cancel the job that is currently printing and -W to have the printer stop after the current job finishes. Both of these parameters are ignored if the printer is on a remote system. Again, use -r to specify text to be displayed to users (when they use the lpstat -p command to check the printer's status). Use the enable *printer* command to restart the printer.

If a printer will be out of service for a while, and you don't want users to keep submitting jobs, use the reject command. If a printer is going to be taken out of service completely, use the lpadmin command to remove it.

If some major problem is plaguing your entire printing system, use the lpshut command to bring everything to a halt while you investigate the problem.

One last command that might be handy when performing troubleshooting or maintenance duties is the lpmove command. This command can move pending print requests from one printer to another. For example:

```
lpmove hplj5 -221 hplj5land -232 laser3
```

In this example, the print job identified by the request-id number 221 will be moved from the hplj5 printer to laser3. The print job identified by the request-id 232 waiting for hplj5land also will be moved to laser3.

Configuring Windows Print Servers

Windows server and workstation/pro operating systems from Windows NT 4.0 through XP and Windows 2003 give you a flexible printing system that can be used to direct user print jobs to a printer that is directly connected to the server, to print queues on other hosts (such as Unix or Linux systems), or to printers that are directly attached to the network. Setup is performed using a wizard that creates a printer in just a few minutes.

Printers and Printing Devices

The terminology used by Windows Servers to refer to the actual physical printer is *printing device*. That HP LaserJet sitting down the hall is a printing device. The term *printer* is used to refer to a logical construct, or an interface to the print device. It might not be apparent why a distinction should be made between the printer and a printing device, but there are a number of good reasons. The main conceptual difference between the two is that they do not necessarily imply a one-to-one relationship. In Figure 45.1, you can see that several *logical printers* can be set up to send print jobs to the same printing device.

Using this kind of setup, you easily can define several different logical printers for a printing device with each printer set up to take advantage of different characteristics of the physical printer. All the logical printers are then pointed to the same physical output device. For example, you might have one logical printer set up to print in a portrait orientation and then another set up to print in a landscape orientation. Users would send print jobs to the printer that matches the characteristics they need, without having to select the necessary configuration options themselves. Other possibilities include configuring multiple printers that select different paper trays or print in draft or letter-quality format. For example, you could create a printer that uses only a tray you keep loaded with letterhead paper.

Another good reason for keeping the printer object and the printing device separate is shown in Figure 45.2. This setup is sort of the opposite of that shown in the preceding figure.

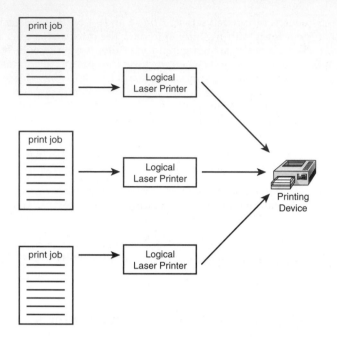

Figure 45.1 In Windows Servers, more than one logical printer can send print jobs to a single physical printing device.

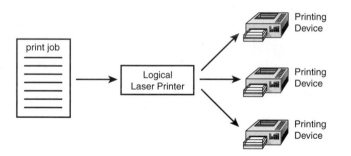

Figure 45.2 A printer pool allows a logical printer to distribute its load over several output devices.

This setup is usually called a *printer pool*. When high print volume is the norm, setting up a printer pool can provide a much faster throughput for end users, who will spend less time waiting for their printouts than if only a single printing device was used. It also eliminates the necessity of having to create and manage multiple logical printers. Using a printer pool makes it easier for you to add print devices without making users aware of it. One of the best features of using a printer pool is that it can be used to eliminate the physical print device as a single point of failure. If a printer begins to malfunction, it can be taken offline and print jobs can continue to be rendered into final format by other printers that are members of the printer pool.

When using printer pools, you must keep several things in mind:

■ Each output printing device should be of the same type or be set up to emulate the same kind of device because the printer driver used by the logical printer is specific to a particular kind of printer.

- When a job is submitted for printing to a printer that uses a printer pool, it's printed on the *first available device*. As long as a printer is available, the user's job doesn't have to wait for another job to finish before it prints.

- Locate all the printers that are part of the same printer pool in a single location. Users won't be happy if they have to walk all over the office to find out where a print job ended up.

Installing and Configuring Printers on Windows Servers

All versions of Windows server operating systems support multiple printing protocols. In this section you will learn how to install and configure printers using Windows NT, Windows 2000, and Windows XP. Although Windows XP Professional is a client operating system, it is included here because it can provide print services in a small network (such as the SOHO environment) where a server operating system is not needed. Windows 2003 server operating systems use similar or the same wizard dialog boxes as used by Windows 2000 computers.

Also, you'll learn what some of the prompts mean and how you can improve printer performance on the network.

Windows NT 4.0

To begin adding a new printer, select Add Printer from the Printers folder that you find under My Computer. The Add Printer Wizard asks you a few simple questions.

Where Will the Printer Be Managed?

This first question can be confusing if you are not familiar with Windows NT 4.0 printing. These are the available choices:

- My Computer
- Network Printer Server

The wizard is *not* asking you where the printer will be *connected*. For example, if you select My Computer, this does not mean that the physical printer device will be connected to the LPT1: port on your server (although it might be). Instead, the prompt is asking you where the printer will be *managed*. If you select My Computer, the necessary drivers for the printer are loaded on the local computer and are responsible for any settings or other management functions for the printer on this computer.

If you select Network Printer Server, the wizard enables you to connect to a printer that is already on the network *or is being offered by another server* (such as a Unix host). The wizard then prompts you to load a driver for the printer, unless one is already loaded on the server that hosts the printer. When you connect to a printer using this method, you can send print jobs to the printer but you cannot manage its properties.

Port Selection

If you chose My Computer as the place where the printer will be managed, the next wizard prompt asks for the name of the port to which the printer is attached. This can be a local port, such as LPT1:, LPT2:, or even COM1:, and so on. You can select to have the printer set up to send the print job to a file instead, although this is a feature more useful for tasks such as capturing the output from an application that doesn't provide such a function.

If you want this logical printer to manage documents that are sent to a printer elsewhere on the network, select Add Port, and then supply the necessary configuration information that the wizard needs in order to create a port for the printer. The following kinds of ports are supported under Windows NT Server 4.0:

- Digital Equipment Corporation Network Port
- Hewlett-Packard Network Port
- Lexmark DLC Network Port
- Lexmark TCP/IP Network Port
- LPR Port

Note

Not all the ports listed here will necessarily be displayed. For the Hewlett-Packard Network Port to appear, you must first install the DLC protocol. For the LPR Port option to appear, you must first install the Microsoft TCP/IP Printing service. Both can be installed by using the Network applet in the Control Panel, after which you will have to reboot the server.

Highlight the port you want to create, and then click the New Port button. Depending on the choice you make, a dialog box appears to prompt you for more information for the specific kind of port you want to create.

Fill in the name you want to give the port, and then select the 12-digit LAN (MAC) hardware address that corresponds to the address of the printer. You can get the address for the HP printer by printing a self-test page, or, if you're really bored, by going through the printer's I/O configuration menus. If no addresses appear on this dialog box, the printer might be powered off or there might be a network error preventing the server from obtaining it. If you click the Options or Timers button, you can customize this printer port further by specifying such things as the logging level that will be performed (information, warning, error) and values for timers associated with the DLC protocol.

Selecting Printer Drivers

After you complete the dialog box for the port you want to use and return to the main dialog box, click the Next button to bring up a dialog box from which you can specify the manufacturer and type of printer. This information is used to determine which drivers Windows NT needs to load for this printer. You also can click the Have Disk button if your printer is not listed and you have a driver from the manufacturer that you can use.

Because the purpose of a print server is to accept print jobs from clients, be sure to load drivers for each kind of operating-system client on the network that needs access to this printer. When the client prints the first time, it downloads the driver from the server so that the print job can be rendered into the correct format for the particular printer.

Giving the Printer a Name

Next, the wizard prompts you to enter a name to use for the printer. This name won't be used as the printer share name; instead, it's a descriptive name for the printer. Use the radio buttons at the bottom of the dialog box to set this printer as the default for this server if applicable. This does not set the printer as the default for users who connect to it over the network; it sets the printer as the default that shows up when you send print jobs from applications while you are logged in to this server locally.

Sharing the Printer on the Network

The last dialog box you see enables the printer to be offered as a printer share for network clients. In this dialog box you must select the Shared radio button, and then give the printer a name that will be displayed to users. Note that the Share Name field defaults to the type of printer and the first eight characters to be available to clients that have restrictions on the length of resource names, such as older MS-DOS clients. You can edit this field and use any name that makes sense to your users. It's usually best to use a name that indicates both the location of the printer and the kind of printer.

This dialog box also can be used to load additional drivers for clients that connect to the printer over the network. For example, if you have Windows 95 clients on your network, you should select Windows 95 from the dialog box. When this type of client must send a print job to the printer, Windows NT Server downloads the driver to the client so that the print job is formatted correctly for the printer. If the driver you specify is not already loaded on the system (for another printer, for example), you are prompted for the location of the driver. When you have finished specifying a share name for the printer and have selected any additional printer drivers you want to load, click the Next button.

Another dialog box asks whether you want to print a test page. This step is highly recommended because if the test page doesn't print, nothing else is going to print. If the test page does not print, review the selections you have made to be sure they are accurate. Or you might have a network problem that needs to be looked into. If this is a TCP/IP-networked printer, for example, you might try pinging the printer to determine whether it's reachable on the network. If you are using another protocol, try printing from a different computer that is configured similarly and determine whether this succeeds. If not, a network problem (such as a router configuration) might need to be resolved.

Print Server Properties, Printer Properties, and Document Properties for Windows NT 4.0 Server

Windows NT 4.0 Server enables you to configure properties for the print server as a whole and configure properties that are specific to each printer you create. You can also configure default properties that are applied to documents printed on the server.

Print Server Properties

To bring up the properties sheet for the print server, choose File, Properties in the Printers folder. There are three tabs on this properties sheet:

- **Forms**—Use this tab to define forms that are available to users who use printers on this server.
- **Ports**—This tab enables you to add, delete, or reconfigure ports (it's similar to the dialog box presented when you created a printer).
- **Advanced**—This tab enables you to set up logging and notifications for the print server, and specify the spooling directory.

Forms are used to define certain properties of the output page that will be printed, including the size of the paper and the margins. Windows NT Server comes with several standard forms already defined, including most standard paper sizes and envelopes. If you have a special form that you have created for your business, such as an invoice format, you can define a new form using the Forms tab.

If you plan to set up several printers but want to get some of the work out of the way beforehand, you can use the Ports tab to create the necessary ports. When you actually get around to creating the printers, you can select the appropriate port rather than create it. This also can be useful in an environment in which one administrator is responsible for network functions and another is responsible for printing. The network administrator who is aware of network addresses used by certain devices can create the ports and send a list to the printer administrator, who can then create and manage the printers that use the ports.

The Advanced tab is an important one to remember for troubleshooting purposes in which the more information you have, the better chance you have of solving your problem. You can enable the following notification and logging categories:

- Log Spooler Error Events
- Log Spooler Warning Events
- Log Spooler Information Events
- Beep on Errors of Remote Documents
- Notify When Remote Documents Are Printed

The Log Spooler Error Events option sets a logging severity level for events that will be placed into the System Event Log. You can use the Event Viewer administrative tool to examine the logged events. If users are complaining that their print jobs are not being printed, enable all three of the Log Spooler check boxes and, after they have attempted to print, review the records found in the Event Log.

Note

Under Windows NT 4.0, the Event Log is made up of three separate log files: System, Security, and Application. The events you can enable on the Print Server Properties page show up in the System Event Log. Matters related to printer security, discussed later in this chapter, show up in the Security Event Log. If applications have been written to use the Windows NT Event Logging service, and if the administrator has enabled the logging of these kinds of events, they might create events in the Application Event Log.

The information recorded in the Event Log helps you determine why the users' jobs are not printing. The Log Spooler Information Events check box also can be used to keep track of the pages printed by individual users.

It can be tedious to use the graphical interface provided by the Event Viewer to review each record. To overcome this obstacle, you can create a comma-delimited file that contains the information found in the file. However, to do this you need the Dump Event Log (DUMPEL.EXE) utility, which can be found in the Windows NT Server 4.0 Resource Kit.

Another useful thing you can do on this tab of the properties sheet is change the spooling directory used by the server. If performance is a problem with the server, you might want to locate the spooling directory on a disk by itself to speed up access. For a low-volume print server, this probably won't be necessary.

Printer Properties

You can access the properties page for any printer by using either of the following:

- In the Printers folder, highlight the printer you want to work with and choose File, Properties.
- In the Printers folder, double-click the printer you want to work with. From the dialog box that appears, select Printers, Properties.

The properties page for a printer is divided into six property sheets that enable you to control a wide variety of properties for each printer on an individual basis:

- General
- Ports
- Scheduling
- Sharing
- Security
- Device Settings

The General tab enables you to modify informational text about the printer that users can view, such as the location of the printer. You also can use this tab to select an existing separator page or create a new separator page. Separator pages can be used to print a page before each user's job so that it's easy for an operator to separate each print job on a high-volume printer used by many users. Separator pages also can be used to send printer-specific codes to a printer that determines how it prints the document. Windows NT Server comes with three separator pages designed for this purpose:

- **PSCRIPT.SEP**—This separator page changes the printer into PostScript mode. No actual separator page is printed.
- **SYSPRINT.SEP**—This page also switches a printer into PostScript mode but does print a separator page.
- **PCL.SEP**—This page switches the printer into PCL mode (HP's Printer Control Language) and prints a separator page.

Note

You might not have to use a separator page to cause a printer to change between PostScript and PCL modes. Many newer printers can autosense the kind of print mode the job requires and make the change automatically. Refer to the documentation for the printer to determine whether you must use a separator page for this purpose.

You can design your own separator pages using escape codes to include information such as the user's name, print job number, date, and any additional text you want on the page.

You also can print a test page from the General tab when troubleshooting the printer. Another useful feature on this page is the New Driver button, which you can use to load an updated printer driver. This might be necessary when a manufacturer releases a printer driver that is more current than the one found on the Windows NT Server source CDs.

The Ports tab is similar to the ports display that you see when you create a printer or when you view ports using the Print Server properties page. Here, however, you can change the port used by this printer, which comes in handy when a printer is moved to a new location and a new network connection is required. You don't have to delete and re-create the printer; just go to the Ports tab and select or create the new port after the printer has been moved. Then, go back to the General tab and print a test page to determine whether the port has been successfully created.

The Scheduling tab enables you to set the time of day that a printer is available for use. Generally, a printer is available 24 hours per day, but you can use this tab to change that if you need to. Note that users can still send print jobs to a printer outside its available time range. Their documents are stored and then printed when the printer is available for use. If you allow users to schedule jobs to be printed later, you also must be aware of the disk space that will be used for spooling the documents that must wait. For large files, such as those containing complex graphics, you'll need a lot of space.

This feature can be used to force certain print jobs, such as lengthy reports, to be delayed until after-hours when ordinary users no longer need the printer. For example, you can set up several logical printers. You can make one logical printer available to your normal workday users and set another to allow printing after hours. Applications that produce voluminous print jobs can send their documents to this latter printer, and users can retrieve their documents the next morning when they come into work.

The Scheduling tab enables you to specify several other configuration options:

- **Spool Print Documents So the Program Finishes Printing Faster**—This allows the application to send a print job quickly because the output is directed to a spooler file rather than directly to the physical printer. Generally, it takes longer to send a job directly to the printer unless it has enough memory to buffer the entire print job.

- **Print Directly to the Printer**—This is the opposite of the preceding option. An application can stall until the printer has finished receiving the entire print job from the user.

- **Hold Mismatched Documents**—This option retains a print job that does not match the current printer settings instead of discarding it. You then can change the printer or disable this option to cause the document to print.

- **Print Spooled Documents First**—Generally a spooled print job begins to print before the document has been completely spooled to a temporary file. This option specifies that jobs already completely written to the spool file will print before those that are still spooling. This setting can override the priority of a spooling print job and allow a completely spooled lower priority job to print first.

- **Keep Documents After They Have Printed**—This setting causes spooled print jobs to remain in the spool directory after they have printed. This can be useful for troubleshooting print problems. You can look at the original print job and possibly send it to another printer to determine whether the original printer is exhibiting unusual behavior when trying to print.

Normally, your documents must be spooled before they print so that users notice a faster response time. However, when troubleshooting, you might want to send documents directly to the printer, bypassing the spooling operation. Also, if space becomes a problem on the disk that holds the spooling directory, you can cause jobs to be sent directly to the printer to avoid using additional disk space. Because this option is selectable by printer, you can set up some printers to use the spool directory and others to send jobs directly to the printer.

The Sharing tab enables you to modify the selections you chose when you created the printer and to either allow or disallow the printer to be shared with network users. You also can use this tab to load additional client drivers when new clients are brought into the network, or to change the share name the printer uses on the network.

The Security tab enables you to set up permissions that control which users or groups can use this printer, and that control auditing features for the printer. Users can be denied access to the printer, be allowed to print and manage documents, or be given full control to the printer. Full control allows users to perform the following functions:

- Print
- Change document settings
- Pause or restart the printer
- Delete print jobs
- Change the priority (printing order) of jobs

- Delete the printer
- Change permissions for the printer

Usually, only print operators or network administrators are given full control over a printer. Most users need only the Print permission. This enables users to send print jobs and control their print jobs, but not those of other users. Auditing can help print operators and network administrators monitor printer usage to determine whether changes in permissions are necessary. The Auditing functions on the Security tab allow you to record events to the Event Log for later review.

▶▶   See Chapter 47, "Auditing and Other Monitoring Measures," to learn more about auditing print events and using the Event Viewer to review the data captured.

The Device Settings tab enables you to configure device-specific values for the printer. This includes information on tray selection, font cartridges, and so on, depending on the features available for the specific printer type.

Managing Printers

After you create a printer, users can connect to it and use it to print. The administrator, or other users who have the appropriate permissions, can view the status of documents waiting to print and can manage the printer. You can access this dialog box by double-clicking a printer in the Printers folder.

Documents that are currently being printed or waiting to print are displayed, showing the title of the document, the user, the size of the print job, the port the printer uses, and the date and time the job was submitted. You can use the Printer menu and the Document menu to manage the printer or any document. The Printer menu allows you to perform the following actions:

- Pause the printer
- Set the printer to be the default on this computer
- Change the defaults for documents sent to this printer
- Change the sharing aspects of the printer
- Remove all documents from the printer
- View or modify properties for the printer

This menu is useful when you're experiencing problems with a particular printer. You can pause the printer, which stops printing but keeps any documents waiting to print, to fix a minor problem and then resume printing after the trouble has been resolved. You also can remove all documents from the printer, which is handy when a user or an application has sent numerous documents to a printer by mistake. You can bring up the Properties page for the printer, discussed earlier in this chapter, and modify items as you see fit.

The Documents menu is used to individually pause, restart, or cancel print jobs. You can selectively highlight individual documents waiting to print and then cancel them.

This view of the printer is most often used by print operators who are responsible for managing printer resources on the network.

Adding a Printer on a Windows 2000 Server

Again, Microsoft provides the Add Printer Wizard to guide you through installing a printer on a Windows 2000 Server. Earlier in this chapter, for Windows NT 4, you learned the basic steps for creating a printer using a TCP/IP port. Now, you'll see the other possible choices you have for a Windows 2000 Server. To bring up the Add Printer Wizard, click Start, Settings, Printers and then double-click the Add Printer icon.

In the same manner as with the Windows NT 4.0 Wizard, you are prompted to create a printer for a local printer or a networked printer. Remember, this refers to *where* the printer will be managed. If you want to connect to a network printer so that the server can send documents to that printer, select the Network Printer check box. However, you won't be able to manage this printer or offer it as a share to other computers. If you want to manage the printer locally (even if it is a printer on the network), select Local Printer and click the Next button.

In the next dialog box, titled Select the Printer Port (shown in Figure 45.3), you choose an existing port by selecting the Use the Following Port option button. The list should include the standard printer ports (that is, LPT1:), as well as any ports you might have created in the past. To connect to a networked printer, however, use the Create a New Port option button. This selection can also be used to create local ports.

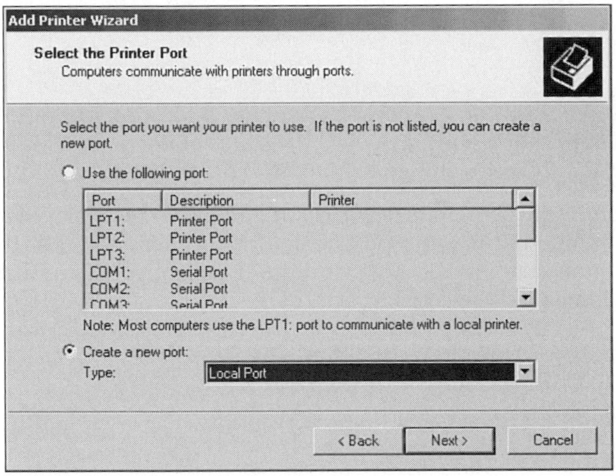

Figure 45.3 You can connect to a printer that is directly attached to the computer or one that resides on the network.

If you select Local Port as the new kind of port to create, you have the following options:

- **Print to File**—You can specify a path and filename to which output is directed when this printer is used by a client. The file is overwritten each time the printer is used.

- **Print to File Share**—You can enter the UNC (Universal Naming Convention) share name of a printer, for example.

- **The NUL Device**—You can use this option to dump printer output into another dimension. Generally, you set up a printer for use with the NUL device to assist in troubleshooting printer connectivity problems without wasting paper.

- **Infrared Port**—This option is available if your computer supports an infrared port. Printers must meet specifications of the Infrared Data Association (IrDA).

Note

Some ports won't appear in your local port selection list, as was pointed out in the Infrared Port option. USB ports also won't show up unless Windows 2000 has detected a printer attached. If they do show up, you can use the port to create additional printers, and manage them as if they were different physical devices with the output all going to the same physical printer.

In addition to using local ports, you can use the Create a New Port option to create ports for printers that reside on the network. The options that you'll find depend on the protocols and services you've installed on the Windows 2000 server. The following additional ports can be created:

- **Standard TCP/IP Port**—This is probably the option you'll use most of the time. Most printers today that support networking also support TCP/IP printing.

- **AppleTalk Printing Devices**—This port type allows you to connect to printers that use the AppleTalk protocol. The AppleTalk protocol has to be installed first.

- **Hewlett-Packard Network Port**—Use this port type for older printers that support the Data Link Control (DLC) protocol. For all practical purposes, you shouldn't have to use this older protocol. If you have a printer this old, it's probably time to replace it! However, Windows 2000 still supports this kind of port, provided you install the DLC protocol.

- **LPR Port**—LPR (Line Printer Remote) is an older TCP/IP-based printing standard that was discussed in the preceding chapter. You can use this to connect to printers on Unix servers, or other servers that support the lpr/lpd printing system. First you'll have to install Print Services for Unix.

- **Port for NetWare**—You can use this port type to connect to NetWare printing resources. The NWLink protocol and Client Services for NetWare must be installed first.

In the preceding list, the most likely choice today is to create a standard TCP/IP port, because almost all printers and printing appliances support it. However, if you need to use one of the other port types, be sure to install the prerequisite protocols or services. For example, to install Print Services for Unix, you can add the component easily by clicking Start, Settings, Network, Dial-up Connections. Next, select Add Network Components. In Figure 45.4, you can see the dialog box that allows you to add networking components. Note that the last check box is Other Network File and Print Services.

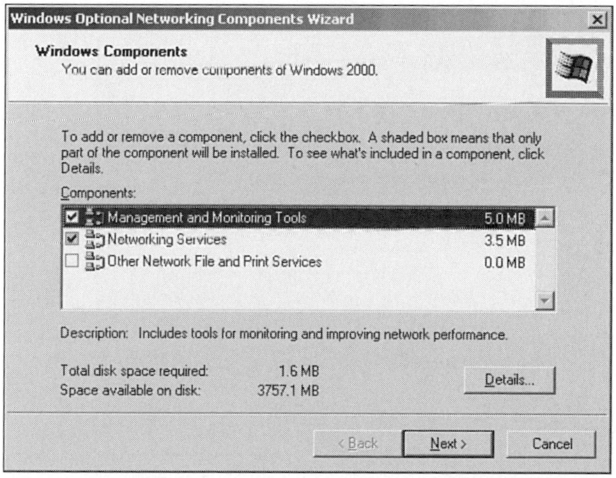

Figure 45.4   You must first install the necessary protocols and services for some printers.

To choose which protocols to install, select the Other Network File and Print Services check box and click the Details button. In Figure 45.5, you see the additional printing services that can be installed on a Windows 2000 computer.

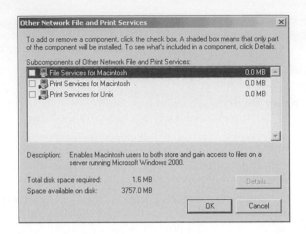

Figure 45.5   You can select which printing service to install from this dialog box.

You can install print services for Macintosh or Unix printers. After you make your selection, you are prompted for additional information, and the service is installed.

To install additional protocols, such as AppleTalk or DLC, use the following steps:

1. Select Start, Settings, Network, Dial-Up Connections.

2. Right-click your LAN connection and select Properties from the menu that pops up. The properties sheet is shown in Figure 45.6.

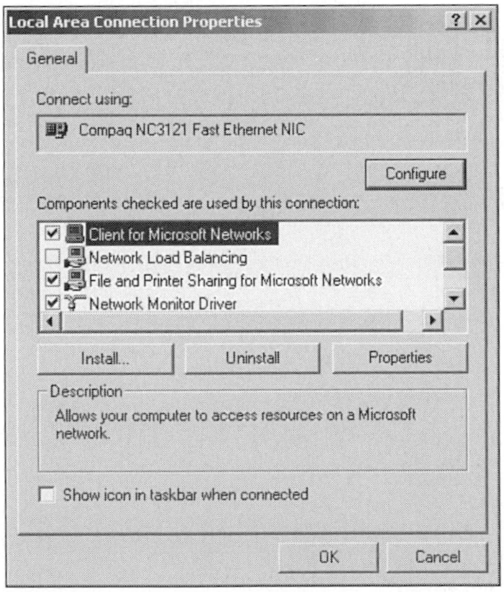

Figure 45.6   You can click the Install button to add additional network protocols to the Windows 2000 server.

3. Click the Install button. A small dialog box pops up and prompts you to install one of the following: a client, a service, or a protocol. Select Protocol and click the Add button.

4. The Select Network Protocol dialog box pops up and allows you to choose the network protocol to be added (see Figure 45.7).

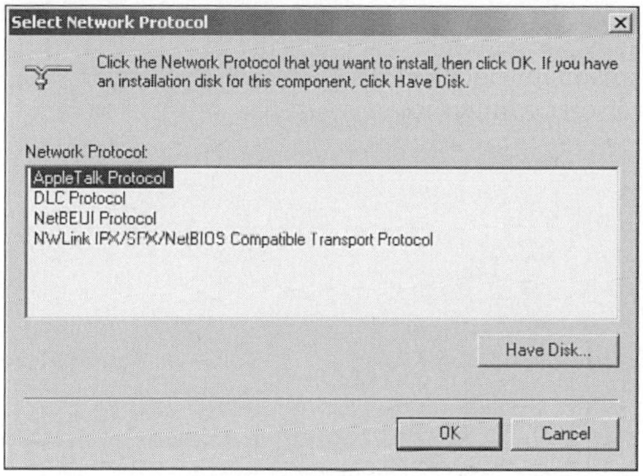

Figure 45.7   You can choose the network protocol to install from this dialog box.

5. Continue to add protocols as needed. When you are done, close the properties page for the local connection, and the protocols should be ready for use.

After you have installed the necessary protocol(s) and service(s), you should see them as options when you elect to create a printer port on a Windows 2000 server. The remaining prompts displayed by the Add Printer Wizard depend on the protocol you've chosen. As with Windows NT 4.0, you also must select the printer manufacturer and the model of the printer. You are prompted to make the printer your default on the local computer and are asked whether you want to share it on the network. Finally, you get to print a test page, and then you're done with the Add Printer Wizard.

Print Server Properties, Printer Properties, and Document Properties for Windows 2000 Server

Just as with Windows 4.0 Server, you can manage Windows 2000 print servers and individual printers. You can also set up default properties for documents. To begin, click Start, Settings, Printers to bring up the Printers window. Choose File, Server Properties. As you can see in Figure 45.8, Windows 2000 adds a new Drivers tab to the Print Server Properties page.

The other standard tabs are there, and work just like they did for Windows NT 4.0 Server. You can design forms, modify ports, and use the Advanced tab to set up logging and other notifications.

The Drivers tab, shown in Figure 45.9, allows you to load additional printer drivers for clients that will access the printer.

To add additional printer drivers, click the Add button. The Add Printer Wizard pops up again. Click Next to go back to the dialog box that allows you to choose a manufacturer and a printer model. Or you can use the Have Disk option to load a driver that is not part of the standard Windows 2000 distribution.

You also can remove drivers by highlighting them and clicking the Remove button. If you need to update a driver, use the Update button. This is a powerful function because, in this one place, you can update a driver that is used by multiple printers. The Properties button allows you to view properties pages specific to the driver you have highlighted. Casual users shouldn't change items on a printer driver's properties page. Make these changes only if you are thoroughly proficient in the printer workings and understand the changes you are making.

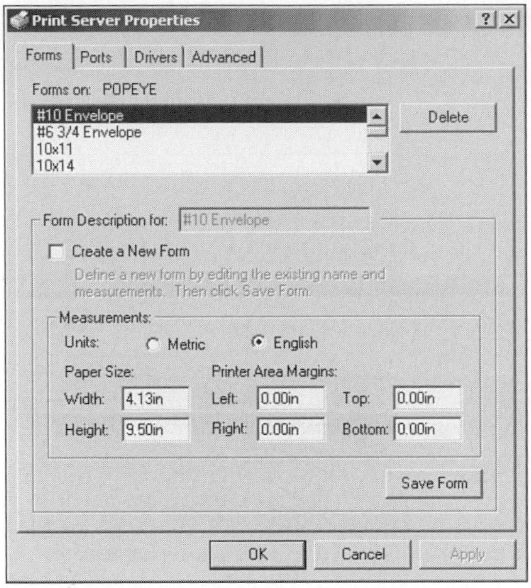

Figure 45.8 The Print Server Properties page allows you to manage global properties for the print server.

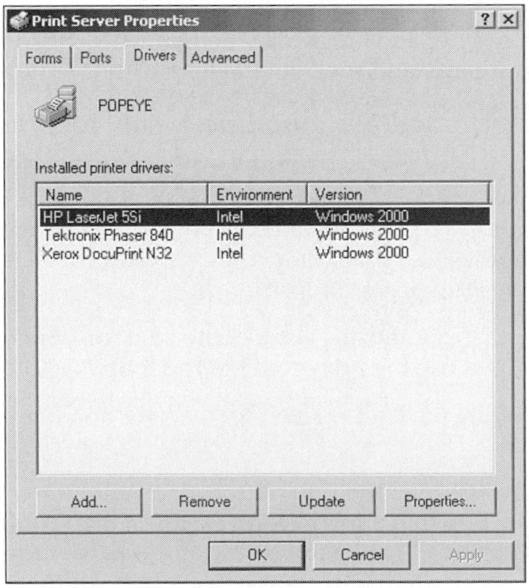

Figure 45.9 You can load additional printer drivers for clients on your network using the Drivers tab.

Printer Properties

Again, the properties page for a printer in Windows 2000 is similar to that used in Windows NT 4.0 Server, but with a few differences, as you can see in Figure 45.10.

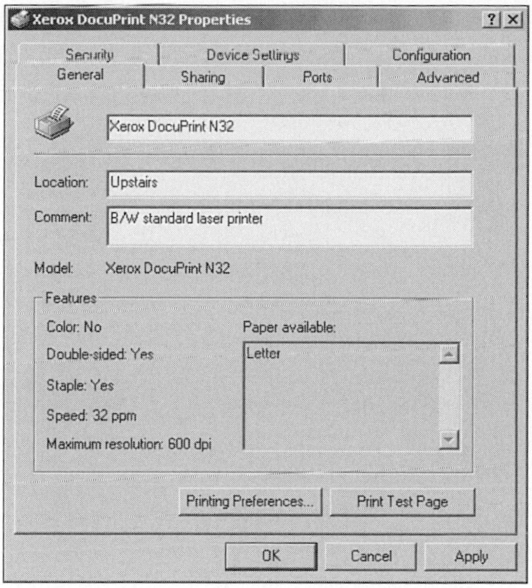

Figure 45.10   You can manage properties for each printer individually.

Note that the Scheduling tab no longer shows up. This function is now located on the new Advanced tab. In addition to the tabs that were available under the Windows NT 4.0 Server version, the following tabs now show up on a printer's properties page:

■ **Configuration**—This tab shows items specific to the printer model, such as additional trays that can be installed and whether a duplex (two-sided printing) module is installed. What you see here depends on the type of printer.

■ **Advanced**—The scheduling functions have been moved to this tab. Other functions, as you can see in Figure 45.11, have also been moved to this page. For example, you use this tab now to select a separator page (this function used to reside on the General tab).

All the other functions found in Windows NT 4.0 are still here; you might have to spend just a minute or two looking through the various tabs to find them.

Managing Printer Properties

For day-to-day printer management, you double-click a printer icon in the Printers folder. You can start, stop, and pause the printer or a particular document. You can also purge the printer of all documents waiting to print or selectively cancel documents.

Publishing Printers in the Active Directory

The Active Directory can hold information about users, computers, and resources such as printers. First, you can publish a printer in the Active Directory if you are logged in to a domain that is part of the Active Directory (for either Windows 2000 or Windows Server 2003). To do so, follow these steps:

1. Bring up the properties for a printer by right-clicking on the printer icon (in the Printers folder).

2. Select the Sharing entry from the menu that appears. Note that a printer must be shared before if it is to be published in the Active Directory.

3. On the Sharing properties page that appears, select List in Directory.

4. To share a printer, on the Sharing tab click on Shared As and fill in the fields, such as the name you want the printer to appear as on the network.

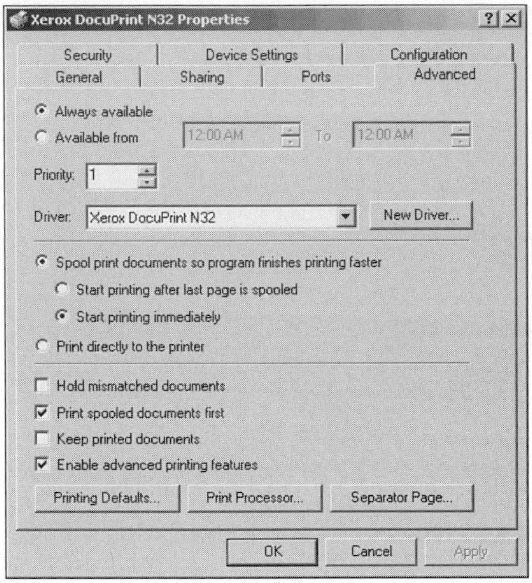

Figure 45.11 The Advanced tab contains functions that used to be on other tabs.

If you want to share a printer that is not managed by a Windows 2000 or Windows Server 2003 computer, the process is a little different. First you must create the printer on the computer (such as a Windows NT Server). The printer share will then be accessible on the network using the Universal Naming Convention (UNC). For example, \\zira\hplj would indicate that a printer named hplj on the computer named zira is being offered to the network as a printer share.

Next, use the Active Directory Users and Computers utility to add the printer to the directory. For Windows 2000, use Start, Programs, Administrative Tools, and then select the Active Directory Users and Computers utility. For Windows Server 2003, click on Start, Administrative Tools, and then Active Directory Users and Computers.

Choose the container object where you want to place the printer. This can be a domain, or a container object beneath a domain, or a container object that holds several domains.

◄◄ For more information about container objects and domains in the Active Directory, see Chapter 31, "Using the Active Directory."

Right-click on the container object, and select New, Printer. In the dialog box that appears, enter the UNC name described previously for the printer you want to publish. Click OK.

Managing Printers Using the Internet Printing Protocol (IPP)

One new feature that Windows 2000 offers is support for the Internet Printing Protocol (IPP) that was discussed in the preceding chapter. In addition to allowing clients to use a browser to connect to a printer on a Windows 2000 print server, you can also use a browser to manage printers.

To use IPP, you must install Internet Information Services (IIS) on the print server as a prerequisite. This can be done during the initial operating-system installation. Or use the Add/Remove Programs icon in the Control Panel and select Add/Remove Windows Components to install IIS later. When you've installed IIS, you'll find a new entry in the Administrative Tools folder: Internet Services Manager.

Managing Access to the Web-Based Printers Folder

As with the other administrative tools, the Internet Services Manager is written as a snap-in for the Microsoft Management Console (MMC). When you first launch the application, you'll see the MMC console tree in the left pane, listing the IIS Web servers that are in your domain. Select a server by clicking it once, and then click the plus sign that appears next to the server to expand the tree. A list of Web sites for the server appears. In the example shown in Figure 45.12, you can see that the Default Web Site has been expanded to show the objects that fall beneath it in the tree. The Printers folder is at the bottom of the list.

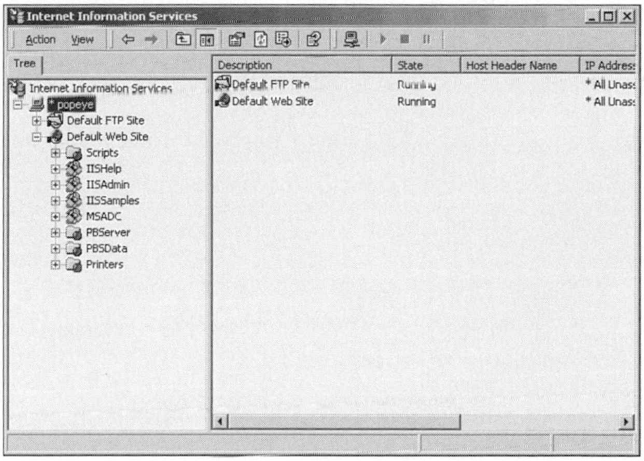

Figure 45.12   You can manage printers using IPP from the Internet Services Manager application.

Right-click the Printers folder and select Properties. In Figure 45.13, you can see the properties page that appears, with the Virtual Directory tab selected.

Note

When first presented with the Properties page for the Printers folder in the IIS MMC management application, some of the items don't seem to relate to printing. That's because, in general, they don't. This is the properties page for managing how printers are presented as a Web page (using the Documents tab), how security is configured to allow or deny access to the printers, and so on. You'll learn more about directly managing individual printers shortly.

For the most part, you can ignore most of this first tab and keep the defaults. If you are running a Web site using IIS, you might have reason to make changes here, but for ordinary printing tasks the defaults should suffice. Leave the virtual directory on the local computer so that information about printers will be stored on the print server. You'll need to leave Read Access enabled so that users can browse for printers. The Log Visits check box can be useful for troubleshooting purposes later.

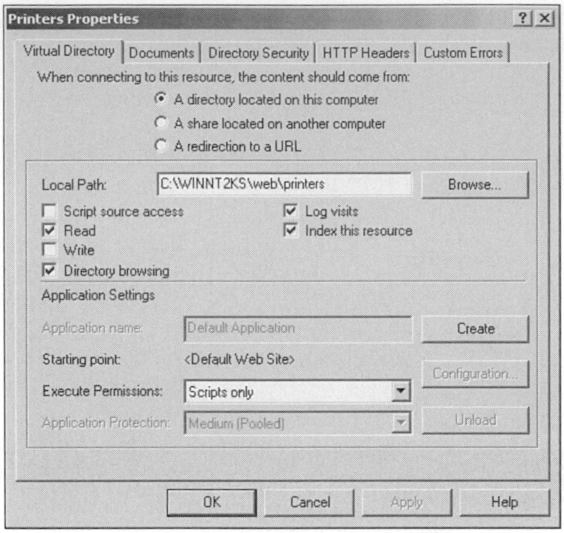

Figure 45.13   You can manage printers via an Internet browser using Windows 2000 and IPP.

You can configure permissions to restrict access to this Web-printing management on the Directory Security tab (see Figure 45.14).

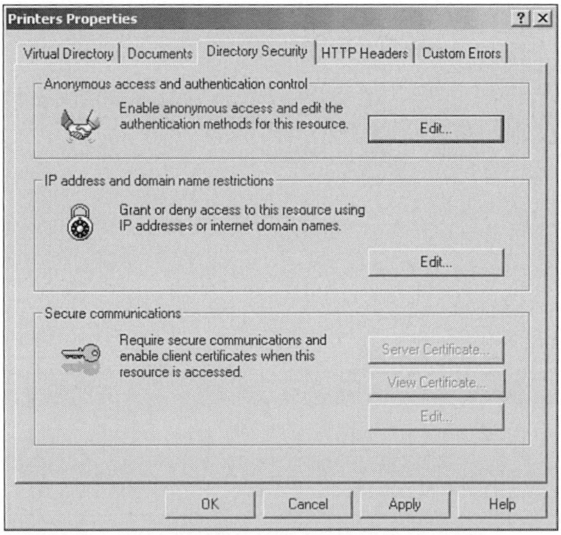

Figure 45.14   You can restrict access to printer management using the Directory Security tab.

If you click the Edit button under Anonymous Access and Authentication Control, you can select the kind of access allowed for managing printers. You can choose the authentication method for users wanting to connect to a printer from the following:

- **Anonymous Access**—This allows anyone to manage printers, without requiring any sort of authentication. You can also configure the account that is used with anonymous access. The default is the account created when IIS is installed: IUSR_*servername*.

- **Basic Authentication**—This method allows for a username/password exchange when connecting to the resource, but sends the information via clear text. For some non-Windows clients, this might be the only kind of authentication you can use. However, keep in mind that sending password information on the network as clear text can pose a security problem.

- **Digest Authentication for Windows Domain Servers**—This method uses a challenge/response mechanism to authenticate the user and is more secure than the basic authentication method. This method is new with IIS 5.0 and sends a hashed value over the network rather than the password.

- **Integrated Windows Authentication**—This last method uses a cryptographic exchange based on the Kerberos method.

You can use the IP Address and Domain Name Restrictions section on the Directory Security tab to further control access. When you click the Edit button for this section, you'll see a dialog box similar to that shown in Figure 45.15.

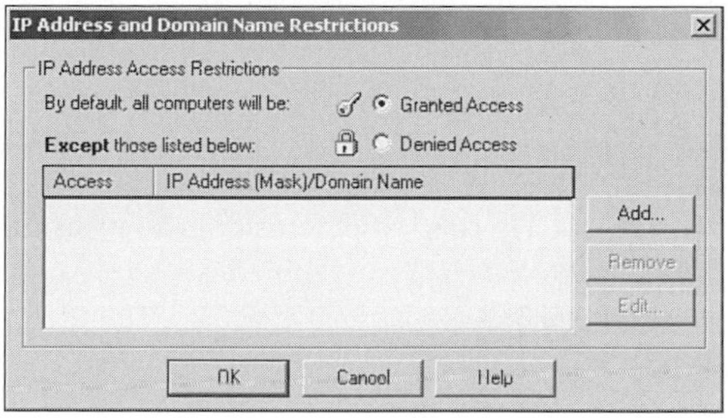

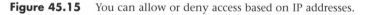

Figure 45.15   You can allow or deny access based on IP addresses.

You can choose to add records for IP addresses that are allowed to use the printer, or you can specify those addresses that are denied access.

To allow access to most users, and restrict just a few addresses, select the Granted Access option and use the Add button to add exclusions. This is the easiest method for granting access if the printer is to be available to most of your users. Alternatively, you can choose the Denied Access option and use the Add button to add IP addresses of those specific computers that are allowed to access the Printers folder on this server.

Figure 45.16 shows the dialog box that appears when you click the Add button. In this example, the Group of Computers option is selected, which is more efficient than entering individual IP addresses. Instead, you specify a network ID and the subnet mask for that network. Thus, you can allow or deny entire groups of computers based on their network address. This is helpful when using DHCP to configure client computers. In that situation, you know the network address for any particular subnet, but you don't know which IP address will be assigned to any particular client. If your network is organized in a logical manner by department, for example, you can control access for different departments if they are each on a different subnet. Simply specify the subnet network address and address mask using this dialog box.

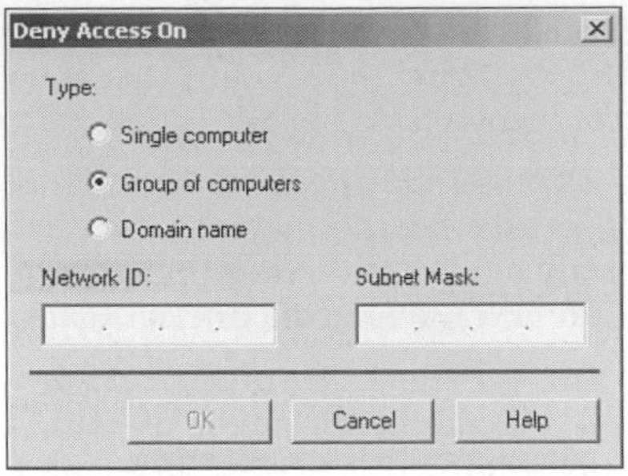

Deny Access On

Type:

- C Single computer
- ⊙ Group of computers
- C Domain name

Network ID: Subnet Mask:

OK   Cancel   Help

Figure 45.16 You can specify an individual address or a particular network using the Add Button dialog box.

Note also that you can use the Domain Name option in the Add Button dialog box, in which case you can control access based on a domain name. This method, however, requires additional overhead and can slow server performance.

Finally, the Directory Security tab allows you to require secure communications using a certificate server. You must have a certificate server on the network for this functionality to be available. This is the most secure form of communications you can choose for managing the Printers folder.

Managing Printers Using a Web Browser

To view the printers on a print server that has been IPP enabled by the installation of IIS, use the URL `http://servername/printers`. In Figure 45.17, you can see a listing of the printers that are shared on the print server Popeye. You can quickly check the status of printers using this URL.

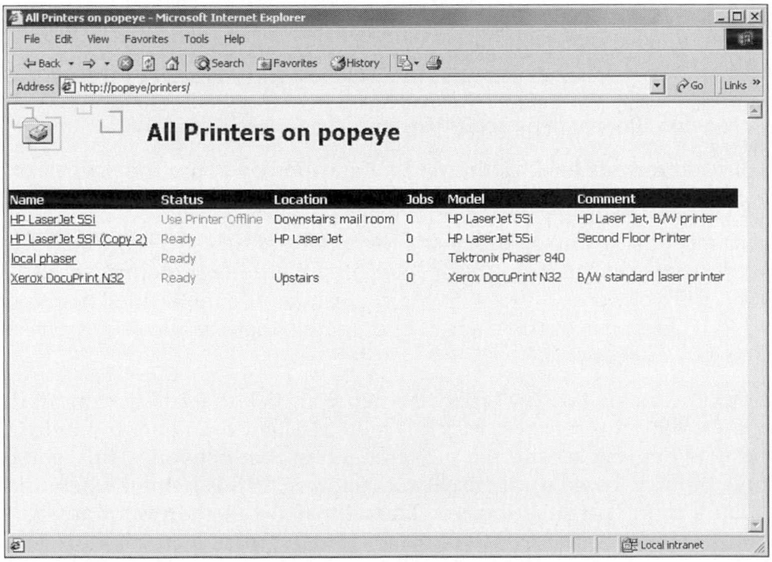

All Printers on popeye - Microsoft Internet Explorer

File   Edit   View   Favorites   Tools   Help

Back ▾ → ▾ ⊗ ⊡ ⚙ | ⚲Search ⚑Favorites ⚙History | ⬛▾ ⬛

Address ⬛ http://popeye/printers/   ▾ ⬀Go Links »

All Printers on popeye

Name	Status	Location	Jobs	Model	Comment
HP LaserJet 5Si	Use Printer Offline	Downstairs mail room	0	HP LaserJet 5Si	HP Laser Jet, B/W printer
HP LaserJet 5Si (Copy 2)	Ready	HP Laser Jet	0	HP LaserJet 5Si	Second Floor Printer
local phaser	Ready		0	Tektronix Phaser 840	
Xerox DocuPrint N32	Ready	Upstairs	0	Xerox DocuPrint N32	B/W standard laser printer

⬛   🖳 Local intranet

Figure 45.17 You can view all the printers shared by a Windows 2000 print server.

To see details about a particular printer, click the printer in this display. Figure 45.18 shows the page that is displayed for a single printer.

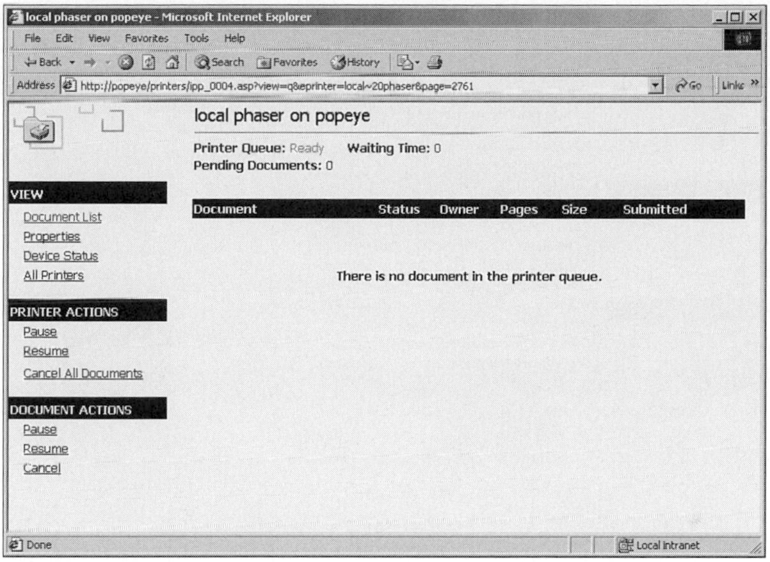

Figure 45.18   You can view information about each printer using a Web browser.

In this figure, the functions available are just about the same as you get when you double-click a printer icon in the Printers folder. However, the display is in Web-browser form instead of the traditional dialog boxes and windows used in the past.

Most of the display is used to show documents waiting to print and status information, such as the owner and when the print job was submitted. On the left side of the Web page, you'll see three sections of options for management purposes:

- **View**—This section provides a listing of documents (the default). You can also choose to view the properties of the printer, view the status of the device, or return to the Web page that lists all printers on the server.

- **Printer Actions**—This section lets you do the normal management functions: pause the printer, resume the printer, or cancel all documents that are waiting to print.

- **Document Actions**—This section allows you to do the same functions on the document level instead of the printer level. Use these options to pause, resume, or cancel a particular document you've first highlighted in the document listing.

Figure 45.19 shows the Properties page for a printer. This is helpful when choosing a printer.

The Properties page for a printer can be used to determine a printer's capabilities. The Comment and Location fields would have been nice to see in this figure. When this printer was created, the administrator was obviously in a hurry.

Finally, Figure 45.20 shows the Device Status page for a printer, which can be useful when troubleshooting. Note the other information you can see from this view, including information from the printer's front panel display, the status of paper trays, and any error messages that might be outstanding for the printer.

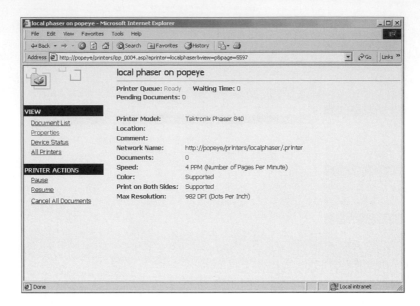

Figure 45.19   Use the Properties page for a printer when trying to decide which printer to use, based on the printer's capabilities.

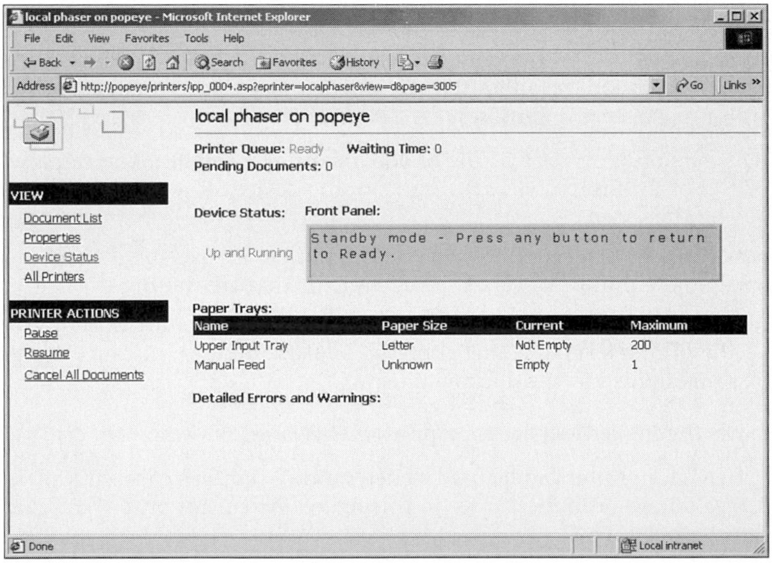

Figure 45.20   You can check the status of the device using this Web-based view.

Because IPP allows you to print to printers literally anywhere on the Internet, it will be more widely implemented in the near future as the standards committee finishes the next version of the specification. Although the usual Windows printer-management utilities allow you to manage printers remotely, by using a browser you can manage printers from just about anywhere, as long as you set up management user access securely.

Installing and Configuring Printing on a Windows XP Computer

Although Windows XP Professional is a client operating system, and not in the same class as Windows server operating systems, it is very popular in SOHO networks that contain just a few computers and do not require a more robust server operating system. If you are operating in the SOHO environment, Windows XP can be configured to share printer(s) as well as file shares. In this section you will find out how to configure a printer on Windows XP Professional—using TCP/IP—to enable it to share printers with other computers.

Windows XP Professional can share a printer that is directly connected to the computer via its physical ports (such as a parallel port, USB, or FireWire port). In addition, like Windows 2000, Windows XP Professional can be used to satisfy client print requests by sending print jobs to printers on other computers, or printers that have their own network connection. If you do not need to use the Windows XP computer as a print server, you can also let clients connect to any printer on the network. Thus, there are three ways you can set up a printer connection in a Windows SOHO network. Each client can make a connection directly to a networked printer (in which case the XP computer is not required to act as a server), a connection can be made directly to a printer physically connected to an XP computer, or a client can print to a shared printer on a Windows XP client that is redirected to a networked printer that the XP computer communicates with. In Figure 45.21 you can see an overview of the choices.

The first scenario demonstrates that network computers can connect to a printer that has its own network connection. This can be an easy solution in a small network where you do not need to control access to networked printers, but rather let clients connect directly to the printers they want to use.

In the second example, a Windows XP computer has a print device connected to one of its ports, and clients send print jobs to the Windows XP computer, which then sends the print job to the physical printer. By using this method, the Windows XP computer can act as a gateway controlling access to the computer. This means that you can create print shares on the Windows XP computer and grant or deny access to individual clients on the LAN.

In the third example, a Windows XP computer can establish connections to printers that are attached to the network. As with the second example, clients send their print requests to the Windows XP computer and it will make the connection to the networked printer. This example also allows the Windows XP computer to control access to the printer.

Note

In the third example shown in Figure 45.21, the Windows XP Professional computer is used to forward print jobs from clients to networked printers. If security is an important issue for your network (and it should be in today's environment), then you should be aware that it may be possible to circumvent the Windows XP computer. If the user of a client computer knows the IP address of one or more networked printers, the user might just decide to side-step the Windows XP computer and create a direct network connection to a printer.

Configuring a Printer Using Windows XP Professional

Tip

If you have a printer that uses Plug and Play, and if the printer uses a USB or FireWire (IEEE 1934) connection—or any other hot pluggable port—then you probably will not have to use the following steps to configure the printer. Instead, if the printer is one that Windows XP Professional recognizes and already has a driver for, you can simply plug in the printer and Windows XP Professional will automatically configure the printer for you. However, you can still use the steps outlined here if you want to bypass Plug and Play. For example, your printer may come with an updated driver and you might want to use the CD that contains the printer driver, and possibly other software, and install the printer manually.

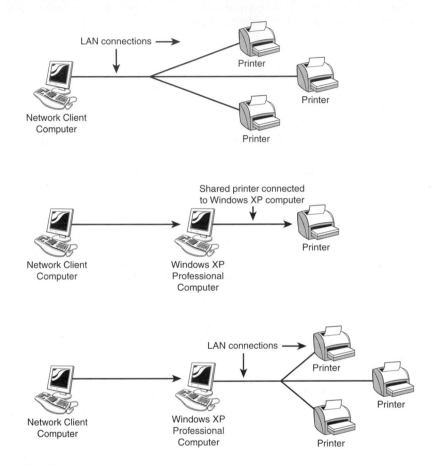

Figure 45.21 There are a few ways you can connect clients in a SOHO network to a printer that uses Windows XP Professional.

Use the following steps to easily configure Windows XP for printing:

1. Click on Start, Printers and Faxes.

2. In the Printers and Faxes window, look under Printer Tasks on the left side of the window and click on Add a Printer. The Add Printer Wizard pops up. Click Next.

3. In Figure 45.22 you can see the Wizard's next dialog box. Here you can use the radio buttons to specify whether you are configuring a printer that is attached to the Windows XP computer, or whether you want to connect to a printer on the network or on another computer. For this example, a printer attached to the XP computer has been selected. In addition, the Automatically Detect and Install My Plug and Play Printer check box is selected. Click Next to continue.

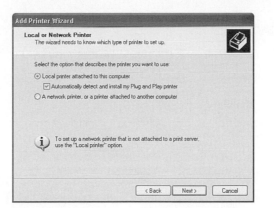

Figure 45.22   This Add Printer dialog box lets you choose to configure a printer attached to the Windows XP computer, or to a printer on the network.

4. The New Printer Detection dialog box pops up and Windows XP tries to locate and install any plug-and-play printers connected to the computer. In Figure 45.23 you can see that Windows XP was successful in finding the printer and installing the printer driver. This dialog box also enables you to send a test page to the printer to ensure that the configuration is correct. Click on the Yes radio button and then the Next button to accomplish this.

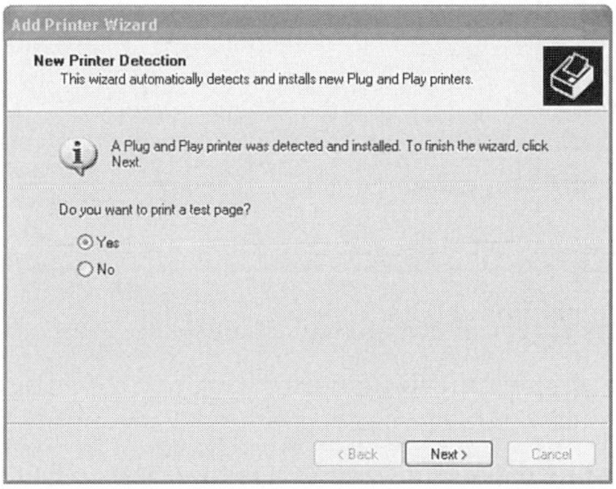

Figure 45.23   The Add Printer Wizard can automatically detect and configure plug-and-play printers that are attached to the computer.

Tip

It is a good idea to send a test page to the printer during the configuration process. If you do not, you cannot be sure that the configuration was properly completed until you send a print job to the printer. You might as well find out at the start if the configuration was successful. If not, you can backtrack and try to determine what went wrong.

5. When the next dialog box appears, click the Finish button. If you have selected the option to print a test page, a test page is then sent to the printer.

6. A small pop-up dialog box tells you that the test page has been sent to the printer. If the page has printed, click the OK button. If not, click the Troubleshoot button.

After you have configured the printer, you can use the Properties pages for the printer to enable sharing the printer with other computers.

Use the following steps to enable sharing the printer with other client computers on the network:

1. Click on Start, Printers and Faxes. In the Printers and Faxes window you will see a printer icon with a short description of the printer next to it. Right-click on the icon. A menu lets you select from many options, depending on the printer.

2. Click on the Sharing menu option, or click on Properties and then select the Sharing tab. In Figure 45.24 you can see the Sharing tab for the printer.

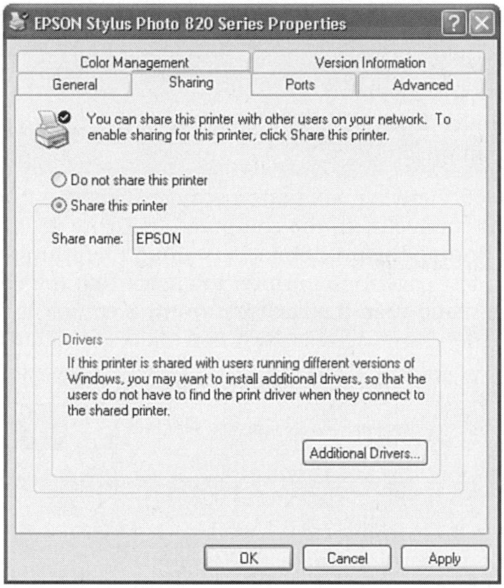

Figure 45.24 This property sheet can be used to enable sharing the printer on the network.

3. In Figure 45.24 you can select the radio button labeled Share This Printer if you want other clients on the network to be able to connect to and use your printer.

4. In the Share Name field enter a name that the printer will be known by on the network.

5. At the bottom of the property sheet shown in Figure 45.24, you can see a Drivers section. If your network uses only Windows XP computers, you can ignore this part of the property sheet. However, if you have other computers on the network, click on the Additional Drivers button. This will allow you to load drivers for other operating systems so that they can use this printer. The current selections include Windows operating systems from Windows 95 through Windows 2000 and Windows Me.

Tip

If you choose to load drivers for other operating systems, Windows XP will prompt you for the location for the drivers you want to install. If the manufacturer of your printer does not include drivers for other operating systems, check its Web site to determine whether a driver exists. In any case, a dialog box will ask you to enter the location for the additional drivers.

6. When you have finished loading other operating-system drivers (or not), click on the Apply button and then the OK button shown in Figure 45.24 to continue.

To ensure that the printer has been properly configured for sharing on the network, use another computer on the network to connect to the printer share and print a document.

In addition to the Sharing tab on the printer's properties sheets, you will find other tabs, depending on the type of printer you have configured on the system. For example, a Color Management tab would be present for a color printer but not for a monochrome laser printer. You might want to check out all of these tabs that are created for your printer to determine whether there are other features you might want to configure.

Printing Under NetWare

Novell Directory Services uses objects in the directory database to represent the functional components of the printing system. As with Windows NT, Windows 2000, and Windows 2003, some terms must be defined:

- **Printer**—This is the physical printer, like the printer device under Windows NT.
- **Print queue**—This is like the logical printer found in Windows NT. Unlike Windows NT, the term *queue* is used. Users send print jobs to a print queue, where they are retained until they print.
- **Print server**—This can be a software print server (such as NetWare's PSERVER.NLM) loaded on a host computer on the network, or a physical print server device connected to the network.

When the administrator creates a Print Queue object in the database, a directory that will hold the spooled files is created automatically. The administrator then specifies the print server that will control the queue, and the printer (physical device) that will render the print job into a finished document. When configuring a NetWare client, you select a print queue. The user does not have to be bothered with other aspects of the system such as the printer or the print server.

Print queues hold jobs waiting to print. A queue can accept documents even if the printer is offline or out of service. The jobs wait in the queue until the printer is restored to service or another printer is assigned to the task. In a manner similar to Windows NT, NetWare print queues can send print jobs to multiple output print devices, and multiple print queues can be established to send output to the same printer.

These three entities—the printer, the print server, and the print queue—do not have to reside on the same host computer. However, to reduce network traffic, it's a good idea in a high-volume printing environment to locate them on the same server. Or else, when a user submits a print job, network bandwidth is used, sending the data to the print queue. Then, more bandwidth is used to send the document from the print queue to the print server, and if the printer is a networked device, additional bandwidth is used to send the document from the print server to the printer.

To create the objects needed for printing in NetWare, you use either the NetWare Administrator or the PCONSOLE utility. The PCONSOLE utility is the recommended route because it has an option that provides a quick setup for all three objects. To use the PCONSOLE utility to set up printing on a server, follow these steps:

1. Log in as an Admin user or a user that has the create, delete, and browse privileges for the container that will hold the printing objects.
2. Run PCONSOLE.
3. Choose PCONSOLE, Change Context. Set your context to the container you want to use for the printing objects.
4. Choose Available Options, Print Queues.

5. Press the Insert (Ins) key to create a new object.

6. Enter the name you want to give to the Print Queue object.

7. A dialog box prompts you for the volume to use for the Print Queue object's spooling directory. Enter an object or use the Insert key to browse for available volumes. When finished, press the Escape key to return to the PCONSOLE menu.

8. Next, create the Printer object. Choose Available Options, Printers.

9. Press the Insert key to create a new Printer object.

10. Enter a name for the Printer object when the dialog box prompts you.

11. Select the newly created Printer object from the Printers list.

12. In the Printer Configuration screen that appears, fill in the configuration information specific to the kind of printer the object represents—whether it uses a parallel or serial port, address restrictions, and so on.

13. While still in the Printer Configuration screen, select the queue you want to use from the Print Queues Assigned field. When finished, press the F10 key to save the information. Press the Escape key to return to the Available Options menu.

14. Select Print Servers to begin creating the new Print Server object. Press the Insert key to create a new object.

15. Enter a name for the new object when the screen prompts you. The object is created. Select it from the Print Servers list so that it can be configured.

16. Select the Printers option from the Print Server Information list. Press the Insert key.

17. A list of Printer objects appears. Select the Printer object you just created. You can continue to add other Print Server objects if you like. Press the Escape key until you reach the main menu of the PCONSOLE utility.

You also can use the Quick Setup feature of PCONSOLE. Choose Available Options, Quick Setup on the PCONSOLE menu. The Print Services Quick Setup screen appears and allows you to fill in the fields on this screen.

Tip

You can use the PUPGRADE utility to upgrade NetWare 3.x servers that are already configured as print servers. Select PUPGRADE, Upgrade Print Servers and Printers; then select the bindery print server you want to upgrade.

Print Queue Object Properties

The Print Queue object is a logical representation of a print queue. It uses a directory (created as a subdirectory under the /QUEUES directory) on a NetWare volume you select when you create the object to store files waiting to print. The following are significant properties of the Print Queue object:

- **Volume**—The volume selected to hold files that are waiting in the queue to print. Choose a volume that has adequate storage for the typical printing volume on the server.

- **Authorized Print Servers**—A list of print servers that can use this print queue.

- **Printers Servicing Print Queue**—A list of printers to which the print queue can send output.

- **Operators**—The users allowed to perform management functions on the queue.

- **Users**—The users allowed to send print jobs to the print queue. Instead of listing individual users for this property, it's much easier to use container objects that include users to make administration tasks easier.
- **Print Job List**—A list of print jobs in the queue. It includes the sequence number for each job, the job ID, the current status of the print job, the form used, and the name of the file to be printed.

Note that the Printers Servicing Print Queue property is used to link the Print Queue object to one or more Printer objects.

Printer Object Properties

The Printer object represents an actual physical printer that will accept print jobs from a print queue. The printer can be connected directly to the network, to a workstation, or to a server.

The properties of the Printer object include a name property, which is established when the Printer object is created. In addition, you can assign values to other descriptive properties:

- Other Names
- Description
- Location
- Department
- Organization

The following are more important properties that affect how the queue functions:

- **Print Server**—Shows the Print Server object to which the printer is assigned.
- **Print Queues**—Lists the Print Queue objects that can send print jobs to the printer.
- **Printer Features**—Contains information such as the kind of printer language understood by the printer and the amount of memory installed. This is a useful feature because users can search Novell Directory Services (NDS) to find a printer that supports the features they need for a particular job.
- **Printer Type**—Indicates whether the printer is a parallel, serial, or other kind of printer, such as one accessed via AppleTalk or Unix.
- **Banner Type**—Can be either text or PostScript.
- **Service Interval**—Defines how often the printer checks with the Print Queue object to see whether there are any jobs to print. The value can range from 1 to 255 seconds, with a default of 5 seconds.
- **Buffer Size in KB**—Defines the size of the data segment sent to the printer. The value can range from 3KB to 255KB, with a default of 3KB.
- **Network Address Restrictions**—Specifies the network address of the printer's network interface or the address of the host computer to which the printer is attached.
- **Service Mode for Forms**—Indicates the policy for changing forms and can be set to Starting Form or Service Mode for Forms. The Starting Form value is the identifying number of a form that the Print Server object expects to be loaded on the printer by default. The Service Mode for Forms is used to indicate whether the form can be changed, and how, or if only the currently mounted form should be used.
- **Notification**—A list of users who are notified when a problem occurs on the printer, such as a paper-out condition.

The Print Server property and the Print Queues property are used to link the three objects that make up the path from the user to the finished print job.

Print Server Object Properties

The Print Server object represents the print server program (PSERVER.NLM), which runs on a server to control the printing process. The only properties that are defined when the Print Server object is created are the Name property (common name) and the Advertising Name, which is used to advertise the service using the Service Advertising Protocol (SAP).

The Print Server object, like the Printer object, also enables you to define descriptive properties such as Department and Location. In addition, the Network Address field displays the address on the network of the print server when it is up and running. The Version property shows the version of PSERVER.NLM that is being used by the print server.

Other important properties include the following:

- **Printers**—Indicates the Printer objects that the Print Server can use to render a print job into its final output form.

- **Operators**—Specifies users who can perform management functions for the server. This can include users, groups, and user templates, as well as Organization or Organizational Unit container objects in the NDS tree.

- **Users**—Specifies users who can use this print server. Again, the values here can also be container objects, so you don't have to list each user individually. Although users only need to be listed as users for a print queue to print, if you list them here also, they can check the status of the print queue.

- **Password**—Allows you to assign a password to this Print Server object so that it cannot be loaded (via LOAD PSERVER) by unauthorized users.

The properties for a print server are loaded into memory when the module PSERVER.NLM is loaded. If you make changes to the object after it is loaded, they do not take effect until the print server is unloaded and loaded again.

PSERVER.NLM and NPRINTER.NLM

On a host that is acting as a print server, the PSERVER.NLM module must be loaded. When it is loaded, the module activates any printers defined by Printer objects that are listed in its Printers property. NetWare allows for both local and remote printers. Local printers are attached to the host print server. Remote printers can be serviced by this Print server but reside on other computers. The NPRINTER.NLM module controls the printer and is automatically loaded for each locally attached printer. Because of this, these printers are called *Autoload printers*.

To load the PSERVER module, use the LOAD PSERVER command:

```
LOAD PSERVER <print server object name>
```

The PSERVER.NLM can support up to 256 printers, up to 5 of which can be connected locally to the server on which PSERVER.NLM is loaded.

The NPRINTER.NLM module must be manually loaded on remote servers (and the program NPRINTER.EXE for remote workstations). When multiple printers are hosted on a single remote server or workstation, NPRINTER must be loaded for each one. The syntax used depends on the computer on which the module will be loaded. For DOS machines, use this:

```
NPRINTER <name of print server object> <name of printer object>
```

For NetWare servers, use this:

```
LOAD NPRINTER <name of print server object> <name of printer object>
```

The NetWare 6.x iPrint Utility

NetWare 6.x introduced many new features that were as impressive as well as useful. Both iFolder and iPrint are among those new features. Because Novell is continuing to evolve its product line and break out some features as separate product offerings, you should be sure to visit its Web site to find out the latest information about any part of NetWare. iPrint, which was delivered with NetWare 6.x, uses both Novell Distributed Print Services and IPP to allow you to print to IPP-enabled printers (whether physically connected to a network or connected to an IPP-enabled server that offers printers to the network).

Although iPrint was introduced in NetWare 6.x, you can also run the software on NetWare 5.x networks if you install Support Pack 2 (or a newer support pack). Because most networks are upgraded to a newer version of the operating system for computers on the network, this backward compatibility enables you to use iPrint on your 5.x network while you contemplate whether to begin an upgrade to NetWare 6.x. Client computers that make use of iPrint need to use Windows NT 4.0/2000/XP, or Windows 95/98/Me—using Internet Explorer 5.x or above, or Netscape Navigator 4.7 or greater.

You can expect to see IPP offered on just about every operating system in the near future. This is because the Internet is becoming the de facto means of exchanging data with computers outside your network. Instead of sending a report, a catalog, or other documents to another company, you can simply establish a connection to a server that supports IPP and print directly to a printer managed by that server. Keep in mind, however, that the receiving end of this data transfer will need to grant access to the printer before you can use it.

Hardware-Based Print Servers—Print Server Appliances

You no longer have to dedicate a network host to act as a print server, either dedicated or otherwise, because it's inexpensive to connect a printer directly to the network using a small hardware-based print server device. These devices range from a size that fits in your hand to larger boxes that look like hubs or routers. In some advertisements, you'll see these referred to as printer appliances, or just print servers. Regardless, the function is the same: to consolidate a number of printers to a single network connection. The device buffers data as it passes between the network and the printer and keeps track of which print jobs are destined for ports attached to the device.

Think about how you will locate printers in relation to users when making purchase plans. How many printers will be located in a single place? For example, if you have a central print room where you keep multiple printers, copiers, and other similar equipment, it might be economical to purchase a more expensive model that supports several printers. If you are placing only one or two printers at strategic locations throughout the enterprise, it might be more economical to buy the small palm-sized devices that can support one or two printers. You should also consider the following:

- **Price**—Especially consider the price per port. However, as these appliances have become more common, price is becoming much less of a factor.
- **Number and kind of printer ports**—You might want to plan for expansion and buy devices that leave an extra port available for future use.
- **Network connection type**—Some models support one connector type, such as RJ-45 or BNC. Some have several types.

- **Management software and supported operating systems**—This is an often-overlooked feature. Does the appliance support the Simple Network Management Protocol (SNMP) or Remote Monitoring (RMON)? Does it use a proprietary management command interface? Do you have to be physically located at the device to manage it via a port, or can you use Telnet to establish a session with the device to execute commands?

- **Upgrade path**—Don't lock yourself in to a print server that can't be upgraded, unless it is inexpensive and will perform the tasks you need for a while to come.

Price might not be an important factor unless you are purchasing a lot of equipment. Take into consideration the number of printer ports that each device makes available. Some devices offer both serial and parallel ports, so be sure to check that the ports are compatible with the kind of printers you have or plan to purchase. Another useful feature for a serial port is the capability to attach a local console terminal for management functions. Although it's preferable to remotely manage the print server from a workstation elsewhere on the network, the capability to attach a local console terminal is helpful when troubleshooting, especially when troubleshooting problems with network connectivity. Troubleshooting printer problems is common, as most network administrators will tell you.

Check to be sure that all ports on a model that offers multiple ports can be used at once. Hard as it might be to believe, some models offer two ports, but only one can be active at any time.

The type of network connection supported by the device is very important. Is it a standard 10Mbps Ethernet connection, a 100Mbps connection, or a Token-Ring adapter?

Note

The IPP is likely to be a major player in the future of network printing. Although the standard drafts for the next version of IPP, as proposed at this time, do not provide a full-featured set of functions that can be used to manage all aspects of the printing process, some print servers do implement some or all of the functions as they currently stand. Don't let buzzwords such as IPP determine your decision when trying to select a print server at this time. Wait until the standard has been more completely defined before using it as a major purchase criterion. Instead, if this feature is important for you now, be sure that the print server has the capability to download new firmware when it becomes available from the manufacturer. Otherwise, use a Windows 2000 server that understands IPP to connect to the printer using another protocol (such as TCP/IP), and use the IPP capabilities of Windows 2000 or Windows 2003 servers IIS to manage the printer device.

Management software is another important factor you should carefully scrutinize when making a purchasing decision. Some print servers have only basic software that runs on a Windows platform. Newer models have the capability to present Web pages on the network so that you can manage them from any workstation that has a browser loaded on it. The information that the management software provides can vary widely from one product to another. The typical status information includes paper-out conditions and whether the printer is online or offline. More advanced management packages tell you whether the toner is low in a laser printer.

Another useful feature for any device on the network, much less a print server, is the capability to be updated with new functionality as technology develops. A print server that uses some kind of rewritable memory (for example, flash memory) that can be updated by downloading new software might save you money in the long run because you won't have to purchase a new device when your needs change.

If you browse the Internet, you'll find a large number of inexpensive print server appliances. You can even find these things in your local computer store. They are handy in an environment such as a small office/home office (SOHO). Typically in this environment, a small hub or switch is used, so available ports might be at a premium. By attaching a print server appliance to one port, you can use it to connect several printers that otherwise would have needed one of those scarce ports.

In larger networks, a print server can serve a similar function, providing a single place to plug in several printers that all reside in a printer room, for example.

Whichever you choose, using a print server appliance, or building a print server using a PC, become familiar with the performance aspects and management capabilities that you'll need when something goes wrong.

System and Network Security

SOME OF THE MAIN TOPICS FOR THIS PART ARE

Basic Security Measures Every Network Administrator Needs to Know

Auditing and Other Monitoring Measures

Security Issues for Wide Area Networks

Firewalls

Virtual Private Networks (VPNs) and Tunneling

Encryption Technology

PART VIII

Basic Security Measures Every Network Administrator Needs to Know

SOME OF THE MAIN TOPICS IN THIS CHAPTER ARE

CHAPTER 46

Keeping a network secure is a time-consuming process that requires a lot of attention to detail. Similar to troubleshooting faulty equipment, maintaining network security is also a time-consuming practice that involves the following:

- Detection of a security breach or network intrusion
- Finding the cause of a security breach
- Finding the method of an intrusion
- Educating users about security on a continual basis

This chapter examines security from two different angles: first, preventive measures that can be used to help keep problems from occurring in the first place, and second, tools and techniques to discover these kinds of problems.

Policies and Procedures

To have security practices that make sense, you must first define—for yourself and the users of the network resources—a security policy that spells out exactly what can and cannot be done on the network. Intruders who might penetrate the network and compromise data or programs do so in many ways. One of those is to exploit "friendly users" who are on the network. Referred to as *social engineering*, this is perhaps one of the most overlooked but most often used method for getting access to a network. Most employees who simply use a desktop computer for word processing and other office activities are especially prone to this kind of security breach.

A good security policy that is enforced—in some cases through means of technological enforcement— can go a long way toward keeping naive users from disclosing information to those who might do harm to your network. *If you don't think your users are vulnerable, just ask someone to call up and say they're calling from the help desk and need to know the user's password.* You'd be surprised how many times this tactic will succeed.

At the same time, you also should establish procedures to follow for routine tasks that are performed on a periodic basis, such as backups, restores, creating user accounts, and the like. When a task is described by a procedure that must be followed, there is less of a chance that something out of the ordinary will be done that can compromise security.

Depending on your site, there are several documents you can use to make users aware of the policies in place for computer and network security. Typically, the human resources department is responsible for having new employees review documents and having them sign the documents to show that they have read and understood them. Documents you might find useful for your site include the following:

- Network connection policy
- Acceptable use statement
- Usage guidelines
- Escalation procedures

Network Connection Policy

This type of document should define the type of system that can be connected to the network. It should set forth the security requirements, such as operating-system features to be used, and a person responsible for approving the attachment of new devices to the network. When configuring a new computer, a switch, or even a router, you should have explicit guidelines as to what is permissible and what is not. For firewalls (see Chapter 49, "Firewalls"), you should have a separate network connection policy that dictates what type of network traffic is allowed through the firewall, in both directions. If allowing users to connect using a Virtual Private Network (VPN), you should also have specific documents detailing how the laptop or other computers they use are configured. Allowing someone to work from home using their own computer is about the worst decision you can make. If the computer is used for personal as well as business work, you open yourself up to all sorts of programs that can infiltrate the computer and attempt to compromise your network, whether or not you use a VPN link.

If the business unit of your company (and not the IT department) decides that certain remote work is confidential, a policy should be put in place that requires a separate computer (such as a laptop, to include mobile users) to be used. By using a company-configured laptop, and not allowing users to make use of the laptop for personal access to the Internet, and disallowing a configuration change, you can make your network more secure. Just keep in mind that if the user is entering your network with his own computer, you will probably have little say over what is downloaded. By giving the user a company computer, and preventing (through a company policy) the use of the computer for personal usage, you can further protect your network.

The use of security programs, such as virus monitoring software, should always be required in today's Internet-centric environment. Any procedures that must be used to obtain a computer account, along with the types of rights and privileges that can be granted to an account, also should be documented here, as well as what network addresses can be used and how they are controlled. Finally, you should explicitly set forth in this document that no connections are to be made to the network without following the procedures in this document, and without notifications made to the proper persons.

It cannot be emphasized enough that you have strict guidelines on how your computers are configured and that users must obtain permission through a written request for any deviances from the established policy. If a program is not supported by your central help desk, it should not be allowed unless a business requirement makes it a necessity. When that becomes the case, you should add the program to your allowable network connection policy documents and educate the help-desk staff on its use. In no situation should you allow users to download software from the Internet and install it on their work computers, on computers that are used in a mobile environment, or on home computers that are used to connect to your corporate environment.

Acceptable Use Statement and Usage Guidelines

A computer is a flexible device. It can be used for many things beyond the tasks that are needed by the ordinary worker during a normal workday. Although some might be concerned with the time that can be lost due to a user accessing a computer for non work-related tasks, there are far more important factors to consider.

As mentioned in the preceding section, one of the most important things you should include is an acceptable use statement. This should state that all computer programs are to be supplied by the company and that unauthorized programs, such as those brought from home, are not to be used on the computer or network. Software piracy is not a victimless crime, as many people seem to think. It is a crime that is punishable by stiff fines and jail sentences. It is important that you make sure that users understand this and that you protect your company from possible litigation by showing that you have made an effort to prevent unauthorized programs from being placed on computers at the site.

Piracy is only half the issue when it comes to unauthorized programs. Computer viruses can easily make their way from one computer to another through floppy disks or by being downloaded from the Internet. Unfortunately, it is usually only after more than one system has become infected that a virus is found or reported. If all software that is used on the company network is first examined, approved, and distributed by a central source, you will have better control over this problem.

Of course, you also should state that users cannot make copies of software or data that is owned by the company and take it home or otherwise use it in an unauthorized manner.

Note

For some tools—such as antivirus products or software-based firewalls—it may be in your company's best interest to negotiate contracts that allow such products to be installed both on office assets and on employees' personally owned home systems. The additional cost can be well worth the investment if it prevents a virus-infected system from connecting and propagating on your corporate network.

In this statement, point out to users that they are required to report any suspicious activity or misuse of network resources. They also should be made responsible for taking necessary measures for protecting data and programs within their scope. This includes not leaving a workstation logged in when they are away from it for extended periods—they should use a password-locked screen saver when away from the computer. Another avenue of infiltration is leaving reports or other output containing sensitive information lying around, and the like. Just because you trust one employee does not mean you trust all employees. For example, if a printout of payroll information is left lying around, do you really think that someone is not going to look at it? If you do not put the rules in a policy statement, users might not realize that these things are a problem.

If dial-up access is granted to users, they should certainly understand that they cannot give information used for this access to anyone else, either inside or outside the company. Many times it has been shown that hackers penetrated a network not through repetitive password cracking techniques, but simply because a user left a password lying around or used one that was so obvious that it could not be considered secure.

All, and I mean all, access to your network should be done through a VPN or a dial-up mechanism that uses a firewall. Although your network policies may absolutely prohibit employees from using company computers for home work (or for mobile users on the road), I can guarantee that you will never be able to enforce this policy. Users will check their own personal email, read the latest news site, and, at worst, download software that may seem innocent, such as programs to play back MP3 files, or others. These things should not be tolerated in a secure network environment. A firewall can only do so much.

Indeed, there is an application on the Internet that can make use of "unused" fields in the IP packet to send one or more characters at a time using otherwise normal IP packets that your firewall will let through. When you consider that several thousand IP packets can be used in a single transmission, you'll see that any hacker intercepting these can gain a lot of information from someone inside your company who appears to be a model employee.

The things you can put into an acceptable use policy are extensive. You must examine the specific types of resources you are trying to protect and think up ways to include them in the statement. Some other items you might want to consider are listed here:

- **Harassment of other users.** What might seem like harmless horseplay in a typical office environment can constitute harassment when it's done over a long period.

- **Threats.** Statements that can be construed as an intention to perform some kind of harmful act should always be treated with the utmost importance and severity.

- **Removal of hardware (or software) from the premises without written authorization.** This includes such things as authorization codes used to activate copies of software that is downloadable from the Internet, as well as copied software. You should not provide "CD burners" for employees who do not have an absolute need for them. Your typical backup procedures for networked disk drive share should be enough to ensure that data is not lost.

■ **Using company email for personal use.** This may seem to be a small matter, but as recent events have shown, just opening an attachment to an email can launch a virus on a computer. In addition, the content of a person's email can sometimes be offensive, especially if the user has gotten onto a "spam" list. Lastly, do you want to pay employees to spend an hour or so each day reviewing their own personal email?

■ **Bringing hardware into the premises without authorization, such as laptop computers.** This is a policy that especially should be applied to vendors and contractors. If they need to perform functions (such as software installation or troubleshooting), then you should, if possible, provide the computer access they need, and be careful to supervise their access.

■ **Attempting to access data not relevant to the user's job, sometimes referred to as "probing" the network.** This is, in my opinion, an offense that you should consider as a reason for firing an employee. There is never a need to go exploring the network. If the user wants to know where data or applications are stored, they should discuss it with management or your help desk.

Employees

Any document that outlines guidelines for using the network should point out to employees that they are to behave ethically on the network. Help-desk personnel, for example, often must access data owned by another person when helping them with a problem. Disclosing information to a third party that is obtained during this type of work is unethical. Administrators and operations personnel often have elevated rights and privileges on the workstations and servers that are distributed throughout the network. They should be made to understand that these privileges include a responsibility to professionally carry out their work without causing problems.

One of the main problems I've encountered with help-desk employees is that they are paid very little compared to others who manage the network. Yet they are a very vulnerable link in the chain. Only constant training and discussions about security can solve this problem because most corporations view the help desk as a minor department, where turnover is frequent because most employees here learn enough to go on to higher-paying jobs.

Vendors and Outside Connections

Another area often overlooked is when outside persons are allowed to access the network. If you have contractors who are brought in to do work that cannot be done by in-house persons, be sure that you have a usage guidelines document for them to review and sign. It should specifically include the fact that information on the network is of a proprietary nature and cannot be disclosed to any outside party, or to any employee in the company who does not have a need to know.

Additionally, the policy document should state that the contractor cannot discuss with others the *type* of information to which they have access. A little information can go a long way when given to the wrong person.

When hardware repair needs to be done, it is sometimes done by a third-party maintenance organization, or perhaps by the vendor who manufactures the equipment. Diagnosing some problems may require that the repairman have access to a logon account. If you maintain a user account just for this purpose, be sure that it is one that can be enabled and disabled so that it is available only when it is needed. For example, the OpenVMS operating system has, by default, a FIELD account that is meant to be used by field service when it needs access to the computer. This account is disabled when it is created and must be enabled by the administrator before it can be used. Because OpenVMS is a widely used operating system, there are a lot of hackers who are aware of this account and also know that many times you will set an easy password for it. Don't make the mistake of leaving this kind of back door open to your network. Disable or remove accounts such as these when they are not needed.

Escalation Procedures

Having a plan of action that should be followed in response to a specific event is a good idea. There should be a specific person or persons in the company who are designated to be responsible for and investigate matters relating to security. A document that sets forth the procedures to be followed for particular security violations will also show users that security is important for the network and that actions will be taken.

A document covering escalation procedures should indicate the kinds of things that are considered a security breach. These can include the following:

- Theft of hardware or software

- Password discovery or disclosure

- Improper disposal of media, including tapes, floppy disks, and printed reports

- Sharing of logon accounts or disclosure of usernames and passwords

- Probing the network to look where one is not authorized

- Interfering with another user's data or account

- Suspected network break-in from outside sources

- Computer viruses

- Physical access violations

Some of these probably seem very obvious when you look at them. To think that you will know how to handle these kinds of problems without a written procedure, though, is a little naive. For example, it is very common for users to allow others to use their account. It's a lot simpler to let another employee use your workstation, when theirs is out of service, than it is to get the appropriate permissions from upper-level management. However, it often happens that when you give someone a password to use on one occasion, it also gets used on another.

When you suspect that the network has been infiltrated from an outside source, what do you do? Shut down the routers? Change all the passwords? Think about this ahead of time and document a list of steps to follow. These steps should include methods used to determine the source of the break-in, as well as procedures to be followed to punish the intruder and reassert ownership of any pilfered information. For example, if information that is confidential has been compromised, what steps do you take to notify the person to whom the information relates? Are there legal matters you need to be aware of that pertain to the data that resides on your network?

Perhaps one of the hardest things a manager has to do is to fire an employee. When someone leaves the company voluntarily and is on friendly terms with management, it is a simple matter to deactivate the user's account and be sure that all access doors are closed. When an unfriendly termination happens, though, you need to have in place steps to follow to be sure you are aware of all access methods that were available to the unfriendly employee. In the case of an employee who is terminated for actions that caused deliberate damage to the network, how do you determine whether any other "time bombs" have been planted? What steps do you take to isolate the resources that were available to this employee until further analysis can be done? Do you need to change passwords on accounts other than the user's—for example, any test accounts or local system accounts to which the user may have had access?

As you can see, network security has far-reaching implications. Knowing what to do in the event of a specific security event will make things easier for you when they happen.

What a Security Policy Should Include

When writing a security policy, you should first perform an inventory of the resources you want to protect. Identify the users who need to access each resource, and determine the most likely place a threat to the resource might come from. With this information, you then can begin to construct a security policy that users will have to follow.

The security policy should not be something that is simply generally understood by everyone. It should be an actual written document. To remind users about the importance of security, you might want to post copies of it around the office so that they will see it on a regular basis.

A good security policy will be composed of several elements, including these:

- **Risk assessment**—What are you trying to protect and from whom? Identify your network assets and possible sources of problems.

- **Responsibilities**—Describe who in the company is responsible for handling specific matters relating to security. This can include who is authorized to approve a new user account up to items such as who will conduct investigations into security breaches.

- **Proper use of network resources**—State in the policy that users are not to misuse information, use the network for personal use, or intentionally cause damage to the network or information that resides on it.

- **Legal ramifications**—Be sure to get advice from the proper sources about any legal matters that apply to the information you store or generate on your network. Include statements to this effect in the security policy documents.

- **Procedures to remedy security problems**—State what procedures will be followed when a security event occurs and what actions will be taken against those who perpetrate them.

Request for Comments (RFC) 1244 ("Site Security Handbook") is a good document to read before designing a security policy. This RFC gives a list of resources found in most networks that are vulnerable to potential security threats. You can download this RFC, along with others, from the Web site www.rfc-editor.org/. These are the five classes of vulnerability vectors:

- **Hardware**—This includes workstations and servers, printers, disk drives, network wiring, and disk drives. This also includes internetworking devices such as bridges, routers, and switches.

- **Software**—Every piece of software you run on any computer in the network is a potential security problem. This includes programs purchased from outside vendors and software created in-house by your own programming staff. Operating systems frequently have to be patched as new bugs are discovered that give an intruder an easy way to infiltrate.

- **Data**—The most important asset on your network is probably the data that is generated or used by your business. You can replace software programs and operating systems. When important data, such as customer lists, sales information, or proprietary trade secrets, is compromised, this can have a significant impact on business.

- **People**—Users, operators, and anyone else who interacts with your network or any device attached to it is a potential security risk.

- **Paperwork**—Often overlooked by many, this is a very valuable resource to hackers. Passwords are written down. Reports are generated that have confidential information contained in them. Often this resource is simply thrown in a dumpster when it is no longer needed. A better approach is to shred or otherwise make it unusable before getting rid of it.

Note

The Post-It Note is—in this author's opinion—one of the single greatest threats to computer security. I can't tell you the number of times I've found Post-It Notes with a username and password stuck to the side of a monitor.

A good security policy that is understood by users will go a long way toward preventing some of the problems you can potentially encounter. Make it a point to review the policy with users periodically, such as at quarterly meetings, and be sure that users understand the responsibilities that go along with having access to the company network.

Physical Security Measures

Preventing unauthorized access to resources means that you must first prevent unauthorized access to the physical components that make up the network. This includes user workstations, servers, network cables and devices, and so on. After the network connection leaves your physical area, such as when you connect to an outside Internet provider, you lose control over the physical aspects of the network. At that point, you must rely on other techniques, such as encryption or tunneling, to maintain security. However, the equipment over which you have control should be closely monitored to ensure that no one is tampering with anything in a manner that might serve to defeat the security policy in effect at your site.

Locking the Door

As silly as it might seem, the simple door lock is an often-overlooked security device. You wouldn't leave your front door at home unlocked all the time, would you? The servers in your network that hold valuable or sensitive data should not be sitting out on a desktop or in an unlocked room where anyone can access them. Routers, hubs, switches, and other devices should be similarly protected. Wiring closets and computer rooms should have a lock on them or be protected by some sort of monitoring on a 24-hour basis. If you have a round-the-clock operations staff, you might not need to lock the computer room. But if that staff consists of only one person during any particular period, get a lock for the door! Ideally, access to these secure areas will be tracked and logged, such as through employee badge readers. With very sensitive systems, you may even want to go as far as securing physical access through biometric authorization systems. Biometric systems, though still in their infancy, can help ensure that someone cannot gain access to a secure area simply by borrowing or stealing a physical token.

Backup media, such as tapes or writable CDs, should be treated the same as live data. Don't back up a server or your own personal workstation and then leave the tape cartridge or CD lying on the desk or in an unlocked drawer.

Uninterruptible Power Supply (UPS)

Keeping data secure can mean keeping it out of the hands of those who are not permitted to view it. It also can mean keeping the data safe from corruption. As more and more business-critical information is being committed to electronic form, it is important to take steps to be sure that it is not unintentionally compromised. A good UPS will pay for itself the first time you have to spend days reconstructing a database or reinstalling programs that become unusable due to a power outage or another problem of this sort.

Most computer operating systems have features that will work with a UPS so that the UPS can perform an orderly shutdown when it detects that power has been lost. If you are using a battery-backup UPS that has only a limited supply of power, an orderly shutdown can save a lot of problems when compared to a system crash.

◄◄ UPS devices are covered in more detail in Chapter 5, "Protecting the Network: Preventative Maintenance Techniques."

Disposing of Hardware and Media in a Secure Manner

When you upgrade your network and bring in new workstations or servers, it is a generous thing to give employees, or an organization such as a school, your old equipment if it is still usable. However, you should establish a policy which dictates that all hard disks are to be erased and, when appropriate, a legal copy of the operating system reinstalled on it. If you leave important information on a computer you give away, don't be surprised when you see it again.

There is also the legal aspect to this. If you give away an old computer system, do you have the legal right to keep the software packages and install them on a new system? Probably not, unless you have a site license or another license that allows you to do so. For that reason, do not give away a computer that has applications installed on it unless you intend to give away the software packages also.

Disposing of used floppy disks, backup tapes, and tape cartridges also poses a potential security threat. It is better to destroy these information carriers than to give them away without being absolutely sure that you have purged them of any recoverable information. A bulk magnetic eraser can be a good security tool to use before disposing of this kind of stuff.

The Two Sides of Security

Locking the computer-room door is a preventive measure intended to keep out those who have no business being there. Preventive measures should be taken for software access mechanisms also. However, no matter how good you are at putting into place the access control mechanisms to protect resources, there is always going to be someone who will try, and possibly succeed, in breaking through. For this reason, you also must be able to keep audit trails of events on the network so that you can determine whether someone is trying to break your security, or whether indeed they have done so.

Before the Fact: Controlling Access

Controlling access to the network is done by several common mechanisms:

- User accounts and passwords
- Physical identifiers
- Resource protections

In many operating systems, the concept of a *resource owner* is important in this scheme. For example, OpenVMS and Windows 2000/Server 2003/XP keep track of the user who creates a resource, such as a file. That owner is able to change the protections applied to the file and can grant others the permissions needed to use the file. To a lesser degree, the same can be said for Unix/Linux operating systems.

Identifying Users

In a homogeneous network in which only one user account and password is required for access to permitted resources throughout the network, system management is not usually a complicated matter. Windows 2000/XP and Server 2003 allow for the creation of areas of control, called domains, that operate as security boundaries. Users in a domain can be granted access to resources on any computer, either server or workstation, that the network administrator wants to give them. In addition, trust relationships can be established between domains when administrators cooperate, making it possible for the user to still use only one username and password to connect to resources throughout the network. From Windows 2000 and more recent Windows versions, group policies can be used to further control access to important resources.

Novell NetWare provides this functionality by giving the user a logon to the network that is controlled by the Novell Directory Services. Each user is represented in the directory by a User object, the properties of which specify information about passwords and connections.

The Unix operating system does not use the concept of a domain. Instead, each Unix host maintains a password file that stores information about each user, including an encrypted password. To access resources on other network hosts, the Unix user must either log on when accessing the computer or use a proxy mechanism. TCP/IP utilities such as FTP and Telnet often send user passwords across the network in clear-text format and are easy targets for interception.

The Unix remote utilities, usually called r-commands because they all start with the letter *r*, are used to perform ordinary network functions such as copying or printing files or logging in to a remote system. This is very useful in the network environment in which a user performs functions on many different machines. These utilities are not necessarily good when looked at from a security standpoint, however. Although the user must have a valid user account on the remote hosts on which these commands execute, the user does not have to provide the password.

Note

Although most Telnet applications still use clear-text passwords for authentication purposes, there are some that use encrypted authentication. If security is of a great concern on your network, be sure to examine the documentation closely before using these utilities on any node in the network. This also applies to other TCP/IP utilities such as the r-commands and FTP.

Instead, an entry in the /etc/hosts.equiv file or the .rhosts file on a remote computer is what determines access. The remote machine trusts the computer on which the user executes an r-command if it can find an entry in either of these files for it. Each entry in the /etc/hosts.equiv file contains a hostname and a username, to identify users and the hosts that are allowed to execute these commands without providing a password. The assumption is that if you have logged in to the remote host, you have already been authenticated. The .rhosts file works in a similar manner but resides in a user's home directory. The remote users entered in this file can perform functions based on the account associated with that user.

Note

Although you'll still find the basic r-commands in most Unix and Linux systems, there is an alternative. The Secure Shell (SSH) utilities offer authentication and encryption for data transfers using utilities that are similar to the r-commands. You can find out more about SSH by visiting the Web site **www.ssh.com/products/ssh/**. You can obtain free versions of SSH by visiting **www.openssh.com/**.

Although this sounds a lot like the Windows NT/2000/Server 2003/XP trust mechanism, it is not. It is quite easy to impersonate a remote node and gain entry into a Unix/Linux system by using the r-commands.

Resource Protections

After a user has been authenticated by the operating system, the next step to access a resource is for a check to be done to see whether the resource has any access controls placed on it. Typically, an operating system will grant access to a resource, such as a file, by granting users the right to do the following:

- Read the file
- Write to the file

- Execute the file
- Take ownership of the file
- Delete the file

These concepts also can be extended to resources such as printers and modems. When granting these rights, most operating systems also enable you to specify which rights are applied to users or groups of users. For example, Windows NT enables you to group users into local or global groups. When you set the access controls on a file, you can specify the access rights by group. Using this method, one group of ordinary users might be able to read a file, while a group of users that manages the file might be granted read and write access, as well as delete access to the file. To prevent programs from being run by unauthorized users, the execute right can be granted or denied to a user or a group of users.

Tip

Starting with Windows NT and continuing through Windows 2003 Server enables you to format a hard disk using the NTFS file system or the standard FAT system that is compatible with DOS and other operating systems, such as Windows 95/98. If you want to provide access controls on individual files and directories under Windows NT/2000/Server 2003/XP and so on, you must format your disk partitions using NTFS. The local access rights that you can assign to files and directories have no effect on FAT partitions. Also, Windows 2000/Server 2003/XP adds a new feature to Windows operating systems that enables you to encrypt individual files on disk. The encryption is done on-the-fly as a file is written or is read, so for a high-security environment this might be a good option to use.

It is important to understand the features of your operating system that pertain to granting rights or permissions. Rights generally enable a user to perform an action. Permissions are placed on resources and define who can access and what kind of access can be made of a resource.

◄◄   For more information on user rights and permissions, and on how they are implemented by different operating systems, see Chapter 43, "Rights and Permissions."

After the Fact: Auditing Use

As you may be aware, there are auditing tools you can use to keep track of resource use, both attempted and successful logon attempts. Here it is important only to note that it is not enough to organize users into groups and grant them resource permissions throughout the network.

▶▶   You can learn more about monitoring successful as well as failed logon attempts by reading Chapter 47, "Auditing and Other Monitoring Measures."

There are several reasons for this. A large user base, combined with multiple servers that hold valuable resources, makes it difficult at times for an administrator who is not familiar with the information resources provided by a specific server to understand the permissions needed. For example, a new user in the accounting department might or might not need access to accounts receivable files or accounts payable files. They might need access to one or the other or maybe both files. A manager in that department would probably be the likely person to make the decision about what files the user should be able to access.

However, if the user is placed into a group, which is generally done to make administration easier, compromises sometimes happen, and the user might be granted access through the group to resources that they do not need to access.

Another reason is that sometimes mistakes are made. It is a fact of life that no one is perfect and that no system for allocating resources is going to get it right 100% of the time. When users are granted the capability to read a file, you can be sure, if the data contained in it is interesting enough, that they will do so.

Indeed, even if a user does not have appropriate access rights to a file, sometimes the user will try to get at interesting information anyway.

For these reasons, a good operating system provides auditing controls that enable you to look back after a security breach to try to determine who did what and where they did it. Unix (and its variants, such as Linux), Windows NT/2000/Server 2003, and Novell all provide features that enable you to record both successful and failed attempts to access resources. They all do it in different ways, and many of these auditing and security features are not enabled out-of-the-box; so if you have multiple operating systems on the network, it will be important that you understand each of them so that you can best enable and use these capabilities.

Passwords

It might not seem like an important thing to mention at this point, but you need to enforce a policy that makes users choose good passwords. And when you do that, you must decide what makes a good password for your environment. Simply put, a good password is one that is hard to guess. When you consider that a standard password-cracking technique used by hackers is to simply try every word in a dictionary, you can begin to understand that luck doesn't have a lot to do with penetrating a network. It comes mostly from lax security that allows doors that are easy to open.

Enforcing Good Passwords

When deciding how passwords are to be constructed, there are a few guidelines you can follow:

- **Use more than one word.** Multiple words "glued" together make a pattern of characters that is much harder for a simple password-cracking program to guess. Don't use words that naturally go together. For example, Atlantabraves is not a good choice; Atlantayoko is a better choice. *Never* use a name of a celebrity or a popular institution.

- **Use nonalphabetic characters somewhere in the password.** This can be numeric characters or punctuation characters, provided that the operating system you use will permit them.

- **In Unix and Windows NT/2000/Server 2003 Server editions as well as Windows XP, passwords are case sensitive.** If you use both upper- and lowercase characters in a password, you can confound many password-guessing applications. Do not, however, substitute numeric characters that resemble alphabetic characters. One of the easiest things a password-hacker application can do is to substitute the letter "O" for zero. Don't fall for that one!

- **Don't make passwords too difficult to memorize.** The last thing you want is to have frustrated users writing down passwords so that they will be able to remember them. If you find this happening, it's time to re-educate the employee. There are many methods in use today that can be used to provide "one password" for all applications on the network. You should investigate these types of applications and, if appropriate for your network, justify the cost versus the cost of a network intrusion. Many of these systems involve smart cards and PIN numbers. Again, although this may be an expensive up-front cost, justify it by the value of your data.

- **Use password history restrictions if the operating system permits it.** This means that the operating system keeps track of a limited number of passwords that the user has previously used and will not allow them to be reused within a certain time frame. A common practice is to change your password when forced to do so and then to change it back to a value that you like and can easily remember.

Be sure that you do not create user accounts and assign them a password that never gets changed by the user. Most operating systems will allow you to set a password to be expired on its first use so that when a new user logs in the first time, he will be required to change his password.

Sometimes it is important to have a password that makes no sense whatsoever. In a highly secure environment this can make sense, in that you want something that is hard to guess. However, remember that when something is difficult to remember it usually gets written down somewhere, which can defeat the purpose of a password altogether. Unix has a command, `passwd`, that can be used to computer-generate a password for a user. For example, the command

```
passwd username
```

displays a list of potential passwords that are generally difficult to guess. The user can select one from this list to use if he is having a difficult time thinking one up. The only problem with this method is in getting the user to memorize the password.

Password Policies

No user account, including one used by an administrator (or root for the Unix/Linux community), should ever be allowed to keep the same password for an extended period. A good idea for passwords is to require that they be changed every 30–60 days, depending on the level of security you need at your site. You also should enforce a minimum length for passwords. Most operating systems will allow you to specify this value so that users cannot change their password to one that is shorter than the size you require.

On Unix systems, you can set the password minimum length by specifying it in a field in the file `/etc/default/passwd`.

On Novell NetWare servers, you can enforce a minimum password length by modifying the object properties of the template object used to create a user account, or by modifying the properties of an individual user object for a particular user.

Depending on the particular operating system, you can enforce other restrictions on passwords or user accounts to enhance security on the network. Some of the capabilities you might find include these:

- **Password expirations**—A password should not be used indefinitely.
- **Password history lists**—This feature prevents a password from being reused within a specified period.
- **Account lockouts**—When a hacker is trying to use the brute-force method to guess a password for an account, you should be able to lock out the account automatically after a specified number of attempts within a specific time frame.

Password Grabbers

About the oldest trick known to those who would want to break into another user's account is the use of a program that imitates the operating system's own logon procedure. This kind of program generally is executed by someone who logs in using his own account on another's workstation. He then runs a program that does nothing but wait until the unsuspecting user tries to log in. The program prompts for a username and password, mimicking the operating system in every respect. However, instead of logging the user on to the system, which the program is unable to do, it simply stores the password in a file and then generates a phony error message.

If the user is not too concerned about security, he will probably never know that he has been fooled. The user might think he has entered his password incorrectly and try again. The second time it will succeed because it is the operating system that is prompting the user this second time. The password grabber program has already done its job and it disappears.

The user who began this fraud simply retrieves the file, thus getting the password, and then can freely log in as that user and cause many problems when it comes to tracking down the real person who is abusing security. Because the perpetrator is now using someone else's username and password, he is difficult to catch.

Note

This subterfuge is one of the reasons Windows NT/2000/2003 Servers, as well as Windows XP, use the key sequence of Ctrl+Alt+Delete to begin the logon process. It is generally difficult to write a program that mimics the Windows logon screen because the Ctrl+Alt+Delete combination of keystrokes is trapped by a processor interrupt, and unless the system has been grossly compromised, any program attempting to pass as the logon screen will fail.

System Daemons and Services

Windows servers have background processes that perform many functions, called *services*. Unix systems also have background processes that work in a similar manner that are called *daemons*. Regardless of what you call them, these processes, which are called background because they do not require interaction with the keyboard but instead execute on the computer waiting to perform some function, can introduce security problems when they are not needed.

You should become familiar with the background processes on any servers in your network and disable those that are not needed. For example, on Unix systems, there are many background daemons associated with the TCP/IP suite of protocols. Some systems might need all of these, whereas some might need just a few or none of them. Table 46.1 lists some of the daemons you might want to look at to determine whether they are needed. If not, disable them.

Table 46.1   TCP/IP Services That Might Not Be Needed on All Systems

Service Name	Description
uucp	Unix-to-Unix copy
finger	Provides information about users
tftp	Trivial file transfer protocol
talk	Allows text communications between users on the network
bootp	Provides network information to clients
systat	Gives out current system information
netstat	Gives out current network information such as current connections
rusersd	Shows logged-on users
rexd	Remote execution utility

It might be that you do need these services. It might be that they need to be configured properly to prevent their misuse. You should read the documentation that comes with your Unix or Linux system to determine the capabilities that these daemons provide and disable them on systems that do not need them.

For example, tftp (the trivial ftp transport application) is a stripped-down version of FTP. It is compact and usually can be easily implemented in an EPROM. For this reason, it is useful in some devices that need to download operating software from a host. However, note that unlike FTP, tftp has no access control mechanisms. This means that a username and password are not used. Because there is no authentication, this can be a real security problem if it is not configured properly, such that it can be used only for its intended purpose.

On Windows servers, you can use two programs that are provided with the Resource Kits to install or run almost any executable program or batch file as a service. These are INSTRV.EXE, which can be used to install an executable, and SRVANY.EXE, which can be used to make other kinds of files into services. On a server that has several users logging in frequently, you might want to make it a regular part of your routine maintenance to review the services running on the machines and disable or remove those that are not installed by the initial operating-system installation or those that did not come from products you have applied to the system.

To do this, you will need to keep an inventory of what runs on each server, but this kind of inventory information can be useful for other purposes, such as when you need to reinstall a server that has been destroyed by a catastrophic failure.

Removing Dead Wood

Every operating system comes with default options installed that you might not be aware of unless you have read the documentation carefully. For example, default user accounts might be created when you install the OS or later install a product. For example, the GUEST account in Windows operating systems is installed by default. You should always disable or remove this account. The Administrator account is also a vulnerable target because it is present on all Windows Server computers from Windows NT through Server 2003. You cannot delete this account, but you can *rename it* so that the hacker's job becomes more difficult. Also, you shouldn't use the Administrator account on a regular basis. Instead, create individual administrative user accounts for each system administrator trusted to perform these high-level tasks. Then put them into the Domain Admins group to allow these users to exercise administrator privileges, while maintaining an audit trail of the actual users who performed certain actions. You should always use separate administrative accounts for your domain administrators. Never use the same account for domain administration as is used for regular user functions. Administrators should be logged in with administrative accounts only when performing activities that require elevated permissions. You can also use group policies to further restrict what each user can do.

Regularly review the user accounts that exist on the network. Use the auditing features provided to determine when an account has not been in use for a long period, and if you can find no reason for its existence, disable it. Maybe someone in another department did not notify you when a user was terminated, or maybe an account was created for an expected new employee or contractor who later changed his mind and did not come on board. New accounts such as these are typically created with a simple password and can leave gaping security holes in your network.

Old programs and files that are no longer needed, or the use for which you are not sure, are also easy targets to cause security problems. As a rule of thumb, if it's not needed, back it up to tape and delete it! If a user finds that something she needs is missing, she will tell you!

When installing a new application product for a user, be sure you know the capabilities of the application. Don't install unneeded optional features that will not normally be used. Read the documentation!

Delegating Authority

In a network of any size other than a simple workgroup, it is usually necessary to delegate authority to other administrators or middle-level management personnel. When you find that you must create accounts that have privileges to perform administrative functions, do not give carte blanche access to every account. Keep track of the exact functions an account will be used for, and grant only the access rights and permissions needed.

For example, if an operator will be performing backup functions on a server, he does not need to have full rights and privileges on the server. Under Windows Servers, you can place the user's account into the Backup Operators user group to give him the capabilities he needs, without compromising all files on the system. If you have users who must be able to add or modify user accounts, check the operating-system documentation and give the users access only to the resources and data files they need.

User Accounts

Generic accounts might seem like a good idea at first thought, but they provide nothing in the way of auditing. If you simply let one or more users share the root account on a Unix system, or the Administrator account on a Windows server, you will have no way of determining who did what when something goes wrong. Indeed, because you can grant the same capabilities to any new account you can create, why not do so?

Give each user who requires elevated capabilities her own account, and grant the necessary privileges to the account. This way you can track each user to be sure she does not abuse her account or use it in a way you do not expect.

When you have more than one user using the same account, there is also the likelihood that the password will be compromised and someone who is not authorized to use the account will do so.

Application Servers, Print Servers, and Web Servers

One particularly common error you can make is to put all your eggs in one basket. Instead of using one server to provide print services or file services or Web services, many administrators use one server to provide all three. This is not necessarily a good idea.

Specialized servers can limit the damage that can be done by intruders and also can make it easier to delegate authority so that a particular administrator can concentrate on a limited set of functions for a certain server. Web servers are particularly prone to attempts by hackers to intrude onto your network. New applications and technologies are being developed and deployed all the time, and the newer they are, the more likely it is that they will have bugs or other loopholes that make them more risky than other applications that run on the network.

Placing sensitive data files on a Web server simply because it is convenient to use the machine's resources is not a good idea if it is also being used as a Web server. Make it more difficult to get at these files by dedicating a file server computer to them instead.

Delegating servers is almost like delegating authority to users. When you divide up resources and partition them into manageable groups, you make it less likely that an attack on one object will result in damage to all objects.

Denial of Service (DoS) attacks are very common on networks now. This kind of attack can be done by a malicious person who takes advantage of a known weakness in a protocol or an implementation of a particular service. One common mistake that administrators make when setting up an FTP site is to place it on an ordinary server.

For example, you might want to have an FTP server that allows customers to log in to your system and download information, patches, or other files. You also might want to be able to let them upload files or messages to your site. If you are going to allow anonymous FTP access, be absolutely sure that the service is configured so that it can access only a dedicated disk or set of disks. Do not allow anonymous access to an FTP service that writes to a system disk or a data disk that is important in your network. It is quite easy for an outsider to simply fill up the disk with meaningless data, causing a system to lock up or crash, depending on the operating system. If an important data disk becomes full, it can cause an extended period of downtime, putting employees out of work for hours while you try to first determine the cause and then remedy it!

Don't Forget About Firewalls

Last, but not least, for this chapter is a quick reminder that a firewall is a necessity for connecting a LAN or larger network to the Internet today. A firewall can serve to prevent the spread of all sorts of trouble that can be perpetuated on the Internet using freely available tools and script files that even high-school kids can download and use to wreak havoc on the network that becomes their target. Using a "demilitarized zone" with a firewall can allow you to provide access to users outside of your network, as well as access by users inside your network. The benefit is that the servers are placed between two firewalls, and access to these types of servers is done on a controlled basis.

▶▶ For more information about firewalls, be sure to read Chapter 49, "Firewalls."

Chapter 49 should be required reading material for any network administrator who cares about security, whether it be a large network or a small office network. Firewall technology can be simple (but easily hacked), or it can be a full-time job for several people in a large network. Justify the cost by comparing what it will cost you if your data is changed, obtained by a third party, or just hacked by some person on the Internet who gets his kicks out of causing you problems!

Auditing and Other Monitoring Measures

SOME OF THE MAIN TOPICS IN THIS CHAPTER ARE

Security for an individual computer system or for the network as a whole requires a two-pronged approach. First you must try to ensure that all applications and data are secured against unauthorized usage. This can mean anything from setting up and enforcing a good password policy to using the access mechanisms (such as resource permissions) provided by the operating system or network software to secure resources or to restrict user activity (by selectively granting or denying rights). However, no matter how good you are at this before-the-fact approach to preventing security breaches, it's almost impossible—short of taking a system off the network and locking it in a room with a guard outside—to be absolutely sure that the system is totally secure. If you are a genius and make use of all the rights and permissions mechanisms at your disposal to secure a system (much less the entire network), an application bug or a disgruntled employee can still compromise a system.

Because you can never be certain that you've covered all your bases, it's also necessary that you follow up on your security configuration by *monitoring* the activities of the system. This chapter discusses the second part of securing your system: auditing techniques.

Note

For information about the mechanisms you can use to try to secure a computer and the network in the first place, see Chapter 43, "Rights and Permissions." You should be sure that you understand how to protect your system using the built-in security measures so that you will have less auditing data to wade through when you are trying to determine whether your security measures are working.

This second approach to securing the network is an important one. You should use all *practical* auditing features to record access to resources and to set up a policy for reviewing the data gathered on a regular basis. The degree to which you will find it necessary to gather information using the various utilities that an operating system provides depends on how important the data is on a system, or whether the system provides access to the network from the Internet. During normal operations, if you were to enable every single type of event auditing on a Windows NT/2000 or 2003 Server, you would end up with a very slow response time and with more data than you could possibly review daily. However, you can strike a compromise, depending on the particular system, and set up auditing that can be used to sufficiently record system activities and increase your audited events during times when you suspect that something might be awry.

Tip

Security issues are always a compromise. You can't lock every door, secure every file or directory, much less prevent users from misusing the system. So be careful to choose the items you monitor. If you suspect that a security incident has occurred, you can then decide to audit a wider range of events for the time required to determine the cause of a security breach. If, however, you operate in a highly secure environment where any security breach can cause damage that cannot be tolerated, then you might want to choose to audit a much wider range of events. In that case, you should configure servers with sufficient storage capacity to store logged event records, and assign one or more of your staff to review the logs daily.

Every major server operating system in use in a business environment today that is connected to a network has the capability to set up auditing for many events. Don't expect to find these capabilities with older client operating systems such as Windows 95 or 98. If you are still using these operating systems, it's time for an upgrade.

But for most operating systems, you can keep track of file and printer accesses, user logins/logouts, and other information that gives you the who, where, what, and when information you'll need for researching when you have reason to believe that a security problem exists. The methods of auditing and the tools used to exploit this data depend on the network or computer operating system. Because most networks are hybrids that have multiple operating systems, it's a good idea to have an employee who is skilled in each OS environment, intimately familiar with the peculiarities of each system.

Unix and Linux Systems

Although Unix was originally developed to be a programmer's operating system and not a business production system, it has been enhanced over the years to include utilities that can track resource usage and access. Today, the various implementations of Unix (along with its cousin Linux) are the primary operating systems used on the Internet for most firewalls and Web servers in the high-end market.

The files discussed here might vary from one Unix/Linux system to the next, but in general most systems have these available for the system administrator's use. The syslog utility covers the widest area of system resources because you can configure it to record messages from many different system utilities, and you can also decide how the utility will notify you of events as they happen.

Other files—such as /etc/utmp and /usr/adm/wtmp—keep track of who is currently logged on to the system and who has logged on to the system in the past. This is an example of Unix and Linux storing files in different locations. For Linux, the files would be /var/run/utmp and /var/log/wtmp.

Understanding each utility or log file and the type of information you can derive from it will enable you to set up a good auditing policy for your systems.

Using *syslog*

The syslog utility can be used to set up logging for many components that make up the Unix operating system. You can set up message logging so that messages from a wide variety of programs can be managed from a central location. To enable syslog logging, you must edit the /etc/syslog.conf configuration file and enter a record that contains a *selector* for each type of message you want to be logged by the facility, as well as an *action,* which is the action the daemon should take for this type of message.

The syslog daemon (syslogd) is usually started when the system boots, by commands placed in one of the rc startup files. This is the syntax for starting the daemon:

```
/etc/syslog [-mN] [-ffilename] [-d]
```

The -f option can be used to specify a configuration file other than the standard /etc/syslog.conf file. The -m option sets a "mark" interval for placing timestamps into the file. Timestamps can be important because they indicate that the logging mechanism is working during periods when no other significant events are logged. The absence of timestamps (if you use them) can be a tip that someone has been tampering with your system. The -d option turns on debugging mode.

The syslog.conf File

The syslog.conf file stores the information that the syslog daemon uses to decide which messages to accept (source and severity) and what to do with them (log file, notify user, and so on). You can use any ASCII text editor (such as VI) to configure this file. Each line should be composed of two components:

- **The selector**—This part of the record is composed of two pieces of information separated by a period. The first part of the selector is the name of the *system component* (or *facility*) from which the message originates. The second part of the selector is the *severity* (or *priority*) of the message. You can place multiple selectors on one line if you separate them with a semicolon.

- **The action**—This tells the daemon what to do when it receives a message that matches the selector criteria.

Table 47.1 lists the facility names you can use when composing the selector portion of the record.

Table 47.1   Facility Names in the *syslog.conf* Configuration File

Source Name	Description
user	Generated by user applications
kern	Kernel messages
mail	Mail system messages
daemon	System daemons
auth	Authorization file (that is, login)
lpr	Line printer spooler system
news	Usenet
uucp	UUCP (not currently implemented)
cron	cron and at utilities
local0-7	Reserved for local use
mark	Timestamp messages
*	All the preceding except for mark

Table 47.2 lists the severity levels you can use as the second component for the selector.

Table 47.2   Severity Levels in the *syslog.conf* File

Severity Level	Description
panic	Panic condition that is usually broadcast to all users
emerg	Same as panic
alert	A condition that needs immediate attention
crit	Warnings about critical situations
err	Other errors not warranting emerg, alert, or crit
error	Same as err
warn	Warning messages
warning	Same as warn
notice	Situations that require attention, but not as important as a warning or another error; not necessarily an error condition
info	Informational messages
debug	Messages generated by programs running a debug mode
none	*Suppresses* messages for this entry

Note that another severity level, called *panic*, has been removed in later versions of Unix/Linux—it's the same functionality provided by emerg. At this time the error and warn severity levels are also considered to be deprecated, which means that although they work now, they will be removed in future versions.

To create a selector, select one of the facilities listed in Table 47.1 and combine it with one of the error conditions listed in Table 47.2. For example:

```
kernel.info
mail.notice
lpr.crit
```

To create the rest of the record, you need to specify an action to take. The action portion of the record is separated from the selector portion by a space character. The `syslog` daemon can deliver the message in these ways:

- Write the message to a log file
- Send it to another computer
- Send it to one or more usernames
- All the above

For example, because kernel events are usually important (the kernel is the heart of the Unix operating system) and need to be looked at immediately, you might want to send them to the computer's console device. To do this, use the following entry:

```
kern.* /dev/console
```

The asterisk tells `syslog` to log all message types generated by the kernel, and the `/dev/console` part of the record specifies the console device (check the documentation to be sure of the exact device filename).

If the message is something important, but not so critical that it needs immediate attention, you can send it to a user whose responsibilities are associated with the application. The following example sends all messages from the mail facility (at a severity level of `info` or above) to the mail administrator named Johnson:

```
mail.info johnson
```

For security reasons, you might want to send important logging messages to another host. This can be a valuable service that the `syslog` daemon can perform. For example, when you are using bastion hosts in a demilitarized zone (DMZ), it's best not to store security logging events on a host computer that might be compromised. Instead, you instruct the daemon to send these events to another server for logging purposes. In a large network, you can dedicate a single host computer to this function and use other security measures to make the computer inaccessible to ordinary users. To send messages relating to kernel events and authorization events to another computer, for example, you might use this:

```
kern.*;auth.* @yoko.ono.com
```

▶▶   You'll find more detailed information about bastion hosts, firewalls, and DMZs in Chapter 49, "Firewalls."

Some message types are more useful for reviewing at a later date to review the overall functioning of the system. Using log files for these kinds of messages is a good idea. To send messages to a log file, specify the log file path in the action field:

```
mail.info;lpr.info;news.* /var/adm/messages
```

Tip

When sending messages to a log file, you can send them all to the same file as shown in the preceding example (`/var/adm/messages`). However, to make administering the logged messages easier, you might want to create several log files and group similar message types together. This way you don't have to search through a large file that might contain a large number of entries to find just a few records of interest. Using separate log files makes it easier to write script files to automate the process of searching for important messages.

Another good reason to use multiple log files is that you can delegate the reviewing of these log files to those employees who are best qualified to review them. A typical Unix system administrator has a lot of things to do during a normal working day. Delegating the review of certain events to subordinates can make the day a much more pleasant experience!

When sending `syslog` messages to a file, don't forget to review the log files periodically. Depending on the severity level you set for each facility, these files can grow to be quite large over a short period. To make administration more efficient, decide on a policy for reviewing, archiving, and deleting log files on a regular basis. You should keep these files available for at least a year. Some intrusions can lie in wait for a trigger before causing your system a problem. If you keep your log files on tape or other offline storage, you can look back through them for what might not have seemed an obvious event when it originally occurred. For legal reasons, keeping log files archived and readily available can help you make your case against an intruder who has spent days, weeks, or months trying to compromise your system.

System Log Files

Unix systems have many log files not related to the `syslog` utility that you can review for security purposes. For example, user logins are recorded in a file, as are usages of the switch user (su) command. When you are new to a system, you should review the documentation to make sure you are aware of all the logging facilities on the computer, where the files are located, and what maintenance procedures are necessary.

Some of the more useful files are listed here:

- **/usr/adm/wtmp**—This file keeps track of all logins, showing the username, terminal, and connect time. System shutdowns (but not system crashes, of course) are also listed in this file. Use the `last` command or the `ac` command to view entries in this log file.

- **/etc/utmp**—This file is similar to the `/usr/adm/wtmp` file, in that it stores information about users logging in to the system. However, this file only shows information about users that are actually logged on to the system currently and is not a historical file.

- **/var/adm/sulog**—This important log file should be looked at often because it records the usage of the su (switch user) command.

- **/var/adm/aculog**—This file records the usage of dial-out utilities, such as `tip` or `cu`.

- **/var/log/cron**—Actions taken by the `cron` scheduling utility are recorded here. This utility schedules events for execution on the system. By reviewing this file, you can determine whether unauthorized users are running procedures.

- **/var/adm/lpd-errs**—This file is used to record messages having to do with the `lpr/lpd` spooling system. Although not really of great concern from a security point of view, it can be a potential tool to use when looking for security breaches, such as determining who printed what.

- **/var/adm/acct**—This is the process accounting file. Use the `sa` command or the `lastcomm` command to view the contents of this file.

Configuring Windows NT 4.0 Auditing Policies

Windows also allows you to set permissions on resources and audit their access. To secure the system, use the following:

- User rights and permissions
- NTFS file and directory access control lists (ACLs)
- Passwords, groups, and interdomain trust relationships

To audit the system, you can configure the events that you want to track and then use the system's Event Viewer to examine the data collected by the system-auditing software.

Setting Up Events to Audit

To set up categories of events to be audited, run the User Manager for Domains utility and choose Policies, Audit. In Figure 47.1, you can see that the Audit Policy dialog box allows you to select which event category to audit and whether to audit successes or failures associated with each category.

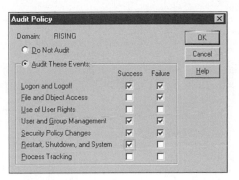

Figure 47.1   Use the Audit Policy dialog box in the User Manager for Domains to configure events to audit.

If you do not want to audit any events, select the Do Not Audit radio button. If you do want to audit, select Audit These Events and check the Success and/or Failure options for each category. The types of events you can set up auditing for are as detailed here:

- **Logon and Logoff**—Tracks users logging in to the system. This also tracks network logins from remote systems.

- **File and Object Access**—Tracks file and directory access and sending of jobs to printers. This category requires you to further define the events for the file, directory, or printer that will be audited.

- **Use of User Rights**—Records when users make use of rights you grant to them when you set up their account with the User Manager for Domains.

- **User and Group Management**—Tracks changes to group accounts, such as creating, deleting, and renaming user groups and passwords.

- **Security Policy Changes**—Keeps track of changes to user rights, and audit or trust relationships.

- **Restart, Shutdown, and System**—Tracks when the system is shut down or restarted, and other events that relate to system security. This category also includes changes to the security event log on the system.

- **Process Tracking**—Records voluminous information about user processes, including when programs are executed, objects are accessed, and programs are exited.

In most cases, you won't want to select success and failure for every category in this list. For example, the data collected when you select Process Tracking can create a large event log file very quickly. You should probably turn on this event-logging mechanism only when you have a definite suspicion about a particular user's activities and then review and purge the log on a regular basis. Another category that can generate a lot of log-file data is the Use of User Rights category.

Other categories, such as users' logins, can be useful and do not take up a lot of space in the log files. The data collected for files and object accesses depends on the specific events you select to audit for them.

File and Directory Events

If you have selected to audit this event category, you need to use Windows NT Explorer to set the specific types of events to audit. To set up auditing on a directory or file, highlight it, right-click, and select Properties. Alternatively, you can highlight the file or directory and select File, Properties.

When the Properties sheet appears, select the Security tab and then click the Auditing button to see a display that looks as shown in Figure 47.2.

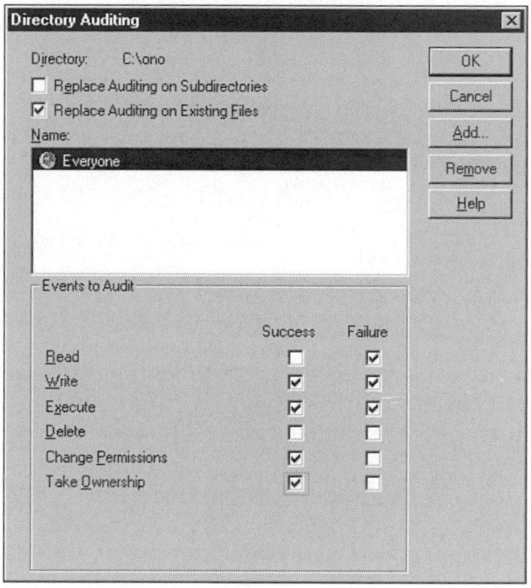

Figure 47.2   Use the Auditing button on the Security tab on the file or directory's properties sheet to set up events to audit.

These are the event types you can audit:

- Read
- Write
- Execute
- Delete
- Change Permission
- Take Ownership

However, because these will be audited by a user or group, you should first click the Add button to add a user or group of users. The Add Users and Groups dialog box (shown in Figure 47.3) displays the current list of user groups. You can use the Show Users button to display the individual users in each group. Select users or groups by highlighting them and clicking the Add button.

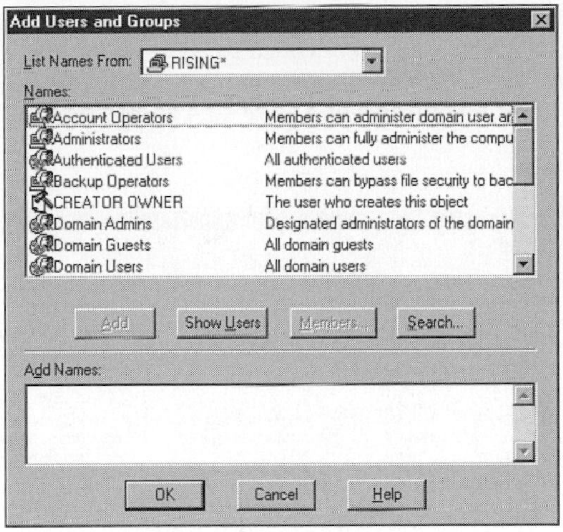

Figure 47.3   The Add Users and Groups dialog box allows you to select which users to audit.

Continue to select users and groups. Click OK when you are finished. After you return to the previous screen, highlight each user or group and select the events to audit for that file or directory on a per-user basis. You also can use the Remove button to remove the auditing configuration for a particular user or group.

You can select success or failure for events. For example, if you selected Success for the Read event type, every time an audited user was able to read this file, a record would be generated in the event log. If you selected Failure, each time an audited user tried to read the file, but did not have the correct access permissions, a record would be created in the event log file.

Printer Events

You select events to audit for printers in much the same way that you do for files and directories. However, instead of using the Windows NT Explorer, you use the properties sheet for the particular printer. You can get to the properties sheet by right-clicking the icon for a printer in the Printers folder. You can add or remove users by using the same type of dialog box. The events you can audit for printers are different and include the following:

- Print
- Full Control
- Delete
- Change Permissions
- Take Ownership

Using the Windows NT 4.0 Event Viewer

The Event Viewer is a utility found in the Administrative Tools folder that can be used to display events from three different log files:

- System
- Security
- Application

The System log file records certain system events, and the Application log file records events generated by many different applications that were coded to write event log messages. The Security log file is used to track events you have set up for auditing purposes. To start the Event Viewer choose Start, Programs, Administrative Tools, Event Viewer. Figure 47.4 shows the Event Viewer with the Security log file selected.

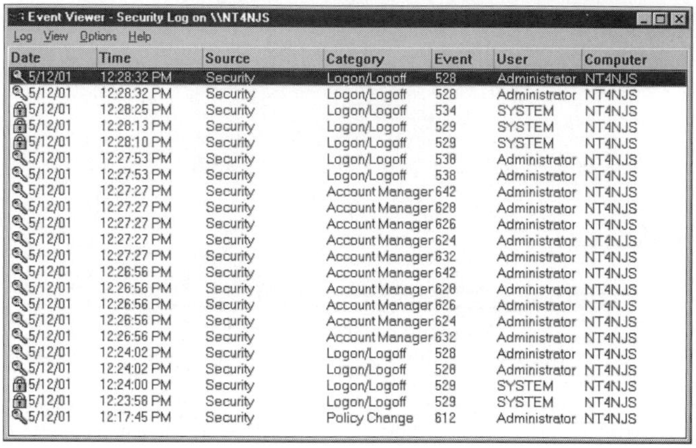

Figure 47.4   The Security log file can be viewed using the Event Viewer.

If the Event Viewer starts up with another log file displayed, such as the Application log file, choose Log, Security to change to the correct display.

This view shows the list of events currently in the log file. To get the detailed record for any event, double-click it. The Event Viewer does not have a reporting capability like the AUDITCON utility in NetWare (which you'll read about shortly). However, you can choose Log, Save As and save the data to either an ASCII text file or a comma-delimited file and use another utility, such as a spreadsheet, to perform further filtering or analysis on the data found here.

You also can change the log file settings by choosing Log, Log Settings. This allows you to set the maximum size the log can grow to, and whether to cycle around and overwrite older events when the file is full. From the Log menu you can also select to clear all the events in the log file, at which time you are prompted to save the current file in a backup file. This is something you should do on a regular basis, archiving the previous log files for a period consistent with the security policy in force at your site.

Configuring Windows 2000 and Windows 2003 Auditing Policies

Windows 2000 and Windows 2003 Servers use the Active Directory to store objects, such as user and computer accounts, as well as security information for the domain. When you promote a Windows 2000/2003 server to be a domain controller in the domain, you can use the Domain Security Policy MMC Snap-in to set up auditing for the domain. With few exceptions, this Snap-in works the same for both Windows 2000 and Windows 2003 servers.

This utility is the first step toward setting up events to audit. You use the Domain Security Policy tool to select the categories of events to audit. You can then select the individual objects (such as files, folders, or printers) that will be audited. After you have selected the kinds of events you want to audit, you need to configure auditing on the resources that you consider important, just as you did in Windows NT 4.0.

Use Start, Programs, Administrative Tools (or Start, Administrative Tools for Windows 2003), Domain Security Policy (Domain Controller Security Settings for Windows 2003) to start this tool. In Figure 47.5, you can see the MMC that is displayed, with the Security Settings object in the left pane of the console expanded to show the various objects that can be used to configure and monitor security for the domain.

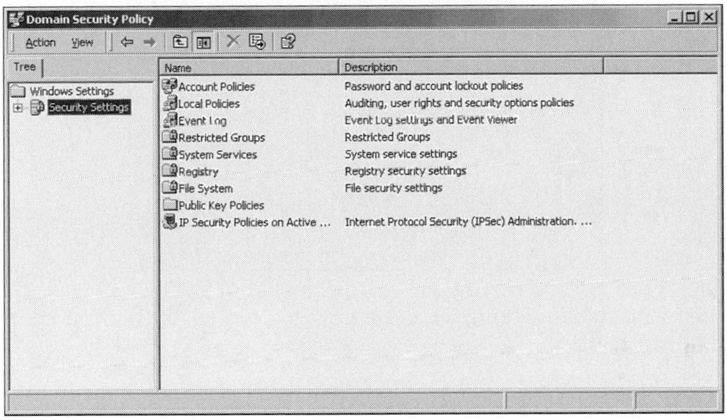

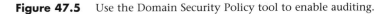

Figure 47.5   Use the Domain Security Policy tool to enable auditing.

Note

The remainder of this section uses examples from Windows 2000 Advanced Server. Windows 2003 Server operating systems can be configured using pretty much the same procedures discussed in this chapter. You will find, however, that there are additional items in the Default Domain Controller Security Settings window. These are specific to the Windows 2003 operating system. However, when you finish reading this chapter, you will find that using Windows 2003 will be easy to learn, because the differences are basically due to the new features that Windows 2003 offers.

In the right pane, double-click Local Policies and then Audit Policy. In Figure 47.6, you can see the events you can set up for auditing for the domain.

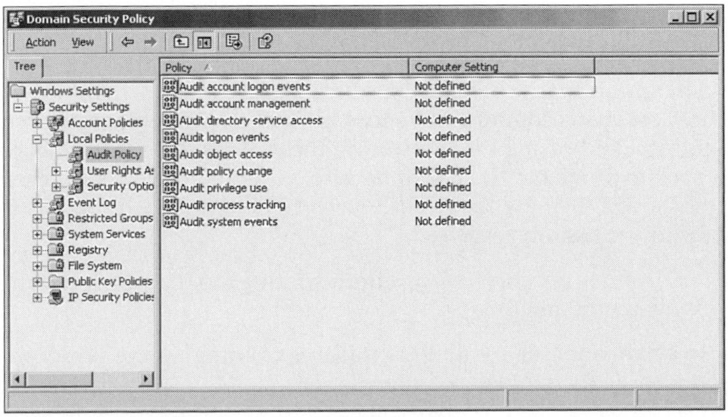

Figure 47.6   Use the Audit Policy object in the left pane to configure auditing.

To enable auditing, first select the kinds of events you want to audit. For example, to enable logging for successful or failed logon attempts, use the category Audit Logon Events. If you double-click this item, you can then select to audit successful or unsuccessful logon attempts (Success, Failure), as shown in Figure 47.7.

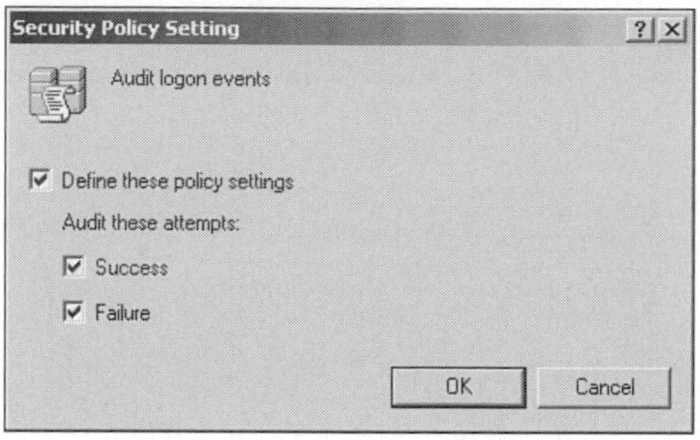

Figure 47.7   When you enable auditing for a category, you can enable both successful access and failed access attempts.

You can choose to audit other categories in this utility, such as changes made to user accounts (Audit account management), and file or printer access (object access). To audit object access on the domain controller, use Audit Directory Service Access. To audit object access on a member server in the domain, select Audit Object Access.

For each category, just double-click the entry in the MMC and select the Define These Policy Settings check box. You can then select either Success or Failure, to decide which kinds of access to audit.

In some environments, it might be desirable to log successful logons so that you can track when users are active on the network. Enabling failed logons can also be useful when you're trying to determine whether someone is attempting to break into your system, or whether a user is having a problem with his account, such as a forgotten password.

Enabling Auditing for Files and Folders

Keeping track of when users log on to the domain or when failed logon attempts occur enables you to track user account usage in the domain. It's also a good idea to keep track of access to important files and folders that reside on your servers. Although the NTFS allows you to grant or deny access with a large degree of precision, it can sometimes be difficult to determine the right combination of user rights and access permissions to use to set up the required access.

For example, the description for the Backup Operators Builtin group you'll find in the Active Directory Users and Computers administrative tool is "Backup Operators can override security restrictions for the sole purpose of backing up or restoring files." Does this mean they can read your files when not using a backup program? No, but to be sure, you can always set up event logging for important files or directories, and then use the Event Viewer to determine when these files or directories were successfully (or unsuccessfully) accessed.

After you've used the Domain Security Policy administrative tool to *enable* auditing for objects, you can *configure specific objects* for auditing.

The simplest way to set up auditing for a file or folder is to bring up the Windows Explorer accessory and use the properties page for a folder or a file:

1. Choose Start, Programs, Accessories, Windows Explorer.
2. Locate the folder or file you want to enable for auditing.

3. Right-click the file or folder and select Properties from the menu that appears. For Windows 2003 Servers, you can also select Sharing and Security from this same menu.

4. Select the Security tab and click the Advanced button that appears at the bottom of the display. This brings up the Access Control Settings properties page for the folder. Click the Auditing tab (see Figure 47.8).

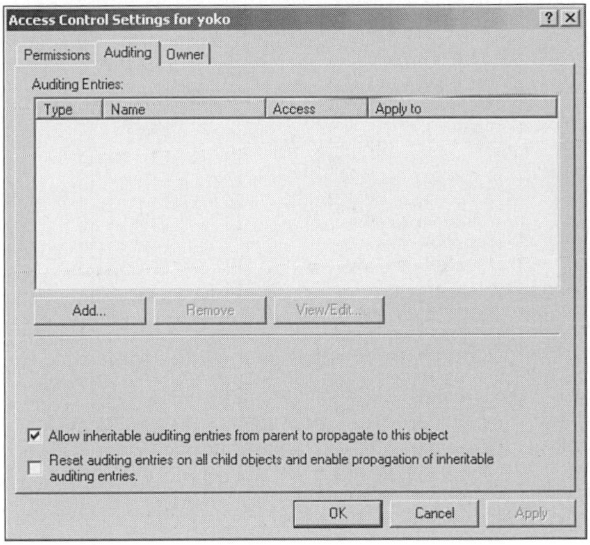

Figure 47.8   The Access Control Settings properties page allows you to control access and auditing for the folder.

5. Click the Add button to bring up the standard Select User Computer or Group dialog box. You can use this dialog box to select the user(s) or group(s) that will generate audit records when access is attempted for the folder. Use the scrollbar to find the user, or enter the name of the user (or group) if you already know it, into the Name field. Click the OK button and the Auditing Entry dialog box appears (see Figure 47.9).

6. This dialog box allows you to select the events to be audited in great detail. Use the Apply Onto drop-down list to choose whether the auditing entry is created for just this folder, the folder and files in the folder, subfolders, and combinations thereof. Use the Access pane to select the action that will be audited by clicking either the Successful or Failed (or both) check boxes.

Tip

Note the Apply These Auditing Entries to Objects and/or Containers Within This Container Only check box at the bottom of the dialog box. Because child objects in the Active Directory inherit attributes from parent objects, you should enable this check box if you want to restrict the auditing entry to just the users or groups you've selected in this particular container (that is, domain, or organizational unit).

Note

In Figure 47.9, the types of access are complicated because on a secure Windows 2000 computer, NTFS is used as the file system. In addition to the traditional access types such as read, write, and delete, you'll see a lot of other things that can be manipulated in the file system, such as changing the permissions or reading and writing extended attributes for the file or folder. Before you begin to select events for auditing, make sure you understand them. You should be well versed in how the NTFS operates before you begin auditing access types that you are unfamiliar with, or you might end up generating literally thousands of entries in the event log. See Chapter 43 for more information on this topic.

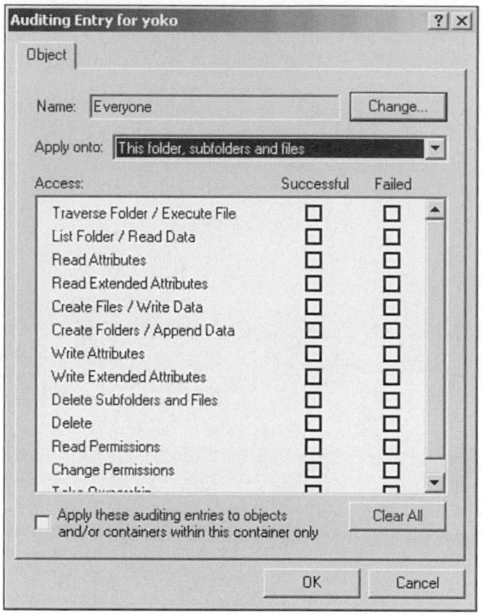

Figure 47.9   After you've selected the user or group whose access will be audited, you can select the event(s) that will generate an audit record.

7. When you've finished selecting the events to be audited, click OK.

8. When the Access Control Settings properties sheet reappears, note the check boxes at the bottom of this dialog box. By default, the Allow Inheritable Auditing Entries from Parent to Propagate to This Object check box is selected. Remember that unless the parent object has blocked inheritance for auditing entries, this is the default in the Active Directory. The second check box resets the auditing entries for all objects that fall under the user or group in the Active Directory.

9. Click OK to dismiss the Access Control Settings properties sheet, and then do the same for the initial properties page for the folder.

After you've set up auditing, you can check the event log periodically to determine which users have successfully accessed the folder or file, and also those that have failed to gain access, depending on which check boxes you have selected.

If all this seems complicated, it is! The Active Directory allows you to finely tune the access permissions, user rights, and auditing for objects that exist in the directory. Obviously, you should structure your file system and user groups with careful planning so that you don't end up with a large number of variables to contend with. If you try to set up auditing for every folder on a user-by-user basis, for example, you'll spend a lot of time setting up auditing every time you add a new user or create a new directory.

Notice also that inheritance can be blocked from above as well as propagated to objects that are beneath the object you are auditing. For example, if you have multiple organizational units in your domain, you can set up auditing based on the domain, and let these auditing records filter down the tree to apply also to the organizational units that fall underneath it. Or you can elect to set up auditing differently for each organizational unit.

Note

The Active Directory can be only as complex as you make it. For many small organizations, a single domain and the built-in containers (that is, Users and Computers) are sufficient for managing a small number of users. For a small home network, you should probably be using a less expensive operating system, such as Windows XP in a peer-to-peer workgroup setup, instead of using the Active Directory.

For more information about container objects in the directory, as well as how the directory is organized, see Chapter 31, "Using the Active Directory," or Appendix D, "The Lightweight Directory Access Protocol."

Enabling Auditing for Printers

The method used for selecting users and groups and the access that will be audited is just about the same for printers as it is for files and folders. You use the same dialog box to select users and groups, and a similar dialog box to select the type of access to be audited. To set up a printer for auditing, use the following steps:

1. For Windows 2000, choose Start, Settings, Printers. For Windows 2003 Server, choose Start, Printers and Faxes. When the Printers window appears, right-click the printer you want to set up auditing for and select Properties from the menu that appears. Select the Sharing or Security tab.

2. Click the Advanced button at the bottom of this properties sheet. The Access Control Settings properties sheet appears. Click the Auditing tab.

3. Click the Add button and the standard Select User, Computer or Group dialog box appears, just as it did when you were setting up auditing for folders in the preceding section. Select the user or group that will be audited and click Add.

4. The Auditing Entry dialog box for printers appears looking a little different from the one used for files and folders (see Figure 47.10).

5. Here the access types are much simpler than they were for file and folder objects. Select one of the first two if you want to track what users print and to keep track of users who manage printers. Note that if you select the Print option, the Read Permissions event is also selected because users must be able to read the permissions you've applied to the printer to determine whether they can print to it. Likewise, if you select Manage Printers, all other events are automatically selected with the exception of Manage Documents, because these other events occur while managing a printer.

6. When you've finished selecting successful and failed events to audit, click OK to dismiss the properties sheet, and then click OK to dismiss the preceding properties sheets.

Logging Shutdown and Startup Events with Windows 2003 Server

Windows 2003 prompts the administrator to give a text message to indicate why the server is being shut down or restarted. This text shows up in the Event Viewer just like any other audited event. Additionally, should the system crash, a similar text message window will pop up after the system boots, allowing you to enter a text message regarding the crash. In this manner, your audit trail can be used to determine what events led up to a crash. If you archive these events to a separate file using the Event Viewer, you can save them for future reference when similar problems occur.

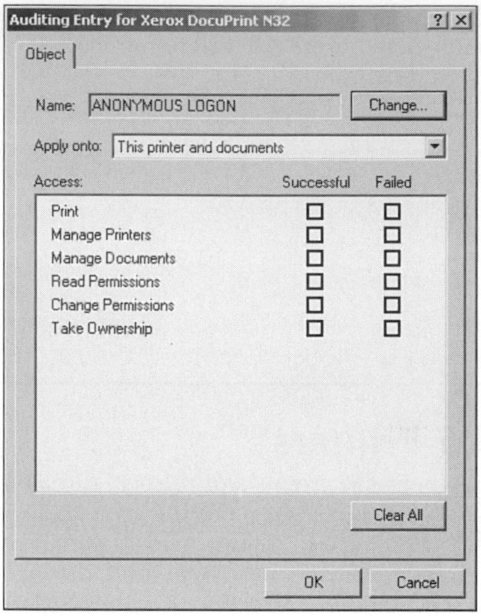

Figure 47.10   Select the type of access to be audited for the user or groups you have chosen.

In Figure 47.11 you can see an example of the Shut Down event dialog box for Windows 2003.

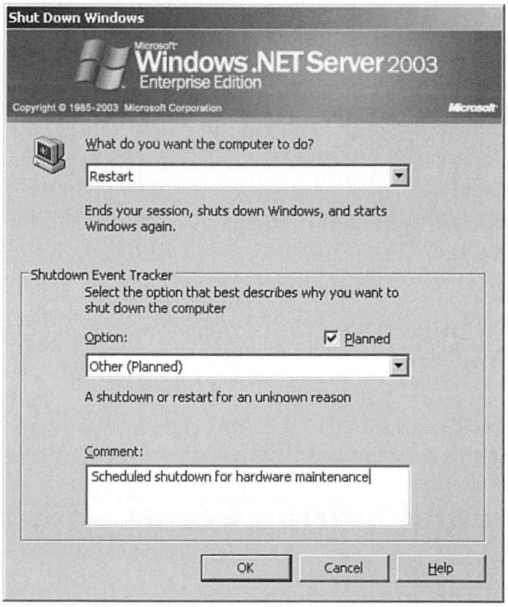

Figure 47.11   You can record an event when shutting down the system.

Using the Windows 2000/2003 Event Viewer

The Event Viewer is another tool you'll find in the Administrative Tools folder. It functions much the same as it did in Windows NT 4.0, although now the MMC is used as the interface, and some additional functionality has been added. In Figure 47.12 you can see the Event Viewer for Windows 2003 with the Security object selected.

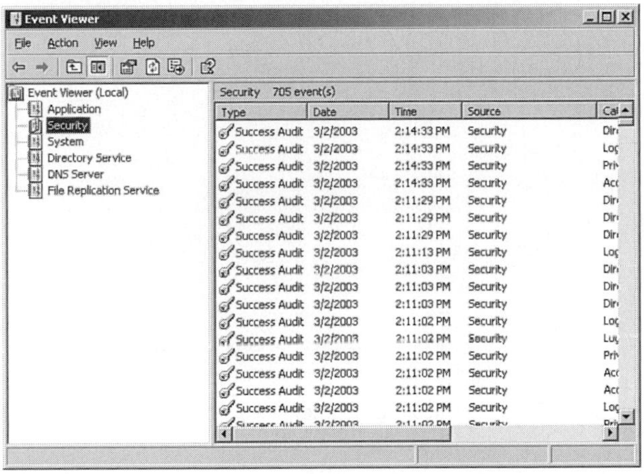

Figure 47.12 The Event Viewers for Windows 2000 Server and Windows 2003 Server now use MMC. This view is from Windows 2003 Server.

In addition to the Application, Security, and System log files, other log files might show up, depending on the services you've installed on the server. For example, in Figure 47.12, the Directory Service, DNS Server, and File Replication Service log files are also listed because they are installed on the domain controller. On member servers that are not domain controllers, your view might be different.

In the right pane of the Event Viewer, you will see a line item for each event in the file. Double-click any event to bring up a properties sheet that contains the detailed information about the event that was logged. In Figure 47.13, for example, you can see an example of a failed logon attempt by the user Administrator on the system.

Notice also in Figure 47.13 that you can use the up- and down-arrow buttons to move through line items so that you don't have to double-click each one to view the details. This can make scanning a set of events easier. Directly under these arrows is a button that looks like two sheets of paper. Clicking this button copies the details of the logged event to the Clipboard. You can then use a word processor or another utility that has a paste function to save or print the details of the event.

Using the Event Viewer Action Menu

You can use a central MMC to manage the event logs from the local computer that you are logged onto. You can also add other computers in your network to the console tree in the left pane so that you can manage their log files from the same place.

Choose Action, Connect to Another Computer. Figure 47.14 shows the dialog box that pops up. Enter the name or IP address of another computer here, and, if you have access to that computer, click the OK button and it will be added to the tree.

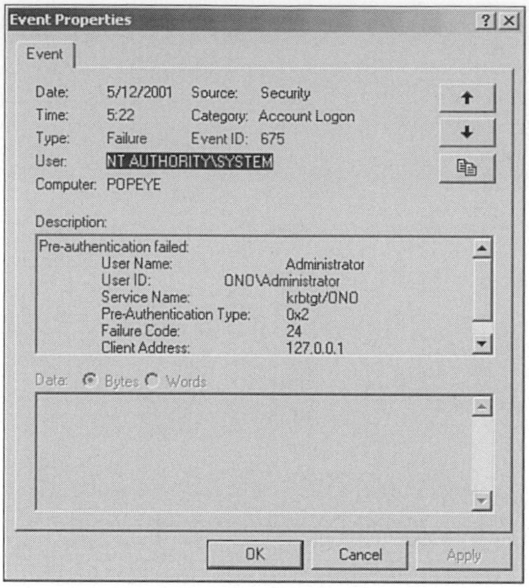

Figure 47.13 Yes, even the administrator can forget his password once in a while.

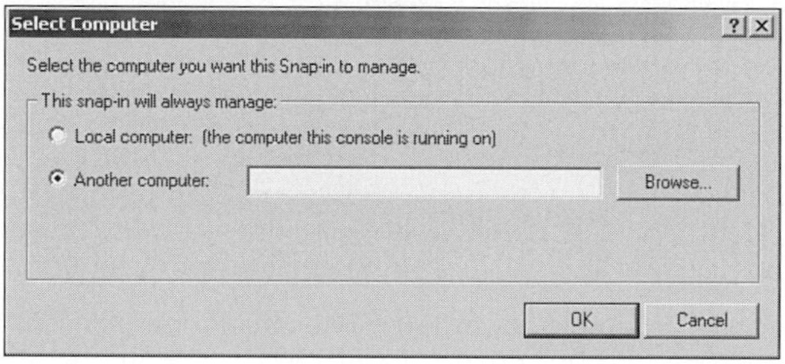

Figure 47.14 You can connect to multiple computers to manage event log files from a central location.

The Action menu also allows you to manage the properties of each log file. You can set the maximum size the log file can grow to, or set whether events should be overwritten when the file becomes full (see Figure 47.15).

The Filter tab allows you to specify information that will be used to narrow down the records you want to look at. You can select the date range, event type, source, category, event ID, and user, among other things. To return the display to show all records in the file, select View, All Records.

Finally, you can use the Action menu to save a log file to another file, export the information in a log file to a text file, rename the log file, create a new log file, or clear all events from the log file.

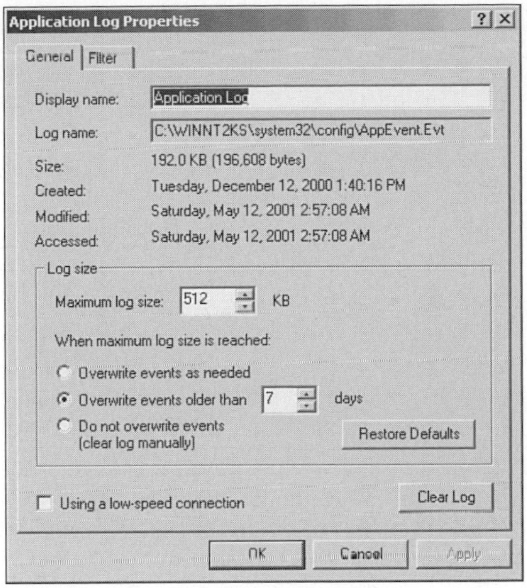

Figure 47.15   Choose Action, Properties to manage a log file.

Auditing Windows XP Professional Computers

Although Windows XP Professional is a client operating system, it can be used in SOHO environments to provide file and print shares for other computers on the network. And Windows XP Professional does include the Event Viewer, which enables you to monitor activity on the computer.

As with Windows NT/2000/2003, you must first set up the events to audit. The interface (the Microsoft Management Console, or MMC) is used to perform this function just as it is in Windows 2000/2003. However, for Windows XP you are auditing actions taken on the XP computer, not events for the domain. This is because Windows XP cannot be a domain controller in the network.

To set up the events to audit, click on Start, Control Panel, Administrative Tools. When the Administrative Tools folder appears, click on the Local Security Policy icon. You will see there (as shown in Figure 47.16) that the local security policy MMC interface looks a lot like the domain interface.

Setting up security policies for such things as the password policy and setting up auditing for the computer are similar to the same tasks for Windows 2000/2003.

You can also use the Event Viewer with Windows XP. In Figure 47.17, you can see an example of this utility. Use Start, Control Panel, Administrative Tools. Click on Event Viewer.

Because Windows XP does not host applications such as DNS, you will not see these items included in the left pane of the Event Viewer. Keep in mind that this is a client operating system. The capability for auditing and viewing significant events, however, is a good feature that makes Windows XP an ideal pseudo-server for small networks that do not need the capabilities offered by Windows server operating systems.

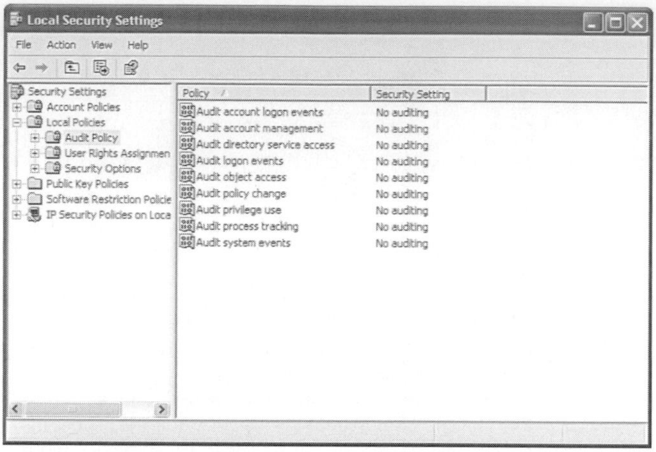

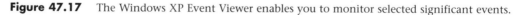

Figure 47.16   The Windows XP Local Security Settings window is similar to the Windows 2000/2003 domain security window.

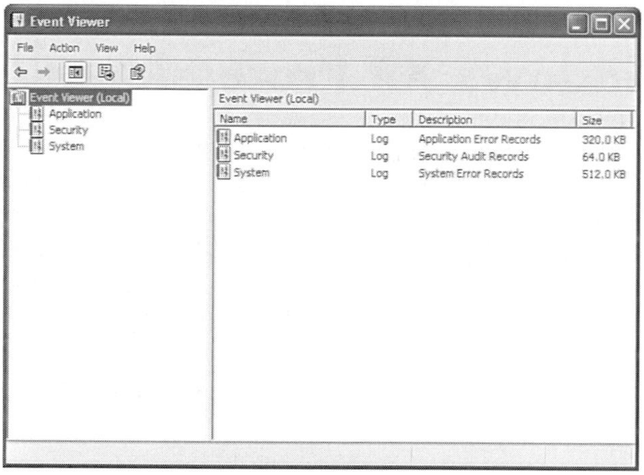

Figure 47.17   The Windows XP Event Viewer enables you to monitor selected significant events.

Novell Security

Novell's NetWare has been around for many years, though it is not the dominant network operating system anymore. Early versions were limited in their capability to keep track of events, but this changed with NetWare 4.x. The most useful tool for older systems is the AUDITCON tool, which can be used to configure and audit a wide range of system events.

SYSCON and AUDITCON

The SYSCON utility that was used in NetWare 3.x was limited in the type of information it could provide to the administrator. It was basically limited to statistical information such as the number of blocks read/written and the services the server provided. In NetWare 4.x the AUDITCON utility provides an advanced tool that is superior to SYSCON in two ways:

- The information is more granular. File-system events, such as access and modifications to individual files or directories, can be tracked. Events are also audited for NDS objects.

- The auditing role has been separated from the administrator's role, enabling an employee other than the administrator to act as the network auditor.

Both of these features are significant advances. The first makes the information gathered more than just statistical. You can now track access and the type of access to individual files or objects. The second can be used to ensure that the network administrators, usually all-powerful people who can do *anything* on the network, are also held accountable for their actions. Network security is not compromised by the auditor, however, because this person does not have to be granted administrator-like rights to objects such as the SYS:SYSTEM directory. The administrator's and the auditor's functions are separated.

Note

The administrator does have some control over the auditor: The administrator has to set up the auditor so that she can perform her functions. After an auditor has been assigned and the account set up, the auditor can change her password, thereby keeping the administrator locked out of the auditing functions. This approach allows the administrator and the auditor to balance each other. The auditor can track the administrator's actions, and the administrator can always change the person designated to be the auditor.

After the administrator has enabled auditing on volumes or containers and designated the auditor, the auditor can use the AUDITCON utility to check the system. Using AUDITCON, the auditor can modify which events are audited on which resources, and can produce reports showing auditing information.

Auditable Events

The precise granularity of things you can audit is what makes AUDITCON a powerful tool. The person who has been set up as the auditor can perform these actions:

- **Audit by event**—This includes file-related events such as open, read, write, and create files or directories. These can be audited for all users (global) or on a per-user basis. You can also audit printer queue events (QMS), server events (such as when it is brought down or restarted), and user events (such as user logins and logouts or the creation or deletion of user objects).

- **File or directory events**—You can select files or directories for which all access will be audited.

- **User**—You can select individual users for which auditable events will be recorded.

Auditing Files

The auditing software uses several places to store its data:

- **NET$AUDT.DAT**—This file can be found at the root of every volume that has auditing enabled. It is always flagged as an open file to prevent anyone other than the auditor from accessing it directly. This file stores binary information in a binary format only for the volume on which it resides.

- **NDS Database**—Auditing for events for the directory (NDS) is stored in the NDS database.

- **AUD$HIST.DAT**—This file is used to keep track of actions taken by the auditor(s). After all, someone has to watch the watcher! When more than one auditor is assigned to the network, each should have a separate user account so that this file can be used to track the actions taken by each auditor, giving still more checks and balances to the system.

■ **NET$AUDT.CFG**—This file contains audit file configuration information and is found at the root of the volume that is being audited. Using the AUDITCON utility, you can change the configuration information stored here, such as the maximum size the audit file can grow to, whether to allow more than one auditor to access the audit file at the same time, and whether dual-level passwords are used, among other things. The dual-level password requires an additional auditor password to be used when changing configuration information.

Note

No system, of course, is perfect. It is easy for the auditor to clear the **AUD$HIST.DAT** file when he has performed some action that was not allowed. However, the new file created after the old one is cleared will record that fact. Thus, although you might not be able to find out what was done, you can still find out that something suspicious is going on.

Using AUDITCON to Enable Auditing

An Admin user can enable auditing on a volume by running the AUDITCON utility. From the main menu, select the Enable Volume Auditing option and enter the password for that volume. If an old audit data file exists on the volume, it is replaced by the new file.

After this has been done, the administrator should give the volume password to the auditor, who should run AUDITCON and change it to a new value that the administrator does not know. Note that if the password is forgotten, the volume must be deleted and re-created if you want to change the password. You cannot recover the password. Also, without the correct password, you can disable auditing on the volume!

To change the audit password, the auditor should run the AUDITCON utility and select Audit Files Maintenance. From the next menu, select Auditing Configuration and then Change Audit Password. When prompted, enter the new password.

Producing Reports

Reports are produced to translate the binary auditing data into a format readable by humans. These reports can be produced by selecting Auditing Reports from the AUDITCON main menu. For security purposes, you should never leave these reports in a directory that can be easily accessed by other users. Instead, view or print the report text files and then delete them. You can always rerun the report later if you need to obtain another copy.

When producing an audit report, you can select events by date, time, and event; you also can choose to include or exclude selected files, directories, or users. This filtering capability makes it easy to get right to the important data when you are troubleshooting a security breach. If you are performing a regular review of the system, you can select all data and spend hours poring through it, but a large volume of data will most likely make it easy to miss an important event. In other words, when performing an analysis of the data, it's best to have a target objective of files or events, or possibly users, you need to keep an eye on.

NetWare 6 Advanced Audit Service

NetWare 6 contains a lot of new functionality that enhances security. For auditing, the utility is called Novell Advanced Audit Service (NAAS). It is a little more complicated to set up NetWare 6 for auditing than Windows or Unix machines, but the utility can catch a lot of events and works with the eDirectory.

An agent is used to collect data on an object, such as a server, and a management NAAS *server* receives this information from agents on the network. The configuration for each NAAS *agent*, as well as the NAAS servers, is stored in the eDirectory. Both the agent and the management server software can be configured by using Console One.

You can also set up NAAS to send email alerts to specified users. Edit the file SYS:\AUDIT\MAILALERT. CFG, and place the name of the SMTP server (outgoing mail server) on the first line, and a list of email addresses on the next line. For multiple email addresses, separate with a space or comma.

NAAS allows you to use Oracle or the Persuasive database that comes as part of NetWare 6.x to store the audit data collected.

Finally, you can configure audit agents for many older NetWare components, such as the various file systems and the eDirectory itself. Creating audit policies and associating them with objects in the eDirectory can be a complex task, due to the many components for which you can audit, as well as the support for older products.

Still, if you are using, or about to migrate to, NetWare 6, you should become intimately familiar with the new auditing feature. You can read the documentation for NAAS at the URL www.novell.com/documentation/lg/nw6p/index.html, and from the list presented select Novell Advanced Audit Service.

Security Issues for Wide Area Networks

SOME OF THE MAIN TOPICS IN THIS CHAPTER ARE

CHAPTER 48

When all you have to worry about are the computers attached to your local LAN and users you know personally, it's easy to implement security policies and keep the network virtually safe from things such as viruses or other malicious programs. A properly trained user base, along with security guidelines that allow only outside programs approved for use on the network, can go a long way toward keeping a LAN safe. Of course, it still pays to regularly use an up-to-date virus-scanning program to be absolutely sure that you've cleaned up your network.

When you connect to the Internet, however, there are so many different ways that your network can be compromised—even when using a very well-secured firewall. At a company that this author consults for, a recent virus attack required over 500 man-hours to resolve. And, all of this was done in less than 24 hours by a dedicated team of network professionals. When you consider the number of personnel involved, you can get an idea of the reason why you should take proactive measures as best you can. Yet, in an enterprise network, you should have a staff that can handle such an attack. The only way to ensure that you can take care of this type of situation is not just to hire the most competent persons, but also to set aside some of your budget for ongoing training. Things change; things change even faster on the Internet.

Note

The SQL Slammer worm of January 2003 was illustrative of how fast things change on the Internet. This worm, capable of infecting the entire Internet within 15 minutes, has been called the Internet's first "Warhol" worm, in reference to the popular Andy Warhol quote, "In the future, everyone will be famous for 15 minutes." By most estimates, the SQL Slammer worm infected over 90% of vulnerable systems within 10 minutes of its first detection. Infected systems doubled every 8.5 seconds, and after only 3 minutes in the wild, the virus was scanning 55 million addresses per second looking for vulnerable machines.

Because of this, and other factors you will learn about in this chapter, it's best to learn about the most recent kinds of attacks and then locate resources to help you stay aware of the latest news. One of the most common misconceptions about firewalls is that they offer complete protection. However, studies bear out the following facts:

- Staying on top of the latest developments in enterprise networking, the Internet, and even a SOHO network can be difficult at times. Part of the misconception may stem from the fact that the term *firewall* has become somewhat of a buzzword, implying that if some type of firewall is in place then all is well. A firewall is not a single technology. Instead, all but the simplest SOHO firewalls are a combination of technologies, some of which are constantly upgraded (such as those that filter specific Web sites or content). Many high-end firewalls must be updated regularly, as new protocol or application loopholes, worms, and viruses are discovered. In a small company, a firewall is a good idea but it is not a panacea. In both SOHO and large networks, a firewall is not a total solution for keeping out viruses. Thus, in addition to a firewall, you should always use a good antivirus program, and keep it up-to-date. In a large company with a staff of technicians maintaining a firewall, you can still *never* be sure that you are completely safe from intrusions. Be sure to keep in mind the following points concerning firewalls as well.

- A firewall can't protect you from your own internal users. Fired or laid off anyone lately? Do you have an employee who was dissatisfied with his last performance review? Do you have an employee or employees who are not trained on a regular basis about computer security (and by that I mean more than once a year)? You might think that just programmers can open back doors to your network. Yet, perhaps the easiest way into a network is called social engineering— just try calling up a user and telling him that you are from the help desk and need to use his password to download a software update. You'd be surprised. Or, maybe you wouldn't.

- Many firewalls are difficult to manage. You can never be sure whether you've done all you need to do to block malicious traffic at the perimeter of your network. In an enterprise network, you should consider devoting at least one or more personnel exclusively to maintaining and managing a firewall. For a SOHO network, don't take for granted a software firewall, much less a cable/DSL router that uses NAT. Email attachments, for example, can defeat a firewall easily. For these types of intrusions, use a good antivirus software (as stated previously) that examines emails as well as files on your computers' disk drives. And be sure to use the update software to continuously stay on top of new virus definitions.

Consider a firewall to be *only* the first line of defense, not the only defense you put up for your network.

This chapter looks at some of the typical problems that can be introduced into your network from the Internet and then at resources you can use to further educate yourself on these topics.

You've Been Targeted!

Too often you are tempted to put in a quick fix and consider a problem solved. However, in the complex matter of network security, you'll find there are no quick fixes. Because a network is composed of many components, hackers, crackers, and detractors have a large number of devices they can target, such as these:

- **Routers**—These devices stand at the perimeter of your network and sometimes perform firewall functions. The main thing a router can do is to block certain IP addresses or ports. This is the basic function performed by a firewall. Routers, though, are easy targets for many reasons. First, a router is your network's connection to the Internet, so it's directly exposed *to the whole world*. Second, routing protocols can be abused when hackers damage the routing table on your router. What good is a router if it doesn't know where to relay network traffic to and from? You learn this in more detail later in this chapter when you read about ICMP redirects. Although there isn't a lot you can do to protect a router from an attack over the Internet, you can take some steps to make it more difficult for potential intruders. You'll learn about that subject later, in the section titled "Protecting Routers." And another thing to consider is denial-of-service attacks. Because your router(s) stand at the periphery of your network, a constant stream of network traffic can be used to overwhelm a router and prevent you from receiving incoming data, much less sending data out onto the network.

- **Host computers**—Servers on your network are supposed to provide data, print, email, or other important services to your users. After a host computer has been infiltrated, however, these services can be corrupted or made unavailable. If a hacker gets past the router or firewall, the host computers on your network are usually the next target. This is one good reason to use a private address space on the internal LAN and save your registered IP addresses for use by the routers and firewall devices that actually need a valid address on the Internet. This technique is known as Network Address Translation (NAT). If the intruder does not know the addresses of computers on your network, the intruder will have more difficulty connecting to them and causing trouble. As a general rule, it's best to *always* hide information about the configuration of all computers on your internal LAN. If you must create a Web presence on the Internet, consider using a demilitarized zone (DMZ) to segment part of your network that interfaces with the Internet from the inside network.

▶▶ For more information on firewalls in general and using DMZs, see Chapter 49, "Firewalls."

- **Applications and services**—There is a great debate on the Internet about open source code. One side of the debate is this: If the actual code for particular applications is known, it's easier for patches or modifications to be made when some hacker detects a loophole in the application or service. The opposite argument goes like this: The bad guys also have a copy of the code and can spend all the time they need looking for vulnerable parts of the code that can be used to their advantage. When you are considering installing mission-critical software on a server, which should you use? I can't really offer an opinion on this because both sides have good arguments. If you use a proprietary program purchased from a vendor, can you depend on the technical support staff of the vendor to help you if the application becomes a target? Microsoft and other vendors regularly post security warnings and patches. Do you install them?

You must pick your vendors carefully—for example, what is the response time when you place a service call for a minor issue? Can you count on vendor support in an emergency, or would you rather have the open source code so that your own staff (and others around the world who use the same code) can immediately begin trying to plug the loophole?

- **Firewalls**—Yes, because most commercial firewall products are well documented, they can be compromised by someone who studies what they protect, and how the firewall does it. Not all firewalls use the same techniques. No single firewall will ever protect you from every threat from the Internet. A skilled staff of professionals, however, can help you mitigate the threats that do get past your firewall.

- **Your network**—If you're the sort of person who enjoys causing problems for other people, attacking the entire network is probably going to give you more pleasure than going after only a few host computers or applications. Think of how expensive it is to a large company such as eBay, CNN, or Microsoft when their networks are taken offline due to an attack. If a hacker can disable your entire network, the damage done can become quite expensive.

Usually, an attack is not as clearly defined as indicated here. Instead, many attacks are sophisticated combinations of several of the previously described varieties.

Computer Viruses, Trojan Horses, and Other Destructive Programs

Computer viruses have been around for a long time. These are programs that travel from one computer to another, using various methods, such as programs that are not what they appear to be. Shareware downloaded from the Internet is a popular method for spreading virus code. You really should seriously enforce a policy for any programs that are installed on any computer in your network. Even software applications from a known vendor should be tested vigorously in a laboratory setting before being deployed on host computers in the network. Shareware, of course, should be evaluated much more closely. Regardless of any policy you decide to implement, it should be clear that viruses are particularly dangerous and sometimes tricky to avoid. The use of antivirus software is a must and should be required protection on any size network where infiltration and data destruction is undesirable—and that includes just about every network, doesn't it?

Note

The term *virus* is used loosely in many publications, as well as within this book, and is meant to include Trojan horses, worms, and other software that can damage your network or data. However, there are some distinctions that will be detailed in the following sections. Keep in mind that the use of antivirus software applies to all types of malicious code and must be regularly updated due to the wide variety of offending programs and the regularity with which they are created and spread.

Trojan horses are programs that an intruder plants on one or more servers in your network. If you have these types of programs, they can be difficult to detect, because many use the same filename as a file that is already part of your operating system or application software. The Trojan horse program is activated by some specific event, such as the arrival of a certain date, or by a user running a program that has been replaced by the Trojan horse. This latter tactic is very popular. Some programs are not what they appear to be.

Worms are usually considered to be self-propagating programs that travel through email as well as by other means. A worm will replicate itself by sending copies of the software to all or most of the addresses in your email address book. A worm travels through the Internet very quickly because of this aspect of its replication. The solution? Don't open email attachments unless you have a good antivirus program (which you have kept up-to-date). After you open an email that contains a worm virus, all heck can break loose, and the friends in your address book will not be inclined to think very well of you!

Other types of destructive programs can attack your network. This is the case in a denial-of-service attack. The perpetrators never have to intrude into your network. Instead, they use one of several methods (which we'll talk about in just a minute) to send massive amounts of network traffic to your network router or server. The server or router becomes overwhelmed and can no longer operate efficiently. Other denial-of-service attacks target specific resources, such as servers or applications.

Trojan Horse Programs

Trojan horses are programs that are planted somewhere in your network to wait for a signal before springing into action. After hackers have gained entry to a server in your network, they can easily plant a program and then run the program, at a time they choose. The program can listen on a selected port waiting for a signal. The program can wait until a certain time has passed. Many methods are used to trigger such a program.

When the signal or time comes, the Trojan horse does its destructive chores. One of the most common techniques for hiding these programs is to give them the same name as some other common program on the computer. Indeed, some Trojan horses are nothing more than modified versions of a standard operating-system file. So what appears to be one thing might be something entirely different. As mentioned earlier, a Trojan horse program also can be activated by other means. The main difference between a Trojan horse program (or a worm) and a computer virus is that the virus is usually activated, does its damage, and then attempts to replicate itself by some means, such as mailing itself to everyone in your address book. Trojan horses are more like bombs waiting to go off.

Computer Viruses

Computer viruses come in all sorts of variations. They have been wreaking havoc on computers even before the Internet became commercial. Before the Internet exploded into the large network it is today, bulletin board services were a popular method for exchanging files, such as shareware programs.

A virus program usually is distinguished by two features. First, the virus replicates itself so that it can be spread to other computers. The method of transport can be a floppy disk that has had its boot sector code modified, or it can be a macrovirus that comes as part of an email attachment that uses the Internet email system to move about. Second, a virus *usually* is created to do something destructive, such as wiping out the contents of a hard disk or damaging some other system resource. However, this second feature is not always present in a computer virus. Some viruses simply display a silly message on the screen to let the user know he's been hit, and then they do no further damage.

Another thing to keep in mind is that a virus has two functions. First, it needs to be transported to another computer to infect. Second, it requires a mechanism to affect the system. In many cases these are implemented as two separate functions. The transport mechanism does just what it says: It finds a method (such as email) to get the entire virus package to another system (such as by using your address book to email itself to others). Then another part of the virus performs some action on your computer. This can range from a malicious action, such as deleting files, to an innocuous one, such as simply presenting a funny message on your screen. The important thing to remember is that viruses are becoming similar to worms, in that they provide a mechanism to propagate themselves, as well as to cause harm to your computer or network.

Now it seems that most viruses are destructive, so you should always use antivirus software on computers in your network. Although deploying an antivirus application on several hundred or several thousand computers can be expensive, especially when you consider that you also must pay for updates from the vendor, the amount of damage viruses can cause if you do get hit greatly justifies this cost. In an enterprise environment you can usually get a large discount for antivirus software. For some packages, you can simply purchase one copy for a small network, and then create file shares for each disk on a computer and configure the antivirus software to check all disks as well as file shares.

Many small network operators install a good antivirus software package and schedule the software to run on an infrequent basis, such as once weekly. If you are using the software for a home environment where the loss of data is insignificant, that might be a good solution, especially if you have a slow Internet connection. However, if you are operating a business from home (SOHO), I suggest that you run the antivirus software daily. You can schedule most products to run at night when you are not using the network. I also recommend that you use any update software on the same daily basis. Viruses are not picky—they don't appear on the Internet on just a weekly basis. They can find their way into your network anytime—even on a daily basis. If you schedule software updates and virus scans to run at off-peak hours for your network, you might just find that you have avoided the latest, greatest new virus.

Tip

Can't decide which antivirus software to buy? Visit **www.symantec.com** and click on Download. There are several products you can download and use for a 15-day trial period. You'll find here a trial version of Norton antivirus software. You can also download a trial version of McAfee's VirusScan software at **www.mcafee.com**. Click on Download, and then the Evaluate button next to the product version you want to evaluate. These are the two most popular products sold in computer stores today. A quick search of the Internet will bring up many more antivirus software packages. Two important factors for most software applications are ease-of-use and support. Consider support to be the most important factor when choosing an antivirus product. The company should be one you can contact via the telephone should an emergency arise, and one whose product enables you to download updates frequently.

How Infections Occur

Viruses and other computer maladies can travel through various routes to get to your computer. One of the most common methods is through the use of email. How many times did you hear on the news last year, "Don't open the attachment if the subject line says..."? Because of the macro capabilities and newer features of modern email clients, it is easy to trick users into launching a program without realizing what they are doing. Many email macroviruses that you receive go through your address book first and mail a copy of themselves to all your friends. Then they go about doing their dirty work on your system. So, as a method of transport, email can be a very lucrative path for a virus to take. If an email offers a link that appears to lead to something that is just too good to be true, it probably isn't true. The old saying "There ain't no such thing as a free lunch" applies here. Anyone who has been on the Internet for a month or more will start receiving spam messages. Although most of these are harmless and can be deleted and ignored, there are always those that just seem to tempt the user in such a way that it must be further pursued. There are many companies that offer anti-spam software.

Tip

Many good antivirus software products on the market today not only can check the files on your computer's disk drives, but also can intercept incoming emails and flag them as candidates for viruses. For example, Norton AntiVirus will query you to "quarantine" a suspect email attachment. You can view it later to decide whether it is actually a virus, or an attachment you need to view. Many products even can warn you if you try to copy a file from a floppy disk to your system. When purchasing an antivirus product, be absolutely sure to define what your needs are, and determine whether they can be met by the software you purchase.

If you set a policy to prevent users from making use of company email for personal purposes, you can prevent a lot of this spam. In this way you also might be able to keep harmful emails from causing you a problem in the first place. Many modern email servers can be configured to check for attachments and prevent suspect attachments from being delivered to the end user. Even Microsoft Outlook Express enables you to set a security level to protect against this threat if your firewall does not. Yet this functionality is usually based on a good antivirus program associated with the email server or firewall, or a content filter that screens known suspicious content.

Still other avenues into the systems on your network exist. For example, as discussed earlier, shareware, freeware, and other demo software downloadable from the Internet can seem a bargain at first. And maybe now and then you find a program that actually fits a business use. However, some programs contain viruses, and the writers of the viruses are just waiting for you to download the program and execute it. The results can show up right away or can be triggered by a signal, such as a certain date, before springing into action.

A good security policy for any site will require that users submit requests to a security team before using software that isn't currently approved. The security team can first run the program through standard antivirus software and otherwise evaluate the security potential of the program. Never allow users to bring floppy disks (or other removable media) from home. This should be spelled out clearly in your company's network security policy.

One of the most useful functions that antivirus software provides is the capability to update itself. For example, Norton antivirus software provides a Live Update function that downloads newer versions of the software components, as well as newer virus definitions. It is a good idea to use this function for a known virus vendor.

Yet, for software vendors that provide the same functionality, can you trust this feature? When it comes to shareware programs, or other small vendors, be wary of automatic updates. If given the choice whether to enable automatic download and installs, select instead to have a choice to review the download before installing it. In this manner you can experiment with the results of such an update in a laboratory setting before deploying it to your network clients.

Your Network Under Fire—Common Attacks

If all you had to worry about were virus and Trojan horse programs, life would be so much simpler. Just deploy a good antivirus application and monitor the alerts or log files the application produces. When a virus does creep into your network, use the appropriate software to remove it. In some situations in which time is of the essence and you don't have time to wait for a vendor to come up with a fix for a newly discovered virus, you can reconstruct the server by either re-creating it on another system or restoring data from backups. You also can reformat the hard disk of the infected system and reinstall your operating system and applications.

However, after the Internet becomes an important part of your business's bottom line, there are other potential problems you need to worry about in addition to virus and Trojan horse programs.

Denial-of-Service Attacks

A denial-of-service attack is characterized by the goal of the attack. The attack's purpose is to cripple routers, servers, or other computers by consuming resources at a pace that makes them effectively unavailable for the ordinary user to perform required functions.

A denial-of-service attack can use different common methods to accomplish its purpose. For example, flooding a server or network with a huge amount of network traffic results in a slow response for all nodes connected to the network. When bogus packets (usually created by an application designed specifically to produce large numbers of packets) are coming into a network or server at a very fast rate, ordinary users will have a hard time getting their legitimate network packets delivered. Indeed, if a router becomes overwhelmed with enough traffic, it might simply start dropping packets because it cannot keep up with the pace. Another method commonly used is to send malformed packets that can cause problems such as buffer overruns and take advantage of other shortcomings in the operating system of the router or server.

Other resources can be targets also. For example, a Trojan horse program can be designed to do nothing except consume CPU cycles as fast as possible when it is activated. Thus, other programs running on the server will slow to a crawl, or possibly not function, if they cannot obtain CPU cycles. Most operating systems allow for the concept of prioritizing certain processes. For example, the operating system itself must have access to the CPU and can interrupt a user process when needed because the operating-system component runs at a higher priority than an ordinary user process. If a destructive program has been planted in your network, and if your password file has been decrypted, it's easy to run a process at a high priority by using an administrative account that has the necessary privileges.

Another method of denying access to resources can take the form of changing configuration information so that the resource will not function properly. Changing router table information, for example, can make sites unreachable. Changing user account information can make it impossible for users to log on to a server. Changing configuration files (or Registry key values, in the case of an operating system such as Windows 2000/2003) can render applications or services unavailable.

Distributed Denial-of-Service Attacks

In the preceding section we talked about denial-of-service attacks. When you have to worry about only one computer trying to overload your system, you can usually block the particular incoming address at the router and then start the process of tracking down the criminal who has damaged your network.

But what do you do if you suddenly find yourself under attack by not one computer but several hundred or several thousand computers? This sort of attack is known as a distributed denial-of-service attack because the "attackers" are multiple computers that can be coming at you from anywhere on the Internet. This is almost the worst thing that can happen to your network from the Internet.

Several years ago a program called Trin00 was developed, and it has been followed by newer versions, such as the Tribe Flood Network (TFN) and Tribe Flood Network 2000 (TFN2K). These are not the only tools that can be used for a distributed denial-of-service attack, but they have been used many times to cause problems on the Internet.

As you can see in Figure 48.1, a distributed denial-of-service attack is an organized attack that uses a central controlling computer to direct other computers to perform the actual attack on your network.

In Figure 48.1 you can see that setting up this sort of attack is not necessarily an easy thing to do. Several steps are involved:

1. The perpetrator first infiltrates other innocent, unprotected computers and plants a program on them to be used later.

2. To make it difficult to track down the source of the original machine that sets off the attack, these infected computers are usually organized into a hierarchy. In Figure 48.1 you can see that a single attacker plants a "handler" program on some of the computers that have been infiltrated and "agent" programs on others.

3. The attacker sends a command to the handlers, who in turn send a command to the computers that actually perform the attack on your network.

4. You suffer! And, of course, you stay up all night with your staff trying to remedy the situation.

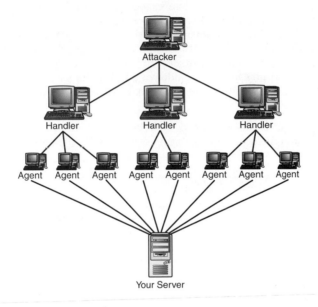

Figure 48.1 A distributed denial-of-service attack can overwhelm your network by using hundreds, if not thousands, of computers to simultaneously launch an attack.

The reason this type of attack is becoming more prevalent is that more and more people are connecting to the Internet—home users as well as businesses. In a business network, you take precautions to secure your computers. Home users rarely secure their computers, not because they're stupid but because they simply are not aware that dialing up to an Internet connection exposes their computers to intrusion from anywhere in the world. With broadband connections such as cable and DSL modems providing an "always online" connection, innocent home computer users might have no idea that while they are peacefully sleeping, some hacker is downloading a program to their computer that's still online.

As you can see, no matter what you do to secure the servers and workstations inside your network, there's nothing you can do about the millions of home users who are connected to the Internet with no firewall protection. It's really a horrifying thing to consider that innocent users connected to the Internet can be unwilling participants in an attack on your network!

Another factor that makes this type of attack so deadly is that the attacker doesn't have to be in any hurry. I can only assume that someone who would perform this attack is doing it for some sick form of pleasure. The hacker can spend hours, weeks, or even months breaking into unprotected computers and planting the seeds of destruction that will be activated later.

SYN Flooding

As you may recall, the SYN (synchronization) bit is used during the initial setup of a TCP/IP connection. It's part of the three-way handshake. When a computer receives a request to open a new TCP session, the initial packet has the SYN bit set. The computer receiving this packet will set aside buffers in memory and create data structures that will be used to manage the TCP session. However, computers are limited in memory and can handle only so many sessions simultaneously.

The SYN-flooding attack just sends the first SYN packet that is intended to begin the setup of a TCP connection. The perpetrator ignores the responses received from the server, leaving half-open connections on the server that is under attack. The SYN-flooding attack sends a constant stream of packets with the SYN bit set. The targeted computer creates the necessary data structures in memory until finally it runs out. Again, the behavior of the computer will depend on the operating system. It might crash, it might hang, or it might simply just slow down and try to keep handling the incoming packets. Even if the system continues to run, the odds of a legitimate user being able to establish a TCP connection become almost impossible. The server is overwhelmed by these half-open connections it is trying to create at a rapid rate.

Whatever the target computer)does, however, there will come a point where no memory is available to run user programs or even to run the operating system itself efficiently.

Note

The SYN flooding is but one of the many denial-of-service attacks that can consume resources on your servers. This type of attack does not have to come from a single computer, however. As you will learn elsewhere in this chapter, a *distributed denial-of-service attack* can be set up by infiltrating a large number of unprotected computers, and then triggering them to start sending the SYN flooding, or other attack methods, to a single site.

The best defense against this sort of attack is to have a good firewall in place that can detect an odd stream of SYN packets coming in at a rapid rate and simply discard them. In addition, newer versions of most operating systems have been patched or modified to detect this rapid incoming flood of SYN packets and alert the administrator.

ICMP Redirects

The Internet Control Message Protocol (ICMP) is used for many purposes, but one important function is to send a message to a router (or a server acting as a router) to tell the router to change entries in the routing table. Once again, if your router doesn't have the correct routing information, it won't be able to deliver network packets. ICMP redirects were created with the best of intentions. Suppose, for example, in Figure 48.2, that Router A sends a packet to Router B as the first hop the packet needs to take to eventually get to Router Z. If Router B knows there is a more direct route (using Router D), it uses an ICMP redirect to tell Router A the more efficient route.

This can happen under many different circumstances. In the simple example shown in Figure 48.2, it's possible that Router A has just been brought back online and knows about Router B, but hasn't yet updated its table to include Router D. In this situation, Router B, which has been up and running for some time, knows of the more direct path, so it sends the ICMP redirect message to Router A telling it to update its routing table.

◀◀   ICMP is covered in Chapter 25, "Overview of the TCP/IP Protocol Suite."

Unfortunately, it's easy to download tools from the Internet that can be used to generate ICMP packets, and this can be used against you to wreak havoc on your routing tables. For this reason, many administrators use filtering rules on routers that connect to external networks to drop any incoming ICMP redirect packets. ICMP redirect messages can be very useful within your network, but you shouldn't trust this information from routers that are not under your control.

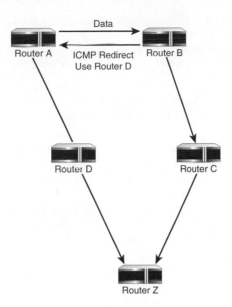

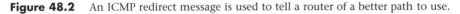

Figure 48.2   An ICMP redirect message is used to tell a router of a better path to use.

The Ping of Death

Almost anyone who has ever dealt with networks has heard of this famous method of attack. The Ping of Death is basically a method of crashing your system by sending a packet that is excessive in size. The ping program is an extremely useful tool and is one of the first tools you should use when trying to determine whether connectivity exists between two machines. However, to sum up the information here, the ping utility sends a small packet (typically 64 bytes in size) to a remote IP address. The packet is an ICMP ECHO packet. The server that receives this packet normally responds with an ICMP REPLY packet. This simple exchange of packets proves that, although you might be having other problems communicating with the remote machine, the network path between the two systems does exist and is working.

However (keeping in mind that TCP/IP was not originally designed with security as a main issue), once again mean people found a way to exploit this utility by simply modifying the ping program to send extremely large packets (say, 65,536 bytes). Most networks won't transmit a packet this large as a single unit. For example, most Ethernet packets range up to around 1,500 bytes. However, larger packets can be sent, using a process in which the original packet is fragmented into smaller packets that can pass through the network devices that connect one computer to another. When packets get fragmented, the receiving end usually stores the information as the fragments come in, and when the last fragment arrives, the data is reassembled into the original packet size. Operating systems typically use registers or set aside memory locations that are sized according to their expected use. If the receiving system knows that it's illegal to create a packet in excess of a certain size, the variable that is set aside (and the buffer space to store the packet) can't hold a number larger than it was created to hold. For example, a single byte (8 bits) can be used in binary to store a number of up to 255. The Ping of Death takes advantage of this by sending a packet (fragmented into manageable chunks) to the target system. When the target system attempts to reassemble the packet, lots of things can happen, depending on the operating system. If a variable overflows (that is, it's not large enough to hold the size of the packet that's being reassembled) or if the buffer space set aside for the packet is not large enough to hold the entire reassembled packet, it is possible for the incoming packet data to cross the buffer boundary and write over other important data.

When this happens, the behavior of the operating system is hard to predict. What area of memory was overwritten? What happens when the variable that stores the size of the packet can't hold the value that the local component of the ping program is trying to store there? Well, usually the computer will hang, crash, or behave in some other undesirable way.

Users have known about this attack method for several years, and most operating systems have been fortified to prevent this attack from succeeding. However, there are still legacy systems (Windows 95, older versions of Unix, and so on) out there performing useful functions. Older systems are extremely vulnerable to this type of attack.

If you are worried about the Ping of Death, check with your vendor to determine whether any patches or firmware upgrades are available to remedy this problem.

Forged Email

Email is probably the most popular application used on the Internet. All people can have an email account, whether or not they have a computer at home. You can sign up for email accounts at several sites, such as Microsoft's Hotmail or Yahoo's email service, and use a computer at your school, at a library, or even at work to access the account.

Email messages, like Trojan horse programs, aren't always what they seem to be. Just because the FROM line contains the name of someone you know doesn't mean that the email actually came from that person. It's a simple matter when configuring an email account to use any name you want. And with the online email services that don't require you to use an email client (these services typically use an HTML interface—a Web browser), it can be difficult to determine where an email actually originated.

There are even programs freely available on the Net that allow you to create bogus email messages that appear perfectly normal in all respects. Although any intelligent person would probably not, in this day and age, open an email attachment from someone they do not know, they most likely would open an attachment from a friend. After all, if you can't trust your friends…

The problem is that email is easily forged and can be used to get a program into your network. As a rule, delete spam and other email from sources you don't recognize.

One of the more insidious things that can be done through email has occurred with alarming frequency in recent years. Worm viruses spread through email can read your address book, replicate themselves by mailing a copy of the virus code to everyone in your address book, and then start wreaking havoc on your system! About the only thing you can do in this situation is to disconnect the computer (or computers) from the network and clean out the mail store with a good virus program. If you have a mail server in your network, disconnect it and do the same. Until you've assured yourself that every computer in your network is free of such worm viruses, don't reconnect to the Internet, or any other part of your corporate network.

Password Protection and SecurID and Smart Cards

Passwords and usernames have been the traditional method for authenticating a user to a computer operating system. There are much better methods you can use for environments that demand a high degree of security, such as smart cards and SecurID cards.

Smart card devices are synchronized with software that runs on the host computer. To log on, the user simply consults the password code, which changes at regular intervals, generated by the smart card. Because the application on the host computer is operating to change the account password using the same algorithm as the smart card, a user's account password can be different every time she logs in. As long as the smart card and the application on the computer are kept in sync, it becomes very improbable for someone to "steal" your password. And most smart cards have passwords that can be used only one time. This means that even if someone happens to glance at the current password on your smart card, after you've used the password to log in, it can't be reused and abused.

SecurID cards are based on digital certificates and require the user to enter a PIN for their use.

Network Back Doors

One of the best reasons I can think of for not allowing noncommercial shareware on a network is that if you can't trust the vendor, you can't trust the application. There are literally thousands of useful programs you can download from the Internet that can be used productively on a network. However, isn't it better to simply purchase a commercial product from a reliable, known vendor who has a good technical support staff?

A back door into a network can be an application that was downloaded by an innocent user who is unaware that the program, in addition to doing what it says it does, also does other things, such as mailing out your user authorization files to some other computer on the Internet.

Shareware programs are not the only method used to create a back door into your network or host computer. Once again, you must consider the amount of trust you have in your users and use good judgment when granting privileges and access permissions to users. Delegating authority to others to make management easier is a great concept. Delegating these privileges to an unhappy employee is not a good idea. The problem is that it's not always easy to tell a happy employee from one who is not. Suppose you have a technician who performs router maintenance activities. You have to trust that the employee is correctly programming the access control lists and other items on the routers.

However, there is an easy solution to this type of problem. Delegate the ability to manage the routers in your network to more than one person and establish a process of regularly reviewing router configurations. Trust no one! But maybe you can trust several people!

TCP/IP and UDP Ports

Ports are used along with an IP address to create a "socket" that uniquely identifies an end point in an IP connection. Whereas the IP address provides a unique identifier for the host computer, the port identifies the specific application for which the connection is to be used. When configuring routers, proxy servers, and other similar devices, use this simple rule: Disable all ports, and then enable only those you actually need to use. In most cases it's easy to disable a port in one direction or in both directions. That is, you can restrict incoming or outgoing network traffic by port. That's why you need to turn off all ports except the ones you specifically use. You don't just lock one door in your house, do you? You lock them all. Even if a particular door is rarely used, it should be locked because you never know when someone is going to try to enter. This analogy holds true for TCP and UDP port numbers.

Using Modems in a Secure Manner

One reason you need a modem on a computer in your network today is to provide remote access capabilities for users who work from remote locations and need access to the corporate network. Allowing individual employees to have a modem on their desktop computer is just asking for trouble. Instead, use a separate server to set up a remote access service, using a reasonable number of modems to satisfy the needs of your remote clients. Remote access servers are typically very configurable—that is, you can provide additional authentication mechanisms, such as callback. With most operating systems, you also can grant dial-in access only to those users who need it. Finally, regularly review any log files created by remote access server modem banks to be sure that you have indeed configured the server correctly and that no unknown users are getting in.

Another solution for remote users is to use Virtual Private Networking (VPN) services. Windows 2000 Advanced Server and Windows 2003 Servers can be set up to allow users to create an encrypted communication tunnel through the Internet. Many routers also provide this functionality. The days of the modem are numbered. Home users in the near future will most likely demand broadband access, using cable or DSL modems rather than the typical modem that connects to the public switched-telephone network.

◀◀ In Chapter 16, "Dedicated Connections," you can find out more about using a digital connection instead of an analog modem for remote users.

Network Probes

A network probe or sniffer is a very useful tool for troubleshooting network problems. You can find software and hardware network sniffers that collect data packets from the network and allow you to examine them to determine what is causing a problem on your network.

Because the purpose of a network probe is to intercept packets and examine them, you can easily see how this could be very damaging when used for purposes other than troubleshooting.

Remember that the less information known about your network by outsiders, the more difficult it is to infiltrate your network. However, when someone has broken in, it's a simple task to plant a program that does nothing except listen to the network and send information back to the person who planted the program in the first place. Using a network sniffer for this purpose enables an outsider to find out all sorts of useful information about your computers, users, and network configuration. For example, you already know it's a bad idea to use FTP, Telnet, and other utilities that use clear-text to send usernames and passwords. However, you might think it's safe to use these inside your network. Well, that's not so. If someone has planted a program in a server on your network and is "probing" the packets that pass around your network, they'll find it very easy to further infiltrate your network by obtaining more user account information, and thus be able to compromise one computer after another. Use safe utilities inside your network as well as for communications on the Internet. An example of this would be to use the Secure Shell utilities.

◀◀ The Secure Shell utilities are covered in Chapter 46, "Basic Security Measures Every Network Administrator Needs to Know."

Spoofing and Impersonation

Just as it's a simple matter to create a program that can construct a steady stream of SYN packets and send them rapidly to your server, it's also easy to create network packets that have false information in other fields of the IP header. For example, you might have a firewall set up to reject packets from known sources of trouble, based on the source IP address found in the header. However, there's nothing to stop the hacker, cracker, or attacker from simply putting in another source address so that your firewall lets the packet through.

IP address spoofing is very easy to do. It's also very hard to detect. One thing a firewall can do, however, is guard against packets that contain a spoofed address, making it appear that the packet originated inside your network. Think about it. If the source address of a network packet falls within the address range of your internal network, it shouldn't be coming in through a firewall interface that's connected to the Internet. It should be the other way around! All good firewalls can be configured to drop packets that arrive from the outside world with an address that makes it look like the packet came from your network.

If It's Too Good to Be True, It Isn't

One of the more prevalent scams that has proliferated on the Internet in the past two years is the claim that you can make a fortune by helping out a civil servant, or the wife of an ex-legislator of a foreign country, usually Nigeria. When you get these emails, don't even try to respond. The scam involves your helping the sender transfer his secret funds to another bank outside the originating country. For a small fee, you can receive a few million in return. Yet, after you get involved, the person encourages you to open an account at a bank he uses (which is simply a Web site, not a bank) and transfer funds to that bank. In this manner he can (1) keep your cash and (2) in some cases gain access to your real account information from your own bank.

This is just one example. Again, if it appears too good to be true, it isn't (true)! The Internet can be a great place to learn about new ideas, to get involved in e-commerce, and so on. It can also be a great place to get fleeced.

Another similar scam is an email that appears to come from a reputable company. Recently, emails from a site that appeared to be Microsoft was passed through the Internet. When you receive a suspicious email, look closely at the address of the email. Check the properties page of the email to see where it was sent from. You shouldn't get emails, for example, from `Microsoft.com`, or `Ebay.com`, unless you have granted them the right to send you emails. Yet, if you get an email from, say, `Microsoft-readnow.com`, don't open it! Check those emails carefully.

Preventative Measures

There are many standard techniques typically used to keep a network up and running. One of these preventative measures is regular backups. If your system becomes infected with virus programs or if you find that data has been corrupted, you'll understand the importance of regular, frequent backups. In addition, it's a good idea to keep offline copies of important data files for an extended period. Simply doing a backup each night and overwriting the tape or tapes the next night will provide you with very little protection. Damage to your system might not become evident until weeks or, in some cases, months after the initial intrusion.

There are also commercial and noncommercial products you can use to help safeguard your system. These include intrusion-detection mechanisms, antivirus programs, and programs that can monitor changes on important servers.

So where should you start when defining the defensive mechanisms needed to protect your network? Let's start at the edge of the network—the router.

Protecting Routers

Routers typically can be configured in several ways. You can attach a serial cable and terminal directly to most routers and perform configuration tasks. Another method is Telnet. Most modern routers allow you to Telnet into the router to perform configuration tasks. Turn this functionality on only when it is needed, and then turn it back off. The same goes for unnecessary protocols and services. In a manner similar to deciding what services you want to allow through a firewall (and in what direction), you should turn off all unnecessary services on a router. You'll have to consult your documentation to find out the particular commands you'll need to use. However, a good document on router security can be found at the following URL:

```
www.cisco.com/warp/public/707/21.html
```

You might want to check vendor Web sites for other router products that are in use on your network to look for similar advice. Additionally, be sure to stay informed of router firmware updates and operating-system updates and patches. As new threats are discovered, a responsible vendor will release information or code that can be used to help improve the security of the routers that stand guard at the edge of the network.

The Network As Target

There are some problems for which there is currently no easy solution. The distributed denial-of-service attack discussed earlier in this chapter is one of those. When the entry points into your network are saturated with an overload of network traffic, there's not much you can do about it. The best tactic you can use when such an attack occurs is to try to block out the address ranges from which the attack is coming. But when your network is being singled out by several hundred other compromised computers, it's rather difficult to quickly program routers to block all of these network addresses. The fact that many large Internet sites have been taken down during the past few years by these kinds of attacks should be indicative of how serious this attack can be. What can you do? Gather all the information you can, and, when the attack is over, try to backtrack to find out where the attack initiated. At this time it might not be possible to do this because one computer can set off others to do the dirty work for them. If you don't have access to the actual computers that perform a distributed denial-of-service attack, you can use the information on those other systems to further research the problem.

So for now, the best solution is to hope that this doesn't happen to you and to use an Internet service provider that has a good technical team that can respond quickly to help block sites that are generating this type of attack. And by all means, if you are targeted, get the authorities involved.

Protecting Host Computers—Encryption and Virus-Protection Software

After an intruder gets past a router, it's usually pretty easy to intrude further by gaining access to host computers on the network. Again, it is so easy to simply put up a router and firewall configuration and assume that your network is safe. However, even if these methods do protect you from outsiders, you still must worry about users who are allowed on the network. A disgruntled employee can do more damage (and probably do a good job of hiding the evidence) than many network intruders. Host security is a very important topic.

You should first start by becoming intimately familiar with the resource-protection and user-authentication schemes used by your computers. For example, many Unix variants provide for a shadow password file that is not easily accessible. When someone breaks into a Unix server, it's a simple matter to download the contents of the /etc/passwd file and spend a few minutes or hours using an automated program to encrypt words in a dictionary, check to see whether they match the encrypted password in the stolen file, and then simply log back into your Unix box using a valid password!

The applications you run on servers or workstations can also make the host computer an easy target. For example, if you are using older versions of FTP or Telnet, you're sending usernames and passwords about your network in clear, easy-to-read ASCII text. A network sniffer (which can be something as simple as a Trojan horse program planted somewhere in your network) can watch for these and transmit them back to the intruder. Because secure versions of these and other related utilities are available, you should always be sure to use the secure versions, even if it means purchasing additional software that already comes with your operating system.

◄◄ You can find more information about standard TCP/IP applications that are particularly vulnerable by reading Chapter 26, "Basic TCP/IP Services and Applications."

If you have an important server that is absolutely critical to your business operations, you might want to consider keeping a "hot spare" around. That is, create another server that is virtually a clone of the important server. If the original server is compromised, place the hot spare into service. This might involve a little time if you have data that needs to be restored to the hot spare before it can be used. However, for servers that contain data that doesn't change often, such as some Web servers, you can have an exact duplicate sitting around just waiting to be used in case the operational Web server becomes compromised.

In this case, however, you need to be sure that the "hot spare" itself has not been compromised. Some malicious code can remain around for many months before causing problems. This is another good reason to use updated antivirus software on a regular, frequent basis.

Another way to protect servers is to use the tools that the operating system provides to protect some services. For example, you'd be a fool to place a directory on your system disk for use as an anonymous FTP site. The last thing you want is to have someone filling up all the space on your system disk. Most operating systems allow you to set quotas that define how much space a particular user account can use on a server's hard drives. Enforcing quotas can help prevent an attack that consists of consuming all the available space on a disk. In addition, you can set alarms to notify you when quotas are being used up at a rate that is faster than what you see during normal operations. It's then an easy matter to track down the source of the data coming into the server and to terminate the user process.

Additionally, protecting computers should also involve software that detects malicious code. Even home PC users are aware of the value of antivirus programs. There are so many vendors of this software that it would be pointless to attempt to list them here. However, when you do choose an antivirus program, there are some things you should consider when making a purchasing decision. For example, does the vendor respond quickly with updates to the software as new viruses are discovered? Does the software have the capability to remove the virus after it has been discovered? Does the software have the capability to scan floppy disks and files transferred to the computer through the network? Of these, the capability to quickly respond to new threats is perhaps the most important. However, your situation might dictate other factors that are more important. Note also that many firewall products now contain some type of virus-detection mechanism.

Using Tripwire

There are many programs you can use to help determine whether your system has been compromised. Tripwire is a very popular program that can be used for this purpose. Tripwire was originally developed in 1992 by Gene Kin and Dr. Eugene Spafford. The Academic Source Release (ASR) version of Tripwire can be downloaded for noncommercial use from Tripwire's Web site. In addition, Tripwire has created commercial versions of the software, including an enterprise manager program (Tripwire Manager) that uses SSL for communications and simplifies management of multiple servers and workstations.

Tripwire is based on the concept of taking a "snapshot" of system resources, such as files, directories, and, in the case of Windows NT, Registry settings. The information gathered by Tripwire is stored in a secure database and is used to compare a server later to determine whether changes have been made and what those changes were. A policy file allows the network administrator to control the types of data that Tripwire monitors and to prioritize certain events using a rule base. In addition, Tripwire can produce reports that make monitoring the system easier for administrators.

Currently, Tripwire runs on the following operating-system platforms:

- Windows NT 4.0, Windows 2000, Windows 2003, and Windows XP Professional
- Solaris (SPARC) versions 2.6, 7.0, and 8.0

- IBM AIX 4.3
- HP-UX 11.0
- Several versions of Linux

Some of the things that Tripwire can monitor are specific to an operating system, whereas others (such as file types and sizes) can be monitored on all platforms. For example, here are a few of the items you can use Tripwire to monitor on Unix systems:

- Addition, deletion, or modification of files, along with file permissions, types, and sizes
- Inode number and number of links
- Owner and group IDs for files
- Modification timestamps and access timestamps

In addition, hash algorithms can be used to ensure the integrity of the contents of files. Tripwire supports several kinds of hashing algorithms, such as CRC-32, MD5, and the SHS/SHA algorithm, among others.

For Windows NT systems, the list that can be monitored includes the standard file components and things such as these:

- File attributes, such as archive, read-only, hidden, or offline
- Create and access times
- NTFS Owner SID, NTFS Group SID, and other NTFS attributes
- Addition, deletion, and modification of Registry keys and the values of those keys

These lists are not all-inclusive. For more information about acquiring an evaluation copy of Tripwire or the Academic Source Release, visit the Web site `www.tripwire.com`.

User Awareness and Training

Social engineering is a term used a lot lately to describe an easy method for gaining access into your network. Put quite simply, are the users of your network trained in security measures? A quick test is to simply have someone from your help desk call a user and ask him for his password. I would bet that in at least half of the cases the users will give out their passwords. A help-desk person shouldn't have to ask this type of question! Instead, if people at your help desk need to access a user account, they can notify the user that they are changing the password temporarily and will notify the user when to reset the password to a value known only to the user.

A password policy should also be in effect to ensure that common names and words are not used. Yet, one must be careful to avoid making passwords so difficult that users have a hard time remembering them. Most operating systems have the capability to keep a history list of passwords to prevent their reuse within a specified amount of time. You'll also find that you can usually set a minimum and maximum password length.

Social engineering also can involve dumpster diving. How secure are the printouts that you throw in the trash can? Do you have paper shredders (and a security policy dictating their use) in place? Even Hollywood stars know that much useful information can be obtained from a trash can! This goes not just for paper materials. When you decommission old tapes or old computer hard drives, do you take the time to destroy any data that is stored on them? It may be well and good to donate old computers to nonprofit organizations or schools, but it's also a good idea to reformat the hard drives and reinstall the operating systems before you do so. Tapes can be made useless by various means, including bulk tape erasers that zap the contents in just a few seconds.

Staying on Top of Security Issues

Your network will never be secure unless you make an effort to keep up-to-date with the latest discoveries concerning security issues. There are many good sites on the Web that you can use as resources to help you get the latest information as well as advice on how to better secure hosts and networks. Keep in mind that those who would do harm to your network are usually one step ahead of you. It's a continual catch-up game. The quicker you find out about a problem, the quicker you can take precautions to protect your network.

49

Firewalls

SOME OF THE MAIN TOPICS IN THIS CHAPTER ARE

CHAPTER 49

You must be on the Internet if you want your business to remain competitive during the next decade. Yet the Internet remains an insecure territory, much like those in the old Wild West days. To help keep your network protected from people who would try to cause you problems, it is unthinkable for a business in today's market to make a connection to the Internet without using a firewall. The term *firewall* is casually tossed around by news reporters and in magazine articles, and it might be difficult for you to understand exactly what a firewall is and what it does. That's because a good firewall is not a single entity, but instead a set of components, each of which has a specific purpose. In this chapter, you'll look at some basic firewall technologies and the problems they help prevent. With this knowledge, you'll be in a better position to make decisions about how best to protect your network.

What Is a Firewall?

A *firewall* is a set of components that stands between your network and the Internet and acts as a gatekeeper, allowing in trusted friends and keeping out known or suspected enemies. A firewall can be a single device, such as a router, computer, or dedicated hardware appliance, which has software capable of making the decisions needed to monitor the flow of data to and from the corporate network and the outside world. A firewall also can be composed of more than one router, computer, or network appliance, each performing a specific function. For small offices/home offices (SOHO)—especially those using a broadband, always-on connection—a simple firewall appliance that you can purchase at the local computer store might be all you need. Just about every device that is called a *broadband router/switch* supports such basic functions as Network Address Translation (NAT), which is covered in this chapter. These inexpensive router/switches do provide some measure of security, but they do not prevent attacks that originate from emails or other locally executed viruses or exploits, especially prevalent in the Windows environment. If you are a home user with a broadband connection, you should install some kind of network appliance between your cable or DSL modem and your computer. Even so, the best protection for SOHO networks is to disconnect your network from your broadband connection when you are not using it. Additionally, as with every computer connected to the Internet, you should be using an antivirus software package on a regular basis, and using the service offered by the manufacturer to keep the virus database up-to-date.

Note

Although this chapter is targeted toward business entities that have valuable data to protect, the information here also can be useful to home users. If you have a broadband connection—be it DSL (digital subscriber line) or a cable modem—for your home computer, you might find yourself either the victim of an attack or an unwitting accomplice to an attack on another larger network. Most of the denial-of-service attacks that have been aimed at popular Web sites involve a multi-tiered attack method known as a *distributed denial-of-service attack*. This type of attack involves breaking into computers of home users and planting the attack program code that will be used later to attack the actual target site. Because many home users are not security conscious, they might have such a program on their computers and never know it. Yet, after infiltrating hundreds, if not thousands, of innocent home computers and installing the attack program, the attacker simply needs to send a command out to these systems to begin an attack on a third party.

Several kinds of firewall technologies are used, and they *generally* can be classified into the following categories:

- Packet filters
- Stateful inspection
- Proxy servers
- Hybrids

Although many vendors offer firewall products (implemented in both hardware and software products), the technology used is so diverse that it's difficult to make direct comparisons between products. The best you can do is carefully review each product and ask a lot of questions before deciding whether it will offer the protection you need for your network. Also remember that even though new security holes are always popping up for firewall products, networks, and computer operating systems (OSs), many times a security breach occurs simply because a particular router or computer is not properly configured from a security standpoint. This chapter covers the basic concepts used for firewall technology. However, as this field continues to adapt and grow, you should be careful when choosing a solution for your network. Evaluate products from many vendors before making a purchase.

Tip

As suggested in Chapter 47, "Auditing and Other Monitoring Measures," in a large network you need to dedicate staff members to exclusively handle firewall duties. A firewall in a SOHO environment is not the same as a firewall in an enterprise network. In larger networks where there are many connections to the Internet, a dedicated staff is required to monitor, update, and fix problems as they occur. In this environment you cannot simply set up a hardware or software firewall and expect that your LAN or network is now secured from the outside world. Just as firewall technology continues to adapt to new conditions, so do hackers and others who may cause harm to your network.

Packet Filters

A packet filter provides the most basic functions of a firewall and can be implemented with a simple router. Indeed, packet-filtering routers were the first type of firewall created to help keep a network safe from intruders. A packet filter examines every network packet that passes through it, and either forwards or drops the packet, according to a set of rules established by the firewall administrator. Just about every router being manufactured today allows you to restrict traffic flowing inward or outward based on the contents of the TCP/IP packet header information.

A packet filter can be configured to block traffic by creating filters for the following:

- **IP addresses**— This includes both source and destination addresses. You can specify individual addresses or ranges of addresses.
- **Protocols**—Typical protocols include UDP (User Datagram Protocol) and the TCP (Transmission Control Protocol).
- **Port numbers**—Port numbers are used to identify connections between applications, such as FTP or Telnet. You usually can specify a range of port numbers, or use filters that allow you to say "greater than" or "less than" a port number.
- **Direction**—Filtering can be done based on whether the network packet is coming into your network from the Internet or being sent out by a user on your network to the Internet.

Note

As indicated, firewalls stand between your network and the Internet. However, in a large corporate network, firewalls are also typically deployed between different networks that exist within the same company. For example, you might place a firewall between the network used by the payroll department and the network that handles manufacturing computers for your company. Think of a firewall as a locked door, which can be used to keep out those who do not belong. Although usernames and passwords provide a general sort of security within your network, it's probably a good idea to isolate network segments that contain sensitive information from the rest of your network. Usernames and passwords are easily compromised. A properly configured firewall is not.

Filtering on IP Addresses

Chapter 25, "Overview of the TCP/IP Protocol Suite," discusses the information found in the Internet Protocol (IP) packet header. To briefly review, the IP protocol is used by other higher-level protocols (such as TCP and UDP) to provide a connectionless best-effort data-delivery service. To do so, the IP datagram encapsulates the TCP or other protocol segment by adding source and destination addresses, port numbers, and other header information before sending the datagram farther down the protocol stack, where it is eventually transmitted on the wire bit-by-bit by the physical components of the network.

The Windows XP Firewall

Windows XP Professional comes with a built-in firewall. However, this firewall is basically a packet filter. It does not include other technologies discussed in this chapter, such as stateful inspection. Yet if you are using Windows XP in a SOHO environment, you should definitely use it. You can turn off selected services based on ports. Ports, as you learned in Chapter 25, are associated with different basic TCP/IP applications, such as Telnet and FTP. You probably won't want to receive incoming Telnet or FTP connections, although you may want to enable outgoing sessions. Log in using a local Administrator account and then click on Start, Control Panel, Network Connections (or Network and Internet Connections using the new Category view of the Control Panel, and then click on Network Connections).

Click once on the network connection you want to modify. Click on Change Settings of This Connection, found on the left side of the window under Network Tasks. When the Local Area Connections Properties sheet pops up, click the Advanced tab. There you'll see a check box you can use to enable or disable Windows XP's firewall. Once enabled, the Settings button will appear at the bottom of the properties page. Click on this button and you can then select which services (Telnet, FTP, and so on) for which you want to allow incoming connections.

Routers can be configured easily to examine the contents of the IP header and drop packets that don't match a set of rules that the network or firewall administrator configures on the router. Perhaps the most obvious example is to filter out packets arriving from the Internet that have a *source* address that falls within the same network address range used on the internal network. Because such a packet, if it were indeed valid, would have to originate inside the network, it shouldn't be coming in from the outside! It is easy to forge IP packets so that the source address, as well as other header information, can be set to anything a hacker desires. A lot of programs are freely available on the Internet to do this.

When a packet with a source address is sent into your network, it's more likely that the destination server or workstation in your network will accept it as a valid packet, thinking it's coming from a user on the local network, and the packet will be processed as usual. Using this method, it's easy to get packets into your network and actually have them delivered, when they should not be.

This is only one example of a good reason to filter packets based on the IP addressing information in the packet header. Because addresses can be forged, and because it's not practical to list all the millions of addresses that are allocated to computers on the Internet and pick and choose, you need to be cautious when using this kind of specific filtering. For example, suppose your network becomes the subject of a denial-of-service attack. You can use a network analyzer to discover the source addresses of the packets, and quickly insert a rule in the router (or firewall product) database that drops all packets that come from the network from which those packets are coming.

▶▶   Network analyzers are discussed in Chapter 53, "Network Testing and Analysis Tools."

Filtering Based on Protocols

In the IP packet, a field is used to indicate the type of protocol the packet is carrying data for. For example, if the IP packet is carrying TCP data, the protocol field in the IP header is 6. If it's carrying an ICMP (Internet Control Message Protocol) message, the protocol number is 1. The capability to filter out certain protocols is useful because many of the protocols in use on the Internet were created many years ago when security was not as much of an issue as it is in today's commercial Internet.

Take ICMP, for example. The Ping utility makes use of ICMP packets to determine whether another host is reachable. An ICMP ECHO REQUEST packet is sent to the address of the host computer in question. If it receives the packet, the destination computer sends back an ICMP ECHO REPLY packet. Sounds simple and safe, doesn't it? Well, it is simple, but not necessarily safe. Inside your network, Ping can be a useful tool for quickly determining that somewhere along the network path something is wrong and a computer is not reachable, whether the destination you are pinging is inside your network or on the Internet.

However, just as you wouldn't give out your credit-card number to a stranger, it's not a good idea to give out *any* information about your network, *especially* the addresses of the computers on the network, to an outsider. And, that's exactly what the ping command can do. It's easy to write a program that sits back and cycles through a range of IP addresses, sending out ICMP ECHO REQUEST packets and looking to see what replies come back. This saves a malicious hacker time because he now knows that an IP address is in use and can proceed to further try to intrude and compromise the system. Because automated tools are available for continuing the hacker's probe, it's imperative that you keep your network address information secret.

If you've ever received those boring telemarketing calls during the early evening hours, you can understand how this works. The telemarketers just cycle through phone numbers until they get someone to pick up the phone and answer. Allowing ICMP ECHO REPLY packets to respond to requests from *outside* your network is the equivalent of picking up the phone. Although you can hang up on a telemarketing call, after a hacker has your network address, she can always try back later when you're not around and use a wide variety of tools to probe your system to determine what is needed to get inside.

For this reason, it's usually a good idea to block incoming ICMP ECHO REQUEST packets. You probably don't want to block outgoing packets of the same sort, because they serve a useful purpose. You can allow users inside your network to Ping other servers on the Internet. For example, suppose you want to place an order with a business that has a Web site, yet it doesn't pop up in your browser when you try to get to its home page. You can use Ping to determine whether the business's computer is on the Net and functioning, and then from there start your troubleshooting efforts to find out why you can't bring up the business's Web page. If you Ping the site and get no response, you can be sure that either it's down or somewhere along the network path a router or another device is not letting traffic get through.

The same goes for you if you offer a service on the Internet. However, in such a case, you should make sure that your Web servers are highly secured and located on a network segment that can limit the damage should these servers be compromised. This network segment is called a demilitarized zone (DMZ), and you'll learn more about that later in this chapter.

Another utility that uses ICMP is Tracert. This command probes the network path and returns a list of all the routers and other intermediary devices it passes through to get to a destination address. Again, this is a useful tool when used properly, but you should block this sort of packet at your firewall. Do you want outsiders to know the addresses of routers and other devices on your network? After an outsider has the address and knows that a computer is online using that address, it's easy to use one of the many hacker tools available on the Internet to begin breaking into the computer.

◀◀ You can learn more about using the Tracert and Ping commands in Chapter 28, "Troubleshooting Tools for TCP/IP Networks."

Filtering Based on Port Numbers

The TCP and UDP protocols use port numbers in their header information to identify applications. Although filtering based on IP addresses blocks all network traffic from a particular source, you can use filtering rules that block only specific ports. Thus, you might allow customers to interact with Web servers inside your network using the ports set aside for WWW activity—port 80, for typical WWW traffic—but block other ports, such as port 23 that is used for Telnet functions.

As another example, you might want to allow some users to use Telnet (port 23) or FTP (ports 20 and 21) to connect to servers *outside* the corporate network while denying this capability to others. You can do this by setting up rules in the packet filter and specifying both a host source address and a port number. Ports are a two-way path. You can block incoming connections, outgoing connections, or both for each port.

Packet filtering is an integral component of most every firewall and has several advantages:

- **Usually inexpensive**—If you use a router to connect to external sources, you already have the hardware—you just need to configure it.

- **Fast**—It does only minimal processing on the header information and does not make decisions based on multiple packets.

- **Flexible**—It is easy, although some would say cumbersome, to configure as many address inclusions or exclusions as you like.

However, there are also several disadvantages to using a packet filter firewall:

- **Packet filters perform no authentication**—A packet is a packet no matter "who" the sender is. The address is the only thing that counts. This is important because IP addresses, ports, and any other part of the packet can be forged using simple tools available on the Internet.

- **Most system administrators don't take advantage of a router's auditing features**— You will most likely not even know that attempts were made to break in to the network; if the router does provide some kind of statistical information, :you won't be able to determine where the attack came from. If you turn on logging for every packet that comes through your router, you'll experience a tremendous slowdown in network response time through the router. Selectively logging events is a better option, but then again you might miss important events. Small SOHO routers do not provide logging, so keep that in mind if you use one.

- **Packet filters operate at the network level**—They are not very effective at stopping sophisticated attacks that are directed at higher-level protocols, such as TCP.

- **Internal network information is not kept from outside prying eyes**—Using ordinary utilities, such as Tracert and Ping, mischievous persons can gain knowledge about your network unless you specifically block the protocol used by these utilities (ICMP).

Note

Although a typical packet filter is fast, more advanced devices offer additional service that can be compute-intensive. Extensive logging is one example. The capability to detect a large number of bad packets coming into the network in a short time can also be useful. Using this technique, packet filters can block access to subsequent packets. This can be useful in a denial-of-service attack.

If you had the choice, which of the following would you choose:

- Allow everything, but deny specific addresses.
- Deny everything, but allow selected known good addresses.

If it's not obvious that the second choice is the best, you need to stop and think about this again.

A good approach for configuring the rules to use on a packet filter is to first *deny all traffic*. Then, selectively enable only those addresses or services that are essential to your business. If you try to do this in reverse—allowing all traffic and then denying specific items—there's no way you can create a set of rules that covers all possible sources of mischief. You might leave out something that didn't seem important at the time you did the configuration, or a new twist on an old technology might creep up and surprise you later.

Intrusion Detection (Stateful Inspection)

A stateful inspection device operates in a manner similar to a packet-filtering firewall in that it also examines the source and destination addresses of every packet that passes its way. However, a packet filter is never aware of the context of any communication. Each packet that passes through it is treated on an individual basis. A firewall that employs stateful inspection techniques attempts to keep track of requests and responses to be sure they match.

This type of firewall maintains tables of information about current connections so that it can determine whether incoming packets are unsolicited or whether they are in response to a request that was made by a user on the internal network. Another name sometimes used for this type of firewall is *dynamic packet filter*.

When a connection terminates, the firewall removes the reference from its internal table so that an external source cannot use it to gain entry again.

Many proprietary stateful inspection firewall products are on the market today. Study the documentation of this type of product before you make a purchase so that you can fully understand how it operates.

Proxy Servers

Proxy servers, also known as application gateways, provide protection for your network at the Application layer. Although packet filters make decisions based on the header information in a packet, they do not understand the application protocols, such as FTP or HTTP. Thus, it's easy for a hacker to exploit known problems with application protocols, and problems can ensue if the packet filter allows the packet to enter the network.

A proxy server can perform this function by managing connections to and from the outside world. A proxy server acts as a "man in the middle" by accepting requests for an application for your users and making that request for them. A proxy server never allows a packet to pass through the firewall; instead, a proxy server follows these steps:

1. Receives an outgoing request from one of your users. It creates a new packet and substitutes the proxy server's own address as the source address, replacing the user's actual source address.
2. The proxy server sends this new packet out onto the Internet on behalf of the user.
3. When a response is received from the Internet server, the proxy server examines the packet to determine whether the data contained in the packet is appropriate for the particular application. If so, it creates a new packet, inserts the data, and places the Internet server's address in the source address field. The packet then is sent back to the original user.

4. The user receives the packet and assumes that it's actually communicating directly with the Internet server—after all, it has the correct addressing information in the header.

Figure 49.1 shows an example of how a typical proxy server functions.

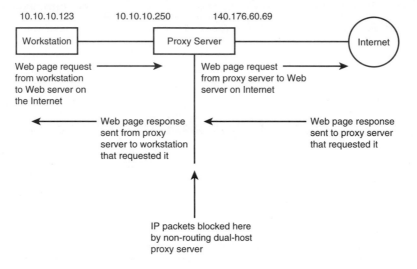

Figure 49.1 A proxy server communicates with the computer inside your network and the Internet server, but it does not allow network traffic to pass directly through the firewall.

Proxy servers also can be used to provide authentication, logging, content filtering, and other security measures. There are two kinds of proxy servers: classical proxy servers and transparent proxy servers.

A *classical proxy server* can be used with any application. The user needs to take a few extra steps to use the proxy server because the application itself was not written to understand the proxy process. A classical proxy server works in the following manner:

1. A client executes a command, such as the Telnet command, to connect to the proxy server.

2. The proxy server receives this request and sends a packet back to the user prompting for authentication information, such as a username and password.

3. The user interacts with this man-in-the-middle by entering the required information.

4. If the proxy server has been configured to allow this user to make use of the service, it prompts the user to enter the target system for the service. For example, after being authenticated by the proxy server, a user could enter username@internetserver.com. In this example, username is the username that will be used to authenticate the user on the Internet server, and internetserver.com is the name of the Internet server to which the user wants to make a connection.

5. The proxy server proceeds to create a packet containing the Telnet request, and sends it out onto the Internet. The Internet server sends back a packet requesting a password (if required) for the service.

6. The proxy server prompts the user to enter the password and passes it back to the Internet server. If the authentication succeeds, the proxy server begins operating as described earlier, by intercepting packets to and from the Internet server, substituting its own address for the user's address when sending packets to the Internet server, and substituting the Internet server's address for packets returned to the client.

After the initial authentication and connection to the service, each side of the communication process thinks it's actually talking to the other. However, because the user must initially authenticate himself to the proxy server, this type of proxy might be undesirable in some environments because some users find these extra steps a burden.

Note

A popular proxy server product called the TIS Internet Firewall Toolkit (FWTK) can be downloaded from the Internet. This kit contains proxy applications for most of the usual Internet services, such as Telnet, email, and FTP, and allows you to create your own specific proxy server applications. You can read more about this package and download it free from `www.fwtk.org`.

A *transparent proxy server* works a little differently. In this case, the application is modified so that it understands that a proxy server is being used. For this to work, you must tell the application the address of the proxy server for each service you want to use. For example, to configure proxy server information in Internet Explorer, you would take these steps:

1. Select Start, Programs, Internet Explorer (or Start, Internet Explorer if this appears in the top portion of the Start menu).

2. Select Tools, Internet Options. When the Internet Options properties page appears, click the Connections tab.

3. At the bottom of the page, click the LAN Settings button to open the Local Area Network (LAN) Settings dialog box (see Figure 49.2).

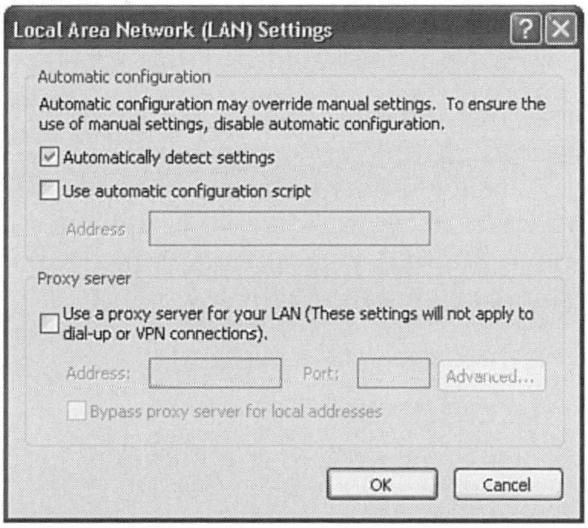

Figure 49.2   The Local Area Network (LAN) Settings dialog box allows you to select automatic configuration of a proxy server or enter the information yourself.

4. In Figure 49.2, the Automatically Detect Settings check box has been selected. If your network is configured to distribute this information automatically, all you need to do is select this check box and click the OK button. Internet Explorer queries the network to determine the proxy server settings and sets them up for you automatically. The Use Automatic Configuration Script check box can be used in a similar manner, but you'll have to get the address for the server that contains the file from your network administrator.

5. To manually configure a proxy server, select the Use a Proxy Server check box, and enter the address or hostname of the proxy server and the port that will be used (typically port 8080). This sets up Internet Explorer to use the same proxy server for all the network services you use.

6. If you want to configure each service separately, click the Advanced button shown in Figure 49.2, and the Proxy Settings dialog box appears (see Figure 49.3).

Figure 49.3   Use the Proxy Settings dialog box when you need to use more than one proxy server for different network services.

7. In Figure 49.3, you can see that Internet Explorer allows you to enter a different proxy server and port for several common network applications. You can use the Exceptions pane to enter hostnames or addresses that should not go through the proxy server. For example, hosts that reside inside your network can be contacted directly, and you don't need to use a proxy server to reach them. If you use this feature, you can enter more than one name or address, separating each entry by a semicolon, and you can use the asterisk (*) character as a wildcard. When finished, click OK.

Standard Proxy Applications

Most off-the-shelf firewall products come with proxy applications for commonly used network applications, such as these:

- Telnet
- FTP
- X Windows
- HTTP
- HTTPS
- Mail (POP and SMTP)
- Socks
- News (NNTP)

Because proxy servers operate at the application level, they are sometimes referred to as *application gateways*. You can set up the gateway using several different topologies. An example of an application gateway is a dual-homed host that runs the proxy software. In this setup, a computer has two network cards, each attached to a different network. Proxy software runs on the host and mediates between the two, deciding what traffic it will allow to flow between the two networks. You can set up a Unix or Windows NT Server computer to perform this kind of function. In Figure 49.4, you see a small network that uses a router to connect to the Internet.

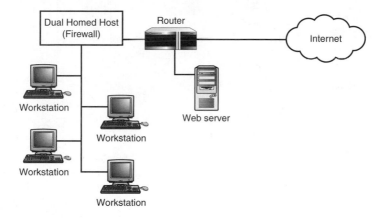

Figure 49.4   A dual-homed host is used to connect the local network to the Internet.

However, the network is not directly connected to the router. Instead, a computer has been designated for this purpose. The dual-homed host has two network cards—one talks to the router and the other participates in the local network. The router can be configured to perform filtering functions while the dual-homed host can supply the proxy functions for any services you want to allow between your network and the Internet. When this host is configured with maximum security measures to provide a defense from external sources, it is sometimes referred to as a *bastion host* or a *screened host architecture*.

As an added advantage, another computer is used to host the company's Web pages so that Internet users can access them without penetrating the interior company network.

You can carry this concept further by using multiple routers to connect to the Internet. Figure 49.5 shows a setup similar to the one just described, but there are two routers between the innermost network clients and the Internet.

The dual-homed host connects the most secure clients to the first router. Between the dual-homed host and the first router are other computers that do not need the same level of restrictions imposed by the proxy server. Again, the Web server sits on the network at a point closest to the Internet, and thus is subject to fewer restrictions than the other computers on this network. The Web server that sits between Router 1 and Router 2 should be treated very cautiously when it comes to security because it's the least-protected computer on the network. As stated earlier in the chapter, the space between these two routers is referred to as the demilitarized zone, or DMZ. Another method of creating a DMZ is to use a router with multiple interfaces and select one interface to use for a network segment that will be the DMZ (see Figure 49.6).

In this example, the firewall/router has three adapters: one for the DMZ, one for your private LAN, and one to connect to the Internet. Traffic from the Internet destined to your FTP or WWW servers is never passed by the firewall to the private LAN segment, but only to those servers residing in the DMZ. Thus, if one of your Web servers is compromised, the computers on your LAN are still safe.

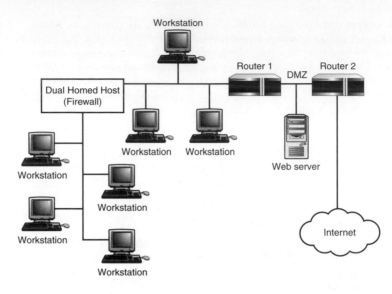

Figure 49.5   Use multiple firewalls to segment users into restrictive and less restrictive networks.

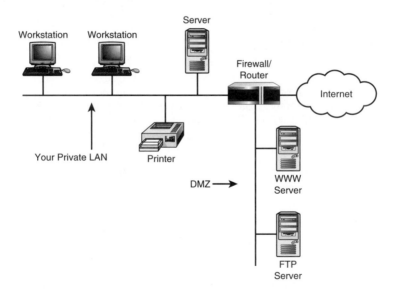

Figure 49.6   A simple DMZ can be created by using a separate LAN segment connected to the router.

Impersonating the End User: Network Address Translation (NAT)

One of the main driving forces behind a new Internet protocol (IPv6) was the assumption that the 32-bit address used by IPv4 was not large enough to keep up with the quickly growing Internet. It was assumed that eventually the entire address space would be used up. Of course, other features of IPv6, such as the security enhancements, also are making it seem as though the Internet eventually will migrate to the newer protocol. However, when you think about how a proxy server works to use its own address instead of the address of the internal network client, it seems that the address space limitation imposed by the 32-bit address is not such a big issue anymore.

Note

IPv6 wasn't designed just to increase the available IP address space. Other features, such as authentication and encryption, among others, are also part of this protocol. IPv4 is the most widely used version of IP today, especially at the LAN level. And some applications have been created to use some of the features that are present in IPv6 on an IPv4 network. However, in a few years you can expect to see IPv6 work its way outward from the core of the Internet to your LAN. Many large corporate LANs already make use of IPv6, if only for parts of their network.

Because only addresses used by the proxy servers need to be valid and registered on the Internet, what prevents you from using any address range on the internal network? This concept, known as network address translation (NAT) is widely used today for just this purpose. The proxy server uses these addresses with valid IP addresses to conduct business for its clients.

You can use practically any address range for the workstations on the LAN. However, RFC 1597, "Address Allocation for Private Internets," specifies a range of addresses that are set aside for private networks. When computers on the inside network need to communicate with each other, they use their actual addresses. The proxy server also has an address that falls within this range so that it can talk to both the private LAN and the Internet.

These ranges of IP addresses are exclusively set aside by the RFC for private networks, and cannot be used on the Internet. These are the address ranges:

- 10.0.0.0–10.255.255.255
- 169.254.0.1–169.254.255.254
- 172.16.0.0–172.31.255.255
- 192.168.0.0–192.168.255.255

Tip

If the preceding address ranges look familiar, you are probably connecting to the Internet via a NAT server. Many ISPs use NAT to conserve the range of valid IP addresses allocated to them. If you buy a cable/DSL router or switch, you'll find that one of the address spaces is used to create a private network for your LAN. Additionally, the range 169.254.0.1–169.254.255.254 is used for Automatic Private IP Addressing (APIPA), which is found in Windows XP, for example.

You can accomplish several things by using these addresses for computers inside your network:

- Your business needs to buy only a small address range from your ISP to use on the firewall or routers that connect your network to the Internet.
- You can now use a huge address space inside your network without having to apply for a large range of addresses from your ISP.
- You can use NAT for address vectoring; that is, you can let the router represent your Web service on the Internet using a single address, yet load balance the incoming requests across several servers inside the network.

Advantages and Disadvantages of a Proxy Server

As with every type of firewall, you can say good and bad things about proxy servers. Their capability to hide the identity of workstations on your network is a definite plus. Packet filters don't do that. Proxy servers are usually highly customizable, and most come with a graphical interface to make the management chores a little more understandable than those that use a command-line set of cryptic instructions.

One thing packet filters usually excel at when compared to proxy servers is speed. Filtering a packet is not much more complicated than any other task a router does. It already must look at the information contained in the header so that it can make routing decisions. Checking a table of addresses to determine which ones are allowed and which are not isn't much different from checking the routing table to decide where to forward a packet.

Note

Some advanced firewalls that provide proxy functions can be configured to support authentication and time-of-day controls. If you have a secure environment in which you need to control who gains access and limit the time of access, look for these features in the documentation before you acquire a firewall.

Hybrids

No one type of firewall that has been discussed can meet the needs of every situation. As mentioned earlier in this chapter, it is often a good idea to have several levels of defense against attack from outside your network. It is easy to segment your network so that it does not appear as one entity to the Internet. You can create several subnetworks, isolate them within your network using internal firewalls, and then enclose the collection of subnetworks with firewall protection from outside intruders.

You also can use more than one firewall between your network and the outside world. In the previous dual-homed host example, this was done because the host served as a proxy firewall that was connected to a router that performed packet filtering.

Most of the quality firewall products on the market today are *not* distinctly packet filters, proxy servers, or stateful inspection machines. Most are hybrids that incorporate the functions of all these firewall technologies, although by different degrees depending on the implementation. As long as you understand the concepts of the functions a firewall performs, you are in a better position to make an informed choice of what will work best for your environment.

Because the firewall has become such an important component of the network, you will find many products that perform other functions related to security that are not easily classified. For example, some firewalls can be used to screen the content of email or other data that passes through the firewall. You can contract with a service provider to obtain a list of known "offensive" or otherwise undesirable sites on a periodic basis and have your firewall block access to these sites. Some firewall products come with built-in virus screening.

Look for the following things when evaluating firewall products:

- Security (of course)
- Performance
- Support
- Price
- Manageability

Caution

A firewall protects you only at the point at which your network connects to an outside network. One of the most common mistakes administrators make is assuming that the network is secure and overlooking the modems that sit on many desktops throughout the enterprise. Even if a modem is used only for dial-out purposes, you still run risks of virus infections and other security problems when users dial out to other sites and download programs or data to their workstations, which are connected to the network. Worse yet, modems used for dial-in purposes, such as remote access for users, present an easy entry point for those who would do harm. If you do allow dial-in access, be sure that users understand the implications of downloading from the Internet using the same computer. If not, viruses and other malicious programs can be downloaded from the Internet, and then transfer themselves to your LAN via the dial-up connection. Most of this can be caught using a good firewall and antivirus programs. However, it can take a few days, or longer, after a new virus is discovered before a remedy is found.

The most important aspect of the firewall is the security it affords your network. Question the vendor about the specific methods used in the product, and whether the product has been evaluated by outside sources.

If you use the Internet connection only for the exchange of moderate amounts of email and an occasional Web-browsing session, performance might not be a significant factor in your choice. However, if you expect heavy demand on the Internet connection, from within or without, check to be sure that the product you acquire can handle the load. Packet filter firewalls provide a higher degree of performance; the trade-off is that they do not protect you as well as a proxy server might if it's configured properly. Because a proxy server is responsible for closer examination of each packet and can be configured to perform other tasks, it is inherently slower than a packet filter.

Support is a critical item to consider. When purchasing an expensive firewall, many vendors include on-site assistance in configuring and setting up the firewall. Additional support, including consulting and hotline help-desk services, is important because the Internet is in a state of rapid growth, and what works today might not be sufficient tomorrow. Unless you have a highly skilled technical staff capable of making decisions about firewall techniques and implementing them, support from the vendor should be a major consideration.

Again, because a firewall is not something you simply configure and forget, the management interface is important. You should look for a product that provides easy access to configuration options so that you can review and modify them as needed. Reporting capabilities should be easy to understand so that you can review data and statistics audited by the firewall. Another important aspect of the management interface is the capability to notify you when something appears to be targeting your network with not-so-good intentions. Alarms that appear onscreen are fine, if you have a round-the-clock operations staff that will be monitoring the screen. The best products will email or page you when specific events occur that you have set a trigger for beforehand.

Finally, in many cases, remote management can be a plus, if it's implemented correctly. Any remote management capability should include a secure authentication technique. The firewall isn't much good if you use a clear-text password when logging in to it remotely. You should proceed under the pretense that someone is always watching what you do on the network.

Price should not be the most relevant factor in your decision. You can download some software firewall products from the Internet free. Some firewalls sell for a few hundred dollars, and some range up into the tens of thousands of dollars. The price of the firewall, however, does not indicate its safety or capabilities. In fact, some of the free firewalls you can get from the Internet are actually quite good. One of the things that the Linux platform excels at is implementing firewall technology. Its robust speed and low overhead make it a good choice for this type of chore. However, no matter what product you choose, be sure you have the skills and know-how to properly configure and operate it.

What to Expect from a Firewall

A common mistake is to assume that a firewall will do more than it can because of its name. In the building trade, a firewall that is used to protect individual units in an apartment complex or a condominium is designed according to rules laid down by the local authorities. In the networking trade, no authorities specify what a product must do to carry the "firewall" label.

In fact, several kinds of applications and devices can be classified as firewalls. Do you need a packet filter? Do you need a device that can perform stateful inspection? Before you answer these questions, first decide what you are trying to protect and what methods you are currently using.

What Do You Want to Protect?

For example, if you have highly confidential information, such as patient records or financial information about customers, you should definitely get some good legal advice on your responsibility in keeping this information from the general public. Keeping important information on a dedicated server that cannot be accessed by ordinary users on your network is the first thing to do. However, assuming that an off-the-shelf firewall application will protect you from outside penetration is being a bit simplistic.

Determine your vulnerabilities and examine your current network. Look at how sensitive data is protected now and look at the means used to access it. Then factor in how your current safeguards will enable you to keep the data secure.

Some information usually is available to everyone in the network. For example, an employee home page that contains information about processes and procedures, such as how to request a vacation or get a purchase order approved, usually will not be considered a high-priority security item. Other information, such as information you keep about your customers, not only is important to your bottom line if you want to keep the customer happy, but also might be confidential, such as a doctor's records about patients. This kind of information should receive your utmost attention when you're trying to decide how it can be accessed after you connect to the Internet. It might be generally available to a large number of employees, depending on your business, or it might be sequestered by OS protections so that only a single department can use this kind of data.

Of course, if you perform your payroll in-house, you are probably already aware of how sensitive this kind of information is. It must be protected from prying eyes both inside your network and outside your network.

Levels of Security

Because different kinds of information are on networks today that need various levels of security, you should carefully structure your network to handle the way information is accessed.

One connection to the Internet, through a firewall, can protect you. However, with one connection and one firewall, you must make sure that the firewall is the most restrictive you need to protect the most sensitive data that you have. One firewall to protect the entire network is one point of failure. One mistake, and the whole network is vulnerable.

Another drawback is that many users resent extremely restrictive access mechanisms and, if allowed, circumvent them.

One method is to segment the internal network and use firewalls not only to keep intruders outside the company from getting access, but also to keep out those internally who might do mischief. Also, by creating different levels of security, you can act to prevent a single security breach that causes extensive damage.

Instead of using a single network, consider creating several smaller networks and using firewall technology to connect them. For example, in-house data that never needs to be accessed from external sources can reside on one network, whereas another network can host machines that provide WWW, FTP, and other services to your external clients. The firewall that connects this network to the Internet would not have to be as restrictive as the one that joins the two networks at your site.

If you have data that is so confidential that its compromise could do severe harm, you should place it on a computer that does not have a connection to the Internet. Remember, there is no way to guarantee that a computer cannot be hacked via a network, short of pulling the plug.

Tip

Remember, firewalls can operate in both directions. Although the first thing that probably jumps into your head when you think about a firewall is that it will keep out unwanted packets, the reverse also can be true. For example, you might want to connect your network to the Internet to allow email or FTP access to and from customers and your employees. You might not want your employees to access Web pages, however, and you can block their outgoing requests to prevent this type of access.

Inexpensive Firewalls for SOHO Environments

For the small office environment it is just too expensive to hire a full-time person to manage an enterprise firewall. However, you can still protect your LAN to a large degree by using a few simple products. There are both hardware and software firewall solutions. For example, cable/DSL routers use NAT, which helps to hide addresses of computers on the LAN so that hackers on the Internet will find it difficult to obtain that information. That's just the first step, however. For example, if your ISP gives you a static address that is valid on the Internet, the cable or DSL modem itself can be the subject of an attack, as well as the attached router. Thus, although clients inside your LAN might not be easy to get at directly, it could be very simple to reconfigure the router using the same type of software you used to set it up in the first place!

Tip

Even if you use NAT and an inexpensive firewall, don't forget that one of the easiest ways to penetrate your LAN is to send a virus or another similar program to you as an email attachment. A good virus-checking program that is kept up-to-date with the latest virus definitions can help prevent this problem. I would recommend that you use a virus-checking program on every computer on your network, because a well-crafted virus can spread easily after it gets onto one machine on the LAN. The price you pay for a virus checker is insignificant when compared to the cost of restoring data, which itself may have been corrupted weeks or months before you discover the virus.

Hardware Solutions

Hardware firewalls are more expensive than software firewalls because the actual hardware itself costs more to produce. Software products can be replicated for a few dollars, including packaging. However, a hardware-based firewall is not beyond the reach of a SOHO environment. You just need to be sure that the firewall you purchase performs well, as described earlier in this chapter, and that the firmware can be upgraded when necessary. The latter may not be possible on an inexpensive hardware firewall, but it is a good feature to look for when making a purchase.

Following is a list of some typical hardware-based firewalls. This is not meant to be an exhaustive list or a recommended list, but instead is presented here to give you an idea of the variety of products available:

- WatchGuard SOHO and Firebox SOHO Security Appliance—www.watchguard.com. This company offers firewalls that range from SOHO appliances to enterprise-scale firewall devices. The WatchGuard Firebox SOHO 6tc, which comes with a 10-user license, can be had for around $500. This product offers VPN functionality, stateful packet filtering, and Web content filtering, among other features. Antivirus software is also included. To purchase this product, read the technical literature at the Web site and then select a reseller, or an online distributor recommended by the company.

- D-Link—www.dlink.com. This venerable manufacturer of inexpensive routers, switches, and other hardware products that fit in well with a SOHO environment also has several SOHO firewall appliances that vary in price and capabilities. Prices range from around $90 to $250. You can make a purchase online at D-Link's Web site, or from many online Web vendors. Even the low end of this line supports VPNs, intruder logging, and stateful inspection, among other features.

- Sonicwall—www.sonicwall.com. From SOHO to enterprise networks, this manufacturer has a solution. At the low end you can get a firewall appliance for about $400–$500. It includes stateful inspection in addition to the other standard firewall techniques, such as packet filtering, VPNs, and proxies. This product is sold through third-party resellers, and the Web site lets you choose by state so that you can find a local reseller. You can also call the sales office to find a reseller.

Tip

Although I don't usually recommend where to purchase network devices or software, I will in this case. After you have read the specifications for a firewall appliance you would like to purchase, it doesn't hurt to search the Internet to find a good price. Most of the discount sites, such as **www.buy.com**, will enable you to get the product at a discount off the manufacturer's suggested retail price. Oh, watch out for those shipping charges, though! Another feature that similar Web sites offer is a rating for each vendor. Don't necessarily go for the lowest price. Read about other users' experiences before you choose a reseller. I also suggest that you visit **www.tomshardware.com**, which is a great site that reviews all sorts of network and computer products. This site's reviews might just help you decide which product to purchase.

Software Solutions

Many firewall solutions are based on software. One of the problems with this approach is that you must purchase a copy for each computer on the network—though this is not *always* the case. You can also set up one of your computers to act as a router for other computers, but this process can be complicated if you are not computer savvy. Yet a software solution that also includes an antivirus program may well be worth the cost. Windows XP also comes with a very basic packet filtering firewall, but this simple firewall does not go far in protecting your LAN. Other techniques discussed earlier in this chapter should be part of a software solution.

Some software firewalls to consider are listed here:

- ZoneAlarm—www.zonealarm.com. You can download a limited version of this firewall for testing, at no cost. This Web site also has a questionnaire that you can fill out if you decide to purchase the product. After you answer a few simple questions, this Web site can suggest which version you should purchase.

- Norton Internet Security 2003—www.symantic.com. Includes intrusion detection, standard application (port) blocking, and other useful features. You can also purchase this product bundled with other Norton products, such as its antivirus software. This product and bundled products are readily available at your local computer store.

- MacAfee Personal Firewall Plus—www.macafee.com. A basic, easy-to-use firewall solution that should be used in conjunction with a separate product for virus protection, such as MacAfee VirusScan Online. You can usually find this at your local computer store, as separate products, or bundled together so that you can save money.

- Sygate Personal Firewall Pro—www.sygate.com. A good solution that offers some features that other similar products do not. Intrusion detection, VPN support, and automatic termination of known Trojan horse programs are part of this firewall, among others.

Using Both Hardware and Software Firewalls

As mentioned earlier in this chapter, Windows XP comes with a simple packet filter firewall. This basic capability simply enables you to block ports (incoming or outgoing) based on basic packet filtering. It doesn't include proxies or stateful inspection. However, if you are using Windows XP, it doesn't hurt to set the settings on XP machines to help to further control access, whether or not you have employed another firewall technique. But don't count on this as the only protection between your computer and the Internet.

To provide a greater deal of security, you might want to use both a hardware and a software solution. Use the hardware firewall appliance as the front end of the network by attaching it to your broadband connection. Then use a software firewall package on computer(s) in your network.

Whichever you choose, keep in mind that no firewall can provide a complete solution to protect a network from outsiders. New viruses, Trojan horse programs, and the like are being created every day. All antivirus and firewall devices/software should have an update feature that you can use to download new software and virus definitions on a frequent basis. This type of service typically comes free for the first year, and then you can pay a small fee for following years.

How Do You Know That the Firewall Is Secure?

The problem with security is that the environment, either internal or external, is always changing. As soon as a bug in an OS or network application is found and exploited by mischievous persons, someone comes out with a fix. As soon as the fix is applied, something else crops up. When you set up a firewall to protect yourself from those who might do harm to your network, you must perform tests to be sure that it does what you think it does.

The problem with testing, however, is that you already know what you are looking for when you create and execute the test. *It's what you don't know that can cause problems.* To keep on top of things, you should continue to monitor the data collected by any auditing or logging functions the firewall provides to make sure that it is working as you expect. Look for attempts to breach the firewall and watch for unusual activity. You might find that you can stop an attack before it succeeds. Using other tools, such as Tracert, you might be able to locate the perpetrator and handle the matter using legal means.

No RFCs define what a firewall *must* do or how it should do it. You can contact several organizations on the Internet to get information about current firewall and security software. Appendix C, "Internet Resources for Network Administrators," contains a list of some interesting sites related to network security and firewalls that might help you decide what kind of protection you need.

Virtual Private Networks (VPNs) and Tunneling

SOME OF THE MAIN TOPICS IN THIS CHAPTER ARE

Security is a big issue both in the corporate network and on the Internet at large. As has been discussed in previous chapters, the basic TCP/IP protocols weren't particularly designed with security in mind. However, over the years many new developments have built on the current TCP/IP base that provide for more secure connections over wide area networks (WANs), such as the Internet. This chapter looks at Virtual Private Networks (VPNs) and the methods they employ to create a private tunnel through a WAN so that you can communicate securely with another computer or network.

What Is a VPN?

Basically, a VPN is nothing more than a secure path through a shared network or WAN that connects two computers, or two networks, so that from the point of view of each endpoint of the connection, they are on the same network. The connection is private because some means have been taken to secure the payload information of the data carried through this virtual tunnel.

A VPN can be a good solution for security issues in many scenarios:

- Employees who work from home and use the Internet to communicate with the company network
- Mobile employees who travel and can dial in to the Internet using a national ISP
- Branch offices using the Internet
- Business partners, customers, or even technical support staff who need access

As this list demonstrates, two basic types of VPNs are used:

- **Remote access VPN**—A connection between a remote computer and the Internet.
- **Site-to-site VPN**—A connection between two networks, which usually is done between two routers, or in some cases firewall/router combinations.

The Mobile Workforce

Many people are on the move in the business world today, and many companies are allowing some employees to work from home. A technique still used today, but which is declining, is to set up a bank of modems and give dial-in access to certain people, such as salesmen, who are always on the move. For a business that needs data connections to branch offices but can't justify the cost of leased lines, modem banks provide the necessary remote connection. You can host a bank of modems under many different operating systems, from Unix (with its efficient kernel and support for large numbers of serial devices) to Windows 2000/2003 (using the remote access service [RAS]). You even can install servers that are basically appliances that act as a front end to provide a bank of modems for dial-in services.

However, maintaining a bank of modems can be expensive because each modem needs a telephone line, which is an ongoing cost. There are several security issues to be considered. For example, what happens if someone discovers the telephone number of your dial-up access? It would then be easy to use a password dictionary attack to break into the network.

However, sometimes a simple dial-in modem is not the best solution. With Internet access in all large and most small cities in the United States, Europe, Japan, and many other countries, the Internet can be a good solution to this problem. You can use a single, high-bandwidth connection (buy what you need) to allow multiple home workers, traveling salesmen, and other mobile workers to connect to your network just as if they were sitting at a desk at the office.

The only problem with this access method is the fact that the Internet is not exactly the most secure place in the world. As a matter of fact, just connecting your company's network to the Internet is a serious task that should be accompanied by careful consideration of how you will control that connection (such as using a good firewall strategy), and how you will segment portions of your network to make sure that intrusions or other security breaches can be minimized.

Note

This chapter uses the Internet as the example of a WAN because it's the most common method used today for connecting to remote sites inexpensively. However, VPN technology can be used across any shared or corporate network. You still can have a bank of modems and let users dial up your local RAS and create a connection through your network.

In a typical LAN (local area network) setting, computers, servers, and other resources are connected using switches (or hubs in older networks that have not yet upgraded to newer hardware). Routers are used to connect LANs so that a logical addressing scheme can be used. The problem with security is that when the IP protocol is used, for example, the payload section of the IP packet carries some higher-level protocol message without any way of encrypting the data. If you can intercept the IP packet, you can easily determine which protocol is being used and get to the information very quickly.

As you can guess, VPNs are made up of two basic components: a tunnel, which is a virtual path through a WAN, and some form of encryption to render the contents of the payload (and possibly the header information of the upper-level protocol) unusable if intercepted.

Protocols, Protocols, and More Protocols!

Because the functions provided by a VPN include tunneling, data integrity, and authentication, it makes sense that a VPN is not created using a single protocol. Instead, several protocols can be used to create a VPN, each performing a particular function. In this section the following protocols are briefly examined:

- Internet Protocol Security (IPSec)
- Point-to-Point Tunneling Protocol (PPTP)
- Layer Two Tunneling Protocol (L2TP)

For the most part, only IPSec should be a major factor in VPNs in the coming years. PPTP was used by Windows NT 4.0 as part of its VPN package, and L2TP has replaced it in Windows 2000 VPNs. L2TP is basically just the PPTP protocol combined with the L2F protocol developed by Cisco. However, most VPN vendors are using the IPSec protocols instead, which are described in greater detail than PPTP and L2TP in this chapter. The IPSec protocols incorporate some of the security mechanisms that were originally designed to be included in IPv6 but have been adapted for use in the existing IPv4 network.

Note

An important factor to consider when it comes to security is that most handheld devices in use today don't support L2TP or IPSec, though some do support PPTP.

IPSec Protocols

As noted previously, IPSec is the emerging standard being adopted by more and more VPN vendors. IPSec was derived from concepts that were originally designed to provide for secure communications in the next generation of the IP protocol, IPv6. However, it might be many years before IPv6 sees widespread adoption because the main driving force behind IPv6 originally was the expected depletion of the IPv4 address space. With techniques such as Network Address Translation, this is not such a pressing problem anymore.

◀◀ For more information about NAT, see Chapter 49, "Firewalls."

Note

No one is really sure when you'll see IPv6. In recent years, it was assumed that NAT, and the enhancement of IPv4 by the addition of protocols such as IPSec, would delay the adoption of IPv6 for some time to come. In the previous year or so, the proliferation of mobile devices (such as PDAs and cellular telephones that are equipped to become Internet devices), along with other emerging wireless technologies, has many people wondering whether the IPv4 address space, along with NAT, will be able to cope. With appliance manufacturers considering making refrigerators, ovens, and other such things capable of Internet connections, IPv6 might become a hot topic once again. Regardless, you will eventually see IPv6 deployed in most LANs, as the Internet continues to expand.

Although Microsoft chooses to use L2TP and IPSec in combination as its VPN solution for Windows 2000, many hardware and software vendors are sticking with a simple IPSec solution.

The good news is that if you decide on an all-IPSec solution, you can be virtually assured that equipment (or software) from one vendor to another will work together. If you have an all-Windows server environment, this might be of no concern. For those who operate multiprotocol networks, IPSec might be the best choice.

IPSec is a standard defined in several Request for Comments (RFC) documents. IPSec is transparent to the end user and can traverse the Internet using standard IPv4 routers and other equipment without requiring any modification because it operates at the Network layer. IPSec is also flexible, allowing for the negotiation and use of many different encryption and authentication techniques.

The three main components of IPSec are the following:

- **Internet Key Exchange (IKE)**—This is the protocol defined in RFC 2048, "Internet Security Association and Key Management Protocol (ISAKMP)," which defines a method for the secure exchange of the initial encryption keys between the two endpoints of the VPN link.

- **Authentication Header (AH)**—This protocol, defined in RFC 1826, "The Authentication Header," provides for inserting a standard IPv4 header into an additional header that can be used to ensure the integrity of the header information and payload as the packet makes its way through the Internet. AH does not encrypt the actual IP payload data, but instead provides a mechanism to determine whether the payload or header has been tampered with.

- **Encapsulating Security Payload (ESP)**—This protocol performs the actual encryption of the data carried in the IP packet so that it cannot be understood by anyone who might intercept your data stream.

Internet Key Exchange (IKE)

IKE defines the mechanism used by the endpoints of the VPN to establish a secure connection and exchange encryption keys and other information pertinent to a secure connection. IKE uses public-key techniques that were discussed in the preceding chapter. If you recall, the public key half of a key pair can be known by anyone, as long as the private-key half of the key pair remains a secret. Thus, each end of the connection can use the other end's public key to encrypt data, which can then be read only by the other end of the connection that holds the private key that can unlock the data.

IKE provides for the establishment of a *security association* (SA), which is the set of data that governs the particular connection. SAs are unidirectional; that is, each side negotiates an SA with the opposite end of the link. Think of it as a contact between the endpoints. The items that are negotiated by IKE for an SA include these:

- **The encryption algorithm to be used on the link**—This can be DES (Data Encryption Standard), triple-DES, and so on.

- **The hash algorithm**—Message Digest 5 (MD5) or Secure Hash Algorithm (SHA) is used to ensure the integrity of data transferred.

- **An authentication method**—Not surprisingly, this is the method that will be used for authentication.

- **A Diffie-Hellman group**—Diffie-Hellman takes its name from the inventors of public-key cryptography. A Diffie-Hellman group is basically a specification in which each group defines the length of the base prime numbers that are used for the key exchange. Group 1 is considered to be easier to break than Group 2, and so on. Both sides of the exchange must use the same Diffie-Hellman group, of course.

▶▶ Encryption is detailed in Chapter 51, "Encryption Technology."

Diffie-Hellman uses a public and private key to form a pair of keys. The public key is used to encrypt data, whereas the private (secret) key of the pair is used by the receiver to decrypt the data. Anyone can discover the public key because it can be used only to encrypt data, and not to perform the reverse process.

Using this process, a master secret key is exchanged so that further encryption can use symmetric encryption, which is much faster than public-key encryption, to protect data on the link.

After both sides have authenticated themselves to the other side, negotiations take place to determine whether AH or ESP will be used, what hashing algorithm will be used, and what encryption algorithm will be used (if ESP is used).

The actual mechanics of this exchange are a little more complicated. The Oakley protocol (defined in RFC 2412) is used by IKE to define such things as the prime number groups that are used for the public-key generation, and to decide whether certificate-based authentication will be used. A security parameters index (SPI) value is used, along with an IP address and the security protocol, to uniquely identify a specific SA. Using IKE, the value for the SPI is a pseudo-randomly generated number.

The Authentication Header (AH)

IPSec consists of the two basic AH and ESP protocols that are used after IKE has established an SA. AH provides a mechanism to ensure the integrity of the IP header and the payload of the IP packet that will be transported across an untrusted link, such as the Internet. When used by itself, AH cannot provide a total guarantee of the entire IP header because some of the fields in the IP header are changed by routers as the packet passes through the network.

◀◀ For more information about fields that make up an IP header, see Chapter 25, "Overview of the TCP/IP Protocol Suite."

The AH is inserted directly after the IP header in an IPv4 packet and is composed of several important fields:

- **Next Header**—This 8-bit field is used to identify the protocol that follows the header. If only AH is being used without ESP, typically this field contains the protocol number for TCP because TCP is the standard packet type used to carry most Internet traffic.

- **Length**—This 8-bit field is used to specify the total length of the AH, and represents the number of 32-bit words that make up the AH.

- **Reserved**—This field is not used at this time, but should instead be zero-filled according to the standard.

- **Security Parameters Index (SPI)**—This 32-bit field contains a number used to identify the SA. A value of 0 indicates that no SA exists, whereas the numbers 1–255 are reserved by the IANA (Internet Assigned Numbers Authority).

- **Sequence Number**—This 32-bit field is used as a counter to keep track of packets that belong to a particular SPI. The counter is incremented once for each packet sent. This is useful for preventing a man-in-the-middle sort of attack.

- **Authentication Data**—This is a variable-length field that contains data used for authentication purposes, such as a digital certificate. If this field does not end on a 32-bit boundary, it's padded to adjust its length.

As mentioned earlier, the AH is used to provide an integrity check to determine whether the actual header or payload has been tampered with during transit. It does this by using a hashing algorithm to provide a digital signature for the packet. AH *does not encrypt the payload data*. If a packet is received and the AH indicates that the packet has been tampered with, the packet is discarded. MD5 and SHA are the two basic hashing algorithms typically used. It is beyond the scope of this book to discuss the details of these algorithms, but rest assured that they are complex formulas that take a variable amount of information and reduce it to a fixed-length unit of data. The hash value can be calculated at each end of the connection to determine whether anything in the packet has changed. Thus, AH provides a method for ensuring the integrity of the packet, but not for keeping its contents secret.

AH can also be used in a Windows environment to ensure that only computers that have certificates administered by the administrator can communicate within the network. The administrator can control the distribution of certificates so that rogue computers (those connected to the network without permission of the administrator) won't be able to use AH as long as certificates are used by computers to authenticate themselves to each other.

For a truly secure VPN connection, ESP must be used.

Encapsulation Security Payload (ESP)

ESP is used to encrypt the payload, or the actual IP packet that is carried in the data portion of the packet. It operates in two modes: transport and tunnel.

In *transport mode*, ESP provides protection for the payload and for headers created by upper-level protocols, such as TCP, that ride inside the IP packet. In this mode, nothing is done to protect the header information of the IP packet that serves as the workhorse to get the data from here to there. This is an efficient method for encrypting the contents of the IP packet in which bandwidth constraints are important.

When operating in *tunnel mode*, ESP is used between two IPSec gateways (such as a set of routers or firewalls) and it protects the IP header information. The entire IP datagram, including the IP header and its payload—usually an upper-level protocol such as TCP or UDP (User Datagram Protocol)—is encrypted and encapsulated by the ESP protocol. New header information is added to the resulting packet that identifies the endpoints of the transfer (the two gateways), but the true source address, destination address, and other packet information carried inside the ESP packet is protected. At the destination gateway, this outer wrapper of information is removed, the contents of the packet are decrypted, and the original IP packet is sent out onto the network to which the gateway is attached.

When in tunnel mode, the ESP header information is inserted directly before the IP or other protocol datagram that is to be protected. The datagram being protected is encrypted (according to methods set up by the SA), and additional headers are added in clear text format so that the new IP datagram can be transported to the appropriate gateway. In other words, the original protocol datagram is encrypted, the ESP header is added, and, finally, a new IP datagram is created to transport this conglomeration to its destination gateway point.

At the receiving gateway, this outer IP header information is stripped off, and according to the parameters defined by the SA, the protected payload of the original datagram is decrypted.

When in transport mode, the ESP header information follows the other header information of an IP datagram. Usually this is an authentication header that has been inserted to protect the integrity of the packet. The upper-level (Transport layer) header information follows the ESP header information. Any information following the ESP header, including the Transport layer headers, is encrypted according to the method described by the SA, and the packet is sent on its way. Note that this method does not use a gateway, so the clear text IP header at the front of the packet contains the actual destination address of the encapsulated datagram. This is the main difference between transport mode and tunnel mode. However, ESP can be used, as just mentioned, in conjunction with AH to protect the integrity of the IP header information.

At the receiving end of the communication path, this clear text header information is saved, the contents of the encrypted packet are decrypted and reassembled with the correct IP header information, and the packet is sent on its way onto the network.

ESP uses both a header and a trailer to encapsulate datagrams that it protects. The header consists of an SPI, such as the one used by AH, to identify the security association, and a sequence number to identify packets, ensure that they arrive in the correct order, and ensure that no duplicate packets are received. The trailer consists of padding from 0 to 255 bytes to make sure that the datagram ends on a 32-bit boundary. This is followed by a field that specifies the length of the padding that was attached so that it can be removed by the receiver. Following this field is a Next Header field, which is used to identify the protocol that is enveloped as the payload.

Additionally, ESP can include an authentication trailer that contains data used to verify the identity of the sender and the integrity of the message. This Integrity Check Value (ICV) is calculated based on the ESP header information, as well as the payload and the ESP trailer. The layout of an ESP datagram is shown in Figure 50.1.

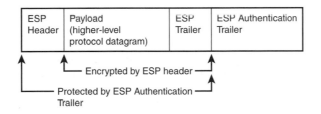

Figure 50.1   The format of an ESP datagram.

As you can see, the ICV attached to the end of the packet is not encrypted. Instead, it is a value calculated on the contents of the rest of the ESP-encapsulated packet. The receiving end of the VPN can recalculate this value to determine whether the contents of the ESP header, or its payload, have been compromised during transit.

The Point-to-Point Tunneling Protocol (PPTP)

The Point-to-Point Protocol (PPP) is an error-checking protocol used for dial-up connections to the Internet. PPP allows for the encapsulation of data packets from multiple protocols for simple transmission across a dedicated link, such as a phone line when you dial in to the Internet. PPP performs no routing functions, but merely encapsulates the protocol packets it receives by attaching its own header and sends them to the other endpoint of the connection.

◄◄   For more information about PPP, see Chapter 15, "Dial-Up Connections."

PPTP extends the capabilities of PPP so that a tunnel can be created through a packet-switched network, such as the Internet, instead of across a serial link. The concepts are similar. PPTP encapsulates another protocol packet and the PPTP packet is then routed through the network. The endpoints that use the PPTP connection don't have to be aware that they are at opposite ends of a large packet-switched network. Instead, it is as if both computers are on the same network.

Note

PPTP is described in more detail in RFC 2637, "Point-to-Point Tunneling Protocol (PPTP)."

Another difference between PPP and PPTP is that PPTP allows for the encryption of the payload portion of the packet so that IP (or other protocol) datagrams can be protected from prying eyes as they travel.

For example, a home user who wants to connect to a server on his company's network first makes a dial-up connection to an Internet service provider (ISP). After the connection is set up, another set of protocol negotiations begins to set up the PPTP tunnel, over the PPP link. The endpoints for the PPP link are the home user and the ISP. The endpoints for the PPTP link are the home user's computer and the company's remote access service (RAS) that uses the Internet. At the RAS endpoint, the PPTP packets are unpackaged and the contents decrypted to reveal the original IP (or other protocol) packet, which can then be sent onto the company network. Thus, the home user can operate as if he were directly connected to the company network.

This protocol was used in Windows NT 4.0, and although it's still supported in Windows 2000, the newer L2TP is the preferred method for newer implementations for Windows clients.

Layer Two Tunneling Protocol (L2TP)

L2TP is the method of choice for Windows 2000 VPNs. The Windows 2000 operating system has the components necessary to create a VPN built into the operating system. This can be an advantage for mobile users who connect via the Internet and need to create a secure connection to the home corporate network.

L2TP is an enhancement of PPTP that uses technology from a Cisco protocol called Layer 2 Forwarding (L2F). The combination of these two protocols is documented in RFC 2662, "Layer Two Tunneling Protocol 'L2TP.'" L2TP uses UDP for sending user data packets as well as for maintenance messages used to manage the VPN connection. Because L2TP itself is only a tunneling protocol, the IPSec protocol, discussed previously in this chapter, is used for the actual encryption that protects the contents of the data traversing the tunnel.

Note

A true VPN should provide both a tunnel, which is a method for encapsulating another protocol datagram or packet, and some kind of encryption to protect the contents of the data being transferred. However, it's possible to create a tunnel that does not use any form of encryption for the data packet. In such a case, L2TP or AH, discussed earlier in this chapter, can provide an integrity check on the header information and packet contents to ensure that they are not altered during transit. This type of tunnel is not a true VPN, but it does provide some sort of security in that you can be assured that the data sent from one end of the connection arrives at the other end in its original format. For security purposes, the data should be sent in encrypted format, using IPSec.

Because UDP packets—rather than TCP packets—are used by L2TP, a session does not exist. Instead, L2TP uses sequence numbers for each message to make sure that packets are ordered correctly from the origination point to the destination.

L2TP Encapsulation

L2TP relies on the PPP protocol. The PPP datagram is encapsulated by L2TP by attaching an L2TP header directly in front of the PPP header. Because L2TP uses UDP, as you can probably guess, the UDP header is prefixed to the result. In Figure 50.2, you can see an overview of how the packet looks at this point.

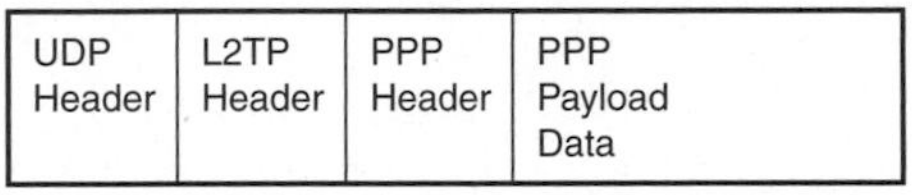

UDP Header	L2TP Header	PPP Header	PPP Payload Data

Figure 50.2   The L2TP protocol transfers PPP datagrams using UDP as a transport protocol.

If you just want to create a tunnel, this level of encapsulation is all you need because the UDP packet will make a best-effort attempt to deliver the packet by passing it to the IP protocol for transmission on the routed network.

However, because a VPN needs to provide some level of security for the payload, the IPSec protocol comes into play. The packet shown earlier in Figure 50.1 is encapsulated by IPSec by attaching the IPSec header and trailer to the packet before it is sent to the IP protocol. In Figure 50.3, you can see the format for the resulting datagram.

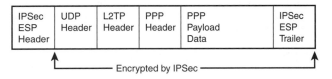

Figure 50.3   IPSec provides the encryption necessary to create a true VPN when used with L2TP.

Finally, UDP passes the resulting packet to IP for transmission on the network, just like any other IP packet. The source and destination addresses used by IP are the addresses of the VPN client and server.

Encryption Technology

51

SOME OF THE MAIN TOPICS IN THIS CHAPTER ARE

CHAPTER 51

This chapter gives you a quick overview of the two basic encryption techniques in use today, and shows how they can be applied to networks to help keep programs and data secure and to prevent unauthorized persons from gaining access. These encryption techniques are known generally as *single-key* encryption and *public-key* encryption. Alternatively, they often are referred to as *symmetric* encryption (single key) and *asymmetric* encryption (public key).

Computers and Privacy

When computers were standalone systems that were easily controlled by a central administrative group, keeping data out of the hands of those who didn't need to see it was already difficult. Usernames and passwords were designed to restrict individual users and their actions, as well as track the actions they performed. File and resource protections enforced by operating systems made it simple to keep most prying eyes out of sensitive files, but where there's a will, there's usually a way, and even operating system resource-protection techniques have their vulnerabilities.

For example, many passwords are either easy to guess or easy to obtain. If you don't enforce a strict security policy in your network, often users will use passwords that are so simple it makes a joke out of using passwords at all. Passwords such as the name of the local football team, a spouse, a child, or even a pet are often used because they're easy to remember. It is a good idea to create passwords using both uppercase and lowercase letters and alphabetic and numeric characters. These techniques can go a long way toward preventing a hacker from using a simple dictionary attack against your network. This kind of attack simply involves using a program that cycles through all the words in a dictionary to see whether any match up to your password. Hackers don't use just any dictionary, but instead can find huge lists of possible passwords (names, city names, baseball teams, and others we've just mentioned) to use. Another type of dictionary attack can be performed on Unix systems if the hacker steals the password file. Because the encryption scheme is known for most Unix systems, the program can simply encrypt every word found in a dictionary and compare it to the encrypted version in the simple /etc/passwd file!

Tip

If you wonder what levels of security passwords afford your network, try calling a user. Tell him you work for the help desk and you need to know his password. Chances are that more than half the time the user will give you his password. So much for password security. This method of breaching security is known as *social engineering*.

When you consider the environment today, with large-scale networks and connections to the Internet, the security issues become even more complex and difficult to manage using simple schemes, such as username/password authentication. Encrypting the actual data files themselves, especially when they are to be transferred across an untrusted network link, can solve a large part of this problem.

Encryption techniques should be seriously considered in an environment in which security is considered an important part of the network and not assumed to be taken care of by the standard username/password mechanism.

What Is Encryption?

Encryption is the process of performing some function on a set of data that attempts to render it in a format that makes it unreadable or unusable by anyone but the intended recipient. A key is required to read something that has been encrypted. This might be a secret key, as is the case with single-key encryption, or it might be a key that can be known by many different people, as is the case with public-key encryption. Some cryptographic methods use the same key for encrypting and decrypting information, whereas others use a separate key for these functions.

Digital signatures and certificates are part of another interesting concept that has become increasingly important in networks today. You'll learn more about that later. First, take a quick look at basic encryption techniques.

Single-Key Encryption—Symmetric Encryption

As its name implies, single-key encryption uses the same key to encrypt and decrypt information. The Data Encryption Standard (DES) is a technology developed by IBM in the 1970s and adopted as a federal government standard in the United States in 1976. DES was thought for many years to be extremely secure. It is still in use in many networks and businesses today. You'll find it in various forms, typically using more than one pass at encryption to secure the data. For example, a technique called *triple-DES* uses three different keys successively to encrypt and then re-encrypt the data. A 56-bit key is used, which results in a little over 72 quadrillion possible key values. You would think with such a large number of possible keys, and using multiple passes, that the data secured by DES would truly be secure.

Note

Actually, DES is a pretty good method for encrypting data, but it's not perfect. Given enough time, it's possible to break the code. Until 1998, it was illegal to export DES cryptographic software outside the United States. It was also in 1998 that a computer was used to break the code, although it took 56 hours to do so. In 1999, a new record was set: approximately 22 hours. With more powerful computer technology now available, DES is just not practical for a high-security environment.

That might have been true a few years ago. However, when you consider that the typical desktop PC today is a lot more powerful than the computers available back in the 1970s when DES was first developed, it's obvious that even this strong form of encryption is vulnerable to being broken, if only by a brute-force method in which every possible key value is tried. The National Institute of Standards and Technology (NIST) has decided not to recertify DES as a standard.

Note

For those who are interested in reading the actual standards documents, DES is specified in ANSI (the American National Standards Institute) X3.92 and X3.106 standards.

The main advantage that single-key encryption has over public-key encryption is that it's computationally fast to implement. The major disadvantage is that you need to protect the secret key.

The New Standard: AES

AES is the name given to the encryption algorithm that was selected by NIST as the new standard for encryption. NIST set the requirements necessary for this new standard, and many candidates submitted algorithms hoping to qualify. The selection that was made is called Rijndael, a block cipher developed by Joan Daemen and Vincent Rijmen from Belgium. This encryption algorithm makes use of variable-length blocks of data and key lengths to encrypt the data. Currently, key lengths of 128, 192, and 256 bits can be used to encrypt blocks of data, also of variable lengths, of 128, 192, or 256 bits. However, the algorithm is extensible, allowing for larger key sizes in multiples of 32 bits. How long this new AES standard will be considered "unbreakable" remains to be seen. However, the longer the key length, the more computational time it will take to break the code because each additional bit adds tremendously to the possible permutations of numbers that can be created using the key.

In December 2001, AES was adopted by the U.S. government as the encryption standard to be used for unclassified documents. The U.S. military uses other, secret encryption technologies for classified documents and communications.

Note

A *block cipher* is a method of taking a block of data and rendering it into ciphertext using some encryption technique. In contrast to this, a *stream cipher* is an encryption method that encrypts individual bits of data in the data stream. Even more complex methods of block ciphers exist. For example, cipher-block chaining involves taking a block of plain text and using the logical **XOR** operation with the previous block of text that has already been encrypted into ciphertext.

If you want to learn more about Rijndael, you can visit the Web site for these cryptographers at www.esat.kuleuven.ac.be/~rijmen/rijndael/, which includes code examples and documentation. It's freely available to anyone who cares to use it. You can also visit the Web site http://csrc.nist.gov/CryptoToolkit/aes/ for more information about AES.

The Problem with Single-Key Encryption

No matter how strong the encryption algorithm used with a single-key encryption method, one thorny problem remains. You still have to find a way to transfer the single known key to the recipient of the message, or establish some method for using an alternating set of seemingly random key selections. If someone trying to intercept your data can determine the single key, it's a simple matter to decrypt the data. However, because most people don't expect their communications to be intercepted and decrypted, sometimes perfection isn't necessary. It's enough to use the best available method and hope that you don't have a hacker (or the government) trying to look into your affairs.

The problem with key transfer, however, exists with AES, DES, or any single-key encryption algorithm. For a large corporation, the exchange of a secret key might involve sending a courier from one location to another to deliver the key. This can be expensive. Of course, if your company is a large financial institution, the cost is miniscule when compared to the value of the data that is encrypted using the secret key. For smaller entities, and for individual users on the Internet, exchanging secret keys in this manner is not a consideration.

To overcome this limitation, another solution was developed, called public-key encryption. Public-key encryption is subject to the same brute-force attack method of trying every possible key that a single-key encryption method is; however, it makes distributing keys much simpler. The difference between single-key encryption, also called symmetric encryption, and public-key encryption is very subtle.

Public-Key Encryption

Whitfield Diffie and Martin Hellman invented public-key cryptography in 1975. Public-key cryptography uses two keys, called a *key pair*, that are mathematically related. One key is used to encrypt the data, and the other to decrypt the data. At first glance, this might seem rather innocuous. In fact, instead of protecting the encryption key and keeping it a secret, the opposite is true. The key used to encrypt the data is the public key that can be shared with many people. You can post your public key on certain places on the Internet so that it's available to anyone who wants to send you a message in encrypted format. It also is common now for users to attach a copy of their public key to emails they send out so that the recipient of the message can use it to encrypt a response to the email. The term *key ring* is used to describe a file that you use to store a set of public keys for others with whom you communicate. Products such as Pretty Good Privacy (PGP) use key rings for just this purpose.

This form of encryption usually is referred to as asymmetric encryption, because more than one key is used. To put it simply, if you want someone to send you a message in encrypted format, you just give her (or anyone else) your public key. Anyone who wants to send you a message encrypts the message using this public key. The difference between symmetric encryption and asymmetric encryption is that the public key that encrypts the data cannot be used to perform the reverse process of decrypting the data that it was used to encode. Instead, a pair of keys is used: the public key that you can distribute freely and a secret key that only you possess. Both keys are mathematically related so that only the secret key can be used to decrypt the message that was encrypted using your public key.

Note

For additional protection, a secret key is often encrypted with an additional password or passphrase that must be entered to make the secret key accessible.

This solves the problem of having to distribute a secret key, because you don't have to. Instead, you can freely publish your public key so that anyone in the world (or on the Internet) can use it. Because this key can be used only to *encrypt* a message, and *can't* be used to unlock the message, you don't have to worry about keeping the public key a secret. Instead, you only need to keep secret the other half of this key pair, and because it is under your control, that should be much easier to do.

Yet, this brings up another question. How can you be sure that the person who has sent you a message is the person he or she claims to be? Because anyone can potentially gain access to your public key—remember, there are places on the Internet where you can publish your public key—how can you be sure, when you receive an encrypted message, that it comes from the person whom the message claims it is from?

Enter, stage left, the *digital signature*. The person who sends you the message can use *her* own secret key to digitally sign the message. You then can use her *public key* to verify that the message most likely did originate from that person. Unless the sender's secret key has become compromised, you can be fairly sure that you've received a message from the person the message claims to be from in encrypted format that can be decrypted only by your own secret key. Throughout this entire process, it's *never* necessary to exchange either party's secret key. The public keys can be known by anyone; as long as the secret keys remain a secret, it's possible to be *reasonably* sure that you've received an encrypted message from the person you think it's from.

One drawback to public-key encryption is that, due to the mathematical relationship between the key pair, the size of the keys is a lot larger than one traditionally used in secret key, or symmetric, encryption. However, the flexibility that public-key encryption provides, and the uses to which it has been put (such as digital signatures), more than makes up for the larger key size. Does it really matter if it takes a few seconds longer to decrypt a message using public-key cryptography when you consider the problems associated with trying to distribute a secret key, and keep it a secret?

Because public-key encryption techniques eliminate the need to share a secret key, a public-key encryption system also could be combined with a secret-key encryption system. That is, a public key could be used to encrypt a secret key for transmission across a network, where it is recovered using the private key at the end of the communication path. From then on, the secret key itself could be used for further encrypted communications. Because secret-key encryption typically uses shorter key lengths than public keys, it's much faster to encrypt or decrypt text using a secret key. Thus, public-key encryption can be used both as a method of encrypted communication and as a method for exchanging secret keys for even faster encrypted communications. To make things even more secure, it's common to change the secret key frequently during the transmission of data, making it even more difficult for anyone who intercepts the data to discover any of the keys. As a general rule, the more data that the interceptor has to work with, the easier it is to use a computer to look for patterns and try to decrypt the data. If the secret key changes frequently (transmitted using public-key technology), the interceptor has less data encrypted with the same key to work with, and the job becomes much more difficult.

RSA Public Key Cryptography

Several algorithms are used today for public-key asymmetric encryption. The most widely known is called the RSA algorithm, named after its inventors, Ronald Rivest, Adi Shamir, and Len Adleman. This method is based on multiplying two prime numbers to come up with the key pair. Further mathematical functions are performed after the multiplication to create the actual key pair, but that is beyond the scope of this book. It's a simple matter to use a computer to come up with a rather large prime number, but it's a difficult computation task to take the result of this multiplication and the subsequent operations performed and determine which two prime numbers were used to generate it.

If you want to learn more about RSA, visit the Web site for the company founded to market this technology: www.rsasecurity.com. The RSA Security Web site is an excellent resource for encryption techniques overall, but also has a lot of information pertaining to the RSA algorithm, which has been licensed to a large number of software and hardware security providers.

Because of the difficulty in cracking RSA-encrypted data, it has been adopted by a large number of vendors, including Sun, Microsoft, and Novell, and is the most widely used cryptosystem today.

Digital Certificates

Digital certificates are used to bind a person's name (or an identity) to a public key. Certificates, then, must come from a trusted authority. The certificate itself is determined to be valid (that is, it was issued by the certificate authority [CA] it claims to represent) by a digital signature. Because the public key of a CA can be known to anyone, it is a simple computational matter to use the CA's public key to determine that the digital signature is valid. After this is done, the certificate itself can be assumed to contain a valid identity (a user, a corporation, or another entity) associated with a public key. Using a digital certificate, you then can obtain the public key for a person and use it to encrypt data to be sent to that person, who then can use his own private key to read your message.

CAs can be trusted companies on the Internet, or you can act as your own CA in your company. Included with Windows 2000 Advanced Server and the family of Windows 2003 servers, for example, is Microsoft's Certificate Services, which can be used within a company that wants to manage its own digital certificates. If you have branch offices and want to use digital certificates to certify public keys used for communicating over the Internet, you can set up your own certificate servers in your enterprise. Or you can use a commercial company (such as VeriSign) and obtain certificates from a third party.

In practice, it also is possible for a hierarchy of certificate servers to be set up, with a single root server being the most trusted certificate server in your enterprise. Then, child certificate servers are created, which can be validated by the end user because the child certificate server itself has a certificate from the root server (or another server in the hierarchy leading back to the root server) that validates its certificate. It's all a game of trust, however. If the secret key of the root server's key pair becomes compromised, it's possible to impersonate the certificate server and all security is lost. Most certificates also are issued with an expiration date, which can be used to ensure that new certificates, created using a new key pair, are in use.

For this reason, should you choose to operate your own certificate server(s) in your network, you need to take extreme security precautions to safeguard the private key. Likewise, if you use a third-party commercial certificate service, you need to read the policy of that company to determine how it verifies the identity of the end users that it issues certificates to. For example, a CA might simply verify the email address of the requestor and issue a certificate. For a software publisher, the CA might conduct some kind of background check and require further evidence before it issues certificates to the company. Before you decide to use a commercial service for issuing digital certificates, be sure you investigate the company's policies for both issuing and revoking certificates.

Note

CAs on the Internet have become numerous in the past few years. If you want to learn more about how commercial certificate issuers operate, visit the Web sites of some of the better-known issuers:

```
www.verisign.com/

www.rsasecurity.com/

www.entrust.com/
```

Be sure to read their policies before you decide to use a commercial CA. Find out what mechanisms they use to verify the identity of the person or entity they issue certificates to. Find out what they do to support revoking certificates that have become compromised, and whether or not they issue certificates that expire after a period of time.

If you'd like to experiment with personal certificates, Thawte (`www.thawte.com`) offers free personal email certificates from its Web site.

Pretty Good Privacy (PGP)

One of the most popular encryption programs on the Internet for a number of years now has been PGP, originally developed by Phillip Zimmerman. PGP uses public-key cryptography and has been ported to many computer platforms, including Unix, Linux, and, of course, all versions of Windows from Windows NT and Windows 95 onward.

PGP Corporation (www.pgp.com) currently markets the commercial version of PGP. Although it charges for the commercial product, it offers a freeware version on its site. In addition, you can download an older freeware version or a command-line version from http://web.mit.edu/network/pgp.html. This freeware version has some, but not all, of the capabilities of the full-fledged product. The freeware product is for noncommercial use only, so it's a good buy (free) for most ordinary Internet users. Also note that the only versions available for freeware download are for the Windows, Unix, and Macintosh platforms. If you want to use PGP in your business environment, you'll need to purchase the commercial version and a license from PGP Corporation.

PGP has been established as an Internet proposed standard through the Request for Comments (RFC) process. RFC 2440, "OpenPGP Message Format," was written in 1998 and details the specification.

An international site devoted to PGP also can be used to download PGP. Visit the PGPi Project International PGP home page at www.pgpi.org/ to learn more about PGP International. The downloads available from this site include support for the following platforms:

- Amiga
- Atari
- BeOS
- EPOC (Psion, and so on)
- MacOS
- MS-DOS
- Newton
- OS/2
- PalmOS
- Unix
- Windows 3.x
- Windows 2000
- Windows Me
- Windows 95/98/NT
- Windows XP

As you can see, various operating systems are supported by the International PGP site, which is working to establish PGP as a standard for encryption on the Internet. In addition to the standard PGP package, which provides for a number of applications, such as document encryption and email, a number of other products also are available, such as PGPdisk (for encrypting disks) and PGPphone (for making secure phone calls on the Internet).

The PGPi Project also is making PGP available in various languages, and also is currently translating the documentation. PGPi is a nonprofit organization dedicated to further developing and distributing PGP technology throughout the world. In addition, for some platforms, the source code is available so that you can examine it before compiling it on your system.

Troubleshooting Networks

SOME OF THE MAIN TOPICS FOR THIS PART ARE

Strategies for Troubleshooting Network Problems

Network Testing and Analysis Tools

Troubleshooting Small Office and Home Office (SOHO) Networks

Strategies for Troubleshooting Network Problems

SOME OF THE MAIN TOPICS IN THIS CHAPTER ARE

CHAPTER 52

Although networks can be composed of many types of physical components, from copper wire or fiber-optic cables to wireless Access Points and network adapters, there are steps you can take to make troubleshooting network problems a little easier, regardless of their composition. Although each device, protocol, or standard that is a part of your network may come with its own tools used for troubleshooting purposes, it's important to realize that you should take a *structured approach* to solving problems on the network. This chapter introduces a few concepts that make life much simpler for a network administrator, including documenting network components, and also documenting problems (and solutions that work).

Note

In other chapters you'll find discussions of specific tools used for troubleshooting. For example, the use of `ping` and `traceroute` for testing IP networks is covered in Chapter 28, "Troubleshooting Tools for TCP/IP Networks." In Chapter 53, "Network Testing and Analysis Tools," we'll look further at some tools that can be used to troubleshoot physical components of the network.

A Documented Network Is Easier to Troubleshoot

One of the oldest abbreviations used on the Internet doesn't have anything to do with a specific protocol or network service. It's RTFM. If you ever get this in response to posting a question on a newsgroup, you can probably guess what the letters stand for. For those who don't know, it's something along the lines of "read the fine manual!" although "fine" is often replaced with a slightly different word. Use of this term is intended to point out that your question is a simple one that you can easily find an answer to, so you should quit wasting bandwidth by your postings.

Documentation consists of the manuals that come with software applications, operating systems, switches, and other network components. The quality of this sort of vendor-supplied documentation can vary widely from one vendor to another. You'll find that many companies, such as Cisco, Microsoft, and Novell, provide a lot of online documentation for their products. Often the documentation you get from a vendor is a simplified booklet combined with more extensive documentation on a CD. One of the most widely used formats for creating user documents is the Adobe Portable Document Format (.PDF files), and you can download the Adobe Acrobat Reader application free from www.adobe.com.

However, after you find yourself with an assortment of documentation—from hard-copy manuals to files on a CD or a Web site—then it's time to consider what you will use to document how your particular network is laid out, from both the physical and the logical point of view. When it comes time to troubleshoot a problem on the network, it's nice to have documentation that enables you to quickly get an answer to such simple questions as "Where are the configuration instructions for that router stored?" or "Just who is that user anyway?"

Note

Documentation made available online via the Internet can serve two purposes. First, you can quickly search and find information in a problem scenario. Second, you can read through any online documentation a vendor provides before you make a decision to purchase the particular software or hardware product. Along the same lines, you can also get an idea of the type of support you'll receive if you review the documentation before you buy. If the documentation isn't up to par, it might not matter how good the product is—support is everything.

For individual applications or operating systems, you can visit USENET newsgroups and participate in (or just lurk around and read) discussions about problems with particular products. You may just find your answer there. If not, you can post your question. One of the things that newsgroup members most dislike is someone posting a question without providing the details that led up to the problem. Provide the details! If you read the newsgroups on a regular basis, you may be apprised of problems before they appear on your network.

Some of the important things you should consider as potential candidates for documenting include the following:

- A logical map of the network. This may or may not match up with the physical way the network is laid out.

- A physical map of the network. This documentation should describe each physical component and illustrate the ways in which the different components are connected.

- Cabling and patch panel information. When you've got hundreds of cables in a wiring closet patching together different physical segments, you'll need to know which cable connects this to that.

- Default settings for computers and other devices on the network. A spreadsheet is good for this. An application that manages servers, network components, and client computers is even better.

- Listings of applications and the computers or users that make use of them, as well as software versions, patch levels, and so on. Be sure to know who to contact for a particular application. If you are a network administrator, you are primarily responsible for the underlying network. If a particular application is failing, but the network is up and running, you need to know who to call. There should always be a contact on your list for application managers. A network manager can do only so much.

- Information about the user accounts, and associated permissions and rights, for the users and user groups on the network.

- A network overview. It's nice to be able to give a new user a document that explains what she needs to know about the network. This should be a short document telling the user such things as which drives are mapped to her computer, and which printers offer what features. This should not be an extensive document such as the physical and logical maps described earlier in this list.

- Problem reports. Keep track of problems as they arise, and document the cause and remedy. No need to solve the same problem twice! This also includes outage reports—keeping track of unscheduled downtime for a computer or network device can tell you over time just how capable the device is.

A logical map of the network shows the relationships between components and the flow of information through the network. A physical map of the network tries to approximate on paper a representation of how each component of the network is connected to the network. For example, a logical map for a Windows network might show computers grouped by domains, even though the computers are not located physically in the same part of the network. A physical map would show the location of each of the computers, the hub or switch to which they are connected, and so on. In general, logical maps can be used to help isolate configuration or application problems, whereas physical maps can be used to isolate a problem that affects only a portion of the network, perhaps a single computer or other device.

You can do the same for any Ethernet or other technology-based network. Knowing the physical layout can be a very important factor in troubleshooting a network problem. For example, Unix and some Linux systems use both NIS (Network Information Systems) and now LDAP (the Lightweight Directory Access Protocol).

Note

You can learn more about NIS in Chapter 30, "Network Name Resolution." You can lean more about LDAP in Appendix D, "The Lightweight Directory Access Protocol." If you want to learn about a specific instance of LDAP, read Chapter 31, "Using the Active Directory."

You can use simple tools, such as Microsoft Paint, to create network mapping documents, or you can buy applications that automate the process. Using an application that is written specifically for creating network maps should be considered for anything but the smallest network. The capability to locate components, update them, and produce easy-to-understand printed documentation is the hallmark of a good network diagramming application. One such tool is Microsoft's Visio, which allows you to create complex network drawings, and includes pictographic elements for most modern network devices that you can easily use.

Inside the wiring closet you can have a tangled mess of wires on a patch panel that haphazardly tie one network link to another. Or you can have an orderly system in which each port on the patch panel is labeled, using a standardized method so that making changes won't be a hit-or-miss effort. The same goes for configuration information for other components of the wiring closet, such as switch ports or routers. In-depth documentation is important so that you can re-create the configuration from scratch if it becomes necessary to replace a device.

Applications should be standardized, which means you shouldn't have multiple applications that all perform the same function. It's much simpler to support a standard application, such as an office suite, than it is to support multiple applications. And, although the same configuration might not be appropriate for every user, you can at least try to create several standard configurations for classes of users. This makes deploying a desktop computer for a new employee much easier. On that odd occasion when you find that something nonstandard is required, document that also, and also document the reasons behind the decision to use an alternative configuration.

Keeping track of which applications are in use and how they are configured serves another purpose. Some applications interact with others, or are tied to specific versions of an operating system. If you have adequate documentation of the applications used on your network, you can better plan for upgrades.

After you've documented the physical components of the network and the applications, what's left? Oh, yes, the users. If not for the users, you would not have a job. Having a document of some sort that shows a user profile can be useful for troubleshooting purposes. If you know only a user's logon username and the name of his computer, you have little to go on when he calls in with a problem. If you can quickly locate more information about the user, such as the applications installed on his computer, or the privileges and permissions assigned to the user account or the computer, then you have valuable information to use to help solve problems. Often you can't get all this information from the user over the phone because many users don't know that much about what resides on their system. They know only the applications they use and how they use them.

Lastly, keep track of problems. Record the symptoms, the tools used to troubleshoot the problem, and the resolution of the problem. This documentation can assist you in the future so you can quickly determine the solution to a problem based on the symptoms reported by the users. You can also use this information to assist in creating documentation that you give to new users. By informing them of problems that have occurred in the past, you can help prevent the same problems from happening again.

Documentation and Maintenance—Keeping Things Up-to-Date

Documentation is an ongoing process. Networks rarely stay the same for a long time. It has been my experience that the larger the network, the faster the rate of change, as users or departments are relocated and new equipment replaces older equipment. So when you consider what means you'll use to create network documentation, be sure to take into consideration that it will need to be updated and you'll need some way for keeping track of changes in an orderly fashion.

Some of the tools you can use to create network documentation include these:

- **Word processors and spreadsheets**—Each of these is beneficial. Word processors enable you to create professional-looking documents that can be easily changed and reprinted. Spreadsheets can be used to locate information quickly and that information can be easily organized by indexing.

- **Online tools**—Use simple Web pages to create online documentation. If you have a specific application that has been customized for your network, create a frequently asked questions (FAQ) document for it and put it online (on your intranet). Additionally, you might shy away from pointing users to FAQs and other documents available on the Internet, unless they are sites known to contain accurate information (such as www.rfc-editor.org). There is a great deal of information, as well as disinformation, on the Internet.

- **Network mapping tools**—Microsoft's Visio and other applications can assist you with developing a complete map of your network. This tool is not inexpensive, but it may prove invaluable in a large installation.

- **Hard copy**—Printed paper documentation. Two words: Read it.

Word Processors and Spreadsheets

These two tools can be useful for creating documentation. You can use either one to gather information about the network and organize it to locate information quickly and easily. Word processing and spreadsheet applications are easy to update, and for instances in which printed documentation is necessary, most of these programs provide excellent formatting and printing capabilities. For example, you can use tables in Microsoft Office's Word program, or possibly a spreadsheet, to create a list of all the network devices and computers that have an IP address assigned to them. If you want to locate a particular item of data, Word enables you to search a document, and spreadsheets allow you to create multiple indices so that important identifiers are sorted to make it easy to locate information.

For a typical LAN today, it's likely that you'll have only a few important devices or servers that have static IP addressing information assigned. It's easier to use DHCP servers to allocate IP configuration information to computers automatically when they boot. To keep track of dynamically assigned IP configuration information, you can consult the DHCP server application to determine what listing or reporting features are available. For computers or devices you configure with static IP information, you can use a spreadsheet to keep track of this information. Then, when it becomes necessary to replace a router or similar device, you can consult the documentation to get the required configuration information to use on the replacement.

Note

The Dynamic Host Configuration Protocol (DHCP) is discussed in detail in Chapter 29, "BOOTP and Dynamic Host Configuration Protocol (DHCP)." If you use the Microsoft DHCP server that comes with Windows 2000 Server and the Windows 2003 family of servers, you can also enter into the DHCP database the static information that you manually configure some of your servers or devices to use. You can do this by entering static IP addresses and setting up reservations using the GUI for the DHCP service. In addition to being sure that the DHCP server doesn't try to use an address that you've already manually assigned to another computer, this enables you to use the DHCP database for reporting and analysis. Microsoft's DHCP server and many others allow you to export data to files, such as comma-delimited ASCII text files, that can be imported into programs such as spreadsheets or other databases.

Many other programs and utilities have "output" capabilities so that you can send their information to a file. For example, on Windows (both workstation and operating-system platforms) from earlier versions to Windows Server 2003 servers, the `IPCONFIG` command can be used to display information about the current IP configuration on the computer. If you use the syntax `ipconfig /all > %computername%.txt`, the output from the command is sent to the file named the same as the computer's name with the `.txt` extension instead of to the screen. The point is that you don't necessarily have to manually create all your documentation. Instead, make use of the tools and utilities provided by the operating system and applications to get the data, and then import it into other programs that make it easier to manage.

Other important things you may want to consider keeping track of for individual computers include the particulars of the hardware that make up the system, any customizations made on the system that aren't part of a standard, and the user(s) of the system. If the computer is a server on your network, it's a good idea to keep track of contact phone numbers for client representatives so that you can keep them informed during any troubleshooting efforts or downtime.

Online and Paper Documentation

The paperless office that was forecast during the early days of the PC revolution in the 1980s has yet to come about. No matter how small PDAs and laptops become, it's generally easier to sit down with a printed manual. Having to stare at a screen for hours at a time can be a lot more cumbersome. Although word processors and other programs are great at making it easy to find information quickly, sometimes the best option is to print things for easier handling.

Today it is not uncommon to find paper documentation being replaced by hyperlinked text files on a Web site. Instead of looking in the index of a book to find the information you need, you can utilize the Web. A Web site can be useful for several reasons. First, for common problems, a simple FAQ document can help end users solve problems themselves so that your help desk doesn't get a call. Second, for those who do sit at a help desk, clicking through a set of links to find information can be faster than having to juggle one or more manuals and talk to the end user on the phone at the same time.

User Feedback Can Improve Documentation

You can easily judge how well your documentation assists end users by soliciting feedback. If you create the greatest looking documents that can possibly be created, that won't matter if the end user can't make sense of the content. After you've created any kind of documentation, be sure to provide a mechanism that can enable users to provide you with questions or comments on the documentation. Take these suggestions into consideration when it comes time to make updates.

Problem-Solving Techniques

After you've got a well-documented network, all you have to do is sit back and wait for problems to occur. Spurious as that may seem, it's true. Sometime, some day, when you least expect it, something out of the blue will knock a server offline, disable a printer, and so on. If you have good documentation, you can tackle the problem and do so from a structured point of view.

The troubleshooting method known as the *problem resolution cycle* builds on accurate documentation for the network and uses a simple question/answer technique to determine what has changed to bring about the problem.

The Problem Resolution Cycle

The problem resolution cycle is a method designed to meet two needs: to solve the immediate problem that prevents the network (or a component of the network) from working, and to provide insights as to the cause of the problem so that it can be avoided or quickly solved in the future. The elements of a structured problem resolution cycle approach are as listed here:

- Accurate and complete descriptions of the symptoms. Determine whether a problem really exists, or whether the user is using the computer or application improperly.

- Understanding how the network functions from a logical and physical point of view.

- Solving the problem instead of creating a makeshift fix.

- Providing a follow-up mechanism for recording and distributing solutions to others who may have a need to know, such as staff at a help desk or a departmental supervisor.

- Development of a solution-tracking system to keep you from having to solve the same problem over and over again.

In most cases, the more data you can collect about a problem, the easier the problem will be to solve. When selecting employees who will serve as help-desk personnel, for example, try to get someone with both good verbal and good listening skills. Although the initial problem report might be something like "I can't print this document," a good help-desk technician can usually walk the user through a series of questions to determine whether other symptoms are present. In the example just given, it would be prudent to ask whether the user can print other documents, or whether the problem is with just the one document. What about different types of documents? If the user can print a spreadsheet but not a word processor document, the problem may be with the application. Another good question would be to ask whether any other users of the printer are having a problem. As you gather more data, you can focus your troubleshooting efforts on the local user PC or the printer. If the user can't print anything but no one else is having a problem, you can begin to troubleshoot the printer configuration (has the user made changes you are unaware of?). Or perhaps the user has lost network connectivity and it's a simple matter to try to ping the computer. You can use utilities such as `ping` or `tracert` to determine whether connectivity exists between the user and the printer or print server. After that, you could start investigating to be sure that the correct print driver is installed, and so on.

◄◄   Utilities such as `ping` and `tracert` are covered in Chapter 28, "Troubleshooting Tools for TCP/IP Networks."

This brings up the network maps mentioned earlier in this chapter. You can quickly locate what hub, switch, or other network device the user's computer is attached to by using a physical map of the network. Using a logical map, you can find other users or computers that make use of the same information flow through the network.

Sometimes things just fix themselves. For example, it may be that the user could not print because a router standing between the user and the printer was overloaded temporarily and was not able to route packets from the user's network segment to the printer. In these situations, don't let sleeping dogs lie. Instead, keep investigating (using your network maps) and try to determine what caused the problem. You can use performance and capacity reporting techniques for servers and network devices. In the next chapter we'll talk about the Simple Network Management Protocol (SNMP) and RMON (Remote Monitoring Protocol) that enable you to gather statistical information about network devices. Find out what caused a problem so that you can anticipate when it might happen again, and try to take measures to prevent it.

Keep track of all incidents in an orderly fashion, and make the information known to others who might encounter the same problem. A help desk should have a log of some sort so that every problem called into the help desk is tracked from the time the call is placed until the problem is solved and the call is closed. Provide feedback to the user about how the problem was solved. This is especially important when you have problems that are self-induced, such as when users try to change the configuration of their computer although they know only enough to be dangerous to themselves!

Don't repeat past mistakes. By tracking problems and recording the troubleshooting effort and the solution to the problem, you make it easier to solve the same, or similar, problems in the future. Your help desk should have a database of some sort (such as a spreadsheet, or perhaps a Web site with documentation linked via HTML code) that can be used to see whether a problem with similar symptoms has been called in before.

Is There Really a Problem?

Sometimes, as noted in the preceding section, problems just fix themselves. There are times when you can't ever find the reason for a particular problem. In many cases, you'll find that sporadic problems are caused not by equipment or software failure, but by users who are not using the system correctly. When any new application is deployed on a network, you need to be sure that the end users receive adequate training for using the application or else you may find that user errors begin to account for many of your help-desk calls. For example, a user may have corrupted files on a hard disk. Should you replace the disk? Should you search for a virus or another harmful program? These sound like logical things to do.

Or you could simply ask whether the user is properly shutting down the computer or just "power cycling" it when he gets stuck in an application and can't find a way out. Some people find that just turning a computer off and back on again is a fine way to start anew, without realizing the problems they may encounter down the line. So, when troubleshooting, try to find out what has led up to the problem. It may be a simple case of user training that needs to be addressed.

I can't stress enough the importance of training new users in the workings of the environment in which they will be placed. If you have configured a desktop in a certain manner, you can't assume that a new employee will be able to make proper use of it. Although it's easy to check someone's résumé to determine what applications they are skilled at using, it's difficult to be sure what the configuration of the application was at their previous place of employment. The same goes for training classes offered by temp agencies and other similar organizations. Although they may have used a standard installation for training purposes, any customizations or configuration changes you make need to be explained to the new user. So, as a general rule, no matter how qualified a new employee may appear to be, it's just an appearance. You should have in place a structured training program and require each new employee to attend, or at least initiate a mentoring system so that one user can teach another.

Tip

Remember that training doesn't stop at new hire orientation. As the network, applications, and so on change over time, retraining should also be a requirement.

Has This Happened Before—What Is the Procedure to Follow?

Keeping track of how problems were solved will keep you from expending a lot of effort solving the same problem again and again. Using documentation that enables a quick lookup of information based on symptoms can help you find older problem reports or perhaps standard help-desk documentation that was written specifically because a particular problem frequently occurs. Indeed, when a problem does occur frequently, it's time to find a better solution to the problem. So by tracking problems and the methods used to troubleshoot and solve the problem, you can not only find it easier to solve the current incident, but also provide a feedback mechanism so that you will know that a particular problem needs a better long-term solution.

For problems that occur on a frequent basis, but that you don't have a lot of control over (such as a user causing errors by not using an application or the network in the appropriate manner), you can at least create a step-by-step outline for solving the problem to make life at the help desk a little less frustrating.

First Things First: The Process of Elimination

If you understand how your network is put together, from both a logical and a physical point of view, then it is possible to use the process of elimination to narrow the focus of your troubleshooting efforts. Some things to think about when trying to pinpoint the cause of a network program include the following:

- What devices—computers, hubs, switches, cables, and so on—are involved? Can you use troubleshooting tools to narrow your search to a single device or a subset of the network?

- If a single computer or device appears to be the only part of the network affected, what is unique about it? If another similar device is up and running, how do the devices differ in their configuration or location in the network?

- If the problem is occurring on multiple systems, what do they all have in common? Are they all on the same network segment? Do they all share a common subnet address? Do they all use the same path through the network to access a device or service that now appears to be unreachable?

- What task was the user performing when the problem occurred? Get specifics about exactly what the user was doing, both up to and when the event occurred. For example, was he using more than one application, printing to more than one printer, or perhaps doing something he should not (like opening an attachment from email that came from outside the local network)?

- Can the problem be reproduced? Walk the user through the same set of steps again and see whether the problem recurs. Next try the same with another user to determine whether the problem is localized to only one computer or is a symptom of a bigger problem or configuration issue.

By narrowing your focus to only the section of the network that experiences the problem, you can more quickly look at the computers and other components of that part of the network to solve the problem. By reproducing the problem, you can be sure that you've isolated the cause. Eliminate the obvious ("Is it plugged in?") and get to the specifics as quickly as you can. Actually, silly as it may sound, asking whether a computer is plugged in is really a very good question. More than once I've come in to work to find that a monitor or another device was off. A quick glance at the power strip can indicate that someone, perhaps a housekeeping employee, may have accidentally unplugged the strip, or flipped the switch to turn off the power.

Auditing the Network to Locate Problem Sources

It is important to know how your network operates from a logical and physical point of view. It's also important to know the capacity of the components of the network, and the degree to which they are utilized. Sometimes problems are simply due to congestion on the network. You can determine these problems by using monitoring software, such as SNMP and RMON, and by baselining your network so that you know what the typical usage patterns are. Knowing when components of the network are stressed close to their usable capacity allows you to plan an upgrade to eliminate the bottleneck, or to reschedule user work habits to make more efficient use of the network.

Pitfalls of Troubleshooting

Above all, when trying to research a problem on the network, remember that you are indeed on a network, and the actions you take can potentially affect other users. When using troubleshooting tools, be sure you first understand how they work and also the correct way to use them. For example, what procedure do you have in place to help users who forget their password? Is a simple call to the help desk all that is required to get the password changed? If so, how does the help-desk technician know who's on the other end of the line? Although it may seem inconvenient to require the user to report to a supervisor or another person who is a delegated local authority to change his password, this technique is more secure than allowing a simple phone call to place your network in jeopardy.

Other examples include using the `route` command to change routing tables. An experienced network technician should do this, and not as a quick fix to solve some network problem that you can't quite put your finger on. If you don't know why the routing problem is happening, don't try to fix it with a quick fix! You might end up causing other routers or computers to use less efficient routes and, in the long run, experience network loss through degradation. Understand the tools you use for your troubleshooting efforts.

In a complex network that involves DNS servers, DHCP servers, and possibly even WINS servers, you should be very careful before making changes on the fly. Again, I want to emphasize that a quick fix may solve the current problem, but can also possibly create another that you don't become aware of until much later, after the damage has been done. Help-desk personnel should be required to contact experienced system administrators before changes are made on these types of servers.

A simple name change in a DNS server, for example, could render a server unreachable for everyone on your network if the wrong address or record type is entered by mistake. Along the same lines, a very common mistake is to use an IP address for a server that falls within the range of the addresses offered by a DHCP server. When the DHCP server allocates that address to another client, everything gets screwed up on the network! Coordinate changes to important network databases and make sure that the person doing the work is fully competent to do it.

Network Testing and Analysis Tools

53

SOME OF THE MAIN TOPICS IN THIS CHAPTER ARE

CHAPTER 53

A network administrator must wear many hats because the network is composed of many elements, implemented in both hardware and software. In a large network environment, many tasks are delegated to those who are particularly adept in a specific technology. However, the administrator who sits at the top of the management ladder needs to understand the principles under which the network functions and the tools that are used to keep it in good working order. This chapter discusses the basic tools used to troubleshoot the underlying structure of the network (such as the cabling), as well as those used to pick apart the semantics of the communication process (packets and protocols).

Basics: Testing Cables

A network consists of end-user workstations connected to servers by what might appear at first to be a tangled web of wires and cables. If the building or campus is wired correctly, however, this is not a jumble of cables joined together in a spaghetti fashion, but is an orderly collection of components much like a spider's web, fanning out to connect everyone in a hierarchical manner. In addition, wireless networking components have added an entire new territory, and tools are currently being developed to address troubleshooting this new area of network technology.

For the most part, when you begin to build a network, the first thing you have to do is install the cables that will connect the servers and workstations. This can be done when a building is being constructed, as is the case in most office buildings today. Or it can involve placing cable ducts in ceilings and knocking out areas of the walls to install faceplates where the cables terminate. Either way, before you begin to connect end users to the network, you first have to test the installed cables to be sure they are performing as expected.

Devices that can be used to test cables (both copper wire and fiber-optic cables) range from very inexpensive handheld devices that a cable installer can use to check his work, to very expensive devices that require a skilled technician to perform the tests and understand the results. Things that are usually tested include the following:

- **Cable length**—The physical network topology restricts the length of certain segments in the network. If you make your own cables, a common error may result from trying to stretch the limits of the topology and create a cable that's just a few meters too long. If a desktop is just a few meters farther from a switch than the standard allows, you may get complaints from that user!

- **Resistance**—Electricity encounters resistance as it travels along a copper wire.

- **Noise**—Interference can come from other cables that are bundled together or from outside sources, such as fluorescent lighting, nearby welding, strong sources of electromagnetic frequencies, and other high-voltage electrical sources located near the network cabling.

- **Attenuation**—As the cable encounters resistance traveling down the wire, and as part of the signal radiates out of the wire, the signal weakens. This is a normal side effect of using copper wiring instead of fiber optics. You can expect copper wiring to work best at the standardized lengths, and take your chances at extending that length.

- **Near-end cross-talk (NEXT)**—From the transmission end of a cable, it is necessary to remove the surrounding material that encloses the copper wires and attach each wire to a pin in the cable connector. Because the strength of signal is strongest at the end of the cable where the electrical signal is generated, there is a greater potential for interference between the wires at this end of the cable.

◄◄ To get a better understanding of the kinds of problems you might experience, see Chapter 6, "Wiring the Network—Cables, Connectors, Concentrators, and Other Network Components."

Two basic instruments are used for testing cables. The first is the simple cable checker, which is used to determine that the cable actually provides an electrical path from here to there. The second is the cable tester, which determines whether the cable has been installed correctly to support the topology of your network, taking into consideration things such as cable length and cross-talk.

Handheld Cable Checkers

A cable-checker device is usually a small battery-operated unit that is used to check STP or UTP cables. This simple test is usually done when cables are first installed as a quick check to be sure that the process of pulling the cables through the ceiling or walls has not damaged them.

If the cable is already attached to a network device, you have to disconnect it and attach it to the unit. A cable checker operates by placing a voltage on a wire and determining whether it can be detected at the opposite end. This can be used to determine whether the cable has a break anywhere along its path and whether you are looking at the same cable on both ends when several cables are traversing a single path. Most cable checkers consist of two components, which you attach to opposite ends of the cable.

Cable Testers

A cable tester is a small step up from the basic checker. This device can be used to measure NEXT, attenuation, impedance, and noise on a line. Some cable testers even perform length measurements, of both the total cable and the distance to a fault on the cable, such as a kink in the wire that is causing reflections of the signal to radiate back to the transmitting side of the cable. Another function you might see is *wire-mapping*, which checks to be sure that the correct wire-pairs in a cable have been mapped to the correct pins on the connector attached to the end of the cable. In cables used for 10BASE-T networks, for example, the standard specifies specific pairs of wires in the cable that must be used for transmitting and receiving data. The actual decisions about which pins are chosen for a particular connector are not made arbitrarily. If the wires are not correctly mapped to the pin-out on the connector specified by the standard, the cable might generate errors due to noise or cross-talk.

Small handheld instruments like these usually have LED lights that indicate a pass or fail condition for the test you are performing. They do not require a keyboard or monitor to display data. Some have a small screen that displays limited text, sometimes showing the suspected type of error that has caused a fail condition. Most are battery powered and can use an AC adapter, which makes them useful portable instruments for installing or troubleshooting cabling.

When you begin to go up the price ladder for these types of instruments, you will find some that can perform more advanced monitoring functions, such as showing network use and Ethernet collisions. Another useful feature to look for if you can afford it is the capability to log data to a memory buffer for later review. Some cable testers are even capable of connecting to a PC or printer to produce a written report. This allows you to leave the device connected for a while to monitor a line.

Depending on the capabilities of the particular device, you can expect to pay from several hundred dollars up to a thousand or more for a good cable tester. When evaluating products, be sure to compare features. Price doesn't always reflect the quality of a device. And you should carefully check the literature and documentation that is available for each device when making a purchasing choice. Although some features, such as the capability to produce a written report, might sound great, do you really need that capability? In a large network, probably so; in a small one, probably not.

Bit Error Rate Testers (BERT)

Data travels through the wire (or the fiber) as a series of signals that indicate a single bit, representing either zero or one. The statistic called bit error rate (BER) is calculated as a percentage of bits that have errors when compared to the total number of bits sampled:

```
                number of bit errors during sampling interval
BER =  ------------------------------------------
                total number of bits transmitted
```

Whereas LAN analyzers operate on data captured from the wire in units of frames (depending on the LAN protocol, such as Ethernet or Token-Ring), a bit error rate tester (BERT) performs a more basic function to determine whether the line is capable of carrying the network signaling at the bit level with a minimum of errors.

This kind of instrument is normally used when installing a connection to a network service provider, and it might be used to demonstrate the quality of service that the provider establishes for your link.

The instrument used to perform this kind of error detection usually does so by generating a specific bit pattern on the line and then checking it at another location to compare the generated signal with that which is received. A *pseudorandom binary sequence (PRBS)* of bits is produced by the instrument. It is pseudorandom because it simulates random data. However, because the pattern is also known by the receiving connection so that it can make the comparison, it's not truly random, but instead is a predefined pattern. Other tests include sequences of specific bits, either zeros or ones, for extended periods, or specific user-defined bit patterns.

When you have a line that exhibits a high bit-error rate, using a slower transmission speed usually improves performance. This is because when you lower the number of errors that occur, higher-level protocols do not have to resend packets as often to compensate. Although one bit error in a frame usually is easily recovered by a network protocol using an error correction code (ECC) technique, multiple bit errors might be all that it takes to cause an entire frame of several hundred thousand bits to be re-sent.

Time Domain Reflectometers

A signal usually propagates down a wire at a constant speed, provided that the impedance of the cable is the same throughout its journey. When the signal runs into a fault in the wire (such as a kink or a splice) or reaches the end of the wire, part or all of the signal is reflected back to its origin. Similar to radar, instruments that use time domain reflectometry (TDR) to make cable measurements are based on precisely timing the signal pulse as it travels through the cable and back.

Of all the instruments you can use to test cables, TDR is one of the most accurate and fastest. It can help locate faults due to various causes, such as these:

- Wires that have been spliced together
- Moisture trapped in the cable
- Cables that have been crushed or have kinks in them
- Short circuits
- Problems in the sheath surrounding a cable
- Loose connectors

You also can use TDR to measure the length of a cable that has no faults. This can be useful for inventory functions because you can even use it to measure the length of a cable while it is still on a reel to determine whether you have enough or need to order additional stock before beginning a major wiring project. TDR can be used to take measurements on twisted-pair cables, coaxial cables, and even fiber-optic cables. Because fiber-optic cabling is the most expensive (but largest bandwidth) media today, you should consider investing in a TDR that supports fiber-optic media if you are planning on a wide deployment of fiber-optic cabling. At the very least, you should expect a third-party installer of a large cable plant to provide such an instrument. You should also make it part of your project plan to record the statistics provided by the installer. Thus, if a future need dictates, you might have a particular cable segment re-evaluated. Be sure to stipulate such things as the performance of any cable segments in your agreement with an installer. If you are performing the installation yourself, be prepared to use a TDR to check a cable segment should performance degrade. For example, for electrical cabling, other devices (even cables) might be installed later that interfere with your original installation. In that case, moving cables to new locations should solve the problem.

The more expensive models of this instrument can be equipped with a CRT or LED display that shows the wave form of the signal and any reflected signals. The more common instrument displays the number of feet to the end of the cable or a fault, and might have an indicator that tells you the type of fault. By showing the number of feet to a perceived defect, you can trace your installed cabling (or unroll your on-the-roll cabling) so that you can get to the point where the defect occurs.

Using a TDR in this method can help you with installed network cabling (where a new problem has been introduced) and help you check out cabling spools before you accept them.

Impedance

When conductors made of metal are placed in close proximity to each other, as in a twisted-pair or coaxial cable, the effect they have on each other is known as impedance. When the wires are perfectly separated by a constant distance, the impedance remains the same throughout the cable. When something happens along the way, such as damage caused by a crushed cable, the impedance changes at that point. Changes in impedance cause parts of the signal to be reflected back to where it started.

Cables that are used in local area networks (LANs) need to be manufactured to strict specifications, ensuring that the dielectric material that separates the wires within the cable remains constant. If there are random variations due to poor manufacturing procedures, the cable will suffer from problems caused by signal reflections, which might render it unsuitable for your network. Thus, TDR can be used not only as a fault-finder when troubleshooting a wiring problem, but also to ensure that you've received what you paid for when you upgrade or expand your network.

Setting a Pulse Width

Most of the good TDR instruments allow you to select the pulse width, which is usually specified in nanoseconds. The larger the pulse width, the more energy that is transmitted from the device and thus the farther down the wire the signal will travel.

A good tip for setting this value is to start with the smallest that the instrument allows and make subsequent measurements, gradually increasing the pulse width. If the fault in the cable is only a short distance away from the measuring instrument, a small pulse width will be adequate to locate it. However, if the fault is minor, a small burst of energy might not be enough to travel to the fault and send back a reflection strong enough to be accurately measured. By varying the pulse width and making several measurements, you can more accurately determine the location of a fault in the cable.

Velocity

Light travels at a constant speed of 186,400 miles per second in a vacuum. When measuring the velocity at which an electrical signal travels through a wire, it is expressed as a percentage of the speed of light, which is considered to be slightly less than 100%, or a value of 1. For example, a twisted-pair cable that has a VOP (velocity of propagation) of .65 would conduct an electrical signal at 65% of the speed of light, or about the speed I drive on the interstate (miles per hour, of course).

Manufacturers usually supply this value to customers, and it will most likely be found on the specification sheet for the cable you are purchasing. Because TDR measures the time it takes for a signal to travel down a wire and make the return trip, you have to know the VOP of the cable being tested before you can make accurate measurements.

If you have cables that you are unsure about, you can test them first to determine the VOP. Do this by measuring a specific length of cable to get its length and then using the TDR instrument to test for the length of the cable, varying the VOP until the tester reads the correct length. Of course, this assumes that the segment of cable you use for this test is in good condition!

Network and Protocol Analyzers

The first level of network testing consists of making sure that the underlying physical cabling structure is performing as expected. The next level is to monitor and test the network traffic and messages generated by the network protocols to be sure that you have a healthy network. Network analyzer products operate by monitoring the network at the Data Link and Transport layers in the OSI reference model.

Note

The OSI reference model separates the components of a network protocol stack into modular layers, each of which performs a specific task for the layer above or below it in the model. Appendix A, "Overview of the OSI Seven-Layer Networking Reference Model," covers this model, discussing each layer in detail. You'll hear terms such as Network layer, Data Link layer, and Transport layer frequently when discussing networking, so it's a good idea to have a basic understanding of what these terms mean and the networking functions they represent.

Again, you will find that the tools you can select for protocol analyzers range from the very inexpensive (free) to the very expensive (several thousand dollars). One difference between these kinds of tools and those used to check cables, however, is that you need to have a good understanding of the network structure and protocols used before you can make meaningful judgments about the data you collect. The LAN analyzer allows you to intercept network traffic as it passes through the wire in real-time and save the data for analysis. A good analyzer should be able to produce meaningful statistics about the traffic on the network, decode the protocols that are used, and provide a good filtering capability so that you don't get bogged down in an overwhelming amount of data.

You should consider many factors when deciding on a network analyzer product. The most basic factor is whether you want a portable device that can be transported to different sites or one or more devices that can be placed at strategic locations in the network to perform continuous monitoring. Other features to consider include the following:

- **Price**—Of course, this is always a factor when purchasing equipment for a network.

- **Software or hardware**—Do you need a dedicated hardware instrument that can perform intense analysis and connect to multiple segments, or can you live with a software implementation that runs on an existing network workstation?

- **Network interface**—Do you need to connect to just a 100BASE-T (or even higher bandwidth devices) environment, or do you need a device that connects to other topologies such as FDDI or Token-Ring?

- **Protocol stack support**—Is your network homogeneous, or does it support multiple network protocols?

- **Statistics**—What kind of statistical data does the instrument support? The most basic is frames-per-second. Others include utilization and usage. Utilization is a measurement of the actual amount of bandwidth that your network media is supporting at any point in time. Usage statistics can tell you what is using that bandwidth—from protocol statistics to such things as the number of collisions on a shared Ethernet segment.

- **Memory and buffers**—Does the instrument provide enough buffering capacity to capture frames on a high-speed network such as 100BASE-T? How about Gigabit Ethernet?

- **Filters**—Does the analyzer provide sufficient filtering capabilities to allow you to look through large volumes of data to get to the frames that really matter?

- **Import and export**—Does the device allow you to save files to a disk or another medium so that you can transfer them to other workstations for further analysis?

A good LAN analyzer allows you to monitor network traffic in real-time mode, using filters to narrow the scope of your view. You can set up capture filters, store part or all of the frames that match in a buffer, and perform further analysis.

Establishing a Baseline

Before you begin to perform monitoring or analysis of the network usage and utilization, you need to establish a set of baseline data. To interpret the statistical data that you can collect using LAN analyzers, you need to have something with which to compare future measurements. Baseline data is used to define the normal operating environment for a system and provides a reference for monitoring and troubleshooting efforts.

Baseline data is useful not only for troubleshooting, but also for planning capacity and measuring the effectiveness of an upgrade. Things you should consider recording in your baseline documentation in addition to values you monitor with a LAN analyzer include such things as these:

- Location of equipment in the network
- Type of equipment in use
- The number and distribution of users
- Protocols in use

Knowing the type of equipment is important because different models of NICs, hubs, and other devices can vary widely in their performance. Knowing where each piece of equipment is located can enable you to create an audit trail for troubleshooting. For example, it is common in a business environment for users and workstations to be constantly on the move.

A simple weekend move, in which you take a few workstations or servers and move them to a different location, might have a dramatic, unexpected impact on the network. Suppose you have two servers that you want to move from a departmental location to a central computer room. When they were located on the same network segment as the users that use them the most, traffic was localized. Placing them on a different segment might cause capacity problems in a backbone link or in a device such as a switch or router that connects the network. If you keep track of hardware and statistical information about its performance and usage, you can usually prevent this sort of thing from happening. At least, you can look back and determine where a problem lies and be in a better position to find a solution.

This same principle applies to the location of users in the network. Different users can make widely differing demands on a single workstation or server. Keep a list of users, the applications they use, and, when appropriate, the time of day they work in situations in which shift-work is performed.

◄◄ In Chapter 52, "Strategies for Troubleshooting Network Problems," you will find additional information regarding analyzing and segmenting groups of users according to their use of network resources.

Understanding the protocols that are used is also important. A simple problem that can be hard to figure out occurs when you move a device to a different network segment and are unaware that it is using a nonroutable protocol. Most routers can be configured to pass these nonroutable protocols (such as NetBEUI), but you need to be aware of this and configure the router accordingly before you make the move.

Finally, baseline data is never going to be something that is cast in stone and unchangeable. Modify your documentation as the network grows or changes so that the data remains useful.

Statistical Data

Although most analyzers provide a wide range of statistical data, the analyzer should be able to give you a few general values.

First, be sure that the analyzer can give you statistics that tell you the utilization of the network. In addition to a real-time graphical display, you should also look for the capability to monitor the network and tell you when *peak utilization* occurs. That is, what times during the day does the network reach its busiest points? Overall utilization calculated over the average workday might not be nearly as helpful as identifying the periods of time when users are working their hardest and getting frustrated with a bogged-down network. Using peak utilization statistics, you can work to resolve the traffic problems by reallocating resources, or perhaps rearranging work habits of the user base.

Another statistic that is found on most analyzers is Frames Per Second (FPS). By itself, FPS isn't a revealing value, but when combined with data showing the size of packets traversing the network, it can produce meaningful data. The larger the packet size used by a protocol, the more efficient the protocol is likely to be. This is because each packet requires overhead necessary to implement the protocol, such as addressing and error-checking information. With a larger packet size, the ratio of overhead to payload is reduced.

Protocol Decoding

The capability to take the raw bits that travel on the network and present them on a frame-by-frame basis is a powerful feature of the analyzer. Looking at a *stream* of byte values isn't very useful when troubleshooting a network problem. Looking at *each frame*, and understanding what kinds of frames are being generated by devices on the network, is a necessary component of a network analyzer.

Look for an analyzer that gives both a summary and a detailed view of the frame. The summary view usually shows just the addressing and header portion of the packet, whereas the detailed view displays every byte contained in the frame.

Filtering

Filtering is a necessary component for any network analyzer. Filtering allows you to set criteria that the analyzer uses when it captures frames, or to selectively search through a buffer of captured data to retrieve only those frames that are pertinent to your troubleshooting efforts. Filters can usually be set to select frames by protocol type, frame type, and protocol address or MAC addresses. Some allow you to search for specific data patterns throughout the entire packet.

Software-Based Analyzers

Software analyzers are the cheapest route for large, complex networks. Because processors have scaled to much greater speeds and network adapters can capture packets from the fastest LAN speeds, software analyzers are now catching up to hardware-based analyzers. And you can find some freeware analyzer products on the Web that perform some or all of the functions you might need in a small network.

Windows NT 4.0 through Windows 2003 servers come with a network monitor tool that enables the local workstation or server to monitor network traffic that is *generated by or sent to* the computer. The version that comes with the Systems Management Server (SMS) allows the network administrator to monitor *all traffic on the LAN*, using a feature referred to as *promiscuous mode*. The Windows 2000 Servers and Windows 2003 Servers network monitor can be found in the Administrative Tools folder.

Both of these products allow you to capture data on the LAN, filter, and troubleshoot many kinds of problems. Because these products run on a workstation, you can use them to collect and store large amounts of information for immediate analysis and long-term reporting. In Figure 53.1, you can see the main window of the Network Monitor for Windows Server 2003 (called the Capture Window).

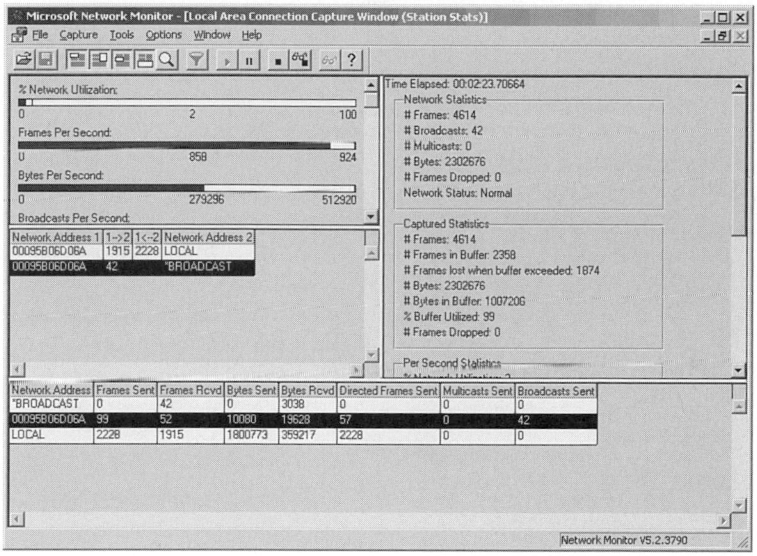

Figure 53.1   The Capture Window shows a summary of the frames that have been captured by Network Monitor.

Tip

If you don't see the Network Monitor in the Administrative Tools folder, you need to install the component. Use Add/Remove Programs from the Control Panel. Select Add/Remove Windows Components, and then choose Management and Monitoring Tools; then, from the details button, select the network monitor.

To begin capturing frames on the network, choose Capture, Start. You can also use the Capture menu to pause or stop the capture process. As frames are captured by the monitor, you can get an idea of what is happening on the network by the continuously updated bar graphs in the Capture Window. To view the actual data being collected, you can stop the capture process by selecting Capture, Stop. Choose Capture, Display Captured Data to view the frames captured (see Figure 53.2).

As you can see, a summary line is provided for each frame that the monitor captured. You can scroll up or down to view all frames in the buffer. At this point, the frames are stored in a temporary buffer. If you only need to view the data for immediate analysis and then discard it, you can do so from this window. If you want to store the data for later analysis, select File, Save As. To view data in a stored file, choose File, Open to read the data in the file into the temporary buffer.

To examine any of the captured frames and view it in detail, double-click it in the summary window. The window opens a Detail pane that shows the kinds of data in the frame. Click the plus sign (+) to expand the list of data contained in the frame. Figure 53.3 is an example of an ICMP (Internet Control Message Protocol) frame generated during a PING operation. By highlighting the ICMP portion of the Detail pane (in the center of this figure), the monitor highlights the data pertaining to this in the data section at the bottom of the figure. By showing the bytes that make up different parts of the frame, the monitor makes your job easier.

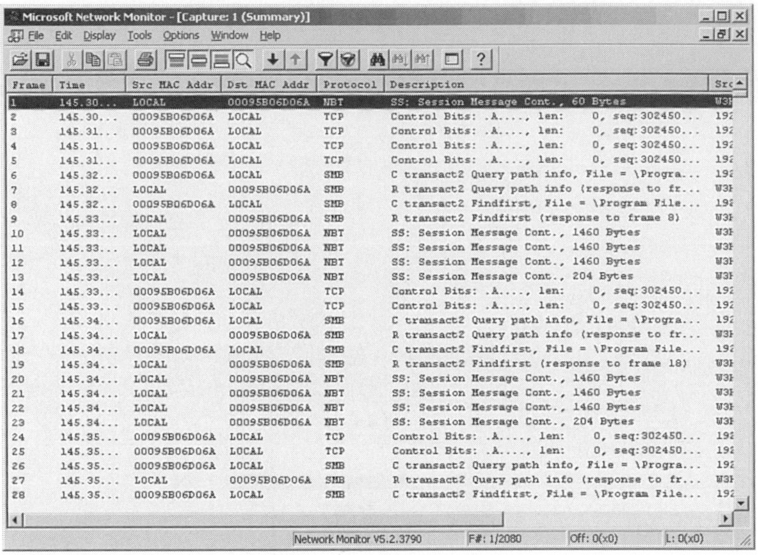

Figure 53.2 The summary view window allows you to examine the captured data.

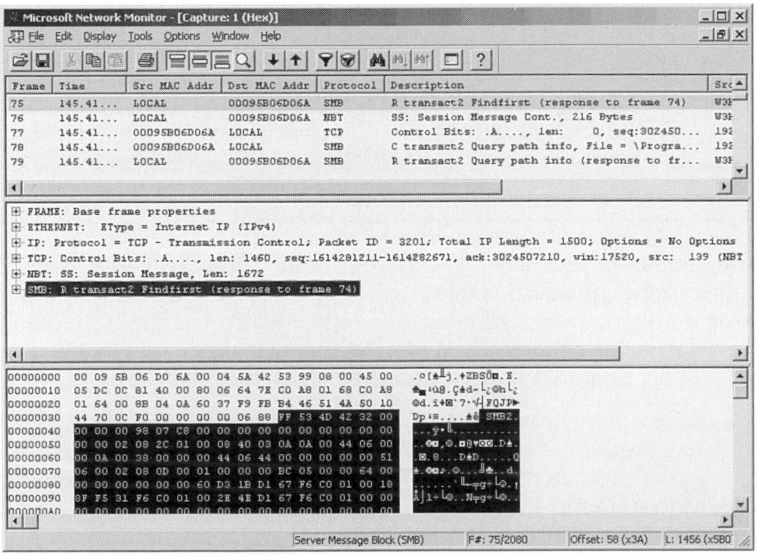

Figure 53.3 You can examine the actual contents of the frame from this view.

Capture and Display Filters

The amount of traffic that passes through even a small network can be overwhelming, but not when you're using a network monitor to watch statistical information about current traffic. When you are troubleshooting, however, it's helpful to be able to filter out the nonessential information so that you can examine only those frames that are pertinent to the problem at hand.

For this purpose, most analyzers allow you to set up a filter that screens out all but the frames you want to view. A capture filter is used to create selection criteria for the frames that will be kept and stored in the temporary buffer, whereas a display filter can be used to further select frames from those that are captured. Select Capture, Filter.

In Figure 53.4, you can see the dialog box used to start creating a capture filter for the Network Monitor.

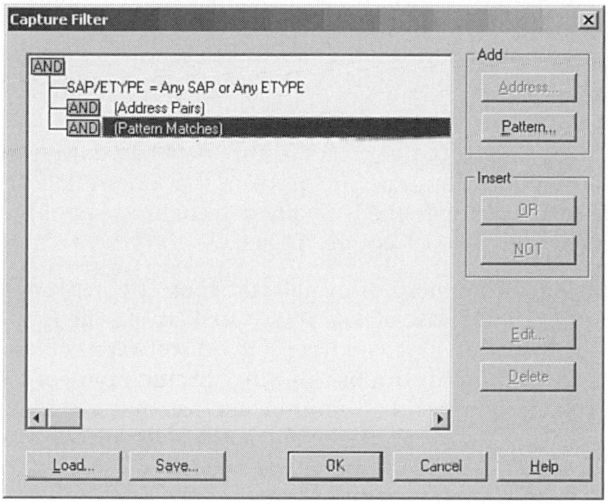

Figure 53.4   Create a capture filter to specify which frames are copied to the temporary buffer.

For a capture filter, you can specify specific protocols, address pairs, or patterns that occur in the frame itself. Figure 53.5 shows the dialog box used to select address pairs, and Figure 53.6 shows the dialog box used to specify a pattern.

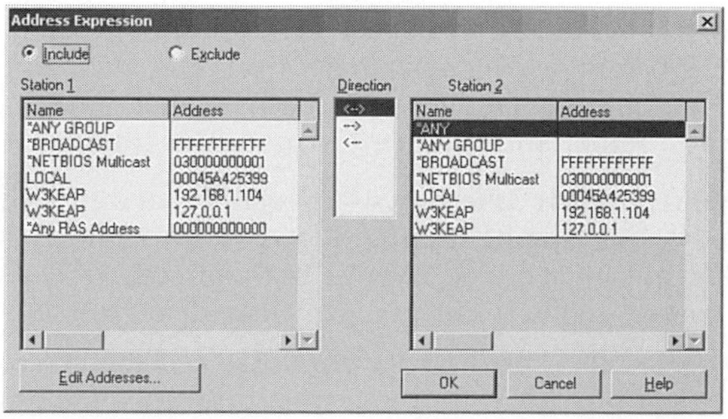

Figure 53.5   You can select the addresses that must appear in a frame in order for it to be selected for capture.

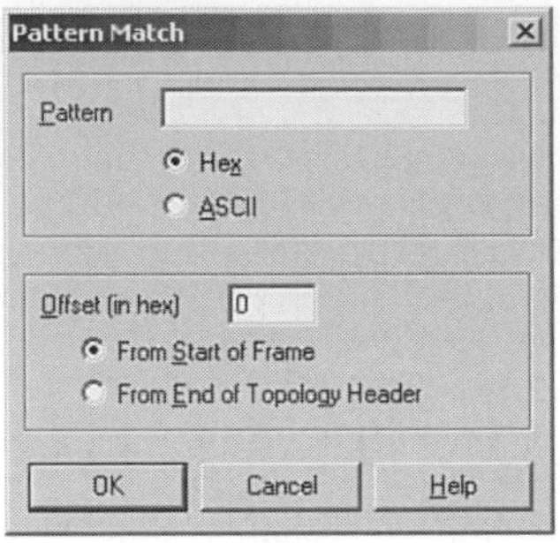

Figure 53.6 Specify a pattern and an offset value for capturing frames based on pattern matching.

When using pattern matching, you can specify a string that must be found in the frame before it is considered a candidate for capture. You can specify an offset value also, which indicates a starting point for the filter in the frame when it searches for the pattern.

Capture Triggers

After you create a capture filter, you can begin to capture data based on it by selecting Capture, Start. When using a narrow filter to look for a specific problem that doesn't occur often, you can set up an event to notify you when a matching frame is finally detected instead of having to sit at the console and wait. To set a capture trigger, select Capture, Trigger.

The Network Monitor allows you to monitor overall traffic on the network by watching the graphs displayed in the Capture Window, and it allows you to look at specific frames to determine where problems exist. Similar to a hardware LAN analyzer, a good software LAN analyzer can be a valuable tool for determining network use or for troubleshooting specific protocol problems. Still, to view all network traffic, you'll need another network monitor, such as that included with Microsoft's SMS, or a third-party-product.

Other Software LAN Analyzer Products

The fast microprocessors used in today's desktop and laptop computers allow for a wide range of software products to provide functionality that used to be primarily the domain of hardware-based analyzers. The preceding section looked at the built-in LAN monitoring tools available as part of the Windows operating system. However, a large market exists for software-based LAN analyzers, and they are usually much less expensive to deploy than their hardware counterparts.

Before investing in a software LAN analyzer, you should try before you buy. Following is a list of a few good products that allow you to either download a demonstration version or order a CD that you can use to evaluate the product before making a purchase. Don't buy the first product you look at. Instead, determine whether the documentation is up to par, whether the company provides good technical support, and, most important, whether the product is intuitive and easy to use.

- **Ethertest LAN Analyzer for Windows**—This LAN analyzer from Frontline Test Equipment, Inc. (FTE), runs on systems ranging from Windows 95 to Windows 2000. You can download a demo of this product at www.fte.com. If you're in the process of deploying Bluetooth technology in your LAN, you might also want to download a demo of FTE's SerialBlue Bluetooth.

- **Observer, Expert Observer, and Observer Suite from Network Instruments**—These products perform everything from simple network protocol analysis to SNMP (Simple Network Management Protocol), RMON (Remote Monitoring) console, and probe reporting. The software also runs on systems ranging from Windows 95 to Windows 2000. Additionally, the Observer product line also includes support for IEEE 802.11a and 802.11b wireless networking. You can download a demo from www.netinst.com.

- ■ **Wildpackets**—An assortment of network analysis tools can be downloaded, ranging from the highly rated EtherPeek LAN analysis tool to AiroPeek for wireless LAN analysis. You can download demos for these and other valuable tools by visiting www.wildpackets.com.

This is only a short list of the large number of products available, and they are not rated as to which is best because it depends on your needs and how your network is laid out. However, you should download the demos listed here so that you can get an idea of what you can expect from a software-based LAN analyzer. If you're going to spend money on such a product, make sure it's an informed purchase.

Hardware Analyzers

This type of instrument can cost as much as tens of thousands of dollars. Hardware analyzers, however, provide functionality in a critical situation that might not be obtainable from a software-based product. A hardware LAN analyzer can be taken to the location where a problem exists and be connected to the network to perform its functions. A hardware instrument will most likely be better able to cope with a high-speed environment, such as 100BASE-T and 1000BASE-T, than a software application that relies on a standard network adapter card to get traffic from the network medium. Hardware analyzers contain special circuitry that is used to perform many functions must faster than can be done via software, and are usually more reliable.

Another thing to consider when comparing hardware to software analyzers is that when you use a PC or a workstation to act as your LAN analyzer, it might be limited as to what the NIC can do. For example, some ordinary adapter cards have built into their firmware a function that automatically discards certain kinds of packets that contain errors. If you are trying to detect what errors are causing problems on your network while troubleshooting, a software product running on a workstation might not be able to help you.

Also, although it's true that network adapter cards can literally see every packet on the network as it zips by, that doesn't mean that the cards are capable of capturing the data and passing it up to higher-level protocols. When a card *does* capture all frames and pass them up the protocol stack, it is operating in *promiscuous mode*. Some cards are designed specifically not to do this, so be sure to check the documentation that comes with the one you might want to use on a workstation that will host LAN monitoring software.

Note

For most typical situations, even in a large network, the functions performed by most hardware-based analyzers can now be performed using software products, such as those discussed in the preceding section. However, for high-speed WAN links, or for situations in which the network topology is complex, involving multiple protocols and services, it might be worth the investment to purchase a hardware-based analyzer. First, try a software product before spending the money on a hardware device. Check out the capabilities of the network adapter(s) you install on a PC or another workstation that will host a network analyzer software product.

Hardware analyzers are expensive because they usually do a very good job and are designed specifically for what they do. Most have built-in disk drives to store captured data, including a floppy disk drive that can be used to exchange data with PC workstations. Be sure that the instrument has enough memory to buffer significant amounts of data. Another feature to look for is a good display so that you can monitor utilization graphically as well as display the contents of individual frames.

A hybrid analyzer that combines the best of the hardware and software products is also available. This type of device implements the capturing and filtering functions in a hardware component that attaches to a workstation, which then provides the display and storage functions. The hardware component has dedicated circuitry and processing power to capture data from the wire, and a software application on the PC is used to filter, calculate, and display the data. This type of device can be external to the PC, although some are implemented as cards that plug into the system's bus.

Simple Network Management Protocol (SNMP)

Building a network today involves integrating products from various vendors. This chapter has discussed tools that can be used to locate faults in the physical elements that make up the network and tools that can be used to monitor the functioning of network protocols.

Yet, so far the tools that have been mentioned are all limited to performing a few specific tasks, and each tool must be used as a separate entity. SNMP was developed to provide a "simple" method of centralizing the management of TCP/IP-based networks. The goals of the original SNMP protocols include the following:

- Keep development costs low to ease the burden of implementing the protocol for developers.
- Provide for managing devices remotely.
- Make the protocol extensible so that it can adapt to new technologies.
- Make the protocol independent of the underlying architecture of the devices that are managed.
- Keep it simple.

The last goal is an important one. Because SNMP is meant to be incorporated into many types of network devices, it was designed so that it would not require a lot of overhead. This makes it easy to create simple devices—such as a bridge or a hub—that can be managed by SNMP, as well as a more complex device such as a router or a switch. Other key factors of the protocol that stick to this goal include the use of the User Datagram Protocol (UDP) for messaging and a manager-agent architecture. UDP is easier to implement and use than a more complex protocol such as TCP. Yet it provides enough functionality to allow a central manager to communicate with a remote agent that resides on a managed device.

The two main players in SNMP are the manager and the agent. The manager is usually a software program running on a workstation or larger computer that communicates with agent processes that run on each device being monitored. Agents can be found on bridges, routers, hubs, and even users' workstations. The manager polls the agents making requests for information, and the agents respond when asked.

Applications designed to be the manager end of the SNMP software vary in both expense and functionality. Some are simple applications that perform queries and allow an administrator to view information from devices and produce reports. Some of the other functions that a management console application might perform include the following:

- Mapping the topology of the network
- Monitoring network traffic
- Trapping selected events and producing alarms
- Reporting variables

Some management consoles, also referred to as network management stations (NMS), can produce trend-analysis reports to help capacity planning set long-range goals. With more advanced reporting capabilities, the administrator can produce meaningful reports that can be used to tackle a specific problem.

SNMP Primitives

Management software and device agents communicate using a limited set of operations referred to as *primitives*. These primitives are used to make requests and send information between the two. The primitives are initiated by the management software and include the following:

- **get**—The manager uses this primitive to get a single piece of information from an agent.
- **get-next**—When the data the manager needs to get from the agent consists of more than one item, this primitive is used to sequentially retrieve data; for example, a table of values.
- **set**—The manager can use this primitive to request that the agent running on the remote device set a particular variable to a certain value.

The following primitives are used by the agent on a managed device:

- **get-response**—This primitive is used to respond to a get or a get-next request from the manager.
- **trap**—Although SNMP exchanges are usually initiated by the manager software, this primitive is used when the agent needs to inform the manager of some important event.

Network Objects: The Management Information Base (MIB)

The primitives just described are the operations that can be performed by the manager or agent processes when they exchange data. The types of data they can exchange are defined by a database called the management information base (MIB). The first compilation of the objects stored in this database was defined by RFC 1066, "Management Information Base for Network Management of TCP/IP-based Internets." A year later, this was amended by RFC 1213, "Management Information Base for Network Management of TCP/IP-based Internets: MIB-II." MIB-II clarified some of the objects that were defined in the original document and added a few new ones. Two other RFCs, 2011 and 2012, added further information for the MIB-II database.

The MIB is a tree of information (a virtual information store). This hierarchical database resides on the agent, and information collected by the agent is stored in the MIB. The MIB is precisely defined; the current Internet standard MIB contains more than a thousand objects. Each object in the MIB represents some specific entity on the managed device. For example, on a hub, useful objects might collect information showing the number of packets entering the hub for a specific port while another object might track network addresses.

When deciding which types of objects to include in the standard, the following things were taken into consideration:

- The object had to be useful for either fault or configuration management.
- The object had to be "weak," which means that it had to be capable of performing only a small amount of damage should it be tampered with. Remember, in addition to reading values stored in the MIB, the management software can request that an object be set to a value.
- No object was allowed if it could be easily derived from objects that already exist.

The first definition of the standard MIB hoped to keep the number of objects to 100 or fewer so that it would be easier to implement. This, of course, is not a factor now.

Because the SNMP management scheme is intended to be extensible, vendors often create their own objects that can be added to the management console software so that you can use them.

An object has a specific syntax, name, and method of encoding associated with it. The name consists of an object identifier, which specifies the type of object to which a specific instance of that kind of object is added. The object identifier is a numeric string of decimal digits separated by periods—for example, ".3.6.1.2.1.1.1". The "instance" of an object is the same, with an additional decimal number following the original object identifier. To make things easier for humans, an object descriptor is used in a text-readable format.

An object can be read-only, read-write, or write-only. In addition, an object can be non-accessible. Syntax types for objects include the following:

- Integer
- Octet String or Display String
- Object Identifier
- Null
- Network Address
- Counter
- Gauge
- TimeTicks
- Opaque

In the first MIB RFC, objects are divided into only a few high-level groups:

- **System**—This group includes objects that identify a type of system (hardware or software).
- **Interfaces**—An object in this group might represent an interface number or an interface type. Other information about network interfaces, such as the largest IP datagram that can be sent or received, is included as objects in this group.
- **Address Translation**—Objects in this group are used for address translation information, such as the ARP (Address Resolution Protocol) cache.
- **IP**—Objects in this group supply information about the IP protocol, including time-to-live values, number of datagrams received from interfaces, errors, and so on.
- **ICMP**—This group includes Internet Control Message Protocol (ICMP) input and output statistics.
- **TCP**—Objects in this group are used to hold information about TCP connections. Instances of these objects exist only while the connection exists. Data contained in these objects includes the number of segments sent or received, for example, or the state of a particular TCP connection (closed, listen, and so on).
- **UDP**—Objects in this group represent statistics about UDP, such as the number of UDP datagrams delivered, or the number of UDP datagrams received for which there is no corresponding application at the destination port.
- **EGP**—These objects are used for the Exterior Gateway Protocol (EGP), and they contain information such as components of each EGP neighbor, and the state of the local system with respect to a neighbor.

In MIB-II, the address translation group was declared to be "deprecated." That is, it should still be supported but might not be in the next version, which is a means for gradually preparing for changes in the protocol. MIB-II, however, adds new objects and functionality that can be used to perform the same functions as those performed by this group, just in a different way.

MIB-II also added new objects to the existing groups. For example, what seems obvious now as necessary information for the system group—a contact person, a system location, and system services—can now be stored in objects in this group.

New groups added by MIB-II include these:

- **Transmission**—Related to the Interface group, this group is used for objects that relate to specific transmission media.

- **SNMP**—A group added for objects needed by the application-oriented working group to collect useful statistical information.

Proxy Agents

Not all devices are equipped with SNMP capabilities. For these devices, another device might be able to handle those functions and acts as a *proxy agent* so that it can still be managed from the SNMP management console. For example, a network card might not be SNMP-enabled, but the host computer can run a process that can monitor the network card and act as a proxy agent, relaying information to the management station. Proxy agents also can be developed to translate between proprietary management software and SNMP. In this case the proxy agent understands the proprietary management capabilities of the device, and communicates with the SNMP management station when necessary.

The Complex Road to SNMPv2 and SNMPv3

The original implementation of SNMP was kept simple and has been widely used throughout the industry. However, it suffers from several limitations. The get/response messaging mechanism allows for the transfer of only one piece of information at a time. The UDP packet is sufficiently large enough to accommodate more data, but the protocol was not built to allow for this. Security is also an issue with SNMP (version 1) because it has no provisions for encryption or authentication.

A committee of the IETF began work on what was to become SNMPv2 in 1994. Work on this second version of the SNMP standard was delayed for years because many could not agree on some of the security and other issues involved. Because of this, several versions of SNMPv2 were created, specifically SNMPv2u and SNMPv2c, each taking a different approach to security issues. In spite of the haziness of the actual SNMPv2 specifications, however, you'll now find that many vendors support some of the functionality that has been described in the many RFCs that relate to SNMPv2. RFC 1901, "Introduction to Community-Based SNMPv2," is the current Experimental Standard that is implemented by some vendors as if it were an approved standard. See also RFCs 1905 and 1906.

One of the good things to come out of the SNMPv2 debate were two new operations:

- **Get-bulk**—This operation allows for the retrieval of a larger amount of information from a single request. This new operation can be used in place of repetitive calls to get-next when transferring large amounts of related information.

- **Inform**—This operation allows for one network management station (NMS) to send traps to another NMS.

For the most part, however, a newer version called SNMPv3 is a more likely candidate for adoption by a wider range of vendors. Although SNMPv1 and SNMPv2 implementations are not compatible with each other, SNMPv3 incorporates the best from both, adding security and other features to the protocol. Actually, SNMPv3 is still being developed, and only some RFCs are considered standards.

RFC 2571, "An Architecture for Describing SNMP Management Frameworks," uses the previous SNMP RFCs heavily, with the following items being the main goals of the RFC:

- Provide an architecture that allows for the standards process for SNMP developments to proceed even when consensus has not been reached for all the specifics of proposed additions.

■ Provide for additional security measures.

■ Modularize each SNMP entity so that each "SNMP engine" can implement the necessary functions to send and receive messages, perform authentication, and perform encryption of messages. Thus, any number of entities can be combined to create an agent, or a management station.

By allowing for a modular approach to SNMP construction, this RFC makes it possible to create new SNMP functionality without having to redefine the entire SNMP standard each time a new feature is added. After all, the "S" in SNMP stands for "simple."

You might want to read these other relevant RFCs when you are evaluating a product and determining how it measures up to the latest in SNMPv3 standards. The following are now IETF standard RFCs, and they apply to different aspects of the SNMP protocol, from version 2 to 3. These are recommended reading for anyone who is involved with purchasing, using, or operating a management console or devices that incorporate SNMP functionality:

■ RFC 1157, "Simple Network Management Protocol (SNMP)," which is considered a "historic" standard, in that it was involved in the process of defining the SNMP protocol.

■ RFC 1643, "Definition of Managed Objects for the Ethernet-Like Interface Types."

■ RFC 3418, "Management Information Base (MIB) for the Simple Network Management Protocol (SNMP)."

■ RFC 3417, "Transport Mappings for the Simple Network Management Protocol (SNMP)."

■ RFC 3416, "Version 2 of the Protocol Operations for the Simple Network Management Protocol (SNMP)."

■ RFC 3415, "View-Based Access Control Model (vacm) for the Simple Network Management Protocol (SNMP)."

■ RFC 3414, "User-Based Security Model (USM) for Version 3 of the Simple Network Management Protocol (SNMPv3)."

■ RFC 3413, "Simple Management Protocol (SNMP) Applications."

■ RFC 3411, "An Architecture for Describing Simple Network Management Protocol (SNMP) Management Frameworks."

Note that these RFC standards are rather recent, although those just listed are now considered standards. However, as complex as the "Simple" Network Management Protocol has become, it is hard to give a general definition of exactly what SNMPv3 is, or will be at this time. The preceding list of RFCs can point you in the right direction when it comes to evaluating manufacturers' hardware/software definitions.

RMON

RMON is a data-gathering and analysis tool that was developed to help alleviate some of the shortcomings of SNMP. RMON works in a similar manner, and its objects are defined in an MIB. It was designed to work much like the LAN analyzer discussed earlier in this chapter. RFCs 1757, "Remote Network Monitoring Management Information Base," and 1513, "Token-Ring Extensions to the Remote Network Monitoring MIB," provide the standard MIB definitions for RMON for Ethernet and Token-Ring networks, respectively.

In SNMP, the roles of the manager and agent are those of a client and server, with the agents being the client of the management console software. In RMON, the agents (often called *probes*) are the active parties and become the server while one or more management consoles can be their clients.

Instead of the management console performing a periodic polling process to gather data and perform analysis from agents out in the field, the agents in RMON perform intelligent analysis and send SNMP traps to management consoles when significant events occur.

Using RMON, the administrator can get an end-to-end view of the network. The types of data collected and the alerts and actions that are associated with RMON are different than those of the standard SNMP type. The objects for RMON fall into the following MIB groups:

- **Statistics**—This group records data collected about network interfaces. A table called EtherStatsTable contains one entry for each interface to hold this data and also contains control parameters for this group. Statistics include traffic volume, packet sizes, and errors.

- **History**—The control function of this group manages the statistical sampling of data. This function controls the frequency at which data is sampled on the network. The historyControlTable is associated with this group. The history function of this group of objects records the statistical data and places the data in a table called the etherHistoryTable.

- **Hosts**—This group tracks hosts on the network by MAC addresses. Information in the hostControlTable specifies parameters for the monitoring operations, and a table called the hostTimeTable records the time a host was discovered on the network.

- **HostTopN**—This group is used to rank hosts by a statistical value, such as the number of errors generated or "top talkers." The TopNControlTable contains the control parameters for this group, and the hostTopNTable keeps track of the data.

- **Matrix**—Data recorded by this group involves the exchange of frames between hosts on the network. Statistics are kept here for data traveling in both directions between hosts.

- **Filter**—This group specifies the types of packets that the RMON probe will capture, such as frame size.

- **Capture**—Although the Filter group specifies the parameters that are evaluated for capturing packets, this group is responsible for capturing packets based on those parameters.

- **Alarm**—This group is used to set up alarms for events that are described in the next group, the Event group. Here you can set the sampling intervals and thresholds that will trigger an alarm. This group reads statistics that have been gathered, and when they exceed the threshold, an event is generated.

- **Event**—When a variable exceeds a threshold defined by an alarm, an event is generated. This group can generate an SNMP trap to notify a network management station or record the information in a log. The Event Table is used to define the notification action that will be taken for an event, and the Log Table is used to record information.

As this list shows, RMON provides a greater deal of functionality compared to SNMP. It allows for the collection of statistical data from all levels of the OSI reference model, including applications at the top in RMON2.

Because Ethernet and Token-Ring networks operate in a fundamentally different way, additional groups are defined in RFC 1513 that are specific to Token-Ring networks:

- **Token-Ring Statistics**—A group to store information about the behavior of the ring, from traffic volume to the number of beacons occurring, ring purges, and other information specific to Token-Ring.

- **Token-Ring History**—Similar to the History group used for Ethernet, this group keeps track of events on a historical basis.

- **Token-Ring Station**—Detailed information about each station on the ring can be found here.

■ **Station Order**—The physical order of stations in the ring can be determined by information stored in this group.

■ **Station Config**—Configuration information for stations is stored here.

■ **Source Routing**—Monitors information about Token-Ring source routing for inter-ring traffic.

Alarms and Events

RMON agents can be programmed to take actions when specific things happen on the network. The Alarms and Events groups provide an important intelligence function.

Configuring an alarm consists of specifying a variable to be watched, the sampling interval, and the event that will be performed when a threshold is crossed. The threshold can be a rising or a falling threshold, or both. For example, an alarm can be set to notify you when something begins to go awry, and to tell you when the situation gets better.

An event that is generated by an alarm can be configured to send an SNMP trap message to one or more management consoles, and store the event in the Log Table. The management station can then take the actions it deems necessary, including retrieving information from the Log Table.

Establishing a Baseline

When making decisions on how to set up alarms and the events they generate, you should consider how the network functions normally. First monitor the network using RMON agents over a long period, noting when variations in traffic or errors occur. Make note of any fluctuations that regularly occur for specific dates or for a particular time of day.

Different network segments might require different sampling intervals and thresholds. For example, a local LAN segment might be subject to wide variations depending on only a small number of users, whereas a major backbone might fluctuate much less as traffic from many segments is blended together. When deciding on a sampling period, it's best to use a shorter interval for a segment that experiences frequent fluctuations and a longer interval for a segment that behaves in a more stable manner.

Response to alarms can be in the form of immediate corrective action, as in the case of a defective device, or a long-term solution such as additional capacity or equipment. Regularly review the baseline values you set, and change them as network usage or topology changes. If alarms and events are not configured to reflect activity that is of a genuine concern, network operators might begin to ignore them, much like what happened to the boy who "cried wolf."

Troubleshooting Small Office and Home Office (SOHO) Networks

SOME OF THE MAIN TOPICS IN THIS CHAPTER ARE

CHAPTER 54

Networking of computers has jumped out of the business/corporate environment to include the home during the past few years. Although inexpensive switches and other networking gear that enables you to interconnect computers at home have been available for several years, they initially were used to allow more than one computer to connect to the Internet for Web surfing or for sharing simple files. It is still possible to use the serial ports on Intel-based systems to establish a point-to-point link with another computer—in essence, a two-node network. However, that method of communication is about the slowest you can achieve, and the limitation of just two computers leaves little room for growing your network. For a small office/home office (SOHO) network, there are various technologies you can use to create a network quickly.

With the deployment of broadband technologies, such as cable and DSL (digital subscriber line) modems, the bandwidth finally is available to make connecting a home office to the Internet a practical solution.

Note

You can learn more about SOHO broadband technologies by reading Chapter 17, "Digital Subscriber Lines (DSL) Technology," and Chapter 18, "Using a Cable Modem." In addition, Chapter 21, "Faster Service: IEEE 802.11a," discusses a new player on the wireless front that is perfect for home networks. The 802.11a standard increases wireless bandwidth from its current 11Mbps (IEEE 802.11b) to around 55Mbps for 802.11a, which should be sufficient for most small networks.

The number of telecommuters—employees who work from home, as well as employees who travel frequently—has been on the rise. A large number of households now have more than one computer or printer, as well as an Internet connection. Because of these and other factors, the Internet is becoming as important to our economy as the telephone switched network (if not more important already).

Another factor that has contributed to using the Internet as a means of communicating with a business network is the increasing use of Virtual Private Network (VPN) technologies, which are discussed in Chapter 50, "Virtual Private Networks (VPNs) and Tunneling." By creating a secure communications path through the Internet, VPNs help reduce the cost of telecommuting, such as long-distance charges. And Windows XP, 2000, and Windows Server 2003 servers all provide VPN solutions in the operating system, so the VPN option is not an extra expense to bear. And when it comes to Unix or Linux, you can pick and choose from a large number of VPN solutions.

SOHO networks usually are composed of only a few computers or other networked devices, so troubleshooting problems on this kind of network is a lot easier than trying to track down problems in a large network. Most of the hardware components are plug-and-play, and even software configuration is a lot simpler than it was a few years ago. However, no matter what kind of networked devices you have in your SOHO environment, invariably a time will come when a document won't print, or a computer can't connect to a resource on another system, and you'll need to spend some time troubleshooting the problem.

Note

Appendix E, "Introduction to Setting Up a SOHO Network," will help you better understand the concepts discussed in this chapter, and it is recommended that you read both of these chapters together. Each has information that will help you understand the concepts in the other. If you know how your SOHO network is set up, and some of the basics about how it operates, you'll be better trained to troubleshoot problems/solutions discussed in this chapter.

In this chapter, we'll look at some common problems you might encounter and methods you can use to troubleshoot them.

Power Troubles

As basic an issue as power might seem, it should be your starting point when you have a device that is not functioning correctly. For example, you might get up one morning and find that although your computer is working just fine, nothing prints. You check the printer and find that it's turned on and has paper loaded; you just can't figure out what the problem might be. Check your hub or switch. Has someone accidentally unplugged the AC adapter that powers the device? Most hubs have a power LED that indicates when the unit is powered up. If you have a power strip, check that too. It's easy, especially in a small office where you don't route cables through the wall, for something as simple as an unplugged device to cause problems. Of course, look to see that no one has switched the power strip to the off position.

You should not use the inexpensive power strips you can find so easily at a discount store. Instead, go to an electronics store (or some of the large home/builders stores) and look for a better power strip. Because a single power strip can do a lot to protect your hardware from damage, all devices, from computers to printers to switches, should be plugged into a power strip that has surge protection as a feature. Again, the low-end strips say they will do this, but in practicality, you get what you pay for. Many of the high-end versions will provide connections for your telephone and even network cables, broadband connections, and even cable interfaces, among others, to further insulate your SOHO network from something like a lightening strike.

If you were even more thorough when setting up your network, you probably bought a small uninterruptible power supply (UPS) and have your power strips or computers plugged into the UPS. Look for any fault lights on the UPS to determine whether it has gone offline due to a power surge or some other malfunction. UPSs should be selected with care, because they implement many of the standard functions of power strips, but provide a lot more in that they are better able to isolate surges, and they can provide battery backups and automatic shutdowns of your servers in the case of a power outage. Small UPS devices can be used in a home network and are not that expensive. And each device usually offers four to six power receptacles, so you can use one UPS for several devices in the SOHO network.

◀◀ For more information on UPS devices, see Chapter 5, "Protecting the Network: Preventative Maintenance Techniques."

Finally, if you are having power problems with all the computers on your network, check the fuse box or power panel in your home or office to be sure that the fuse or circuit breaker at that point hasn't disconnected the power.

Computer Configuration Issues

If you use a broadband connection to the Internet, you'll probably have a switch/router appliance connecting your small LAN to the cable or DSL modem. These inexpensive devices allow your LAN to share a single Internet connection (that is, a single IP address) on the Internet, while providing for separate addresses for each computer on the LAN.

DHCP (the Dynamic Host Configuration Protocol) allows the router/switch to automatically configure your computer with the network addressing information it needs when it boots up. When you add a new computer to the LAN, you need to be sure that it's configured to use DHCP. Otherwise, if you've configured a static address on the computer, you need to be sure that the following are true:

- The address is compatible with the addresses of other computers on your network.
- The address is not already in use by another computer on the network.

Tip

Although you might consider yourself a network guru just because you have a network at home, don't try to step on your own toes. That is, if you decide to assign static IP addresses to some computers in your network, such as a server, then be sure to enable your DHCP service to use an address range which doesn't include that address. Or, if your switch allows, enter a record for the static address. This can be useful when you're connecting to the Internet yet maintaining an internal Windows domain-based network.

You can check your computer configuration easily. For Windows 2000, for example, follow these steps to configure your computer to use DHCP:

1. Select Start, Settings, Network, Dial-up Connections.

2. Right-click Local Area Network and select Properties from the menu that appears.

3. Scroll down in the Components section of the properties sheet shown in Figure 54.1, highlight Internet Protocol (TCP/IP), and click the Properties button.

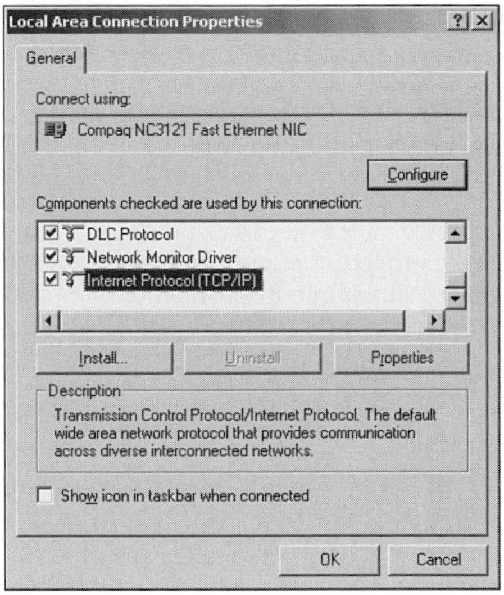

Figure 54.1 Select the Internet Protocol to troubleshoot network address issues.

4. The Internet Protocol (TCP/IP) Properties sheet pops up, as shown in Figure 54.2. If you are using DHCP, be sure that the Obtain an IP Address Automatically option is selected. Unless your Internet provider has told you otherwise, the Obtain DNS Server Address Automatically option should also be selected.

5. If you configured your computers with static addresses, select Use the Following IP Address, and the IP Address, Subnet Mask, and Default Gateway fields should contain the appropriate values. If you chose to use DHCP (automatic configuration), you will not see the IP address, DNS servers, and so on that were assigned by the switch. To see these details, you must run IPCONFIG /ALL from the command line, as described in step 7.

6. If all looks okay in the configuration screens, check out what address your computer is actually using. Choose Start, Programs, Accessories, Command Prompt for Windows 2000 (or Windows 2003 servers), or Start, Programs, Command Prompt for earlier versions of Windows.

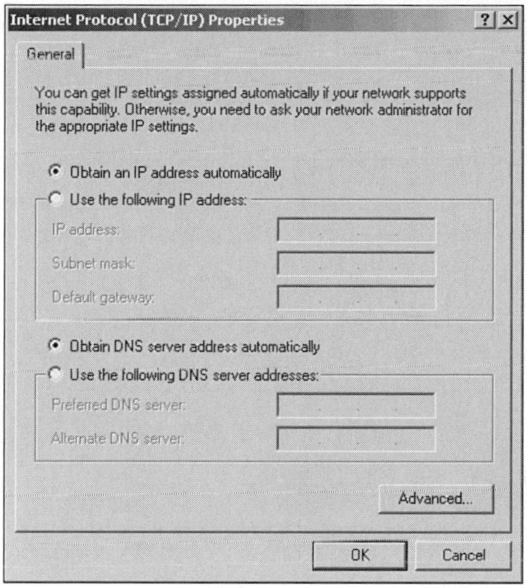

Figure 54.2 Be sure you have the correct IP configuration information filled in for this dialog box.

7. From the command prompt, issue the command IPCONFIG /ALL for Windows NT/2000/XP or Windows 2003 servers operating systems (you can use WINIPCFG to find the same information for Windows 95/98). The response to this command will include a lot of information, so look for the IP address and the subnet mask. Try using the ping command (described in Chapter 28, "Troubleshooting Tools for TCP/IP Networks") from another computer to determine whether it can bounce packets off this address. If not, you probably have unplugged the computer from the network (either at the network card end or at the switch/router or hub).

Another possible cause of the problem is that you are using an address that is not in the same network or subnet as the other computers. It doesn't matter if all the cables are connected to the hub or switch and each computer's network card if you have misconfigured IP addresses or subnet masks. For example, a computer with an IP address of 10.10.10.1 is not going to talk to a computer with an address of 140.176.222.1, no matter how long you try, unless you go through a router that has been configured to pass this information. The network adapter card detects the data you try to send back and forth, but because the protocol stack knows that it's destined for a different network, those packets are ignored and never passed up to the Application level.

Figure 54.3 shows an example of using a switch/router to connect to the Internet through a cable or DSL modem.

In this example, the Internet service provider (ISP) has assigned an IP address to your connection (140.176.200.123). Because you have more than one computer, you went to the local computer store and bought a small switch/router designed to work with broadband connections. Note that the switch/router is plugged into the broadband modem using one port, and plugged into your LAN using another port. To keep track of both connections, the switch/router uses a different address on the port that connects to your LAN.

In this example, the IP address is 10.10.10.1. The switch/router uses the address range of 10.10.10.0 through 10.10.10.254 to allocate IP addresses to computers on the LAN. This means that Computer C has an invalid address, which was configured as a static address.

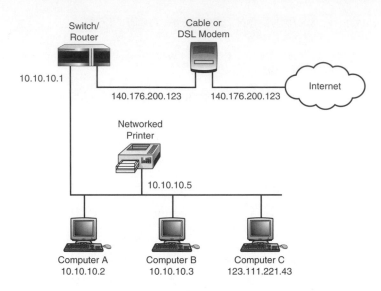

Figure 54.3   Connect to the Internet using a cable or DSL modem and a router/switch. Note that the IP address for Computer C is not valid on the LAN and can't pass through the switch/router.

Yet, when computer A (10.10.10.2) on your network wants to send or receive data to or from the Internet, the switch/router knows that the IP address of the Internet server is different from the LAN address (the 10.10.10.0 address space). Thus, Computer A knows that it must send the data packet to the default gateway, which is the switch/router (10.10.10.1).

When the switch/router receives the data packet, it substitutes its own valid Internet address (140.176.200.123) in the packet header and sends it to the Internet through the broadband modem. When a response is received back from the Internet connection, the switch/router removes the 140.176.200.123 address from the packet header and puts Computer A's address (10.10.10.2) in the header so that it can be delivered to Computer A.

The important thing to keep in mind here is that addresses used inside the network are not valid on the Internet. The switch/router must use sleight of hand to act as a "man in the middle" for you so that, although you have multiple computers on your LAN, the switch/router makes the cable or DSL modem think you have only one. The switch/router keeps track of which computer on the LAN sends out requests and makes sure that packets are routed back to the correct computer.

Note

You can learn more about reserved IP address spaces that you can use in your local network but that are not valid on the Internet. Chapter 25, "Overview of the TCP/IP Protocol Suite," covers this topic in detail.

When Computer A wants to talk to Computer B, it compares the address of Computer B (10.10.10.3) with its own address. Because the address falls in the same network address space, it doesn't send the packet to the default gateway. Instead, it just broadcasts a packet on the LAN knowing that Computer B will see the packet and pick it up.

So far, everything is working as it's supposed to. However, let's suppose you just brought a computer from work to your home office (Computer C) and plugged it into your network. At work, the computer had been configured with a static address of 123.111.221.43. When you try to send or receive data from Computer C, nothing happens because of the following:

- Computer C has an IP address that does not match the addresses on the LAN, so the other computers just ignore the packets that Computer C sends out.

- Computer C was configured at work to use a different default gateway address, so it can't even get a packet to go through the router/switch.

The point is that if your switch/router allows for DHCP and you set up each computer to use DHCP, things should work just as you expect. If you try to mix and match computers with different subnets on the same LAN, you're going to have trouble.

Note

Broadband services come in all sizes and shapes. Just check out Chapter 16, "Dedicated Connections." If your service provider is using DSL, you might have to connect a small device to your telephone outlet before you can plug in a telephone. This device prevents telephone interference from causing problems with the frequencies used on the copper wire by the DSL service. And the reverse is also true. These filters can keep the DSL frequencies from interfering with and degrading the voice channel. Not all DSL services require this sort of device. If your service does, when you buy a new phone for a different room, be sure you obtain another of these devices. Don't just plug in the phone and expect all to be well. A ringing phone or a phone off the hook can cause enough interference to make the DSL connection sporadic or nonfunctional for this kind of connection.

Component Problems—You Can't Get There from Here

Just as in a large corporate network, you might have a problem with one or more components that make up the network. Network cards go bad, as do hubs and switches (and even individual ports on a hub or switch). Always keep handy the minimal documentation that comes with your computer(s), network card, hub, switch, router, and other devices so that you'll know what the LEDs mean when you start troubleshooting.

For example, most network adapters have two LEDs you can examine. One is called the link LED and the other is used to indicate activity on the network. If both of these LEDs are off, you might have a bad network card. Before you make that assumption, however, try moving the cable that plugs the card into the hub or switch/router to a different port and see whether that makes a difference. Check the LEDs on the hub or switch/router to determine whether they have link or activity LEDs. Try switching the patch cable that runs between the network adapter and the port on the switch. Above all, read the documentation to understand what the LEDs mean for your specific product.

Another thing to think about is that many small hubs or switches have an "uplink" port that allows you to connect the device to another one when you want to expand your small LAN. The pinout for this port is not the same as it is for the other ports. The transmit and receive pins are swapped. If you need to plug a computer into an uplink port, you can usually do so, but there will probably be a small button or switch you need to use to change it from an uplink port to a standard port.

Secure Those Cables!

A common problem with small offices or home offices is that you are not using a structured wiring plan. That is, you just string cables from here to there and plug things in. If you have a twisted-pair network cable lying on the floor near your desk, use tie-wraps, scotch tape, or anything else that you can to make sure that the cable doesn't just lie on the floor where you can roll over it with a chair. Even stepping on a twisted-pair network cable can be enough to cause it to have problems carrying the network signal. Secure those cables so that they aren't mangled by accident.

Note

A friend of mine had a pet rabbit at home that was occasionally let out of the cage. Rabbits, in case you don't know, like to chew on just about anything (my friend no longer has the rabbit). Be sure to keep your network cables (not to mention electrical cords) safe, even from your pets!

If you suspect a problem with the cable, trace it from the network card back to the hub or switch/router to be sure that it hasn't been damaged. Never try to "stretch" a cable or pull too hard on it when you are moving things about. This too can damage the cable and cause it to generate so many errors that the network becomes unavailable to the attached computer.

Firewall Problems

If you have installed a router/switch device between your network and a broadband Internet connection, be sure to read the manual thoroughly and understand how the device should be configured. Many come with default settings, but you need to fill in some information, such as the address of the broadband link, if your service provider gives you a static address. In most cases, the provider will be using DHCP also, so you won't have to make any changes. If you do have to make changes, write them down and keep the information handy for later troubleshooting efforts.

Earlier in this chapter, you read that it's not a good idea to mix computers you use for play with those you use for business on the same network. If you do, you are just asking for trouble. If you play Internet games—those that allow you to interact with other users playing the same game on the Internet—you might be instructed to change the port settings on a small switch/router that also functions as a firewall. If you start playing around with opening, disabling, or forwarding ports, keep track of the changes you make. If something stops working after you've made a change, undo the modification and see whether the changes you've made have caused the problem.

Remember that the firewall capabilities of a small switch/router are minimal and are designed to protect you from simple attacks from the Internet. It might be that the default settings are very stringent, and if you end up making changes that relax the firewall settings, you might also be opening a door that can allow bad things into your small LAN.

◀◀   For more information about how firewalls work and the features that are important, see Chapter 49, "Firewalls."

Keeping Your Network Healthy

Another good reason to keep your entertainment computers separate from your business LAN is that you don't want to be surfing the Web, find a neat program, and download a virus or some other bad program that will start to eat up things in your network. This is yet another reason other people shouldn't be using your business computer to access the Internet. Additionally, if you have children who want to use the Internet, you might want to buy them their own computer and provide a separate Internet connection. The shorthand is like this: Play games on your play computers; do business on your business computers. If at all possible, it's not a bad idea to adopt this policy. With computer prices falling and the fact that many people keep older computers after upgrades, this may be more feasible than ever.

And, of course, because business is business, back up your files on a regular basis. Above all, it's worth the cost to buy a good antivirus software package and keep it updated. The cost is a tax deduction and it will save you a lot of grief if something bad does get loose in your network.

For the safety of your network, a good antivirus program should be used to scan all disks on all computers on your LAN on a very frequent basis—such as nightly when you are asleep. A good antivirus program should also download updates (new virus definitions) frequently. Keep in mind that if you don't keep your virus definitions up-to-date, then when one gets loose in even a large network, much less a small one, it can wreak havoc as it quickly spreads.

Lastly, a good antivirus program should detect malicious attachments when you are sending and receiving email, and should check removable media (such as a floppy disk) and block you from copying files if the removable media contains a virus or some other threatening program.

Wireless Networking Problems

The newest, latest, and maybe greatest approach to SOHO networking environments is to remove the cables altogether. It's now quite inexpensive to buy a small wireless Access Point (AP) and install wireless network cards in the computers in your small or home office. This allows you, for example, to use a laptop and take it from the living room to the kitchen to the basement, or wherever you feel most comfortable working. Heck, if it's a nice day outside, you might as well take the laptop out to the deck in the back yard, work from there, and get a tan at the same time!

◄◄   Wireless is a fairly big topic; for more information on wireless networking solutions, see Chapters 19 through 24.

You should keep a few things in mind when using wireless networking, however. Both in a small office and at home, you're likely to have a microwave oven sitting around somewhere. Although this is usually not a problem, it is possible for a microwave oven to interfere with the wireless transmissions of your network. This should be easy to troubleshoot. Just turn the darn thing on and determine whether the computers in your LAN can still talk to each other.

Another problem is that wireless networking is bounded by how far you can be from the AP. Although you might be able to communicate with the AP from the living room, the signal might not reach the basement, or it might not be strong enough to penetrate the brick wall that separates the backyard deck from the AP. Experiment to see whether moving the computer closer to the AP fixes the problem. If it does, you can always buy one or more APs, place them in strategic locations around the home or office, and use ordinary twisted-pair cables to join the APs to a switch/router that connects you to the Internet.

Note also that other wireless devices, such as 2.4GHz cordless telephones or 2.4Ghz wireless security cameras like the ones on those annoying pop-under ads, can interfere with wireless networks. This is a simple thing to troubleshoot. Just make a phone call and watch file transfers from one computer to another creep to a halt.

For wireless connections, be sure to use the management application that allows you to check/configure the Access Point, and do the same for each wireless network adapter in the network.

Before you call your cable or DSL provider, you should carefully go over every aspect of your LAN and determine how each computer is configured. ISPs don't make a lot of money off individual customers—it's the large aggregate of happy customers who have no problem that pays their bills. A single call from you might negate an entire year's worth of what you are paying them.

So, to be a nice player, check such things as network addressing, cables, and other things mentioned in this chapter as a start. For example, the first thing to do is take an adapter that is known to be good (that is, it's working on one computer) and substitute it for one that you suspect is bad. Check the adapter configurations on both computers. If you suspect that a network cable is the problem, swap it with one that is working.

This procedure of swapping parts that are known to be in good working order might be the quickest way to solve the problem. Remember that if the problem does lie on your end of the line, it can likely be fixed more quickly if you find it yourself than if you have to wait days for the provider to send someone to your site.

When All Else Fails

If you've tried everything in this chapter and you can send and receive data on your LAN, but not to or from the Internet, there is an important tool that can help solve this problem. Every office (and most every home) has this tool: the telephone. Pick it up, call your ISP, and find out whether the problem is on its end. Simply dial the ISP's customer service line and be persistent.

Provided that you have thoroughly checked out your end of the connection first, never take "it's not our problem" for an answer. If it was working and now it's not, your ISP should be able to at least troubleshoot the problem from its end. If the problem can't be solved on the phone, request that the ISP send someone out to prove to you that the cable or DSL modem is working as it should. The problem today is that ISPs that provide broadband access to the Internet are growing so fast that it's hard to find qualified technical personnel to troubleshoot the customer problems that happen. It's easier to make you struggle through level after level of automated touch-tone response menus and then let you talk to some script-reader who just screens calls, looks up things in a database, and spits out a canned answer. Be sure you get through to someone who knows his stuff and can get the problem fixed.

Upgrading Network Hardware

SOME OF THE MAIN TOPICS FOR THIS PART ARE

Upgrading from ARCnet to Ethernet or Token-Ring

Upgrading from Token-Ring to Ethernet

Upgrading Older Ethernet Networks

Upgrading from Bridges and Hubs to Routers and Switches

Adding Wireless Networking to a LAN

PART X

Upgrading from ARCnet to Ethernet or Token-Ring

SOME OF THE MAIN TOPICS IN THIS CHAPTER ARE

Of the networking technologies still widely used today, ARCnet is the oldest. It was created at Datapoint Corporation in the 1970s and is a token-passing system similar in some ways to Token-Ring. For small networks, ARCnet is a reliable technology that is easy to configure. However, also like Token-Ring, only a small number of manufacturers produce ARCnet equipment when compared to Ethernet. Along with its slow network speed (2.5Mbs), this makes it a prime candidate for an upgrade to newer technology.

Note that there are places where ARCnet is still a viable solution. It is still widely used in factory environments where the network needs to provide a controlled, deterministic access to the network for all devices. In industrial automation scenarios, this is a major requirement. Timing can be a very important issue when dealing with modern machine tools and industrial robots, the gathering of statistical information, and so on. In that case, if ARCnet is not holding its own, you can find other networking solutions, such as Token-Ring, which also provide a deterministic access method to the network. If you are running ARCnet in an old (and I mean old!) office environment, it's time you came into the twenty-first century and upgraded to Ethernet.

ARCnet Overview

Because it is a token-passing system, ARCnet is a deterministic network technology that is useful in situations in which a predictable throughput is required. Limitations of ARCnet include the fact that it operates at a rate of 2.5Mbps and can be used to create a LAN of up to only 255 computers. This might have once been an acceptable number of nodes for a factory floor setting, but in the large automated factories of today, this is a small number indeed. Although methods can be used to bridge ARCnet LANs together, other solutions can prove cheaper. Another benefit of upgrading from ARCnet to either Ethernet or Token-Ring is the increased management tools you'll have at your disposal to monitor and troubleshoot network performance and problems.

◄◄   For a detailed discussion of how ARCnet works, including the network frame and message types used, see Chapter 13, "The Oldest LAN Protocol Is Still Kicking: ARCnet."

Upgrading to Ethernet or Token-Ring

You probably can safely assume that any conversion from ARCnet is going to require replacing network adapter cards, hubs, and, most likely, network cables—in other words, just about everything but the workstations and servers. You'll have to be sure that any specialized devices, such as industrial machinery that uses a network connection, can also be used with a newer technology. It might be a simple matter of swapping out a component card as you do with a PC, or it might involve upgrading firmware or even the replacement of some machinery. These costs must be taken into consideration when you are creating a budget to justify the upgrade.

If you have used Category 3 or better cables, you might be able to reuse the cables, but you will need to modify the connectors to use the appropriate cable pairs and pin-out specifications for 10BASE-T. Ethernet does not support daisy-chaining using twisted-pair wiring, however, so if you have an existing ARCnet LAN that is composed of multiple segments of this sort, you will have to purchase new cabling for an upgrade. If you currently use hubs, you might get by with rewiring the connectors and replacing the hub with an Ethernet hub or switch. However, because you're going through an upgrade from such an old technology, now might be the time to consider running new Category 5, 6, or better cables. This is especially true if you are installing Fast Ethernet and expect to upgrade this to Gigabit Ethernet in the future. For all practical purposes, any future advances in network bandwidth will not use Category 3 cabling, so it's usually better to bite the bullet and expend the money required to replace cables at the same time.

Tip

If you want to plan for the long run, it might even be a good idea to upgrade your cable plant to fiber-optic cables. Although most network adapter cards that have fiber-optic receptacles operate at gigabit or 10Gb speeds, there are now many on the market that can be used for Fast Ethernet (100Mbps) connections until you have a need to upgrade to faster communications. You can use a search engine online to find these manufacturers, and the price of these cards is not inexpensive—usually $150 and up. However, pulling network cables is a much more expensive proposition, so adapter cards will probably be the least expensive component in this kind of upgrade. By the time you decide to upgrade to gigabit speeds, the price of those adapters will have come down dramatically. One site you might want to visit online for more information is `www.unicomlink.com/products/network_equipment/nic_cards.htm`

◀◀ Chapter 6, "Wiring the Network—Cables, Connectors, Concentrators, and Other Network Components," contains an in-depth discussion about the differences in copper cables and fiber-optic cables, including the different types of each.

If you are replacing ARCnet with Token-Ring equipment, you'll also probably have to use new network wiring. The distances that Token-Ring networks cover vary a little from one vendor's products to another. They also are more expensive than Ethernet components. However, like ARCnet, Token-Ring networks can provide a deterministic, maximum access time for nodes on the network. In the past, if timing was critical in your environment, Token-Ring was probably a good upgrade path. However, modern versions of Ethernet currently operate at much larger bandwidths, and in an environment where timing is critical, Ethernet can meet the challenge today.

Although pulling new wiring (both Ethernet cabling or Token-Ring cabling) is a labor-intensive task, if you opt to install new high-grade cable now, it's an investment that will last for many years.

ARCnet normally is used to create small LANs. A few manufacturers sell bridges that can be used to connect the 255-node LANs into larger configurations. Most ARCnet LANs operate at the standard 2.5Mbps rate. Other versions, such as ARCnet Plus, can be used at up to 20Mbps. To decide which Ethernet technology you want to use, examine the current layout and identify important nodes and the bandwidth you think they will need. Try to locate bottlenecks that occur in the current topology, if any.

Here are some questions to ask yourself:

- Which servers do most nodes in the LAN use?
- Where should devices that require a quick response time be placed in the network?
- Which servers get the heaviest use in terms of network bandwidth? Would you benefit from Fast Ethernet or Gigabit Ethernet switching for these servers?
- Can any groups of users and servers be segmented? Are there any groups of users that should be isolated behind a firewall for security purposes? A firewall is unnecessary unless the servers that connect to automation devices are also connected to a more typical office LAN.
- If this upgrade is the result of merging with another network, what kind of interconnection will be made? Which users on each network will be allowed access on the other network?

ARCnet provides a physical LAN that uses a token to allow access to the network medium. Because no prioritization is built into the protocols used, every node on the LAN must process each packet sent out on the wire. Conversion to a simple Ethernet broadcast domain seems to be a simple task. However, you'll need to look closely at the distances between hubs on the current LAN and those distances between workstations and these hubs.

Because ARCnet allows for up to 2,000 feet between active devices, you'll need to make decisions based on the kind of Ethernet technology to which you're upgrading and whether or not it can span the distance you require. You can use Fast Ethernet or Gigabit Ethernet with fiber links to connect switches at larger distances than is possible using coaxial cable, which is rarely used today, or twisted-pair wiring. If your factory floor is small, you should have no trouble locating switches or hubs to service a large number of network nodes. In a large campus environment, you'll need to set up a router or two and segment your network into subnets. This not only cuts down on local segment network traffic, but also makes it easier to manage the network from an administrative point of view. You could also use a cascade of switches to connect geographically distant devices.

Laying Out the New Network

Ethernet offers many solutions to help build networks that range from 10Mbps to gigabit speeds. What you use depends on the current needs of the network, the projected usage for at least three years, and the distances to be covered.

In a small network, such as an office setting, where there are from two to a few dozen computers, a simple solution is to replace the current ARCnet hubs with one or more Ethernet switches, run new cables to the workstations, and equip each workstation with a new Ethernet network adapter card. This kind of a swap-out can be done easily over a weekend without causing downtime for network users. To facilitate the process in a minimal amount of time, you can do a lot of work in advance, such as installing the new cabling and preparing the faceplate and other hardware at the user's desk and simply hooking things up when you get some downtime. This type of upgrade can be very useful in a large network, or a network that requires a 24/7 operation schedule.

Tip

Currently, many 24/7 networks use several technologies to attempt to maintain operations with no downtime. For example, using clusters, in which two or more servers operate together, prevents a single server from being a point of failure. Other methods include multiple network cards and other redundancy built into the entire network, from routers to duplicate lines of cabling, and so on. Most of these techniques are covered in various chapters throughout this book.

When the LAN is larger, however, you might need to sit down and think about how users utilize network resources before you decide on a migration plan. For example, ARCnet enables you to place a workstation up to 2,000 feet from an active hub. Ethernet's 10BASE-T allows a maximum distance of only 328 feet. If your network has multiple workstations that are using cables that extend the maximum distance allowed by ARCnet, then you will not be able to perform a simple swap-out and replace ARCnet hubs with Ethernet switches. Instead, you will have to look at the geography of your building and decide on locations for switches that can be used to stay within the 10BASE-T limit of 328 feet. The end result is that you will probably use additional switches to extend the distance covered by Ethernet, or use fiber-optic cabling to connect a series of switches over a greater distance. Again, you can solve this problem with a mix-and-match solution by installing Ethernet switches that connect to a fiber-based Fast or Gigabit Ethernet pipe, while allowing switch ports for 10Mbps and 100Mbps computers.

Figure 55.1 shows an ARCnet LAN that uses two active hubs and one passive hub. On the first active hub you can see that there are five workstations, all of which are placed the maximum distance from the hub, 2,000 feet. The passive hub, however, can be no farther from the active hub than 100 feet, and the workstations connected to it are also bound by this limit.

The workstations in this layout are more than 300 feet from the second active hub, which is within the Ethernet 10BASE-T limit of 328 feet. It is a simple matter here to replace this second active hub with an Ethernet switch, and then replace the cables that connect the workstations to the switch and the network adapters in each workstation.

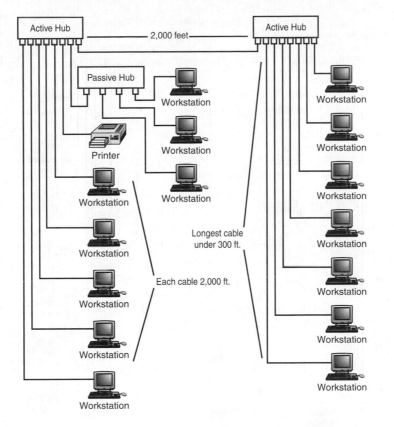

Figure 55.1 ARCnet allows the LAN to span distances of up to 2,000 feet between hubs.

The first active hub, however, poses a problem because it has workstations that are beyond the distance limitation 10BASE-T/100BASE-T technology imposes (see Figure 55.2). Here, a solution might be to replace the active hub and the passive hub with an Ethernet switch, and connect the printer (and the workstations attached to the passive hub) to the new switch. From here you can run an additional link to another switch that is situated closer to the other workstations.

To connect these three switches, you need to use a fiber-optic link to span the distance. When you are looking at switches to purchase, be sure they have the correct ports needed to connect Category 5 (or greater) cables as well as fiber. Twisted-pair cables, such as those used by 10BASE-T and 100BASE-T, typically use an RJ-45 jack, whereas fiber-optic cables typically use an ST or SC type connector. Be sure that the device you choose for a replacement supports the number and kind of ports needed for these connectors.

The purpose of this example is to show that in addition to swapping out the networking equipment when you upgrade to Ethernet, you must pay close attention to the differences between the current ARCnet topology and that of the technology to which you are upgrading. Pay close attention to the limits imposed and compare them with the current layout of user workstations and servers. You will probably find that additional switches will be needed when the ARCnet network is stretched to its limit and needs to be converted to Ethernet.

The same process is required for conversion to a Token-Ring network. You'll need to get the specifications for the hardware (MSAUs, cabling, network cards, and so on) and lay out a topology that can accommodate the nodes on your current network.

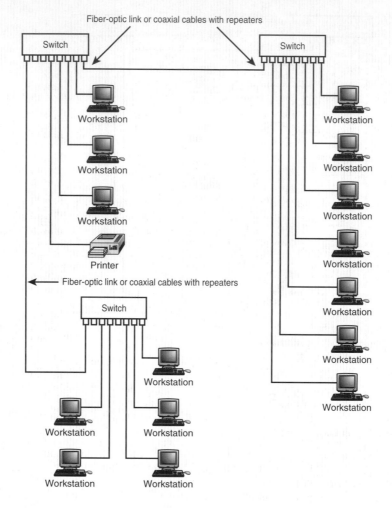

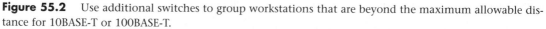

Figure 55.2   Use additional switches to group workstations that are beyond the maximum allowable distance for 10BASE-T or 100BASE-T.

Solving Performance Problems

Another consideration for the upgrade path is what kind of interconnecting devices you need to use. In a very small network, one or more 10/100Mbps hubs or switches will probably suffice and be an easy upgrade. ARCnet is not known for having a large bandwidth (2.5Mbps for the standard ARCnet), so if this speed sufficed before upgrading, it's unlikely that you will have to worry about bandwidth problems afterward. Even if the ARCnet bandwidth usage is becoming saturated (at about 65% of the total possible 2.5Mbps), a simple 10Mbps or 100Mbps Ethernet LAN handling the same number of nodes will probably show dramatic improvement.

Speed is another reason you might choose Ethernet over Token-Ring. Although some vendors sell equipment that can be used to run Token-Ring at very fast speeds, the standards on this technology have pretty much stalled in the past few years, so you shouldn't expect to see a lot of vendors devoting research dollars to come up with faster products. Instead, if performance is a problem, a well-planned network of Fast or Gigabit Ethernet to connect switches with ports dedicated to important network nodes might prove a more viable solution than Token-Ring.

As always, though, you should be looking to the future. For example, it is typical that when upgrading an old LAN you will be upgrading not just the physical infrastructure, but also the end-user applications used on the network. Although a simple word processing program that was marketed 10 years ago might not require a lot of network bandwidth to run from a server, the needs of newer versions might seem gigantic in comparison. If end-user workstations are also being replaced, you might find it easier to install a copy of the application on each workstation, assuming that it has much more hard disk storage space than its predecessor (and the cost of additional licenses doesn't prove prohibitive). If you plan to continue serving applications from an application server, you might find it necessary to use Ethernet switches and possibly a higher-bandwidth technology than 10Mbs Ethernet.

The same goes for factory automation devices, which are a lot more complex today than 20 years ago. Faster processors and more specific tasks mean that network communications on the factory floor is a field that will be growing and evolving rapidly during the next few years.

◄◄ Switches come in many sizes and support varying numbers of ports and bandwidth. You can learn more about switches, and thus how to deploy them in a network, by reading Chapter 8, "Network Switches."

Connecting servers that need a large amount of bandwidth to a switch, in full-duplex mode, can help in this situation. Whether you need to use a switch port or a hub for each user workstation depends on the current user work habits, along with a projection of network use you expect after you upgrade applications.

Upgrading from Token-Ring to Ethernet

SOME OF THE MAIN TOPICS IN THIS CHAPTER ARE

Token-Ring networks have been around for about the same length of time as Ethernet. These two network technologies accomplish the same thing, in that they allow devices on the network to exchange data in an orderly fashion. The methods they employ to accomplish this task, however, are fundamentally different. Because of the different methods used to mediate access to the network, the hardware used for Token-Ring and Ethernet networks is not generally interchangeable. That is, you cannot simply pick up a workstation that is configured on an Ethernet network and move it to a Token-Ring network without some hardware changes.

The Future of Token-Ring

Token-Ring networks have been around for about 20 years. When the technology was first developed, PCs were not as an important a business tool as they are today. The main rationale for hooking a PC to a corporate network in the early days was to provide access to larger computer systems, such as mainframes and minicomputer systems. In that kind of scenario, most of the data flow was within a small workgroup of computers with only a small percentage of network traffic from PCs traveling over a backbone to a larger wide area network.

In today's client/server atmosphere, in which intensive traffic loads can be generated by applications such as multimedia or Web servers, this might not be the case. Some vendors, however, produce Token-Ring equipment that operates at speeds faster than the 4Mbps and 16Mbps standard speeds (such as 100Mbps), so this might not be the case in your network. Such faster equipment comes with a price, and as Ethernet bandwidth continues to grow, you probably should consider upgrading to Ethernet rather than upgrading a slower Token-Ring network to a faster one. One of the reasons, besides the cost, is that the future of Token-Ring is uncertain at this point.

Tip

There are hard-core Token-Ring gurus who do not want to see the technology go away. Because faster, newer Ethernet equipment has already incorporated functionality that makes it a better choice than Token-Ring, Token-Ring will not see a lot of new feature development. For the curious, there is the Wireless Token-Ring Protocol (WTRP). You can find out more about this at `http://eecs.berkeley.edu/~ergen/WTRP/wtrp.ppt`. And who would you expect to be selling WTRP? Just visit `http://pc.ibm.com/us/accessories/comms.html`. It seems that some companies never give up. You probably won't find WTRP hardware for home or SOHO use. You won't even find it in your local computer store. If you need this type of hardware, scan the Web or use the IBM URL just mentioned.

Some might argue that Token-Ring has built-in mechanisms for handling heavy traffic loads because its basic frame structure includes bits set aside for prioritization. However, in reality not many manufacturers have implemented priority-based schemes using these bits. Although there have been some technological improvements in Token-Ring over the years, they are a far cry from the changes that have been made to Ethernet standards.

If your network is already made up of Token-Ring equipment, you will have to justify maintaining that environment. Today, Ethernet far surpasses Token-Ring in the LAN area. When justifying the cost of upgrading a Token-Ring network to Ethernet, consider the following:

- The cost of the hardware portion, both now and in the future. Can you be sure that there will be a sufficient number of vendors producing Token-Ring devices in the future to keep prices in a reasonable range? Will there be enough vendors involved to promote the development of new and innovative additions to the technology? Ethernet devices, from network cards to switches, along with most other equipment, are much cheaper than equivalent Token-Ring items. The large marketplace of Ethernet vendors makes it easy to get quality devices that are targeted to specific markets. For example, Ethernet network adapter cards can be had for under $100, and usually for under $20. Small switches for a departmental LAN are available for a few hundred dollars, and even smaller ones (four ports) are now going for $50–$100.

- Will you be able to continue to find technicians who are proficient in Token-Ring technology, or will you find yourself spending additional funds training new employees? Because it is so pervasive in the world today, Ethernet gives rise to better support options—from vendor support to the pool of technicians that you hire to manage your network.

- Will you be forced to find some kind of interoperability solution in the near future if your business merges with another that already has a large installed base of Ethernet equipment?

- Ethernet has been an ongoing project of the IEEE 802 Committee. Whereas most Token-Ring equipment still runs at 4–16Mbps, Ethernet can span from 10Mbps or 100Mbps on the desktop, to gigabit (and now Gigabit Ethernet) in larger networks. IEEE 802.5 does provide for a 100Mbps Token-Ring network adapter, but don't expect the cost to be cheap. In May 2000, the IEEE 802.5 committee decided to "hibernate," saying its business was complete. Since then some new developments have been done on creating standards for faster Token-Ring networks. You can visit the Web site at `www.8025.org/`, where you'll find that a gigabit standard was completed (P802.5v), but that "there are no known implementations."

To put the preceding point more succinctly, it appears as if Token-Ring is at the end of the road. There are fewer and fewer manufacturers each year of Token-Ring networking gear, and there is little incentive to produce new equipment—if you can find a gigabit Token-Ring network adapter, this author would like to be informed!

Phasing Ethernet into the Token-Ring Network

If you've decided that you are going to have to embrace the Ethernet network in your Token-Ring shop, the next step is to decide on a plan for making the change. The most disruptive method would be to simply go ahead full force and swap out all the hardware at one time and hope for the best. Depending on your circumstances, that might be the only choice you have. The issue that will help you make this decision is whether you can segment your network into functional components where you can identify which end stations need to communicate with which stations. Why? Because of the fundamental differences between Ethernet and Token-Ring, it can be very difficult in many cases to make the two work together.

There are translational bridges and other internetworking devices you can use to connect Token-Ring LANs to an Ethernet LAN or a backbone joining the two. Using a backbone to provide a high-speed transport to both kinds of networks is not terribly complicated. Asynchronous Transfer Mode (ATM), for example, can be used to carry both kinds of traffic. But without some kind of translation capability to account for the difference in the frame formats, a network of this sort can be limited to allowing Token-Ring stations to talk only to Token-Ring stations, and Ethernet nodes to talk only to Ethernet nodes.

Differences That Make Translation Difficult

There are several reasons why it is not an easy task to make a perfect translation device that can allow Token-Ring and Ethernet nodes to communicate with each other:

- Canonical versus non-canonical bit ordering
- Embedded MAC addresses
- Frame size
- Notification of delivery (Token-Ring status bits)
- Token-Ring routing (RIF) information

These issues are discussed in more detail over the course of the next three sections.

Bits and Frames

The most basic difference between these two networking technologies that becomes apparent lies at the beginning of the network transport process: They interpret the ordering of bits for addressing purposes in the opposite direction. That is, although they both use a six-byte MAC address to uniquely identify a network adapter on a LAN, Ethernet considers the first bit in the serial stream to be the low-order bit (the canonical method), whereas Token-Ring considers the first bit to be the high-order bit (the non-canonical method).

This problem can be easily addressed with a hardware device, such as a bridge or router, that reorders the addressing bits depending on what kind of network is attached to the port on which the frame is to be sent. However, there are cases, such as in the Address Resolution Protocol (ARP), where MAC addresses ride in portions of a frame in addition to the addressing fields. Designing a hardware device that can determine all the cases in which this is possible is a daunting task. And, when such an attempt is made, latency factors enter the picture because the device is forced to read much more of the frame than just the header fields that contain the source and destination fields.

Frame size is another important factor. Ethernet networks use a frame size that can be up to approximately 1,500 bytes, whereas Token-Ring uses a frame size that can be a lot higher, possibly up to 17.8KB on a 16Mbps Token-Ring LAN. If the higher-level protocol being transported on the LAN does not allow for fragmenting packets (as TCP/IP does), it is necessary to force the entire network to use the lowest common denominator of Ethernet's 1,500-byte frame.

Notification of Delivery

Token-Ring uses three bits in its frame to notify the sender of what happened to the frame after it was sent out onto the ring. The Address Recognized bit is set when a station recognizes that it is the intended destination of the frame. The Frame Copied bit is set if the destination station can copy the frame from the wire into an internal buffer. The Error bit is used to indicate that some kind of error was encountered in the frame somewhere along its travels. Using the information these status bits signal, the sending station can determine whether it needs to retransmit the frame.

Ethernet doesn't worry about such things. It provides a "best effort" delivery system and depends on the higher-level protocol whose traffic it is transporting to decide whether the frame was able to successfully navigate the network to its destination.

When a translational device is being designed, how are these bits to be handled when a Token-Ring frame is sent out onto an Ethernet network where there are no built-in mechanisms for storing this kind of information? There are differences in how these bits are handled from vendor to vendor, and you must be aware of how their devices handle this situation. For example, some simply set the Frame Copied bit when the frame is received at the device, but not the Address Recognized bit, whereas others set both bits before sending the frame back onto the ring. When the frame makes its way back to the sending station, how is it to interpret these? Because the translational device is not the final destination of the frame, the higher-level protocol must be able to cope with this.

Routing Information

Token-Ring uses source-routing bridges (SRB), whereas Ethernet uses transparent bridges. In the source-routing algorithm, an "explorer" frame is sent out through the network to discover a path to the destination computer. When more than one path exists in the network, the frame is duplicated and is able to travel more than one path. As the explorer frame travels from bridge to bridge to its destination, it compiles a list of addressing information that details the route it has taken. This information is stored in the Routing Information Field (RIF). When it reaches its destination, it can use this routing information to travel back to the sending station, which can then decide from the multiple frames that come back to it which route it wants to use to communicate with the destination station.

There is simply no concept like this in an Ethernet network. Transparent bridges don't perform this "routing" function like SRB devices do. They simply keep a table of MAC addresses as they learn which segment a device is on and try to send out frames only on the port on which the destination MAC address is known to exist.

A translational device can sometimes be made to work by caching the information in the RIF before it translates the packet from Token-Ring format to Ethernet format. When a frame with a unicast address returns, the translation bridge can check its cache and reconstruct the Token-Ring frame from the data stored there before outputting it on the Token-Ring network.

However you look at it, trying to create a gateway between these two fundamentally different kinds of networks is not an easy task. If you need to gradually phase Ethernet equipment into an existing Token-Ring network, you might have to deal with the incompatibilities and incur the expense of translational devices that might or might not solve all the problems. If you can localize your users and the servers that they use into units that can be swapped out all at once, the process becomes much easier to implement.

Replacing All Token-Ring Equipment

In a small LAN, swapping out all the Token-Ring hardware and replacing it with Ethernet equipment might be feasible. If you carefully plan the implementation around users' work schedules, you can minimize disruptions on the network. Before beginning, you should inventory the existing equipment to see what must be replaced and what, if any of it, can be retained.

For the most part, however, you'll likely find yourself replacing the cabling from the desktop to the wiring closet, older routers, multi-station access units (MAUs and MSAUs), and other connectivity equipment. Some of your infrastructure may be salvageable, however. For example, the backbone wiring of your network may be adaptable to the new topology of your network. Similarly, other parts of your current network may not be sufficient for an Ethernet network. For example, if Token-Ring MAUs are distributed throughout an office instead of being situated in a wiring closet, you may have to run new cables from a wiring closet to each desktop. Recabling a network can be both time-consuming and expensive.

Each situation will require a good inventorying of existing equipment to see how it fits into an overall plan.

Tip

Another possibility to think about is using wireless networking for small islands of users where stringing cables to the desktop may be very expensive. Section V, "Wireless Networking Protocols," is worth reading if you are interested in learning whether wireless networking is appropriate for part or all of your network.

Switches and Routers

Some of the newer routers and switches that have come onto the market in the past few years have the capability to operate with either Ethernet or Token-Ring networks. If you are contemplating a change-over in the near future, this should be a consideration when you're making any current purchases. Buying a more expensive device now, that you can use now and still use when you upgrade the network in the near future, can save you money in the long run.

If you have been using a gradually phased approach for your upgrade (that is, you are upgrading in small chunks), the router or switch that is currently operating as a translation device might easily be reconfigured to work just fine in an all-Ethernet network. Read the documentation for each device to determine what steps need to be taken. If you cannot find the information readily available in the documentation that came with the equipment, check with the manufacturer. Many times a simple download of a new version of the device's firmware can solve this kind of problem.

Network Cabling and Connectors

Most new installations of network cabling are of the Category 5 (or better) twisted-pair type. This cable can support ordinary Token-Ring 4MB or 16MB networks as well as Ethernet networks running at speeds from 10Mbps to 100Mbps with no problems. You will need to consult your network map to be sure that any existing cabling infrastructure for the LAN does not violate any of the distance or nodes-per-segment rules that apply to Ethernet. If the existing cables have been installed for quite some time and are of a grade not equal to Category 5, you should probably replace them.

The connectors used for Token-Ring and Ethernet may be different on your network. Ethernet networks based on 10BASE-T or 100BASE-T typically use an RJ-45 connector. Although this kind of connector also can be used on a Token-Ring network, the wires used and the pins to which they are attached on each end will be different from the pin-out used on Ethernet networks. Changing these requires time for making the actual physical wire-to-pin changes. Additionally, even more time is needed for testing the cable to be sure that the connectors have been properly installed and will function with a minimum of errors on the new network.

Network Adapter Cards

Token-Ring and Ethernet network adapter cards are different at a very basic level and are not compatible. Token-Ring NICs usually cost much more than Ethernet cards. One of the reasons is that Token-Ring NICs take on more responsibility for managing transmission of data on the local LAN than Ethernet cards do. Remember that Token-Ring cards wait for a token before transmitting data. Ethernet cards can just start talking any time they sense that the network media is free. When making a change-over, it will be necessary to acquire a new card for each end-user workstation, as well as for any servers on the network.

Upgrading Older Ethernet Networks

5 7

SOME OF THE MAIN TOPICS IN THIS CHAPTER ARE

One of the most expensive parts about installing a network is the task of pulling network cables. You not only have to make sure that you meet local building codes, but must also spend many hours (and labor is expensive) in dropping cables so that you can install a faceplate at the user's cubicle or office. From there on, it's an easy task! For modern Ethernet such as 100Mbps, you just run a short cable from the faceplate on the wall to the user's computer.

The original Ethernet specifications used coaxial cabling instead of twisted-pair wiring or fiber-optic cables. If you're still using an older network, it might be time to upgrade. Don't get me wrong: If you have a specialized environment, such as automation control on a factory floor, you might not need to upgrade this type of network because data transfers will be miniscule when compared to an office network. However, this chapter assumes that you have an office network, which can eat up network bandwidth at tremendous rates. Not only do you have to provide file servers for such mundane tasks as word processing and other data files, but newer applications such as live video streaming can send 10BASE-2 and 100BASE-T networks to the history pile.

Older 10BASE-2 networks used a coaxial cable (referred to by those in the field as *thicknet*) as a backbone, and tapped into this cable (using what is popularly called a *vampire tap*) to drop a smaller coaxial cable (again with a nickname, *thinnet*) to each user's workstation. In an office environment, this type of network is untenable today. Worker productivity is measured in hourly costs. Even a few minutes downloading a document from a file server or creating a report based on data on a remote server costs you money. For an office network, it's time to upgrade.

Note

Of all the types of installed networks today, factory automation probably is the least you need to worry about when it comes to upgrading to the latest whiz-bang technology. These systems tend to be stable and usually use shielded cabling due to the nature of the factory floor, which can contain hundreds of machine tools that can interfere with simple twisted-pair cables. Upgrades to software for management consoles tend to be few and far between. If it works, why change it?

For example, one of the oldest networking technologies, ARCnet (covered in Chapter 13, "The Oldest LAN Protocol Is Still Kicking: ARCnet"), is still providing network services to something you will find in everyday life: point-of-sale terminals. In your local hamburger joint (I mean in your local fast food restaurant), do you need to upgrade to the newest version of Ethernet every few years? It doesn't take a lot of bandwidth to take orders, display them on screens for the hired help, and keep track of transactions performed at the cash register.

The topic of this chapter is the office LAN and network enterprise network. Newer applications, from video conferencing to employees who like to waste time browsing through the Internet, require much more bandwidth than older Ethernet technologies such as 10BASE-2 can provide.

Upgrading from 10BASE-2 or 10BASE-T

Twisted-pair wiring pretty much replaced 10BASE-2 many years ago and was, for a long time, the networking solution of choice. Hubs allowed for centralization of wiring and switches helped localize errors due to faulty cables or network adapter cards.

100BASE-T and gigabit Ethernet solutions are now the de facto standards for creating a new network. If you're creating a network from scratch, it's best to start with the latest and greatest if your budget allows.

Like 10BASE-2 networks, you should ask yourself why you would even want to operate a 10BASE-T network. If you already have one in place, continuing to add new hubs, switches, and routers may make sense, provided this limited bandwidth (10Mbps) can satisfy the demands of your users/applications. However, 100BASE-T (also known as *Fast Ethernet*) has been around for more than 5 years, and is now the most widely used version of Ethernet between the wiring closet and the user desktop.

◀◀ For more information about network topologies and how the physical network should be laid out, see Chapter 3, "Network Design Strategies."

For this reason, this chapter skips upgrading from 10BASE-2 to 10BASE-T because such an upgrade really isn't a good investment. If you're going to swallow the expense of pulling new cabling to replace older coaxial cabling, there's no reason to go to 10BASE-T today. Category 5 cabling can handle both, and almost every network adapter card produced today can operate at 10Mbps as well as 100Mbps. After you've upgraded the cable plant, you might as well go for the added bandwidth of 100Mbps instead.

The rest of this chapter quickly looks at some of the things to consider when planning to replace an older Ethernet network with more modern technology.

Hardware and Software Factors to Consider for 10BASE-2, 10BASE-T, and 100BASE-T

Obviously, it's the hardware that you'll have to replace when making this kind of upgrade. Network protocols, such as TCP/IP, don't care what the underlying physical network is made up of as long as they can get data segments from one place to another. However, you might still be using older software, and if so, you might want to consider upgrading it in addition to the hardware when you plan for this kind of upgrade. As discussed in other parts of this book, Novell's NetWare has basically lost the LAN environment to Unix and Windows NT/2000 and Windows 2003 servers, much less the Windows XP client XP, and even the most recent versions of NetWare can use IP. For NetWare 6, IP is the main protocol, given the emphasis that Novell now puts on Internet access. For the network that you use, whether it be a built-in technology as with Windows or Unix/Linux or an add-on product such as NetWare, the IP protocol remains an underlying factor.

For a historical overview, 10BASE-2 and 10BASE-T have more differences than just the type of cables they use. Although both of them use the same messaging technique (CSMA/CD), their topologies are basically different: 10BASE-2 uses a bus topology, whereas 10BASE-T (and 100BASE-T) installations use a star topology, implemented by a switch, although you might find an older hub still being used. The distances that can be covered by cable segments are also different. The network adapters transmit signals at different speeds. When preparing for an upgrade, check your network inventory to determine which parts of the hardware you'll have to upgrade in addition to the cabling. The major considerations that need to be researched when upgrading from 10BASE-2 to a twisted-pair network are as follows:

- **Network cables**—The fundamental difference between 10BASE-2 and 10BASE-T/100BASE-T is the move from coaxial cable to twisted-pair wiring, usually Category 5 cables, although newer cabling is now being deployed.

◀◀ For more about cables and other relevant components, refer to Chapter 6, "Wiring the Network—Cables, Connectors, Concentrators, and Other Network Components."

- **Network topology**—You'll be going from a linear bus topology to a star topology. The distances covered by 10BASE-T/100BASET are shorter than those allowed using 10BASE-2. But because of the star topology and the uses of switches, you'll actually find it easier to greatly extend the reach of your network.
- **Network adapters**—Older network adapters might have only a BNC connector on them. You'll need cards that provide an RJ-45 jack for 10BASE-T or 100BASE-T. This connector looks much like an ordinary telephone jack, but is slightly larger.
- **Network cable connectors**—Instead of BNC connectors, twisted-pair cabling uses RJ-45 connectors.

■ **Hubs and switches**—Although a 10BASE-2 network allows you to use multiport repeaters, no central wiring devices are actually *required*. For a 10BASE-T/100BASE-T network, you need (at a minimum) a hub to act as a wiring concentrator. Although a lone hub might suffice for a small network with a limited number of users, you should really consider using switches instead because they enable you to further extend the distances covered by a LAN. And it is very unlikely you'll find a hub for sale today.

◄◄ To learn more about how hubs and switches function, see "Bridges, Repeaters, and Hubs," on the upgradingandrepairingpcs.com Web site and Chapter 8, "Network Switches."

For example, if you're using a multiport repeater, replacing it with a more functional hub or switch seemed a natural thing to do a few years ago. However, remember that the topology rules for 10BASE-2 and 10BASE-T networks specify different maximum cable segment lengths, so you might have to relocate wiring closets or make other accommodations if your current distances are too long:

■ Maximum segment length for 10BASE-2: 185 meters

■ Maximum segment length for 10BASE-T/100BASE-T: 100 meters

■ Maximum number of devices on a 10BASE-2 hub segment: 30

■ Maximum number of devices on a 10BASE-T/100BASE-T hub segment: 2 (but one of these is the hub, so effectively, just 1)

◄◄ Chapter 14, "Ethernet: The Universal Standard," covers in more detail the different cabling distances you'll need to consider.

Today, however, using switching technology to replace hubs is about the only option you have today. As stated earlier, you'll find it difficult, if not impossible, to find a hub on the market today. They are legacy devices. If you're going to upgrade your network, consider a switch to be a hub replacement. That doesn't mean you need to discard hubs in small segments of your LAN if you already have them. Indeed, if you connect a few computers that have minimal bandwidth requirements to your LAN, there's really no need to replace a hub with a switch. It all depends on how your users make use of the network. If no one is complaining with a hub connection (which you'll most likely have connected to a switch upstream), don't worry about replacing it. Today it's usually the applications that drive the need for additional network bandwidth. If it's working now and no one is complaining, don't change it.

The main consideration here is the topology requirements used for earlier Ethernet networks. If the cable doesn't provide the distance or bandwidth requirements you need today, you'll have to replace the cabling to accommodate modern networks. In a small LAN environment, this usually isn't the case. In a larger environment, you might have to replace cabling to reach the distances you need, yet still provide the same bandwidth that older equipment (such as hubs) can give to users.

Network Cables

Because 10BASE-2 uses thinnet coaxial cabling, the first upgrade issue you must address is getting the appropriate network cabling.

This should be the simplest decision you have to make. Although it's quite possible to use Category 3 wiring to construct a 10BASE-T (and even a 100BASE-T) network, the only good reason I can think of to do so would be that you already have the wiring in place and can use it with few modifications. Other than that, if you're going to install a 100BASE-T network to replace a network based on coaxial cables, you would be better served to go ahead and use Category 5 cabling or better. Why? Further down the road you might find yourself upgrading to Gigabit Ethernet or even 10 Gigabit Ethernet.

Both of these technologies require Category 5 cables or higher. Although it might seem like Gigabit Ethernet is something that's far in the future, keep in mind that many network administrators didn't think that video on demand would be a requirement today. It's easy to underestimate the network bandwidth that you'll need for future requirements. And because installing the cabling is one of the most labor-intensive (and thus expensive) components of a network upgrade, I recommend that when you decide to upgrade cabling, you go for the latest to protect your investment farther into the future. Indeed, I'd say that your network backbone should already consist of fiber-optic cabling because Gigabit and the newly ratified standard for 10 Gigabit Ethernet operate best using these cables. Both can use ordinary copper cables, but only for very short distances—usually in the wiring closet.

The amount of cable you need might work out to be a lot more than you used for the 10BASE-2 network. Remember that in the bus topology that thinnet (coaxial) networks such as 10BASE-2 use, you can daisy chain one workstation to another using a linear bus. A 50-ohm terminator terminates each end of the bus. The total amount of cable needed is simply the sum of all the cables that are daisy chained together. When using a hub or switch, you can have two workstations sitting right next to each other, both having a 100-meter twisted-wire cable going back to the hub. Because of this, the total amount of cabling you'll need is generally a lot more than you did when you installed 10BASE-2 technology. Yet consider that the cost of twisted-pair wiring is now a lot less expensive that it used to be. The economics of scale always provide for this.

If you instead use a multiport repeater on an existing 10BASE-2 network, and if only one computer is attached to each port, you'll find that replacing the cables is a simple matter of stringing Category 5 (or greater) cables through the same route used by the current coaxial cables. Then all you need to do is replace the repeater with a switch. If you have segments on a multiport repeater that have more than one computer attached, you'll have to plug each computer into a separate port on a switch. Another possibility is to place these computers on a separate switch and connect it to the network backbone.

Note

Another consideration is how you originally installed your coaxial cables. Different jurisdictions have laws that state how electrical and network cables can be installed. They're generally encased in a conduit of some sort, such as a metal pipe. Trying to place several hundred Category 5 cables in a small space that originally contained just one or two coaxial cables might be a problem. Consider this when designing the topology of your new network.

Because you must string cable from a central location to each workstation, you need to have a place you can use as a wiring closet to store the switch and any other interconnecting equipment used to join the LAN to a larger network. Again, if you were using a multiport repeater in your 10BASE-2 network, all you need to do after stringing the cables is to replace the multiport repeater with a switch. Also keep in mind that if you're simply upgrading a small office LAN (5–10 computers), you can use an inexpensive off-the-shelf switch from your local computer store and simply place it out of the way somewhere convenient in the office.

For all practical purposes, consider making backbone connections using fiber-optic cabling. Doing so will give you a much faster connection between LANs today and better prepare you for the future. Keep in mind that the old 80%/20% rule no longer applies. This rule stated that 80% of network traffic remained in the local LAN and 20% was sent to another segment of the LAN. Today, it's more typical to centralize large servers in a computer room and keep LANs separated by switches. Because computers on the LAN need to access these servers, and they might be separated by multiple switches or even routers, you should consider the 80%/20% rule to be reversed. Now 80% of network traffic is directed outside of the local LAN.

Network Adapter Cards

If you had the foresight to purchase the kind of network adapter cards called *combo cards*, which have connectors compatible with both BNC connectors and RJ-45 connectors (see Figure 57.1), this is one piece of hardware you might not necessarily have to replace. The minimum requirement for the NIC is that it have a receptacle to which you can plug in the RJ-45 connector end of the cable to connect the adapter to a hub. However, if you plan to incorporate switches into the network and want servers to use full-duplex connections, you'll probably have to get a newer card for these computers (most older cards supported only 10Mbps and not 100Mbps). Older combo cards enabled you to upgrade from BNC connectors (used by 10BASE-2) to 10BASE-T. Newer cards use the standard RJ-45 jack and allow for 10/100Mbs communications. And today, most of these cards support auto-negotiation and Wake on LAN (WOL) technologies. So, if you're still using combo cards, you can continue to use them, but will most likely be limited to a 10Mbps bandwidth on the network for the workstations that use them.

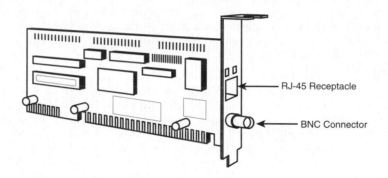

Figure 57.1   A combo card contains connectors for both thinnet coaxial cables (BNC connectors) and a receptacle for an RJ-45 jack used with twisted-pair wiring.

◄◄   To learn about the latest developments in network adapter cards, including technologies such as auto-negotiation, WOL, and even newer stuff such as PC Cards and wireless network adapters, refer to Chapter 7, "Network Interface Cards."

If you're going to have to upgrade a large number of workstations to newer NICs, think carefully about the future when you make this purchase. No matter what your budget is, there's absolutely no reason to buy a 10Mbps network card, if you can still find one. At the bare minimum, a 10/100Mbps card that can support your older network as well as Fast Ethernet is the best choice to make. Why? Because the price of network adapter cards has fallen so low that you can now find 10/100Mbps cards (depending on the features they support) for less than $20–$30, and for even less at some computer stores and online retailers. If you purchase in quantity from a catalog reseller, you might even find greater reductions in price. Network adapter cards in this range are now commodity items. You can even buy them at department stores such as Wal-Mart.

Network Cable Connectors

As already pointed out earlier in this chapter, a 10BASE-2 network uses a different kind of connector than a 10BASE-T/100BASE-T network does. You should pay attention to the details when ordering connectors (if you plan to make cables yourself) or when ordering ready-made cables that have the connectors attached. When upgrading to twisted-pair wiring, I've already suggested that you use Category 5 cabling (or greater) instead of a less capable variety, such as Category 3. This enables you to use the cabling later when you decide it's time to install 100Mbps segments on part or all or part of the network. Keep in mind that Gigabit Ethernet adapters are already available and the standard for 10 Gigabit Ethernet has just been approved. Although you might not find these speeds required for a workstation connection, they will probably figure into server and backbone connections in just a few years or even less. And because predictions of this sort tend to be conservative, think proactively and investigate the costs of these cards and the switches/routers that support them! Better to pay the more expensive up-front cost now than have to switch out a lot of cards at a lower price in the future.

Connectors, like cables, can exhibit different performance characteristics depending on how they're manufactured. Be sure that the RJ-45 connectors you choose are compliant with the specifications for Category 5 cables. Inferior connectors can cause a lot of trouble later (such as noise or near-end cross-talk), causing you to spend a lot of time troubleshooting. When constructing your own cables, be sure that you follow the specifications when attaching the jacks to the cables. Many noisy cables are created simply because too much wire is left exposed at the end of the cable where the cable is attached to the connector.

◄◄   In Chapter 6, you'll find more information about cables and connectors and the problems you can encounter when they aren't manufactured correctly.

Bridges, Hubs, Repeaters, and Switches

To extend the length of a LAN based on 10BASE-2 technology, the standard technique is to attach multiple segments with a bridge or a multiport repeater. A repeater works similar to a hub: It simply makes one large broadcast domain out of the various cable segments that are connected to it. A bridge connects two segments, but is capable of learning MAC addresses. Therefore, a bridge can reduce traffic by passing on frames to segments only if their destination isn't on the local segment from which they originate.

▶▶   For more information about bridges and how they operate, see "Bridges, Repeaters, and Hubs" on the upgradingandrepairingpcs.com Web site.

You can use bridges on a 100BASE-T network for the same purposes you would use them in 10BASE-2. They can group similar users on local segments, reduce traffic on individual segments, and extend the length of the local area network. Bridges can perform other functions related to performance as well, such as discarding packets with errors and reducing noise. Newer layer 3 switches accomplish much of the same function by reducing traffic between segments and between specific ports on the switch. Since the previous edition of this book was published, the price of switches has decreased dramatically. Because of this, and its superior performance capabilities on anything but a very small network, I advise using a switch rather than a hub. Hubs should be considered to be legacy devices. You probably won't be able to find hubs on sale anymore because switches have replaced them and offer much better performance.

Network applications are becoming more data intensive than ever before as computers become faster and more memory is added. A switch creates a small collision domain (that is, just the switch and the computer attached to a switch port) and can drastically reduce network congestion.

Note

For more information on how switches work and how they can be used to improve performance in your network, refer to Chapter 8. Hubs are now becoming difficult, if not impossible, to find. Even in small networks, switches are now the wiring concentrator of choice. Hubs share bandwidth among all the network segments attached. Switches limit the collision domain and give the full bandwidth to each computer attached. If you're still using an old hub you bought just a few years ago, you should go ahead and upgrade to a switch.

Also, in anything but a small network, you might need to use more than one switch to connect user workstations to the network. If you're planning ahead for a future migration to 100Mbps networking, you'll find that a multitude of switches operate at both 10Mbps and 100Mbs. Look at the cost difference and decide whether making an investment in a 10/100Mbps device now will save you money in the future. Most switches support both speeds, as well as auto-negotiation to determine what types of devices are attached to each port.

A more important factor to consider when evaluating a switch is to find out whether it comes with management software that's compliant with SNMP and RMON standards. Check to find out whether each port can be set to a different speed. If it can, make sure that you know whether it's autosensing or if you must manually set it to operate at one speed or the other.

◄◄ The Simple Network Management Protocol (SNMP) and RMON (Remote Monitoring) are discussed in detail in Chapter 53, "Network Testing and Analysis Tools."

If your existing network already uses a router to connect to a larger network, be sure that the hub or switch has a receptacle that can be used for the router connection. Most routers made today accept cables terminated with several different kinds of connectors, even 10BASE-2, so this probably won't be a problem. However, you should check this as you do all aspects of the network when making an upgrade plan. Note also that the connection between the switch and a router might need to provide for a larger bandwidth than the connection from the switch to the user's desktop. Although 10Mbps or 100Mbps might be suitable for some end-user applications, when you aggregate this bandwidth and add up the amount of network traffic that will be needed on the entire network, you might want to consider a switch that can use a faster connection—such as fiber-optic cables—when it connects to another hub or a router.

◄◄ For more information about using routers to join individual network subnets, refer to Chapter 10, "Routers," and Chapter 37, "Routing Protocols."

Connecting Networks That Use Different Cables or Topologies

Because switches, like routers, can be found with different kinds of ports that are used to link them (uplink ports), it's possible that you can incrementally upgrade your network, depending on such factors as the size of the broadcast domain and the number of users on each network segment. For example, you might want to replace one multiport repeater with a hub or switch in one department, while leaving another existing multiport repeater in place for a while.

If you need to maintain backward compatibility by keeping a multiport repeater on the network for a while during the upgrade process, you can use a hub or switch that has a BNC port and connect the two using thinwire Ethernet cables. Or you can connect each of these two devices to separate ports on a router, and create different subnets on your network.

◄◄ Subnets, and how to calculate subnet addresses and subnet masks, are covered in Chapter 14.

Other Possibilities

This chapter covered the basic components that you need to change when converting a network from 10BASE-2 to 10BASE-T and 100BASE-T, which are the most prevalent network standards in place today. However, in addition to the cables, connectors, network adapters, and other devices, a change such as this one might warrant further research into the larger network to which you're connected. In many cases, the local LAN is in reality part of a much larger network. When you have resources that are frequently accessed and lie outside the local LAN, you might need to look at the big picture when making decisions about the local area network. Consider the following:

- Do you need to replace the equipment that has been used to connect to the larger network?
- Are you currently using a bridge that can be replaced by a switch to improve performance?
- Do you have multiple small LANs that can now be merged into a single larger LAN connected by multiple switches?

Upgrading the Network Backbone to Gigabit Ethernet

Today Gigabit Ethernet has arrived, in a big way. You won't find many people using Gigabit to the desktop yet (although in some high-end environments, such as video production, you just might). But as a backbone transport, Gigabit is an ideal replacement for Fast Ethernet or other protocols used to transfer high-bandwidth traffic.

The initial cost for implementing Gigabit Ethernet as a backbone transport doesn't have to be a large expense. Consider what happens when you replace local switches and network adapter cards—a large expense can be involved due to the high number of workstations and switch ports required.

However, if you're replacing a switch that consolidates traffic from these existing switches, you have only to replace these switches and possibly the cabling between these switches. Consider the collapsed backbone topology discussed in Chapter 2, "Overview of Network Topologies." You don't replace every departmental LAN switch. Instead, a collapsed backbone means that department level switches all feedback to a single larger switch that controls traffic between each of the departmental switches. So, if the departmental switches satisfy your users' needs, you'd have to replace only the central switch that connects them. Gigabit (and now 10 Gigabit Ethernet) is ideal for network backbone transport. You can use this technology to connect backbone switches to others in different buildings in a campus environment, and further localize network traffic. It will still be a few years before it's used to the desktop.

Using Gigabit Ethernet for High-End Servers

Another upgrade you might want to perform using Gigabit or 10 Gigabit Ethernet is for server connections. A single file server connected to a switch can be limited by the total bandwidth of all the workstations that connect to it through a single switch or a cascade of switches. For a high-end server, the CPU(s) and disk array (which could even be a fast storage area network) might not be the bottleneck where performance is concerned. Instead, you might find that you need to use multiple network adapter cards and make several connections between the switch and the server. Whether or not this is the situation, upgrading the server by using Gigabit Ethernet cards can dramatically increase performance. The switch can perform buffering between lower-bandwidth workstations and the server that's now equipped with much faster adapter cards.

A good way to determine whether the network card is the bottleneck is to use a good network analyzer to determine the utilization of the connection between the computer and the switch. If it's approaching 80% (in a full-duplex connection), you should definitely consider replacing the network card.

The other component you'll have to replace is the switch to one that supports Gigabit Ethernet. That doesn't mean you have to replace any downstream switches because they will feed into the new switch, with network traffic being funneled into the server by the new switch that supports both Gigabit Ethernet as well as Fast Ethernet ports for connections to the other switches or workstations.

Gigabit Ethernet to the Desktop?

Ethernet adapters that you can use in desktop workstations are available now. However, there's no reason to consider placing them into a typical user's workstation. Unless you also replace the switches between the workstation and the server(s) it uses, the switches that lie in between become a limiting factor.

But if your business involves such things as video editing or other high-end graphics applications, swapping out old adapter cards and switches might be a good idea. The main thing to consider here is whether the workstation can handle the Gigabit Ethernet bandwidth that the adapter provides. Again, use performance monitoring to be sure that the TCP/IP stack or the CPU of the workstation is not a limiting factor that makes the Gigabit Ethernet card merely something to talk about. If the workstation can't process the bandwidth that the card can deliver, you're wasting money! Use the cash in other parts of the network (such as the backbone)!

Gigabit Ethernet Can Cover the Distance

One of the main reasons for replacing network backbone segments with Gigabit Ethernet (and 10 Gigabit Ethernet) network adapters and switches is that the backbone carries a much larger amount of network traffic today than departmental switches do. Each local LAN switch merely needs to make connections for workstations that probably use very little of the 100Mbps bandwidth for the majority of the time. Yes, when you're using FTP to download a file from a remote server, it can be frustrating because of the time involved. But if most of the work performed on the server falls into the typical office scenario type of work (word processing, spreadsheets, presentations), the network bandwidth usage is sporadic and you don't need to use Gigabit Ethernet to make a connection to the network for this type of workstation.

However, when you consider consolidating network traffic from hundreds, if not thousands of workstations and the file and print servers they use, Gigabit Ethernet (and now 10 Gigabit Ethernet) is a viable solution. First, the technology provides a much faster bandwidth. Second, when using fiber-optic cabling (copper cabling is pretty much confined to the wiring closet for these technologies), the distances you can cover are measured in kilometers instead of meters. You might find that you can connect buildings that are much farther apart without having to use an intermediary switch or router due to the distance that Gigabit Ethernet technologies can cover. For example, when using single-mode fiber optic cabling with a 1300-nanometer laser, you can cover distances of at least 10 kilometers.

10 Gigabit Ethernet Is Becoming Economically Feasible

The standard for 10 Gigabit Ethernet was finalized in 2002. Just as Gigabit Ethernet equipment is now available that conforms to the established standards. In 2002, the 10 Gigabit Ethernet was finished. For this reason it might be considered as a replacement for older backbone technologies mentioned earlier in this chapter. Gigabit Ethernet is the more cost-effective technology today.

Upgrading from Bridges and Hubs to Routers and Switches

SOME OF THE MAIN TOPICS IN THIS CHAPTER ARE

CHAPTER 58

You can use many kinds of network devices to expand a local area network (LAN) or to connect it to a wide area network (WAN). They range from simple repeaters to devices with more intelligence, such as bridges, routers, and switches. For the most part, traditional bridges have been replaced with switches. Both segregate network traffic to specific ports, but switches do so on a computer-by-computer basis, whereas traditional bridges do so based on LAN segments.

Note

Hubs, low-end repeaters, and simple bridges are generally not the best choice for networks today. Instead, switches have pretty much replaced them in the marketplace. Where hubs or multiport repeaters still exist, they're being replaced as applications and workstations require more and more bandwidth. For more information about these legacy devices, see "Bridges, Repeaters, and Hubs" on the **upgradingandrepairingpcs.com** Web site.

As a small LAN grew in the past, it was common to use bridges to segment a few small workgroups. Bridges were used to isolate local traffic among groups of users and thus cut down on the overall traffic on the LAN. However, depending on the kind of network (for example, ARCnet, Ethernet, or Token-Ring), there are limits to how many bridges (repeaters) could be used in a LAN. In addition to their usefulness in solving network traffic congestion problems, you can use routers or switches to solve several other problems: expanding the LAN beyond the size that bridges allow and connecting the LAN to other LANs to create a larger local network, or for a connection to a WAN, such as the Internet. In short, switches and routers offer the following benefits:

- Switches enable you to expand the LAN because they greatly limit the collision domain and switch traffic from one port to another, avoiding broadcasting packets unnecessarily on ports that don't have a route to the packet's destination.

- Routers enable you to connect to a much larger collection of networks, such as the Internet, and enable you to organize a large LAN into a hierarchical address space and many subnets.

◄◄ You can find out more about how routers and switches function by reading Chapter 8, "Network Switches," and Chapter 10, "Routers."

A traditional bridge has just about outlived its usefulness in a modern network. Instead, switches (which are really glorified multiple bridges all in one box) and routers can be used to better segment a LAN and limit unnecessary network traffic on local LAN segments.

Note

The term *bridge* is used in this chapter to refer to a legacy device that connects several network segments and is used to limit network traffic to local segments.

Other types of bridges exist that are important in networking today. For example, there are translational bridges that can convert frames from one format to another, enabling you to connect different types of LANs. Another example is a SCSI-to–Fibre Channel bridge that enables you to connect legacy SCSI devices to a Fibre-Channel network, thus preserving your investment in older disks, tape drives, and so on.

In this chapter, the possibilities offered by upgrading to switches and routers are discussed, along with information you must consider when bringing such devices into your LAN.

Growing Beyond a Small LAN

Several chapters in this book cover the basic devices used to interconnect network segments: repeaters, bridges, switches, and routers. Each of these devices builds on the one previous to it so that together they span a continuum of functionality that you can use to solve problems with a LAN or WAN. Standard bridges were developed to enable you to extend the reach of a LAN and to limit traffic to local segments, therefore building on the function of repeaters. Switches took this concept further by enabling each workstation or server to have its own physical LAN segment, thus limiting the broadcast domain (just the workstation and the switch). Routers enable you to extend the reach of a LAN by connecting it to a wide area network.

Note

A switch that operates in full-duplex mode eliminates the collision domain between the switch port and the device attached to it. Instead of using the same set of wires for transmitting and receiving data (half-duplex), full-duplex switches use separate wires for transmitting and receiving, so both ends of the path can be sending information at the same time. Thus, a switch port and network card operating in full-duplex mode can essentially double the network bandwidth.

To quickly summarize:

- *Repeaters* are simple devices that connect network segments (usually two segments). They repeat all traffic and thus do nothing to help segment network traffic patterns. Repeaters are used to expand a LAN when it grows beyond the limitations imposed by a single network segment. Multiport repeaters function in the same way, but resemble a hub in that more than one segment can be connected to a multiport repeater. However, multiport repeaters are typically used in much older environments that use coaxial cables for the network media and use BNC connectors. Most hubs have RJ-45 jacks and receive twisted-pair wiring with RJ-45 modular connectors. If your network still uses repeaters of this type, you're long overdue for an upgrade.

- *Bridges* are similar to repeaters except that they apply a little intelligence to the packet-forwarding process: Bridges learn MAC addresses of devices on each segment when they make an initial transmission. From then on, a bridge will not pass traffic to another segment if it knows the recipient is on the segment local to the transmission. Bridges are helpful for expanding a LAN and can be used to group collections of computers and servers that commonly interact to lower overall bandwidth consumption.

- *Routers* work like bridges in that they're selective about which packets get forwarded on which ports. However, whereas bridges operate at layer 2 of the OSI reference model (the Data Link layer) and look only at the flat namespace provided by the MAC addresses, routers operate at layer 3 (the Network layer) and make decisions based on the addressing scheme provided by a higher-level networking protocol. Bridges are typically used to create larger local area networks. Connecting a LAN to other LANs or to a larger WAN can be done using a router.

- *Switches* are the current technology for connecting network LAN segments as well as for connecting individual network nodes to the network. Switches operate like bridges in that they keep track of which network node is located on each port by remembering MAC addresses. When retransmitting an incoming packet, the switch will send it out only on a port that will get it to its destination, provided that it has already learned the destination's MAC address. Whereas bridges usually have only two ports, switches are like hubs and contain many ports. Most switches will allow for full-duplex operation, thus effectively doubling the available network bandwidth for a single node connected on a segment. In a sense, a switch operates like a collection of bridges. And don't forget that you can connect one switch to another to further localize network traffic. A LAN today can consist of multiple layers of switches that eventually connect to a router.

From this summary, you can see that it's easy to use repeaters or bridges to grow the small LAN, but when it becomes necessary to expand beyond certain limits or when it becomes necessary to make a connection to a larger LAN, you must incorporate routers or switches. Growth is not the only reason you might want to use a router or switch, however. These devices also can be used in a small LAN. For example, a small LAN that's experiencing network traffic congestion might find relief by replacing the hubs in the LAN with switches to cut down on the overall network traffic. Indeed, if you look at the price of a switch today, the benefits you will achieve in network bandwidth are well worth the price. When users begin to complain about network response time in a network that uses hubs, you should definitely consider replacing hubs with switches.

In addition to connecting LANs to larger networks such as the Internet, routers can be used in a campus LAN to allow network administrators to logically group network segments using the addressing scheme provided by TCP/IP (subnetting), for example.

Segmenting the Network Can Improve Performance

You might need to segment devices on the network for many different reasons. These include the following:

- **Topology limitations**—You need to add more nodes to the network but the expansion will break distance limitations or maximum nodes-per-segment rules. This is usually the case only in older Ethernet LANs where the broadcast domain was constrained by the round-trip time.

◀◀   For more information about topology limitations, refer to Chapter 14, "Ethernet: The Universal Standard."

- **Networking protocol limitations**—Address space is fragmented and you need to connect segments that have different network addresses. This can happen when two companies merge and both already have an address space in place for their respective networks. It's much easier to simply place one or more routers between the two networks than it is to reassign network addresses to the many devices on the network. When using DHCP to configure workstations, this might not be a limitation, provided that you have an address space that can accommodate all the devices that will be placed on the larger network.

- **Network bandwidth limitations**—When a few high-performance servers or workstations consume too much of the segment's available bandwidth, it's time to segment the LAN (create additional subnets) and thus limit network traffic to smaller segments that contain fewer devices.

- **Security reasons**—An Ethernet adapter set to *promiscuous mode* can intercept all packets that are sent out on a particular segment, for example. You need to place a few high security workstations on their own segment, yet allow some kind of connection to the rest of the network. Keep in mind that in an Ethernet network that uses hubs as a wiring concentrator, every device on the hub (or hubs) can see every network frame that's broadcast on the LAN. It isn't difficult to download a program from an Internet source to read every packet that passes through the network.

Note

Security is an important topic in computer networks today. For more information about the issues you should consider, refer to Chapter 46, "Basic Security Measures Every Network Administrator Needs to Know," and Chapter 48, "Security Issues for Wide Area Networks." Other chapters that might help you understand how to protect your network include Chapter 49, "Firewalls," and Chapter 50, "Virtual Private Networks (VPNs) and Tunneling."

- **Geographically distant connections**—It's best to segment each geographic location to ensure that unnecessary traffic isn't being sent across the remote connection and wasting valuable bandwidth. Some routers provide a dial-up function so that a dedicated link isn't necessary, providing an inexpensive way to use routers to connect branch offices.

Depending on which combination of these reasons applies to your situation, a router or switch might be the solution you need to segment the network.

Connecting Remote Locations

When a business expands geographically, you'll find that using bridges to connect remote locations isn't a feasible solution. There are many different technologies from which you can choose today—from simple dedicated lines to ATM and Frame Relay—to connect geographically distant locations. For these connections, you'll find it necessary to incorporate routers or switches. You'll also find these methods of transport expensive. Today, it isn't unreasonable to consider connecting the local network to the Internet with a router that provides virtual private network (VPN) capabilities. Thus, by using an inexpensive connection to the Internet (far cheaper than using leased dedicated lines), you can still provide a secure channel to remote branch locations.

◀◀   ATM (Asynchronous Transfer Mode) and Frame Relay are very common protocols used to send data across long distances. You can learn more about these in Chapter 16, "Dedicated Connections."

When to Use a Router

Routers are similar to bridges only in the fact that they can both be used to connect multiple network segments. Whereas bridges make all their decisions based on the MAC address of a particular network packet, routers access the addressing information provided by a higher-level protocol to decide how to best forward a packet. Using the OSI reference model (see Appendix A, "Overview of the OSI Seven-Layer Networking Reference Model"), you can see that the bridge operates at layer 2, the Data Link layer, whereas routers operate at layer 3, the Network layer. With bridges, the address space is flat: It's simply the MAC addresses associated with nodes on each segment, each one unique. For protocols operating at the Network layer, the address space becomes more complicated because there must be a mechanism for identifying the network as well as the individual node.

Note

To be more specific, routers operate at layer 3 of the OSI model by using higher-level addresses (such as IP) to make routing decisions. However, when the network frame reaches a router that can deliver it to its final destination, the router uses the MAC address to communicate with the destination node connected to the router's port. The Address Resolution Protocol (ARP) is used on local segments to translate between IP addresses and MAC addresses. For more information about ARP, refer to Chapter 25, "Overview of the TCP/IP Protocol Suite."

When to Use a Switch

Switches are one of the fastest growing categories of network equipment. They can act as a wiring concentrator for a LAN just as a hub does, but they also can make available a much larger bandwidth to clients because they selectively forward traffic from one port to another based on the destination address of each packet. When you use a switch with only one node attached to each port, you are in effect creating a collection of broadcast domains that consist of only two network nodes: the switch and the client node connected to the port. For network adapters and switches that support full-duplex operation, the effective bandwidth is doubled for each client and there is no broadcast domain between the two.

From Bridges to Routers

Routers are inherently slower than bridges when it comes to forwarding network packets. This is because a router must read further into each network frame to get Network layer addressing information, whereas a bridge merely looks at a fixed location for the MAC address. Hubs, bridges, and switches can be set up in a short amount of time and usually require little or no configuration.

Routers require that the network administrator configure networking information for each port that's used. The command set available to configure a router is quite large because it's a very flexible device and can be confusing for a novice. The kinds of information you need to configure a new router are

- A list of the network protocols for which you'll be using the router. For example, TCP/IP or IPX/SPX.
- The routing protocol that you'll use for each network protocol. For example, RIP.
- Whether or not you'll need to set filters to block certain addresses or IP or UDP ports—a technique used to create a simple firewall.
- Information about the address space used on each segment the router will connect.

◄◄   For additional information about routing protocols, refer to Chapter 37, "Routing Protocols."

Network Protocol Issues

In many networks, more than one network protocol is used on the same medium. To do their job, routers need configuration information about each protocol for each port. For example, because each port on the router connects to a different network segment, each port must have a unique network address that it can use to communicate on the segment. If you plan to restrict some segments for security or other reasons, you'll need to create a set of access control lists (ACLs) for each port, which indicate which frames are allowed through, in both directions.

◄◄   Using routers to restrict network traffic is often referred to as *packet filtering*. For more information about this technology, refer to Chapter 49.

When using a router to connect to a larger WAN, you'll probably be faced with having to configure a port on the router that uses a WAN protocol, such as Frame Relay, in addition to protocols you're already familiar with on your network. With a WAN connection, you'll have to coordinate your activities with other system administrators to ensure that the router is configured with the correct information for the larger network.

Network Addressing Issues

Because the router makes decisions based on a higher-level networking protocol, such as IP, you'll have to take into consideration your current address space when you decide to introduce a router into the network. If you're adding new segments to the LAN and have the freedom to choose a new network address, this can be an easy task. If you're going to take an existing LAN and use a router to separate it into more manageable segments, you have two possible choices. You can use your original network address for one segment and create new networks on the remaining segments or you can use subnetting.

Note

To connect to the Internet, you'll have to obtain an IP address that is valid on the Internet. Due to the rapid growth of the Internet, the addresses supported by IP version 4 (IPv4) are slowly becoming exhausted. When IPv6 becomes widely implemented, the fields that store IP addresses will increase from 32 bits to 128 bits. This single factor will increase the available addresses from 2^{32} (about 4.29 billion) to 2^{128} (about 340 undecillion—and for reference, 1 undecillion is a 1 followed by 36 zeros!) so that just about every grain of sand on the Earth can have its own IP address. Until then, it's becoming more common to use a set of reserved IP addresses that are valid only on your local network, and to use fewer IP addresses to access the Internet. The technique called network address translation (NAT) makes this possible. This method also helps to keep outsiders from gaining knowledge about the addresses of your clients, and that helps increase security at your site. To understand how NAT works and the addresses you can use on the local network, refer to Chapter 49.

Regardless, you'll have to then reconfigure each client with new addressing information. If you're using DHCP, the process is made simpler because you can make the changes at a central location and have clients request the new information after the changes have been made. DHCP is the most prevalent method used today to configure workstations and other non-server devices on a network.

If you're going to use a router to connect your LAN to a larger corporate network, you might not have to make any addressing changes on your network, depending on the company's overall network plan. You'll still have to configure the ports, however. If you're going to connect the LAN to the Internet, using a router configured as a firewall might be something to consider.

Other Router Management Issues

Routers are very much like smart PCs that have been customized to perform the routing function efficiently. They have CPUs, memory, and I/O ports just like an ordinary PC. They also have an operating system, which is subject to periodic updates by the manufacturer. So, in addition to learning how to configure the router, you'll also need to become familiar with the commands used for such functions as saving a copy of the system image to a server for backup purposes and performing troubleshooting and testing.

Managing a network that uses routers can seem a difficult task at first. However, by enabling you to organize your network according to the hierarchical network address spaces used by upper-level network protocols, the initial configuration problems will be worth the effort.

Tip

The best way to learn how to configure your router is to read the documentation. The most popular routers today for LANs are made by Cisco Systems. Its documentation site, which you can reach online at http://www.cisco.com/ univercd/home/home.htm, provides documentation for almost all of Cisco's products. On this page, select Cisco IOS Software and you'll find a wealth of information about router setup and configuration. Because of the in-depth content, you can use this site to learn not just about configuring Cisco routers, but also the concepts behind protocols and other information that can be helpful no matter what kind of router is used on your network. For students, this is an excellent source of information.

Using a Router to Segment the Network

Like bridges, routers can be used to isolate traffic between network segments. Unlike bridges, routers further reduce network bandwidth use because they do not pass broadcast messages from one segment to another unless programmed to do so. A router also does not have to take time to learn which nodes are connected to each segment. The information it needs is configured in advance—the administrator assigns protocols and addresses to each port. Routing protocols also use various methods to update each other about network topology as it changes.

One very important reason why routers are used to help organize a network into segments is that routers enable you to connect many network segments. Whereas bridges are limited to a few thousand nodes, depending on the topology used, routers can enable the LAN to be connected to an infinitely larger WAN, such as the Internet.

The internal processing that routers must perform make them slower than bridges (although that might not be the case with most high-end routers being manufactured today), which need to examine only a small amount of data in the packet header. Although this performance difference will not be noticed on network segments with only moderate traffic use, you might find that you need to place routers at only strategic locations throughout the network, retaining switches for connecting other computers or network segments. Remember that you can connect individual computers to a switch port or use the port to connect to other switches.

The method you use will depend on the usage patterns that can be monitored for each segment and the cost of the links used to connect different segments. Another thing to consider is that many of the high-end routers available today operate at what is called "wire speed." That means they can route packets at virtually the same speed as the network medium, with just the very slightest delay for processing time.

Connecting to a Larger WAN or the Internet

When connecting the LAN to a WAN, a router is required. When connecting to the Internet, for example, you cannot use a bridge or a repeater. The Internet is composed of a hierarchical IP address space and a router is needed to participate in this hierarchy. Or you might plan to use a dedicated line of some sort to connect to a larger corporate network. In that case, placing a router between your LAN and the WAN hardware, such as an ATM switch connection, will help reduce the traffic that crosses the expensive dedicated connection by keeping local traffic confined to the local network segments.

Note

There are two situations in which a router is not needed to make an Internet connection. The first is if you have a modem-based dial-up connection. Although it's possible to set up routing tables in operating systems such as Windows and Unix/Linux, this isn't really a practical method for connecting a small office LAN to the Internet due to the very limited speed.

The other situation is when you use a broadband connection, such as a cable or DSL modem. In this case, you can connect the high-bandwidth modem to a single computer and then set up routing tables so that other computers can send and receive traffic through the computer, which operates as a router. However, there's a better idea in a Small Office/Home Office (SOHO) environment or a home environment where everyone from the parents to the kids have their own computers: Purchase an inexpensive 4–6 port router (for less than $100 in most cases) that you can connect to the cable/DSL modem. These types of routers require very little knowledge about computers and can usually be set up in less than a half-hour. For more information about configuring a SOHO environment, see Chapter 17, "Digital Subscriber Lines (DSL) Technology," Chapter 18, "Using a Cable Modem," and Chapter 54, "Troubleshooting Small Office and Home Office (SOHO) Networks."

Although you'll certainly have to configure the ports that connect the local LAN and the WAN interface, you might have to reconfigure addressing information on clients. For example, if you're already using a valid TCP/IP network address, possibly a subnet of the corporate network address space, you'll need to configure only routers.

If your business has just been acquired by a larger concern, however, you might find that your LAN has been assigned a new subnet by the larger corporation. In such a case, you'll probably have to plan on downtime for end users in order to make changes to important servers, such as Domain Name System (DNS) servers. DHCP servers (which workstations can find themselves) are used to translate between user-friendly names (such as http://www.twoinc.com) and IP addresses. Although DHCP can dynamically assign configuration information to workstations, important servers, such as DNS servers or gateways to other networks (usually routers), must have a static (unchanging) address. This is because part of the configuration information that DHCP supplies to clients is those addresses! If the address of a DNS server changed with every reboot of the server, you would have to reconfigure the information on each workstation client—a tedious effort even in a small network!

By using DHCP, you can overcome client configuration headaches such as this. Just reconfigure the DHCP server with the address range for the new subnet, add in the DNS servers and default gateway, and reboot your client computers. This is a simple explanation of the information supplied by DHCP servers. Indeed, you can use DHCP to provide configuration information for many other network parameters.

◄◄   For more information about using DHCP and how it works, refer to Chapter 29, "BOOTP and Dynamic Host Configuration Protocol (DHCP)."

From Bridges to Switches

Switches can be useful for solving network problems related to traffic congestion and network segmentation. For example, they can be used as replacements for hubs at the LAN level. In Figure 58.1, you can see a small LAN that uses two hubs. The three servers for this network share a common broadcast domain with all the other users on the network.

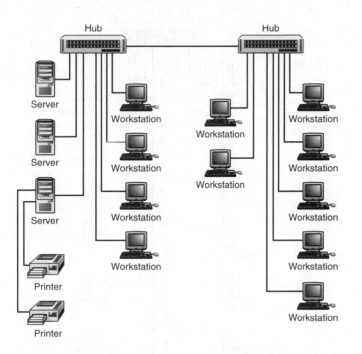

Figure 58.1   Hubs do nothing to limit network traffic on the LAN.

When this older LAN was first installed, there was more than adequate bandwidth available and users were satisfied with the response time. Over time, however, each server was replaced with a more powerful model, and some of the end users' workstations were replaced with high-performance machines and new database software that relies on information stored on the servers.

Network traffic has increased considerably, users are dissatisfied, and the network administrator must take action. Because the main problem is the traffic exchanged between the servers and the high-performance end-user workstations, a switch can be a simple solution. There are two simple solutions you could devise using switches. In Figure 58.2, you can see that both of the 8-port hubs have been replaced with a single 16-port switch.

Tip

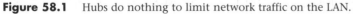

Throughout this book, I keep emphasizing that hubs are now legacy devices. For large networks, this is true. If you're using a small inexpensive hub for a SOHO network and you don't experience a slow network response time, there is no reason to "switch." However, when contemplating any new network installations or an upgrade, there's absolutely no reason today to consider purchasing a hub because switches are around the same price as hubs (even at the high-end level).

Indeed, you'll find it difficult to find larger hubs on the market anymore, except by vendors who want to support older networks.

An exception to this rule is that in a larger LAN, you might still use a hub (connected upstream to a switch) for a few users whose bandwidth is minimal. In that case, replacing a perfectly good hub would cost more in labor costs—much the cost of a replacement switch. Therefore, in larger LANs, hubs can still be used in very small departments that don't have high-bandwidth needs.

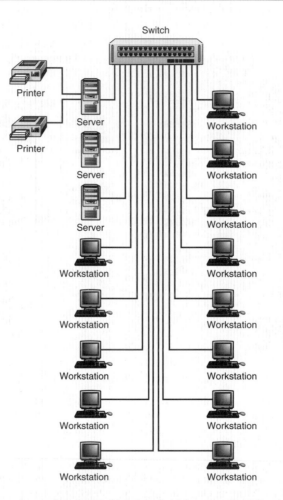

Figure 58.2 A switch can be used to isolate high bandwidth network nodes.

This layout gives each node that is connected to the switch a full 10Mbps network connection or more likely 100Mbps, depending on your hardware. If you can't afford to replace older 10Mbps network cards (which is a possibility in a large network with a few hundred or thousands of computers), you might not need to worry. Most modern switches support autosensing, so they can detect both 10Mbps as well as 100Mbps traffic, and you can thus connect both types of network adapter cards to the switch. Even switches that support autosensing don't always work with older network adapters, so you can use the management software that accompanies the switch to manually set ports that don't behave as you would expect. Check your network traffic using a switch's built-in monitoring software to ensure that you're obtaining the maximum bandwidth that the switch port and network card enable you to use. Otherwise, you should disable the autosensing function and set both the switch port and the network card to the desired speed.

Each connection on a switch is a broadcast domain with only two end nodes: the connected workstation or server and the switch. In this solution, the server nodes were equipped with full-duplex network adapters, effectively doubling their available network bandwidth. Provided that the switch is capable of handling the traffic load, individual users on the workstations that make only moderate use of the network should notice a better response time through the switch, as compared to a hub connection.

The servers and high-performance workstations should also notice better performance, but their network traffic is no longer broadcast on the segments of the other moderate users, effectively isolating this traffic. For example, in Figure 58.3, you can see another solution discussed a paragraph or so earlier. Here, a hub is used for the workstations that use the network only moderately.

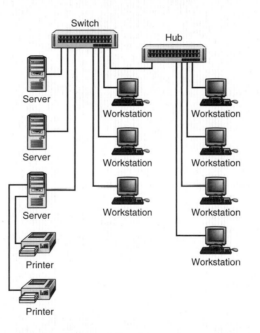

Figure 58.3   Traffic on the hub is not hampered by the traffic generated by the other high-performance servers and workstations.

Here each of the three servers that are responsible for much of the bandwidth use has been placed on a separate port on the switch. Again, full-duplex network adapters were installed to further increase the available bandwidth to each server. The three high-performance workstations also were placed on separate switch ports so that their network use does not directly interfere with other nodes. A hub was retained for connecting moderate network users. Because these nodes do not generate a lot of network communications, placing them on a hub connected to the switch should allow them fast communications among themselves while still allowing access to the other servers and workstations.

Adding Wireless Networking to a LAN

59

SOME OF THE MAIN TOPICS IN THIS CHAPTER ARE

CHAPTER 59

Wireless networking is one of the fastest growing segments of the networking industry that your end users will probably be aware of. Because the IEEE 802.11b Wi-Fi standard has recently helped to bring some order to the chaos of non-interoperability that has existed these past few years, the price of wireless LAN equipment has fallen dramatically and it has become much easier to implement. However, you should consider whether you really need to use wireless networking in your LAN before you decide to implement it. Wireless networking isn't a solution looking for a problem. Indeed, there are many problems that wireless networking can solve. If you have the need, you should consider using a wireless solution. If you simply have eager users that want fun new things to play with, you should reconsider and think about the management, security, and troubleshooting tasks you'll have to deal with.

One particular environment that can benefit greatly from wireless networking is the small office/home office (SOHO) network. Wireless networks are easier to install than having to run cables everywhere.

Note

In addition to the popular 802.11b standard, two newer standards were recently approved: IEEE 802.11a, which provides a faster transmission rate than 802.11b but operates in a higher frequency radio spectrum, and 802.11g, which operates in the same radio spectrum as 802.11b. Don't be confused by the letters following the 802.11. The b standard was approved before the a standard. The 802.11a standard does give you a much faster network—up to 54Mbps as compared to 11Mbps for 802.11b. However, for most small SOHO networks, 11Mbps is more than you need at this time. The 802.11g standard also provides for a 54Mbps data transmission rate. You can read more about both of these standards in Chapters 20, "IEEE 802.11b: It's Here and It's Inexpensive," and 21, "Faster Service: IEEE 802.11a."

Why Go Wireless?

Wireless networking has its place in the home, small office, and enterprise environments. You can use an inexpensive access point to create a network of just a few computers, or you can use multiple access points (APs) throughout a large company to further enable mobility of your networked clients.

There are many good reasons to use wireless networking. First, it's a quick way to set up a peer-to-peer network that is needed for only a short period of time, such as in a home office where you only have two or three computers that need a link and you don't want to be running network cables through your walls. For the home environment, wireless networking may be the perfect choice because it not only eliminates the necessity of pulling cables, but also gives you flexibility in where you locate your equipment. For example, although you might have set aside a portion of your house to use for your home office, it's nice to be able to take the laptop into the living room (or out on the deck in the back yard) and work while you're watching that favorite TV show. Wireless networking makes this simple.

Another use for wireless technology is the trade show environment. If you need to network several computers and possibly a printer or two, an ad hoc network using a wireless access point can be a quick way to get your booth up and running in a hurry. This also can be used at a client site if you're in the consulting business and don't want to connect your computers to your client's network. Indeed, it can be an easy way to get your computers into the client's office because they'll have no up-front work to do to provide you with networking services.

Finally, you can use a wireless network to extend the reach of your existing LAN. Access points can be connected to a wired LAN to provide an ingress point for wireless clients. However, just because it's possible doesn't mean it's necessary. Some places in a corporate network that you might find wireless network APs a good idea include

- **Conference rooms**—Users often bring laptop computers to meetings to take notes. Using wireless networking in a conference room can allow that laptop to locate information that exists elsewhere on the LAN that might be useful during the meeting. No more "I'll get back with you on that" excuses.

- **Temporary workgroups**—An access point can be useful when you need to bring in temporary workers, using space that's otherwise not wired for network access. Because many manufacturing plants have seasonal peaks and slumps, this might be an ideal way to quickly set up new clients on a network without the expense of having to go through the process of providing switches and cable runs to all parts of your building. Instead, a single cable run can be used for an AP that can serve a variable number of clients on an as-needed basis.

- **Mobile users**—For users who mainly work with a laptop and are usually on the road—such as salespeople—a wireless solution might be a good idea. When the user returns to the office for a short time, a docking station can serve to connect the laptop to the wired network. However, a docking station basically means reserving a desk as well and overhead can be expensive in today's competitive market. Instead, a single office with a few desks and an access point can serve a large number of transient workers.

- **Factory floor**—Laptops are not the only computers that can be used in a wireless network. Many PDAs and other small handheld devices are available that can use Wi-Fi network cards. On a factory floor, where mobility is important, it's easier to use a small portable device than it is to set up a series of PCs throughout the plant. Because many manufacturing plants need to reconfigure the factory floor on a periodic basis to retool for new products, wireless networking can again prove to be a cost saver.

◄◄   In Chapter 20, you can find information on how to extend a network with wireless technology.

Another place that wireless networking can serve a useful purpose is for outdoor activities. I've worked at many places that have outdoor locations that employees can use at lunchtime. These areas also can be comfortable places to hold meetings. Sometimes just getting out of the office can boost employee morale and taking the network outside can, as noted previously, make meetings more productive. There are many other uses for wireless networks, and new ideas are being created every day.

Note

In addition to the deployment of wireless networking in the SOHO and enterprise corporate environment, you can expect to find wireless networking proliferating into public spaces. At this time, many hotels already offer wireless networking for clients, along with the plug-in dial-up access that has become the norm. Major hardware vendors have announced plans to wire public spaces (airports, malls, and so on) with wireless access points during the next few years. Perhaps some day soon you'll be able to use your laptop computer (or whatever smaller network devices come along) wherever you go, using a single nationwide provider.

Choosing Locations for Access Points

Just as you need to test new network configurations or PC configurations in a laboratory before rolling them out for production usage, you need to evaluate the placement of access points should you decide to get into wireless networking. Wi-Fi provides for roaming capabilities, but it also enables you to restrict users to selected access points if you choose to do so. First, decide how you want to use wireless networking and which users it can be used by in a productive manner. Next, decide how many access points you need and where to place them.

You'll have to do some experimentation. Read the vendor's documentation to get the basics of the coverage area that the product is capable of, keeping in mind that this is only a general figure. For example, you'll find that most access points are capable of covering larger distances outside, rather than inside, because there are fewer structural components, such as bricks or steel beams, that can block the signal. You should take a vendor's specifications about its particular product with a grain of salt. Your mileage can vary.

If you use wireless networking inside and want to cover the entire building, you'll have to test to see exactly how far the coverage is for each access point. Also note that several factors can influence the performance you'll get no matter where you place the AP. For example, each AP is capable of supporting only a limited number of users before the available bandwidth begins to become saturated. Wireless networking at 11Mbps is faster than the standard 10BASE-T network connected to a basic hub. Yet it's nowhere near as fast as having a dedicated connection to a Fast Ethernet switch. There will come a point where too many users competing for too little bandwidth will provide too little performance to make wireless networking practical. IEEE 802.11a operates at a higher bandwidth and can accommodate a larger amount of users and network traffic.

Another thing to consider is source of interference, such as microwave ovens and other wireless devices. If you employ Bluetooth devices, you need to be careful because the technology is still new and despite some of the literature you may read, it's still inconclusive whether Bluetooth (or HomeRF for that matter) can interfere with Wi-Fi communications. All three use the same ISM radio frequency band, and although hopping around on different frequencies and using direct spread spectrum technologies might serve to reduce the chance of interference, don't count on there being no interference at all. Instead, if you use multiple technologies, go back to your lab and test the devices to see what kind of throughput you are able to achieve. Another popular device is the 2.4Ghz cordless telephone. These telephones operate in the same band as some wireless networks and can cause problems when used in the vicinity of wireless networking devices.

And keep that microwave oven in the break room well shielded! You can purchase an inexpensive device at most consumer discount stores that can measure the amount of microwave radiation that's leaking from a microwave oven. You might find that simply replacing an old microwave oven with a newer model cures any interference problems. And because most work places don't need a top-of-the-line microwave that can zap a baked potato in just a few minutes, go with a low-end model that uses less power.

Security Issues

Using wireless technology opens up the possibility of security breaches. Thoroughly read the documentation that comes with your choice of devices to find out what kind of security features can be enabled. It's probably best to associate the wireless network adapters you buy with one or more access points, depending on the work habits of the user. Also note that many devices come with default settings and that these are known to anyone who owns a similar device or who cares to look up the information on the Internet. For example, you might be required to designate a password or group name for each wireless adapter that matches the one used by the access point. This assignment is usually done using a direct connection to the router and filling in a few HTML forms.

Similarly, a configuration CD or utility comes with most wireless adapters enabling you to modify their configuration to match that of the access point.

Change any default settings used to match up wireless adapters and access points to use a value other than the default. Use the security features of your operating system to monitor wireless users. For example, I'd be more concerned with a Windows 2000 user's resource access permissions if the client computer uses a wireless network card than I would if it were wired directly to the network. Keep in mind that Wi-Fi devices can implement the Wireless Equivalency Protocol (WEP) for security. However, the weaker 40-bit key used by WEP doesn't provide a lot of security. Some wireless networks can be configured to encrypt using a stronger 128-bit WEP key, but even this level of encryption is vulnerable to a number of workarounds. It should suffice for most situations because in most situations you don't expect someone to be attempting to tap into your network. However, where security is a critical issue, WEP in its present form isn't something you should bet your business on.

The Wi-Fi Alliance has already released specifications for a successor to WEP. The Wi-Fi Protected Access standard is more secure and most vendors are expected to provide software/firmware to upgrade older models to use this new security functionality. Considering the value of data, buying WPA or adding it at a later time is probably a good idea. Remember that it's easier to eavesdrop on a wireless network because you don't have to make any connections to a cable, as in a wired network. Radio waves are out there for anyone within range of your technology to pick up. So, keep security in mind and look for WPA when buying new devices.

The Protected Access standard will provide a more secure encryption algorithm and enhanced user authentication. The latter was a very weak point for WEP. Next in line for wireless security is the IEEE 802.11i standard.

◄◄ You can learn more about wireless security in Chapter 24, "Other Wireless Technologies."

In any case, it's easy to set up auditing for important resources and to review them using the Event Viewer in Windows 2000 and Server 2003. No matter how safe you think your network is, there's no excuse for not auditing (and checking the audits) to ensure that your security measures are working. Looking for such things as a large number of login failures can alert you to someone trying to break into your wireless network. Unix and Linux (using the syslog utility) can also be used to look for system auditing information. The syslog utility can be configured to also send alerts, by email and other means, so that you can be informed quickly of any possible security breaches (or attempts).

◄◄ For more information about auditing, see Chapter 47, "Auditing and Other Monitoring Measures."

Another cause for concern is that wireless networking enables the computer to be mobile. A user can take his computer home. Although you might be able to stop users from downloading prohibited Internet files at work, you can't always police what they do at home. It's a simple matter to pop out the wireless networking adapter and pop in a modem (or better yet, simply use a wireless access point at home also, because it is so inexpensive). As with any computer that leaves the company premises, a regular audit of software on the system should be performed, and your security policy should state what the computer can—and cannot—be used for. Of course, this should be a standard procedure for all computers on your network.

Migration and Integration

PART XI

Migrating from NetWare to Windows 2000 or Windows Server 2003

SOME OF THE MAIN TOPICS IN THIS CHAPTER ARE

When Windows NT 3.51 was released, the default network protocol during installation was Microsoft's implementation of Novell's IPX/SPX protocol, NWLink. It easily can be assumed that at that time Microsoft perceived that Novell was its most important competitor in the network operating system marketplace. With Windows NT 4.0, the TCP/IP protocol suite, along with the Internet Information Server and a host of utilities for creating applications for the Internet, moved that focus away from Novell to the then-fast-growing Internet market.

Yet, over the years, Windows has continued to dominate the desktop, from Windows 95 to 2000 Professional and now to Windows XP. So one has to consider what benefits there are to pay for Novell's NDS (now the eDirectory) and related networking products, when most of the functionality that Novell provides is already present in Windows 2000 and Windows 2003 Servers. Novell has recently concentrated its efforts on a new and improved NetWare 6.0. But whether that remains the focus of the company is somewhat in doubt. Parts of NetWare 6.x have been broken out for sale as separate products, such as iPrint and iFile. And as new versions of NetWare have been released, there has been an inconsistency in the Web server that comes bundled with the package. NetWare has also decided to head toward the Linux route and offer future versions that run both in native NetWare mode and on top of the Linux kernel.

Microsoft cannot be absolved from any blame here either. Each generation of Internet Information Services comes with new features, and also gets rid of older features, given time. And with 2003 Server features now being introduced, you can expect that Microsoft will try, as Novell, IBM, and others have, to conquer the Internet desktop. This is the future of networking and the Internet.

This chapter covers ways to migrate your network from Novell NetWare to Windows 2000 by doing the following:

- Examining features of the Windows operating system that help provide connectivity between Windows and NetWare computers.

- Looking at Microsoft Windows Services for NetWare 5, which can be very useful, along with other tools for performing a migration to Windows NT or Windows 2000.

You can take a gradual approach, slowly integrating Windows into important roles in the network, or you can take the all-at-once approach. The former probably would be cheaper in the long run (you can lose NDS servers by attrition and you don't need as many people devoted to the migration if you have more time). And, if you take the slow road, you can learn from your experiences. The latter approach might be a lot more costly, because you'll need to have a larger team of trained professionals to get the job done quickly. Using the all-at-once approach also is riskier. If something goes wrong, or if your capacity planning or organizational planning is faulty, you'll need a good back-out plan (and probably another job).

Note

When planning any migration or upgrading project, you should carefully consider your choices and experiment in a lab situation to ensure that your solution works, among other things. Chapter 4, "Upgrading Strategies and Project Management," may be useful reading before this chapter.

Windows Protocols and Services

Although earlier versions of NetWare use Novell's IPX/SPX network protocols, the TCP/IP protocol suite is supported with NetWare versions 5.x and 6.x. Microsoft Windows NT 4.0 and Windows 2000 also support Microsoft's implementation of the native NetWare protocol under the name NWLink.

You can configure a Windows server to use the NWLink protocol, and it then can be used as a server for NetWare clients. If you're taking the gradual approach for your migration, this is the easiest way to introduce Windows servers into older versions of NetWare. Otherwise, if you already are using TCP/IP on your NetWare clients, Windows also has a full-featured TCP/IP protocol stack and supports many related protocols and services, such as DHCP and DNS, as well as the Active Directory, which can be used to replace most functions provided by Novell Directory Services (which was named NDS, and is now called the eDirectory).

Windows 2000 provides two basic services that allow NetWare and Microsoft clients to access servers that reside in both environments. These tools are listed here:

- **Client Services for NetWare (CSNW)**—This tool enables the Microsoft client to directly connect to a service offered by a NetWare server.

- **Gateway Services for NetWare (GSNW)**—This utility also enables a Microsoft network client to access file and print shares offered by NetWare servers. The services are provided to the Microsoft clients through a gateway Windows NT Server computer that is used to communicate with the NetWare servers.

Looking first at these two services and then exploring some other utilities you can use to further integrate Novell NetWare with Microsoft Windows computers will help you understand this migration path.

Client Services for NetWare (CSNW)

This service can be installed on Windows NT Workstation and Windows 2000 Professional computers to enable them to connect to file and print services provided by NetWare servers on the network. By using CSNW, you can begin by gradually adding Microsoft Windows 2000 Professional and XP Professional clients to your network, and they can access services on your existing NetWare network. This can allow you the time to hone your Windows networking skills, while still allowing users access to the same NetWare resources they are used to.

Installing CSNW on Windows 2000 Professional Clients

To install CSNW on Windows 2000 Professional or Windows XP, these are the steps to follow:

1. Click Start, Settings, Network and Dial-Up Connections.
2. Right-click the Local Network icon and select Properties from the menu that appears.
3. From the Local Area Network Properties sheet General tab, click the Install button. The Select Network Component Type dialog box pops up. Click once on Client to highlight it, and then click the Add button.
4. In the Select Network Client dialog box, click Client Service for NetWare and click OK.
5. When the Select NetWare Logon dialog box appears, fill in the fields for the preferred server if you are going to use the client to connect to a bindery-based NetWare server. If you are going to use the service with NDS, click the Default Tree and Context button and enter the NDS tree and context names. If you want to use a logon script, select Run Login Script. When you've made your selections, click OK.

When you have finished, you'll be prompted to reboot the computer. You can do so at that time or wait until a more convenient time for the reboot. After you've rebooted your workstation, you'll be able to connect to the preferred server or authenticate yourself to another.

Caution

If you have previously installed Novell's client software on a Windows 2000 Professional or Windows XP Professional computer, you'll have to uninstall that client before you can install Microsoft's version. The two are not compatible and will not run on the same computer at the same time.

Gateway Services for NetWare (GSNW)

Microsoft employs two methods to enable its networking clients to connect to services offered by a NetWare server. Client Services for NetWare, discussed in the previous sections, allows each client to make connections directly to NetWare servers, just as though they were ordinary NetWare clients. This method has advantages, in that only the Microsoft client and the NetWare server are involved in processing the exchange of data. However, in a network where the interaction between Microsoft clients and NetWare servers will not be large, and many clients might need to make the connection at one time or another, a better solution might be the Gateway Services for NetWare (GSNW) product. Another benefit of using GSNW is that, because the gateway server makes requests on behalf of the clients, the users would not need to have logon accounts on both Windows and NetWare networks.

Keep in mind that accessing resources through the gateway service will be a little slower than access by clients that have the CSNW service installed. If you have clients on the network that have differing needs to access NetWare resources, you can install CSNW on those that most frequently use those resources, and let others use the gateway service.

Note

Gateway Services for NetWare uses Microsoft's implementation of IPX/SPX, called NWLink, to communicate with NetWare servers. For Windows 2000 and Windows 2003 Servers the NWLink protocol is installed automatically when you perform the GSNW installation.

When using GSNW, a Windows 2000 or Windows 2003 Server acts as a link between Microsoft clients and the NetWare Server. Microsoft clients continue to use the Server Message Block (SMB) protocols to access network resources, with the gateway server performing the bridging function to the NetWare servers, which use the NetWare Core Protocol (NCP) for file and print functions.

The gateway server does this by redirecting a drive to the NetWare volume. It then offers the drive as a share to Microsoft clients. You can treat this share just like any other share offered by the server, when it comes to management utilities.

Another feature that GSNW provides is the capability for the Windows 2000 and 2003 Servers that are hosting the gateway software to make direct connections to NetWare services, just as workstations do when using the Client Services for NetWare product. A local user on the server can elect to connect to NetWare resources without offering them to other clients through the gateway.

Installing GSNW on Windows 2000 Server

You must be a member of the Administrators group on the Windows server to install the gateway service. Use the following steps to install GSNW on a Windows 2000 or Windows 2003 server:

1. Click Start, Settings, Network and Dial-Up Connections (or Start, More Programs).

2. When the Network and Dial-Up Connections window appears, right-click the local area connection icon that you want to use for the service. From the menu that appears, select Properties.

3. From the Local Area Connection Properties dialog box that appears (see Figure 60.1), click the Install button.

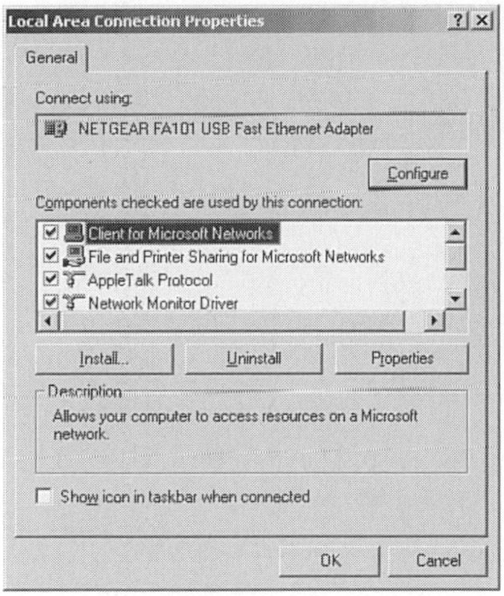

Figure 60.1 Click the Install button on the Local Area Connection Properties page to install the GSNW service.

4. The Select Network Component Type dialog box appears (see Figure 60.2). Click once on Client to highlight it, and then click the Add button to add a new service.

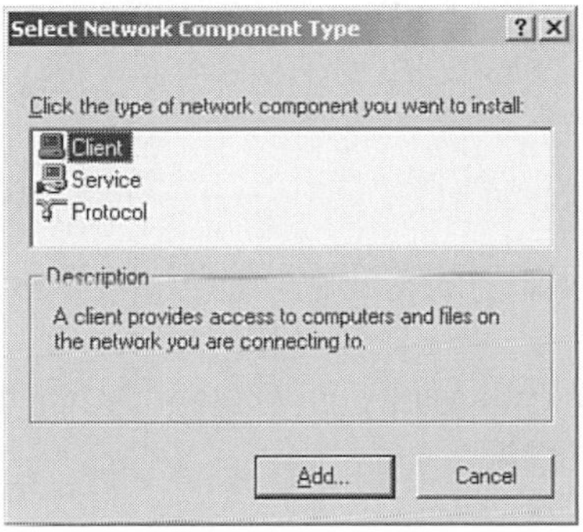

Figure 60.2 Use the Add button to add the new service.

5. When the Select Network Client dialog box appears (see Figure 60.3), highlight Gateway (and Client) Services for NetWare, and then click the OK button.

6. Use the Select NetWare Logon dialog box (see Figure 60.4) to choose a preferred server (if you are using a bindery-based NetWare network), or select the radio button labeled Default Tree and Context (if you are using NDS) and fill in the appropriate information. When finished, click the OK button.

Note

If you do not have available at installation time the necessary information for logging on to a NetWare server or NDS, you can perform this step after you've installed GSNW and rebooted the Windows 2000 Server.

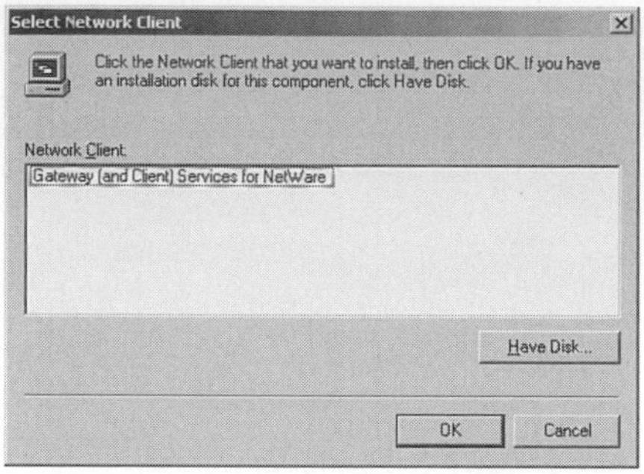

Figure 60.3   Select the gateway service and click the OK button.

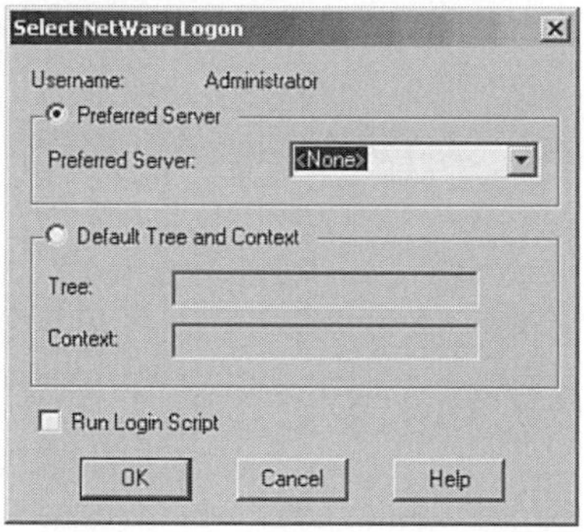

Figure 60.4   Choose the method you will use to log on to the NetWare server or NDS.

7. Finally, you are prompted to restart your computer before the changes you have made will take effect.

After the server reboots, using the following command at the command prompt should display a list of servers available to your gateway:

```
net view /network:nw
```

After you reboot, you'll notice that, in addition to installing the gateway service, these NWLink components also have been installed for you:

- NWLink NetBIOS
- NWLink IPX/SPX/NetBIOS Compatible Transport Protocol

You can see these in the Properties page for the local area connection.

Configuring GSNW on Windows 2000 Server

After you have installed the software and have entered the authentication information needed to access services on the NetWare network, there are several things you need to do to make NetWare resources available to your Microsoft clients. First, you must be sure that there is a user account on the NetWare network that has the needed access rights to the resources for which you want to create a gateway. On the NetWare side, there must also be a group named Ntgateway that has the needed rights for the resources. The NetWare user account that you will use must be a member of this group.

To create the gateway, you must take the following actions:

- Enable gateways on the server that is running the GSNW software. This needs to be done only once to establish the gateway.
- Activate each file or print resource gateway. This must be done for each resource you want to offer to Microsoft clients.

To enable a gateway, double-click the GSNW applet that is now found in the Control Panel, shown in Figure 60.5. Click the Gateway button to bring up the Configure Gateway dialog box (see Figure 60.6).

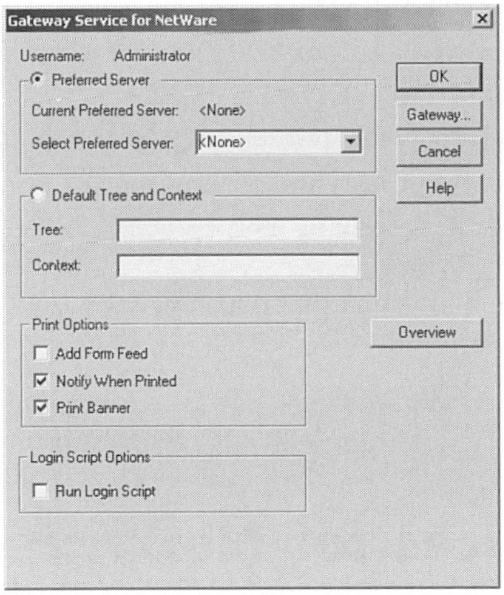

Figure 60.5   The GSNW applet in the Control Panel enables you to configure the gateway service.

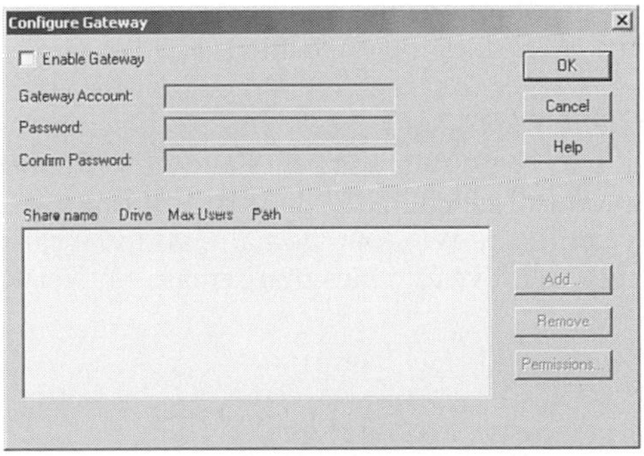

Figure 60.6   Use the Gateway button on the GSNW dialog box to bring up the Configure Gateway dialog box.

In the Configure Gateway dialog box you will again have to enter a method and the information required to access the resources you require on a NetWare server. This is in addition to the account that you supplied when the Windows 2000 Server was first rebooted after the gateway service was installed. That first logon information is used to enable the Windows 2000 server to log on as a user to the NetWare account. The second account will be used here to actually access the needed resource.

After you supply a gateway account and password and type the password again in the confirm box, click the Add button to add a NetWare file share resource that you want to add to the gateway.

You also can place comments in the appropriate field and elect to limit the number of simultaneous users that can connect to the share when it is offered to Microsoft clients through the gateway.

Setting up a printer that allows Microsoft clients to send documents to NetWare printers or print queues through the gateway is performed in a manner similar to setting up other printers in Windows 2000. The difference is that you must correctly specify the port for the printer. To make a NetWare printer available through the gateway, follow these steps:

1. Click Start, Settings, and then Printers.

2. From the Add Printer Wizard dialog box that appears, select My Computer. Do *not* select Network Printer Server.

3. The next dialog box shows available printer ports on the server. Click the Add Port button.

4. Depending on the network protocols and services installed on the computer, you then are shown a list of printer ports that can be added. Select Local Port from this list and click the New Port button.

5. Finally, in the Port Name dialog box that pops up, enter the UNC pathname that is used to designate the NetWare Printer resource (*servername**printername*).

The remainder of the Add Printer Wizard works just as it does for any other printer. You must select a driver for the printer and specify the name to be used when it is offered as a share on the Microsoft network.

Microsoft's Services for NetWare Version 5.0 (SFN)

Besides the client and gateway services (and the NWLink-compatible transport protocols) that come with Windows 2000, you can purchase an additional product called Services for NetWare Version 5.0 (SFN). The CSNW and GSNW products enable your Windows clients to connect to and use resources that reside on NetWare servers. SFN does the opposite. It enables you to let NetWare clients access resources that reside on Windows NT/2000 servers. When you first start to introduce Windows clients into your NetWare environment, CSNW and GSNW make replacing desktop systems for your users an easy task. When it comes time to begin migrating files and other services from NetWare servers to Windows servers, SFN gives you the capability to do this. You can use SFN to grant access to NetWare clients to newly created services in the Windows domain, and you can finish off the migration by using the File Migration Utility to move any files that remain on NetWare servers to Windows 2000 servers.

SFN gives you the following features:

- File and Print Services for NetWare 4.0 (FPNW)
- Directory Service Manager for NetWare (DSMN)
- Microsoft Directory Synchronization Services (MSDSS)
- File Migration Utility (FMU)
- File and Print Services for NetWare version 5.0 (FPNW version 5)

Of these, the first two are intended mainly for use with Windows NT 4, whereas the last three are exclusively for use on Windows 2000/2003. Version 5 of SFU contains the earlier versions of FPNW and the Directory Services Manager for NetWare so that you don't have to buy both versions 4 and 5 of this product. It's all on the 5.0 CD.

Comparison of Windows 2000/2003 and NetWare File Permission Rights

When using FPNW 5.0, trustee rights for directories for NetWare clients can be mapped to those used on Windows 2000/2003 systems, as shown in Table 60.1. Table 60.2 shows the same thing in reverse, or how FPNW5 translates Windows 2000/2003 permissions for directories to NetWare directory rights.

Table 60.1   Mapping NetWare Trustee Rights to Windows 2000/2003 Permissions in FPNW5 for Directories

NetWare File Rights	Windows 2000/2003 File Permissions
Read (R)	Read (RX) (RX)
Write (W)	Write (W) (W)
Create (C)	Write (W) (W)
Erase (E)	Delete (D) (D)
Modify (M)	Write (W) (W)
File Scan (F)	Read (R) (R)
Access Control (A)	Change Permissions (PO) (PO)

Table 60.2   Mapping Windows 2000/2003 Permissions to NetWare Trustee Rights in FPNW 4.0 for Directories

Windows 2000/2003 Directory Permissions	NetWare Directory Rights
List (RX) (not specified)	Read, File Scan (RF)
Read (RX) (RX)	Read, File Scan (RF)
Add (WX) (not specified)	Write, Create, Modify (WCM)
Add and Read (RWX) (RX)	Read, Write, Create Modify, File Scan (RWCMF)
Change (RWXD) (RWXD)	Read, Write, Create Modify, File Scan (RWCMF)
Full Control (All) (All)	Supervisor (S)

For files, Table 60.3 shows the mapping done by FPNW from Windows 2000/2003 to NetWare, and Table 60.4 shows the mapping done from NetWare to Windows 2000/2003. Note that Windows 2000/2003 Server uses directory permissions to grant the Create and File Scan equivalent rights that NetWare uses as file rights.

Table 60.3   Mapping NetWare File Trustee Rights to Windows 2000/2003 Server File Permissions

NetWare File Rights	Windows 2000/2003 File Permissions
Supervisor (S)	Full Control (All)
Read (R)	Read (R)
Access Control (A)	Change Permissions (PO)
Create (C)	Write (W)
Erase (E)	Delete (D)
Modify (M)	Write (W) (W)
Write (W)	Write (W)

Table 60.4 Mapping Windows 2000/2003 Server File Permissions to NetWare File Trustee Rights

Windows NT File Permissions	NetWare File Rights
Read (RX)	Read, File Scan (RF)
Change (RWXD)	Read, Write, Create Modify, File Scan (RWCMF)
Full Control (All)	Supervisor (S)

Besides having to translate between the rights and permissions used on each system, FPNW5 also translates between the different kinds of file attributes that both systems use at the file level. Table 60.5 shows the translation mapping that FPNW performs.

Table 60.5 Mapping File Attributes Between Windows 2000/2003 and NetWare

NetWare File Attributes	Windows 2000 File Attributes
Read Only (RO)	Read Only (R)
Delete Inhibit (D)	Read Only (R), or remove user permissions to delete the file
Rename Inhibit	Assigned at the directory level by removing the user's permission to write to the directory
Archive Needed (A)	Archive (A)
System (Sy)	System (S)
Hidden (H)	Hidden (H)
Execute Only (X)	Execute (E)
Read Audit (Ra)	Audit Read, Audit Execute
Write Audit (Wa)	Audit Write, Audit Delete

However, FPNW 5.0 *does not* provide support for the following NetWare attributes:

- Don't Compress
- File Migrated
- File Compressed
- Immediate Compress
- Can't Compress
- Purge
- Index FAT Entries
- Transactional Tracking
- File Migrated

The Shareable attribute can be set only on a per-server or global basis when using FPNW 5, and cannot be set on an individual file.

You should carefully examine how security is currently enforced for clients on the existing NetWare network before beginning to decide how to offer file shares from a Windows NT Server. Understanding the mapping between the two systems can prevent unexpected access violations or errors from compromising security on the network.

Installing File and Print Services for NetWare Version 5.0 (FPNW 5.0)

To install FPNW 5.0 on a Windows 2000 server, follow these steps:

1. Right-click My Network Places on the desktop. From the menu that appears, click Properties.

2. In the Network and Dial-Up Connections window (see Figure 60.7), right-click Local Area Connection and select Properties from the menu that appears.

Figure 60.7   Right-click the Local Area Connection icon and select Properties.

3. Click the Install button on the connection's Properties page (see Figure 60.8). The Select Network Component Type dialog box pops up and prompts you for the component type to install. Select Service and click Add.

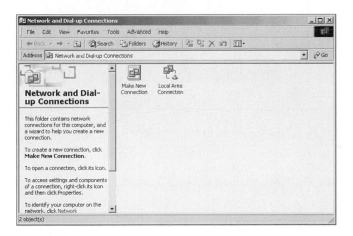

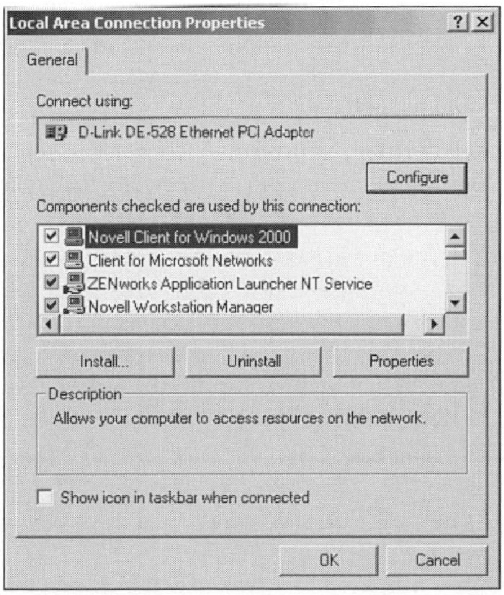

Figure 60.8   Click the Install button on the Properties page for the local connection.

4. The Select Network Service dialog box appears (see Figure 60.9). Click the Have Disk button.

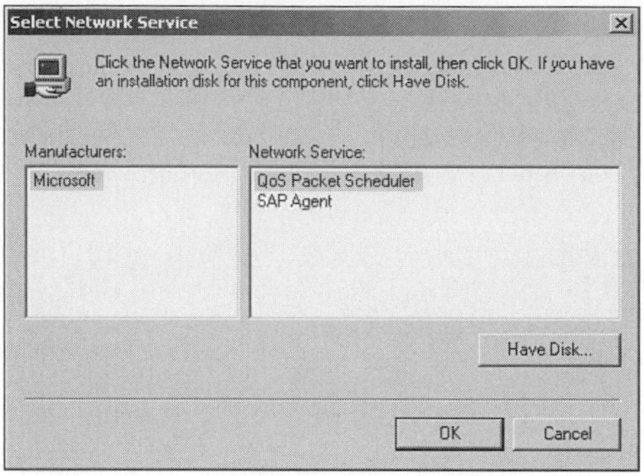

Figure 60.9 Use the Have Disk button to install the FPNW service.

5. The Install from Disk dialog box prompts you to enter the path for the service. Enter the drive letter for the CD-ROM drive that contains the SFN disc, followed by the pathname \FPNW, as shown in Figure 60.10, and then click the OK button.

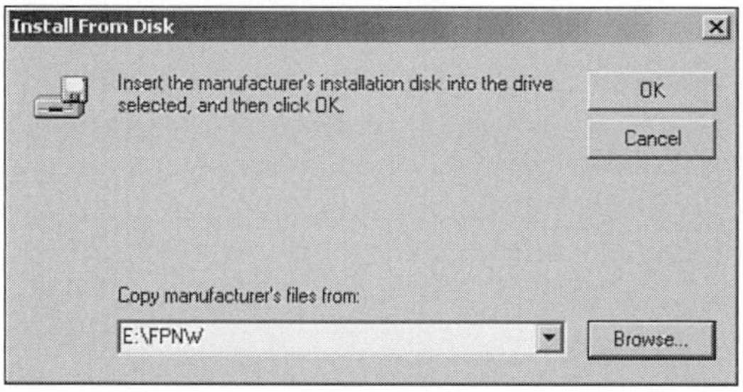

Figure 60.10 Enter the path that contains the FPNW files.

6. The Select Network Service dialog box prompts you for the service to install. The only service that appears in this dialog box is File and Print Services for NetWare. Highlight this service and click OK.

7. The Install File and Print Services for NetWare dialog box pops up (see Figure 60.11). Enter the necessary information for the volume you want to create for NetWare users, along with the password that will be used for the FPNW supervisor user account that will be created. You also can use the Tuning section on this dialog box to determine how memory use is allocated to users of the service. Click OK when you've supplied the necessary information.

Note

If you are installing FPNW in a domain, another dialog box will pop up and ask you to enter the password that will be used to run the service. In a domain setup, *use the same password on all domain controllers that you set up to offer FPNW to NetWare users.* Click OK to dismiss this dialog box.

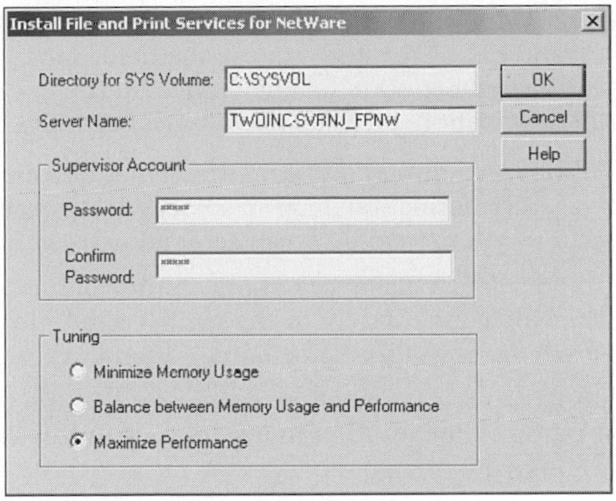

Figure 60.11   Enter the information for the services you want to offer to NetWare clients along with a password to be used by the account that will be used to manage the service.

   8. When the Local Area Connections Properties sheet reappears, click Close. You'll be prompted to restart your server before the FPNW service runs. You can click Yes to reboot immediately, or simply wait until a more convenient time by clicking No.

   9. If you chose to wait until later for the reboot, click the Close button that appears on the Local Area Connection Properties dialog box.

You'll find an icon in the Control Panel titled FPNW that can be used to manage the service. In Figure 60.12, you can see the File and Print Services for NetWare dialog box used in version 5.

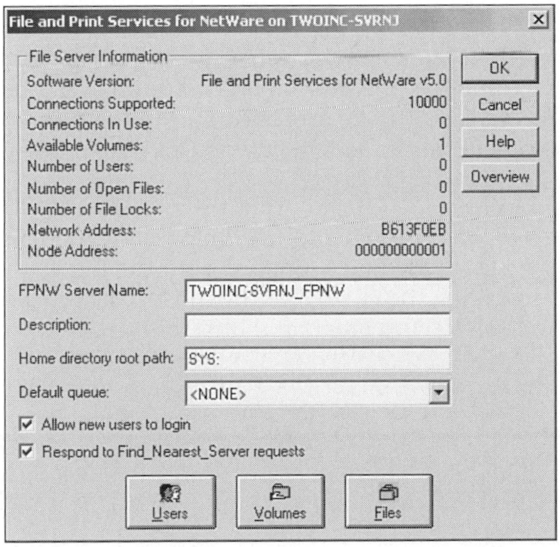

Figure 60.12   The FPNW dialog box, accessed from the FPNW Control Panel icon, enables you to manage the FPNW service.

Statistical information is displayed in the File Server Information section, showing data about the current connections, open files, and so on. You also can use the fields under this section to set up a print queue, a home directory path, or a description for the service on this server. Three buttons at the bottom allow you to view more information about users, volumes, and files:

- **Users**—This button brings up a display showing the names of connected users, the network address and login time, and information about resources being used. You can use this dialog box to send messages to users or to disconnect one or all users from the service.

- **Volumes**—This button displays a dialog box showing the volumes you have set up to share with FPNW clients, showing connected users, the connection time, and information about file opens. You also can use buttons in this dialog box to disconnect one or all users.

- **Files**—This button displays information about each open file, the user who opened it, locking information, and the path to the file. You can use buttons in this dialog box to close a file or all files currently open.

Microsoft Directory Synchronization Services (MSDSS)

This utility improves on Directory Service Manager for NetWare (DSMN) but is for use with the Active Directory instead of the Windows NT 4.0 SAM database. MSDSS provides for a *one-way* synchronization with NetWare 3.x binderies and the Active Directory (AD). MSDSS also gives you the capability for either one- or two-way support for synchronization between NDS and AD. Finally, MSDSS allows you to create a file that can be used by the File Migration Utility (FMU), discussed later in this chapter, so that NetWare trustee rights and ACLs are propagated to Windows 2000 servers when you decide to move files from NetWare servers to complete the migration to Windows 2000.

However, to use MSDSS there are a few prerequisites:

- MSDSS can be installed only on a Windows 2000 server acting in the role of a domain controller. Remember that domain controllers contain the Active Directory database, and it is this database that stores user account/password information that is to be kept synchronized.

- You will need to obtain a copy of Novell's Client for Windows 2000. If you've just upgraded a Windows NT 4.0 server that had the previous version of Novell's client installed, you won't need a new copy. The old copy will be upgraded during the Windows 2000 upgrade process. If you need to get a copy of the Novell client, you can obtain one from www.novell.com/download/index.html.

Novell has released several versions of its client for Windows NT/2000. Because differences exist from one version to another, read the release notes supplied with the file you download from Novell and follow the instructions for installing the client. For the most part, you simply need to extract the files to a temporary directory and run a setup program that takes only a few minutes, after which you'll need to reboot the server.

Note

If you have already installed Microsoft's Client Service for NetWare, you'll get a prompt when you try to install Novell's client. When asked whether you want to remove Microsoft's version, answer Yes to continue the installation of Novell's version of the client. The two are not compatible.

When the server reboots, you are presented with the Novell logon box instead of the familiar Windows logon box.

When using MSDSS to perform synchronization between NDS and AD, you create sessions that specify the NDS and corresponding AD objects that will be kept in sync. You can create a one-way session in which changes made to the Active Directory object will be propagated to the NDS object. However, one-way synchronization does not work in reverse. That is, with a one-way synchronization, changes made to an NDS object do not get copied back to AD. In this type of setup, you should use the Active Directory administrative tools and utilities to perform directory management. From a migration standpoint, this allows you to keep NDS on the network while you gradually educate your network administrators on using the AD tools. After your staff is comfortable using AD, you can use MSDSS to migrate all the required NDS information to AD, and then decommission the NDS servers.

Installing MSDSS

To install MSDSS after you've installed the NetWare client from Novell, follow these steps:

1. Insert the SFU CD into your local CD-ROM drive.

2. Click Start, Programs, Accessories, Windows Explorer.

3. In the left pane of the Explorer, double-click My Computer. The SFU CD shows up in the left pane of the Explorer display.

4. Double-click the SFU icon. You see two folders, one named FPNW and one named MSDSS. Double-click MSDSS.

5. Inside the MSDSS folder, you now see an MSDSS icon that is used to start the Windows Installer. Double-click the icon.

6. The Windows Installer copies files to your system directory, and you then are prompted to reboot the computer.

After you've installed MSDSS, you'll find that the Active Directory server now has a new program in the Administrative Tools folder called Directory Synchronization.

Creating One-Way Synchronization Sessions

You create *sessions* that define the synchronization between NDS and AD objects. The objects must be container objects, such as organizational units (OUs), and not individual leaf objects, such as a single user in the AD. Before you start the New Session Wizard, you should decide which NDS and AD container objects you want to synchronize. This does not create these objects for you. For example, suppose you have an existing NDS object that contains user accounts for the manufacturing department of your business that you want to eventually migrate to AD. You should create a new OU and give it a meaningful name before you start the New Session Wizard. Or you can simply choose to use a container object that already exists in your AD database.

To create a one-way synchronization session, follow these steps:

1. Click Start, Programs, Administrative Tools, and then Directory Synchronization. The Microsoft Management Console (MMC) snap-in called MSDSS pops up on your screen.

2. In the left pane of the MMC, you can right-click on MSDSS and select New Session from the menu that appears. Alternatively, you can click once on MSDSS in the left pane, select the Action menu, and then select All Tasks, New Session (see Figure 60.13).

3. The New Session Wizard pops up and displays information about the task that you are about to start. That is, you will migrate objects from NDS to AD and, if you want, establish a synchronization schedule. Click the Next button.

4. The New Session Wizard prompts you to select either NDS or a Bindery as the source for the initial migration using a drop-down menu (see Figure 60.14). Under this menu, you can elect to perform a one-way or two-way synchronization, or to simply do a one-time migration from the NDS or bindery source to AD.

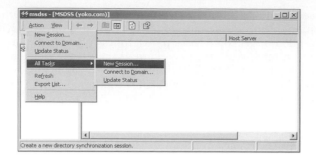

Figure 60.13   Use the MSDSS MMC snap-in to create a new session for synchronization.

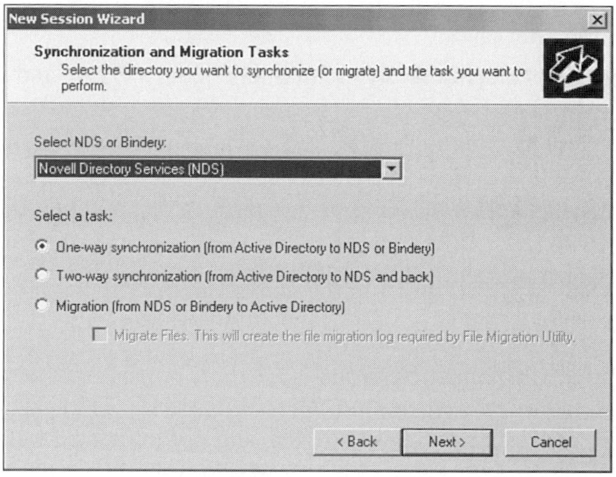

Figure 60.14   Select NDS or Bindery, and then choose to perform synchronization or a one-time migration.

5. Select the radio button for One-Way Synchronization (from Active Directory to NDS or Bindery), and then click Next to continue.

6. The next dialog box lets you select the AD container and the domain controller that stores information about this session, and is responsible for performing the synchronization tasks (see Figure 60.15). Click Next to continue.

Note

If any container objects are child objects to the AD container (organizational unit) you select for synchronization, synchronization will be performed for the selected container object and all of its child container objects as well. If you want to enter the container object in the Active Directory Container field, use the LDAP URL syntax instead of using the Browse button—for example, **LDAP://yoko.com/DC=yoko,DC=com**. In the Domain Controller field, the server on which you are running the New Session Wizard is the default. Click the Find button if you want to search for another domain controller in your network to use instead. For more information about LDAP, container objects, organizational units, and so on, see Chapter 31, "Using the Active Directory."

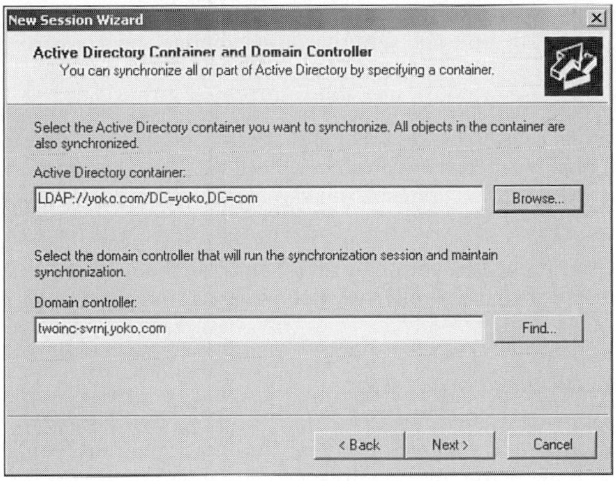

Figure 60.15 Enter the AD container object that will be used for this synchronization session (or click the Browse button to find one), and then enter the domain controller that will manage this session.

7. Next, a similar dialog box prompts you to enter the name of the NDS container object that you want to synchronize with the AD object you selected in step 6. Again, the NDS container must already exist, and any child objects of the container also are synchronized with the AD container object. The Browse button can be used, or you can use the NDS or bindery syntax to specify the NDS container object—for example, NDS://Tree1/O=ono/OU=mfg for an NDS object or NWCOMPAT://*servername* for a bindery server. Enter an NDS username and password that can be used to access the NDS object or bindery, and click Next.

The remaining dialog boxes for the New Session Wizard prompt you to do several things. First, the Initial Reverse Synchronization dialog box can be used if you want to import NDS objects into the Active Directory (a reverse synchronization) after the wizard finishes. Using this dialog box, you first can import NDS information so that you do not have to enter it manually into AD. Because we're just setting up a one-way synchronization, this initial reverse synchronization can be used to populate your AD database with NDS objects that then will be managed using AD administrative tools and utilities.

Because NDS passwords cannot be imported into AD during a reverse synchronization, you can select one of the following methods to set user passwords for user accounts that are initially added to AD during a reverse synchronization:

- **Set passwords to blank**—The first time a user logs on to AD, the user will not have to specify a password and can set the password to a value he wants. Note that this leaves your migrated user accounts vulnerable to security problems unless properly coordinated. If you use this method, follow up to be sure that each user has logged in and changed his password.

- **Set passwords to the username**—This is the default. Again, be sure to follow up and be sure that user passwords are changed after the initial migration.

- **Set passwords to a random value**—A random value is chosen for each account. A file is created in the directory *systemroot*\System32\Directory Synchronization\Session Logs that contains the user account names and the random passwords that were created. The file has an extension of .pwd, and after the synchronization process is finished, you can look in the Event Viewer to get the name of the file. Using this method, a help-desk technician can distribute passwords to users in a more secure manner than using the other options in this list.

■ **Set all passwords to the same value that you specify**—All accounts have the same password. Once again, follow up to be sure that users change their password to a different value.

The default is to set all the user account passwords imported into AD to the user account's username.

Another dialog box can be used to create specific mappings between AD and NDS objects. This can be useful when the child objects of an AD container object are not organized under the parent object in the same order as they are in the AD object. You can create an object mapping table that stores these relationships.

The New Session Wizard finally asks you to enter a name for this session, which you can use later to manage the session, or make changes to it. After you enter a name to use for the session, click the Finish button.

Creating Two-Way Synchronization Sessions

In the preceding section, you learned how to create a one-way synchronization that could be used to import NDS objects into the Active Directory. From that point forward, you should use the AD administrative tools to manage the objects. However, you also can use the New Session Wizard to set up a two-way synchronization process. To do so, use the same Directory Synchronization utility found in the Administrative Tools folder, and start the New Session Wizard. When the Synchronization and Migration Tasks dialog box pops up (refer to Figure 60.14), select two-way synchronization (from Active Directory to NDS and back) instead of the one-way synchronization.

You will have to supply similar information for the AD and NDS containers, as well as access information, just like you did for a one-way synchronization. You also can choose to perform an initial reverse synchronization, or you can elect to do this later.

One-Time Migration

Using a one- or two-way synchronization enables you to import NDS objects into AD so that you can manage your network resources (users, printers, and so on) using the administrative tools designed to work with the Active Directory. After you no longer have any need to keep NDS servers on your network, you can use the one-time migration option to simply import the data from NDS (or from bindery servers). The process is just about the same as a one-way synchronization, but after you have imported the data, changes made to objects in the Active Directory *will not* be propagated back to the NDS or bindery servers. Using the synchronization method, you can gradually migrate your network from NDS to AD. Using the one-time migration option, you can complete the process and turn off your NDS servers.

Again, you use the MMC MSDSS snap-in Directory Synchronization that is found in the Administrative Tools folder to begin a one-time migration. Use the New Session Wizard, as described earlier, to start the process. However, when the Synchronization and Migration Tasks dialog box appears (refer to Figure 60.14), select the Migration (from NDS or Bindery to Active Directory) radio button. You'll have to supply the same type of access information for the AD and NDS objects that will be migrated, and you can select an additional option: Migrate files from the NDS or Bindery servers to Windows 2000 servers. The check box for this function, also shown in Figure 60.14, *does not actually perform the file migration*, but instead creates a file that is used by the File Migration Utility, which we'll get to next. When you've decided it's time to get rid of those NDS servers, use this option to create the file, and then invoke the File Migration Utility.

File Migration Utility (FMU)

This is the second tool that Services for NetWare 5.0 provides that you can use only on Windows 2000 Server. FMU is used to migrate files and directories from NetWare volumes to Windows 2000 disks, while keeping intact security permissions. You can use this tool with both the IPX/SPX and TCP/IP protocols.

When you migrate files from NDS to Windows 2000, the MSDSS utility discussed in the preceding sections can be used to create a file that FMU uses to maintain user and group relationships and rights associated with files and directories. Before using FMU, be sure to read these sections! MSDSS maps organizational units (OUs) and organizations from NDS to the Active Directory by creating local security groups for every NDS OU and organization.

FMU is installed when you install MSDSS. To start the actual file migration process, click Start, Programs, Administrative Tools, and then File Migration Utility. The File Migration Utility Wizard, shown in Figure 60.16, pops up and performs some preliminary functions. When it has finished, the Next button becomes available. Click Next and you'll see a large property sheet that has tabs (see Figure 60.17), each of which can be used to perform a step in the migration process.

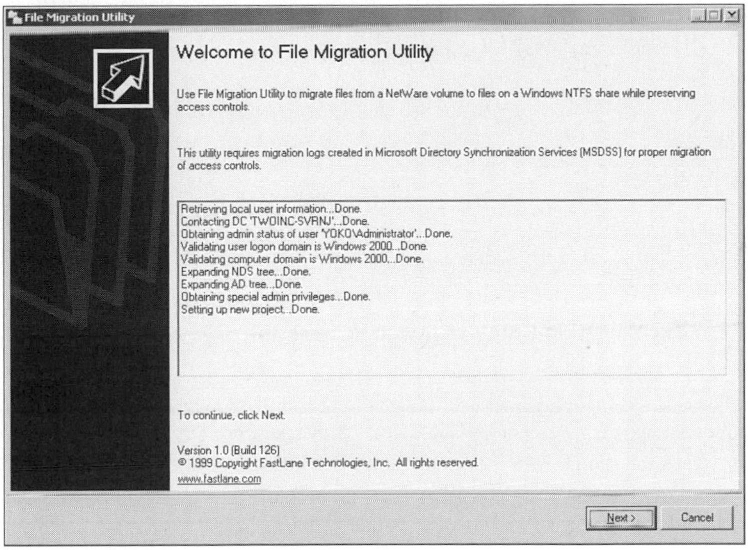

Figure 60.16   The File Migration Utility performs a few preliminary functions before you begin the migration process.

In the Step 1 tab, you must enter the full path for the migration log that you created using MSDSS. You can use the Browse button to locate the file if you don't recall where it was created. After you locate the file, click the Load Data button to read in the file. Note that at the bottom of the screen you'll see a display called Steps Completed, with boxes numbered 1 through 5. If you do not have time to complete the entire migration process in one session, or if you have to stop and rethink the process, you can look here to see what you've done so far. You can use the Allow Step Completion in

Any Order check box if you want to perform steps out of order. Each time you click the Next button you move to another step. Using this check box, you can bring up any of the steps. The View Maps and Access Rights buttons enable you to view how access rights are mapped between Windows 2000 and NetWare access rights. This might be necessary, for example, if you have a file that has the NDS Modify right associated with it. By default, this maps to the Windows Read right. You can change this to the Write right if you want to by using the Access Rights button.

Click the Next button to continue.

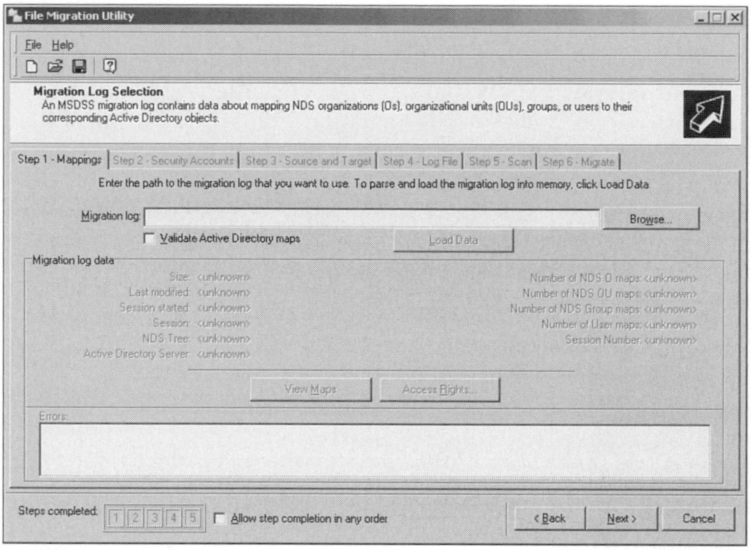

Figure 60.17 The File Migration Utility steps you through the migration process.

Note

The default location for the migration log that MSDSS creates is *systemroot*\System32\Directory Synchronization\Session Logs. Look for the log file on the same server on which you performed a one-time migration.

The Step 2 tab shows you the Active Directory account that you used to log in to the Windows 2000 server (see Figure 60.18). Use the NetWare Connections button to show any current connections you have made to NetWare resources. If you have yet to log on to NDS or a bindery server, use the Log On to Novell button to do so at this time. Enter the required NDS or bindery account name and password, and click Next.

Step 3 enables you to select the source and target of the migration task (see Figure 60.19). Use this step to select the NDS or bindery volume or directories that you want to migrate to the Windows 2000 server. Under Target, select the Windows 2000 file shares or directories that will be used as the location for the files to be migrated. When you've finished making selections, click on Map and then, of course, click the Next button.

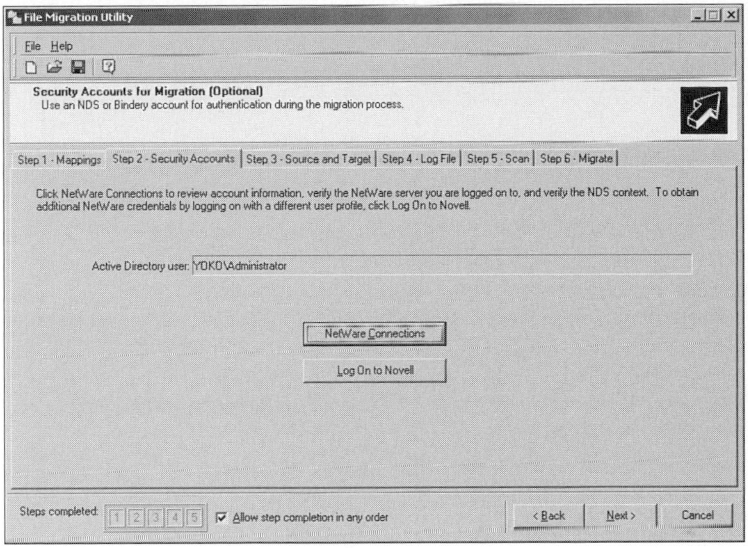

Figure 60.18   In Step 2 you review your Windows logon and can log on to the Novell network if you have not yet done so.

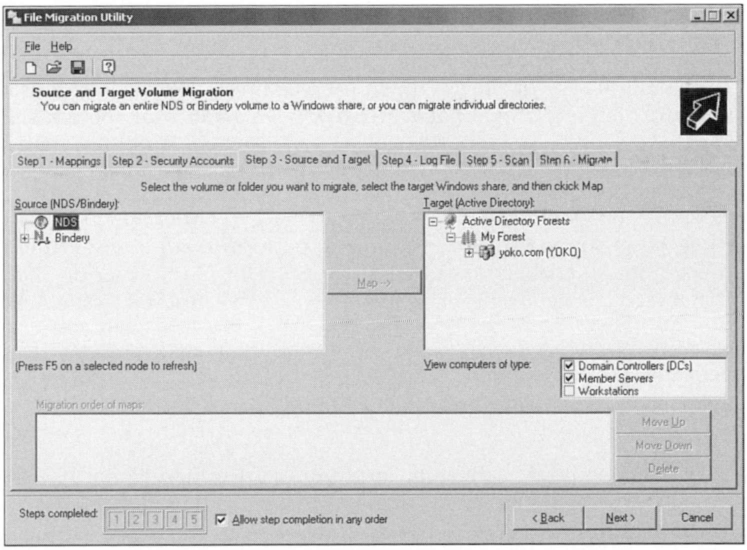

Figure 60.19   In Step 3 you select the source and target for the files and directories you want to migrate.

Step 4 enables you to create a log file and select options for generating the log file that will be created during the migration process (see Figure 60.20). Use the check box labeled Enable Logs, and then you can fill in the remaining fields shown in this figure.

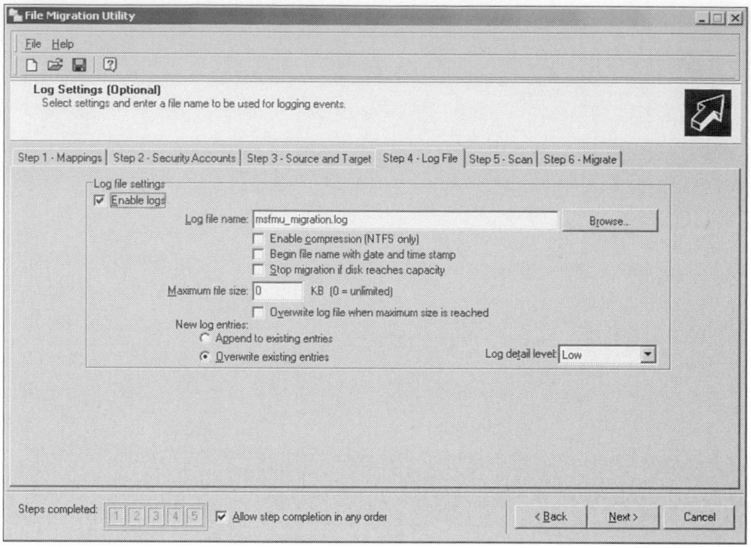

Figure 60.20 You can configure how the log file will be generated during the migration using Step 4.

If the migration will involve a lot of files, you can help reduce the size of the log file by using the Enable Compression (NTFS only) check box. If you want to append a date and timestamp in the log-file to determine when a file was actually migrated, use the next check box. The Stop Migration If Disk Reaches Capacity check box does just what it says!

You also can set a maximum size for the log file in the Maximum File Size field, or leave it at the default of zero to allow the file to grow to any size. If you set a value for this field, the check box underneath it, Overwrite Log File When Maximum Size Is Reached, should be used so that the process will continue if the log file exceeds the size you set.

The radio buttons under New Log Entries enable you to elect to either append new entries or over-write existing entries when you use the same log file to perform migrations at different times. The Log Detail Level drop-down menu enables you to select the amount of information that is logged for each file. When you've finished configuring the log file, click Next to proceed to the next step.

Step 5 is used to scan the volumes and directories you selected as sources from NDS or NetWare for the migration (see Figure 60.21). Click the Scan button and the program counts the directories and the files within them, and checks that the correct access rights are associated with each volume (or directory/file).

If any errors occur, you can choose to continue and simply use a manual method for copying the files or directories. However, if a large number of errors is encountered, the FMU utility will stop and you'll need to rethink your migration. Go back to the previous steps in the process to see whether you've entered any incorrect information or ignored access rights required to access the NDS or bindery data.

Another thing that can cause errors during the migration process is opened or locked files on the NetWare server. You might want to perform Steps 1 through 5 and save the actual migration (Step 6) until a time when you can obtain downtime for your NetWare servers to ensure that all files and directories that are to be migrated are accessible. For example, to perform the migration, you must be logged on to the Windows 2000 server with an account that is a member of the Domain Admins group.

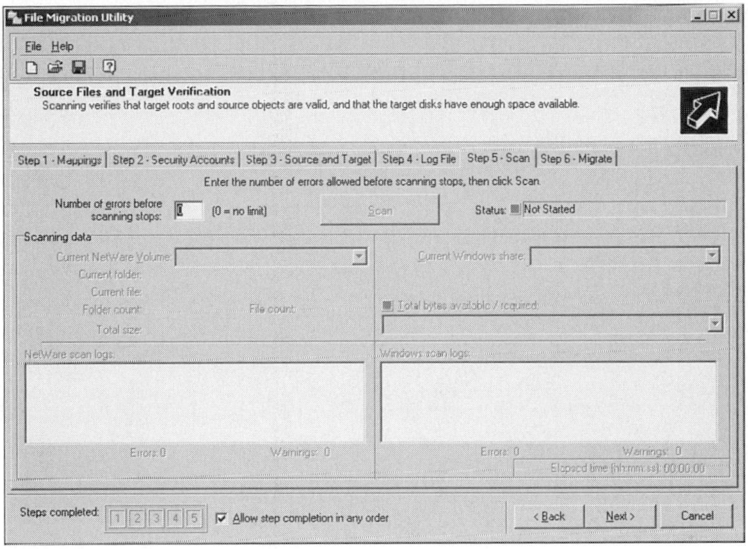

Figure 60.21   Step 5 allows you to perform a scan to check for errors before you do the actual migration.

Finally, when you are ready to perform the actual data transfer, Step 6 enables you to start the process. On the Step 6 tab (see Figure 60.22), click the Migrate button. Depending on how much data is to be transferred from NetWare to Windows 2000, the process can take just a few minutes or many hours.

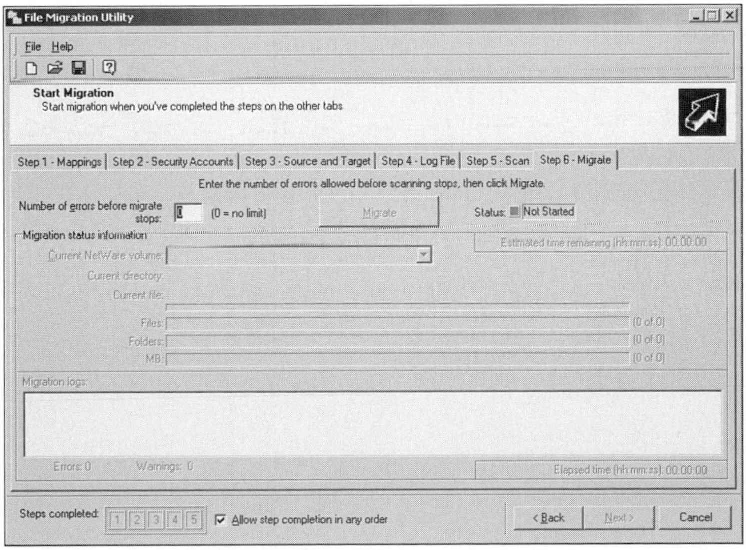

Figure 60.22   Use Step 6 to perform the actual file migration.

After you've migrated your files to Windows 2000 servers, you should perform testing to be sure that your clients can connect to the Windows 2000 servers and that the files and directories are set up as you planned. After everything checks out, consider the migration a success and decommission those NDS servers!

Migration and Integration Issues: Windows NT, Windows 2000, Windows 2003, Unix, and Linux

SOME OF THE MAIN TOPICS IN THIS CHAPTER ARE

CHAPTER 61

It would be difficult to find two operating systems that differ more from each other than Unix and Windows. Unix has been around for a much longer time than Windows and has yielded an offspring: Linux. What started out as a developer's operating system (Unix) has evolved over the years into a stable platform that runs on more hardware platforms than perhaps any other operating system, from Alpha Servers and Sparc Stations and to even "Intel Inside" systems.

Many large Web sites use either Unix or Linux to run their Web servers. Even Microsoft has been known to use Unix/Linux to run some of its Web services, until users discovered it. After that, these servers were replaced with Windows servers!

Windows 2000/2003/XP, on the other hand, are graphically oriented operating systems that now run on only one platform: Intel-compatible chips (such as AMD). If you want to run Windows 2000/2003 or Windows XP, you'll have to replace those very good Alpha Server systems (which also run Unix, Linux, and OpenVMS, by the way—so you might be able to put them to other uses).

The alternative is to stay with using Windows NT 4.0 on those older systems, if they still provide the capabilities you need and if you don't have any application requirements that require you to upgrade to a newer version of the operating system. If this is the case with your network, it's time for you to map out a long-term strategy to remove obstacles that keep you from upgrading, such as applications that will not run on a newer version of the operating system, whether it be a Microsoft OS or a Unix/Linux OS.

Microsoft usually does not support its own legacy operating systems for a long time. For example, certification examinations are phased out rather quickly so that MSCEs are required to upgrade their skills every couple of years to keep pace with the releases of the latest OS versions. Although the same can be said, to some extent, for the Unix/Linux community, an upgrade path is generally easier for these operating systems. The kernel of the Unix/Linux operating system might change to enhance performance, but the administrative tools you're familiar with can easily be recompiled and used on newer versions of Unix/Linux.

Note

If you're stuck with a vertical market application, such as a doctor or lawyer's office application, you can usually skip a generation of an operating system. A *vertical market application* is one that serves a specific purpose, often available as a packaged (or *turnkey*) solution that includes hardware, operating system and, application(s). In many cases, the vendor of this type of application software will continue to provide upgrades as operating system upgrades come to market. However, that isn't always the case. As the old saying goes, if it isn't broke, don't fix it. It's common to see vertical market applications skip one or two generations of an operating system. If this is the case with your applications, the vendor will most likely provide an upgrade path because vertical market applications and the support costs are not inexpensive, and retaining existing customers is important.

Windows 2000/2003 Support for Unix Protocols and Utilities

Windows operating systems now support many protocols and utilities that were originally created for the Unix Environment. The first that comes to mind, and perhaps the most important, is the TCP/IP protocol suite. This includes not just the TCP/IP protocols, but other associated protocols and utilities.

Many of the technologies that began in the Unix world have evolved into standards that have been implemented on other platforms over the years. For an example, see the `lpr`/`lpd` printing system and TCP/IP stream printing. Both of these started out on Unix platforms and are now supported not only by Windows, OpenVMS, and other operating systems, but also by printers from Hewlett-Packard (and most other major printer vendors) and print server appliances made by a number of other vendors. When adding Windows computers to a network that consists mainly of Unix or Linux servers, printing can be the least of a network administrator's worries. It's a simple matter to configure Windows NT 4.0/2000/2003 server operating systems to direct printer output to a Unix system that manages print queues. It's also a simple task to configure clients to use a printer that understands the `lpr/lpd` protocols or TCP/IP stream method. And, of course, you can also configure Windows 2000/2003 servers to operate as a print server using these protocols.

◄◄ If you need to learn more about printing protocols, such as `lpr/lpd` or TCP stream printing, refer to Chapter 44, "Network Printing Protocols."

Other technologies that were either first developed in or adopted by the Unix world, which Windows and Linux also support, include the following, among others:

- The TCP/IP networking protocol suite, including the standard utilities and troubleshooting tools
- BOOTP and the Dynamic Host Configuration Protocol (DHCP)
- Support for the Network Information System (NIS), developed by Sun Microsystems, and adopted by many other Unix/Linux vendors (refer to Chapter 30, "Network Name Resolution")
- The Domain Name System (DNS)

This chapter covers the protocols and utilities that these diverse operating systems have in common as well as tools that can be used to fill in the gaps in a multiprotocol environment.

TCP/IP

When Windows NT 3.51 was first brought to the market, the default network protocol was IPX/SPX. Basic TCP/IP protocols and utilities were there if you wanted to use them, but at that time Microsoft perceived its main competitor in the client/server market to be Novell's NetWare. When NT 4.0 was released, the default networking protocol had been changed to TCP/IP. Because the Internet had begun to take on a higher degree of importance during the time frame in which NT 4.0 was being marketed, this was a natural path for the operating system to take. TCP/IP is the network protocol suite that's used throughout the Internet to connect computers from a wide range of manufacturers running many different operating systems. For example, you can find TCP/IP on every Unix or Linux variant currently on the market as well on most every operating system from IBM, from OS/2 to mainframes, along with any other major operating system vendor. Of course, by the time Windows 2000 was released, TCP/IP had become the de facto standard networking protocol for all Microsoft products. It's included with Windows 2000/2003, as well as Windows client operating systems, Me and XP, as well as the client version for Windows NT and Windows 2000.

Note

The next generation of NetWare will be based on both the current NetWare kernel as well as Linux. This will provide backward compatibility for existing customers who cannot at this time upgrade to a Linux-based version of NetWare, as well as offer new functionality to NetWare, because Linux is a fast-rising star in the operating system community.

In a network that consists of Unix servers, TCP/IP can be used by Windows clients to access resources on these servers. The most common method provided by the TCP/IP suite of applications for executing commands on another computer is Telnet. For exchanging files, use the FTP utility. Other applications, such as the SSH (Secure Shell) utilities, can be incorporated into the network to allow for additional security.

Telnetxxx

Windows NT/2000/2003/XP comes with a Telnet *client*. Although Windows XP does not come with a Telnet server application, you can add this functionality by installing Services for Unix (SFU version 3.0), which is discussed later in this chapter. SFU can be installed on Windows NT/2000/2003 and Windows XP. So, for those who operate a small LAN, you can install a Telnet server on Windows XP Professional, along with many other Unix utilities and commands, for a small fee.

Windows XP is also making inroads into the corporate market. But it has been available for more than two years now, and sufficient time has passed to work out the bugs and add additional features to the OS.

Tip

If you're considering an upgrade to Windows Server 2003, you might want to wait before jumping onto the band-wagon. When any new major version of an operating system is released, there are problems. This is inevitable due to the complexity of writing code for an operating system, much less performing extensive beta testing for a wide variety of applications. It's best to wait until at least the first service pack is released. It's also a good idea to subscribe to the many Windows/Unix/Linux newsgroups so that you can find out about features/bugs early adopters are experiencing.

Windows NT/2000/2003 Servers do provide a Telnet service, but it isn't enabled by default. You must have the TCP/IP protocol networking components installed in order to use the server. This can be done during the system installation or by using the Components button in the Add/Remove Software Control Panel utility. To start the service on a Windows 2003 Server computer, use the following steps:

Note

The examples and figures in this chapter are based on Windows 2003. Windows 2000 might look a little different, but the steps described in the examples are pretty much the same.

1. Click Start, All Programs, Administrative Tools, and then Services. A list of services available on the computer is displayed in the right pane.
2. Scroll down in the right pane until you find the Telnet service.
3. Right-click on the Telnet service and select Properties (or just double-click on the Telnet service).
4. From the General properties tab (see Figure 61.1) you can select how you want to start the Telnet service. The drop-down menu labeled Startup Type enables you to select Automatic (start when the system is booted), Manual (start the service when you want to use it), or Disabled (to prevent the Telnet service from being used). In this example, the Automatic option has been selected.

If you've selected either Automatic or Manual to start the service, you must start the service by clicking on the Start button shown in Figure 61.1. If you have chosen the Manual option, then you can close the dialog box and then re-open it and start the service when you wish by using the Start button. If you've chosen the Automatic option, the service will automatically start the next time you reboot the server. Notice also that there are Stop/Pause and Resume buttons on this General tab. The Start and Stop buttons do exactly what they say: They stop and start the service. However, if you use the Pause button, administrators and members of the Server Operators group can still use the service and establish a Telnet connection with the server. This can be useful when you don't want ordinary users making Telnet connections to the machine while you're performing maintenance chores, for example. Use the Resume button to allow the service to continue servicing other users (provided you haven't stopped the service).

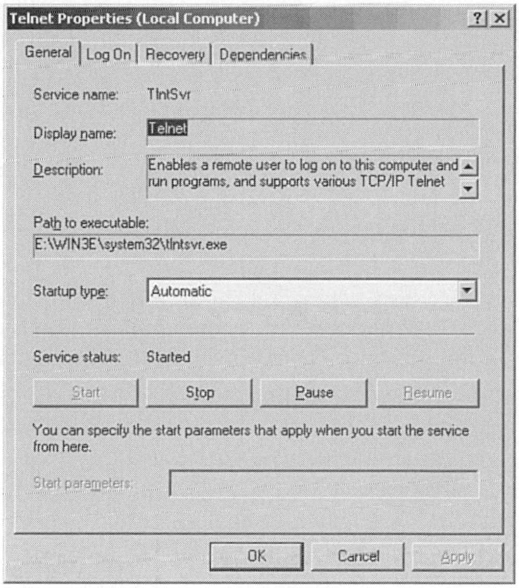

Figure 61.1   You can choose how to start the Telnet service using the General tab.

Also in Figure 61.1, you can see that there are several tabs, each of which is used for a different set of properties that you can configure for the service. Using the General tab, you can change the display name for the service and the description of the service.

Tip

If one or more of the options (start, stop, pause, and so on) appear grayed out (unavailable), it's because the current state of the Telnet server does not enable you to make the selection. For example, if the Telnet service has already been started, the Start button will not be available. Similarly, if the service is stopped, the Stop button will be grayed out and not available.

The Log On tab functions the same as for other services. You should be familiar with how services work on Windows 2000/2003 before using this tab or the Recovery tab. For example, using the Log On tab, you can select the user account that the service is run under. The AUTHORITY\LocalService account is typical for the Telnet service as well as many other services for Windows 2003. For Windows 2000, the LocalSystem account is generally used for running services. At the bottom of the Log On tab, you can choose a hardware profile for which the service can be enabled or disabled. Select the particular hardware profile you want to modify and use the Enable or Disable button.

The Recovery tab, shown in Figure 61.2, determines how the service will be restarted if the service fails for some reason.

The options available on the Recovery tab are

- **First failure**—Your options are to take no action (leave the service unavailable), restart the service, run a program (one other than the Telnet service, for example), or restart the computer. Using the restart option, Windows 2003 will attempt to restart the service. Selecting the Restart the Service option can be used if you suspect that the service was stopped because of some other problem with the server, and if you've selected the automatic startup type for this service.

- **Subsequent failure**—The options here are the same as for the First Failure drop-down list. However, the option you choose here will be used for each failure that occurs after the first failure. This can be modified by setting a value for the next field.

- **Reset fail count after**—If you leave this value at the default of 0, after the second failure, the next failure will take the action specified in the First Failure field. Otherwise, you can set the number of days that the service must run successfully before the failure count is reset to the First Failure field. A higher number of days will cause the service to use the action set in the Subsequent Failure field for that number of days. After the number of days you specify, the First Failure option will be used.

- **Restart service after**—Use this field to set the number of minutes that the system will wait before attempting to restart the service. This value applies to both the First Failure and Subsequent Failure options, provided that you've selected the Restart the Service option.

- **Run Program**—If you've selected Run a Program for either the First or Subsequent Failure fields, you can enter a program or a script file that will be run after a failure. This can be useful if you want to write a script file that notifies you that the service has failed, for example. You can use the Browse button to select a program or script file to run or just fill in the field labeled Program.

- **Command line parameters**—Use this field to provide command-line parameters that will be passed to the program or script file, if you have chosen the Run Program option.

- **Append fail count to end of command line**—The number of failures can be passed to the program or script file using this field. For example, you might want the script file or program to know how many times the service has failed and take a different action based on this value.

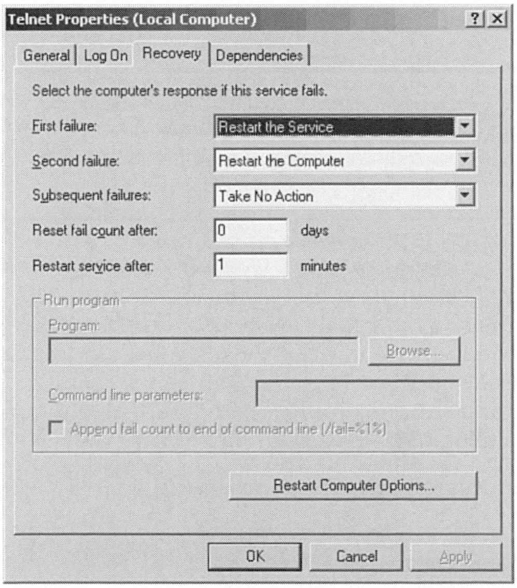

Figure 61.2 You can use the Recovery tab to decide what actions to take if the Telnet service fails.

The Restart Computer Options button enables you to specify the number of minutes after which the computer will restart, if you have chosen that option in the preceding fields. In Figure 61.3, you can see that you can also enter a message to display to users on the network who are using the Telnet service to inform them that the service is either not available or being restarted, depending on the options you selected on the Recovery tab. Use the Restart Computer Options button on the Recovery tab to display this dialog box.

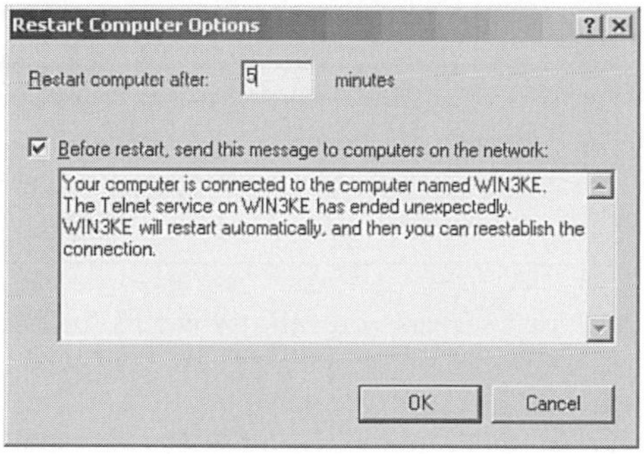

Figure 61.3   Select the number of minutes after which the computer will be rebooted after the service fails, and enter a text message to send to users currently using the Telnet service.

The last tab, Dependencies, is used to list the other services that must be running before the Telnet service can be started. If one of these services fails, for example, the Telnet service itself can fail. And if there is a problem in restarting one of these services after the computer reboots (if you chose that option), the Telnet service will not restart. In this case, you should check the Event Viewer to determine the reason that a service that Telnet depends on isn't restarting. If the Telnet service fails because a dependent service fails, you might consider using a script file to check for and restart dependent services.

Managing Windows 2000 Telnet Server

After you've started the Telnet server service on the Windows 2000 Server, you can manage the server by using the Telnet Server Administration utility found in the Administrative Tools folder. As you can see in Figure 61.4, the interface to the Windows 2000 service utility is simple. You have the options of listing connected users or terminating users and the ability to start or stop the service.

Figure 61.4   The standard Windows 2000 Telnet server uses a simple interface for management purposes.

Option number 3 enables you to view current default settings that are stored in the Registry for the server. This option can be used to allow trusted domains access to the server, provide a logon script, and set the number of log failures before a user is locked out. An important feature you can use is one that forces users to use the more secure Windows NT NTLM authentication instead of the typical clear-text username/password method that is found in many typical Telnet server implementations. This should definitely be used in an all-Windows environment. However, Unix clients do not, by default, support this authentication method.

Note

The default Telnet server that comes with Windows 2000 Server allows for a maximum of two simultaneous Telnet sessions. If you need to allow more users to establish Telnet connections to the server, you'll have to use the Telnet server provided by the Microsoft Services for Unix (SFU) package instead. SFU is discussed later in this chapter and supports as many as 63 client sessions.

There are excellent third-party Telnet servers you can use with Windows. If you intend to make heavy use of Telnet on your network, it's worth investigating these competing products to determine which Telnet server is right for your needs. Don't forget, however, to look first at the server that you can get from SFU. Because SFU is available for about $100—and you can install the products on as many Windows computers in your LAN as you want, with no additional fee—this more robust Telnet server (along with many other Unix-based utilities) is a bargain.

Telnet provides a character-cell terminal emulation that can be used to run applications that do not depend on the features provided by either the Windows GUI or its equivalent in the Unix world, the X Window System. For example, it's easy to telnet into a Unix system to perform system administration tasks using a command-line interface provided by a shell. Script files can be edited and run remotely by using a Telnet session. Telnet is pretty much the standard for many operating systems for remote administration on a command-line basis. You can telnet to many different systems, each using a different operating system, and execute commands that are specific to that system. For example, from a Windows or Unix/Linux computer, you can telnet to an OpenVMS server, another Windows server, as well as all the various flavors of Unix/Linux. After the Telnet session has been established, just remember to use the commands that are appropriate for the operating system of the host you've established a session with. Telnet is a powerful application for system/network administrators who manage computers in the network that use different operating systems. Telnet servers have been imbedded in the firmware of many devices other than computers. For example, most printers, print servers, switches, and so on can be accessed using Telnet. This capability usually presents you with a menu to perform tasks specific to that device.

However, not all Windows administrative utilities have a command-line counterpart. And even when they do, you often find that the command-line version doesn't provide the full capabilities that the GUI version does. The same, of course, applies to other operating systems. For example, although you can telnet to a Linux box from a Windows system, you might not be able to use all the system utilities offered in the KDE/Gnome and other X Window System GUI interfaces that can be used on Linux.

However, Telnet and FTP are perhaps the two most useful applications now available on most operating system platforms.

Managing Telnet on Windows 2003 Server

When using the Windows 2000 Telnet server application, you saw that the Command Prompt was used with a menu to enable you to manage the Telnet server. For Windows 2003, a command-line interface is also used, but you'll have to specify the option you want to manage instead of using a menu. The basic command used for all of these options is the `tlntadmn` command. If you enter just the `tlntadmn` command at the Command Prompt, with no qualifiers, a display (see Figure 61.5) shows you the current configuration of the Telnet server.

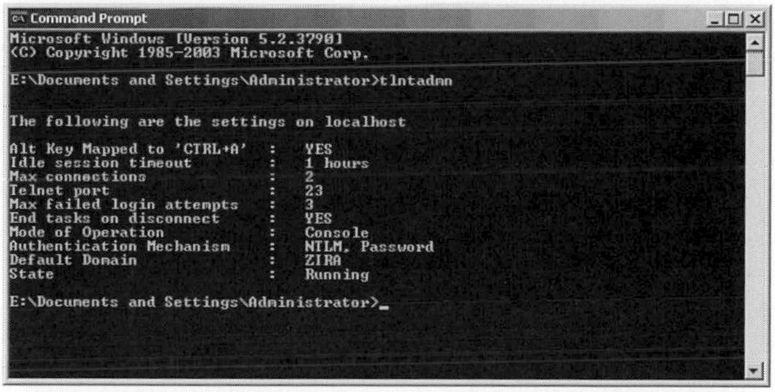

Figure 61.5   Use the `tlntadmn` command with no command-line parameters to display the current configuration of the Telnet server.

The syntax for this command varies depending on the function you want to perform. In the following examples, brackets are used to indicate optional components. You can use one or more of the command-line options listed here. The basic functions are

```
tlntadmn [\\remoteserver] [start] [stop] [pause] [continue] [-u username -p password] [-s]
[-k (sessionid | all)] [-m (sessionid | all) "message"]
```

- **\\remoteserver**—Specifies another server that you want to administer instead of the local computer's Telnet server.

- **start/stop/pause/continue**—These options operate in the same manner as detailed previously when using the Administrative Tools Telnet service tool.

- **-u username and -p password**—These command-line parameters can be used to specify a username and password that's valid on the remote server. Note that the user account must be an administrator account or an account that's a member of the Server Operators group.

- **-s sessionid**—Use this parameter to list information about a session.

- **-k sessionid | all**—Kill a session or use all to kill all sessions.

- **-m sessionid | all "message"**—Send a message to a particular user (using the session ID) or to all users. Enclose the message in quotation marks.

There are other command-line options you can use in addition to these basic ones. Use the help function to see all the possible options you can use with the `tlntadmn` utility.

Figure 61.6 shows an example of using two of these commands. The first command (-s) lists the current session of a remote user who has used Telnet to connect to the server. The second command (-k sessionid) shows an example of how to use the session ID (under the column ID) to kill that connection. You can also see information about the session, such as the domain name of the initiator of the session, the username, the IP address, as well as the date/time that the session was established and the amount of idle time (time that no commands were being used by the remote user).

The File Transfer Protocol

Like the Telnet server, Windows NT/2000/2003/XP comes with an FTP client. For Windows NT 4.0 through Windows 2003, the FTP server is provided by installing Internet Information Services (IIS).

◄◄   Chapter 26, "Basic TCP/IP Services and Applications," covers the actual mechanics of FTP in greater detail.

Figure 61.6 This is an example of using the -s and -k command-line options.

The FTP Client

The FTP client can be utilized easily from the Command Prompt and uses the standard syntax that's common to other FTP clients, with a few exceptions that you might not notice. For example, although many Unix/Linux servers require that you log in by using the command User <*username*>, the Windows version prompts you for the username after you issue the FTP command as well as the password for the account name you enter. This is a minor difference, but it's important to note that although FTP is defined by a set of RFCs, some vendors add their own features to make the utility simpler to use.

The FTP server for Windows NT through Windows 2003 Server is a component of IIS, which is included as part of the installation procedure for Windows 2000. For Windows NT, you can use the icon that appears on the desktop of a Windows NT Server to install IIS or, better yet, download the newest version from Microsoft. IIS has been enhanced many times since its first release. Windows 2000 users will find that IIS is included on the server installation CD, but again, check for a newer version at Microsoft's Web site. An important reason for this is that newer versions have fixed problems with previous ones. Of course, the reverse is also true in some cases. One problem is fixed by a newer version, but might introduce a new set of problems! In Figure 61.7, you can see an example of using the Windows 2000 FTP client.

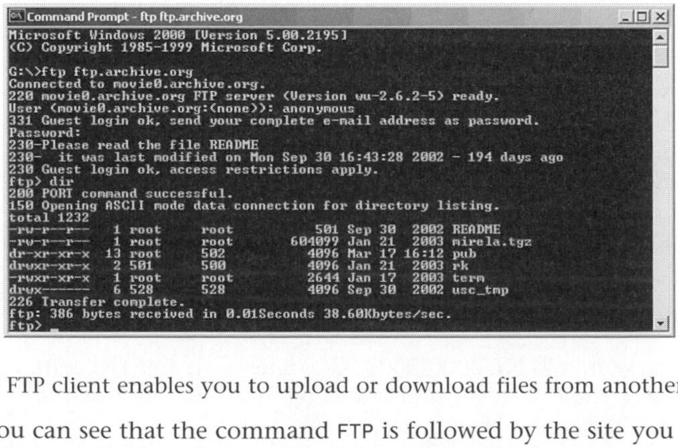

Figure 61.7 The FTP client enables you to upload or download files from another server.

In this example, you can see that the command FTP is followed by the site you want to make a connection to. If the site is available only to authenticated users who have an account on the server, you have to enter a valid username and password for that server. Another method for logging into many sites is to use the username anonymous. The convention for using this login is to use your email address for the password prompt. After you've logged in to the FTP server, you can issue commands that are available on that server. For example, the commands ls and dir will usually produce a listing of files and directories for the main directory that's set up for your login type. When using Unix/Linux or Windows clients, you can use the CD command to change to another directory until you find the data that you need to use. Notice that for most implementations of FTP, you must use lowercase characters for the commands and use the exact lowercase or uppercase syntax for a particular file. You can then use commands such as the following:

- **get**—Use this command to retrieve a file from a remote server. For example, get *filename*.
- **put**—Use this command to send a file to a remote server. For example, put *filename*.
- **mget**—This command can be used with wildcards (such as * and ?) to retrieve multiple files that match the wildcards.
- **mput**—This command works like mget, but enables you to send multiple files to the FTP server using wildcards.
- **hash**—If you care to watch the progress of an operation such as sending or receiving a file, this command will print hash marks (#) to show you the progress of the operation.
- **binary/ascii**—These commands specify the type of file you want to receive or send. ASCII files consist of simple text files, whereas binary files are usually executable files (application files, word processing files, and so on).
- **prompt**—This command might not be available on all implementations of FTP. This command is generally used with the mget or mput commands. When using these commands with wildcards, you might be prompted to specify yes or no (Y/N) before sending a file. The prompt command eliminates these prompts and just downloads or uploads all files matching the file specification.
- **quit**—This command is used to exit the FTP client.

Tip

Wildcards are used by many operating systems to indicate that you're specifying certain characters that a filename must contain and at the same time specifying that other characters can be anything. The asterisk (*) wildcard means that any characters (and any number of characters) can be substituted for the filename. For example, using the filename of Yoko*.txt will retrieve (or send) any file that starts with Yoko, ends with .txt, and contains any number of characters between Yoko and the dot (.) delimiter.

Another wildcard, the question mark (?) can be used to specify a specific number of characters that can be used to match a get or put operation. For example, the filename secret???.txt means that the file must start with the text secret and be followed by just three characters and the filename extension .txt. Contrast this with the * wildcard which allows for any number of characters following those you specify.

Additionally, you can specify the * wildcard in a manner such as *.mpeg2 to send or receive any file that ends with the file extension of .mpeg2, no matter how many characters make up the first part of the filename. The same goes for using the ? wildcard, although it still specifies that only filenames that contain the same number of question marks will be sent or retrieved.

Managing the FTP Service on a Windows Server 2003

To manage the basic FTP server on a Windows 2000/2003 server, follow these steps:

1. Click Start, All Programs (Programs for Windows 2000) Administrative Tools, Internet Services (IIS) Manager.

2. The MMC console starts with the IIS snap-in. Click on the IIS server you want to manage (in this example, FTP sites).

3. Right-click on the FTP site you want to manage (the Default FTP site in our example) and select Properties.

4. The properties pages for the FTP server can then be used to configure the server (see Figure 61.8).

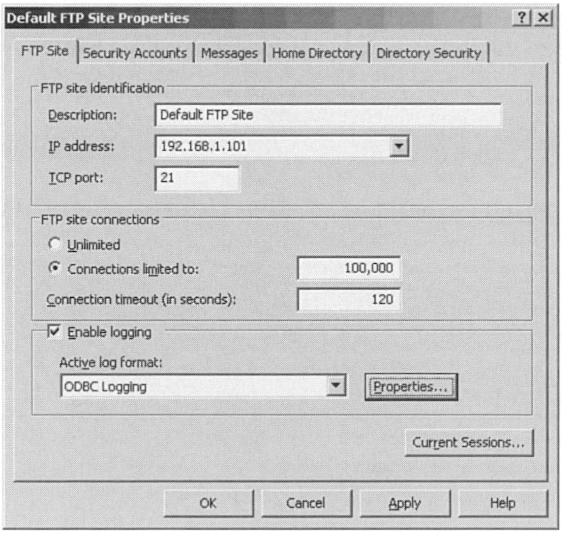

Figure 61.8 You can configure the FTP server using these properties sheets.

The Default FTP Site Properties page appears in this figure with the first tab (FTP Site) selected. You can use the Description field to change this from `default` to a more meaningful name. This can be useful if you're using the MMC to manage multiple FTP sites on the same server or on other servers. The IP Address field can be used to select an IP address that the FTP service will use when listening for incoming requests, and the TCP Port field can be used to set which TCP port will be used for the service. In this example, the standard TCP port number of 21 is shown.

Other fields on this tab are fairly self-explanatory, enabling you to set the maximum number of users that can be connected to the server simultaneously and the number of seconds after which an idle session will be automatically disconnected from the server. At the bottom of this first property page, you can also enable logging for the service. The Active Log Format drop-down menu enables you to choose from

- **Microsoft IIS Log File Format**—This is a standard ASCII text file format. If you use this format, the information that's stored in the log file is fixed.

- **W3C Extended Log File Format**—This also is an ASCII text file, but one that you can customize to select what events to log. This is the default format for the IIS FTP server.
- **ODBC Logging**—This can be used to direct logging data to an ODBC-compliant database.

The Properties button to the right of this drop-down menu enables you to further configure properties for the log file. For the Microsoft IIS log file format, there's not much you can configure. The data that is written to the log file is a standard set of data. You can use the Properties button to configure when a new log file is created—this can range from hourly, daily, weekly, or monthly. Or you can set a maximum size to which the file can grow before a new file is created. Additionally, you can set the location of the log file. The default is %WinDir%\System32\LogFiles, where %WinDir% is a variable that resolves to the Windows system directory.

For the W3C extended log file format, you have many more options. In addition to being able to configure the same options about how or when a new log file is created and the location of the log file, this format has an additional tab labeled Advanced.

There are far too many data items to discuss in this chapter, but you need to be aware that you can create a customized log file that stores just the information you need. You might find that on an anonymous FTP server, you don't care much about what data is stored in the log file, whereas on a server that provides for a secure logon, you might want to collect extensive data about the users of your system. To find out the meaning of each of these logging options, click the Help button and a brief description of each item will be displayed.

Caution

When using an FTP server that requires authentication using a username/password, you can usually be sure that a malicious user won't abuse your site. However, when using anonymous FTP, you need to be aware that a simple hack is to use this anonymous account to fill up the allocated space so that other users cannot use the anonymous login. For more information about this topic, see Chapter 46, "Basic Security Measures Every Network Administrator Needs to Know."

Other tabs on the FTP Site Properties page include

- **Security Accounts**—Use this tab to allow or disallow anonymous access to the FTP server. If you allow anonymous FTP connections, you also can configure the user account that will be used for these connections.
- **Messages**—This tab enables you to input text that's presented to the user when logging in to and upon exiting the service. You also can enter a message that will be displayed to users who try to log on to the server when the maximum number of user sessions has already been reached.
- **Home Directory**—This tab enables you to configure the home directory for this FTP service. You can select a directory that's local to the server or a directory that's offered as a file share from another computer. If you choose the file share option, you'll be prompted to enter authentication information needed to connect to the file share. The default directory is c:\inetpub\ftproot. Here you can select whether the directory can be read, written to, or both. You also can select to allow logging for this directory. Finally, this tab can be used to specify how directory listings are displayed to users. You can choose between the standard MS-DOS format and the standard Unix format.
- **Directory Security**—This tab is important because it enables you to decide which computers (or IP addresses) will be allowed to connect to the service. You can choose to allow all computers access and then specify a number of specific computers to exclude from access, or you can choose to deny access to all computers and then add in only those specific addresses you want to allow to use the service.

When using the Directory Security tab to allow or deny access to the FTP service, remember that some computers use a proxy server. This is typically found when the computer to which you want to grant access is on the other side of a fire-wall. In this case, the address of the firewall (acting as a proxy server) uses its address when sending connection requests instead of the actual address of the client computer. If you allow (or deny) access in this manner, any computer that uses the proxy server will be allowed (or denied) access.

As you can see, the FTP service enables you to control who can access your server and to log each visit in detail. You can create additional FTP sites on the same computer. For example, if you have multiple network adapters or if you assign multiple IP addresses to the same adapter, you can create additional FTP sites on the same server. To add additional FTP sites on this server:

1. Highlight the computer server's name in the left pane of the MMC console.

2. Click on Action, select New, and then FTP Site.

3. A wizard appears and prompts you through creating the site, enabling you to enter the necessary information, such as a description of the site, the IP address to use, and so on.

Of course, after you've created an additional site, you can further refine how it operates by using the properties pages for that site.

The Dynamic Host Configuration Protocol and BOOTP

Most Unix environments, which use TCP/IP for networking, use DHCP servers to provide network configuration information to clients on the network. DHCP is not a proprietary solution, but is based on standards that are defined in RFCs 2131 and 2132. Microsoft clients using TCP/IP can also use DHCP servers. Additionally, Windows 2000/2003 have a highly configurable DHCP server that supports options provided for in the RFCs as well as a few that are specific for Microsoft clients.

Tip

There are a few other proposed standards RFC documents that apply to DHCP. For more information, search the database at www.rfc-editor.org.

If you're bringing Windows-based client systems into an existing Unix environment, configuring each Windows client with the address of a DHCP server will be simple. In an existing Windows network, you might want to stick with the Microsoft DHCP server. Because DHCP is based on Internet standards, most of the implementations you find will be compatible with both operating systems.

Bringing Unix clients into a network that uses Microsoft DHCP servers can cause even some seasoned Unix administrators to worry. DHCP servers have been around for quite a while on Unix networks, running on Unix servers, and Microsoft's DHCP server is a relatively new creature on the market. However, because Microsoft's DHCP server is built using the standards set forth in the relevant RFC documents, you should have no reason to worry. The graphical interface Microsoft's version offers makes it even easier to manage the server and should be considered an advantage over some other products.

The DHCP server that you can install on Windows NT 4.0 through Windows 2003 is a full-featured implementation that can be used to support clients no matter what their operating system. The configuration information that a DHCP server sends to clients is itself configurable through the use of DHCP options. Each option describes a parameter that can be configured for the client from information the DHCP server can provide.

◀◀   For more information about how BOOTP and DHCP function and how they can greatly simplify network administration tasks, refer to Chapter 29, "BOOTP and Dynamic Host Configuration Protocol (DHCP)."

Microsoft's DHCP server provides support for the options defined in RFC 1533, "DHCP Options and
BOOTP Vendor Extensions." In addition, it enables the administrator to define custom options when
needed. This ability to create customized options makes the server flexible in a networking environment that consists of different client types. Additionally, it's possible to set up the Microsoft DHCP
service to run on a Windows 2000/2003 cluster, and thus provide redundancy for the network without having to divide the address space into separate scopes and place each scope on a separate server.

Before there was DHCP, there was BOOTP, which functions in a manner similar to DHCP. The BOOTP
protocol is mainly used by diskless workstations, usually in a Unix network, to request addressing
configuration information and to download an operating system. Microsoft's DHCP server enables the
administrator to create records in a BOOTP table that can be used to satisfy requests from this kind of
client. When the DHCP server receives a BOOTP request from a client, it looks up the client in the
table. If a record for that client is found, the server returns three pieces of information to the client:

- **Boot Image**—A generic filename for the boot file
- **File Name**—The path to the boot image on a TFTP (Trivial File Transfer Protocol) server
- **TFTP Server**—The server from which the client can download the boot file

The Microsoft DHCP server responds to BOOTP clients with the information they need to download a
boot file from another server. Unlike the standard DHCP lease, the BOOTP client does not have to
renew the IP address periodically as regular DHCP clients do. Instead, a BOOTP client is managed like
clients who use reserved DHCP addresses. Additionally, Windows 2000/2003 DHCP server allows for
many other options that can be used by BOOTP clients, as provided for in the RFCs.

DNS

DNS is the standard method used on the Internet to resolve host IP addresses to friendly names that
humans find easier to remember. Microsoft NT 4.0/2000/2003 provide a DNS server that is based on
RFC 1053 and can be used by both Microsoft clients and other clients that have been created based
on this standard. This includes, of course, most Unix and Linux clients. Additionally, with Windows
2000/2003, Microsoft's DNS server supports dynamic DNS, which is defined in RFC 2136, "Dynamic
Updates in the Domain Name System (DNS UPDATE)." This enables clients to use DHCP to obtain an
address, and then have that address automatically registered with the DNS server. This feature can be
very useful if you have many mobile clients that move among different subnets. Manually updating a
DNS server for every move could be a daunting task in a large network.

◀◀   Chapter 30 covers the implementation of DNS.

If you already have a DNS server running on your network, you might wonder why you would want
to use Microsoft's DNS server when you add clients that are not running Unix or Linux. The answer is
simple: In addition to providing support for dynamic DNS, Microsoft's DNS server provides a WINS
(Windows Internet Name Service) lookup feature that can further simplify network administration
chores. It provides a service similar to what DNS does, but with an interesting twist. Microsoft's DNS
server has the capability to query a WINS server when it cannot resolve a name or address based on
the information contained in its database.

Although DNS is basically used to perform IP address/name translations, WINS was developed to provide name resolution services for NetBIOS names. When a WINS client computer boots, it registers its
NetBIOS name(s) with the WINS server along with its current network address. Sounds a lot like
dynamic DNS, doesn't it? If you incorporate DHCP into the network, you'll be relieved of having to
keep track of IP addresses for Microsoft clients as well as maintaining an address space when clients

move or new clients are added to the network. Enabling Microsoft clients to use the WINS service eliminates the manual task of administering a name server to keep track of additions or changes to the network.

If you plan to move your network toward using only Windows 2000/2003 and Windows XP, you probably won't need WINS any more. It's provided with Windows 2000/2003 only for backward compatibility with earlier Microsoft operating systems. It's possible to use both WINS and DNS in the same network with Windows 2000/2003 and earlier systems. However, in a network that includes Unix, Linux, and Windows clients, you really don't need WINS any more if the Windows clients are all Windows 2000 or above (such as Windows Me/XP as well as Windows Server 2003).

Applications

Does every user need a desktop computer in the first place? Years ago, when typewriters were the main "word processor," they weren't deployed on every desktop—that's what administrative assistants were used for. Today, other applications, such as email, are essential for many users. However, that isn't always true for every employee. For managers who have administrative assistants, a single desktop computer can suffice in many cases. And the administrative assistant—who is often already responsible for receiving emails and passing on important ones to the managers—can perform this function. Is it really necessary to put a computer on every desktop?

I've found it to be typical in many corporate environments to deploy a wide array of applications to all desktops, or to segmented groups of user desktops, that are never used and aren't required for the user to perform his job function. Does every user in your company need every application for which you have purchased a site license? But the downside to this is that it might be more expensive to tailor desktops on a user-by-user basis than by groups or the entire enterprise as a whole. It's a balancing act. Which is less expensive? Configuring (and paying for) applications that not every user needs, or spending your budget for administrative and help desk personnel to determine just what applications a user *does* need? I like to refer to this as *application overload*.

Both the Windows and Unix/Linux operating systems have their own strengths and weaknesses, and each can be used to solve certain problems more effectively than the other. By integrating these two systems into the same network, you can take advantage of each one's best capabilities and enhance performance of the services provided to users.

For example, Microsoft makes the majority of its profits based on sales of operating systems and the Microsoft Office suite of products. There are many alternatives. One of these is offered by two different organizations. The OpenOffice initiative is an open source suite of applications that, although not as sophisticated as Microsoft Office, is free. And the spreadsheet and word processor applications can read/write files based on Microsoft formats, for the most part. In a recent test, I found that the OpenOffice spreadsheet program does a better job of printing these files to fit-to-page than Microsoft Office does in some cases.

Visit the Web site `http://www.openoffice.org`. You'll even find a Mac OS X version at this site. If you want to purchase similar software, with enhancements and support from the vendor, you can contact Sun Microsystems using the URL `www.sun.com`. There you'll find StarOffice, which can be installed on Solaris, Linux, as well as Windows systems. This product isn't free, but does have a respected vendor backing it, so you can expect to get a good amount of support if you decide to adopt it in your network.

Whichever you choose, OpenOffice and StarOffice both provide a subset of the functionality of Microsoft's Office product. Unless you need all the bells and whistles provided by Microsoft Office, consider this alternative. And because Microsoft Office products continue to incorporate new features that many users don't need, you might find that OpenOffice and StarOffice are all that you need for your business. This book was written using all three.

There are two approaches you can take to integrating these two kinds of systems in one network. First, you can use the features Microsoft provides for the Windows environment, which were derived from standards that were developed in the Unix world—such as TCP/IP and the standard suite of utilities that have been written around it (FTP and Telnet, for example). Second, you can use third-party applications, such as Samba, that have been created to allow Windows Server Message Block (SMB) and Common Internet File System (CIFS) functionality to be installed on Unix/Linux platforms. This last approach seems to be the path that Microsoft will be taking in the near future, heralded by the release of the Microsoft Services for Unix (SFU) version 3.0. SFU provides components from Microsoft and other vendors that can make life easier for a Unix administrator who inherits a network of Windows clients.

◄◄ Refer to Chapter 35, "File Server Protocols," for more about Samba, SMB, and CIFS.

Microsoft Windows Services for Unix 3.0

Instead of trying to tackle the enormous job of developing still more applications to make it easier to integrate Unix and Windows into a cohesive network, Microsoft chose to take advantage of developments by other vendors and instead released the Windows NT Services for Unix Add-On Pack. This set of applications contains in-house applications developed by Microsoft as well as products licensed and bought from other companies. Now simply called Services for Unix (SFU) Version 3.0, this optional software, which sells for about $100, contains applications that were developed by Microsoft and other vendors, but that can be bought as a single package.

Not all the services available in SFU 3.0 are discussed in this chapter, but Table 61.1 can give you an idea of what types of software are available in SFU 3.0 and which platforms they can be used on.

Table 61.1   Services Provided by the SFU 3.0 Package

SFU Component	Windows 2000/2003	Windows XP
Basic Utilities	Yes	Yes
Unix Perl	Yes	Yes
Interix GNU Utilities	Yes	Yes
Interix GNU SDK	Yes	Yes
Client for NFS	Yes	Yes
Server for NFS	Yes	Yes
Server for PCNFS	Yes	Yes
Server for NFS Authentication	Yes	Yes
Gateway for NFS	Yes	No
Server for NIS	Yes (DC Only)	No
Password Synchronization	Yes	Yes
Telnet Server	Yes	No
Windows Remote Shell Service	Yes	Yes
User Name Mapping	Yes	Yes
Interix SDK	Yes	Yes
ActiveState ActivePerl	Yes	Yes

Tip

Although the price for SFU 3.0 is inexpensive, you can still try it before you buy it. At **www.microsoft.com**, search for **SFU 3**; from the results, you'll be able to go to the home page for Windows Services for Unix 3.0. You can also try the link **http://www.microsoft.com/windows/sfu/default.asp**, although URLs at Microsoft's Web site tend to change now and then.

You can download a copy of a 120-day trial version. Other vendors sell similar software, so it would be prudent to check out SFU 3.0 against what competitors are offering, especially because many parts of SFU 3.0 were licensed from third-party vendors.

In addition, you'll find many other components, such as support for Sun's Network Information System (NIS) among others.

SFU 3.0 can be run on Windows NT 4.0 (with Service Pack 6a installed), Windows 2000 and 2003, and even Windows XP Professional (which was a surprise to me). In this chapter, Windows XP will be the example. Perhaps the best thing about SFU, besides its price, is that *you can install it on as many computers in your network as you want*. You don't have to buy a license or additional copies of the software for each computer.

Installing SFU 3.0

Installing SFU 3.0 is a simple task, as explained in this section. Note that some of the dialog boxes and steps in the following text might not appear during your installation. This example is based on installing all components of SFU 3.0. If you select less than all components, only dialog boxes for those components will appear. To begin the installation:

1. Insert the CD and wait for the Installation Wizard to appear. If the CD does not automatically run, execute the setup.exe program on the CD. Click Next to continue the installation.

2. The next wizard dialog box asks you to enter customer information (your name and organization name). After you click Next, the End User License Agreement (EULA) dialog box appears. Read the licensing information, click the I Accept The Agreement radio button, and then click Next.

3. You're then presented with a dialog box asking whether you want to select the standard installation or a custom installation. I suggest you select the custom installation because doing so gives you the ability to select just the components you want to install. For example, you might want to install the new Telnet server and the Interix system and not install other components. Using the Custom Installation radio button, you can make choices in the next dialog box.

4. In Figure 61.9, you can see the Selecting Components dialog box (if you chose to perform a custom installation). Some of the entries in this dialog box can be expanded by clicking on the plus sign (+) to reveal additional components. To get a brief description of each component, click once and read the text that appears at the bottom of the dialog box under the Description label.

5. Use the arrow button (pointing downward) to reveal the options for each component. The options you can select are a) Will be installed on local hard drive, b) Entire feature (including all subfeatures if any) will be installed on the local hard drive, or c) Entire feature will not be available. An icon that looks like a hard drive will be displayed for each component you select to install. A red X will appear by a component you've chosen not to install. Click Next.

6. Some features preclude installing other features. If you choose to install both the Client for NFS as well as the Gateway for NFS, for example, a warning box will inform you that you must select one or the other. Dismiss the warning box and re-select the option to install.

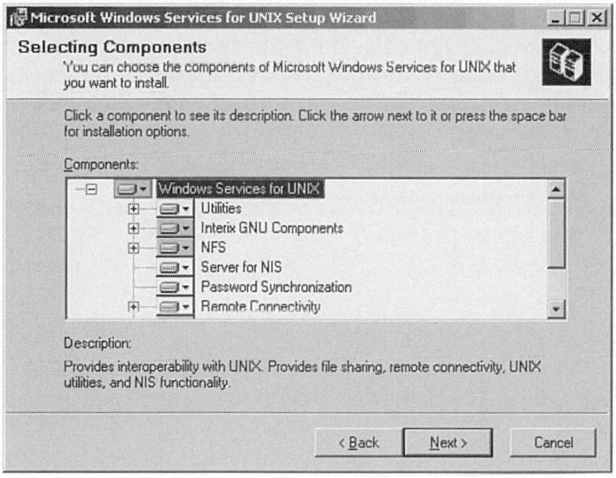

Figure 61.9 This dialog box enables you to select which components to install when performing a custom installation.

7. If you chose to install the Interix GNU SDK (software development kit), the next wizard dialog box gives you information about the GNU license. If you accept these licensing terms, click Next. If you don't accept them, click Back and deselect that option.

8. Figure 61.10 shows another license dialog box; this one appears if you chose to install ActiveState Perl. This license is presented as an option because the component is provided by a third-party software developer instead of Microsoft. Click I Accept the Agreement radio button and then click Next to continue. Otherwise, click the Back button to deselect this option.

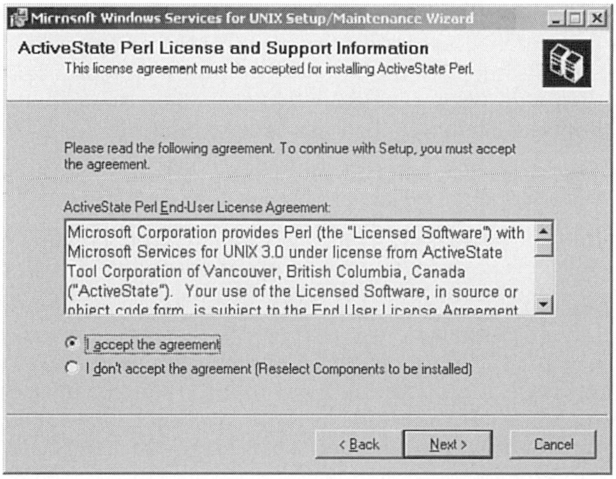

Figure 61.10 Some components of SFU 3.0 are provided by third-party software developers and require you to accept the terms of their license before you can install that component of SFU.

9. Figure 61.11 shows an important dialog box that might be displayed, depending on which components you chose to install. You can enable the `setuid` options for programs that run under the Interix system, and change Windows default from case-insensitive behavior to case sensitive. This is because the Unix and Linux operating systems use case-sensitive filenames. For example, `MyFile.txt` is not the same file as `MYFILE.TXT`.

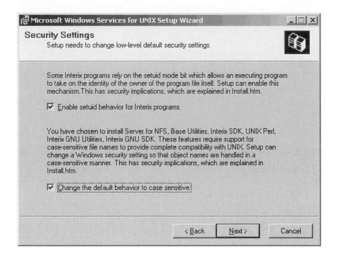

Figure 61.11 Select options that enable certain features to behave the same as if they were running on a Unix/Linux computer.

10. If you've decided to install username mapping, a dialog box will ask you to enter the name of the server that runs this service. You can enter the server name here or enter it at a later time if you don't know the name of the server. Click Next.

11. If you chose to install the NIS/Password Synchronization component, the next wizard screen informs you that this feature will need to be installed on all replicas of domain controllers in your domain and that the Active Directory schema will be changed. Remember that changes to the schema cannot be deleted, although they can be disabled.

12. In Figure 61.12, the wizard lets you choose the hard drive and directory path that will be used to install the SFU components. Make your choices and click Next.

13. A wizard screen will show the progress as the installation of SFU components are installed. After the selected components have been installed, the services for SFU will be started. This can take a few minutes, depending on the services chosen and the hardware of your server.

14. Finally, a wizard screen will inform you that the SFU components have been installed, and that some services, such as `cron` and some of the Interix daemons (background processes similar to services in Windows operating systems), have not been started. To start these, use Start/Administrative Tools/Services for Windows XP or Windows 2003 (or Start/Programs/Administrative Tools/Services for Windows 2000) to start or stop the new services that have now been added to Windows.

After the installation has finished, you have to restart your server to make all components available.

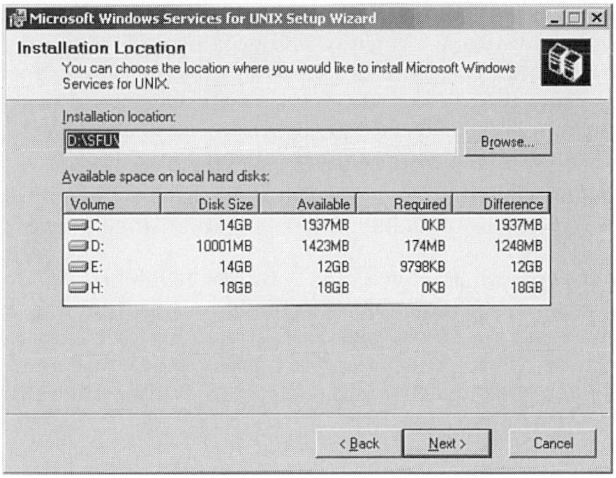

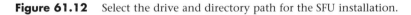

Figure 61.12   Select the drive and directory path for the SFU installation.

Network File System

The NFS client allows Windows clients to connect to NFS file systems hosted on Unix servers. The client can connect to the file system exported by a Unix server using several methods. The simplest method is to use the Windows Explorer Accessory; click on My Network Places, and select the server you want to connect to from the right-side pane. Then use Tools, Map Network Drive to make a drive letter to the NFS file share. You also can use the command line to connect to NFS file systems. To make matters simpler for a network that's composed of both Unix and Windows users, several syntaxes are supported:

- **net use**—The standard Windows net use command can be used to connect just as you can to a normal Windows file share. The specification of the resource to which you want to connect can be expressed as a standard Windows file share (net use * *server**sharename*), or you can use a format that's similar to using the Unix mount command (net use * *server*/*sharename*). Note, however, that the second (Unix) syntax will result in the connection being set up more quickly.

- **mount**—Those of you more familiar with NFS might prefer to use the mount command. Again, you can use either the Windows or Unix format to specify the resource to which you want to connect; for example, mount *server*/*sharename* * or mount *server**sharename*.

In the preceding syntax examples, the asterisk character causes the next available drive letter to be assigned to the resource. You also can specify a particular drive letter. In either case, after the connection has been made to the NFS resource, you can then use Windows applications to access files on the resource just as if they were Windows file shares.

SFU also provides for these:

- **Server for NFS**—Use this to allow Unix clients to access file shares on Windows NT through Windows 2003 computers using standard Unix NFS commands. After this component is installed, you can offer a Windows directory as a file share by clicking on the NFS Sharing tab that's located on the properties page for a directory using Windows Explorer. Alternatively, you can use the command line to offer a directory on a Windows server to create the NFS share. The syntax for this is nfsshare *sharename=drive:path*.

- **Gateway for NFS**—Use this when your Windows clients need to make only moderate use of Unix NFS file systems. By using a gateway, you need to load SFU on only a single server, and it acts as a gateway, making the connections to Unix NFS file systems for Windows clients. The Windows clients connect to a file share offered by the gateway. If your Windows clients will be using NFS resources heavily, load the SFU client software instead so that the gateway does not become a bottleneck in a bandwidth-limited network.

- **Server for PCNFS**—This component enables a Windows NT or Windows 2000/2003 Server to act as a PCNFSD server. This provides for authentication when connecting to NFS resources.

Using these components, you can grant access to both sets of clients—Unix or Windows—to files stored on the other's systems. One limitation you should note for the gateway service is that you're still stuck with the drive letter limitation. Suppose that your network has a large number of Unix servers and each exports an NFS file system. For each connection, the gateway server will use one of its drive letters that could normally be mapped to a regular Windows file share.

The Korn Shell

The Korn Shell commands that SFU gives to Windows NT/2000/2003 and Windows XP enable you to use existing script files that run on Unix systems. For users trained on Unix systems, the Korn Shell commands make it much easier to add Windows computers to their flock of computers that must be administered. Table 61.2 lists the most useful commands provided by SFU.

Table 61.2 Korn Shell Unix Commands Provided by the Add-On Pack

Korn Shell Command	Use
sh	Invokes the Korn Shell.
basename	Removes a pathname and leaves just the filename.
cat	Similar to DIR; shows files in the directory. Also can be used to concatenate files.
chmod	Administers file permissions.
chown	Administers file ownership.
cp	Copies files.
cron	Executes commands found in the user's crontab file at the times specified.
cut	Cuts selected fields from each line of a text file.
date	Displays the current date and time.
diff	Compares two text files and displays lines that are different.
dirname	Extracts pathname from string.
dos2unix	Converts a DOS-style text file to a Unix-style text file.
du	Displays disk use of one (or more) files or directories.
find	Searches directories to find files matching a Boolean expression.
grep	Searches files for a pattern.
head	Copies n number of lines from a file to standard output.
kill	Sends a message to a process; can be used to delete the process.
ln	Creates a link to a file (hard link).
ls	Lists a directory.
mkdir	Creates named directory in mode 777.

Table 61.2 Continued

Korn Shell Command	Use
mount	When Client for NFS is installed, mounts an NFS file system.
more	Displays contents of file, one screen at a time.
mv	Moves a file.
nice	Runs the user's command at a lower priority.
od	"Dumps" the contents of files.
paste	Pastes text from one file into another.
perl	An interpreted language printenv. Displays the current environment.
ps	Displays a list of processes currently running.
pwd	Displays the current directory ("print working directory").
rcmd	Executes a command or a shell on a remote computer system.
renice	Changes the priority of a process.
rm	Removes a file entry from a directory.
rmdir	Removes a directory.
sed	Copies a file to standard output while making edits according to a script.
sdiff	Formats the output from the diff command so that the lines of text that differ appear side-by-side.
sleep	Pauses (sleeps) for a specified number of seconds.
sort	Sorts contents of one or more files.
split	Splits a file into separate pieces.
strings	Searches for strings in a *binary* file.
su	Changes the user ID of the current shell.
tail	Similar to head; sends lines from a file to standard output, starting at a specified location in the file.
tar	Tape Archive utility that creates or extracts files from a tape archive.
tee	Transcribes standard input to standard output and makes copies in filename.
top	Displays a list of processes making the most use of CPU time.
touch	Updates the modification or access time of a file.
tr	Replaces all occurrences of one set of characters with another set of characters.
uname	Displays system information (name, operating system, and so on).
uniq	Finds repeated lines in a file.
unmount	If Client for NFS is installed, use this command to dismount an NFS directory.
uuecode (uuencode)	Encodes and decodes a binary file into a 7-bit ASCII text file.
wait	Waits for a process to terminate.
wc	"Word Count"; displays a count of lines, words, or characters in a file.
which	Identifies the location of a given command that will execute.
vi	Screen-oriented text editor.
xargs	Creates an argument list and executes a command.

Tip

Although SFU 3.0 provides a great deal of functionality to Windows that appeals to Unix/Linux administrators, there are other products that can offer similar functionality. Some are comprehensive, such as SFU, whereas others offer partial solutions. For example, see `http://www.cygwin.com` for a Linux set of utilities that you might find more useful in your Windows environment.

Some of these commands, such as `mkdir` and `find`, are already familiar to Windows NT users. However, their functions in the Korn Shell might differ from those provided by the standard Windows implementation. For Unix administrators, the addition of these commands can make moving into managing Windows NT and Windows 2000/2003 computers a simpler transition. You can use the Unix commands listed in Table 61.1 and, at the same time, become familiar with the Windows Script Host (WSH). WSH enables you to create scripts using VBScript or JScript so that you aren't stuck using only the familiar MS-DOS commands that have been the mainstay for creating script files on Windows systems for more than 20 years. In addition, SFU provides an implementation of Perl that can be used with WSH.

Password Synchronization

In Version 1 of SFU, the password synchronization feature enabled you to configure a group of Unix servers so that when a user's password was changed on a Windows NT server, the change was propagated to the user's accounts on those target Unix servers. Because the application ran only on the Windows NT computer, it was a one-way service. That is, changes made on the Unix servers were not sent back to the Windows NT computer.

Versions 2 and 3 of SFU now make this functionality a two-way street. To use this SFU component, you'll need to load the Password Synchronization service on the Windows 2000/2003 Server (or NT) and, additionally, you'll have to run a daemon (called a Single Sign-On Daemon, or SSOD for short) on each Unix box that will participate in the password-update process. SFU Version 3 comes with versions of the daemon that have been compiled for the following variants of Unix:

- HP-UX 10.3+
- Sun Solaris 2.6+
- IBM AIX 4.3+
- HP (formerly Digital, and then Compaq) Tru64 Unix
- Red Hat Linux

However, if your Unix isn't in this list, you can still use the synchronization daemon. SFU comes with the source code and makefiles that you can use to compile a version for your particular system. The SSOD daemon is the background process that receives password changes from Windows computers. Another program, called the Password Authentication Manager (PAM), is used on the Unix server to send password changes made on the Unix system to Windows systems.

There are a few things about the synchronization process to consider before you deploy this service in your network. First, if your Windows computers are participating in a domain, you'll have to run the service on all the domain controllers in that domain. If you use Windows NT or Windows 2000 in a workgroup (or simply as standalone computers), you'll have to run the service on each computer if you want the passwords to stay synchronized among all the Windows computers.

Note

Although most large Windows NT and Windows 2000/2003 networks use the Active Directory to make managing network users, computers, and resources an easier task, you can still run Windows NT/2000/2003 as standalone computers. In that situation, each computer stores user and computer account information locally instead of in the Active Directory. That's why you must run the Password Synchronization service on each Windows computer if you don't use a domain or an Active Directory model for your network. Each computer must be capable of receiving password changes and applying them to the local database. In a domain-based environment, where users log on to the domain, only the domain controllers need to run the service.

Another caveat you must keep in mind is that Unix account names and passwords are case sensitive. Therefore, you'll have to create accounts on your Windows and Unix systems that are exactly the same. If you already have accounts set up in your network that have users with different account names on different systems, you'll have to pick a single account name for the user and then re-create the account on each computer so that they all match.

Finally, in addition to providing the capability to synchronize passwords between the Windows systems and those that are stored on individual Unix computers (in the /etc/passwd file, for example), you also can synchronize passwords with Unix networks that use the Network Information Service (NIS). Just install the SSOD on a master NIS or NIS+ server.

User Name Mapping

If you have an environment in which users already have accounts on both Unix and Windows NT/2000/2003 servers that aren't the same, SFU provides a component that can be used to map the different usernames. You can map usernames in a one-to-one manner or in a one-to-many manner. For example, you can create an entry that maps the name togletree to TOGLETREE. Or if you want the user to be able to access multiple user accounts, you can map the user's account name to several different account names. This second feature proves very useful if you have an assortment of Unix servers and each server has a different name used for an administrative account. You can map a single Windows NT/2000/2003 user account name to each of the user accounts on the various Unix servers. Or you can use this multiple-mapping feature to map the typical Unix account called *root* to more than one Windows administrative account.

The advantages of multiple mappings might not seem very intuitive at first, but let's consider an example. Suppose that you want to enable the Unix administrator in your network to manage some, but not all, of your Windows-based systems. You can create a user account on each Windows computer and grant it the necessary rights and permissions. Then map the root account to these new account names. That way you don't have to simply map root to Administrator, which would give access to all computers in the domain.

One final note about username mapping: It isn't a substitute for password synchronization. Remember that password synchronization, discussed in the previous section, requires that user account names be exactly the same on the computers that are participating in the synchronization process. User Name Mapping is simply another tool you can use to manage users who have accounts on both systems. If you're creating a network from scratch or if you can easily create user accounts on all of your systems that are the same, you probably won't need to use User Name Mapping and simply can let the users have a single account name on all systems, keeping passwords synchronized. Password synchronization will not work to synchronize passwords for accounts that are linked using User Name Mapping!

New Telnet Server and Client

SFU also includes a Telnet server for Windows servers, and a character-cell–style client application that greatly improves on the simple GUI Telnet client that comes with the standard Windows client operating systems. That makes it easy to use Telnet to log in to Windows server computers to perform system administration tasks or run character-cell–based user applications.

However, if you're using Windows 2000/2003 computers, this new Telnet client is already on your computer. It's now the standard client for Windows 2000 computers. Simply use the `telnet` command at the Command Prompt. Alternatively, click Start, Run, enter **telnet**, and click OK. If you use the `telnet` command at the Command Prompt, you can specify a target computer on which you want to establish a session. If you use the Start, Run method, you'll find the client starts up in console mode, as shown in Figure 61.13.

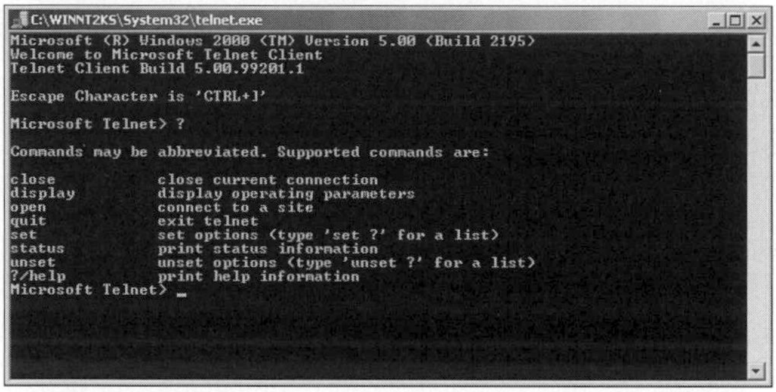

Figure 61.13   The new Telnet client will start in console mode if you use the Start/Run method to start the program.

For those not familiar with console mode, it simply means that the client is ready to accept configuration commands or open a session with a remote system. In Figure 61.13, you can see that the ? character has been used to display the help text that you can access while in console mode. If you simply want to telnet to a remote system, use the open *<remotesystem>* command. After you exit the remote system, you can return to console mode by holding down Ctrl and then the right-bracket (]) key.

Note

After you use the **open** command to start a Telnet session with a remote computer, you can use the Ctrl+] key sequence to escape to console mode. This can be useful if you need to use the **display** command to show your current configuration, such as the terminal emulation type. Suppose that you open a session and find that certain keys don't seem to work as you expect. You can escape to console mode, check your current settings (using the **display** command), and then use the **set** command to change to a different terminal type. Then simply use the **close** command to close the session you started, and use the **open** command to re-establish a session with the remote system. The terminal types that you can emulate using the **set** command are ANSI, VT100, VT52, and VTNT.

Some users who are accustomed to using the GUI Telnet client might not appreciate you giving them a simple character cell type of Telnet client. However, the new version is actually faster than the older GUI client and offers more features than its predecessor.

Although Windows server operating systems come with an excellent Telnet server (as described earlier in this chapter), SFU also provides a Telnet server that will run on Windows NT/2000/2003 servers.

The new server also supports logging to the Windows event log or to a separate log file, and you can choose which events you want to store in the log file. Instead of using the Internet Services Manager to manage and configure the Telnet server, you can load the SFU snap-in for the Microsoft Management Console (MMC) or you can use a command-line utility, tnadmin. Both methods enable you to configure the standard options discussed earlier in this chapter. This includes selecting which authentication method to use, enabling logging, setting the maximum number of connections (remember that the Windows server versions allow for only 2 simultaneous connections, whereas this SFU version allows for up to 63), and other parameters.

ActiveState ActivePerl 5.6

Web site administrators will be glad to see this SFU component because it's used on a lot of Web servers. Additionally, Perl can be used for other functions, such as automating system management procedures. The version included with SFU is Perl 5.6, ported to the Windows NT/2000/2003 platform. Your Windows clients also will be pleased because this port of Perl provides support for the Windows Script Host (WSH). By including Perl with the SFU package, it becomes easier for Unix or Web administrators who are already familiar with the language to manage systems or Web sites that run on Windows servers. WSH enables those coming from the Windows camp to continue to use JScript, VBScript, and other procedural languages with which they are used to working.

Samba

Samba is a set of applications that's freely available on the Internet. Samba enables you to set up Unix servers that can act as file servers for Microsoft clients that use the older SMB (server message block) protocol.

◄◄   Chapter 35 covers the Microsoft Server Message Block (SMB) protocol along with Samba.

Using Samba, you can make resources running on high-performance Unix/Linux servers available to Microsoft clients on the same network. The reverse is also true. You can offer file shares to Windows clients when those files (or printer) shares exist on Unix/Linux systems.

You can obtain Samba, as well as documentation for Samba, from www.samba.org.

Sun Network Information System

NIS is used on Unix networks to keep important system files, such as the password file, synchronized among a group of servers. Remember that on Unix systems, each server has a password file, a user group file, and other important files that are managed locally on each server by default. This is similar to using a Windows computer in a standalone manner where each Windows computer has its own user account database.

NIS uses a database of maps that contain entries for the files the system administrator chooses to keep synchronized. For redundancy purposes, a master NIS server can be used along with slave NIS servers that receive updates from the master server.

SFU version 3.0 contains a component that can be used to allow a Windows 2000/2003 domain controller to operate as a NIS server. The Windows server can operate as either a master or slave NIS server. However, if it is to operate as a slave server, the master NIS server on the network must also be a Windows server. This is due to the way NIS is implemented in Windows 2000/2003: The information that Unix NIS servers store in a map database is stored in the Active Directory. The Active Directory schema is extended to include a class for each NIS map. Then objects are created based on this class for each map entry.

NIS uses its own protocol to send updates from a master NIS server to slave servers. The Active Directory, on the other hand, has its own method for replication information to other Active Directory replicas. The two methods are not compatible. That's the reason why a Windows domain controller cannot be made a slave NIS server to a Unix master NIS server. However, Microsoft does provide support for the NIS protocol so that Unix systems can become slaves to a Windows 2000 master NIS server! So, if you decide to integrate NIS into the Windows 2000 portion of your network, you'll have to make a Windows domain controller the master NIS server.

The advantages of using NIS should be obvious. On Unix networks, NIS relieves the administrator of having to manually coordinate important system files on multiple servers. By incorporating the SFU NIS server into the network on a Windows domain controller, you can use the tools designed around the Active Directory to manage not only your Windows users but also users on your Unix systems.

Another advantage to using a Windows-based NIS server is that the Active Directory is a hierarchical database, whereas the NIS database format is a flat namespace. You can place NIS maps into any container in the Active Directory, such as an organizational unit (OU). You can probably figure out from this that you can support multiple NIS domains in the same Active Directory database.

Migrating from Windows NT 4.0 to Windows 2000, Windows 2003, and Windows XP

SOME OF THE MAIN TOPICS IN THIS CHAPTER ARE

CHAPTER 62

This chapter covers two types of upgrades: upgrading servers and upgrading users' desktop workstations. Windows NT 4.0 Server can easily be upgraded to Windows 2000 or Windows 2003. Windows NT 4.0 Workstation can be upgraded to Windows 2000 Professional or Windows XP Professional. This chapter examines the need for upgrading your operating system and applications. Perhaps the more difficult upgrade will be from Windows NT 4.0 to Windows 2000 or one of the Windows 2003 servers. This assumes that you'll be using Active Directory, which was not part of an all–Windows NT 4.0 network. Active Directory requires you to make some choices and acquire additional skills to manage users and resources.

Upgrading Windows NT 4.0 Workstation or Windows 2000 Professional, or to Windows XP from either of these, does not present much of a problem.

Although you can use both Windows 2000 and 2003 servers without the Active Directory, doing so is not advisable at this time unless you currently use another directory service. LDAP directories are becoming more important every year because they can be used to manage not just your network, but also interoperation between other networks. Unless you're operating a very small LAN that you don't see changing for a few years, it's time to bite the bullet and upgrade. The new features, after you learn them, are one benefit. New applications that make use of directory services are another.

Do You Need to Upgrade the Operating System or Applications?

Although Windows 2003 and Windows XP are the newest operating system releases from Microsoft, you still might want to consider upgrading to Windows 2000 first. There are many reasons for this, including the fact that Windows 2000 has been around for a few years and, with the appropriate service packs applied, it has attained a good degree of stability. Another good reason to stick with Windows 2000 is application compatibility. Some older applications might work under Windows 2000, but not under Windows 2003 or Windows XP. Of course, your vendor might provide updates to applications to make them compatible with the newer operating systems. But having to upgrade a lot of applications at the same time you're upgrading operating systems will require careful planning, testing, and a lot of work.

Another peripheral reason why you might want to consider Windows 2000 over Windows 2003/XP is the availability of trained personnel. Even though Microsoft will likely begin to rescind support (and user certifications) for older operating systems shortly after Windows 2003 starts to gain momentum, that doesn't mean that you'll find a lot of people who are trained on the newer OSs. And just because people are certified for a new operating system doesn't necessarily mean that they're qualified to satisfy your every need when it comes to support. Perhaps the most important thing that I've found to be indicative of an employee's abilities is *experience*, not certification examinations. There are a lot of people who are very experienced (trial by fire, so to speak) with Windows 2000. It's one thing to read a book about how to drive a car and then pass a written test. It's another thing to get into a car and drive it. Experience counts.

The same goes for your administrative staff. I would not consider passing a certification exam to be all that's required to hire a new employee. Experience counts. If you want to hire employees who understand Windows 2003, it would be a good idea to look at their résumés to see that they have some experience with Windows 2000 (and the Active Directory) first.

Windows 2003/XP will be around for a few years, just as Windows 2000 has started to be accepted by many Windows sites (and Windows 2000 has been around in one form or another since 1999). So, if you want to wait and perform this upgrade later—or perhaps skip the Windows 2003/XP generation— a later upgrade might save you a lot of money in a large organization. One consideration is that some of the features of Windows 2003 variants (and there are four versions of Windows 2003) might be something that your organization can reap great benefits from. If that's the case, consider training your in-house employees on Windows 2003 and then using a laboratory of computers to ensure that the solutions they envision do indeed work.

Note

Just as upgrading to a newer operating system might not be necessary until it has been widely accepted by the marketplace, the same goes for applications. Although Microsoft Office and the various operating systems released in the past few years make up the larger percentage of Microsoft's sales, this author still uses Office 97. I find that Office 97 also runs very well on Windows 2003. Do I have any need to upgrade to Office XP or Office 2000 or XP if all I need is a basic word-processing program? Why should you upgrade if the products you're using now satisfy your requirements? If you skip a few generations of operating systems and applications, it will likely be more difficult to upgrade. But consider this fact: Will it be easier to continually upgrade as each new OS or product is brought to market? Will it be less expensive? Another thing to look at when using Microsoft products (as opposed to Linux and other open source products) is how the licensing cost will impact your bottom line. Microsoft is continually changing its licensing policies, mainly due to market pressure.

There's one good reason to go ahead with the upgrade to the Windows 2003/XP platforms: support. This issue can be a minor one if you've already prepared your own support infrastructure, such as keeping personnel trained. One inexpensive way to do this is to subscribe to Microsoft's MSDN (Microsoft Developer's Network). MSDN gives you a superset of the documentation and knowledge articles that you can get from `msdn.microsoft.com`. Even though the articles on the Web site may be aged out over time, you can always turn to your CDs (or DVDs, if you chose that option) to find support for Windows 2000 as the next few years go by. Microsoft also offers a subscription to TechNet, which is a scaled-down version of the MSDN subscription. I suggest that you subscribe to one or the other as your budget permits. In a large network, the MSDN subscription is a small cost to pay for the many benefits (from programming to operating systems) you'll get.

Tip

Another option you might want to consider is the Microsoft Action Pack. This is a subscription that supplies Microsoft Partners with operating systems, Exchange Server, and a few other software items. If you do not need the development tools that come with an MSDN subscription, you can at least preview newer operating systems and some software by becoming a Microsoft Partner. You can sign up as a partner by becoming a reseller, or even a consultant. See the Web site at **www.members.microsoft.com/partner/salesmarketing/**.

If you already have trained personnel for the current operating system and applications, support isn't that much of an issue for your network. Yet, Windows 2003/XP might be a good choice mainly because of the additional functionality and security improvements they provide. For example, Windows XP Professional has a new user-friendly GUI (although you can choose to revert to the classic Windows interface). Other important features of Windows XP Professional include a solution to what is called (in Microsoft documentation) *DLL hell*. Applications that now overwrite DLLs (dynamic link libraries) in the Windows NT/2000/2003/XP environment are now stored in application-specific directories, so the core DLLs located in the system files directory remain untouched (except by Microsoft updates, of course). This can solve a lot of headaches for network administrators who are deploying new applications. So, if your network adopts new applications frequently, upgrading might be a good choice as opposed to a network that requires only minor upgrades for applications.

Windows XP also has many other new features, some that make the user experience easier and some of which solve problems that exist in Windows 2000. For example, the capability to set checkpoints and roll back to a previous state on the computer is an important one. This feature is called *System Restore*. If you or a user makes a change to the desktop's configuration or installs an application that causes problems, it's easy to simply use System Restore to go back to the previous configuration of the desktop without having to remove programs and diagnose other configuration changes. System Restore enables you to create these checkpoints yourself (for example, just before you make the changes), and automatically creates checkpoints on a periodic basis and when some changes are made to the operating system or applications. However, it's best to create a checkpoint yourself (a simple matter) before making changes to the desktop computer.

Tip

For more information about DLL hell and System Restore, see *Platinum Edition Using Windows XP*, published by Que Publishing (ISBN 0789727900).

System Restore is not a free lunch. It works by saving critical system files, including Registry settings, on the hard disk so that it will have the necessary information to restore your computer if you choose to roll back to a previous state. If disk space is important, this feature might not suit your environment. System Restore requires, at a minimum, 200MB of disk space. However, you can change this to a larger value to keep old restore points around for a longer period of time.

There are many other features that Windows XP offers for desktop users that go far beyond the scope of this chapter. You might want to check out these features on Microsoft's Windows Web pages for Windows XP. There are many white papers and other documents available on Microsoft's Web site. Some changes are cosmetic—such as stacking multiple instances of a single program into one item on the toolbar when the toolbar has become overpopulated—to the new interface—to the capability to enable another user to take control of the desktop and assist a user with problems. Many of these new features are also offered by third-party products. However, if you have not yet invested in these kinds of products, you might find the features that Windows XP offers for desktop users—not to mention the features to make life easier for your help desk staff—worth the upgrade.

Windows 2003 Server(s) are another story altogether. You'll find Windows 2003 Server Standard Edition, Windows 2003 Enterprise Server, and Windows 2003 Web Server. And there's always the new 64-bit Windows 2003 Datacenter Server. If you're contemplating an upgrade to the higher end of this line, please check out the specifications and benefits you can achieve from this upgrade. Keep in mind that the 64-bit Datacenter server offers greater computing capacity, but lacks some of the improvements that you'll find in the other Windows 2003 server products and the capability to run some applications.

With all that said, let's now get on upgrading to Windows 2000 and then Windows 2003 if your network consists now of Windows NT 4.0.

Tip

Whatever you decide, check Microsoft's Web site and examine all the white papers and other documentation available to determine whether you'll benefit from an upgrade to Windows 2000 or Windows 2003, much less Windows XP.

Upgrading to Windows 2000 Server

Fortunately, when you upgrade your network to Windows 2000, you don't have to jump in and do it all at once. The Windows 2000 Active Directory is backward compatible with previous Windows NT Server domain controllers, so you can upgrade your Windows NT 4.0 Servers in a time scale convenient to your own timetable. The Active Directory that comes with Windows 2000 adds additional functionality. And, for your desktops, Windows 2000 Professional is more intuitive and easier to use than Windows NT Workstation.

You can choose to upgrade only a few servers at a time while you test the waters on the migration to Windows 2000, also called *mixed mode*. When you get ready to make the final change into an all–Windows 2000 network (native mode), you can simply click the switch. Otherwise, you can remain in a mixed network consisting of both Windows NT 4.0 domain controllers as well as Windows 2000 domain controllers. Note, however, that you won't gain all the benefits that the Active Directory can provide while you operate in mixed mode. When you convert your network to an all–Windows 2000 network, you'll gain a large number of features (offered by the Active Directory) that can make managing the network a much simpler set of tasks. However, after you make the switch to a native-mode network, you can't go back! It's a one-time conversion that you cannot easily undo.

When you do make the decision to upgrade your domain controllers to Windows 2000 and switch to an all-2000 network for your domain controllers using the Active Directory, there's still one way you can back out if you must. You can create an additional domain controller for each domain (a backup domain controller or *BDC*) before you change over to an all-2000 network, and then take that domain controller offline (power it off!). If for some very good reason you need to revert a domain to Windows NT 4.0, you can shut down the Windows 2000 domain controllers (and thus the Active Directory), power up the BDCs, promote them to be primary domain controllers, and keep your fingers crossed. You might have some problems with user workstations that were members of a Windows 2000 domain, but these can usually be resolved by changing their domain membership. However, this method is not recommended except as a very last resort.

The more time that passes between switching to native mode and attempting a rollback, the more problems you're likely to run into. Remember, the BDC has a snapshot of your domain from the point at which you power down the machine. Any domain object changes that are made between powering down the last BDC and going native mode—including, for example, adding new computer accounts, changing user accounts, or even changing user passwords—must be redone if you roll back. Because the BDC would not be aware of those changes, it would be as if they had never occurred.

In the past, Windows domains were used to group resources and users into manageable units for administrative control. The Active Directory provides for enhanced security mechanisms, such as the capability to delegate security administration and a new method of grouping users and resources: the organizational unit (OU). These two features can make it easy to reduce the number of domains you have in an existing network as you migrate to a network that eventually will be managed totally using the Active Directory.

Note

Before you jump right into this chapter, it's highly recommended that you first review several other chapters. If you aren't familiar with how domains are used in pre-Windows 2000 environments and how users and resources are managed, you should read Chapter 40, "Windows NT Domains," and Chapter 43, "Rights and Permissions."

If you're new to the Active Directory and how it functions to store information about users and resources for the network, you should read Chapter 31, "Using the Active Directory," and Chapter 41, "Windows 2000 and Windows Server 2003 User and Computer Management Utilities."

The tools associated with the Active Directory are vastly different from those used in previous versions of Windows operating systems. In Windows 2000 and the family of Windows 2003 servers, domain controllers are peers in a domain, and there are no primary domain controllers (PDCs) or BDCs as was the case with Windows NT 4.0 and earlier versions. You'll find that the Administrative Tools folder is now populated with utilities based on the Microsoft Management Console (MMC), which you can use to manage the data stored in the Active Directory.

This chapter examines some of the things you should consider before performing an upgrade and shows you an example of how you can create a domain controller in a Windows 2000 network.

Before You Begin

You must consider several things when you are deciding how to arrange your domains for the migration. These include the following:

- **Existing namespaces**—Do you already have registered Internet domain names in use at your company? Do you have more than one namespace; that is, `acme.com` and `acme-mfg.com`? The Active Directory names domains use DNS (Domain Name System)-style names such as these, rather than NetBIOS-style names.

- **Number of users in the network**—Although the Active Directory is scalable to many millions of objects, hardware capacity and network bandwidth will still limit the numbers of objects that any particular domain can handle efficiently. You might find that for branch offices, for example, it's easier to create a separate domain to reduce the amount of data in a single domain. This can also cut down on the multimaster replication used by the Active Directory across slow links.

- **Structure of the organization**—Many existing Windows NT networks use domains to model the business's organization structure. In the Active Directory, the OU can perform this function.

- **Geographical separation**—If you have a large enterprise with many users separated into distinct geographical sites, you can use either multiple domains to accommodate them or choose to use Active Directory sites and a single domain. As noted earlier, keep in mind the bandwidth used to connect to remote sites when deciding to use a single domain or multiple domains. Replication traffic can consume valuable bandwidth over slow links.

Windows NT Domain Controllers and Member Servers

One of the annoyances with Windows NT 4.0 was that to create a PDC or BDC, you had to do so when you *first installed the operating system*. That is no longer the case with Windows 2000. In fact, as discussed earlier in this chapter, there are no primary or backup domain controllers. There are only domain controllers, each of which holds a full copy of the *domain's* Active Directory database. Updates, such as adding new users or changing passwords, can be done using *any* domain controller in the domain. For Windows NT 4.0, you had to make these changes on a PDC and either wait for the data to be replicated to BDCs or force a push of the data to synchronize the domain controllers. Updates made to domain controllers in Windows 2000 can be made at any domain controller, and updates are propagated using multimaster replication to all other domain controllers in the domain.

Also, remember that in the Active Directory domain names are expressed as DNS-style names. That is, instead of naming a domain `acme`, for example, you should use a name such as `acme.com`, which is a DNS-style name. When you create a tree of domains in the Active Directory, you must use a hierarchical DNS naming scheme so that you maintain a contiguous namespace.

Even though your domains now use a DNS-style name, you're still asked to provide a NetBIOS-style name when you upgrade a server to an Active Directory domain controller. This NetBIOS-style name will be used for down-level clients—for example, any NT 4.0 Workstation systems that are left on the network.

Note

Although you could use a DNS server in a Windows NT 4.0 network, it was not a requirement. Microsoft developed the Windows Internet Naming Service (WINS) that could be used in a similar fashion, although it mapped NetBIOS names to IP addresses, whereas DNS performs mappings of DNS-style names to IP addresses. In Windows 2000/2003 networks, a DNS server (which must be capable of accepting dynamic updates) is required because clients use it to locate domain controllers, as well as register their own information when they boot. For more information about DNS and WINS, see Chapter 30, "Network Name Resolution." You still can use WINS in a Windows 2000/2003 network, but it isn't needed unless you have pre-Windows 2000 clients that depend on NetBIOS name resolution to function on the network. Additionally, some applications, such as System Management Server (SMS), might require WINS. Check your documentation for all applications before deciding on a no-WINS solution.

Each domain in the tree is a subdomain of the topmost domain. The domain tree provides a two-way transitive trust relationship between *all* domains that exist in a single Windows 2000 tree. In Windows NT, trust relationships had to be established between domains, with one trust relationship created for each direction that you wanted to trust. In other words, you could trust one domain, or it could trust your domain, or two trust relationships could make the trust relationship mutual.

In the Active Directory, inheritance of security rights flows downward from the top of the tree. So, you can assign users administrative access rights and permissions at a single point in the tree and therefore grant them the same rights for child objects farther down the tree. Access control lists (ACLs) can help you further refine the delegation of authority in the Active Directory.

When you have a network that's composed of disparate namespaces, you can create separate trees and group them into a *forest*. Recall that a forest is a collection of domain trees. In this type of organization, each domain tree represents a contiguous namespace, but other disjointed namespaces exist in the network. A domain forest is used in a similar manner to a domain tree, in that users still can be granted access rights in domains that are contained in other domain trees. The main difference between a domain tree and a forest is the disjointed namespaces (that is, different DNS-style names that can exist when you merge two or more businesses together). Additionally, although domains that exist within the same domain tree have implicit transitive trust relationships, you must create trust relationships between domains that exist in different trees in a forest before you can begin to grant users access to resources in other domain trees. Later in this chapter, you'll learn how this has changed in Windows 2003. This simple feature could be a deciding factor in which version of Windows Server operating systems you choose for your upgrade.

Replication of Directory Information

Active Directory domain controllers replicate, through multimaster replication techniques, all changes to the Active Directory database for their domain to all other domain controllers in the domain. Domain controllers for *other domains* in the domain tree do not receive these replication updates because they're responsible only for the portion of the directory database that concerns objects in their respective domains.

◄◄ For more information about multimaster replication, see Chapter 31.

However, all domain controllers in a particular domain tree do receive replication updates that concern the *metadata*, which defines the domain tree. For example, when a new domain joins a domain tree or when a domain is detached from one part of the tree and reattached at another part, this information is replicated to other domain controllers in the domain tree.

Modeling the Directory Structure After Your Business Organization

The main points to consider when grouping users and resources are how you want to administer them and what this will do to affect the network traffic associated with logon authentication and directory information replication.

Do you want to create a network that allows centralized or decentralized control? In Windows NT, domains were used to enable you to group users and resources into convenient, manageable units that share a common security policy. With the X.500 naming hierarchy adopted by the Active Directory, you might find that you now can get by with fewer domains, while using other methods, such as organizational units, to make administration more flexible.

Having a single domain and using OUs to divide users and resources for administrative control purposes is a good idea if the network is connected by high-speed links. If your network is widely dispersed over a large geographical distance (or via slow links), you should take into consideration the replication traffic that will occur when changes are made to the database if a single domain is used. If frequent changes to the database occur, you might want to consider using separate domains for users and resources in different locations so that only the domain tree metadata becomes the object of replication.

For example, suppose that a manufacturer has just decided to upgrade all its business sites to Windows 2000 and use the Active Directory to manage resources. The sales office is located in New York and two manufacturing sites are located in Dallas. The user base at the Dallas site has a much higher turnover rate than that of the New York site. Because users at each site mainly access only resources local to their site, it makes sense to use two domains, one for each geographical site. Using two domains also keeps replication traffic between the sites to a minimum because the frequent changeover of users at the Dallas site does not need to be replicated to the New York site.

Later, the company decides to open another manufacturing plant in San Antonio. A high-speed leased line is installed between the Dallas and San Antonio sites because the plants will be sharing a lot of information between them. The Dallas domain is expanded to include the San Antonio users. However, a separate OU is used for each of these sites so that users can be dealt with easily by the local managers for each site. Because both of these OUs reside in the same domain, controlling user access to domain resources is a simple task no matter where the user is located.

Domains Are Partitions of the Active Directory

A domain in the Active Directory is basically a partition of the entire domain tree namespace. The namespace consists of all domains in the domain tree of which the domain is a member. In the Active Directory, each domain controller in the domain holds a complete replica of that domain's partition of the directory database. Each domain is responsible for holding directory information about users, resources, and other objects defined in the domain. The *global catalog* enables users in other domains in the domain tree the ability to quickly locate resources that are entered in other partitions, or domains, of the tree.

Note

You aren't stuck with your initial decision when you set up a domain tree or forest. The Active Directory uses a unique number, the globally unique identifier (GUID), to identify each domain in the network. Because this identifier is used throughout the network to uniquely identify the domain, the directory enables you to add, delete, and change domain names easily as your organization or network changes. Because each domain can be easily identified by its GUID, you can make changes to the shape of the domain tree or forest by moving domains around and reattaching them at different points to match your current needs. In the Windows 2003 Active Directory, you can use drag-and-drop utilities to rearrange domains in a tree.

Another important characteristic of a domain is the domain security policy. You define certain characteristics of the security policy, such as the password history and account lockout values, on a domain-by-domain basis. However, you cannot assign different account policies, such as lockout values, on an OU basis.

Organizational Units Allow for Delegation of Control

Organizational units are container objects in the Active Directory. A *container* object is an object that can hold other objects in the directory. An OU can hold other organizational units and container objects, as well as leaf objects in the directory. *Leaf objects* are the endpoints in the tree structure of the directory and hold information about such things as users, printers, applications, and other resources.

Tip

In the Active Directory, you can use the OU to subdivide portions of the directory. By doing so, you can reduce the number of domains that you need. You can delegate authority to manage OUs to only those administrators who need such access. Thus, OUs can be used not only to partially replace domains, but also can be a very useful method for controlling rights and access for day-to-day management chores.

In Windows NT, you use a domain to group users and resources so that they can be managed as a unit. Within a domain, you can grant certain users the rights to perform system management and administrative tasks, such as creating user accounts or adding computers to the domain. However, this administrative control is domainwide. For example, if you grant a user account the right to modify user accounts, that user can modify any user account in the domain.

OUs enable you to further subdivide a domain and grant those same user rights based on the OU instead of the entire domain. This finer granularity of control can make it possible for you to get by with fewer domains in situations in which you want to use a large number of user groupings for administrative control purposes. Instead of creating a domain for each of the accounting, human resources, and manufacturing departments, you can create one domain and assign administrative privileges by OUs created within the domain to allow each department to control its own users and resources.

Migration Considerations: Centralized Versus Decentralized Management

When planning the domain layout for your organization, you should consider the type of management control (centralized versus decentralized), security policies, and the network infrastructure. When deciding whether to use many or fewer domains as the basis for dividing resources and users, consider what happens on the domain level. Each domain controller in a domain holds a complete copy of the domain's portion of the directory database. Replication between domain controllers happens only within a domain. That is, when you add a new user, file, or print resource, the information is replicated via multimaster replication to all other domain controllers in the domain. The information is *not* replicated outside of the domain to the domain controllers in other domains (although some attributes are stored in the global catalog). Thus, by using a larger number of domains for geographically dispersed networks, you can reduce replication traffic.

Security policy also is implemented on a domain basis. If different departments in your business have widely varying security requirements, you might need to use the domain as a tool for organizing users and resources. You cannot define different password history values or set a security policy of how strong a password must be based on the OU.

Delegation of Administrative Rights Reduces the Need for Multiple Domains

In Windows NT, several built-in domain groups were used to grant administrative rights to users. Those included the all-powerful Domain Admins group, whose members can perform all administrative functions in the domain (unless the local administrator chose to take the Domain Admins group out of the Administrators group), down to the Account Operators and Backup Operators groups, which have access to only specific management functions. Although having these built-in user groups made it easy to grant specific users only a portion of the administrative rights that are possible in a domain, the drawback is that these rights exist throughout the domain. For example, if a user is a member of the Account Operators group, that user can potentially modify any user account in the domain (other than the Administrator accounts).

The Active Directory provides for the capability to delegate the assignment of administrative rights, down to the level of the OU. Because user accounts are not stored in the Registry-based SAM (Security Accounts Manager) database anymore, but are instead objects in the directory database, you can grant or deny administrative privileges on specific portions of the directory tree.

Two important concepts to understand about administrative privileges in the Active Directory are

- Per-property access rights
- Inheritance of access rights

Each object in the Active Directory can have an ACL attached to it, which defines who is allowed to perform what functions on the object. This access can be defined down to the property (or *attribute*) level. That means you can grant a specific user the ability to manage all aspects of user account management for a particular container object (OU), or the ability to modify selected properties of user objects within the container, such as the users' passwords or default directories.

Each object in the directory is made up of specific attributes, called *properties*. Each property is a single type of information about the object. You can grant or deny administrative privileges on each and every property of a particular object type. To make things even easier, you also can grant or deny administrative privileges on groups of properties. The *property set* attribute of the schema defines groups of properties that can be administered together. If the default definitions of this attribute do not meet your needs, you can modify the schema.

Caution

As explained in Chapter 31, you should think carefully before modifying the schema. Changes to the schema cannot be undone. Although you can disable objects or attributes that you add, this applies only to new instances of these objects or attributes and not those created before you made schema changes. In other words, don't change the schema unless you have an absolute need to do so. The objects that are provided with the Active Directory should satisfy most business needs.

Inheritance of access rights is another concept that makes delegating administrative authority more convenient. If you think of the Active Directory as a hierarchical structure organized in a tree fashion, you can pick a particular point in the tree and grant access rights to a user from that point to objects farther down the tree. The administrative rights flow down the tree to include other container objects and finally down to the end leaf objects of the tree. When a new child object is created in the directory tree, the access rights that apply to the container object that holds the child object are included with the default access rights created on the child object. This is true unless you place ACLs on specific objects or OUs to prevent this inheritance.

This method of inheritance allows for faster authentication time when the operating system must determine access rights. It isn't necessary to trace back up the hierarchy through all parent objects to determine the access rights of a particular child object. The child object contains all the information that's required to perform an access right check.

Implementing a Migration to the Active Directory for Windows 2000

As with any major network upgrade project, you should be sure to carefully plan ahead. Develop a written master plan and schedule for the migration and review it on a frequent basis. Some of the items to consider in a migration plan include

- **Back-out procedures**—For any big changes you make on a particular server, be sure that you plan a method to back out of the change if it doesn't function as you expect. *Always* maintain up-to-date backups of key systems that can be used to make a full restoration without seriously impacting the user base.

- **Alternative plans**—Sometimes there's more than one way to affect a solution to a problem. If you can make note of more than one method of accomplishing a particular task, such as the capability to schedule users or resources for the project, that flexibility will enable you to adapt to changes in the project schedule.

- **Assign users and resources carefully**—When you make decisions about which personnel are going to be used to execute portions of the project plan, be sure to keep in mind the existing workload of the person and how participating in the upgrade migration plan will affect his or her job. Again, it is a good idea to have a backup person or backup resource you can use if unforeseen events limit a person's capabilities.

- **Nonproduction testing**—As discussed in other chapters, test your plan in a laboratory setting! Nothing is ever as it seems to be (there goes my existential thought). You should always test any network modification using all the possible usages you can think of before deploying changes to any network, whether it be one based on a Windows network, or another, such as NetWare, Unix, or Linux.

- **A well-defined team structure**—There should be a migration team that has a designated leader and assigned duties and areas of responsibility for each member. Nothing makes executing a migration plan more difficult than personality conflicts that can arise from the nonspecific assignment of duties to team members.

Start by Upgrading Primary Domain Controller

When you decide to upgrade your network to a Windows 2000 Active Directory–based network, you'll need to plan the order in which servers and workstations will be upgraded. The Active Directory–based Windows 2000 domain controller is backward compatible with Windows NT 4.0 domain controllers, so upgrading the PDC is transparent to the users and domain controllers that are still operating under Windows NT 4.0. Backup domain controllers in the domain see the new Active Directory domain controller just as if it were a PDC in the Windows NT 4.0 domain. One consideration to keep in mind is that after you upgrade a server to be a Windows 2000 Active Directory domain controller, you can't, in the same domain, promote a Windows NT 4.0 BDC to become a PDC. The new Active Directory domain controller provides this capability as far as Windows NT 4.0 BDCs are concerned, and you can have only one PDC in a Windows NT 4.0 domain.

Upgrade the Domain's PDC and Then Any BDCs

When you upgrade the PDC to become an Active Directory domain controller, you're prompted to either join an existing domain tree or create a new domain tree. If this is the first Active Directory domain controller in the network, you have to create a new domain tree. The operation is a simple, painless one—no complicated setup or configuration is required to create a domain tree.

After you've created the first Active Directory domain controller from the domain's PDC, you'll have a mixed network environment that still can function normally from the user's standpoint. That is, users still can authenticate using the BDCs that remain in the domain. However, because the BDCs do not yet recognize the Active Directory database, but instead see it as a PDC, you still can't create new security principals, such as user accounts, on the BDCs. This is the normal way in which a Windows NT 4.0 network functions. You will have to do so on the new Active Directory domain controller just as you did when it was a PDC.

The new Active Directory domain controller uses the single-master replication method to inform any existing BDCs of changes to the security database. After you promote one or more BDCs to become Active Directory domain controllers in the domain, you can update the security database on any of those new domain controllers because they're all equal peers in the network with other Windows 2000 domain controllers. Multimaster replication is used only between the new Active Directory domain controllers. Existing Windows NT 4.0 BDCs continue to function as if the network were still composed of nothing but Windows NT 4.0 domain controllers.

However, after you've finally converted *all* your Windows NT 4.0 BDCs to be Active Directory domain controllers and have made the switch to the native-mode Windows 2000 Active Directory, only multi-master replication will occur from that point on. This implies that *you will no longer be able to add Windows NT Server 4.0 domain controllers to the domain*. If you're uncertain about the migration, leave at least one Windows NT 4.0 BDC in the domain and operate in a mixed environment until you're sure that the changeover is working as you expect, and you have no need to downgrade back to a Windows NT 4.0–based network.

Tip

You should always keep a "back door" open when implementing new technology. When you make the final decision to go with the Active Directory and forego the Windows NT PDC/BDC networking method, keeping an old BDC around can be a lifesaver if something goes wrong. To provide this open door using a BDC, you don't have to keep the old BDC online in the new network. Instead, before you make the final switch, take a BDC offline. That is, turn it off or disconnect it from the network. Keep it around for a few months until you're absolutely sure that you don't need to downgrade out of the Active Directory. If some disastrous event occurs that forces you to back out of the upgrade, the BDC will not contain any changes that are made after it is taken offline, but it will be a good place to start when trying to recover your old network.

However, you must consider that that this is a short-term solution. In a large network, computers will change their own computer passwords, and thus render this capability almost useless for the long term. You should also take into consideration your password policy. How often do you require that users change their password? In either of these cases, using this back door can cause more problems than it solves.

After you have made the switch and all *domain controllers* are based on the Active Directory, all clients, including those down-level non–Windows 2000 clients, will be capable of taking advantage of the transitive trust relationship that's created between all domains in the domain tree. This is because the trust relationship is created between domain controllers, which perform authentication functions, not by the individual workstations or other clients in the network. That means you can proceed to upgrade all your BDCs to Windows 2000 Active Directory domain controllers and then, as you find opportunities to schedule the required downtime, you can upgrade client machines, such as Windows NT 4.0 Workstation clients, at a more leisurely pace.

Adding Other Domains to the Active Directory

In a multidomain network, you'll first create a domain tree using one of the domain controllers in an existing domain or you can even create a new domain from a fresh install to serve as the first domain in a new domain tree.

When you later decide to upgrade other domains in your network to use the Active Directory, you can still create a new domain tree or you can choose to join the existing domain tree. Again, the operation is simple. To join an existing domain tree, you need only supply the name of the parent domain where you'll attach the new domain to the tree.

Several things occur when you join an existing tree:

- The domain's current SAM database is migrated to the Active Directory database.
- The Kerberos security software is installed and is then used to create a two-way trust relationship with the parent domain to which the domain has been attached in the tree structure.
- A domain controller in the parent domain supplies configuration information, such as the Active Directory schema, to the child domain and then informs other domain controllers about the addition of the new child domain.

Upgrade the Master Domain First

In the master domain model, all user accounts reside in the master domain and resources are created in separate resource domains. When you upgrade a network that's based on a single domain, there isn't much choice: first upgrade the PDC and then upgrade the domain's BDCs.

Note

If you're starting from scratch—that is, you're running Windows NT 4.0 in a standalone or workgroup mode and don't have a PDC—you can still create a domain controller for your Windows 2000 network. After you've installed Windows 2000 Server or upgraded a Windows NT 4.0 server to Windows 2000, you can then use the command **dcpromo** to promote the server to be a domain controller. The process is not as complicated as you might think. Simply bring up the Command Prompt (from the Start menu, choose Programs, Accessories, Command Prompt) and enter the command **dcpromo**. The Active Directory Installation Wizard pops up to guide you through the process. This command can also be used in Windows 2003 servers.

In the master domain model type of network, you should choose to upgrade the master domain first and then upgrade the resource domains. At the completion of the basic upgrade, you use the Active Directory Installation Wizard to install the Active Directory (see Figure 62.1).

The next few dialog boxes prompt you to create a new domain tree or create a child domain in an existing tree (see Figure 62.2). If you choose to create a new domain tree, you're prompted to create a new forest or create the domain in an existing forest. Because this is the first server being upgraded to Windows 2000, you should create a new forest.

The wizard then prompts you for the domain name that you want to use. You have to specify it as a fully qualified DNS name, however (see Figure 62.3).

The wizard then asks you to enter a NetBIOS-compatible name for the new domain. Previous versions of Windows use this name for the domain until you've finished the migration and are running a Windows 2000–only network.

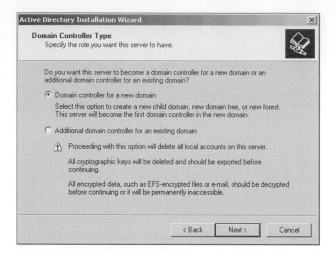

Figure 62.1 The Installation Wizard guides you through the process.

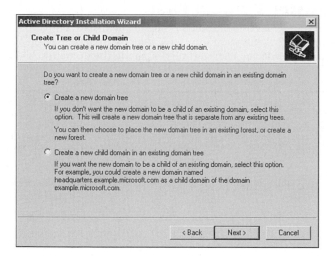

Figure 62.2 If this is the first controller to be upgraded, you create a new domain tree.

The wizard then asks you where you want to create the files that will serve as the database for the directory and for a device to store the log file for the directory (see Figure 62.4). If your domain is large, you should specify a different device for each of these files to improve performance.

The next dialog box prompts you to enter a path that will be used to store files that are replicated to other domain controllers in the domain. As you can see in this figure, the path must point to a directory that is located on an NTFS partition. You cannot use a FAT partition for this.

If you are not yet using a DNS server in the domain, the wizard will prompt you to install Microsoft's DNS Server. Click the OK button to dismiss this dialog box. The Configure DNS dialog box pops up and asks whether you want to install DNS now or wait until later. For Active Directory to function correctly, a DNS server is required. It's best to go ahead and elect to install Microsoft's DNS at this time because the Active Directory must register resource records that clients will use to locate domain controllers.

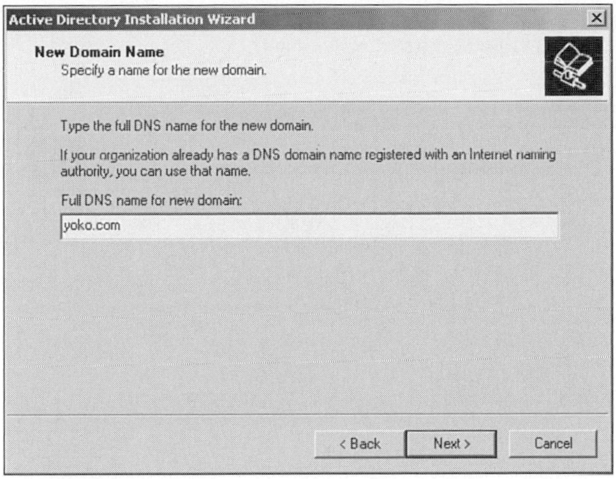

Figure 62.3   Use a fully qualified DNS name when prompted by the wizard.

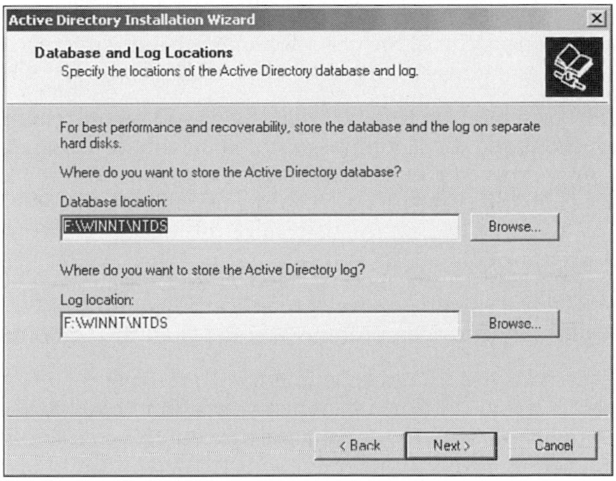

Figure 62.4   Enter the paths that will be used to create the Active Directory database and log files.

The next dialog box is an important one. If you're planning on a gradual migration where you will keep pre–Windows 2000 clients on the network for a while, you'll need to run Windows 2000 in mixed mode so that the Windows 2000 domain controller can act as the PDC in the domain for these down-level clients. You can see this dialog box in Figure 62.5.

Note

If your network is small and you plan to upgrade all your servers and workstations at the same time, you should select the second option in Figure 62.5.

The wizard then prompts you to enter a password that will be used as an administrator password for this server if you need to start the computer in Directory Services Restore Mode. Finally, you'll see a summary dialog box that shows the options you've selected. Scroll through this dialog box to re-examine your choices and, if they're correct, click Next.

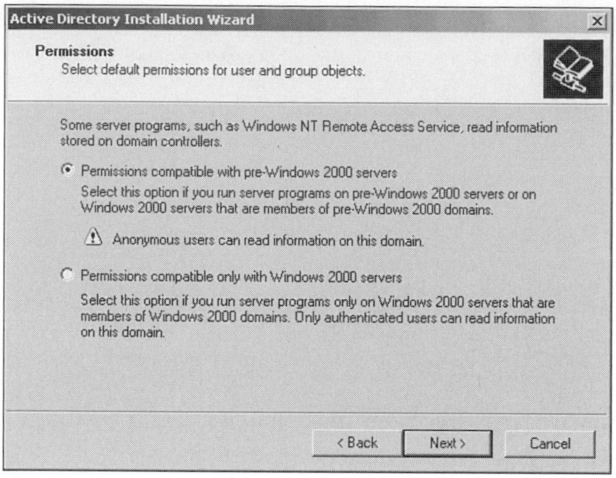

Figure 62.5 For a gradual upgrade, take the first selection so that down-level clients will have permission to access the Active Directory as if it were a PDC.

An informational dialog box appears telling you that the wizard is configuring the Active Directory. Depending on your selections and the information stored on the server when it was operating in Windows NT 4.0 PDC mode, this could take some time. Existing data stored in the Windows NT 4.0 Security Accounts Manager (SAM) database needs to be migrated to objects in the new Active Directory. Drink a cup of coffee or two. At the bottom of this dialog box, you'll see the processes that are being performed, such as installing DNS and configuring databases for the Active Directory.

As a last step, the wizard adds shortcuts to several tools in the Administrative Tools folder that you can use to manage the directory and then prompts you to restart the computer.

After upgrading the first server, you should experiment with it to get used to the new tools and review your plans for the other servers in the domain. When you're sure that you want to proceed, upgrading backup domain controllers is done in the same way except that you don't create a new domain for the BDCs. When upgrading servers in other domains that you want to place into the same domain tree, you can choose to create a child domain and construct the fully qualified domain name according to where you want to place the domain in the tree.

Upgrade the BDCs Next

After you've upgraded the Windows NT 4.0 PDC to become a Windows 2000 domain controller, your network will be operating in what is called mixed mode as long as other Windows NT 4.0 (or prior versions) backup domain controllers exist on the network. To continue your migration, use the same steps on each BDC as you did to upgrade and promote the PDC. After you've upgraded all down-level domain controllers to Windows 2000 domain controllers, you can switch the network to native mode.

A domain administrator using the MMC Active Directory Domains and Trusts snap-in must perform this function. This step should not be done until you're absolutely sure that you no longer need to employ Windows NT 4.0 domain controllers in the network. After the switch is made, there's no going back!

To take this final step and make the switch to a native-mode Windows 2000 domain network, follow these steps:

1. Click Start, Programs, Administrative Tools, and then Active Directory Domains and Trusts.

2. Right-click the domain name you see in the left pane of the MMC console and select Properties from the menu that appears. Alternatively, click once on the domain name and select Properties from the action menu.

3. On the General tab of the Properties page, click Change Mode, and then click Yes when prompted.

That's it. There's no going back (unless you've saved a prior Windows NT 4.0 PDC or BDC offline for recovery purposes). You'll now be operating in an all–Windows 2000 environment.

Upgrading Windows NT 4.0 or Windows 2000 to Windows 2003 Servers

You don't have to upgrade to Windows 2000 before upgrading to Windows 2003. You can skip a generation and upgrade directly from Windows NT 4.0 to Windows 2003. Performing an upgrade from Windows NT 4.0 to Windows 2003 isn't much different from upgrading to Windows 2000, other than a few caveats. The upgrade process depends on three major factors.

Note

Although this chapter discusses upgrading to Windows 2000 and the family of Windows 2003 servers, there's an important distinction to be made when upgrading. Windows 2000 has been available for several years, and many large businesses are just now upgrading to that operating system from Windows NT. If you want to upgrade from Windows NT or Windows 2000 to the family of Windows 2003 servers, be sure that you've examined the benefits that you will gain from the upgrade. As stated earlier in this chapter, you might want to skip Windows 2000 and wait a few years for Windows 2003 servers to stabilize before making such an upgrade. It all depends on the features you need offered by the operating system platforms, as well as the number of trained personnel you have who can handle either operating system.

First, the hardware you're using for hosting Windows NT 4.0 might not be up to par if you want to upgrade to Windows 2003. Windows 2003 servers and the Active Directory they come with have additional features that weren't available in Windows 2000. If you choose all or some of these new features, you might find that you're using a lot of CPU power and disk space. So, you might have to upgrade the hardware or even purchase new servers. If you're going to purchase new server hardware, a clean install might be a good idea. Yet, if you want to preserve existing applications and settings on your current Windows NT 4.0 servers, you might have to copy your disks to a new computer and then proceed with the upgrade.

Second, as discussed earlier, more than one version of the Windows 2003 Server operating systems is available:

- Windows 2003 Server, Standard Edition
- Windows 2003 Server, Enterprise Edition
- Windows 2003 Server, Web Edition
- Windows 2003 Server, Datacenter Edition

Note

You must install Service Pack 5 on your Windows NT 4.0 servers before you can upgrade to Windows 2003.

The upgrade path is not as simple as it seems at first. The current version of Windows NT 4.0 you're now using determines which version of the Windows 2003 server operating systems you can upgrade to. You cannot perform an upgrade to a version of Windows 2003 that's considered to be a downgrade of the operating system. For example, you cannot upgrade from Windows NT 4.0 Enterprise Server to Windows 2003 Standard Edition. Check Microsoft's Web site before planning on upgrading to a Windows 2003 server to decide which will work.

Considering the additional functionality and performance offered by Windows 2003 operating systems, this might be a crucial factor when making a decision to upgrade or perform a new installation. For budgetary purposes, upgrading is less expensive than a fresh install. Yet, for large networks, this can be a significant cost. For a small network, this might not be a concern at all.

Additionally, Windows 2003 Datacenter Edition is not available as an upgrade—you must perform a fresh install to use this edition. You also must purchase (or have available) a machine capable of 64-bit processing (such as an Itanium processor) instead of the usual Pentium (32-bit) CPU. Datacenter is based on the 64-bit processor model and is considered to be the high end of the Windows 2003 server family.

Hardware Requirements for a Windows 2003 Upgrade

As mentioned in the last section, you need to check your current hardware to determine whether it can meet the requirements necessary to run Windows 2003. See Table 62.1 for the requirements.

Table 62.1 Hardware Requirement Recommendations for Windows 2003 Operating Systems

Windows 2003 Operating System	Minimum/ Recommended CPU Speed	Minimum/ Recommended Memory	Support for Multiprocessor Systems	Disk Space
Windows 2003 Standard Edition	133MHz, 550MHz	128MB, 256MB	Up to four processors	1.5GB
Windows 2003 Enterprise Edition	133MHz (x86); 733MHz for Itanium	128MB for x86; 256MB for 64-bit Itanium	Up to eight processors	1.5GB for x86; 2GB for 64-bit Itanium
Windows 2003 Datacenter Edition	400MHz for x86; 733MHz for Itanium	64GB for x86; 512GB for Itanium	Minimum 8, maximum 32 for x86; 64 for Itanium	1.5GB for x86; 2GB for Itanium
Windows 2003 Web Edition	133MHz, 550MHz	128MB, 256MB	Up to two processors	1.5GB

In Table 62.1, the values given for Itanium processors are assumed to be 64-bit CPUs. The disk space requirements are for the finished installation process. Additional disk space might be required during an upgrade process. If you want to exceed NTFS's current limit of 32GB, you must perform a clean install (that can handle disk partitions larger than 32GB), not an upgrade. For FAT partitions, you must also either do a new installation or convert to NTFS, if doing so is appropriate for the version of Windows 2003 you want to upgrade.

Anyone who has ever upgraded or installed a new version of a Windows operating system should already know to check the Microsoft Web site to determine whether other components of your hardware (such as network adapters, printers, and so on) have been tested and added to the hardware compatibility list (HCL). If you don't see all of your hardware components on the list, be sure to check the vendor's Web site to see whether the vendor has created a new driver or software for Windows 2003.

The Application Compatibility Toolkit Application

Microsoft has a toolkit you can use to assist you in determining whether your system is adequate for an upgrade or install of Windows 2003. You can download this from the Web site `www.microsoft.com/windowsserver2003/compatible/appcompat.mspx`.

After you've downloaded this application, run the program to install it on the computer you want to upgrade or perform a fresh install on. The first screen the wizard presents just tells you that you that you're running the toolkit application. Click Next to continue.

The next wizard dialog box contains the standard license dialog box. Click the I Accept the Terms of This Agreement radio button and then click Next. The third wizard screen enables you to select whether only the current user or any user can run the program. Make your choice and click Next.

The fourth screen displayed by the wizard enables you to select where this application's files will be stored. You can take the default (recommended) or enter a directory you choose. Click Next (you guessed that, right?) to continue. The next screen enables you to review the choices you have made. Click Back to make changes or click Install to begin the installation. The files for this application will then be copied to the directory you selected and a text document will appear, describing how to use the toolkit as well as references to other utilities you can use.

The tools included in this kit are beyond the scope of this chapter and might change over time. It's highly suggested that you read this documentation and select the appropriate tools or documents that pertain to your particular environment. You can also read the documents found in the Windows 2003 CD \Docs folder to review the major applications that have been tested and are supported by Windows 2003.

As you can see, upgrading to Windows 2003 might be an easy task, but determining whether your applications will work with the newer operating system can be time-consuming.

What Role Will Your Server Perform?

Windows 2003 operating systems enable you to determine what role your server will be used for in the network. Obviously, a domain controller will service user logons and other related services. Servers that are not domain controllers can be used to provide file or print services for the network, as well as

- Application servers
- Database servers
- Web servers
- Certificate servers
- Firewalls
- Remote access servers

Domain controller servers, however, are used for the following functions:

- To store a copy of the domain's portion of the Active Directory database
- To perform multimaster replication so that all domain controllers within a domain are updated with the most recent changes to the Active Directory database for the domain

- To provide for delegation of administrative functions to administrators for a particular domain
- To provide resources to the network that can be used by users in other domains that exist in the AD tree or forest
- To authenticate users who log on to the network

As you can see, servers that are domain controllers are used for important security services in the network. Member servers (those servers that are not domain controllers) simply offer the services, such as file and print services, to the network.

Tip

Unlike Windows NT 4.0, you can promote a member server in a Windows 2003 network to become a domain controller. You can also demote a domain controller to become a member server. Neither of these role changes requires a new installation of the operating system.

An Example of Upgrading Windows 2000 Server to Windows 2003 Server Standard Edition

To upgrade from Windows 2000 Server (with the Active Directory installed) to Windows 2003 Server Standard Edition, use the steps outlined in this section. First, be sure to read any text files labeled Readme and so on. Many services (Windows 2000 components) are not compatible with Windows 2003, each depending on the edition you're upgrading to. As displayed later in this sample upgrade, you might have to exit the upgrade procedure to fix these problems by removing certain components. As well, some third-party applications might not be compatible with Windows 2003; the upgrade process will continue, but these will be disabled. As mentioned in the previous section, running the Compatibility Wizard can help you prevent this problem from occurring in the first place.

Tip

Before you begin an upgrade, one of the most important things you should think about is the Active Directory. The Windows 2003 server family will extend the schema to include new objects and attributes, and this requires that your current directory be prepared. Before starting the upgrade, insert the Windows 2003 CD, switch to the \i386 directory, and execute **adprep /domainprep**. This program will prepare the domain controller for the upgrade. Next, to prepare the forest for the upgrade, use **adprep /forestprep**. This command will modify your Active Directory forest and depending on the amount of data, its execution might take a while.

When you're ready to begin the upgrade, insert the Windows 2003 Server CD and select Install Windows 2003, Enterprise Edition from the typical Windows installation window (see Figure 62.6).

The next window (see Figure 62.7) should also look familiar if you've done a previous installation or upgrade. The default selection here is to upgrade your current Windows version to Windows 2003. You can also opt to install a new installation using the current disk/partition, or by selecting a different one later in the process. To perform a new installation, select it from the drop-down menu in this dialog box. In this case, the upgrade option is selected and will be used.

The next dialog box requires you to accept the license agreement. Read the license agreement and then, if you still want to upgrade, click on I Accept This Agreement and then the Next button.

As with all Windows installations, you must enter the key code that is found on the jewel case that came with your CD. Enter the code and click Next to continue.

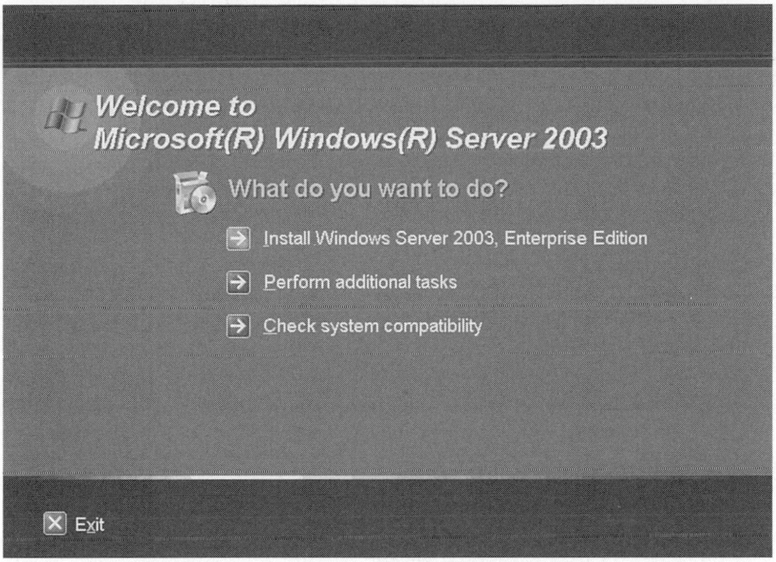

Figure 62.6 Use the Install selection on the standard Windows window to upgrade from Windows 2000 to Windows 2003.

Figure 62.7 Use this window to select whether you want to upgrade your current Windows server or install a new version from scratch.

An important dialog box appears next (see Figure 62.8). It's assumed that the server you're upgrading is connected to the Internet. If that isn't the case, click on the radio button labeled No, Skip This Step and continue installing Windows. If you have an Internet connection currently working on the Windows 2000 server you are upgrading, select the first radio button, Yes, Download the Updated Setup Files (Recommended) and then click Next. This enables the installation procedure to download any new files that have been created since the CD was manufactured. By selecting this option, you'll end up with the latest version of Windows 2003.

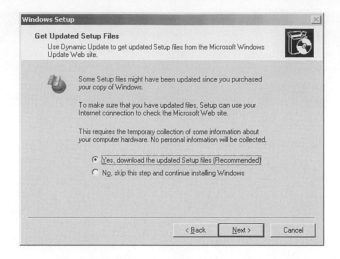

Figure 62.8 If you're connected to the Internet, select the first radio button.

The Report System Compatibility dialog box, shown in Figure 62.9, will inform you of problems with application or previous Windows component applications that will not function correctly using Windows 2003. You can elect to continue or to exit the upgrade at this time. If you see a red X next to a component, you must exit the setup procedure and remove those applications or components. Click the Details button for each to get instructions on how to do so. If the application or component has a yellow triangle with an exclamation point next to it, the installation will continue but the feature will not be available under Windows 2003. All of these dependencies will vary depending on the edition of Windows 2003 you're installing.

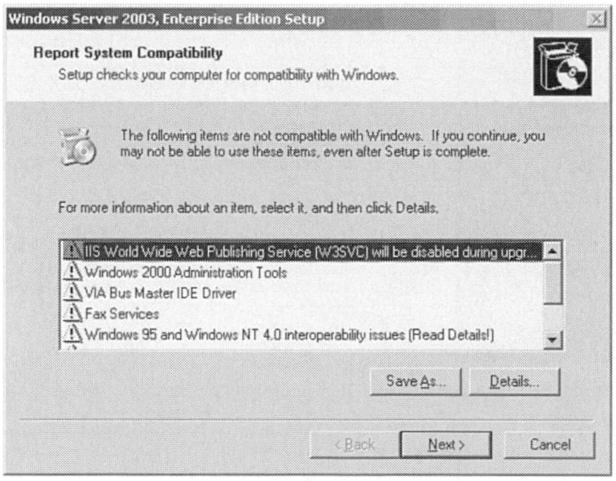

Figure 62.9 Not all Windows components or applications can be upgraded.

Setup will next copy installation files to your computer and then restart. After the restart, the traditional stages of a Windows upgrade/installation will be performed (the first two have already been completed):

- Collecting information
- Dynamic update

- Preparing installation
- Installing Windows
- Finalizing installation

When the system finally reboots, you will find that any compatible applications still work. Those applications that don't work require an upgrade (check your vendor). If you use this server to offer services to clients, you should practice this installation with those application services in advance in a laboratory to ensure that you can continue to satisfy clients after the upgrade.

The interface for Windows 2003 Server Standard Edition isn't that much different from the one for Windows 2000 Server. However, you will notice some new features as well as some changes under the Administrative Tools folder. The last are due to the new features offered by Windows 2003.

Should You Use Windows 2000 Professional or Windows XP Professional?

The decision of which operating system you should choose as a target should be based on several factors. For the most part, I think the decision should be based on the applications currently used and potential hardware you'll use in the near future. For example, although Microsoft always provides an upgrade path for its applications to ensure that you can expend a large budget to upgrade both their operating systems as well as applications, that might not be the case for third-party applications. This also might not be the case for newer hardware—an operating system upgrade will require new device drivers, which might not be available from Microsoft, much less the hardware vendor.

You should evaluate the benefits that you can obtain from upgrading to a new operating system and possibly applications (which might or might not be compatible with newer Microsoft operating systems). Keep in mind the costs involved. Microsoft tends to drop or charge more for support for older operating systems and applications. If you have trained personnel on older systems, you might want to skip a generation or two of both operating systems as well as applications. For Enterprise customers, these are valid options to consider.

Caution

Although upgrading to a newer operating system might not seem to be feasible to your company due to a cost/benefit analysis or even because of application compatibility, there is another very important factor to consider. Before upgrading to a new operating system, the general consensus is to wait for a while to see whether the new version is a stable one, generally after security patches or service packs have been issued.

But that doesn't mean that you should stay at an earlier version for a long time unless financial constraints force you to, as mentioned in this chapter. The main problem with this is that with an operating system that has been in use for a few years is probably going to be more vulnerable to penetration and damage by hackers. A known operating system, for which the vendor stops generating security patches, can be an easy target for these malicious persons.

Upgrading for SOHO Clients

You can upgrade a Windows NT Workstation computer to Windows 2000 Professional or Windows XP Professional and maintain domain membership at any time. However, if you're performing an upgrade from Windows NT or Windows 2000 servers to Windows 2003 servers, it might be a good idea to perform that upgrade first. When you're sure that your servers are properly configured and that the Active Directory has been installed, you can upgrade clients at your leisure.

This is not an absolute, just a suggestion. Why? If you operate in a mixed network environment, the client workstations that have been upgraded to Windows 2000 (or Windows 98 or Windows 95 clients that have the appropriate Active Directory client software installed) can use some of the new features provided by the Active Directory. This includes the capability to query the database to locate resources throughout the domain tree. Those clients will then use DNS as their locator service, while any remaining clients that are not Active Directory–aware will continue to use NetBIOS names. The version of the Active Directory that is supplied with Windows 2003 supports many new features. For example, you can enforce a larger number of items for security or to manage a user's desktop using group policies.

Yet, for clients before Windows 2000, you will find that there is a great deal less you can do to enforce group policies and control the desktop. Windows 95 and Windows 98 are considered ancient operating systems, along with MS-DOS. If you still have these clients in a SOHO network, and your applications work, you might find them useful when it comes to the cost of upgrading to newer versions. Keep in mind, however, that the longer you wait, the more it will cost you later to invest in newer operating systems, much less applications. This last point, applications, is perhaps the most important one. Operating systems are not cheap for a SOHO environment, but if you have more than just a few applications from different vendors, you might want to explore the cost of upgrading those applications. It might be the case that you cannot upgrade directly from older Windows operating systems to the newer ones. Many applications don't allow you to skip several generations of operating systems.

So, should you upgrade to Windows XP? Not necessarily. However, you should check the Web site (if there is one) for the vendor of your applications to determine what the upgrade path will be. If you have to upgrade from Windows 98 to Windows 2000 Professional to Windows XP, you'll incur a significant cost for both the applications as well as the interim operating systems. For example, can you still find Windows 2000 Professional for sale at your local computer store now that Windows XP has replaced it? Does your application vendor support upgrading from Windows 95 or 98 to Windows XP? I don't mean to suggest that you upgrade to every operating system Microsoft releases. However, I do recommend that you keep track of what your application vendor is doing, and possibly skip one generation of operating systems. For more than one generation, I repeat: Check what your application vendor says!

A last word for SOHO clients: If you use just a few applications, should you consider an upgrade at all? If you're using a vertical market application, follow the upgrade path that your vendor *requires*, and not necessarily the path they recommend. If a vertical market vendor wants to keep your business, you can almost be guaranteed it will help you with future upgrades. Vertical market applications are not inexpensive. Money talks, so to speak.

63

Migration and Integration: NetWare, Unix, and Linux

SOME OF THE MAIN TOPICS IN THIS CHAPTER ARE

CHAPTER 63

Although Unix and Linux can be considered close cousins, trying to find similarities between them and Novell NetWare is not an easy job. Unix/Linux and NetWare systems are very different from each other, so when you're considering a migration from one to the other, or integrating the two into a heterogeneous network, it requires some diligent planning. In this chapter, we will look at some of the key differences between Unix/Linux and NetWare and discuss a few scenarios in which integrating these two different systems can be accomplished.

Why Use Unix or Linux?

NetWare has been around for many years, and other than ARCnet it is perhaps the oldest PC networking technology still in existence on a wide scale. NetWare, however, has been deployed in large networks that span great geographical distances, as well as in small departmental LANs for many years. There exists a large user base and a sizable population of trained network administrators. Many applications have been developed by vendors to make use of Novell's Directory Service (NDS, now the eDirectory, and referred to in the rest of this chapter as directory services when discussing NetWare). However, using Linux in a NetWare environment to provide services to NetWare clients, to protect the network through a firewall, or to give technical users a Linux desktop does make sense in some situations.

One good integration scenario is the small LAN. For example, consider a small company that originally created a LAN to link several Intel-based Web servers that use a Windows operating system. Business has grown and it's time to upgrade. The choices are more powerful Intel-based systems running a Windows variant or Linux boxes. In this case, Linux has the edge because it is not limited to the Intel platform. You'll find both Unix and Linux running on many hardware platforms. Recent partnerships between Red Hat and hardware manufacturers enable Linux to scale to larger enterprise servers. However, if the existing LAN uses NetWare (which means you have Windows systems in your network), exchanging information with Unix and Linux Servers will require some new networking skills. By using fast Unix/Linux boxes to run your Web servers, databases (such as Oracle), and other CPU-intensive applications, you can still keep your Windows desktop machines. Novell does incorporate technology (most notably in the 6.x versions) that goes a long way toward enabling connectivity between Unix/Linux and NetWare.

Another reason you might consider bringing Linux into your small LAN is that it's basically free. You can buy inexpensive versions from many vendors, such as SuSE, Caldera, or Red Hat, that have sprung up to cater to the Linux community, or you can download a version from a Web site, usually free. If you have an experienced Unix staff at your site, Linux will be much cheaper to implement than NetWare. Without the experienced staff, however, it might become more expensive when it comes to support and engineering. However, the various vendors just mentioned also provide support for their Linux versions, and you can find a lot of information on the Internet by searching for Unix or Linux "how to" documents.

Tip

In addition to Web resources for "how to" documents, don't forget the man (manual) pages that both Unix and Linux have. For example, if you go to the help page for Red Hat Linux, you are referred to the man pages, sorted by functions. If you know a command but need a quick look at the syntax, you can simply enter **man <command>**. Some of the man pages are very technical in detail, but you can usually find what you need quickly.

Key Differences Between Unix/Linux and NetWare

The most obvious difference that should come to mind when looking at NetWare and Unix/Linux is that the latter systems are computer operating systems and NetWare is a network operating system. NetWare clients can include many different platforms, usually ones that have their roots in MS-DOS or Windows of some kind. Yet, no matter on which platform you use NetWare, it basically only provides support for network resource sharing. You can use native NetWare servers, or you can use Windows servers in the same network to offer application, print, and other services to users. Authentication services are provided, as are mechanisms for granting or denying access to data. This is especially the case when using the eDirectory. Or the underlying server operating system (such as Windows 2000/2003) can also be used to enforce access permissions and user authentication.

File Sharing

NetWare excels at providing file servers on the network. Either the bindery-based NetWare 3.x or the directory services versions can be used to exercise a great deal of control over file and directory access for one or more servers on the network. By using directory services, you can distribute files throughout the network on multiple servers. Clients can be authenticated by bindery-based servers, or directory services, and access the resources they need. Using a bindery-based system of servers works best when local users need access to only one or two servers. In a larger network this might not be a good idea if resources are spread out among many servers. This is because the bindery servers require a user account/password on each server, and keeping these synchronized on a lot of servers can be a headache for the user. If you need to manage a large number of servers, which has users needing resources on different servers, then directory services is a better choice because it allows the user to log on to the network using directory services and gives management a single place to manage users and resources.

Unix and Linux do not come with file shares or directory services. Instead, you must substitute NFS, the Network File System, which was originally developed by Sun. Access permissions can be controlled using the standard mechanisms provided by Linux. You can set up NFS so that users must log on to each server to mount the exported file system, or you can hide the authentication process from users by using proxy mechanisms built in to most NFS implementations.

◄◄ For more information about NFS, see Chapter 35, "File Server Protocols." To learn more about how Linux and Unix systems use resource access permissions, see Chapter 43, "Rights and Permissions."

Printer Sharing

NetWare is capable of providing support for many kinds of printing technologies and protocols, including the `lpr/lpd` and TCP stream printing protocols used by Unix and Linux. Novell Distributed Print Services enables printing from Unix to NetWare, as well as from NetWare to Unix, by using a generic NetWare gateway. Additionally, third-party printer manufacturers can develop gateways that can provide additional features for their printers.

User Authentication

If the NetWare version you currently employ uses bindery-based authentication services, you are familiar with having to log on to each server when you need to access a resource. Similarly, Unix and Linux use a file called `/etc/passwrd` that resides on each system. Users must have an entry in this file that can be used when they log on to the server. Linux does not natively support a directory service yet (though an open source directory service is available on the Web), so providing a single logon for the network will not be something you get out of the box. Most Unix operating systems, however, support NIS (Network Information System) for small LANs or NIS+ for larger networks. This software was originally called Yellow Pages, but the name was changed to NIS due to trademark reasons. NIS coordinates password and other information on the network between Unix servers. There are several open-source versions of NIS that can be found on the Web, some of which are intended for use with Unix, and others for Linux.

Note

The `/etc/passwrd` file is a simple text file, although the password is encrypted for each user. Another file, called the shadow password file, is usually employed on modern Unix/Linux systems because all the data in the file is encrypted. Using the text version can open up the entire system should the file become available to an intruder.

Moving User Accounts

To establish NetWare user accounts on the Linux server, you must manually configure them. There are no widely available utilities or tools you can use to perform this function. However, the typical Unix/Linux password can be used as a reference for the kind of information you'll need in order to create user accounts on Unix/Linux systems. If you only need to create a few user accounts for just system administrators, for example, the process will be simple. If you need to create a large number of accounts, possibly for client workstations, you probably will find it necessary to produce a report from the NetWare system and use this to make the entries or create a script file that can be used for this purpose.

◄◄ The Unix/Linux password file is covered in Chapter 42, "Managing Unix and Linux Users."

And if you are using NetWare 5.x or 6.x, the Native File Access Pack feature enables Unix, Windows, and Macintosh clients to access NetWare servers. This feature doesn't require you to install NetWare client software on the client systems, and can be integrated with the directory services.

NetWare, particularly the 4.x and higher versions that support directory services, keeps track of a lot more information for a user account than is done on Unix/Linux systems that use just the `/etc/passwrd` file. Because of this, and the simplicity of the `/etc/passwrd` file, you won't have to do a lot of work to create new user accounts on the Linux system. However, you might find that the trade-off is that you need to examine security (file permissions, for example) and other aspects of your Unix/Linux system to ensure that your users are afforded the same access.

Networking Protocols

The TCP/IP protocol is the standard used on the Internet and most LANs. It has become increasingly popular for use in all kinds of networks in just the past few years. For example, early versions of Windows NT would install the IPX/SPX protocol by default. Starting with Windows NT 4.0, the default became TCP/IP. This has stayed the same for Windows 2000/2003 and Windows XP.

NetWare's legacy protocols (IPX/SPX) aren't used a lot anymore, since NetWare adopted TCP/IP a few years ago. Unless you have an older version of NetWare that still uses IPX/SPX, it would be a good idea to upgrade the NetWare servers to at least version 5.0, which does support IP.

Applications

Unfortunately, if you have a large investment in application software that was written (or compiled) for a Windows platform or NetWare's native servers, you will need to purchase new versions of your existing software or purchase new software. If you have internally developed applications for which you have the source code, you might need to make only minor changes and recompile the source code on a Unix/Linux system. The C language (and its descendants) is the programming language of choice for Unix/Linux, so if your in-house applications were written in C, then this task may be somewhat easier.

Unix systems are marketed by most every major computer manufacturer. As the popularity of Linux continues to grow, many vendors have started to think about producing Linux versions of their products as well as Unix versions. You won't find Microsoft Office there yet, but you will find competing products. If you can use the file conversion capabilities that come with most products of this type, you might find that changing to a new product is not that painful, short of a little user training.

One important competing product is Sun's StarOffice. This application was originally offered as a free download. However, Sun now charges a very small price for the software. If you want a version that is almost the same, but lacks just a few features that StarOffice provides, you can get the open-source OpenOffice suite. OpenOffice is distributed by most Linux vendors (such as Red Hat). Because Linux is more likely to be used as a desktop replacement for Windows systems, OpenOffice is a bargain. And OpenOffice's word processing, spreadsheet, and other programs are compatible with Microsoft Office versions, for the most part.

StarOffice is available for the following platforms:

- Linux (x86)
- Solaris Intel
- Windows 95, 98, NT, and Windows 2000 and Windows Server 2003
- Solaris on SPARC

You should regularly check the OpenOffice Web site to keep up with new ports of this office suite to other platforms.

The applications that are provided with Sun's StarOffice include the following:

- **StarOffice Writer**—A professional word processing program.
- **StarOffice Calc**—A spreadsheet.
- **StarOffice Impress**—A graphics presentation program.
- **StarOffice Draw**—A graphics drawing program.
- **StarOffice Base**—A database for the suite.
- **StarOffice Schedule**—A scheduling application to keep your appointments in order.
- **StarOffice Mail**—An email client.
- **StarOffice Discussion**—A news reader program.

As you can see, StarOffice offers just about the same applications you'll find in Microsoft Office. Because of its price and availability on multiple platforms, you might find integrating Linux into an existing Windows environment to be less costly than you had originally anticipated. Or, if you do have a Unix desktop computer, StarOffice is easier to use than many Unix utilities that provide similar functionality.

You can learn more about the StarOffice Application Suite at the following URL:

`wwws.sun.com/software/star/staroffice/6.0/`

OpenOffice can be found at this site:

`www.openoffice.org/`

OpenOffice is available in several languages, and you'll even find a version for Windows. So you can run the same office suite for Unix/Linux users as well as for Windows clients on your NetWare network.

If you already have a large investment in Microsoft applications, you can use one of the alternatives to StarOffice or OpenOffice. You can purchase software that emulates Windows and runs some of those applications on a Linux computer.

For example, a company called CodeWeavers (www.codeweavers.com) sells a product called CrossOver Office. You can download an evaluation copy from its Web site before you decide to make a purchase. If you decide that this product works well on your Linux computers, you'll find that it is very inexpensive: just under $60. Although CrossOver Office doesn't run every Windows application, CodeWeavers is working to add additional applications. Some of the Windows applications depend on the version of the product you buy. The following applications that were written for Windows 97, Windows 2000, and Windows XP using CrossOver Office include:

- Microsoft Word
- Microsoft Excel
- Microsoft Internet Explorer
- Microsoft Visio
- Microsoft PowerPoint (Windows 2000 version only)
- Microsoft Outlook (Windows 2000 version only)
- Microsoft Access (Windows 2000 version only)

In addition, some non-Microsoft products are also supported:

- Adobe Photoshop
- Lotus Notes
- Quicken

At the CodeWeavers Web site you can also find a list of applications that can be run, but may encounter a few bugs. These applications are still under development, however, and support for them will be added in future versions of CrossOver Office.

NetWare for Linux

Linux is an open-source product supported by many individuals on the Internet, along with several new startup companies that have begun to produce additional utilities and products for the Linux community. In particular, Caldera produced NetWare for Linux, which can be installed on its version of Linux, as well as those from Red Hat Linux and some other variants. Although the product probably should not be used as a substitute for NetWare in a large environment, it is suitable for providing NetWare services to a few clients in a LAN. You might also use it when performing a migration to Linux when you have a few clients that need to continue using NetWare for some period. You can move your files and printers to Linux servers, configure NetWare for Linux, and then allow those few clients to make use of it. Also, in 2002, Caldera, which had acquired SCO, changed its name to The SCO Group. You can visit its Web site at www.caldera.com or www.sco.com.

NetWare for Linux provides functionality for the following:

- Novell Directory Services (now called the eDirectory)
- NetWare File Services

- NetWare Print Services (and NetWare Distributed Print Services)
- NetWare Client support
- NetWare user account security and authentication

The installation can be performed on a Caldera Linux system quickly using a setup file or manually on other Linux systems. To update the Caldera version, you need only to change your directory to the installation CD and enter the following command:

`./update.NWS4L`

When the procedure finishes, you need to reboot. Other commands that are useful include these:

- **nwserverstatus**—Shows status information about the Linux NetWare server.
- **/etc/rc.d/init.d/netware start**—Starts the NetWare server.
- **/etc/rc.d/init.d/netware stop**—Stops the NetWare server.

You also can install Caldera NetWare for Linux client on Linux systems. This allows Linux clients to connect to the Linux server that runs the NetWare services or to an actual NetWare server. In this way, both ordinary NetWare clients and Linux clients can share the same information. Some useful commands for the client include the following:

- **nwlogon *<netware user name>***—Log on to NetWare if using NDS. You also can log on to a particular context using the nwlogon command and connect to a specific NDS tree.
- **nwlogin -s *<server>* -b -u *<NetWare username>***—Log on to the server when using the bindery instead of NDS.
- **nwlogout -s *<server>***—Log off the particular server.
- **nwlogout -t *<tree>***—Log off a particular NDS tree.
- **nwwhoami**—Display status information about your process, showing the NDS trees to which you have connected, the username used, and so on.
- **nwprint *<filename>***—Allow the client to submit files to print.

Accessing files on a NetWare-enabled Linux server is done in the same manner as for other files in the Linux file system. The NetWare files appear under the /NetWare/bindery directory (if using bindery services) or the /NetWare/NDS directory (when using NDS).

Appendixes

Overview of the OSI Seven-Layer Networking Reference Model

SOME OF THE MAIN TOPICS IN THIS APPENDIX ARE

When discussing different network devices or software components of a network, it is common to use, as a reference point, a model that the International Organization for Standardization (ISO) created. The Open Systems Interconnection (OSI) Seven-Layer Networking Reference Model was originally developed as a blueprint for creating the additional network protocols that the ISO developed. However, these protocols were written during a time when a lot of computer horsepower was required to implement them, and they were never widely adopted. Some companies, such as Digital Equipment Corporation's DECnet, did move toward OSI standards.

With the explosion of the Internet, and also of its requisite protocols, TCP/IP became the overall standard for most local area (and wide area) networks instead of the OSI protocols. TCP/IP is based on a network model that has fewer layers, as discussed in Chapter 25, "Overview of the TCP/IP Protocol Suite." This appendix looks at the OSI reference model because it is still generally referred to when discussing networking technology.

It's Only a Model!

The OSI networking model is just that—a model. It's a reference you can use when discussing networking with colleagues. The model specifies seven layers, which you can think of as separate modules, each of which performs a specific set of functions. Each layer in the model communicates with adjacent layers in the model using a standard defined interface. Therefore, the internal workings of each layer can be left up to the vendor to develop. All that matters is that all the layers work together, no matter which vendor provides them. For example, network adapters and network cabling fall into the bottom layer, the Physical layer. Network cards are designed to work with the software that falls into the next higher layer, the Data Link layer.

Figure A.1 shows how the layers of the model interact with one another, from two ends of a network connection.

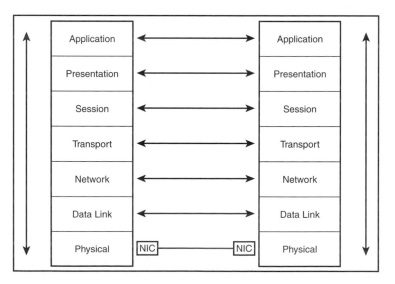

Figure A.1   Each layer in the OSI reference model provides functions to adjacent layers in the model.

As you can see in Figure A.1, arrows show the flow of information down the stack from one computer. When the information reaches the Physical layer, the components at that layer act to deliver the data to the remote system. At the remote system, the Physical layer receives the electrical (or light) impulses, converts them into the appropriate message format, and passes the information back up the stack so that the data eventually reaches the application for which it was intended.

Also in Figure A.1 you can see that arrows point both ways between the layers on one system and the corresponding layers on the other system. This implies that from a logical point of view, each layer in the model performs functions as if it were talking directly to its corresponding layer at the remote system. Each layer is unaware of what is going on in layers underneath it or how the message is delivered to the matching layer on the remote machine.

For example, TCP breaks up large messages into smaller messages called *segments*. These segments are then passed to lower layers that encapsulate them in IP datagrams and then into a physical layer protocol, such as Ethernet. On the receiving end, the TCP software does not have to know that Ethernet, Token-Ring, or any other technology was used to deliver the message. Instead, the TCP software on the remote system receives the segments that the TCP software on the sending system originally sent.

Encapsulation

Most layers attach information to the data that they pass to lower layers. This data is called *header information*. For example, an IP datagram contains header information such as the source and destination IP addresses and port numbers. When the IP datagram is passed down the stack, it can be encapsulated in an Ethernet frame. An Ethernet frame adds its own header information (see Chapter 14, "Ethernet: The Universal Standard"). Here, instead of IP addresses, physical MAC addresses are used in the Ethernet header.

On the receiving end of the communication, the Ethernet header information is stripped off before the remaining data is passed up the stack. At the IP level the IP header is removed and the data is passed back up to the TCP software, and so on. Thus, each layer on each computer actually sees, with few exceptions, only the header information that was attached to the original message by the corresponding layer on the other machine. This is how the layers logically interact, regardless of how layers above or beneath operate internally.

The following sections describe the functions that are performed at each layer, starting from the bottom (Physical layer) and working up to the top. An important point to remember is that some vendors combine two or more layers into a single software application. As mentioned, the OSI Seven-Layer Reference Model is just that, a model. It's a way to discuss networking technologies in a rational manner that professionals can understand. It does not mean that all networking products must conform to this model!

Physical Layer

The Physical layer comprises the physical components that make up the networking hardware of the network, including the network adapter, connectors, network media (copper wires or optical cables), and so on. To sum it up in a simple sentence: The Physical layer gets the data from here to there. This layer covers both electrical and mechanical aspects of the network. For example, the method used to encode data into electrical or light signals on the network media is decided at this layer.

Data Link Layer

The Data Link layer serves several functions, which the IEEE has divided into two sublayers. The first is the Logical Link Control (LLC) and the second is the Media Access Control (MAC). As a whole, the Data Link layer is responsible for transmitting data from one place to another and doing some minimal error correction. The purpose of the LLC is to provide Service Access Points (SAPs) that devices can use to send information. The MAC component takes care of transmitting the data and correcting errors.

The Data Link layer is responsible for putting together the Ethernet frame, for example. This includes formatting the header information into the correct fields and placing the data in the right place. Functions operating at this layer also determine the order in which bits are interpreted (that is, big- or little-endian), and add checksum information used to ensure that the frame arrives intact at its destination.

Bridges are network devices that operate at this level in the model. Bridges examine the MAC addresses of packets and use that information to decide whether to forward a packet to another port.

Network Layer

The Network layer provides an important functionality to a network protocol stack. Here, protocols are created that manage how packets are delivered on the network or routed to another network. For example, the Internet Protocol (IP) resides at this layer. IP addressing works at this level. Remember that IP addresses have two components: a network ID and a host ID. Therefore, packets can be delivered on the local LAN (using the host ID) or routed to another network (using the network ID). This layer is also responsible for breaking larger messages into smaller ones that fit into the frames created at the Data Link layer. This size is called the Maximum Transmission Unit (MTU). At the receiving end, the Network layer reassembles these into the larger original message before passing the data up to the Transport layer. The easiest way to remember this layer is to remember that it provides for addressing and routing.

It should be obvious that traditional routers operate at this level. Routers use a protocol's network address to determine on which port a packet is to be forwarded.

Transport Layer

Whereas the Network layer is responsible for routing data packets, protocols at the Transport layer take on the duty of making sure that those packets actually get delivered, and in the correct order. For example, the Transmission Control Protocol (TCP) can be found at this layer. TCP uses IP (at the Network layer) and tracks which segments get lost in the network and cause IP to retransmit segments as necessary.

Although this layer can provide for retransmissions for lost packets, it does not have to. For example, the User Datagram Protocol (UDP) is found at this layer. UDP also uses IP to get its messages delivered. However, UDP does very minimal management of the messages it sends. It does not acknowledge packet delivery, but it does respond to ICMP messages, such as those designed to throttle back transmissions when they are arriving at the receiving end at too fast a rate.

Session Layer

The Session layer is responsible for deciding the format of the data transmitted. Session protocol examples are the remote procedure call (used by NFS and other applications). Another way to think of the Session layer is that it functions to allow processes on networked computers to talk to each other. TCP and NetBIOS are both protocols that reside at the Session layer.

Presentation Layer

The Presentation layer interprets the actual data that is being exchanged. For example, different systems can use different methods to represent floating-point numbers or other data. The order of bits in a byte is translated at this level. The necessary conversions take place at this layer. It is at this layer that translations from different character-encoding methods take place. For example, when one computer uses ASCII characters and another computer uses IBM's EBCDIC encoding, translations between these two methods of representing characters are made at the Presentation layer.

Application Layer

The user comes into the picture in the Application layer. Without applications that need to use the network, we network administrators would be out of a job. Examples of network components that reside at this layer include firewalls or networked file systems (such as NFS). End users can recognize Application layer components as programs that they use every day, such as email and FTP.

Networking Glossary

10BASE-2—10Mbps networking using a smaller, more flexible coaxial cable than 10BASE-5. Devices on the network connect to the cable using BNC connectors. Also known as thinnet.

10BASE-5—10Mbps networking using a coaxial cable larger than one used by 10BASE-2. To attach a network drop to connect a device to the coaxial cable, the cable is tapped by punching a hole through the cable. Also known as thicknet.

10BASE-T—10Mbps networking using twisted-pair wiring. A wiring concentrator such as a hub or switch is used to connect devices on the LAN.

100BASE-T—100Mbps networking using twisted-pair wiring. Also known as Fast Ethernet. A wiring concentrator such as a hub or switch is used to connect devices on the LAN.

10Gigabit Ethernet—Ethernet operating at 10 billion bits per second. Defined by IEEE 802.3a.

Accelerated Graphics Port (AGP)—A PCI-based port that enables you to connect a graphics card that supports advanced features.

Access Point (AP)—See *Wireless Access Point*.

Active Directory—An LDAP-based directory and directory service that contains information such as user accounts, computer accounts, and links to network resources. The Active Directory is used on Windows networks but can interoperate with some other LDAP directories.

Active monitor—A node on a Token-Ring network that initializes and monitors the traffic on the ring. The active monitor detects error conditions and can reset the state of the ring. There can be only one active monitor on the ring at any point in time. If the active monitor fails, another node in the ring can be promoted to that position.

Ad hoc wireless network—A wireless network that does not use a Wireless Access Point (AP). Instead, each computer that is part of the ad hoc network can establish a connection with others in the network without using an AP or a wired network. See also *Wireless Access Point* to contrast this with a network that uses an AP.

Address Resolution Protocol (ARP)—The protocol used to probe a LAN to discover the MAC address of a computer based on an IP address. The arp command can be used for many other purposes, such as viewing and managing the current table of MAC addresses stored in the local ARP cache.

AGP—See *Accelerated Graphics Port*.

American National Standards Institute (ANSI)—ANSI was founded in 1918 and is the major standards organization for the United States. ANSI is also a member of other standards organizations, such as ISO.

American Standard Code for Information Interchange (ASCII)—An assignment of alphabetic characters (both upper- and lowercase) and certain other symbols (such as punctuation marks) to a numeric format. For many years ASCII was the standard means used to represent text in computer systems. Newer systems expand on this concept to include other languages that use additional symbols/characters, such as Unicode.

American wire gauge (AWG)—The wire gauge is the standard for sizing wires in the U.S. Wire size is based primarily on the current carrying capacity of the wire set by the National Electrical Code. As the wire gauge increases, the physical diameter of the wire decreases.

ANSI—See *American National Standards Institute*.

APIPA—See *Automatic Private IP Addressing*.

Arbitrated Loop—A loop topology used by Fibre Channel. Up to 126 nodes can be placed on a single loop, or 127 if the loop connects to a switch. Each device on the loop must contend for access on the loop; thus data transfers can be initiated by only one device at a time.

ARCnet—An older LAN protocol, similar to Token-Ring, limited to 255 nodes. ARCnet is still in use in point-of-sale registers, as well as factory automation applications. The main benefits of ARCnet are due to its simplicity: Little setup is required, other than assigning an address to each device.

ARP—See *Address Resolution Protocol*.

ARPANET—The predecessor to the Internet.

ASCII—See *American Standard Code for Information Interchange*.

Asynchronous Transfer Mode (ATM)—A switched protocol that sets up a dedicated path through the switched network and uses a small fixed packet size (53 bytes), usually referred to as a cell. By limiting the size of the cell to a known size, hardware switches can route ATM cells much faster than protocols that use frames or packets, which can vary in size. See also www.atmforum.com/.

ATM—See *Asynchronous Transfer Mode*.

Attenuation—The decrease in magnitude of the signal as it travels through any transmitting medium, such as wire or glass. Attenuation is measured as a logarithm of the ratio between the input and output power or between the input and output voltage of the system, expressed in db (decibels).

Audit trail—A mechanism by which an operating system can record user activity. In most cases the administrator of the system needs to set up which actions to record.

Automatic Private IP Addressing (APIPA)— APIPA enables computers to obtain IP addressing automatically when no DHCP server is present on the LAN. The computer that needs to obtain configuration information automatically selects an address from the range 169.254.0.0 through 169.254.255.255 and then broadcasts an ARP packet containing this address. If no other computer responds that the IP address is already in use, the computer will configure itself using that IP address. If the address is in use, another is selected and the process is repeated.

Autosensing—The capability of a network adapter to detect the speed of the network to which it is attached (such as 10Mbps versus 100Mbps). This enables you to use a mobile computer without having to change the bandwidth settings when moving from one network to another. However, some network adapter cards and switch ports that claim to support autosensing may not work well together. The operating system usually allows you to select the mode of operation for a network adapter card. If the autosensing selection doesn't work, specify the correct setting.

AWG—See *American wire gauge*.

Backbone Cabling System Structure— Connections between multiple telecommunication rooms, equipment rooms, and entrance facilities.

Backup Window—The time required to perform backups on a computer system, such as servers in a network. This term implies that the system should be used exclusively by the backup program, and that users cannot access the server at the same time. This concept is becoming outdated as many large data centers require a 24/7 uptime. Storage Area Networks (SANs), along with certain RAID techniques, can be used to create backups without interrupting user access. Additionally, a newer technology "snapshot" technique can be used. Using the snapshot technique, users can read data files that are being backed up, but changes are stored separately. After the backup has finished, the changes can be applied to the original data.

Bandwidth—The range (or width) of frequencies used for transmission of a signal on a network media. This is expressed in hertz (Hz) as a difference of frequencies.

Bindery—A server-based database used by NetWare clients to authenticate and access resources on a server. The bindery has been superceded by NDS (or the eDirectory) by most new implementations of NetWare.

Bit Error Rate (BER)—A calculated value as a percentage of bits that have errors when compared to the total number of bits sampled.

Bit Error Rate Tester (BERT)—A diagnostic device that performs a more basic function to determine whether the line is capable of carrying the network signaling at the required bit level with a minimum of errors.

Bluetooth—An inexpensive networking technology (operating in the 2.4GHz radio frequency) designed to connect devices such as keyboards, cellular phones, and computers over short distances.

BOOTP—The Bootstrap Protocol that enables diskless workstations and other network devices to discover their IP address and other configuration information, and download an operating system.

Bridge—A bridge is basically a repeater with a little intelligence. Bridges can store MAC addresses in a table in memory. Because of this, after a bridge has received a transmission from a particular computer, subsequent transmissions intended for that computer do not have to be repeated on all segments connected by the bridge, but only on the physical network segment on which the target computer resides. Using this technique, bridges help to reduce broadcast network traffic and reduce bandwidth usage. Other types of bridges can include such functions as translating different network protocols to allow data transfers between two dissimilar networks.

Bridge Tap—An open circuit on the local telephone loop caused by the removal of service from another site, without removal of the connection to the loop. The "dangling" bridge tap acts as an antenna and can cause problems with digital services, such as xDSL.

Bus—When a bus is applied to networking topologies, a single cable connects multiple computers (or other network-enabled devices). When applied to computer mechanics, a bus is a physical path that joins a computer's CPU, memory, and peripheral devices (such as PCI cards).

Cable modem—Used by cable TV companies to enable part of the bandwidth of their network to be used to provide Internet access to their customers.

CAP—See *Carrierless Amplitude Phase modulation*.

CardBus—The next generation of PCMCIA cards. CardBus devices enable new features, such as direct memory access and a 32-bit data path, and operate at a greater speed than PCMCIA cards. CardBus also consumes less power than its predecessor, which is important when it's used in a laptop using battery power. In most cases, CardBus devices are backward compatible with PCMCIA cards, depending on the manufacturer.

Carrier Sense Multiple Access/Collision Avoidance (CSMA/CA)—A method used in wireless networks by clients wanting to gain access to the shared bandwidth. A small packet is first transmitted to let other devices on the network know that a packet is about to be transmitted. This technique does not eliminate collisions, and thus produces additional overhead. It is used by older AppleTalk networks, as well as some wireless networks. See also *Carrier Sense Multiple Access/Collision Detect*.

Carrier Sense Multiple Access/Collision Detect (CSMA/CD)—A method used by early Ethernet devices to contend for access to the network media. Carrier sense means that a node wanting to transmit data first listens to the network media to determine whether another transmission is in progress. Multiple access implies that many computers can try to access the media at any point in time. If two nodes on the media start transmitting at approximately the same time, a collision occurs. Collision detect means that a node is able to detect whether its transmission occurred while another was also being sent. Each node involved in a collision will back off for a pseudo-random interval before listening to the network media and again attempting a transmission.

Carrierless Amplitude Phase (CAP) modulation—A technique used by xDSL lines for transmitting and receiving data. CAP uses a broad frequency spectrum for receiving data, and a smaller frequency range for uploading transmissions. Compare to Discrete MultiTone (DMT), which divides the frequency spectrum into 256 units to make recovery from errors easier.

Channel Service Unit (CSU)—Used in leased lines to provide the basic functions needed to transmit data across the line, such as a keepalive signal, loopback capabilities, and statistical information.

CIDR—See *Classless Interdomain Routing*.

CIFS—See *Common Internet File System*, as well as *Server Message Block*.

Cladding—A material used in fiber-optic cables to reflect light back into the glass or plastic core.

Classless Interdomain Routing (CIDR)—Also known as supernetting (as compared with subnetting). CIDR removes the restrictions for the Internet core routers, as well as for ISPs, by doing away with the traditional class system used for IP addresses. Instead of a traditional subnet address (such as 255.255.0.0), CIDR postfixes a value (such as /18) to specify the number of bits to be used for the network address, with the remainder being used for the host address. Thus a Class A or Class B address, both of which enable a huge number of host computers, can be used to provide for many networks, instead of a single network, and thus help to conserve the limited address space provided for by IPv4.

Client—In computer networks the term *client* is generally used to refer to a computer that accesses resources on another computer called a server.

Coaxial cables—Cables used by early networks to connect computers. Both thinnet and thicknet cables were common, with these descriptions indicating their diameters. See *10BASE-2* and *10BASE-5*. Note also that cable TV providers still make use of coaxial cables. So if you are using a cable modem, it is very likely that

the last mile between you and your cable company travels across this type of cable.

Collision domain—A collection of networked devices on a legacy Ethernet network that share a common network media. Each device on the shared media must contend for access to the media; hence, collisions can occur when more than one device attempts a transmission at approximately the same time. Switches have replaced hubs and other devices that propagated this shared network media, so the collision is pretty much a thing of the past for modern Ethernet networks.

Common Internet File System (CIFS)—The file/print server protocol that superseded the Server Message Block (SMB) protocol. Like SMB, CIFS uses TCP/IP as a transport protocol to exchange messages and data with other computers.

Cost—When referring to routers, synonymous with metric or hop.

CRC—See *Cyclic redundancy check*.

Cross-talk—The electrical signal in a copper wire not only travels down a particular wire, but also *radiates out* perpendicularly and can interfere with other copper wires in the same cable or bundle. This interference is called cross-talk.

CSMA/CD—See *Carrier Sense Multiple Access/Collision Detect*.

CSU—See *Channel Service Unit*.

Cut-through switch—A switch that begins transmitting the incoming frame on the outgoing port after it receives the header information, or about 20 or 30 bytes from the incoming port. The switch needs to determine only which port to output the frame—the *destination address* (hardware address), which is contained in the frame header.

Cyclic redundancy check (CRC)—A value calculated according to a specific mathematical algorithm. The CRC value can be derived from header or payload information in network packets and frames. The receiving end of a network communication can perform the same calculation and compare it to the original value to determine the integrity of the data the CRC covers.

Data Over Cable Service Interface Specification (DOCSIS)—A specification created by CableLabs to assist in standardizing how cable modem service operates. CableLabs also certifies hardware so that DOCSIS-labeled devices can interoperate. See also www.cablemodem.com.

Data Service Unit (DSU)—Used on a leased line for translating between the data encoding used on the line, such as the time-division multiplexed (TDM) DSX frames that are used on a T1 line, and the serial data format used on the local network. DSUs also perform other functions such as error correction. A DSU usually has RS-232C or RS-449 connectors that can be used to connect to data terminal equipment (DTE), which then provides the actual physical connection to the LAN. The CSU and DSU used for leased lines are often combined into a single device today.

DECnet—A set of proprietary network protocols developed by Digital Equipment Corporation, and still available on computers running the OpenVMS operating system.

Demilitarized zone—A section of a network that consists of a firewall that connects it to the Internet, as well as another firewall that is used to protect the internal LAN. Those computers lying between these two firewalls are said to be in the demilitarized zone, and are less protected than those on the internal LAN. This technique is often used to provide access to Web servers (or other similar servers) that require some degree of security, while protecting LAN clients with a further degree of security offered by the second firewall.

Denial-of-service attack—An attack on your computer or network, designed to cripple routers, servers, or other computers by consuming massive resources. When this happens, the affected devices are unable to perform their normal actions.

DFS—See *Distributed File System*.

DHCP—See *Dynamic Host Configuration Protocol*.

Dialectic—An insulating material used to help prevent interference between two conductors. Typically a plastic or other nonconducting material that is used to separate cables in a bundle of wires.

Digital subscriber line (DSL)—DSL makes use of frequencies above the 4MHz voice channel on ordinary telephone lines. Standard DSL provides a larger download capacity and a smaller upload capacity. However, this technology is also referred to as xDSL, because many providers offer services that can vary in the upload/download bandwidth. There are also several methods used for signaling on DSL lines, such as CAP (Carrierless Amplitude Phase modulation) and DMT (Discrete MultiTone).

Digital Subscriber Line Access Multiplexer (DSLAM)—A device that concatenates multiple digital lines (such as DSL) and multiplexes the signals across one or more higher bandwidth interfaces, such as ATM or Frame Relay.

Directory—A term used to refer to a collection of files, and possibly other subdirectories that can also hold files and other subdirectories. When used in reference to the Active Directory or another LDAP database, the directory is the database that holds the objects that the directory service manages.

Directory services—A collection of programs that manage a directory database, such as the Active Directory or Novell's eDirectory.

Discrete MultiTone (DMT)—An xDSL technology that divides the frequencies (above the 4MHz voice channel) into 256 channels. Because each channel can be independently monitored, channels that interfere with the transmission of data can be isolated. DMT is the preferred method for DSL technologies. See also *Carrierless Amplitude Phase*.

Disparity—A term used by Fibre Channel to describe the number of ones or zeros transmitted on the network media. If the transmission over a short period consists of more zeros than ones, it is called *negative disparity*. If it consists of more ones than zeros, it is called *positive disparity*. If the number of ones and zeros is approximately the same, it is called *neutral disparity*.

Distributed Coordination Function (DCF)—Another name for CSMA/CA.

Distributed denial-of-service attack—Similar to a denial-of-service attack, this sort of attack is conducted by more than a single source. For an example, see *Trojan horse*. This type of attack uses hundreds, if not thousands, of infected computers to launch an attack on a single source at the same time, making it difficult to defeat by simple blocking of IP addresses or ports.

Distributed File System (DFS)—Similar to Sun's NFS, a method that enables Windows computers to share file systems by mounting all or part of a remote computer's file system so that it appears as if the remote files are part of the local file system.

DMT—See *Discrete MultiTone*.

DMZ—See *Demilitarized zone*.

DNS—See *Domain Name System*.

DOCSIS—See *Data Over Cable Service Interface Specification*.

Domain Name System (DNS)—A hierarchical system for resolving network names and hostnames to IP addresses. DNS is the heart of the Internet for name translations. Each domain contains two (or more) DNS servers, which are authoritative for a particular domain. When resolving a network name, DNS servers query other DNS servers that reside up the hierarchy until the authoritative DNS server is found, or until another DNS server that caches (stores in a short-term table in memory) the name resolution is located. Note the difference between this and a DNS server, which hosts the DNS database.

DSL—See *Digital subscriber line*.

DSLAM—See *Digital Subscriber Line Access Multiplexer*.

DSU—See *Data Service Unit*.

Dynamic DNS—A DNS server that can accept updates dynamically from a client on the network. Older DNS servers required that the network administrator manually enter information for each IP address to network name translation. Dynamic DNS works with DHCP to enable networks that change frequently to maintain updated information. See also *Dynamic Host Configuration Protocol*.

Dynamic Host Configuration Protocol (DHCP)—A protocol that is used to allow a client computer to obtain addressing, as well as other configuration information, from a central DHCP server. This relieves the network administrator from having to manually configure every client in the network. See also *Dynamic DNS*, which enables a client that receives configuration from a DHCP server to update the DNS server on-the-fly.

Dynamic packet filter—See *Stateful Inspection*.

E_Port—An expansion port used to connect a Fibre Channel switch to another Fibre Channel switch.

EBCDIC—See *Extended Binary-Coded Decimal Interchange Code*.

eDirectory—The name given to an enhanced version of Novell Directory Services (NDS) beginning with NetWare version 6. The eDirectory is also backward compatible with NetWare 5. Many features of the eDirectory can be used by other operating systems, such as Unix and Windows. See also *Novell Directory Services*.

EISA—See *Extended Industry Standard Architecture*.

Electromagnetic interference (EMI)—Signal interference between copper cables in a bundle of cables. High-frequency signals traveling through a copper wire tend to flow more rapidly near the outer edge of the cable, and radiate a signal at a 90-degree angle. This is also known as radio frequency interference (RFI).

EMI—See *Electromagnetic interference*.

Encryption—The process of performing some function on a set of data that attempts to render it in a format that makes it unreadable or unusable by anyone but the intended recipient. See also *Single key* and *Public key encryption*.

Ethernet—The most widespread LAN protocol. Ethernet was originally a baseband protocol, based on research by Robert Metcalf. That technology was further refined by Digital Equipment Corporation, Intel, and Xerox (DIX). Today, Ethernet technology has evolved to incorporate other technologies, such as switches, higher bandwidths, and other features that have made it still the main choice for a business, enterprise, and home network. Ethernet is also the current standard protocol for wireless networks.

Extended Binary-Coded Decimal Interchange Code (EBCDIC)—A method for encoding alphabetic, numeric, and other symbols using 256 binary numbers. EBCDIC was developed for use in IBM's mainframe operating systems. However, PCs developed by IBM use ASCII or Unicode for this purpose today. EBCDIC is usually used today by IBM mainframes, and is not a widely adopted standard for computers today.

Extended Industry Standard Architecture (EISA)—A computer bus created to compete with IBM's proprietary Microchannel bus. EISA operates at 8MHz, like the ISA bus, but it allows for a 32-bit path, enabling more data to be channeled through the bus.

F_Port—A port on a Fibre Channel switch used to connect to a device.

Fabric—Used to describe a network that is transparent to network nodes that traverse a network composed of many interconnecting devices.

Far-end cross-talk—The transmitting end of a cable pair produces a strong electrical signal. However, because the signal attenuates, or becomes weaker, as it passes through the copper wire (or fiber-optic cable), interference between copper wires at the endpoint can distort the signal, because the signal is usually weaker at the endpoint of a connection. This is why the specifications allow only a *very small amount of exposed copper wire* when a cable is connected to an actual connector (such as an RJ-45 jack). Otherwise the exposed copper cables, which have been stripped of the protective dialectic insulator, can interfere with each other at the endpoint of the transmission.

Fast Ethernet—See *100BASE-T*.

FDDI—See *Fiber Distributed Data Interface*.

FEXT—See *Far-end cross-talk*.

Fiber Distributed Data Interface (FDDI)—A dual-ring topology that enables network traffic to pass from one node to another. Although this technology is still in use, it has been superseded by newer technologies. One advantage that FDDI offered during its prime is that a problem caused on one of the dual-rings (such as a cable break or a malfunctioning node) could be corrected by the ring-wrap capability built into FDDI. This enabled communications to continue using the other ring, effectively isolating the problem until it could be resolved. FDDI can be used on both single- and multi-mode fiber-optic cabling. Speeds range from 10Mbps to 100Mbps.

Fiber-optic cables—Cables that contain a glass or plastic core surrounded by a material that reflects light back into the core. Fiber-optic cables can be classified into two categories. Single-mode cables contain a small core (9 to 12.5 microns), whereas multi-mode cables have a larger core (usually 50 to 62.6 microns). Single-mode fiber works best over long distances, and multi-mode fiber is generally used for shorter distances.

Fibre Channel—A serial form of communications protocol used today mostly by storage area networks (SANs), among others. Between any two devices, there are two connections—one to transmit and one to receive data. The two cables are swapped so that the transmitter of one device is connected to the receiver of the other end of the connection. SANs use Fibre Channel to provide (usually over fiber-optic cables) faster access to storage devices, over longer distances, than can be accomplished using the standard SCSI architecture. Fibre Channel is also used by other technologies for data transmissions.

File Transfer Protocol (FTP)—A protocol/utility that enables network devices to send/receive files, as well as obtain a list of files on another device.

Firewall—A combination of technologies designed to protect a network from another network. For example, a firewall can be placed between your network and the Internet, or between departments in your own network. Firewalls use techniques such as packet filtering, stateful inspection, proxies, and content filtering, among others.

FireWire—Described by IEEE 1394, a high-speed serial bus (usually between 100Mbps and 400Mbps) that can connect up to 63 devices to a computer. Like USB, FireWire is hot plug-and-play, enabling you to connect or disconnect devices (such as computer peripherals or consumer devices) without requiring a reboot of the computer.

FL_Port—A port that connects an Arbitrated Loop to a Fibre Channel switch.

Frequency—A measurement of the number of times a periodic action occurs in a measure of time. In terms of alternating current, this is the number of cycles per second and is usually expressed in hertz (Hz).

Frequency Hopping—Transmitting data by rapidly changing the radio frequency on a predetermined basis. Used by some wireless protocols to help avoid interference between devices using the same radio spectrum.

FTP—See *File Transfer Protocol*.

Full-duplex—Communications between two network nodes that occurs in both directions simultaneously. See also *Half-duplex*.

GID—A numerical value used by Unix/Linux systems that identifies a user group to which the user account belongs. The file /etc/group contains a listing of user groups and the numbers associated with them. Group membership can be used to make managing access to system resources, such as files and directories, an easier task, because access can be granted to the group as a whole instead of individual users.

Gigabit Ethernet—Ethernet that operates at 1 billion bits per second, defined by the IEEE 802.3 standard.

Half-duplex—Communications between two network nodes in which only one side of the link can transmit at any point in time.

HBA—See *Host Bus Adapter*.

HomeRF—This specification was originally intended to be used for home wireless networks. Later the specifications were extended to enable the same functionality that was already provided by the IEEE 802.11b and 802.11a standards. HomeRF products are on the market today, but they should be considered in context of the IEEE standards mentioned. See also www.homerf.org.

Hop—A term used to describe the number of routers (or number of seconds) a network packet will pass through to reach its destination. This value can be manipulated to force network traffic to use a specific route. See also *metric* and *cost*.

Horizontal Cabling System Structure—Connection from the telecommunications outlet in the work area, terminating in the telecommunications room.

Host Bus Adapter (HBA)—The term given to the adapter card that connects a computer to a Fibre Channel SAN. The HBA differs from an Ethernet card in that the HBA performs more functions than the Ethernet card, which frees up CPU cycles for other duties.

Hostname—The name of the network device. The command hostname can normally be used to discover the name of the current host.

HOSTS file—A file used to translate hostnames to IP addresses. Although it's still useful in some situations, the Domain Name System (DNS) has replaced this functionality on most networks, though the HOSTS file can still be used to force a translation that is different from that stored in a DNS server.

HTML—See *Hypertext Markup Language*.

HTTP—See *Hypertext Transfer Protocol*.

Hub—A device that concentrates wiring of a LAN into a star formation using twisted-pair cables so that each device is connected to a port on the hub. Hubs are similar to multiport repeaters, but were first designed for use with 10BASE-T connections, whereas repeaters used the older thinnet (10BASE-2) Ethernet connections (coaxial cabling). In addition, later developments added features to hubs that could isolate segments that were transmitting corrupt data, and enable the use of SNMP for management purposes. Hubs have been replaced by switches in most cases for both SOHO and enterprise networks.

Hypertext Markup Language (HTML)—A programming language that is used to create Web pages using a set of defined symbols that describe how text, images, and other data should be presented to the user accessing a Web site using a browser.

Hypertext Transfer Protocol (HTTP)—A protocol that uses TCP/IP to receive and respond to requests for data using the World Wide Web. Although much of the data transferred using HTTP consists of HTML pages, other technologies are also transferred using HTTP.

ICMP—See *Internet Control Message Protocol*.

ICMP redirects—The Internet Control Message Protocol can be used to manipulate routing tables, usually by sending "destination unreachable" messages to a router. This type of attack can make it difficult for your network to communicate with other networks because the routing table can become inaccurate due to this sort of attack.

IEEE—Institute of Electrical and Electronics Engineers. This professional society is responsible for many standards, including networking standards. See http://ieee802.org/.

IEEE 802 LAN/MAN Standards Committee—An IEEE committee that is responsible for creating standards for local and wide area networking. This committee was formed in 1980 and was originally called the Local Network Standards Committee.

IEEE 802.11a—A wireless network protocol developed by the IEEE, operating in the 5GHz radio spectrum, and providing a bandwidth of up to 54Mbps.

IEEE 802.11b—A wireless network protocol developed by the IEEE, operating in the 2.4GHz radio spectrum, and providing a bandwidth of up to 11Mbps.

IEEE 802.11g—A wireless network protocol developed by the IEEE, operating in the 2.4GHz radio spectrum (like 802.11b), providing a bandwidth of up to 54MHz. Most 802.11g devices can interoperate with 802.11b devices, which might give it a marketing edge over 802.11a in the future. The larger bandwidth in the 2.4GHz spectrum is accomplished by using a more sophisticated technique for encoding data.

IEEE 1394—See *FireWire*.

Ifconfig—This command used on Unix/Linux systems is similar to the Windows ipconfig command. However, this command goes far beyond displaying configuration information and can be used to configure network interfaces.

iFolder—A technology used by NetWare to allow access and synchronization between data from remote clients and servers. This is usually employed by mobile clients to ensure that data on servers/clients remain synchronized.

IMAP—See the *Internet Message Application Protocol*.

Industrial, Scientific and Medical (ISM) Radio Frequency Band—A radio frequency band that has been set aside worldwide (for the most part) to be used for specific purposes. This frequency range doesn't

require a radio operator's license for the user. This is the frequency range that was chosen to be used for wireless networking based on the IEEE 802.11b and IEEE 802.11g standards.

Industry Standard Architecture (ISA)—The name given to the original PC bus, created in the 1980s. This computer bus operated at 8MHz, using a 16-bit data channel to connect components to the computer's memory and CPU.

Integrated Services Digital Network (ISDN)—A digital connection that consists of a B-channel, which carries voice and other data, and one or more D-channels, which transmit control and signaling information. Primary Rate Interface (PRI) consists of one D-channel, and two 65Kbps B-channels (for a total bandwidth of 128Kbps). Primary Rate Interface services can provide for up to 23 B-channels (or 30 B-channels in Europe), greatly increasing the bandwidth.

Internet—The worldwide interconnection of many networks, which evolved from the ARPANET.

Internet Control Message Protocol (ICMP)—A protocol that uses UDP packets for many diagnostic purposes for the TCP/IP protocol. See also *ping* and *traceroute*.

Internet Message Application Protocol (IMAP)—A protocol that enables users of email to view, download, or delete email messages from an email server. Whereas the POP3 protocol downloads all email messages from the email server to the client's computer, IMAP enables the user to leave messages on the server as well as viewing the subject headers and the message and attachments. The user can also explicitly delete messages from the server.

Internet Printing Protocol—A new development that enables clients to send print jobs to printers across the Internet.

Internet Protocol—The workhorse of the TCP/IP protocol suite. IP is a connectionless, unreliable protocol that makes a best-effort to get data from one location to another. IP provides the hierarchical address space that makes routing between networks possible. TCP, UDP, and other protocols in the TCP/IP suite use IP to route data through the Internet and intranets. The upper-level protocols that use IP are responsible for providing the mechanisms that ensure reliable delivery of data.

Internetwork Packet Exchange—A NetWare protocol that is used to transfer data between multiple NetWare networks. See also *Sequenced Packet Exchange*.

Interrupt Request (IRQ)—IRQ is a hardware component of the computer that devices can use to send an *interrupt* signal to the CPU in an attempt to get the attention of the processor. This is accomplished using a hardwired interrupt request line connected to the processor. Although many devices require their own interrupt request value (a numeric value), some devices today can share the same request number.

Intranet—A collection of networks connected by routers that compose a private network. Compare to *Internet*.

IP—See *Internet Protocol*.

Ipconfig—This command can be used on Windows computers (from Windows NT and above) to view current IP and other configuration assignments. Other features of this command can be used to release/renew DHCP configuration information, among other things.

IPP—See *Internet Printing Protocol*.

iPrint—NetWare's implementation of the Internet Printing Protocol. See also *Internet Printing Protocol*.

IPX—See *Internetwork Packet Exchange*.

IRQ—See *Interrupt Request*.

ISA—See *Industry Standard Architecture*.

ISDN—See *Integrated Services Digital Network*.

ISO—The official international name for the International Organization for Standardization. It is a Greek-language prefix that reflects their function. ISO means equal, the same, and so on. ISO is not an abbreviation or acronym.

LAN—See *Local area network*.

LDAP—See *Lightweight Directory Access Protocol*.

LED—Light-emitting diode. A low-power semiconductor device that produces light when electricity is applied. LEDs are commonly used on network adapter cards and other network devices (such as hub or switch ports) to indicate whether certain functions of the device are working correctly. LEDs can also be used in place of lasers to transmit data on fiber-optic cables.

LIFA—See *Loop Initialization Fabric Address*.

Lightweight Directory Access Protocol (LDAP)—A directory and directory services based on the OSI directory protocols (X.500). LDAP-compliant directories can be accessed by clients running different operating systems, provided that the client software has been created. LDAP uses the directory structure described by X.500, but the protocols and services provided by X.500 were scaled down to lessen the overhead required by the client and server.

LIHA—See *Loop Initialization Hard Address*.

LILP—See *Loop Initialization Loop Position*.

LIP—See *Loop Initialization Primitive*.

LIPA—See *Loop Initialization Previous Address*.

LIRP—See *Loop Initialization Report Position*.

LISA—See *Loop Initialization Soft Address*.

LISM—See *Loop Initialization Select Master*.

LMHOSTS file—See also HOSTS file. This file is used on Windows systems to provide translation between hostnames and IP addresses on older Windows operating systems that used NetBIOS names. The Windows Internet Name Service (WINS) was developed to automate this process. DHCP can assign an IP address to a Windows client, and WINS can dynamically register this name/address translation. However, today most Windows operating systems use a DNS server.

Load coil—A device used on analog telephone circuits to amplify a voice circuit. Because these devices can interfere with frequencies nearing the 4MHz voice boundary on an ordinary telephone line, you may not be able to get DSL service.

Local area network (LAN)—A small network used to connect network devices over short distances, such as in an office.

Logical topology—The logical path through the network that data can take from one place to another. See also *Physical topology*.

Loop Initialization Fabric Address (LIFA)—The first frame used in assigning addresses on a Fibre Channel Arbitrated Loop. Devices that were assigned an address by a Fibre Channel switch can register their addresses using this frame.

Loop Initialization Hard Address (LIHA)—The third frame used in assigning addresses on a Fibre Channel Arbitrated Loop. Devices that have hardware-assigned addresses can register their address using this frame.

Loop Initialization Loop Position (LILP)—The last frame sent around a Fibre Channel Arbitrated Loop to let each member know the position of all other devices on the loop.

Loop Initialization Previous Address (LIPA)—The second frame used in assigning addresses on a Fibre Channel Arbitrated Loop. Devices that remember their previous address can register that address using this frame.

Loop Initialization Primitive (LIP)—Frames used during the initialization of a Fibre Channel Arbitrated Loop.

Loop Initialization Report Position (LIRP)—A frame used during the initialization of an Arbitrated Loop enabling devices to report their position on the loop. After this information has been gathered, the loop master sends the Loop Initialization Loop Position (LILP) frame around the loop so that all devices know the position of all other devices on the loop.

Loop Initialization Select Master (LISM)—The procedure used to select a temporary loop master that will coordinate address assignment during the initialization of a Fibre Channel Arbitrated Loop.

Loop Initialization Soft Address (LISA)—The last frame used to assign addresses on a Fibre Channel Arbitrated Loop. Any device that was not assigned an address using the previous frames can select an address from those not yet assigned.

Loop Master—A device on a Fibre Channel Arbitrated Loop that is temporarily selected to coordinate addressing and reporting functions during the initialization of the loop.

Lpr/lpd—Line printer remote/line printer daemon. These Unix utilities enable sending print jobs to remote computers. Today TCP stream printing is generally used for this purpose.

MAC address—See *Media Access Control*.

MAN—See *Metropolitan Area Network*.

Media Access Control (MAC)—A sublayer of the OSI Data Link layer. The MAC sublayer creates the frames to be transmitted on the physical network media. The MAC address is one that is typically burned into a network adapter card by the manufacturer, and it creates a flat address space. MAC addresses are used to communicate on a network LAN, whereas IP addresses are used to communicate between devices on different LANs, using a router.

Media access unit (MAU)/multistation access unit (MSAU)—Similar to an Ethernet hub, these devices centralize wiring in a Token-Ring network. The capabilities of the MAU or MSAU exceed those of a simple hub, however, in that misbehaving ports can be isolated so that communications can continue on the ring. Also, these devices do not broadcast all traffic received out on all ports at the same time as a simple hub does. Instead, the MAU or MSAU maintains the ring topology of the network, and passes frames from one port to the next.

Mesh topology—A network in which every device has a connection to every other device in the network. For practical reasons, this includes just the switches and servers that connect clients to the network. A mesh topology provides a great deal of redundancy to a network. This can be an important building factor for a network that requires 99.999% uptime. This topology can also be used to describe the topology of many wireless networks.

Metric—This term is a synonym for the hop count that limits the number of routers a network packet can pass through before being dropped. This term is also referred to as the "hop count" or the "cost" of a particular route. This value is used in distance-vector routing protocols to assign a value (usually 1) to a router. You can manipulate this value for different routes to a particular destination, forcing traffic to that destination to use a route you prefer.

Metropolitan Area Network (MAN)—A network that is larger than a LAN but smaller than a WAN. Typically, this designation is used to describe a network that covers the geographical distance of a city, or another similarly sized geographical area.

Microchannel—IBM's proprietary bus created to attempt to recapture the PC market from clone manufacturers that used the ISA and, later, the EISA bus. The PCI bus eventually replaced these buses.

Microsoft Management Console (MMC)—A generic interface tool introduced in Windows 2000 that enables many management utilities to use a common interface. The basic utilities are set up and available in the Administrative Tools folder, but new tools can be created by loading Snap-ins.

MMC—See *Microsoft Management Console*.

Modem—This used to be an acronym for "modulation/demodulation," but it now has entered the English language as a word. Modems enable computers to send digital information across an analog line (such as a telephone connection) to another modem. Modems are used to connect to the Internet, or to business networks. Broadband connections, such as DSL, are slowly replacing these devices.

Monitor bit—Used by a workstation that acts as the *active monitor* for a Token-Ring network to determine when a frame has been around the ring more than once.

Multi-mode fiber-optic cabling—Coaxial cabling that uses a larger glass or plastic core than single-mode fiber-optic cabling. Instead of a single wavelength of light, multi-mode cabling injects more than one wavelength of light, each at a different angle to help prevent one wavelength from interfering with another.

Multi-Protocol Label Switching (MPLS)—Used by a Layer Three switch. A packet enters the MPLS network through an *ingress LSR* (label switching router), which attaches a label to the packet and exits the MPLS switched network through an *egress LSR*. The ingress LSR performs the necessary processing to determine the path a packet will need to take through the switched network. MPLS makes IP seem like a connection-oriented protocol. That function is usually provided by TCP.

NAS—See *Network Attached Storage*.

NAT—See *Network Address Translation*.

NDIS—See *Network Driver Interface Specification*.

NDS—See *Novell Directory Services*.

Near-end cross-talk—Interference that occurs between two twisted pairs measured at the same location; it usually occurs between wires in a twisted-pair cable. One of the conditions that can introduce this interference is a crushed cable, so care must be used when pulling network cabling and attaching connectors. See also *far-end cross-talk*.

Negative disparity—See *disparity*.

NetBEUI—Short for NetBIOS Extended User Interface. A means for transmitting data packets on the local network used early on by IBM, Microsoft, and other LAN providers. NetBEUI is a LAN (nonroutable) protocol and uses other protocols (such as TCP/IP) when traversing networks that consist of multiple LANs connected by routers.

NetBIOS—Short for Network Basic Input/Output System. Created by IBM and used by Microsoft and other early LAN operating systems, NetBIOS gives the application programmer a standard interface called a Network Control Block (NCB). Whereas TCP/IP uses IP addressing, NetBIOS uses a naming convention that can include unique names or group names. The underlying transport protocol (such as NetBEUI or TCP/IP) is transparent to NetBIOS. Used for many years in Windows operating systems, it is now supported mainly for backward compatibility for older applications. Newer versions of Windows, and other operating systems, typically use TCP/IP. The Windows Internet Naming Service (WINS) is used to translate between NetBIOS names and IP addresses. See also *SAMBA*, which is an open-source alternative to this protocol.

Netstat—A command used on Windows and some Unix/Linux systems to obtain statistics about the TCP/IP protocols that are in use on the computer.

NetWare—A network operating system developed by Novell.

Network Address Translation (NAT)—NAT allows you to use one or more IP addresses that are valid on the Internet, while using a reserved address space for the computers on the LAN. The NAT server (such as a router/switch) uses its valid Internet address to translate between the private network address and one valid on the Internet.

Network analyzer—A device that monitors the network at the Data Link and Transport layers in the OSI reference model, enabling you to locate protocol errors, among others. Some operating systems, such as Windows servers, contain a scaled-down version of this type of device. For Unix/Linux you can use the tcpdump utility to perform similar functionality. However, a good network analyzer offers other features that make the device worth the cost.

Network Attached Storage (NAS)—Storage devices (disk/tape) attached to the same network used by client computers. Contrast this with a Storage Area Network (SAN), which uses a separate network for storage.

Network Driver Interface Specification (NDIS)—A network driver interface created by Microsoft and 3Com Corporation.

Network File System (NFS)—Developed by Sun Microsystems, this set of protocols enables the network administrator to mount file systems from one computer onto a mount point on another computer. This makes it appear to the other computer as if the file(s) were part of the local file system. See also *Distributed File System*.

Network Information System (NIS)—A service developed by Sun Microsystems that enables clients on a network to obtain information from other computers, using a single sign-on. NIS+ was developed to enhance security. NIS code was released by Sun to the public domain and has been ported to a wide variety of operating systems.

Network interface card (NIC)—Network hardware that links a computer or workstation to the network media. Also known as network adapter card.

Neutral disparity—See *disparity*.

NEXT—See *near-end cross-talk*.

NFS—See *Network File System*.

NIC—See *network interface card*.

NIS—See *Network Information System*.

NL_Port—A port that connects a device to an Arbitrated Loop.

Node—A term generally used to describe any type of device connected to a network, such as a computer, bridge, server, or router.

Novell Directory Services (NDS)—A directory service used generally by Novell NetWare. NDS stores user accounts and links to network resources, among other data. NDS was renamed and given additional functionality with the release of NetWare 6.0, and has been renamed the eDirectory.

Nslookup—Use this command followed by a hostname or an IP address to get information about a particular host from a DNS server in your network.

NTFS—A file system used by Microsoft server operating systems starting with Windows NT. More recent client operating systems, such as Windows XP, also support NTFS. NTFS enables support for large disks, encryption, expanded security permissions, and data compression, among other features.

ODI—See *Open Data-Link Interface*.

Open Data-Link Interface (ODI)—A network driver specification created by Novell and Apple.

Open Shortest Path First (OSPF)—A routing protocol that uses Link State Advertisements (LSAs) to exchange routing information. Compared to RIP, OSPF takes into consideration other cost metrics, such as the speed of a route, the traffic on the route, and the reliability of the route. Additionally, OSPF does not suffer from the 15-hop limitation that RIP employs, and it uses subnet masks, which RIP does not.

Open Systems Interconnection (OSI)—A set of protocols developed in the 1980s that was designed to be implemented on computers from various hardware platforms, to provide seamless interconnection. See also the *OSI Reference Networking Model*.

OSI—See *Open Systems Interconnection*.

OSI Reference Networking Model—A seven-layer model created by ISO, designed to describe specific functional modules and interfaces on which network protocols could be created. Used today to teach the concepts of networking. Contrast this with the DOD (Department of Defense) or DARPA model, which was created earlier and is used to describe TCP/IP.

OSPF—See *Open Shortest Path First*.

Packet filter—A basic firewall that filters incoming and outgoing network traffic based on information in the IP header, such as IP addresses and ports.

Patch panels—Provide a means of rearranging circuits so that adding, subtracting, and changing workstations is made easier. Patch panels are where the circuits are connected and reconnected, typically in a telecommunications closet.

PCI—See *Peripheral Component Interconnect*.

PCMCIA—Small cards that can be used in laptops and other small computers. The acronym does *not* stand for "People Can't Memorize Computer Industry Acronyms," which is a popular phrase used to remember the acronym. Instead, PCMCIA is the Personal Computer Memory Card International Association, which originally defined the specification. See also *CardBus*.

Peripheral Component Interconnect (PCI)—The standard bus used on most modern PCs and minicomputers. PCI offers faster data transfer rates (33MHz) and wider (32- or 64-bit-wide) data paths than earlier computer interconnect hardware, such as ISA and EISA. Devices on the PCI bus can also use a feature called *bus mastering*, whereby a card can take control of the bus and directly transfer large amounts of data to system memory without using the CPU. PCI cards also use a smaller footprint, as compared to PCI's predecessor, EISA.

Permissions—On many computer systems, this term is used to grant or deny access to system resources, such as files or printers. See also *Share-level permissions* and *User-level permissions*.

Physical topology—The physical layout of a network media (such as copper and fiber-optic cables and, more recently, wireless equipment) and the devices that are connected in a network.

Ping—A TCP/IP utility that uses ICMP ECHO/REPLY packets to determine whether a particular network device is reachable. Another related troubleshooting tool is TRACEROUTE/TRACERT, depending on your operating system.

Plain old telephone service (POTS)—This term is used to refer to service provided by the older analog telephone network.

Point Coordination Function (PCF)—A method used by wireless clients to gain access to the network bandwidth by exchanging frames (RTS/CTS) with an Access Point.

Point-to-Point Protocol (PPP)—This protocol allows two endpoints of a connection to establish a communications channel. PPP is typically used by an ISP to allow a dial-up user to connect to a modem at the ISP to provide Internet access for the dial-up client.

Point-to-Point Tunneling Protocol (PPTP)—Similar to a VPN when it comes to a secure "tunnel" through the Internet. Companies that have many locations can use PPTP (if offered by their ISPs at each location) to get a secure "tunnel."

POP3—See *Post Office Protocol Version 3*.

Positive disparity—See *disparity*.

Post Office Protocol Version 3—The current protocol used by many ISPs for downloading email from their servers to clients. Contrast this with IMAP, which can leave messages on the server until the user explicitly deletes them. POP3 downloads the emails to the users' computers and they are then no longer available on the POP3-based server.

POTS—See *Plain old telephone service*.

Power distribution units—Used in minicomputers and mainframe computers to condition the incoming power. Usually employed by using two or more units so that if one fails, the others continue to supply a stable, conditioned power supply to the computer. These devices are used to provide redundant power to a high-end server, and are usually connected to separate power sources. Because of this, the failure of one power supply does not bring a server down, because other power supplies can continue to provide electrical current to the other power distribution units.

PPP—See *Point-to-Point Protocol*.

PPPoE—The Point-to-Point Protocol over Ethernet.

PPTP—See *Point-to-Point Tunneling Protocol*.

Pretty Good Privacy (PGP)—A public key encryption set of utilities originally developed by Philip Zimmerman. PGP is widely employed on the Internet, though initially U.S. government restrictions disallowed exporting the technology. Both commercial and freeware versions are available. For the freeware version, see `http://web.mit.edu/network/pgp.html`.

Another Web site, dedicated to international distribution of PGP, can be found at www.pgpi.org/.

Protocol—An agreed-on set of methods for establishing communications between two or more nodes on a network, and for exchanging data or messages. In many instances, such as that which occurs with encryption technology, protocols must be negotiated to a level that both ends of the connection can understand. TCP and IP are perhaps the two most understood, and widely used, networking protocols in use today.

Proxy server—A firewall technique in which the firewall acts as a go-between for your network and another network, such as the Internet. The proxy server replaces the client's IP address with its own before sending a packet. When a response is received, the proxy server replaces its IP address with that of the client and sends the packet back to the client.

PSTN—See *Public switched telephone network.*

Public key encryption—An encryption method that uses two keys: a public key and a secret key. The message is encrypted by the public key, and decrypted by the secret key. This means that the public keys can be published on the Internet. The sender need only use the public key to encrypt and send a message to the holder of the private key for this transaction. The recipient can then use his secret key to decrypt the message. The key combination is a mathematical calculation that enables only the holder of the secret key to decipher messages sent that are encoded by the public key, which anyone can use. Compare this to using a single encryption key known by both parties to a secure connection. Using public key encryption means that both sides of the data exchange do not have to arrange some other means (such as a diplomatic pouch) to exchange the single encryption key. Indeed, the Secure Sockets Layer (SSL) uses public key encryption to begin the process of exchanging a single encryption key used for the remainder of the communications process.

Public switched telephone network (PSTN)—The telephone network in use today. The PSTN consists of myriad devices that interconnect many smaller telephone networks, and it is mostly made up of digital lines until that last mile to your home or office. Contrast this with POTS (plain old telephone service), which is the voice-grade service you get from your telco. In some cases these terms are used interchangeably, but that is incorrect.

R-utilities—A set of utilities developed by University of California at Berkeley that simplifies many tasks usually associated with other TCP/IP utilities. Today these utilities have for the most part been superceded by SSH utilities that provide the same capabilities but incorporate security mechanisms that make them less vulnerable than the original R-utilities.

Radio frequency interference (RFI)—See *electromagnetic interference (EMI).*

RAID—First defined as "redundant array of inexpensive disks," this has now been redefined as "redundant array of independent disks," because disks are not inexpensive as they used to be. RAID technologies are common today and cover a large territory. Different RAID levels can provide access speed (striped sets) or redundancy (mirror sets or striped sets with parity). To carry this concept further, a stripe set composed of mirror sets can provide the best of both of the others. If a disk in a mirror set fails, the other disk in the mirror enables the disk volume to maintain operations until the failed member has been replaced. When a striped set with parity is used, performance is reduced because the parity stripe (which is spread across all members of the stripe set) needs to be calculated each time a client accesses the data.

Repeater—A repeater joins physical network segments and amplifies the signal it receives on one port before it transmits it on other ports. Because the repeater does not check on the contents of the data it receives or retransmits, frames that are corrupted by noise and other factors can also be repeated. A repeater that connects more than two network segments is usually called a multiport repeater. The development of the hub replaced the multiport repeater for all practical purposes, because it performs the same functions, and can include additional features.

RFI—See *electromagnetic interference (EMI).*

Rights—On most computer operating systems this term is used to indicate actions the user can perform on the computer.

Ring topology—A physical topology that connects each node to its upstream and downstream neighbors. That is, each node in the network is connected to another node, and eventually the last node in the ring connects back to the first node. This can be accomplished by connecting cables from one node to the next, or by using a wiring concentrator (such as a MAU or MSAU when used in Token-Ring networks) that make the ring topological connections internally. All communications on the ring pass through every other node until the destination is reached.

RIP—See *Routing Information Protocol.*

RMON—See *Simple Network Management Protocol.*

Router—A device that operates at the OSI model third layer, the Network layer. The Network layer offers a logical address space, which makes it easier to organize networks and route traffic between networks. This overcomes the flat address space provided by lower-level devices that use Media Access Control (MAC) addresses. Each router contains two or more network interfaces. One or more of these interfaces can be used to connect the router to a wide area network, while other interfaces can be used to connect to local network segments. Routers receive input from one network interface, and then make routing decisions based on which interface can best get the packet to its eventual destination. Routers can also be used to configure such things as packet filtering, an important concept used by firewalls.

Routing Information Protocol (RIP)—A protocol uses routers to decide which port to use when sending a network packet to its eventual destination. RIP is a distance/vector protocol. RIP judges the best route to a destination based on information in the routing table that contains the distance (in hops) and vector (direction) to the destination. RIP routers also exchange data to update routing tables among themselves.

SAMBA—An open-source implementation of the Server Message Block (SMB) network communication protocol, which has been updated to include the Common Internet File System (CIFS)—the predecessor to SMB. SAMBA is a freeware product that has been ported to many operating systems so that communications with Windows operating systems can be accomplished easily. See www.samba.org.

SANs—See *Storage Area Networks*.

Sequenced Packet Exchange (SPX)—A NetWare protocol that ensures that packets sent via IPX are delivered in an orderly, session-oriented manner.

Serial Line Internet Protocol (SLIP)—An older method used to establish a connection between two devices, typically two computers. SLIP has been replaced for the most part by the Point-to-Point Protocol (PPP).

Server—A computer that offers resources to other computers, usually referred to as clients. For example, a server may offer file or print shares for use by clients.

Server Message Block (SMB)—A protocol developed by IBM and adopted by Microsoft to exchange messages and provide for client/server resource access. SMB is still used by some applications and in Windows operating systems. Other operating systems adopted SMB to provide compatibility with Microsoft operating systems. SMB was enhanced and renamed the Common Internet File System (CIFS). SAMBA is an open-source version of the protocol.

Shadow Password File—Used on Unix/Linux systems to provide a password file (which stores user account information) that is protected so that only the root account (or an application that runs under root, such as the logon process) can access the file. This file prevents a hacker from obtaining the information contained in the typical world-readable /etc/passwd/ file and using tools to decrypt account passwords. On many Unix/Linux systems this file is /etc/shadow.

Share-level permissions—Permissions that grant access to all files/subdirectories offered by a file share on the network. Note that on many systems, selected files or subdirectories can be further protected by using user-level permissions. For example, you can use share-level permissions on an NTFS partition on a Windows server but restrict access to selected files and directories by applying user-level permissions.

Simple Mail Transfer Protocol (SMTP)—The current method for transferring emails from one email server to another. After the transfer is completed, users can use IMAP or POP3 to view and manage emails.

Simple Network Management Protocol (SNMP)—An extensible protocol used to monitor a wide variety of network devices. (RMON, or Remote Monitoring Protocol, is an extension of SNMP.)

Single key encryption—Encryption techniques that use a single, secret key to encode and decode the information. Using this technique, it is necessary for both ends of the communication to establish a mechanism for obtaining the single encryption key.

Single-mode fiber-optic cabling—A fiber-optic cable that conducts a single wavelength of light, provided by a laser or light-emitting diode (LED). Because only a single wavelength is used, there is no interference with other wavelengths, so a single-mode fiber-optic cable is able to transmit a signal across a longer distance than a multi-mode fiber-optic cable. Single-mode cabling has a smaller glass or plastic core than multi-mode cabling, and can be used to transmit data over a longer distance than multi-mode cabling.

SLIP—See *Serial Line Internet Protocol*.

Small Computer Systems Interface (SCSI)—A parallel architecture that enables the connection of disk and tape devices to a server or high-end workstation. See also *Storage Area Networks* and *Network Attached Storage*, which use a serial connection to storage devices.

Small office/home office (SOHO)—A small network usually confined to a single office or a small home office network. In the SOHO environment only a small number of computers are configured on the LAN, and simple router/switches are used, along with software-based firewalls for protection from intrusions from the Internet. Inexpensive hardware firewalls are also available for this purpose, and require little management compared to high-end enterprise network firewalls.

SMB—See *Server Message Block*.

SMTP—See *Simple Mail Transfer Protocol*.

SNIA—See *Storage Networking Industry Association*.

SNMP—See *Simple Network Management Protocol*.

Social engineering—A simple method for obtaining information about your network, such as user accounts and passwords. A typical event is to call a user and tell him that you are someone from the help desk and that you need his password to perform some action on his behalf. A good security policy can help prevent this sort of intrusion.

SOHO—See *Small office/home office*.

Spread Spectrum—A wireless transmission technique that uses a signal that is a combination of a pseudo-noise signal and the actual information modulated on an RF (radio frequency) carrier. Mixing two different signals to produce only one for transmission causes the data to be masked by the seemingly random signal that it is combined with. Note that because the actual data and seemingly random "noise" are transmitted at the same time, a larger bandwidth is used than would be used by the data signal alone. The recipient of this signal simply masks out the pseudo-noise signal to recover the actual data.

SPX—See *Sequenced Packet Exchange*.

SSH—Secure Shell. This is also known as the Secure Socket Shell. This protocol provides a more secure environment for the traditional R-utilities. The current SSH utilities include slogin, ssh, and scp. End-to-end transfers of data using these connections are protected by a secure login mechanism as well as encryption of the data transfers. The most current version of these utilities is defined by the Internet Engineering Task Force (IETF) as version SSH2.

Star topology—A network topology in which a central wiring concentrator is used. Each computer on the network is cabled to a single concentrator (such as a hub or switch). It is at this wiring concentrator that communications between devices on the LAN (or MAN/WAN in some cases) are accomplished. An example of this topology is 100BASE-T Ethernet using a switch.

Stateful Inspection—A firewall technique that keeps track of outgoing requests and matches incoming responses. This firewall mechanism helps keep unsolicited traffic from entering your network.

Storage Area Networks (SANs)—A network used by servers to access high-speed, high-bandwidth storage. SANs provide many functions. A much larger number of disk/tape devices can be stored on a SAN than can be attached to a server using SCSI or other protocols. In addition, storage on a SAN can be accessed by more than a single server. Contrast this with NAS, which must compete with other network clients and servers on a production LAN.

Storage Networking Industry Association (SNIA)—An industry association devoted to storage technologies, specifically NAS and SANs.

Store-and-forward switch—A switch that buffers a frame in its memory before beginning to send it out to the appropriate port. The switch can connect two different topologies, such as 10Mbps and 100Mbps networks, without having to worry about the different speeds. This type of switch can check the integrity of the frame, allowing it to discard damaged frames and not propagate them onto other network segments. See also *cut-through switch*.

Subnet—A subset of an IP address class. For example, you can divide a Class C IP address class into several subnets by borrowing bits from the host address portion of the IP address to create two or more subnets on your network. The subnet mask is used for this purpose. Contrast this with Classless Interdomain Routing.

Subnet mask—Thirty-two bits that are used to describe which bits of an IP address are used to identify the network address and which bits are used to identify the host address (your computer or other network device). Keep in mind that an IP address is used to specify both the network and the host address, and the subnet mask determines which bits represent each of these.

Switch—A device that is similar to a hub, in that it works as a wiring concentrator. However, instead of broadcasting all incoming data on all other ports, a switch makes connections between the data on the incoming port to a port that can deliver the data to its destination. Switches have replaced hubs in modern networks.

SYN flooding—An older form of attack against a server. This attack depends on the three-way handshake used by TCP/IP to set up a connection. The SYN bit in the TCP packet causes the server to set aside memory resources for the connection. By sending a large number of SYN packets, and not responding to responses from the server, it is easy to overrun the server's memory, and thus render it useless. Many modern operating systems have patches that prevent or limit this sort of attack.

Syslog—A Unix/Linux daemon (background process) that records significant events as configured by the administrator. Syslog provides an audit trail for these operating systems.

T-carrier—Used to describe digital services that range from T1 lines (1.544Mbps) to T4 lines (274.186Mbps). T1 provides 24 separate channels that can be used to send voice or data from one place to another using two pairs of wires. Each of the 24 channels can transmit at a rate of 64Kbps. In Europe this service is known as E-carrier. However, the channels supported vary. For example, the E1 line carries 30 channels.

TCP—See *Transmission Control Protocol*.

Tcpdump—A third-party utility commonly used in Unix/Linux operating systems to capture and view current TCP/IP packets and statistics. This popular utility is included with many Unix/Linux operating systems. A similar version for Windows clients is called windump. See `http://windupm.poltio.it`.

TDR—See *Time domain reflectometry*.

Telecommunications closet—The central wiring point for a floor. The telecommunications closet can contain both network devices and concentrators, as well as telephone equipment.

Telnet—A protocol/utility used to establish remote terminal sessions.

TFTP—See *Trivial File Transfer Protocol*.

Thicknet—A term commonly applied to 10BASE-5 coaxial cabling, which was used in the first Ethernet networks.

Thinnet—A coaxial cable (10BASE-2) that has a smaller diameter than 10BASE-2 coaxial cables.

Time domain reflectometry (TDR)—A method of measuring cable length or locating faults by timing the period between a test pulse and its reflection from an impedance discontinuity on the cable. TDR measuring instruments can enable you to determine the approximate location of a problem on a cable.

Time to Live (TTL)—A concept used by many protocols. This value generally indicates the seconds, or number of hops, that a network packet can travel through the network before it is dropped. This ensures that a misconfigured routing topology does not endlessly route a packet.

Token-Bus—Similar to Token-Ring, except that all workstations connected to a bus can hear all transmissions that are made. However, the addressing for members on a Token-Bus preserve the integrity of the ring topology, passing the token (or data) frames from one node to another in an orderly fashion.

Token-Ring—A LAN technology that passes a token frame from one node in the network to another, in an orderly fashion. When a node on the LAN needs to transmit data, it waits until it receives the token frame and then constructs a frame containing the data to be sent, along with destination and originating addressing information. The data frame then travels through the ring until it reaches the originator. The originator can check flags in the frame to determine whether the receiving node was able to intercept the data and complete the transfer. The IEEE 802.5 working group was formed to develop standards for Token-Ring networks. Today, these networks make up only a small percentage of installed LANs.

Traceroute—A TCP/IP utility that uses ICMP ECHO/REPLY packets to discover the routers (or gateways) along a path to a destination device. This utility increments the TTL (Time to Live) value starting at one, and then adding one to each subsequent probe to determine each device along the path. This utility might be considered to be an advanced Ping utility. Traceroute is also known as tracert for some operating systems.

Tracert—The Traceroute command used by Windows and some other operating systems from MS-DOS 6.2 through Windows 2000 and Windows XP. Newer versions of Microsoft operating systems use Traceroute.

Transmission character—In the context of Fibre Channel, a 10-bit character chosen for transmission to assist in maintaining neutral disparity. Eight-bit values are encoded into one or two possible transmission characters to maintain neutral disparity.

Transmission Control Protocol (TCP)—A connection-oriented, reliable protocol that uses the Internet Protocol (IP) to transmit data through a network. TCP establishes sessions with the remote host and uses various techniques, such as acknowledgments, to ensure that data is reliably transferred between the two endpoints of a communication.

Trivial File Transfer Protocol (TFTP)—This is a stripped-down version of FTP that is generally used for uploading files to a router, and other similar equipment. It does not use any authentication or error correcting mechanisms. TFTP should not be used on a production network.

Trojan horse—A program similar to a virus. However, a Trojan horse file usually resides on the infected computer until some event sets it into action. This can be a specific date, or an external signal sent by another computer. For example, a Trojan horse program can be planted on many thousands of computers that do not use a firewall or antivirus protection. At a later date a signal can be sent to enable each copy of this file to begin a distributed denial-of-service attack on another computer. Many Trojan horse programs disguise themselves using a filename that appears to be relevant to the operating system they've infected.

TTL—See *Time to Live*.

Twisted-pair cables—Also referred to as unshielded twisted-pair cables, because no shielding is required to protect the integrity of the signals. The twisting of the individual pairs of the cable is significant—twisting the wire couples the electromagnetic fields equally, thus helping to cancel out any interfering signals.

UDP—See *User Datagram Protocol*.

UID—A numerical value used by Unix/Linux systems to identify the user when running processes or evaluating access to files and other system resources. A value of zero for this field is used to indicate the *superuser*, or a user who has the same privileges as root. On some systems, values from 1 to 99 are reserved for use for system processes, such as background daemons.

Unicode—A method used to assign numeric values to alphabetic, numerical, and symbolic characters. Compared to ASCII, which was a standard used early in the computer age, Unicode supports many languages, and is made up of 34,168 characters. See also *American Standard Code for Information Interchange* and *Extended Binary-Coded Decimal Interchange Code*.

Uninterruptible power supply (UPS)—A power source, usually powered by batteries, that provides power when the main source of power fails. For enterprise servers, a UPS, coupled with diesel generators, can maintain computing services indefinitely. For smaller units, a battery can suffice and can communicate with the server to perform an orderly shutdown of the server so that no data is compromised.

Universal serial bus (USB)—A high-speed bus that can be used to attach a large number of computer peripherals or consumer electronics devices to your computer. The initial specification supported up to 12Mbps.

Uplink port—A port on a hub, a switch, a router, or another network device that is used to connect it to another similar device to increase port density for a LAN.

UPS—See *Uninterruptible power supply*.

USB—See *Universal serial bus*.

User Datagram Protocol (UDP)—A connectionless, unreliable protocol that uses IP to send messages through a network. Contrast this with TCP, which also uses IP but is a connection-oriented, reliable protocol.

User-level permissions—Permissions placed on files and directories that allow or deny specific users access to resources in a network. See also share-level permissions.

Virtual LAN (VLAN)—A method that uses network switches to connect a number of devices to one or more switches. A virtual LAN lets the network administrator select which LAN a computer or device will belong to. Because a switch is a wiring concentrator device, this virtual capability means that you do not have to use separate switches for each LAN segment. Instead, you can connect multiple clients to the same switch(es) and use software to designate which virtual LAN a computer or device is a member of.

Virtual Private Network (VPN)—A secure path through a shared network or WAN that connects two computers, or two networks, so that from the point of view of each endpoint of the connection, they are on the same network. The connection is private because some means have been taken to secure the payload information of the data carried through this virtual tunnel. Many different protocols are used to create VPNs, so check the documentation provided with your operating system, or third-party VPN solution, to determine what security is offered by this technique.

Virus—Similar to a virus that attacks a human (or any other living species) a computer virus tends to (1) disrupt normal activity on the computer, if only to present a message, (2) duplicate itself so that it can infect other computers, and (3) disguise itself as another program. Email viruses are very common, and you can usually protect yourself by using a good antivirus program, and by using an automatic update feature to download new virus definitions frequently.

VLAN—See *Virtual LAN*.

VPN—See *Virtual Private Network*.

W3C—See *World Wide Web Consortium*.

Wake On LAN (WOL)—Part of the Wired for Management (WfM) Initiative, WOL enables a administrator to send a signal to a network adapter and boot a computer that has been shut down. This capability is useful in environments where a large number of computers need to be booted after-hours so that patches and other software upgrades can be downloaded to computers without interrupting the normal workday of a user.

WAN—See *Wide area network*.

WEP—See *Wired Equivalent Privacy*.

Wi-Fi—The Wireless Ethernet Compatibility Alliance (WECA) was formed specifically to promote products from different manufacturers that are subjected to stringent testing to ensure interoperability. The brand name chosen by WECA that will be used for these products is Wi-Fi ("Wireless Fidelity").

Wi-Fi 5—A term used to describe IEEE 802.11a networking technology. See also *Wi-Fi* (for 802.11b wireless networking terms).

Wide area network (WAN)—A network technology that connects LANs or MANs over a large distance. WANs can use various protocols, such as ATM and Frame Relay.

Windows Internet Naming Service (WINS)—A name resolution service used by Microsoft operating systems to translate NetBIOS names to IP addresses. WINS is still used today because of application dependencies, but for the most part the Domain Name System (DNS) server is used by most Windows (and other) operating systems to translate DNS names to IP addresses. Note that Microsoft's DNS server can be configured to query a WINS server if it cannot resolve a name.

Winipcfg—This command can be used on older Windows operating systems (such as Windows 95/98) to view IP and other configuration systems. Similar to the ipconfig command for later Windows operating systems.

WINS—See *Windows Internet Naming Service*.

Wired Equivalent Privacy (WEP)—Used in early implementations of Wi-Fi networks. WEP is a weak encryption technique that was designed to provide the same security as a wired network. However, wired networks also are usually protected by physical security measures. Today WEP should be used only for wireless networks in which security is not a great issue.

Wired Protected Access (WPA)—The IEEE 802.11i specification is intended to overcome the vulnerabilities of the Wired Equivalent Privacy (WEP) security that came with earlier wireless products. WPA uses authentication techniques, and a constantly changing encryption key, and thus may provide a more secure wireless environment.

Wireless Access Point (AP)—A wireless network device that is used as a central point between wireless clients wanting to transmit data on the network. The AP can be used with wireless clients as a standalone device, or the AP can be connected to a wired network. Contrast this with an ad hoc wireless network that does not use an AP.

WLAN—Wireless LAN (local area network). A small network that uses wireless networking as all or part of the LAN.

WOL—See *Wake On LAN*.

Work Area—The termination point of the network at a user's workspace.

World Wide Web Consortium (W3C)—An industry group whose purpose is to promote the Web, by producing standards, and software that can be used as a reference model for creating interoperability between Web products.

Worm—A worm is similar to a virus in that it infects a computer and then uses resources on that computer, such as your email address book, to replicate itself on other computers. Today, worms can reside in memory and travel through your network or the Internet at a very rapid rate.

WPA—See *Wired Protected Access*.

xDSL—See *Digital Subscriber Line*.

Internet Resources for
Network Administrators

SOME OF THE MAIN TOPICS IN THIS APPENDIX ARE

APPENDIX C

This appendix contains a few good Web sites that can be useful if you are responsible for administering a network. This is not an exhaustive listing, but just some of the Web sites that I use frequently.

Standards Organizations

Request for Comments

www.rfc-editor.org

Many of the technologies in this book are detailed in standards documents. Request for Comments (RFCs) documents are the result of an ongoing process to develop and enhance protocols for the Internet. Because it is an ongoing process, not every RFC defines a standard. Instead, some are drafts, some are simply informational, and others are considered to be the current standard. This site is mentioned in several places in this book, but it is mentioned here in case you missed those chapters.

The Institute of Electrical and Electronics Engineers (IEEE)

www.ieee.org

The IEEE, an organization that has been around for a long time, establishes standards for many areas of technology. One area is computers and networking. Some of the 802.x standards are available online in PDF format. Others you can order through the site's bookstore. Most of the basic LAN/MAN/WAN documents, however, are included online for no cost. If you want to get into the details about many networking products, be sure to visit this site.

ISO

www.iso.org

The International Organization for Standardization—also known as ISO—is an organization that coordinates many standards throughout the world. Whereas the IEEE works on standards that cover many areas related to the electrical field of protocols and products, the ISO works to coordinate standards for everything from credit cards and smart cards to steel, tools, food products, and so on. The one area the ISO does not cover is electrical and electronic engineering standards. These types of standards are covered by the International Electrotechnical Commission (IEC). However, information technology standards are a joint effort between the ISO and the IEC.

The ISO is composed of members from all over the world. Each country is allowed one representative standards body for the country, known as a member body of the ISO. Correspondent members come from countries that do not yet have a representative standards body of their own, and that receive information from ISO but do not participate in the development of new standards. A subscriber member is one from a very small country whose economy and other factors do not permit the creation of a standardization body for the country.

As noted elsewhere in this book, the term ISO is not an acronym. This term was chosen from the Greek root meaning "the same," or "equal" (such as in the term *isometric*). Thus, the ISO name can be used worldwide, in many different languages, without having to use a different acronym for each country.

The World Wide Web Consortium (W3C)

www.w3.org

This is the organization that helps to develop standards for protocols, software, tools, and other things to enhance the Internet. This site contains a large number of standards and projects. It is well worth a visit if your network connects to the Internet. Before you decide to deploy a new Internet technology, it would be a good idea to get all the information you can. For example, one of their sites,

`www.w3.org/Security/Overview.html`

details many developments concerning security on the Web, and also has links to other sites that cover a wide variety of security issues.

The Storage Networking Industry Association (SNIA)

`www.snia.org`

Learn about SANs and NAS at this site. You can also view the requirements for SNIA certifications. Large networks are consuming an ever-increasing amount of storage, and this site can help you learn about the technology.

Network Hardware and Software Manufacturers

Cisco Systems

`www.cisco.com`

The name of this manufacturer is known to just about every network administrator who operates a network. Cisco's Web site is a treasure trove of information relating to routers, switches, wireless devices, and so on. If you want a detailed explanation of Cisco operating systems and software, this is the place to go. If you just want to learn about a particular networking technology, you will likely find educational material here using the search function. There is so much information to be found at this vendor's site that it would take years to read all of it. A highly recommended site.

IBM

`www.ibm.com`

This is the site of the largest computer manufacturer in the world today. For reference purposes, however, IBM has a series of informational documents called "Redbooks." These cover a wide range of computer and networking technology. You can use the search function on the main page to find hardware, software, and some articles. For Redbooks, use the following URL:

`www.redbooks.ibm.com/pubs/pdfs/redbooks/`

Juniper Networks, Inc.

`www.juniper.net`

Juniper is a manufacturer of high-end network switching equipment, and its products are geared toward a large enterprise network, as well as larger entities, such as Internet Access Point providers. Unless you have limitless amounts of cash, you won't be using this site to purchase hardware for a SOHO network. Juniper offers technical books, training, and certifications.

HP

`www.hp.com`

In the past few years HP has acquired Compaq Computer Corporation, which acquired the venerable Digital Equipment Corporation. You can use the search function at this site to find informational articles and documentation for hardware manufactured by all three of these companies. And, as with most vendors, this is the place to visit to download new drivers, as well as patches for operating systems and other applications.

Microsoft

www.microsoft.com

This name is known around the world. Microsoft dominates the desktop today, and its office suite is also the most widely used product of that sort. You can use the search function available at the preceding URL to find home pages for all of Microsoft's main products. Additionally, Microsoft offers a service for developers called the Microsoft Developer's Network (MSDN). This is a paid service that you should consider subscribing to if you want to do a lot of in-house support for applications, operating systems, and development tools relating to Microsoft products. You can also subscribe to another service, called TechNet, which gives a smaller subset of the information available from MSDN. MSDN also enables you to receive betas of operating systems as well as 120-day evaluation copies of finished products. In an enterprise network, both of these can be very important sources of information.

However, for those who cannot afford an MSDN subscription (and it is not inexpensive for a single person), you can find a great deal of content available online at

http://msdn.microsoft.com

Additionally, you can use the following URL to keep up-to-date on recent new projects that Microsoft is working on:

www.research.microsoft.com

You can download some of the software for new projects from this link, and for those who are interested, you'll also find a jobs link here.

NETGEAR

www.netgear.com/

This site, along with the next one, is a good place to check out hardware such as routers and switches, including wireless devices. If you operate a SOHO network, you are probably familiar with these manufacturers, because a lot of their equipment is readily available at computer and electronics stores. One good reason to visit this Web site, and the next two, is to compare products before you make a purchase. Another good reason is that you can download drivers for some hardware.

LinkSys

www.linksys.com

This is another manufacturer that produces everything from consumer-level routers and switches to some high-end devices, such as gigabit Ethernet hardware. One caveat, however, is that Cisco has entered into an agreement to acquire LinkSys. Still, the URL listed here should still work for quite some time because LinkSys will be a subsidiary of Cisco.

Anixter

www.anixter.com/

This is one of the largest distributors for cables, connectors, computer racks, patch cords, and so on. To assist customers, Anixter has a technical library that contains information on standards, such as the ANSI/TIA/EIA-569 standard for wiring a network in your building. Many white papers written by Anixter and various vendors are also found here. If you are upgrading an older network, or starting from scratch, Anixter can not only sell you the products you need, but tell you how to use them.

RedHat

www.redhat.com

RedHat is one of the more popular Linux variants used by commercial organizations. You can download the current version or purchase a packaged copy of the software. There is a searchable database of articles that can be useful for learning about Linux, or for diagnosing problems. You can also sign up to receive email from RedHat. And if you want to be a beta tester for new versions of RedHat, you'll find a link at this site. You will also find documentation for current and past copies of their documentation.

Samba.org

www.samba.org

Samba enables Unix/Linux computers to easily connect to Windows platforms. At this top-level site you can select the country you live in, and then read documentation and recent news, as well as download the software. Samba is discussed in Chapter 35, "File Server Protocols." Most of these sites enable you to download both compiled versions for your operating system and binary code that you can examine and compile for your own system.

Wireless Networking

Open Mobile Alliance (AMA)

www.openmobilealliance.org/

This is a worldwide organization devoted to promoting standardization of mobile devices and applications, which includes wireless networking. AMA works with other organizations to accomplish this effort. AMA also works to perform interoperability testing for hardware/software vendors.

In particular the WAP Forum falls under this organization. For more information about WAP, see Chapter 24, "Other Wireless Technologies." There is a link on this Web site for the WAP Forum, or you can use the following link to go directly to that Web site:

www.wapforum.org/what/technical.htm

The Wi-Fi Alliance

www.weca.net

The name of this organization has changed recently (which explains the "weca" portion of the URL listed here. However, if you are interested in 802.11 wireless standards, this is the site to visit. You'll learn how the name Wi-Fi was chosen, and find out about the many vendors that are part of this organization. The Wi-Fi Alliance conducts many events, from conferences to documentation. Perhaps the most important function is the testing of hardware from members to ensure interoperability so that if you purchase Wi-Fi devices from various vendors, you can be sure that they will work together. At this Web site you can find out which vendors and products have been certified.

The Wi-Fi Alliance is also involved in establishing public hot spots so that you can use your wireless computer or other device on a public network. You can use a locator service at this site to find hotels, airports, and other places where the service is offered.

The IEEE

www.ieee.org

The IEEE organization was mentioned earlier in this appendix. In addition to creating standards for wired networks, the IEEE has also been responsible for defining standards for wireless networks, under the IEEE 802.11 series of documents. For example, you can find online many of the recent standards for 802.11b, 802.11a, and 802.11g, which are the predominant standards today for wireless networking products. When making purchases for products based on these standards, check to be sure that they are based on the IEEE standards. The Wi-Fi Alliance brand can also assist you in choosing products, because they test for interoperability between products that are based on these standards.

Security

CERT Coordination Center (CERT/CC)

www.cert.org

This is a great site to visit to learn about new vulnerabilities on the Web. Information about viruses, bugs in important software products, and new attack programs can be found here. CERT is funded by the U.S. government and operates out of Carnegie Mellon University. CERT provides training courses and publications relating to security issues. If you want to keep yourself up-to-date, you can subscribe to the CERT Advisory Mailing List (highly recommended). In many cases, CERT quickly publishes fixes to security problems that occur on the Net. If you are a network administrator, or in a position of security administration for a network, you should definitely bookmark this Web site.

Computer Incident Advisory Capability (CIAC)

www.ciac.org

This is another Web site operated by the U.S. government, specifically the Department of Energy. It functions much like CERT, by detecting and reporting on potential security issues on the Internet, and applications that are vulnerable to attack. CIAC offers training classes, and links to articles relating to security issues.

Forum of Incident Response and Security Teams (FIRST)

www.first.org

An international organization (of which CIAC is a member) is composed of both governmental organizations and academic ones, and is used to coordinate security incidents among these various members. Without a central focal point, many separate organizations would be working on similar problems or the same incident separately. FIRST enables member organizations to communicate with each other and thus speed up the process of disseminating information and resolving security issues on the Internet.

NTBugtraq

www.ntbugtraq.com

This is a valuable resource for those operating Windows operating systems. Although it was first set up to report on security issues relating to Windows NT, it has continued to grow to encompass the newer Microsoft operating systems and software. NTBugtraq is basically just a mailing list that you can sign up for to receive current security issues relating to Microsoft products. If you use any Windows products in your network, then this list (along with Microsoft's own mailing list) is a must for the network administrator. This mailing list is a two-way proposition. You can read about security issues, as well as post your own observations. There is also an archive of older posts that can be very useful for those who are just starting to learn about security issues relating to Microsoft products.

Symantec Security Response

securityresponse.symantec.com

This site is operated by a vendor of antivirus and other software. Similar to the previous sites, this site offers information about the latest viruses, as well as advisories about programs that expose your network to attack. The site's Threat List and Virus Encyclopedia link can give you a lot of information about recent malicious programs. Because this is a vendor site, you can also find links to purchasing vendors' products, as well as tools that can be used to remove certain virus, work, and other similar programs.

OpenSSL Project

www.openssl.org

This site is dedicated to creating and supporting an open-source toolkit that you can use to develop Secure Sockets Layer (SSL) as well as Transport Layer Security (TLS) applications. You can find source code as well as documentation at this site. For more information about SSL, see Chapter 38, "The Secure Sockets Layer (SSL) Protocol."

Internet Firewalls: Frequently Asked Questions

www.interhack.net/pubs/wfaq

This FAQ contains voluminous information about firewalls and how you can use them to assist in protecting your network. The FAQ was created by Matt Curtin and Marcus J. Ranum. Ranum was one of the original developers of early firewalls, so he should know what he is talking about. This FAQ is an *excellent* place to start learning about firewall techniques, as well as what they can or cannot do to protect your network. This site is a must for anyone who works with firewalls, whether a hardware or a software solution. To make things easier to understand, this FAQ contains diagrams that help to explain the concepts covered in this FAQ.

The Firewall Toolkit (FWTK)

www.fwtk.org

The Firewall Toolkit consists of proxy applications that an advanced user or administrator can use to construct a firewall. This Web site provides the needed information. Chapter 49, "Firewalls," contains information about proxies and how they work. In that chapter you can learn the difference between proxies and packet filters, among other firewall techniques.

This Web site gives you the software needed to construct your own proxy applications. You can download the source (coded in the C language) from this site, as well as documentation and tutorials that can assist you if you want to use the FWTK in your network. Another note: Marcus J. Ranum, along with others at Digital Equipment Corporation, were instrumental in creating the first proxy-based firewall. It is available as a commercial product in addition to the software you can download from this site. The FWTK was developed as a marketable product by Digital, and was used by the U.S. government when it was first put online and needed some sort of protection for its connection to the ARPANET.

The Lightweight Directory Access Protocol

SOME OF THE MAIN TOPICS IN THIS APPENDIX ARE

APPENDIX D

A few years ago the term *directory services* was understood by few, even though Novell's directory, NDS, and Banyan Vines StreetTalk products had been around for many years. Microsoft was quick to tell you that Windows NT 4.0 Server had a directory service, but it was just the same old Security Accounts Manager database with a few extras added. In Windows 2000, Microsoft finally got around to creating a true directory based on the Lightweight Directory Access Protocol (LDAP). NetWare 6.x has improved in the directory field by enabling an interface for NDS that acts as a go-between to allow native LDAP access to what is now called the eDirectory. In this appendix you will learn about the LDAP, and the history behind directory services that led to the development of a lighter version of directory services that is the de facto standard today for networks as well as many Internet services.

A Quick Introduction to LDAP

During the 1980s when PCs were first being accepted into the corporate environment, the computer room, which contained large proprietary mainframe or minicomputers, was in control of computer system managers. Simple terminal devices, such as the VT100 (a landmark in computer history itself), were attached to these large computers; access mechanisms, such as user accounts and passwords, along with file protection schemes, were used to control access to data. Applications were managed from a central location, and any interaction between computers was also the domain of computer system managers.

The introduction of the PC gave users the capability of managing their own applications and data files. PC networks were the next logical step, and suddenly computer system managers became network administrators and realized that the chaotic environment that came with distributed management was plagued with many problems.

At about the same time, many large businesses found it necessary to support multiple proprietary computing platforms, based on things such as application availability and maintenance costs. Supporting multiple operating systems and hardware platforms produced a dilemma: Users needed to access data on different computers, and each department (and sometimes each user) required setting up different access control mechanisms. In addition, locating the services (or applications) that each user needed became a complex task.

To try to conquer this collection of proprietary systems and distributed data, the X.500 set of protocols was proposed. X.500 encompassed network protocols as well as a method for storing information about resources, applications, users, and other data so that a network based on different systems could be easily managed. Although the X.500 protocols were never widely adopted, they did lay the groundwork for what was later to become the Lightweight Directory Access Protocol.

I can't remember who said it, but it is true that one of the best things about standards is that there are so many to choose from. This is especially the case when it comes to directory services. What started out as a good idea—X.500—spawned all sorts of development of protocols and services that eventually led to the development of LDAP.

The X.500 Protocols and Standards

In 1993, the International Telecommunications Union (ITU) approved the X.500 standard. This later was adopted also by the International Organization for Standardization (ISO). All that said, just what is X.500 and why is it so important for directory services today?

Basically, the X.500 set of standards was developed to provide a common *namespace* that could be used by various applications so that common data could be consolidated into a single hierarchical namespace. For example, an earlier standard known as X.400 was developed to help standardize email applications on the Internet. Initially, development on X.500 protocols and services was developed to interface with X.400 email-compliant systems so that different products could equally access important information, such as email addresses. However, the hierarchical structure of the namespace described by the X.500 standard was so elegant that it didn't take long for developers to realize that it could be used to organize all kinds of data.

X.500 is a general term that covers several complex protocols using the hierarchical namespace to access a database. The problem is that when X.500 was developed, the protocols that were proposed were too cumbersome and required too much computing overhead to ever be practically employed on small personal computers. Instead, these protocols were created to run on minicomputers and mainframe computers that were still the mainstay of corporate computing.

Other standard protocols were developed along with X.500, such as the OSI networking protocols. However, by the time anyone got around to actually trying to create a market for the OSI-related protocols and services, the Internet had already been pretty much standardized on the TCP/IP protocol suite. In addition to the OSI protocols, the OSI seven-layer Network Reference Model (described in Appendix A, "Overview of the OSI Seven-Layer Networking Reference Model,") was created so that network protocols could be discussed in terms that compartmentalized the functions that a computer network performs.

Once again, TCP/IP has become so predominant that even the OSI reference model is a bit dated. Indeed, TCP/IP is based on an earlier model (as described in Chapter 25, "Overview of the TCP/IP Protocol Suite").

Yet, you don't throw the baby out with the bath water, as the old saying goes. There were some good ideas in the OSI protocols, and the namespace provided by X.500 was an excellent solution looking for a problem. After the Internet went commercial and larger corporate networks were created, it became apparent that some kind of logical organization was needed to manage diverse kinds of information.

The Domain Name System (yet another child of the TCP/IP protocol suite) was created to handle resolving host computer and network names to IP addresses, and it is still used today on the Internet. However, when it comes to managing users and data and resources on networks, the term "directory services" is where it's at today.

Novell Directory Services (NDS) was a leader in this kind of technology for several years. NDS is widely deployed still today (reincarnated as the eDirectory), although the newer versions of NetWare have finally accepted TCP/IP as a transport protocol. Microsoft spent several years promising that the Active Directory would solve just about every problem a network administrator could dream of. Of course, we now know that any kind of directory service is going to be complex to manage due to the many types of applications it is used for and the kinds of information that need to be stored in the database.

Acronyms, Acronyms, Acronyms!

But in the beginning there was X.500 and the protocols that were developed to work with it. These were the main protocols developed for X.500:

- Directory Access Protocol (DAP)
- Directory System Protocol (DSP)
- Directory Information Shadowing Protocol (DISP)
- Directory Operational Binding Management Protocol (DOP)

DAP, DSP, DISP, DOP, Duh? Well, let's get a little more specific, and throw in a few more acronyms.

The DIB and the DIT

The Directory Information Base (DIB) is the actual database and the data stored by the directory. Every record in the database is an object that holds some kind of data. Objects are collections of attributes that store the actual values of the properties of objects that are records in the database.

The DIB can be a small database that is hosted on a single computer, or it can be a large, distributed database that resides on many computers. Because the database is organized in a hierarchical fashion, it is easy to locate an object, no matter on which server it actually is stored.

The treelike structure that organizes the objects in the database is called the Directory Information Tree (DIT). At the top of the tree is the entry called the root object. In Microsoft's case it's called the Top abstract class. But the name really doesn't matter. The point is that you can start at a single entry point in the tree structure (the top) and locate an object—using a carefully constructed name—by traversing the branches that make up the tree, until you finally get to the leaf object that contains the actual data you are looking for. In addition to leaf objects that store the real data (as object attributes), there also are container objects in the tree structure that hold other container objects and also leaf objects. Using container objects makes it easy to group objects that have something in common. Another type of object in the DIT is the alias object, which is used to give a nicer name to some other object in the tree to which the alias points.

The DUA, DSA, and DAP

The Directory User Agent (DUA) is the client application that is used to access the database (DIB) that is organized by the tree structure (DIT). The DUA queries the database to find the information that the client application needs to obtain. Specifically, the DUA can perform the following tasks:

- Read some or all of the values for attributes of a particular object in the database.

- Compare a value with an attribute of an object in the database to see whether they are the same.

- List objects that are subordinate in the tree structure to an object specified by the DUA.

- Search the database, either all or a portion of it, to find objects that have attributes matching values supplied by the DUA. A search can return more than one object to the DUA, depending on the criteria that the DUA supplies for the search filter.

- Abandon the search or any other request that the DUA has previously made to the directory database.

- Add an entry, or a new object, to the database, provided that the necessary access permissions allow this.

- Modify an object (well, one or more of its attributes) in the database, again provided that permissions allow for it and also provided that the new value the DUA wants to give to an attribute is allowable by the syntax associated with the attribute.

- Remove an entry from the database, provided that the client application has permission to do so.

- Modify a distinguished name (DN).

Of course, to make matters more complex, DAP is the protocol that governs how the DUA interacts with the DSA. The DSA is the server side of this equation. So basically, you have the Directory User Agent interacting with the Directory Access Protocol that talks to the Directory System Protocol to get all this done. It's that easy to remember: DUA uses DAP to talk to the DSA, which does all the work the DUA wants done in the directory! The DOP protocol was developed for administrative purposes to manage operational bindings between different DSAs.

The DN and the RDN

The final item in this list might seem insignificant, but it is not because of the method used to name objects in the DIT. Each object has a "common" name, also called the *relative distinguished name (RDN)*, which does not have to be unique in the DIT. For example, you might have several objects in the directory named HPLASERJET. However, the *distinguished name (DN)* for an object is its common name (or its RDN), concatenated with all the common names of the objects in the directory that are above it. The relative distinguished name doesn't have to be unique in the directory structure, but the full distinguished name, by the very nature in which it is formed, must be unique.

This is why it is so easy to locate objects in the directory. If you know the object's distinguished name, you essentially have a path through the tree that leads to the object you want to find.

The Schema

If you have read Chapter 31, "Using the Active Directory," or Chapters 33, "Overview of the Novell Bindery and Novell Directory Services," and 34, "Expanding and Enhancing NDS: NetWare's eDirectory," you probably are aware that to create objects consisting of attributes and organize them into a tree structure, you must have rules about how this all fits together. The *schema* is this set of rules. The schema is similar to a dictionary in that it defines object classes, which then are used to create the actual objects in the tree. The schema also defines the attributes, and the kinds of data each attribute can hold (the syntax). The schema defines whether certain attributes of an object are mandatory or optional.

The Lightweight Directory Access Protocol

Now that all this is perfectly clear in your mind, let's talk about LDAP. Throw out most of the acronyms in the first part of this chapter and you're left with a clever method of naming and organizing data in a directory database. The only problem is that implementing DAP, DSP, DISP, DOP, and all those other protocols is just too complex, and a lot of the functionality can be performed by simpler protocols. That's why LDAP was developed. It's "lightweight" compared to the overhead involved in the original directory service protocols. If Microsoft had decided to implement the original X.500 directory service as envisioned by the original developers, Bill Gates would still be trying to get Windows 2000 out the door, much less Windows XP.

Because the Internet is standardized on TCP/IP, it was decided that a new set of protocols, also based on TCP/IP, could be developed that could query, add to, and modify a database that was based on the X.500 tree structure. Version 2 of LDAP (described in RFC 1777) was the first practical implementation of LDAP, whereas version 3 (described in RFC 2251) more fully delineates the client/server nature of the functions that are performed for accessing the directory database. Microsoft's Active Directory supports both LDAPv2 and LDAPv3. LDAPv3 provides for additional operations that were not supported in the earlier versions of LDAP and allows for paging and sorting of information. Additionally, LDAPv3 is *extensible*, that is, it defines a concept called *extended operations*, so that future developers can implement operations that are not provided for in the current protocol. This extended operations capability allows a vendor to customize his version of LDAP applications, yet still allows his product to interact with other LDAPv3-compliant products (more or less).

Tip

The next version of LDAP, version 4, is already being readied for use. This version uses XML technology and will go a long way toward making different directories interoperate more easily. You can learn about other features being considered for LDAPv4 by doing a quick search of the Internet.

Another interesting thing that LDAPv3 does is to allow the schema to be defined in the directory. Unlike the Domain Name System (DNS), which usually is implemented as a flat file that must be read into memory when the service is started, LDAPv3 allows for the very definitions of the object classes and related attributes to be defined in the directory. This might not seem important at first, but just think about it. Because the definition of all the classes and attributes is stored in the directory itself, applications can query the database to find out just what kinds of objects it contains.

Note

Ever have one of those nights when you had guests who just didn't know when it was time to go home? The next time that happens, try pulling out some of the following RFCs and reading them out loud:

RFC 2252, "Attribute Syntax Definitions"

RFC 2253, "UTF-8 String Representation of Distinguished Names"

RFC 2254, "The String Representation of LDAP Search Filters"

RFC 2255, "The LDAP URL Format"

RFC 2256, "A Summary of the X.500 User Schema for Use with LDAPv3"

RFC 2247, "Using Domains in LDAP X.500 Distinguished Names"

Actually, these documents, available through a quick search on the Internet, can give you more insight into the details of how LDAP works. They also can put you to sleep.

The LDAP Protocol

LDAP requests and replies are sent as an LDAP Protocol Data Unit (PDU) using either TCP or UDP to get from here to there. The kinds of functions that LDAP can provide include the following:

- Connecting to an LDAP server and authenticating the client to the server.
- Searching the directory and doing something with the results that are returned to the client.
- Managing memory on the client and handling any errors that pop up.

Binding to the Server

The client uses a *bind request* to make a connection to the LDAP-based directory database server. This must be done before the client can begin to query the directory for information. The request should contain the version number of the LDAP protocol the client uses, the name of the directory object to which the client wants to bind, and the information that is used for authentication. The server can respond in several ways (all described in the RFCs), but it basically comes down to one of the following:

- **Operations error**—In other words, this is how the server tells the client, "You screwed up."
- **Protocol error**—The server doesn't use the same version of LDAP that the client wants to use.
- **Authentication method not supported**—LDAP allows for many different authentication schemes, and this is the message sent back when the server doesn't use the one that the client wants to use.
- **Strong authentication required**—Similar to the preceding item, the server is telling the client that a strong authentication method must be used if you want to get any data from this server.

- **Referral**—This is sort of like when your doctor hasn't a clue about what's wrong with you, so he refers you to another doctor. The server is telling the client that it doesn't have the object, or information, that the client is requesting, but gives the client a referral to another LDAP server that might have the info.

- **SASL bind in progress**—The LDAP server is requesting that the client send in another bind request using SASL.

- **Inappropriate authentication**—The client wants to use an "anonymous bind" but the server won't allow it.

- **Invalid credentials**—The server can't process the authentication information sent by the client, or perhaps the client has forgotten the password.

- **Unavailable**—Just an information message to tell the client that the server is shutting down.

Searching the Database

After the client has successfully binded with the server, it can send in a request to search for the data required by the client application. The client can specify where in the directory tree the search should begin, because searching the entire directory database is not very practical in most large databases. This means that the client must have at least some information regarding the kind of object about which it wants more information. The client's request also can specify the maximum number of objects it will accept back from the server in response to the search. If the client specifies a zero number of objects, the server can send back all the data it finds that matches the search criteria. Of course, the server can have limits for this set by the administrator of the database.

In its request, the client can specify how much time it wants the server to spend on the search, and again, zero means "Take all the time you want; I'm in no hurry." The client can query the server to return the types of attributes of the objects found, or both the attribute types and their values. Finally, the client can specify a filter to be used for the search and a list of the attributes it would like to receive, provided they are found in the database.

Adding, Modifying, or Deleting Information in the Directory

The client also can add information to the database, as long as it has the necessary permissions to do so, by specifying the distinguished name (so that the database will know exactly where in the database to put the new object) and values for all the mandatory attributes for the particular object class of which the client wants to create an instance. Take into consideration that for the addition to succeed, the relative distinguished names that make up the portion of the distinguished name that should be superior to the object in the tree must already exist.

To modify or delete an object from the database, the client again must specify the distinguished name of the object so that the server can locate it in the database. If the client just wants to modify an object, it must use one of several methods. It can add one more value to an attribute, delete one or more values for an attribute, or replace values for attributes of an object. But there is an exception to this: The relative distinguished name (RDN) of the object (its common name) can't be modified with a simple modify request, and neither can the relative distinguished names of objects above it in the hierarchy be modified. Instead, a special modify DN operation is used. This is because changing one of the RDNs can cause the object to be moved to a new location in the tree. This affects both the object and any child objects that exist under it in the tree.

Comparing Information in the Directory

The compare operation allows the client to simply supply the values for selected attributes of an object and ask the server to compare them with the actual values stored in the object and the method to be used for the comparison. Although the same thing could be accomplished by having the client read the database and make the comparison itself, this method can be used for things such as comparing passwords and other authentication information.

LDAP Directories

LDAP is now found in just about every medium to large-scale network today. If you are running NDS (or the eDirectory) or Microsoft Windows 2000 or .NET Server, then using LDAP can make managing the network a much simpler task than trying to manage separate islands of data stored on many computers. In today's business environment where companies are merging, using LDAP to store user and application information is almost a necessity. LDAP enables the network administrator to consolidate information into a logical hierarchical database, a much simpler task than in years past.

Windows 2000 and NetWare Are Not the Only Choices You Have

In past years the two primary contenders for your network dollars have been Microsoft and Novell. Although NetWare 6.x still includes NDS, now called the eDirectory, it appears that Novell is moving away from its core application services and directory services. Although the eDirectory will probably be around for a few more years to accommodate existing users, the company appears to be focusing now on Internet services, as evidenced by its iPrint and iFolder products. While Microsoft is trying to pull together a wide assortment of technologies by using the Active Directory, Novell is now trying to break apart its offerings into separate pieces so that you can choose what you like. The marketplace will determine who will succeed in this ongoing saga.

Yet, as a network administrator, you need not feel that you are constrained by Microsoft or Novell. Directory services are going to be here for quite some time until someone thinks up a better way to make locating and using network resources an easier task. Many other vendors, such as Netscape, jumped into the fray early on, and you will find that if you do not want to be locked into any particular vendor, there are other solutions. Another popular directory server product, iPlanet, was recently acquired by Sun Microsystems, and is now part of the Sun Open Net Environment–Sun ONE.

Using a search engine, you can find a large number of software vendors that now offer LDAP directory servers. If you don't want to make a large investment in a directory server, or you just want to learn about directory services, you can download the source code and documentation for the OpenLDAP directory server at www.openldap.org.

Sticking to Standards: Interoperability Between Directories

LDAP was developed to be a standard method for accessing a directory database. Just as TCP/IP allows data transfers and interoperability between different operating systems, the goal of LDAP is to do the same thing for directories.

However, while the structure of the database (the schema) and the protocol for a directory server are defined by the LDAP standards, that doesn't guarantee that all directory server products will easily interact with one another. This will probably change in the future as directories become more important in the corporate environment.

Import and Export Utilities

The LDAP Data Interchange Format (LDIF) is a specification that lets you export data from an LDAP-compliant directory to a flat-file, and then import the data into another directory. LDIF enables you to specify a point in the directory structure from which the export will be performed, and you can also filter selected objects or attributes. Most directory server products support LDIF, including Microsoft's Active Directory and Novell's eDirectory.

Metadirectories

In some cases you might find it desirable to maintain different directory servers instead of using LDIF to import data into a single server. For example, following the acquisition of another company, it may be impractical to integrate data into a single directory server product. Or it may be that each directory server provides features, all of which you want to keep. Another reason for maintaining multiple directory products is the cost of training network personnel on new applications. By keeping the same directories in place, business as usual can continue in today's fast-paced business world. Lastly, one of the features that a metadirectory product can provide is the capability to interface with data stores other than LDAP-based directories. Some applications, such as email products, were not written to work with LDAP servers but can be easily managed using a metadirectory product.

Introduction to Setting Up a SOHO Network

SOME OF THE MAIN TOPICS IN THIS APPENDIX ARE

APPENDIX E

Most of this book has dealt with high-end technologies, but a significant portion has been directed toward the small office/home office (SOHO) audience. The reason for this is twofold. First, from computer consultants to eBay sellers and to many other types of home businesses, small home-based business has been booming. The Internet has led to the blooming of many new businesses that only the Web can provide or use to entice customers. These types of businesses lend themselves to the small office setting and, more economically, to a portion of a house. A single computer is very often insufficient when a small business begins to grow past the entrepreneur who founded the company, however. When you have two or more employees who need to access a computer, you'll save money by installing a low-cost network instead. This scenario assumes that the employees will need to frequently use a computer.

If you just turned to this chapter because you wanted to set up a network quickly, you can usually do so by following the directions included with one of the many "kits" that provide a small network-in-a-box solution, although this convenience usually comes at a premium.

If you want to *understand* your SOHO network so that you will be better able to plan the network as well as troubleshoot it, some of the other chapters that would make good reading before this one are the following:

- Chapter 7, "Network Interface Cards"
- Chapter 8, "Network Switches"
- Chapter 15, "Dial-Up Connections"
- Chapter 17, "Digital Subscriber Lines (DSL) Technologies"
- Chapter 18, "Using a Cable Modem"
- Chapter 54, "Troubleshooting Small Office and Home Office (SOHO) Networks"
- Part V: "Wireless Networking Protocols"

You don't have to read these chapters to get value out of the following content, but familiarity with the listed chapters will make you pretty much a whiz at quickly determining the cause of a SOHO network problem.

Assessing Your Requirements: What Do You Need?

First and foremost it should be stated that there are many third-party providers of application software that can assist your business. This ranges from accounting software to inventory control, and beyond. However, *many* small businesses operate in one of two basic situations:

- A vertical market (such as a doctor's office) in which a third-party vendor supplies software (and perhaps hardware) as a turn-key solution for a particular market solution.
- An office for which no particular vertical market exists. Instead, the business is based on standard programs, such as word processors, databases, and spreadsheets.

The third situation that could be added to this is one in which your SOHO business is large enough to hire a network employee (not likely in most cases) or a consultant to help you out (a better decision, provided that the rates are reasonable). The reason this last situation is not part of the preceding list is that a consultant (now usually called a contractor, as in other businesses) may recommend one of the two items discussed previously. The consultant may agree that the vertical-market approach is good for your situation, or that the second is a better idea. In either scenario, the consultant can help you configure the standard office programs you will use.

There are several things to think about when using vertical-market software:

- In a vertical-market situation you may be constrained by your contract to use only software installed by the vendor. This makes sense only when you consider that the last headache the vendor needs is for you to install new software that may compromise its application. You may even be prohibited from connecting the SOHO network it provides with other computers already in your office. It might even limit your access to the host operating system, giving you access only to run the application.

- Another problem with using vertical-market software is that the support may or may not be what you expect. If you are evaluating a package like this for your office, be sure to ask about support options, additional assistance in training employees, and the costs these will entail. You should make sure that both you and any employees (if any) are both allowed to look over the demos of the software to determine whether it is suitable for your environment. In general, a small office has fewer requirements than a larger office that must keep track of many items. Accounting rules, inventory data, customer databases, and other types of data stores are very important, and you don't want to overwhelm any employees with software that takes a large number of steps to perform a simple task. If you are a sole proprietor, you don't want to bog yourself down trying to memorize complicated software! You'll spend forever reading the documentation, and then *paying* for a support call.

When it comes down to vertical-market software, you may have no choice. For a SOHO business you can't invest hundreds of thousands of dollars (or even much more) developing applications that are specific to your needs. In this case, be sure to "shop around" and get information (and usually happily provided demos and a free lunch) from vendors of such software. In addition, always try to negotiate the price on these types of applications. Although you may not be able to call up Microsoft and ask to get $75 off the price of Office, vertical-market vendors are another matter. Generally, the development effort is already a sunk cost. The application exists, and duplicating usage documents and distribution media is the lowest portion of the cost.

If you are using off-the-shelf applications (such as Microsoft Office or accounting applications), you'll find that when your business expands, most temp agencies will be able to find someone to assist you during "boom" times as long as you are using standard packages. This can be a great benefit for a small business that ramps up during holiday seasons. For most of these standard applications, there are schools that offer courses that teach the skills, and many educational software packages that do the same.

Note

This type of solution works best for an office environment. For a specialized business, you may get by with the forms provided by the office software. Or you may find it necessary to use the vertical-market software. A standard Windows PC today will allow you to install a wide variety of applications, from common business functions such as accounting, inventory, and payroll processing to some off-the-shelf applications that are specialized to certain professions. Are they as good as the vertical-market versions? Please email me and let me know your experiences!

Training is very important when it comes to using a computer, or when introducing new systems to employees of a small business. If you do opt for a class on a particular software application, consider the following types of training and/or certification:

- From a vendor of the application. Many companies, from Novell to Microsoft, offer classes and training certifications for their products.
- From computer consultants who perform on-site training. Look for a competitive price, and references.

- From a local community college. You would probably be surprised how many two-year colleges (tech schools, vocational schools—they're all similar) teach computer courses, many devoted to specific popular applications. This formal education may be useful in getting your foot in the door for a job. You might just find it useful to take one or two classes that relate to commonly used applications instead of opting for a longer course of study.

- Read the manual! This is the oldest technique, the history of which I won't go into here. However, many people buy an expensive book before even thinking about looking at the available documentation for the computer, network hardware, and software applications that they buy. That may be because you want to understand how this network you can easily create operates. This book gives you a good broad overview of the topic of networking, but when it comes down to it, you've got to read the documentation for your specific products!

After all this discussion, sit back and think of the applications your small business needs in order to accomplish all tasks necessary, with the least amount of software. The problem with using multiple applications that store the same type of data is that you now have more than one application to update when customer or order changes occur.

Keep in mind, as pointed out earlier, that many temp agencies, which are a great support for a small business, have workers already trained in the basic office applications. Got a mess you need cleaned up? Call in a temp! Did an employee (or a friend who was helping you out) just leave? Call a temp! Are you under investigation for scandalous accounting practices and need assistance shredding evidentiary documents? Call a temp! These services are not to be underrated in the SOHO environment. Many times a small business needs help only for a particular issue, or to assist in peak-season times. In these sorts of situations, a temp agency can be worth the cost when you consider the revenues to be gained or lost.

Applications Drive Hardware Purchases

A vertical-market application can come in two flavors: The vendor supplies the hardware in addition to the software, or the vendor supplies just the software. In the latter case, if you understand computers and their capacity, you can create your own network instead of paying much higher prices for vendor-supplied hardware.

Tip

Don't get me wrong when I suggest that you provide your own hardware over that of a particular vendor. The vendor knows their application better than you do. And in a busy office environment, paying the extra cost to have someone else come in, install the hardware and software, and then train your staff can be well worth it. For example, in a SOHO you should never need a full-time network administrator—part-time, perhaps, or an on-call consultant. Instead, in cases in which the expertise is low, and the vendor-supplied features can take the place of an extra employee or a part-time one, then the vertical-market hardware/application/support solution might just be the thing for your network. Although the application needs to be able to suit your office and accounting needs, support is the key issue.

If you have the in-house expertise, you can design your own network. This is usually the case with many of you who have purchased the now-basic networking devices such as small hubs, switches, and routers. You are already familiar with these devices and the cables needed to connect them. It doesn't take a genius to figure out these things, because high schools are now turning out prospective employees who can do this sort of simple networking. It's easy to set up a small network.

Switches and small routers now enable you to connect several computers in a SOHO environment and allow you to make a single Internet connection and share it with your other computers. Using a router, and possibly a software firewall, you can do a lot to protect your private network from external attacks. This is not a perfect solution when compared to high-end firewalls, but due to the minor expense involved, simple things like regular backups of data can be all that is required to recover data.

The hub is now practically considered legacy equipment. If you are using one in a SOHO environment, and are satisfied with the network throughput, then don't worry! If throughput is starting to cause problems in your small network, upgrade to a switch. A small switch today (four ports) will cost you about what a small hub did about two years ago.

Note

Some of the most popular vendors for routers for DSL/cable modem routers/switches for the SOHO market are D-Link, Linksys, and NETGEAR. (Yes, D-Link and Linksys sound similar, but they are two different companies.) These are the major brand names you'll probably see at your local consumer electronics store. Yet as other manufacturers start to enter the market, it would greatly benefit you to do a Web search to check the features of these and other companies' offerings for SOHO networks. You can visit D-Link at **www.dlink.com**, Linksys at **www.linksys.com**, and NETGEAR at **www. netgear.com**. Keep in mind that even discount stores are offering their own brand names for these products. As long as they have a free return policy, you might investigate the much less expensive products. I bought several 10/100 network adapter cards recently for less than $14 each.

Even the wireless hubs (called Access Points because many wireless devices contend for access to the network through the Access Point) and wireless network adapter cards are dropping rapidly in price, at least for the slower IEEE 802.11b standard. The IEEE 802.11a standard was finalized in 2002 (and supported by the Wi-Fi brand), and is faster (around 55Mbps on average) compared to 11Mbps for IEEE 802.11b. However, the slower wireless network equipment can be a good solution in many cases. For years the desktop standard was 10BASE-T, or 10Mbps. At 11Mbps, low-end equipment can be sufficient for a small network. This is perfect for a small SOHO that exchanges word processing documents, accesses a central database, or otherwise is involved in fast—but not voluminous—data transfers. Like I say, if it was good enough to stick around for many years, before Fast Ethernet, then it must have some benefit, especially in small networks.

◀◀ For more on wireless connections, which can be a great help in a SOHO environment—especially because there are no wires to connect except to your broadband ISP, if you are connected to the Internet—see Part V of this book.

Typical Office Applications

Microsoft Office, throughout the range of supported versions, is the most widely sold and used office application suite today. At one time (over seven years ago), WordPerfect ruled the word processing domain. Yet, with features that rivaled some typesetting software, in the short run, Microsoft Word overcame WordPerfect. And because Microsoft Office was then offered with a suite of applications, it became possible for Microsoft to take over this market for the most part.

Yet there are alternatives. For example, Corel still produces WordPerfect Office 2002 to compete with Microsoft's hold on the marketplace. Besides Corel's entry, there are two variations on a theme: OpenOffice and StarOffice. OpenOffice is a free, downloadable version of an office suite intended to be an alternative solution to Microsoft Office; SUN's StarOffice 6.0 Suite adds functionality but will cost you around $100. The more user licenses you purchase for StarOffice, however, the lower the cost per user.

When you compare this cost to Microsoft Office, along with support costs and required upgrades, then StarOffice or OpenOffice may just be a good solution if all you want right now is to have basic office applications. This is not meant to denigrate Linux, which already, in all flavors, comes with a large variety of other applications, from sound to graphics, and many others. The emphasis on OpenOffice is because one of the things that has kept larger corporations tied to Microsoft for so many years has been the applications, not the operating systems. If the OS works, and requires minimal maintenance, then the applications will drive the marketplace in the long run.

Tip

If you want to contact the organization responsible for creating the OpenOffice suite of applications, visit the Web site `http://openoffice.org`. This organization is responsible for developing and distributing the latest open software for OpenOffice.

SUN offers its own version of OpenOffice, with some enhancements, and calls the product StarOffice. Like the free download of OpenOffice, StarOffice provides an alternative to the Windows desktop if you are well versed in the Linux operating system. OpenOffice and StarOffice both allow you to save documents, spreadsheets, and so on in various formats (including Microsoft Office), so this may be a good choice for a small organization that includes someone skilled in Linux. Otherwise, I recommend the easier-to-use Windows operating systems to create small networks.

Should You Use Freeware or Shareware Applications?

One of the biggest headaches of a large network manager is the installation by users of unapproved applications, and these applications usually are downloaded from the Internet. Although free software may sound too good to pass up, consider the following facts and considerations:

- You get what you pay for. Support for freeware or shareware applications is usually available at a minimal cost, but the support you receive is not what you'd get from most major application vendors.
- Can you rely on the application? Does it perform all the functions you need? Will it be a "kludge" in which you have to enter data more than once for separate applications? For example, if you use a shareware general ledger program, will it take automatic input from your accounts payable application from another vendor?
- Does the application come with adequate documentation? Is it understandable?
- Are there any undesirable capabilities of the application? Read the fine print—the licensing and privacy statements. Does the application gather any information about you and upload it to the vendor's site?

Perhaps the most important issue to discuss about freeware/shareware is the black-box/crystal-box argument. The black-box argument is that if you buy software from a reputable company, and the source code is known only to the company, then you are better protected against someone who has the code and might find and exploit bugs, or back-doors that can be a security issue.

The crystal-box argument is that if everyone has the source code, the application is scrutinized by a large number of people in the open source community, so the odds of finding and fixing bugs or other problems is greatly enhanced. With so many people evaluating the code, problems will, in theory, be found quicker and then be more easily solved.

The other side of this argument is that the "bad guys" also have the code, and you never know what they'll be up to.

Should You Make Copies of Applications You Purchase or Obtain from Others?

You should always make one or more backups of any CDs or floppy disks that come with an application you buy. You should read the licensing information to see whether it can be installed on more than one computer.

Making backups of software you have purchased is a good idea and likely to be in line with the vendor's license agreement. However, using copies of your friend's software or downloading it from community shareware sites is called piracy, and in the SOHO environment it seems to be, if not a common practice, one that does occur frequently. Large companies are more likely to get audited, but that doesn't mean a small operator like you can't go to jail if you get caught using software you have no right to use. In addition, don't forget to register shareware if you plan to use it outside of the stated evaluation period. The vendor might be smaller, but the penalties are just as high.

Operating Systems: Should You Choose Linux over Windows or Unix?

Using Unix or Linux in a SOHO environment will be best implemented using a vendor-installed version, or having in-house Unix/Linux support, or at least a consultant. This assumes that the entrepreneur in a small business is acquainted with Unix/Linux. Most SOHO environments cannot afford a full-time employee to devote to operating-system tweaking and such. This does not apply, however, if your business is oriented toward products for just this type of environment.

Although the preferred operating system is a Windows version for a SOHO network, if you are a computer professional yourself (whether or not your business involves computers), then you might find yourself more comfortable using Unix or Linux. Yet you may also find yourself consumed by business activities and need a consultant part-time, to do what you could otherwise do yourself.

If you are going to use Unix/Linux as your desktop operating system, consider that there are several popular vendors of each. The most popular vendor of inexpensive (free) Unix is FreeBSD. This operating system was created based on the BSD Unix operating system. That version of Unix was developed by the University of California, Berkeley. The FreeBSD version runs on Intel and AlphaServer hardware platforms.

Tip

FreeBSD is a very popular operating system. You can download it from **www.freebsd.org**. Source code is also available from this site, along with other important links.

However, today it seems that the Linux operating system is making small, but steady, inroads into the business environment. Once used as simple network firewall devices, Linux has grown to a large industry, and there are many applications (mostly open-source that you can get for no charge) being ported to this operating system. Another benefit that Linux sports is its capability to run on low-end hardware platforms. Thus, older computers that may be at the expected end-of-life for a Windows operating system might run Linux at a satisfactory speed for a desktop, if not a server, depending on the hardware.

Note

Even Microsoft, according to industry gossip, is courting the idea of releasing its own version of Linux, or at least of releasing versions of its top software applications, from Office to Exchange, that run on Linux. A few years will tell.

If you decide to use Linux, perhaps the most widely used are these:

- **Red Hat Linux**—This is probably the best seller (or downloader) today. Red Hat Linux has scaled from the lowest current Intel- or AMD-processor to high-end IBM mainframes. It is one of the few Linux vendors who are profitable today. Visit www.redhat.com.
- **Mandrake Linux**—Another very popular version of Linux. Visit its site at www.mandrake.com.

- **Debian GNU/Linux**—This vendor has chosen to use the Linux operating-system kernel (the guts of the operating system that controls everything else) and add to it application packages from the GNU project. This is the reason for the name of this Linux version. Debian is free, so that's a bargain. You can download the OS or obtain other information at `www.debian.org`.

- **SuSE**—If you need to support other hardware platforms, such as older AlphaServer computers, that are now becoming replaced by other computers, then SuSE might be simply a temporary solution to lower costs by using earlier Intel or AlphaServer systems that otherwise would go unused as they are replaced. Visit `www.suse.com`. Because SuSE, like Red Hat, runs on both small-end servers and high-end performers, it can be a scalable solution as your small business grows.

When it comes to other office-productivity applications, you should evaluate the choices between those products and your business. It may be that your choice works best on a Windows machine or a Linux computer.

Graphics, Video, and Other Network-Intensive Applications

A small office usually requires standard business applications, such as word processing. It is also possible that one or two computers are devoted to special applications, such as engineering or programming, depending on your business. But accounting functions must be done, and word processing, billing, and so on must be accomplished at the same time. Earlier in this chapter you learned about the simple office network. If you have larger network needs, you will have to plan for them and provision the correct network equipment.

SOHO Network Topologies

In Figure E.1 you can see two types of SOHO networks, each of which is connected to the Internet.

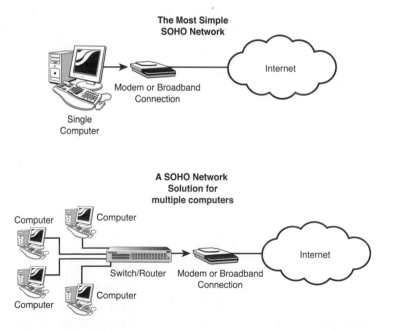

Figure E.1 There are several topologies for creating a SOHO network.

In some cases you might not want to connect your SOHO network to the Internet. Instead, you might choose to use a separate computer for that connection (if it is required) and use it for general emails to company contacts. This approach will suffice to provide customers with an Internet presence, but will lack the capability to coordinate external contacts with internal network capabilities, such as fulfilling an order and billing the customer. As you can see, there is a lot to be gained from connecting at least part of your SOHO network to the Internet. Using a firewall will usually suffice, but again, an inexpensive firewall is not as good as an enterprise firewall. So if you want to expose part of your network, do it with several firewalls.

Note

You can find out more about firewalls in Chapter 49, "Firewalls." There are many types of firewall technology, and you should understand them before trusting your small business with a hardware or software firewall product. For example, Windows XP and Windows 2003 Server have a simple built-in firewall—limited to port and IP address restrictions. The standard TCP/IP ports are there by default: Telnet, FTP, and so on, and you can define other ports by number.

A third topology uses wireless connectivity instead of copper cables. If you operate your business from home and don't want to go punching holes in the wall and spending endless time stringing network cables from one room to another, then wireless may be a great solution for your business. Unless you have no need for an Internet connection, the only cable in a wireless network that you'll need is one to connect the Access Point to your Internet connection (such as a cable or DSL modem). Even if all the computers in your SOHO are located in the same room, wireless may be a good choice if you don't want to go tripping over cables running here and there.

The installer of the cable/DSL modem should configure it and your main computer to work well. After that you will have to move the connection from that computer and attach it to the Access Point.

Caution

Some cable/DSL modems come with an RJ-45 receptacle, and this is usually the case with an Access Point (as well as other cable/DSL routers). Some cable/DSL modems come with a USB connection. In that case, connecting it to a single computer is easy. Finding an Access Point or router that can connect to a USB port can be difficult and, as they come to market, expensive. Be sure to check with your ISP—find out what kind of termination will be done on your premises. If possible, request an RJ-45 jack/receptacle.

Another way around this is to connect the cable/DSL modem directly to a computer, such as Windows Server, and use the routing and Internet sharing capabilities of these operating systems.

To configure an access point, most DSL or cable modems enable you to connect an RJ-45 terminated network cable to your PC and/or Access Point. From there you can use a browser (the URL is given in the hardware's installation manual) and then configure such things as an ID that the Access Point and computers that access it will use. Another thing you can configure here is security using encryption. This can keep others from intercepting your network communications. Use this feature to lessen the chance that someone can listen in on your network traffic. After it's configured, disconnect the cable and hook up the access point to your cable/DSL modem (or a router port connected to the modem).

Installing a wireless adapter is as easy as installing a regular network adapter. Just unscrew the protective slot-protector on the PCI card section and gently insert your new network card. For notebooks, you may just need to insert a PC card. In addition, USB to Wireless Ethernet adapters are available for around $100. These devices are a type of external network card; installation is as simple as plugging a cable in to the USB port on your notebook or desktop and then loading the software. You may have to use a CD or a floppy to configure the network adapter (and load a driver for the operating system). When configured, your wireless network is ready to go.

In Figure E.2 you can see the layout of a simple wireless network for a SOHO.

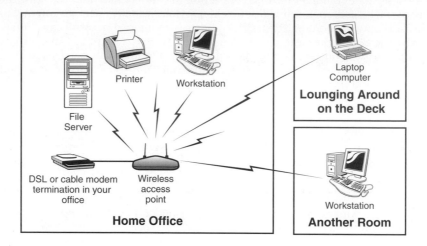

Figure E.2 Using a wireless network in the SOHO environment.

Tip

Another thing to consider when incorporating wireless networking is that most wireless access points for the SOHO market have four or more RJ-45 ports. This means you can use standard network adapters for some computers and connect them to the AP, while using wireless adapters for others. This is a great solution if you have servers or client computers that generally stay in the same place (use a wired connection), while other computers (such as laptops) can be moved around and use the wireless connection.

Using wireless in any kind of office offers you mobility when using a laptop computer. It offers easy relocation should you decide to move a computer from one place to another. And the price is now down so low that wireless (IEEE 802.11b) equipment is very inexpensive. The major trade-off is 11Mbps versus 100Mbps with typical network adapters and cables. If you decide a year or so later that 11Mbps is just not fast enough, by then IEEE 802.11a hardware will cost about what the IEEE 802.11b equipment costs, and a few minor replacements (network adapters, Access Point) will upgrade you to a much faster environment (around 55Mbps for IEEE 802.11a).

Backup Solutions for a SOHO Network

One of the most important things you can provision in your SOHO network is a means to create regular backups of your data. Applications, as mentioned earlier, should always be copied (and the copy used, with the original safely stored elsewhere). Most software licenses allow you to make backup copies; you just can't give these backups to your friends as "evaluation copies."

But you do need to back up data files and other information on a regular basis. The frequency will be determined by weighing the cost of having to re-enter the data (or lose it). It used to be common practice to use a tape drive to back up an entire drive from a PC. Today, with disk drives with capacities of over 180GB, it may not be practical to wait a few days for a backup to complete—or use a more expensive tape drive costing thousands of dollars. You can still use an expensive tape drive if you just want to copy a few important data files, or you can use a low-cost CD burner to do the same. CD burners can use both write-once and read/write media, and at their price-point now, they are a viable means for creating backups for a SOHO environment.

Another method you can use is to copy data from one computer to another. If you have a second drive installed on another computer, you can create a nightly batch job to copy files to that other computer. You can use this method to copy data from a set of more than two computers, ensuring that all important data files are safely stored in more than one place.

If lightning strikes, however, be sure your surge protector or UPS is capable of withstanding this kind of event, or you could still lose it all!

Networking equipment is so inexpensive today that using a single computer and exchanging data with other business associates of other computers at your SOHO is now just impractical. A small network should cost less than a few hundred dollars (depending on the number of network adapters and cables you have to buy). The technology has become so simple that just about anyone who can read a few pages of documentation can have a SOHO network up and running in a few hours or less.

INDEX